ALASKANA CATHOLICA

St. Therese of Lisieux, "the Little Flower,"
letting fall a shower of roses upon the village of Kaltag. Note
her Indian features! The painting by Father John B. Baud,
S.J., hangs in Kaltag's St. Teresa's Church. *LR.*

ALASKANA CATHOLICA

A History of
the Catholic Church
in Alaska

A REFERENCE WORK IN THE FORMAT
OF AN ENCYCLOPEDIA

By
Louis L. Renner, S.J.

SOCIETY OF JESUS
Oregon Province
2005

ISBN 0-87062-342-7
Library of Congress Catalog Card Number 2005020143

Library of Congress Cataloging-in-Publication Data
Renner, Louis L., 1926-
Alaskana Catholica : a history of the Catholic Church in Alaska : a
reference work in the format of an encyclopedia / by Louis L. Renner.
    p. cm.
Includes bibliographical references and index.
ISBN 0-87062-342-7 (hardcover : alk. paper)
    I. Catholic Church—Alaska—History—Encyclopedias. I. Title.

BX1415.A4R46 2005
282'.798'03—dc22

                                        2005020143

Design and production by
THE ARTHUR H. CLARK COMPANY
P.O. Box 14707
Spokane, WA 99214

Dedicated to
SAINT THERESE OF LISIEUX
"The Little Flower"
Patroness of the Alaska Mission

TABLE OF CONTENTS

PUBLICATION SPONSORS

Publication of ALASKANA CATHOLICA *was made possible, in large part, by the many kind and generous friends, whose names are listed here below. May Saint Therese of Lisieux, "the Little Flower"—patroness of the Alaska Mission, and to whom this history of the Catholic Church in Alaska is dedicated—obtain special blessings and favors for them!*

Albino, Mr. Joseph Xavier

Anne, Congregation of the Sisters of Saint (Lachine, Q.C.): In honor and memory of the works of the Sisters of Saint Anne in Alaska

Anonymous #1: A.M.D.G.

Anonymous #2: In memory of Father George E. Carroll, S.J.

Anonymous #3: In memory of Bishop Michael J. Kaniecki, S.J.

Anonymous #4: In honor/memory of Alaska Mission Volunteers and Bishop Michael J. Kaniecki, S.J.

Anonymous #5: In memory of Father William J. Loyens, S.J.

Armitage, G.T. and E.A. and family: In memory of deceased family members

Baker, Father Kenneth W., S.J.

Bergquist, Father Patrick D.: In memory of Bishop Michael J. Kaniecki, S.J.

Berman, Angela McMillan

Bernet, John W. (Jack): In memory of Charles J. Keim

Betz, Madeleine: In memory of Robert K. Betz

Bez, Nicholas J.: In memory of Magdalene Bez

Bichsel, Mr. Tom: In memory of George Bichsel

Boone, Brother Kirby, C.F.X.: In memory of Frank and Martina Boone

Bradley, Father Theodore X.

Brennan, Geoff and Maura

Brother Joe Prince Jesuit Community, St. Marys, Alaska

Burbank, Glenda: In memory of Edna and Norman Grant

Burdick, Mr. and Mrs. John L.

Butler, John A. and Anne M.

Cardy, Father William E., O.F.M.: In memory of Mary Therese Cardy

Carlin, Mrs. Della: In memory of Donald W. Carlin

Case, Father Richard D., S.J.: In honor of Father Louis L. Renner, S.J.

Conwell, Father Joseph F., S.J., and Mrs. Gertrude Doyle (sister): In memory of Father James U. Conwell, S.J.

Crandall, Mrs. Blanche: In memory of Mitchell Crandall

Creedican, Elizabeth (Gustin) and family: In memory of Maurice and Tommy Creedican

Cronin, Father James D.

Cruikshank, Ms. Jewell M.: In memory of Father William J. Loyens, S.J.

Cusick, George and Anne

Daniggelis, Paul: In memory of Urbici Soler y Manonelles, Catalonian sculptor

de Lima, Jay and Ginger: In memory of John J. May

DeLong, Mr. and Mrs. Louis F.: In memory of Patricia DeLong Freeman

Demientieff, Daisy A.: In memory of Mike and Kenny Demientieff

Desso, Father Leo C.: In memory of Wilfred Desso

de Verteuil, Father Jack: In memory of Bishop Michael J. Kaniecki, S.J.

Doogan, James P. and Barbara: In memory of Father Cornelius K. Murphy, S.J.

Douglas, Kathleen Renner: In memory of Mary Jean Renner and Selma Sandgren

Douglas, Reimer and Kathleen, Alex and Daniel

Dykema, Michael and Shelley

Dykema, Ken and Deb: In memory of Albert Dykema

Engh, Father Michael E., S.J.: In honor of Richard Mahan

Extension Magazine: In honor/memory of Catholic Extension benefactors of the Alaskan Missions.

Fairbanks, Diocese of: In honor of those who give to the Missions by going to the Missions. In honor, too, of those who go to the Missions by giving to the Missions.

Falsey, Father James E.: In memory of William P. and L. Marjorie Falsey

Fienup-Riordan, Ann: In memory of Father René Astruc, S.J.

Finnerty, Mr. Robert W.: In memory of Ingeborg Finnerty

Fitz-Patrick, Father David M.

Franciscan Friars, Northern Alaska

Gallagher, Father Richard J.: In memory of Mr. and Mrs. John Gallagher

Gallagher, Father Thomas N., S.J.: In honor of "Deka Haroleen" and companions, and Mary Kathleen Kameroff

Gavora, Donna L.: In memory of Father William J. Loyens, S.J.

Geraghty, Mr. and Mrs. Patrick, Jr.: In honor of Father Louis L. Renner, S.J.

Gerchman, Mr. Carl F.: In memory/honor of Alaskan missionaries past and present

Gorges, Father Peter F.

Gould, Tom and Lillian

Graafstra, Tom and Julie Renner Graafstra: In memory of Selma Sandgren

Grey Nuns of the Sacred Heart, St. Mary of Kodiak

Gustin, Mrs. Rose

Hartmann, Father Edward J.: In memory of Mr. and Mrs. E. Hartmann

Hassannia, Ali and Helen: In memory of Florence, Clarence and Robert Perlatti

Hassannia, Jeff and Crissie, Ali and Brianna

Hebert, Father Daniel J.

Hemmer, Father Joseph, O.F.M.: In honor of Virginia Kalland

Hidy, Rev. Ross F.: A friend in the Lord, and Head of the Lutheran History Center of the West

Hilcoske family

Hinsvark, Father John A.

Holy Mary of Guadalupe Parish, Healy, Alaska: In memory of Father Paul B. Mueller, S.J.

Hughes, Mary: In memory of Jerry Hughes

Hursh, Steve and Nancy, Kimberly and Lori: In honor of William and Bernice Renner

Hutchinson, Mr. John M.

Jacobson, Father James E., S.J.

Jauhola, Carl and Geraldine

Jalbert, Mr. and Mrs. Roland: In memory of our parents

Jesuit Community at 1500 Birchwood Street, Anchorage, Alaska

Jesuit Community at Gonzaga University, Spokane, Washington

Jesuit Community at Santa Clara University, Santa Clara, California

Jesuit Fathers of St. Rita's Church, Tacoma, Washington: In honor of Father Louis L. Renner, S.J., and in memory of Father William J. Loyens, S.J.

Johnson, Frank and Betty: In memory of Dorothy Richards and Victoria Johnson

Johnson, Meg: In memory of Sister Margaret Jane

Johnson, Robert and Rosemary: In memory of Rosemary C. Johnson

Jones, Dr. Eliza: In memory of my children: Charlene, Vern, Ben, Jr., Julie

Journal Graphics, Portland, Oregon

Kangas, Ivan and Katie: In honor of Mary Huxley

Kaplan, Dr. Lawrence D. and Janice Dawe

Kari, Dr. James M.: In honor of Father Louis L. Renner, S.J.

Keenen, Mrs. Celene M.: In memory of David Keenen

Kelly, Mike and Cherie: In memory of Hal and Helen Kelly, and Jim and Betty Haynes

Kettler, Bishop Donald J.

Kolb, Father James M., C.S.P

Kolvenbach, Father Peter-Hans, S.J.

Konda, Father Bernard A.: In memory of Matt and Irene Konda

Langlotz, Robert: In memory of John Robert Langlotz

Laudwein, Father James R., S.J.

Lauinger, Mrs. Clementine: In memory of Katherine Curtis

L'Ecuyer, Rosalie

Levin, Mrs. Catherine: In memory of Robert T. Levin

Little Sisters of Jesus, Nome

Lynn, Jacqueline B.

Maddock, Father Andrew L., S.J.: In memory of Father William J. Loyens, S.J.

Martinek, Father John B.

McAdoo, Patricia: In memory of Deacon William Tyson

McAleer, Mr. Joseph J.

McCarthy, Paul and Lucy

McGuirk, Donald and Thelma: In memory of Father Frederick A. Ruppert, S.J., and M.A. and Hazel McCorkle

McLean, Mac and Diane: In memory of Eziekel McLean

McMahon, Susan

McMillan, Duncan and Julie: In honor of Father Louis L. Renner, S.J.

Meany, Father Neill R., S.J.: In memory of Bishop Robert L. Whelan, S.J.

Menard, Marcia K.: In memory of Ray E. Menard, Sr.

Mielke, Mary Joeann Monagle: In memory of Pope John Paul II

Mitchell, Magdalen M.: In memory of my parents Joseph and Jane Cloherty

Mohrmann, Eric J. and Patricia A.

Morris, Sister Joan, O.S.F.: In memory of Jane Morris Browning

Morrison, Robert and Frances: In memory of Mildred Morrison

Mount, Helen R.: In memory of George and Clara Reeves, parents

Muckenthaler, Stella: In honor/memory of all the Jesuits who served in Alaska

Mueller, Walter J.: In memory of Eleanor M. Mueller

Murkowski, Governor Frank H. and Nancy

Mynarski, Florence M.: In honor/memory of the Mynarski family

Naparagamiut (Hooper Bay), Little Flower of Jesus parish

Nigro, Father Armand M.: In memory of Frank and Margaret Nigro

O'Keefe, James and Virginia: In memory of Most Rev. Joseph O'Keefe

Olson, Wallace M.: In memory of Father William J. Loyens, S.J.

Ornowski, Father Gerald, M.I.C.

Partridge, Capt. Alan J., U.S.A.F.

Partridge, Brian and Cheryl: In honor of Father Louis L. Renner, S.J.

Partridge, Daniel and Katie Ponsford Partridge

Partridge, Gayle

Popp, Charles F.: In memory of Bishop Michael J. Kaniecki, S.J.

Post, Roger and Bonita: In memory of Father Arthur Lopilato, S.J.

Quashnock, COL and Mrs. Joseph M., Ph.D.

Ray, Dr. Dorothy Jean: In memory of Dr. Verne F. Ray

Renner, Albert and Joanne: In memory of our parents

Renner, Andrew M.

Renner, Brian and family

Renner, David and Valerie

Renner, Greg and family: In memory of grandparents

Renner, John F.

Renner, Leonard and Martha

Renner, Mark and family

Renner, Michael J. and Karen O.

Renner, Richard and Mary Ann: In memory of Pope John Paul II

Renner, Robert Louis and Marie Renner

Renner, Tom and Debbie: In honor of Richard and Mary Ann Renner

Renner, Mr. and Mrs. William J. and Bernice E.

Riedel, Mr. Charles E.: In memory of Father William J. Loyens, S.J.

Ross, Gary W.: In memory of John and Rose Renner

Sander, Father Timothy L., O.S.B.: "In gratitude for the years I spent in Alaska"

Schwietz, Archbishop Roger L., O.M.I.

Shaw, George F. and Dorothy

Shirey, Father Joseph E., S.J.

Spils, Mrs. Marge: In memory of Richard W. Spils

Staskanis, Beverly

Stepovich, Mike: In memory of Matilda Stepovich

Sundborg, George and Mary

Tero, Father Richard D.: In honor/memory of the Tero family

Thompson, Daniel and Yvette: In memory of Father Francis W. McGuigan, S.J.

Toussaint, Don A. and Wilda M.

Travers, Rev. Patrick J.: In honor of Rev. Louis L. Renner, S.J.

Ulz, Ken and June: In memory of Frances Cleary and John and Emma Ulz

Van Flein family: In memory of Helmut Van Flein

Valerius, Cyril H. and Joan M.

Walter, Jim and family: In honor of Benefactors of the Missionary Diocese of Fairbanks

Weber, Msgr. Francis J.

Weber, Richard and Bette

Welborn, David and Pat

Welp, Mrs. Mary Ann

Westerheide, Kathleen H.: In memory of Alexander G. and Dorothy N. Westerheide

Whittaker, Dr. and Mrs. John R.: In memory of Dorothy B. Whittaker

Wieber, Mary

Wood, Thomas F.: In memory of Eurana G. Wood, mother

Wyatt, Mrs. Ruth M.: In memory of Glenn E. Wyatt

Zahler, John, Vicki, Amy and Matthew

FOREWORD

Slush beneath the runners of a dog sled indicates a change from what was, at the beginning, a sub-zero degree trek. Almost overnight, it seems, a "spring break-up" has occurred. The thoughtful driver of the sled ponders, considers the route, and envisages what might lie ahead.

Around 1970, long-time missionary Father Segundo Llorente, S.J., perhaps sensing even then "a spring break-up," wrote that the Alaska Missions deserve a historian familiar with conditions, as they were before the turn of the twentieth century, and as they are at the present time. Unfortunately, there seems to be no such person. Anyone attempting such a history will have to depend on the writings of the early ones, the missionaries. They lived and worked under conditions that exist no longer.

Father Louis L. Renner, S.J., a historian who has experienced Alaska since 1958, has come along to do just what Father Llorente was hoping would happen: record that history. Grasping the significance of the sound of slush, Father Renner has judged that, as the new century and new millennium begin, it is not only a good time, but also a *must* time to stop and consider the journey so far.

ALASKANA CATHOLICA is the result of what a thoughtful person, ruminating about the changes felt and witnessed, translates into vignettes of historical importance. Whether one wants to review the trail, or plan a new one, what is written here sets up probabilities, possibilities, and accomplishments of inestimable value. The author of this volume of precious data has culled and pulled together scenarios, strategies, and strengths of a time now gone. He has done much pondering. In sitting with this material, he has also been able to focus, at times, on the immediate, that which he currently sees. Occasional vagaries of wind and mist rise to allow

him glimpses of the trails and experiences about which others will write.

In helping to bring the Christian Faith to the people of the Great Land, missionaries lived and recorded history. Beginning with the presence of the Russian Orthodox Church in Alaska, heralds and heroes of this Church had tagged trees, as it were, and planted markers indicating "trails" that they had broken, re-marked, and re-charted for over one hundred years. After the purchase of Alaska by the United States in 1867, in the vacuum left by the withdrawal of Russia, various Protestant Christian Churches valiantly continued to make and record history in the North, through various good works: child care for orphans, health care for the sick, education, proclaiming the Gospel.

Beginning in 1873, messengers of the Roman Catholic faith set out on their own Alaskan trip, often enough into a veritable unknown. Father Renner has laid out, in encyclopedic format, the tortuous, but "happy trail" of this Roman Catholic missionary trek of multiple drivers. That trek could lead to isolated settlements, follow interminable sloughs, end at nomadic camps or subterranean homes. The travelers could also find themselves along spectacular beauties of coastal waters, forested mountains, wandering rivers. Fields of ice could be shadowed by storms or made magnificent by the Aurora Borealis. As varied and as dangerous as the stages of the trek could be, there was a *constant*: the felt presence of God sensed in a unique and gripping way. In all of this, records of immense social and historical value have been written and preserved.

Speaking of his Jesuit confreres, Father Llorente commented: "In those small and faraway villages the missionary trained in logic and theology had no one with whom to converse on a high level.

Some were extraordinary men able to cope with the demands of the North, others found Alaska unbearable from the beginning and maneuvered themselves out of it rather early. Still others found that they had no particular call of the North in them, and managed to leave." What is true of the Jesuits can also be said about any priests and Brothers, and, indeed, of the Congregations of women Religious. As with all Christian missionaries, those bringing the Catholic Faith were deeply concerned about caring for orphans, health care for the sick, education, proclaiming the Gospel. There was great joy in bringing the Mass and the sacraments to the people and to be part of evolving ministries, such as, concerns for justice, opportunities for job training, housing improvements, leadership formation. *ALASKANA CATHOLICA* records the beginnings of these efforts. It would take another book, even a series of volumes, to bring all the more current people and ministries into a focused historical limelight.

Father Renner's work shows individuals, extraordinary or not, ministering through the passing decades of the 1800s and 1900s, even as Alaska developed from District, to Territory, to State. Dog sleds gave way to snowmachines. Ice movements and eroding riverbanks caused early mission churches to be relocated; the smoke and whistles of stern-wheelers faded from the Alaskan scene; "kicker boats" tended fish camps and trawlers fed the ocean catch to canneries. Early missionaries are gone. New ones carry on, feeling their way, guided by a Spirit that responds to needs of the time.

A log book of any trip records the details: names, dates, events, places, landmarks, directions. Pondering what has been and what may lie ahead allows one to remain on course, or to choose new routes, to camp a while, or to adapt to another season. Father Renner, confident that 1) there is a great story to be told and 2) the story is great because of the people who were part of it, opens for the reader the "log book" of this Roman Catholic missionary trek. Careful scholarship regarding biographical and other historical facts, a bit of humor, and insightful appreciation about many of the significant "drivers," guides, camps, villages, and events have resulted in *ALASKANA CATHOLICA*, an enjoy-able, encyclopedic collection of biographical and historical material covering, in particular, the beginnings of more than 125 years of the journey of the Catholic Church in the Great Land.

Any such proposed writing project could have daunted Father Renner. However, he realized that much of the necessary research had been done by him. Over many years, he had diligently searched for old notebooks and diaries. He had studied and transcribed them. Having been the long-time editor of *The Alaskan Shepherd*, his office files already held articles he had written about many missions and personalities. He had, to his credit, other historical essays and reports about the North, as well as all the experiential and factual material he had gathered for the three books he had published. Additional information for the proposed project was available to him in several archival repositories and, to a certain extent, from actual "Alaskani," aging missionaries replete with stories garnered through their years in the Great Land. Tentatively, he began to sketch out the possible structure of such a work, to speak of its pros and cons, to incorporate suggestions, to accept offers of assistance for what was becoming truly a mammoth work. When discussions centered more and more on the concept of a biographical encyclopedia, a tentative schema developed; articles, including those about places and general topics, began to be compiled. Expressions of encouragement for *ALASKANA CATHOLICA* to move from proposal to actuality came from many who knew of Father Renner's writing gifts, organizational skills, and energetic capabilities.

Early in 2002, affirmation for his proposed project came in a letter from his Provincial: "I mission you to continue your work writing a history of the Catholic Church in Alaska." As scholarly work demands time and atmosphere, Father Renner accepted to become a scholar in residence with the Gonzaga University Jesuit Community, in Spokane, Washington. Although he was out of Alaska by mid-June, Alaska was not out of him. Material that he had brought with him, his proximity to the Jesuit Archives at the university, and his Jesuit confreres, especially nearby former Alaskan missionaries, with minds overflowing with stories of the North, provided a balm when the ache for the North was strong. That same "ache" provided the adrenalin that pushed the history project along.

In reading this finished work, this "log book" compilation of journeys traced and missions accomplished, it will become evident that much of *ALASKANA CATHOLICA* truly records a time in history that is fast disappearing, or totally gone, as of the year 2004. Father Renner has, indeed, felt "the slush beneath the runners of the dog sled" and most fittingly responded. A long winter, with all its marvels, has passed. New seasons, new treks, new stories await.

Love reaches back in grateful thanks to the people who made all this happen, and to the God Who smiled with pride at the stamina, inventiveness, and welcoming hearts of the people of the North.

SISTER MARGARET CANTWELL, S.S.A.

PREFACE

For over a quarter of a century, on a part-time basis, I spent countless hours in research and in writing books and articles, most of them biographical and historical in nature, about people and things at the same time Catholic and Alaskan. However, in June 2002, this kind of research and writing became my full-time assignment, given me by my Jesuit Provincial Superior, Father Robert B. Grimm. On February 26, 2002, he wrote to me: "Now is the time for you to take up a new mission. On behalf of the Society, I mission you to a ministry of scholarship. I mission you to continue your work of writing a history of the Catholic Church in Alaska, and ask you to go to Gonzaga University Jesuit Community as a scholar in residence to carry out this ministry." (Archival materials relating to the Catholic Church in Alaska are housed in the Foley Library at Gonzaga University in Spokane, Washington.)

In 1979, from Moses Lake, Washington, Father Segundo Llorente, S.J., wrote to me: "Writing is an all-consuming activity, an exhausting one. Reading is a pleasure. Readers should bear this in mind." At times, writing has, indeed, been for me an all-consuming, exhausting activity; and often also a frustrating one, as I dealt with critical archival materials that had gone through floods and fires, were written in a faded scribble nearly indecipherable, lacked reference points as to time and place, lacked completeness, were unsigned, and the like. Nevertheless, I must admit that, in general, I have found research and writing a very satisfying occupation, a pleasure. I hope readers of the contents of this volume will find the reading of them a pleasure.

In 1895, Father Paschal Tosi, S.J., Prefect Apostolic of Alaska at the time, ordered that the grave of Lt. John J. Barnard, a British naval officer slain and buried at Nulato in 1851, be fenced in and that the cross and inscription be renewed. He ordered this, "lest the memory of a brave man be forgotten." Many "brave" men and women—living and deceased, clerical and lay, Native and non-Native—have been and are makers of Alaska's Catholic history and heritage. One of the main intents of this volume is to keep alive for posterity their memory by the telling of their stories, by the recording of their lives and deeds.

For many years, booksellers, scholars, and historians had urged me to write a general history of the Catholic Church in Alaska. Fellow Jesuits had encouraged me to produce biographies of Jesuit Alaskan missionaries. They assured me: "You are the one to do it. If you don't do it, it will never get done." Dr. Dorothy Jean Ray—anthropologist, historian, universally recognized expert on Alaska Native arts, and editorial co-author with me on my first book, *Pioneer Missionary to the Bering Strait Eskimos: Bellarmine Lafortune, S.J.*—had all but demanded that I compile a history of the Catholic Church in Alaska. On April 15, 2002, after she had learned that I was being assigned full-time to write what, at the time, I was already tentatively referring to as *"ALASKANA CATHOLICA,"* she wrote, "I'm happy, happy that you will be beginning solid work on 'Alaskana Catholica,' and I do hope I'll live long enough to see its completion." Dr. Ray's words imply that I had an immense task facing me.

In a 1998 letter, Father Armand M. Nigro, S.J., a classmate of mine, who himself had served for several years in Alaska, had already written to me with a like implication: "I hope you will live long enough to write the mini-biographies of all the Jesuits who served in Alaska. The four you sent me are excellent. I hope you'll have them all published in one volume. Won't that be a great gift and legacy, an historical treasure!"

In her book, *A Legacy of Arctic Art*, Dr. Ray referred to me as "the foremost authority on Catholic history in Alaska, writing history at its purest, almost exclusively from archival sources." Father Nigro urged me to consider devoting myself totally to the kind of writing in question here. Still, it was not I, who proposed myself as the one to write this history. It was Father Grimm, my Provincial Superior, who took the initiative in this whole matter and "missioned" me to write *ALASKANA CATHOLICA*. This put everything within the framework of Jesuit obedience, and assured me that all was in keeping with the will of God for me. Reassuring, too, I found the words of St. Paul, "I am confident that He Who began a good work in me will also bring it to completion." With peace of mind, I happily relocated to Gonzaga University, on June 10, 2002, and began, in ideal surroundings and under most favorable conditions, the writing of *ALASKANA CATHOLICA*.

Despite the Catholic Church's presence in Alaska for roughly a century and a half, no general, comprehensive history of it had ever been written prior to *ALASKANA CATHOLICA*. This is not to say that the writing of such a history had never been contemplated, nor that brief historical sketches and monographs of people, places and time-periods had not been produced.

As early as January 14, 1925, Father Julius Jetté, S.J., wrote to his Father Provincial, Joseph M. Piet, "What I have begun to write is the complete history of the Alaska Mission." Two years later, on February 24, 1927, at Akulurak, Father Jetté died, leaving a manuscript scarcely begun. In 1953, Father Joseph F. McElmeel, S.J., wrote: "It is my hope that the mountain of good material which we have in the Alaska archive will soon be put to good use. The stories of such men as Lucchesi, Sifton, Rossi, Jetté, *et al.* should be given to the world." In his book, *When Jesuits Were Giants*, published in 1999, historian Cornelius M. Buckley, S.J., referring to former Jesuit missionaries in Alaska, wrote, "Whole biographies beg to be written." What he said of Jesuit missionaries can equally well be said of many other Catholic Alaskans.

As I began the full-time ministry of writing *ALASKANA CATHOLICA*, I was heartened by the thoughts that I had for over four decades called Alaska home, had met all its Catholic bishops—except for its first, Bishop Joseph R. Crimont, S.J.—and knew many of the veteran Alaskan missionaries and many of Alaska's Native people well. Having traveled extensively throughout much of Alaska, I had spent time on its Bering Strait islands, hiked its high country, boated and floated its rivers, and was familiar with its natural wonders. And I had read widely, researched in-depth, and written about many people, places, and things Alaskan. In mind and heart, I was thoroughly "Alaskanized." I felt myself qualified and ready to write a Catholic-Alaskan, an Alaskan-Catholic history.

ALASKANA CATHOLICA reflects my esteem and respect for people and matters both Catholic and Alaskan. In keeping with my intentions and hopes, may it inform, interest, and inspire the living, while it, at the same time, keeps alive and honors the memory of the dead.

FATHER LOUIS L. RENNER, S.J.

INTRODUCTION

A pioneer Jesuit Alaskan missionary spoke true, when he wrote: "There was a good deal of misery and very little poetry in our early missions in Alaska." I hope that readers of *ALASKANA CATHOLICA* will find the reading about some of that misery anything but a miserable experience and that they will delight in the occasional touches of poetry that writing about Alaska and its people inevitably brings with it.

ALASKANA CATHOLICA is intended to be "user friendly." It is in the format of an encyclopedic dictionary, containing diverse topical and biographical entries arranged alphabetically. A time-line at the beginning, along with an alphabetically arranged list of entries, and an index, are meant to make for quick easy reference. All entries are cross-referenced. Boldface font indicates this. Every item in the extensive bibliography at the end of the volume is numbered. Numbers in boldface font at the end of entries refer the reader to the corresponding numbers of the bibliography.

To the extent possible, names of photographers and sources of photographs are given. Unknown photographers and sources are herewith nevertheless gratefully acknowledged.

I deliberately chose the encyclopedia-dictionary format, because this enabled me to treat each topic as a mini-history and each biography as a mini-biography having its own chronologically arranged sequence of events, its own beginning, middle and end. The entries, though obviously never exhaustive, are complete in themselves, able to stand on their own. This has, admittedly, led to some redundancies or repetition, but it saves the reader an undue amount of page flipping. In keeping with the intent of being "user friendly," few abbreviations are used and exact dates are supplied. In a given entry, the full name of a particular person is, as a general rule, given only the first time it occurs.

Most of the entries in *ALASKANA CATHOLICA* were obvious choices. A number of them, however, were chosen rather arbitrarily, as representative of a certain class or group of people. *ALASKANA CATHOLICA* is designed to be inclusive rather than exclusive. It offers biographical sketches of many who helped make the Catholic Church in Alaska, and of some in Alaska who were made by the Catholic Church in Alaska. While certain sketches may, in the eyes of some readers, seem to have as their subject persons of little importance, those persons may well be heroes in the eyes of their own people. Readers who know something about the history of the Catholic Church in Alaska will notice some glaring omissions. This was not by choice on my part. In some cases, there was simply no data available; in others, the person in question opted not to be included. I made every effort to solicit basic biographical data from them, or to dig it out myself whenever possible. That this was generally the case is attested to by Bishop Michael W. Warfel's question to me, after I submitted to him my entry about him for his approval, whether I had ever worked for the C.I.A.

ALASKANA CATHOLICA has as one of its aims to offer readers something more than just bare-bones reference data. Accordingly, some entries about a given individual or place or program have a story, or a "tapestry" woven out of mission diary entries, attached to them. These are intended, in addition to providing readers with historical information and interesting reading, to provide them also with a kind of "you are there" experience of times past and of places remote to them.

A word about what by some might be considered "orthographical niceties." I purposely tended to do more capitalizing of words than was customary, as the third millennium dawned. I felt it desirable to distinguish, for example, between Church as institution and church as building; between Brother/Sister as Religious and brother/sister as sibling; between Father as priest and father as parent; between Religious as member of some Order/Congregation and religious as a common adjective; between Order/Congregation as established Church group and order/congregation as command/gathering; etc. Traditionally, Catholics have referred to their parishes as, for example, St. Leo's, St. Rita's, St. Patrick's, or even simply as St. Pat's. As of the year 2004, it had become common practice to drop the possessive endings. Throughout *ALASKANA CATHOLICA*, I have tended to adhere to the more traditional, more familiar form. Furthermore, I have not drawn sharp distinctions between priest as rector, pastor, quasi-pastor, associate pastor, assistant pastor, or as visiting or supply priest. Nor have I always distinguished between a parish, a quasi-parish, a mission or, a dependent station, or between a church and a chapel. In many cases, the distinction, if there was one, was virtually meaningless. The same might be said as to whether a given church was blessed or dedicated; and if dedicated, whether it was dedicated "under the title of," or "in honor of," or to some saint or mystery or title of Our Lord or Mary. Again, the differences between the various expressions, where there actually were differences, were relatively insignificant.

Proper names of places, as well as both the first and last names of some of the early, foreign-born missionaries to Alaska, have been spelled variously in books, on maps, and in manuscripts. Some of the names of these missionaries took on, in the course of time, a more or less standardized, Americanized spelling. In any case, throughout *ALASKANA CATHOLICA*, I have consistently used the same spelling for proper names of places and people. Americanized last names of people are generally used. Both the original names and the Americanized names of a given individual are mentioned in the biographical sketch of the person in question, for example, Antonio Chiavassa/Anthony Keyes, Bartolomeo Chiaudano/Bartholomew Keogh, Johannes Sifferlen/John Sifton, and Filiberto Tornielli/Philibert Turnell.

I considered adding a glossary of terms, but felt it to be unnecessary. The meaning of most of the expressions is clear from the context in which they occur, or can be found in any collegiate dictionary. The one notable exception is "tertianship," occurring in the biographical sketches of almost every Jesuit priest. Tertianship, also known as "the third probation"—the first probation being a brief period of postulancy, and the second that of the two-year novitiate proper—constitutes the last stage of the Jesuit training process. It begins with a 30-day retreat, as did the novitiate. While making his tertianship, a Jesuit studies in depth the Constitutions of the Society of Jesus, undertakes various apostolic works, reflects on his life and call as a Jesuit, and, in general, rekindles some of the fervor supposedly lost since his novitiate days. All this he does under the direction of an older, experienced Jesuit, known as the Tertian Instructor.

Entries in a typical encyclopedic dictionary are produced by many different authors. This is not the case here. All the entries in *ALASKANA CATHOLICA* were written by me. Material for them was, to be sure, derived, in varying degrees, from a great variety of sources, published and unpublished. The bibliography reflects many of the sources to which I am indebted. I drew liberally upon obituaries of Oregon Province Jesuits by Father Neill R. Meany, S.J. A few of the entries are virtual reprints of articles that first appeared in *The Alaskan Shepherd*, a newsletter that I produced for over 20 years which was sent out to the benefactors of the Missionary Diocese of Fairbanks. Many of the entries are, in varying degrees, simply autobiographical sketches written in the third person, sketches solicited and adapted by me.

ALASKANA CATHOLICA is dedicated to St. Therese of Lisieux, the patroness of the Alaska Mission. My life-long devotion to her was implanted in me when I was in the fifth grade and attended the weekly "Little Flower Devotions" in Holy Rosary Church in Tacoma, Washington. In October 1964, I had the privilege of offering Mass at her altar in the Carmelite convent in Lisieux. I herewith acknowledge unique indebtedness to her spiritual assistance with *ALASKANA CATHOLICA*.

In addition to St. Therese, I owe a singular debt of gratitude also to Dr. Dorothy Jean Ray, who for years urged me to write a history of the Catholic Church in Alaska and who gave me valuable help when I finally began it. I acknowledge here, too, with heartfelt gratitude, the pains-taking, meticulous care Alaska historian Sister Margaret Cantwell, S.S.A., my chosen editorial collaborator, lavished on the manuscript. As I produced the entries, I sent them, batch after batch, to my classmate and fellow Jesuit, Father Armand M. Nigro, who read them and fed back important corrections and suggestions. *Tante grazie*, Caro Armando! Without the considerable help of Father Peter F. Gorges, entries relating to the Diocese of Juneau would simply not have become what they are. Know me deeply grateful, Peter. And special thanks, also, to Father Richard D. Tero for his long-time interest in and support of my writing endeavors. Thanks, Dick—and smooth sailin'!

Had not Father Provincial Robert B. Grimm, S.J., assigned me to the writing of *ALASKANA CATHOLICA*, and his successor Father Provincial John D. Whitney, S.J., continued to assign me to the writing of same, there would be no *ALASKANA CATHOLICA*. So, to them, for the confidence they placed in me and for their total, unstinting support while I was engaged in producing this history, likewise my sincerest thanks.

I herewith acknowledge very sincerely the help given me by a host of generous, supportive archivists: Jesuit Fathers Clifford A. Carroll, Neill R. Meany, and Wilfred P. Schoenberg, past archivists of the Jesuit Oregon Province Archives at Gonzaga University in Spokane, Washington, and present archivist thereof, David A. Kingma, C.A; Sister Margaret Cantwell, S.S.A., C.A., archivist of the Archives of the Sisters of St. Ann in Victoria, B.C., Canada; Father Richard D. Case, S.J., archivist of the Diocese of Fairbanks Archives, Fairbanks, Alaska; Father Joseph Cossette, S.J., archivist of the *Archives de la Compagnie de Jésus* in St. Jérôme, Quebec, Canada; Loretta Greene, C.A., archivist of the Sisters of Providence Archives in Seattle, Washington; Father Donald A. Hawkins, archivist of the New Orleans Province Archives in New Orleans, Louisiana; Deacon Gary Horton, archivist of the Diocese of Juneau Archives; Monte G. Kniffen, C.A., archivist of the Redemptorist Archives in Denver, Colorado; Father Liborio L. LaMartina, S.J.,

archivist of the Maryland Province Archives, Baltimore, Maryland; Very Rev. Steven C. Moore, archivist of the Archdiocese of Anchorage Archives; Francis E. Mueller, S.J., past archivist of the Diocese of Fairbanks Archives; Brother Daniel J. Peterson, S.J., archivist of the California Province Archives at Los Gatos, California; and Julianne Ruby, archivist of the Ursuline Center Archives in Great Falls, Montana.

I owe a special debt of gratitude to the many who graciously favored me with an autobiographical sketch: Allie, Aloralrea, Anderson, Bates, Bergquist, Beuzer, Boone, Boulet, Bugarin, Burik, Busch, Cardy, Case, Cochran, Cronin, Delmore, Desso, de Verteuil, Dibb, Falsey, Fitz-Patrick, F. Fox, Frister, Gallagher, Gorges, Gurr, Hargreaves, Hartmann, D. Hebert, Hemmer, Hinsvark, Hoelsken, Jacobson, Kelliher, Kestler, Kolb, Konda, Jos. Laudwein, Levitre, Lopilato, Macke, Martinek, McGuigan, McMeel, F. Mueller, O'Malley, Ornowski, Pepin, Perreault, Peterson, Provinsal, Radich, Ruzicka, J. Ryan, Sander, Saudis, Shirey, Strass, Tam, Tero, Tozzi, Travers, and G. Wood.

I thank sincerely also a large number of others who helped make *ALASKANA CATHOLICA* the reality that it is: Sr. Diane Bardol, G.N.S.H.; Sr. Carol Bartol, G.N.S.H.; La Rae Bartolowits; Mary G. Beck; Sr. Marie Anne Brent, S.H.F.; Fr. Gerald Brunet, O.M.I.; Annemiek Brunklaus; Mary Joe Burgener; Fr. Anthony S. Coca, S.J.; Dcn. Walter Corrigan, Jr.; Beverly Dalzell; Thomas Fitterer; Claire Fitzgaireld; Rt. Rev. Wesley W. Izer, S.D.B.; Robbie Izzard; Sr. Jill Jaeb, O.S.U.; Ray Lizotte; Fr. John J. Morris, S.J.; Little Sister Odette; Sr. Francis Xavier Porter, O.S.U.; Renamary Rauchenstein; John Roscoe; Sr. Joyce Ross, R.S.M; Fr. Paul Scanlon, O.P.; Sr. Zita Simon, O.P.; Patricia Walter; Barbara Walters; and Teena Woscek. I owe a particular debt of gratitude to Kent Sturgis of Aftershocks Media/Epicenter Press Inc. for his most valuable and much appreciated suggestion regarding the placement of photographs. Fr. Leo C. Desso needs to be thanked for kindly granting permission for the use of images that appeared in the St. Michael's Parish, Palmer, Alaska, Golden Jubilee book.

For providing me with the ideal working atmosphere and furniture for my writing project which I enjoyed in room 311 in Jesuit House on the campus of Gonzaga University, I express fraternal thanks to Father James M. McDonough, S.J. I thank all my fellow Gonzaga Jesuits who heartened me with their prayers and interest, as I carried out my "mission." A word of special thanks goes to Brother Edward S. "Bud" Jennings, S.J., for his prayers and abiding concern for its successful outcome.

I thank Vicki Craigen sincerely for setting me up so well with the computer that expedited the writing beyond my fondest expectations. And sincere thanks to Joe Previtali and Michael Rorholm for the gracious, much-appreciated computer-related help they unstintingly gave me. Bill Lockyear, I thank you sincerely for the expertise and dedication you brought to contract matters. Darlene Allred and Maria Howe, know me truly grateful for the painstaking care with which you tracked donations from benefactors helping with the publication costs of *ALASKANA CATHOLICA*.

Penultimately, and with sincere apologies, I thank all the many whose help I have here, inadvertently, failed to acknowledge, even though they, too, played an important role in the making of this history.

My final, and ultimate, expressions of sincerest, heartfelt gratitude—gratitude so richly merited—go out to Mr. Robert A. Clark and to Ms. Ariane C. Smith of the of The Arthur H. Clark Company. Bob and Ariane, without the professionalism and care you brought to the production of *ALASKANA CATHOLICA*, it would simply not be the book that it is. I am so deeply grateful to you!

FATHER LOUIS L. RENNER, S.J.

CHRONOLOGY

1779
Franciscan Fray Juan **Riobó**, chaplain on a Spanish exploration ship, offers the first Mass ever celebrated in **Alaska**, near present-day **Craig** in Southeastern Alaska on May 13.

1847
Alaska ceases, ecclesiastically speaking, to be a "no-man's land," when Modeste **Demers** is consecrated Bishop of Vancouver Island and given jurisdiction over that island and over all British and Russian possessions as far north as the "glacial sea."

1862–63
Oblate Father Jean Séguin, entering Alaska from the Canadian North, spends the winter at Fort Yukon, and in the spring travels downriver as far as Nuklukayet (**Tanana**).

1867
The United States purchases Alaska from Russia. It takes possession on October 18.

1868
Father Joseph **Mandart** visits **Sitka**, February through July.

1870
Oblate Father Émile Petitot visits Fort Yukon briefly during the summer.

1872–73–74
Oblate Bishop Isidore Clut and future Oblate Father Auguste Lecorre experience a fruitless winter at Fort Yukon. In the spring of 1873, Bishop Clut returns to Canada, while Father Lecorre goes to **St. Michael**, where he spends the winter of 1873–74, before returning to Canada.

1873
Father Charles **Seghers** becomes Bishop of Vancouver Island, and makes his first trip to Alaska, visiting Sitka and **Unalaska**.

1877
Bishop Seghers and Father Mandart arrive at **Nulato**, on July 31, to spend the year there.

1878
Bishop Seghers and Father John **Althoff** visit Southeastern Alaska.

1879
Father Althoff is appointed resident priest of the newly established St. Rose of Lima parish, **Wrangell**, on May 4. He builds the first Catholic church there. Bishop Seghers again visits Southeastern Alaska.

1880
The 1880 U.S. census of Alaska shows a population of 33,426 people with only 430 of them being non-Alaskan Natives. Bishop Seghers becomes Archbishop of Oregon City on December 20.

1882
Father Althoff offers the first Mass in **Juneau**, on July 17. Father William **Heynen** visits Sitka.

1883
Father Patrick Healy, S.J., on board the U.S. Revenue Cutter *Corwin*, captained by his brother, Michael Healy, visits the west coast of northern Alaska. He is the first Jesuit to set foot in Alaska, but not as a missionary.

1885

Archbishop Seghers again visits Alaska. Father Althoff begins to reside in Juneau. In Sitka, Father Heynen transforms an old carriage barn into St. Gregory Nazianzen Church and offers the first Mass in it on December 13.

1886

In Juneau, three Sisters of St. **Ann** open a hospital in September and a school in November. Archbishop Seghers is shot to death at Bishop Rock near Nulato on November 28.

1887

Jesuit Fathers Paschal **Tosi**, Aloysius **Robaut**, and Aloysius **Ragaru**, and Jesuit Brother Carmelo **Giordano** enter Alaska. Father Ragaru takes up station in Nuklukayet (Tanana). Father Tosi founds St. Peter Claver mission at Nulato.

1888

Father Tosi builds the first church at Nulato. Father Robaut founds **Holy Cross Mission**. Three Sisters of St. Ann arrive at Holy Cross on September 4.

1889

Father Joseph **Tréca**, S.J., founds the Nelson Island mission of St. Alphonsus Rodriguez, at **Tununak**. The first Catholic church in Juneau, dedicated under the title of the Nativity of the Blessed Virgin Mary, is blessed by Bishop John Lemmens of Victoria on July 9.

1892

At **Ohagamiut**, a mission house dedicated to St. Ignatius Loyola is built.

1892–93

Father Tosi is in Europe to recruit priests for Alaska, and in Rome to visit Pope Leo XIII.

1894

Alaska becomes a Prefecture Apostolic, in July, with Father Tosi as its first Prefect Apostolic. St. Joseph's boarding school, staffed by four Sisters of St. Ann, opens at **Akulurak**.

1895

Alaska is separated from the Diocese of Vancouver Island. Jesuits, in the person of Father John **René**, take over ministry in Juneau. Two Sisters of St. Ann open a school in **Douglas**.

1896

Our Lady of the Mines Chapel opens in Douglas on December 8.

1897

Father René replaces Father Tosi as Prefect Apostolic. The Sisters of St. Ann build a hospital in Douglas.

1898

St. Mark's parish in **Skagway** is founded. Father Tosi dies on January 14. St. Ann's Hospital opens in Douglas on March 19. The mission at St. Michael is established. St. Joseph's boarding school at Akulurak is closed for lack of pupils. In the summer, Father Francis **Barnum**, S.J., on the U.S. Revenue Cutter *Bear* visits the High Arctic, the first Jesuit missionary to do so.

1899

In **Eagle**, Father Francis **Monroe**, S.J., establishes St. Francis Xavier's mission. Father René visits **Nome**, the first priest to do so, in August. Three Sisters of St. Ann open a day school at Nulato on November 2.

1900

A new church, dedicated to St. Michael, is built at St. Michael. Father Monroe opens a hospital in Eagle. Our Lady of the Mines Church opens in Douglas on December 24.

1901

Father Aloysius **Jacquet**, S.J., establishes St. Joseph's parish in Nome, builds a church and rectory. The new church is blessed on November 17.

1902

The Sisters of **Providence** arrive in Nome to staff Holy Cross Hospital on June 19.

1903

Mass is offered for the first time in **Valdez**, by Father Philibert **Turnell**, S.J., on August 15. Father Monroe's hospital in Eagle is closed. St. Ignatius Mission at Ohagamiut burns on November 30.

1904

Father Joseph **Crimont**, S.J., becomes Prefect Apostolic of Alaska in May. A permanent mission, dedicated to St. Aloysius, is opened at Tanana. The first Mass ever offered in **Fairbanks** is celebrated in the District Court House by Father Monroe on July 2, before he goes on to establish Immaculate Conception parish and build a church. At **Kokrines**, Father Ragaru builds a house with a small room added to serve as a chapel. The Brothers of Christian Instruction of Ploermel (**F.I.C.**) first begin serving in Alaska, at Holy Cross Mission. In **Ketchikan**, the old schoolhouse is purchased and converted into Holy Name's Church. The Sisters of Providence open St. Joseph's Parochial School in Nome on October 5. The first Mass offered in the newly-built Immaculate Conception Church, Fairbanks, is celebrated on November 1.

1905

Three **Ursuline** Sisters arrive at Akulurak to staff St. Mary's Mission boarding school. St. Francis Xavier's parish in Valdez is established. Holy Angels Mission for the Eskimos opens in Nome.

1906

At Holy Cross Mission, the new Holy Family Church is finished. In Nome, the new Holy Cross Hospital opens. In Fairbanks, St. Joseph's Hospital is dedicated on November 25.

1907

At **Marys Igloo**, Our Lady of Lourdes mission is opened. At **Hamilton**, a church is built.

1908

St. Francis Xavier's Church is built in Valdez, St. Joseph's Church in **Cordova**, and a new St. Rose of Lima Church in Wrangell replaces the 1879 building. At Kokrines, the Episcopal church is bought and converted into a Catholic church by Father Julius

Jetté, S.J. The Ursuline Sisters establish a mission, "St. Ursula's-by-the-Sea," at St. Michael. Father Joseph **Chapdelaine**, S.J., establishes St. Bernard's mission at **Stebbins** in October.

1909

Seven Sisters of St. Benedict temporarily staff St. Joseph's Hospital in Fairbanks.

1910

Father Edward **Brown**, S.J., builds a new Nativity of the Blessed Virgin Mary Church in Juneau, and Father Matthias Schmitt, S.J., builds the first Sacred Heart Church in **Seward**. The Sisters of Providence begin to staff St. Joseph's Hospital, Fairbanks, in October.

1911

Brother Ulric **Paquin**, S.J., freezes to death near St. Michael on January 27. Father Monroe builds a chapel and residence at **Iditarod**. A new prefabricated church is put up at Marys Igloo, and a new residence for priests and Brothers at Holy Cross Mission. Immaculate Conception Church, Fairbanks, is relocated across the Chena River in November.

1912

The Jesuit mission field of northern Alaska is transferred from the French-Canadian Province to the California Province. A new St. Mary's Church is built at Akulurak. **Ruby** is provided with a new chapel.

1913

The Kokrines mission is closed. **Little Diomede** Island is visited for the first time by a Catholic priest, Father Bellarmine **Lafortune**, S.J., in June.

1914

The **Pilot Station** mission, named for St. Charles Spinola, is established. At Akulurak, boys, too, begin to be admitted into the boarding school.

1915

At Nulato, a new St. Peter Claver Church is constructed. In **Anchorage**, the first Holy Family

Church is built through the efforts of Father William **Shepherd**, S.J.

1916

The Sisters of St. Joseph of Peace–Newark open "Seward General Hospital" on January 25. Holy Family parish is established in Anchorage. Father **Hubert Post**, S.J., visits the village on **Little Diomede** Island, and builds a chapel at **Teller**. Father Lafortune, on the *Bear*, visits **King Island** for the first time. Alaska becomes a Vicariate Apostolic on December 22.

1917

The flooding and cave-in of the Treadwell mines on Douglas Island occurs on April 20–21. Father Crimont is consecrated a bishop and becomes Alaska's first Vicar Apostolic on July 25.

1918

The first ordination of a Catholic priest in Alaska takes place in Juneau, when G. Edgar **Gallant** is ordained by Bishop Crimont on March 30. The **Pilgrim Hot Springs** property is transformed into Our Lady of Lourdes Mission. St. Joseph's Grade School and Holy Cross Hospital in Nome close, and the Sisters of Providence leave Nome. Father Monroe builds **Nenana**'s first Catholic church. "St.-Ursula's-by-the-Sea" convent at St. Michael burns on December 9.

1919

"Seward General Hospital" closes on June 7. Ursuline Sisters arrive at Pilgrim Hot Springs on August 16. The new St. Ann's School in Juneau is dedicated.

1920

Chapels are built at **Haines** and **Galena**. Sisters of St. Ann leave Douglas.

1921

The **Mountain Village** mission, dedicated to St. Lawrence, is established. The first Mass in the new church is offered on October 7.

1922

In Sitka, the second St. Gregory of Nazianzen Church is built by Father Aloysius **Roccati**, S.J.

1923

In Ketchikan, on February 22, Bishop Crimont blesses Little Flower Hospital, and the Sisters of St. Joseph of Peace–Newark take charge of it. Father Frederick **Ruppert**, S.J., freezes to death near Pilgrim Hot Springs on December 15.

1924

At **Chaneliak**, St. Margaret's Mission is established by Father John **Sifton**, S.J., on November 26.

1925

St. Therese of Lisieux is declared patroness of the Alaska Mission by Bishop Crimont. Fire destroys the house of the Sisters and girls at Akulurak on June 12.

1926

In Douglas, Our Lady of the Mines Church burns. Father Philip **Delon**, S.J., builds a church at Upper **Kalskag**. At **Paimiut**, a mission is built. At Akulurak, the Sisters and girls move into their new quarters on December 9.

1927

At **Kashunuk**, Sacred Heart Mission is established and a church built by Brother John **Hess**, S.J., and crew. Father Martin **Lonneux**, S.J., builds a chapel at Tununak.

1928

At **Hooper Bay**, Little Flower of Jesus Mission is established and a church built by Brother Hess and crew. Immaculate Conception Church in Fairbanks receives stained-glass windows.

1929

On **King Island**, Christ the King Church is built by Father Lafortune. At **Kotzebue**, St. Francis Xavier's Mission is established and a church built by Father William F. Walsh. St. Mary's Church at Akulurak burns on August 15.

1930

At **Scammon Bay**, Blessed Sacrament Mission is founded by Father Francis **Ménager**, S.J. A new Fathers House is built at Nulato. The *Marquette Missionary* crashes at Kotzebue, killing Fathers Delon and Walsh, and Ralph Wien on October 12.

1931

In Skagway, the cornerstone of Pius X Mission is laid on August 30. At **Nightmute**, Brother Hess builds Our Lady of Perpetual Help Church.

1932

On Little Diomede Island, St. Jude's Mission is founded by Father Lafortune. Blessed Sacrament Chapel is built at Scammon Bay by Father **John Fox**, S.J. The Kashunuk mission is moved to Old **Chevak**. At Hooper Bay, the Sisters of Our Lady of the **Snows** are founded by Father Fox on August 5. Classes begin at Pius X Mission School on October 18.

1933

The new St. Mary's Church at Akulurak is blessed on December 7.

1934

Father Paul **Deschout**, S.J., reestablishes St. Joseph's Mission at Tununak. In Nome, the Eskimo workshop built by Fathers Lafortune and **Van der Pol** in 1905 is demolished.

1935

In **Palmer**, the first Mass is offered on May 26.

1936

The new St. Jude's Church on Little Diomede is completed.

1937

The St. Michael's log church in Palmer is dedicated on July 24. A new St. Joseph's Church is built at Tununak.

1937–38

Father Bernard **Hubbard**, S.J., and his party spend the winter on King Island. The statue of Christ the King is placed atop the island and blessed on October 31.

1938

A mission is built at **Keyaluvik**. Father Fox builds a convent at **Hooper Bay**. The new Holy Name Church in Ketchikan is dedicated on November 24.

1939

Father Walter **Fitzgerald**, S.J., is consecrated Coadjutor Bishop of the Vicariate of Alaska on February 24. Providence Hospital in Anchorage opens on June 29. At **Aniak**, Father Ménager builds the first St. Theresa's Church. Msgr. Gallant offers the first Mass ever celebrated in **Yakutat** on August 24.

1940

The new St. Rose of Lima Church at Wrangell is finished on June 2.

1941

The Pilgrim Hot Springs Mission is closed by Father Edmund **Anable**, S.J., on July 31. The chapel at the **Shrine** of St. Therese near Juneau is dedicated on October 26.

1942

At the old site of **Chefornak**, Father Deschout builds St. Catherine of Siena Church. Father Ménager, the first priest to do so, takes up station in **Bethel** on August 16.

1943

The first Immaculate Conception Church in Bethel is built by Father Ménager. At Kashunuk, the semisubterranean church, dedicated to the Sacred Heart, is built by Father Jules **Convert**, S.J.

1944

In **Kodiak**, St. Mary's parish is established and Griffin Memorial Hospital is taken over by the **Grey Nuns** of the Sacred Heart in November.

1945

In Nome, by bringing together two military surplus buildings, Father Anable constructs the second St. Joseph's Church, opened on Easter Sunday 1946. Bishop Crimont dies in Juneau on May 20; Bishop Fitzgerald automatically succeeds him as Vicar Apostolic of Alaska. At **Marshall**, the new chapel of the Mother of God is blessed by Bishop Fitzgerald. Bishop Fitzgerald suppresses the Sisters of Our Lady of the Snows effective as of August 5. Crimont Hall in Skagway burns on November 16.

1946

Holy Name Grade School opens in Ketchikan. Immaculate Conception Grade School opens in Fairbanks. The first St. Joseph's Church in Nome is sold to the U.S. Smelting, Refining and Mining Company and moved to the outskirts of town and converted into a warehouse. Father Norman **Donohue**, S.J, builds Blessed Sacrament Church at Scammon Bay.

1947

Bishop Fitzgerald dies on July 19. The new St. Charles Spinola Church at Pilot Station is blessed on August 15. At **McGrath**, the Quonset hut church, dedicated to St. Michael, is formally opened on November 16.

1948

Father Francis **Gleeson**, S.J., is appointed Vicar Apostolic of Alaska on January 8, consecrated bishop in Spokane, Washington, on April 5, and installed in Juneau on May 30. In **Dillingham**, Holy Rosary Mission is opened by Father George **Endal**, S.J., on April 22. Jesuit Brothers George **Feltes** and Aloysius **Laird**, the first Alaskan missionaries ever to enter Alaska exclusively by road, drive from Spokane to Fairbanks in the spring. The new Holy Family Church in Anchorage is completed in October.

1949

New churches are built: at **New Knock Hock**, by Father Donohue; at Ruby, by Father James **Spils**, S.J.; and at Nightmute, by Father Deschout.

1950

Father Endal builds Holy Rosary Church in Dillingham. "Our Lady of the Snows" becomes the official name of the Nulato mission. At New **Chevak**, the first Sacred Heart Church is built by Father Henry **Hargreaves**, S.J. At **Tok**, Father John **Buchanan**, S.J., begins to build the log chapel, the original part of the present Holy Rosary Church, in July. The new Dillingham church burns on November 15.

1951

The new addition to St. Joseph's Hospital in Fairbanks is blessed on March 18. At Alakanuk, Father Segundo **Llorente**, S.J., builds a new St. Ignatius Loyola Church. St. Mary's Mission is moved from Akulurak to **Andreafsky** on August 3. The new Immaculate Conception Grade School building in Fairbanks is blessed on September 3. Father Dermot **O'Flanagan** is consecrated bishop for the newly established Diocese of Juneau on October 3, and installed as the first Bishop of Juneau on October 7.

1952

The **Little Sisters of Jesus** establish a Fraternity in Nome. Father Hargreaves moves the church from Keyaluvik to **Newtok**. At **Unalakleet**, Father Convert builds Holy Angels Church. At Chefornak's new site, a new St. Catherine of Siena Church is built. St. Theresa's Church in Nenana burns on December 19.

1953

A new Fathers House is built at Nulato. Father Convert builds a new St. Michael's Church at St. Michael. A log church, dedicated to Our Lady of the Angels, is built in **Kenai**. At **Emmonak**, a new Sacred Heart Church is built. In Nenana, the burnt church is replaced, on the same foundation, with a new one. At Holy Cross Mission, high school classes are taught for the first time on the Yukon River, by Sister Anne Rita, S.S.A., and William **Loyens**, S.J., in the fall.

1954

The Little Sisters of Jesus establish a Fraternity on Little Diomede Island. Bishop Gleeson visits Little Diomede Island, the first Major Superior to do so, on May 2. At **Barrow**, Father **Thomas Cunningham**, S.J., builds St. Patrick's Church out of a military surplus Quonset hut. A parochial school opens in Kodiak.

1955

Father Endal's school in Dillingham burns on March 26. Fathers Hargreaves and **John Wood**, S.J., build a new Blessed Sacrament Church at Scammon Bay. Father Wood also builds a new Holy Family Church at **Newtok**. Monroe Catholic High School opens in Fairbanks. Bishop Gleeson and Father James **Conwell**, S.J., move into Loyola Hall, Fairbanks, on December 10.

1956

The missions of northern Alaska become quasi-parishes. The first high school graduation at St. Mary's Mission, Andreafsky, takes place. The new Immaculate Conception Church in Bethel and the new St. Bernard's Church at Stebbins are finished. Monroe Catholic High School in Fairbanks is dedicated on September 2. The Holy Cross Mission boarding school is officially closed on September 14. A nucleus of Holy Cross students and staff, in "Operation Snowbird," move to **Copper Valley School** on October 14. Volunteers, forerunners of the future **Jesuit Volunteer Corps**, begin to serve at the newly-opened school.

1957

At the first high school graduation at Copper Valley School, Anna Patsey and Teddy Mayac graduate. The **Paimiut** mission burns. A new church is built at Mountain Village. St. Anthony's parish in Anchorage is established by Bishop O'Flanagan on August 28.

1958

The Little Sisters of Jesus build a house on Little Diomede Island. The Byzantine Rite parish of St. Nicholas of Myra is established in Anchorage by Bishop Nicholas Elko. Father Vsevolod Roshko begins his seven-year ministry in Dillingham by building the small Church of the Protective Stole of the Blessed Virgin Mary.

1959

Alaska becomes the 49th state of the union on January 3. Monroe Catholic High School in Fairbanks graduates its first senior class in May. Pius X Mission School in Skagway closes. A new St. Joseph's Church is built at Tununak. St. Nicholas of Myra Church in Anchorage is blessed by Bishop Nicholas T. Elko on September 13.

1960

The mission on King Island closes in the spring. St. Anthony's Church in Anchorage is dedicated on June 13. The Little Sisters of Jesus establish a Fraternity in Fairbanks. Father Paul **Linssen**, S.J., drowns in a boating accident at the mouth of the Kuskokwim River on September 21. Father

Llorente is elected to the State House of Representatives in November. The new St. Michael's log church in McGrath, built by Father John Wood, is ready for the Christmas Mass.

1961

Redemptorist Fathers from the Oakland Province, California, begin ministry on the Kenai Peninsula. Central Catholic Junior High School in Anchorage opens on September 18.

1962

At **Koyukuk**, a new St. Patrick's Church is finished. At **Teller**, a building purchased by Father Lawrence **Nevue**, S.J., is transformed into St. Ann's Catholic Church. The Diocese of Fairbanks is established and Bishop Gleeson appointed its first Ordinary on August 8. Holy Rosary Mission School in Dillingham closes in September. In the Mendenhall Valley, near Juneau, the mission of St. Paul the Apostle comes into being. The move into the new Providence Hospital in Anchorage is made on October 26. In **Soldotna**, in the new Our Mother of Perpetual Help Church, Christmas Mass is celebrated for the first time.

1963

Bishop Gleeson is installed as the first Bishop of Fairbanks on February 21. A fire at St. Mary's Mission, Andreafsky, causes major damage on March 26. Bishop O'Flanagan solemnly blesses the new St. Andrew's basement church in **Eagle River** on May 12. The new Our Mother of Perpetual Help Church in Soldotna is dedicated in May. Our Lady of Guadalupe Church is built at **Russian Mission**.

1963–64

Father Pasquale Spoletini, S.J., builds a "Catholic Center" at Kotzebue. A gymnasium is built at St. Mary's Mission Boarding School.

1964

The "Good Friday" earthquake strikes Alaska on March 27. Father George **Boileau**, S.J., is consecrated Coadjutor Bishop of Fairbanks at Copper Valley School on July 31. People of Nightmute move and found the new village of **Toksook Bay**. The new St. Peter the Apostle Church at **Ninilchik** is dedicated. The new St. James Church at **Seldovia** is ready for the Christmas Mass.

1965

Bishop Boileau dies on February 25. The groundbreaking ceremony for Ketchikan's new Holy Name Grade School takes place on April 11. Angus **McDonald** is ordained a priest by Bishop Gleeson on April 24. He is the first priest to be ordained in and for the Diocese of Fairbanks, and the only priest to be ordained in Immaculate Conception Church, Fairbanks. The new St. Joseph's Church in Cordova is blessed on May 1. A new Immaculate Conception Church is built at Upper Kalskag by Father **Paul Mueller**, S.J.; as is a new St. Teresa's Church at Kaltag by Father Convert. The church is moved from **Chaneliak** to **Kotlik** by Father James **Plamondon**, S.J., in the winter of 1965–66.

1966

The Archdiocese of Anchorage is established on February 9. Father **Joseph Ryan**, its first archbishop, is consecrated bishop on March 25. Holy Family Church in Anchorage becomes a Cathedral and Archbishop Ryan is installed as Archbishop of Anchorage on April 14. St. Benedict's Church in Anchorage is established by decree on May 26. Sacred Heart Cathedral in Fairbanks is dedicated on June 17. The new Our Lady of the Lake Church at **Big Lake** is dedicated in July. The new St. Teresa's Church at Kaltag, the new St. Peter the Fisherman Church at Toksook Bay, and the new St. Ignatius Church at Alakanuk are finished. A new St. Michael's Church, and a nearby rectory, are built in **Palmer**. The old Holy Cross Hospital in Nome is taken down by Father Paul Mueller. In Ketchikan, classes begin to be held in the new Holy Name Grade School. The St. Francis Xavier's Mission in Valdez becomes a parish in November.

1967

Jesuit Father General Pedro Arrupe visits Alaska in April. The Archdiocese of Anchorage, by official decree, is placed under the patronage of St. Joseph the Worker on April 28. Central Catholic Junior High School in Anchorage closes. At **Northway**, St. Ann's Chapel is relocated. The new Sacred Heart Church in Seward is dedicated by Archbishop Ryan on August 6. Fairbanks is severely flooded in mid-August. A new Sacred Heart Church is finished at Emmonak. The log church, dedicated to St. Aloysius, is constructed in Tanana by Father Charles **Saalfeld**, S.J. A new Our Lady of Guadalupe Church at Russian Mission replaces the old. At **Willow**, St. Christopher's parish is established. At Barrow, a new prefabricated rectory is put up by Father McDonald. Hubbard Memorial School opens in Anchorage. St. Andrew's parish in Eagle River is established on October 16. The new Our Lady of the Lake Church at Big Lake burns in November.

1968

Father Robert **Whelan**, S.J., is consecrated Coadjutor Bishop of Fairbanks on February 22. The new St. Mary's School in Kodiak is dedicated on May 7. The new Our Lady of the Angels Church in **Kenai** is dedicated on May 25. St. Ann's Hospital and St. Ann's School in Juneau close. The new St. Francis Xavier's Church in Valdez is dedicated on June 20. St. Paul the Apostle Mission in Juneau is declared an independent mission by Bishop O'Flanagan in June. Bishop O'Flanagan resigns as Bishop of Juneau in June. St. Joseph's Hospital in Fairbanks closes at midnight on June 30. The new St. Anthony's Church in Anchorage is dedicated on October 27. Fire destroys the church at Big Lake in November. Bishop Whelan becomes Bishop of Fairbanks on November 30.

1969

Jesuits move into the Birchwood residence on February 8. J. Michael Hornick is ordained a priest in Westerville, Ohio, on May 17. He is the first priest to be ordained for the Archdiocese of Anchorage. Hubbard Memorial School in Anchorage closes. Father Andrew Eördögh, S.J., takes down the Holy Family Church at Holy Cross. At **Umkumiut**, Father John **Hinsvark** builds Christ the King Church. The diocesan chancery building in Fairbanks is completed, as is the first Sacred Heart Church in **Wasilla**.

1970

Father Francis **Hurley** is ordained a bishop on March 19. The Diocese of Juneau begins publication of its diocesan newspaper, *The Inside Passage*. The Church of the Nativity parish is established at St. Marys. Our Lady of the Angels in Kenai and Our Lady of Perpetual Help in Soldotna achieve parish status on October 9. The **Eskimo Deacon Program** is formally inaugurated in Bethel on October 16.

1971
Copper Valley School closes. New rectories are built at Marshall and **Nunam Iqua** (Sheldon Point) by Brother John **Huck**, S.J., and Richard **McCaffrey**, S.J. In Hoonah, the new Sacred Heart Church is built. Radio station **KNOM** goes on the air on July 14. Bishop Hurley is appointed Ordinary of the Diocese of Juneau on July 20, and installed as the second Bishop of Juneau on September 8. Holy Spirit Retreat House (renamed "**Holy Spirit Center**" in 1999) is established. Brother Huck drowns in a boating accident on the lower Yukon on October 8. The new St. Bernard's Church in **Talkeetna** is dedicated by Archbishop Ryan on October 20.

1972
At Chefornak, St. Catherine of Siena Church burns on March 4. In Yakutat, St. Ann's Church is built. In St. Marys, Father Convert builds a parish center. St. Paul the Apostle Mission in Juneau is declared a parish. Bishop O'Flanagan dies in La Mesa, California on December 31.

1973
The new St. Gregory of Nazianzen Church in Sitka is dedicated by Bishop Hurley on September 3. The residence at 1127 Koyukuk Street in Fairbanks is acquired by the Diocese of Fairbanks. Fire blackens the inside of St. Peter's Church in Douglas in June.

1974
Alan Carl Abele is ordained a priest in Holy Family Cathedral, Anchorage on May 1. This is the first ordination to the priesthood in Anchorage. Father Louis **Renner**, S.J., visits King Island in June, and offers the last Masses celebrated there. Holy Family Church in Newtok burns in August. At St. Mary's Mission only the four-year high school is retained. A storm devastates King Island Village, Nome, in November. The new Our Lady of the Snows Church in Nulato is dedicated on November 10.

1975
St. Peter's Church in Douglas, damaged by the June 1973 fire, is rededicated in January. The Little Sisters of Jesus build a house in Nome. A new Holy Family Church is built at Newtok. At Marshall, Alvin Owletuk, the first Eskimo to be ordained to the permanent diaconate, is ordained on February 8. St. Elizabeth Ann Seton parish in Anchorage is established on Easter Sunday 1975. In **Homer**, the new log church, dedicated to St. John the Baptist, is blessed by Archbishop Ryan on June 21. St. Nicholas parish in **North Pole** is established on September 28. The new St. Therese of the Child Jesus Church in Skagway is dedicated on October 3.

1976
Archbishop Ryan's term as Archbishop of Anchorage ends on January 1. Bishop Hurley is appointed Archbishop of Anchorage on May 4. Immaculate Conception Church in Fairbanks is listed on the National Register of Historic Sites. The former Copper Valley School burns. The new St. Catherine of Siena Church at Chefornak is blessed in November. The new parish center for Our Lady of Guadalupe parish in Anchorage is dedicated on December 12.

1977
A new Little Flower of Jesus Church is built at Hooper Bay by Father Bernard **McMeel**, S.J. St. Mark's University Parish, Fairbanks, is established on March 3. Sister Josephine **Aloralrea**, O.S.U., makes her final profession on September 22. In Juneau, St. Ann's Nursing Home is established by Archbishop Hurley.

1978
On Little Diomede Island, a new St. Jude's Church is built by Father Thomas **Carlin**, S.J., and Jesuit Brothers Ignatius **Jakes** and James Lee. The new Holy Family Church at Newtok is dedicated by Bishop Whelan on July 26. The St. John Neumann Mission at **Cooper Landing** is dedicated by Archbishop Hurley on August 13. The new St. Nicholas Church in North Pole is dedicated by Bishop Whelan on December 3.

1979

Sacred Heart parish in Wasilla is established in January. Bishop Whelan blesses the new St. Jude's Church on Little Diomede Island on March 7. Father Michael **Kenny** is ordained a bishop on May 27 and installed as the third Bishop of Juneau on June 15. In Fairbanks, the new two-story Immaculate Conception Grade School is built.

1980

A new church in **Healy** is begun. St. Elizabeth Ann Seton Church and the new parochial school in Anchorage are dedicated.

1981

Pope John Paul II visits Anchorage on February 26. Archbishop Hurley dedicates the new St. Andrew's Church in Eagle River on May 27. In Haines, the new Sacred Heart Church is built by Father **James Ryan**.

1982

In Healy, Bishop Whelan dedicates the new Holy Mary of Guadalupe Church on May 30. The Unalakleet mission is raised to parish status by Bishop Whelan. Bishop Kenny dedicates the addition to St. Ann's Church in Yakutat on October 24.

1983

Bishop Whelan dedicates the new Sacred Heart Church at Chevak on April 13. Bishop Gleeson dies on April 30. The Brother Francis Shelter opens in Anchorage.

1984

Father Michael **Kaniecki**, S.J., is ordained Coadjutor Bishop of Fairbanks on May 1. Pope John Paul II visits Fairbanks on May 2 and blesses the cornerstone for the new Holy Name Church to be built in Ketchikan. Holy Mary of Guadalupe in Healy is formally established as a parish by Bishop Whelan on October 28.

1985

In Kaltag, Father James **Sebesta**, S.J., is "dressed" for Edgar **Kalland** at a "stickdance" on April 13. The vacated Pius X Mission building in Skagway burns. Bishop Kaniecki becomes Ordinary of the Diocese of Fairbanks on July 28. In Fairbanks, the Monroe Foundation, Inc. is created. The new Holy Name Church in Ketchikan is dedicated on October 20. In Galena, the new St. John Berchmans Church is built.

1986

The House of Prayer in Fairbanks opens on April 20. The Franciscan Friars begin ministry along the middle Yukon River. Bishop Kaniecki dedicates the new St. Theresa's Church at Aniak on September 14. The residence on Koyukuk Street in Fairbanks begins to serve as the Episcopal Residence. Soldotna's Our Mother of Perpetual Help Church becomes Our Lady of Perpetual Help Church.

1987

The oratorio, "Obedient Unto Death," composed by Father Normand **Pepin**, S.J., is premièred in Fairbanks on April 12. St. Mary's Mission High School closes in May. Cathedral of the Nativity of the Blessed Virgin Mary parish in Juneau and St. Peter's parish in Douglas merge into one parish on July 1. Bishop Kaniecki dedicates the new St. Lawrence Church at Mountain Village on August 23. Jesuits stationed in Fairbanks move into the new Kobuk Street residence in the summer. The roof of St. Elizabeth Ann Seton Church in Anchorage collapses on December 23.

1988

The new St. John Berchmans Church in Galena is dedicated on May 22. At Koyukuk, the old generator building is transformed into a new St. Patrick's Church to replace the old. The Little Sisters of Jesus close their Fraternity in Fairbanks and establish a new one in Anchorage.

1989

In Holy Cross, the new Holy Family Church is dedicated on May 17. In **Delta Junction**, the new Our Lady of Sorrows Church is dedicated on September 17.

1990

In Anchorage, a new St. Elizabeth Ann Seton Church is completed.

1991

The Archdiocese of Anchorage founds the Nativity of Jesus parish in Magadan, Russia, on January 4. The new St. Mary's Church in Kodiak is dedicated on March 10. The new Resurrection Chapel in Anchorage is dedicated on April 7. The Diocese of Fairbanks hosts a Tekakwitha Conference at St. Mary's Mission in late April. The new St. Raphael's Church near Fairbanks is dedicated on May 12. The new St. Mary's Church in Kodiak opens for services.

1992

In **Klawock**, the first St. John by the Sea Church is blessed by Bishop Kenny on April 28. Father Andrew **D'Arco** is killed in an accident at Aniak on May 27. Bishop Kaniecki blesses the new Monroe Junior High School. Construction on the second St. Patrick's Church in Barrow begins. A rooming-house is built in Nome for KNOM radio staff members.

1993

New churches are built in Bethel, Nome, and Unalakleet. Bishop Kaniecki dedicates the new St. Patrick's Church in Barrow on March 28, and KNOM's new Keller Broadcast Center on April 23. In Alakanuk, St. Ignatius Church is moved away from the eroding riverbank. The new Holy Cross Church in Anchorage is dedicated by Archbishop Hurley on September 12.

1994

Bishop Kaniecki dedicates the new St. Joseph's Church in Nome on March 19. In Juneau, the new Cathedral Parish Hall is completed. Sacred Heart Cathedral in Fairbanks receives a new roof during the summer and a new steeple on October 12.

1995

The new Church of the Holy Angels in Unalakleet is dedicated on January 29. Bishop Kenny dies suddenly in Jordan on February 19. The new Immaculate Conception Church in Bethel, built by Father McCaffrey, is dedicated by Bishop Kaniecki on April 30. At Pilot Station, the new St. Charles Spinola Church, designed by Deacon Paul **Per-reault**, is dedicated, likewise by Bishop Kaniecki, on December 10. A new rectory is built at St. Nicholas parish, North Pole. The Paulist Fathers leave North Pole. The new Our Lady of Perpetual Help Church in Soldotna is dedicated.

1996

The new St. Patrick's Church in Anchorage is built. Father Michael **Warfel** is ordained a bishop by Archbishop Hurley and installed as the fourth Bishop of Juneau on December 17.

1997

The new Immaculate Heart of Mary Church at Marshall is dedicated on December 5.

1998

The new Our Lady of Guadalupe Church at Russian Mission is dedicated on October 18.

1999

The new Sacred Heart Church in Wasilla is dedicated in February. The Archdiocese of Anchorage begins publication of its archdiocesan newspaper, *Catholic Anchor*, on April 30. New entry ways are built onto the east and south entrances of Sacred Heart Cathedral in Fairbanks. The Tok parish complex is enlarged by the addition of a new rectory. Construction of a school chapel and major renovations at the Catholic schools complex in Fairbanks are begun and are carried well along. Holy Spirit Retreat House in Anchorage is renamed Holy Spirit Center.

2000

Holy Family Chapel at the Catholic schools complex in Fairbanks is dedicated by Bishop Kaniecki on April 14. Bishop Kaniecki dies at Emmonak on August 6. The Great Jubilee 2000 celebrations take place in the Carlson Center, Fairbanks, on August 26–27. The new St. Christopher's Church in Willow is dedicated on June 23. A new rectory is built at Healy.

2001

Roger **Schwietz**, O.M.I., succeeding Archbishop Hurley upon the latter's resignation, becomes the new Archbishop of Anchorage on March 3. Archbishop Schwietz dedicates the new St. Christopher's by the Sea Church at **Unalaska** in May. In St. Joseph's Church, Nome, Ross **Tozzi** is ordained a priest on July 14. This is the first ordination to the priesthood to take place in Nome.

2002

Father James **Kelley** dies in an airplane crash some 30 miles west of Dillingham on March 23. The new St. Paul the Apostle Church in Juneau is dedicated on June 2. The new St. Christopher's Church in Willow is dedicated on June 23. Msgr. Donald **Kettler** is ordained and installed as Bishop of Fairbanks on August 22. In Fairbanks, the Jesuits move out of Jesuit House in September. The new St. Bernard's Church at Stebbins is dedicated by Bishop Kettler on November 6.

2003

The St. Mary's Mission complex on the Andreafsky River is sold by the Diocese of Fairbanks to the CIUNERKIURVIK Corporation; transfer date, July 15, at midnight. The Kateri Tekakwitha Center in Galena is dedicated on August 31. In Anchorage, ground is broken on September 21 for a new Our Lady of Guadalupe Church.

2004

The new St. Michael's Church in St. Michael is dedicated by Bishop Kettler on November 7.

LIST OF ENTRIES

Akulurak/Andreafsky; Alakanuk; Alaska; Allie, Fr. Stanley J.; Aloralrea, Sr. Josephine, O.S.U.; Althoff, Fr. John J.; Anable, Fr. Edmund A., S.J.; Anchorage; Anderson, Fr. David J., S.J.; Andreafsky/Akulurak; Aniak; Ann (Sisters of St.); Arvinak; Astruc, Fr. René, S.J.

Babb, Fr. William H., S.J.; Baker, Fr. Harley A.; Bakewell, Fr. Anderson E., S.J.; Balquin, Fr. Don M.; Baltussen, Fr. Peter L., S.J.; Barnum, Fr. Francis A., S.J.; Barrow; Bartles, Fr. Charles A., S.J.; Bates, Fr. Urban M., O.P.; Baud, Fr. John B., S.J.; Bayusik, Fr. Robert E.; Benish, Br. Robert L., S.J.; Bergquist, Fr. Patrick D.; Bernard, Fr. Joseph, S.J.; Bethel; Beuzer, Fr. Vincent J., S.J.; Big Lake; Boileau, Bp. George T. , S.J.; Boone, Br. Kirby, C.F.X.; Bougis, Fr. Peter, S.J.; Boulet, Sr. Marie Teresa, O.P.; Brown, Fr. Edward H., S.J.; Buchanan, Fr. John R., S.J.; Bugarin, Fr. Fernando T.; Burik, Ms. Mary T.; Burke, Fr. William T., S.J.; Burns, Fr. Eugene P., S.J.; Busch, Dr. Thomas A.

Camille, Fr. Rogatien, S.J.; Cardy, Fr. William E., O.F.M.; Carlin, Fr. Thomas F., S.J.; Carlo, Dr. Poldine; Carroll, Fr. George E., S.J.; Carroll, Fr. John B., S.J.; Case, Fr. Richard D., S.J.; Cataldo, Fr. Joseph M., S.J.; Chaneliak (Chaniliut); Chapdelaine, Fr. Joseph A., S.J.; Chefornak; Chevak; Cochran, Fr. Paul M., S.J.; Concannon, Fr. John A., S.J.; Convert, Fr. Jules M., S.J.; Conwell, Fr. James U., S.J.; Cooper Landing; Copper Valley School; Cordova; Corrigal, Fr. Robert F., S.J.; Council; Cowgill, Msgr. Francis A.; Craig; Crimont, Bp. Joseph R., S.J.; Cronin, Fr. James D.; Cunningham, Br. Bernard I., S.J.; Cunningham, Fr. Edward J., S.J; Cunningham, Fr. Thomas P., S.J; Custer, Fr. Arnold L., S.J.

D'Arco, Fr. Andrew P.; de Verteuil, Fr. Jack; Delmore, Fr. Eugene P., S.J.; Delon, Fr. Philip I., S.J.; Delta Junction; Demers, Bp. Modeste; Deschout, Fr. Paul C., S.J.; Desjardins, Fr. Joseph-Alphonse, S.J.; Desso, Fr. Leo; Devine, Fr. Edward J., S.J.; Dibb, Fr. William C., S.J.; Dillingham; Donohue, Fr. Norman E., S.J.; Douglas; Dunfey, Fr. Ronald K.

Eagle City; Eagle River; Edmond, Sr. M. George, S.S.A.; Eline, Fr. S. Aloysius, S.J.; Emmonak; Endal, Fr. George S., S.J.; Eskimo Deacon Program; Esmailka, Mr. Harold.

F.I.C. (Brothers of Christian Instruction); Fairbanks; Fallert, Fr. Francis J., S.J.; Falsey, Fr. James E.; Feltes, Br. George J., S.J.; Fink, Fr. Louis B., S.J.; Fitzgerald, Bp. Walter J., S.J.; Fitz-Patrick, Fr. David M.; Forhan, Fr. John, S.J.; Fox, Br. Francis J., S.J.; Fox, Fr. John P., S.J.; Frister, Fr. Jerome A.

Galena; Gallagher, Fr. Thomas N., S.J.; Gallant, Msgr. G. Edgar; Giordano, Br. Carmelo, S.J.; Gleeson, Bp. Francis D., S.J.; Glennallen; Gorges, Fr. Peter F.; Greif, Fr. Harold J., S.J.; Grey Nuns; Gurr, Fr. John E., S.J.

Haffie, Fr. Lawrence N., S.J.; Haines; Hamilton; Hansen, Br. John F., S.J.; Hargreaves, Fr. Henry G., S.J.; Hartmann, Fr. Edward J.; Hatrel, Fr. Thomas J., S.J.; Healy; Hebert, Fr. Daniel J.; Hebert, Fr. Joseph L., S.J.; Hemmer, Fr. Joseph,

O.F.M.; **Hess**, Br. John, S.J.; **Heynen**, Fr. William L.; **Hinsvark**, Fr. John A.; **Hoch**, Fr. Matthew E.; **Hoelsken**, Fr. Mark A., S.J.; **Holy Cross Mission**; **Holy Spirit Center**; **Homer**; **Hoonah**; **Hooper Bay**; **Horwedel**, Br. Edward J., S.J.; **Hubbard**, Fr. Bernard R., S.J.; **Huck**, Br. John, S.J.; **Hurley**, Archbp. Francis T.; **Huslia**.

Iditarod.

Jacobson, Fr. James E., S.J.; **Jacquet**, Fr. Aloysius, S.J.; **Jakes**, Br. Ignatius J., S.J; **Jesuit Volunteer Corps**; **Jesuits in Alaska**; **Jetté**, Fr. Julius, S.J.; **Jones**, Dr. Eliza; **Judge**, Fr. William H., S.J; **Juneau**.

Kalland, Mr. Edgar; **Kalskag**; **Kaltag**; **Kaniecki**, Bp. Michael J., S.J.; **Kashunuk**; **Kekumano**, Msgr. Charles A.; **Kelley**, Fr. James F.; **Kelliher**, Fr. Vincent P., S.J.; **Kenai**; **Kenny**, Bp. Michael H.; **Keogh**, Br. Bartholomew, S.J.; **Kestler**, Fr. Theodore E., S.J.; **Ketchikan**; **Kettler**, Bp. Donald J.; **Keyaluvik**; **Keyes**, Fr. Anthony M., S.J.; **King Island**; **Klawock**; **KNOM**; **Kodiak**; **Kokrines**; **Kolb**, Fr. James M., C.S.P; **Konda**, Fr. Bernard A.; **Kotlik**; **Kotzebue**; **Koyukuk**.

Lafortune, Fr. Bellarmine, S.J.; **Laird**, Br. Aloysius B., S.J.; **Lapeyre**, Br. Martial O., S.J.; **Laudwein**, Fr. James R, S.J.; **Laudwein**, Fr. Joseph E., S.J.; **Lemire**, Br. Alphonsus, S.J.; **Levasseur**, Fr. William G., S.J.; **Levitre**, Fr. J. Albert; **Linssen**, Fr. Paul H., S.J.; **Little Diomede**; **Little Sisters** (of Jesus of Brother Charles of Jesus); **Llorente**, Fr. Segundo, S.J.; **Lohagen**, Sr. Scholastica, O.S.U.; **Lonneux**, Fr. Martin J., S.J.; **Lopilato**, Fr. Arthur, S.J.; **Loyens**, Fr. William J., S.J.; **Lucchesi**, Fr. John L., S.J.; **Lunney**, Msgr. John A.

Macke, Fr. Paul B., S.J.; **Mandart**, Fr. Joseph M; **Manley Hot Springs**; **Manske**, Fr. James J.; **Markham**, Br./Fr. Aloysius J., S.J./dio. priest; *Marquette Missionary*; Marshall (Fortuna Ledge); **Martinek**, Fr. John B.; **Marx**, Fr. John J.; **Marys**

Igloo; **McCaffrey**, Fr. Richard L., S.J.; **McDonald**, Fr. Angus R.; **McElmeel**, Fr. Joseph F., S.J.; **McGrath**; **McGuigan**, Fr. Francis W., S.J.; **McIntyre**, Fr. William T., S.J.; **McMeel**, Fr. Bernard F., S.J.; **McMillan**, Fr. William, S.J.; **Melbourne**, Fr. David A.; **Ménager**, Fr. Francis M., S.J.; **Miller**, Msgr. James F.; **Monroe**, Fr. Francis M., S.J; **Mosey**, Fr. Raymond W.; **Mountain Village**; **Mueller**, Fr. Francis E., S.J.; **Mueller**, Fr. Paul B., S.J.; **Muellerleile**, Fr. Ernest H.; **Murphy**, Br. Alfred T., S.J.; **Murphy** Fr. Cornelius K., S.J.; **Muset**, Fr. Paul, S.J.

Nawn, Fr. Francis X., S.J.; **Nayagak**, Dcn. Michael; **Nenana**; **Nevue**, Fr. Lawrence A., S.J.; **New Knock Hock**; **Newtok**; **Nightmute**; **Ninilchik**; **Nome**; **North Pole**; **Northway**; **Nulato**; **Nunam Iqua**.

Oalaranna, Mr. John Charles; **Oblates of Mary Immaculate** (O.M.I.); **O'Brien**, Fr. Charles, S.J.; **O'Connor**, Fr. Paul C., S.J.; **O'Flanagan**, Bp. R. Dermot; **Ohagamiut**; **O'Malley**, Br. Gerald J., S.J.; **O'Neill**, Fr. Edward C., C.Ss.R.; **O'Reilly**, Fr. Patrick J., S.J.; **Ornowski**, Fr. Gerald S., M.I.C.

Paimiut; **Palmer**; **Paquin**, Br. Ulric, S.J.; **Parodi**, Fr. Aloysius, S.J.; **Pepin**, Fr. Normand A., S.J.; **Perreault**, Dcn. Paul V.; **Perron**, Fr. Joseph, S.J.; **Petersburg**; **Peterson**, Fr. Charles J., S.J.; **Pilgrim Hot Springs**; **Pilot Station**; **Plamondon**, Fr. James W., S.J. (Ret.); **Poole**, Fr. James E., S.J.; **Post**, Fr. Hubert A., S.J.; **Post**, Fr. John A., S.J.; **Prange**, Fr. Francis B., S.J.; **Prince**, Br. Joseph J., S.J.; **Providence** (Sisters of); **Provinsal**, Fr. Thomas G., S.J.

Radich, Sr. Kathleen M., O.S.F.; **Ragaru**, Fr. Aloysius, S.J.; **René**, Fr. John B., S.J.; **Renner**, Fr. Louis L., S.J.; **Riobó**, Fray Juan A. Garcia, O.F.M.; **Robaut**, Fr. Aloysius J., S.J.; **Roccati**, Fr. Aloysius J., S.J.; **Rosati**, Br. John B., S.J.; **Roshko**, Fr. Vsevolod; **Rossi**, Fr. Crispin S., S.J.; **Ruby**; **Ruppert**, Fr. Frederick A., S.J.; **Russian Mission**; **Ruzicka**, Br. Robert J., O.F.M.; **Ryan**, Fr. Gerard T., C.S.Sp.; **Ryan**, Fr. James P.; **Ryan**, Archbp. Joseph T.

Saalfeld, Fr. Charles A., S.J.; **Sander**, Fr. Timothy L., O.S.B.; **Saudis**, Fr. Richard B.; **Scammon Bay**; Schwietz, Archbp. Roger L., O.M.I.; **Sebesta**, Fr. James A., S.J.; **Seghers**, Archbp. Charles J.; **Seldovia**; **Seward**; **Shageluk**; **Sheldon Point** (see Nunam Iqua); **Shepherd**, Fr. William A., S.J.; **Shirey**, Fr. Joseph E., S.J.; **Shrine** (of St. Therese); **Sifton**, Fr. John B., S.J.; **Sipary** (Ivan and Maggie); **Sitka**; **Skagway**; **Snead**, Msgr. James P.; **Snows** (Sisters of Our Lady of the); **Soldotna**; **Spils**, Fr. James C., S.J; **St. Michael**; **Stebbins**; **Stolz**, Fr. Joseph G.; **Strass**, Fr. Richard G., C.Ss.R; **Sulzman**, Fr. F. Merrill.

Tainter, Fr. Daniel J., S.J.; **Talbott**, Fr. Raymond L., S.J.; **Talkeetna**; **Tam**, Mr. Patrick, C.W.; **Tanana**; **Teller**; **Tero**, Fr. Richard D.; **Tiulana**, Mr. Paul; **Tok**; **Toksook Bay**; **Tomkin**, Fr. Joseph, S.J.; **Tosi**, Fr. Paschal, S.J.; **Tozzi**, Fr. Ross A.; **Trapper Creek**; **Travers**, Fr. Patrick J.; **Tréca**, Fr. Joseph M., S.J.; **Tununak**; **Turnell**, Fr. Philibert, S.J.; **Twohig**, Br. James, S.J.; **Tyson**, Dcn. William.

Umkumiut; **Unalakleet**; **Unalaska**; **Ursuline** (O.S.U. Sisters).

Valdez; **Van der Pol**, Fr. John B., S.J.

Warfel, Bp. Michael W.; **Wasilla**; **Whelan**, Bp. Robert L., S.J.; **Wickart**, Br. Carl F., S.J.; **Wilhalm**, Br. Peter P., S.J.; **Willebrand**, Fr. Aloysius G., S.J.; **Willow**; **Wood**, Fr. Gregg D., S.J.; **Wood**, Fr. John J., S.J.; **Wrangell**.

Yakutat.

ABBREVIATIONS

The following abbreviations are found in the captions of some images.

BH: Photo by Father Bernard R. Hubbard, S.J.

BR: Photo by Father Brad R. Reynolds, S.J.

DFA: Photo courtesy of Diocese of Fairbanks Archives

DJA: Photo courtesy of Diocese of Juneau Archives

JOPA: Photo courtesy of Jesuit Oregon Province Archives, Foley Library,
         Gonzaga University, Spokane, Washington

LR: Photo by Father Louis L. Renner, S.J.

LRC: Photo in the Father Louis L. Renner, S.J., Collection

MK: Photo by Bishop Michael J. Kaniecki, S.J.

PP: Photo by Deacon Paul V. Perreault, P.E.

St. Mary's Church, Akulurak.
JOPA-152.2.01.

AKULURAK/ANDREAFSKY

The first Catholic mission among the Eskimos in **Alaska** was founded in 1889, at the village of **Tununak**, on Nelson Island. From the very beginning of that mission, it was hoped that a school would be part of it. The school at **Holy Cross Mission**, which was serving mainly Indian children in predominantly Indian country, prompted the Jesuits to intensify their efforts to bring into being a similar school in Eskimo territory. However, the remoteness of Nelson Island relative to other Jesuit missionary activity in western Alaska made it difficult to supply and ill suited to serve as a center of missionary activity in a district stretching along the Bering Sea coast from the mouth of the Yukon to that island. Accordingly, in 1892, that mission station was relocated some 200 miles north, to Kanelik, a site on Kanelik Pass, a channel near the south mouth of the Yukon. The Kanelik site, however, lying low, was prone to flooding. The following year, therefore, it was abandoned in favor of a site some two miles away on the west bank of the Akulurak River. The Akulurak Mission dates from the year 1893, and Fathers Joseph M. **Tréca**, S.J., and Francis A. **Barnum**, S.J., are rightly recognized as its founders. The mission was intended to have a boarding school, but to be also a center out of which priests would travel to villages and camps scattered throughout that vast district to evangelize the people.

In 1894, a boarding school, under the patronage of St. Joseph, was opened at Akulurak. To the Eskimos scattered across the tundra in the Yukon-Kuskokwim Delta in 1894, the two-story log building erected on the banks of the sluggish Akulurak River seemed gigantic. The contrast with their semi-subterranean, sod-covered dugout dwellings

was especially startling. And the strangely costumed Sisters of St. **Ann**—Zephyrin (Superior), Benedict, Pauline and Prudence—who had come to run this boarding school, were a rare curiosity. The Eskimos were suspicious of them and their school. Parents were reluctant to allow their children to attend it. Still, at one time there were as many as 30 boarders at the school. Ultimately, however, if only indirectly, the Sisters were, in reality, forced to leave by the shamans, who told parents that, if they allowed their children to attend the school, they would die. The Sisters left it in 1898. During the year 1896–97, Fathers Barnum and Joseph M. **Cataldo**, S.J., were at Akulurak. They were followed for two years by Fathers Aloysius **Parodi**, S.J., and **John A. Post**, S.J. For several years the Akulurak mission was closed, with only an occasional visit to the district by a priest from Holy Cross Mission or **St. Michael**.

In 1902, Father Anthony M. **Keyes**, S.J., and Brother James **Twohig**, S.J., returned to Akulurak. They were received more favorably by the survivors of the epidemic that had decimated that whole region in 1900, taking with it also the majority of the elderly and more aggressive shamans. The mission school reopened in 1905. Since the parish in Nome, which had come into being 1901, was named for St. Joseph, the Akulurak mission was given a new name, that of St. Mary's. From 1905 on, the mission school was staffed primarily by the **Ursuline** Sisters. Jesuit priests and Brothers played a secondary, a supporting role in the school.

During its first year, St. Mary's Mission operated only a day school. The boarding school opened in 1906. The diphtheria epidemic that swept the coast in 1906 killed many people and left in its wake many orphans. It also helped to weaken further, on the part of shamans and the Eskimo people, resistance to newcomers and new institutions. There was now no longer a shortage of children to be cared for and schooled. At first, only girls attended the reopened boarding school. Beginning in 1914, however, boys, too, began to be admitted. Boarders at St. Mary's generally numbered between 75 and 100, and usually girls outnumbered boys by a large margin. As a rule, children stayed at St. Mary's for an average of about five years. Some, especially orphans, stayed as long as ten to sixteen years. The great influenza epidemic of 1918 likewise left many orphans for whom St. Mary's offered providential care.

The first three Ursuline Sisters to serve at St. Mary's were Mother Laurentia Walsh (Superior), and Sisters Mary Claver Driscoll and Dosithée Leygonie. Mother Laurentia was Superior of St. Mary's for over 30 years. Concerning her, Father John B. **Sifton**, S.J, wrote from Akulurak on June 6, 1927: "We all admit that she is too much of a policeman—and yet, stern Mother that she is, she made this place." This same Mother Laurentia was not above getting her hands dirty. Of her, Father Sifton wrote that she, while at fish camp, took upon herself "the sloppiest job of all, washing the fish, as the boys piled them into the box." After her death, a mission boat was built and named for her, the *Laurentia*.

Along with the Ursuline Sisters, it was the Jesuit Brothers who were the mainstay of St. Mary's Mission. They prefected, instructed and trained the boys. With the help of the boys, they provided the firewood, driftwood scattered along the banks of the Yukon, for the mission's 14 stoves. They played a key role, when it came to setting up fish camp, tending the fish wheels, and hauling the fish to the tables, on which the Sisters and girls cut and prepared them for the smokehouse or the brine. The mission needed around 20,000 fish, for its own needs and to trade for vegetables with the mission at Holy Cross. The Brothers helped with the Akulurak gardens, but these produced little other than turnips. Robert L. **Benish**, the last Brother to garden at Akulurak, wrote, "The garden finally sunk into the ground." The Brothers also hunted, helped haul water, maintained and operated the mission boats, built and maintained mission buildings, built dogsleds, and helped keep the mushing missionaries on the trail. Outstanding among the Brothers, both for the number of years they served at St. Mary's Mission and the quality of their service, were Benish, Bartholomew **Keogh**, **Alfred T. Murphy**, Twohig and Peter P. **Wilhalm**.

Life at St. Mary's Mission was a basic, demanding life for all living it. At times, it could be harsh, and even heartbreaking. During the earlier years, Mass at St. Mary's was offered in the mission chapels. As more and more people began to settle near the mission, a church was needed. The first one was built in 1912. On June 12, 1925, the building housing the Sisters and the girls burned to the ground. By December of the following year, however, they were able to move into their new quarters. On August 15, 1929, the church was destroyed by fire, and needed to be replaced by a new one. It took four years before the new one was ready to be blessed, on December 7, 1933. In addition to fires, sickness, accidents, and untimely deaths also brought sorrow to the hearts of the people at St. Mary's Mission. But, all in all, the mission, an oasis on a vast stretch of wilderness tundra, brought more joy than sorrow into the lives of those who staffed it, of those to whom it was home, and of those who visited it. To missionary priests stationed at St. Mary's and working out of there, it was also "the hope for the future."

By 1928, Father **John P. Fox**, S.J., could write to his Father Provincial, "We have at present 28 boys and 59 girls. The children are doing pretty well, and I guess our hope for the future has to be placed in these children." At St. Mary's, the boys and girls were given a rudimentary schooling in the three R's and practical training for everyday living in their Native environment. The girls were trained in childcare and homemaking. The boys were taught carpentry, sled building, and the maintenance and operation of motorized boats. The school intended also to ground its charges in the basics of the Catholic Faith. For these reasons it was inclined to have more attend it for shorter periods of time than fewer for longer periods. All in all, it can be said of St. Mary's boarding school that, in terms of its basic aims during its years of existence at Akulurak, it flourished.

Evangelization of the Akulurak district met with less success. Too few priests were available for that. Generally, those assigned to the district were preoccupied with the mission itself. The language, Central Yup'ik Eskimo, was a problem for most of them, at least initially. In 1917, Father Aloysius J. **Robaut**, S.J., wrote to his Father Provincial from Akulurak: "In my judgment nothing, or rather nothing good, has been accomplished here in the spiritual line except baptizing the people, whilst the damage done to the Indians [*sic*] in the same spiritual line is very great. They are now so indifferent, careless and also averse to religion, that, without a miracle, or a very saintly missionary, I see no chance whatever of ever succeeding to make good, practical Christians out of these people around us."

While Father Robaut was rather harsh in his judgment of the people and, implicitly, of the missionaries who had been and were working in the Akulurak district, he did recognize, as an excusing cause, the fact that many of the people were living "far from the Mission," and were, consequently, "only visited once in a while by the fathers." In defense of the Fathers and of their seemingly little success in making "good, practical Christians" out of the people, he conceded that the people "are all

plunged into superstitions from the sole of their feet even to the top of their head. It is simply impossible for the father to do anything solid, especially if you add to it the incredible difficulties, hardships, suffering and dangers, even of life, and the excessive expenses, which the winter traveling in this country is fraught with."

The general situation in regard to the evangelization of the people in Akulurak's outlying villages seems to have improved little during the following decade. After one year in Alaska, in a 1928 letter to his Father Provincial, Father Fox described the people whom the Akulurak mission was to evangelize as "merely baptized pagans." He went on to write, "What we need here is a Father who has nothing to do but keep traveling from village to village to instruct and encourage the natives in the practice of their religion."

Generally, there were two priests assigned to Akulurak: one to "hold down the fort," the other to travel from village to village. The Akulurak district stretched from the mouth of the Yukon some 200 miles down to Nelson Island and included around 20 settlements. In fairness to the missionaries who had served the district before Father Fox was assigned there, it must be said that they did, as a

t. Mary's Mission, Akulurak. rsuline Sisters Laurentia and osithée and Father John L. ucchesi, S.J., are in the oreground. *JOPA-152.1.02.*

1907
Johanna-M.Dosithee-Lucy

(*above*) Central Yup'ik Eskimo girls in class at
St. Mary's Mission Boarding School, Akulurak, 1907. *JOPA-104.12.*

(*below*) A group of Central Yup'ik Eskimo children from
St. Mary's Mission Boarding School, Akulurak, enjoy a tea break while on
a berry-picking excursion sometime in the late 1940s. *JOPA-506.5.01.*

matter of fact, travel from village to village to instruct the people and encourage them in the practice of the Faith, but that they, too, faced the basic problem: too many villages and encampments to be visited and too few priests to do the visiting.

During the years of its existence for over half a century, many priests served for longer or shorter periods of time at St. Mary's Mission and in the Akulurak district. Among those who were stationed there for longer periods were, in addition to its founder, Father Tréca, Jesuit Fathers: Anthony M. **Keyes**, John L. **Lucchesi**, Sifton, Norman E. **Donohue**, Segundo **Llorente**, and Paul C. **O'Connor**.

Early in its history, the advantages and the disadvantages of the location of St. Mary's were already being weighed one against the other. It was quite favorably located, inasmuch as it was relatively central to the district it served; and it was fairly accessible from the lower Yukon, in spite of "around 52 tortuous turns" and the shallows in the Akulurak River. It was also close to the major salmon runs that headed up the Yukon to spawn. The tundra terrain, however, on which the mission buildings stood, gave the whole complex anything but stability. Buildings were forever shifting, sinking into the tundra, with the result that wide cracks between every part of every building were constantly opening up, leading to major heat loss. During thaws and the summer months, lakes formed under the buildings. With no hills and no trees near, the mission was at the mercy of every wind and blizzard. Ropes had to be strung between buildings to keep people going from one to another from being swept away. Getting enough firewood for the mission stoves was never-ending, tedious, and expensive work. Providing enough water safe for drinking and general purposes was a constant concern. Any attempt at gardening was, as stated above, mostly a wasted effort.

As early as 1916, Father Philip I. **Delon**, S.J., Superior at Akulurak, wrote of the buildings there that, except for the 1912 church, they were "no more than a conglomeration, not to say a heap, of structures put up now and then, now in this fashion, now in that, as necessity demanded, so full of cracks that they are scarcely able to keep out the winds and the rains, the ice and the snow." Two years later, major

Superiors decreed that the mission be moved or closed. Many years, however, were yet to elapse, and many more meetings were yet to be held, before the mission was, not closed, but finally relocated.

Various causes delayed the eventual relocation of St. Mary's Mission. The influenza epidemic of 1918 left behind many orphans in the Akulurak district. Then the Great Depression of the 1930s made monies for the Alaskan missions almost nonexistent. From 1929–40, the Akulurak mission had its own reindeer herd, another reason for staying at Akulurak.

But, the main reasons for moving the mission continued to be valid, and talk about moving it to a more favorable site continued. In February 1949, an historic meeting took place at St. Mary's. Present were Bishop Francis D. **Gleeson**, S.J., Vicar Apostolic of Alaska as of 1948, and Harold O. Small, S.J., Provincial of the Oregon Province. Also attending the meeting were: Jesuit missionary Fathers Jules M. **Convert**, Paul C. **Deschout**, Donohue, Fox, Llorente, Martin J. **Lonneux**, Francis M. **Ménager**, O'Connor and James C. **Spils**. At that meeting it was unanimously decided that the mission should be moved to a new site, to the site on the Andreafsky River, where it stands today. On June 18, 1948, Father Lonneux had written to Bishop Gleeson, "I nearly 25 years ago wanted to rebuild at Andreafsky."

In the spring of 1950, Father Spils, who was put in charge of construction of the new St. Mary's Mission, wrote in the diary he kept of the building project: "On June 4, Trinity Sunday, at 7:00 P.M. the *M.S. Seghers* runs up the Andreafsky River to the site chosen for the new location of St. Mary's Mission." Building supplies were not yet at the site. Finding suitable gravel was still a major concern. With him Father Spils had as helpers two of his nephews, four young men from Holy Cross, and men from the area. As construction began, other men and priests from the area formed and led crews to help with construction. For a time, Bishop Gleeson served as cook. (A photo shows him on a caterpillar, but that, by his own admission, is posed.) Suitable gravel was found. Construction moved ahead rapidly. From late October to early March, it was suspended. Father Spils and Harold **Esmailka** were the first to return to the site, on March 5. Others, too, soon returned; and, a little less than five months later, the building, two and a half years after the decision to relocate St. Mary's, was ready for occupancy.

On August 3, 1951, Father Llorente wrote in the Akulurak house diary: "Friday—1st Friday—Aug. 3. Mass at 5. All receive Holy Communion. We leave in perfect calm weather at 10 to 6 A.M. 100 children, 3 Sisters, 2 Brothers." All these persons, plus mountains of personal belongings and baggage of every kind, were transported up to the new mission on the two mission boats, the *Sifton* and the *Laurentia*, the latter pushing the barge belonging to Holy Cross. The *Hyack*, a boat belonging to the trader George Sheppard, also pushed a barge as part of the convoy. There were "no mishaps of any kind" along the way. The weather continued to be "perfect." Father Llorente recorded the arrival of all at the new mission: "We arrive at Andreafsky at 9:45 P.M. Friday Aug. 3—a memorable date. The flag is run up the tower. We all go to the chapel to thank God. Then we look over the wonderful building, so ably put up by Father Spils in the face of almost insurmountable difficulties." The day after the move, it rained "pitchforks." On August 15th, Feast of the Assumption, the new mission was formally dedicated.

It was that "wonderful building" especially that made the "New St. Mary's," as it was soon commonly called, so attractive. But, there were also real trees and rolling hills at the site. The crystal clear Andreafsky River flowing past its doorstep provided an endless supply of good water, and easy access to the nearby Yukon. All this was in sharp contrast to the Akulurak setting, which was described by adjectives such as "barren," "desolate," "remote," "a boundless expanse," "barren wilderness." When Rocky Mountain Mission Superior George de la Motte, S.J., first saw the old St. Mary's at Akulurak, he exclaimed, "What a solemn funeral!" As the years went by, the site of the new St. Mary's proved ever more to have been very well chosen indeed.

In many respects, life at the new St. Mary's, especially during its earlier years, resembled that of the old. The Ursuline Sisters and Jesuit Brothers continued to be the mainstays of the mission. But the larger building with much more classroom space

noticeably improved teaching and learning. New buildings soon constructed at the mission complex afforded additional, less congested, living space and made for more comfortable living. The student body, while still consisting predominately of boarders of an elementary school age, began to have more and more day scholars in it, as more and more people began to build homes near the mission. Soon there were more people at the new mission site than had been at the old. In 1955, the post office of "St. Marys" was established. In 1967, "St. Marys" was incorporated as a first class city. In the year 2000, it had a population of an even 500.

As for Akulurak, soon little remained there after the mission was relocated. The post office, opened in 1924, was closed when the move was made. The buildings were taken down, board by board, and the lumber salvaged for reuse elsewhere. In a relatively short time, except for the cemetery, there was little left at what, for generations, had been a thriving center of human habitation.

In the early 1950s, shortly after the move to the Andreafsky site, a Native Sisterhood, the Oblates of St. Ursula—also referred to as the "Little Sisters"—came into being there. They were founded and trained, for the most part, by Sister Antoinette Johnson, O.S.U. Sister Antoinette was the last Superior of the Ursuline Sisters at Akulurak and their first at the new St. Mary's. The Native Sisterhood, though it had only a few members during its existence of less than a decade, did, nevertheless, gain some recognition during its short life span. The Sisters were well received by their own people, and they were sought out, especially as catechists, by priests serving in Eskimo villages.

On March 26, 1963, when the new St. Mary's Mission was only 12 years old, fire broke out in the building that housed the priests, Brothers and boys, along with the gymnasium and machine shop. The building was totally destroyed. A short circuit in a little room serving as a broadcasting station was suspected as the cause of the fire. With a great effort on the part of all at the mission and in the village, and a change in the wind, the flames were kept from spreading to the main building. Before long, a new gymnasium was up, and more spacious buildings were ready to house the Fathers, Brothers, and boys.

Later on, a "Volunteers House" was added. During its heyday, St. Mary's Mission High School owed much of its success to the competent and dedicated service of numerous members of the **Jesuit Volunteer Corps**.

A change of place frequently brings with it other changes, some minor, some major. In time, the grade school at St. Mary's Mission was phased out. By 1974, only the four-year high school remained, with an average enrollment of 125 students. The curriculum was expanded to include the Central Yup'ik Eskimo language, sewing, boat and sled building, and Yup'ik culture and traditions in general. Educational standards were raised. The gymnasium at the school brought with it an athletic program. Basketball was big. Ursuline Sisters continued to be the principal teachers at St. Mary's. They were said to be the "stabilizing influence that held the school together." But, Jesuit priests and many Jesuit lay volunteers, too, served as high school teachers and staff members.

For two decades, the big mission chapel was at the same time also the church for the people of the village of St. Marys. However, in order to give the people not immediately related to the school a sense of self-identity as a parish, Father Convert,

in 1970, founded the Church of the Nativity parish and, in 1972, built a church-parish center in the village. With the founding of a parish in St. Marys, St. Mary's Mission and St. Mary's Mission High School became virtually synonymous.

Education at St. Mary's Mission High School was based on "a firm belief that Christ is central to all of life." The school stressed also "cultural values, human knowledge, a search for truth, and a spirit of service and leadership." The school had, as one of its primary aims, to graduate students who could go on to college, and eventually return to their villages and assume leadership roles. Its basic philosophy was enthusiastically shared by faculty, supporting staff, and students alike. While St. Mary's fostered Eskimo dancing and did offer Central Yup'ik Eskimo language courses and other courses geared to preserve traditional cultural values, it was by the late 1970s equivalently a college preparatory school. In 1980, Robert L. **Whelan**, S.J., Bishop of **Fairbanks** at the time, could write: "Throughout the years, St. Mary's students have proved to be a credit to the Church and to their school. The name that the graduates have made for themselves at the University of Alaska has made people realize that St. Mary's is a very special kind of school." Given the success the

St. Mary's Mission Boarding School ca. 1960.
Eskimo children are playing on the frozen Andreafsky River. *DFA*.

Church of the Nativity, St. Marys. *DFA.*

school was enjoying at that time, it is hard to believe that within less than a decade it would be closed.

In 1976, the settlement of the Molly Hootch case resulted in the passage of a law by the State of Alaska that mandated high schools in even relatively small villages. By the late 1970s, over 100 high schools had been built in rural Alaska. Boys and girls of high school age now had the option of attending high school in their own village. Most of them, the brighter ones among them included, chose to do so. As a consequence, fewer grade school graduates applied for admission to St. Mary's; and, in many cases, those who did apply were poorly prepared for the kind of education St. Mary's offered. Some turned out to be, in fact, "real problem children," even though every effort had been made not to accept those already identified as such. Given fewer applicants, the school could no longer be as selective as it had been previously. All this resulted in a less qualified student body, with, consequently, lower morale among the students and the school staff. It was a downward-spiral situation.

On January 27, 1987, Michael J. **Kaniecki**, S.J., then Bishop of Fairbanks, announced that St. Mary's Mission High School would close at the end of the 1986–87 school year. While acknowledging the school's "glorious record and a history to be proud of," Bishop Kaniecki acted on the findings of a special task force and the advice of his consultants. Of his decision to close St. Mary's, he said: "This is not an easy decision for me to make, for I am well aware of the tremendous influence St. Mary's has had in the lives of so many students, families and teachers; and, so, there is real sadness about this announcement. On the other hand, I am a realist and I see clearly that the data presented to me supports my decision, in fact, dictates it."

Dr. Judith Kleinfeld, a professor at the University of Alaska-Fairbanks and the author of an extensive, in-depth study on St. Mary's, called the closing of the school "the passing of a very bright era in Native education." Sister Angie Pratt, O.S.U., supported the decision to close the school, but found the closing "an emotional heart-break."

In an official document issued on the occasion of the closing of St. Mary's, the Alaska State Legislature stated: "The members of this body are proud to honor the many mission workers, past and present, who have devoted much of their lives providing for the many homeless children during the early years of the mission and a quality education to rural Alaskan students during the past 84 years."

"The many mission workers" who served at both the old and at the new St. Mary's are far too numerous to mention all by name; however, certain ones must be singled out and mentioned by name. At the new St. Mary's, Brother Benish continued the good work that he had begun at the old. Along with him and the other Brothers of old St. Mary's—Keogh, Twohig, and Wilhalm—must be mentioned also Brothers Gerald J. **O'Malley**, S.J., and Ignatius J. **Jakes**, both of whom served for many years as competent and devoted custodians and maintenance men at the new St. Mary's. Deserving of mention, too, are laymen Moses John and George Sipary. For many years, Moses worked as a carpenter and maintenance man at the new St. Mary's, while George headed up the kitchen crew.

In addition to Sister Antoinette, a major figure at both the old and new missions, three other Ursuline Sisters stand out for the number of years they served at the two mission sites, and for the wholehearted devotion they brought to their service during those years. Each of the three spent at least 35 years serving at St. Mary's. They are Sisters Thecla Battiston, Lucy Daly and Scholastica **Lohagen**.

The three together served at St. Mary's for a grand total of 123 years!

The following Jesuit Fathers were Superior at the new St. Mary's: Ménager (1951–53), O'Connor (1953–59), James E. **Poole** (1959–64), René **Astruc** (1964–70), **James R. Laudwein** (1970–81), **Joseph E. Laudwein** (1981–82), James A. **Sebesta** (1982–84), Thomas N. **Gallagher** (1984–86), and Richard D. **Case** (1986–87).

On April 26, 1991, at the Alaskan Regional Tekakwitha Conference held at St. Mary's Mission, after Native American Father Paul Ojibway, S.A., had prayed for general forgiveness, and that the Lord might forgive all the assembled and that they all might forgive one another, Bishop Kaniecki rose before the assembled—made up largely of Native Americans—and very humbly and sincerely admitted his personal shortcomings as bishop of the Diocese of Fairbanks, and asked for pardon, forgiveness, and prayers for himself. On behalf of the Church, he then apologized to America's Native peoples for the pain, the hurt the official Church and its missionaries had caused them by not always having been sensitive to and respectful of Native spiritualities and the richness of Native cultural values. For these offenses, too, he humbly, sincerely asked pardon and forgiveness. Many silent tears were shed. "This was a very powerful experience for everyone present," wrote one Native American about Bishop Kaniecki's apology and plea for forgiveness.

On September 29, 1991, the last day of the **Eskimo Deacons** retreat, in the St. Mary's Mission chapel, the deacons, mindful of Bishop Kaniecki's earlier apology and on their own initiative, decided to accept it officially and formally. They chose Eskimo Deacon William **Tyson** to speak for them. During the liturgy which concluded the retreat, at the end of the penitential rite, Bishop Kaniecki sat down in front of the altar and Deacon Tyson, placing his right hand on the bishop's head, solemnly said in Central Yup'ik Eskimo: "We accept your apology in the name of all the Natives who are around us, and we forgive everything that needs to be forgiven."

After the closing of St. Mary's Mission High School, the St. Mary's Mission complex, while still owned by the Diocese of Fairbanks, served as a residence for Jesuits, as a center for workshops, retreats, and meetings, and as the headquarters for the Rural and Native Ministry Training Programs. The complex was sold in 2003 to CIUNERKIURVIK Corporation, transfer date, June 10th. All buildings were sold. Thereafter, the diocese leased the building housing the Jesuits, a house for the Sisters, and space for the Rural and Native Ministry Training Programs, as well as some storage and office space. The cemetery, the last resting place of, among others, former mission personnel Sister Scholastica Lohagen, O.S.U., Brother Alfred T. Murphy, S.J., and Father René Astruc, S.J., was turned over to the City of St. Marys.

16, 57, 64, 76, 129

ALAKANUK

The Central Yup'ik Eskimo village of Alakanuk is located at the east entrance to Alakanuk Pass, the major southern channel of the Yukon River. It is approximately eight miles southwest of **Emmonak**. The name of the village derives from the Yup'ik word *alarneq*, meaning "wrong way," or "a mistake," a name aptly applied to a village located amidst a maze of watercourses. A village was reported at the site in 1899. When Father Segundo **Llorente**, S.J., first saw Alakanuk, in 1936, it was a village of only seven small cabins. A post office was established there in 1946. In 1950, Alakanuk had a population of 140. During the 1950s, people from the Black River region, notably from **New Knock Hock**, moved to Alakanuk. By 1960, it had a population of 278; by 1979, 575; and by the year 2000, 652.

For several generations the ancestors of today's Alakanuk people were evangelized by priests stationed at **Akulurak**. In 1904, Jesuit Fathers Joseph M. **Tréca** and Anthony M. **Keyes** saw to the building of a church, dedicated to St. Ignatius, at Alakanuk.

The village of Alakanuk first appears in the Oregon Province catalog in 1943, but under the name of "Alaranak." In 1943, Father Llorente built a new church there. During the years 1943–46, Alakanuk was visited out of Akulurak by Father Norman E. **Donohue**, S.J. Father George S. **Endal**, S.J., was in residence in Alakanuk for the years 1946–48. It

St. Ignatius Church, Alakanuk. *LR.*

was then again served out of Akulurak, by Father Donohue, until 1950; and then by Father Llorente, also out of Akulurak, during the year 1950–51. In 1951, Father Llorente took up station in Alakanuk. The following year, the spring flood swept the church buildings downriver. However, that same year he built a new church, with priest's quarters. On September 23, 1952, he was able to write: "Last evening I moved to my new quarters, cooked supper and slept under a solid roof. It has been a tough summer, living like a tramp, eating peanuts and crackers, same checkered shirt from June to September and so on, but now I feel like a soul taken from purgatory to heaven. I love this church."

In 1963, Father Llorente was replaced at Alakanuk by Father William T. **McIntyre**, S.J. It was he who oversaw the building, in 1966, of what was, as of the year 2004, still serving as Alakanuk's church. Father Francis X. **Nawn**, S.J., replaced Father McIntyre in 1968 and served the Alakanuk parish until 1983. There was no priest stationed at Alakanuk during the year 1980–81, while Father Nawn was on sabbatical leave. He was followed by Father Thomas J. **Hatrel**, S.J., at Alakanuk till the time of his death, in **Anchorage**, on May 5, 1988. Father Hatrel lies buried at Alakanuk.

Father René **Astruc**, S.J., ministered to the peo-

ple of Alakanuk during the year 1988–89, as did Father Thomas N. **Gallagher**, S.J., 1989–90. They were followed by Father Henry G. **Hargreaves**, S.J., at Alakanuk 1990–92. Beginning in 1992, Father Thomas G. **Provinsal**, S.J., was Alakanuk's priest. He made it his home base until the year 2002, when he began to serve it out of Emmonak.

Eskimo Deacons, too, have ministered and are ministering at their Alakanuk parish: Damien Keatoak (deceased and buried at Alakanuk), Joseph Phillip, Emmanuel Stanislaus, Denis Shelden, and Clyde Smith.

The following School Sisters of Notre Dame also have been engaged in pastoral ministry at Alakanuk: Rose Andre Beck, Ann Christine Pendleton, Michael Marie Laux, Ann Brantmeier, Cynthia Borman, and Susan Michelle Dubec. Sister Mary Anne Kollmer, O.P., began ministry in the Alakanuk parish in 1999.

Monica Shelden-Murphy served faithfully and competently as Alakanuk's Parish Administrator from 1990 to 1995.

Alakanuk's Eskimo elders remember when Alakanuk Pass was a slough so narrow they could throw sticks across it. When the new church was built in 1966, it was set so far back from the bank, that it was hardly visible from the slough. However, the village of Alakanuk, located on a river delta formed by centuries of deposition of sand, silt and loam from the Yukon River, sits on anything but *terra firma*. In the course of the years, the normal current, spring flooding, and the wave action of boat traffic led to a steady widening of Alakanuk Pass, as the unstable banks were eroded. By the mid-1980s, the people of Alakanuk began to show concern for their church, as the waters kept eating away the ground on which it stood. By the early 1990s, it was imperative that the church be moved.

The people of Alakanuk are resourceful and self-reliant, but moving a building the size of St. Ignatius Church would be a major undertaking. They looked to diocesan headquarters in **Fairbanks** for suggestions. Michael J. **Kaniecki**, S.J., Bishop of Fairbanks at the time, suggested the church be moved in the depth of winter, when the road could be flooded, paved with a sheet of ice, and the building, on a sledge made of logs, dragged by a bulldozer to the new site. This plan was adopted, and proved to be a very workable one. On March 23, 1993, under the leadership of Charlie Hill—a Finnish Lutheran from Black Duck Lake, Minnesota, who had served the Alaska missions generously for some years— and his son, Doug, the church was moved with no major incidents to its present site.

64, 105, 147

ALASKA, CATHOLIC CHURCH IN
Part I: Evolvement of Ecclesiastical Jurisdiction

Alaska (spelled variously during earlier times) is the name the Native inhabitants of the Aleutian Islands, the Aleuts, gave to the land mass lying to the east of their ancestral homeland. It translates basically as "the Great Land." Comprising 591,004 square miles, this massive peninsula at the northwestern extremity of the North American continent is nearly one-fifth the size of the rest of the continental states. Relative to the Greenwich meridian, Alaska is the USA's northernmost, westernmost and easternmost state. "Discovered" in July 1741 by Vitus Bering sailing under the Russian flag, Alaska was known as "Russian America" up to the time of its purchase from Russia by the United States in 1867 for $7,200,000. Organized as a Territory in 1912, Alaska was admitted into the Union in 1959 as the forty-ninth state.

According to reliable records, the first formal act of Christian worship in what is today the State of Alaska took place on Ascension Day, May 13, 1779, when the Franciscan priest, Father Juan **Riobó**, a member of a Spanish exploratory expedition sailing out of San Blas, Mexico, celebrated Mass near present-day **Craig** in Southeastern Alaska. Alaska remained, in terms of Roman Catholic ecclesiastical jurisdiction, a "no-man's land" until 1847, when Modeste **Demers** was consecrated the first bishop of Vancouver Island, Canada, and given jurisdiction "over the island of that name and all British and Russian possessions as far north as 'the glacial sea.'"

The first Catholic missionary priest to enter Alaska was a member of the Missionary **Oblates of Mary Immaculate**, Father Jean Séguin, who, coming from Canada, spent a fruitless winter, 1862–63, at Fort Yukon. In 1870, Oblate Father Émile Petitot visited Fort Yukon briefly. Two years later, Oblate Bishop Isidore Clut and Father Auguste Lecorre (still a diocesan priest) traveled to Fort Yukon in hopes of establishing a permanent mission there. Owing to an Anglican presence there, they met with little success. In the summer of 1873, the two went down the Yukon River to **St. Michael**, where they were favorably received and enjoyed a modest degree of evangelizing success. Father Lecorre spent the winter of 1873–74 at St. Michael. In the summer of 1874, when he learned that Alaska was under the jurisdiction of the bishop of Vancouver Island, he returned to Canada. It was at the invitation of, and thanks to, the support of François X. Mercier, a French-Canadian Catholic from Montreal and agent of the Alaska Commercial Company, that the Oblates entered Alaska from Canada and were able to achieve some limited, evangelizing result.

While Oblate missionaries were active in northern Alaska, diocesan priests from Vancouver Island were visiting Alaska's Southeast in hopes of establishing missions. In 1867, Father Joseph M. **Mandart** made a brief trip to the Panhandle, and, in 1873, Charles J. **Seghers**, newly consecrated Bishop of Vancouver Island, as of June 29, 1873, made his first of five trips to Alaska, visiting **Sitka**, **Kodiak** and **Unalaska**. In 1877, accompanied by Father Mandart, he traveled to the northern interior, arriving at **Nulato** in August. The two spent the next twelve months there, engaged in missionary activity at Nulato and in the surrounding area. In May 1879, Bishop Seghers founded a mission at **Wrangell** and put Father John J. **Althoff** in charge. In 1885, Seghers, now an archbishop, established a mission at Sitka with Father William L. **Heynen** in charge.

In 1886, Archbishop Seghers, rightly honored as "the Apostle of Alaska," set out for Alaska on what was to be the last journey of his life. He had with him two Jesuit priests, Fathers Paschal **Tosi** and Aloysius J. **Robaut**. The party had as its goal the establishment of missions in Alaska's northern interior, especially at Nulato, which Archbishop Seghers fondly remembered from his earlier stay.

The archbishop, the two Jesuits, and a Catholic layman, Francis Fuller, left Victoria on July 13, 1886. On September 7, via the Chilkoot Trail, they arrived at the confluence of the Stewart and Yukon Rivers, still in Canada. It was decided that the two Jesuits would spend the winter there, while Seghers and Fuller would push on downriver toward Nulato. It was getting late in the season for river travel, but Archbishop Seghers was most eager to get to Nulato, driven, as he was, by the fear that Octavius Parker, an Episcopal priest rumored to be at St. Michael, might arrive there before he did and take over the area.

As Archbishop Seghers and Fuller, who had already given clear signs of mental instability soon after the party left tidewater, made their way down the Yukon, their boat, traveling conditions, and Fuller's mind deteriorated rapidly. On October 4, they arrived at the confluence of the Yukon and Tanana Rivers, where they abandoned their boat and waited for the river to freeze solid enough for sled travel. On November 19, they again set out for Nulato. On November 27, with Nulato still a good distance away and travel difficult because of deep snow, the party camped. Early the next morning, the demented Fuller fired a shot into Archbishop Seghers as he bent over to pick up his mittens. He died instantly.

The following spring, 1887, Fathers Tosi and Robaut came down the Yukon into Alaska, where they learned of Seghers' death. Immediately Father Tosi sailed for the Pacific Northwest to confer with the Rocky Mountain Mission Superior, Father Joseph M. **Cataldo**, S.J. When Archbishop Seghers was given Fathers Tosi and Robaut for the trip north in 1886, they were intended simply as traveling companions. There was no intention to commit Jesuits to the Alaska Mission. Divine Providence ordained otherwise. Upon Father Tosi's urging, Father Cataldo decided then and there that the Jesuits would, for the time being, take charge at least of parts of Alaska. A long-term commitment would need Rome's approval. Armed with all the faculties the Vicar General of Vancouver Island could give him, Father Tosi returned to Alaska in the summer of 1887 to organize the systematic development of missions in northern Alaska. In 1892, during a private visit with Pope Leo XIII in Rome, Father

Tosi so moved him with his account of Alaska that he told Father Tosi: "Go, and make yourself the pope in those regions!"

Formal ecclesiastical jurisdiction within the whole of Alaska first came about in 1894, when the Holy See separated Alaska from the Diocese of Vancouver Island and made it a Prefecture Apostolic with Father Tosi as Prefect Apostolic. At the same time, Alaska became an independent mission, entrusted to the Jesuits, with Father Tosi as General Superior. Failing health led to his being replaced as Prefect Apostolic in 1897 by Father John B. **René**, S.J. He, in turn, was replaced, in 1904, by Father Joseph R. **Crimont**, S.J. In 1916, Alaska was raised to the next ecclesiastical level, that of a Vicariate Apostolic. The following year, Father Crimont was consecrated a bishop to serve as Alaska's first Vicar Apostolic. (It was Bishop Crimont, who, in 1920, five years before she was declared a saint, placed the whole Alaska Mission under the protection of St. Therese of Lisieux.) Upon his death in 1945, he was succeeded by his coadjutor, since 1939, Bishop Walter J. **Fitzgerald**, S.J., who died two years later. He was followed in 1948 by Francis D. **Gleeson**, S.J., Alaska's last Vicar Apostolic.

From time to time, beginning already during the Bishop Crimont years, Alaska's vastness and its varied geographic and ethnic makeup prompted those in authority, both in Rome and in Alaska, to consider the desirability of dividing it into several ecclesiastical districts. In 1951, Rome decreed the erection of Alaska's first diocese, the Diocese of **Juneau**, comprising at the time Alaska's Panhandle, a coastal region consisting in large part of many heavily forested, mist-shrouded islands sculptured by glaciers, and inhabited by a mix of many peoples. These included some of Alaska's first peoples, such as the Haida and Tlingit Indians. This first diocese also included much of Southcentral Alaska. Dermot **O'Flanagan**, a long-time diocesan priest in Alaska, was consecrated its first Ordinary by Bishop Gleeson, in **Anchorage**, on October 3, 1951. This was the first consecration of a Roman Catholic bishop in Alaska.

Up to 1951, all of Alaska's ecclesiastical leaders after Father Tosi had made Juneau their headquarters. When the Juneau diocese was established, Bishop Gleeson moved to **Fairbanks**, where he continued on as Vicar Apostolic of the rest of Alaska. In 1962, however, the vicariate became the Missionary Diocese of Fairbanks (directly under the *Propaganda Fidei* in Rome) with Bishop Gleeson as its Ordinary. In 1966, the 138,985-square-mile Archdiocese of Anchorage was established with **Joseph T. Ryan** as its first archbishop. This left the Juneau diocese with 37,566 square miles and the Fairbanks diocese with 409,849. (The additional 4,604 Alaskan square miles found subsequently by geographers have yet to be claimed by one or other of the three dioceses.)

Bishop O'Flanagan resigned the See of Juneau in June 1968. For two years, Archbishop Ryan administered it. Bishop Gleeson retired in November 1968, and was succeeded as Bishop of Fairbanks by Robert L. **Whelan**, S.J. (Although Bishop George T. **Boileau**, S.J., never exercised ecclesiastical jurisdiction in Alaska, his name should be mentioned here. He was consecrated Coadjutor Bishop to Gleeson with right of succession on July 31, 1964, and died February 25, 1965.) In 1970, Francis T. **Hurley** became auxiliary bishop to Archbishop Ryan and administrator of Juneau as his vicar. In 1971, he was named Ordinary of the Juneau diocese. In December 1975, Archbishop Ryan became Coadjutor Military Vicar of the U.S. Armed Forces. The following year, Bishop Hurley became Archbishop of Anchorage and administrator of Juneau. From 1979 to 1995, the year of his sudden death in Jordan, Michael H. **Kenny** was Juneau's Ordinary. Michael W. **Warfel** succeeded him as Ordinary of Juneau in 1996. When, in 1985, Bishop Whelan retired as Ordinary of Fairbanks, Michael J. **Kaniecki**, S.J., ordained a bishop on May 1st of the previous year as his Coadjutor, began his 15-year term as Ordinary of Fairbanks. In the Eskimo village of **Emmonak** near the mouth of the Yukon River, on August 6, 2000, Bishop Kaniecki died suddenly of a massive heart attack, leaving the Fairbanks diocese without a bishop until August 22, 2002, when Donald J. **Kettler** was ordained and installed as Bishop of Fairbanks. On January 18, 2000, Roger L. **Schwietz**, O.M.I., was appointed Coadjutor Archbishop of Anchorage. He succeeded Archbishop Hurley as Archbishop of Anchorage on March 3, 2001, when the latter resigned.

Part II: Apostolic Works

The first women Religious to undertake apostolic works in Alaska were the Sisters of St. **Ann**. In 1886, they opened a school and a hospital in Juneau. By the time they left Alaska over a century later, they had staffed schools and hospitals in various other places, but it was especially at **Holy Cross** on the Yukon that they had their greatest impact in Alaska, serving there continuously for decades as teachers—along with Jesuits and, for a few years, with Brothers of Christian Instruction (**F.I.C.**)—and nurses. The Holy Cross Mission was founded in 1888 by Father Robaut, who died there in 1930 and lies buried there. In northern Alaska, however, it is Nulato, founded in 1887 by Father Tosi, that rightly claims primacy. Inseparably connected with the name of Nulato is the name of Father Julius **Jetté**, S.J. It was at Nulato that Father Jetté, who spent over 25 years in northern Alaska and was hailed as "the most distinguished scholar in Alaska," began work, in 1898, on his monumental dictionary of the Koyukon Athabaskan Indian language. He never lived to see it in print. A century later, the Alaska Native Language Center at the University of Alaska-Fairbanks published this mammoth work of 94 introductory pages and 1118 pages of text under the title of *Koyukon Athabaskan Dictionary*.

Evangelization among the Central Yup'ik Eskimos of western Alaska began in 1889 with the founding of the mission on Nelson Island by Father Joseph M. **Tréca**, S.J., "the Apostle of the Tundra." At **Akulurak**, near the south mouth of the Yukon, St. Joseph's Mission and Boarding School, staffed by Sisters of St. Ann and Jesuits, was opened in 1894. It was closed four years later. The mission at St. Michael dates from 1898. (At St. Michael lies buried Jesuit Brother Ulric **Paquin**, who froze to death on the trail, while bringing building supplies from St. Michael to **Stebbins** by sled and dogteam.)

The **Nome** parish was founded in 1901 for the whites and Eskimos of the area. The Sisters of **Providence** operated a hospital there from 1902 to 1918, and a day school from 1904 to 1918. The **Little Sisters of Jesus** began their stay in Nome in 1952. In 1971, Nome's Catholic radio station, **KNOM**, founded by Father James E. **Poole**, S.J., went on the air. Now the oldest Catholic radio station in the U.S., it has been winning top awards ever since.

Immaculate Conception parish in Fairbanks was founded in 1904 by Father Francis M. **Monroe**, S.J., "the Alaskan Hercules." A hospital followed two years later. This was staffed briefly by Sisters of St. Ann, then by Benedictine Sisters, then, from 1910 to 1968, by the Sisters of Providence. When Immaculate Conception Grade School in Fairbanks opened in 1946, it was Sisters of Providence that staffed it; and when Monroe Catholic High School in Fairbanks opened in 1955, Sisters of Providence, along with Jesuits and lay men and women, members of the **Jesuit Volunteer Corps**, served on its faculty for many years.

In 1905, the boarding school at Akulurak, now staffed by **Ursuline** Sisters, along with Jesuits, was reopened under the new name of St. Mary's. The school flourished until 1951, when it was moved into new facilities built by Father James C. **Spils**, S.J., and crew at the new site on the **Andreafsky** River. There, still staffed by Ursulines and Jesuits, assisted by many dedicated members of the Jesuit Volunteer Corps—who, at the time, were serving also in many other places throughout Alaska—it continued to prosper until the 1980s. It graduated its last class of high school seniors and was closed in the spring of 1987.

In Alaska's north, other missions, schools, programs continued to come into being. In 1918, the **Pilgrim Hot Springs** Mission and boarding school north of Nome began to care for many children left orphaned by the influenza epidemic of that year. The mission, staffed by Ursuline Sisters and Jesuits, closed in 1941. Father Frederick A. **Ruppert**, S.J., lies buried there. He froze to death, in December 1923, while on the trail with sled and dogteam headed for the mission with oranges for the orphans for Christmas.

The mission on **King Island** was founded in 1929 by Father Bellarmine **Lafortune**, S.J. It was he who, during the course of his 44 years in the Seward Peninsula area, had founded, among others, the Pilgrim Springs mission. By the time he had built the church on the island and had spent his first winter there, most of the King Islanders were Catholic, having been received by him into the Church during their summer sojourns in Nome. The **Kotzebue** mission, the first Catholic mission north of the Arctic Circle, was also founded in 1929, by the diocesan priest Father William F. Walsh. Father Walsh, along with Father Philip I. **Delon**, S.J., and pilot Ralph Wien, died the following year in the crash of the new mission airplane, the *Marquette Missionary*, at Kotzebue.

The last mission of major importance to be established in northern Alaska is that of St. Patrick's at **Barrow**, established in 1954 by the legendary Father **Thomas P. Cunningham**, S.J. Father Cunningham, widely know as "Father Tom," pioneered also the mission on **Little Diomede** Island, and served on King Island.

In 1956, **Copper Valley School**, near **Glennallen**, opened. It was staffed by Sisters of St. Ann, Jesuits, and numerous lay volunteers. Its founder, Father John R. **Buchanan**, S.J., intended as the primary purpose of the school that of preparing Alaska Natives for college and for positions of leadership in Alaska. As did the other Catholic schools in northern Alaska, Copper Valley School, too, had the strong support of Bishop Gleeson, a promoter of education on all levels. (For a time he had four priests on the faculty at the University of Alaska-Fairbanks.) Copper Valley School closed in 1971.

Bishop Gleeson is given credit not only for a supporting a tradition of solid Catholic education in northern Alaska, but also for the restoration of the permanent diaconate in the United States. Upon his urging, the United States bishops petitioned Rome, in 1968, for approval of the restoration of the permanent diaconate. Approval was given. Under Bishop Whelan, Bishop Gleeson's successor, the Diocese of Fairbanks' **Eskimo Deacon Program** came to full flower. In the year 2000, there were 18 Native deacons, all Eskimo, and 7 urban deacons serving in the Fairbanks diocese. The deacons, a nucleus of diocesan priests, Franciscan Friars (serving in Alaska's northern interior since 1986), and men and women Religious of various Communities have all served to lessen the long dominance in northern Alaska by Jesuits as apostolic workers and helped the diocese along its road to becoming a diocese of age.

Meanwhile, pioneer parishes and apostolic works

were being founded also in Alaska's Panhandle. The Wrangell parish dates from 1879, the parishes of Sitka and Juneau from 1885. The **Skagway** parish was founded in 1898. Skagway's Pius X Mission, a boarding school founded by Father G. Edgar **Gallant**, opened in 1931. The **Ketchikan** parish was founded in 1903. In 1923, the Sisters of St. Joseph of Peace–Newark began operating a hospital there. The Daughters of St. Paul had a bookstore apostolate in Anchorage during the last decades of the 1900s.

In Southcentral Alaska the parishes of **Seward** and **Valdez** were established in 1905, that of **Cordova** in 1908, that of Anchorage in 1915. Anchorage's Providence Hospital under the care of the Sisters of Providence opened in 1939. Parochial schools, a retreat house (**Holy Spirit Center**), and social outreach programs have been part of the Anchorage scene for decades. The parish of **Kodiak** came into being in 1944. That same year the **Grey Nuns** of the Sacred Heart took over the management of the hospital in the city of Kodiak. A Catholic grade school has flourished there for decades. The **Dillingham** parish dates from 1948. For some years there was also a Catholic day-boarding school in Dillingham.

Needless to say, during the latter half of the twentieth century many additional parishes and apostolic works, too numerous to mention, came into being in all three of Alaska's dioceses. While Catholic Alaska is not overly impressive in terms of numbers (according to the 2000 *Official Catholic Directory*, the Archdiocese of Anchorage had 20 parishes and 8 missions serving 31,071 out of a total population of 396,801; Fairbanks had 46 parishes and 7 missions serving 17,068 out of total population of 155,224; and Juneau had 10 parishes and 10 missions serving 6,049 out of a total population of 73,302), it has achieved a certain degree of maturity, and its three dioceses resemble for the most part other U.S. dioceses. However, the geographic and ethnic makeup of Alaska gives rise to some major differences. Many communities are "bush" communities, communities widely separated from one another and unconnected by roads. They can be reached only by airplane, boat, or snowmachine. At certain times of the year, Little Diomede Island is

accessible only by helicopter. To save time and to cut costs, several of Alaska's bishops and many of its priests have flown and do fly their own airplanes. The Anchorage and Juneau dioceses have relatively few Alaska Native Catholics, while Fairbanks has many, most of them Athabaskan Indians and Central Yup'ik Eskimos.

From the day they first set foot in Alaska to the present, Catholics have, in all areas of life, whether in academia, in the business world, or in the arts, been part of mainstream Alaskan life. This is strikingly evident, above all, in the area of politics. Among the more prominent Catholics in Alaska's political life have been: Mike Stepovich, Alaska's last territorial governor; William A. Egan, the State of Alaska's first governor; Walter J. Hickel, twice Alaska's governor and Secretary of the Interior under President Nixon; Frank H. Murkowski, U.S. senator and governor of the State of Alaska; Lisa Murkowski, U.S. senator; George Sullivan and Tom Fink, mayors of Anchorage; Edward Merdes, President of the International Junior Chamber of Commerce and Alaska State senator.

The past, as prologue to the future, is easier to record than the future to predict. However, as the third millennium begins to unfold, it can safely be assumed that many of the traditional ministries of the Catholic Church in Alaska (schools, hospitals, social works) will continue to be ever more in the hands of the laity. In all three of Alaska's dioceses, sincere, positive, on-going efforts are being made to prepare, to train, to empower lay men and women, Native and non-Native, to take on ministerial roles in the Church at all levels short of those open only to ordained ministers. It can safely be assumed, too, that the Catholic Church in Alaska—while not losing sight of its primary mission, namely, to prepare people for a "kingdom not of this world"—will continue to take an active interest in and will try to influence policies and legislation concerning matters ethical, social, medical, educational, ecumenical, and environmental. However, when it comes to salvation history, to the story of grace at work in the hearts of individual souls, the historian does well to leave the future to the prophet.

ALASKA—as "the Great Land," as "the Last Frontier," as the 49th State of the Union—is still young, still on the road to full maturity. And what is true of the State of Alaska is true also of the Catholic Church in Alaska.

47

(This entry, somewhat modified, is reprinted here with the kind permission of The Catholic University of America Press, 620 Michigan Avenue, N.E., Washington, D.C., 20064. It was first published in the New Catholic Encyclopedia, Second Edition: Vol. 1, pp.207–211.)

Father Stanley J. Allie.
Courtesy of Fr. Allie.

ALLIE, Father Stanley J.

Stanley J. "Stan" Allie was born, the sixth of eight children, on March 29, 1930, in Newcomb, New York, very near the source of the Hudson River. Both his parents, from the Province of Quebec, Canada, were French-speaking. His father was a foreman of various lumber camps for a period of about 45 years. When Stan was three years old, the family moved to North Creek, New York, a small town, also located on the Hudson River, 28 miles south of Newcomb. In the North Creek public schools, he received all of his elementary and secondary education. He graduated from North Creek High School in June 1948, having majored in mathematics. In an honest vein, he wrote many years later, "I think it would be more accurate to say that I majored in basketball, baseball, and social life."

Stan's biggest dream in life was to learn to fly. At age sixteen, in a J3 Cub, he soloed, having paid for all of his flying lessons out of his own pocket. For lack of funds, however, his flying as a youth was severely limited.

After graduating from high school, he tried to enlist in the Air Force Cadets, only to be told that he could not be accepted without two years of college. That was a great disappointment to him, because his parents could not afford to send him to college. He, therefore, at the age of eighteen, worked from July 1948 to September 1949 for a chain grocery store, the A&P, "Atlantic and Pacific Tea Company."

By his own admission, Stan was only an average student. "Still," he wrote, "I always had a great attraction for the priesthood. But, there was a great struggle going on inside me, because of the great dream I had to become an airline pilot." Nevertheless, during the summer of 1949, he decided that he should at least give the idea of the priesthood a chance. He applied to Edmund F. Gibbons, Bishop of Albany, to be accepted as a candidate for the priesthood in the Diocese of Albany, but was turned down, because he did not have four years of Latin. However, after Stan's pastor asked the Rector of St. Andrew's Minor Seminary in Rochester, New York, to give Stan a chance, he was admitted to that seminary and did so well in Latin, that he was accepted by Bishop Gibbons. Stan then spent two years at St. Andrew's, taking college level courses, after which he entered Our Lady of Angels Major Seminary, at Niagara University, for courses in philosophy and theology. He was ordained a priest on May 31, 1958.

During his first summer as a priest, Father Allie was assigned to Blessed Sacrament parish in Bolton Landing, New York. From September 1958 to June 1967, he served as assistant priest at St. Catherine of Siena parish in Albany, New York. Next he found himself at St. Francis De Sales parish in Herkimer, New York, for about a year, and then at Our Lady of Victory parish in Troy, New York, also for about a year.

Around this time, the idea of helping out in the Archdiocese of **Anchorage, Alaska**, came to Father Allie. **Joseph T. Ryan**, former priest from the Diocese of Albany, was now Archbishop of Anchorage. Father Allie decided to write to him to see if he could use him. He began his letter, paused to gather his thoughts, glanced out the window next to his desk, and, in his words, "I couldn't believe my eyes, for there was Archbishop Ryan walking across the parking lot to enter the rectory to visit the pastor. That was all I needed to make me feel that, perhaps, God was trying to give me a message. The rest is history."

Not sure that he could take the ruggedness of Alaska, Father Allie volunteered to help out in the Archdiocese of Anchorage for only one year. Shortly after arriving in Alaska, however, he fell in love with it, and realized that it was the place for him. What was at first intended to be a one-year stay, turned out to be a stay of 30 years of full-time active ministry.

From the middle of July 1969 to March 1970, Father Allie served as an associate pastor at Anchorage's Holy Family Cathedral parish. On March 8, 1970, he was assigned as the first pastor of **Talkeetna** and visiting priest to its dependent missions: **Trapper Creek**, **Willow**, and **Big Lake**. Fortunately, the archdiocese at the time owned a Cherokee 180. He, being a pilot, having obtained his private license while at St. Francis De Sales, had the plane assigned to him to cover his missions. Over 30 years later, he wrote, "This became one of the most exciting times of my life."

Not long after coming to Alaska, Father Allie set about improving his flying skills by obtaining additional pilot ratings such as commercial pilot license, instrument rating, instructor rating, land and sea rating, and multi-engine rating. He earned the instructor rating, so that he could help those unable to afford flying lessons to obtain their private license.

During Father Allie's first year on the Talkeetna assignment, he offered Mass wherever space could be found. The two-bedroom house trailer provided for him in Talkeetna was soon too small for the number of people coming to attend Mass in it. In 1971, he was finally able to build a combination church and social center there. The church was named for St. Bernard of Menthon, who trained St. Bernard dogs to rescue people lost or in trouble in the Swiss Alps. The name was thought very appropriate, since Talkeetna is the staging area for climbers of Mount McKinley, Denali, "The Great One." At that time, about a third of his congregation was not

Catholic, but they were always welcome. Usually about 45 people attended Sunday Mass.

Talkeetna was still pretty much a bush area, when Father Allie first began to live there. On three different occasions, bears tried to break into the rectory, without success. They did, however, succeed to break into the church. Often, in the winter, when temperatures dropped into the minus 50 range, he would find as many as a dozen moose lying against the church building trying to keep warm. He would have to shoo them away from the front door, so that he could enter to offer Mass on week days.

Four miles west of Talkeetna is the settlement of Trapper Creek. Both are located on the Susitna River. The two are only four miles apart, as the raven flies, but the road linking them at that time was built in such a way that it was a 60-mile round-trip from one to the other. Father Allie commuted to Trapper Creek in his airplane, landing on the rough highway. It took him only four minutes from take-off to touch-down. During those days, there were only a handful of people at Trapper Creek, homesteaders on land given them by the Federal Government. There were no telephone or electrical services. People communicated by radio. Mass was offered in a very small log cabin, 14×14 feet. A gasoline lantern hanging from the ceiling provided light; a wood-burning barrel stove heat. A stack of three orange crates served as an altar. "It was a great Faith experience," he wrote. After about two years, he had a "basement" church built at Trapper Creek.

Regarding Willow and Big Lake, Father Allie wrote: "On weekends I would fly to Big Lake, located 56 miles south of Talkeetna, on Saturdays from Talkeetna to offer Mass in a public grammar school, located only a couple hundred yards from a rough airstrip. In the winter months, I would often offer Mass in a tourist hotel located on the lake. On Sunday morning, I would fly to Willow and Trapper Creek to offer Mass, and then at Talkeetna at four in the afternoon."

In the summer of 1974, Father Allie was transferred to St. Benedict's parish in Anchorage. He remained there for ten years as pastor. At this time the parish was growing so fast that, within a few years, it was split in three, bringing about the two new parishes of St. Elizabeth Ann Seton and St. Paul

Miki. Even after the splitting, the parish continued to grow, so much so that he had to build a new church to accommodate the congregation at St. Benedict's.

In the summer of 1984, Father Allie became pastor of St. Elizabeth Ann Seton parish. On December 23, 1987, right at the Offertory of the noon Mass, the roof of the church collapsed. Fortunately, all got out, with only ten seconds to spare, so that there were no fatalities. "I thought my building days were over," wrote Father Allie, "but that was not to be the case. I had to build another church."

In the summer of 1990, Father Allie was appointed pastor of Sacred Heart parish in **Wasilla**. There he found the same situation he had had, when he first came to St. Benedict's. The area was growing so rapidly that the original church, built in the latter 1960s, "was bulging at the seams." He had no choice but to build a new church. Dedication took place in February 1999. This was the fifth time that he, as a pastor, had to see to the building of a new church.

On July 1, 2000, Father Allie went into a well-deserved retirement, making his home in Wasilla. Three years later he wrote, "I have enjoyed every minute of it." However, even though retired from full-time pastoral ministry now, he continued to help out with weekend Masses at Talkeetna, Trapper Creek, Willow, and Big Lake. "I am back right where I started, at least on weekends" he wrote, adding, "Thanks be to God I no longer have the responsibilities as pastor. Being a pastor is extremely challenging and rewarding, but there comes a time when you realize that it is time to hang it up and leave things to the next generation." On May 31, 2003, with a grateful heart, he celebrated the 45th anniversary of his ordination to the priesthood.

15

ALORALREA, Sister Josephine Theresa, O.S.U.

Josephine Theresa (Igilan) Aloralrea was born to Andrew (Anegellegneq) and Juliana (Nimegulrea) Aloralrea in a sod house at **Kashunuk** shortly after midnight on December 28, 1946. Her twin sister Elizabeth (Betty) Fermolye was born shortly before midnight. Her extended Central Yup'ik (Čup'ik) Eskimo family lived off the land by traveling to sea-

sonal campsites in the vicinity of Kashunuk and Old **Chevak**.

In the 1920s and '30s, Josephine's father helped and guided Father Francis M. **Ménager**, S.J., and the Ivan **Sipary** family, catechists and builders of mission structures, in the Yukon-Kuskokwim Delta. Josephine's mother had a remarkable memory and told her children detailed stories of early missionary and catechetical activities in Kashunuk and the general area. She kept the memory of her husband alive by telling his story to her children. Through the telling of traditional Čup'ik stories, she taught her children the moral lessons contained in those stories. Long after her parents had departed this world, Josephine recalled how they had "lived and taught their strong faith in the presence of God, Who is compassionate and present in all of life." From the example of her mother's and her maternal aunt's both giving birth to boys, contrary to reasonable expectations, she learned, too, that "God is for us and we are often surprised by new life entering into our experience, when we thought it was impossible."

As a toddler, Josephine came close to a premature, watery death. She and her twin sister were with their mother on a berry-picking outing near a pond. At one point, and just in time, Betty cried out in alarm, as she watched her twin sister floating face down in the pond. Their older brother, Gregory, with a wooden pole used to snag a shot seal, reached out and saved Josephine.

Josephine grew up in the traditional, subsistence way of life of Eskimo people living along the Bering Sea coast. With her extended family, she traveled to the various seasonal camps: spring camp, fish camp, berry camp. One summer, the mission boat, the *St. Patrick*, skippered by Father **John J. Wood**, S.J., came to their fish camp and brought her family to their berry camp in Old Chevak. On board were **Ursuline** Sisters and members of the Native Sisterhood, the Oblates of St. Ursula, from St. Mary's Mission on the **Andreafsky** River. Years later, Josephine remembered how the Sisters prayed at the cemetery and put ripe salmonberries on plates that had been left on graves and how impressed she was by the manner in which the Sisters related to her family in a gentle and lighthearted way. She remembered, too, how the Oblate Sisters visited the

Sister Josephine Aloralrea, O.S.U.
LR.

family fish camp near New Chevak, taught vacation bible school classes in Chevak, and asked her and the older children to teach basic prayers to the younger children.

Josephine's mother was a devout Catholic, who took her children to daily Mass and prayed the family rosary with them. Later, as an Ursuline Sister, Josephine was to write, "The Church was the center of the people's lives in Chevak." Her uncle, Deacon Michael **Nayagak**, an exemplary member of the **Eskimo Deacon Program**, was a prayer leader for the community in the absence of a priest.

For her elementary schooling, Josephine attended the Bureau of Indian Affairs school in Chevak. Leaving her home village, a village she described as "a safe and fairly peaceful place in which for families to bring children up," Josephine went on to attend St. Mary's Mission High School. Her years at the boarding school, from 1964–68, she found "a positive experience," one that expanded her world. The Ursuline Sisters were her teachers, and dorm and chore supervisors. Along with the rest of the students, she took seriously her studies and assigned household chores. With pride, she related in later years how the Chevak students took part in a Yup'ik dance with the St. Mary's villagers. She had praise for "the strong feeling of community among the diverse groups of people at the boarding school."

During her last years at St. Mary's, Josephine read two books that had "a lasting impact" on her life: Thomas Merton's *No Man Is an Island*, and St. Theresa of Avila's *Interior Castle*. Both books expanded her "sense of God." She was moved by how the two spoke about God as one very much involved in their lives. It was at this time that she first became interested in Religious life and consulted a priest about it. He told her, "It is between God and you." This left her "hanging in the air to reflect on the Yup'ik word for God, '*Agayun*'"— the mysterious provider for all essential human needs.

One day, in the sacristy of the school chapel, Josephine comforted a young girl student from **Kaltag**, who was crying because she felt misunderstood by the Sister in charge of her dorm. On that occasion, the thought of making a difference in the lives of young Alaskan Native women entered Josephine's mind. Also, while in her last year at St. Mary's, she heard a white woman from **Anchorage** warn her class by telling them about a Native woman who was found outdoors during the cold of winter apparently victimized by local military men. That account of such inhumanity toward her people shattered Josephine's view of a safe, sheltered world. Those experiences of harsh reality, along with her spiritual reading, brought her to the conclusion that God was calling her to serve Him and her people as a member of the Order of St. Ursula.

Leaving the only world she had ever known for one still almost wholly foreign to her at the time was for Josephine anything but easy. Members of the **Jesuit Volunteer Corps** serving at St. Mary's made negative comments, letting her know that they thought her decision to become an Ursuline Sister rather overly ambitious for a Čup'ik young woman. Her protective mother, who had heard about the hard life led by Sisters at the missions of **Holy Cross** and **Akulurak**, would not speak to her for a week. Moreover, being a widow, she felt her daughter was abandoning her for good. From a childhood friend in **Hooper Bay**, Josephine received a letter inviting her to "consider settling down." She wrote him to tell him she had other plans. Her twin sister, Betty, however, respected her decision.

Josephine applied to be accepted as a member of

the Western Province of the Ursuline Sisters of the Roman Union and was accepted. After working for Rural-Cap as a food stamp representative in Chevak for a short time, she traveled to Santa Rosa, California, where, living with a family, she attended Santa Rosa Junior College. At first, she experienced "culture shock, feeling not quite at home."

On September 8, 1969, Josephine was received as a postulant into the Ursuline novitiate at Santa Rosa by the Mother Provincial, Sister Teresita Rivet. On March 9, 1970, she received the Ursuline habit and began her novitiate. Sister Celeste Dempsey, who had once visited some of the fish camps of the Chevak people, was her formation director. Whenever Josephine suffered bouts of homesickness, Sister Celeste comforted her and told her to look to the future, to when she would again return to Alaska to serve her people. Sister Josephine spent part of the second year of her novitiate back at St. Mary's helping a group of bright young Native students read. Years later she recalled how "they took advantage of my quiet demeanor and lack of experience in the classroom. Some of them, however, became my good friends."

For the whole of her canonical year as a novice, Josephine was at the novitiate in Santa Rosa. In the course of that year, she learned how to meditate and pray the Divine Office with the rest of the community. She also studied theology, Church history, and read some contemporary Catholic authors. During her second year as a novice, as a part of her "ministry experience," she was assigned to work with Sister Sally Ann Nash, O.S.U., in **Toksook Bay**. Out of there, she visited **Tununak** and **Newtok**. She felt very much at home with the Yup'ik people, many of whom knew her father from the days when he accompanied the missionaries in that region. With gratitude, she recalled, many years later, the "wonderful Yup'ik hospitality, generosity and kindness" shown her while among her own people. Except for her ministry experience in Alaska, she found novitiate life in general "a very traditional, cloistered convent lifestyle." Nevertheless, in her post-novitiate years, she had praise for "the spaciousness of Religious life."

On May 13, 1972, at St. Mary's, Josephine made her temporary profession as a Religious. In doing so, she made history. As of the year 2004, Sister Josephine was the only member of the Central Yup'ik Eskimo people to become a member of the Ursuline Order. The month after her temporary profession, she was assigned to Our Lady of Loreto community in Novato, California. By December 1976, she had her B.A. degree from the Dominican College in San Rafael, California. In 1994, she received her M.A. degree in Religious Education from the University of San Francisco. Two years later, she took part in a seminar, "Development and Self-Determination among the Indigenous Peoples of the North."

Sister Josephine spent the first half of the year 1977 in an inner-city parish in Los Angeles working among Afro-Americans. Back at St. Mary's, on September 22, 1977, she made her final profession as an Ursuline Sister. A month later, she found herself in the Holy Land and Rome, thanks to an unused ticket from a tour group.

Throughout much of the 1970s, Sister Josephine had taught on and off at St. Mary's. In the early 1980s, she was there full-time teaching Old and New Testament courses to high school freshmen, and serving as a counselor and dorm supervisor. She spent the year 1984–85 studying with Amerindians at Kisemanito Centre in Grouard, Alberta, Canada. From time to time, she also attended Tekakwitha Conferences held in various places across the nation. At these she was exposed to traditional spiritual rituals and ways of America's Native peoples. This enabled her to incorporate the traditional ways and values of her Yup'ik culture into her classes at St. Mary's. She introduced Yup'ik dancing into the Sunday liturgy. In addition to her work at St. Mary's High School, she also served as a "parish Sister" at the St. Marys village parish from 1985–87. Sister Josephine taught at St. Mary's until the school closed in May 1987. Father **James R. Laudwein**, S.J., administrator of St. Mary's Mission High School while Sister Josephine taught there, remembered her as "popular with our Yup'ik students."

By the time Sister Josephine left northwestern Alaska, she had been involved also with the Ecumenical Consultation for Ministry Training in Alaska. She and Cecilia Martz developed a course entitled "Yup'ik/Čup'ik Traditional Life-Ways," which they presented to catechists, Yup'ik deacons, and Moravian pastors. The Yup'ik people felt empowered and affirmed by those programs.

In 1987, after taking care of her ailing mother in Chevak, Sister Josephine went to Santa Rosa to work as a pre-kindergarten assistant and as a substitute Religion teacher at the Ursuline High School there. In the early 1990s, she moved to Oakland, California, and worked for the Indian Education program and the Oakland school district in a multicultural child-development center geared mainly to Native American children from nursery to sixth grade. Along with ministers of other denominations, she served also as a member of Bay Area Native American Ministry, whose mission statement read: "This ministry seeks to serve members of one of the world's oppressed communities as they work for healing from the physical, emotional, and spiritual problems which have continued to have devastating and multi-generational consequences."

In the Bay Area, Sister Josephine also did volunteer work at the American Indian Family Healing Center, sharing with people there the values of her traditional Čup'ik way of life. She was invited to speak about her cultural heritage at the Pacific School of Religion, Graduate Theological Union, in Berkeley, California. She was a member of the Nunamta Yup'ik/Eskimo Dance Troupe. In 1994, the troupe, along with other Native American performers, made a tour of California universities. In 1997, it performed in Australia. As a troupe member, she lectured in various U.S. cities on Yup'ik spirituality and performed as an Eskimo dancer at the Kennedy Center for the Performing Arts and in the Library of Congress. In summary, Sister Josephine wrote, "My experience with the Nunamta Yup'ik/Eskimo Dance Troupe has diversified my identity as a member of the Roman Union of Ursuline Sisters."

During the year 1997–98, Sister Josephine and thirteen other Ursuline Sisters from literally all over the world made their tertianship in Rome. During the first part of this, they spent some time in northern Italy, making pilgrimages to places and shrines sacred to their Order. In Brescia, they visited the shrine of their foundress, St. Angela Merici. Sister Josephine spent

Father John Althoff.
LRC.

the second part of her tertianship among Navajo Indians in Arizona and New Mexico.

In April 1999, Sister Josephine was interviewed, and hired, by Michael W. **Warfel**, Bishop of **Juneau**, to serve as Parish Administrator of St. Ann's parish in **Yakutat**. In November 2003, he was able to write concerning her presence in Yakutat: "Sr. Josephine has been a true blessing to the parish of St. Ann's, as well as to the entire community of Yakutat. She has provided a pastoral presence to meet the pastoral and spiritual needs of the people. Having her in residence in Yakutat has been a stabilizing element for the church there."

As of the year 2004, Sister Josephine was still happily serving the Lord and His people in Yakutat.

ALTHOFF, Father John J.

John J. Althoff was born in Haarlem, Holland, on May 5, 1853. He arrived in Victoria, British Columbia, Canada, in 1878, to serve as a member of the Diocese of Vancouver Island. On May 4, 1879, Charles J. **Seghers**, Bishop of Vancouver Island, put him in charge of the mission at **Wrangell, Alaska**. For the next four years, Father Althoff made Wrangell his headquarters, but he also made periodic visits to the Cassiar mining district on the Stikine River and to **Sitka**. In 1882, he was transferred to Nanaimo, Vancouver Island. When **Juneau** was less than two years old, he visited that gold mining town. On July 17, 1882, in the "Log Cabin Church," he offered the first Mass celebrated in Juneau and, that same day, recorded Juneau's first Catholic baptism.

In November 1885, Father Althoff took up residency in Juneau. There he set to work at once to build a church. He was responsible for bringing to Juneau the Sisters of St. **Ann** in 1886, who, that same year, began to run a hospital and a school.

Father Althoff was stationed in Juneau from 1885–95. During those years, he visited Wrangell from time to time. While in Juneau, he earned for himself the honorific nickname of "the miners' friend."

After his Juneau years, Father Althoff worked in Nelson, British Columbia, and served, at the same time, as Vicar General of what was then the Diocese of Vancouver Island.

Father Althoff died at Nelson on December 30, 1926. Of him and Father William L. **Heynen**, Joseph R. **Crimont**, S.J., Vicar Apostolic of **Alaska** at the time, said: "These two men were the pioneers of the Church in Southeastern Alaska."

15, 16

ANABLE, Father Edmund A., S.J.

He was a man of well-forged steel. One who knew him for many years said of him that he had a "penchant for efficiency," that he was a "born boss," because he knew not only the *how* of things, but also the *why*. "Anytime, anytime!" were his words, when someone needed a favor he could render. People had trouble with his last name, misspelling it even on the cake he cut into as he celebrated the fiftieth anniversary of his ordination to the priesthood. He was fiercely loyal to God and the Church. He was a fisher of men, and he was a fisher of fish. He was a frontier priest.

Edmund A. Anable was born in Utica, New York, on November 13, 1903. His father was a railroad conductor all his life. His mother he described as "a housewife, in the best sense of the word." There were five boys and two girls in the family. Four of the boys became priests; one of the girls a Sister.

Edmund Anable was attracted to the foreign missions during his high school years. As a freshman at New York's Fordham University, he applied for admission into the Society of Jesus and was accepted. He entered the novitiate at Poughkeepsie, New York, on March 18, 1924. After completing his two-year noviceship and classical and humanities studies there, he made his philosophical studies at Woodstock, Maryland. From 1930–33, he taught biology and algebra at St. Joseph's Prep School in Philadelphia. It was during those teaching years that his thoughts began to turn to **Alaska**. Upon his arrival back at Woodstock for theological studies, he volunteered for Alaska. He was ordained a priest on June 21, 1936. After a fourth year of theology at Woodstock and his year of tertianship at Poughkeepsie, he traveled west and sailed for Alaska in the summer of 1938. That marked the beginning of a long and distinguished missionary career in Alaska. His first assignment took him to the heart of the Central Yup'ik Eskimo country, to St. Mary's Mission, **Akulurak**, where he arrived on August 7, 1938.

One of Father Anable's more unusual accomplishments at Akulurak was the designing and building of a new mission boat. During his second year there, his local Superior, Father Paul C. **O'Connor**, S.J., told him that the old mission boat was falling apart and that he wished Father Anable to replace it with a new one. In remote Alaska, with few resources at hand, this presented him with a daunting challenge indeed. However, providentially, one of his boyhood hobbies had been the building of model ships. "So," he wrote years later, "I took a log from the woodpile outside and carved a hull on a scale of half an inch to the foot, showing what a mission boat should be according to my ideas. Father O'Connor accepted it, and I then spent several months drawing plans and sending orders for the building materials to come in on the first boat in the summer. Brother George J. **Feltes**, an excellent mechanic, did the same for the metal work and the engine. And, finally, we had a fifty-foot flat-bottomed boat, which did yeoman work for the next twenty-five years." The boat, named after Father John B. **Sifton**, S.J., General Superior of the Alaska Mission for many years, was launched in the summer of 1941. Father Anable, however, did not witness the launching. As of March 16, 1941, he had been at the **Pilgrim Hot Springs** Mission as Superior there.

Soon after his arrival at the Hot Springs mission, Father Anable sent a report to Joseph R. **Crimont**, S.J., Vicar Apostolic of Alaska at the time, on its physical condition. On the basis of that report, Bishop Crimont instructed Father Anable to close the mission. This he did on July 31, 1941.

Father Anable was then assigned the task of going to the Lower 48 States to beg monies for the missions. A year later, after preaching and begging in churches all across the country, he returned to Alaska to present Bishop Crimont with $28,000.

Father Anable spent the year 1942–43 at **Holy Cross Mission**. In June 1943, he was appointed pastor of St. Joseph's parish, **Nome**. The church he found there was by that time over 40 years old, and showing its age. Though the parish had only $273.00 in the bank, he began planning for a new church-rectory building. From the military he bought two plywood buildings located several miles from Nome, had them moved into town onto church property, and, with the help of two Eskimo men working for minimum wages, started to transform the two buildings into a new church-rectory structure. It took him a full year—and a trip to the hospital—to complete the complex. The new church was ready for the Easter Sunday Mass of 1946.

In late 1947, Father Anable was appointed pastor of Immaculate Conception parish in **Fairbanks**. For some years, the members of that parish had been agitating for a parochial school. Bishop Walter J. **Fitzgerald**, S.J., Bishop Crimont's successor, as one of his first acts in office, gave the order that a Catholic school be started in Fairbanks. Immaculate Conception Grade School opened in the basement hall of the church in 1946 with a kindergarten and grades one through four. As grades were added, a school building became imperative. The city had for sale six empty barracks, which had been used by construction crews, when they built the airport. Under Father Anable's leadership, these were bought and moved to a school site, where a construction crew transformed them into a school building with eight classrooms and a principal's office. The new school complex was opened in 1951.

Father Edmund A. Anable, S.J. *LRC.*

In 1952, Francis D. **Gleeson**, S.J., Catholic bishop in Alaska since April 5, 1948, appointed Father Anable to be Mission Procurator, based in Seattle. His principal responsibility now was to purchase and ship supplies to the various missions in northern Alaska, as well as to raise needed funds. Churches in the Lower 48 were no longer as open to a begging missionary as they had been a decade earlier. "Could funds be raised within Alaska itself?" Father Anable asked himself.

Recalling the great salmon runs he had witnessed in the lower Yukon River region and the relatively low wages paid Natives for working in canneries outside that region, Father Anable saw the possibilities of benefits to both the Alaskan missions and the Native people in a cottage salmon industry. "In our first summer," he wrote, "we—for lack of a better way—cut, hung, dried and smoked several thousand pounds of delicious salmon, which we were able to sell in Fairbanks for a dollar a pound." With these funds he next purchased a small canning machine. During the second summer, now at the new St. Mary's Mission on the **Andreafsky** River, Father Anable's crew put up over a thousand cases of canned salmon. These were sold through a broker in Seattle. Soon the salmon cannery proved to be a real success story. By 1959, the year Father Anable turned the cannery over to Father René **Astruc**, S.J., it was putting out 15,000 cases a season. The Native fishermen, instead of being paid

85 cents per fish, as they had been by commercial packers less than ten years earlier, were now getting $5.00 per fish, and the missions realized a return of almost $100,000. Father Segundo **Llorente**, S.J., attributed the cannery's success to Father Anable's "talents and many sophistications, perhaps the greatest of which was his penchant for efficiency. Wherever he showed up, things began to move and no nonsense was tolerated. With a shade over his eyes, he could work under a bright bulb for hours, till he was satisfied that the plan was flawless and so would be its execution. His power of concentration was truly remarkable."

In the meantime, Bishop Gleeson had been looking for some cheaper way of getting supplies to the missions. With Father Anable leading the way, a flat-bottomed tugboat and a large steel-hulled barge were obtained and converted into a riverboat, the *Cabna* (Catholic Bishop of Northern Alaska). The boat itself was a success, but a series of mishaps and the difficulty of finding a reliable crew for it led to its being sold after operating only two seasons.

In 1963, Father Anable was again assigned pastor of Immaculate Conception parish in Fairbanks. To end his building days, he saw to the construction of the combination gymnasium-parish hall building at Monroe Catholic High School and a thorough renovation of Immaculate Conception Church. From 1966–67, he served as Rector of the newly built Sacred Heart Cathedral.

Father Anable spent his last fully active years in the ministry, the years 1967–81, almost exclusively in fund-raising, in soliciting monies for the missions through a direct mail program. As part of this program, he edited *The Alaskan Shepherd*, a bimonthly newsletter sent to benefactors. From its inception, this fund-raising program was, and continued to be, the principal source of funds needed to support the missionary works of the Diocese of Fairbanks.

In 1981, after 44 years of working either in or for Alaska, Father Anable, with the blessing and gratitude of his bishop, Robert L. **Whelan**, S.J., and Jesuit Superiors, decided to go into semi-retirement. He chose Florida in hopes of finding some relief from arthritis. He drove to Daytona Beach to do part-time parish work there. Though generally distracted by building projects, he had been, nevertheless, a competent, devoted, highly respected pastor in Alaska. People of a more conservative bent especially took to him. For two months he found parish work in Daytona Beach "great." Then, one morning, he woke up with the realization that Florida was simply not Alaska. A homesick Father Anable phoned for permission to return home. Permission granted, he started the return trip to Fairbanks the following day.

Father Anable was to spend eight more years in Alaska. On March 18, 1984, in Immaculate Conception Church, he celebrated a Mass of Thanksgiving for his 60 years in the Society of Jesus. Asked, on that occasion, about his plans for the future, he answered: "There are, of course, no plans for the future. God has been most good to me and has taken care of me all these years of my unusual, interesting life as a missionary. I am most confident He will continue to do so. I look forward to the day, two years from now, when I may celebrate my 50th anniversary as a priest of God."

A man of action all his life, Father Anable found semi-retirement difficult. Accordingly, on a regular basis, he began to offer Sunday Mass for the elderly in the Golden Towers, a home for the retired. From time to time, he helped out in various parishes with Masses and confessions. He was always a ready volunteer to drive people to or from the airport. He ran errands for the Jesuit community he lived in. Occasionally he cooked dinner for them. The sport fishing he so enjoyed in his younger days was now too much for him. He generally kept a low profile, spent much time in his room reading spiritual writings, or Louis L'Amour westerns.

By 1989, Father Anable was beginning to need special care. So, after calling Alaska home for over half a century, he went to the Jesuit Regis Retirement Community in Spokane, Washington. Soon after his arrival there, however, he had to be transferred to St. Joseph Care Center, where he ended his days in the care of the Sisters of Providence. He died peacefully of natural causes, in his 89th year, on June 24, 1992, and lies buried in the Jesuit cemetery at Mount St. Michael's, Spokane.

Holy Family Cathedral, Anchorage. *Courtesy of Fr. Donald J. Bramble, O.P.*

ANCHORAGE

Anchorage, **Alaska**'s largest city, was first referred to as "Ship Creek." Located along Knik Arm at the head of Cook Inlet, it was established in 1913 as the construction camp and headquarters for the proposed **Seward** to **Fairbanks** Alaska Railroad. The name was derived from that of Knik anchorage, immediately off shore from the new camp. Anchorage's estimated population in 1917 was 6,000. In 1920, it was officially 1,856; in 1930, 2,277; in 1939, 3, 495; in 1950, 11,254; in 1967, 44, 237; and in the year 2000, 260, 283. The Anchorage post office was established in 1914.

The Catholic Church was not long in coming to Anchorage. The first visit to the new city by a Catholic priest took place on June 22, 1915, when Father William A. **Shepherd**, S.J., 41 years old and stationed in Southcentral Alaska since 1912, arrived there and stayed for two weeks. Later that summer, he was formally assigned to Anchorage. The date for the official beginning of the Catholic Church in Anchorage is given as that of September 12, 1915, when he offered Mass in "Crist House," a rooming house at the corner of Fourth Avenue and "K" Street. Construction of a modest wooden church, the first church edifice in Anchorage, began two days later at a site between Fifth and Sixth Avenues, on "H" Street. On October 17, 1915, Father Shepherd offered Masses for the first time in the new church.

In keeping with the wishes of a generous benefactor, the church was dedicated under the title of Holy Family. From the outset, the small church had to be extended a number of times. Anchorage grew so rapidly that, even while Father Shepherd was still pastor, there was already talk of a hospital. This was to come, but not until several decades later.

Father Shepherd left Anchorage in 1919 for **Ketchikan**. He was replaced, just before Christmas 1919, by Father Aloysius J. **Markham**, a diocesan priest. For eight years, from 1901–09, Father Markham had served at **Holy Cross Mission**, not as a priest, however, but as a Jesuit Lay Brother. Father Markham, while not an old man—he was born in Washington, D.C., on May 1, 1867—was not a well man. When he was ailing, or out of Anchorage, Father S. Aloysius **Eline**, S.J., came down by train from Fairbanks to tend Holy Family parish. During the 1920s, Father Philibert **Turnell**, S.J., too, helped out at Holy Family. He offered the first High Mass offered in Anchorage, on Easter Sunday 1922. Father Markham, in poor health, left Alaska in 1929. His last assignment in life was that of chaplain at Marylhurst College, Oswego, Oregon, where he died on January 7, 1933.

During the years 1928–31, Father George H. Woodley was pastor of Holy Family. While he was taking flight training on the east coast, Father Godfrey Dane, S.J., stationed in Southeastern Alaska at the time, substituted for him. Father Woodley died accidentally on October 12, 1931, while hunting in Alaska. The funeral Mass offered for him in Anchorage was the first such Mass offered in Anchorage for a priest. Father Dane, who followed Father Woodley as pastor of Holy Family, left Anchorage in 1933.

In 1933, there appeared on the Anchorage scene the best remembered of all the priests in the early history of Anchorage. This was Father Robert Dermot **O'Flanagan**. He came to Anchorage on a temporary basis, to replace for a few months Father Dane, who needed rest and medical attention. Little did Father O'Flanagan realize then that Anchorage would be his home for 18 years and, eventually, his final resting place.

In the mid-1930s, there was already talk about replacing the original Holy Family Church with a bigger, more substantial structure. However, the effects of the Great Depression were still being felt. Money was in short supply. Then came World War II. This diverted people's attention in other directions; but, at the same time, drew people to Anchorage. The aging, wooden church became woefully inadequate to handle the increased numbers attending Masses there.

Following the war, amidst prosperity and optimism, a drive for a new church was renewed with a fervor born of necessity. Adequate funds for the new church were soon raised. Compared to the little 1915 church, the projected new church would be enormous. It would have a full basement and a 40-foot tower. Its white cement exterior would, in all seasons, reflect the sub-arctic sun in all its moods. Soon construction began. By Sunday, December 14, 1947, its basement was ready enough to accommodate over 200 attending the Advent liturgy. Ten months later, in October 1948, the new church was a concrete reality. Less than 20 years later, Holy Family Church became an archdiocesan cathedral. In late 1969, the main entrance to the cathedral was modified and enlarged. On February 26, 1981, Holy Family Cathedral was honored by the presence in it of Pope John Paul II.

Father O'Flanagan left Holy Family parish in 1951 to become the first bishop of the newly estab-

The first Holy Family Church and rectory, Anchorage.
JOPA-420.01.

lished Diocese of **Juneau**. He was succeeded as pastor by Father Harley A. **Baker**, who had been assistant pastor since 1949. Of immediate concern to him as pastor was to bring into being a catechetical program. To him fell also the responsibility for the completion of the church, the providing of a new rectory, and the nurturing of the dream for a Catholic school. In 1959, Father Baker was transferred to Juneau to serve there as Chancellor of the Juneau Diocese. In the late summer of that year, Monsignor G. Edgar **Gallant** became pastor of Holy Family parish. He served as such until January 7, 1967, when Father John A. **Lunney** was named to that position. He was succeeded in 1970 by Father Francis A. Murphy. A year later, Father Richard B. **Saudis** took over as pastor. He was followed in 1972 by Father Edward J. Stirling, C.S.Sp., who, for health reasons, left in 1973. For a short time, Father Thomas E. Power filled in for him.

After July 5, 1974, members of the Western Province of the Dominican Fathers, Oakland, California, served as pastors and assistants at Holy Family Cathedral. The following served as pastors: Bede Wilks, 1974–77; Lawrence Farrell, 1977–83; Kent Burnter, 1983–86; Martin Diaz, 1986–91; Bede Wilks, 1991–95; LaSalle Hallissey, 1995–98; Paul Scanlon, 1998–2000; Joseph Sergott, 2000–02; and Donald Bramble, 2002 to the present (2004). It was Father Scanlon, the Dominican Father Provincial in the early 1970s, who arranged for the Dominican Fathers to staff Holy Family. Along with the Dominican Fathers, the following deacons served at Holy Family parish: James W. Hostman, 1982–90; Felix M. Maguire, 1990–99; and Gerry Grewe, 1999 to the present (2004).

Soon after Holy Family parish was established, there was renewed talk now of the need for a hospital, now of the need for a school in Anchorage. The need for a hospital seemed the greater. In the mid-1930s, Father O'Flanagan brought up the subject of a hospital with Joseph R. **Crimont**, S.J., Vicar Apostolic of Alaska, and the Sisters of **Providence**. On July 22, 1937, the Sisters accepted the responsibility of erecting and operating a hospital. Sister Stanislaus, first Superior in Anchorage, and Sister Isadora arrived in Anchorage on March 25, 1938. That same year witnessed the blessing, on September 9th, of the cornerstone for the new hospital at

the site selected for its construction, the square block between Eighth and Ninth Avenues and "L" and "M" Streets. The following year, on June 29, 1939, Providence Hospital, described in the *Anchorage Daily Times* as "Alaska's Finest Hospital," was formally dedicated and opened. But, given the rapid growth of Anchorage's population owing to World War II and the closing in September 1944 of the Government-owned Alaska Railroad Hospital, Providence Hospital was soon inadequate.

By 1952, the demand for a broadened scope of medical services and accompanying facilities was apparent. Apparent, too, was the fact that the "L" Street facility and location were too limited to meet this demand. Land for a modern, much larger hospital was acquired on June 19, 1958, at the Goose Lake site. On May 15, 1960, the groundbreaking ceremony for the new, enlarged, 175-bed, $6,000,000 hospital took place. By the middle of 1962, the new hospital was almost finished. Moving day was October 26, 1962. By the end of 1962, the hospital in the Goose Lake area was functioning smoothly. The old hospital on "L" Street, remodeled and renamed "St. Mary's Residence," became a nursing home.

The new Providence Hospital, both as a physical structure and a human institution, did not have to wait long, before it was subjected to a test severe beyond anyone's imagining. On Good Friday, March 27, 1964, at 5:36 P.M., Anchorage was struck by the full force of an earthquake registering 9.2 on the Richter scale. The building withstood the force of the quake remarkably well, considering the severity of the quake. Off-duty staff members of all departments not at the hospital returned immediately to help receive the injured and care for them. There was comfort for a stunned and broken city to hear the news via emergency radio broadcasts that Providence was operating and caring for casualties. After much repair work on the building and restocking of supplies, a degree of normalcy soon returned to Providence. In the decades that followed "the Good Friday Earthquake," many major improvements and expansions were made at Providence Hospital to make it the highly regarded modern medical facility that it was as of the year 2004.

While the Catholic Church was striding forward on the medical front, it was moving forward also on the parochial front. By the early 1950s, it was evident to many that Holy Family Church was no longer big enough for the number of parishioners it was expected to care for. Additional parishes were needed in Anchorage. On August 28, 1957, Bishop O'Flanagan, whose Diocese of Juneau included also Southcentral Alaska, and, therefore, Anchorage, canonically established St. Anthony's parish on Mountain View Drive. That same month, Father Robert L. **Whelan**, S.J., arrived to see to the construction of a church and rectory, and to serve as the first pastor of St. Anthony's. After a simple blessing of the church by Father Whelan on Sunday, November 17, 1957, he offered the first Mass celebrated in St. Anthony's. On the evening of the Feast of St. Anthony of Padua, June 13, 1960, Bishop O'Flanagan solemnly blessed and dedicated Anchorage's second parish church. This initial church was replaced by a new and bigger edifice with a modern hexagonal design. Groundbreaking ceremonies for this church were held on July 16, 1967. The new combination church-parish hall building was formally dedicated on October 27, 1968. Father Whelan was St. Anthony's pastor until 1968, when he was replaced by Msgr. Francis A. **Cowgill**. In 2000, he was followed by Father Thomas Wynne, O.M.I., for a year. His successor was Father Steven C. Moore, Administrator, with Father Nelson R. Marilag as Parochial Vicar. As of the year 2004, Father Fred T. **Bugarin** headed the parish. Deacon Dennis D. Foreman served at St. Anthony's during the late 1980s and early 1990s. Deacon Theodore W. Greene began serving there in 1989 and was still serving there as of the year 2004.

In connection with St. Anthony's, it should be mentioned that in 1981 it began to host Anchorage's Korean Catholic community, with Msgr. Cowgill offering Masses in Korean for it. Ten years later, the community was stable enough to construct a small center on the parish grounds. Thereafter, Korean priests and nuns served the community on a regular basis. As of the year 2004, it enjoyed the services of its pastor, Father In Yong Shin, and of Sisters Magdalena Yu and Dorothea Han.

In the same year, 1957, that St. Anthony's was being canonically established, a tiny wooden chapel, named for St. Juliana—in keeping with the wishes of a benefactor, who contributed toward the chapel's establishment through the Catholic Church Exten-

sion Society—was put up in Spenard, an area still outside the Anchorage city limits. The little chapel was subsequently moved to a site on Jewel Lake Road, where it was replaced by a larger wood-frame church. On May 8, 1966, what was up till then St. Juliana's Church was dedicated under the title of St. Benedict. The parish of St. Benedict was established by an official decree dated May 26, 1966. Father James P. **Snead** was its first pastor, from 1966–70. He was followed by Father J. Thomas Connery, 1970–74. From 1974–84, Father Stanley J. **Allie** was pastor. Msgr. Francis A. Murphy was pastor for the year 1984–85, and Father H. William Goehring for the years 1985–89. During the first four of those years, he had as his associate pastor Father William C. **Dibb**, S.J. Father Alfred W. Giebel began serving as pastor of Benedict's in 1989, and was still doing so as of the year 2004. Sister Kathleen O'Hara, R.S.M., was a pastoral associate at St. Benedict's during the late 1980s and early 1990s. Throughout the 1990s, St. Benedict's had the services of Deacon Ray W. Allor.

In 1958, the Byzantine Rite parish of St. Nicholas of Myra was established by Bishop Nicholas T. Elko of the Eparchy of Pittsburgh. The parish church was constructed on Arctic Boulevard out of an old mess hall purchased from the Air Force. After modifications, the hall was blessed as a church on September 13, 1959. Pioneer pastors of St. Nicholas parish were Fathers Robert E. **Bayusik**, John Kasarda, and Michael Artim. Father Joseph Hutsko was pastor from 1985–89. He was followed by Father Stephen Greskowiak. As of the year 2004, the parish numbered 70 families and was served by Father Wesley W. Izer, S.D.B. Among the former parishioners of St. Nicholas parish, Maggie **Sipary** holds a place of special respect.

By 1960, the Catholic Church in Anchorage had parishes to provide for the needs of the soul, and a hospital to provide for the needs of the body, but still no school to provide for the needs of the mind of the young. For years there had been talk about opening a parochial school. Holy Family parish had bought land for the site of such a school already in 1949. Talk for establishing a Catholic school intensified during the later 1950s. In 1960, Holy Family and St. Anthony's parishes, assured that they would have a teaching staff provided by the Sisters

(*above*) Holy Cross Church, Anchorage, dedicated on September 12, 1993. *Photo by Ms. Nina Stafford-Wenrich.*

(*right*) The first St. Anthony's Church, Anchorage. *JOPA-421.02.*

(*below*) St. Elizabeth Ann Seton Church, Anchorage, completed in 1990. *Photo by Joshua Sanders.*

Sister Mary Clare, P.B.V.M., arrived in Anchorage on June 29, 1967. On July 22nd, she became Director of Catholic Charities for the Archdiocese of Anchorage. At the time, she was the only woman in the United States to hold that office. The following month, she distinguished herself, as she brought relief to victims of the mid-August flood that hit Fairbanks. From 1967–74, she served also as Co-Director of Religious Education at St. Michael's parish, Palmer. *Courtesy of St. Michael's parish, Palmer.*

of Providence, went ahead with a plan to build a junior high school to accommodate grades seven, eight and nine. The plan left open the possibility of expansion later, so that a new class level could be added each year to create eventually a full-fledged junior-senior high school. Construction began in the spring of 1961. On September 18, 1961, the school, named Central Catholic Junior High School, opened with 107 seventh graders. The faculty consisted of four Sisters of Providence: Mary Armella (Regina Tessier, principal), Esther (Lauretta Frawley), Mary Maurice (Mary Florence Gaetz), and Patricia Maureen (Patricia Rivest).

Central Catholic, as new classes were added year after year, continued to grow. By the spring of 1965, however, those principally concerned for the school's future came to a consensus that, chiefly for financial reasons, the plan to complete a senior high school program was no longer feasible. When the 1965–66 academic year began, the tenth grade was

no longer offered. Central Catholic closed altogether in the spring of 1967. During the next two years, Sisters of Providence staffed Anchorage's new Catholic primary school, Hubbard Memorial School, housed in the same facility that had housed the junior high school. Hubbard Memorial, named for Father Bernard R. **Hubbard**, S.J., closed in 1969.

But the Catholic people of Anchorage would not be denied Catholic schools. In 1980, St. Elizabeth Ann Seton Catholic School was established with 102 students in grades kindergarten through four. At the beginning of the school year 2003–04, it had 165 students in grades kindergarten through six. As of that year, too, Holy Rosary Academy, a private school, and Lumen Christi Jr./Sr. High School in St. Benedict's parish were also flourishing

February 9, 1966, was a day of major importance not only for the Catholic Church in Anchorage but also for the whole Catholic Church in Alaska. On that day the Archdiocese of Anchorage, a 138,985-square-mile area comprising the Third Judicial Division of Alaska, was officially established. The new archdiocese was created from territory detached from the Dioceses of Fairbanks and Juneau. **Joseph T. Ryan**, consecrated a bishop on March 25, 1966, was the first Archbishop of Anchorage. Holy Family Church became a cathedral at 10 A.M. on Thursday, April 14, 1966, when Archbishop Ryan formally took possession of the church as the seat of the new archdiocese, the Catholic Metropolitan See of Anchorage. By an official decree, issued on April 28, 1967, in Rome, St. Joseph the Worker was declared the patron of the new archdiocese.

Several years after Archbishop Ryan came to Anchorage, social and catechetical ministries began to flourish in the archdiocese. The Sisters of the Presentation of the Blessed Virgin Mary, in 1969, opened Catholic Charities offices in the city and were involved with religious education in **Palmer** and **Wasilla**. The Sisters of Mercy directed catechetical ministries in the city parishes. In 1969, too, Sister Dorothy Forest, a Sister of St. **Ann** in Alaska since 1952, began to coordinate religious education programs among the Native youth living in Anchorage, and to engage in ministry to the sick in the Native hospital and extended care facilities, to Native urban elders, to alcoholics, and to the incarcerated. By the end of the 1960s, "St. Francis House," subsequently known also as "St. Francis Shelter," and as "Brother Francis Shelter," had come into being in Anchorage. Its mission was from the outset to serve as an overnight shelter for homeless men and women and to supply food and clothes to the needy. As of the year 2004, Anchorage and **Kodiak** each had a flourishing "Brother Francis Shelter."

At the time the Archdiocese of Anchorage was created, it had a Catholic population of around 18,000, out of a total population of around 130,000. It was served by 23 priests. J. Michael Hornick was the first to be ordained a priest for the archdiocese, on May 17, 1969, in Westerville, Ohio. Alan Carl Abele was the first to be ordained a priest for the archdiocese in Anchorage, by Archbishop Ryan, on May 1, 1973. The ordination took place in Holy Family Cathedral.

In 1970, Our Lady of Guadalupe parish was established. The initial Mass of this parish was offered on Sunday, October 11, 1970. For the first five years of Our Lady of Guadalupe's existence, Sunday Masses were offered in the Turnagain Methodist Church on Northern Lights Boulevard; then, for a year, in the Turnagain Public School. Msgr. John A. **Lunney** was the first pastor of the parish, from 1970–94. (From 1994–97, he stayed on as pastor emeritus.) On Sunday, April 18, 1976, he presided, as ground was broken for the long-awaited multipurpose parish center at the Wisconsin Street site. The new Our Lady of Guadalupe center was dedicated on December 12, 1976. It was not until September 21, 2003, that ground was broken for a real church structure to accommodate the multicultural parish, estimated at approximately one third Filipino, one third Hispanic, and one third Anglo. Along with and after Msgr. Lunney, the following served as pastors or associate pastors at Our Lady of Guadalupe: Father Arthur **Lopilato**, S.J., 1989–96; Father Michael W. **Warfel**, 1995–96; Father **Daniel J. Hebert**, 1997–2001; and Father Vincent Blanco, 2001 to as of the year 2004.

At the end of July 1971, the formation of a new parish, St. Patrick's, to serve Anchorage's Muldoon area, was announced. Msgr. Francis A. Murphy was appointed its first pastor. As such, he served from 1971–84. During the years 1981–84, he had as his assistant Father Hebert. Archbishop Ryan was the

Pope John Paul II in Anchorage, February 26, 1981. *LRC.*

principal celebrant at the first Mass offered, on October 10, 1971, in St. Patrick's parish. It was offered in the muli-purpose room of Chester Valley School, where St. Patrick's parishioners met until their church, meant to become a parish center later on, was built in 1977. Father Richard D. **Tero** was pastor of St. Patrick's from 1984–92. He was assisted by Father Charles B. Crouse. Father Steven C. Moore pastored St. Patrick's from 1992 to 2001. It was he who saw to the building of the new church in 1996. Father Scott Medlock, in 2001, followed Father Moore, and was pastor of St. Patrick's as of the year 2004. Throughout most of the 1970s, Sister Joyce A. Ross, R.S.M., also served the parish, as did Deacon Kenneth E. Donohue, during the late 1980s and early 1990s. Deacon Felix M. Maguire was serving at St. Patrick's as of the year 2004.

The year 1971 saw the coming into being also of Holy Spirit Retreat House at the corner of O'Malley Road and Hillside Drive. In 1999, this was renamed **Holy Spirit Center**.

In 1975, to accommodate the increased number of parishioners served by St. Benedict's parish, two new parishes were established: St. Paul Miki and St. Elizabeth Ann Seton. At first, church services for the St. Paul Miki parish were held at Oriental Gardens Restaurant on the Old Seward Highway, and those for St. Elizabeth Ann Seton at O'Malley School. In 1978, it was determined that the number of people served by the two parishes did not justify the existence of two separate parishes. Accordingly, they were merged into one, St. Elizabeth Ann Seton. The church and school buildings of St. Elizabeth Ann Seton parish, located on Huffman Road, were dedicated in 1980. On December 23, 1987, the roof of the church collapsed during the noon Mass. Although the church was destroyed, all got out safely. A new church was completed in 1990. In November 1999, the parish witnessed the completion of its new $3 million multi-purpose facility. At the beginning of the third millennium, there were more than 1,300 families registered in the parish. The following priests served St. Elizabeth Ann Seton parish: Father J. Thomas Connery, 1975–78; Father Ernest H. **Muellerleile**, founder of the parish and its first pastor, 1975–84; Father Stanley J. **Allie**, 1984–90; Father Daniel J. Hebert, 1990–97; Father Justin Dzikowicz, O.S.B., 1997–98; Father Scott Medlock, 1997–2000; and Father Craig Loecker, 2001 to the present (2004).

Another rather dramatic change for the Church in Alaska took place nine years after the creation of the Archdiocese of Anchorage. In 1975, Archbishop Ryan was named Military Ordinary. His duties as Archbishop of Anchorage ended on January 1, 1976. On July 8, 1976, Francis T. **Hurley**, Bishop of Juneau at the time, was installed as the second Archbishop of Anchorage. For a quarter of a century, Archbishop Hurley headed the Anchorage Archdiocese. When it celebrated its 25th Anniversary in 1991, its Catholic population numbered just over 25,000 out of a total population of 332,373. It was being ministered to by 41 priests.

On Sunday, July 22, 1984, the site for the future Holy Cross Church at Lake Otis Parkway and Lore Road was dedicated. On that day, in the Abbott Loop Public School, Mass was concelebrated by Arch-

Father David J. Anderson, S.J. *BR-CD 0309-B235.*

bishop Hurley and Father Muellerleile to mark the founding of Holy Cross parish. Father Muellerleile was its founder and first pastor, from 1984–2001. The new Holy Cross Church was formally dedicated on September 12, 1993, by Archbishop Hurley. Father Hebert became pastor of Holy Cross parish in 2001 and was its pastor as of the year 2004. The parish was blessed with the services also of Deacons Robert Larroque and William Finnegan.

The Archdiocese of Anchorage began publishing its archdiocesan weekly newspaper, *Catholic Anchor*, on April 30, 1999. As of the year 2004, John Roscoe had been its only editor.

Archbishop Hurley was succeeded, on March 3, 2001, by Archbishop Roger L. **Schwietz**, a member of the Missionary **Oblates** of Mary Immaculate. By that time, the Catholic population of Anchorage numbered 32, 364 out of a total population of 370, 376. Under his leadership, the Archdiocese of Anchorage continued to experience steady growth and maturing as an ecclesiastical province of the Church.

15, 16, 40, 180

ANDERSON, Father David J., S.J.

David J. Anderson was born, one of five boys, on March 20, 1964, in Rapid City, South Dakota. His father was a banker, his mother a homemaker. For his elementary and secondary education, David attended public schools in Rapid City. From 1982–86, he studied at Gonzaga University in Spokane, Washington, earning a B.A. degree in Psychology and Religious Studies. On August 23, 1986, he entered the Jesuit Novitiate of St. Francis Xavier in Portland, Oregon. After completing his two-year noviceship, he returned to Gonzaga University for two years of philosophical studies. From 1990–93, he taught Religion at Gonzaga Preparatory in Spokane. His theological studies were made at the Jesuit School of Theology in Berkeley, California, from 1993–97. He was ordained a priest in St. Aloysius Church, Spokane, on June 7, 1997, by Bishop William S. Skylstad. In June 1998, after serving for a year at St. Joseph's parish in Seattle, Washington, he arrived on Nelson Island, **Alaska**. There he made his headquarters at **Toksook Bay**, out of which he tended also the villages of **Tununak** and **Nightmute**.

Father Anderson's interest in Alaska was first awakened in 1982, when he, a freshman at Gonzaga University, listened to Father Vincent J. **Beuzer**, S.J., "tell stories about Jesuit priests and Brothers working in the Alaska bush and traveling by dogteam and small airplanes." While growing up, Father Anderson "spent lots of time with family and friends in the Black Hills, which fostered a love for nature and the outdoors." Asked, several years after his arrival on Nelson Island, whether he liked Alaska and hoped to stay, he answered, "I'm enjoying my ministry among the Yup'ik people very much and would like to stay." As of the year 2004, he was still happily serving the three Nelson Island villages.

ANDREAFSKY See AKULURAK!

ANIAK

The Central Yup'ik Eskimo village of Aniak is located on the south bank of the Kuskokwim River at the head of Aniak Slough in the Yukon-Kuskokwim Delta. No twentieth century settlement was

St. Theresa's Church, Aniak. *DFA.*

started there, until Tom L. Johnson homesteaded the site, in 1914, and opened a general store. The simultaneous arrival of Willie Pete and Sam Simeon from **Ohagamiut** marked the first settlement of Eskimo families in modern Aniak. A post office was established in the village in 1914. In 1939, Aniak had 122 inhabitants; in 1950, 142; in 1960, 308; in 1970, 205; in 1979, 355; and in the year 2000, 572.

Catholic baptisms were performed in the Aniak area long before a permanent Catholic mission was established there. Some of Aniak's Catholic people have their Catholic roots in **Holy Cross** and at **Paimiut**. Father Francis M. **Ménager**, S.J., built a church at Aniak in 1939. After he took up station in **Bethel** in 1942, he visited Aniak on a regular basis from 1942–48.

The following Jesuit Fathers served Aniak's St. Theresa (Little Flower) parish out of Bethel: Segundo **Llorente**, 1948–50; Norman E. **Donohue**, 1950–53; Lawrence N. **Haffie**, 1953–56; Pasquale M. Spoletini, 1956–57 and 1958–59; Henry G. **Hargreaves**, 1957–58; **John J. Wood**, 1959–60.

After 1960, Aniak began to be served, still by Jesuit Fathers, but now not always out of Bethel, as follows: Wood, out of **McGrath**, 1960–62; William T. **McIntyre**, out of McGrath, 1962–63; Hargreaves, out of Bethel, 1963–64; Robert F. **Corrigal**, out of Bethel, 1964–65; **Cornelius K. Murphy**, out of

Bethel, 1965–66; Corrigal, out of McGrath, 1966–67; Corrigal, out of **Kalskag**, 1967–70; different priests out of Bethel, 1970–75; and Michael J. **Kaniecki**, out of Holy Cross, 1975–84.

Father Andrew P. **D'Arco**, priest of the Diocese of **Fairbanks**, made Aniak his headquarters from 1984 to the time of his tragic death there on May 27, 1992. It was he who led the way in the construction of the new Aniak church, dedicated on September 14, 1986.

During the years 1992–2000, Father William E. **Cardy**, O.F.M., made Aniak his headquarters. Beginning in the year 2001, and as of the year 2004, Father Maciej Napieralski, a priest from Poland serving in the Diocese of Fairbanks, did likewise.

17

ANN, Sisters of St.

They were the first women Religious to set foot in what is today the State of **Alaska**. The first of their number landed in Southeastern Alaska late in the 19th century. By the time they celebrated their first

100 years in the North, 246 of them had served there. Some served for only a year, many served for many years. But the 246 were not faceless numbers. They were so many individuals, each with her own distinctive personality, calling, talents and aspirations. They served mainly as educators and nurses, staffing schools and hospitals. Twelve of their number lie buried in the North. They were the Sisters of St. Ann, members of the Religious Congregation founded for the education of children from farms and small settlements in 1850 at Vaudreuil, Quebec, Canada, by Blessed (beatified in Rome, on April 29, 2001) Marie Anne Blondin, known in the West and North as Mother Mary Ann. St. Ann, the mother of the Blessed Virgin Mary, is their heavenly patroness.

The United States bought Alaska, Russian America, from czarist Russia in 1867. Less than 20 years later, on September 11, 1886, three Sisters of St. Ann, pioneer Sisters Mary Zenon, Victor, and Good Counsel, stepped ashore in **Juneau** to open St. Ann's Hospital for accident-prone miners. They had gone north at the request of Archbishop Charles J. **Seghers** and Father John J. **Althoff**, the priest then in charge of Juneau. Before the year was out, the

Sisters of St. Ann at Holy Cross Mission.
Courtesy of Sisters of St. Ann Archives, Victoria, B.C., Canada.

Sisters opened also St. Ann's School. In the late 1890s, the Sisters initiated similar institutions in nearby **Douglas**. In 1920, both St. Ann's Hospital and St. Ann's School in Douglas were closed as a result of the cave-in, on April 21–22, 1917, of the Treadwell Mines on Douglas Island.

The **Jesuits** first arrived in Alaska in 1887. The following year, Father Aloysius J. **Robaut**, S.J., founded **Holy Cross Mission**. A boarding school was to be the heart of this, and the Sisters of St. Ann were asked to staff it. They accepted, and, on September 4, 1888, Sisters Mary Stephen, Pauline, and Joseph Calasanctius disembarked at Holy Cross. That date marked the beginning of roughly a century of harmonious collaboration in Alaska between the Sisters of St. Ann and the Jesuits. In 1939, Bishop Joseph R. **Crimont**, S.J, Vicar Apostolic of Alaska, traveled to Lachine, Quebec, Canada, to celebrate a jubilee Mass for the Sisters of St. Ann, on the feast of St. Ann, July 26th. The original three at Holy Cross attended that Mass!

The Sisters began life at Holy Cross in a tent. In her book, *The Voice of Alaska*, Sister Joseph Calasanctius left an account of the beginnings and early years at Holy Cross. It was not long before Holy Cross, with its mission, boarding school and hospital, was, in very large part thanks to the Sisters of St. Ann, a flourishing establishment, soon known as "the smile of the Yukon."

The success of the undertaking at Holy Cross encouraged the Jesuits to open a similar mission in Eskimo territory, at **Akulurak**, near the south mouth of the Yukon. For staffing, they looked to the Sisters of St. Ann already at Holy Cross. In 1894, Sisters Zephyrin, Pauline, Prudence, and Benedict went downriver to Akulurak. Efforts at Akulurak, however, met with little success. The Sisters were unable to win the trust of the people, because the shamans had prejudiced the people against them. In 1898, they left Akulurak.

The Jesuits first undertook missionary work among the Koyukon Athabaskan Indians of Alaska's interior in 1887, when they established the mission at **Nulato** on the middle Yukon. Twelve years later, on November 2, 1899, Sisters Stephen, Antonia of Jesus, and Didace went to Nulato to continue to run the school started by the Jesuits. With but several brief interruptions, Sisters of St. Ann served in that village with distinction, primarily as schoolteachers, until 1983. Among the more illustrious of

Sisters of St. Ann on the Copper Valley School staff during the year 1963–64,
left to right: M. Alice Therese, Mary Eulalia, Mary Ida, Kathleen Mary,
Mary Agatha (Superior), and Christine Marie. *LRC.*

SR. M. HOLY CROSS
1787

their one-time pupils, Poldine **Carlo** and Harold **Esmailka** stand out.

Fairbanks, founded in 1901, first saw Sisters of St. Ann in 1906, when Sisters Stephen, Mary of the Heart of Jesus, and Pauline went there to staff, but only for a year, the newly opened St. Joseph's Hospital. Fairbanks again benefited from the presence of the Congregation between the years 1968–1983, when Sister Judith Morin worked in campus ministry at the University of Alaska-Fairbanks, and Sisters Alice Therese and Joyce Snyder worked among the Hispanic people, the young, the poor and the homeless. Because of her great kindness and help to the poor and needy, Sister Alice Therese became known as "the Mother Theresa of Fairbanks."

In 1932, the Sisters of St. Ann accepted to serve in a second location in Southeastern Alaska, at **Skagway**, in a school built by Father G. Edgar **Gallant**. That school, Pius X Mission, attempted to do for Southeastern Alaska what Holy Cross Mission was doing in the northern interior. Sisters Martin of Tours, Adolphus, Pudentienne, and Julien were the Skagway pioneers. The Sisters of St. Ann staffed Pius X Mission until December 1959, when it closed. During the mid-1940s, they cared for the tuberculosis patients in sanatoriums in Skagway and **Sitka**.

"Our buildings and much of our equipment was nothing so much as a great junk pile," wrote Father

(*left*) Sister Mary of the Holy Cross, S.S.A. Born Margaret Mary Demientieff on October 10, 1900, she had the distinction of being the only Holy Cross-born person to make a life-time commitment to Religious life. She entered the Congregation of the Sisters of St Ann in 1923. Though part Alaskan Native, she spent most of her long life as a Sister ministering outside of Alaska, mainly in British Columbia, Canada. She died in Victoria, B.C., on November 17, 1986. *Photo by Gibson's Studio, Victoria, and courtesy of Sisters of St. Ann Archives, Victoria.*

(*right*) On Juneau's Fifth Street, the Church of the Nativity of the Blessed Virgin Mary and the parish rectory stand to the left of the three-level St. Ann's School. The 1914 and 1933 hospital wings front Sixth Street. The 1954 concrete wing extends from the 1914 wing. The living quarters of the Sisters of St. Ann abut on the 1933 wing. An apple tree stands in the courtyard. *Courtesy of Sisters of St. Ann Archives, Victoria, B.C., Canada.*

John P. Fox, S.J., Superior of Holy Cross Mission in 1956. The physical condition of Holy Cross and the prospect in the early 1950s of statehood for Alaska and the need, therefore, for well-trained Native leaders led to the closing of Holy Cross as a boarding school and the establishment of a new educational institution by the Jesuits. A site near **Glennallen** was selected, and, by the fall of 1956, the new school,

Copper Valley School, was a budding reality. Again the Sisters of St. Ann were called upon to collaborate with the Jesuits in the bold, forward-looking enterprise. In mid-October of that year, a nucleus of 26 Holy Cross students, along with Sisters Alice Therese and Edward of Jesus, made the move from Holy Cross to the new school, where they were met by Sisters M. George **Edmond**, Agatha of the Angels, and Freda, already there. The school grew and prospered until the late 1960s. It prepared many students for university studies and leadership roles. Various factors brought about its closure in 1971.

During roughly the last quarter of the 20th century, the Sisters of St. Ann, now no longer committed to staffing large institutions, such as schools and hospitals, undertook a variety of pastoral ministries in Northern and Southcentral Alaska. They spent years in some towns and villages, and traveled to many others, in their efforts to train Native people as catechists and Church leaders. In the big cities, they showed concern for the religious education of Native youth and for the integration of Native people into city parishes. They ministered to urban minority groups, worked in the prison apostolate, and cared for the sick and dying in hospitals and extended-care facilities. For her long years of distinguished service in the North, both on the missions and in the cities, Sister Ida Brasseur, who first came to Alaska in 1946, received the Catholic Church Extension Society's 1980 Lumen Christi Award as "Home Missionary of the Year."

In 1986, the Sisters of St. Ann celebrated 100 years of service in Alaska. On that occasion, the Fourteenth Alaska Legislature in Juneau paid them tribute and honored them in a formal document for having always striven for excellence in education and for having prepared leaders in the State of Alaska. "The Sisters nurtured," concluded the citation, "befriended and empowered throughout a century of pioneering service in Alaska. The Fourteenth Alaska Legislature is proud to commend the Sisters of St. Ann on behalf of the generations of Alaskans who have looked upon the Sisters as symbols of faith, integrity and courage." Ten years later, the last of the Sisters of St. Ann to serve in Alaska left. They were Sisters Gaetana Cincotta and Anne Eveline Paquette.

16, 30, 32, 41, 144

Father René Astruc, S.J.
BR-961914.

ARVINAK

Arvinak was a small Inupiat Eskimo settlement near the **Pilgrim Hot Springs** Mission. A chapel was built there in 1929–30. This was dedicated under the title of Our Lady of Victory. Priests stationed at Pilgrim Springs visited Arvinak on a regular basis until 1940.

ASTRUC, Father René, S.J.

By the time he had spent over four decades on the **Alaska** Mission, he had become truly a tricultural man. Though he retained his French citizenship and his affiliation with the French Province of the Society of Jesus—and never lost that charm, urbanity, reserve that graces France's finest sons—he was thoroughly at home and at ease with American ways. In addition, he had so become a part of the Central Yup'ik Eskimo way of life that he was given an Eskimo name and, at a potlatch ceremony held to honor him, was, while standing ritualistically on a silvery seal skin, officially and formally "presented" to the assembled Eskimo community as "one of the family."

René Astruc was born on September 17, 1924 in Versailles, France, the second of nine children. While attending secondary school, he came across a Jesuit mission magazine in which he read several articles written by his fellow countryman, Father Joseph **Bernard**, S.J., missionary among Alaska's Seward Peninsula Eskimos from 1906–15. It was these articles, richly illustrated with high quality photographs, that first aroused René Astruc's interest in the Alaska Mission. An exchange of letters with Father Jules M. **Convert**, S.J., French Jesuit missionary serving the Eskimo people of the Yukon-Kuskokwim Delta, further heightened his interest in Alaska.

On April 4, 1945, René Astruc entered the Jesuit novitiate at Laval, France, with the stated purpose that he be assigned to minister in Alaska. He made his philosophical studies at Vals-près-Le Puy, after which he taught for a year in Poitiers. In September 1950, he found himself at **Holy Cross Mission** on the lower Yukon River. In the fall of 1951, he began theological studies at Alma College, Los Gatos, California. He was ordained a priest in Spokane, Washington, on June 19, 1954. After a final year of theology at Alma College, and ten months of tertianship at Paray-le-Monial, France, he was back in Alaska.

From September 1956 to January 1962, Father Astruc served near and at the mouth of the Yukon: first at **Stebbins** and **St. Michael**, then at **Chaneliak**, **Hamilton**, and **Kotlik**.

By the early 1960s, the era of travel by dogsled was coming to an end. Father Astruc obtained a snowmachine for himself, which enabled him to cover all of his mission stations for Christmas, something he could not have done by dogsled.

Looking back on his early years in Alaska, Father Astruc wrote: "Without the constant help of the people of the villages, I would never have made it." Barely had he arrived in Alaska as a priest, when, at Stebbins, he was faced with the task of finishing a church-building project. "I had no experience in building," he recalled in an interview, "I had to rely on the people to finish the job. They were generous with their time and most patient with me." With their help the building was completed. Describing himself as "a city boy" when he first came to Alaska, he acknowledged 40 years later his great indebtedness to the Eskimo people of the Yukon-Kuskokwim Delta for all the various kinds of help they had given him, when he first came among them, wholly innocent of every aspect of their lives and culture. "They also provided me," he recalled, "with transportation during the winter, helped me with my boat and mechanical chores in the summer, scolding me, when it appeared I was taking chances with

rough weather. I learned so much that in a few years I felt comfortable in those villages."

It was at Chaneliak that Father Astruc first experienced traditional Eskimo dancing. Some of those dances he remembered to his last days. "Of course," he wrote, "the people wanted the priest to dance with them, and I guess I very hesitatingly and bashfully took my first steps on the floor. Once again the people were so kind and generous with their encouragements."

That Eskimo dancing and potlatch celebrations are alive and well in the Catholic villages of the lower Yukon regions today is due, in very large part, to Father Astruc. While still a bush missionary, and especially during his years as Superior of St. Mary's Mission Boarding School on the **Andreafsky** River, 1964–70, he encouraged Eskimo dancing among the people and students, and himself became a proficient dancer. In February 1996, in appreciation for what he had done to foster Native cultural traditions, he was "potlatched" and officially made an honorary Central Yup'ik Eskimo, the first non-Native to be so honored. By then, he had already been given an Eskimo name. Ten years earlier, in 1986, the grandmother of a child he was baptizing asked him, "What your Eskimo name?" "I don't know," he answered. Whereupon she formally gave him the name *Nucang'in*, the name of a man from the lower Yukon known for his patience and kindness who had died about the time Father Astruc first came to Alaska.

Here it should be mentioned that, in the mid-1990s, Father Astruc played a key role, was the "primary catalyst," in bringing about a major exhibit of Yup'ik Eskimo masks, the *Agayuliyararput* (Our Way of making Prayer) exhibit. This consisted of masks from some of the leading museums in the western world. The intent of the exhibit was to bring the masks, both as historical museum pieces and as part of the living tradition of Yup'ik masks, back to the people who had created them, and then to the general public. Concerning Father Astruc's part in making the exhibit a very successful reality, Dr. Ann Fienup-Riordan, a noted anthropologist who made a specialty of western Alaska cultures and who wrote the text for the exhibit, said simply, "Without his connection, it never would have happened."

During the first part of 1963, after holding station on the middle Yukon, at **Galena** and its dependent villages, Father Astruc was assigned to Holy Cross, where he served from June 1963 to the spring of 1964. Having helped run the salmon cannery at St. Mary's Mission during the summers of 1962, '63, and '64, he was thought by his Superiors to be the logical man to head the mission boarding school. This he did from 1964–70. Of those years he wrote, "Wholly unexpectedly I was asked to stay at St. Mary's and be responsible for the mission school. Nothing had prepared me for that work. All my education had taken place in France, and I had no experience. But, with the help of the **Ursuline** Sisters and members of the **Jesuit Volunteer Corps**, I lasted six years. I have the best memories of those years and meet my former students with joy, especially those who have risen to positions of responsibility in their region, those teaching and those who have learned to dedicate themselves to the young people of their villages."

Father Thomas E. Ambrose, S.J., who was at St. Mary's for a time while Father Astruc was there, wrote concerning him: "He was a most far-seeing man. While he set the educational policy of the school, he saw to it that the students developed skills that would enable them to make their way in the industrial, commercial world, into which he knew they would move after graduation. At the same time, he insisted that they retain many fine social customs and ways of the Eskimo tradition."

In a certain sense, Father Astruc can be considered also as the founder of the Church of the Nativity parish in the village of St. Marys. At his request, an additional priest was added to the mission staff with the charge that he care for the villagers and lay the foundation for a village parish independent of the mission.

During the early 1970s, Father Astruc assisted a layman, Paul Dixon, with adult education projects geared to help people of the Eskimo villages come to grips with The Alaska Native Claims Settlement Act.

From 1973 on, Father Astruc began to devote virtually all of his time to the Yup'ik **Eskimo Deacon Program**. For over 20 years he was its full-time director. Under his talented, enlightened directorship, it flourished beyond all reasonable expectations. His contribution to the program was described by Michael J. **Kaniecki**, S.J., Bishop of **Fairbanks**, as

"both unique and monumental, of great benefit not only to the Diocese of Fairbanks, but to the continuing development of the diaconate in the United States and, indeed, in the universal Church as well." As director of the program, Father Astruc saw 52 Eskimo men from 18 different villages ordained to the permanent diaconate. Among these, two stand out: Michael **Nayagak** and William **Tyson**.

Father Astruc's love for and dedication to the Yup'ik Eskimo people and his respect for their cultural traditions did not go unrecognized or unappreciated. As has been noted above, he had been given an Eskimo name and formally adopted by the Yup'ik Eskimo people as "one of the family." Nor did his total dedication to the Eskimo Deacon Program go unrecognized or unappreciated. In 1996, Bishop Kaniecki, at the annual Eskimo Deacon Retreat, formally presented him with a special award created by the National Association of Deacon Directors to honor him "in recognition of his outstanding contributions to the development of the Native Deacon Program in the Diocese of Fairbanks." The NADD saw fit to create the award in light of what Bishop Kaniecki had written to them: "I simply cannot say enough for Father René's dedication and commitment to our deacons and their wives. It is not easy traveling the distances we have up here, and in all kinds of weather, to present a workshop. The task is made even more difficult when you realize you are forced to work through an interpreter. Father René is very conscious of the importance of inculturation, and has consciously, prudently, and wisely worked to make this a Yup'ik Deacon Program, by making the Eskimo culture part and parcel of both the training, and, with my permission as bishop, truly reflected in liturgical worship."

In October 2001, Father Astruc was honored by the Alaska Humanities Forum as "A Friend of the Humanities" during an awards ceremony presided over by Alaska State Governor Tony Knowles. The award was given in recognition of his many years of service in western Alaska, and "especially his work in building bridges between the Catholic Faith and the spiritual world of the Yup'ik Eskimo."

In 1996, Father Astruc retired from the Alaska Mission for a while, and returned to his native France. He wanted to be closer to family members, and to take on a new ministry while he, now in his early 70s, was still young and able enough to do so. However, after less than two years in France, he felt himself drawn irresistibly back to Alaska. He was, of course, most welcome to return to Alaska. Accordingly, during the latter part of 1998, he returned and undertook pastoral ministry in the villages of Kotlik and **Mountain Village**.

In June 2001, in Anchorage, Father Astruc was shocked to learn that he had kidney cancer. The news was, at first, devastating, but, after an evening spent in prayer with his Superior, Father Mark A. **Hoelsken**, S.J., he said he was "granted the grace to move forward," to see that "death is the most natural thing to do and there really is nothing to fear." He was never afraid thereafter. He spent the summer months in Spokane getting needed medical attention. In early October, he returned to Alaska with the intention of returning to his two villages. However, while in Anchorage, a medical checkup revealed that he was too sick to return to the bush. He was then and there hospitalized, since he was not expected to live through the end of the month. Immediately, members of his family came from France to bid their last adieus. From many villages of western Alaska came scores of people to assure him of their prayers and say tearful, bedside farewells. A special waiting room had to be set up in the hospital to accommodate them. He was bombarded by e-mail letters and telephone calls. People, without exception, were very much edified by his resigned, cheerful acceptance of his condition. Their visits to him brought them peace. Near the end of October, Father Louis L. **Renner**, S.J., received an urgent phone call from Father Hoelsken in Anchorage telling him to write up and e-mail to him an obituary article, since Father Astruc was "not expected to make it through the weekend." The Jesuits had already bought food for the wake. The attending physician said a sad goodbye, before leaving on a scheduled trip. That was in October 2001.

An item under date of July 5, 2002, in the Archdiocese of Anchorage's newspaper, *The Catholic Anchor*, began: "Jesuit Father Rene Astruc, who served most of his 48 years as a priest in Western Alaska, died June 28 of kidney cancer. He was 77." Remarkably, seemingly miraculously, Father Astruc

outlived the dire predictions of his imminent death by eight months. His one remaining kidney began to function again. He was moved to the Mary Conrad Center rest home in Anchorage. There he continued to receive visitors, to read, to listen to music, to pray, to celebrate and concelebrate Mass, to share laughs with friends. And there he continued also to carry on a real apostolate by his edifying example, by his patient listening to people, by hearing confessions, and by "saying a good word now and then." Of the rest home he said, "It's just like a small village here." It was there that he died, alone, except for the presence of a nurse logging some records for the night. He died around 10:30 P.M., on June 28, 2002. Father Hoelsken and several close friends had intended to keep vigil with Father Astruc. "But," in the words of Father Hoelsken, "his passing caught all of us flat-footed."

Father Astruc had asked to be buried in St. Mary's Mission cemetery, next to members of a family that was especially dear to him. Accordingly, full wake and funeral ceremonies in the traditional style of the Yup'ik people were planned to be held at St. Marys. However, for the sake of the many friends he had had in Anchorage, a funeral Mass was celebrated in Holy Family Cathedral on Tuesday evening, July 2nd. Father Hoelsken was principal celebrant. Archbishop Roger L. **Schwietz**, O.M.I., presided. Many priests concelebrated. The church was filled. "It was a remarkably joyful occasion," wrote Father Hoelsken.

Father Astruc's body was flown to St. Mary's the following day, July 3rd. A two-day wake followed. Many people came from nearby villages, some by boat or plane, to take part in the traditional Native wake ceremonial, to sing and eat and pray. The funeral Mass—delayed several times to enable Joel Astruc, Father René's brother coming from France, to be present—was held on Saturday, the 6th, in St. Marys city hall to accommodate the huge crowd that had come from near and far.. "Once again," according to Father Hoelsken, "it was a grand and joyful celebration." After the Mass of Christian Burial, good Father René Astruc was buried in the mission cemetery "in a clearing among the willows beyond the garden."

BABB, Father William H., S.J.

William H. Babb was born in Brockton, Massachusetts, on December 3, 1904. He graduated from Boston College High School in 1922. On September 7th of that year, he entered St. Charles Novitiate of the New Orleans Province of the Society of Jesus at Grand Coteau, Louisiana. He studied philosophy at Mount St. Michael's in Spokane, Washington. From 1929–32, he taught at Jesuit High School in New Orleans, after which he made his theological studies at St. Mary's, Kansas. He was ordained a priest at St. Mary's on June 23, 1935. After making his tertianship in Cleveland, Ohio, he spent a year at the Gregorian University in Rome. In 1941, he began to serve as a chaplain in the U.S. Navy. As such, he was stationed successively at Group 59 Marine Corps Air Station, Eagle Mountain Lake, Texas; HQ. Air FMF, Pacific; and Marine HQ., Squadron 3, c/o FPO, San Francisco. He separated from the Navy in February 1946. For some years thereafter, he was out of the Society of Jesus.

Father Babb first arrived in **Alaska** in March 1951. He spent the years 1951–53 in **Juneau**. In 1953, he moved to **Fairbanks**, where he was assistant pastor at Immaculate Conception parish from 1953–59. When Monroe Catholic High School opened in Fairbanks in 1955, he did some limited teaching there for a short time. From 1959–74, he served at the Diocesan Curia as Vice-Chancellor, Chancellor, Vicar General, Diocesan Treasurer, and as a member of the Matrimonial Tribunal. In 1969, he was readmitted to the Society of Jesus.

Father Babb left Alaska in 1974. For two years, until his health worsened, he was engaged in pastoral ministry at Immaculate Conception parish in Albuquerque, New Mexico. He spent the last years of his life at the Sacred Heart Residence of the Little Sisters of the Poor in Mobile, Alabama. During those years, he was very active in assisting the Sisters as their bookkeeper.

On August 10, 1984, after he had been hospitalized for some days in Mobile's Providence Hospital, Father Babb died there of heart failure. He lies buried in the Jesuit cemetery at Spring Hill College, Mobile.

BAKER, Father Harley A.

Harley Andrew Baker was born in **Skagway, Alaska**, on August 15, 1913. He was the first Alaska-born man to become a priest for the Vicariate of Alaska. Ordained a priest, on May 31, 1941, by Bishop James McFadden in St. John's Cathedral, Cleveland, Ohio, he celebrated his first Solemn High Mass in St. Mark's Church, Skagway, the same church in which he had been baptized and made his first Holy Communion. He had also been confirmed in it, by Joseph R. **Crimont**, S.J., Vicar Apostolic of Alaska at the time. Skagway, too, was his first assignment as a priest. As assistant pastor to Father G. Edgar **Gallant**, he served there, spending much of his time at Skagway's Pius X Mission, until 1949, the year he became assistant at Holy Family parish in **Anchorage**.

In 1951, when Holy Family's pastor, Father Dermot **O'Flanagan**, became Bishop of the newly established Diocese of **Juneau**, Father Baker replaced him. Of immediate concern to him as pastor was to bring into being a catechetical program. To him fell also the responsibility of seeing to the completion of the new church, the providing of a new parish rectory, and the nurturing of the dream for a Catholic school. "When we consider the leakage," he said, "especially of the children, and the great number of children who do not come to catechism classes, I am feeling more and more that a

Father Harley A. Baker.
LRC.

parish school is the only solution." He was not to see the realization of his dream for a Catholic school. However, before his decade at Holy Family was up, he had the satisfaction of seeing the new church completed, the new parish rectory built, and the new parish hall finished. And he had the satisfaction, too, of having assisted with the establishment of the new St. Anthony's parish in Anchorage and that of St. Andrew's at Chugiak–**Eagle River**.

In 1959, Father Baker was transferred to Juneau, to serve there as the Chancellor of the Juneau Diocese. Five years later, in **Douglas**, at the age of 54, he died of an apparent heart attack on September 22, 1965.

Funeral services for Father Baker were held in the Cathedral in Juneau on September 28th. Msgr. Gallant, who had been Father Baker's "mentor" in Skagway, and who had succeeded him as pastor of Holy Family parish in Anchorage, offered the funeral Mass. Father Baker lies buried in the city of his birth, Skagway.

15

BAKEWELL, Father Anderson E., S.J.

Anderson E. "Andy" Bakewell, was born in St. Louis, Missouri, on September 18, 1913. There he was educated at Sacred Heart Academy, at St. Louis University High School, and at St. Louis University. After two years of post-graduate work at S.L.U., he applied to enter the Society of Jesus. However, for health reasons, he was turned down. Determined to become a Jesuit, he set about building up his health. He began mountain climbing, and developed a deep and personal interest in the work of the American Geographical Society of New York, and, in particular, in Field Research.

In the summer of 1935, the University of Michigan conducted an expedition into Mexico, and Andy was invited by its leader to become a member of the party. On the slopes of Colima Volcano, in the depths of the rain forest, he found what he had set out in hopes of finding: a rare python snake. This he donated to the University of Michigan. In 1939, he was an invited member of a scientific expedition to the Saint Elias Mountains in Canada's Yukon Territory. That same year, he and two others climbed Pico Cristóbal Colón, the highest peak in Colombia, South America. In 1941, he was again in the Saint Elias Mountains, helping gather scientific data, and climbing the previously unclimbed Mount Wood.

By this time Jesuit Superiors came to the conclusion that Anderson Bakewell did, after all, have health enough to join their ranks. On September 8, 1942, he entered the Maryland Province Novitiate at Wernersville. In 1947, he was with the first group of Maryland Province Jesuits sent to India. There, still a seminarian, he attempted a climb of Mount Everest and continued collecting snakes for scientific purposes. In Kurseong, on November 21, 1951, he was ordained a priest.

As a newly ordained priest, Father Bakewell asked to be assigned to "the most difficult mission in India." For five years he served among the Native peoples of Raj Anandpur and Gomo. The jungle atmosphere and the eating of native foods, however, led to sickness and a breakdown in his health. He had to return to the United States.

In Washington, D.C., he was charged with raising funds for Loyola Retreat House. This, for ten years, he did successfully, using his connections with various embassies, the diplomatic corps, the White House, the Pentagon, and the upper echelons of the Department of Defense, the Army and the Navy. During summers he did scientific research in the High Sierras.

Father Anderson E. Bakewell, S.J. *LRC.*

While Father Bakewell was on that Washington assignment, the American Geographical Society of New York and the Arctic Institute invited him to join another expedition to the Saint Elias range. On that expedition, an inspiration came to him: just across the border, in **Alaska**, was where he should be. When the expedition returned to the States, he lost no time in requesting Superiors for permission to become a missionary again, this time in Alaska.

However, before Superiors even had time to act upon his request, he was invited to join an airborne scientific expedition, to take part in an around-the-world flight, the Rockwell Polar Flight, with transits of both the North and the South Poles.

As the only clergyman on board, Father Bakewell prepared a "Prayer of Thanksgiving" while flying over the South Pole. This, before the end of that historic flight, he recited in the name of all on board:

> Father, at the inception of this flight, we asked you to bless this aircraft and preserve it from accident or loss. We asked you to appoint an angel from on High as an escort for us; to shield us as we circled this planet over the hostile environment of both poles, penetrated the stratosphere, and journeyed through the kingdom of clouds across five oceans and the Antarctic Continent in search of the knowledge of Your creation. You have done all that we asked; we are sincerely and humbly grateful. May You and Your Son and the Holy Spirit be praised forever. Amen.

From 1967–76, Father Bakewell was in Alaska, as pastor of the **Delta Junction** parish and its two dependent missions, **Tok** and **Northway**. This meant that he had to spend much time at the wheel, driving his Ford Mustang, often on roads in very poor condition, and in all kinds of weather. But, he was now surrounded by wilderness, and close to those Saint Elias Mountains that he had come to know and love. He made a retreat camped in the wilds. He found satisfaction in being in the wilds with G.B. "Nikki" Threlkeld, a naturalist and painter of wildflowers, to protect her with his rifle against bears.

As a pastor, Father Bakewell was on the conservative, devotional side. The people liked him and were well satisfied with his ministrations. Much as he loved Alaska and his assignment, he had, however, to leave it, in 1976. Severe arthritis mandated a change to a less severe climate. He moved to Santa Fe, New Mexico, where he spent the remainder of his eventful life as an in-house chaplain: one year at St. Vincent Hospital, then 21 years at the Discalced Carmelite Monastery. He died in Santa Fe, in his 87th year, of cancer, on October 13, 1999, and was buried at Calvary Cemetery in St. Louis.

BALQUIN, Father Don M.

"But why **Alaska**?" his mother wanted to know, when he told her that he would be going to Alaska to minister to the people there as a priest. Why would a young man want to trade his native land, the tropical Philippine Islands, for the taiga and tundra of northern Alaska? The answer to the question we have from the man himself. Referring to his twofold vocation, he said of it, "I don't have an exact answer. It wasn't I, who designed everything, but God Himself. All I know is that I was enjoying my teaching career in the Philippines, when, suddenly and mysteriously, my plan changed. I consider my vocation to serve in Alaska and as a priest a divine call."

Don M. Balquin was born the fifth of ten children and the oldest of the boys on May 26, 1958, in Santo Domingo, a town in the Province of Albay, Republic of the Philippines. His parents saw to it that their children were from early childhood on given a solid grounding in the Catholic Faith. By the time Don left his native land in 1986, he had earned a B.A. in the field of sociology and an M.A.

Father Don M. Balquin. *LRC.*

in Developmental Education, and had taught sociology for more than four years at Trinity College, Quezon City, Metro-Manila.

What occasioned Don's coming to the USA? On some of his free days, while still in university studies, he had helped an American missionary priest working with people on one of the remote islands off the coast of Albay. About this same time, the Pallottine Society from the United States was recruiting candidates in the Philippines. Given these two contacts, along with his rich Catholic background and his naturally generous heart, it was not long before he felt himself drawn to the priesthood. In September 1986, he left the Philippines for New Jersey, there to join the Pallottine Society.

As a member of the Pallottines, Don received a thorough grounding in philosophy and theology, earning an M.A. in Divinity. He was also exposed to a variety of Church ministries, and came to know and admire different diocesan priests, their spirit and their work. Still discerning his vocation, he could write by 1992: "I am being drawn to the diocesan priesthood. I say this with deep conviction. My decision to be a diocesan priest did not occur overnight."

After leaving the Philippines, Don joined the Diocese of **Fairbanks** in 1992. In his own words: "By then I had been led to the realization that my call-

ing was to serve in the remote and isolated regions of the world." During the summer of that year, he worked for the diocese in **Nulato** and **Kaltag**, remote, isolated Athabaskan Indian villages on the middle Yukon River.

Don was ordained a deacon on January 3, 1993, in Sacred Heart Cathedral, Fairbanks, by Michael J. **Kaniecki**, S.J., Bishop of Fairbanks. Of the event he wrote: "It was memorable, as the ordination was supposed to take place the day before. But, owing to a snowstorm and a power outage, the ceremony was held the next day. Nevertheless, it was a joyful occasion." Five months later, on June 6, 1993, he was ordained a priest.

During the year 1993–94, Father Don, as he was always affectionately known, served as associate pastor of Sacred Heart Cathedral parish. That year he also made week-long trips every month to **Tanana**, another Indian village on the middle Yukon. He spent a week in **Barrow**, to get acquainted with the Catholic community there, a large part of which was Filipino. In addition, from the earliest days of his priesthood, Father Don offered Mass every fourth Sunday of the month for the Filipino-American Catholic community in Fairbanks. One member of that community said: "Father Don has this infectious joy, the joy of the Lord that bubbles out. We love and appreciate him and all that he does for the Filipino community."

After that year in Fairbanks, Father Don was given what turned out to be his last assignment as a priest in the Diocese of Fairbanks. He was appointed pastor of the parish in **Delta Junction** and of its two dependent missions, **Tok** and **Eagle**. To cover this vast area, he had, at first, an Isuzu Trooper. This gave him good service, until, one day, while he was making his once-a-month trip to Eagle and driving the Taylor Highway, a 160-mile stretch of notoriously rough road linking Eagle with a junction on the Alaska Highway, . . . But, hear him tell it:

On July 19, 1994, on my first trip back from Eagle, I was driving the Taylor Highway at mile 32. I'd been driving for four hours on that rough, rocky, dusty road, when, suddenly, my Trooper, after hitting a washboard, spun out of control. I tried controlling it by applying a hard brake, but to no avail. Before I knew it, I found myself in a ditch, my Trooper facing in the opposite direction and lying on its side. Fortunately, I had my seatbelt on. The cassette tape I was playing stopped, and the last line I heard was "Let us be gentle and humble," sung by the Weston Priory Benedictines. The sun roof was collapsed, allowing me to crawl out, before the oil and gasoline started to spill out and I had an explosion to fear. The jagged edges of the sun roof caught the side of my arm, creating a small, gaping wound. A kind couple picked me up, and took me to Tok, where I called people to inform them about the accident, the bishop first. I did not need medical attention, but I was badly shaken. The Trooper was totaled. That incident, however, did not faze me from traveling the Taylor again. Nor did it dampen my desire to proclaim the Good News to the people in Eagle. Now, every time I pass mile 32, I either stop or slow down, reminding myself to be thankful to God for sparing my life from that accident.

During the summer months, Father Don generally drove to Eagle about every six weeks. During the winter months, when the highway was closed, he flew there in a bush plane.

In contrast to Eagle, Father Don was able routinely to visit Tok, a two-hour, 108-mile drive down the Alaska Highway from Delta Junction. That highway is open year-round. He generally made the trip to Tok every other Sunday, and on all major Church feasts. Weather and road conditions were always a concern. "My temperature cut-off," he wrote, "is thirty below zero. Colder than that is dangerous, as metals in the vehicle act 'funny' in extreme cold, and the engine might get frozen."

Despite its woes, and because of its natural wonders, Father Don loved Alaska. "This is Alaska!" he wrote in one of his letters. "I came up here in May 1992, and have ever since loved this place."

The beginning of this biographical sketch of Father Don shows that he, personally, could not account for his presence as a priest in Alaska with "an exact answer." He attributed all to God Himself, acknowledging that God designed everything affecting him according to a "mysterious divine plan." Little did Father Don realize, when he wrote those words, that his earthly life, so full of vitality, optimism, and cheerfulness, would—in keeping with that mysterious divine plan—soon be at an end.

In early November 1998, exploratory surgery in Seattle revealed that Father Don was suffering so seriously from cancer of the liver and gall bladder that remedial surgery was no longer deemed a viable option. In spite of his cancerous condition, however, he, in early 1999, took his previously planned tourist trip to Eastern Europe. With friends, he visited Prague, Dresden and Vienna. He left Europe "full of treatment memories." From mid-March to mid-April, he was in Tijuana, Mexico, for "an alternative treatment." So confident was he that the treatment would produce positive results, that he took a two-month vacation in the Chicago area and on the East Coast. But, his condition did not improve. Chemotherapy in Fairbanks came next. He then visited home and family in the Philippines, went back to Fairbanks, then again, for the last time, back to the Philippines. There, in his hometown of Legaspi, surrounded by family and caring friends, he, just 42 years old, died peacefully in the Lord.

He was a little man, but his passing left a big hole in the lives of many.

157

BALTUSSEN, Father Peter L., S.J.

Peter L. Baltussen was born in Maastricht, Limburg, Netherlands, on February 11, 1896. After studying at the Apostolic School in Turnhout, Belgium, he came to the United States and entered the Jesuit novitiate at Los Gatos, California, on September 17, 1915. After completing the two-year noviceship, he spent a third year at Los Gatos studying the classics. From 1918–21, he studied philosophy at Mount St. Michael's, Spokane, Washington, before going on to teach at St. Ignatius High School in San Francisco. He spent the year 1924–25 studying theology at Valkenburg, Limburg, Netherlands, and the years 1925–28 studying theology in the city of his birth, Maastricht. He was ordained a priest on August 15, 1927, and later made his tertianship at Amiens, France, 1928–29.

Father Baltussen arrived in **Alaska** in October 1929 to serve at the **Pilgrim Hot Springs** Mission. While there, he became an able dog-musher, and routinely made trips to the nearby Eskimo settlements of Marys Mountain and **Arvinak** to minister to the people there. As a practical man, he worked with Jesuit Lay Brothers John **Hansen** and Peter **Wilhalm** to make needed improvements at the mission.

He and Brother Hansen, using a long coil, installed a hot water heating system. Father Baltussen became Superior of the mission on August 4, 1930.

Transferred to **Kotzebue** in September 1931, Father Baltussen found his year there anything but pleasant. On March 14, 1932, he wrote to Father Paul P. Sauer, S.J., the man responsible for getting supplies to the Alaska missions: "This house is in an awful shape. I will not live in this place another winter. God alone knows what I have gone through this last winter. I have had enough of this hell. I have not undressed to go to bed since Thanksgiving. Many a night I did not even dare go to bed for fear that I might freeze."

Father Baltussen left Kotzebue on August 24, 1932, to spend the years 1932–34 back at Pilgrim Springs, again as Superior there. After leaving the Springs in May 1934, he returned to the Pacific Northwest. For ten years he taught high school Religion and Latin, first at Gonzaga in Spokane, then at Bellarmine in Tacoma. Serving on the Indian missions in Montana filled the last ten years of his life. He died at Big Sandy, Montana, on April 28, 1955, and lies buried in the Jesuit cemetery at Mount St. Michael's.

BARNUM, Father Francis A., S.J.

"Father Barnum brought a nine-foot American flag, which we put in front of our tent," wrote Father William H. **Judge**, S.J., on July 4, 1891, from **St. Michael**, **Alaska**, where Father Barnum had arrived five days before. Author Alice Henderson, who met Father Barnum at St. Michael a few years later, wrote that his ancestors came to this country in 1629, "so he is thoroughly American *if* a Jesuit." If Father Barnum was anything, he was thoroughly American—and that proved to be his undoing as a missionary and linguist in Alaska.

Father Barnum, the first American-born priest to serve in Alaska, spent only six years there, but his sparkling and colorful personality, his farsighted proposals and initiatives, and his writings merit for him an honored place in the annals of the North. He proposed reindeer herds for the various missions, a pottery industry for Nelson Island, a doctor of medicine to serve as a lay missionary. His writings constitute a mine rich in data of interest to histori-

ans, ethnohistorians, cartographers, geographers, and geologists. It is in the field of linguistics, however, that he made his major and most lasting contributions.

Francis Aloysius Barnum was born of wealthy parents on January 23, 1849, in Baltimore, Maryland. There his father owned Barnum's Hotel, one of the great hostelries of the South. After attending various elementary schools and spending over a year in Paris, where he became fluent in French, Francis Barnum, in 1864, enrolled in Loyola College, a school in Baltimore conducted by the Jesuits. Two years later, he transferred to Georgetown University in Washington. Then, in 1868, he returned again to Loyola. On February 11, 1867, he was baptized and received into the Catholic Church. He never gave a reason for his conversion.

About this time, Barnum applied for admittance into the Society of Jesus, and was accepted. Before entering the novitiate at Frederick, Maryland, which he did on September 20, 1870, he spent his last year of independence traveling widely. The 20-year-old Barnum had already been abroad at least three times. This time, on his own, he traveled not only all over Europe, but continued on to the Holy Land and Egypt. There he followed the Nile from the delta to its source, a trip he painstakingly recorded in his journal.

Barnum's father had died in 1865, and less than eleven months after Francis entered the novitiate, his mother also died. This necessitated his leaving the novitiate, on August 24, 1871, to take care of the younger Barnum children and manage the estate. Domestic cares, however, did not claim all his time. During the ten years before he re-entered the novitiate, he traveled to Europe three times, once via Buenos Aires, on a barkentine. He simply loved to travel. As an old man, he was able to count 56 ocean voyages.

Barnum spent the year 1876–77 at the University of Virginia studying medicine. The following year he was in Florida growing oranges. By April of 1879, he was "burnt out," so, being a restless spirit, he went on a "tramp through Louisiana." He next went west, to Leadville, Colorado. In Kansas City, as he carefully recorded in his notebook, he resolved to re-enter the novitiate at Frederick. This he did on July 17, 1880.

In January 1881, novice Francis Barnum made the 30-day-long Spiritual Exercises of St. Ignatius of Loyola. On July 31, 1882, he formally became a member of the Society of Jesus by taking the vows of perpetual poverty, chastity, and obedience. He was then sent to teach at Boston College. In September 1885, he went to Woodstock, Maryland, for theological studies. On August 27, 1887, he was ordained a priest by James Cardinal Gibbons.

Father Barnum knew that, by becoming a Jesuit priest, it would cost him, quite literally, a small fortune. His younger brother, Dr. Zenus Barnum, died on April 23, 1882, leaving a will that read in part: "If within twelve months after my decease my brother Frank Barnum shall withdraw from the priesthood and from any and every order and society connected with the [Catholic] Church, I direct that the net income of said rest and residue of my estate be paid Frank Barnum." Father Barnum did not withdraw, and so he forfeited considerable wealth.

After spending his first year as a priest doing parish work and teaching at St. Joseph's School in Troy, New York, Father Barnum spent the following year prefecting the small boys at Georgetown. From August 1889 to September 1890, he traveled

Father Francis A. Barnum, S.J. *JOPA-1057.01.*

throughout the eastern states as an itinerant preacher. In the summer of 1890, he accompanied home for vacation some wealthy Mexican students attending Georgetown. He spent three months in Orizaba, Mexico, where he made an eight-day retreat, and collected books and "many vivid impressions." Father Barnum was famous for "noticing," and most of what he noticed he also recorded in his ever-present journal.

When, in 1884, Archbishop Charles J. **Seghers**, Bishop of Vancouver Island, visited Boston College, Father Barnum informed him of the desire he had of serving in Alaska. The archbishop was willing to have Father Barnum come north with him, but the latter's Superiors denied permission. Several times more he petitioned to be allowed to go to Alaska, but to no avail. He let the matter drop.

In 1890, quite unexpectedly, Father Barnum received the news that he was to go north. By Christmas 1890, he was at Colville, Washington, and by April 10th, in San Francisco. From there, liberally outfitted for Alaska by his sister Annie—who had hurried to San Francisco from Paris to see him off—Father Barnum, on June 4, 1891, on the *St. Paul*, sailed for Alaska. He arrived at St. Michael on June 29th. Before he could disembark, "a boat came off and there was great excitement among our party wondering who would be here to meet us." In the boat was Father Paschal **Tosi**, S.J., General Superior of the Alaska Mission. Little did Father Barnum suspect at that first friendly meeting how difficult Father Tosi was soon to make life in Alaska for him.

Of Father Barnum's arrival in Alaska, Father Judge wrote: "Fr. Barnum delighted all on the steamer with his pleasant manners, great general knowledge and pleasing conversation. The captain took a great liking to him and the [Alaska Commercial] Company's head man, who came up with him, congratulated Fr. Tosi on getting such a man."

Father Barnum volunteered to serve at the mission in the Central Yup'ik Eskimo village of **Tununak** on Nelson Island. After tenting for two weeks at St. Michael, he—along with Jesuit Lay Brother **Bernard I. Cunningham** and Jesuit Father Joseph M. **Tréca**, who had founded the Nelson Island mission two years before—left St. Michael to sail some 350 miles across "the storm tortured coast" to Tununak in an 18-foot rowboat Father Tosi had purchased for them. The boat, lacking centerboard, bowsprit, rigging and sail, was ill-suited for sailing, even after makeshift modifications had been made.

The *St. Michael*, the small mission-owned sternwheeler, towed their "yacht," as Father Barnum humorously described the simple rowboat, to the mouth of the Yukon. From there on, the three were left to shift for themselves. After a week's journey and several near disasters, the boat, with its travel-worn trio and woebegone sail, limped to the landing at Tununak, its destination and the scene of Father Barnum's first missionary activity in Alaska. "It was a cheerless journey," he summarized.

What Father Barnum found upon his arrival at Tununak was no longer a virgin field for missionary activity, but a field with the Faith planted and taking root. Nowhere in his writings did he state anything like a philosophy of evangelizing peoples of another culture. He took for granted the legitimacy of his missionary work among the Central Yup'ik Eskimos.

Writing in his customary graphic, often witty, manner, Father Barnum described the Tununak mission residence as a "hastily constructed edifice in the homemade style." It had been put together from driftwood in September 1889, by Fathers Tréca and Tosi. He had his bunk up above in among the provisions, in "a little cockloft scarcely high enough in the center to stand upright." Driftwood was used for heating the place. It was never adequately warm. In retrospect he wrote, "The native abodes were in every way more comfortable and far warmer than our miserable hut, and I have often wondered since, why we never had sense enough to make use of one of them."

What seems to have tried the early-day missionaries more than anything else, more even than the intense cold and the primitive living conditions, was the "death-like" silence and gloom of the long subarctic winter. It was mainly to this that Father Barnum ascribed what he termed "polar anaemia." This mental disorder, this "insidious malady," afflicted severely, if only temporarily, some of his fellow missionaries, Father Tréca among them.

There is nothing in Father Barnum's writings to suggest that he ever considered himself to have fallen victim to "polar anaemia." Given his buoyant, extroverted disposition, and his lively interest in everything about him, one would hardly expect him to suffer from mental depression. In fact, he seems to have been quite immune to "polar anaemia," for not even the silence and introspection that were part of the 30-day retreat he made in November during his first year at Tununak were able, in his case, to precipitate this "insidious malady."

Father Barnum found sanity and satisfaction in his cheerful service of God and neighbor, and, to a high degree, in a natural escape, the study of the difficult Eskimo language. "Our chief mental relaxation," he wrote, "was derived from the study of the language, and in discussing the many problems it presented."

The language in question here is Central Yup'ik Eskimo. Father Barnum, however, referred to it as "Innuit." From the outset of his years in Alaska, he devoted much time to the compilation of a grammar and dictionary of Central Yup'ik Eskimo. His facility for picking up an unfamiliar language bordered on genius. Still, he found pioneering in that language difficult and progress slow. More than once all the work of months had to be done over. "With no books or opportunities for any intellectual or scientific work" to help him in his linguistic studies, he was left to his own devices.

Throughout his Alaskan years, Father Barnum kept working on his Eskimo grammar. He seemed to sense that his Superiors were not happy with him as a missionary and that he might, therefore, be recalled at any time. This gave urgency to his linguistic efforts. In August 1894, he wrote to his friend at Georgetown, "I have devoted myself solely to Innuit. I am getting near the threshold of Innuit."

After his year at Tununak, Father Barnum was assigned to **Holy Cross Mission** on the Yukon. On August 28, 1892, he joined Fathers Tosi, Tréca, and Aloysius J. **Robaut**, S.J., founder of that mission, as they went to the place upriver from **Nulato** where Archbishop Seghers had been shot to death, on November 28, 1886. There the three erected a memorial to "that noble-hearted herald of the Cross," as Father Barnum hailed him, and offered Masses. Father Barnum, though always ready to catch and record an historic moment, also had personal reasons for wanting to honor the memory of the slain archbishop. He felt he owed his call to Alaska to him, and had once hoped to accompany him on his historic journey north in 1886. At that time, he had written to a friend:

Fiat voluntas! I have seen Rev. Fr. Provincial and spent one full hour with him. I begged and pleaded for all I was worth; he was proof against every plea I could produce. Now there only remains patience and resignation. How I wish I was with Father Tosi! The route is the very one I would have selected. Crickee, it makes my veins throb.

Though formally assigned to Holy Cross, Father Barnum spent a good part of his second year in Alaska at a new mission site on the Kanelik Pass, a channel at the south mouth of the Yukon. The site proved to be a poor one, and was abandoned after a year. Both Fathers Barnum and Tréca had advised against it, but Father Tosi gave them "a peremptory order to settle there." Of Father Tosi, Father Barnum wrote, "It was not in his nature to accept any advice." In 1893, while Father Tosi was on a lengthy trip to Europe and elsewhere and Father Tréca Superior in his stead, the Kanelik house was taken down and the logs rafted and towed to a new site on the **Akulurak** River. Here, in the reassembled structure, the Fathers lived in relative comfort.

In December 1893, Brother Thomas Power, S.J., skipper of the Holy Cross mission boat, wrote:

Father Barnum is doing in Alaska an immense amount of work for the glory of God. His ways are very taking, and one cannot come in contact with him without loving him. He is not only a good missionary, but an excellent scientist. Wherever he goes he maps out the country with great care. Neither is his work limited to paper. He has, in truth, rendered an important service to all who travel from Holy Cross to the Kuskokwim by cutting a trail across the mountains that lie between these stations. This trail is now known as Barnum's Pass.

During his years in Alaska, Father Barnum spent much time in looking for suitable mission sites, in visiting Native villages, and in exploring the Yukon-Kuskokwim Delta. The editor of *Alaska–Yukon Magazine*, who reprinted Father Barnum's article, "The Yukon Delta Region," said of it, "No better description of the Yukon Delta has ever been printed."

In a letter written in 1893, Father Barnum revealed his strong pro-America bias, his farsightedness, and

his penchant for "schemes." He was disappointed that Father Tosi, upon his return to Alaska, did not bring back two or three English-speaking priests. The Alaska Mission was at that time entrusted to the Rocky Mountain Mission, which was, in turn, subordinate to the Province of Turin in Italy. Father Barnum wanted to see the Alaska Mission coupled to some American province. "The mission," he wrote categorically, "would succeed much better under Americans."

In July 1894, the Alaska Mission was raised to a Prefecture Apostolic and Father Tosi was appointed Prefect Apostolic. He was now both the Jesuit Religious Superior and the Vatican's official representative in Alaska.

Father Barnum spent a second winter at Akulurak. Then, on July 5, 1895, he went south with the understanding that he was going to collect money for the Alaska Mission and to publish some of his writings. Father Tosi, however, understood otherwise. To Father Barnum's close friend at Georgetown, Father J. Havens Richards, S.J., he wrote:

I recommend to your kindness not to let him print anything. I don't think proper at present to have printed his Malamute [Eskimo] catechism, as it is not complete and theologically exact—so also his grammar and dictionary. It will take yet two or more years before it will be worthy of having it exposed to the public. It is true that the good Father worked very hard, and what he has is good, but very deficient and incomplete, particularly in way of writing. In two or more years, with the help of other Fathers, he may be able to make a good work and worthy of the public.

None of Father Barnum's linguistic works were published at this time. In light of some subsequent remarks Father Barnum himself made, Father Tosi definitely showed the better judgment this time. It was part of Father Barnum's nature to rush into print.

The Tosi-Barnum interrelation, so replete with misunderstanding, and often with ill will on both sides, was one of those sad, enigmatic relationships that exist all too often between two persons of superior qualities who are forced by their responsibilities to interact closely.

Father Tosi was replaced as Prefect Apostolic of Alaska in March 1897, by Father John B. **René**, S.J. The Tosi thorn was now out of Father Barnum's side, but he had little cause for joy, for his days in

Alaska were already pretty well numbered. He spent the winter of 1896–97 at Akulurak, having returned from his journey south by way of the Chilkoot Pass and the Yukon River. From St. Michael he wrote on July 3rd: "Father René said he would leave me at St. Michael's where I could complete the Innuit grammar and dictionary. One more year would be well spent on this." However, in another letter, written that same summer, he gives a more plausible reason why his stay in Alaska was extended: "Two of our Fathers have broken down, and no new recruit has come. I cannot leave now, as the mission is too much crippled."

In that same letter, Father Barnum revealed something of his more intimate personal side. After commenting on the Klondike gold discovery and the adverse influence of miners on the Natives along the Yukon, he went on to write:

> Now children whom we have raised so carefully and whom we counted on would intermarry and form a [Christian] settlement around the missions are being ruined. It is enough to break one's heart. I almost wish an epidemic would sweep over Holy Cross while the children are yet innocent.

Shocking as this passage is to modern ears, it leaves no ambiguity about Father Barnum's scale of basic values.

While at St. Michael during that summer of 1897, Father Barnum was visited by writer Alice Henderson, as mentioned above, who wrote:

> I met Father Barnum, and stopped for a talk. He is delightful company, and so full of information that one cannot be with him for five minutes without learning something. He is small, slight, with an intellectual, refined face, smiling but rather cynical in expression. He insists he is happy and content—and he ought to know—but he looks as if he would be more in place in the luxurious library of his old home down South, flashing his ready wit at dinner parties and controlling affairs.

During his last summer in Alaska, Father Barnum was able to realize one of his long-cherished dreams, a visit to the Arctic coast, "to see what prospects there were for mission work." On the U.S. Revenue Cutter, *Bear*, as guest of Captain Francis Tuttle, he left St. Michael on July 7, 1898, returning on August 24th. A week later, he took leave of his friends and sailed south, ostensibly to prepare his manuscripts for publication. The real reason, however, we find in his "Notebook." Under date of September 1, 1898, he wrote, "I left Alaska—recalled by Fr. Purbrick." But it was really Father René—and before him Father Tosi—who was behind Father Barnum's being recalled from Alaska. He had tried already the previous year to have him recalled. Father Purbrick, as Father Barnum's Father Provincial, merely carried out Father René's wishes. Father Barnum was never to see Alaska again.

Having returned to Georgetown, Father Barnum devoted his time to readying his grammar for publication. In 1901, Ginn and Company published his *Grammatical Fundamentals of the Innuit Language*, a large octavo volume of 384 pages. From the preface, we learn much about the difficulties under which he worked to produce it. "Much of this work," he wrote, "has been done in the gloomy underground abodes of the Innuit. Many words were taken down while traveling by dog sled over the ice fields, when the very act of making a hurried note in the intense cold meant a degree of misery which the written account but feebly expresses."

Father Barnum's grammar received widespread attention. Scholars at the Smithsonian Institution and at the Royal Danish Geographical Society spoke well of it. But there were also dissenting voices, mainly among his fellow Jesuit Alaskan missionaries. He conceded some validity to their fault-finding. In self-defense, however, he wrote to one of them:

> I felt always that my notes were very incomplete, and I hoped on my return to Alaska that I would be able to make many more discoveries and improvements. I *did not want* to publish the book till it promised to be more perfect. Now when I found that I *was not* allowed to return by Fr. René, then I felt that my notes were at least worth saving by being printed. [Father Barnum's emphasis]

For what reasons was Father Barnum recalled from Alaska and never allowed to return, in spite of his requests to be allowed to return? As late as 1915, he was "still alive to things Alaskan." What is clear from various letters is that Father René was the immediate obstacle to his return to Alaska. What is also clear is that Father Barnum's return never gained the approval of "headquarters," the Jesuit Generalate in Rome.

The Father General of the Jesuits at the time was Luis Martín. Influenced by Father Tosi, who, according to Father Barnum, "possessed a domineering and most irascible disposition," he opposed Father Barnum's return.

Animosity between Fathers Barnum and Tosi began to build almost from the day the two first met. This was based on deep-seated personality differences, but even more on fundamentally different cultural backgrounds and on basically opposing views as to the best means to be employed to make the Alaskan missionary enterprise succeed. Wrote Father Barnum: "In great measure this [Tosi's authoritarian, unimaginative manner of governing] was owing to Fr. Tosi's ignorance of American ways and his reluctance to adopt means which were new to him." From the outset, then, the door to mutual understanding and reconciliation between Father Tosi, the Italian, and Father Barnum, virtually a *Mayflower* American, was hermetically sealed.

Father Barnum could also be quite outspoken in his views. Father Julius **Jetté**, S.J., wrote to him in 1903, "I have been guilty of the same crime as you: telling the truth too plainly to Princes and Prelates, as you express it elegantly."

Word of Father Barnum's ways and views, too plainly expressed and out of harmony with those of princes and prelates Father Tosi and Father René, did not take long to reach Rome. As early as July 1896, Father General Martín had formed his opinion of Father Barnum. He wrote to Father Tosi that he was requesting Father Barnum's recall to his province, and that the Provincial of the Maryland province had agreed to recall him. Father Martín assured Father Tosi that he, Father Martín, was acting all the more willingly in the matter, since he knew from Father Tosi's letters that he, Father Tosi, wished Father Barnum recalled.

In a letter to Father Louis L. **Renner**, S.J., Father Edmond Lamalle, S.J., of the Jesuit Generalate Archives in Rome, sheds further light on this subject. "As far as Fr. Francis Barnum is concerned," wrote Father Lamalle,

the motives for his being recalled from Alaska are anterior to the Prefecture Apostolic of René. Father Tosi already desired his departure, which was decided by Father General, Luis Martín. It is certain that Father René was opposed to Father Barnum, but the princi-

pal opponent of the latter was Father General himself, who found that Father Barnum scattered his attention to too many irrelevant projects, and also made too much noise.

Father Lamalle's letter further paraphrases and summarizes Barnum-related archival materials. In some instructions, written in August 1897, Father Martín directed the newly appointed Prefect Apostolic René, a notably weaker personality than Father Tosi, not to allow himself to be manipulated by any Jesuits under him. Father Martín definitely had Father Barnum in mind, for he brought up his case and raised the question of his possibly staying on in Alaska. Should it be decided, however, after consultation, Father Martín instructed, that Father Barnum was to be allowed to stay on in Alaska, he was to be cautioned to use more prudence and restraint. "For there [in Alaska]," wrote Father Martín, "we need men who work much, but speak little." On March 11, 1898, he gave Father René further instructions to the effect that the Fathers on the Alaska Mission should not allow themselves to be distracted by any occupations other than the care of souls and the sacred ministries. All scientific investigations, whether of an historical or ethnological or geographic nature, were to be given secondary place to the care of souls, and in such a way that, if there were any men in Alaska who had such investigations more at heart than the conversion of souls, such men were to be removed from Alaska. Father Lamalle adds his own gloss to this: "Father Barnum is not mentioned by name, but manifestly there is question here of his proposals and practices."

Among the proposals referred to here was one Father Barnum made in a 13-page letter written in July 1894, to the Father Assistant of England. He proposed a program of scientific research and insisted on its urgency. Some time later, he proposed to Father Jetté "a grand plan," part of which called for a comparative study of major American Native language groups.

Such, then, according to the most reliable sources, are the real reasons why Father Barnum was recalled from Alaska and never allowed to return, much as he wanted to. From the outset, his views and ways of proceeding were deemed unbefitting the kind of missionary considered necessary in Alaska at the time. His plans and schemes were thought to be too far-fetched by the transatlantic mentalities of the time. He roamed too far and wide, spoke too much, and made too much noise. The not-too-subtle implication was that he neglected his missionary work. In sum, his Superiors did not consider him a good choice for the Alaska Mission. His ever-active, inquisitive mind and the very richness, breadth and depth of his personality became his undoing as an Alaskan missionary.

Though Father Barnum was now out of Alaska, much of his heart continued to remain there. Throughout the remainder of his life he never lost contact with the Alaska Mission. He kept collecting Alaskana. Letters flowed to and from Alaska. He continued to suggest schemes and innovations, as he had from the beginning. During his first year in Alaska, he had already proposed the drying and burning of peat as a fuel. Today this is considered wholly feasible. He had a scheme for a clay pottery industry. Near Tununak he had found "excellent pottery clay." After he had "experimented with some and had had great success," he suggested that teachers and equipment be brought to develop a ceramics works. He anticipated quality Native art, "since the people already possessed much artistic talent." Seventy years later, just such a project was launched. He also urged that the various missions acquire reindeer herds. Several decades later, Akulurak, Holy Cross and Nulato each had a large herd.

Though Father Barnum remained singularly attached to Alaska and things Alaskan, he was never embittered by his exile. Being a spiritual man, and an obedient man, as well as congenial and cheerful by nature, he continued on in his priestly life with genuine enthusiasm and dedication. During the 23 remaining years of his life, he had 17 different assignments. Going from place to place, he put heart into his work: librarian at Georgetown and Woodstock, chaplain of various prisons, hospitals, and welfare institutions. He went on business trips for his Order to Jamaica, Cuba, New Mexico and Florida.

Father Barnum spent the last six years of his life at Georgetown as archivist and museum curator. Among his prized acquisitions was the bearskin Archbishop Seghers had used as a bed. In a showcase he placed a football helmet between two bishops' miters. When asked why the incongruous juxtaposition, he answered that it was "just for contrast, to make people ask questions."

Father Barnum's pleasant wit and disarming playfulness removed him so far from the picture of a frustrated old man that his confreres would have had difficulty identifying him with the deep pathos of some of his private writings. His comments on articles published by Father Tosi would have been unkind had they not come from so kind a man. "But, then," wrote one of his admirers, "who can measure what his removal from Alaska cost him, and who can blame him for acquiring somewhat of a fixation on the affairs that brought about his exile from the land of his heart?"

At Georgetown University, on November 3, 1921, septuagenarian Father Francis A. Barnum, S.J., "a polished gentleman, endowed with rare conversational powers, an extraordinary linguist, an apostolic man, a man of boundless wit and humor, died piously in the Lord." He lies buried in the Georgetown University cemetery.

5, 94, 122, 174

BARROW

Seen from the air, facing the Arctic Ocean, with vast stretches of treeless tundra behind it, the town of Barrow, home to 4,581 inhabitants in the year 2000, mostly Inupiat Eskimos, appears to cling to the land's very edge. This northernmost U.S. city, 330 miles above the Arctic Circle, takes its name from Point Barrow, ten miles to the northeast, which was named, in 1826, for Sir John Barrow. The settlement's Eskimo name is *Utqiagvik*, "the place to hunt snowy owls." There has been a Barrow post office since 1901.

Christianity was first brought to America's arctic regions in 1890, when the Presbyterian Church established a mission at Barrow. The first Catholic missionary to enter the high arctic was Father Francis A. **Barnum**, S.J., who spent a short time there in the summer of 1898, "to see what prospects there were for missionary work." It was not until 1954 that a permanent Catholic presence began in Barrow, when, in May of that year, Father **Thomas P. Cunningham**, S.J., began to build St. Patrick's Mission. The church consisted of one abandoned World War II military Quonset hut and the living quarters of a second such. The two huts were obtained from the Air Force locally. The material for the central structure connecting the two huts was salvaged at Umiat and flown in by the Air Force.

Father Cunningham was resident pastor of the Barrow parish from 1954 until his sudden death there on September 3, 1959. Barrow's Cunningham Street is named for him. During the years 1959–61, DEWline (Distant Early Warning) chaplain, Father Joseph L. Asturias, O.P., tended the Barrow parish on a part-time basis. From 1961–64, it was DEWline chaplain Urban M. **Bates**, O.P., who did likewise. Father James E. **Poole**, S.J., was resident pastor for the year 1965–66. He was followed by Father Angus R. **McDonald**, who lived in Barrow from 1966–71. He was responsible for getting a new rectory building, a prefabricated structure, put up in 1969.

During the year 1971–72, Father McDonald was either out of **Alaska**, or living in **Fairbanks**, from which he commuted, from time to time to Barrow, a round-trip of 1,012 air miles. Father McDonald offered his last Mass in Barrow on May 14, 1972. From 1972 to the year 2000, Father **Francis E. Mueller**, S.J., was pastor of the Barrow parish. No flock in Alaska has ever been served by one and the same pastor for a time longer than that. On a regular basis, generally every other week, he commuted to Barrow from Fairbanks for stays of varying durations.

By the mid-1980s, the parishioners of St. Patrick's and Father Mueller had come to the conclusion that the old Quonset hut church was much too small for Barrow's Catholic community and woefully lacking in basics such as running water, toilet facilities, an efficient heating system. It was no longer a safe place for holding services. In 1990, pastor and people of St. Patrick's committed themselves to replacing the old church. The rectory building was sold

The first St. Patrick's Church in Barrow—built by Father Thomas P. Cunningham, S.J., in 1954—as it appeared on October 23, 1982. *LR.*

and moved off the premises. On Easter Sunday 1992, the last Mass was offered in the Quonset church. In the spring of that year, it was torn down, and construction of the new, the present, church, with living facilities for a priest, begun. By Christmas 1992, the new St. Patrick's complex, though not yet completely finished, was ready for Midnight Mass. On Sunday, March 28, 1993, the new church was formally dedicated by Michael J. **Kaniecki**, S.J., Bishop of Fairbanks at the time. He was assisted by Father Mueller and Father Louis L. **Renner**, S.J.

After Father Mueller's resignation as pastor of the Barrow parish in the spring of the year 2000, it was visited at irregular intervals and for varying lengths of time by priests stationed in Fairbanks.

During the summer of 1967, Sisters Pauline Higgins and Carrie Thompson, Sisters of **Providence** stationed in Fairbanks, taught catechism in Barrow to children.

139, 169

BARTLES, Father Charles A., S.J.

Charles A. Bartles was born in Shreveport, Louisiana, on January 10, 1936. There he attended St. Vincent's Grade School, 1941–47, and St. John's High School, 1947–52. On July 30, 1952, he entered the New Orleans Province of the Society of Jesus. He made his novitiate and classical and humanities studies at St. Charles College in Grand Coteau, and at Loyola University in New Orleans, 1952–56; then his philosophical studies at Spring Hill College, Mobile, Alabama, 1956–59. He studied theology at St. Mary's, Kansas, 1962–66. On June 7, 1965, he was ordained a priest. During the year 1966–67, he made his tertianship in Cleveland, Ohio. From 1967–71, he worked as a counselor at Jesuit High in Tampa, Florida. After a year as guidance counselor at Campion College in Kingston, Jamaica, 1971–72, he worked as an instructor and counselor at Marist School in Atlanta, 1972–78.

Father Bartles was restless as a classroom teacher. He was characterized by a high official in his Province as "self-willed," and as "quite self-sufficient with somewhat of an independent streak. He deplores living in a large community and has an urgent need to live a rather simple, frugal life in his personal expression of religious poverty." This and his strong desire to engage in mission work he made known to his Father Provincial.

In the summer of 1978, Father Bartles arrived in **Nulato**, a Koyukon Athabaskan Indian village on the middle Yukon River. Here he found what he had been looking for: missionary work, a chance "to live a poor life among poor people, sharing their simple, subsistence lifestyle." He quickly got to know the people, and developed good relationships with them, especially with the elderly. At Nulato, he also had good outlet for his practical skills. He was a physicist by training. He was a pilot. He knew how to butcher a moose. He was a skilled cook. After he had been at Nulato for some time, he could say in an interview: "My life here so far after three and a half years has been most gratifying and fulfilling." He was heartened by the fact that he could also say "I find, too, that up here there is a tremendous amount of trust placed in the men." He was edified by the strong prayer-life among his fellow mis-

The present St. Patrick's Church, Barrow. *LR.*

sionaries, and by the fact that "the older men seem indefatigable in their service."

In early October 1980, Father Louis L. **Renner**, S.J., traveled to Nulato with Father Bartles to spend a few days there with him. "Charlie and I," wrote Father Renner afterwards, "wandered through the village, but we made slow progress, for everyone we met wanted to greet and chat with him after his absence of two weeks. They really miss him, when he is away, and chide him about it. He has a wonderful, easy way with people, young and old."

On May 8, 1982, Robert L. **Whelan**, S.J., Bishop of Fairbanks at the time, wrote to Father Bartles: "By this letter I appoint you as Pastor of St. John Berchmans Church in **Galena** and St. Francis Regis Church in **Huslia**, together with St. Patrick's Church in **Koyukuk**. This appointment is effective on 1 July 1982." Being a pilot with an airplane at his disposal, this appointment was "a natural" for Father Bartles.

In Galena, Father Bartles found himself faced with a formidable challenge. The church building, with small living quarters tacked on to it, that awaited him in Galena had stood there since 1923. It was not originally built as a church. It was a one-time saloon barged downriver from **Ruby** and turned into a church. By 1982, it had long since been much too small, and it was ready to crumble into the Yukon. Moreover, it was in "old town," whereas most of the Galena people were by then living at "new site," several miles upriver. A new, larger church at new site was badly needed, and the people had been raising funds for it for some time before Father Bartles came to Galena. By energizing the Galena Catholic community, by interesting others, by soliciting volunteer help, and by putting his own considerable personal energy into the whole church project, he was able to bring about a new St. John Berchmans Church and rectory at new site. By the first Sunday of Advent 1985, the year he left Galena, this was ready for its first Mass.

During his years both at Nulato and at Galena, Father Bartles was blessed to have co-working with him Sisters of St. **Ann**. Unfortunately, he did not recognize this special blessing. He, who so cherished the freedom and trust he himself enjoyed, did not find it in him to concede the same to the Sisters. This caused them considerable pain, and also

led to a certain degree of alienation between him and the people.

After leaving Galena, Father Bartles spent some time at Jemez Springs, New Mexico. Then, motivated by his experiences along the middle Yukon, he went on to get training as a substance-abuse counselor at Hazleton, Pennsylvania. He next spent two years, 1986–88, in **Bethel**, Alaska, as a counselor. From there he went on to spend happy years working in Campinas, Brazil, as Director of Treatment and Training Counselors at Instituto Souza. In 1993, he returned to the States for medical tests. On July 28, 1993, he collapsed as he was entering the parking lot of University Hospital, New Orleans. There he died. The cause of his death was given as "cardiac arrhythmia." He lies buried at St. Charles College in Grand Coteau.

101

BATES, Father Urban M., O.P.

Francis Patrick (Urban Mary) Bates was born on March 29, 1915, to Patrick and Isabelle Jane McKernan Bates at Eagle Grove, Iowa. He was the oldest of four children, two boys and two girls. While Francis was a young child, the family moved a number of times. He graduated from St. Mary's parochial school, in Peru, Illinois, in June 1928, and from North Division high school in Milwaukee, Wisconsin, in January 1932. He then went to work in a local auto parts manufacturing firm for four years. In May 1936, he began working as a clerk for a local sheet metal, furnace, and air conditioning wholesale firm. His father died in March and his mother in October 1936. That same October, he became a substitute letter carrier for the Milwaukee post office. During those years, he was also involved with the Catholic Youth Organization, the local Catholic Worker Holy Family House, the Dominican Third Order. He was a charter member of the St. Gabriel League of Post Office and Federal Employees. Meanwhile, he earned his commercial pilot, single engine, land and sea ratings.

In October 1941, Francis registered as a conscientious objector in the draft and was given 4-F status, reporting for duty at the Civilian Public Service Camp at Stoddard, New Hampshire. From there

Father Urban M. Bates, O.P. *LRC.*

he was transferred to a temporary camp in Oakland, Maryland; subsequently, he was sent to a camp in Vahalla, Michigan. In January 1944, he changed his status, and was drafted into the U.S. Navy and sent to the Great Lakes Navy Training Center. After finishing basic training, he, as a member of a medical unit, was sent to serve on Truk in the Caroline Islands. In March 1946, with an honorable discharge, he returned to civilian life and to his former position with the Milwaukee Post Office.

In the fall of 1946, Francis enrolled in the Jesuit-sponsored St. Philip Neri School for Delayed Vocations, in Boston; and, in September 1947, he entered the Dominican novitiate of the Western Province at Kentfield, California. A year later, having taken the Religious name of Urban Mary, he made his first profession of vows at St. Albert's College in Oakland, California. He remained there for three years of philosophy and four of theology. Archbishop John J. Mitty ordained him a priest in St. Mary's Cathedral, San Francisco, on June 13, 1953.

Father Bates spent 1955–57 at Blessed Sacrament parish in Seattle, Washington; 1957–58 at St. Dominic's parish in San Francisco; 1958–59 at Holy Rosary parish in Portland, Oregon; and 1959–61 at St. Vincent Ferrer parish in Vallejo, California.

Father Bates began serving in northern **Alaska** on July 5, 1961, as a chaplain on the DEWline (Distant Early Warning). In October, he visited Arliss II Ice Island, floating at the time in the Arctic Ocean near Wrangel Island. In May 1964, after three years on the DEWline, he returned to Blessed Sacrament parish in Seattle for a second tour of duty. In April 1968, he became pastor of St. Dominic's parish in Benicia, California.

On June 22, 1971, Father Bates was transferred to St. Albert's College in Oakland to prepare himself for ministry in one of the Western Province's missions, Ocosingo, Chiapas, Mexico. In July and August, he made a five-week trip to Europe, visiting Italy, England, and Ireland. He arrived at Ocosingo on January 9, 1972, to minister at San Jacinto parish. On September 30, 1975, he was reassigned, to St. Dominic's parish in Eagle Rock, California, a northern suburb of Los Angeles.

Father Bates returned to Alaska in 1977 to be pastor of St. Mary's parish in **Kodiak**, beginning on August 27th. A year later, on August 31st, he became pastor of Holy Family parish at **Glennallen**. As of January 1, 1984, he served at a number of parishes and missions north of **Anchorage: Wasilla, Talkeetna, Willow**, and **Trapper Creek**. On September 8, 1991, he began living in the Dominican residence at Holy Family Cathedral in Anchorage. On weekends, as a "supply priest," he traveled to parishes without resident pastors to bring the people the Mass and Sacraments. Up until a few weeks before his death, he ministered to prisoners in Anchorage jails.

Father Bates died peacefully in his sleep, on September 9, 2003, in Anchorage. He was known for his extraordinary personal kindness. A fellow Dominican, who knew him well, hailed him as "a great missionary, Dominican friar, and priest." Father Urban M. Bates, O.P, lies buried in St. Dominic's Cemetery in Benicia, California.

BAUD, Father John B., S.J.

For over a quarter of a century he made the oldest Catholic mission in northern **Alaska** his headquarters. His skilled fingers fashioned wood-carvings, carnival style, for merry-go-rounds and puppet shows to entertain and teach children. Out of sheet metal he fashioned the mission's stoves. He was a painter in oils beyond the rank of amateur. He was a gifted musician. No other Jesuit Alaskan missionary caused the people he served as much pain as he caused his; yet, few were more loved by their people than he was loved by his. He was regarded by all as a devoted, exemplary missionary, as "one of the warmest personalities in all Alaska."

Jean-Baptiste Baud was born in Lyons, France, on August 11, 1897. From 1903–11, he attended the Christian Brothers grade school in Lyons, then, for a year, the Clerical School there. After that, from 1912–15, he attended the Apostolic School of the Jesuit Province of Lyons in Lanzo, Italy. During World War I, from 1915–19, he was in the French Army, serving for a time as a member of the "Blue Devil" Division in Syria. After the war, he came to America and entered the Jesuit novitiate at Los Gatos, California, on November 28, 1919. After completing the two-year noviceship and two years of classical and humanities studies there, he went to Mount St. Michael's, Spokane, Washington, for three years of philosophical studies, 1923–26. He became a U.S. citizen in 1926—but he retained his love for "la Belle France" all his life.

John Baud spent the year 1926–27 at St. Ignatius High School in San Francisco teaching Latin and music. He next taught for two years in Yakima, Washington, teaching, among other subjects, music. During the year 1929–30, he was at **Holy Cross Mission**, Alaska, prefecting boarding school boys. From 1930–34, he was at Weston College, Weston, Massachusetts, for theological studies. He was ordained a priest on June 20, 1932. Back in his native France, at Paray-le-Monial, he made his tertianship, 1934–35.

In the spring of 1935, Father Baud returned to Alaska to begin 27 years of uninterrupted missionary work at and out of **Nulato**. After helping out in **Fairbanks** for several months, he arrived at Nulato on July 9th. From 1940 on, until he left Nulato, he was Superior of that mission. During his earlier Alaskan years especially, he regularly visited villages above and below Nulato, principally **Galena**, **Koyukuk**, and **Kaltag**. Having no dogteam of his own, he relied on others for winter travel. Between break-up and freeze-up, when the Yukon River was open, he traveled up and down it on Nulato's "mission chapel boat," the *Seghers*. It was built in 1936 by Brother Edward J. **Horwedel**, S.J., so that the priest could visit the people not only in their

Father John B. Baud, S.J. *JOPA-862.02.*

villages, but also at their fish camps. Father Baud always regretted that he could not visit the outlying stations more often and for longer periods of time. The Sisters of St. **Ann** stationed at Nulato as schoolteachers had been assured that they would have daily Mass on a more or less regular basis, and he was faithful to that assurance.

For the most part, Father Baud's Nulato years were happy, satisfying years. Two realities, however, marred those years: too frequent and too excessive "drinking" on the part of his flock, and the celebrations of the traditional "stickdance," or "Feast for the Dead." He was the last of the missionaries to consistently and vehemently oppose the "stickdance." In the Nulato house diary he recorded that he "preached against it in the church," that he "gave a good scolding to the people for bringing back old superstitions." In his mind and heart, he was convinced that the dance was superstitious, idolatrous. One Christmas, he announced to his people that all who intended to go to confession would have to promise to stay away from the dance, or absolution would be denied them. Very few were willing to promise. They complained he was spoiling their Christmas. He answered that, on the contrary, they were spoiling God's Christmas. Many came to the Midnight Mass, but more than half the congregation left, not staying for the second Mass as they normally would have. "It was awful for the heart of the priest," he wrote in the diary, "to hear the slamming of the door every time someone decided to leave the church. What a sad Christmas." Sad for all concerned. Obviously, the people were torn between the Catholic Christmas celebrations and the time-honored "stickdance" ceremonials.

Fortunately, given the kind of man and priest that Father Baud was, hard feelings and strained relations between pastor and people were always soon overcome. The people could not help but esteem and love him, for they knew from his total dedication to them that he, in turn, esteemed and loved them.

Poldine **Carlo**, in her book, *Nulato: An Indian Life on the Yukon*, recalled how Father Baud for Christmas

> froze colored water in a foot-sized can and put it out overnight before midnight Mass. The altar boys would light the candles that were placed inside this frozen ice. These were placed along the road leading to the church. They were just beautiful—all colors of the rainbow. There was always so much excitement during this time, because we just felt the full meaning of the birth of our Lord.

Father Baud showed special concern for the children and youth of Nulato. In 1946, he organized for them "The Club of St. John Bosco," and two years later he provided the club with a clubhouse of its own. "All the children and even big ones," he wrote in 1951,

> are welcome to come every evening of the week to gather in that building, there to spend the time interestingly in reading or playing decent games or little amusement like dances or having shows, etc. It has been very prosperous lately and we hope that it will continue the same, as it is a great help to keep the people happy and the children occupied with something interesting and decent.

He himself made board games for the children to play on, and, in general, fostered the manual arts.

Years after Father Baud had left Nulato, one of those former club members recalled the games—monopoly, checkers, dominoes, Parcheesi—and the dances. "Father Baud," he wrote, "our most favorite missionary, started to learn to dance too."

June 20, 1957, was a memorable day for Father Baud and the people of Nulato. On that day, he celebrated the 25th anniversary of his ordination to the priesthood. Present for the occasion to celebrate a Mass of Thanksgiving with him were: Bishop Francis D. **Gleeson**, S.J., Vicar Apostolic of Alaska; Father Henry G. **Hargreaves**, S.J., General Superior of Jesuits in Alaska; his fellow countryman, Father Jules M. **Convert**, S.J.; and Fathers James W. **Plamondon**, S.J., and Wilfred P. Schoenberg, S.J. On that day, when asked about his long years at Nulato, he said, "I like it here. I do not care to go—no time. I want to stay right here." In 1962, however, Father Baud's long tenure at Nulato came to an end. While still there, he wrote to Father Paul C. **O'Connor**, S.J., "I am being dethroned from the little kingdom of the Nulato mission."

In 1962, Father Baud received his second Alaskan assignment as a priest. He was named to **Copper Valley School**, to serve there as "Spiritual Father," as student counselor, as a teacher of Religion, and, in keeping with his artistic talents, as an instructor in art. He and Sister Kathleen Mary (Margaret Cantwell), S.S.A., combined their ideas and enlarged the Art Department.

When Father Baud arrived at the school, it was in dire need of a school bus. Hearing that such a bus could be obtained by redeeming 1,500,000 Betty Crocker coupons, he, in 1963, launched a Betty Crocker coupon drive. Response to the drive was dramatic. Coupons poured in. Within less than two years there was much rejoicing and cheering, as "Betty Bus" arrived at Copper Valley School, courtesy of General Mills and of Father Baud's coupon drive.

Regarding his stay at the school, Father Baud said in an interview, "It is a joy to be here." In a letter to General Mission Superior, Father George T. **Boileau**, S.J., he wrote, "The dear Lord has been flooding my soul with His consolations."

Father Baud spent the year 1965–66 at St. Mary's Mission on the **Andreafsky** River. There, too, he served as "Spiritual Father" and as teacher of Religion. From 1966–68, he was chaplain of Griffin Memorial Hospital in **Kodiak**. He was a happy man in Kodiak, referring to it as "this wonderful place." During the summer of 1968, he made a trip to his homeland, the first since he had left it in 1935, to visit his remaining family members. For a short time, during the latter part of 1968, he served also as chaplain of Ketchikan General Hospital in **Ketchikan**. Suffering from severe pains, he was sent to Seattle for a medical examination. "Inoperable cancer" was the finding. Father Baud died in Providence Hospital, Seattle, on December 6, 1968, and lies buried in the Jesuit cemetery at Mount St. Michael's.

The day after Father Baud's death, the Oregon Province Provincial, Father John J. Kelley, S.J., wrote to Father Baud's sister in Lyons: "I know you will be pleased to know that Father John was held in very high esteem by all his brothers in Alaska and here in the Oregon Province. He was an example to us all and was always most priestly in his dealing with everyone. We will all miss him."

142

BAYUSIK, Father Robert E.

Robert E. Bayusik was born to John J. and Susan Churma Bayusik in Bridgeport, Connecticut, on March 1, 1927. After serving in the U.S. Army, he attended Sts. Cyril and Methodius Seminary in Pittsburgh, Pennsylvania, from 1952–58. He was ordained a Byzantine Rite priest by Bishop Nicholas T. Elko on June 1, 1958. That same year, he was sent to **Anchorage, Alaska**, where he founded St. Nicholas of Myra parish and built a church and rectory. In September 1959, Bishop Elko traveled to Alaska to bless the new church. Father Bayusik served as pastor of St. Nicholas of Myra parish until 1962. In 1960, he was nominated Outstanding Man of the Year by the Anchorage Chamber of Commerce and Outstanding Young Priest by the Pittsburgh archdiocese. While in Anchorage, he co-founded the Anchorage Council of the Knights of Columbus. In 1963, he was sent to administrate St. John's Church in Barnesboro, Pennsylvania. He remained there until 1966. In September 1966, he became pastor of Sts. Peter and Paul parish in

Portage and of St. Michael's parish in South Fork, both in Pennsylvania. He remained pastor of those two parishes until his death, at Altoona Mercy Hospital, on October 21, 1991. Father Bayusik lies buried in Sts. Peter and Paul Cemetery, Portage.

15

BENISH, Brother Robert L., S.J.

He spent 40 years among the Eskimos of western **Alaska**. He was known as "the tundra baker." For long years he was a successful gardener, a competent ham radio operator, a reliable U.S. postmaster. It can safely be said that the Fighting Irish of Notre Dame never had a more avid fan than him. He was an enthusiastic fisherman. He was an exemplary Jesuit missionary Lay Brother.

Robert L. Benish was born in Spokane, Washington, on November 11, 1920. He was one of nine children, and the family was poor. As a child and young boy, he attended public grade and high schools. Tuition costs at Catholic schools put them out of reach.

It was during his high school days that Robert first became interested in Alaska. In the school library he found a copy of Jesuit Father Paul C. **O'Connor**'s book, *Eskimo Parish*. No sooner had he read the book, than he was convinced that Alaska was the place for him, and that becoming a Jesuit was the way to get there.

When Robert talked to the Jesuits about becoming a priest in their Order, they asked him to attend Spokane's Gonzaga University for two years, since, by his own admission, his grades were "nothing to brag about." This he did. Again, his grades stayed unimpressive. Nevertheless, he did apply for admission into the Society of Jesus, indicating that he was quite content to be a Jesuit Lay Brother.

He was accepted into the Order in 1941, and told to arrive at the novitiate at Sheridan, Oregon, before the end of June to begin his six months of postulancy. He arrived a day late. He had been working on the Northern Pacific Railway bridge construction crew in Spokane and had to wait until payday to be able to afford the trip to Sheridan.

After finishing his six-month postulancy and two-year noviceship, he, on January 1, 1944, took

Brother Robert L. Benish, S.J. *LRC*.

the simple, but perpetual, vows of poverty, chastity and obedience that constituted him a member of the Society of Jesus. In the course of those two and a half years, every time the Father Provincial came to the novitiate, Brother Benish told him of his great dream of one day serving in Alaska. But, in spite of the fact that he had taken his vows, he still had to wait two more years at Sheridan, before he was given the green light to go to Alaska. It was during this time that, from an older Brother and by doing, he learned the art of baking.

In the summer of 1946, Brother Benish sailed on the *S.S. Aleutian* from Seattle to **Juneau**, arriving there of August 6th. From there, on an Alaska Airlines plane, he flew to **Anchorage** and **Fairbanks**. A bush plane brought him to **Holy Cross**, where he spent about a week. While at Holy Cross, he showed the boys who baked the bread how to use dried yeast instead of potato yeast—and "a few other tricks."

A sternwheeler then took him down the Yukon to **Marshall**, where he boarded the mission boat, the *Sifton*, which brought him to St. Mary's Mission, **Akulurak**, a place he had searched for on maps while at Sheridan, but could not find. Thirty years later he still remembered the exact hour of his arrival at Akulurak: 9 P.M., October 1, 1946. Many years after Brother Benish's arrival at Akulurak, Father Segundo **Llorente**, S.J., Superior of St. Mary's at

the time, wrote: "Brother Benish descended on us at Akulurak like a ray of sunshine. The boys loved him, and knew that he loved them." Brother Benish was a man who radiated sunshine.

Soon after his arrival at Akulurak, Brother Benish found himself in the mission bakery. Here, too, as at Holy Cross, "there was a problem with potato yeast. It gave everything a rather unpleasant sour smell and taste. And, since the mission was too poor to spend much money on luxuries, like sugar and lard, the bread dried quickly." Again he introduced the use of dried yeast, and "the bread improved greatly."

At Akulurak, Brother Benish's main assignment was that of prefect of the boys. This meant being with them virtually around the clock. It meant eating with them, sleeping in the same dormitory with them, praying with them, going hiking, picnicking, berry picking with them, teaching them practical skills, working with them. Above all, it meant working with them.

One of Brother Benish's jobs at St. Mary's was to see to it that there was always enough firewood on hand for the mission's many stoves. This he did with the help of the bigger boys. On the *Sifton* they went up the Yukon, gathered drift logs, rafted them up, and towed them down to the mission. There they sawed them up and split them into stove-size pieces.

On laundry days, or on Saturday bath days, it was Brother Benish and his boys who provided the hot water. From a hole chopped through the ice on the river they carried enough water to fill a huge cauldron—"it must have been about five feet across"—beneath which they made a roaring fire to bring the water to a boil. They then transferred the hot water to tubs for baths, or for laundry. According to Brother Benish, "They had a very simple laundry process: scrub boards, plungers, big tubs, and a couple of hand cranks for wringing the clothes out."

The big annual adventure for Brother Benish and his boys was the trip to the spring fish camp. This meant both a change of scenery and some fun. It took them four to five hours on the *Sifton* to reach the camp. There they got the three fish wheels into working order and properly positioned in the slough, ready for the beginning of the salmon run. When the run began, the *Sifton* made a quick trip to the mission to get some of the Sisters and older girls to help process the fish. Salmon, primarily king salmon, whether salted away in barrels, or canned or dried or smoked, were a year-round staple in the mission diet. Mission personnel and dogs alike depended on it. "We had to have fish," said Brother Benish. "The very minimum we needed was 18,000." Fish were needed also to exchange for vegetables with Holy Cross.

While life at fish camp was, for the most part, pleasant, it was also hard work, made the more so by the mosquito nuisance. "We had a big dock there," recalled Brother Benish,

> and we'd put a big canvas tent over it. There we had our sliming or cleaning tables. We cut the fish, hung them up, turned them over, and when they reached a certain point, we'd haul the fish into a great big fish house. There we smoked them with willows. It was a rather hard time for everyone involved, because, when the fish came, we had to work and work and work. And in the summer there was hardly any darkness, so we had long hours.

Brother Benish spent only five years at what was later referred to as "Old St. Mary's." On August 3, 1951, the whole St. Mary's Mission operation, after flourishing for close to sixty years near the south mouth of the Yukon, was moved into newly constructed buildings at its present site on the right bank of the **Andreafsky** River several miles upstream from where it empties into the Yukon. Various factors led to the mission's being relocated: poor drinking water, difficulty in getting supplies and firewood to the place, very unfavorable gardening conditions, but especially the dilapidated state of the buildings. Some of them were literally sinking into the tundra.

At the "New St. Mary's," Brother Benish continued to serve as prefect of the boys. To this role he added also those of ham radio operator, postmaster, gardener, and baker. By 1956, he had his ham radio operator's license. His call number was KL7BIA. He was the first St. Mary's postmaster, an office he held from 1951 to 1970. For over 30 years, by using old wooden boats, wash tubs, barrels cut in two, and the like, he raised vegetables for the mission in abundance. From 1961 on, he was the chief baker at St. Mary's.

The fall of 1972 had a special treat in store for Brother Benish, described as "perhaps the Fighting Irish's greatest fan." Mission Superior, Father **James R. Laudwein**, S.J., and members of the St. Mary's staff got together and hatched a plot to surprise him. On the sly, they, with the help of the whole school and village, raised enough money to send him to South Bend to see Notre Dame play Miami on November 11th. The Notre Dame Athletic Department was in on the plot and cooperated fully. Brother Benish was given a grand tour of the campus, got to sit on the stage with the players during the pre-game pep rally, and, from a choice seat on the 35-yard line, was able to take in every detail of the game. The Fighting Irish, too, cooperated. In a close, thrilling game they downed Miami, 20 to 17, and so won a trip to the Orange Bowl. The whole exciting affair had, indeed, come to him as a complete surprise. Only after he had had plane and game tickets in hand, had he realized that anything was afoot. By Tuesday after the game, he was back at St. Mary's. He had promised to be back in time to bake the pies for Thanksgiving Day.

About this time, Brother Benish felt that he needed a longer break from his many, endless duties at St. Mary's. Accordingly, in 1975, it was decided that he should take a year off, go to Anchorage, and take courses in cooking and baking at the Community College there. In the fall, he took a class in cooking. But it was baking that really interested him. So, in January, he enrolled in the head baker's classes. Concerning them, he said: "The teacher showed me a lot of short cuts, some tips on pies and cakes and bread baking and flours. I really enjoyed those classes and got a lot out of them. The only thing I didn't enjoy was that crazy frosting stuff. I was just all thumbs."

When Brother Benish left St. Mary's for Anchorage, it had not yet been determined what he would do after his year there. But, before that year was over, he was informed that St. Mary's wanted him back. He was only too happy to return. His many friends, his radio set, his bakery, his garden, his fishing cabin up the Andreafsky were all waiting to welcome him home.

The students of St. Mary's dedicated two of their yearbooks to Brother Benish: "for being a very dedicated person," and "for helping to maintain the mission not only with his work, but also with his sense of humor and constant spirit." That was their way of showing their appreciation for all he had done for them, as well as for the parents of some of them, for, by the early 1980s, he was able to say, "I'm presently on my second generation of kids." In the course of his long years among the Eskimo people of western Alaska, Brother Benish did much with and for them. Above all, he left them an edifying example of a Christian life well lived.

During the latter part of 1987, Brother Benish went into semi-retirement, moved from St. Mary's into the newly constructed Jesuit House in Fairbanks. Two years later, with his mind and memory beginning to slip noticeably, this one-time Consultor to the Jesuit Superior of the Alaska Missions went into full retirement. On October 24, 1989, he moved into Jesuit House at Gonzaga University. There, in the infirmary, on April 24, 1991, he died peacefully in his sleep. He was buried several days later in the Jesuit cemetery at Mount St. Michael's, only a short distance from where he had been born.

112

BERGQUIST, Father Patrick D.

Patrick D. Bergquist was born the fourth of seven children to John J. Bergquist and Mary Ellen Fitzgerald on July 1, 1960, in Ottumwa, Iowa. In 1968, the family moved to Iowa City, where Patrick's father taught at the University of Iowa College of Dentistry and his mother worked as a pharmacist at Mercy Hospital. In 1972, his father took the chair of the Periodontics Department at the University of Maryland. The family then moved to Timonium, Maryland, near Baltimore. The large family was very close-knit and supportive of one another's interests and gifts. They were also quite involved in the life of their parish, St. Joseph's, in Cockeysville, Maryland. Education and a career in a professional field were held in high esteem in his family.

Patrick, after graduating from Dulaney Senior High School in May 1978, went on to attend Western Maryland College, from which he graduated with a B.A degree in Philosophy in May 1982. Dur-

ing his college years, he was involved in the Catholic Campus Ministry Program. In 1980, he first began to discern that he might be called to Religious life. While home for Christmas, he spoke with his pastor, Msgr. Paul Cook, whom he found very supportive.

Interested in rural missionary work, Patrick went on a "vocation discernment week" in the summer of 1981 with the Glenmary Home Missioners, headquartered in Cincinnati, Ohio. Upon graduating from college, he joined the Glenmary formation program. In the fall of 1982, he entered the Glenmary collegiate program at the University of Dayton. After spending a semester "in community," he worked at Holy Family Mission in Fayette, Alabama. There he helped the pastor and parishioners build a church. This experience was to prove most helpful to him years later. In the summer of 1983, he entered the Glenmary novitiate in Cincinnati. As part of the novitiate program, he spent the latter half of 1983 at St. Mary's Mission in Franklin, Kentucky. After the novitiate program collapsed, because his fellow novices left it, he was sent to St. Mark's Mission in Clarksville, Georgia.

About this time, Patrick, realizing that he was not, after all, being called to be a Glenmary Missioner, returned home to Timonium to reflect further on what his call in life might be. He concluded that he was called to the priesthood. After working for a year as Director of Religious Education at St. Thomas Aquinas parish in the inner city of Baltimore, he applied to be accepted into the formation program of the Archdiocese of Baltimore and was accepted.

In August 1984, Patrick began his studies for the priesthood at St. Mary's Seminary and University in Baltimore. It was while he was in his second year of theology at St. Mary's that he first entertained the thought of one day serving in the Missionary Diocese of **Fairbanks**. He thereupon began corresponding with Father David M. **Fitz-Patrick**, at the time Rector of Sacred Heart Cathedral, Fairbanks, and with Michael J. **Kaniecki**, then Bishop of Fairbanks. In the summer of 1986, Patrick made his first visit to **Alaska**. However, he did not yet feel ready to commit himself to switching dioceses.

Patrick returned to Baltimore to finish his studies. In May 1989, he graduated from St. Mary's Seminary with a Master of Divinity degree and a Pontifical Bachelor of Sacred Theology degree. As part of his formation program, he spent a two-year internship in the inner city parish of St. Francis of Assisi in Baltimore. In his own words, during that internship he "learned the ins and outs of parish life and ministry, and also acquired a great love for people, especially for the disenfranchised and marginalized of society." At the end of his internship, he was ready for Holy Orders. On February 19, 1990, he was ordained a deacon; and, on May 26th of that same year, a priest. He received both ordinations at the hands of William Cardinal Keeler.

Father Patrick D. Bergquist.
Courtesy of Fr. Bergquist.

Father Bergquist's first assignment as a priest was that of an associate pastor at Our Lady of the Fields parish in Millersville, Maryland. Serving with an experienced pastor of many years, he discovered and experienced at first hand his new role and identity as a parish priest. During the next five years, still as an associate pastor at Our Lady of the Fields, he soon became, first and foremost, a seasoned sacramental and pastoral minister. Among other ministries, he founded a prison ministry, a young adult ministry, a bereavement ministry, various youth ministries, and an ecumenical social outreach program.

During his fourth year at Our Lady of the Fields, Father Bergquist, one morning while at prayer, once again felt called to serve the Lord and His Church on the missions in northern Alaska. Whereas prior to that time he had felt himself ill prepared for such a ministry, he now, with four years of experience in priestly ministry behind him, felt himself sufficiently qualified to serve the Church in the North. He again contacted Bishop Kaniecki. With the permission of a gracious Cardinal Keeler, he visited northern Alaska a second time, with a view to possibly serving there one day.

Beginning in January 1994, Father Bergquist experienced periods of ministry at Sacred Heart Cathedral parish in Fairbanks, at St. Joseph's parish in **Nome**, and in the villages of **Stebbins** and **St. Michael**. These exposures to ministry in urban and rural Alaska convinced him that he was, indeed, called to serve in Alaska. After returning to Our Lady of the Fields parish, he asked Cardinal Keeler to release him for three years to the Diocese of Fairbanks. This the cardinal did.

In late August 1995, Father Bergquist began his formal ministry in Alaska as the Rector of Sacred Heart Cathedral. Two years later, desiring to experience life and ministry in the Alaskan bush, he was assigned pastor of St. Berchmans parish in **Galena** and visiting priest to its dependent station, St. Francis Regis mission in **Huslia**. He found working with the Koyukon Athabaskan Indian people both a new and an exciting ministry, keeping it in the back of his mind as something he would like to do in the future, if he found himself in the Diocese of Fairbanks on a permanent basis. To his regret, his three-year, "on loan," stay in the North came to an end all too soon. In July 1998, he had to return to the Archdiocese of Baltimore, where he then served for a brief time in the parish of Our Lady of Mt. Carmel in Essex, Maryland.

The "call of the North," however, gave him no rest in the East; and, after getting permission from Cardinal Keeler for an undetermined leave of absence from the Archdiocese of Baltimore, he soon found himself back in Alaska again. In October 1998, he became pastor of St. Raphael's parish just to the north of Fairbanks. As of the year 2004, he was still serving in that capacity. Within half a decade, he saw the parish nearly double in size. In the year 2002, the parish undertook to build a new parish center of over 8,000 square feet.

After much prayer and discernment on his part,

Father Bergquist decided that he wanted to serve God's people in Alaska on a permanent basis. In February 2002, he was formally incardinated into the Diocese of Fairbanks.

BERNARD, Father Joseph, S.J.

He was "a natural" for the **Alaska** missions. He was a loyal son of his native France, and a loyal son of the Society of Jesus. He was an excellent photographer. For close to 50 years, he was an exile at heart. He was too resourceful for his own good.

Joseph Bernard was born on January 10, 1875, at La Fontaine de l' Orme, Commune of Touillon, Canton de Montbard, Department de la Côte-d'Or, France. His schooling he received at the hands of the Jesuits: first in Paris, in the rue de Madrid, 1880–84; then at St. Ignatius College in Dijon, 1884–94. In 1894 he entered the Jesuit novitiate at Gemert, Holland, as a member of the Champagne Province of the Society of Jesus. During the year 1896, he put in his mandatory year of military service in the French Army. He took his vows on October 10, 1897, at St. Acheul, Amiens. At the end of 1897, he went to St. Joseph College, in Lille, to study the natural sciences. At the same time, he began his "regency" period, his several years of teaching, there. In 1899, he was sent to the Collège de Notre-Dame de Boulogne to finish it. In October 1900, he began his philosophical studies at St. Helier on the Isle of Jersey, England. While there, he met Father George de la Motte, Superior of the Rocky Mountain Mission, who accepted him as a volunteer for Alaska. At the end of 1900, Joseph was sent back to Gemert to finish his philosophical studies. In 1901, he was assigned to help found the new College of St. John Berchmans in Florennes, Belgium. From there he left, on August 20, 1903, for the United States. In October 1903, after spending a short time at St. Ignatius Mission, Montana, he went to Spokane, Washington, for his courses in theology. He was ordained a priest in the old St. Aloysius Church, Spokane, on May 31, 1906. At the beginning of July, he sailed out of Seattle for **Nome**, Alaska, where he arrived on August 3, 1906.

Upon his arrival in Nome, Father Bernard immediately began his study of the Eskimo language, Inu-piaq, and his work among the Nome and Seward Peninsula Eskimos. Father Bellarmine **Lafortune**, S.J., was his able mentor. During the latter half of 1906, Father Lafortune started to make regular trips to **Marys Igloo**, some 60 miles north of Nome. By 1907, there were 35 Catholics there. On April 8, 1907, Father Bernard made his first trip to Marys Igloo "to see about buying a house to establish a mission among the Natives there." He returned on the 12th. In his autobiographical sketch, he wrote, "In April, Father Lafortune sent me further north to found at Marys Igloo a new mission, which I named 'Our Lady of Lourdes.'" In the Nome house diary, however, we read, under date of November 25, 1907: "Rev. Fr. Fortune returned home from Mary's Igloo after having spent about two months there establishing the new mission there among the Natives." It was Father Lafortune who established that mission, but it was Father Bernard who first began to reside there.

In September 1908, Father Bernard moved to Marys Igloo. After Nome, this was the first mission on the whole Seward Peninsula to have a resident priest. He soon made of it a viable, flourishing mission center. By dogteam he traveled out from there to visit Eskimo villages and settlements scattered throughout the Seward Peninsula and as far north as **Kotzebue**. He became an accomplished musher; and, wherever he went, he was warmly received by Eskimos and whites alike. His friendly, outgoing nature made him a welcome guest, wherever he found himself. On his travels he always had his camera with him. It was a good one, and he knew how to use it. At Marys Igloo, and at the various villages he visited, he took excellent photographs. Many of these were made into postcards and became items for collectors. His travels, and his dogteam, especially his leader, Spot, gave him much pleasure, and much material for his photos, writings, and lectures. He considered his dogs his Religious community, and himself as their Father Superior. His writing style was lively and engaging. He had an excellent command of English, both written and spoken. The reader was made to feel present to and part of what was being written or lectured about. The young Father Bernard was a happy, enthusiastic missionary at Marys Igloo and in the surrounding area. He found

Father Joseph Bernard, S.J.
JOPA-512.A3.

the people to be "very moral, very friendly clans."

In July 1909, Father Bernard left Alaska for Canterbury, England, to make his tertianship. While in Europe, he found time to make lecturing trips to France, Belgium and Switzerland to raise funds for his Alaskan mission. Using 120 glass slides as props, he became a dynamic, highly entertaining lecturer, much in demand. He proved to be a successful fund-raiser. He returned to Marys Igloo in the summer of 1910, able to tell his Eskimo congregation there that his lectures had netted him enough cash to purchase a collapsible panel church from the American Portable House Company in Seattle, and that it would arrive on the next freighter. The church was put up the following year. He also hoped soon to have an orphanage at Marys Igloo.

Father Bernard left Alaska rather suddenly, on June 16, 1915, to answer the call to arms in his native France. French civil authorities called all patriots to the defense of their country, and Religious authorities cooperated. Inducted into the

French Army as an interpreter and orderly officer, he served with the British forces on the Ypres and Vosges Mountains fronts. During the latter part of his three and a half years in the Army, he served as a delegate of the American Red Cross in Lille. He was discharged from the Army in August 1919.

When Father Bernard learned that the influenza epidemic of late 1918 had swept through Marys Igloo, and that most of the adults and many of the children there had died, or were orphaned, he was deeply distressed. Some of the children that did survive were sent to **Teller**, and he initiated a correspondence with them that continued nearly to the end of his life.

When Father Bernard left for France, he had every hope of returning to Alaska again after the war. But, despite his pleading for years with his Superiors for permission to return, he was never allowed to return. In his autobiographical sketch he gives as the reason that, owing to the war, there was a shortage of priests in France. However, in a letter to Prefect Apostolic Joseph R. **Crimont**, S.J., dated May 24, 1915, Father John B. **Sifton**, S.J., Alaska Mission Superior, writing with a certain pique, gives different reasons: "Of course, it goes without saying that Fr. Bernard did not consult me about his response to the call to arms." In that same letter, he writes also about Father Bernard's "unscrupulousness in handling money." It should be mentioned in passing that Father Sifton was born into this world as Johannes Sifferlen and was during his early life a German citizen. He may have, at least subconsciously, resented Father Bernard's going off to fight against his former homeland.

But, it is fairly certain that the basic reasons for Father Bernard's not being allowed to return to Alaska, in spite of his persistent plea to be allowed to do so, were his ways of dealing with money matters. The Provincial of the California Province, Father Francis C. Dillon, S.J., under date of April 14, 1921, wrote him frankly:

> The one serious charge against you, as far as the province is concerned, is that you are too independent. You left your work in Alaska without permission, and while there, collected and used money, and ran affairs without ever giving an account to superiors or asking advice or permission in the management of the Mission.

It seems not to have been a matter of ill will, of "unscrupulousness," on Father Bernard's part. It seems, rather, that he did not have a clear understanding of what, at the time, were but vaguely formulated policies concerning missionaries and money and accountability.

After the war, Father Bernard worked for a time with American soldiers stationed in France. He then began a fruitful, 32-year-long career as a retreat master and a preacher of popular missions in France and Switzerland. At the same time, he kept living in the past, and his thoughts and his heart continued to be in Alaska. He kept sending religious articles there; kept corresponding with people he knew there. As late as June 28, 1955, he wrote, "My heart is still up in the great North with my dear Eskimos. I am still in touch with Teddy Kunuluk, my former altar boy." In his old age, as his eyesight failed and death seemed not too far off, he wrote, "My only wish would be to go back to Mary's Igloo, to die there and be buried in that cemetery on the hill opposite my igloo."

Towards the end of his life, he wrote to the editor of a newsletter: "If you mention my death in your paper, please don't give me any praise. The missionaries who were in Alaska before me, they alone deserve it."

Shortly before he died, he wrote:

> I have spent my life as a kind of rolling stone for the Lord. I have not accomplished much. I leave behind me many words and much noise, but little solid good for the salvation of souls and for the glory of my Lord Jesus. I have not used well the talents He has given me. I must, therefore, in all sincerity repeat the words of the publican, "Have pity on me, oh Lord, a sinner! I entrust myself wholly into thy great mercy."

Father Joseph Bernard died far from the Alaska and far from the Eskimos he had loved, and had loved to the end. At St. Albert's College, in Louvain, Belgium, on May 3, 1962, his long life—a life unfulfilled in his own eyes—came to a peaceful end.

20

BETHEL

The Central Yup'ik Eskimo town of Bethel is located on the right, the northwestern, bank of the Kuskokwim River, in the Yukon-Kuskokwim Delta. It lies beyond the tree line. It is a port city, accessible to ocean-going vessels. It is also an airline hub, serving 48 villages in the Delta. As a regional center for the Delta, Bethel has the only hospital, community college, and court system. State and Federal offices are home-based in Bethel. The Alaska Commercial Company had a store at the site as early as 1880. This was called "Mumtrekhlagamiut Station." The name was derived from a small Eskimo village on the opposite side of the river, *Mumtrekhlagamiut*, which freely translates as "smokehouse people." In 1885, Moravian missionaries founded a mission near the store and called the place Bethel, after the biblical name. Bethel's population numbered 33 in 1890, 110 in 1910, 221 in 1920, 278 in 1930, 376 in 1940, 651 in 1950. By 1992, these figures had soared to 4,674; and by the year 2000, to 5,471. The Bethel post office was established in 1905.

Jesuit missionaries traveling between **Holy Cross Mission** and **Tununak**, on Nelson Island, visited the Kuskokwim drainage already around 1890. In 1891, Father Paschal **Tosi**, S.J., visited the Kuskokwim and contracted to have a mission dwelling erected at **Ohagamiut**. The following year, Father Francis A. **Barnum**, S.J., visited the central sector of the river. However, except for the mission at Ohagamiut, served by Father Aloysius J. **Robaut**, S.J., no Catholic mission stations were established on the Kuskokwim until the early 1940s. During their first half century in northern Alaska, Jesuit missionaries merely visited, from time to time, the lower Kuskokwim, mostly out of Holy Cross, but also out of Tununak, **Akulurak**, and **Hooper Bay**.

In 1941, Father Francis M. **Ménager**, S.J., staked out a claim in Bethel; and, on August, 16, 1942, he took up residency there. The following year, he built a small church next to what is commonly referred to as "Honey Bucket Lake." At that time, there were about 25 Catholics in Bethel. During his years in Bethel, Father Ménager did a considerable amount of traveling up and down the Kuskokwim, visiting, among other places, **Aniak**, **McGrath**, and **Kalskag**. His successors at Bethel likewise visited these places, along with a fair number of minor ones. Since around 1970, **Russian Mission** and **Marshall** on the Yukon River, too, have been visited out of Bethel.

The present Immaculate Conception Church: built by Father Richard L. McCaffrey, S.J., and dedicated in 1995. *PP.*

In 1948, Father Segundo **Llorente**, S.J., replaced Father Ménager at Bethel. Finding the small cabin residence too small and depressing, Father Llorente acquired two Quonset huts. One of these he used for his living quarters, the other for storage. Of his two years in Bethel he said, "I found Bethel quite agreeable."

From 1950–57, Father Norman E. **Donohue**, S.J., held station in Bethel. Seeing the need for more bedroom space to accommodate missionaries passing through Bethel on their way to and from the coast, as well as the need for a bigger church to accommodate Bethel's growing Catholic population, he saw to it that "a real building" was put up, in 1955–56, to take care of both of those needs. In 1957, Father Donohue was succeeded by Father Henry G. **Hargreaves**, S.J.—who was, eventually, to serve Bethel's Immaculate Conception parish far longer than any other priest. His first term there ended in 1964. During the year 1963–64, he had with him Father George T. **Boileau**, S.J. Father Hargreaves began serving in Bethel again in 1998, and continued to so until 2003, the year he left Alaska.

The following Jesuit Fathers also were pastors in Bethel: **Paul B. Mueller**, 1964–65; **Cornelius K. Murphy**, 1965–68; John E. **Gurr**, 1968–74; Hargreaves again, 1980–87; Richard L. **McCaffrey**, 1987–98; and Eugene P. **Delmore**, 1998 to the latter part of 2004. On April 30, 1995, the new Immac-ulate Conception Church, built by Father McCaffrey, was formally dedicated. Father John A. **Hinsvark**, priest of the Diocese of Fairbanks, was pastor of the Bethel parish from 1974–80.

The following Jesuit Fathers served or resided in Bethel, either as assistant pastors or as visiting priests to outlying villages: Lawrence N. **Haffie**, 1953–56; Pasquale M. Spoletini, 1956–57 and 1958–59; **John J. Wood**, 1959–60; Robert F. **Corrigal**, 1963–65; Gurr 1980–83; Thomas N. **Gallagher**, 1987–89; and Hargreaves, back again, 1998 to 2003. Father Andrew P. **D'Arco**, priest of the Diocese of Fairbanks, was assistant pastor, 1983–84.

Other Jesuit Fathers resided in Bethel, while serving in various capacities: Charles J. **Peterson** (Director of the **Eskimo Deacon Program**), 1970–73; Gallagher (Counselor of Native high school boarding students), 1972–78; Richard D. **Case** (Director of the Center of Spirituality and Theology for the Development of Ministries), 1984–85; Charles A. **Bartles** (Counselor in the Alcohol Treatment Program), 1986–88; and Edward A. Flint (working in the Phillips Alcoholism Treatment Center), 1990–94.

Eskimo Deacons, based in Bethel, have also served and are serving the Bethel parish: Nick Charles (deceased and buried in Bethel), Bob Aloysius, Peter Aluska, Sr., and Brian McCaffery.

In the course of the years, many members of the **Jesuit Volunteer Corps,** too numerous to mention

The second Immaculate Conception Church, Bethel, built by Father Norman E. Donohue, S.J., in 1955–56. *MK.*

all by name, have also served in various capacities and were continuing to serve, as of the year 2004, in Bethel. Rosalie Elaine L'Ecuyer, after serving there for two years as a member of the JVC, continued to serve there as a "diocesan volunteer," from mid-1982 until June 30, 1988.

Though he was never stationed in Bethel, it was in Bethel, in "the House of God," that Father Paul H. **Linssen**, S.J., found his last resting place.

64

BEUZER, Vincent J., S.J.

Vincent J. "Vince" Beuzer was born—the middle child, having one older and one younger sister—to Vincent John and Augusta Caterina Obit Beuzer on August 24, 1927, in Everett, Washington. He was baptized in St. Joseph's Church in Wenatchee, Washington, on November 6, 1927. Shortly thereafter, the family moved to Tacoma, Washington.

Vince's parents were both born and raised in "the old country," in the province of Udine, Italy, and identified themselves as "Italians of Austrian descent." Their citizenship after World War I was Italian, but their first language was Slovenian. In Tacoma, his father owned and operated a family cor-

ner grocery store. The family lived in a house next door to it. This was but two blocks from Sacred Heart Grade School. There, from the Sisters of Providence, Vince received his elementary schooling, during the years 1933–40. He completed the third and fourth grades in one school year. When he was in the eighth grade, he was in the same classroom as Louis L. **Renner**.

During his grade school years, as well as during his high school years, Vince, when not in class, was busy at the store: chopping stove wood, unloading groceries, stocking shelves, waiting on customers, and delivering groceries to homes.

From 1940–44, Vince attended Tacoma's Jesuit-staffed Bellarmine Preparatory. There he participated in a variety of extracurricular activities: elocution, debate, drama, and writing for the school paper. At Bellarmine, as at Sacred Heart, he was a top student and a superior athlete. He lettered in varsity basketball during his senior year. At age sixteen, as valedictorian of his class, he graduated with an Honor Classical diploma, having taken four years of Latin and two of Greek. He was awarded a scholarship to what was then still Seattle College for the year 1944–45.

During the summer of 1945, Vince took courses in mathematics to prepare himself to enlist in the

U.S. Navy. But, after summer midterm examinations and a short break, he decided to join the Jesuits. His parents were not only surprised at his decision, but thought that he, not yet eighteen years old, was too young and too inexperienced in life to make such a decision. They felt that the Jesuits should have consulted them before accepting him as a candidate. He, for his part, however, was convinced that he had a genuine vocation to the priesthood in the Society of Jesus. For some years there was pain on both sides, until his parents became reconciled to his being in the Jesuits. On August 14, 1945, just as the country was celebrating V.J. (Victory over Japan) Day, he arrived at the Jesuit Novitiate of St. Francis Xavier at Sheridan, Oregon.

Father Vincent J. Beuzer, S.J. *BR-CD 0308-A112.*

After completing his two-year noviceship and taking the simple vows of poverty, chastity and obedience, "Brother Beuzer," as he was now known, spent an additional two years at Sheridan studying the classics and humanities. Those four years were for him "not a struggle," he recalled years later. He next spent three years, 1949–52, at Mount St. Michael's in Spokane, Washington, studying philosophy. It was not long before he changed his academic major from English to philosophy. In 1952, he received his M.A. in philosophy.

From 1952–55, "Mr. Beuzer," as he was now known, taught English, Latin, Greek, and Religion at Seattle Preparatory, an all-boy Jesuit high school in Seattle, Washington. He also coached the frosh basketball team, and in the school bus hauled athletic teams to and from games. By his own admission, he "thrived on those years of activity."

Mr. Beuzer began his four years of theological studies at Alma College, Los Gatos, California, in 1955. On June 14, 1958, at the end of his third year, he was ordained a priest in St. Aloysius Church in Spokane. He left Alma College with a Master of Sacred Theology degree in 1959. After spending a year as Vice-Principal at Seattle Preparatory, he made his tertianship at Manresa Hall, Port Townsend, Washington. He took his final vows at Campion Hall, Oxford, England, on August 15, 1962.

Father Beuzer spent the years 1961–64 taking courses in Systematic Theology at the Gregorian University in Rome. He found those years "memorable because of the excitement and energy generated by the Vatican Council just then taking place." He was in Rome to witness the death of Pope John XXIII and the election of Pope Paul VI. From an academic standpoint, however, his years in Rome turned out to be less than satisfying. He found his classroom experiences and thesis-related research work at the Gregorian "discouraging." He was ill advised in the choice of a thesis subject and received little help from his director in doctoral studies. He left Rome without completing a doctoral dissertation. It was of little comfort to him to have become quite fluent in Italian during his Rome years.

From 1964–86, Father Beuzer was a member of the Jesuit Community at Gonzaga University in Spokane and taught in the Theology/Religious Studies department. He was Chair of the department from 1970–75. As such, he developed a way of "Double-Majoring" students. This greatly increased the number of majors in the Religious Studies department.

During the years 1973–79, Father Beuzer served as Rector of Gonzaga's Jesuit Community. In that capacity, he instituted the Wednesday Jesuit Community Evenings. These began with a Mass liturgy at 4:30 P.M. and were followed by socializing and dinner. It was he who hired Marcia Renouard to serve as a receptionist at the Jesuit Residence. She was the first woman to have her office in the Jesuit

Residence, and served the Jesuit Community most competently and faithfully until 2003.

The year 1979–80 saw Father Beuzer taking sabbatical leave. From 1983–86, he was involved primarily with Gonzaga University's innovative programs: Christus, Credo, and Mater Dei Institute. Along with Jesuit Fathers Armand M. Nigro and John J. Evoy, he was co-founder of the Mater Dei Institute. One of the chief focuses of these programs was the preparation of older men for the priesthood. Under his leadership, these programs truly flourished.

While at Gonzaga University, Father Beuzer's principal area of teaching was the New Testament. He also taught the Practicum in Spiritual Direction. Along with his teaching responsibilities, he served also as a spiritual director, especially for post-graduate students, and as a member of retreat teams that gave the Ignatian Spiritual Exercises to groups of bishops, priests, and women Religious in all parts of the United States and Canada. He was a member of Retreats International and of Jesuit Retreat and Renewal ministry.

In early June, 1986, Father Beuzer learned that he was being appointed Executive Director of Holy Spirit Retreat House—renamed **Holy Spirit Center** in 1999—in **Anchorage**, **Alaska**. On September 8th of that year, he officially assumed the directorship of the retreat house. This belonged to the Archdiocese of Anchorage, but its management and ministry was entrusted to the Oregon Province of the Society of Jesus. Upon his arrival at the retreat house, he found that "the challenges were many: personnel, financial, buildings and maintenance, and, of course, spiritual ministry." Under his energetic directorship, many improvements, major and minor, to the physical plant were made. After several years a balanced budget was in place.

Meanwhile, on the spiritual side, Father Beuzer and Kathryn Gallagher, Director of Ministry, began offering the Ignatian "19th Annotation Retreat in Everyday Life." Numerous "Challenge" groups, involving adult lay ministry associates as facilitators, were formed. Almost from the outset, many turned to Father Beuzer for personal spiritual direction. This led him to inaugurate a program for the formation of many lay spiritual directors. In 1991,

a Saturday men's group, involving some 20-plus men, began to meet bi-weekly from 7 A.M. to 9 A.M. for Mass, continental breakfast, and an hour of Faith-sharing. As of the year 2004, this group was still in full vigor.

Toward the end of his tenure as Executive Director of the retreat house, Father Beuzer was able to hire Father Paul B. **Macke**, S.J., to assist with spiritual direction and pastoral counseling. In 1998, when Father Macke succeeded him as Executive Director, Father Beuzer took sabbatical leave. In September 2000, he returned to Anchorage in the position of Spiritual Director and Coordinator of the two-year formation program for spiritual directors, "Seeking The Spirit I." From 1996 to 2002, living now in the 1500 Birchwood Street Residence, Father Beuzer served also as Religious Superior of the Anchorage Jesuit Community.

During the early part of the third millennium, Father Beuzer conducted a Deacon-Wives retreat in Tampa Bay, Florida, after which he, at the invitation of the Mercy Sisters, did spiritual ministry for six weeks in Australia and New Zealand. He next gave the Lenten Retreat at St. Olaf's parish in Poulsbo, Washington. From there he traveled to Africa, where, along with Father Nigro, he spent 30 days giving retreats and performing other spiritual ministries for the Sisters of Jesus of Nazareth in Zimbabwe. As of the year 2004, he was still making Anchorage his home and engaged in retreat work and spiritual direction.

BIG LAKE

The town of Big Lake is located on the shore of Big Lake, which is 13 miles southwest of **Wasilla** and 18 miles north of **Anchorage**. In 1967, Big Lake had a population of 74; by the year 2000, this had increased to 2,635.

Although Big Lake's Catholic community, Our Lady of the Lake, was, as of the year 2004, canonically a mission of Sacred Heart parish in Wasilla, it never functioned as a mission. Rather, it always stood as a "parish" in its own right, financially and pastorally. In the year 2004, its canonical pastor was the pastor of Sacred Heart, but it was being administered by a laywoman, Mrs. Katherine Bishop. As

Pastoral Administrator, Mrs. Bishop ministered to the parish in all ways except sacramentally. In the absence of a priest, she presided at liturgies and performed all other duties in keeping with correct pastoral procedure for a lay person.

Our Lady of the Lake Church is located on nine and a half acres on South Big Lake Road. This tract of land was bought by Mr. Ed Beech in the 1960s, and donated to the Archdiocese of Anchorage. The first church, built under Msgr. John A. **Lunney**, pastor of the Palmer parish at the time, was dedicated in July 1966. Unfortunately, this burned to the ground in November 1967.

Until the new church was built in the latter 1970s under Father **Gerard T. Ryan**, C.S.Sp., people met in the Big Lake Elementary School and in a local bar for services. Mr. Beech was contractor for the new church and donated his time and talent. Mr. Leo Brueggman, owner and operator of Blue Bear Drilling, donated a new water well. The Catholic Church Extension Society helped finance the building of the new church and rectory. Parishioners donated time and labor. In the late 1980s, parishioners, under the direction of Father Thomas E. Power, built the Catechetical Center.

When, in 1996, the Miller Reach Fire devastated the community of Big Lake, Our Lady of the Lake parish became a center for disaster and relief help. The National Guard set up Quonset huts for supplies and built picnic tables. Our Lady of the Lake began a food bank that served the community at large until 2000, when it was closed. The Quonset huts were removed during the summers of 2000 and 2001. During the summer of 2002, all the parish plant buildings were repainted.

The following priests have served Our Lady of the Lake parish: Father Stanley J. **Allie**, out of **Talkeetna**, 1970–74; Father Ryan, also out of Talkeetna, 1974–79; and Father Power, 1981–90, except for the year 1984–85.

The following Parish/Pastoral Administrators, too, have served the parish: Deacon Louis Hoffman, 1993–99; Deacon David Schutt, 1999–2000; and Mrs. Katherine Bishop, as of the year 2004.

15

BOILEAU, Bishop George T., S.J.

He was the second Catholic priest to be consecrated a bishop in **Alaska**. (Father Dermot **O'Flanagan** was the first.) To him, as priest and as bishop, young people were of major concern. People of all Faiths were his friends. His spirit of ecumenism was reflected on his coat of arms: "One body in Christ." People, recognizing in him a "true shepherd of the flock," had the highest expectations of his episcopacy. Less than seven months after his consecration, what was mortal of him was laid to rest in the **Fairbanks** Clay Street Cemetery only a few blocks from where he had spent virtually all of his Alaskan years. Ernest Gruening, senator of Alaska at the time, noted his passing in the *Congressional Record*, referring to him as "one of the great citizens of my state, one of the best known, best loved members of the Catholic clergy in Alaska."

George Theodore Boileau was born in Lothrop, Montana, on September 10, 1912. He attended the Bonner, Montana, public grade school, 1918–26; Missoula's Loyola High School, 1926–30; and Montana State University, 1930–34. There he was a member of the Honorary Dramatic Society, of the Glee Club, and of the debate team. From 1934–36, he taught at Hogeland High School in northern Montana.

George entered the Jesuit novitiate at Sheridan, Oregon, on September 5, 1936. After completing his two-year noviceship, he spent two additional years there studying the classics and humanities. From 1940–43, he made his philosophical studies at Mount St. Michael's in Spokane, Washington. The year 1943–44 saw him teaching at Gonzaga University in Spokane, and the year 1944–45 prefecting the boys at **Holy Cross Mission**, Alaska. His theological studies he made at Alma College, Los Gatos, California, from 1945–49. He was ordained a priest in San Francisco on June 13, 1948.

After making his tertianship at Port Townsend, Washington, 1949–50, Father Boileau returned to Alaska in the summer of 1950. He spent several months doing pastoral work in and around **Dillingham**, then began to serve as assistant pastor of Fairbanks' Immaculate Conception parish. He was soon recognized as a preacher and speaker above the ordinary. In 1952, he became pastor of Immaculate Conception parish. As such, he served also as Superintendent of Catholic Schools in northern Alaska, ministered to students attending the University of Alaska–Fairbanks, and did some teaching in Fairbanks' Immaculate Conception Grade School. In 1959, he organized a summer school foreign language program for any and all interested in learning either French, or German, or Latin, or Spanish. While pastor, he was also a member of various civic organizations. The Boy Scouts of America received his special attention. In recognition of his service to them, he received some special BSA awards.

In February 1963, Father Boileau was appointed General Superior of Jesuits in Alaska; and, on April 21, 1964, Coadjutor Bishop, with right of succession, to Francis D. **Gleeson**, S.J., Bishop of Fairbanks. At **Copper Valley School**, near **Glennallen**, on July 31, 1964, he was consecrated bishop by

Francis Cardinal Spellman. Father Boileau himself had chosen the site, giving his reason for doing so: "Because I want to be among the people I have lived with and with whom I will be associated in the land of my fellow missionaries and co-workers."

Sister Margaret Cantwell, S.S.A., who was at Copper Valley School, when Bishop Boileau was consecrated, shares the following:

> The evening before the big ceremony, he went into the kitchen, where Sister Ida [Brasseur, S.S.A.] was still finishing up things. I remember the glow that was there. He was looking at the two small loaves of golden-crusted bread that Sister Ida had made for the ceremony the next day. They were meaningful to him, as he was a poet and a spiritual person. They were meaningful to Sister Ida, because her religious name is that of Sister Mary Ida of the Eucharist. Bread is always special for her. The bishop-to-be and Sister Ida were having a good talk, and then Father Boileau, awaiting *his* consecration the next day, broke one of the loaves and shared it with Sister Ida. This was a beautiful happening.

In the fall of 1964, Bishop Boileau attended a session of the Second Vatican Council. Accompanied by Brother Carl F. **Wickart**, S.J., he then did some "touristing" in Switzerland. In Oberammergau, Germany, the two were joined by Father Louis L. **Renner**, S.J. The three then, in a new Volkswagon station wagon Bishop Boileau had had delivered to him in Rome, drove from Germany, through Luxembourg, and on to Belgium and northern France, stopping to see major sights along the way. In Belgium and France, they visited the families of Alaskan Jesuit Fathers William J. **Loyens** and René **Astruc** respectively. In Paris, Bishop Boileau bought several paintings. (Bishop Boileau was endowed with a fine aesthetic sense, collected works of art, and himself did some painting and literary writing.) On the evening of October 28th, the three arrived in Lisieux, where they spent their last night in Europe together. That evening, they were given a private tour of the great Basilica of the Little Flower. The next morning, at the altar-shrine of Ste. Thérèse in the Carmelite convent, Bishop Boileau and Father Renner each offered Mass. After the Masses and breakfast, the three drove on to Le Havre. There, final farewells said, Bishop Boileau and Brother Wickart boarded ship for the United States. Father Renner took the train back to Germany.

In Holy Family Chapel at Copper Valley School, newly ordained Bishop George T. Boileau, S.J., blesses the congregation at the end of his first Mass as bishop. *DFA.*

In late February 1965, a great many people were shocked to learn of the sudden death of Bishop Boileau. He had delivered a lecture at Seattle University and was to leave the next morning for Spokane. At his sister's place, in Riverton, near Seattle, where he had spent the night, early in the morning of February 25, 1965, as he was putting on his coat, he was stricken with a heart attack that brought instant death. Solemn Pontifical Masses of Requiem for the repose of his soul were celebrated in Seattle and Fairbanks.

In Fairbanks, the memory of Bishop Boileau lives on, concretely, in "Boileau Hall," the gymnasium at the Catholic schools complex. These simple biographical data paint but a very inadequate portrait of the man, the priest, the bishop that was George Theodore Boileau, S.J.

Brother Kirby Boone, C.F.X.
Courtesy of Br. Boone.

BOONE, Brother Kirby, C.F.X.

James Anthony Boone was born on June 11, 1926, in Nelson County, Kentucky, near New Haven, and about ten miles from where Abraham Lincoln was born. His parents were Frank Boone and Mary Martina Bowling. He had one sister and ten brothers. In 1929, the Boone family moved to Louisville, Kentucky, to get away from the one-room schoolhouse and the hardships of farming during the Great Depression. In Louisville, James attended Holy Family elementary school and St. Xavier high school. He graduated from St. Xavier in 1944. In 1947, he attended the University of Louisville and St. Louis University "to try out college life." He later earned a B.A., in 1953, and an M.A., in 1968, both from the Catholic University of America in Washington, D.C. In the course of time, he also became a certified counselor and school administrator.

In 1945, James was drafted into the U.S. Army Air Force. After completing his basic training at Sheppard Field, Texas, he was assigned to radio mechanic school at Scott Field, Illinois. At the end of the six-month course at Scott, he was appointed a teacher there. In December 1946, he was honorably discharged. His acceptance of the teaching appointment had "guaranteed" him an early discharge.

James entered the Xaverian Brothers on February 15, 1948. After completing his six-month postulancy at Fort Monroe, Virginia, he took the Religious name of Kirby, and began his two-year noviceship. The second year of his noviceship he made at the Congregation's scholasticate in Washington, D.C. He took his temporary vows on August 15, 1950, and his final vows three years later.

From 1953–60, Brother Kirby taught in Bardstown, Kentucky. He then taught at Flaget High School in Louisville, from 1960–74, serving as principal during his last six years. For the years 1974–76, he was at St. Francis Indian School, Rosebud Reservation, South Dakota. During the following ten years, he was at Mount St. Joseph High School in Baltimore, Maryland, serving as principal from 1980–86. He next spent the years 1986–88 at Holy Family High School in Ensley, Alabama. He was back again at the Rosebud Reservation as Director of Religious Education, 1988–90.

In the summer of 1990, Brother Kirby went north, to **Alaska**. By that time, he had had a great variety of work experiences. During his pre-Xaverian years he had worked in cornfields, and had been a paperboy, a service station attendant, a cafeteria busboy and cook, a grocery clerk, and a surveyor's helper. In the military, he was a radio mechanic and a teacher. As a Xaverian Brother, he had served as a high school teacher, a principal, an athletic director, a coach of track, football, and swimming, and a summer camp counselor.

"In the summer of 1990, on the Yukon River banks and vicinity, a dream and a wish came true," wrote Brother Kirby as the third millennium began. It was in July 1990 that, as Pastoral Minister in **Ruby**, he began his long years of service to the Diocese of **Fairbanks**. From the outset, he found Ruby "a beautiful location to wonder, wander, and serve." During his first year there, he served full-time, making himself available to the people "around the clock." The following two years, he served part-time in Ruby and part-time in **Galena**.

A number of years after Brother Kirby began his Ruby ministry, he was able to write:

> My position in Ruby as pastoral minister has brought with it more than one occasion of major joy and consolation. Let me recount one such. It has to do with an old Ruby sourdough, who made his Profession of Faith and his first Holy Communion on Christmas Day, 1993. I was privileged to play a part in his finding the Faith and its blessings in so formal a manner. But, of course, it was a kindly Providence that first set him on the path that eventually brought him so much peace of heart and happiness in his old age.

The "old Ruby sourdough," in his mid-80s at the time, was Albert Yrjana.

Beginning in 1993, while still making his headquarters in Ruby, Brother Kirby began to serve also as "Coordinator of Ministries for 13 Villages." They were: **Galena, Huslia, Holy Cross, Kaltag, Koyukuk, Kotzebue, McGrath, Nome, Nulato**, Ruby, **St. Michael, Stebbins**, and **Tanana**. In 1996, while retaining his role of coordinator, he was assigned to Tanana, to serve there as Pastoral Minister. As coordinator, he visited each village twice a year for several days, mostly to observe and listen on behalf of Michael J. **Kaniecki**, S.J., Bishop of Fairbanks at the time. Brother Kirby reported his observations and findings back to the bishop. As coordinator, he also organized regional meetings every fall and spring for parish ministers and people from the 13 villages.

In 1999, Brother Kirby, by then freed of his role of coordinator, began to serve the Tanana parish, now as Pastoral Minister, now as Pastoral Administrator. At the same time, on six-week rotations, he served also as Pastoral Administrator of the McGrath parish.

Throughout his years of ministry in the villages of northern Alaska, one of Brother Kirby's chief "operating objectives" was, in his words, "to empower the people, to get them to realize that they are a priestly people, as St. Peter proclaimed." He found them to be talented, graced, and quite capable and worthy to be Eucharist Ministers and presiders at liturgies when no priest was present.

Brother Kirby considered it a personal privilege to have been called to ministry among the people of northern Alaska; and, as of the year 2004, he was hoping to continue on in that ministry as long as he was able. He had a major knee operation on October 23, 2003, but came through it well enough to be able to return to Alaska six weeks later.

10

BOUGIS, Father Peter C., S.J.

Peter Bougis was born on March 31, 1860, in Les Sables-d'Olonne, in the Ardennes Mountains of France. He entered the Society of Jesus on August 28, 1879. From 1881–84, he studied philosophy at Woodstock College, Maryland. Then, after spending a year as a French teacher at Holy Cross College, Worcester, Massachusetts, he was sent to St. Peter's Mission, Montana. He began his theological studies at Woodstock in 1888. After completing his first year there, he continued at St. Helier on the Isle of Jersey, England, before going on to complete them at Chieri, Italy. It can be assumed that he was ordained to the priesthood in 1890 or in early 1891. As a priest, he spent 1891–95 among the Indian peoples of Montana, at Holy Family Mission in Chouteau County. He made his tertianship at St. Stanislaus, Florissant, Missouri, 1895–96.

From 1896 to 1905, Father Bougis served as pastor of the Catholic community on **Douglas** Island, **Alaska**. As such, he visited **Wrangell** and **Sitka**. In 1898, he made two lengthy visits also to **Skagway** and Dyea. There was no church in Douglas, when he first took up station there. He offered Mass in a private home. However, on December 8, 1896, a chapel, dedicated to Our Lady of the Mines, was ready for public services. This was soon much too small, so Father Bougis set about putting up a real church, "a new one that henceforth caught the eye of tourists and passengers bound for **Juneau** as it threw into the shade the churches of all other denominations in the area." This church was ready, on December 25, 1900, for the Christmas Mass. After almost a decade in Douglas, Father Bougis became pastor of St. Mark's parish in Skagway. As such, he served from 1905–08, the year he left Alaska. According to Father Philibert **Turnell**, S.J., who followed him as pastor of Skagway, Father Bougis spent his Skagway years "to the great spiritual advantage of the congregation and with general satisfaction."

Years after Father Bougis had left Alaska, Jesuit historian Father Gerard G. Steckler wrote: "All through Southeastern Alaska, Father Bougis' name is still held in veneration, especially at Douglas Island and Skagway, where as a popular missionary for a dozen years he endeared himself to all and in a quiet way wrought wonders."

Father Bougis spent the remaining years of his life, except for the years 1911–14, which he spent back at Holy Family Mission and in Missoula, Montana, in San Francisco. He died at Los Gatos, California, on March 27, 1920.

BOULET, Sister Marie Teresa, O.P.

Helen Boulet was born on July 31, 1920, the fourth daughter in a family of five girls and one boy, in Green Bay, Wisconsin. She was baptized in St. John the Evangelist parish on August 15th of that year. She attended the parish school for the first six grades. Early in her seventh grade, the school building was condemned. Thereafter she attended public schools through her senior year in high school. Given the Great Depression years, her family could not even think of sending her to a private school. She spent her entire childhood in Green Bay.

While religion was not a frequent subject of conversation in her home, it was definitely taught, by example. It is to that good example that Sister Marie Teresa credits her vocation to the Sisterhood. By the time she was in junior high school, there was already little doubt in her mind as to what she planned to do with her life.

Helen Boulet finished high school in June 1937, and then spent one year doing office and lab work for a pharmaceutical company, while her application to join the Sinsinawa Dominican community was being processed. The Sinsinawa Dominicans are a Third Order Dominican community founded to educate young women. From its beginning, the community was dedicated to education. She had no personal knowledge of that community, but relatives had, and their admiration for it sparked her interest. Learning that the Sinsinawa Dominicans had two schools in Green Bay, she became acquainted with the Sisters of one of them. She found them gracious and welcoming, and thus thrived on their manifest love and concern.

On September 8, 1938, after having said her good-byes to family and friends, Helen, accompanied by one of the Sisters, left to begin her postulancy at Sinsinawa Mound in the southwest corner of Wisconsin. The next two years of her life were to be filled with study, prayer and formation in the spiritual life.

On August 4, 1939, Helen received the Dominican habit and a new name, Sister Marie Teresa. Then began her canonical novitiate year, a year devoted to the understanding of the rules and constitutions of the Order and the deepening of her spiritual life. The year ended with her profession of temporary vows on August 6, 1940. By the end of that August, Sister Marie Teresa and her "crowd" had received their first mission assignments and were dispersed throughout the United States. Her first assignment was St. Rose of Lima School in Milwaukee, Wisconsin. There she spent the next six years teaching classes of 45 to 50 second graders. She found "preparing the little ones for their first Holy Communion the most satisfying part of those years."

Sister Marie Teresa devoted the year 1946–47 to earning a post-secondary school degree at Edgewood College in Madison, Wisconsin. In 1947, she was assigned to Corpus Christi School in New York City. She found this assignment "a whole new experience." For eleven years, she taught, and learned to love, the children of different cultures and nationalities there. The school was considered a model school of its kind. Visitors from various colleges and universities, especially from Columbia

University, and from neighboring parishes, came to observe it in operation.

During the years 1958–60, Sister Marie Teresa taught in Muncie, Indiana, and then in Rockwell, Iowa, 1960–62. This latter assignment was another new experience for her. Rockwell was a small, farming town of around 600 people. There she taught some 25 pupils ranging from fifth to eighth grade. After Rockwell, she spent a year at Winnetka, Illinois; and then, in the summer of 1963, she moved to St. Mary's grade school in Portage, Wisconsin. There, for six years, she taught the eighth grade, and social studies in two other grades, and was principal.

Next Sister Marie Teresa was assigned to Holy Rosary School in Minneapolis. There her idea of one day serving in **Alaska** began to take shape. Alaska had been a dream of hers ever since her high school days, when she heard Father Bernard R. **Hubbard**, S.J., talk about his experiences in the cold North. The thought that the founder of the Sinsinawa Dominicans, Samuel Charles Mazzuchelli, had advocated working among Native Americans heartened her enough to raise the question of being a missionary in Alaska with her Sister Provincial. To her pleasant surprise, the latter encouraged her to look into the matter of needs and opportunities in Alaska. It was learned that a principal was needed for Immaculate Conception Grade School in **Fairbanks**. By this time, however, Sister Marie Teresa had already been assigned to Sioux Falls, South Dakota, for the school year 1973–74. During her Christmas vacation, she made a trip to Fairbanks for an interview. The need for a principal was still there. In the eyes of all parties concerned, she was the one to fill the position.

Early in July 1974, Sister Marie Teresa arrived in Fairbanks. At that time Immaculate Conception Grade School was still staffed in large part by members of the **Jesuit Volunteer Corps**, who made up in enthusiasm for what they lacked in experience. Most of them had just received their academic degree and teacher's certification. She found working with them both an inspiration and a challenge.

For the really great Alaskan adventure Sister Marie Teresa did not have to wait very long at all. Early in 1975, she was approached by the Diocesan Director of Religious Education about teaching summer religion classes on **Little Diomede** Island. This offered her an opportunity to see bush Alaska beyond her wildest dreams. On June 11th, she and Father Louis L. **Renner**, S.J., flew by jet from Fairbanks to **Nome**. There they met Sister Judy Tralnes, C.S.J.P, her teaching partner. The following day, in a small bush plane, under marginal flying conditions, the three flew to Wales to await a boat from Little Diomede. During summers, at that time, Little Diomede could be reached only by boat. Toward morning of their first, and only, night at Wales, a crew of Diomede hunters landed there in a traditional Eskimo skinboat, an *umiaq*. Around noon of that day, the 13th, on sleds towed behind snowmachines, the two Sisters and Father were brought out to the edge of the shore-fast ice, where boat and crew were ready to take them on board for the 26-mile crossing to the island. Space in the boat was shared by the three, the crew, and several walrus carcasses. Keeping an eye glued to his compass, for the day was shrouded in fog, the captain, with signals from the lookout man in the bow, deftly steered the boat around ice floes still partially clogging Bering Strait. The three-hour trip, except for several wide-of-the-mark shots fired at a walrus, was uneventful—but shiveringly cold.

In the Little Diomede village of Ignaluk, the two Sisters taught classes every afternoon to the children. They spent the mornings in preparing classes and in getting acquainted with the people on the island. Father Renner offered Mass every day, and visited the people. After five weeks on the island, the Sisters returned to Fairbanks.

Sister Marie Teresa remained in the Fairbanks schools until June 1978. That summer, she moved to **Holy Cross**, Alaska, where she worked in Holy Family parish, of which Father Michael J. **Kaniecki**, S.J., future Bishop of Fairbanks, was, at the time, pastor. As he was a pilot with an airplane at his disposal, she flew often with him to various villages in the area. At Holy Cross, she gave religious instructions to the children, and became part of the Catholic community.

In June 1983, Sister Marie Teresa returned to Fairbanks. For the next four years, she worked as secretary at Monroe Catholic High School. It was her first real contact with senior high students, and, in her own words, she "enjoyed it immensely."

In August 1987, her community offered Sister Marie Teresa a sabbatical. She spent the first semester of that in a renewal program for women Religious at St. Stephen Priory in Dover, Massachusetts. The second semester she spent taking courses in religious studies at her community's Edgewood College. After her sabbatical, in August 1988, she returned to Fairbanks to be a partner to Robert L. **Whelan**, S.J., retired Bishop of Fairbanks, in operating the House of Prayer. In their quiet, deeply spiritual ways, the two were a perfect match up. One witty wag, rather perceptively, referred to them as "The Blessed Couple." After Bishop Whelan retired to Spokane, Washington, in 1995, Sister continued on at the House of Prayer, now as assistant to Father Normand A. **Pepin**, S.J. Early in the year 2000, Sister Marie Teresa, too, went into retirement. On May 9, 2001, she went south to reside at her Motherhouse in Sinsinawa. In December 2003, she came through "hip surgery with flying colors and hardly any pain," according to Sister Alita Lisbeth, O.P. "She was such a darling in the hospital that they would ask to bring in staff for training sessions with her."

On Palm Sunday, April 4, 2004, Sister Marie Teresa, in the words of Sister Alita, "celebrated her own 'triumphal entry.' She peacefully let out her last sigh and went home to God." She lies buried in the Motherhouse cemetery at Sinsinawa Mound. A well-attended memorial Mass was celebrated for her in Holy Family Chapel at the Catholic Schools complex in Fairbanks on June 16, 2004, by Father Pepin.

91, 113

BROWN, Father Edward H., S.J.

Edward Howard Brown, was born on May 15, 1860, in Baltimore, Maryland. He belonged to a well-known Catholic family, and enjoyed from his earliest years all the advantages that religion and culture could bestow. There were eight sons and one daughter in the family. Edward was educated first at Loyola College in Baltimore, then at Georgetown University in Washington, D.C. He belonged to the

Father Edward H. Brown, S.J.
JOPA-856.01.

class of '79, and was universally admired for his "gentle manners and sterling qualities."

Edward Brown entered the Jesuit novitiate at Frederick, Maryland, on July 31, 1879. He took novitiate life very seriously, perhaps too much so for his physical well-being. He began to develop headaches at an early stage of his Jesuit career. Headaches were to plague him throughout his life. After completing his training at Frederick, he went on to three years of philosophical studies at Woodstock, Maryland. These were followed by three years of teaching at Georgetown, then two more years of teaching at Fordham University in the Bronx, New York. In 1889, he returned to Woodstock for theological studies. His headaches, however, forced him to cut short his stay there. After two years at Woodstock, he went to Holy Cross College in Worcester, Massachusetts, hoping that a change of place might bring him relief. In 1893, he volunteered for the Rocky Mountain Mission, and was accepted. In the West, he studied theology privately for another year, and, in 1894, was ordained a priest in St. Aloysius Church in Spokane, Washington.

During his first three years as a priest, Father Brown served as the Father Minister and as the Prefect of Discipline at Gonzaga College in Spokane. Following that, he made his tertianship at Florissant, Missouri, 1897–98, after which he was Prefect of Studies and Discipline for six years: two at

Gonzaga and four at Seattle College in Seattle, Washington. He was an impressively tall, stately man and, at the same time, a man endowed with a kindly, sympathetic heart. According to a fellow Jesuit, he was also "enthusiastic as a high school boy about all student athletics." In brief, he was ideally suited to fill the role of a Prefect of Discipline.

On August 14, 1904, Father Brown arrived in **Juneau, Alaska**, to become pastor of Nativity of the Blessed Virgin Mary parish there and to serve as Chancellor of the Prefecture Apostolic of Alaska. He served in this dual capacity until he left Alaska on September 25, 1913, on the steamer *Northwestern*. From time to time, during his Juneau years, he brought the Mass and Sacraments also to **Douglas**, **Petersburg**, **Wrangell** and **Ketchikan**.

Father Brown was loyal to Juneau. Many years after he left it, he was still gratefully remembered, not only as a devoted parish priest, but also as "a man of strong will and sterling character, who took an active interest in civic affairs, gaining the respect of citizens both Catholic and non-Catholic." With his own hands, beginning in 1906 and finishing in 1908, he built a trail to the summit of Juneau's Mount Roberts. He made safe the difficult climb to the top and constructed benches at scenic spots and at regular intervals. For some years, the trail was affectionately referred to as "Father Brown's Trail." The name was subsequently changed to "Mount Roberts Trail."

In 1908, Father Brown was in Wrangell for a time to help with the construction of Wrangell's new St. Rose of Lima Church. In 1910, he saw to the construction of a new Nativity of the Blessed Virgin Mary Church in Juneau and to the laying of the foundation for a new rectory. John F. Mullen, Vice-President of a Juneau bank and a member of the Juneau parish at the time, wrote of Father Brown, "He was meticulously careful in planning the church and in carrying out his plans. He was exacting in the kind of material and workmanship that was employed." He made the decorating of the church and its neatness his personal concern, often cleaning it himself.

During the years 1911 and 1912, Father Brown worked closely with Sister Mary Zenon, S.S.A., on the construction of a new hospital building in Juneau. According to her, he was "a man of no ordinary stamp, so enthusiastic about the building of the new hospital, and worked, or rather overworked, so courageously that he was obliged to lay down the burden of his pastorate and return to Seattle to recuperate his health."

In 1913, shortly before Father Brown left Alaska, he was appointed chaplain of Alaska's First Territorial Senate. The appointment was tendered in the light that he would confer honor on that body, rather than that the position would be an honor to him.

When Father Brown returned to the Pacific Northwest in late September 1913, he was "a physical wreck, a martyr to his zeal and charity," according to one of his fellow Jesuits. However, with proper medical care and nourishment, his health improved to the point, where he was able to do light priestly work in Tacoma, Washington, in Spokane, and in Pendleton, Oregon. A few years before his death, he suffered a paralyzing stroke which nearly ended his life.

After Father Brown recovered sufficient strength to resume his active life, he was sent to Our Lady of Lourdes Hospital in Pasco, Washington. He found the hospital in wretched financial condition. By sending out hundreds of letters, typed out on an "old battered typewriter, patched by himself," and by collecting thousands of dollars owed for services rendered, he saved the Sisters from bankruptcy. But, it was his ministry to the sick and to the Sisters that left the Sisters inconsolable when he died, rather unexpectedly, in their hospital, on Sunday, June 21, 1925.

That Sunday morning, Father Brown offered Mass and heard confessions as usual. About 9:30, he felt a violent pain in his chest. The doctor was summoned, but could give him no relief. Soon the parish priest arrived to administer to him the Last Rites of the Church. In a clear voice, Father Brown answered all the prayers for the dying, and remained conscious to the last. He expired in the early afternoon. It was the feast of St. Aloysius, to whom he had had a life-long devotion. His passing was mourned not only by the Sisters, to whom he had been so devoted, but also by the people of Pasco, in general. "Always a polished gentleman, with a vivid way of telling a story," he had been a prominent figure in Pasco, often invited to address civic or social organizations. Father Brown lies buried in the Jesuit cemetery at Mount St. Michael's on the outskirts of Spokane, Washington.

BUCHANAN, Father John R., S.J.

John R. "Jack" Buchanan was born in Chicago, Illinois, on August 5, 1915. When he was still a boy, the family moved to Spokane, Washington. There he came to know the Jesuits, when he attended Gonzaga High School and played quarterback on the football team. He entered the Jesuit novitiate at Sheridan, Oregon, on July 30, 1933. He studied philosophy at Mount St. Michael's, Spokane, 1937–40, then taught for two years at Seattle Preparatory. Having volunteered for the **Alaska** missions, he spent the years 1942–44 prefecting the boys at **Holy Cross Mission**, before going on to four years of theological studies at Alma College, Los Gatos, California. He was ordained a priest on June 16, 1947. After another year of theology at Alma College, and a year of tertianship at Auriesville, New York, he returned to Alaska.

Father Buchanan, known more commonly as "Father Jack," was, at first, slated to work among the Eskimos of the lower Yukon River, but was assigned instead to a vaguely defined area of some 74,000 square miles northwest of Alaska's Panhandle. A government nurse, Marie Bronson, took credit for bringing about this change in his assignment. In 1982, in **Fairbanks**, she told Father Louis L. **Renner**, S.J., that it was she who convinced Francis D. **Gleeson**, S.J., Vicar Apostolic of Alaska at the time, of the urgent need for a priest in that vast region. However, in a letter to Father Jack, dated September 20, 1949, Father James U. **Conwell**, S.J., writes to the contrary: "The government nurse thinks your appointment was the fruit of her visit. Needless to say, it was not." Whatever the full truth of the matter might be, one thing is certain: a priest for the area assigned to Father Jack was long overdue.

When Bishop Gleeson assigned Father Jack to that area, an area that included 17 Indian villages and many small white camps and communities, he

Father John R. Buchanan, S.J. *LRC.*

gave him $500, a '39 Chevy truck, and his blessing. More he could not afford.

Father Jack made **Tok**, "The Gateway to Alaska," his headquarters, but spent most of his time on the road visiting his widely-scattered little flocks at **Northway**, Copper Center, **Delta Junction**, **Glennallen**, Gulkana, Chitina, **Nenana**, and Suntrana-**Healy**. While living out of his truck in Tok, he built himself a cabin, a crude 8 × 10-foot structure, for the winter of 1949–50 out of materials he had begged and salvaged from near and far. In the early 1950s, again while living in his truck, or in a tent, he went on to build chapels at Tok, Northway, and Copper Center. The materials for these chapels, too, he, for the most part, begged or "scrounged." Because of his begging, scrounging ways, he was soon affectionately referred to all up and down the highway as "the pack rat priest." The locals got accustomed to his audacity and creativity, when it came to acquiring essential materials and raising money. In the Tok Lodge, he set up a "swear box" to collect fines from those who had a loose tongue. At another bar, he held a box-lunch sale. The people arrived quietly and apprehensively, not knowing just what to expect of a priest. Father Jack sidled up to the bar, ordered a shot of whiskey, and the bidding began. Six hundred dollars was raised, and in the process he acquired new friends. Among his many benefactors, one stood out: Bing Crosby.

From the famous singer, Father Jack received just the truck he needed to make his rounds.

In his letters to Bishop Gleeson, Father Jack made known some of his very real frustrations: lack of adequate worship spaces, lack of money, lack of time to attend to his own spiritual nourishment, too much time spent on the road, too much time spent in building and on material concerns. In general, there was always simply too much to do and too little time to do it in. In spite of all the obstacles to his ministry, undaunted, never losing his enthusiasm and zeal, he carried on, all the while putting up buildings and ministering to his people.

In 1955, Father Jack left his highway ministry to play a major role in the realization of a dream he had had ever since he began that ministry. The story of that dream and its realization is told in the entry entitled **Copper Valley School**.

In the 1964–65 Oregon Province Catalog, Father Jack is listed as still being stationed at Copper Valley School and as serving as "procurator, buyer, and part-time beggar." In 1965, he made his headquarters in **Anchorage**, where he continued to provide supplies for the Alaska missions until he left Alaska in 1966. He received his mail first in Seattle, then in nearby Renton, but he spent most of the rest of his life on the roads of the American West, obtaining supplies for needy groups in the western states. According to a friend, he kept gathering food and necessities for the poor, "little pockets of folks, nuns, schools, parishes, living out of his car, barely keeping enough for himself."

The aftermath of Vatican II left Father Jack disillusioned and bewildered by what he considered irresponsible vagaries in thought and practice. From the prominence into which he had been thrust during his heroic efforts to build Copper Valley School, he gradually dropped from view and embraced the hidden life. The end to the life of Father John R, Buchanan, S.J., "the pack rat priest," once featured in *Newsweek Magazine*, came quickly. In St. Elizabeth's Hospital, Yakima, Washington, on November 26, 1988, he died of a cerebral hemorrhage. He lies buried in the Jesuit Cemetery at Mount Saint Michael's, Spokane.

Father Fernando T. Bugarin.
Courtesy of Fr. Bugarin.

BUGARIN, Father Fernando T.

Fernando—commonly known as "Fred"—Tiburcio Bugarin was born in the Philippine Islands, on the Island of Luzon, Province of Isabela, to Fernando Bugarin, Sr., and Eufemia Tiburcio, on December 12, 1948. In 1962, his father moved to **Anchorage**, **Alaska**, where his brother Felix, Fred's uncle, had been at home for some years already. The following year, Fred joined them. His mother died in the Philippines.

In his youth, Fred was a member of St. Juliana's parish in Anchorage's Spenard district. At first this was a mission of Anchorage's Holy Family parish. St. Juliana's ceased to be, when St. Benedict's parish was established in May 1966.

For part of his schooling, Fred at first attended Central Catholic Junior High School, in existence from 1961–67. He then went on to complete his secondary schooling at Anchorage's West High School, graduating in 1967. It gave him satisfaction in retrospect to realize that Central Catholic had, in God's Providence, produced at least one priestly vocation, his.

There were two, more or less obvious, directions that the new graduate could go. With the Vietnam War raging, military service seemed a likely option; the other, college. He opted for neither. With memories of the missionary work done in his native Philippines by the La Salette Fathers, he seriously considered joining them as a third option. At the end of the summer of 1967, he approached Msgr. Francis A. Murphy, Archdiocesan Director of Vocations, to tell him of his intentions to join the La Salette Fathers and go back to the Philippines. "I can't remember," Fred said years later, "exactly what the persuasive Monsignor told me, but somehow I ended up in Dallas, Texas, at Holy Trinity Seminary, preparing to become a priest for the Archdiocese of Anchorage."

In Anchorage's Holy Family Cathedral, on January 25, 1975, Archbishop **Joseph T. Ryan** ordained Fred to the priesthood. A large delegation of Filipino-Alaskans attended the ordination ceremonies and rejoiced to see one of their own become a priest of God. His sister, Kathy, did one of the readings.

As a newly ordained priest, Father Bugarin assisted at St. Benedict's parish, Anchorage, during the year 1975–76. He was Parish Administrator during the years 1976–78. During the year 1978–79, he was stationed in **Palmer**, out of which he cared for Sacred Heart mission in **Wasilla**. In January 1979, Sacred Heart became an independent parish. Father Bugarin, residing now in Wasilla, served as its first pastor, from 1979–81. It was he who built St. Jude Center in Wasilla. He was Archdiocesan Director of the Permanent Diaconate Program and Office of Ministries from 1981–1987.

About this time, Father Bugarin felt, in his own words, "another call surfacing from deep inside, from a passion from my past not forgotten." It was a time for him as a young priest "of deep personal conversion, and discernment." With the permission of his Ordinary, he spent seven months, during the year 1987–88, at the East Asian Pastoral Institute at the Ateneo de Manila, Philippines. There his eagerness for service among the poorest of his own people was confirmed. After receiving a "mission orientation" at Maryknoll, New York, during the last quarter of 1988, and attending the Maryknoll School of Language and Culture in Davao City, Philippines, during the first half of 1989, he began a seven-year ministry in his native land.

From August 1989 to May 1992, Father Bugarin served at St. Joseph's parish, a remote parish in Bayog in the Province of Zamboanga del Sur, Ipil Prelature. For his second assignment in the Philippines he was sent to the Mati diocese in the Province of Davao Oriental. There, in the remote barrio of Barangay Calapagan, Lupon, he started Holy Rosary parish, a parish responsible for 23 base Christian communities.

Father Bugarin left the Philippines in April 1996. Looking back on his seven-year missionary experience with the Maryknoll Fathers among the poor of rural Philippines, he found that it had provided him an occasion to refocus his priesthood and his priorities. His subsequent pastoral ministry was indelibly marked by that third-world experience. The words "justice" and "preferential option for the poor" had taken on new meaning for him.

After spending May and June 1996 at Maryknoll, New York, and July and August 1996 at Maryknoll House in Seattle, Washington, Father Bugarin returned to the Archdiocese of Anchorage in September. He spent the month of October as assistant pastor at St. Anthony's parish in Anchorage. In November 1996, he began a six-year term as pastor of St. Mary's parish in **Kodiak**. During his Kodiak years, he concentrated his outreach ministry on the immigrants who came from all parts of the world looking for work in the fish processing plants. He soon became involved in community organizing and networking with various service agencies bringing help to the needy and under-served.

In March 2003, Father Bugarin was named pastor of St. Anthony's parish in Anchorage. There, too, he found ample opportunity to put to use the pastoral skills he had learned from his experiences as a missionary in the Philippines and that had served him so well in Kodiak.

On August 23, 2003, he wrote to Father Louis L. **Renner**, S.J.: "The journey continues—the journey to that fullness of life promised by the King I follow and serve."

15

BURIK, Miss Mary Therese

Mary Therese "Tweet" Burik, the sister of an older brother, Edward, was born in Cleveland, Ohio, on May 9, 1933, to Frank Burik and Mary Cecilia Berilla Burik, both offspring of parents who had come from Czechoslovakia. Her father died, when she was two and a half years old. Her mother then took

Miss Mary Therese Burik.
MK.

the two children to Byesville, Ohio, to live with their maternal grandparents. For her elementary schooling, Tweet attended the Byesville public school; for her secondary schooling, St. Benedict High School in nearby Cambridge, from which she graduated in 1951.

With diploma in hand, and, in her words, "a strong determination to straighten out the government," she went to work for the Federal Housing Administration in Washington, D.C. She remained there for 12 years, "struggling to climb the bureaucratic ladder." Then, in 1963, "realizing that money, power, and a steady job were not everything," she left her satisfying, high-positioned secretarial job to answer the "Call of the North" by volunteering her services to the Catholic Church in **Alaska**. As a member of the **Jesuit Volunteer Corps**, her intention, at the time, was to spend only one year in Alaska. However, at the first of her three major stations in Alaska, St. Mary's Mission boarding school on the **Andreafsky** River, she stayed on for four happy years.

In 1967, Tweet, answered another call, a call to go farther north, to **Nome**, there to help Father James E. **Poole**, S.J., get radio station **KNOM** on the air. In this, because of her sharp business sense, along with exceptional managerial skills, she proved to be of inestimable help to him. The station went on the air in 1971. She remained at the station, first as a non-salaried volunteer, then at a nominal salary, to serve as its Business Manager. Occasionally, in some of her "more flamboyant moments," as she wrote, she would even go on the air, announcing and spinning records. As volunteers came and went at KNOM, it was she who provided stability and kept the domestic side of the whole operation running orderly and smoothly. In April 1978, she was honored with the Alaska First Lady's Volunteer of the Year Award.

In 1985, Tweet, having by then enjoyed over a decade of "fantastic years" at KNOM, and having become a recognized "legend" there, received yet another call. This one came from Bishop Michael J. **Kaniecki**, S.J., requesting her to be his Executive Secretary in **Fairbanks**. Though very reluctant to leave Nome, she, nevertheless, "after much thought and prayer," decided to make the move to Fairbanks, motivated in part by the thought that, as Executive Secretary, she would be rendering important service to the Church, and, at the same time, providing some kind of financial future for herself. In her new position, she would receive a modest salary and the various benefits that come with a full-time employee position.

From 1985–99, Tweet served competently and faithfully as Bishop Kaniecki's Executive Secretary. For some years, during the early 1990s, she was engaged also in prison ministry. On a monthly basis, on Saturday afternoons, she and Father Louis L. **Renner**, S.J., conducted a non-sacramental service at the Fairbanks Correctional Center for such inmates as cared to attend it. For recreation, she, among other things, played cribbage or pinochle, went bowling with friends, or went for drives in her new car sporting a "Tweet" license plate. Occasionally, she and friends went on a fly-in fishing expedition with Bishop Kaniecki.

On April 27, 1999, Tweet suffered a serious accident, falling down a flight of steps in her apartment and striking her head on the doorknob below. Her life was all but despaired of. She was flown to **Anchorage**, where she was hospitalized for weeks. She then returned to Fairbanks to undergo lengthy rehabilitation therapy. Memory loss was a major concern. Given her strong determination to recover, she eventually made a remarkable comeback. Sooner than anyone could reasonably have expected, she was able to return to her apartment, and even to drive again.

Having known Bishop Kaniecki from the time she first arrived in Alaska, long before he was ordained a bishop, and having been his Executive Secretary for 14 years, Tweet, understandably, was deeply saddened, by his unexpected death, on August 6, 2000.

In December 2000, the Diocese of Fairbanks, at a special Mass and luncheon, honored and thanked Tweet for her long years of service to it and its people. Although she was not able to resume her secretarial position, she did volunteer work around the diocesan chancery. As of the year 2004, beginning every day in the House of Prayer chapel with morning Mass and Communion, she continued doing volunteer work for the diocese, as well as some minor salaried work in the diocesan archives.

86, 116

BURKE, Father William T., S.J.

William T. "Bill" Burke, the oldest of ten children, was born in Hammond, Indiana, on January 2, 1935, to Thomas and Sally Burke. His father, a welder-pipefitter, converted to Catholicism from German Lutheranism some years after William's birth. His mother was a life-long, most devout, daily rosary-praying Catholic. In Hammond, Bill received his elementary education at St. Joseph's Grade School and his secondary education at Bishop Noll Institute, from which he graduated in 1952. From 1952–56, he attended Loyola University in Chicago. He next spent three years working for Parke-Davis Pharmaceutical as a Medical Detailer. During those three years, he never dated, but went dancing many a Saturday night. Toward morning, he would slip out, buy some bait, and go fishing. He attended the Sunday evening Mass in his parish, where he was treasurer of the Holy Name Society.

On September 1, 1959, Bill entered the novitiate of the Chicago Province of the Society of Jesus at Milford, Ohio. After completing his two-year noviceship, he spent an additional year there studying the classics and humanities. His philosophical studies he made at St. Louis University, from 1962–65. He next spent a year teaching at Brebeuf Preparatory in Indianapolis. During the summer of 1966, he earned his Master of Education degree at

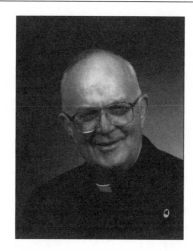

Father William T. Burke, S.J.
Courtesy of Fr. Burke.

St. Louis University. He then went on to four years of theological studies at the Bellarmine School of Theology at Loyola University in Aurora, Illinois. There he was ordained a priest on May 29, 1969. Before he left Loyola, he had earned his Master of Divinity degree.

Father Burke spent the year 1970–71 back at Brebeuf Preparatory teaching biology and English, and the following year in graduate studies in microbiology at Stritch Medical School in Maywood, Illinois. Even though he was by now an experienced teacher and well prepared for the academic life, he did not feel himself drawn to the classroom. It was work in parishes that attracted him. Parish work he described as "my first love in the Society."

During the year 1972–73, Father Burke did parish work at St. Mary's parish in Riverside, Illinois, and, from 1973–75, at St. Ignatius parish in Sacramento, California. Both of these assignments he "thoroughly enjoyed." When investigating the possibilities of one day serving in **Alaska**, he wrote, on December 15, 1980, in a letter to Thomas M. McCarthy, S.J., staff member of the Oregon Province Provincialate: "People like my liturgies, my singing (not a bad voice), me (I hope not in that order). And so I like them and normal everyday parish activities." Father Burke was, indeed, blessed with a fine singing voice, and he used it very effectively in his liturgies. His love of singing came to him at an early age from his mother. While in high school, he had played the clarinet in the high school band.

After his happy, but short, career in parish work, Father Burke was asked to serve at the Jesuit Provincial Residence in Oak Park, Illinois, as Director of Development, raising funds for providing care for senior Jesuits. This he did from September 1975 to June 1981. Regarding this assignment, he wrote, "For me that was God's Will, and I said 'yes,' though my heart was not in it. I tried to do the job as best I could." Of Father Burke as a fund-raiser, his Provincial, Father J. Leo Klein, S.J., wrote, "I'm sure he found it as hard as anyone else would have, but that never stopped him from putting his full generosity and energy into the project." During his last two years at Oak Park, Father Burke served also as Father Minister of that Jesuit community. "His two years as minister for the Oak Park community," wrote Father Klein, "are typical of his cheerful fidelity to vital but hidden labor for the sake of his fellow Jesuits. I am grateful for his example in our midst."

But, all the while, it was to parish work that Father Burke was being drawn, and preferably parish work in Alaska. "Why Alaska?" he wrote in that same letter to Father McCarthy, "My vacations since scholastic days have always been at Maryvale Villa in Fraser, Colorado—8,700 feet above sea level. I prefer the cold weather, and I like to fish. I want to do parish work, and also enjoy my hobby."

From June to September 1981, Father Burke found himself in **Nome**, Alaska, replacing Father Paul B. **Macke**, S.J., pastor of St. Joseph's parish at the time. During his summer in Nome, Father Burke—described as "a state of the art fly fisherman, who ties his own flies"— hooked many a fish in the waters near Nome, and, in turn, got thoroughly hooked on Alaska.

After spending a sabbatical year, 1981–82, upgrading his theology at the Jesuit School of Applied Theology at Berkeley, California—and, while there, shedding 75 pounds as a member of, and counselor to, Overeaters Anonymous—Father Burke was back in Alaska. Starting on August 2, 1982, he began to serve as pastor of Our Lady of Sorrows parish in **Delta Junction** and of its dependent missions, **Tok**, **Northway**, and **Eagle**. He also visited Mentasta Lodge and Chicken occasionally. To make the complete circuit of those five stations, he had to drive somewhat over 500 miles. Many another man would have found the long hours on the road rather tedious. Father Burke, for his part, knew how to shorten them: by enjoying the awesome wilderness scenery in that part of Alaska, or by stopping along the way from time to time to cast a fly or two on some placid side stream, or by putting his poetic talent to work to express the joy and wonder of it all in verse.

By the time he left Alaska, Father Burke saw three books of his poetry published, as well as many of his poems published in various prestigious literary journals. Many of his experiences in Alaska and with Alaska's people found expression in verse. He found the long dark days of winter, when "It's four P.M. and dark as death in Tok," conducive to writing poetry, and to tying flies. While some of his poems reflect moods of melancholy and sadness, by far the majority of them give expression to his personal optimism, positive outlook on life, and his close friendship with nature and its loving Creator. He experienced God as loving him through nature. Much of his poetry is about life, about being "fully alive," and "life-giving." Though very close to nature, he was even closer to "family": his immediate personal family, his family of fellow Jesuits, and his family of parishioners.

After his first two years on the Delta Junction assignment, Father Burke wrote, "I love it here. I need to be doing things that are life-giving, that make me feel more fully alive. Solitude is fully alive for me, a silence with God's presence filling it. For me, that's nature, fly fishing, liturgy, small talk with friends, reading, reflection and prayer, poetry and music, and the people."

Father Burke's Delta Junction assignment came to an end in 1987. He spent the summer of that year in **Anchorage** training for hospital chaplaincy work and doing his internship at Providence Alaska Medical Center. From September 1987 to July 1989, he was stationed in **Fairbanks**, engaged in hospital chaplaincy ministry there. At the same time, he served as visiting priest to Catholic communities living along the "Railbelt" (the communities strung out for 110 miles along the Parks Highway and the Alaska Railroad from **Nenana** all the way to Cantwell) chief among them Nenana and **Healy**.

From August 1989 to June 1990, Father Burke was in Spokane, Washington, at Deaconess Hospital getting training in Clinical Pastoral Education. He received his CPE certification in 1991. From June 7, 1990, to September 2001, he was a member of the Pastoral and Spiritual Care Department at Providence Alaska Medical Center, Anchorage.

After nearly 20 years in Alaska, Father Burke left it, in the summer of 2001, and took on a new, two-part assignment in Missoula, Montana: half-time associate pastor at St. Francis Xavier's parish, and half-time certified priest-chaplain at St. Patrick Hospital.

On February 2, 2002, Father Burke wrote to Father Louis L. **Renner**, S.J.: "The reason I left Providence: Change of administration in the department. I knew they were going to make changes I didn't like. Hated to leave, but couldn't stay. I'm enjoying my new career. Missoula is a great place to do some fly fishing."

121

BURNS, Father Eugene P., S.J.

Eugene Patrick Burns was born in Boston, Massachusetts, on November 22, 1908, to Eugene Burns and Hannah Dwyer Burns. He entered the novitiate of the New England Province of the Society of Jesus at Shadowbrook, Lenox, Massachusetts, on July 30, 1928. After completing his two-year noviceship, he spent an additional two years there studying the classics and humanities. From 1932–35, he made his philosophical studies at Weston College, Weston, Massachusetts. He spent the year 1935–36 earning an M.A. degree in French at St. Louis University. He then taught French at Boston College High School in Dorchester, Massachusetts, during the year 1936–37. His theological studies he made at Weston College from 1937–41. He was ordained a priest on June 22, 1940. During the year 1941–42, he made his tertianship at St. Robert's Hall in Pomfret, Connecticut. On February 2, 1942, he took his final vows.

From 1942–46, Father Burns taught Latin, English and French at Fairfield Preparatory in Fairfield, Connecticut. He next spent nine years, 1946–55, teaching the same subjects at St. Philip Neri School for Delayed Vocations in Boston. The years 1955–59 saw him occupied as a professor of French at Collège Notre Dame de Jamhour in Beirut, Lebanon. For some time during those years, he served also as an Auxiliary Chaplain to the American Fleet. He then returned again to St. Philip Neri School to teach the same subjects he had taught during his first stay there. From 1963–67, he was a professor of English and Theology at Al-Hikma University in Baghdad, Iraq. After spending the year 1967–68 teaching French at Boston College High, he returned to Al-Hikma for several months as a professor of English. In November 1968, the Jesuits were expelled from Iraq.

At the invitation of Archbishop **Joseph T. Ryan**, Father Burns arrived in **Anchorage, Alaska**, on January 26, 1969. From January 30, 1969, to January 31, 1971, he was assistant pastor at St. Benedict's parish in Anchorage. From February 1, 1971, to July 30, 1971, he was an assistant at Holy Family Cathedral parish in Anchorage, and from July 31, 1971, to August 17, 1977, pastor of St. Francis Xavier's parish in **Valdez**. During his Valdez years, he cared also for the **Cordova** parish during the year 1973–74. While in Valdez, he served also as Port Chaplain and as Alaska Pipeline Chaplain.

From the latter part of 1977 till 1986, Father Burns lived in Anchorage, at 7528 on Stanley Drive. In addition to being chaplain to the Sisters of St. **Ann**, also living on Stanley Drive, in a convent at 7538, he was part of the archdiocese's Ministry of Caring Program. As such, he ministered to people living in the Anchorage Pioneers Home, in the McLaughlin Youth Center, in the Alaska Psychiatric Institute, and in Our Lady of Compassion Care Center. His ministry extended also to numerous shut-ins.

Father Burns left Alaska in 1986. During the last two years of his life, he lived at the Campion Residence, formerly Weston College, and did some pastoral ministry. There he died, on August 27, 1988.

When Father Burns left Alaska, Francis T. **Hurley**, Archbishop of Anchorage at the time, wrote of him: "He was not in the public limelight. He focused on the task assigned, and moved quietly and effectively among the people he served. For nine years he brought the Mass and the sacraments to people, not as a functionary, but with the patience and kindness one seeks in a priest. His light shone to many."

BUSCH, Dr. Thomas A.

When he first arrived in **Nome**, **Alaska**, in 1970, as a volunteer to help get station **KNOM**, the "Alaska Radio Mission" of the Diocese of **Fairbanks**, on the air, he was hailed as "that key man." For 30 years, his official title was that of General Manager of KNOM, but he was, at the same time, also the station's chief engineer, system operator, fund-raiser, development director, as well as one of its main announcers, show hosts, and disc jockeys. He was voted "Broadcaster of the Year" by the Alaska Broadcasters Association, was inducted into its hall of fame, and was twice elected its president. Both he and station KNOM under his leadership were the recipients of numerous citations and awards. "Radio is my life," he readily admitted. For his apostolic work at KNOM, his alma mater conferred on him an honorary doctorate.

Thomas Anthony "Tom" Busch was born in Philadelphia, Pennsylvania, on November 1, 1947—45 years to the day of his father's birth. His mother was diabetic. After several miscarriages, she prayed to St. Thomas Aquinas to be blessed with a child, and pledged that, if it were a boy, he would be named for the saint. An only child, Tom was raised in a modest housing development in Rosemont, Pennsylvania, and schooled at Waldron Academy in nearby Merion Station by the Sisters of Mercy. Tom's childhood hobbies included scouting, astronomy, electronics, and playing in the dense 40-acre neighborhood woods. One of his fond childhood memories is the one about how John F. Kennedy once held him by the shoulders and begged his forgiveness. Nine-year-old Tom was with his mother, who was taking him on a tour of the U.S. Capitol. In the rotunda, a man accidentally bumped into Tom, steadied him, and said "Excuse me!" It was the future president.

On New Year's Day 1959, Tom's parents gave him a pink clock radio, which they had won at a party the night before and had no use for. Tom began at the bottom of the AM dial, listening to various stations, until, a few days later, he reached 990, the rock-and-roll station WIBG. He was immediately captivated, both by the music and by a thrill for radio broadcasting. "They were talking right to me," he recalled as an adult. One day, a few mornings after

Dr. Thomas A. Busch. *Courtesy of Dr. Busch.*

he had written a fan letter to the morning deejay, he heard his name on the air. "It made my whole week," Tom remembered, crediting the announcer, Joe Niagra, with inspiring him eventually to pursue broadcasting as a life's career.

At Jesuit-staffed St. Joseph's Preparatory in Philadelphia, Tom was active in Our Lady's Sodality and the school's inter-racial council. Summers, he worked for a landscape architect, "swinging a grub hoe all day, every day." Although he did not consider his voice sufficiently resonant, after graduating from high school, he landed a job at WLDB-AM in Atlantic City, New Jersey. The job of "announcer" there was, technically, a very challenging one, demanding extremely fast tape checking and editing. But the job involved only limited speaking over the air.

His first night at Boston College, also Jesuit-staffed, Tom visited the campus radio station, and was soon named "Director of Engineering Personnel," a title without duties. At the same time, he hosted a weekly radio show, produced shows for others, and announced newscasts. During his second year at Boston College, the college station appointed him Chief Engineer. In the summer, WLDB named him its Chief Announcer. Actually, he was the only announcer, but his boss thought "Chief

Announcer" "might look good on a resume some day."

While attending Boston College, Tom continued to be involved in radio. During the school year 1967–68, "using about three miles of cable," he completely remodeled the campus station's two studios. In December 1968, his father died. The Vietnam War was still raging in 1969, the year Tom graduated from college—with a B.A. degree in Psychology, and after having earned a First Class Radiotelephone License, the highest commercial FCC certification. He was now eligible for the draft, and anticipated being almost certainly drafted in January 1970. Being at heart a pacifist, bordering on a conscientious objector, he dreaded the very thought of going to war.

In 1969, while he was living in Atlantic City, Tom drove every Saturday night to Philadelphia to spend Sunday with his mother. On Saturday November 8th, however, moments before leaving for his mother's home, Tom felt a sudden and intense urge to drive to Boston instead. He called his mother and his friend in Boston, told them of his intentions, and headed north. "It was," according to Tom, "a life-changing decision."

Before reaching his buddy's house that night, Tom stopped by the Boston College radio station. "It was pure Holy Spirit," he termed the event many years later. A few minutes earlier, another of his college pals had dropped into the station. This was seminarian Richard L. **McCaffrey**, S.J., who had just returned from a year of teaching at **Copper Valley School** in Alaska. After regaling Tom with tales of grizzly bears, northern lights, minus-60 degree temperatures, McCaffrey mentioned that Father James E. **Poole**, S.J., in Nome was seeking a broadcast engineer to build his proposed new radio station in Nome. "Immediately I knew that I had to go there," said Tom in retrospect. "I knew it was something I wanted to do, something for me." He applied to Father Poole, was accepted, and was granted an occupational deferment from his draft board. On February 2, 1970, Tom found himself in **Anchorage**, Alaska. There, following Father Poole's directive, he met Augie Hiebert, pioneer Alaskan broadcaster, who was handling the federal paperwork connected with the station to go on the air the fol-

lowing year under the call letters of KNOM. "I had no idea at the time how great this man was," said Tom of Augie, "nor what good friends we would become." Augie handed Tom a stack of files five inches thick and said, "It's all yours."

Almost 20 years later, Tom recalled his Anchorage to Nome flight:

A brilliant moon reigned over the Arctic night that February 8, 1970, as a lone Alaska Airlines 727 ferried me and a handful of other passengers across 500 miles of Alaska wilderness to remote Nome. It was crystal clear; and yet, I couldn't see a single light on the ground the entire trip. It was so remote, more isolated than I'd ever imagined. What was I getting myself into?

On February 9th, Tom's first full day in Nome, Father Poole and Tom, in the mission's beat-up Chevy station wagon, set out to visit the projected station's transmitter site. "Once we were rolling on Nome's dirt streets," wrote Tom, "I noticed that the car's suspension was gone. After a few miles, I no longer wondered why there were three spare tires in the back." With the Alaskan tundra to the left and the forbidding ice of the frozen Bering Sea just off to the right, they drove the three washboard miles to the site. As the two were facing the vast, barren, snow-covered tundra, Father Poole told Tom, "This is the transmitter site." At that point, the awesome challenge of putting a radio mission station on the air in Nome hit Tom "like a punch in the gut." Back in town, Tom was shown the small old house in which the main studio was intended to be. "My confidence in the whole project continued to slip," wrote Tom years later. As Father Poole proceeded to show him the facilities and plans for the projected station, Tom, in his own words, "felt like I had signed onto a rapidly sinking ship," and apologized for his lack of faith. However, it was time to go to work, time to help Father Poole make what looked like an impossible dream become a concrete reality.

The most daunting radio-related task was blasting and shoveling out the 20-foot deep hole in the frozen tundra needed for the foundation of the 236-foot radio tower. Week after week, for twelve hours a day, Tom, helped at first by a hired-on old local miner, then by a dynamite expert, and a fellow volunteer, John Pfeifer, kept at it. "It was backbreaking labor," wrote Tom years later. "What kept me going was daily Mass in the shack which the **Little Sisters of Jesus** had fixed up among the **King Island** Eskimos at Nome's east end."

What also helped keep Tom going during that first very difficult year in Nome was his being accepted by the people of Nome, and especially by the King Island children. Shortly after he arrived in Nome, the King Island Eskimo Dancers performed for some tourists. Tom was in the back of the hall. As the first male volunteer for the radio mission, he was a fascination for the young children, but they were afraid to touch him. When the leader of the dancers called for one of the tourists to join the dancing, the kids all pointed toward Tom, and yelled "Him, him!" His awkward dance over, a thoroughly embarrassed Tom sat down. "All of a sudden," Tom remembered, "I was surrounded by an ocean of little kids, all trying to grab me, jump on top of me. I had been accepted." After that, he was like a pied piper to the King Island kids. He found their attachment to him "very healing."

Tom's earlier years in life had been "intensely prayerful ones," but by the time of his first years in Nome, his interest in religion had, by his own admission, "waned." Still, after work, he attended Father Poole's daily Mass. "It was comforting," he found, noting that he enjoyed especially being alongside the handful of King Island elders and the Little Sisters of Jesus who daily attended the Masses.

During his first year in Nome, Tom was tutored evenings in Morse Code by Leigh Birkeland, a member of a roving crew of construction workers helping out the Diocese of Fairbanks at the time. Soon Tom, proficient to 30 words a minute, had his amateur radio license. (In 1998, he finally upgraded to Extra, the highest class.) From Brother John **Huck**, S.J., another member of that construction crew, Tom learned enough carpentry to enable him, during the crew's absence, to stud out, wire, apply dry wall, and finish many of the walls in the new radio station.

Many problems unique to the Arctic delayed the station's going on the air. But, in spite of the delays, and after much hard work on the part of Tom and other volunteers, the new radio mission station KNOM was finally able to sign on, at 5 P.M., on July 14, 1971, a memorable day in the annals of the Catholic Church in Alaska. With that signing-on, Tom rightfully considered his personal mission in Nome, that of serving as chief engineer, designer, and supervisor of the radio station project, essentially accomplished.

While covering the first Iditarod Trail Sled Dog Race, in 1973, Tom was offered the position of Chief Engineer for KIAK Radio in Fairbanks. After Father Poole and he had located a replacement for him, Tom moved to Fairbanks, where he not only installed and maintained the equipment at KIAK, but also deejayed 20 hours a week, recorded commercials, produced investigative news documentaries, and read the 5 P.M. news. "Suddenly," to quote Tom, "I was earning more money than I could ever imagine. The work was super. I loved almost every minute of it. There were perks: travel, free lunches. I enjoyed the company of many friends, the work, the excitement of the trans-Alaska pipeline boom. My career was on the upswing. It was a very happy time for me." Several times he flew to Nome to help clean and adjust the KNOM transmitter. Meanwhile, Father Poole was trying to woo him back to KNOM, where he needed a full-time professional station manager. "But," said Tom, "becoming KNOM's manager was the farthest thing from my mind."

"By this time," Tom, recalling that period in his life some years later, humbly admitted , "my agnosticism had metamorphosed into a quiet atheism. I simply did not believe. The idea of God seemed absurd. It really was not a big deal to me."

"And then," to hear Tom tell it, "I was knocked off my horse." To describe what happened to him on that occasion, Tom, 20 years later, used the term "near death-like experience." According to Tom, the experience began one evening, as he slipped into bed following a pleasant, ordinary day. "It came out of nowhere. Suddenly, I felt depressed and anxious. And then, very, very depressed and anxious. And angry. And fearful." Within moments, his spirit was burdened by "every negative emotion you can name, at a highly amplified intensity." He tried to lift himself with positive images, "little girls in crinoline dresses running in fields of wheat, the seashore, a deep forest." He found all of them, everything repulsive. He wondered if he might have been drugged, or be suffering from some kind of brain incident.

"I was frozen in place," he continued the account of the event. "I knew that I could get out of bed, but I'd never make it to the telephone to call for help. Instead, I knew that I would throw myself out the window and kill myself to end the intense mental pain. That thought horrified me all the more. The pain cannot be described."

As his negative emotions intensified, Tom felt himself moments from what appeared to be, by his own admission, "an inevitable suicide." "I was desperate," he said, "so desperate that I cried out, 'God, if you exist, please come to me right now, and I will be yours for the rest of my life.'"

Shaking his head, Tom went on to tell how,

Just then, the most incredible thing happened. The sensation was of being lifted upward with great speed. A moment later, I found myself looking at an immense globe of intense light, brighter, more pure, than anything I could ever imagine. Instantly, I felt a river of incredible love from the light entering my body. It is beyond description; a thousand times more powerful, more joyful, more ecstatic than anything I've ever encountered on this earth.

Tom had no doubt in Whose presence he was. Experiencing "an abiding sense of peace," he returned love for love. In his mind, he heard the words, "If you ever again doubt I exist, remember this moment!"

A few days after his "conversion," reminiscent of the conversion of St. Paul, Tom happened to be asked again by Father Poole to consider being Station Manager of KNOM. The salary he proposed was upped to about a third of what Tom was earning in Fairbanks. After praying over the matter, and reflecting on how the Lord had guided his life up to that time, Tom came to the conclusion that the Lord's will for him was Nome. In June 1975, he found himself there as General Manager of KNOM. (The new title was given him to allay the fears of his mother, who saw in his return to Nome a serious blow to what she thought was a promising career. Tom was KNOM's first permanent, salaried employee.) Looking back on his decision to return to Nome, Tom, said, "I chose Nome, and it turned out to be another miraculous choice. I thank God daily for that."

One of the first things Tom did, upon his return to KNOM, was to impose a much-needed rigid programming format. In general, he brought more discipline and order to the overall operation of the station.

In September 1975, a new group of volunteers arrived at KNOM. Among them was **Pilot Station**–born Florence Francis from St. Marys, Alaska. When she was a child, she had known Father Poole. Her role at KNOM was to serve as Eskimo translator, secretary, and part-time deejay. This she did, for the year 1975–76. By the end of September 1977, she was back in Nome; now, however, as Mrs. Thomas A. Busch. On September 3rd, in the St. Mary's mission chapel, the two had been married. Father Poole was the principal celebrant of the nuptial Mass. Four area priests and Robert L. **Whelan**, S.J., Bishop of Fairbanks at the time, were concelebrants. Tom's mother and two aunts, his entire family, along with about ten people from Nome, were present. According to Tom, "It was really something!"

Now a married man, Tom was an unusually busy man. In addition to his responsibilities at KNOM, in his spare time, he was active also in Nome's Library and Museum Association, holding the office of president, starting in 1976. As her time allowed, Florence helped out at the station. In 1979, Florence bore the couple a son, Stephen; and, in 1981, a daughter, Kathleen. Tom was present for both deliveries, as Florence's Lamaze coach. "I know that it's a completely natural and normal process," Tom said of the deliveries, "but it struck me as absolutely magical and magnificent. It still does. They were the two most wonderful moments of my life."

In 1979, Tom was elected to the Board of Directors of the Alaska Broadcasters Association; and, in 1982, at the age of 34, he became the statewide group's president. In June of that year, he had the honor of introducing the ABA's convention speaker, Walter Cronkite, before an audience of 600 at Anchorage's Sheraton Hotel, an event broadcast on statewide television. Following his first term as president, he remained the group's secretary for nine years. He was named president of Nome's preschool association in 1985, and led a drive to construct the group's first building in 1987. In 1992, Tom was re-elected president of the ABA and elected president of Nome's Rotary Club.

In 1989, Florence began to work at KNOM as the station's business manager. On July 4th of that year, Tom, with his son Steve at his side, found himself walking on the main street of Provideniya, in the Soviet Far East. This was his first trip there, but his KNOM voice had often been heard there. "What began as a simple educational and goodwill trip," he wrote,

> quickly grew into something nobody had anticipated. People who were strangers at first meeting soon became fast friends. As we were leaving the Soviet Union, we were hugging our hosts, sobbing. We had developed family bonds. The experience, not just for us, but for all the Soviets and other Americans involved, was too magnificent, too intense to explain any other way than as an outpouring of grace, as an answer to the millions of prayers offered for world peace and international harmony and goodwill.

During the 1990s, Tom saw to it that the whole KNOM operation finally had the kind of buildings it really, and rather desperately, needed. On April 15, 1992, the volunteers were able to move into a new, safe dormitory. The following year, in April, the new Keller Broadcast Center was dedicated. In August 1997, KNOM's new 25,000-Watt transmitter was housed in a new, safe, shielded building. The final need, at the transmitter site, was a new building to house the new emergency generator. By 1999, this, too, was a reality. At the end of that decade, a grateful Tom could write: "For the first time ever, KNOM finally has safe, secure, energy-efficient buildings, with all the tools needed to serve our listeners. It is wonderful."

In the course of the years, awards and honors kept coming to radio station KNOM and to Tom Busch personally. In 1997, he was inducted into the Alaska Broadcasting Hall of Fame; and, in August 1998, he was the first North American to be honored by Unda World's Agnellus Andrew Award. He was in Montreal, Quebec, Canada, to accept that award.

Radio-minded and civic-minded as Tom was during the 1980s and 90s, he was, before all else, family- and Church-minded. While the children were growing up, both he and Florence—of whom Tom said, "In my own mind, she is ever-present and largely responsible for keeping me whole and on an even keel"—limited outside activities as much as possible, in order to concentrate on raising their children in a peaceful, loving family environment. Once the children were in school, both Tom and Florence became increasingly more active in their local parish, as Eucharistic ministers, lectors and lay presiders.

On May 24, 2004, Tom Busch became "Dr. Busch," when his alma mater, Boston College—"praising an esteemed son's admirable response to Jesus' call to 'Bring the Good News to the ends of the earth,'"—proudly declared Thomas Anthony Busch Doctor of Humane Letters, *honoris causa*.

As of July 2004, Tom and Florence anticipated moving into their new and permanent home in Anchorage "in early 2005." In Anchorage, Tom was to continue on as KNOM's principal fund-raiser. Norman Eric "Ric" Schmidt was to take over as KNOM's General Manager.

"Tom Busch, a talented and dedicated man," to quote *Our Sunday Visitor*, "is an exceptional Church servant." The Church in Alaska, and the people of northwestern Alaska, have been blessed, and continue to be blessed, as of the year 2004, in having the dedicated services of a man of the caliber, the competency, the generosity of KNOM's and Nome's Tom Busch.

14, 86, 116, 134

CAMILLE, Father Rogatien, S.J.

Rogatien Camille was born in Nantes, France, on August 12, 1863, and entered the Jesuit novitiate of the French Province at Aberdovey on October 9, 1882. He made his tertianship at Florissant, Missouri, during the year 1898–99. He arrived in **Alaska** in the summer of 1899. Before the end of that summer, he joined Father Francis M. **Monroe**, S.J., at **Eagle**. Being full of zeal and ambition, he was, however, greatly disappointed in finding himself in a place, where there was not work enough for even one priest. He spent the year 1900–01 in **Juneau** as assistant to Father John B. **René**, S.J., before going to **St. Michael**. From mid-November 1901 to mid-July 1902, Father Camille was in **Nome**. During his stay in Nome, he visited **Teller** and Gold Run between April 3rd and April 12th.

Father Camille spent the remainder of his life at St. Michael. His ministry style was that of a stay-at-home pastor. It was at St. Michael that he died, unexpectedly, on July 29, 1907, after an attack of apoplexy. Father Anthony M. **Keyes**, S.J., was present to administer the Last Anointing. Father Camille was apparently a very popular priest; for many, including the Russian Orthodox priest, came to his funeral. One month later, to the day, Father Peter C. **Bougis**, S.J., wrote from **Skagway** to Joseph R. **Crimont**, S.J., Prefect Apostolic of Alaska at the time: "Last night I had a conversation with a Catholic man who buried good Fr. Camille. He had seen him full of health a half hour before his death, cutting wood and jolly; and it is in that occupation that he dropped dead of heart failure. They made him a coffin; someone recited the funeral service, and such was the humble end of a truly good man."

Father Camille lies buried in the cemetery at St. Michael, Alaska.

CARDY, Father William E., O.F.M.

William Edward Cardy, the oldest of five children, was born on Chicago's Northwest Side on June 7, 1945, to Donald K. Cardy and Yvonne M. Crowley. He was baptized on July 1, 1945, at St. Ignatius parish, Chicago. He attended Queen of All Saints Elementary School from K–2nd grade, and St. Mary of the Woods Elementary School for grades 3rd–8th. At St. Mary's, he was taught by Franciscan Sisters. To their influence he traced his first inclinations to one day being a Franciscan priest.

As a young boy, William loved all sports, especially running, baseball and basketball. He also loved the outdoors and animals, especially birds. Often he would roam the Forest Preserve just west of his home to look for new birds to add to his bird-sighting list.

In August 1959, William, influenced more immediately by a piece of Franciscan seminary promotional material his father had placed on the family kitchen table, entered St. Joseph Franciscan Seminary in Westmont, Illinois. There he made all of his high school studies and his first year of college. For the three remaining years of his collegiate studies, he attended the recently built Our Lady of the Angels Franciscan Seminary in Quincy, Illinois. In Teutopolis, Illinois, between his second and third year of college, he participated in a full year of novitiate training for the Franciscan Order. He received his B.A. in Philosophy degree from Quincy University in 1968. The next year, 1969, he made his solemn profession as a member of the Franciscan Sacred Heart Province, headquartered in St. Louis, Missouri.

For his theological studies, William attended the newly formed Catholic Theological Union in Chicago. From June 1971 to December 1971, he served

Father William E. Cardy, O.F.M.
Courtesy of Fr. Cardy.

as a deacon at St. Anthony's parish in Parma, Ohio. After four years of intensive study, he received his Master of Divinity degree, on June 2, 1972. The following day, he was ordained to the priesthood.

For the first three years of his priestly life, Father Cardy was associate pastor at St. Joseph's parish in San Antonio, Texas, an Hispanic parish of about 2400 families. In addition to teaching in the elementary school there, he also assisted at many baptisms, weddings, and funerals, and heard thousands of confessions.

In 1975, Father Cardy was assigned Assistant Director of Novices at St. Paschal Friary in Oak Brook, Illinois. He found this "a most challenging job." In 1976, he and the novices were asked to move some 500 miles north to St. Agnes Friary and Parish in Ashland, Wisconsin. There, with five men who had just completed their one-year noviceship, he, at his Province's request, established an Apostolic Year of Formation as a kind of second year of novitiate. This concentrated on apostolic work suited to the novices. After one full year at Ashland, he was requested to move the whole training program to Indianapolis, Indiana, to Sacred Heart Friary and Parish. This was larger and, therefore, more capable of housing the increasing numbers of young Franciscans. Moreover, Indianapolis, being much larger than Ashland, offered many more possibili-

ties for supervised apostolic work. He served in Indianapolis as Director of the Apostolic Year of Formation and associate pastor of Sacred Heart parish from 1977–81.

In July 1981, Father Cardy was appointed pastor of two parishes: St. Philip's in Stone Lake, Wisconsin, and St. Ignatius in New Post, Wisconsin. At the same time, he assisted at St. Francis Mission in Reserve, Wisconsin. At these latter two places, he was among the Ojibwa Indians. In 1984, he was a member of the Wisconsin Ad Hoc Commission on Racism. In his own words, he "very much enjoyed serving and learning from the Ojibwa people." During his final months among them, he was formally honored by them and given the name *Mikisi Mikwin*, "Eagle Feather." He served that northern Wisconsin area for five full years, from 1981–86.

In 1985, the Franciscan Friars of Sacred Heart Province were invited by Michael J. **Kaniecki**, S.J., Bishop of **Fairbanks**, to consider ministry among the Koyukon Athabaskan Indian people living in villages along the middle Yukon River in **Alaska**'s northern interior. After the Father Provincial of the Friars visited the area under consideration, and deemed it a field fitting for Franciscan ministry, he made known to the members of his Province that he was looking for volunteers "ready, able and willing to answer the call to Alaska, not a place for babes in the woods, but a mission demanding a great deal of self-giving and dedication."

Father Cardy, for one, heard and answered the call. On July 1, 1986, he, along with three other Friars, arrived in Fairbanks. His first assignment in Alaska was that of pastor of both Our Lady of the Snows parish in **Nulato** and of St. Teresa's parish in **Kaltag**, and of visiting priest to St. Patrick's mission in **Koyukuk**. It was not long before he found himself sharing the subsistence lifestyle of the Native people. Fishing for salmon, hunting moose, and picking berries were not mere pastimes, but ways of putting food on the table. Water for drinking and washing was hauled by bucket from the clear Nulato River two miles away. When the Yukon was paved over with ice and snow, he traveled it from village to village on a snowmachine; when it was open, by boat with an outboard motor. The year after his arrival in Nulato, he had the joy of celebrating with his people the centennial of the founding of that mission. While at Nulato, he also had the questionable joy of living through "the great cold of January 1989," when for weeks the temperature hovered between minus 40 and minus 70 degrees.

After six years on the middle Yukon—where he was by then known to be a Franciscan and not, as some people thought at first, a "Sanfriscan"—Father Cardy, in 1992, was appointed pastor of St. Theresa's parish in **Aniak**, a Central Yup'ik Eskimo village on the middle Kuskokwim River. As such, he served regularly, too, as visiting priest to **Kalskag** and **Holy Cross**. Occasionally, he visited also Crooked Creek, a village upriver on the Kuskokwim. He found this ministry to be a very demanding one, given all the travel involved and the considerable amount of manual labor that village life brings with it. He found himself "repairing steps, patching roofs, shoveling snow, painting outhouses, emptying honey buckets, cutting up fish, keeping outboard motors and snowmachines running, transferring heating oil from drums to tanks, and doing countless other mundane, down-to-earth tasks." At the same time, however, having "truly become part of the village family," he found his "tri-village, hands-on" ministry also a consoling, satisfying one. "I feel it a privilege," he wrote on the occasion of his silver jubilee as a priest, "a grace, to be near the people of my villages, as they, assisted by their faith, navigate through many of life's difficulties."

The year 1998 is one Father Cardy long remembered. The highlight of that year for him was the six-day trip to the Holy Land he made as companion to Bishop Kaniecki. This was the first time he crossed the Atlantic. Together, the two walked where Jesus walked.

Father Cardy spent eight years on the Aniak–Kalskag–Holy Cross assignment, from 1992 to the year 2000. This turned out to be his longest assignment in Alaska. Throughout it, he was blessed to have as co-ministers competent and loyal Sisters. After leaving the area, he graciously and gratefully acknowledged his indebtedness to them, mentioning them by name. They were Sisters Susan Michelle Dubec, S.S.N.D.; Linda Hogan, C.S.J.;

Anne Eveline Paquette, S.S.A.; Margaret Cantwell, S.S.A.; Maureen Freeman, C.S.J.; Paul Bernadette Bounk, C.S.J.; Anne Hogan, S.S.J.; and Frances McCarron, I.B.V.M. During his last years at Holy Cross, he had the able assistance of Jim and Mary Jean Smith, a lay couple.

In the summer of 2000, Father Cardy was assigned pastor of Our Lady of Sorrows parish in **Delta Junction** and as visiting priest to its dependent station, **Tok**. Through no fault of his own, it turned out to be, in his own words, "a very painful 100-day assignment." Because of certain internal parish problems at Delta, he was asked to withdraw from that assignment. He then relocated to Fairbanks, where he visited the prison, the hospital, and nursing homes in the area. His main duty, however, was to assist at St. Nicholas parish in **North Pole**.

Throughout his 16 years in Alaska, Father Cardy never missed a day of work. In the fall of 2002, he took a sabbatical leave. During this, he came to the conclusion that the time had come for him to undertake a new ministry elsewhere. He was assigned to the Franciscan Retreat Center in Dittmer, Missouri.

17, 18

CARLIN, Father Thomas F., S.J.

Thomas F. Carlin was born in Philadelphia, Pennsylvania, on January 17, 1939. There he attended St. Bonaventure and St. James grade schools, 1945–53; St. Joseph's Preparatory, 1953–57; and St. Joseph's University, 1957–61. He then tried the Maryknoll Seminary in New York for a year, after which he joined the **Jesuit Volunteer Corps**, and, as a member thereof, went to **Alaska** to teach Grade 8 at Immaculate Conception Grade School, **Fairbanks**, from 1963–64. There he realized his vocation to the Society of Jesus. He entered the Jesuit novitiate at Sheridan, Oregon, on September 7, 1964. On September 8, 1966, he took his vows, then went on to Mount St. Michael's, Spokane, Washington, for a year of philosophical studies. After that, he taught at Gonzaga Preparatory, Spokane, 1967–68. He was back in Alaska, at **Copper Valley School**, for the years 1968–70. His four years of theological studies he made at Woodstock College, New York City,

Father Thomas F. Carlin, S.J. *BR*-897735.

1970–74. He spent the year 1974–75 teaching Religion at Monroe Catholic High School, Fairbanks. He was ordained a priest by Robert L. **Whelan**, S.J., Bishop of Fairbanks, on September 4, 1976, at Elkins Park, Pennsylvania.

Father Carlin began his priestly ministry in Alaska at **Chevak**, 1976–77. At the University of Alaska–Fairbanks the following year, he studied the Inupiaq Eskimo language. Next he was stationed on **Little Diomede** Island, for the years 1978–83. During his first year there, with the considerable help of Jesuit Lay Brothers Ignatius J. **Jakes** and James J. Lee, he built a new church. From September 1981 to June 1982, he made his tertianship in Spokane, after which he again returned to Little Diomede. From 1983–85, he was pastor of St. Joseph's parish in **Nome**.

Father Carlin's approach to life was intense and rigid, with a tight grip on rules and regulations. He made decisions with great deliberation and difficulty. It was, therefore, with considerable personal delight on the part of Father Louis L. **Renner**, S.J., that, on July 2, 1984, he watched Father Carlin, as he, in a rare moment of total relaxation, excitedly cast for and hooked silver salmon off a bridge half way between Nome and **Council**. The trip to Council was made to oblige a woman who had begged Father Carlin to drive her to her home there. The fishing interlude took place when the two priests were on the way back to Nome.

From 1985–87, Father Carlin was out of Alaska, engaged in pastoral work, first at West Yellowstone, Montana, then at St. Luke's parish in Woodburn, Oregon. In July 1987, he returned to Alaska to take up station in **Kotzebue**. There, as at his other posts, he laid much stress on catechizing, especially as it concerned children. He devised his own plan of teaching. His people found in him a compassionate, caring priest.

In 1995, Father Carlin was assigned to minister to the people of **St. Michael**, **Stebbins**, and **Unalakleet**. While on that assignment, he contracted cancer. Being a very private person, he put off making known the rapidly deteriorating condition of his health, until it was too late. On his own, in July 1999, he went to Fairbanks, where he spent a few weeks in the Jesuit Residence, and then a few days in the Fairbanks hospital. On the 24th, accompanied by Father **Joseph E. Laudwein**, S.J., he was medivaced to Spokane in a plane piloted by Father James A. **Sebesta**, S.J. He died in the Gonzaga University infirmary the following day, the 25th. He lies buried in the Jesuit cemetery at Mount St. Michael's, Spokane.

CARLO, Dr. Poldine

At her baptism she was named for a Sister of St. **Ann**. As an octogenarian she was awarded an honorary doctorate. She sang songs in her Native language at the burials of two of northern **Alaska**'s bishops. The memory of the death of her son inspired her to write a book. Being wholly bicultural and bilingual, she was equally at home in small Native villages on the Yukon River and in northern Alaska's largest city.

Poldine Carlo was born to James Demoski and Priscilla Stickman at **Nulato** on December 5, 1920. (Her first name derives from that of Mother Mary Leopoldine, General Superior of the Sisters of St. Ann, who visited Nulato shortly after Poldine's birth.) Poldine's father drowned, on October 12, 1922, while he was crossing the Yukon River in a canoe to check his fishwheel. When Poldine was eight years old, her mother died of tuberculosis. Consequently, Poldine was raised by her grandparents, Joseph and Anna Stickman—"two of the

Dr. Poldine Carlo.
Courtesy of Dr. Carlo.

most powerful medicine people along the Yukon"—both in the Catholic Faith and, in part, "in the old beliefs and old ways." Throughout her long life she remained most loyal both to the Catholic Faith and to what is best in the Koyukon Athabaskan Indian way of life.

Her earliest education Poldine received at the hands of the Sisters of St. Ann, who staffed the Catholic grade school at Nulato. In an interview she recalled "I stayed in the fifth grade for five years, because they didn't have a sixth, seventh, or eighth." Many years later she still remembered the name of her grade school teacher "dear Sister Mary Claude. She had a heart of gold."

When Poldine was 16, she left the "peaceful, happy life" of Nulato to attend school briefly in Eklutna, Alaska. After that, she worked as a nurse in the hospital at **Tanana** for three years. It was there, at a St. Patrick's Day dance, that she met her future husband, William Carlo, a gold miner. The two were married in **Ruby** on March 19, 1940. The first of their eight children, five boys and three girls, was not long in coming. Concerning motherhood, Poldine wrote in her book, *Nulato: An Indian Life on the Yukon*, "When you are going to have a baby, you are not afraid. The thought of something going wrong never enters your mind. You are a woman. This is expected of you. This is your thing."

Nor is it expected of a woman and mother that she should take lightly the sudden death of one of her children. The whole Carlo family was deeply saddened, on October 3, 1975, when their son and brother, Stewart Allen, was killed suddenly in an automobile accident. Three years later, in 1978, the above mentioned book, dedicated to the memory of Stewart Allen, was published.

The Carlo family first lived in Ruby, from 1940–55, while they worked at a gold mine on Ophir Creek. They then made their home in **Galena** for two years, before moving on to **Fairbanks**. By living in Fairbanks, the children did not have to be sent away for high school. It was in Fairbanks that Poldine herself, although she had "learned a lot from the missionaries," and was already past her fiftieth birthday, earned, after only three months of schooling, her high school diploma. As a counterbalance to Fairbanks city life, the Carlos spent summers in Rampart mining gold and fishing.

Two years after Poldine and William had celebrated their fiftieth wedding anniversary, William died, in Fairbanks, on March 22, 1992. He was buried at Nulato five days later.

On May 13, 2001, Poldine Carlo became "Dr. Carlo," when the University of Alaska–Fairbanks, at its commencement ceremony, conferred upon her the honorary degree of Doctor of Laws. She was awarded the degree in recognition of her "efforts to preserve Alaska Native cultures and to promote their impact on public policy for the State." Recognized, too, on that occasion were the facts that she had helped to create the Alaska Native Languages Program at the UA–F, that she was a founding member of the Fairbanks Native Association, and that she had, in general, contributed greatly to the preservation and handing on of traditional Koyukon Athabaskan cultural values. The citation issued at the time the honorary doctorate was granted her stated that "she is considered a living cultural treasure."

In Catholic circles, too, Poldine was for many decades recognized and highly admired for her deep faith and dedication to the Church. At the burial ceremonies both of Bishop Michael J. **Kaniecki**, S.J., and of Bishop Robert L. **Whelan**, S.J., it was she who led the singing of songs in the Koyukon language.

"For me," Poldine said at the end of an interview

held on June 20, 1987, "life has been beautiful. I have never known what it is to have a depressed feeling. There is so much for me to do in life. There just isn't enough time." As of the year 2004, life was still beautiful and good for Poldine, and she continued to be most grateful to God for that.

19

CARROLL, Father George E., S.J.

Obituary notices identified him as "everybody's friend," as "a lovable person, so friendly and sweet."

George E. Carroll was born on January 30, 1905, in Warrenpoint, County Down, Ireland. His father died when he was still a boy. His mother supported her seven children, George and his three older brothers and three younger sisters, mostly by cooking up and selling marmalade made from orange peelings collected by the children. Throughout his long life he always had a fondness for marmalade.

His grade and high schooling George received from the Presentation Brothers. For two years then he worked as a cashier in a bank. On September 14, 1927, having already been accepted for the California Province as a volunteer for its missions in **Alaska**, he entered the novitiate of the Society of Jesus at Tullabeg, Ireland. After two years there, he spent a year at Rathfarnham Castle, County Dublin. In 1930, he came to the United States to continue his studies at Los Gatos, California. After one year, he went on to spend three years in philosophical studies at Mount St. Michael's, Spokane, Washington. He next taught chemistry for three years, 1934–37, at Gonzaga University and Gonzaga High School, Spokane. From 1937–41, he studied theology at Milltown Park, Dublin, Ireland. There he was ordained a priest on July 31, 1940. He made his tertianship at Rathfarnham Castle, 1941–42. After returning to the United States, he taught Mathematics at Seattle College during the year 1942–43.

Father Carroll first went to Alaska in 1943. He had initially become interested in Alaska as a young boy, when he saw photos of Seward Peninsula Eskimos taken by Father Joseph **Bernard**, S.J. **Holy Cross Mission** was Father Carroll's first

Father George E. Carroll, S.J. *LR.*

Alaskan assignment. There, for three years, he was Father Minister, catechism teacher, and visiting priest to nearby villages. While at Holy Cross, he gained some notoriety by taking dips in holes chopped through the ice on the Yukon.

During Holy Week of 1946, Father Carroll was sent, unexpectedly, to **Kotzebue** to replace Father Paul C. **O'Connor**, S.J., who was in need of medical attention. Father Carroll spent the years 1946–51 at Kotzebue. As did priests there before him, so he, too, found this a difficult assignment, not so much because of the remoteness and the harsh climate of the place, but because of the religious indifference of many of his parishioners and lax morals of the whole community, in general.

In October 1951, Father Carroll "got a rushed call at Kotzebue" to go to **King Island**. Thereupon he began to minister to the King Islanders, on their island during the winters and in **Nome** during the summers, until April 1960. In 1997, the story of his arrival at King Island was made into a highly successful musical, *King Island Christmas*.

One winter day, while on King Island, Father Carroll came close to losing his life. He was out sliding with the youngsters. On one trip down from high up on the island, he lost control. The next thing he knew, he found himself in his quarters with bruises, a big bump on his head, and several cracked ribs.

He had no recollection whatever of what happened between the time he was flying down the steep slope out of control and the time he came to his senses in his living quarters at the far end of the small chapel. People who witnessed his scary adventure assured him that he had acted quite normally throughout the whole of it, and that he had even stopped briefly to pray in the chapel.

While Father Carroll found his winters on King Island exciting and satisfying ones, they did take their toll on him. The April 26, 1960, entry in the Nome house diary reads: "Fr. Carroll arrived from K.I. about 11:45 A.M. by Munz Airways. Fr. C. was not himself—physically and mentally worn out." After being together for almost ten years, the King Islanders and Father Carroll were of one mind and one heart. Twenty-five years after he left the island, he was still offering Mass on the Feast of Christ the King for those King Islanders living in **Fairbanks** and in **Anchorage**.

Father Carroll spent the years 1960–63 as assistant pastor of St. Joseph's parish in Nome. After almost 20 years among the Eskimo people, he then found himself, from 1963–69, ministering to the Koyukon Athabaskan Indian people of the middle Yukon River region. He was stationed at **Galena**, out of which he cared also for the villages of **Huslia** and **Ruby**. At the same time, he served as auxiliary military chaplain to the Galena and Campion Air Force Bases. Long after he had left that area, people from there kept asking anyone who knew him, "And how is Father Carroll?"

Father Carroll spent the 1970s ministering as assistant pastor of Sacred Heart Cathedral in Fairbanks, and the 1980s, his last decade in Alaska, offering home Masses, visiting faithfully the elderly, shut-ins, the sick in the hospital and in the convalescent home. In spite of his own health problems (he had had both hip joints replaced, had undergone major eye surgery, and had had a kidney removed) he was always upbeat, cheerful, cheering others up with his inexhaustible wellspring of Irish wit and stories. His many friends—and he had only friends—kept the phone and the doorbell ringing for him. He was available at all hours for any callers. There was a tremendous energy about him. Generously he did the grocery shopping for the community in which he lived, and regularly he took a turn as cook on weekends. Stews seasoned just so and sour milk raisin bread were among his specialties.

On April 12, 1989, on an Alaska Airlines jet, accompanied by Father Louis L. **Renner**, S.J., Father Carroll left Alaska to spend the remainder of his days in the infirmary at Gonzaga University, Spokane. There, on September 6, 1990, while listening to his mail from family and friends being read to him, he lapsed into a coma and died peacefully.

To his dying day, Father George E. Carroll, S.J., remained an ardent Notre Dame football fan, a staunch Republican, a tribute to his Irish origins, a faithful Jesuit, and, above all, a truly priestly priest. He lies buried in the Jesuit cemetery at Mount St. Michael's, Spokane.

171

CARROLL, Father John B., S.J.

John B. Carroll was born in Steir Horn Neck, St. Mary County, Maryland, on March 8, 1866. He entered the Jesuit novitiate at Frederick, Maryland, on August 13, 1885. During the early 1890s, as a member of the California Province, he studied philosophy at Gonzaga College in Spokane, Washington, and, during the latter 1890s, theology at St. Ignatius Mission, Montana. He was ordained a priest on May 19, 1899. As a young priest, he worked among the Indians of Montana. He arrived in **Nome**, **Alaska**, on August 18, 1905, and served there till August 30, 1908, when Superiors recalled him to work again among the Indians of Montana. Father Bellarmine **Lafortune**, S.J., wrote in the Nome house diary that Father Carroll was recalled "to our regret." Father Carroll was a well-liked, zealous priest while in Nome, in spite of the fact that he saw that gold-rush city as a place where "gold abounded, and wickedness did still more abound." At St. Leo's parish in Tacoma, Washington, he spent the last four years of his life. He died in San Francisco on August 7, 1920.

Father Richard D. Case, S.J.
Courtesy of Fr. Case.

CASE, Father Richard, D., S.J.

Richard D. Case was born in Seattle, Washington, on May 9, 1942. His elementary schooling he received at St. Joseph's Grade School; his secondary, at Jesuit-staffed Seattle Preparatory. After graduating from high school in 1960, he attended the University of Washington for a quarter, then Seattle University for two and a half years. There he majored in business and economics. While attending Seattle University, he qualified as a flight instructor and taught flying at Renton Airport for two years. From June to August 1963, starting and ending in Seattle, he made an 80-day trip around the world, visiting Japan, Southeast Asia, India, Africa, South and Central America.

On September 7, 1963, Richard entered the Jesuit novitiate at Sheridan, Oregon, following in the footsteps of his brother, Frank, who had entered the Jesuits seven years earlier. After completing his two-year noviceship, Richard spent a third year at Sheridan studying the classics and humanities. During the years 1966–69, he made his philosophical studies at St. Louis University in St. Louis, Missouri. While making them, he earned an M.A. degree in economics. In the fall of 1969, having obtained his Washington State Teacher's Certificate from Gonzaga University in Spokane, Washington, he began a three-year teaching assignment at Gonzaga

Preparatory in Spokane. His theological studies he made in Amsterdam, in the Netherlands, from 1972–75. He was ordained a priest in Seattle on June 21, 1975, by Archbishop Raymond G. Hunthausen. After spending his first summer as a priest serving as a chaplain at Providence Hospital in Seattle, he returned to Gonzaga Preparatory to teach Religion and work in the campus ministry program.

In the summer of 1970, Father Case, not yet a priest then, had been sent to **Alaska**, "to learn about the missions." In **Fairbanks**, he participated in the Upward Bound program at the University of Alaska–Fairbanks as a tutor-counselor for Native American high school students. Years later, he recalled: "Fairbanks seemed a bit isolated and wild. Just over the hills, in any direction, was open tundra, with no roads and no population. Quite frankly, the vastness of the state frightened me a little." However, after he was introduced to bush Alaska by pre-eminent Jesuit pilot Father James A. **Sebesta** that same summer, he came to see the wilds of Alaska in a new light. The summer of 1971, he again spent time in Alaska, this time with Father William C. **Dibb**, S.J. The experiences of those two summers sparked in him a love for Alaska and its people, and convinced him that his calling as a priest was to serve the people of Alaska.

Father Case began his missionary career in Alaska by first ministering in **Emmonak**, from June 14 to August 3, 1976. Beginning in August 1976 and continuing to July 1977, he lived in Fairbanks and attended classes in Central Yup'ik Eskimo at the University of Alaska–Fairbanks. During that year, he flew to **McGrath** every other weekend to hold services. In the spring of 1977, he spent two months there. In July 1977, he began serving the villages of **Chevak** and **Newtok**, a ministry he was obliged to leave in December 1978, when he was called to Spokane to begin his tertianship in January 1979. With a mandate to care for the people of the villages of **Tununak**, **Toksook Bay**, and **Nightmute**, he returned to Alaska in July 1979. This assignment lasted until 1984. During the years 1983–85, he headed up a special Diocesan Planning Task Force. This entailed travel to meetings taking place in a considerable number of different towns and villages.

From 1984–87, Father Case was Director of the

Center for Spirituality and Theology for the Development of Ministries. As such, he resided in **Bethel** for the first year, then at St. Mary's Mission on the **Andreafsky** River for the following two years. On July 31, 1987, he was named Rector of the Jesuit Community at Bellarmine Preparatory in Tacoma, Washington. However, before his normal three-year term there was up, he found himself at Gonzaga Preparatory, having been hired, in 1989, by the Board of Directors of that school to be its president. When his term as president ended in 1995, he took time out for a sabbatical.

By 1996, Father Case was again back in Alaska, now as Director of the **Eskimo Deacon Program** and assisting with the Native Ministry Training Program. Residing at St. Mary's Mission, he served in those two capacities for four years.

On August 6, 2000, Michael J. **Kaniecki**, S.J., Bishop of Fairbanks, died unexpectedly. Four days later, on August 10th, Father Case was serving the Diocese of Fairbanks as Diocesan Administrator, having been chosen for that position by the Diocesan Consultors. As Diocesan Administrator, he had, from the outset, the respect and confidence of the diocesan priests and of his fellow Jesuits. Overnight the chancery staff, too, warmed to his good-natured and approachable demeanor. Lucy Dalsky, veteran chancery member, spoke for all, when she said: "After the bishop's death, we felt truly orphaned, but Father Case brought a sense of tranquility, peace, and unity that soon convinced everyone he was the ideal savior in the middle of tragedy."

Father Case saw his role as Diocesan Administrator as essentially a caretaker role. "My job," he told a reporter, "is to keep out of the way of good people, and let them do their work." When, on October 23, 2001, Michael W. **Warfel**, Bishop of **Juneau**, was appointed Apostolic Administrator of the Diocese of Fairbanks, he asked Father Case to continue the day-to-day administration of the diocese as his assistant, with the authority and power equivalent to that of a Vicar General. On August 22, 2002, the day Donald J. **Kettler** was ordained and installed as Bishop of Fairbanks, Father Case became Chancellor of the Diocese of Fairbanks, a position he held until August 31, 2004. On December 1, 2004, he was assigned the pastoral care of the villages of **Galena**, **Nulato**, **Koyukuk**, and **Huslia**.

CATALDO, Father Joseph M., S.J.

A town in Idaho, and a street in Spokane, Washington, are named for him. He knew the warmth of sunny Sicily and the sub-arctic cold of northwestern **Alaska**. He was familiar with the numerous Indian tribes of America's Pacific Northwest, with the Koyukon Athabaskan Indians of Alaska's interior, as well as with the Inupiat Eskimos of Alaska's Seward Peninsula. He was a master linguist. He was a Superior much of his life as a priest. A slight man, he reminded the Indians of a dried salmon, hence they nicknamed him "Dried Salmon." Not expected to live into old age, he died at the age of 92; and, according to historian Father Segundo **Llorente**, S.J., "passed into history as one of the great Missionaries of all times."

Joseph M. Cataldo was born, on March 17, 1837, at Terrasini, Sicily. In spite of poor health in his youth, he was allowed to enter the Jesuit novitiate of the Sicilian Province on December 23, 1852. He received part of his early Jesuit training in Rome. There he volunteered to serve on the Jesuits' Rocky Mountain Mission. He went on to complete theological studies in Louvain, Belgium, where he was ordained a priest on September 8, 1862. Immediately after his ordination, he came to America, to Boston, to learn English.

During his first winter in America, Father Cataldo developed an illness that was diagnosed as tuberculosis. In 1863, his Superiors sent him to Santa Clara College, California, to recover his health. The California climate agreed with him, so much so that by 1865 he saw fit to volunteer again for the Rocky Mountain Mission. He was accepted, and assigned to work among the Coeur d'Alène and Spokane Indians. Ultimately, however, he became most closely associated with the Nez Percé of present-day Idaho. For them, and in their language, he wrote a prayer book and a life of Christ.

From June 16, 1877, to March 24, 1893, Father Cataldo was General Superior of the Rocky Mountain Mission. In 1883, he founded Gonzaga College, in Spokane, Washington. In 1885, Charles J. **Seghers**, Archbishop of Vancouver Island at the time, appealed to him in hopes of attracting Jesuits to the Alaska Mission. Despite the opposition of his advisors, who feared the loss of personnel from their own field of responsibility, Father Cataldo allowed Fathers

Paschal **Tosi** and Aloysius J. **Robaut** to accompany the archbishop north in 1886 on what was to be the last journey of his life. The two were allowed to accompany him simply as trail companions, "on loan," "only for a visit," and "to scout out the country." It was not intended that they stay in Alaska on a permanent basis. Nevertheless, in the spring of 1887, when Father Tosi learned of the fatal shooting of the archbishop on November 28, 1886, and reported the matter to Father Cataldo, the latter, then and there, took it upon himself to have the Jesuits take on the responsibility of the Alaska Mission. The decision, however, was subject to the approval of the Father General in Rome. Upon learning the circumstances of the events of 1886–87, Father General, Anthony Anderledy, gave his approval.

Not only did Father Cataldo embrace the Alaska Mission as part of the Rocky Mountain Mission, but he "assigned" himself to serve in Alaska for a total of three years. He spent part of the summer of 1896 at **Holy Cross Mission** and the winter 1896–97 at **Akulurak**. From September 1901 to July 1902, he was at **Nulato**, among the Koyukon Athabaskan Indians. He immediately set about learning the local Native language and produced a Koyukon–English dictionary.

On August 1, 1902, Father Cataldo arrived in **Nome**. There, on December 23rd, by the celebration of his golden jubilee as a Jesuit, he was, providentially, to help dispel the cloud of ill will and bitterness that still hung over the Nome Jesuits and their work because of the Father **Jacquet** affair.

In Nome, Father Cataldo found himself among the Inupiat Eskimos. Being the linguist that he was, he began immediately to learn their language, Inupiaq Eskimo, and to evangelize them. He was the first Jesuit to come in contact with the Inupiat Eskimos. On July 16, 1903, Father Bellarmine **Lafortune**, S.J., arrived in Nome, with Holy Cross his intended first Alaskan assignment. "However," he wrote from Nome some years later, "Rev. Fr. Cataldo, seeing the number of Eskimos who were around here without pastor, stopped me and obtained the Superior's permission to keep me here. That permission was granted to him, and so it happened that I stayed here. From that time on, I had the charge of the Eskimos." Father Cataldo postponed his trip to Spokane for two weeks to teach Father Lafortune what he knew of the Nome Eskimo dialect.

When Father Lafortune's fellow Jesuit Alaskan missionary, Father Martin J. **Lonneux**, S.J., wanted to give him the honorific title of "Catholic Apostle of the Seward Peninsula and Bering Strait Eskimos," Father Lafortune objected vehemently. To Father Lonneux he wrote, on June 12, 1922: "You are wrong to call me the apostle of the Eskimos, and I want that to be taken out of your history entirely. Father Cataldo is the one who started the work among the Eskimos here. In spite of his old age, he tackled the language, and became able to teach them the rudiments of religion. The first Catholic Eskimos were instructed and baptized by him."

After his year in Nome, Father Cataldo was back once more among the Indians of the Pacific Northwest for another quarter century. Even into his 80s, he continued to be a tireless, fearless traveler, from Indian community to Indian community, in all kinds of weather, over all kinds of roads and trails. With each passing year, he increased his knowledge of, and sensitivity to, the Native peoples, their languages, and their cultures. For his honesty and devotion to them, the people he dealt with, no matter in what capacity, respected him.

Father Cataldo died, in Pendleton, Oregon, on April 9, 1928, in his 92nd year of life and in his 75th year as a Jesuit. He was first buried in Pendleton, then later reburied in the Jesuit cemetery at Mount St. Michael's, by Spokane. So great was his priestly service to Alaska and the Northwest that the editors of the *Gonzaga University Quarterly* of 1928 excused themselves from a full obituary with the remark that his accomplishments "dazed our scribes, and left them mute admirers of what they could not express."

CHANELIAK (CHANILIUT)

The Central Yup'ik Eskimo village of Chaneliak was located two miles southeast of Pastol Bay, near **Kotlik**, virtually at the northern mouth of the Yukon River. During the early 1900s, it was visited from time to time by priests stationed at **Akulurak** or **St. Michael**. Baptisms took place at Chaneliak as early as 1899. On November 26, 1924, Father John B. **Sifton**, S.J., more or less formally opened a mission station at Chaneliak by having a building put up there. "In the winter of 1925," wrote Father Martin J. **Lonneux**, S.J., some years later, "I visited Fr. Sifton in this place and nearly froze to death. Father himself told me that the building was put up by a native during his absence and was a fiasco. The material was second hand lumber too and, as the supply was far short, only one board was put on the inside. When I succeeded Fr. Sifton in 1928, and came here in winter, I could not warm up the building enough and there was always frost on the walls of the sanctuary. On windy days, I had a hard time to prevent the cruets from freezing." In an attempt to provide some insulation, Father Lonneux covered the inside walls with oil cloth.

Chaneliak was never a real village, according to Father Lonneux, "but a sort of winter camp." When he first started to go there, only five houses and the church building occupied the site. Then a government school was built there. By 1938, Chaneliak had grown considerably, to 24 houses. To accommodate the greatly increased population, Father Lonneux enlarged the church, dedicated to St. Margaret, and built priest's quarters and a shop on to it.

Until 1954, Chaneliak continued to be served by priests stationed at St. Michael. During the year 1954–55, Father Paul H. **Linssen**, S.J., ministered there out of **Hamilton**. The following year, he resided there. From 1956, until it ceased to exist entirely (around 1965), after most of the people had moved to Kotlik, it was again served out of St. Michael, mainly by Father René **Astruc**, S.J. The church was taken down in the early 1960s and the lumber salvaged for use in Kotlik.

St. Margaret's Church and school, Chaneliak. *JOPA-172.1.01.*

CHAPDELAINE, Father Joseph A., S.J.

Joseph A. Chapdelaine was born in Canada on March 10, 1868. He entered the Society of Jesus on September 23, 1889, and was ordained a priest on July 27, 1902. In 1907, he went to **Alaska**, where he spent the years 1907–09 at **St. Michael**, the year 1909–10 at **Akulurak**, and the years 1910–17 again at St. Michael. While stationed both at Akulurak and St. Michael, he made missionary excursions to outlying villages. He made regular visits to **Stebbins** and **Unalakleet**. Three weeks after Father Chapdelaine departed St. Michael for his home Province of French Canada, Father Anthony M. **Keyes**, S.J., wrote in the house diary of that station: "The people talk very highly of Fr. Chapdelaine as a man of mortification to a fault and of great zeal for the Natives." Father Chapdelaine died in Montreal on April 28, 1936.

CHEFORNAK

The Central Yup'ik Eskimo village of Chefornak is located at the junction of the Keguk and Kinia Rivers, a little southeast of Nelson Island, in the Yukon-Kuskokwim Delta. According to the 1990 census, it had a population of 320, virtually all Catholic. Ten years later, it had 394.

Chefornak first appears in Catholic Church records in 1937, when Father Paul C. **Deschout**, S.J., baptized many children and adults there. St. Catherine of Siena has, from the outset, been the patron saint of the Chefornak parish. The present village was formed in the early 1950s, when people relocated from the old Chefornak village site, two miles distant, to the new one, because the Bureau of Indian Affairs chose this high ground on which to build the school. The old village site flooded at least once annually. The first Chefornak church was built around 1952. This burned to the ground on March 4, 1972. The present church, built by the people themselves, without any outside funding sources, was begun in the fall of 1975, and blessed in November 1976.

Father Deschout, greatly assisted by some outstanding catechists, interpreters and translators, was the principal missionary to all the Nelson Island area villages, Chefornak included. In the 1940s, he wrote: "I am miles away from my beloved nest on Nelson Island at a place called Chfrnk (without vowels), where there is no teacher, no postmaster, no white man, but a fine group of natives, and all of them Catholic, keeping me on the go. The men-folk are away now for mink. The women-folk are wearing out the floor of the church. Can't keep them out of church, daily communicants, etc. . . the Eskimos here are living saints." From 1937–56 and 1960–61, out of **Tununak**, Father Deschout ministered to the people of Chefornak.

The following Jesuit Fathers, too, have ministered to the people of Chefornak: Paul H. **Linssen** (out of Tununak), 1956–58, and (in residence), 1958–60; James E. **Jacobson** (in residence), 1961–66; Francis J. **Fallert** (out of **Toksook Bay**), 1974–75; Norman E. **Donohue** (in residence), 1975–83; Thomas G. **Provinsal** (in residence), 1986–91; Eugene P. **Delmore** (in residence or out of Toksook Bay), 1991–94; Paul M. **Cochran** (in residence or out of St. Marys), 1994–97, and 2000 to the present (2004); Mark A. **Hoelsken** (in residence and out of St. Marys), 1997–2001.

Father John A. **Hinsvark**, priest of the Diocese of Fairbanks, was in residence in Chefornak from 1966–74, and ministered in Chefornak out of **Hooper Bay** from 1983–86.

Eskimo Deacons, too, have served and are serving their Chefornak parish: Cyril Alexie, David Erik, David Panruk, and Joe Avugiak.

Sisters Jeannette LaRose and Patricia Richard, both Sisters of St. **Ann**, split their time during the years 1983–88 between Chefornak—"a real gem on the tundra," in the words of Sister Jeannette—and **Nightmute**. Regarding their mission in those two villages, Sister Jeannette wrote, "It is to impart Adult Religious Education, to prepare catechists, and to minister in any other way opened to us at the moment." As need arose, the two also did some substitute teaching in the school, "our favorite way of reaching the children."

Mention must be made here also of Agnes Kairaiuak, competent and faithful parish administrator at Chefornak beginning 1990.

When Father Donohue died, on October 24, 1983, in **Anchorage**, the people of Chefornak requested that he be buried in Chefornak, saying, "We were his family; he is one of us. We ask that his body be laid to rest in our village." Their request was granted.

St. Catherine of Siena Church, Chefornak. *DFA.*

Along with the story of Chefornak, must be re-told here also the story of Chefornak resident, Agnes Matthew, "forever a child of God." The story was first told by Father Provinsal in 1988.

~

The small bush plane approaching Chefornak is still but a tiny speck on the distant horizon, but already Agnes Matthew is hurriedly making her way up to the landing strip to meet this plane—as she does every plane. By the time the plane circles and lands, a small group of villagers has gathered at the unloading zone to meet and greet arriving passengers, and to pick up eagerly awaited packages and mail. Walking with short, cautious steps, her toes pointed inward, her smiling, ruddy face turned down and away into the fingers of her right hand, Agnes moves along the edge of the little crowd. She is waiting, expectantly, longingly, for her mother to arrive. (Her mother died in an Anchorage hospital many years ago.) Agnes is now 48 years old, but, gifted with the mind of only about a five-year old, ever a child on this earth—until, someday, forever a child of God in the kingdom of heaven.

Agnes Matthew is probably in the best physical condition of anyone in Chefornak. She spends much of her time out of doors. Often she can be seen running about with the little girls in a friendly game of tag, her lightly clenched fists jabbing the air as she gives gleeful chase or takes flight in feigned terror—her rather ponderous, shambling gait in marked contrast to the lithe sprints of her playmates.

When her playmates are in school, Agnes can be seen patrolling the village boardwalks—and this in all kinds of weather. She prefers the teeth of the stiff northeast wind to the stuffy indoor air of overheated houses, and solitary roaming to tea sipping and soap opera watching. Even in the dark of winter, and even in blizzard conditions, her lone phantomlike form can be seen moving about the village.

There is a knock on my door. I open it, and find two small girls staring at me. The older one pulls her little cousin back out of the way, and they allow Agnes to enter ahead of them. When Agnes comes to visit me, she almost always first recruits several tykes to serve her as a vanguard. She is not really afraid of priests, but simply too shy to come alone.

Generally her little companions also stay on. They go into our game and toy room to play a while. I continue to work at my desk, as Agnes visits with me, chattering about her adventures and how this or that playmate tagged her too hard. I ask her if she would like to join me in a cup of coffee. Politely she accepts my offer. As we sip away, she again and again asks me if she might bring up the gifts at today's late-afternoon Mass. And daily she asks about her birthday: Is it close, or is it far? Soon she hears a plane approaching. She wants to run off to meet it. I dissuade her by whispering to her the secret that soon George might come and then we can play cards. She sits down again. When Agnes has "something important" to tell me, she squints severely, cups her hands around her mouth, and whispers the words. Her secrets are hard to hear—but it is harder still to ignore them.

Soon George does indeed come, and we play a card game. Suddenly she reminds me that no music is coming from the tape recorder. She enjoys whatever she hears, be it Perry Como or something out of Aida. She asks only that the music be not too loud. As soon as a selection is over, she says, "Next!"

Before Agnes ends her visit and card playing, she glances around to see if anything is out of place or in disorder. If so, she sees to it that everything is made right again. Sometimes she asks for the broom, and then she goes into the church to sweep the floor and to straighten up the hymnals and prayer books.

It is nearing the time for the daily afternoon weekday Mass. I ring the first bell. Soon Agnes is in the porch

AGNES MATTHEW: FOREVER A CHILD OF GOD

Agnes Matthew in St. Catherine of Siena Church, Chefornak,
posing with the ciborium containing hosts to be consecrated during a Mass.
Photo by Fr. Thomas G. Provinsal, S.J.

of the church, eager to help get things set up. She fetches the Sacramentary from the sacristy chest and hustles it to its place near the presider's chair. Soon she is back to bring the Communion breads and the ciborium to the little table standing just inside the church entrance. However, when children come in, she begins to play with them and tell them little stories. They giggle with her. Pretty soon the noise gets to be a little much for those at prayer inside the church, and I remind her that she must be quiet. Touching her forefinger to her tightly compressed lips, she goes to her usual place. There she waits for Mass to begin. She is now serious, silent, expectant.

The homily and prayers of general intercession are over. The moment for the bringing up of the gifts for the Holy Sacrifice has come. Back by the church door, on a little table, the hosts lie in the shiny ciborium set next to the cruets holding the wine and the water. I prepare the chalice and paten on the altar table, then step around to wait for the gifts to be brought forward. Agnes is sitting near the door, her forearms resting on the brown wooden ledge of the pew in front of her. She glances about to see who will take up the gifts. She waits. Others wait. Then, with hushed, whispering voice and jerky gestures, she beckons to one of the folks near her to help her bring me the gifts. Grasping the ciborium firmly with both hands, she confidently and triumphantly leads the two-person procession up the aisle. Reverently she releases the ciborium into my hands, and with eyes cast down returns to her place to

await the moment of Holy Communion. This small, gift-bearing ritual is, along with receiving Holy Communion, her supreme daily delight. Every day she asks me at least a half dozen times if she might: "Tonight itrachik?" Agnes, remarkably, is bilingual. At times she intermingles her native Central Yup'ik Eskimo language with English. This phrase translates roughly, "Will bring something in."

After Mass, Agnes reminds me that she must get the book from near the presider's chair. And, if there was no altar boy in attendance, she then takes the snuffer and "turns off" the waxen candles on the altar and by "the little house," her name for the tabernacle. Next she draws my attention to any other details in the sanctuary and sacristy that I may have overlooked and need to be taken care of. Agnes always shows a general concern for neatness and orderliness in our parish church. Finally, we turn off the lights and head home: I to watch the Alaska State Evening News on bush Alaska's one-channel satellite TV hookup, Agnes to have supper. She lives with and is cared for lovingly by her brother Peter Matthew and his wife Mary.

A final reflection: Manifestly, but mysteriously, Agnes has a mature affinity with the Christ of the Sacrament. And Christ greets her with the same intimate communion with which He greets any of us, saint or sinner. In a special way, the Supreme Lord and Shepherd embraces tenderly Chefornak's precious lamb, Agnes Matthew—forever a child of God.

In the home of Sister Rose Beck, S.S.N.D., in Chevak,
after a Confirmation liturgy, Bishop Michael J. Kaniecki, S.J.,
relaxes with a gleeful group of young Chevakers. *LR.*

CHEVAK

The Central Yup'ik Eskimo village of Chevak is located on the right bank of the Ninglikfak River, 17 miles east of **Hooper Bay**, in the Yukon-Kuskokwim Delta. The village is sometimes referred to as "New Chevak" to distinguish it from "Old Chevak," a site on the north bank of the Keoklevik River, 9 miles east of Hooper Bay. Old Chevak, being prone to flooding, was abandoned in favor of the new site in 1950. The name Chevak refers to "a connecting slough" on which Old Chevak was situated. New Chevak became the site of the post office in 1951. The population of Chevak, virtually all Catholic, sustained steady growth, from 230 in 1950, to 315 in 1960, to 387 in 1970, to 488 in 1979, to 598 in 1992, to 765 in 2000. The people of Chevak are noted for their resourcefulness, for their readiness to help themselves, for being "in control of their own destiny."

The mission in the village of Old Chevak was dedicated to St. John the Baptist. That mission is first mentioned in baptismal records for 1928. In the 1930s, people from **Kashunuk** began to move to Old Chevak, because of flooding problems at Kashunuk. It was Father **John P. Fox**, S.J, who established the mission at Old Chevak, in 1935, and had a new church and living quarters erected there by 1937. Some of the lumber used for these came from the partially dismantled Kashunuk mission. Old Chevak was served by priests stationed at Hooper Bay. New Chevak's earlier residents were mainly people who had lived in Kashunuk, and then in Old Chevak.

In 1950, Father Henry G. **Hargreaves**, S.J., with Ivan **Sipary** as foreman, and many helping hands, built a church at New Chevak. This church was dedicated to the Sacred Heart, under which title the Kashunuk mission had been dedicated. In the summer of 1982, while Father Thomas G. **Provinsal**, S.J., was pastor of Chevak, the foundation for a new church was laid by Brother Ignatius J. **Jakes**, S.J., who oversaw its construction. The men of Chevak, together with a skillful, dedicated lay volunteer, James McCroy, and Father Louis L. **Renner**, S.J, rendered noble service in hauling building materials from the boat landing to the construction site.

Sacred Heart Church, Chevak.
Photo by Fr. Gregg D. Wood, S.J.

The new church was formally dedicated on April 13, 1983, by Robert L. **Whelan**, S.J., Bishop of **Fairbanks.**

The Catholic community of Chevak has been ministered to mostly by Jesuits priests. Some made it their headquarters. Some visited it on a regular basis. Some served it for a relatively short time; others for a fair number of years. They were Fathers Hargreaves (1950–52), **John J. Wood** (1952–59), Bernard F. **McMeel** (1959–64), Francis X. **Nawn** (1964–68), William T. **McIntyre** (1968–70), James E. **Jacobson** (1970–76), Thomas F. **Carlin** (1976–77), Richard D. **Case** (1977–79), Thomas G. Provinsal (1979–86), priests from St. Mary's Mission **Andreafsky** (1990–91), Mark A. **Hoelsken** (1991–96), **Gregg D. Wood** (1996 to the present, 2004). Father John A. **Hinsvark**, priest of the Diocese of Fairbanks, tended Chevak's Sacred Heart parish, 1986–90.

Eskimo Deacons, too, have served and were serving their Chevak parish as of the year 2004: David Boyscout, Jacob Nash, and Frank Smart. Deacon Michael **Nayagak** died within weeks of his scheduled ordination to the priesthood. He lies buried in the Chevak cemetery.

School Sisters of Notre Dame Rose Andre Beck, Ann Brantmeier, and Lu Ann Jacobs were engaged in pastoral ministry in Chevak for a significant total of years.

24, 108, 207

COCHRAN, Father Paul M., S.J.

Paul Martin Cochran, the younger of two sons, was born in Walla Walla, Washington, on June 24, 1962, to Keith and Marianne Cochran. He was baptized at St. Patrick's parish in Walla Walla, his home parish until he entered the Society of Jesus 20 years later. He grew up on a wheat farm north of Walla Walla. His elementary and secondary schooling he received in Walla Walla's public schools. His living at the end of the school bus route allowed him to do plenty of reading and homework while commuting to and from school. He spent his weekends and summers working on the farm, helping with the various chores and harvest activities. This hands-on work enabled him to learn many practical and mechanical skills. He soon became adept at fixing various kinds of machinery, and, later on, also various kinds of computers.

Although Paul and his brother were not able to attend Walla Walla's Catholic schools, because the family farm was too far out of town, they did, nevertheless, receive a solid grounding in the Catholic Faith. Their parents taught them as much by example as by word. Grandparents, on both sides, by the example of their own devout lives, helped instill in the boys a deep love of God and Church.

After his graduation from Walla Walla High School in May 1980, Paul began studies in engineering and accounting at Gonzaga University in Spokane, Washington. During his second year at Gonzaga, he, in his own words, "sensed a strong and persistent call to Religious and priestly life." On August 28, 1982, he entered the Jesuit Novitiate of St. Francis Xavier in Portland, Oregon. During the course of his two-year noviceship, he had, as one of his "experiments," a six-week stay on the Coeur d'Alene Indian Reservation in Idaho. This disposed him favorably toward the prospect of one day living and working as a priest among Native Americans. It proved to be the first step along the path that eventually led him to apostolic ministry in **Alaska**.

After completing his noviceship and taking his vows, Paul was sent to Gonzaga University for further studies, especially in philosophy. By 1987, he had earned a B.A. degree in Philosophy, with a minor in Computer Science, an area that had held his interest since high school days.

From 1987–90, Paul was on the faculty of Bellarmine Preparatory School in Tacoma, Washington. There he taught in the Community Service Program and in the Computer Science Department, and assisted with retreat work. During two of his summers while in Tacoma, he lived and worked in Tacoma's L'Arche Community. He looked back upon this as "one of the greatest blessings" of his three years in Tacoma; for, as he wrote, "the warmth and openness of the core members of L'Arche helped me to see some of the deeper mysteries of God's love for people whom the world does not value or esteem."

In 1990, Paul began his theological studies at Regis College in Toronto, Ontario, Canada. From 1991–92, he was Student Council President at Regis. In the spring of 1993, he received his Master of Divinity degree from Regis, and was ordained to the transitional diaconate at the Jesuit parish of Our Lady of Lourdes in Toronto. With some sadness on his part, he then bade farewell to Toronto, and moved to the Jesuit Weston School of Theology in Cambridge, Massachusetts. There he completed his theological studies with Master of Arts and Master of Theology degrees. On June 18, 1994, he was ordained a priest in St. Joseph's Church, Seattle, Washington.

While in theological studies, Paul spent a summer living with, and being mentored by, Father Michael J. McHugh, S.J., on the Blackfoot Indian Reservation in Montana. About this same time, he came into close contact also with Father Theodore E. **Kestler**, S.J., General Superior of Jesuits in Alaska. Both brought him to consider seriously a future pastoral ministry among Native Americans. It was Father Kestler who "opened the door" to Alaska for Paul and "charted the direction" of his subsequent priestly ministry there.

Shortly after his ordination to the priesthood,

Father Paul M. Cochran, S.J.
BR-CD 0309-3274.

Father Cochran, in the summer of 1994, found himself in western Alaska, on Nelson Island, as "visiting priest" for the villages of **Chefornak**—at which he made his headquarters—**Newtok** and **Toksook Bay**. But for some limited initial contact with fellow Alaskan Jesuit missionaries and the "gentle mentoring" of veteran Alaskan missionary Father Henry G. **Hargreaves**, S.J., he was, almost from the outset of his ministry to the Central Yup'ik Eskimo people, pretty much on his own. However, given his early life on the farm and his training as a Jesuit, he quickly adapted to life and work in a different culture. He respected and took to the people, finding it "a joy to be fully present to them." They, in turn, took to him, especially the children. "Can we visit?" he commonly heard from the other side of his door shortly after he had returned to a given village. They were, of course, always welcomed in, to visit and play.

During Father Cochran's first year on Nelson Island, one of the Eskimo deacons, good-naturedly, to be sure, referred to him as "the rookie priest." On the first anniversary of his ordination, he was given the Yup'ik name of *Ungusraq*, an elder's name, to signify a transition in his life and in the lives of the people.

After "three wonderful years" among the Nelson Islanders, years that he found both an ongoing "blessing and a challenge," Father Cochran received a call from his Superior, "You're needed and wanted in another area and program. Please gather your things and move to the Yukon River area." Although ever ready to hear and heed his Superior's call, as a call coming from the Lord Himself, Father Cochran, by his own admission, found making the requested move "a difficult thing to accept and do." He had, by now, made many friends on Nelson Island, and all indications were that he had done very commendable pastoral work there.

In the summer of 1997, Father Cochran entered upon his new assignment: part-time team member of the Native Ministry Training Program—headquartered at the one-time St. Mary's Mission boarding school on the **Andreafsky** River—and visiting priest to the villages of **Marshall** and **Russian Mission**. In 1999, he left the NMTP to be full-time visiting priest to Marshall, Russian Mission, **Pilot Station**, and to tend the St. Marys parish in the fall and winter.

During the year 2000–01, Father Cochran made his nine-month tertianship at Weston, Massachusetts. For his "ministerial experience" he chose to be in Africa, to see and share in the the work that the Society of Jesus was doing there. The Regional Superior of Nigeria quickly accepted his offer to do priestly ministry, and assigned him to the bustling parish of St. Joseph in Benin City, a parish of over 12,000 parishioners. The resilience of the people, in spite of their poverty and the hardships of daily life in Africa, and the powerful expression of their Faith through song and dance had a profound, lasting impact on Father Cochran. He offered to return to Africa, to help the Jesuits build up a self-sustaining Province of the Society of Jesus there. However, in the summer of 2001, he found himself happily back in Alaska again, back again where he had first begun his Alaskan ministry, at Chefornak and Newtok. As of the Year 2004, he was still visiting priest to those two villages.

Along with being assigned visiting priest to Chefornak and Newtok, Father Cochran was made responsible also for the production of "The Lord Be With You!"—a weekly program broadcast over the Catholic radio station **KNOM**, **Nome**. The program, founded in 1990 by Father Charles J. **Peterson**, S.J., as kind of an extension of the Native Ministry Training Program, consisted, originally, of reflections on the given Sunday's gospel reading as a way to help deacons and lay preachers in villages prepare their homilies. As more and more lay Eucharistic ministers began to take various leadership roles in parish liturgies, the program, under Father Cochran's production, addressed itself also to their needs. The program was broadcast four times a week, as well as made available also on e-mail. In the course of time, it came to appeal also to a more general listening audience.

CONCANNON, Father John A., S.J.

John Aloysius Concannon was born in St. Paul, Minnesota, on January 10, 1890. His parents were Michael F. Concannon, a railroad engineer, and Briget A. Joyce. In St. Paul, he attended a public grade school, and then Gretin High School, from 1900–02. From 1903–06, he studied at Seattle College High School, and, from 1906–09, at Seattle College. He was a member of the College's first graduating class. In later years, he recalled, with a twinkle in his eye, that he was among the top third of that class, adding, "Of course, there were only three of us." His skill in college as a baseball player would have secured him a position in the Pacific League. But, instead of pursuing a career in baseball, he entered the Jesuit novitiate at Los Gatos, California, on November 13, 1909. After completing his two-year noviceship, he spent two more years there studying the classics and humanities. Next followed five years, 1913–18, of teaching and prefecting boarders at Gonzaga High School in Spokane, Washington. "I had a kid with a real good voice in my public speaking class," he related years later. "His name was Bing Crosby."

After his years of teaching and prefecting, John Concannon went on to make his philosophical studies at Mount St. Michael's, Spokane, Washington, from 1918–21. His theological studies he made at Oña, Spain, from 1921–23, and at the Pontifical Seminary in Naples, Italy, from 1923–25. He was ordained a priest at Oña, on July 30, 1923. His tertianship he made at St. Stanislaus, Parmadale, in Cleveland, Ohio, during the year 1925–26.

On August 27, 1926, Father Concannon, having volunteered to serve on the **Alaska** missions, arrived from Seattle on the *Victoria* at **Nome** to be assistant to Father Bellarmine **Lafortune**, S.J., pastor of St. Joseph's parish there. Father Concannon spent one year in that capacity. In the course of that year, he made a number of trips to the **Pilgrim Hot Springs** Mission to give retreats. On February 2, 1927, he took his final vows as a Jesuit at the Springs.

In early September 1927, Father Concannon received word that he was to go to **Nulato**. For two weeks, he was detained in Nome by stormy weather. When he finally reached **Holy Cross Mission**, he was told by his Superior, Father Philip I. **Delon**, S.J.—who saw in him "much more of a college man than a missionary," as he wrote to the Father Provincial—to stay there. This Father Concannon did, for three years, from 1927–30. He never did serve at Nulato. At Holy Cross, he did well with the children, making a specialty of teaching catechism to the older boys. He also traveled to outlying villages.

The year 1930–31 saw Father Concannon back

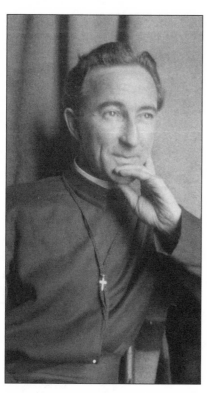

Father John A. Concannon, S.J.
JOPA-1058.01.

in the Northwest, in Seattle, at St. Joseph's Church. The following year, he was again in Alaska, as Superior at the Pilgrim Hot Springs Mission. After one year there, he spent the year 1932–33 at **Kotzebue**. Then he was in Seattle again, at Seattle College, from 1933–36. After spending the year 1936–37 as assistant pastor of St. Stanislaus parish in Lewiston, Idaho, he returned once more to Alaska, to be pastor of the Nome parish for a year. He arrived in Nome on October 25, 1937, and left it on September 2, 1938. This was his last assignment in northern Alaska.

From 1938–42, Father Concannon was assistant pastor at St. Leo's parish in Tacoma, Washington. Next he assisted again at the Lewiston, Idaho, parish, from 1942–45; then he was pastor there, from 1945–51.

Father Concannon returned to Alaska, in 1951, to minister in **Ketchikan**: as pastor of Holy Name parish, as chaplain at Ketchikan General Hospital, and as visiting priest to outlying communities. In 1960, he left Alaska. He was now 70 years old.

From 1960, until his death, except for the year 1963–64, when he again served as hospital chaplain in Ketchikan, Father Concannon was the live-in hospital chaplain at St. Joseph's Hospital in Tacoma, Washington. Until the very last years of his life, he was, as a hospital chaplain, "energy itself." Every morning, after spending time in prayer, he made the rounds of the hospital to visit the patients, to "pass a cheerful minute or two" with each of the hospital's bedridden patients. "God love you, now," were his parting words to each. Being the kind man that he was, kind words came to him readily, and he made friends easily.

During the course of his long years of residency in St. Joseph's Hospital, Father Concannon became "a tradition" there. Even when he was no longer able to move about as energetically as he once did, the Sisters wanted him to stay on, in semi-retirement. He himself wished to die in the hospital. His wish was granted. In the morning of October 16, 1975, after he had watched a World Series baseball game on television the evening before, he died peacefully. He lies buried in the Jesuit cemetery at Mount St. Michael's.

CONVERT, Father Jules M., S.J.

As a young missionary in **Alaska** he traveled from mission to mission by dogteam. He was the first Jesuit priest to fly an airplane in Alaska. Near the Bering Sea coast, he built an igloo–church–residence. He was a cannery worker, a union organizer, a strike leader among Eskimo cannery workers in the Bristol Bay fishery. He helped his people organize co-op stores in their villages. He was an innovator. He was General Superior of Jesuits in Alaska. Affectionately, his fellow Alaskan Jesuits called him "Uncle Jules."

Jules M. Convert, born in Bourg-en-Bresse, France, on April 12, 1910, entered the Lyons Province of the Society of Jesus at Yzeure on October 8, 1929. After completing the two-year noviceship and two years of classical studies there, he studied philosophy, from 1933–35, at St. Helier on the British Isle of Jersey. From 1935–37, he taught at St. Joseph University in Beirut, Lebanon. While there, he also served in the French Army for a year. In October 1937, he began theological studies at Alma College, Los Gatos, California. He was ordained a priest in San Francisco on June 27, 1940. After a fourth year of theology at Alma College, he made his tertianship at Port Townsend, Washington.

Father Convert went to Alaska in 1942. After spending the summer as Father Minister at **Holy Cross Mission**, he went to **Hooper Bay**, a Central Yup'ik Eskimo village on the Bering Sea coast in western Alaska, to assist Father **John P. Fox**, S.J., and, in his own words, "to begin learning the ropes" of missionary work among the Eskimo people in that region. In 1943, he took up station at **Kashunuk**, where, out of driftwood and sod, he and the people built a semi-subterranean "igloo church" with attached priest's quarters. While stationed at Kashunuk, he also visited, by dogteam, the villages of **Scammon Bay**, Old **Chevak**, and **Keyaluvik**. In 1947, Father Convert played a major role, when he and the villagers of Kashunuk, along with their igloo church, relocated to Old Chevak, in order to be on higher ground, away from the frequent floodings and blocks of ice pushed in from the sea. The Kashunuk mission was dedicated to the Sacred Heart of Jesus. While Father Convert was there, Louis L. **Renner**, at the time an aspiring Alaskan missionary at the Jesuit novitiate at Sheridan, Oregon, kept him amply supplied with pictures and badges of the Sacred Heart.

After two years at Old Chevak, Father Convert, in 1949, was entrusted with the care of the villages of **St. Michael**, **Stebbins**, and **Unalakleet**. At this latter village, he built a chapel–residence. In the early 1950s, he also helped out ailing Father Martin J. **Lonneux**, S.J., by occasionally visiting **Chaneliak**, **Hamilton**, **Kotlik**, and Bill Moore Slough. Father Convert became a U.S. citizen in **Nome** on April 20, 1951.

During his first decade in Alaska, Father Convert spent a series of summers in the Bristol Bay area. While still in his philosophical studies, he had become interested in socio-economic questions. He had continued reading in the fields of sociology and economics also while at Alma College, little knowing then how valuable the knowledge acquired in these sciences would be to him during his early years in Alaska.

In 1946, Eskimos from the Yukon-Kuskokwim Delta began to be recruited by cannery owners in the Bristol Bay salmon canneries. Some of the missionaries working among those Eskimos feared that they would come under a bad influence while at the canneries and so make more difficult the work of the missionaries. They felt, therefore, that recruitment of "their" Eskimos should be discouraged. Father Convert opposed their "salvation by isolation" attitude. He took the opposite view, pointing out that this was the first opportunity the Native people of the Bering Sea coast had to share the benefits derived from the utilization of the natural resources of their land. In 1947, with the encouragement of Bishop Francis D. **Gleeson**, S.J, he went to Bristol Bay as "chaplain" to the Eskimos working in the canneries. By 1949, the situation there had changed. People felt concerned about a communist takeover of the unions. With Bishop Gleeson's permission, Father Convert became a priest–worker, a co-worker with the Delta Eskimos in the Libby's Cannery. Then, in his own words, "the fireworks began." Force of circumstances led to his becoming, by turns, first a union organizer, then a union delegate, and, finally, a strike leader.

In April 1954, Father Convert was appointed

Superior of Holy Cross. As such, he played a major role in the moving of the boarding school program from Holy Cross to what became **Copper Valley School**. In September 1956, he became pastor of **Kaltag**, responsible also for the villages of **Huslia**, **Koyukuk**, and Unalakleet. At Kaltag, as he had done at Stebbins, he helped the people organize a Native co-op.

In Tacoma, Washington, in 1958, Father Convert earned his pilot's license at Oswald's Flying Service. Flying instructions were given him at no cost, as they were given subsequently to other Alaskan Jesuit priests seeking a pilot's license. This was the Oswalds' way of showing their gratitude for what Bishop Gleeson (still "Father" Gleeson at the time), as Rector at Bellarmine High School, had done to make possible the schooling of their boys during the darkest days of the Great Depression. Father Convert became the first Jesuit priest to fly in Alaska. Henceforth, he made the rounds of his mission stations in his own plane, a Piper Super Cub.

In 1964, Father Convert was appointed General Superior of Jesuits in Alaska. He continued, however, to live at Kaltag. The following year, he oversaw the construction of a new church–residence there. In 1967, on orders from the Jesuit Father General, he left Kaltag and made **Fairbanks** his headquarters. When he left the office of General Superior in 1968, he was satisfied that he had done much to clarify the Bishop-Jesuit Superior relationship.

As Mission Superior, Father Convert, under date of June 6, 1965, addressed a lengthy letter to "All Snow Vehicle Operators." The letter began, "Dear Fathers: In view of the two recent accidents, I wish to formulate some definite directives to insure your safety at all times." The winter before he wrote that letter, both Father William C. **Dibb**, S.J., and Father William T. **McIntyre**, S.J., were hospitalized for many weeks owing to frozen feet they suffered during separate mishaps. In that letter, Father Convert wrote in great detail about machines and their maintenance, about travel, clothing, emergency supplies, emergency signals, and the like. "In an emergency," he urged, "keep cool, so you won't freeze to death!" He signed off with "Placing you all under the special protection of the Good Angels. . . ."

After taking a mini-sabbatical in France, from March to August 1968, Father Convert took over as pastor of **Teller** and its dependent mission station, **Little Diomede**. In 1969, he was back again on the middle Yukon, serving as pastor first at **Nulato**, then at Kaltag, with visits to Koyukuk.

Father Convert spent his last decade in Alaska back once more among the Delta Eskimos. At St. Marys on the **Andreafsky** River, in June 1970, he founded the new Church of the Nativity parish. In so doing, he gave the Catholic community of the village of St. Marys an identity separate from that of the mission school. In the summer of 1972, he built the St. Marys parish center to house the worship area and the residence. His final Alaskan years were spent at St. Marys.

By 1979, the years and high blood pressure had begun to take their toll on Father Convert. In **Anchorage**, his doctor told him not to return to the bush and its cold and sometimes rather primitive living conditions. Instead, he was advised to "take the little pills faithfully, and don't work too hard; take it easy."

Since Father Convert still belonged to the French Jesuit Province that had "loaned" him to the Alaska Mission back in 1937, its Superiors thought best for him to return home to a gentler climate. With a heavy heart, and after many sad good-byes, he left for France in mid-June 1979. There, after some months of visiting relatives and friends and relaxing, he took an agreeable parish assignment at Cormaranche-en-bugey, Hauteville. On October 8th, he celebrated his golden jubilee as a Jesuit. He served at Cormaranche till 1986, when failing health necessitated his move to the Jesuit retirement home in Francheville, near Lyons. For several more years he continued to help out occasionally in various nearby parishes. Finally, poor health forced total retirement upon him. During his years back in France, he was visited from time to time by his very close friends, fellow Jesuit Alaskan missionaries, Fathers William J. **Loyens** and René **Astruc**. Their visits did much to brighten the evening and twilight years of Father Convert's life. To those two confreres in particular, he continued to be, after as before, "Uncle Jules."

Father Convert died in Francheville, in his 86th year, on July 28, 1995. He is remembered as a man who possessed a keen, penetrating, orderly mind. He was not a scholar. Alaskan conditions demanded that he be the practical man that he was. He quickly learned to drive a dogteam, how to keep engines and boats running, how to put up and remodel buildings, how to maintain and fly an airplane—in general, how to survive the rigors of missionary life in bush Alaska. As Mission Superior, and, in general, he carried on a voluminous correspondence. This reveals a warm-hearted, sensitive man, with a gracious sense of humor. He was a "fighter," especially when it came to social issues or matters that concerned his fellow Jesuits, but he did his fighting without rancor or alienating people. His intelligence, practical skills, and personal spirituality earned him the respect and friendship of most, especially of his brother Jesuits. "Father Jules M. Convert, S.J.," wrote one of them, "was endowed with all the charm the French have every right to lay claim to."

It must be mentioned that in the summer of 2003 several men came forward alleging that they had been sexually abused by Father Convert, while he was stationed in rural Alaska in the 1950s to the 1970s. Law suits were filed against the Diocese of Fairbanks and the Society of Jesus, Oregon Province. As of the summer of 2004, the Society of Jesus—seeking a pastoral response to these painful allegations—had settled with the original complainants, though the Diocese of Fairbanks remained in litigation. The charges arose only many years after Father Convert left Alaska.

24, 70

CONWELL, Father James U., S.J.

James Urban Conwell was born in Chewelah, Washington, on July 30, 1912. He had two sisters, one of whom became a Franciscan Sister of Perpetual Adoration. His younger brother, Joseph, also became a Jesuit priest. James attended Holy Rosary Grade School in Chewelah for the year 1918–19, then Our Lady of Lourdes, in Spokane, Washington, 1919–20, and St. Xavier, Spokane, 1920–26. His secondary education he received at Gonzaga High School, in Spokane, 1926–30.

James entered the Jesuit novitiate at Los Gatos, California, on July 15, 1930. After one year there, he—as one of the so-called "twelve apostles"—moved north to the newly opened novitiate at Sheridan, Oregon, for his second year of noviceship and two years of humanities and classical studies. From 1934–37, he studied philosophy at Mount St. Michael's, Spokane, after which he spent three years teaching at Gonzaga High School. His theological studies he made at Alma College, Los Gatos, California, 1940–44. He was ordained a priest in San Francisco on June 12, 1943. Father Conwell's academic records show him to have been almost a "straight-A" student. He spent the year 1944–45 teaching Latin and Greek to the collegians, "the Juniors," at Sheridan. His tertianship he made at Port Townsend, Washington, 1945–46.

Of Father Conwell, Father Mark A. Gaffney, S.J., who was with him at Sheridan at the time, said: "Father Conwell seems to be a fine priest. He is likeable around here, and immensely so. He is a painstaking man, working on details; also a sympathetic man, open to suggestions. Everyone seems to like him." Several other evaluators found that Father Conwell could be "stubborn," when it came to interpreting Canon Law. Given these character traits, Father Conwell was well qualified to be the "desk missionary" that he was, in **Alaska**, for almost 15 years.

From 1946–48, Father Conwell served in **Juneau** as Chancellor of the Vicariate of Alaska. Those were critical years for the Church in Alaska, inasmuch as Walter J. **Fitzgerald**, S.J., Vicar Apostolic of Alaska at the time, was, by 1946, already virtually incapacitated by failing health. He died on July 19, 1947. His successor, Francis D. **Gleeson**, S.J., was not consecrated bishop until April 5, 1948. To bridge this interregnum, Father Conwell was appointed "Vicar Delegate" by Father Paul C. **Deschout**, S.J., General Superior of the Alaska Mission, who considered him to be of "Episcopal timber." Father Deschout's confidence in Father Conwell proved to be well founded, as Father Conwell attended to the affairs of the vicariate with meticulous and compassionate care. This meant a great deal to people, especially to the priests who needed answers to questions of many kinds from "headquarters."

Father Conwell's correspondence for all his years

in Alaska shows him to have been a man who attended without delay, painstakingly, and sympathetically to all the many demands made upon him in his role as Chancellor. Questions concerning fine points of Canon Law were addressed to him. Marriage cases were referred to him for solutions. He was turned to, when people had questions concerning church property. The men in the bush confidently relied on him, when they needed such things as altar linens, books, household items, a watch repaired, a doctor's appointment, or just about anything that he, in the city, might be able to provide. These matters he always took care of promptly and with gracious good will. His letters are models of clarity and neatness. After attending to the business in question, he commonly rounded them out with news items, especially about fellow Jesuits, that he knew would be of interest to his correspondents.

In hopes of being a more qualified Canon Lawyer, and a better Chancellor and marriage tribunal officer, Father Conwell spent the year 1948–49 in the chancery office of the Archdiocese of Portland, Oregon. He then returned to Juneau for the years 1949–51, to serve as Chancellor and right-hand man to Bishop Gleeson. When Bishop Gleeson moved the vicariate headquarters north to **Fairbanks** in 1951, Father Conwell, still in his role as Chancellor, made the move with him.

While serving as Chancellor, Father Conwell was not exclusively a "desk missionary." Until 1958, he also helped out in the Fairbanks parish and taught in the newly opened Catholic high school in Fairbanks. During this time, he also made trips to outlying towns and villages, especially to **Tanana**, where he offered Mass and administered the Sacraments.

While continuing on as Chancellor, Father Conwell took on a new, an even more demanding assignment. On July 1, 1958, he was named Superior of the recently founded **Copper Valley School** (grade and high school, with accommodations for boarders) near **Glennallen**, some 300 road-miles southeast of Fairbanks. Fulfilling his role as Chancellor and as Superior of the school was for him a formidable challenge. From the outset of his stay at Copper Valley, he delighted to be with the children, especially the younger ones.

Father James U. Conwell, S.J. *JOPA-991.19.*

But, alas, his days at the school were already numbered. That same year, he was found to have a cancerous kidney. This was removed. Soon the other one, too, was found to be cancerous. He left Alaska in the earlier part of 1959 and began to live with the Jesuit community at Gonzaga University. "I am down here to die," he told people. He was in and out of the hospital. Nevertheless, in October of that year, accompanied by his brother, Father Joseph F. Conwell, he made one final trip to Alaska, to Copper Valley School, to wind up affairs there and to pack up a few belongings. On arriving back in Spokane, he kept up a steady correspondence with his many Alaskan friends, young and old, despite his weakened condition.

Father Conwell's health continued to deteriorate steadily. He said his last Mass on Easter Sunday 1960. In June, Father Louis L. **Renner**, S.J., after visiting him in the hospital, could say that this was the same, but much enfeebled, Father Conwell he had known in Alaska; for the mind, the personality, the matter-of-fact manner of the man were all still there.

Father Conwell understood the value of suffering. "Death? It doesn't scare me!" he assured visitors. He died in Sacred Heart Hospital on July 12, 1960. Those who saw him immediately after death found that "he looked very peaceful."

Father Conwell lies buried in the Jesuit cemetery at Mount St. Michael's, Spokane.

COOPER LANDING

The roadside community of Cooper Landing, named for gold prospector Joseph Cooper, is located on the Sterling Highway on the upper Kenai Peninsula 30 miles northwest of **Seward**. It originated around 1900 as a gold mining camp. In 1967, Cooper Landing's population numbered 88; in the year 2000, 369.

It is very likely that, beginning in the fall of 1950, when the road from Seward to **Homer** was opened, Father Martin G. Borbeck, S.J., stationed in Seward, began making more or less monthly visits to Cooper Landing, offering Mass in private homes, and that his successor in Seward, Father Arnold L. **Custer**, S.J., continued this practice.

In 1961, Redemptorist Fathers from the Oakland Province came to **Alaska** to provide pastoral care for the Catholic communities on the Seward Peninsula. The first three, all headquartered in Seward to begin with, were Fathers Edward C. **O'Neill**, pastor of the Seward parish, James Van Hoomissen, and Robert L. Woodruff. Out of Seward they began to care for the Cooper Landing Catholic community, offering Mass, at first, in the living room of Mark and Dolores "Dodie" Wilson. History honors Dodie as the one person who did most to make the Cooper Landing church a reality. The logs of the peninsula's youngest Catholic church, named after Redemptorist St. John Neumann, were set in place in 1977 by volunteers led by Joe Harvath. The church was formally dedicated on August 13, 1978, by Francis T. **Hurley**, Archbishop of **Anchorage**. Redemptorist Father Daniel D. Debolt, pastor of Sacred Heart parish in Seward from 1972–77, contributed much of his time and skills toward the construction of the new church. In 1982, Betty and Harold Fuller donated a log cabin, which served subsequently as a rectory. Throughout its history, and as of the year 2004, the Cooper Landing mission was served by the pastors of the Seward parish.

Next to St. John Neumann Church stands a squat log structure, the Marian shrine dedicated under the title of "Our Caring Mother for the Handicapped" on August 15, 1999, by Archbishop Hurley. On Sep-

St. John Neumann Church, Cooper Landing.
Photo by Annemiek J. Brunklaus.

tember 14, 2003, Roger L. **Schwietz**, Archbishop of Anchorage, and Francis T. Hurley, Archbishop of Anchorage Emeritus as of March 3, 2001, along with Fathers Peter F. **Gorges** and Richard D. **Tero** concelebrated the 25th anniversary of the dedication of St. John Neumann Church. Present at that anniversary Mass were also Deacon Walter Corrigan and some 50 parishioners and visitors.

COPPER VALLEY SCHOOL

It began as a dream. It was in operation a scant 15 years. For multiple decades it has been for many little more than a bitter-sweet memory. Its founder was idealist enough to "dream the impossible dream," yet realist enough to translate that dream—by the grace of God and the generous cooperation of fellow dreamers—into concrete reality. To those who knew and loved it best, that school in the valley was known affectionately simply as "Copper."

By around 1950, the buildings of the **Holy Cross Mission** boarding school were in such a state of dilapidation that Father **John P. Fox**, S.J., could write: "Our buildings and much of the equipment was nothing so much as one great junk pile." Moreover, the Yukon River had by then so changed its course, that a wide sandbar had formed in front of the mission, which made landing supplies there difficult and expensive. At the same time, Father John R. **Buchanan**, S.J., was dreaming of having a school—a college prep school for the training of Alaskan Natives for leadership roles in a changing society—in his territory, a vaguely defined 74,000-square-mile wilderness area northwest of Alaska's Panhandle. At a meeting held in Fairbanks in January 1955 to discuss matters involving the two schools, he argued forcefully that a school in his area would meet both his school needs and, at the same time, solve the Holy Cross school dilemma. He was persuasive. Then and there, Bishop Francis D. **Gleeson**, S.J., Vicar Apostolic of **Alaska** at the time, and his consultors determined that, instead of rebuilding at Holy Cross, the school there should be "moved" to Father Buchanan's area and become one and the same with his dream school.

The confluence of the Copper and Tazlina Rivers near **Glennallen** was the site selected for what was to blossom into Copper Valley School. From the U.S.

Department of the Interior a 462-acre tract was purchased at $3.00 per acre. In 1954, Father Buchanan and Father James C. **Spils**, S.J., were assigned to the school project. The former was to procure the building materials; the latter to oversee construction.

By this time Father Buchanan had built four chapels in his territory, the materials for which he had, for the most part, obtained free of charge from friends and strangers alike. He had by then made a fine art of begging, of "scrounging." Trucks loaded with donated building supplies began to roll toward the school site. Some of them came up the Alaska Highway, with Father Buchanan himself at the wheel; others came out of Anchorage with supplies acquired on the spot or barged up from Seattle. Much of the material originated in Idaho, was donated by Father Buchanan's classmates, Jim and Larry Brown, owners of the Pack River Lumber Company in Sandpoint. Glass, paint, cement and a mold for making concrete blocks on the site were also donated. Numerous volunteers, many of them from Army and Air Force bases, got involved in the procurement and trucking of supplies, and in the building of the new school. It was one grand effort, orchestrated, on the one hand, by Father Buchanan, "the pack rat priest," and, on the other, by Father Spils, "God's builder."

Under the leadership of Father Spils, construction of what was eventually to be a $5,000,000 school complex began in 1954. The school plan, drawn up by architect Ned Abrams, resembled a rimless, seven-spoked wheel, with a central recreation area as its hub. Six of the buildings were oblong and of concrete block construction, while the seventh was a T-shaped frame structure. The school was completed in 1962, when the hub area was "capped" with a dome.

In the fall of 1956, the school was in rudimentary readiness to receive its first students and staff. How to get those at Holy Cross from there to Copper Valley? An "old friend" of Father Buchanan's, Nelson David, then president of Alaska Airlines, came to the rescue with "Operation Snowbird." On October 14, Stinson bush planes shuttled 26 children, two Sisters of St. **Ann**—Sisters Alice Therese and Edward of Jesus—Jesuit Lay Brother John **Hess**, and Jesuit seminarian Thomas N. **Gallagher** from Holy Cross to **Aniak**. From there a DC-4 Star-

Aerial view of Copper Valley School near
the confluence of the Copper and Tazlina Rivers. *DFA.*

liner flew them the 540 miles east to the Gulkana airport, twelve miles from Copper Valley School. There they were met by, among others, Sister M. George **Edmond**, S.S.A., the Sister Superior.

As school was late getting started, teachers and students strove to make up for lost time. A few local children came as day scholars or as weekly boarders. The school was planned from the outset as a college prep school, but, because some of the students transferring from Holy Cross were still in the grades, CVS opened also as a grade school. This was phased out, as students moved on into high school.

From its very beginning, the school was remarkable for its warm family spirit. This was fostered by the fact that all lived and worked under fairly primitive conditions, but especially by Sister M. George Edmond, Superior of the Sisters and principal of the grade school, and by Father Francis J. **Fallert**, S.J., the principal of the high school. Father Spils described the atmosphere of the school as that of a "pioneering family."

In principle and, generally, in practice, the CVS student body was made up of roughly three quarters Alaska Natives from all over Alaska and one quarter non-Natives. The intent was that the non-Natives not dominate the Natives, but, instead, help them to adjust to the white-dominated culture in which they would find themselves sooner or later.

High standards of learning and teaching were set at the school's inception. They were taken as the norm and maintained, for the most part, throughout the 15 years of the school's existence. Having identified itself as a college prep school, Copper offered courses in Religion, Latin, French, German, History, Algebra, Physics and English. Sisters of St. Ann, Jesuits, and qualified lay volunteers made up the faculty. It had a well-stocked library, and home economics and physics labs, as well as equipment for secretarial training. It had a gymnasium and a stage. Sports, music, and drama were major components of life at Copper. The school had many student clubs, a chapter of the National Honor Society, a Civil Air Patrol group for boys and girls—and even a Hunting Club, that helped put fresh meat on the table. With its sodalities, retreats, and liturgies, it strove to give its students a solid grounding also in the Catholic Faith. Its facilities were not state of the art, still positive results were obtained, goals

achieved. Graduates routinely went on to higher education, college degrees, professional careers. Fondly, nostalgically they remembered their years at Copper, and gratefully they acknowledged their indebtedness to it.

Ten years after CVS opened its doors to its first students, rumors in and around Copper were confirmed, in February 1966, with the announcement that Rome had created the Archdiocese of **Anchorage** from sections of Alaska carved from both the Diocese of **Juneau** and the Missionary Diocese of **Fairbanks**. The school was now in the Anchorage archdiocese, and ceased, therefore, to be under the jurisdiction of Bishop Gleeson—this, in spite of the fact that he, in a letter to the Apostolic Delegate, Aegidius Vagnozzi, dated December 6, 1964, had made known his sincere wish that the school remain under his jurisdiction. "Since the loss of the plant,"

Jesuit seminarian John R. Buchanan on the bank of the Yukon River at Holy Cross Mission, 1942–44. *JOPA-800.21.*

wrote Bishop Gleeson, "would be a serious loss to the educational effort of the Diocese of Fairbanks, I think that boundaries had better be set that would leave this installation within the jurisdiction of Fairbanks." **Joseph T. Ryan**—a priest of the Albany diocese and who had never been to Alaska—was named the first Archbishop of Anchorage.

The latter half of the 1960s brought with it much worldwide and national change and unrest, both in society in general and in the Church. The Second Vatican Council, which ended in 1965, left the Catholic world with a host of new ideas and mandated changes. There was also the war in Vietnam, with its domestic repercussions. College campuses were in turmoil. Traditional patterns of behavior were being widely questioned. Authority was being challenged, and breaking down. Remote as CVS may have seemed to be from Rome, Hanoi, colleges and universities, all these social changes and upheavals quickly made themselves felt there also. Students, teachers, and staff were not immune to them. In addition, the State of Alaska made changes at this time in its educational policies. A boarding home program in the cities enabled Native students to get a high school education closer to home. All these new influences brought about differing views, dissatisfaction, unrest, disharmony, a sharp drop in enrollment at Copper. Disciplinary problems cropped up. All this led to a loss of a common, shared sense of purpose. The vision and the will and resolve that got the whole Copper Valley School wheel rolling in the first place was, all too quickly, being distorted and eroded. By about 1970, the possibility of closing the school was being seriously considered by Archbishop Ryan and his advisors. The principal reason advanced for doing so was the high cost of running it. Copper Valley School was closed in May, 1971.

In a letter to the "Benefactors of Copper Valley School," dated March 11, 1971, Archbishop Ryan gave his reasons for the closing: "the rising cost of maintaining the School, the difficulties that have been encountered in securing the services of competent and trained Volunteers, the falling off in Religious Vocations of Sisters, the failure of the greater number of students to pay tuition." He cited, too, "a great drop in enrollments in the student body." He emphasized that the closing "has been made nec-essary because we can no longer meet the financial, economic or educational requirements of the present." He stressed—in his own defense, one senses, and in anticipation of the criticism the closing would inevitably occasion—that he deeply deplored the necessity of closing the school, that every possible approach had been exhausted, and that the decision had been reached upon the recommendation of his advisors, both clerical and lay.

Seven weeks earlier, at the end of January, Archbishop Ryan had convened a meeting in Anchorage to discuss the future of the school. Present at that meeting were his consultors, Robert L. **Whelan**, S.J., Bishop of Fairbanks, and Bernard F. **McMeel**, S.J., Jesuit Superior in Alaska. All present, except for these latter two, thought the closing of CVS was necessary. "Subsequently," wrote Bishop Whelan to Father Louis L. **Renner**, S.J., on March 29, 1984, "before the announcement was made, Archbishop Ryan offered Copper Valley School both to the Diocese of Fairbanks and to the Jesuit Fathers, debt free, offering us a free hand in the operation of the school. Both Father McMeel and I, however, felt that we did not have the personnel available to accept the offer." Staffing would have presented a challenge, true; but the most basic reason for Father McMeel's non-acceptance of the operation of the school was that he was unable to take at face value the "free hand" assurance.

In a February 12, 1971, letter Father McMeel expressed to Archbishop Ryan under what conditions the Jesuits would take over the operation of the school. Responding to Father McMeel's letter in a letter of his own, dated March 11, 1971, Archbishop Ryan wrote:

> You insist, Father, on "the granting of canonical status for the Jesuit community resident at the school" as a condition for your acceptance of the school. You say that "we feel that we would need a certain degree of autonomy in the operation of the school, in selecting staff, in determining policy, etc., if we were to make a go of it." You have decided that canonical status is a "requisite" for your successful operation of the school. And thus you continue to denigrate my position as the Ordinary of the Archdiocese and my responsibility in the sight of God for the school and its students. Were I to turn Copper Valley School to you as you have insisted that it must be done, there would be no guarantee whatsoever that my responsibility for souls would be honored.

Clearly we have here a case of mutual distrust: the one party was not convinced that it would have a "free hand" in the operation of the school, the other that it would have a "guarantee" that its responsibility for souls at the school would be honored.

In August 1974, Copper Valley School and countless items of all kinds were auctioned off. The auction drew a large crowd of bargain-hunters and of just plain curious people. Three Glennallen men, friends of the school, formed a partnership on the spot and bought the school and sixty acres with an option for the other 402. The three men struggled to make payments, but then had to let the school go to a group of Anchorage businessmen, who envisioned a shopping mall with theater at the site. Such a turn of events brought much pain and sorrow to those who had originally brought about the "Miracle of Copper Valley School," and to all who loved the school and had been part of it—whether as students or teachers or supporting staff—during its relatively short, meteoric existence. It was with a certain sense of relief, then, that they learned that, in the summer of 1976, fire, rumored to be arson, swept through the school and left of it little more than blackened concrete blocks and twisted steel. It was an ending they could accept. By then Copper had more than justified its existence.

After the fire, Father Spils, the school's builder, said to a lamenting Sister M. George Edmond: "George, God decides the duration of a work. Copper Valley School is finished. We will not talk about it anymore."

15, 16

CORDOVA

The town of Cordova is located on the southeast shore of Orca Island in Southcentral **Alaska**. It was so named by William J. Heney, builder of the Copper River and Northwestern Railroad about 1906. A post office was established there in 1906. The town had its origin as the railroad terminus and ocean shipping port for the copper ore shipped from the Kennecott Mines up the Copper River. In 1967, the town had a population of 1,128; in the year 2000, 2,454.

The official Catholic Church came to Cordova in June 1908, in the person of Father Matthias Schmitt, S.J. By September of that year, he had a church, dedicated to St. Joseph, built. From the founding of the Cordova parish, and over the years, the priests responsible for it made their headquarters variously in Cordova, in **Valdez**, and in **Seward**. This is true of Father Schmitt, in that Southcentral Alaskan area from 1908–10, and of Father John B. **Van der Pol**, S.J., there from 1910–19, as well as of many of their successors. During his tenure in Southcentral Alaska, Father Van der Pol wrote to his Father Provincial concerning Cordova: "A railroad town with little of the large and generous Alaskan spirit. Devotion and piety, about nil. Support, barely enough to live." During the Van der Pol years, Jesuit Fathers John T. Corbett and Alphonsus Fletcher also served for short periods of time in Cordova.

Father William **McMillan**, S.J., had charge of the Cordova–Valdez parishes from 1919–33. From 1919–25, he resided in Valdez; from 1925–33, in Cordova. Father Timothy O'Sullivan Ryan was in Cordova from 1934–39. He was followed by Father David A. **Melbourne**, in Cordova from 1939–59. For a time, around the mid-1950s, he was assisted by Fathers Emeric Kovach and Ronald K. **Dunfey**.

After Father Melbourne came Father John A. **Lunney**, in Cordova from 1959–66. During his years there, to keep the parish in the limelight of town happenings, he issued periodic press releases. These thanked parishioners involved with parish activities and singled out faithful altar boys for recognition. This limelighting helped build up his congregation. To further stir up the Faith of his people, he saw to it that they had a better physical plant. The old 1908 church was on a hill and, therefore, inaccessible for many parishioners, when gale-force winds struck the town. For years, a Quonset hut in a more accessible area had served as the parish church. A push for a new church came from within the town itself, when, on May 2, 1963, fire gutted the nearby Cordova business area. Although no church property was involved, the fire made Father Lunney and parishioners aware of how truly vulnerable to fire the old 1908 church structure was and of how inadequate the low, dark and damp Quonset church was becoming.

St. Joseph's Church, Cordova. *Photo by Richard Collins.*

An earlier St. Joseph's Church, Cordova. *JOPA-422.01.*

On December 1, 1963, a parish drive to raise funds was launched for the construction of a new church. The devastation caused by the March 27, 1964, earthquake and the consequent tidal waves added further incentive and urgency to the drive. Construction of a new parish plant began in September 1964. Though far from finished, the new St. Joseph's Church was ready for limited use by December 22, 1964. It was formally dedicated on May 1, 1965.

During the year 1966–67, Fathers John J. **Marx** and Peter Houck, O.S.B., were in Cordova. They were followed by Father Segundo **Llorente**, S.J., in Cordova from 1967–70. The Trappist monk, Thomas Merton, who visited him there, wrote in his diary, "Fr. Llorente—a remarkable person, a legend in the region [of Alaska]."

Father Anthony Neff was in Cordova, 1970–71; Father Daniel Crowley, 1971–73; Father Eugene P. **Burns**, S.J, 1973–74; Father J. Thomas Connery, 1974–75; Father Melbourne—though officially retired—1975–83; Father **Daniel J. Hebert**, 1983–84; Father Robert Rietcheck, C.Ss.R., 1984–87; and Father Alfred L. Galvan, 1987–89. After that Cordova was served by visiting priests. Father Tom Killeen, O.M.I., was resident pastor as of the year 2004.

Sister Peggy Glynn, O.P., was in residence in Cordova from 1989–99, serving as Pastoral Administrator. She was followed in that role by Cordova resident Mrs. Sharon Frost.

15

CORRIGAL, Father Robert F., S.J.

He was a good Irishman, and a good Central Yup'ik Eskimo; and he was a good social worker, and a good Jesuit priest. The combination of these seemingly conflicting factors gave him great joy and, at the same time, great heartache throughout much of his life. There was "war in his soul."

Robert F. "Bobby" Corrigal was born in **Bethel**, **Alaska**, on September 7, 1928, to Central Yup'ik Eskimo Anna "Nusta" Petluska and Neil Corrigal, straight from County Cork, Ireland. He was orphaned at a relatively early age. He spent his boy-

hood in Bethel, before going on to attend the mission boarding school at **Holy Cross**. In 1942, when Jesuit seminarian **Cornelius K. Murphy** left Holy Cross, he took Bobby Corrigal south with him, to Butte, Montana, where he gave him a home with the Murphy family. After finishing his secondary education at Butte's Central Catholic High School, Bobby entered the Jesuit novitiate at Sheridan, Oregon, on September 7, 1946. There, upon completing the two-year noviceship, he took the vows of poverty, chastity and obedience. He spent two more years at Sheridan, studying the humanities and classics, before he moved to Mount St. Michael's, Spokane, Washington, for three years of philosophy. From 1953–56, he taught Latin, English, Religion, and typing at Seattle Preparatory. For several years there, he was also in charge of "the property room," caretaker of athletic equipment. He was a very conscientious teacher, especially when it came to correcting papers. At times his Superior had to command him, quite literally, to go to bed at night at a decent hour. During the summer of 1953, he spent "two short months" helping Father John B. **Baud**, S.J., build a new Fathers House at **Nulato**. He proved to be "just a grand helper," in Father Baud's words. From 1956–60, he made his theological studies at Alma College, Los Gatos, California. He was ordained a priest—the only Eskimo ever to become a priest—on June 13, 1959, in Spokane. Father Corrigal spent the year 1960–61 making his tertianship at Port Townsend, Washington.

In 1961, Father Corrigal returned to Alaska to teach English literature and social ethics and to be counselor at St. Mary's Mission High School, **Andreafsky**. Next he was associate pastor of Immaculate Conception parish in his hometown of Bethel, from 1963–65. In 1965, he was appointed pastor of **Russian Mission**, **Pilot Station**, and **Marshall**. To cover those missions, along with those of **Aniak** and **McGrath**, more effectively, he obtained his pilot's license, in 1966, in Tacoma, Washington. He proved to be an adequate pilot. Being a short, though beefy man, he fit easily into the small Piper Super Cub he flew.

Father Corrigal, too, was caught up in the general social, cultural and ethnic unrest and turmoil of the late 1960s. He saw a need for more social work on the part of the Church. Concerned also about the poor medical care his people were getting, and, wanting to help them in a more direct way himself, he went on to study medicine in Las Vegas, Nevada. There his close friend, Father William J. Bichsel, S.J., visited him. He found him living in a garage and "studying his heart out." But the pre-med courses were just too difficult for him. He then went on to study for a master's degree in Guiding and Counseling at Eastern Washington State College, getting this in 1973. As associate pastor, 1973–74, of Immaculate Conception parish, **Fairbanks**, he was also counselor of Native students attending the University of Alaska–Fairbanks. When it came to counseling, Father Corrigal was a natural. He was a compassionate listener, "just a real open guy," according to Father Bichsel, and, between sips of coffee, also a tireless talker.

After that Fairbanks year, Father Corrigal moved to **Anchorage**, where he began to work closely with Alaska Native people. In 1979, he accepted a position with Fluor-Alaska, Inc. and Cook Inlet Native Association to establish a counseling program for Alaska Natives employed in the Trans-Alaska Pipeline project. When the pipeline was finished, he returned to Bethel to work with the Alaska Village Council Presidents, counseling Natives interested in higher education. Then, in 1984, he returned again to Anchorage, where he worked with the Alaska Housing Authority until his fatal illness. In that capacity he counseled tenants, wrote the newsletter, and encouraged and promoted healthy community relations between tenants and management.

By 1979, Father Corrigal had already taken off the Roman collar and disappeared, to a large extent, off the Jesuit and official Church "radar screens." On February 3, 1981, Father Henry G. **Hargreaves**, S.J., wrote from Bethel to Father **Francis E. Mueller**, S.J., in Fairbanks concerning Father Corrigal, "I've seen him once, when he dropped into the house. He doesn't show up for anything around here. He said people are asking him if he is married, or why he isn't married, but he says he is still a priest." Offered a chance by Father Hargreaves to say Mass in the Bethel church to show the people that he was still a priest in good standing, Father Corrigal declined the offer, claiming that peo-

Father Robert F. Corrigal, S.J. *JOPA-1059.01.*

ple would say that priests were running the villages and that he, by functioning as a priest, might leave himself open to that criticism and hurt his work with the Natives.

But, as the 1980s unfolded, changes were coming about in the Church and in society in general, even as Father Corrigal fought his own personal and social battles—as well as his battle with aggressive cancer. The Church and Native cultures were coming to understand one another, to fuse. Father Corrigal was blessed to see these changes during the last few months of his life. They helped him to bring to an end the private, interior struggles he had now endured for years. Peace returned to his mind and heart, as he saw that the official Church, too, shared his basic concerns about people, about their social, cultural and spiritual needs. He came to realize that he could be, at the same time, a good Eskimo Native and a good Irish white man, and a good social worker and a good Jesuit priest. The Church and the Society of Jesus had never written him off. In his last months he turned to his Jesuit brothers for companionship. He received the Sacraments of the Church. He became especially close to his longtime friend, Father Vincent J. **Beuzer**, S.J. The two had studied together, and taught together at Seattle Preparatory. Father **James R. Laudwein**, S.J., Father Corrigal's Superior since 1986, showed much understanding and compassion for him during his last months. He said of him, "His role was prophetic in many ways. He was on the cutting edge of the change that's happening now. And he is still doing things in a very priestly way." Many of Father Corrigal's friends said that he was born 20 years too soon to be the kind of priest he wanted to be.

In Anchorage's Alaska Native Medical Center, on May 20, 1988, Central Yup'ik Eskimo and Jesuit priest Father Robert F. Corrigal died peacefully in the Lord. The "war in his soul" was over. He was 60 years old. He lies buried in the Catholic plot of Anchorage's Angelus Memorial Park Cemetery.

COUNCIL

Council (City), located on the left bank of the Niukluk River and about 70 miles northeast of **Nome**, came into being in the fall of 1897, when gold was discovered in that area of the Seward Peninsula by Daniel B. Libby and party. A year later, this typical miners camp consisted of about 50 log houses and had a population of around 300. The Council post office was established in 1900, but discontinued in 1953. The population fluctuated noticeably over the years, reaching a high of around 2,000 in the early part of the 1900s and a recorded low of nine in the 1950s.

Council was first visited by a Catholic priest, when Father John B. **Van der Pol**, S.J., spent two weeks there, from the 6th to the 20th of March 1902. He found 50 Catholics out of a population of around 450. From July 1902 to July 1904, Father Edward J. **Devine**, S.J., was responsible for the Catholics in Council. He visited them often, sometimes staying in Council for periods of two to three months. In 1903, he built himself a log cabin and began to build a log church. However, having been promised a ready-made church from the States, he discontinued building. A notation in the Nome house diary reads: "Council does not prove to be a successful field. There are entanglements. Fr. Devine is deceived by a dreamer, who promises him a church ready-made from the States. He leaves the log church unfinished, to the dissatisfaction of many of the Catholics."

After Father Devine left **Alaska**, in July 1904, Council was visited only at infrequent intervals by priests from Nome.

Msgr. Francis A. Cowgill.
Photo by Ward Wells.

COWGILL, Msgr. Francis A.

Francis A. Cowgill was born in Spokane, Washington, on June 27, 1927. After completing studies at St. Thomas Seminary in Denver, Colorado, he was ordained a priest there on June 7, 1952. Having volunteered for **Alaska**, he was assigned to the newly created Diocese of **Juneau**.

His first appointment was that of principal and teacher at Pius X Mission Grade and High School in **Skagway**. At that time, Father G. Edgar **Gallant** was still the man in charge of all things Catholic in Skagway. In addition to appointing the newly ordained Father Cowgill principal and teacher, he also put him in charge of the mission's 25 dairy cows. His idealism a bit shattered, the young priest made clear to Father Gallant that he was not ordained to be a dairyman, and offered to butcher the troublesome cows rather than milk them every day.

Soon after Father Cowgill came to Skagway, his keen business sense suggested to him a program that would bring some financial support to the school and, at the same time, help the boys. He introduced them to lapidary work and silver designing. The fine jewelry produced by them in their "hobby-shop" was displayed for and sold to tourists. Father Cowgill left Skagway in 1959. His leaving Pius X Mission saddened the Sisters of St. **Ann**, who had found in him "a good friend and supporter of their work."

From 1959–64, Father Cowgill served as assistant pastor to Father Gallant at Holy Family parish in **Anchorage**. Meanwhile, he was also involved with Catholic Charities, the Christian Family Movement, the Catholic Youth Organization, and the establishment of Hubbard Memorial School. He was pastor of St. Mary's parish in **Kodiak** during the years 1964–66. He had the distinction of being the only certified bowler on Kodiak Island. As such, he gave bowling lessons to the young.

When the Archdiocese of Anchorage was established on February 9, 1966, Father Cowgill became its first Chancellor, a position he held until 1969. At the same time, he served also as Secretary of Education, and helped to operate Anchorage's Catholic Junior High School. He was elevated to the rank of Monsignor in October 1966. On October 17, 1967, he was appointed the first pastor of the newly established St. Andrew's parish in **Eagle River**. His stay there was a short one, lasting only four months.

From 1968 to the end of his life, Msgr. Cowgill was pastor of St. Anthony's parish in Anchorage. In the early 1970s, his deftness in the area of fiscal matters being well known by then, he was named Archdiocesan Financial Secretary. On the occasion of Pope John Paul II's visit to Anchorage on February 26, 1981, one of Msgr. Cowgill's proudest achievements was helping coordinate the visit and so arranging everything that, after it was over, the archdiocese, instead of being burdened with a huge deficit, came out $3,000 ahead.

When many Koreans began to come into the area of St. Anthony's parish in the late 1970s, Msgr. Cowgill responded immediately to the request of Francis T. **Hurley**, Archbishop of Anchorage, to be the host parish for them, himself offering Mass in what limited Korean he had learned. According to one member of the Korean community, "No matter how sick he was, he would always do the Korean Mass for us if we needed him. He was like a real father to us; he kind of spoiled us."

As pastor of St. Anthony's, Msgr. Cowgill, in addition to his public roles, ministered also in many private ways known only to the individuals involved. He was a sought-out confessor and a trusted counselor to his fellow priests and parishioners young and old. At least six young priests were sent to him as associate pastors by Archbishop Hurley, so that he might be a model and mentor to them. He was known, too, for his "marathon story-telling."

Despite failing health, Msgr. Cowgill continued to serve as pastor of St. Anthony's up to the time of his death on October 16, 2000. He died of an apparent heart attack. In his homily, Archbishop Hurley summarized: "Msgr. Cowgill was a dedicated servant of God who loved his people and was firmly rooted in his earthly mission."

Msgr. Francis A. Cowgill lies buried in the Catholic plot of Anchorage's Angelus Memorial Park Cemetery.

15, 16

CRAIG

The town of Craig, 60 miles northwest of **Ketchikan**, is located on Craig Island, just off the west coast of Prince of Wales Island. Its name derives from that of Craig Millar, who, in 1907, built a mild-cure salmon packing plant on the site. The town's present name was adopted in 1912, when its post office was established. It was incorporated as a first-class city in 1922. In 1939, with a population of 231, Craig had a salmon cannery, a sawmill, and a Customs Office. Currently, fishing is still the town's primary industry, with lumber harvesting a close second. Its population numbered 273 in 1967, and 1,397 in the year 2000.

Official Catholicism first touched Alaska 25 miles from present-day Craig, on Ascension Thursday, May 13, 1779, when Franciscan Friar Juan Antonio García **Riobó**, assisted by fellow Franciscan priest Matías de Santa Catalina, and secular priest Cristóbal Antonio Díaz, offered a Mass of Thanksgiving at Port Santa Cruz, Suemez Island, Bucareli Bay. The three were members of the Don Ignacio de Arteaga exploratory expedition that had sailed north from San Blas, Mexico, on the two frigates *La Princesa* and *La Favorita*. The diary of the commander of the expedition records that some 60 Natives attended that Mass and that a few Native children were baptized. On July 3, 1979, to celebrate the bicentennial of that historic event, Father

Richard D. **Tero** offered Mass on the site of that first Mass.

Already as early as July 1913, Father William A. **Shepherd**, S.J., alerted his Superiors that there were Catholics in the towns of Craig and nearby **Klawock** that were asking for pastoral care. In 1925, Bishop Joseph R. **Crimont**, S.J., designated northern Prince of Wales Island as a mission of St. Rose of Lima parish in **Wrangell**. However, it was not until two decades later that priests from there began to visit Craig and Klawock with any kind of regularity. In 1946, Father Matthew E. **Hoch**, pastor in Wrangell from 1942–59, began to make intermittent visits to Craig, numbering at the time "about 10 Catholics." Father Hoch is rightly regarded as the founder of the Craig parish, St. John by the Sea.

After Father Hoch, priests stationed at Wrangell and **Petersburg** continued to visit Craig from time to time. From 1973–76, Father Jerome A. **Frister** visited it as a fly-in priest out of **Ketchikan**; then, from 1976–79, out of Wrangell. While Craig has never had a resident pastor, it did begin to be visited with some regularity after Michael H. **Kenny**, Bishop of Juneau, assigned full-time ministers to Prince of Wales Island.

In 1974, Sister Marguerite Gravel, C.S.C., began pastoral ministry at Craig and at other communities on Prince of Wales Island. This she continued to do for roughly a decade. She was followed by Sister Nadine Grogan, S.N.J.M. It was she and Father Michael Nash who "began the real history" of the Catholic community at Craig. Assigned on September 1, 1983, Father Nash was the first priest to serve Prince of Wales Island and the surrounding island communities. Flying his own plane out of Thorne Bay, "he made pastoral outreach a reality in that area." He left the area in 1988. St. John by the Sea became a parish in the late 1980s. It should be noted here that all the Catholic communities on Prince of Wales Island are part of the one St. John by the Sea parish.

Sister Laetitia Lariviere, I.H.M., arrived on Prince of Wales Island in 1987, and Father James Blaney, O.M.I., less that a year later.

Father Blaney left the area in 1999, and Sister Laetitia the following year. Father Edward Matthews, O.M.I., was there for the year 1999–2000. Father Jean-Paulin Engbanda Lockulu and Sister Zita Simon, O.P., began ministry in Craig in the year 2000. In June 2003, Father Lockulu was transferred to **Sitka**. He was replaced by Michael W. **Warfel**, Bishop of Juneau, serving as pastor; Father Edmund J. Penisten as Parochial Vicar; and Sister Zita as Parish Administrator. On July 15, 2004, Father Perry M. Kenaston became pastor of St. John by the Sea parish.

CRIMONT, Bishop Joseph R., S.J.

He was the last Prefect Apostolic of **Alaska**, and the first priest to be consecrated a bishop for Alaska. As a child he was of such delicate health, that he was expected to die young. He lived to be almost 90 years old. He was the first Jesuit Father Rector in the Pacific Northwest. He had a singular devotion to St. Therese of Lisieux, to whose intercession he attributed many favors, even miracles. Only a book-length biography could begin to do justice to the man and to his long life's accomplishments.

Joseph Raphael Crimont was born on February 2, 1858, in the French town of Ferrières, near Amiens, France. When he was three years old, his parents, with their three boys and two girls, moved to Amiens, so that the children could get a good education. His mother died soon after the move. The family was poor and adequate food was not always on hand. In later years, Bishop Crimont blamed his small stature on the poor diet of his childhood. When he was about to enter the Jesuit school at Amiens, the priest who knew him well said of him, "As for little Crim, I don't know. He has very little health, but he has the stuff to become a saint."

At the age of eleven, Joseph attended the Apostolic School in Amiens. The object of this school was to train boys who showed signs of having a vocation to the priesthood or to Religious life, or to a combination of both. A year later, he started to attend the Jesuit school of La Providence, also in Amiens. There, in 1873, he met for the first time Francis M. **Monroe**, who was soon to be his fellow Jesuit and lifelong friend.

On August 14, 1875, Joseph entered the Jesuit novitiate at St. Acheul, Amiens. He was ordained a sub-deacon in September 1882, in Louvain, Belgium. His health at this time was so poor that there was little hope for his life. A doctor who examined him gave him less than a month to live. However, help came from a wholly unexpected quarter. Just at this time, Don Bosco, the Apostle of Youth and founder of the Salesian Order, came to Lille, where Joseph was stationed, to establish there an institute for poor boys. In Lille, he stayed with the Jesuits. Joseph was appointed to serve his Mass. After the Mass, Joseph said to him, "Father Bosco, I have a favor to ask of you." He then went on to tell him of his hopes of one day becoming a missionary, and of the doctor's verdict that there was no hope for him. Father Bosco, since canonized, assured him of his prayers and that Joseph's hopes of becoming a missionary would one day be realized.

In 1884, Archbishop Charles J. **Seghers**, under whose jurisdiction Alaska fell at the time, came to Liège, where Joseph was now teaching in the Jesuit college, to give a lecture there. Joseph heard the lecture. Then and there he saw where his missionary aspirations were to be realized. He volunteered for the missions of the American West, and two years later landed in New York. After two years of theological studies at Woodstock, Maryland, he was ordained a priest, on August 26, 1888. There followed another year of theology at Woodstock and a year of tertianship at Drongen (Tronchiennes), Belgium. Next Father Crimont spent four years among the Crow Indians of Montana.

In 1894, Father Crimont, now in his 37th year, sailed for Alaska. Upon arriving at **St. Michael**, he was met by a very much surprised Father Francis A. **Barnum**, S.J., a former classmate of his at Woodstock. Father Barnum urged him not even to get off the boat, telling him, "You are not made for this kind of country. In a few weeks you will be dead." Father Barnum's words fell on deaf ears. By August 1894, Father Crimont was at **Holy Cross Mission**. He spent the years 1894–1901 at Holy Cross, which he was later to describe as "the smile of the Yukon." One of the Sisters of St. Ann, who was with him at Holy Cross, said of him that he was "the soul of the mission family." He showed special solicitude for the children. "Always be loving and patient with the children," he counseled.

In 1901, Father Crimont was called out of Alas-

ka to be president of Gonzaga College in Spokane, Washington. He held that office from October 1901 to May 1904. As president, he was more concerned with the college's academic program than with its athletics. In 1902, in recognition of the growth of the college and the personal ability of its president, the Jesuit Father General in Rome raised the canonical status of Father Crimont from that of Superior to that of Rector. This gave him the distinction of being the first Jesuit Rector in the American Northwest. When, on May 26, 1903, President Theodore Roosevelt, while on a visit to Spokane, stopped by Gonzaga College, Father Crimont was his principal host. Two months later, Father Crimont helped break ground for a new addition to the college building. On Pentecost Sunday, May 22, 1904, the Gonzaga Jesuits were startled by the news that their Father Rector had been appointed to succeed Father John B. **René**, S.J., as Prefect Apostolic of Alaska. That same evening, Father Crimont, whose three years at Gonzaga were said by one historian to have "moved along so serenely that they seemed like months instead of years," departed Spokane for Alaska.

From 1904–07, Father Crimont made his headquarters in **Juneau**; then, from 1907–11, in **Fairbanks**. Then it was Juneau again. From 1911 on, Juneau remained his home base until the end of his life. In both of those cities, during the winter months, he, as Prefect Apostolic, attended to the many duties incumbent upon him in virtue of that office. At the same time, he also did much pastoral work in the respective parishes. During the summers, in his capacity as Prefect Apostolic, he traveled extensively throughout Alaska, visiting, by turn, the widely-scattered towns and missions on official Church business.

The year 1917 was a year of major importance not only for Father Crimont, but also for the Church in Alaska. On December 22, 1916, Alaska was raised to the next ecclesiastical level, that of a Vicariate Apostolic; and, on February 15, 1917, Father Crimont, as was to be expected, was appointed Vicar Apostolic of Alaska. In St. James Cathedral, Seattle, on July 25, 1917, he was consecrated a bishop by Alexander Christie, Archbishop of Oregon City. When he first received word that he was to be Alaska's first bishop, he wrote to his Superior: "If it is God's will to glorify Himself in me by choosing this helpless pauper and raising him from the dust and placing him among the princes of the Church, let it be so. I did not ask for it, nor expect it. I am not scared, and do not refuse it."

On his coat of arms Bishop Crimont placed "*la rose effeuillée*" (the rose unpetaled). This he did to honor, and to thank for many personal favors received, Sister Therese of Lisieux, who, in 1919, was still four years from being beatified and six from being canonized. Father Julius **Jetté**, S.J., thought this to have been an over-hasty move on Bishop Crimont's part. To his fellow missionary in Alaska, Father Crispin S. **Rossi**, S.J., Father Jetté wrote, on December 26, 1919, referring to the holy Carmelite nun: "Though I admire her virtues and holiness, I cannot help thinking that our good Bishop has made a rather hasty move in selecting a 'patron saint' that is not yet beatified." Bishop Crimont was in Rome in 1925 to see Sister Therese canonized and to hear her decreed by the Sacred Congregation for Missions "Queen and Patroness of Alaska." On that trip he also led a pilgrimage to Lisieux. St. Therese, "the Little Flower," has been the official patron saint of the Alaska missions ever since, and the rose has appeared on the coats of arms of all subsequent bishops of northern Alaska.

Even though a bishop now, Bishop Crimont's personal lifestyle continued to be simple and frugal. He routinely gave away gifts he received. During the winters he spent most of his time in Juneau. He was often seen shoveling snow off the walks. When he attended the furnace, he took his ring off and put it in his pocket. When not traveling outside of Alaska to attend various meetings, to raise funds for the missions, or to receive needed medical attention, he spent long hours at his desk. He carried on a voluminous correspondence, doing all his own writing in a penmanship described as "exquisite." Many of his letters are still extant. Recipients cherished and kept them, because he had brought to them "an unusual gift of expression, a kind of personalized beauty of phrase and depth of feeling." And in Juneau, in addition to taking care of his duties as bishop, he again did much pastoral work, both in the city itself and in nearby towns. During

Bishop Joseph R. Crimont, S.J.
JOPA-940.16.

the summers he continued to move about the vast territory under his ecclesiastical jurisdiction to administer the Sacrament of Confirmation, to bless new churches, and, in general, to take care of business calling for his attention as bishop.

In August 1920, while on a Confirmation trip to the **Pilgrim Hot Springs** Mission, Bishop Crimont, now 62 years old, came close to losing his life. On the 18th, accompanied by Father Frederick A. **Ruppert**, S.J., he traveled from **Nome** to "the Springs" by "dogomobile"—a cart on railroad tracks pulled along by a team of dogs. "After various vicissitudes," in the words of Father Ruppert, they finally arrived at the mission. Writing in the mission house diary, Father **Hubert A. Post**, S.J., tells what those "vicissitudes" were:

Bishop Crimont paid us a nice visit, but it came near costing his life. He came by dogomobile, but from the track to this place there is a very hard "mush" over the tundra. Had he not found Fr. **Lafortune** on his way to Nome, and persuaded him to turn back, he might never have reached us alive. With Fr. Lafortune as guide, they made Hot Spring Station about 2 P.M. Thence they had still 8 miles to make and his Lordship, being not strong, had to stop several times to catch his breath. Fr. Ruppert came ahead, but he too found the road heavy and got lost in the willows, after swimming the ice-cold waters of the Pilgrim. We were about to retire, when the Brothers heard someone calling for help. They answered the call. They were told that Fr. Ruppert was lost in the willows and swamps. They lit a lantern and went in search. When getting nearer to the Father, he begged them to go at once across the river and help the Bishop. Finally they reached us about a quarter of twelve.

In 1937, Bishop Crimont again traveled to Rome. There he had a long audience with Pope Pius XI, who called Alaska "the most difficult mission." When the two compared ages and found they were practically of the same age, the pope told the bishop, "the ice preserves you."

But not even the ice could preserve "little Crim"

Prefect Apostolic Joseph R. Crimont, S.J., in Nome ca. 1915. *Photo by Fr. Joseph Bernard, S.J./JOPA-512.C56.*

forever. Inexorably, accidents—twice he fell and broke ribs—long and hard years in Alaska as priest, as Prefect Apostolic, as Vicar Apostolic took their toll. By 1938, he was eighty years old and in failing health. He petitioned Rome to give him a Coadjutor with right of succession. His petition was granted. In Spokane, on February 24, 1939, he consecrated Father Walter James **Fitzgerald**, S.J., a bishop, to be his Coadjutor Bishop with right of succession.

It is the well-founded belief of Jesuit historian Wilfred P. Schoenberg, S.J., that Bishop Crimont would have been much happier consecrating a man of Euro-French origins as his successor. Bishop Fitzgerald, son of Irish immigrant parents, was the first native son of the State of Washington to become a bishop. According to Father Schoenberg, "Crimont, totally out of character, received his coadjutor coldly, gave him directions that appear to have been harsh. He could not get himself to accept Fitzgerald graciously at Juneau." It was a case of the older, European mentality meeting up with a more modern, American mentality. In Bishop Crimont's defense, Father Schoenberg wrote, relative to the bishop's attitude toward Americans, "With all his grace and charm, he never came to fully appreciate the American personality. A European to the core, he retained certain unpleasant reservations regarding Americans, prejudices he would have been shocked to discover in himself. He never realized they were there. Because of his native sweetness of disposition, they seldom came to the surface."

On July 29, 1942, Bishop Crimont, now the oldest bishop in America, celebrated his Silver Episcopal Jubilee in St. James Cathedral, Seattle, where he had been consecrated bishop twenty-five years previously. Three years later, at the age of 87, in St. Ann's Hospital, Juneau, on May 20, 1945, he died. The Governor of Alaska at the time, Ernest Gruening, hailing Bishop Crimont as a "great Christian man," ordered flags throughout Alaska to be flown at half-mast for three days.

On October 30, 1938, Bishop Crimont had had the joy of blessing and laying the cornerstone of the chapel at the **Shrine** of St. Therese, near Juneau. A year later, on October 26, 1941, he had offered the first Mass in it. It was in the crypt beneath this chapel that this "great Christian man," predicted by Don Bosco to be a missionary, found his final resting place.

16, 174

CRONIN, Father James D.

James D. Cronin was born on February 2, 1920, in Central Falls, Rhode Island. When his mother died three days after his birth, diversity began to mark his life. He was given to his maternal grandparents to be raised for the first six years of his life. Being of French heritage, they spoke only French. James could speak no English, until he began school. Upon the death of his grandparents, when he was six, he went to live with his father, who had re-married, and his sister, and half-sister, and two half-brothers. He then started the first grade at St. Matthew's School in Central Falls; but, before the school year was over, the family moved to Pawtucket, Rhode Island, where he attended Sacred Heart School. From 1934–38, he attended a public high school in East Providence, Rhode Island, where the family was then living.

Upon completing his primary and secondary schooling, James wanted to enroll in the seminary division of Providence College, in Providence, Rhode Island, but was not accepted, because he knew no Latin, a requirement at the time. He went to work full-time in a market. But he also returned to high school, to study Latin. Unsuccessful in the attempt, he concluded that he did not have a vocation to the priesthood.

While trying to learn Latin, he became acquainted with the Christian Brothers (Brothers of the Christian Schools), and decided that he might have a vocation to that Congregation. On July 1, 1939, he entered their novitiate in Barrytown, New York; and, on September 8, 1940, he took his first vows as a Christian Brother.

Always true to his motto—"Here I am, Lord; send me!"—Brother James, for the next 34 years, served in various capacities, such as procurator, teacher, prefect-counselor of orphans and boys from broken homes, director general of the Motherhouse in Barrytown, dean of students, and the like. His assign-

ments took him to a diversity of places: Washington, D.C.; Troy, New York; New York City; Detroit, Michigan; and Santa Fe, New Mexico.

Around 1960, Brother James volunteered for the African missions, but was considered to be too old. Soon after the Second Vatican Council, while he was at the College of Santa Fe, his yearnings for the priesthood re-surfaced. Early in 1973, he contacted Francis T. **Hurley**, Bishop of **Juneau** at the time, and requested him to "take me in!" The bishop invited him to visit **Alaska** that summer.

Brother James arrived in Juneau on July 1, 1973, and was assigned to live with the pastor of the Cathedral parish. He was also asked to visit all the nine parishes in the diocese, and to spend a few days with the priest in charge of the given parish. This was so that the priests could look him over, and he them. After a few weeks, he returned to Juneau. There the bishop had a report in hand from each of the pastors. The reports were all favorable. "The bishop," in the words of Father Cronin, writing in retrospect, "gave the green light, and I applied to Rome for my dispensation of vows, which I received on August 15, 1973. After signing the papers, I had a strange feeling of being 'a nothing.' I was neither a Brother, nor a priest."

During the latter quarter of 1973, priest–candidate Cronin served a kind of "apprenticeship" under Father James F. **Miller**, pastor of Holy Name parish in **Ketchikan**. There he was ordained a deacon by Bishop Hurley in November 1973. On his 54th birthday, February 2, 1974, in his home parish of St. Martha, in East Providence, Bishop Hurley ordained him a priest. "So," Father Cronin wrote, "within eight months, I was a Brother, a 'nothing,' a deacon, and a priest! Thanks to the education received while in the Brothers, all this became possible."

Bishop Hurley, before accepting Brother James as a candidate for the priesthood in the Diocese of Juneau, had asked him to contact one of the professors at Detroit's Sacred Heart Seminary regarding classes preparatory to the priesthood. After three weeks of meetings, both the professor and he agreed that they were both wasting their time. The professor wrote to Bishop Hurley, assuring him that Brother James was, unquestionably, ready for the priesthood.

At the time of his ordination to the priesthood, and thereafter, Father Cronin was often asked the question, "Why did you leave the Brothers for the priesthood?" His answer: "The MASS! The most important thing in my life is the Mass!" His answer to the question as to why he chose Alaska: "Because the Diocese of Juneau has only six priests." These two considerations were enough to motivate him to become a priest, in Alaska. At the same time, he conceded that "taking leave of the Brothers—after enjoying 34 years of happiness and joy with them and the many students who came under my direction—was no easy matter."

After his ordination to the priesthood, Father Cronin spent a few more months in Ketchikan, now as assistant pastor. In May 1974, Bishop Hurley paid him a visit there, and mentioned to him that a priest was needed for St. Therese parish in **Skagway**. True to his motto—"Here I am, Lord; send me!"—Father Cronin accepted to become pastor of the Skagway parish, as of May 15th.

"In Skagway," he wrote, "I had my work cut out for me." He had only the rectory in which to offer Mass. A few people came on Sundays. For his daily weekday Masses, during his first year in Skagway, only his friendly dog was present. Convinced that to stir up the Faith of the Catholic community of Skagway and to get the people to attend Mass more faithfully a decent church building was needed, he asked Bishop Hurley to be allowed to build a new church. "Go to it!" the bishop told him.

However, there was little money on hand for a new church structure. Labor costs in Skagway were high. But, there were "the good Christian Brothers." And there was financial assistance from the Catholic Church Extension Society to be counted on. The cement foundation was poured; pre-cut lumber was ordered; and, on June 30th, eight Brothers and two laymen arrived to build the church. "This caused the people of the parish to come out of the woodwork; and even the non-Catholics pitched in, because of the Brothers." When the Brothers left at the end of August, the church was 90 percent complete. On October 3, 1975, Bishop Hurley was there to dedicate it. The new church, as had been hoped, and anticipated, drew people back to a more regular practice of their Faith.

When, on July 8, 1976, Bishop Hurley became Archbishop of **Anchorage**, Father Cronin, in his own words, "lost truly a great friend."

In 1977, after three years in Skagway—"long enough for any priest," Father Cronin wrote—he was appointed Rector of Juneau's Cathedral of the Nativity of the Blessed Virgin Mary parish and Chancellor of the diocese. This he found, "a most active, interesting and enjoyable assignment."

During his Juneau years, Father Cronin served also as Director of the Diocese of Juneau's Deacon Program. As such, he was responsible for putting together the curriculum. Given his many years of experience in the academic life as a Brother, he found this "a most enjoyable" aspect of the program. Under his tutelage, the diocese had the joy of seeing nine deacons ordained. Father Cronin is given credit, too, for reactivating the Juneau Council of the Knights of Columbus, inactive since World War II.

Toward the end of his Juneau years, Father Cronin had a heart attack, which put him in the hospital both in Juneau and in Seattle. After a new "valve job and by-pass," he was back on the job in six weeks.

The Lord had more work for Father Cronin to do in Alaska. After his eight years in Juneau, he was, in 1985, now of retirement age. Nevertheless, he was assigned to St. Gregory of Nazianzen parish in **Sitka**. His two years in Sitka he described as "like being on the Riviera! Everything seemed to have been done here, and I spent most of my time being nice to the people and children."

In April 1987, Father Cronin, recalling the happy days he had spent at the College of Santa Fe, and with the approval of Michael H. **Kenny**, Bishop of Juneau at the time, retired to his beloved city of Santa Fe. For over a decade, he served there as chaplain at the College of Santa Fe and at St. Michael's High School. He also helped out in the local parish and at the two communities of Brothers. "In short," he wrote, "you might say, I became a Mass priest with few or no responsibilities."

While in semi-retirement in Santa Fe, Father Cronin was awarded the Papal Benemerenti Medal in recognition of his "exceptional accomplishments and services to the Church, to education, and to his fellowman."

In the earlier part of the year 2003, Father Cronin

left Santa Fe to return "home," to Narragansett, Rhode Island, to be near the remaining members of his family. There, in April, 2003, he was accepted into a Christian Brothers nursing home. From there, in a letter to Father Louis L. **Renner**, S.J., dated April 18, 2003, he wrote: "I am now 83 years old, and it's time to get ready to meet my Lord."

CUNNINGHAM, Brother Bernard I, S.J.

He was described as "the best house builder in **Alaska**." He spent only a decade in Alaska, but is to be numbered among the pioneer Jesuits who served there. He is credited with finding the high bank of the **Akulurak** Slough on which St. Mary's Mission was built. The Eskimos traded fish and game for calico at the mission. In the absence of a yardstick, the missionaries measured the yard by holding the calico with both hands and opening their arms wide. He was a six-footer with long arms. The Eskimos insisted that he do the measuring of the calico.

Bernard I. Cunningham was born on March 17, 1838. He entered the Society of Jesus on August 15, 1875. On June 10, 1890, along with the saintly Father William H. **Judge**, S.J., he sailed from San Francisco on the *St. Paul* for Alaska. He arrived at **St. Michael** on July 13th. After a year at St. Michael and **Holy Cross Mission**, accompanied by Fathers Francis A. **Barnum**, S.J., and Joseph M. **Tréca**, S.J., he sailed to "the Coast Mission," **Tununak**, on Nelson Island.

Brother Cunningham spent the year 1891–92 at Tununak, then a year at Kanelik Pass, a temporary mission site near the south mouth of the Yukon River, then two years at Akulurak, before moving up the Yukon to serve at **Nulato** and Holy Cross. He spent the year 1898–99 in Dawson, Yukon Territory, Canada. He was at the bedside of Father Judge, when he died, on January 16, 1899. In the spring of that year, Brother Cunningham returned to Alaska to serve again at Holy Cross and St. Michael.

Brother Cunningham left Alaska in 1901, and died in Spokane, Washington, on February 20, 1912. He lies buried in the Jesuit cemetery at Mount St. Michael's, Spokane.

CUNNINGHAM, Father Edward J., S.J.

Edward J. Cunningham was born on May 19, 1881, in Harrison, New Jersey. Having heard Father Joseph M. **Cataldo**, S.J., preach about the **Alaska** Mission, he felt inspired to join the Society of Jesus. He entered the Jesuit novitiate at Los Gatos, California, on July 24, 1903. After completing the two-year noviceship, he spent three additional years at Los Gatos studying the classics and humanities. He spent the year 1908–09 teaching at St. Ignatius High School in San Francisco. Next he studied philosophy at Gonzaga College, Spokane, Washington, from 1909–12. Talented in music, while at Gonzaga he was a member of the band and orchestra. Later, in Alaska, he trained some of the boys to accompany others while they sang. From 1912–17, at Santa Clara University in California, he taught music, among other subjects. He made his theological studies at Woodstock College, Maryland, from 1917–21. He was ordained a priest at Georgetown University, Washington, D.C., on June 29, 1920. His tertianship he made in Cleveland, Ohio, 1921–22.

Father Cunningham went to Alaska in 1922, and spent the years 1922–28 at **Holy Cross Mission**. While at Holy Cross, he did a considerable amount of traveling to its dependent mission stations. "I carry about as part of my baggage," he wrote, "50 pictures, 20×28 inches, done in beautiful and striking colors, [depicting] such subjects as the Life of Christ, the Sacraments, the Ten Commandments, the Apostles Creed, and the simple natives never tire of looking at them and hearing them explained." Not able to speak the Central Yup'ik Eskimo language, he communicated through an interpreter.

Father Cunningham spent the year 1928–29 at **Paimiut**. Though handicapped by his inability to speak the Native language, he put his heart into his ministry at Paimiut and won the esteem of the people. He next spent two years at **Mountain Village**; then he was back again at Holy Cross for the years 1931–34. He was a Mission Consultor from 1928–33. He was in **Juneau** for the year 1934–35. Before returning to northern Alaska, he spent several months, in 1935, traveling to some of the eastern States to raise funds for the missions. Dressed in fur parka and mukluks, he would stand in the vestibule of various churches asking for alms for Alaska. His efforts met with "excellent success."

Father Edward J. Cunningham, S.J.
JOPA-1060.01.

Father Cunningham spent the last years of his life as Superior of the **Pilgrim Hot Springs** Mission. He arrived there in October 1935. When he heard that the mission might possibly be closed, he volunteered to go to St. Lawrence Island to start a Catholic mission there. On January 23, 1941, however, a heart attack put an end to his life, and to his dreams. He lies buried at the Hot Springs mission.

Father Cunningham's one-time Major Superior, Father Philip I. **Delon**, S.J., described him to his Father Provincial as "an excellent man." Bishop Walter J. **Fitzgerald**, S.J., said of him that he "was very devoted to the Alaska Missions."

CUNNINGHAM, Father Thomas P., S.J.

He was born restless and preordained to a life of high adventure. A fellow Jesuit missionary described him as "one of the most loved, versatile and dynamic missionaries ever to serve the **Alaska** missions." He was an expert on polar ice conditions. When he died at **Barrow** after 24 years in the Far North, he was acclaimed a folk hero in Catholic New Zealand, and read into the *Congressional Record* as "a noble and gallant figure, a

devoted servant of God and of his fellow men." *Time* and *Newsweek* magazines, too, noted his passing.

Thomas Patrick Cunningham was born in New Zealand of Irish immigrant parents on February 24, 1906. His childhood, according to his brother, "was uneventful. He was always full of life, and ready for fun." On March 4, 1924, he was received into the Irish Province of the Society of Jesus in Sydney, Australia. After completing the two-year noviceship in Sydney, he sailed to Ireland, in August 1926, for a year of classical studies at Rathfarnham Castle near Dublin. In September 1927, he began philosophical studies at the Jesuit college of Eegenhoven, near Louvain, Belgium. While there, he volunteered for the Alaska mission and was accepted. He arrived at Mount St. Michael's, Spokane, Washington, on October 1, 1929, for his final year of philosophy. On September 7, 1930, he stepped ashore at **Holy Cross Mission** on the Yukon River, where he spent one year, before going on to theological studies in Montreal. He was ordained a priest on August 12, 1934. A year later he arrived in **Nome**, Alaska, to serve there as pastor of St. Joseph's parish.

During his year in Nome, Father Cunningham, though busy with routine pastoral duties, devoted four hours daily, except Sundays, to the study of Inupiaq Eskimo. By March 1936, he could write, "the language is no longer the illogical puzzle it used to be." He was soon well known and liked in Nome and the surrounding area, by Eskimos and whites alike. All called him "Father Tom." One of his parishioners echoed the sentiment of all Nome: "Fr. Tom seemed to fit right in with the people of Nome and the Eskimos. He had great public relations; knew everyone in Nome."

Although Father Tom had expressed a "great desire to labor in the **Kotzebue** district," he was next assigned to **Little Diomede** Island. On October 13, 1936, on the *North Star*, he sailed for that tiny islet in the middle of Bering Strait. Father Bellarmine **Lafortune**, S.J., who knew from personal experience what the Little Diomede assignment entailed, considered Father Tom particularly well suited for that station. "He has lots of pep," wrote Father Lafortune, "and lots of experience on the sea and with boats. Moreover, he begins to speak Eskimo, and that goes to the heart of the natives more than anything else."

On Little Diomede, too, Father Tom devoted much time to the Eskimo language. He soon became quite fluent in it. He also became an expert seal and walrus hunter. From time to time he visited Big Diomede Island, or entertained visitors from there. During the year 1939–40, he was away from the island he called his "first love" to make his tertianship at Mont-Laurier, Quebec. He became a U.S. citizen on October 1, 1941.

During World War II, Father Tom took on what he described as "a couple of extra-curricular jobs" for the Army Intelligence Department. Sickness on his part caused him to spend the winter of 1942–43 ministering to the Eskimos in and around Nome. In the late fall of 1942, the ship *Crown City*, with military cargo on board, got impaled on an uncharted crag 25 miles west of Nome and five miles off the Seward Peninsula coast. Despite her critical military cargo, Army officials wrote her off as beyond salvage. That winter, as Father Tom was returning to Nome from **Teller** with his dogteam, he swung out over the sea ice and boarded the ship to size up the situation. Upon his arrival in Nome, he went immediately to the commanding officer at the Army base to assure him that he would see to it that the cargo on the *Crown City* would be brought ashore, if he were furnished enough manpower. The Army, having been convinced by Father Tom that he was familiar with pack ice and its behavior, supplied the needed manpower, Eskimo and military. Led by him, they set to work. He himself operated the winch on the ship, hoisting cargo out of the hold and lowering it down to the Eskimos on the ice, who hauled it ashore. After a few weeks of feverish activity, under truly adverse conditions, most of the military supplies were safely at the base. One morning Father Tom called an abrupt halt to the whole operation and ordered all ashore at once, although a fair amount of desirable matériel still remained on the ship. By this time he was familiar with Bering Sea ice conditions, knew how to "read" the ice, how to listen to and feel its movements, something he could do very well in the steel hull of the ship. He also seemed to have a sixth sense for ice behavior. The military offered to pay him for his services, but

Father Thomas P. Cunningham, S.J., about to return to Little Diomede Island in the early 1940s. *JOPA-973.01.*

he refused payment, asserting that he was doing no more than his patriotic duty. He was generously thanked for his "invaluable services" and given a Citation of Commendation by the Army's commanding officer in Nome.

The year 1943–44 was Father Tom's last full year on Little Diomede. As early as 1941, he had had hopes of becoming a military chaplain. "Just sort of figured it was the patriotic thing to do," he wrote his Father Provincial. He received his commission in the U.S. Army on January 11, 1945, and, after graduating from Chaplain School on March 17, 1945, was assigned to Nome. On September 20, 1945, he arrived at Hickam Field, Hawaii. He had requested an assignment in the Pacific Theater in hopes of visiting his aging parents in New Zealand, whom he had not seen since 1924. By mid-November, he was on New Caledonia. While there, he was granted a temporary leave and authorized to visit his family. After a few days with them, he traveled to Brisbane, Australia, "for the purpose of coordinating chaplain activities." For Christmas he was back on New Caledonia, which he found "dreadfully hot." His duties next took him to Manila, Honolulu, Guam, Saipan, and Japan, before he wound up in Korea for a four-month tour of duty there, from March 29 to July 20, 1946. After Korea, he returned

Father Thomas P. Cunningham, S.J., in early 1951, offering Mass on an altar made of carved snow blocks on the polar ice cap north of Barter Island with members of the 10th Air Rescue Squadron attending. *U.S. Air Force photo/JOPA-973.52.*

to Japan for five weeks, at which time he made a 10-day retreat with the Jesuits in Tokyo. On September 9, 1946, he was released from active duty to take accumulated leave, and on October 11, 1946, he left the Army with a "superior" rating, making him one of very few retiring officers to receive a rating above "excellent."

Father Tom, upon returning to Alaska in the latter part of September 1946, went at once to Little Diomede, where he found "little change." Soon thereafter, he was back in Nome to assume charge of the parish there and of all its dependent stations. He hoped to spend the summer of 1947 at Teller. However, around mid-July Father Lafortune, while saying Mass in St. Joseph's Church, Nome, collapsed at the altar. Father Tom went to Nome to tend to him. On July 29th, he and Father Edmund A. **Anable**, S.J., accompanied Father Lafortune on a flight to **Fairbanks**. Father Tom was now the obvious choice to replace Father Lafortune on **King Island**. He landed there on October 4, 1947.

No sooner was Father Tom on the island, than he was teaching school there for the Bureau of Indian Affairs. In addition to that, he continued Father Lafortune's long-established tradition of catechizing, visiting the sick, and sharing in village life. But, unlike Father Lafortune, he also joined the men in hunting. "On Wednesday and Saturday," he wrote, "I hunt in the afternoons, as I need to eat too. All hunting is done on moving ice, and it is sometimes dangerous and always cold and miserable." In reality, he did not have to hunt. He would have been, and was, given meat, just as Father Lafortune had been. Father Tom hunted because he needed to hunt, was a hunter at heart, and a good one. One King Islander said of him, "He's tough man, that one! He go hunt on ice, just like us. All alone. He come back with something every time. Ahhhh! Father Tom!"

From his earliest days in Alaska, Father Tom felt very strongly that one should speak Eskimo, when among Eskimos. On King Island, as on Little Diomede, he kept studying the language. He produced several rather scholarly manuscripts on Eskimo. For the Alaska Air Command serving in the Arctic he produced a 108-page phrase book.

During his King Island years, Father Tom recorded faithfully in the house diary, started by Father Lafortune, information concerning weather, hunting, ice conditions; church, school, catechism attendance; the health of the people, births, baptisms, marriages, deaths and burials. Almost every facet of King Island life found itself, sooner or later, in the diary.

On June 5, 1948, Father Tom's first winter on King Island came to an end. He had hopes of spending the summer on Little Diomede, but found no way of getting there. Instead, he spent the summer in Nome. On October 18th, along with the King Islanders, he left Nome on a government ship for his second winter on King Island.

"The New Year came and went with a minimum of noise and much happiness," wrote Fr. Tom in the diary on January 5, 1949. The following day, however: "Bad news today. Three of our men floated away northward on the ice. They were seen to be in danger but could not be aided." Father Tom wired the Army in Nome and requested them to help locate the three and to drop them food and sleeping bags. For the next several days, the weather was "terrible, the worst blizzard of the winter, visibility nil." When the weather improved, the Army began a four-day search for the missing men, but in vain. After two weeks on the treacherous ice, "the ice that never sleeps," one of the men made it to shore on the mainland and was rescued. The other two perished on the pack ice.

On March 17, 1949, a footnote to Alaskan bush aviation history was written, when Tex Ziegler made the first landing on top of King Island. He came to take Father Tom to Little Diomede. They left the following day. "The operation was hazardous," Father Tom noted in the diary.

During the summer of 1949, Father Tom, who had been in the Army Officers' Reserve Corps since October 1946, was on active duty, stationed at Marks Air Force Base, Nome. By October 2nd, he was back on King Island for what was to be his last winter there. On January 1, 1950, he wrote in the diary, "A nice, mild day ushered in the new year." The year 1950 was to bring about a significant change in his life.

On February 17th, Father Tom received a wire informing him that he had been transferred from the Army Officers' Reserve Corps to the Air Force Reserve. He himself had requested the transfer. On June 30, 1950, in his own boat, he left King Island for the last time. He was scheduled to go on active duty the next day. At first he intended to put in only the normal 60 days that he owed as a reservist. However, the U.S. Air Force wanted more—and so did Father Tom. From October 30, 1950, to July 29, 1952, he was on active duty with the U.S. Air Force. What the Air Force wanted from Father Tom was not only his "chaplain activities," but even more his knowledge of the Arctic. He was by now an expert on the behavior of pack ice and on arctic survival.

During his first year in the Air Force, Father Tom was stationed at the Air Force's 5005th hospital, Elmendorf AFB, **Anchorage**. He was called away frequently from this primary assignment to conduct "chaplain activities" and to give lectures on arctic survival at various military posts. In early February 1951, he received special orders to proceed to Barter Island. He and the "Polar Ice Pack" crew arrived there the first week of February. Detained there by bad weather, he scouted out the Eskimo settlement on the island, and learned that he could "converse easily enough with the local natives, and they seemed surprised to find military personnel speaking Eskimo." At Barter Island, he may well have recalled what he wrote to his Father Provincial two years earlier that he had "always had the ambition to begin a mission along the arctic coast east of Barrow."

On February 20th, the weather had improved enough to allow Father Tom and Captain Marion F. Brinegar to fly out over the polar ice cap to find a suitable floe on which to set up the proposed experimental station. Roughly 200 miles north of Barter Island they found such a floe, and camp "Polar Ice Pack" was established the same day with Captain Brinegar and Father Tom in charge of the eight-man project.

From this arctic oasis, Father Tom wrote to friends: "My special job is safety, which means scouting around the area a distance of 3 to 5 miles per day, and trying to ascertain from the cracks in the ice just when we will have to pack up and leave in a hurry. A lot of this is pure malarkey, of course, but it does the men good, when I come home and say we are safe for another 48 hours." For 17 days everything at the polar ice pack camp went more or less as anticipated. However, on March 10th, a 150-foot-wide crack opened up near the camp, and on the 12th all were safely evacuated. When several days later flights over the area were made, no trace of the camp could be found.

Soon after his return to Elmendorf, Father Tom gave a conference on "Eskimo Life," which, according to a "Letter of Appreciation" he received after the conference, provided his audience with "a keen insight into life in the Far North." The conference was "unique for its color and human interest." He had spoken with "an authority that evoked the admiration of the entire student body." Of Father Tom as lecturer, Father Segundo **Llorente**, S.J., wrote: "The minute he entered a room with people, he filled the room with his presence and began to 'take over.' Nobody resented it; on the contrary, all were pleased to be in his company. Somehow he gave the impression that he was speaking with authority."

One might think that Father Tom's tour of active duty as a chaplain was one long, uninterrupted round of high adventure, of hobnobbing with top military brass, of honors. True, his 21 months in the Air Force were anything but commonplace or monotonous. He did move easily and often with top ranking officers. Still, numerous papers and letters in his archive file show that he always attended painstakingly to ordinary, routine chaplain business, that he was always ready to help anyone in need, and that he had time for all, especially "the underdog." "Whenever anyone was in trouble or needed help," wrote one who knew him well at that time, "Father Tom had a way of just happening along." Captain Cunningham, military chaplain though he was, remained at the same time, and always, Father Tom, the simple, approachable priest.

On July 29, 1952, Father Tom returned to civilian life. He spent August visiting radar sites for the Alaskan Air Command, and September and October helping out in the Fairbanks parish. On November 5th, in an Air Force plane, Father Tom, who had felt himself drawn to missionary work in the Arctic ever since he first came to Alaska as a priest, was flown to Kotzebue for the winter 1952–53. On board

he had with him his recently purchased team of seven dogs, along with sled and harness. He anticipated that his winter in Kotzebue would be a time for him to make long-range preparations for his projected new field of missionary work along the arctic coast. From April 15th to the 27th, he was in Barrow making further preparations for the establishment of a mission in the high Arctic. During that winter, he also made trips to Little Diomede and Nome.

On March 26, 1954, Father Tom was able to write friends, "The church in Point Barrow is practically finished, and I have had close contact with the wandering Eskimos." The following month he was back on Little Diomede. On April 15th, when the **Little Sisters of Jesus** were on the island with him, he wrote to Father James U. **Conwell**, S.J.: "The more I see of these nuns, the more I am in favor of them. The only difficulty right now is the confusion of languages. I use four languages a day and that's hard on the tongue. Never imagined life on Diomede could be so complicated." On May 2nd, Bishop Francis D. **Gleeson**, S.J., Vicar Apostolic of Alaska at the time, landed on the ice at the foot of the island. This was the first time a major Superior set foot on that island, and it was a great occasion for the Little Diomeders. Thirty people were confirmed in an impressive ceremony. Thirteen children made their first Holy Communion. The singing was excellent. When Father Tom left the island a week later for Nome, Fairbanks, and points north, he was never to see Little Diomede, his "first love," again, but he left it with his missionary work there well done.

On May 16, 1954, Father Tom wrote that the work at Barrow was "progressing nicely," and that "eventually, by putting out lots of effort and determination," he would be able to introduce Catholicism north of the Brooks Range, "which is the reason I came to Alaska in the first place."

A rather diverse ministry faced him, when he took up station at Barrow. There were the white Catholics in Barrow itself: construction workers, military personnel, people connected with the school, the hospital, the U.S. Weather Bureau, and the Civil Aeronautics Administration. Soon he was to minister also to the men working on the Distant Early

Warning radar sites, the DEWline. He was also expected to make converts among the Eskimos in Barrow and outlying villages. To cover his vast arctic parish, he planned to travel by dogteam and on military planes. He was still in the Air Force Reserve at this time.

During the summer of 1954, Father Tom was preoccupied with getting his mission complex in Barrow built. This was constructed out of salvaged lumber and two military surplus Quonset huts. Despite weather "altogether cold and miserable," the 12 x 24-foot living quarters, also used as a temporary chapel, were ready for occupancy by November 1st. While building, he received a "surprise amount of volunteer labor," but he himself did most of the carpentry work and all of the wiring.

As a missionary to the arctic slope Eskimos, Father Tom had little to show. By this time most of those northern Eskimos had already embraced some form of Christianity.

On July 1, 1955, Father Tom, still in the Air Force Reserve, was promoted to the rank of major.

Throughout the summer and fall of 1955, Father Tom was busy beyond words. In addition to putting the finishing touches to his church and living quarters, he traveled almost constantly along the arctic coast, mostly to DEWline sites. He made frequent trips to Fairbanks and Anchorage. On August 10th, he wrote from Barrow to George T. **Boileau**, S.J., his Religious Superior and close friend: "Tomorrow I have a Mass here, at the flagship, and at the camp. Monday I have Mass on another ship, plus a lecture in the evening to all Navy personnel in the vicinity. Tuesday I have Mass on an icebreaker, and a lecture in the evening to about 70 scientists. Wednesday I have the regular weekday Mass at the camp and a character guidance talk to all Army and Air Force men in the vicinity."

When the Air Force was planning to establish a semi-permanent scientific station on the drifting pack ice in the Arctic Ocean as part of the international scientific effort in connection with the 1957 International Geophysical Year, it called on Father Tom to help with the planning. On October 12, 1956, he wrote friends, "They want me to be in charge of the locating and constructing, and remain until the camp is underway. I know I can do the job, provid-

ed I am given sufficient leeway. I am promised enough rank to be impressive." Responsibility for locating a suitable ice floe for what was variously called "Operation Ice Skate," "Project Ice Skate," and "Drift Station Alpha," for setting up camp, for guaranteeing reasonable safety, for choosing the final personnel, and for making final decisions in all emergencies rested solely with Father Tom.

In late March 1957, a floe approximately 600 miles north of Barrow was selected as the site for a camp intended to house nine civilian scientists and eleven Air Force members. The camp was expected to last about 18 months. Scientists were to study the Arctic Ocean: its currents, bottom, salinity, temperatures, marine life, and the like. On Easter Sunday, April 21, 1957, Father Tom celebrated morning Mass at Drift Station Alpha, then flew south to Barrow for evening Mass. The next day he flew north again.

On May 21st, the American flag was planted at Drift Station Alpha and the station pronounced a "going concern for the United States." After the ceremony, the commander of the Alaskan Air Command presented Father Tom and two airmen with the USAF Commendation Ribbon for "meritorious achievement in this most hazardous venture." To Father Tom, the commander said, "Father Tom, in utter humility I say this is your field of honor. I commend you for rendering exceptionally meritorious service as a technical advisor on Arctic conditions to Project Ice Skate Task Group."

With the camp established and operational, Father Tom returned to Barrow. However, throughout the whole time Drift Station Alpha was occupied, he was on call in case of an emergency. From April 4, 1957, his first night on the ice, to September 1, 1958, he spent a total of about 250 days on the polar ice cap. His presence was reassuring to the men there.

At 11:15 A.M., on September 23, 1958, Father Tom landed at Drift Station Alpha for what turned out to be his last stay there. In the gloom of early November, he and the men at the station made national headlines: "Ice Island Carrying 21 Breaks Apart," "Rescue Planes Set Out to Aid Group on Floe," "20 Men Airlifted from Polar Floe." On Sunday, November 2nd, the floe on which Alpha was located was lashed by a polar storm so violent that it broke in two. The section with the runway, which alone made travel to and from the floe possible, broke away from the section on which the camp was pitched. Alpha had to be abandoned without delay. However, owing to high winds, no plane could come to the rescue for four days. On Thursday, November 6th, two planes did arrive. Seventeen minutes after they landed, all Alpha occupants, ferried from the camp floe to the landing floe in a 16-foot boat powered by a 40-horse outboard, were on board and ready for takeoff. Most of the scientific data collected were also on board. Father Tom, one of the first to land at Alpha, was the last to step off it. On November 16th, he and other rescued airmen appeared on the nationally televised Ed Sullivan TV program. Sullivan singled out Father Tom, wearing the uniform of an Air Force major, as "the man with the know-how."

Father Tom was now a national figure, described variously as "hero of northern near-tragedy," "padre of the arctic ice," "indomitable Jesuit priest," "expert on polar ice conditions." Friends wrote him how thrilled they were to see him on the Ed Sullivan show. He was teased good-naturedly about being a national TV celebrity, and about having played hopscotch at the North Pole. A fellow Jesuit complimented him on having added to the glory of the Church by his "exemplary though adventurous and charmed life." Officials high in the National Academy of Sciences and in the Air Force, too, expressed "warm and sincere thanks for meritorious service rendered under extremely adverse and hazardous conditions." One of the pilots involved with Project Ice Skate wrote, "There is no question about the fact that Father Tom was a great morale builder on Station A. The mere fact that he was there and knew so much about the Arctic was reassuring. He worked as hard and probably kept longer hours than most of the men. And, of course, he ministered to all the men irrespective of their faith."

No sooner was Drift Station Alpha abandoned, than the Air Force looked again to Father Tom for his polar expertise for a new drift station it was planning. But, by the early spring of 1959, drinking had again become a problem in his life, and his Superiors hesitated at first to let him take part in yet another arctic venture. However, because it was

thought that he would be helping out for only a month, and because the Air Force insisted on his services, he was allowed to serve one more time as a special advisor. By April 14, he was again out on the ice, having "specific responsibility for providing guidance on all matters concerning camp layout and construction, arctic survival, and arctic safety" from the Commander of the Alaskan Air Command. So totally in charge of the safety of the station, Ice Station Alpha II, was he that he could write, "I can also close up the whole works, no questions asked, if I should think it necessary."

What inspired such confidence on the part of the Air Force in Father Tom's judgment in matters polar ice was, according to one of the pilots involved, his ability "to make such accurate predictions of just where and when Station Alpha would crack. The original map he drew predicting cracks was almost a duplicate of one which was kept to show where the cracks actually were."

The 12th of August, 1959, marked the 25th anniversary of Father Tom's ordination to the priesthood. He himself made little of the occasion. However, from the archbishop of the Auckland archdiocese he received assurances of "prayers, felicitations and wishes." A grade school classmate of his wrote to him, "May I wish you great joy, happiness and every blessing. May God spare you for many more years to carry on the wonderful and heroic work you do amongst your people in the far distant North." But, it was not in the designs of Divine Providence to spare Father Tom for many more years—not even for another month.

"Fr. Cunningham, Arctic Priest, Dies," read a headline in the September 5, 1959, issue of the *San Francisco Chronicle*. Again his name was in the headlines of newspapers across the nation and on nationwide radio broadcasts, but this time it was to announce his death. At Barrow, in his Quonset hut dwelling, after morning Mass and breakfast, on September 3, 1959, without benefit of last rites, Father Tom's colorful life came to an abrupt end, at the age of 53. "Coronary occlusion," the nurse said.

On Friday, September 4th, the commanding officer of the Air Force in Alaska dispatched his personal plane to Barrow to bring Father Tom's body to Fairbanks for burial. On Monday, the 7th, the body—lying in a simple gray casket, unadorned except for a small crucifix, which well symbolized his life and work—was moved into Immaculate Conception Church at 4 P.M. to lie in state. That evening many lay people, priests and Sisters gathered there to pray the rosary and to recite the Office for the Dead. The body, dressed in priestly vestments and bathed in the mellow light of six flickering candles, was left in the church overnight. The following morning at 10 o'clock, a Solemn Pontifical Requiem Mass was celebrated by Bishop Gleeson. The church was crowded to capacity. There was a military honor guard. A chorus of military chaplains sang the responses. The 49-star flag was draped over the casket.

Many who attended the Mass were also present at the graveside ceremonies in the Clay Street Cemetery. After the Latin *Benedictus* was chanted, taps sounded. The military honor guard fired off a three-round rifle salute. Airmen folded the flag and presented it to Bishop Gleeson. The body of Father Thomas Patrick Cunningham was lowered down to lie next to that of Father Bellarmine Lafortune, who, 24 years before, in Nome, had introduced him to the Eskimo apostolate. What Father Cunningham wrote in the King Island diary about Father Lafortune at the time of the latter's death can fittingly be written about Father Cunningham himself, "He was a good man to have in this world."

36, 115

CUSTER, Father Arnold L., S.J.

Arnold L. Custer was born in Aberdeen, Washington, on April 11, 1910. In Portland, Oregon, he attended St. Ignatius Grade School, and in Spokane, Washington, Gonzaga High School. On July 18, 1929, he entered the novitiate of the California Province of the Society of Jesus at Los Gatos, California. After completing his two-year noviceship, he spent two additional years there studying the classics and humanities. From 1933–36, he made his philosophical studies at Mount St. Michael's in Spokane. He next spent the years 1936–39 teaching at Marquette High School in Yakima, Washington. His theological studies he made at Alma Col-

lege, near Los Gatos, during the years 1939–43. He was ordained a priest on June 13, 1942, in St. Mary's Cathedral in San Francisco.

During the year 1943–44, Father Custer served as the Father Minister at the Jesuit novitiate at Sheridan, Oregon. The following year, he was Vice-Superior of St. Paul's Mission at Hays, Montana. He then made his tertianship at Manresa Hall in Port Townsend, Washington. From 1946–50, he was stationed at St. Ignatius Mission, Montana. He was pastor of St. Thomas parish in Harlem, Montana, from 1950–52.

From 1952–61, Father Custer served as pastor of Sacred Heart parish in **Seward**, **Alaska**, and as visiting priest to its dependent stations on the Kenai Peninsula, among them: **Kenai**, **Homer**, and **Ninilchik**. Given the considerable distances between his posts of responsibility, he spent a great deal of time on the road, driving, in the words of Father **Paul B. Mueller**, S.J., who helped him out at times, "a somewhat dilapidated and ill-functioning Volkswagen Transporter, which rides more like a bucking bronco than a vehicle." In that vehicle, Father Custer would drive around his Seward parish to pick up the children and bring them to the church for catechism classes. He himself taught the older children. On Wednesdays he would drive to Homer and take a plane to **Seldovia**. There he would offer Mass in some family's living room, spend the night sleeping on the front room couch, then fly back to Homer, hop into his Volkswagen, drive up the peninsula to Anchor Point, offer Mass again in someone's home, spend the night there, before driving several hundred miles back to Seward. While night-driving near Kenai in 1956, he had a bout with a bull moose. He described this as his "biggest excitement in Alaska." The huge animal smashed the windshield of his Volkswagen. "We all survived," he said, "but the car took a worse beating than the moose."

On April 6, 1954, Father Custer wrote to his Father Provincial, Harold O. Small: "Last night the Catholic Ladies surprised me by presenting me a new wrist watch for my birthday. The watch is a yellow gold Elgin and a gold expansion bracelet—price $70.00. I thought it too rich looking. I could exchange it for a stainless steel case. May I accept the watch or exchange it for another?" Father Small's answer: "Keep it as is."

In 1961, Father Custer, "the Priest of the Peninsula," was assigned to St. Anthony's parish in **Anchorage**, where he served for a year as assistant pastor to Father Robert L. **Whelan**, S.J. As such, he regularly visited St. Anthony's dependent mission, St. Andrew's, at Chugiak.

In 1962, Father Custer was reassigned to St. Paul's Mission at Hays, Montana, to serve there as Vice-Superior. In 1966, he fell victim to a debilitating stroke. Needing therapy for his semi-paralyzed condition, he was taken to the Benedictine Nursing Home at Mount Angel, Oregon. A year later, he was transferred to Mount St. Joseph Nursing Home in Portland. Despite all efforts to restore mobility to his arm and leg, and to brighten his understandable intervals of depression, he gradually wasted away, lapsing finally into a lingering comatose condition from which he never emerged.

He died at Mount St. Joseph Nursing Home on Sunday, March 2, 1969, and lies buried in the Jesuit cemetery at Mount St. Michael's. (His brother Ephrem—younger by five years—a Jesuit Lay Brother, died nine years after him.)

After Father Custer died, one of his fellow Jesuits wrote: "Fr. Custer was a gentle, honest, hidden soul—one of those Jesuits about whom you never hear, but who pursues the will of God with love and determination through all kinds of weather. As a Religious he was a pattern of observance; as a priest, of zeal and solicitude. Perhaps his greatest suffering came from his shy nature and the consequent feeling of inadequacy that sometimes gnawed at his spirit. Yet he never refused the responsibilities that faced him, but went wherever he was sent and did the best he knew how. His passing reminds us that in this super-sophisticated age we can still learn much from the meek and humble of heart."

D

D'ARCO, Father Andrew P.

Andrew P. D'Arco was born on May 21, 1950, in the Bronx, New York. In the fall of 1977, he went to **Fairbanks** as a member of the **Jesuit Volunteer Corps**. During the school years 1977–79, he taught mathematics, science and Religion at Immaculate Conception Grade School. He spent a summer helping out with manual labor in some of the remote villages in **Alaska**. It was those experiences that engendered in him the desire to become a priest and to serve Native peoples in bush Alaska. In September 1979, he began four years of theological studies at Mount Angel Seminary, St. Benedict, Oregon. He was ordained to the diaconate on June 5, 1982, in Fairbanks, and to the priesthood on June 4, 1983, in St. Thomas Aquinas Church in Rio Rancho, New Mexico. In both cases, Robert L. **Whelan**, S.J., Bishop of Fairbanks at the time, was the ordaining prelate.

Father D'Arco spent his first year as a priest as associate pastor in **Bethel**. After that he served as pastor of **Aniak**. As such, he cared, too, for its dependent missions, **Holy Cross** and **Kalskag**. In addition to these, he visited also some of the small settlements on the Kuskokwim River upstream from Aniak.

According to Sister Margaret Cantwell, S.S.A., who worked closely with Father D'Arco, "He could be difficult to work with, but he could also be understanding and compassionate. People in crises found in him a gentle, helpful friend. In celebrating the Sacrament of Reconciliation, he was a Christ-like shepherd and healer."

Father D'Arco was totally at home in the villages, loved the people and bush life. With almost equal fervor, he loved plants, flowers, and birds.

Father D'Arco was a man of many talents. He was handy with tools, and had an eye for what needed

Father Andrew P. D'Arco.
LRC.

to be repaired or replaced. He led the way in the construction of the new church at Aniak, witnessing its dedication on September 14, 1986. He did important maintenance work in the living quarters at Holy Cross. On May 17, 1989, at Holy Cross, he witnessed the dedication of the new Holy Family Church.

Being a generous man, Father D'Arco was always ready to lend a hand. This led to his tragic death, at the age of 42, on May 27, 1992, at Aniak. He was helping a friend build a hangar, when trusses fell upon him, killing him instantly. He lies buried in the State of his birth, New York.

de VERTEUIL, Father Jack

Jack de Verteuil was born on February 11, 1942, in Trinidad, British West Indies. In 1953, the family immigrated to Canada. In 1965, he graduated from King's College, London, Ontario, with a B.A. degree in English and History. "The years from 1965–87," in his words, "were a quilted patchwork

Father Jack de Verteuil.
*Photo by Barbara
Walters.*

of work and study: teaching high school in the Yukon Territory and Central, B.C.; work at an asbestos mine in the Yukon; stock room clerk for Simpson-Sears in Vancouver, B.C.; and then a social worker for Catholic Community Services, also in Vancouver."

During one of his teaching years, Jack was intrigued by a colleague's statement: "While man can invent many wondrous things, he cannot invent himself." This remark led to a deep interest in philosophy and theology on Jack's part. Impressed by the missionary work being done in northern Canada by the Missionary **Oblates** of Mary Immaculate, he joined that Congregation, in the late 1970s. In 1982, he obtained a Bachelor of Theology degree from Newman Theological College, St. Albert, Alberta, Canada. However, realizing that he was not called to be an "Order" priest, he left the Oblates and went to Spokane, Washington, where, in August 1987, he entered Mater Dei Institute. Sponsored by Gonzaga University, the institute offered a seminary program for older men aspiring to the priesthood. Mater Dei was founded by Jesuit Fathers Armand M. Nigro, Vincent J. **Beuzer**, and John J. Evoy, its first Rector-President. Jack singled Father Nigro out as one who was especially helpful to him on his journey to the priesthood.

In 1988, Jack earned his M.A. degree in Spirituality from Gonzaga University and was ordained a deacon. He spent his diaconate year, 1988–89, at St. Michael's parish in **McGrath, Alaska**. There he lived through "the great cold of January 1989." He saw the temperature plummet to a record low of minus 76 degrees. For weeks, no planes flew.

On October 28, 1989, Jack was ordained a priest for the Diocese of **Fairbanks**, in Sacred Heart Cathedral, Fairbanks, by Michael J. **Kaniecki**, S.J., Bishop of Fairbanks at the time. Father de Verteuil spent his first year as a priest at St. Nicholas parish in **North Pole**. In 1990, he was appointed assistant pastor of St. Joseph's parish in **Nome**. As such, he served also as visiting priest to St. Joseph's dependent stations: **Teller**, **Little Diomede** Island, and **Unalakleet**.

In 1994, Father de Verteuil became pastor of the so-called "Railbelt"—the communities strung out for 110 miles along the Parks Highway and the Alaska Railroad from **Nenana** all the way to Cantwell. For the first two years, he made his headquarters in Nenana, out of which he visited Anderson, Clear Air Force Radar Station, **Healy**, Cantwell, and Denali National Park. In 1996, he began to make his headquarters in Healy, visiting the above mentioned places out of there. It was not long before he recognized, and gratefully acknowledged, deep indebtedness to both Sister Agnes Wilcox, S.M.S.M., long-time Pastoral Administrator of the Nenana parish, and to Barbara Walters, Pastoral Administrator of the Healy parish since 1980, the year of its founding. He came to regard both as "the two *keys* to successful ministry on the Railbelt."

An avid downhill skier, as well as an enthusiastic professional sports fan, Father de Verteuil, as of the year 2004, found relaxation on the slopes, or in front of a TV set watching the Houston Oilers or the Montreal Canadiens or the Toronto Blue Jays. He found peace and relaxation, too, in taking "Sibir," his Siberian Husky, on long wilderness walks. Punning on his first name, he admitted to being "a jack-of-all-trades, and a master of none." First and foremost, he has been a committed priest of the Lord.

DELMORE, Father Eugene P., S.J.

Eugene Patrick "Gene" Delmore, the oldest of eleven children, was born on January 17, 1938, in St. Vincent's Hospital in Billings, Montana, to Michael Delmore and Ellen Linehan Delmore. Michael was a devout man; so much so, that, on their wedding day, Ellen became a Catholic. Michael worked as an engineer for the Northern Pacific Railway. For his elementary schooling, Gene attended Fratt Memorial, a grade school in Billings staffed by Sisters. For his first two years of high school, and for part of his third, he attended Central Catholic High School, likewise in Billings. During his junior year, in 1954, the family moved to Seattle because of his father's promotion to district freight agent. The family, now numbering eleven—with twins on the way—"all piled into one coach car," as Gene remembered the move years later, "and," quoting his father, "it was the biggest departure from Montana since Chief Joseph went to Canada."

In Seattle, Gene's father, having attended Jesuit-run Marquette University in Milwaukee, Wisconsin, and thinking that some of that "good Jesuit discipline" which he had experienced would be good also for Gene, sent him to Jesuit-staffed Seattle Preparatory. Gene, in spite of having had neither Greek nor Latin, nor being, by his own admission, "an especially good student," survived the college-prep curriculum, and graduated from Seattle Prep. During his senior year, he made a retreat at Port Townsend, Washington, in the course of which he "received the confirming graces" that made him sure he wanted to be a Jesuit priest rather than a diocesan priest. On August 14, 1956, he entered St. Francis Xavier Novitiate at Sheridan, Oregon. After completing his two-year noviceship, he spent an additional two years there studying the classics and humanities.

From 1960–63, Gene made his philosophical studies at Mount St. Michael's in Spokane, Washington, completing them with an M.A. degree in philosophy. During the summer of 1963, he taught some courses in ethics at Gonzaga University, in Spokane. He next spent three years teaching at Jesuit High School in Portland, Oregon. From 1966–70, he made his theological studies at Regis College in Toronto, Ontario, Canada. In the course of those studies, he began doing retreat work in that general vicinity. He was ordained a priest in Seattle on June 14, 1969.

In 1970, Father Delmore began his ministry as a priest at Seattle University, serving there as a member of the campus ministry team. At the same time,

Father Eugene P. Delmore, S.J. *BR-897932.*

he became quite involved with the Marriage Encounter and the Engaged Encounter movements. For three years, while on the Seattle University staff, he lived in a small community, whose members shared the cooking. From this experience he learned the art of cooking, which was to stand him in good stead during his years in **Alaska**.

During the year 1976–77, Father Delmore made his tertianship in Hazaribagh, Bihar State, India. After that "third world experience," he returned to Seattle University. While there, he was asked by his good friend, Father William C. **Dibb**, S.J., if he could assist him during the Lenten season of 1977 at Sacred Heart Cathedral parish in **Fairbanks**, Alaska. With the approval of Father William J. **Loyens**, S.J., Provincial of the Oregon Province at the time, and former General Superior of Jesuits in Alaska, Father Delmore was able to accept the invitation. At the end of Lent, a letter writing campaign was begun to keep him in Fairbanks. Asked by Father Loyens, "Did you like the experience?" Father Delmore said simply, "Yes." To that, Father Loyens, "Then stay there."

Father Delmore went on to spend five years at Sacred Heart Cathedral parish: as assistant pastor from 1977–80 and as pastor from 1980–82. In 1978, he started the Alaska chapter of the Engaged Encounter program. "Those were busy years, full of many changes," he remembered years later.

Interested in giving retreats since the time of his

theological studies, Father Delmore, in late1982, requested that he be allowed to go into retreat work. Accordingly, he was assigned to Holy Spirit Retreat House—renamed **Holy Spirit Center** in 1999—in **Anchorage**. From late 1982–85, he was deeply involved "doing retreats, and lots of pastoral ministry to surrounding parishes, especially **Wasilla**, **Palmer**, and on the Kenai Peninsula." An avid outdoorsman, and member of the Alaska Hiking Club, he loved the Kenai, and spent his summer vacations there. Accompanied by his dog, Jill, and armed with his fishing pole, he spent many an hour on the banks of the Kenai's Russian River. In the winter, he found escape and relaxation in cross-country skiing on the slopes of the Chugach Mountains rising right above the Retreat House.

Beginning in 1980, Father Delmore served as a Consultor to the General Superior of Jesuits in Alaska. In 1985, Father James A. **Sebesta**, S.J., his General Superior at the time, suggested that he consider getting "some bush experience," so as to be better qualified as a Consultor. Father Delmore was faced with a difficult decision, knowing that to get some bush experience he would have to leave his "city roots," with all the conveniences and comforts attached thereto. Nevertheless, in December 1985, he began his long years of ministry in rural Alaska, as pastor of **Mountain Village** and **Pilot Station**.

During his first weeks in the villages, Father Delmore felt himself like "a lamb among wolves," in his own words. Knowing little about building maintenance and the practical aspects of everyday village life, he had, at first, a rough time of it. Some wondered out loud, "Will this greenhorn make it in the bush?" But, being sure that he was called to ministry in the bush, he was determined to make believers out of them.

It was not too long before Father Delmore was quite at home as a village pastor. Because of his gentleness and evident love for them, the people soon came to appreciate his pastoral presence among them and to accept him as one of their own. He shared their lives and their lifestyle. He fished, and hunted moose with them. In an open skiff, powered by an outboard motor, he plied the Yukon River and its sloughs, when they were ice-free. Between freeze-up and break-up, he traveled them by snowmachine. Before he left Mountain Village, he had the joy, on August 23, 1987, of seeing the new St. Lawrence Church, which he had helped construct, dedicated.

In 1987, Father Delmore was asked to take charge of the "Center of Theological Studies," located at the recently closed St. Mary's Mission boarding school on the **Andreafsky** River. This he did, while, at the same time, serving as visiting priest to Mountain Village, Pilot Station, and the St. Marys parish. As head of the CTS, along with Sisters Pauline Igoe, O.P., and Angela Fortier, C.S.J., he traveled to various villages in the Yukon-Kuskokwim Delta, conducting workshops. In 1989, the CTS was discontinued. As visiting priest, he continued to tend the villages of Mountain Village and Pilot Station, and the added villages of **Marshall** and **Russian Mission**.

In 1991, Father Delmore was assigned to the Nelson Island villages of **Toksook Bay**, **Tununak**, **Nightmute**, **Newtok**, and **Chefornak**. This assignment entailed almost constant travel. In 1994, "after three exhausting years on the trail," in his words, he was granted a sabbatical year. The first semester of this he spent with the Manresa Jesuit Community in Spokane, and the second at the Arrupe Jesuit Residence in Seattle. During that "wonderful year," he attended classes at both Gonzaga and Seattle Universities.

His sabbatical over, Father Delmore returned to Alaska in June 1995. From that date to the end of 1997, he served as pastor of Mountain Village and **Kotlik**. In January 1998, he became pastor of Immaculate Conception parish in **Bethel**, and of its two dependent stations, Marshall and Russian Mission. This assignment entailed far less traveling than did his previous assignments. "It's nice," he wrote, "not to have to live out of a suitcase all the time." He considered himself most fortunate to have with him, from the outset of his Bethel assignment, Father Henry G. **Hargreaves**, S.J., as his assistant priest. Father Hargreaves generally served as visiting priest to the two villages on the Yukon. Concerning Father Delmore, Father Hargreaves wrote, on March 21, 2001, to a Jesuit friend in California, "Fr. Gene Delmore is pastor, and a great one at that. He is very personable and gets on well with the people."

As of the year 2004, Father Delmore was still pastor of the Bethel parish. As such, he regularly visited Bethel's large public health hospital. He also reached out to the unfortunates in Bethel's prison and halfway house. He continued to be deeply concerned about the matter of training and involving Native people as leaders in Church affairs. Like the Native people he had served for so many years, he had become a specialist, when it came to offering hospitality. With Bethel's being a transportation hub, people were constantly coming and going. Many of them sought hospitality at Immaculate Conception Church. It was not long before Father Delmore became known for his gracious hospitality. He enjoyed the reputation of always having a pot of beans on the stove for people to partake of after the daily noon Mass.

A life of ministry and service as demanding as Father Delmore's was throughout most of his years in Alaska could not, obviously, have been sustained without a solid spiritual foundation. Not surprisingly, his public ministry and personal spiritual life were founded on the Spiritual Exercises of St. Ignatius Loyola, with which he became so very familiar as a maker and director of many retreats. There are certain parts of the Exercises in which he found particular spiritual strength and support, foremost among them being the "Contemplation to Obtain Divine Love," and the Ignatian principle of "Finding God in All Things." He and his ministry were supported, too, by an intense personal devotion to the Holy Spirit. "Increasingly," he wrote, "in my ministry, I see the need to affirm again and again the creative, life-giving presence of the Holy Spirit."

DELON, Philip I., S.J.

For seven years he was General Superior of the **Alaska** Mission. He saw the desirability of the Mission's having its own airplane, and was instrumental in getting one, though he himself was apprehensive about flying. It was in the fatal crash of the mission plane that he lost his life.

Philip Isidore Delon was born in Laborie Rouge, Dordogne, France, on April 22, 1876. He volunteered for the Rocky Mountain Mission, was accepted, and, on July 26, 1892, entered the Jesuit novitiate at DeSmet, Idaho. He made his philosophical studies at St. Ignatius Mission, Montana, then taught there for a year, before going on to teach for three years at Gonzaga College in Spokane. He taught mainly the sciences, mathematics, and French. He studied theology at St. Louis University, and was ordained a priest there on June 26, 1906. After two years at Los Gatos, California, where he made his tertianship and served as assistant to the novice master for a year, he was assigned to the Indian Mission of the Holy Family, Montana, for a year. He spent the years 1911–15 as pastor of St. Francis Xavier's parish in Missoula, Montana.

Father Delon, whom Father Segundo **Llorente**, S.J, described as "a man of much zeal, like a good Frenchman full of energy, a bit of an idealist with the effervescence of a boiling pot, always planning," went to Alaska in 1915, arriving in **Nome** on August 2nd. His first Alaskan assignment was St. Mary's Mission, **Akulurak**. He began his three-year stay there on August 17th. He was Superior of that mission during the second of his two years there. In 1918, he was appointed Superior of **Holy Cross Mission**; and, on September 15, 1923, he became General Superior of the Alaska Mission. As such, he continued to make Holy Cross his headquarters, out of which he traveled far and wide, by boat and

Father Philip I. Delon, S.J. *JOPA-1061.01.*

dogsled, in every kind of weather, founding new missions: among them **Kashunuk**, **Hooper Bay**, **Nightmute**, and **Kotzebue**. He was compared to Junipero Serra, because of the many missions he founded in northern Alaska between 1923 and 1930, the year of his death. In his letters to his Father Provincial, Joseph M. Piet, S.J., he was constantly making known his needs for qualified men to staff those missions, for men who, among other things, could "learn the lingo." He attached great importance to this, and himself seems to have had an adequate command of Central Yup'ik Eskimo. A reading of his official letters reveals Father Delon to have been a shrewd evaluator of men and a level-headed judge of situations.

Father Delon held the position of Superior almost the whole of his priestly life, much as he kept hoping all along to be freed of the burdens of that office. His correspondence reveals him to have been a model Superior, not too permissive, yet gentle and caring for his "subjects." He made his visitations faithfully, gave his subjects an adequate hearing and the benefit of the doubt. If one "really selected his own status," as did Father Martin J. **Lonneux**, S.J., he was ready to see in it the hand of Divine Providence for some greater good. He knew what his men were going through, as he himself had spent much time on the trail. One day, while on the winter trail to an Eskimo village, and thinking he could not reach it before total darkness set in, he decided to camp for the night. He woke up the next morning to find an Eskimo semi-subterranean dwelling buried in the snow within only ten feet of where he had slept.

Father Delon's official reports to his Father Provincial were expansive, forthright, objective. He was more ready to accept the blame himself for shortcomings of whatever kind than to assess it. He was patient with human weakness and tried always to see the bright side of things, to build up downcast spirits, to encourage. And he knew how to value "that inexplicable feminine intuition" that he encountered in the **Ursuline** Sisters at Akulurak and in the Sisters of St. **Ann** at Holy Cross. As a Superior, his mind was open to new ideas, to innovations, such as the introduction of typewriters, radios, communicating by telegram, and traveling by air. It may sound trite to say that Father Delon, as a man, and as a Superior, was genuinely a man of faith,

hope, and charity, but, in his case, this can be said without qualification.

In March 1929, Father Delon had pilot A.A. Bennett fly him around to visit various missions. The ease with which he was able to make the rounds sold him on the idea that the Alaska Mission should have a plane of its own. He proposed the matter to Father Piet and Joseph R. **Crimont**, S.J., Vicar Apostolic of Alaska at the time. Both saw the merits of his proposal. The following year, on July 19, 1930, Father Delon found himself airborne, in the newly acquired mission plane, the *Marquette Missionary*, flying out of New York, headed west. At the controls of the plane was Brother George J. **Feltes**, S.J., who had earned his pilot's license just the year before. Their final destination was Holy Cross, the designated home base for the plane. From Seattle the plane was shipped by boat and train to **Fairbanks**. There Ralph Wien, an airplane mechanic, a pilot, a man at home in Alaska, was hired on to serve as co-pilot. The trio arrived at Holy Cross on September 18th. After Holy Cross, came stops at Nome and at **Pilgrim Hot Springs**. On October 9th, the *Marquette Missionary* made its first landing in Kotzebue, where Father Delon visited with Father William F. Walsh, pastor of the Kotzebue mission, and went over parish business with him. In his day-to-day account of events involving the plane, Brother Feltes wrote: "October 12th: Sunday, Father Delon and Father Walsh finished their last work on earth."

In the afternoon of that fateful Sunday, October 12, 1930, Father Delon wanted to take a trip to Deering, a small village not very far from Kotzebue, to attend to some business there and to show Father Walsh some of his mission territory. Father Walsh had come to Kotzebue only the previous year. He welcomed the opportunity to see Kotzebue and his mission territory from the air. However, when the plane was about to take off for Deering, some snow-flurries blew in. By the time they had cleared out, it was too late in the day to make the flight to Deering. But, since the plane was already warmed up and ready to fly, it was decided that Ralph Wien, because he was already at the controls, should take the two priests up for a short swing around Kotzebue. To keep the plane load lighter, Brother Feltes decided to stay on the ground. The Kotzebue airstrip was not very long.

"Ralph took off with the two fathers and got off nicely with some room to spare," reported Brother Feltes in a telegram to Father Piet. He then went on to describe the pre-crash nature of the short flight. And then he reported how the plane "went into a straight dive for the ground and struck it head on and the plane stood straight up on its nose with the motor buried in the ground." All three passengers were killed upon impact. Throughout the rest of his long life, Brother Feltes remained unshakable in his conviction that it was "an error of human judgment" that led to the crash.

Our Lady of Sorrows Church, Delta Junction. *Photo by Fr. John B. Martinek.*

Father Delon, it seems, had a premonition of his death. He had left sealed instructions at Holy Cross for the administration of the missions in the event of his death. Two years earlier, he had written to Father Piet the words, "much as I dread being up in the air."

The bodies of the two priests were shipped south immediately after the fatal accident. Father Philip I. Delon, S.J., lies buried in the Jesuit cemetery at Mount St. Michael's, Spokane.

92

DELTA JUNCTION

Delta Junction, on the right bank of the Delta River, is located at the junction of the Alaska and Richardson Highways, some 100 miles southeast of **Fairbanks**. In the year 2000, Delta Junction had a population of 840.

The Catholic Church began to establish itself in Delta Junction in the early 1940s, when Ray Stirewalt gave the Catholics of Delta Junction a building and some land on Buffalo Lane. The building was remodeled into a simple church. Army chaplains from nearby Fort Greely offered Mass in it for a time. In 1952, "a new mission church" was completed. For some years, during the early 1950s, Father John R. **Buchanan**, S.J., served Delta Junction's Catholic community out of **Tok**.

In 1961, Father Joseph L. Asturias, O.P., took up residency in Delta Junction. "I never was able," he wrote "to build the church Bishop **Gleeson** wanted. I lived in a small trailer beside the little wooden church just off the hotel grounds." In November 1962, Father Asturias was replaced by Father Patrick S. Duffy. In the early 1960s, Father William A. Zorichak, the Army chaplain at Fort Greely, arranged to have an old World War II barracks building shipped from Eielson Air Force Base to what became the site of the new Our Lady of Sorrows Church on Deborah Street. The building furnished some of the materials for the new church. Concrete blocks used in the construction of the new church were made from gravel hauled to **Copper Valley School**, there made into blocks, and then hauled back.

Father Duffy left Delta Junction in 1963. For the next four years, until Father Anderson E. **Bakewell**, S.J., arrived in November 1967, Our Lady of Sorrows parish was without a resident pastor. Father Bakewell was to be the first resident pastor in the new church–rectory complex. He lived in the Nissen Apartments, until the new church–rectory was completed. He left Delta Junction in 1976.

From 1976–79, Father **Joseph L. Hebert**, S.J., routinely visited Our Lady of Sorrows parish, out of Tok. He was followed by Father Lawrence A. **Nevue**, S.J., who visited it, likewise out of Tok, during the years

1979–81, and then was in residence for the following year. Father William T. **Burke**, S.J., was resident pastor of Our Lady of Sorrows from 1982–87.

In 1987, Father **Joseph E. Laudwein**, S.J., became pastor of Our Lady of Sorrows. He, too, saw the need, as did his predecessors, for a larger church. He was instrumental, in his own words, "with the skillful and generous cooperation of parish members," in bringing about a beautiful new and larger church. This is connected to the old parish complex by an enclosed corridor. The new Our Lady of Sorrows Church was solemnly dedicated by Michael J. **Kaniecki**, S.J., Bishop of Fairbanks at the time, on September 17, 1989.

Father Laudwein was replaced as pastor of the Delta Junction parish in 1994, by Father Don M. **Balquin**, who served that parish until 1998. During the years 1999 to 2002, the Delta Junction parish was visited at irregular intervals out of Fairbanks by Fathers William E. **Cardy**, O.F.M.; Timothy L. **Sander**, O.S.B.; and J. Albert **Levitre**. In the year 2002, Father John B. **Martinek**, headquartered in Delta Junction, began to serve as pastor of Our Lady of Sorrows.

DEMERS, Bishop Modeste

Alaska was first officially and formally recognized by the Catholic Church as an ecclesiastical province in 1847, when Modeste Demers was consecrated the first Bishop of Vancouver Island, Canada, and entrusted with the evangelization of that island and of "all the British and Russian possessions as far north as the glacial sea." While Bishop Demers is honored as the cofounder of the Church in Oregon and as founder of the Church in British Columbia, there is no documentary evidence to indicate that he paid anything more than passing attention to Alaska, known at that time as "Russian America." He was totally lacking in the resources needed to do missionary work in the North.

Modeste Demers was born on October 11, 1809, at St. Nicholas, Quebec, Canada. He was ordained a priest on February 7, 1836, and left for the Oregon country two years later. In 1842, he began missionary work among the Indian tribes in the interior of British Columbia. On November 30, 1847, he

Bishop Modeste Demers. *LRC.*

was consecrated Bishop of Vancouver Island. The following year he made a trip to Europe to find support for his priestless and penniless diocese. Still trying to find clergy and Religious for his diocese, he interested the young Congregation of the Sisters of St. **Ann** to leave St. Jacques, Quebec, in 1858, for Fort Victoria on Vancouver Island. Unknowingly, this providential move on his part was the prelude to the future Alaska/Yukon ministry of the Sisters of St. Ann.

Bishop Demers died, as a consequence of a stroke, on July 28, 1871, and is buried in St. Andrew's Cathedral in Victoria.

DESCHOUT, Father Paul C., S.J.

Paul C. Deschout was born of Flemish parents on January 4, 1900, in Tielt, West Flanders, Belgium. In Turnhout, Belgium, he attended the Apostolic School for four years of high school and two years of college. With a view to serving as a missionary priest in **Alaska**, he applied to be accepted into the California Province of the Society of Jesus. On November 1, 1919, he entered the novitiate at Los Gatos. After completing his two-year noviceship, he spent a third year there studying the classics and humanities. He spent the years 1922–25 at Mount St. Michael's, Spokane, Washington, in philosophical studies. After teaching at St. Ignatius High School in San Francisco during the year 1925–26, he moved on to four years of theological studies at

Woodstock College, Maryland, and Louvain, Belgium. He was ordained a priest at Louvain on August 24, 1929. After his fourth year of theology, he went to Alaska.

On August 28, 1930, Father Deschout arrived, "just from Europe," according to the mission diarist, at St. Mary's Mission, **Akulurak**, where he was to spend his first four years in Alaska. There he immediately applied himself to learning the Central Yup'ik Eskimo language. Gifted linguistically, he soon had a good grasp of the language and left some manuscripts in it. When he was General Superior of the Alaska Mission, he, in a letter dated August 29, 1948, urged Father Harold O. Small, S.J., Oregon Province Provincial at the time, to insist that the Jesuit missionaries in Alaska "not too easily give up the study of the native language."

In addition to devoting much time to the study of the language while at Akulurak, Father Deschout, shortly after his arrival there, began also to travel often to the widely-scattered villages in the area. While at Akulurak, he routinely played the organ and directed the singing. His musical gifts served him well throughout his long years among the Eskimos.

On August 28, 1934, Father **Hubert A. Post**, S.J., noted in the Akulurak diary: "The *St. Patrick* pulled out for **Hooper Bay** having aboard good Fr. Deschout, who is to spend a year on Nelson Island and then go to tertianship. We will miss him very much." Father Deschout spent the year 1934–35 on Nelson Island, at **Tununak**. Father **John P. Fox**, S.J., who accompanied him there, wrote, "I turned the mission over to Father Deschout in 1934, a big day in Tununak history. They spent an hour in thanksgiving in church, when I arrived with the new pastor, after coming out to meet us in full procession." Since Father Deschout did not keep a house diary during that year on Nelson Island, little is known about his doings. It can be safely assumed, however, that he carried out the routine work of a missionary in that situation.

Father Deschout made his tertianship at Port Townsend, Washington, 1935–36, then returned to Nelson Island, where he was to spend all his years as a missionary in Alaska. Making Tununak, which he described as "my beloved nest on Nelson Island," his main station, he visited, on a regular basis, its

Father Paul C. Deschout, S.J. *JOPA-946.01.*

two dependent stations, **Nightmute** and **Chefornak**. Unfortunately, he did not keep a house diary there either. However, he left a rich legacy of letters, that describe well his life and ministry on Nelson Island. His letters are always positive, optimistic, upbeat, written from the heart. They sparkle with witticisms, he himself often adding the "ha, ha!" There is a charming informality about them. The bishop is often referred to as "the Bip," or as the "big boss." Superiors in general are the "big guns." His Father Provincial, Leopold J. Robinson, S.J., is addressed as "Robbie," referred to as "Big Chief." Commonly Father Deschout signed his letters simply as "Pablo." In turn, he was addressed as, "Pablo, my boy." French and Latin phrases are sprinkled generously throughout his correspondence. All this was at a time when strict formalities were still the general norm. Even during the six years he was General Superior of the Alaska Mission, he did not take himself too seriously. Business matters were, often enough, of a very serious nature, but he was able to treat them with a light touch.

Father Deschout led a simple lifestyle, not unlike that of the people among whom he lived and worked. In 1946, he visited the Jesuit novitiate at Sheridan, Oregon. There the assembled young Jesuits had occasion to ask him what he ate for breakfast, and for lunch, and for dinner. In each case he answered the question with one and the same word. When they were astonished at this, he said,

"But *feesch* eez gooot!" As a relief from his basic diet of fish, he greatly welcomed, with profuse expressions of gratitude, an occasional chunk of Swiss cheese from his Father Provincial.

Father Deschout raised his own dogs, which he needed for his routine trips to his dependent stations, and for his infrequent trips to his Jesuit neighbors at Hooper Bay and Akulurak. It was written of him that "he always smiled with kindness to everyone he met on the trails." For summer travel he had an open skiff with an outboard motor, "a kicker."

On Nelson Island, where he had "a really very edifying bunch of Christians," Father Deschout lived pretty much in isolation. On April 17, 1939, he wrote to his Father Provincial, William G. Elliott, S.J., that there was no post office on the island and that mail was very irregular. "To get Christmas cards in August," he wrote, "is *regular*." As a happy hermit on Nelson Island, he could write: "the work here is my consolation. Outside of that I've got nothing." Still, the musician and choir leader in him longed for an organ. On July 25, 1944, he wrote to Father Elliott, "I surely would like an organ that plays true. The missions may have their drawbacks, but one leads a happy life here and very close to the Lord." Anticipating getting the organ, he concludes his letter with "oodles of thanks!" When Father Deschout made his simple needs known, he always did so with expressions of resignation and with sentiments of heartfelt gratitude.

No other Alaskan missionary ever, with the possible exception of Father Bellarmine **Lafortune**, S.J., vis-à-vis the King Islanders, was so wedded to his flock as Father Deschout was to his Nelson Islanders. It was truly a mutual love affair. While his success in bringing about such a relationship rested in large part on the fact that he did genuinely love his people and mastered their language, it rested, in no small part, also on the fact that he did not present Catholicism as a threat to their traditional way of life. He was shrewd enough to play on points of similarity between the positive, life-renewing aspects of traditional Native beliefs and the Catholic Faith. He was highly successful as a missionary also, because of the genuine respect he had for the traditional Native culture and attitudes. To Father Fox he wrote in 1938, "I encouraged the Eskimos to keep up their old prac-

tices and dances because they were used as a source of amusement and everyone loved them, and they were innocent enough, they weren't superstitious or anything like that."

As of March 28, 1944, Father Deschout was General Superior of Jesuits in northern Alaska. As such, he continued to stay on at Tununak, where he had "430 souls" to care for, during the winters. During the summers, he went "around a bit to see if the monks say their prayers." As General Superior, he was concerned that so few of the priests knew "the lingo." He urged that priests be sent to the Bristol Bay area, to **Dillingham**, to establish a Catholic presence there and to minister to the Bering Sea coast Eskimos working seasonally there in the canneries.

On May 20, 1945, Joseph R. **Crimont**, S.J., Vicar Apostolic of Alaska, died. He was succeeded as such by his Coadjutor, Walter J. **Fitzgerald**, S.J. The latter, however, was by that time already in very poor health, virtually a "lame duck." For two years, consequently, there was a leadership vacuum in the Vicariate of Alaska. This made Father Deschout's position as General Superior somewhat ambiguous, complicated. Then, on July 19, 1947, Bishop Fitzgerald himself died. Father Deschout, by this time in his third year as General Superior, now automatically became also Vicar General of the Vicariate of Alaska. As such, he was now the "big gun," the "big boss," with major decisions to make. For the most part, however, he let the *status quo* be the order of the day.

Father Deschout's main concern as Vicar General was for a new bishop, and sooner rather than later. "The great cry of the missionaries," he wrote in a letter to "Dear Robbie," dated March 30, 1947, "is for a good, healthy, holy missionary bishop living with us on the missions." Did he himself, perhaps, aspire to become that missionary bishop? Far from it, for in that same letter he wrote, "I will be a happy boy to re-enter in the rank and file of good missionaries." When he learned that his name was on the list of three candidates proposed to Rome to fill the position vacated by the death of Bishop Fitzgerald, he became, as he wrote, "very nervous," was greatly troubled, hoped and prayed he would not be Rome's choice. So concerned was he about this possibility, that he brought the matter up with

Father Provincial Robinson and asked for his advice on it. Father Robinson wrote him that he, as Provincial, having prayed over the matter, could, *coram Deo* ("before God"), assure Father Deschout that, if nominated, he could in good conscience refuse the nomination. This put Father Deschout's mind and heart at rest. "Am I relieved!" he wrote.

As Vicar General, Father Deschout lived temporarily in **Juneau**. From there, he wrote on July 23, 1947, "Here I am, like a fish out of water, most lonesome for my Eskimos and machinating how to get back to them as soon as possible." His cares as Vicar General came to an end, when, on April 5, 1948, Francis D. **Gleeson**, S.J., became the new Vicar Apostolic of Alaska. Another of Father Deschout's great concerns also came to an end, when, on October 3, 1951, Father Dermot **O'Flanagan** became the bishop of the newly established Diocese of Juneau. For six years, Father Deschout had been urging, "pleading and crabbing," that there should be two bishops for Alaska, one for the Panhandle in southeastern, the other for the missions of the North. He was convinced that unless there were two, the missions of northern Alaska would continue to receive less than the needed attention.

On November 1, 1950, Father Deschout's term as General Superior of Jesuits in northern Alaska came to an end. How happy he was to return full-time again to his people on Nelson Island! Commenting on Father Deschout's term of office as General Superior, Father Francis M. **Ménager**, S.J., wrote, "[Father Deschout] endeared himself to all by his wonderful Religious spirit, his genial ways and his affectionate heart."

In spite of his fairly numerous trips away from the island as General Superior and Vicar General, Father Deschout remained at heart "the hermit of Nelson Island." On January 27, 1950, while he was still General Superior, Father Paul C. **O'Connor**, S.J., saw fit to write to James U. **Conwell**, S.J.: "A note of confidence—just received a letter from Pablo. It did not sound good at all. That guy has been too long alone. I wish the bishop would change him so that he would be around Ours [fellow Jesuits] for awhile. Living 15 years alone is an abnormal situation even for a saint. Several government people told me that Pablo is going completely native—

'has missed too many boats,' as one told me." But, Father Deschout continued on as missionary on Nelson Island for another ten years.

By around 1950, modern inventions had made their way also to Nelson Island. Some time in the early 1950s, Father Deschout was struck on the head by a whirling snowmachine propeller. He needed to be hospitalized. The blow caused some brain damage. He also had a stroke sometime in 1952. Accordingly, for health reasons and to remove him from his isolated condition on Nelson Island, he was sent to Hooper Bay for a time. From there he wrote to Bishop Gleeson on June 1, 1953, about his "lonesomeness for Nelson Island," which, he found, far from decreasing was increasing and "torturing him." In his early 50s, he was still a relatively young man, but his mental and physical health was no longer what it had been.

About this same time, Father Deschout sought permission from higher Superiors to visit his family and friends in his native Belgium. He had not seen them since 1930. Permission was graciously granted, and he had a wonderful visit during the summer of 1953. By Christmas, he was again back in Tununak, having been brought there from **Bethel** by "faithful dog teams, 6 strong." He saw humor in the fact that, on his return trip from Belgium, he had spent more time traveling by dogsled than he had by plane.

From Tununak, he wrote, on May 14, 1954, to Bishop Gleeson: "Whole town is *daily* at Mass and H. Communion. They return at 7 P.M. for rosary in common, evening prayer and hymns. Nelson Is. is a paradise. These people are simply wearing out the church's floor. This is my 20th yr. here and 25th yr. as a priest. I'll be everlasting grateful to you for sending me back here."

For stroke-related health reasons, Father Deschout found himself at St. Mary's Mission, **Andreafsky**, during the latter part of 1955. From there he wrote to Bishop Gleeson, on December 18, 1955, "With my health returning, my strong desire to return to Nelson Is. is daily more felt. My stroke of Nov. 12 is about finished. So here I am asking, begging you for permission to return to Nelson Is." In April 1956, he was in Seattle for a medical examination, after which the doctor told him, "You can return to Alaska any day." Bishop Gleeson gave him permission to return to Nelson Island. On May 13, 1956, he wrote the bishop from the village of Chabutnuak, near Nelson Island, "I am here, the happiest man in Alaska. A real springtime for me. God bless the day you were consecrated!"

In 1958, Father Deschout visited family and friends in Belgium for a second time. In early 1961, he was again, for health reasons, back at St. Mary's Mission. Strokes kept afflicting him. Still, according to Father James E. **Poole**, Superior of St. Mary's at the time, he was "determined to go back to the Island, but he can hardly make it about this place." In late December 1961, Father Deschout saw Nelson Island for the last time. In 1934, shortly after he first set foot on that island, he told Father Fox, that he would consider it "the greatest grace of his life" to spend the rest of his days with those people. There was great sorrow all around, when Father Deschout left Tununak for good.

During the early part of 1962, Father Deschout was in **Ketchikan**, to help out as hospital chaplain there and to attend to his own health. In all respects, it was not a happy situation. Again he begged, in spite of his severely damaged health, to be allowed to go back either to Nelson Island or to Belgium. He was allowed to make a third visit to Belgium; but, alas, he was simply no longer the man he had been earlier. In mind and body he was a changed man. He kept falling down, suffered mental lapses, was irritable, impossible to please. A later examination by a doctor revealed that he was suffering from a "degenerative disease of the nervous system." The visit was a sad affair for him, but more so for his family and relatives. Nevertheless, as his nephew, a Belgian Jesuit priest wrote, his relatives "took every care of him with admirable solicitude and complaisance."

Even after this third visit home, Father Deschout continued to beg, even writing a series of letters to the Father General in Rome, to be allowed to make yet another visit to Belgium, with the possibility of staying there permanently. Both his mental and physical condition had by now deteriorated noticeably. Members of his family, including his nephew, urged that he not be allowed to return, giving as reasons that he fell frequently, suffered mental lapses,

and was very difficult to live with, and that they had neither the personnel nor the facilities to care for him. At the same time Father Deschout was begging to be allowed to return to Belgium, he was begging, too, to be allowed to return to Nelson Island, stressing how sorely his people must miss not having the Mass and Sacraments in their own language. His letters of the early 1960s especially, letters written with tears of the heart, make for heart-rending reading. By contrast, letters Superiors wrote to him in response to his entreaties, letters showing great compassion and understanding on their part, make for uplifting reading.

By now, the whole matter was in the hands of the Father Provincial of the Oregon Province, under whose jurisdiction Father Deschout came. He assigned him to Sheridan, Oregon, where he spent the last years of his life in restless, unresigned retirement. Up to the very last year of his life, he continued to plead to be allowed to return to his Nelson Island paradise.

In October 1964, Father Louis L. **Renner**, S.J., met Father Deschout's sister in Belgium. She knew well the status of her brother's health and of his discontent at being confined to the novitiate at Sheridan. It broke her heart to think about it. Father Renner was able, however, to console her to some extent by assuring her that the man who had visited her in 1962 was, by then, already a broken man, not the real Father Deschout, and that the real Father Deschout, the truly great Alaskan missionary, was the one remembered and esteemed by all who knew of him.

Father Deschout died in St. Vincent's Hospital in Portland, Oregon, on February 12, 1966. He lies buried in the Jesuit cemetery at Mount St. Michael's.

After Father Deschout's death, one of his fellow Jesuits wrote: "Those of us who saw him in his prime in 1936 and then again in 1963 found it hard to believe that he was the same man, for in his prime he had been every inch a perfect, enterprising, zealous, enthusiastic and well-organized missionary."

DESJARDINS, Joseph-Alphonse, S.J.

Joseph-Alphonse Desjardins, French Canadian, was born on September 3, 1867. He entered the

Society of Jesus on July 31, 1886, was ordained a priest in Montreal in 1899, and came to **Alaska**, as a volunteer, in 1908. After spending a year at **Holy Cross Mission**, he served among the Koyukon Athabaskans: at **Nulato**, from 1908–13; and at **Ruby** and **Kokrines**, from 1913–15, when he left Alaska. In his book, *EN ALASKA: Deux mois sous la tente*, he gives an account of a two-month period he spent with the Nulato Koyukon, while they were on a fall hunting outing in the Kaiyuh Mountains region. His style is concrete and such as to make the reader feel present to the events being described. Father Desjardins died on May 1, 1962, four months short of his 95th birthday. He is remembered for his air of reserve, for his soft voice, his sense of compassion for one and all, for his accessibility to all at any time. He seemed so happy to render service, that one never needed to fear he was intruding upon him.

28

DESSO, Father Leo C.

Leo C. Desso, one of eight children, was born on May 19, 1935, in Colchester, Vermont, but spent his early youth in Winooski, Vermont, where he attended public elementary schools and received his religious education by attending Confraternity of Christian Doctrine classes. He graduated from high school in Key West, Florida, in 1954.

Leo worked for the Raytheon Company in Waltham, Massachusetts, from 1956–65. During those years he also taught elementary catechism classes at St. Charles Church in Waltham and was in the process of discerning his calling in life. In the Boston archdiocesan newspaper, *The Boston Pilot*, he came across on advertisement placed by the Brothers of Charity of Immaculate Heart of Mary headquartered in Banning, California, inviting men to join their community. This Leo did in 1965.

As a Brother, Leo was at first assigned to work with juvenile delinquents at Boys Town of the Desert in Banning. Later he worked in the community's facility in Beaumont, California. For a time he was his community's Vocational Director and Assistant Superior. He attended the San Jacinto Community College from 1969–72.

Father Leo C. Desso.
Courtesy of Fr. Desso.

Around 1970, **Joseph T. Ryan**, Archbishop of **Anchorage**, **Alaska**, seeking Brothers to help him in his archdiocese, visited Brother Leo's community. Three Brothers went North in February 1972. Brother Leo joined them the following August. At first he worked at Holy Spirit Retreat House— renamed **Holy Spirit Center** in 1999—assisting Father Vincent J. **Kelliher**, S.J. From the Retreat House, Brother Leo went on to do catechetical work in the archdiocese and to serve at St. Patrick's parish, Anchorage. At the same time, he continued his education at the Anchorage Community College. In 1975, he graduated with a degree in sociology, with emphasis on social services.

About this time, Archbishop Ryan asked Brother Leo if he would consider studying for the priesthood for the archdiocese. In September 1975, Brother Leo began his seminary training at Holy Trinity Seminary in Irving, Texas, and at the University of Dallas. On April 28, 1979, he was ordained a priest in St. Stephen's Church in Winooski by Francis T. **Hurley**, Archbishop Ryan's successor.

In 1979, Father Desso was assigned to St. Patrick's parish, Anchorage, as associate pastor to Msgr. Francis A. Murphy. As such, he was involved with youth ministry and oversaw both the elementary and secondary religious education programs. The following year, he became associate pastor to Msgr. John A. **Lunney** at Our Lady of Guadalupe parish, Anchorage. There, too, he was responsible for the religious education program. In 1982, he took over as pastor of St. Bernard's parish in **Talkeetna** and as visiting priest to its dependent missions at **Trapper Creek** and **Willow**.

From 1984–89, Father Desso was pastor of St. Mary's parish in **Kodiak**. There the children attending St. Mary's School became a special concern of his. He also laid plans for a new church, and, before he left, was involved in its architectural design.

In September 1989, Father Desso was appointed pastor of St. Andrew's parish in **Eagle River**. From the outset, he encouraged the parishioners to assume ownership in the parish and to take part in social activities that involved the whole family. He instituted a high school religious education program and a youth ministry program. A volley ball court was built, as well as a playground for younger children to play on after Sunday services. While at St. Andrew's, he was a member of the Knights of Columbus, serving as chaplain of their Council. He later became a 4th Degree Knight, and served as chaplain of the Joseph T. Ryan Assembly, before going on the become State Chaplain for the Knights of Columbus in Alaska.

Father Desso became pastor of St. Michael's parish in **Palmer** in 1999. As of the year 2004, he was still serving in that capacity—and joyfully celebrating his silver jubilee as a priest.

15

DEVINE, Father Edward J., S.J.

Father Edward J. Devine, S.J., was born on March 3, 1860, at Pointe Bonnechère, County Renfrew, Ontario, Canada. He entered the Society of Jesus on September 4, 1879. On July 14, 1902, he arrived in **Nome** to assist in the parish and to take over caring for the Catholics at **Council**. During his two years in Nome, he visited Council on a regular basis, sometimes staying there for two or three months at a time. In 1903, he built himself a cabin at Council and began to build a church, which, however was never finished.

Father Devine was a careful observer and an able writer. While on the Seward Peninsula, he contributed a series of informative articles, his "Alaskan Letters," to the *Canadian Messenger of the Sacred Heart*. With Montreal as his destination, he left Nome on July 23, 1904. He died in Toronto in 1927.

DIBB, Father William C., S.J.

He spent a total of 38 years in **Alaska**, serving in all three of Alaska's dioceses. He ministered to Alaska's Native peoples, as well as to its non-Natives. He served in many of Alaska's villages, and in Alaska's largest cities. As a marine on Pacific islands, he knew at first-hand the bloody, senseless horrors of war. His hobbies were people—and classical music. People often, erroneously, added an "s" to his name. But then, there was something plural about the man.

William C. "Bill" Dibb was born in Salem, Oregon, on August 18, 1925. He was raised in Seattle, where, for eight years, he attended mostly Catholic grade schools, foremost among them St. Joseph's, staffed by Sisters of the Holy Names. In January 1944, he graduated from O'Dea High School, staffed by the Christian Brothers.

From February 25, 1944, until July 29, 1946, Bill served in the U.S. Marine Corps. He spent most of his tour as a marine overseas, in the Southwest Pacific, in the Central Pacific, and in north China. His tour of duty took him to such places as Pearl Harbor, Guadalcanal, the Palau and Ryu Kyu Islands, Okinawa, and Guam. He took part in the amphibious landings made on the islands of Peleliu and Okinawa. The memories of the horrors of war he witnessed on Peleliu stayed with him all his life. Before being discharged from the marines at Sand Point Naval Station, Seattle, on July 29, 1946, he was a patient in the hospital in San Diego, then again in the hospital in Seattle.

Back in civilian life, Bill attended Seattle University from September 1946 to August 1949. On August 15, 1949, he entered the Jesuit novitiate at Sheridan, Oregon, where, after completing his two-year noviceship, he spent two additional years studying the classics and humanities. In 1952, he moved to Mount St. Michael's, Spokane, Washington, for three years of philosophical studies.

Bill's course of Jesuit training next took him to Alaska, to **Holy Cross Mission** on the lower Yukon River. He went north as a volunteer, having entered

Father William C. Dibb, S.J.
JOPA-1062.01.

the Jesuit Order with a view to one day serving in an overseas mission field. He spent the year 1955–56 teaching in the mission high school and prefecting the "little boys." When, in 1956, the Holy Cross school was, in part, relocated to near **Glennallen** and became **Copper Valley School**, he relocated with it. In the fall of 1957, he began his theological studies at Alma College, Los Gatos, California. In Spokane, on June 11, 1960, in St. Aloysius Church, he was ordained a priest by Bishop Bernard J. Topel. After finishing his fourth year of theology at Alma College, Father Dibb went to Port Townsend, Washington, to make his tertianship.

Father Dibb's first assignment as a priest in Alaska took him to **Dillingham**, where, from 1962–64, he was Superior of Holy Rosary Mission School and pastor of the Dillingham parish. At Dillingham, he found that "the condition of the place and operation defied description; utterly exhausting, just to keep head above water." To make the school a more efficient instrument of education, he, always a man more concerned with quality than quantity, reduced the number of its grades from twelve to six.

Father Dibb took his final vows as a Jesuit at Copper Valley School on February 3, 1964. The following month, on March 27, 1964, the devastating "Good Friday" earthquake struck Southcentral Alaska. Having had his ham radio operator's license already since 1959, he was able, on the night of the

earthquake, to provide an important "link," by functioning as a relay between **Valdez** and **Fairbanks**, from where relief came to Valdez.

In July 1964, Father Dibb left Dillingham to take charge of the mission at **Mountain Village**, as well as of its dependent stations, **Marshall**, **Russian Mission**, and **Pilot Station**. On December 31, 1964, while traveling on a snowmachine between Marshall and Pilot Station, he accidentally drove into an overflow on the Yukon, with the result that he froze his feet, suffered third degree frostbite. Rescued that same night, he was brought to Pilot Station, and, on the following day, to **Bethel**. On January 4, 1965, he was evacuated to the U.S. Air Force Hospital at Elmendorf AFB, **Anchorage**. From this he was discharged on March 15. He was next admitted to Anchorage's **Providence** Hospital, where he remained, except for a two-week period in June, until August 14, 1965, after which he continued his recuperation at St. Anthony's parish, Anchorage.

During his months of recuperation in Anchorage, Father Dibb came to the determination that he should be assigned to Anchorage "to set up an urban apostolate for Alaska Natives." To do this he had the blessing of Father Jules M. **Convert**, S.J., at the time General Superior of the Jesuits in Alaska. Accordingly, with genuine enthusiasm, he began to plan and to prepare himself for that apostolate. However, it was not meant to be. Rather abruptly, around mid-September 1965, he was assigned to Copper Valley School "to function as Father Minister, Vice-President, or what have you?" While at Copper Valley School, he did some teaching and some pastoral work. He saw to the material well-being of the school. He spent Christmas in Valdez. In June 1966, he conducted a retreat for a mixed group from Anchorage.

At the request of **Joseph T. Ryan**, newly-appointed Archbishop of Anchorage, Father Dibb returned to Dillingham in July 1966 to serve as pastor of the parish and as visiting priest to the outlying communities of Clarks Point, Ekuk, and Naknek. He was also auxiliary chaplain at the King Salmon AFB. In June 1968, he was assigned by Father Convert to Anchorage, where he hoped to pursue his long-cherished dream of "developing an urban Alaska Native Project." But, in his hopes of meeting the needs of Eskimo and Indian people living in Anchorage, he was totally frustrated. Giving the reason for this, he wrote: "I should have known that the Anchorage Ecclesiastical Establishment, from the Archbishop down, was unalterably opposed to the concept of a ministry devoted to the Alaska Natives living in Anchorage." His stay in Anchorage lasted only a year. During that frustrating year, however, he was instrumental in acquiring for the Anchorage-based Jesuits the 1500 Birchwood Street residence. As the third millennium dawned, this residence was still housing Jesuits, and accommodating countless Jesuits and lay volunteers passing through Anchorage.

By June 1969, Father Dibb was again at Mountain Village, attending to the mission there and to its dependent stations, Marshall and Pilot Station. Before being assigned to those villages, he had told Robert L. **Whelan**, S.J., the new bishop of the Diocese of Fairbanks, that he thought he would survive in those villages only if the living quarters— "which," according to him, "were about the worst in the Bush at the time"—could be fixed up. No help in this regard was forthcoming. Finding life in those villages under those conditions "extremely difficult," Father Dibb requested a change.

From June 1970 to June 1972, Father Dibb served as pastor of **Nenana**. As such, he was responsible also for other "Railbelt" communities—communities strung out for over 110 miles along the Parks Highway and the Alaska Railroad from Nenana to Cantwell. Included among the communities he cared for, in addition to Nenana and Cantwell, were Anderson, Clear Air Force Site, **Healy**, Suntrana, Usibelli, and McKinley Park. He spent much time on the road, often under extremely poor weather and road conditions. Summarizing his two-year Nenana assignment, he wrote, "This was an exhausting, but fruitful and pleasant assignment."

Pleasant, too, Father Dibb found his August 1972 to August 1973 year at St. Joseph's parish in Seattle, the parish of his boyhood days. In December 1972, he made a Marriage Encounter weekend. This marked the beginning of his ministry to married people, a ministry that was to occupy him during much of the rest of his life.

From September 1973 to June 1974, Father Dibb was enrolled in the School of Applied Theology at Berkeley, California. He found that academic year an "exciting, revitalizing and rewarding year," for which he was "most grateful."

On July 28, 1974, Father Dibb arrived in Fairbanks. His new assignment there: to serve as Rector of Sacred Heart Cathedral parish. This was, at the time, technically, the one and only parish for the whole of Fairbanks and the North Star Borough. It soon became evident to him that he found himself in a "not workable situation." With his urging, St. Nicholas Parish in **North Pole** came into existence in September 1975. On July 1, 1976, Immaculate Conception parish, founded in 1904, and much later joined to Sacred Heart Cathedral parish, again became a separate parish. The following year, St. Mark's University Parish was formally established as an extra-territorial parish. Father Dibb resigned as pastor of Sacred Heart Cathedral parish in August 1979.

While Rector of the Cathedral parish, Father Dibb served also as a Diocesan Consultor, as Diocesan Liaison Person with the Charismatic Renewal Movement, and as Vice-President of Catholic Community Resources. In 1975, he introduced Marriage Encounter to the Diocese of Fairbanks, and, in 1976, to the Diocese of **Juneau**. During the summers of 1976–78, he helped with the training of diocesan deacons and seminarians. He was President of the Tanana Valley Conference of Churches for the year 1977–78.

During the latter part of 1979, Father Dibb began to offer Masses in the Two Rivers and Fox schoolhouses for people living on the northern outskirts of Fairbanks. Throughout his years in the active ministry, he felt strongly that "we should be building communities of Faith. This is the challenge we face." By offering Masses for and ministering to the people of what was, at the time, called "the Catholic Church North," from 1979 to 1983, he was doing just that, building a community of Faith. A few years later, St. Raphael's parish, with its new church, became the visible, concrete embodiment of that community of Faith.

On September 23, 1983, Father Dibb arrived in Juneau to operate a House of Prayer and to offer monthly Sunday Masses at **Yakutat**. However, health concerns made his Juneau stay a short one. In January 1984, he went to Jemez Springs, New

Mexico, for a six-month rehabilitation program. Of this he wrote, "It was God's way of saving my life, because I 'flunked' the treadmill test, the passing of which was a prerequisite for the Cardio-vascular Exercise Program that was part of the overall program." Serious heart and artery problems calling for surgery put him in the hospital in February 1985, and again in May 1999.

The year 1985 found Father Dibb back in Anchorage, living and helping out at St. Benedict's parish. There he was "very pleased" with the growth of a prayer community, which sponsored a monthly "Healing Mass." After a stay of several years at St. Benedict's, he began, in June 1988, to work for the Diocese of Anchorage, and out of Anchorage, as a "sacramental minister." As such, he visited and offered Masses in the parishes of Glennallen, **Cordova**, Valdez, **Kenai**, Dillingham, King Salmon, Naknek, Clarks Point, and **Unalaska**. From late September 1990, until July 2, 1991, he tended the **Seward** parish.

From 1991–95, Father Dibb was in charge of St. Michael's Parish in **McGrath**. By 1994, he was into the Retrouvaille ministry, another ministry he was to be engaged in for most of the rest of his life. It was a ministry very much in keeping with his nature "as a sensitive people person," as a man ready to come to the rescue of anyone in need. After spending the year 1995–96 in Anchorage working out of Holy Spirit Retreat House—renamed **Holy Spirit Center** in 1999—where he resided as a "Retrouvaille Minister," he moved to Fairbanks, where he continued on in the Retrouvaille ministry, and, at the same time, served as the Superior of the Fairbanks Jesuit community. In the year 2000, he became a member of the Jesuit Regis Community in Spokane, living there in semi-retirement, slowed down somewhat by failing eyesight, but still serving as a "pastoral minister." As of the year 2004, he was still serving as such.

15

DILLINGHAM

Dillingham, a commercial salmon fishing town and supply and transportation center for the general area, is located on Bristol Bay, at the junction of the Nushagak and Wood Rivers, 360 miles southwest of **Anchorage**. The Dillingham post office was established in 1904. In 1992, Dillingham's population numbered 2,017; and in the year 2000, 2,466.

The Catholic Church was late in coming to Dillingham. By the time it came, the general area was already heavily Moravian and Russian Orthodox. The first Catholic baptism recorded for Dillingham took place on July 18, 1946, when Father George S. **Endal**, S.J., traveling there from his station on the lower Yukon, baptized the infant son of Domingo and Mary Floresta, Domingo Jr. It was Domingo Sr., a Filipino, who had asked for a Catholic priest to come to baptize his son. A little less than two years later, Father Endal again traveled to the Bristol Bay area, this time to stay, and to found a mission there. He arrived at the Army Air Base at Naknek on April 22, 1948. On April 27th, he arrived in Dillingham. He gave April 22, 1948, as the date of the founding of the Dillingham mission. This mission he dedicated to "Our Lady of the Holy Rosary of Fatima."

Soon after his arrival, Father Endal "visited around and tried to size up the situation." Even though he found only some 30 Catholics, he began to look for "a suitable location whereon to build the new church and residence." At the same time, he determined also to open an elementary school. On September 20th of that year, he began teaching around 20 children in a schoolhouse, located between Dillingham and the Kanakanak Hospital, that the "Government" had abandoned two years previously. He was not a great success at this, having five different grades to teach. Still, in hopes of attracting people to the Catholic Faith, he continued to make teaching his principal work. At the same time, he was working to get a church and rectory built. For this he found, in Dillingham, "a very nice location on which to build a church."

During the year 1949–50, Father Endal spent a great deal of time on constructing both a new church and a new school. He began to offer Mass in the new, though far from finished, church on Christmas Eve 1949. He hoped to have the new school, located near Squaw Creek, ready to open in September 1950, but in this he did not succeed.

Before the year 1950 was out, the new church, still in the process of being built, burnt to its foundation on November 15th. A chimney fire was responsible for the loss. The fire left him with only the clothes on his back After making the basement of his as yet unfinished school habitable, he made that his temporary home. The school opened in 1951. It was staffed in large part by lay volunteers. It continued to operate through to the end of the school year 1965–66.

In the summer of 1951, in addition to being preoccupied with completing the school and church buildings, Father Endal was again, as he had been the previous summer, involved in ministry to the Bristol Bay cannery workers, and in matters concerning the labor unions. During his early years in Dillingham, he was almost overwhelmed with work of every kind. For the summer of 1950, however, he was fortunate enough to have the assistance of Father George T. **Boileau**, S.J. And, on December 28, 1952, Father Harold J. **Greif**, S.J., arrived. Though he made Dillingham his headquarters, he did spend much time away, tending to the pastoral needs of outlying communities such as Clarks Point, King Cove, King Salmon, Levelock, Cold Bay, Naknek, South Naknek, Ekuk, and Iliamna. In so doing, he freed Father Endal from having to travel. Father Greif left the area in 1967.

During the summers of the late 1940s and early 1950s, Father Jules M. **Convert**, S.J., too, was in the Dillingham area, but he devoted all of his time to ministering to cannery workers and to matters involving the workers and the labor unions.

The first Confirmations in the Bristol Bay area took place in September 1953. On the 16th, Bishop Francis D. **Gleeson**, S.J., confirmed 15 in Dillingham. The following day, he confirmed 13 at Clarks Point, and, the next day, 8 at the Naknek airbase. Four of these were from Naknek village. Father Greif assisted him at those Confirmations.

Throughout his Dillingham years, from 1948–62, Father Endal's main concern was his school. He was the sole teacher at it until 1953, when he was joined by a co-teacher, Miss Mary Ann Mandy. From that year on, until its closing in 1966, unmarried volunteer lay women did most of the teaching.

In 1958, Father Vsevolod **Roshko**, priest of the Byzantine/Eastern Rite, came to Dillingham to found an Eastern Rite mission there. He was in Dillingham for seven years, built a small Byzantine church there, but made few converts. During the school year 1959–60, he taught Russian to the nine students attending Father Endal's high school.

On March 26, 1955, tragedy struck the Dillingham mission for the second time. A fire started in the lean-to that housed the generator, and soon the school building was up in flames. "The loss was almost complete." Classes, however, continued to be held in two small buildings near the burnt-out mission school structure. Rebuilding began immediately and on a grander scale, in the summer of 1955; and, by the fall of that year, the new building, though not yet nearly finished, was opened for classes. It was greatly enlarged in 1958. High School classes began to be taught in the fall of 1959, but they were discontinued after the 1961–62 school year. The whole school closed in the spring of 1966. The last year of its operation, it had 24 boarders and 21 day students.

In September 1962, Father William C. **Dibb**, S.J., replaced Father Endal at the Dillingham mission. It was he who decided that high school classes should no longer be offered by the school. His two years at Dillingham were not easy ones for him, having, as he did, to contend with major disharmony among the school's faculty and with a sub-standard physical plant.

Father Dibb left Dillingham in July 1964. He was replaced by Father Norman E. **Donohue**, S.J., who arrived there the month before. He left Dillingham in June 1966. When the Archdiocese of Anchorage was established, on February 9, 1966, the line dividing the Dioceses of Anchorage and **Fairbanks** was drawn in such a way that Dillingham fell within the boundaries of the former. At the request of **Joseph T. Ryan**, Archbishop of Anchorage at the time, Father Dibb returned to Dillingham again, for the years 1966–68. With the school closed by now, he was able, during his first year, to devote all of his time to pastoral ministries in Dillingham, since Father Greif was still in the area; then, during his second year, also to the surrounding area. During those two years, Father Dibb had with him, in his own words, "two superb older Lay Volunteers, Mr.

John Schmid and Mrs. Martha Schuler, who were more than devoted to their work and valued and appreciated by the people in the Dillingham area." Both had served as members of the **Jesuit Volunteer Corps** at **Copper Valley School**, and the experience they had gained there they brought with them to Dillingham. Before the start of the 1964–65 school year, Sister Jeannette LaRose, S.S.A., of the CVS staff, spent some time in Dillingham helping to get the school there "up to par."

During the last two years of the 1960s and throughout the 1970s, a considerable number of different priests were stationed in Dillingham or visited it, for longer or shorter periods of time. Among them were Fathers: John J. **Marx**; Timothy J. Daley, M.M.; Peter Houck, O.S.B.; Thomas Creagh; Alan C. Abele; John H. Smyth, C.M.; and Richard D. **Tero**. Father Richard K. Smith, O.S.A., a capable priest-pilot flying a Cessna, ministered in Dillingham and the Bristol Bay area from 1978–83. Father John Tyma, O.S.A., did likewise, from 1983–86.

From 1991 to 2002, Father James F. **Kelley**, a retired Navy chaplain and pilot, served the Dillingham parish and several dozen outlying communi-

ties. Father Kelley died on March 23, 2002, when the single-engine Piper Cherokee 140 which he was piloting, crashed into a mountain during a snowstorm. He was on his way to celebrate Palm Sunday Masses in the Togiak area. After Father Kelley's death, Father LeRoy Clementich, C.S.C., began to serve the Dillingham parish, out of Anchorage.

During the 1970s, two Sisters of St. **Ann**, Ida Brasseur and Margaret Cantwell, traveling as a "Rural Ministry" team, visited Dillingham on a regular basis. Sister Ida was appointed administrator of the Dillingham parish in 1977. Before transforming, with the help of some devout local women, a little free-standing Thrift Shop into a neat little church, the Sisters had for a parish "church" only a room in the old, vandalized school building. For her ministrations in Dillingham and small rural communities, Sister Ida received the Catholic Church Extension Society's 1980 Lumen Christi Award as "Home Missionary of the Year."

After Father Tyma left Holy Rosary parish in May 1986, Sister Marie Ann Brent, S.H.F., began to serve the Dillingham Catholic community, as Pastoral Administrator, until 1993. When she came to

The Dillingham church, school, living quarters complex as it appeared in 1962. *JOPA-519.2.57.*

Dillingham, she "inherited" the new church building, which had been completed by Father Tyma. In the absence of a priest, she presided at the Liturgy of the Word and held Communion services. She also provided a Religious Education program for children and adults, served as an Emergency Medical Technician III with the State of Alaska, and was an on-call chaplain at the Kanakanak Hospital.

15

DONOHUE, Father Norman E., S.J.

He was a thoughtful, quiet man, gentle and sweet of disposition, with a subtle, refined sense of humor. At the time of his death, he had spent 42 years in **Alaska**, six of them on the middle Yukon River among the Koyukon Athabaskan Indians and most of the rest on the Bering Sea coast in Western Alaska among the Central Yup'ik Eskimos. As General Superior of all Jesuits in Alaska, he resided for six years in **Bethel**.

Norman E. Donohue was born in St. Paul, Minnesota, on December 27, 1907, to Edward Donohue, a grocer, and Claire Frances Isaacs. She was Jewish, and throughout his life it pained her son, whenever he heard anything unkind said of the Jewish people. He had one sister, no brothers. The family moved to Seattle in 1911. There the boy was schooled during the first grade at Isaac Stevens School, then at St. Joseph's Grade School, staffed by the Sisters of the Holy Names, and at the Jesuit-staffed Seattle Preparatory School. As a boy and youth, he was considered "different," extremely quiet, not a mixer, uninterested in sports or social activities, preferring to "sit and think a lot." After he graduated from high school in 1924, he worked for two years as a Western Union Telegraph bicycle messenger.

On July 15, 1926, Norman Donohue entered the Jesuit novitiate at Los Gatos, California. He proved to be a good Religious, faithful to the rules, a hard worker. His thoughts he kept mostly to himself, content to listen on the periphery of any group gathered for conversation. After completing the two-year noviceship and two years of classical and humanities studies at Los Gatos, he went to Mount St.

Michael's, Spokane, Washington, for three years of philosophical studies. From 1933–36, he taught at Bellarmine Preparatory School in Tacoma, Washington. For four years, 1936–40, he studied theology at Alma College, near Los Gatos. He was ordained a priest at Santa Clara, California, by Archbishop John J. Mitty on June 16, 1939. After making his tertianship at Port Townsend, Washington, 1940–41, Father Donohue began his long missionary career in Alaska.

"I arrived in Alaska on August 12, 1941," he wrote in his account of his early years in Alaska,

by boat from Seattle. After stops in **Juneau**, **Anchorage** and **Fairbanks**, Fr. **McElmeel**, the Jesuit Superior, who happened to be in Fairbanks, had me fly to **Tanana** to take care of the parish there, while I waited for the sternwheeler to take me downriver. Bishop **Fitzgerald**, then Coadjutor, came upriver on that boat and informed me that I was assigned to **Holy Cross**. I arrived there the 6th of September, and worked as assistant to Fr. **Spils**. Visited **Paimiut** around Thanksgiving and Christmas, about a week each time. Towards the end of January I left for **Akulurak** to replace Fr. Frank **Ménager**, who went to **Hooper Bay** to replace Fr. **Fox** temporarily. I assisted Fr. **Llorente** at the school and in visiting the district. Beginning around the fall of 1944, Fr. Llorente stayed at the school, and I did all the traveling. I was based at Akulurak, but spent most of the time visiting the surrounding villages and settlements. I was in charge of building a log schoolhouse in **Alakanuk** (summer, 1944?). In 1946, Fr. **Endal** was put in charge of the northern part of the Akulurak district, while I took care of the southern part plus **Scammon Bay**, where I built a tiny church–rectory. In 1947 Scammon Bay reverted to the Hooper Bay parish, Fr. Endal went to **Dillingham** in the spring of 1948, and I resumed my duties as circuit rider for the entire Akulurak district. In 1948 I began a church-residence at **New Knock Hock** assisted by William **Tyson** as catechist and teacher of a small school we began there at that time.

Father Donohue wrote the above account of his early years in Alaska in February 1978. It was easy enough for him to write such a laconic, factual account, but this reveals little of the personal challenges he had had to meet and come to grips with by then. Given his shy, impractical nature, his early years on the Alaska mission were for him anything but easy. He suffered much from the cold. He knew, before he went to Alaska, that his fingers were, by

Father Norman E. Donohue, S.J. *DFA.*

his own admission, "very sensitive to cold." Still, he volunteered to serve on the Alaska missions. From the outset, he made every effort to be a good missionary.

In a letter to Bishop Francis D. **Gleeson**, S.J., Vicar Apostolic of Alaska at the time, dated October 5, 1948, Father Fox wrote: "Brother **Murphy** reports that Fr. Donohue had a hectic time at New Knock Hock. On the second trip there Fr. swamped his little speed boat and landed as a 'Refugee' at Black River. Fr. Donohue is a very talented man for books, and a good religious that will never give up once he starts something. But he is woefully lacking in practical talent, and I think it is positively dangerous to let him boat around alone."

Soon after his arrival in western Alaska, Father Donohue began to study seriously the Central Yup'ik Eskimo language. He gained an adequate intellectual knowledge of it, and a certain proficiency in speaking it, but his accent was such that it brought laughs from the Natives. This was more than his shy, sensitive nature could take, so he generally used an interpreter. In reality, Father Donohue got along well with the Eskimo people, and had, in his own words, "a deep and true love for these people." He played a piano accordion "to bring more joy," as he wrote, "to the hearts of my isolated flock, and to accompany the hymns with music

even in the most remote igloos." Visiting his isolated, widely-scattered flock involved him in many a misadventure. More than once his boat got away from him. More than once he lost his dogteam. On one occasion, overtaken by nightfall while still on the trail, and not sure of the way, he headed with enthusiasm toward a distant light. It never drew nearer. It turned out to be a star low on the horizon.

Father Donohue served in the Akulurak district until 1950. Then, in recognition of his deep personal spirituality and his unquestioned intellectual gifts, he was chosen to succeed Father Paul C. **Deschout**, S.J., as General Superior of Jesuits in Alaska. When Father Deschout learned of Father Donohue's appointment, he wrote to the Father Provincial, "The choice of Fr. Donohue is inspired. He is a clever man, and a spiritual man and—what I consider of vital importance—an American." Father Donohue was Superior from November 1, 1950, till January 1957. During those years he served also as the pastor of the Bethel mission and outlying stations. A new church with rectory was built in Bethel, while he was there.

After his term as General Superior and years in Bethel, Father Donohue next served at Hooper Bay, with Scammon Bay as a dependent station, 1957–64. He spent the years 1964–66 as pastor at **Dillingham**, and as the man in charge of the boarding school there. For the year 1966–67, he was at **Copper Valley School**, where he helped out in the school in various capacities and, at the same time, visited Catholics in that general area and offered Mass for them.

From 1967 to 1974, Father Donohue was, for the first time, stationed among the Koyukon Athabaskan Indians. Making now **Kaltag**, 1967–69, now **Nulato**, 1969–74, his headquarters, he served those two villages, along with their dependent station, **Koyukuk**. Nulato and Kaltag are the two villages in which the "stickdance," the traditional Koyukon "Feast for the Dead," is held. In the eyes of some of the earlier Jesuit missionaries this was at least tinged with "superstition." Being, on the one hand, sensitive about such a matter, and, at the same time, on the other hand, sensitive to the feelings of the people, Father Donohue resolved what was for him a dilemma by simply being in the other village, when the ceremonial was being held in the one. Thus, he had neither to condone, nor to condemn.

After his years on the Yukon, Father Donohue returned to the land of the Central Yup'ik Eskimos. He was in the village of **Tununak** from August 1974 to July 1975. Then he moved down the coast to the last scene of his labors, **Chefornak**, where he held station from 1975 to the year of his death, 1983.

Throughout his life, Father Donohue was, in a word, otherworldly. His voluntary, life-long sense of poverty bordered on the drastic. When he was alone, his standard fare consisted mainly of oatmeal, raisins, canned butter and pilot crackers, which he described as his "staff of life." Gratefully he accepted occasional gifts of seal meat from his Eskimo parishioners. Hot water sufficed him as a beverage. For the benefit of guests, however, he would splurge, bring out instant coffee and fig Newtons held in reserve for that purpose. Being a deeply spiritual man, he spent many hours throughout his life in prayer and adoration before the Blessed Sacrament. By his later years as a missionary, he had become a true mystic. In the chapel of the Bishop's Residence–Chancery building, Fairbanks, Father Louis L. **Renner**, S.J., chanced to find him one day deeply absorbed in prayer, sobbing gently, tears moistening his cheeks. Always ill at ease in the public eye, except when exercising his ministry, he was not built for this world. He was created to walk straight into heaven. This he surely must have done, when, shortly after injuring himself in a fall down some steps in Anchorage, he died there on October 24, 1983. At the request of the people of Chefornak, who said, "We were his family; he is one of us," his body, which had held so little importance in his own eyes, was transported there. In the cemetery at Chefornak, he was laid to rest on the Feast of the Holy Souls.

The following true story by Father Donohue was found among his papers after his death.

～

Around January 1946 I was traveling by dogteam in the area south of Akulurak, and had reached a village called Kalvaryak. There I heard of a baby to be baptized at a "two family" village at the southeast base of Kuzilvak Mountain. Next morning was beautiful. The temperature was 35 below, but I did not know that, since the settlement had no thermometer. I decided to go to that village, Nunapikpuk, baptize the baby, and

return to Kalvaryak. Ordinarily I always carried a heavy load, but this time, as I was to return to Kalvaryak for the night, I took only the requisites for baptism.

The trail was good, the dogs enjoyed the lack of load, and the cold made them lively. About half way I had to stop to adjust one of the harnesses. During the process, the lead dog turned off the trail at right angles, so that the sled turned over. This jerked out the anchor bar. I failed to notice this; I was enjoying the sunshine too. I chased the leader back to the trail and started for the sled, when suddenly the team took off. Thinking the sled was held by the bar, I did not react in time. I took off after the dogs, not greatly worried even then, for the sled was still on its side, and would certainly soon get caught on a bush. Unfortunately, the opposite happened: the flying sled hit a bump and righted itself, and the dogs were "off to the races!"

I followed on foot, trusting the dogs would stop when they reached Nunapikpuk. A couple of hours of walking brought me there, and then my worries really began. The dogs were not there, had not even been seen. It is contrary to all sled-dog psychology to pass a village without stopping. A village means a rest, excitement, maybe a meal. Perhaps in their exhilaration, riderless sled and all, my dogs had gone on to the next village, Kassigilok, where I not infrequently stopped. However, I knew something the dogs could not know: there was nobody living in Kassigilok at this time!

To make matters worse, only one of the two men living at Nunapikpuk had a dogteam, and he was away with it, not expected to be back till the next day. Nothing for it but to continue on to Kassigilok on foot. This was at the season of the shortest days, and there would be no question of returning to Nunapikpuk for the night, unless I should find the dogs. I would have to depend on getting into a cabin at Kassigilok.

My friends at Nunapikpuk gave me a lunch, and I was off again on foot, alone with my thoughts. They were not particularly happy thoughts. Most of my walking that day had been along the Black River on a fairly well-beaten trail. When I came to the turnoff, a shortcut to Kassigilok, there was no sign of fresh tracks. The dogs, however, could have continued on by way of the river, so there was nothing for it but to go on and hope. I reached Kassigilok in perhaps three hours, just at sunset. No dogs in sight. But I had no time to worry about dogs then. I had to get inside, and fast.

Both cabins were padlocked. The door of one was proof against any housebreaker. I had thought of breaking a window, but about that time I had no desire of extra ventilation during the night. The door of the other cabin was too much for my bare hands, but I saw a broken shovel protruding from the snow, and with its help I finally succeeded in prying off the hasp. The inside was not exactly a camper's delight, but Providence had provided the minimum for survival. There was a very little wood in the porch, the heel of a loaf of bread, a bit of butter, a piece of dry fish, a little oatmeal, a kerosene lamp with a little oil. Most surprising and best of all, there was a sleeping bag.

The wood range had too small a firebox to heat the house. With everything frozen, there was no hope of making the place comfortable. But I built a fire, ate a scanty supper, pulled the bed right beside the stove, crawled into the sleeping bag, and tried to sleep. Oh, yes, one other valuable item I found there was an alarm clock. I set the alarm for one hour later. When it went off, I arose, replenished the firebox, reset the alarm for one more hour, and retired again. This process I kept up all night. Sleeping bag, stove and all, I was still too cold to sleep much.

Next morning I consumed the remainder of the food, wrote a note of explanation to the owner of my hotel, and resumed my travels as soon as it began to get light. I meant to return to Nunapikpuk, but took the river trail this time, always watching for some place where my wandering dogs might have turned off. As I headed back up the river, I saw a trail turning off to an isolated cabin which I had never visited. Unlikely that my dogs would have gone there, but I had to explore every possibility. This detour would lengthen my trip several hours, but I would probably be able to get the Eskimo there to give me a ride back to Nunapikpuk. But that was not my week: here, too, the man of the house was away. I rested a bit and resumed my journey to Nunapikpuk.

The people of Nunapikpuk had been worrying about me. The man with the team had returned just ahead of me. The night before they hung a lantern out on the river just in case I should have found my dogs and be returning late with them. The night ahead was just the contrary of the preceding. I was in a tiny igloo, maybe ten feet square, with the parents and six children, the oldest a boy about eleven, the youngest the infant I had started out to baptize. I was given the boy's top-decker for the night. Of course, it was too short, and I had no bedding, so I was almost as cold as I had been at Kassigilok.

Next morning the two men of Nunapikpuk started hunting for my team, but very soon my host from two nights back at Kalvaryak arrived with his team. When I had not returned the first night, he suspected trouble; and when I had not returned the second, he was sure of it. It was decided I would return with him, watching out for any place where my dogs might have turned off the trail. At one place we decided to take a different route, but my guardian angel must have given me a very sharp poke; for, on reflection, we turned back to my original trail. When we were two miles from where the dogs had originally run away, my guide discovered tracks at the end of a wind-swept lake. Almost certainly this was the trail of my team. They had wan-

dered off the trail, I suspected, shortly after leaving me, and the bare ice had left no tell-tale tracks.

The trail of our wandering team now led us a winding course over the tundra. I had every reason to expect that at the first clump of bushes the dogs would have become tangled up, a fight would have ensued, and I would find only a mass of blood, hair, harness, and dead dogs. However, my leader had been smarter this time. For a long ways he carefully skirted all bushes. Finally their trail disappeared into a fringe of bushes bordering a small slough. The dogs had negotiated even these bushes; but just as they emerged from the other side, the sled had turned upside down, burying the points of the runners in the snow and bringing the race to an end.

I crawled through the bushes, and there they were! One had wriggled out of his harness, but had found nothing better to do than to lie down beside his teammates. Naturally they were almost as glad to see me, their meal ticket, as I to see them, for they had had nothing to eat for nearly three days. For my part I was so glad to find them safe and sound that I was willing to let bygones be bygones.

Our first move was to return to Nunapikpuk, where I baptized the baby who had been the innocent occasion of all my trouble. He died a year or two later, so he knows all about it now, and I trust he has been praying for his Father in Christ these many years.

DOUGLAS

The town of Douglas is located on the northeast coast of Douglas Island, from which it takes its name, on Gastineau Channel, 1.8 miles southwest of **Juneau**. To begin with, it was a suburb of the city of Treadwell. The two were established in the early 1880s as the result of mining activity in the area. Douglas became an incorporated city in 1902. For a time, the Treadwell–Douglas community was the most flourishing in **Alaska**. The flooding and cave-in, on April 20–21, 1917, of three of the four Treadwell mines, to which Douglas owed its prosperity, dealt the community a severe blow. Several times, serious fires destroyed much of the original town. In 1935, a bridge spanning Gastineau Channel was built. In 1967, Douglas had a population of 1,042.

The Catholic Church established itself in the Treadwell–Douglas community during the latter half of 1896. Father Peter C. **Bougis**, S.J., offered his first Mass there, in a private home, on July 19, 1896. A small chapel, 22 × 14′, dedicated under the patronage of Our Lady of the Mines, began to serve as a place of worship on December 8th of that year. This soon proved to be much too small. In the fall of 1899, the foundation for a new church, 70 × 32′, was laid. This opened its doors for the first time on December 24, 1900. The Catholic Church properties were located on St. Ann's Avenue, which was actually in the city of Treadwell. The city of Douglas began at the bottom of the hill. When the mines closed, after the cave-in, Treadwell ceased to exist, and the city of Douglas was enlarged to include what used to be the residential area of Treadwell, including St. Ann's Avenue and the properties located on it.

As in Juneau, so in Douglas: the Sisters of St. **Ann** were active there one year before the Jesuits. In 1895, two Sisters of St. Ann—Sisters Mary Frances and Mary Febronia, living in Juneau on the weekends and in Douglas Monday through Friday—taught school to Catholic children in what was called "the Bear's Nest," a long and low primitive structure. A new school building, 30 × 24′, was completed the following year. On March 19, 1898, St. Ann's Hospital opened. On February 17, 1916, a large wing added to the original building opened.

Father Bougis was the pioneer priest in Douglas, serving there from 1896–1905. Among his parishioners he found men from over a dozen different countries, prompting him to wish he had the gift of tongues. He, in turn, was followed by Jesuit Fathers Edward H. **Brown**, John B. **Van der Pol**, and Henry A. Gabriel. Father Joseph Bruckert was in Douglas from 1908–17. Father Michael M. O'Malley was there for the year 1917–18, and Father Philibert **Turnell** for the year 1918–19. Father Van der Pol was the last Jesuit to reside in Douglas, doing so during the year 1919–20.

The Treadwell Mines catastrophe in April 1917 brought with it a significant drop in Douglas' population. The Sisters of St. Ann left Douglas in 1920. For close to 40 years then, Douglas was treated as a mission and served by Jesuit priests stationed in Juneau. Notable among them was Edward C. Budde who visited the Douglas mission during the years 1933–43. The last Jesuit to do so was Father Joseph F. **McElmeel**, during the years 1952–57.

In passing, it should be noted that four Douglas parishioners became Sisters of St Ann. Three were members of the Doogan family: Ann Marie became Sister Mary Joseph Raphael, Marjorie became Sister Mary Kevin, and Theresa became Sister Miriam Jude. Frances Cashen became Sister Mary Philippa.

In 1926, a fire destroyed the original Our Lady of the Mines Church. The new church which replaced this was named for St. Aloysius, in keeping with the wishes of a generous donor. It was known as St. Aloysius Church until 1966, when its name was changed to St. Peter's Church. In June 1973, a fire in St. Peter's burned the organ and blackened the corpus on the crucifix. That crucifix subsequently came into the possession of Juneau's Cathedral parish, where it is usually displayed in the sanctuary during Lent. The refurbished St. Peter's Church was rededicated in January 1975.

From 1957 to the mid-1960s, Douglas was served out of Juneau. During the latter half of the 1960s, Father James J. **Manske** resided there. During the first half of the 1970s, Father John J. **Marx** did likewise. He was followed by Father Edward Cunningham, O.M.I., from 1974–78. Fathers Everett Trebtoske and Dennis P. O'Neil were in Douglas during the early 1980s.

On July 1, 1987, the Douglas parish ceased to be a parish. It was merged with Juneau's Cathedral of the Nativity of the Blessed Virgin Mary parish. Father Jerome A. **Frister** was Douglas' last resident pastor, from 1983–85. Father Bernard A. **Konda** served it out of Juneau during the last two years of its existence as a parish. He celebrated the last Mass in St. Peter's Church.

16

DUNFEY, Father Ronald K.

Ronald K. Dunfey was born in Boston, Massachusetts, on April 29, 1922, to Frederick A. Dunfey and Sara MacGillivray. He was ordained a priest in Brookline, Massachusetts, on June 7, 1952, for the Diocese of **Juneau**, by Dermot **O'Flanagan**, Bishop of Juneau at the time. Not long after his ordination, he drove to **Alaska** in a jeep. With him he had the future Alaskan priest, John A. **Lunney**. It was in large part to Father Dunfey that Father Lunney attributed his interest in Alaska and his desire to serve there as a priest.

Father Dunfey's first assignment in Alaska was Holy Family parish in **Anchorage**. As part of his ministry there, he served as chaplain at the local jail. His duties were to visit the prisoners daily and to be available to give spiritual assistance. Distressed by the deplorable conditions for the detention of juveniles, he pressed for better facilities. His interest in the plight of juveniles motivated him to find foster homes for problem boys. He also tried to establish "a home for homeless boys and those in trouble with the law." People of the area supported him in his project. However, his dream for a "Boys Home" remained only that, an unrealized dream. Money donated toward it was returned, to the extent possible. The reason no such home came into being was that Father Dunfey was transferred to **Cordova-Valdez**, by Bishop O'Flanagan. At the time of his transfer, he was characterized by the

The complex of Catholic buildings in Douglas appears in the foreground in this 1910 photo. Prominent are the church and the school, and the hospital with the recently added annex. Across Gastineau Channel, clustered at the foot of Mount Juneau, is Juneau, the state capital of Alaska. *Photo by E. Andrews of Douglas, Alaska, and courtesy of Sisters of St. Ann Archives, Victoria, B.C., Canada.*

bishop as "a hardworking, zealous priest, highly thought of in Holy Family Parish."

Throughout his life, Father Dunfey was concerned about wayward youth, down-and-outers, the alcohol addicted, the "street people." At times his personal lifestyle resembled that of the people of his concern.

Over the years, Father Dunfey served also in the middle Yukon River villages of **Tanana** and **Ruby**. In Ruby, an artist painted a portrait of Father Dunfey, "the unkempt, bearded friend of the alcoholic."

During his last active years as a priest, Father Dunfey "did street ministry" in Juneau, working with the homeless. He is remembered also for offering Mass during the summer months at the **Shrine** of St. Therese.

In 1992, Father Dunfey retired from active ministry and took up residency in Fairbanks, where he lived in a simple apartment until his death. Described as a "voracious reader," during his retirement years he spent much time on the University of Alaska–Fairbanks campus, either in the library, or hanging around with skiers or mountain climbers. It was his custom, throughout much of his life, to spend time with the unchurched and with fallen-away Catholics. At the time of his death, he had an extensive library: philosophy, theology, history, and anthropology. In the first of the two house fires he survived earlier in his life, he lost many books.

Father Dunfey died, in Fairbanks, on April 13, 1996. Four days later, in St. Raphael's Church, near Fairbanks, his life was celebrated at a Mass of Christian Burial. Father James M. **Kolb**, C.S.P., his long-time friend, who knew him well, and described him as "both an interesting and complicated person, with a tender ego under all his bluster," was principal celebrant. Many priests concelebrated. A few days later, in Juneau, another one of his close friends, Msgr. James F. **Miller**, celebrated another Mass of Christian Burial, after which Father Dunfey was laid to rest in the Juneau cemetery.

EAGLE CITY

Eagle City is located on the left bank of the Yukon River at the mouth of Mission Creek, six miles west of the Alaska–Canada boundary. It is at the end of the Taylor Highway. Eagle came into being in 1874, when the trader Moses Mercier built a log-house trading post, called "Belle Isle," there. The post operated intermittently until 1898, when a mining camp was set up to accommodate miners in the area. The site, then with a population of around 800, was platted and named "Eagle City" for the American eagles nesting on nearby Eagle Bluff. In 1899, the U.S. Army established its presence by building Fort Egbert. The Eagle post office was established in 1898, and the **Valdez**–Eagle telegraph line was completed in 1903. In 1899, Eagle became the seat of government of the Third Judicial District of Alaska. It was incorporated as a first-class city in 1901. At the beginning of the 1900s, the new little town had a population approaching 2,000, and entertained hopes of a bright future. However, as with many gold-rush communities, Eagle's heyday was brief. Its population declined rapidly to less than 200 by 1910, as gold-seekers moved on to richer grounds. The court moved to **Fairbanks** in 1904, and the Army withdrew its garrison from Fort Egbert in 1911. The population of Eagle City numbered 383 in 1900, 178 in 1910, 54 in 1930, 55 in 1950, 168 in 1990, and 129 in the year 2000.

The Catholic presence in Eagle dates from August 10, 1899, when Father Francis M. **Monroe**, S.J., arrived. For $300 he bought a site in the most favorable part of town. On it were two log cabins. The larger cabin became his residence and chapel. The mission was placed under the patronage of St. Francis Xavier. Soon he bought more lots, until the mission owned seven. Most of the ground he turned into a garden. The yield of his gardens provided him with nearly the only means of livelihood.

Toward the end of the summer of 1899, Father Rogatien **Camille**, S.J., joined Father Monroe in Eagle. But, as there was little for him to do in Eagle, he left it the following summer for **Juneau**.

In late 1900, Father Monroe opened a small hospital in Eagle. This was closed in 1903, when civilians began to be admitted to the military hospital.

During his five years in Eagle, Father Monroe recorded 12 baptisms, 2 marriages, 5 burials, and one man received into the Church. In June 1904, he left Eagle to establish Immaculate Conception parish in Fairbanks.

Over the years, the Catholic people of Eagle have been served, at irregular intervals, by priests stationed in Dawson, Fairbanks, **Delta Junction**, and **Tok**.

96

EAGLE RIVER

Eagle River, **Alaska**, on the Glenn Highway 13 miles northeast of **Anchorage**, is the home of the Catholic parish of St. Andrew's. Plans for a new church at the nearby community of Chugiak were drawn up as early as 1953, but the celebration of the first Mass there did not take place until the Saturday before Thanksgiving Day, 1955. On that day, U.S. Army chaplains, Father Gerard J. Gefell and his twin brother, Father Joseph G. Gefell, sang a Mass in the hall of the Chugiak Volunteer Fire Company. The altar consisted of a sheet of plywood on two sawhorses. A military Mass kit supplied all other essential needs.

On August 28, 1957, Dermot **O'Flanagan**, Bishop of **Juneau** at the time, established St. Anthony's parish in Anchorage. This included the Eagle River–Chugiak area. Father Robert L. **Whelan**, S.J., pastor of St. Anthony's, soon began to visit the Chugiak area. That same year the Church acquired a plot of land at Mile 14 on the Glenn Highway. Several years of increased activity led to the construction of a 64 × 34′ basement foundation at the site. On Easter Sunday, April 14, 1963, Father Whelan offered Mass in this new basement church. On May 12, 1963, Bishop O'Flanagan solemnly blessed it.

St. Andrew's remained a mission of St. Anthony's parish until October 16, 1967, when **Joseph T. Ryan**, Archbishop of Anchorage, designated the area north of Fort Richardson and south of the Matanuska–Susitna Borough as the parish of St. Andrew. The next day, Msgr. Francis A. **Cowgill** was appointed the first pastor of the new parish. Four months later, however, Father Joseph E. **Shirey**, S.J., replaced him as pastor. Early in his pastorate, he started the Legion of Mary. Father Shirey, in turn, was replaced by Father Peter Houck, O.S.B., on June 7, 1972. During those years, a small mobile home and a miniature "Husky House" was home for the priests.

In January 1976, Father Alfred W. Giebel became pastor of the rapidly expanding St. Andrew's parish. The mobile home and "Husky House" were by then becoming a maintenance problem. Accordingly, the parish decided to build a rectory on top of the basement church. This project was rapidly completed, but it was soon obvious that the basement church was not big enough to accommodate the people moving into the area.

By early 1980, plans for building a major new church structure were underway. On August 14th, footings were started. Contractors completed the block work, but most of the construction was accomplished in the course of the winter by a parishioner labor force. Parishioners also made the altar, the ambo, stands for the baptismal font and tabernacle, the Transfigured Christ, and the Stations of the Cross. On May 27, 1981, Francis T. **Hurley**, Archbishop of Anchorage at the time, with a multitude of priests as concelebrants, formally dedicated the new St. Andrew's Church. Nearly 500 people were present for the Mass and dedication ceremonies.

On August 15, 1989, Father Leo C. **Desso** became pastor of St. Andrew's parish. His tenure as pastor witnessed further explosive parish growth, as the town of Eagle River itself grew. Father Desso is remembered at St. Andrew's for having encouraged much lay involvement and leadership in the parish. He led the parish in an increased participation in charitable causes, and actively sought to involve youth in parish activities.

Father Leo Walsh was installed as pastor of St. Andrew's on July 4, 1999. With his guidance, the parish benefited from several important changes. Communion under both species was introduced, an additional Mass was added for Sunday mornings, and the former rectory was converted into meeting rooms and office space. Under his leadership, the parish set as its priorities: liturgy, education, and evangelization.

Growth, and more growth, marked St. Andrew's parish from its beginning. As it began the 21st century, it was poised to welcome its 1,000th family.

15

EDMOND, Sister M. George, S.S.A.

In the annals of the North, her name deserves to be recorded, and written large. She was widely recognized as a pioneer Alaskan missionary and educator. Because of her understanding of Native culture and values in the context of Catholic teaching, the archbishop of **Anchorage** described her as "a pioneer of indigenous theology." She was characterized as "an instigator of new ideas." The whole length of the Yukon River owed its first high school primarily to her initiative. It was she, who first introduced lay volunteers to the missions of northern **Alaska**. Being recognized as "an energetic, vibrant, valiant woman," as "a woman of compassion," she was accorded, both in life and in death, highest honors.

Sister M. George Edmond (née Lucienne Babin) was born of French-American heritage on May 2, 1907, in Three Rivers, Massachusetts, St. Ann's Parish. She had three brothers and a younger sister. Her basic education she received from the Sisters of St. **Ann**: in St. Joseph's Elementary School and Notre Dame High School. She earned a High

School Teacher's Certificate at the University of Montreal and a Baccalaureate in Education at Anna Maria College, Paxton, Massachusetts.

After working as a secretary, Lucienne Babin, at age 21, entered the novitiate of the Congregation of the Sisters of St. Ann in Lachine, Quebec, Canada, in 1928. One of her first tasks there was to type the French translation of *The Voice of Alaska* by Sister M. Joseph Calasanctius, one of the three foundresses of **Holy Cross Mission**, Alaska. Throughout her life her finger tips were very familiar with the keyboards of typewriters, pianos, and organs. She made her Religious profession in 1930, and took as her name in Religious life that of Sister Mary George Edmond. Her first assignment as a Religious took her to Holy Family School in Montreal, where she taught for two years.

In 1942, Sister M. George Edmond was named Sister Superior, even though she was the youngest member of that community at the time, at Kahnawake (Caughnawaga), an Iroquois Indian Reservation across the St. Lawrence River from Montreal. During her 14 years as teacher and Superior at Kahnawake, she became a much-loved personage and leader, not only among the school population, but also throughout the whole Reservation. Kahnawake offered few physical comforts; still, she found her years there satisfying, happy ones.

In 1946, Sister M. George Edmond was asked by her Mother Provincial to consider leaving Kahnawake and going to Holy Cross, Alaska, there to be Sister Superior. At that time she was in questionable health, and her mother's death seemed imminent. Had she chosen to decline the "Obedience" to go to Holy Cross, her doing so would have seemed understandable to many. For the woman that was Sister M. George Edmond to even consider doing so was never an option. In a spirit of the deep faith that characterized the whole of her life, and of Religious obedience, she embraced the new assignment wholeheartedly.

Sister M. George Edmond first set foot on Alaskan soil in **Juneau**, when she disembarked from the Canadian Pacific Princess boat that had brought her there. From Juneau she flew on a DC-3 to Anchorage, and from there, on another DC-3, to **McGrath**. From McGrath it was Oscar Winchell, veteran pilot

Sister M. George Edmond, S.S.A. *LRC.*

and mail carrier, who flew her, in a red four-seater plane, the last lap of her journey to Holy Cross. Weather conditions at the time were poor; but, after bumping through air pockets and fighting headwinds and rain, they landed safely in the meadow at Holy Cross. No one was there to meet the plane. Given the adverse weather conditions, people at the mission neither expected nor heard the plane. Arriving at the mission, however, Sister M. George Edmond was given a warm welcome. Among those welcoming her was James C. **Spils**, S.J., the Father Superior of Holy Cross at the time. This first meeting marked the beginning of a long association between the two.

Ever a compassionate woman, Sister M. George Edmond, upon her arrival at Holy Cross, was moved to tears, when she observed the real poverty that pervaded much of life at the mission. Then and there, unashamed to beg, she began to write unceasingly—a practice she was to continue throughout her years in Alaska—to friends and potential benefactors in hopes of getting the help needed to better the local living conditions. In her eyes, it was not a matter of charity but of basic justice that those who have should share with those who have not.

Sister M. George Edmond spent nine years, from 1946 to 1955, at Holy Cross, all of them as Sister Superior. During those years she was responsible for many improvements at the mission. It was she who was primarily responsible for the coming into being of a high school at Holy Cross. Opening in 1953, this was the first high school on the Yukon River. She herself taught classes in Home Economics. As her duties as Sister Superior allowed, she also typed up the mission newsletter, *Northern Winds*, played the organ in the church and in the Sisters' chapel, operated the baking machine that produced altar breads needed near and far, and, above all, was a real mother to the Sisters and the many Indian and Eskimo children at the mission.

Around 1950, change was in the wind in the Catholic mission fields of northern Alaska. There was new thinking regarding the schooling of Alaska's Native youth. Father John R. **Buchanan**, S.J., initiated plans for the opening of another mission high school, a college preparatory school, that would educate Alaska Natives to be leaders in their communities. From the outset, Sister M. George Edmond was involved with the planning of the school and its curriculum. To prepare herself for what lay ahead, she requested, and was granted, a sabbatical leave for studies at St. Jacques, a Home Economics specialty school in the Province of Quebec, and at Anna Maria College.

While in the East, Sister M. George Edmond aroused great interest in the educational aspect of Jesuit missionary activity in Alaska. Through numerous formal and informal talks, lectures, slide shows, and appearances on radio, she gained much spiritual and material support for Holy Cross and for the new school, to be known as **Copper Valley School**, about to come into being. She proved to be a dynamic, captivating, persuasive lecturer. While in the East, she also initiated contacts with federal government officials, to whom she made known the needs of the many orphans and abandoned children being cared for, without any remuneration whatsoever, at Holy Cross. Before returning north, she recruited the first lay volunteers for Alaska. It is thanks to her initiative in the matter of lay volunteers that the flourishing **Jesuit Volunteer Corps** soon came into being.

In 1956, Sister M. George Edmond was named Sister Superior of Copper Valley School. The boarding school, located in the wilds of Alaska at the confluence of the Copper and Tazlina Rivers near **Glennallen**, was barely habitable, when she first arrived there. It was still in the process of being built. Father Spils was in charge of construction. Nevertheless, in mid-October of that year, it was ready enough to allow her to welcome a nucleus of students, along with two Sisters of St. Ann, from Holy Cross. In addition to serving again as Sister Superior, she served also as principal of the grade school and as teacher of her specialty, Home Economics. She served also as organist, counselor, public-relations person, purchasing agent, and secretary, as well as occasional cook, seamstress, and laundress.

A quarter of a century after those difficult beginnings, Sister M. George Edmond recalled an encounter she had had one day with Father Spils:

One day, as I was struggling, Father Spils came by. "How goes it, George," he asked, with a concerned and friendly look. My spirits were very low that day, and I turned away to hide my tears. Emotion was overcoming me, so I sought the sanctuary of my room, a corner behind a butcher-paper wall. Soon there was a knock on the 2 × 4s. "May I come in?" It was Father Spils, sensing something was wrong. After he had pushed aside the paper wall, he entered and said, "Sit down on that box! Do you remember the day you took your vows? How happy you were to give all to God." Then he went on to talk about St. Peter and of how he had followed the Lord. He recalled the Gospel incident, where Jesus says: "Someday, Peter, you will be led, where you do not wish to go." After assuring himself that I was listening, Father exclaimed: "Well, damn it, this is it!" He stomped out, and I shook off my discouragement and got on with the business in hand.

Sister M. George Edmond left Copper Valley School in 1962 to serve at the Kamloops Indian Residential School in British Columbia, Canada. In the summer of 1965, however, she returned again, once more as Superior of the Sisters, and as assistant in the high school office. She also taught several Home Economics courses. One of the Sisters of St. Ann, who was there at the same time, said of her, "She was the heart of this Copper Valley endeavor. The children knew and loved her. Her presence was a comfort to anyone who might show signs of loneliness." In recognition of her "daring determination, her intensely human approach to people and problems, and her courageous facing of daily trials," the students of Copper Valley School dedicated their 1965 yearbook to her.

During the years 1967–76, Sister M. George Edmond served successively in Prince George, British Columbia (1967–68); as Superior of St. Ann's Academy in Marlborough, Massachusetts (1968–69); as Provincial Superior of Saint Marie Province of the Sisters of St. Ann, Marlborough (1969–73); and as Director of Services at St. Ann's Provincialate, Marlborough (1973–76).

In 1976, Sister returned to Alaska for the fourth time in 30 years. She became a member of the community of Sisters of St. Ann living in Anchorage. For six years the one-time secretary served as part-time secretary for the Diocesan Office of Religious Education, as a gracious hostess, always at home, to many, as well as an occasional organist for various parishes. Her chief work, however, consisted in helping Sister Margaret Cantwell with the writing of the history of the Diocese of Anchorage. This massive manuscript remained unpublished. She collaborated with Sister Margaret also with the production of *North to Share*, a history of the Sisters of St. Ann in Alaska. This has been published. To these two monumental works Sister M. George Edmond contributed, in addition to highly appreciated moral support, her guidance, the verification of countless data, the typing for endless hours of the manuscripts. All this she found to be "a true labor of love."

On July 24, 1980, Sister M. George Edmond celebrated the 50th anniversary of her Religious Profession. On October 14th of that same year, in recognition of her missionary work, she was presented the *Pro Ecclesia et Pontifice* medal from Pope John Paul II. The Holy Father also imparted his Apostolic Blessing upon her, "for her selfless commitment to God's people, especially in Alaska."

Sister M. George Edmond left Alaska in 1982, for Mount St. Mary Hospital, Victoria, B.C. After spending the years 1982–84 there, she returned to Anchorage for the years 1984–86. For the year 1986–87, she was back at Mount St. Mary Hospital. After that she returned to the Motherhouse in Lachine, where she spent the years 1987–92. In 1992, she was transferred to Marlborough to reside in the infirmary there. It was there, on February 4, 1999, that her long, fruitful life came to a peaceful end. Honors came to her in death no less than in life. On May 16, 1999, her Alma Mater, Anna Maria College, conferred upon here, posthumously, the honorary degree, Doctor of Laws.

16

ELINE, Father S. Aloysius, S.J.

In **Fairbanks, Alaska,** he was said to have done "yeoman's work as a diplomat spreading friendship among non-Catholics and being loved and admired by all in the city." He had "a knack at conversions and bringing back fallen-away Catholics." He was known for his "unremitting care of and attention to the poor." The "welfare of every sourdough" was of concern to him. He was "the consultant of doctors, lawyers, politicians, and even ministers." In the confessional, he was "most generous in priestly forbearance with the weak." Given his quiet, gentle, scholarly nature, he would seem to have been a poor choice for a rough frontier town such as Fairbanks. And yet, it was precisely those qualities that made him the perfect choice for Fairbanks. He was esteemed, especially by the men, for being "a man's priest."

S. Aloysius Eline was born on February 5, 1878, in Milwaukee, Wisconsin. There he attended grade and high schools, and Marquette University. He graduated from Marquette in 1897, and taught there from 1898 to 1900. During the year 1902–03, he was a teacher at Gonzaga College in Spokane, Washington. In 1903, he entered the Jesuit novitiate at Los Gatos, California. After completing his two-year noviceship, he remained there for a third year to study the classics and humanities. For the years 1906–08 he was back at Gonzaga, serving as General Prefect of Discipline. He then spent three more years at Gonzaga, not as a faculty member, but as a student of philosophy. From 1911–14, he taught at Santa Clara University in California. His theological studies he made at St. Louis University in St. Louis, Missouri, from 1914–18. He was ordained a priest in 1917. He taught again at Santa Clara during the year 1918–19. The following year found him back at Los Gatos, for his year of tertianship.

On September 10, 1920, Father Eline arrived at **Nulato.** Eight months later, in a letter to his Father

Father S. Aloysius Eline, S.J. *DFA*.

Provincial, Joseph M. Piet, S.J., he was able to write, "I have spent a very happy eight months here. One enjoys more peace of soul here in one week than could be experienced outside in a lifetime. My sole regret is that I could not have given myself to work in Nulato some years ago." From time to time, he traveled out of Nulato to its dependent stations up- and downriver.

After less than a year at Nulato, where he found the work "not uncongenial," and the climate "most invigorating," Father Eline had to leave it, on August 12, 1921, for Fairbanks, where Father Francis M. **Monroe**, S.J., was ailing and needed an assistant. After a year in Fairbanks—where, according to Father Crispin S. **Rossi**, S.J., writing to Paul C. **Deschout**, S.J., he was "doing wonders"—he was back again at Nulato, for the years 1922–24. During this stay there, he took up farming, "cultivated a quarter of an acre, just to keep from going crazy; but the results were nil—but I didn't go crazy, as far as I know." He missed the companionship of his peers and their stimulating conversation. There is a fine touch of humor in his letters.

During the years 1924–26, Father Eline was once more in Fairbanks. The next two years, 1926–28, he spent at Gonzaga University, serving as treasurer and Prefect of Discipline. In September 1928, he returned to Fairbanks, where he was to spend the

rest of his remaining years. From 1933–38, along with his pastoral duties, he served as a Consultor to the General Superior of the Alaska Mission.

One who knew Father Eline well during his Fairbanks years said of him that "he continually effervesced with priestly happiness and contentedness," and that "he was always neat in dress with a noticeable priestly preciseness." During his more active years, he was accustomed to take a daily walk to the post office, and to make "the grand tour of the town." It was more than a matter of picking up the mail or getting a little exercise. It was his way of meeting and keeping in touch with the old sourdough, the miner, the trapper, the bartender and his customers, the shop-keeper, the Alaska Native. People of all Faiths, and of none, experienced his personal concern for them and their concerns. His charity to the needy he kept "quite hidden." Not infrequently he would go to a store, order a quantity of food, and have it delivered to some needy family without his name on the delivery slip. Once he won a ticket for a trip outside. He had the bank send the value of the ticket, $150.00, in a check to the Sisters of **Providence** operating St. Joseph's Hospital in Fairbanks. He signed his gift, "An Old Sourdough."

While Father Eline clearly preferred the company of men, he had, nevertheless, a special "priestly respect, kindness, and regard for the good Sisters of Providence." Year after year, he gave them their annual retreat. One year, he won a new automobile in the town raffle. This he presented to the Sisters for their own use. When he was late in starting Mass for the Sisters, he would go without breakfast as a self-inflicted penance. The Sisters, in turn, lavished the most tender care upon him during the last years of his life. From December 1940 until his death, he was a virtual invalid, laid up "with a bad heart condition" in one of their hospital rooms.

Early in the morning of April 20, 1943, Fairbanks lost its "most beloved resident." He died shortly after receiving the Sacrament of the Dying. "The end was peaceful." His last request was that his remains not leave church property prior to burial. He wanted his fellow priests to prepare him for the open-casket wake, the funeral Mass and the burial. His wishes were honored. Vested as a priest, he lay in state; and so vested, he was buried in the Clay

Street Cemetery in downtown Fairbanks. According to reports, more non-Catholics than Catholics attended the funeral and burial services.

EMMONAK

The Central Yup'ik Eskimo village of Emmonak, more exactly, *Imangak*, meaning "black fish," located near the mouth of the Yukon River on the north bank of Kwiguk Pass, was originally called "Kwiguk." A post office was established there in 1920. During the 1950s, people from the Black River region, notably from **New Knock Hock**, moved to Emmonak. Later commercial salmon fishing became a major industry in the village, and the Northern Commercial Company built a cannery there. In 1964, the cannery was washed away by floods. Erosion was threatening the whole village. In 1964–65, it was, therefore, relocated 1.4 miles to the north of the original site. The new location was named Emmonak. In 1939, Emmonak had a population of 42; in 1960, 180; in 1970, 439; in 1990, 642; and in the year 2000, 767.

For generations the ancestors of the people presently living in Emmonak were evangelized by priests stationed at **Akulurak**. The names "Kwiguk" and "Imanok" first appear in the Oregon Province catalog for the year 1951–52, the year Father Segundo **Llorente**, S.J., began to visit them on a regular basis, out of **Alakanuk**. He saw to the building of a new church, dedicated to the Sacred Heart of Jesus, in 1953. Father Llorente served the villages of Alakanuk and Emmonak until 1963. Referring to the people of Emmonak, he wrote, "The years I spent with those people were—seen in retrospect—years of peace and great satisfaction."

Father William T. **McIntyre**, S.J. replaced Father Llorente in 1963. He, too, made Alakanuk his headquarters, and out of it served Emmonak. While he was pastor of the Alakanuk and Emmonak parishes, Brother John **Huck**, S.J., and Thomas V. Karlin—a former Trappist Brother and an expert cabinetmaker—built the new church in Emmonak. The first Mass in it was offered in September 1967. Father Francis X **Nawn**, S.J., served Emmonak, likewise out of Alakanuk, during the years 1968–77.

Beginning in 1977, the following Jesuit priests also served the Emmonak parish: Fathers Henry G. **Hargreaves,** René **Astruc**, James J. **Strzok**, and Thomas G. **Provinsal**. It was Father Provinsal who was at the side of Michael J. **Kaniecki**, S.J., Bishop of Fairbanks at the time, to administer to him

Sacred Heart Church, Emmonak. *MK.*

the Last Rites of the Church as he lay dying, felled by a fatal heart attack, near Emmonak's Sacred Heart Church, on the Feast of the Transfiguration, August 6, 2000. As of the year 2004, Father Provinsal—home-based in Emmonak since 2002—was caring for Sacred Heart parish.

Father Declan Caulfield, a priest from Ireland, was in Emmonak for the year 1994–95.

Eskimo Deacons, too, have ministered and were, as of the year 2004, ministering in their Emmonak parish: Stanley Waska (deceased and buried at **Hamilton**), William Trader, Bart Agathluk, and Raymond Waska.

The following School Sisters of Notre Dame also ministered in Emmonak: Mary Beck, Cynthia Borman, Jean Paul Zagorski, and Michael Marie Laux. **Ursuline** Sister Cecilia Huber did likewise.

In 1981, Patrick C.W. **Tam** began serving in Emmonak as Young Adult/Youth Minister. In more recent years, and as of the year 2004, he served, out of Emmonak, as Director of Adult Faith Development in the Yukon-Kuskokwim Delta.

64

ENDAL, Father George S., S.J.

When his Father Provincial asked him if he would be willing to go to **Alaska**, he answered that he was not interested in Alaska, that he dreaded the cold, did not think he could stand it, and that as an 11-year-old boy he had dreamt of being a missionary in China. However, being the obedient Jesuit that he was, he told his Father Provincial that he would go to Alaska, if he wanted him to. He did, and Alaska it was. Sixty years after he first set foot there, his life's trail came to an end, in Alaska. No other Jesuit had ever spent so many years in the North.

George S. Endal was born in Tacoma, Washington, on February 25, 1902. He entered the Jesuit novitiate at Los Gatos, California, on July 31, 1918, and, after completing the customary course of training and studies, was ordained a priest, on August 24, 1932, in Lyons, France. On June 24, 1936, he arrived at **Holy Cross Mission**, to begin a career of priestly ministry in Alaska that was to last fully six decades.

At Holy Cross, Father Endal found himself, owing to the regular Superior's frequent and long absences, "the de facto Superior, totally green and unprepared." The mission boarding school had 125 Eskimo and Indian children and was staffed by four Jesuit Lay Brothers and eight Sisters of St. **Ann**.

After two years at Holy Cross, Father Endal was assigned to serve for eight years at **Mountain Village** on the lower Yukon. While there, he was responsible also for nearby villages, among them **Pilot Station** and **Marshall**. To these he traveled with his own dogteam in winter. During summer months, he visited his villages and fish-camps on a little barge he built to serve him as transportation, housing, and a floating chapel. While at Mountain Village, he had, according to his successor, Father **John P. Fox**, S.J., "the practice of giving absolute priority to the seriously sick, regardless of time or inconveniences involved." In his old age, Father Endal remembered his Mountain Village years as "the happiest years of my life." In August 1946, he was transferred to **Alakanuk** to attend to that village and others near the mouth of the Yukon.

About this time, Eskimo men from villages in western Alaska began spending their summers working in salmon canneries in the Bristol Bay area. It was felt important by Father Endal, as well as by fellow priests and Superiors, that some priest be with them there. On December 15, 1947, Father Paul C. **Deschout**, S.J., General Superior of the Alaska Mission at the time, wrote to Oregon Province Provincial, Father Leopold J. Robinson, S.J.: "Endal is the man for the job. He has the zeal of 10 of us, and the sailors and fishermen of Bristol Bay will knock some prudence in him."

On April 27, 1948, Father Endal arrived in **Dillingham** to establish an official Catholic presence in that fisheries center. As the pioneer priest there, he put up a number of buildings to serve as residence, chapel and school. He himself taught school, both as a substitute teacher in the public school and in his own Holy Rosary Mission School. Twice fire destroyed his buildings. Resolutely he rebuilt. He lived in the basement of one of his new buildings under rather Spartan conditions. His Father Provincial, who visited him in Dillingham, advised him "to put a floor and heat in the basement to safeguard his health." To help him "bring

God's grace and American culture to the residents of Bristol Bay," as he put it, Father Endal recruited lay volunteers to staff his boarding school.

Meanwhile he was not neglecting the cannery workers. From 1949–62, the year he left Dillingham, he served as assistant agent of the Cannery Workers' Union, Local 46. In so doing, he had contact with all the canneries, "both as a union official and as a Church official." His principal concern was that the workers, especially the Alaska Natives, get a fair deal and that their spiritual needs be met.

In 1962, Father Endal took up station at **Nulato**. The two years he spent there were his first and only years among Alaska's Indian people. Of his Nulato years he wrote: "I found the Athabaskan Indians very open to the priest and a pleasure to work with." On August 15, 1964, he arrived in the Eskimo village of **Hooper Bay** on the edge of the Bering Sea to begin a four-year assignment there. While at Hooper Bay, he was pastor also of **Scammon Bay** and **Chevak**. For three years, he served also as Hooper Bay's postmaster, a position he happily turned over to Mrs. Alice Napoleon, an Eskimo woman, who filled it competently for many years.

In September 1968, Father Endal arrived in **St. Michael**. For the next 14 years he made this his headquarters and attended to its spiritual needs, along with those of its dependent mission stations, **Stebbins** and **Unalakleet**, which he visited on a regular basis.

By early 1982, Father Endal was 80 years old, had been a priest almost 50 years, had spent almost 50 years in Alaska. He was beginning to feel the weight of those years, and, therefore, asked to be relieved of his responsibility for the St. Michael and Stebbins parishes, and be allowed to live in Unalakleet, being responsible for that community alone. In keeping with his wishes and recommendations, Robert L. **Whelan**, S.J., Bishop of Fairbanks at the time, raised the Mission of the Holy Angels in Unalakleet to the rank of a parish and appointed Father Endal its first resident pastor. At the time, Unalakleet's Catholic population numbered around 40, but by then he had, to quote him, "formed friendly relations with most in that Protestant [Covenant] village."

In Unalakleet, where, in his words, he "had built up a good library," he lived in a tiny room without benefit of refrigerator, or shower, yet, according to one of his parishioners, "he prided himself in his personal appearance and grooming. He lived a wonderful example of humility."

On August 24, 1982, Father Endal celebrated the 50th anniversary of his ordination to the priesthood with a Mass of Thanksgiving. This was followed by a little party, at which cake and juice were served. "Joshua Hickerson, aged 3, helped Father blow out the 5 candles on the cake," noted Father Endal in the Unalakleet diary.

Exactly 50 years after Father Endal's 1936 arrival at Holy Cross, he wrote, on June 24, 1986, a little item he entitled "My Fifty Years in Alaska." Of this he said that it was "a hymn of praise to Almighty God, Who allowed His servant to be sifted as wheat only to sustain him in ways which add to His glory of being faithful in patience, long-suffering and mildness." Looking back on his long years in the villages, years of almost complete isolation, he said that he learned total dependence on God: "There was no one to consult. When things had to be done, when emergencies arose, I had to make the best decisions I could. I learned to lean on God. On the loneliest days He was always with me."

During his five years in Unalakleet, Father Endal had a considerable amount of time to himself. Much of this he spent in prayer, often before the Blessed Sacrament. But he had by no means become a recluse. He was active in matters concerning local education and had a lively interest in politics. According to one who knew him well, he "never shied away from a lively political debate. He loved to follow current events, and subscribed to many periodicals. He enjoyed them so much that he kept them all."

Father Endal was a voracious reader, as well as a prolific writer, especially of letters. His reading fed his writing; his writing was based on, supported by, what he read. He could express his views forcefully and fearlessly, whether on matters sacred or profane, whether in letters to editors of local newspapers or in letters to princes and prelates in high places. Legislators, state and national, heard from him, as did Jesuit Superiors, local and all the way up to Father General in Rome, as did bishops and archbishops, and the Holy Father himself. Father Endal was intimately familiar with all relevant constitutions, official documents, decrees, laws, teachings, as well as with Sacred Scripture, and he knew well how to cite sources: chapter and verse, page, paragraph and line. He could be judgmental, but his "judgmentalism" was born of a fierce loyalty to and love for the Church, the Society of Jesus, the Constitutions of state and country.

Five years after retiring to Unalakleet, Father Endal felt he wanted no longer to be alone. With his Superior's permission, he applied to be received into the **Anchorage** Pioneers Home, where he hoped to spend his last active days carrying on whatever ministry he would be capable of and that demand might suggest. He entered the Home on January 13, 1987. There he found "living conditions excellent, a spacious room, a good bed, private toilet and bath with shower, maids to keep the room clean and bed made, three adequate meals a day, even building heat. It is like staying at a rich resort, with money no consideration."

One might think that the octogenarian would now finally take his ease, be content to do little more than pray, read, eat and sleep. But, instead, he ministered in many ways. In his room and in the Pioneers Home chapel, Father Endal regularly said Mass for Home residents. He led them in rosaries and Holy Hours. He made retreats and guided others in retreats. He heard confessions, prepared people for and gave them first Holy Communion, anointed the sick, officiated at funerals. The year before he died, he officiated at the marriage of an elderly Pioneers Home couple.

In the Home, he continued to read and carry on what he termed his "ministry of correspondence." His room resembled a mini-library, complete with a set of the *Catholic Encyclopedia*, the *Britannica*, the *Great Books*, and "other books of worth," as he described them. An *Anchorage Times* reporter found Father Endal to be "an unassuming man in a black windbreaker and clerical collar" and that "books and magazines pile up by his neat bed. He reads and files, then reads some more."

In August 1989, Father Endal again made the *Anchorage Times*, by taking part in an anti-abortion protest sit-in at an Anchorage clinic. Ever a man

of his convictions, and having "the Church's support" to take part in that rescue operation, when invited to move away, he refused. He was arrested. At his trial he was charged with "criminal trespass." He denied the charge on the basis that what he had done was not a criminal act, was rather "a praiseworthy deed," something he felt in conscience he needed to do. In his favor, he cited both the Declaration of Independence and the U.S. Constitution. He was, nevertheless, convicted, and, in 1990, "did time," served a 15-day sentence at an Anchorage halfway house. He opted to be jailed rather than pay a $250 fine. During his time in jail, the 89-year-old Father Endal maintained "a twinkle in his eye and a smile on his face," saying that he "felt free as a bird."

Though well into his 90s, Father Endal was determined to continue to carry on an active ministry. "He wants to die at the altar is the impression he gives most of us Catholics here," wrote one who knew him well, adding, "and he has served us well, over and above what God would expect of him." Meanwhile the people of Unalakleet wanted him to be there, when their new church, a church for the building of which he himself had raised a considerable amount of money, was to be dedicated. And he was there, that January 29th, 1995, in Unalakleet, where he was fondly remembered as "an enduring spirited strong man, who took time to listen and speak with all who approached him."

But, even strong Alaskan men come sooner or later to the end of their life's trail. Strong though he was, Father Endal was not to see the end of the second millennium, and he sensed as much. In 1992, in response to a request from his Father Provincial that he write an answer to the question "Where do you see yourself in the year 2000, and what do you see yourself doing?," he wrote: "My present age is 90. By the year 2000 most probably I shall have said 'Good-bye' to my companions in this vale of tears and gone to my eternal reward. So, I see myself hopefully in heaven in union with St. Ignatius and all of our Jesuit saints."

It was in the evening of November 15, 1996, in **Providence** Hospital, Anchorage, that Father Endal, fortified for his last journey by the Sacraments of the Church that he had served so long and so well, said his last good-byes to his companions and to this "vale of tears," and rendered his soul to God. A major stroke three days earlier had signaled the beginning of the end for him. For some time already, he had expressed to his Father Superior his readiness and desire "to return to God." He said he could not figure out why the good Lord was putting off taking him.

Father Endal was one of the last of a band of great pioneer Alaskan Jesuit missionaries. After his death, one of his many admirers wrote, "We are happy that he is with Our Lord in that place of which he so often spoke, Paradise." Another said, "I'm sure he has many stars in his crown." Michael J. **Kaniecki**, S.J., Bishop of Fairbanks at the time, summarized, "When one speaks of determination, conviction, and loyalty to the Pope and Holy Mother Church, Father George Endal's name jumps to the foreground. Yet, what comes even more to the forefront is the fact that he was truly a man of prayer, a faithful Companion of Jesus."

His last resting place Father George S. Endal, S.J., found not in far-off China, but in Alaska, in the Catholic plot of Anchorage's Angelus Memorial Park Cemetery.

154

ESKIMO DEACON PROGRAM

Among the very first of them, all "men of good reputation," were men with Greek names like Timon, Nicanor, Stephen, Prochorus. Among those of our day, likewise all men of good reputation, were and are men with Central Yup'ik Eskimo names like **Nayagak**, Owletuk, Keatoak, Avugiak, Agathluk. These men and countless others have one thing in common: they have ministered, or are ministering as of 2004, to the people of God by virtue of the sacramental grace of the sacred order of the permanent diaconate. This third grade of sacred orders is as ancient as apostolic times, and as modern as post-Vatican II times.

In its Constitution *Lumen Gentium*, the Second Vatican Ecumenical Council decreed that "the diaconate can be restored as a proper and permanent rank of the hierarchy." Francis D. **Gleeson**, S.J., still

Bishop of **Fairbanks** in 1966, is credited by Francis T. **Hurley**, former Archbishop of **Anchorage**, with bringing up before the "competent territorial bodies of bishops," to quote the words of Vatican II, in this case the bishops of the United States, the matter of the permanent diaconate. According to Archbishop Hurley, "soft-spoken Bishop Gleeson's pastoral concern for his people made the rest of the bishops take notice of the permanent diaconate." Bishop Gleeson requested that the National Conference of Catholic Bishops petition Rome for approval of the restoration of the permanent diaconate in the United States. On May 8, 1968, Rome was petitioned, approval was given, and the restoration of the permanent diaconate in the United States became a reality. It was now within the power of the local Ordinary, within the sphere of his own jurisdiction, to approve and ordain candidates to the permanent diaconate.

While Vatican II assigned the restored diaconate a "proper and permanent rank of the hierarchy," regarding it as more than just a temporary solution to the "priest shortage" problem, much of the impetus to revitalize in the local churches, including the missionary Diocese of Fairbanks, the order of the permanent diaconate came, *de facto*, from a feared, or actual, shortage of priests.

"The Church in Alaska has reached a critical stage," wrote Father John J. Morris, S.J., in a 1967 letter to the bishops of Alaska at the time and to the bishop of Spokane. On the premise that "the shortage of priests is going to continue to make itself felt," he proposed "a center for the training of lay deacons, a training program" at Gonzaga University in Spokane, Washington. The following year, he wrote to his fellow Jesuits that, in his opinion, "the single most powerful force we can bring to bear, the single most important and far-reaching effort we can make is to establish a permanent diaconate program [in **Alaska**]." He felt such a program to be "worth the total dedication of a priest." Although the initiative, the push, to begin the permanent diaconate program in Alaska came mainly from Father Morris, he was not, as it turned out, to be the priest to bring that "total dedication" to the program. Father Charles J. "Chuck" **Peterson**, S.J., was to be that priest. Jesuits then serving in Alas-

Diaconal history in Alaska was made on February 8, 1975, in Marshall, when Alvin F. Owletuk of Marshall was ordained to the permanent diaconate by Bishop Robert L. Whelan, S.J., assisted by Father Charles J. Peterson, S.J., Director of the Eskimo Deacon Training Program. Here newly ordained Deacon Owletuk is being presented to his people. *DFA*.

ka were wholly in support of the program. On September 30, 1969, Father **John P. Fox**, S.J., a wise and practical man with over 40 years of missionary service in northern Alaska, wrote to Robert L. **Whelan**, S.J., Ordinary of the Diocese of Fairbanks: "Lay Diaconate? The sooner, the better." It should be noted here that a man, once ordained a deacon, is no longer a layman, but a cleric. Hence, it is not correct to speak of "lay deacons," or of a "lay diaconate."

By July 31, 1970, after a series of meetings, the Eskimo Deacon Program had taken concrete shape to the point where Bishop Whelan saw fit, upon the recommendation of his consultors, to appoint Father Morris director of the program. However, since he was then serving in the Mission Office in Portland, Oregon, and was, therefore, outside Alaska most of the time, Father Peterson, who showed interest in the program and was stationed in **Bethel**, was appointed co-director. During the first deacon training workshop, held in Bethel in October 1970, it soon became evident to Father Morris that he and Bishop Whelan, two men of quite different temperaments, would not be able to work well together. He saw, too, as he wrote years later, that "Chuck was very capable and would do a fine job. I had no difficulty in backing off, and seeing Chuck take over the program." Giving credit where credit was due, Father Peterson, with equal magnanimity, wrote in a 1973 issue of the program's bulletin, "Father John Morris was the original spark of our collective fire."

At its inception, the Native diaconate program had as its aim to meet the diaconal needs of the three major Native American groups represented in the Diocese of Fairbanks: the Athabaskan Indians of the Great Interior, the Inupiat Eskimos of northwestern Alaska, and the Central Yup'ik Eskimos of western Alaska. However, in spite of the best intentions and genuine, sincere efforts on the part of all concerned, the program had, as of the year 2004, produced only Central Yup'ik Eskimo deacons.

It was under Bishop Whelan that the Eskimo Deacon Program came into being and began to flourish. Throughout 1969 and 1970, he and priests serving in the Eskimo villages talked about and stressed the need among the Central Yup'ik Eskimo people for men willing to commit themselves to work generously and untiringly for the Church and the people in their respective villages. From the outset of the program, it was clearly understood that candidates for the permanent diaconate were to be only such men as were approved and proposed by the parish council and the people of their village, and who offered themselves freely. The wives of the candidates had to give their consent and pledge their support, before a given candidate could be seriously considered.

From the outset of the program, candidates have invariably had feelings of not being worthy, or of not being talented enough, for the diaconal office.

However, they all accepted the call to serve as deacons, because their communities asked them to serve as their deacons and assured them of their support. They have been motivated, too, by a spiritual call and desire to serve, to minister, to attend to the spiritual, liturgical needs of their communities.

Where to train the Eskimo candidates for the permanent diaconate? Some knew almost no English, could neither read nor write. They were family men with families to support by hunting, fishing, and seasonal work. Thoughts of sending them to training centers in the Lower 48 were soon quickly dismissed. It was decided—and, in retrospect, wisely decided—that the training of the candidates would take place right there, in Central Yup'ik Eskimo country. There would be a series of workshops. For a given workshop all would gather in some designated village. And there would be "homework," while they were in their home villages. The priest in the village would be the tutor. "The bush priest," wrote Father Morris on July 31, 1970, "is the critical element in the success or failure of the program. It absolutely will not burst into full bloom without you in the bush becoming a 'seminary professor.'" There were no objections on the part of Rome to this workshop-homework approach.

The Eskimo Deacon Training Program was more or less formally inaugurated on October 16, 1970, in Bethel, when seven deacon candidates took part in the first of that lengthy series of workshops that led eventually to their ordination to the permanent diaconate. The original seven were: Leo Moses and Michael Nayagak of **Chevak**, Henry Albert of **Tununak**, Nick Therchik of **Toksook Bay**, James Gump and Joseph Lake of **Hooper Bay**, and Nick Charles of Bethel. Others soon joined the group, until the original group of candidates numbered 20. That first workshop was a great success. "The beginning of our program of study and training was beautiful," wrote Father Peterson.

The key roles played in the program's success, especially during its early years, by Fathers Morris and Peterson are a matter of record. It should be noted, however, that its overall success—beginning already with the planning stages and during the first 15 years of its existence, 1970–85, the years he was Ordinary of the Diocese of Fairbanks—was, in large part, due also to Bishop Whelan. It was never without his enthusiastic, whole-hearted support. He took a personal interest in it, regularly attended training sessions, sitting on the floor alongside the candidates. He carried on a warm, personal correspondence with each one of them. His was a hands-on approach, but the touch was always gentle.

Bishop Whelan was present at that first Bethel workshop. It was he who welcomed the Eskimo deacon candidates to the "very special meeting." He asked them to look upon themselves as having "a special vocation, a calling from God in the Church to do much for the spiritual life and sanctity of our Eskimo people." Right after the meeting, he wrote that he was "extremely pleased and edified with the response received from the seven men" who were at the meeting, and with the "willingness and generosity" they manifested.

From the outset, those responsible for the Eskimo Deacon Program manifested cultural and anthropological concerns, gave thought to the matter of adaptation, inculturation, indigenization. There was concern especially about putting parts of Scripture and the whole of the liturgies and rituals into the Native language. With few reservations, they were given permission by Rome and by Bishop Whelan to do what they thought best in these matters.

At the second workshop, also held in Bethel, the deacon candidates were again urged to be "men of prayer" and to continue to lead daily prayers, and especially the prayers at Mass, in both Eskimo and English. Present at that second workshop, in addition to the seven who attended the first one, were, among others, William **Tyson** of St. Marys, and Larry Chiklak of **Kotlik**. Because of their skills as translators and interpreters, William was elected discussion leader and Larry recording secretary.

At that second workshop the topic of liturgical art was discussed, notably a design for the vestment to be worn by a deacon, when bringing Communion to the sick or when conducting services in the church. A vestment designed after the traditional Eskimo parka was modeled by William Tyson. This design was agreed upon and approved by Bishop Whelan. On the outside of the vestment, over his chest, the deacon wears a simple cross hung loosely from the neck.

Prior to that second workshop, the men who attended the first one all received letters of appointment to the office of "lay-deacon" from Bishop Whelan and were installed in their respective village churches in a public ceremony of appointment. Giving the deacon candidates and the diaconal role a high profile early in the program did much to enhance their status among their people.

New men joined the diaconal candidates at the third workshop, bringing the total number of candidates to twenty-one. It was decided at that workshop that the program would no longer admit new applicants into that "first group." Some of these had by then already as much as four months of practice, of personal formation, and the benefit of three workshops behind them.

The fourth workshop took place in mid-April 1971, again in Bethel. Its intent was "to move into deeper questions which lead to deeper understanding." It was recognized that to raise the type of questions that lead to a deeper understanding called for "a stronger and more intimate spiritual life." To foster that spiritual life, a mid-August "husband and wife deacons' retreat" was held at St. Mary's. This was the first such retreat of what became a series of annual such retreats. It proved to be a deeply moving experience for all involved. Father Fox, helped by William Tyson as interpreter and translator, was its director. "The retreat spirit grew as a stream flows," wrote Father Peterson, "gently and powerfully."

In May 1971, at "the Tununak Conference," William Tyson, Elizabeth Beans of St. Mary's, Leo Moses of Chevak, Paul Albert of Tununak, and Fathers Francis J. **Fallert**, S.J., and John A. **Hinsvark** met for the purpose of producing an acceptable translation of the Mass and of the Communion liturgy presided over by the deacons. What they produced was judged "a major achievement." Adeline Panruk, Mary Tunuchuk, and Agnes Kairaiuak, three women from Chevak, deserve most of the credit for that major achievement, for they had laid the foundation of the translation that was in the end approved at the Tununak Conference. It was left to William Tyson to attend to fine points concerning orthography, and to type up the Eskimo translation.

At the fifth workshop, also held in Bethel, the Sacrament of Baptism and the liturgical practice of Baptism were focused on. The proceedings of this fifth workshop were taped, as were those of subsequent ones. The tapes were reproduced and distributed to all the deacon candidates for home study and reflection, and as "a way of bringing the brotherhood and spirit of the workshops" into their homes and villages.

Immediately after attending the sixth workshop, held in Bethel, January 20–23, 1972, Bishop Whelan wrote, in a letter addressed to the parish councils of the parishes having deacon candidates:

> Every time I have been with them, I have been edified by their dedication and seriousness of purpose. All of us, you the people, our deacon candidates, and I your Bishop, have been given the opportunity of bringing something new and life-giving to the Church in our diocese. I am proud of what has been accomplished by these men in the short period of a year and a half.

In September and October 1972, Father Peterson visited ten villages to see the deacon candidates at work in their respective villages and to learn from them what kinds of study and training were most needed before ordinations could take place. The eighth workshop focused on the "meaning, the duties and privileges of ordination."

The ninth workshop, held January 23–27, 1973, took place not in Bethel, but in Toksook Bay. The deacon candidates themselves had suggested holding the workshops in different villages, with the host village doing the inviting. Participants came to Toksook Bay by snowmachine, mail plane, and charter plane. Some were flown there by Father James A. **Sebesta**, S.J., in the diocese-owned Cessna 180. On several evenings of this workshop, Eskimo dances were held, a first.

Workshop number ten, held March 21–24, 1973, was hosted by the people of **Emmonak**. It laid heavy emphasis on New Testament studies and Holy Orders. At this workshop, Father Peterson announced that he would be away for a year, in India, to finish his formal training as a Jesuit. After a discussion involving all the assembled was held, Bishop Whelan appointed Father Hinsvark as the new director of the Eskimo Deacon Program. Father René **Astruc**, S.J., who had for some time been involved in a low-key way with the program, was appointed co-director.

The eleventh workshop was held in Hooper Bay, in October 1973, and focused on the pastoral care of the sick.

On March 12, 1974, deacon candidate Michael Nayagak wrote (through another) to Bishop Whelan: "Whenever we have meeting, deacons and priests, I always happy. I feel very happy, just way down in my heart." No one embodied the spirit of the whole diaconate program better than Michael Nayagak. If the Eskimo Deacon Program has a patron saint, it is Michael Nayagak.

By late summer 1974, Father Peterson, back from India, was again involved with the deacon training program. His primary responsibility was to see to the ongoing training of the original group, still numbering eighteen. Father Astruc took charge of the training of the second group, a new group, organized by Father Hinsvark, numbering ten. Father Hinsvark continued on in the program as coordinator of the activities of both groups.

In December 1974, the original group met for its 13th workshop, in **Chefornak**. The main topics covered at it were Scripture, the Sacrament of Reconciliation, and Homily Preparation. From its inception, the Eskimo Deacon Program focused on the liturgical role of the deacon. Bishop Whelan considered this more important than the roles of witnessing and service. At this workshop, on December 11th, eleven deacon candidates took a major step toward their ordination to the permanent diaconate, when they stepped before Bishop Whelan to receive from him the symbols of office: the Lectionary for the ministry of Reader and a plate of bread for the ministry of Acolyte. They had all freely requested these ministries. It should be noted here that the candidates were not rushed along the road to ordination. In retrospect, it is evident that much of the Eskimo Deacon Program's extraordinary success has been due, in large part, to a policy adopted at the outset of not ordaining candidates, before they had a sound formation and were ready and willing to be ordained.

On the evening of February 8, 1975, in **Marshall**, Native diaconal history was made in the Diocese of Fairbanks, when Alvin F. Owletuk, a Central Yup'ik Eskimo living in Marshall, was ordained to the permanent diaconate by Bishop Whelan. Sixteen deacon candidates took part in the ceremony. The following morning, Deacon Owletuk performed his first official act as a deacon, when he baptized four children.

The new, or second, group met in **Scammon Bay** the middle of January 1975, for its first workshop. At this workshop they were appointed extraordinary ministers of Communion, the first step on the road to the permanent diaconate. It met next at **Stebbins**, then again at **Alakanuk**.

By November 15, 1975, Bishop Whelan had ordained 11 Eskimo men to the permanent diaconate. There were still 19 in training. During 1976, he ordained nine of these. One of them was Stanley Waska, one of the first of the Eskimo deacons to go to his reward. In dying, as in living, he did the whole Native diaconate program much honor.

Stanley Waska was born on January 17, 1917, in Kwigmiut. He married in 1939, and became the father of eight children, of whom only one lived to adulthood. Stanley's wife died in 1950. He never remarried. In the early 1970s, living in Emmonak now, he was "elected' by his people to serve them as a permanent deacon. He was remarkable as a deacon for his faithfulness to his diaconal ministry and for his loyalty to the Church. Even in summer, at the height of the fishing season, he left his camp every Saturday and boated to Emmonak, so that the people left in the village could have Sunday services. He barely knew how to read, and spent hours each week preparing the reading of the Gospel and his homily. He was very faithful in bringing Communion to the shut-ins and the sick. Lengthy preparations preceded each baptism. After performing his first baptism, that of his grandson, when entering it in the record book, he, with a smile on his face, added, "grandpa."

Deacon Waska was very much appreciated as a preacher, particularly at funerals. Neighboring villages often sent for him to come to them to preach the funeral homily. When his own turn to die came, he remarked that, although he had enjoyed his work as a deacon and would gladly have continued it, he was not afraid to die. Shortly before he died, he had gone to Bethel for a checkup. While waiting at the airport to return home, he unexpectedly suffered a heart attack. He was taken back to the hospital, where he refused any special means to prolong his life. Early the next morning, December 5, 1986, a First Friday, always a special day in his life, he died very peacefully, holding his crucifix. (Deacons Stanley Waska and Michael Nayagak both had a special devotion to the Sacred Heart of Jesus, served parishes dedicated to the Sacred Heart, and died on a First Friday of a month, a day when the Sacred Heart is honored in a special way.) Stanley Waska lies buried in **Hamilton**.

January 26, 1977, was a memorable day for William Tyson and the whole Eskimo Deacon Program. On that day, in Anchorage, Archbishop Jean Jadot, Apostolic Delegate to the United States, ordained William to the permanent diaconate. "It was a very happy occasion for us," wrote Bishop Whelan to Agnelo Cardinal Rossi in Rome, "and I feel that Archbishop Jadot had a favorable impression of the Eskimo deacons whom he met." It was the "preparation and formation of these men to their high calling" that impressed the Archbishop.

On October 13, 1977, Bishop Whelan wrote to Mike Saclamana, an Inupiat Eskimo from **King Island** living in **Nome** at the time, inviting him to attend the workshop scheduled to take place from October 31 to November 4 at Alakanuk, to observe and to inform himself concerning the Eskimo Deacon Program. This, in itself, may seem to be a minor detail to note, but it is noted to show that in late 1977 there was still hope that the Native diaconate might be established among groups other than just the Central Yup'ik Eskimos.

On July 26, 1978, the first man of the second group, Nicholas Tommy of **Newtok**, was ordained in that village's newly dedicated and blessed church. By the end of the year 1979, the total number of Eskimo men ordained to the permanent diaconate stood at twenty-six.

In 1985, Michael J. **Kaniecki**, S.J., succeeded Bishop Whelan as Bishop of Fairbanks. From the outset, he adopted the Eskimo Deacon Program as his own and gave it his careful attention. He likened the deacons to his right hand; and he told them, "You are my eyes and my ears in the villages."

The Eskimo deacon candidates of the 1980s and the 1990s differed markedly from the earlier ones. Among other respects, they were bilingual and literate. Consequently, a new kind of training and schooling, more formal and systematized, was possible and introduced. At the same time, the program's traditional goal of establishing a truly indigenous, a genuinely "Native," Catholic Church continued to be stressed. A more formal procedure for admitting candidates to the program and to the order of diaconate was put into place. For his work with the Eskimo Deacon Program and his six years of service on the Bishops' Committee for the Diaconate, the National Association of Permanent Diaconate Directors presented Bishop Kaniecki with its 1990 award, "in recognition of the outstanding services rendered in developing religious leadership within the diaconate movement in the United States."

In 1973, as stated above, Father René Astruc was appointed co-director of the Eskimo Deacon Program. He soon took over as director of the program, a post he held for two decades, until 1996. That year Father Richard D. **Case**, S.J., became the program's director. After the death of Bishop Kaniecki, on August 6, 2000, Father Case was elected Administrator of the Diocese of Fairbanks. Soon thereafter, Father Mark A. **Hoelsken**, S.J., became the program's director.

On August 22, 2002, Donald J. **Kettler** was ordained Bishop of Fairbanks. On November 3rd of that year, in the village of **Nightmute**, he had the joy for the first time of ordaining an Eskimo man to the permanent diaconate. That man was Ignatius Matthias. As Bishops Whelan and Kaniecki before him, so Bishop Kettler, too, took the Eskimo Deacon Program to heart.

124, 145, 148, 178, 193

ESMAILKA, Mr. Harold

"He's just a wonderfully nice guy." "No one in the state has one bad word to say about him." "He's respected all over for his honesty." "He built everything he has by sheer hard work and determination." These are but some of the remarks made about him

On July 28, 1985, in Sacred Heart Cathedral, Fairbanks, following the Mass at which Michael J. Kaniecki, S.J., was installed as Bishop of Fairbanks, Harold and Florence Esmailka, Sister Ida Brasseur, S.S.A., and Father Louis L. Renner, S.J., have something to smile about. *Photo by Jimmy Bedford/LRC.*

by his fellow "airplane guys." His pastor of many years, Father Joseph **Hemmer**, O.F.M., said of him: "He fosters a great vision of the Church, seeing the Church as alive and productive in imparting and enhancing divine life. He shows a constant concern for all Church needs, whether spiritual or temporal." His origins were humble, but before he was fifty years old, he was, thanks to his innate drive and keen business sense, a millionaire. However, being wholly unpretentious by nature, and gratefully aware of the ultimate source of his success, he would have been the last one to boast about "having made it," about "having arrived." His life's story, a story of unfailing faith and fidelity to God and neighbor, is as interesting as it is inspirational.

Harold Esmailka was born of Koyukon Athabaskan Indian ancestry on the south bank of the Yukon River, in a wood-cutting camp (wood for steamboats), 11 miles above **Kaltag**, on October 6, 1930. As an infant, he was adopted by Peter and Martha Esmailka, who gave him all the love and care any child could wish for. From his earliest years, though living in the village of **Nulato** on the middle Yukon, he was trained in "the old ways," the traditional Native subsistence way of life. This consisted mainly in hunting, fishing, trapping, gathering. However, he was also exposed to "book learning," inasmuch as he attended the day school at Nulato run by the Sisters of St. **Ann**—when he was not in some fishing, hunting or trapping camp.

On June 1, 1942, Harold's adoptive father died. Shortly before his death, he urged Martha, who had spent some time downriver at the **Holy Cross Mission** boarding school, to send Harold and his sister, Mary, down to that school. Recalled his mother many years later: "The Father [John B. **Baud**, S.J.] came to me and asked, 'Are you going to send those kids down, Martha?' 'I got nothing. How will I send them down?' I told him. He just start to laugh. 'You get ready with them and God will take care of it,' he told me." That summer, Harold and his sister found themselves at Holy Cross.

From time to time, Harold visited his mother, but the visits were short ones. Brother George J. **Feltes**,

S.J., a master mechanic and teacher of "shop," wanted him back at Holy Cross to learn to be a mechanic. Harold proved to be a good learner, and it is to Brother Feltes and the training that he received from him that he attributes, in very large part, his success in life. (When, in 1983, Brother Feltes left Alaska to retire in California, Harold, as an expression of his indebtedness to him for the training he had received from him, gave him an extremely generous monetary gift.) In the spring of 1951, Harold, well grounded in mechanics in general, and in engine maintenance in particular, and thinking airplanes, left Holy Cross to join the Army. Before joining the Army, however, he spent the months of March and April as a member of the building crew led by Father James C. **Spils**, S.J., working on the construction of the new St. Mary's Mission boarding school on the banks of the **Andreafsky** River. He did all the wiring in the big building. Helping build St. Mary's was, in part, his way of showing his gratitude for what Father Spils and Holy Cross had done for him. Harold served in the Army from May of 1951 to May of 1953. While in the Army, when on furlough, he visited Holy Cross, rather than Nulato, for to him Holy Cross was "home."

After Harold had served his two years in the Army, his brother, Eddie Hildebrand, got him a job working for the Morrison-Knutson Construction Company. Harold became a member of the Operating Engineers Union 302. He worked out of that Union for ten years, from 1954–64. As a Union laborer, he worked for a time at heavy construction in **Fairbanks** and on Johnson Island in the Pacific. By 1954, though he had not yet learned how to fly, he had earned enough money to buy his first airplane, an Aeronca Chief with a 65-hp. engine.

By 1957, Harold had his Super Cub. In it, on Christmas Day 1958, he flew Father James W. **Plamondon**, S.J., from **Koyukuk** upriver to offer the Christmas Mass at **Ruby**. Harold himself was spending the winter at Nulato. Bertha, his sister, and her family were living in Ruby. He spent the night with them. That night it snowed. The next morning he ran up to the Northern Commercial Company store to borrow a push-broom to sweep the snow off the wings of his plane. It was at the store that he first laid eyes on Florence Lorine Gurtler, home

for the holidays from **Copper Valley School**, which she was attending at the time. On November 5, 1960, in Nulato, with Father John B. Baud, S.J., officiating, Harold and Florence were married. In Florence, Harold found a most capable and likeminded partner, whether there were concerns of faith or of family or of business. The couple made their home in Ruby.

In 1964, Harold and Florence bought the store there from Johnny May, and began, as co-owners, to operate it as "The Ruby Trading Company." (The name of the store was not an arbitrary one. Up until the latter 1960s, about 75 percent of its transactions were conducted through barter: fish, furs, fire wood, and services for store goods.) They bought the store, because Harold's sister, Bertha, and her husband, Claude, who lived in Ruby, were killed in a boating accident and left behind a large family that needed somebody to provide for them. Harold and Florence helped to take care of the children the first winter after the death of their parents. (Regarding Johnny May, it is worthy of note that, in 1989, when he was suffering from cancer, Harold and Florence moved to Fairbanks to take care of him, so that he would not have to be put into a care home. They nursed him back to passable health, then took him into their Ruby home until his death in 1995.)

Children were not long in coming to Harold and Florence. Harold, Jr., nicknamed "Punky," was born on August 10, 1961. Taking after his father, inasmuch as he, too, was mechanically inclined and airplane-minded, he earned his pilot's license while still in his teens. Unlike his father, however, who was never involved in a serious airplane accident, Harold, Jr., though a naturally skilled pilot and gifted athlete, lost his life, in 1979, when the plane he was piloting crashed, killing him and two others onboard. In addition to leaving behind his parents, Harold, Jr. left behind also three sisters: Cynthia, Ginger, and Agnes, or "Aggie" (adopted), and a brother, Thomas, or "Tommy."

As in the case of most families with children, so in the case of the Harold and Florence Esmailka family, there were times of great joys, and times of great sorrows. Apart from the tragic death of Punky, there was the drowning death of Tommy. Sad as this event was, Harold and Florence, being both people of deep faith, were inclined to see in this the intervention of a kindly Providence. Tommy was severely afflicted with apoplexy. In 1996, Aggie, Ruby's postmistress at the time, was brutally murdered, while on duty in the post office. The perpetrator of the crime was apprehended and convicted. The crime being a federal offense, the death penalty was legally justified. Harold, however, in keeping with his nobility of character and deep faith, urged that the culprit's life be spared. His wish was granted. Said Harold, "We're not vindictive people." Grateful for having himself been adopted into a loving and caring family, he adopted Aggie's oldest daughter, 15-year-old Jenasy. A few years later, he generously paid for her training as a professional nurse. Daughters Cynthia and Ginger, after receiving a good formal education and hands-on practical training, went on to happy marriages and successful business ventures. It was in large part Harold, who helped them get started in business.

In 1988, Harold and Florence adopted as their son a new-born infant boy, whom they named John Charles. The following year, they adopted as their son another new-born infant boy. Him they named James. In both cases the natural mothers wanted very much that Harold and Florence be the adoptive parents of their infant sons.

"Family" and "business," in that order, are the key words without which one could not even begin to write a biographical sketch of Harold Esmailka. And "business" means, of course, primarily "airplane-related business."

Harold's business ventures began with one airplane. At first he flew charter flights out of **Galena**. Before long, he had a fleet of Cessna 207s. In 1974, Wien Air Alaska subcontracted him to haul mail from Galena to outlying villages. He went on to buy, develop and sell various air services, among them Vanderpool Flying Service, Vanderpool Air Taxi, Aniak Flying Service, Grayling Air Service, and Alaska Air Central. In the spring of 1982, he sold the company he owned at the time, but remained on for a year as its president and Chairman of the Board, "to make sure the business remained stable."

In 1983, identifying the little boy, Harold, in a photo, his adoptive mother, with a touch of maternal pride—and, one senses, an admonition to humility—said, "He's the big shot now!" By 1984, Harold's Air Service was a reality. It serviced 63 villages and had a fleet of 28 aircraft. This included a turbine DC-3, the only certified one in the world at the time, and a helicopter. After Harold's Air Service, came Friendship Air Service and Tanana Air Service, both owned by Harold and under his leadership. Given Alaska's weather extremes and wild, rugged terrain, and the countless hours and air miles flown by his fleets of commercial planes, it is remarkable, and cause for much gratitude on his part, that there was only one fatality involving a commercial plane of his. One of his pilots, flying an Islander, 22JA up the Nowitna River was killed, while attempting to land on a sandbar.

As late as the year 2002, Harold, already into his 70s, was still in the airplane business, as owner of Tanana Air Service. What motivated him? Was it simply that operating such a business was in his blood, or that the revenue it generated was timely, given the fact that he and Florence had to provide for the two young adopted boys mentioned above? Most likely it was a combination of both.

Harold's life's story is, unquestionably, a success story. He made the most of his natural gifts and of the training he received early in life. In Florence he was blessed with a highly competent, supportive wife. But Harold, being a man of deep faith and close to the Church all his life, recognized beyond the shadow of a doubt that it was to God that he ultimately owed his life's successes and blessings, and that, therefore, to Him alone the ultimate debt of gratitude was owed.

Harold's spirit of gratitude manifested itself in many concrete, tangible ways. Having himself been adopted into a loving and caring home, he, in turn, over the years, adopted four children and provided them with a like home. When his adoptive mother was in her later years, he insisted that she let him build her a comfortable, modern home. In 1982, when the small priest's quarters at one end of the Ruby church needed additional space, he was one of several who saw to it that a bedroom was built and the costs taken care of. In 1984, shortly after Michael J. **Kaniecki**, S.J. was ordained Bishop of Fairbanks, he received from Harold a Cessna 207.

It was Harold who played a key role in seeing to it that the new much-needed Ruby church became a reality in 2004. Thanks to Harold's generosity, priests, Sisters, and Brothers on official Church business for decades flew as his guests on his airplanes. At times of major feasts, he and Florence had a special eye out for the needy of the village. Having generously received, Harold generously gave. The full extent of Harold's charities is known to God alone, and that is the way Harold wanted it.

The village of Ruby, his Native people, and the State of Alaska, too, were well served by Harold.

He was a member of the Ruby City Council, of the School Committee, of the Dineega Corporation, of Alaska Air Carriers, of the Denali State Bank Board, of the Monroe Foundation, Inc., as well as a member of many other committees. He supported local creative artists by commissioning works from them. He was a financial partner, not surprisingly, of the newly founded magazine, *Alaska Flying*.

Harold Esmailka: as of the year 2004, still a credit to the people of his origins, still a credit to his Church, and still a credit to his Creator and Lord.

F.I.C.: Brothers of Christian Instruction of Ploermel

The Brothers of Christian Instruction (in Latin, *Institutum Fratrum Instructionis Christianae de Ploermel*, hence their distinctive initials, F.I.C.) is a Religious Congregation that emerged from the union in 1820 of a group in Brittany founded by Gabriel Deshayes in 1816 at Auray with another started by Jean-Marie de La Mennais in 1819 at St. Brieuc. The congregation, sometimes called also the La Mennais Brothers, was originally founded to teach in elementary schools. Later its members undertook to teach also on the secondary and college levels.

The Brothers first came to the United States in 1903, to open a school in Plattsburgh, New York. Already the following year, on August 21, 1904, one of the Brothers, Constantin-Marie Roulin, arrived at **Holy Cross Mission**, **Alaska**. For the next five years he was in charge of the boys, supervising them day and night. He was not their classroom teacher. In him the boys had a shrewd psychologist, and, still more, a kind-hearted man.

In 1905, Brother René-Maurice Allory joined his confrère in Alaska, but not at Holy Cross. His first assignment was to teach school at **Kokrines**. After a short year there, he went downriver to join Brother Constantin-Marie at Holy Cross. Brother René-Maurice was described in a biography of Brother Constantin-Marie as "one of the most brilliant students, as well as the most cheerful. Quickly he learned the English language, which he spoke and wrote with fluency. Furthermore, he was an excellent teacher, and a soul profoundly religious with a heart of gold."

Brother René was recalled from Alaska in 1908; Brother Constantin-Marie the following year. Their change of status was brought about by the fact that in 1907 the Alaska Mission was transferred to the Jesuits of the French-Canadian Province. The excellent work by these two Brothers was acknowledged and appreciated. With their departure, the first chapter of service rendered in Alaska by the La Mennais Brothers came to an end.

The second chapter of their work in Alaska began after a lapse of 66 years. In 1975, Brothers Normand Berger and Albert Heinrich came to **Nome** to serve there as volunteers. Brother Normand was chief engineer at the Catholic Radio Mission, **KNOM**, and music director in the parish. Brother Albert was news director at the station, and helped with parish visitations. He left Nome in 1982 to teach school in Tokyo, Japan. Brother Normand left Nome in 1985, took up flying, became the first professional pilot in his Congregation, and flew for the missions in Africa. There, in February 1989, he died in a fatal airplane crash.

Brother Raymond Bérubé began serving in Nome in April 1979, as head of maintenance. This was a very demanding responsibility, given the dilapidated condition of the old radio studio and parish buildings. Brother Raymond left Nome in 1990.

In 1988, Brother Phillip Drouin came to Nome. He soon won the hearts of many Nomeites with his friendly greetings and home visits. He celebrated his golden jubilee as a Brother of Christian Instruction in 1992. On that occasion, the Alaska Legislature honored "this remarkable man of God" with a formal document recognizing his positive contributions to the lives of the people of Nome. He was honored as Nome's "Street Minister," because of his tireless efforts to help the homeless and troubled. Brother Philip left Nome in 1998. He was the last of his Congregation to serve in Alaska.

Brother René-Maurice (Pierre Allory), F.I.C., was at Kokrines 1905–06 and at Holy Cross Mission 1906–08. This photo of him was taken by Brother Albert Heinrich, F.I.C., at Josselin, France, on July 5, 1980, less than four months before Brother René-Maurice's 96th birthday. *LRC.*

FAIRBANKS

The city of Fairbanks, located on the right bank of the Chena River near where it enters the Tanana River, was founded in 1901, when a trading post was established there by E. T. Barnette. It was first called "Barnette's Cache"; but, in 1902, the name was changed to honor Charles Warren Fairbanks, Senator from Indiana and later Vice President of the United States under Theodore Roosevelt. Fairbanks began as the supply center to the mining region to its north after gold was discovered there in 1902 by Felix Pedro. It soon became the commercial and transportation hub of north and central **Alaska**. Its population was 3,541, in 1910; 1,155 in 1920; 2,101 in 1930; 3,455 in 1939; 5, 771 in 1950; and 30,224 in the year 2000. The Fairbanks post office was established in 1903.

The history of the Catholic Church in Fairbanks began on July 1, 1904, when Father Francis M. **Monroe**, S.J., first arrived there. Standing alone on the banks of the Chena River that day, he found himself, in the words of one historian, "penniless, landless and forlorn." But he wasted no time on self-pity. The day after his arrival, he offered the first Mass celebrated in Fairbanks, in "a private house." On the 3rd, a Sunday, he offered the first public Mass celebrated in Fairbanks, in the District Court building. No sooner was he in Fairbanks, than he set about raising money and acquiring land suitable as a church site. On the south side of the Chena, at

Front and Dunkel Streets, he found what he was looking for. Gifted with architectural drawing and carpentry skills, he himself set about building what today still stands as Immaculate Conception Church. The first public Mass to be offered in the structure, measuring 30 × 65 feet, was celebrated on the Feast of All Saints, November 1, 1904. The year 1904 marks the founding of Immaculate Conception parish, Fairbanks.

Concerned not only for the soul, but also for the body, Father Monroe built a hospital, named for St. Joseph, on the north side of the Chena and a little downstream from the church. By November 18, 1906, the 40-bed hospital was ready to admit its first patients, 35 of them. Sisters of St. **Ann** were part of the hospital staff from September 30, 1906, to June 23, 1907. They were replaced by Benedictine Sisters, who helped staff the hospital for the next three years. On October 1, 1910, Sisters of **Providence** took charge of St. Joseph's Hospital. They operated and staffed it until it closed in 1968. Additions were made to the hospital in 1935 and 1950.

With the church and the hospital on opposite sides of the Chena, Father Monroe found himself spending too much time commuting between the two. The two structures needed to be side by side. In 1909, he discussed the problem with Father Joseph R. **Crimont**, S.J., his Superior. "Move the church!" was Father Crimont's directive. Though not a professional engineer, Father Monroe was resourceful, and a man possessed of practical good judgment. He determined that the church could be moved across the river next to the hospital. Townspeople were skeptical, thinking such a move impossible. But, Father Monroe had a plan, as simple as it was ingenious.

When the Chena froze solid enough to bear the weight of the church, he drew two parallel lines 30 feet apart on the ice. Holes were cut through the ice at eight-foot intervals along these lines. Upright logs were wedged into these holes and left to freeze in solid. The following day, the tops of these were sawed off two feet above the ice, making strong supports for heavy timbers. On these the church was rolled diagonally some 400 feet across the frozen river to its present site. There the building was raised up high enough to allow for a full basement. That was in late November 1911. In the course of the following years, until he left Fairbanks in 1924, Father Monroe continued to make notable improvements to the church.

In the early spring of 1912, the rough work on the basement parish hall was completed, and a two-story structure, 34 × 36 feet, was added for priests and Brothers. Brother Joseph Coté, S.J., came to Fairbanks that summer and assisted greatly by doing all the wiring, the painting of the residence, and much of the plumbing work.

In the early spring of 1914, the roof of the church was given a steeper pitch. The additional five feet in height made possible a choir loft. At the same time, a belfry was added to the front elevation of the church, and a bigger than life-size statue of Our Lady of the Immaculate Conception was placed above the front doors. The whole interior of the church was later finished with fleur-de-lis embossed decorative tin. Father Monroe was depending on Brother Coté for this task, but he was recalled by his Superior in Canada, and Father Monroe had to do much of the work himself, until Brother Thomas Callahan, S.J., came and rendered much assistance.

During the winter of 1921–22, Father S. Aloysius Eline, S.J., was in Fairbanks, where Father Monroe was ailing and needed an assistant. From 1924, the year Father Monroe left Fairbanks, until 1926, and from 1928 until 1941, when, because of failing health, he became assistant to Father Joseph F. McElmeel, S.J., for a year, Father Eline was the much loved, highly respected pastor of Immaculate Conception parish. Despite temperatures of 60 degrees below zero, he began his term as pastor with the Forty Hours Devotion, the first time that devotion had been held in Alaska. During those days, he sang a High Mass every morning, with the Sisters from the hospital and some of the parishioners forming the choir. Father Eline, after being a virtual invalid for several years in St. Joseph's hospital, died there on, April 20, 1943. He lies buried in the Fairbanks Clay Street cemetery.

During the years 1926–28, Father Patrick J. O'Reilly, S.J., served as pastor of Immaculate Conception parish. It is thanks to his efforts that the church has the beautiful stained glass windows that so brighten it to the present day. It is thanks also to his efforts that the church did not burn to the ground, in March 1927, and that it has a brick chimney and a concrete porch. A reliable history manuscript in the Jesuit Oregon Province Archives informs us:

Sacred Heart Cathedral, Fairbanks. *MK.*

During the Novena of Grace in March the chimney in the parish rectory caught fire. The chimney was a stovepipe from the furnace going through three floors of the frame structure. Father O'Reilly, who was alone in the house at the time, fought the blaze for 30 minutes, and eventually got it under control. Accordingly, in the summer of 1927, he built a brick chimney, 38 feet high. He rented an old brick machine, and, with the help of a laborer, made the bricks out of cement and very fine sand and gravel. He built also a concrete porch, and laid 900 square feet of cement walk.

After Father O'Reilly, Father John F. Hayes, S.J., spent a short time as pastor of the parish, from November 1928 to August 29, 1929. His contribution to the changing aspect of the church structure was the building of the back stairs and the converting of one of the upstairs rectory rooms into a small chapel. Today this room, with a glassed-in front looking out into the sanctuary, and outfitted with a loud-speaker, serves as "The Baby Room."

Father William G. Elliott, S.J., was pastor of Immaculate Conception parish for the year 1942–43. While in Fairbanks, he also organized the Sodality of the Blessed Virgin Mary. "Fairbanks is blessed to have him here," wrote Bishop Walter J. **Fitzgerald**, S.J. From 1939–45, Bishop Fitzgerald made his headquarters at Immaculate Conception Church; and, when not traveling, rendered the parish many useful services.

During the 1940s, the following Jesuit Fathers also served Immaculate Conception parish as pastors: Joseph A. Balfe, Louis B. **Fink**, Clifford F. Allbutt, Donald G. McDonald, and Edmund A. **Anable**. They had as assistants, Fathers Joseph A. Farrell, John W. Laux, and McElmeel.

It was while Father McDonald was pastor of Immaculate Conception parish, from 1946–47, that Immaculate Conception Grade School, at the request of the parishioners, came into being. Classes began in the basement of the church on September 3, 1946, with kindergarten and grades one through four. Fifty-five children were enrolled. Two Sisters of Providence, Joan of Providence and Ignatia Marie, were the first teachers. Each succeeding year, the next higher grade was added. The first grade eight class, numbering eight, graduated in 1951.

By 1951, the school had long since outgrown its basement facilities. That spring and summer, Father Anable, who had replaced Father McDonald as pastor in late 1947, supervised the construction of the new school. This was built in Slaterville, out of six used barracks bought from the city. The new school had eight classrooms and a principal's office. For almost three decades, the barracks school served its purpose well. The years, however, exacted their toll. The school simply needed to be replaced. This was

Immaculate Conception Church being moved across the frozen Chena River in November 1911.
Tony Tronseth Collection/University of Alaska–Fairbanks Archives.

done in 1979 with the construction of a new two-story building.

In 1952, Father George T. **Boileau**, S.J., became pastor of Immaculate Conception parish. One of his priorities was to see to the bringing about of a Catholic high school. Named for Father Monroe, Monroe Catholic High School had its beginnings, as did the grade school, in the basement of Immac-ulate Conception Church, in the fall of 1955, with an enrollment of nine students in the freshmen class. Father Bernard F. **McMeel**, S.J., was its first principal. On September 2, 1956, the new high school, built next to the grade school, was dedicated and ready to receive its first freshmen and sophomore classes, numbering 32. Father Lewis N. Doyle, S.J., was now its principal, and Sister Dorothy, a Sister

Immaculate Conception Church, Fairbanks, 2002. *Photo by Patricia Walter.*

The Diocese of Fairbanks chancery building being blanketed by the snows of winter. *LR.*

The House of Prayer, Fairbanks. *LR.*

Holy Family Chapel at the Catholic schools complex, Fairbanks. *PP.*

of Providence, was the first Sister to teach in it. To begin with, Monroe had for a gymnasium only a small, unheated Quonset hut. This was replaced in 1966 by the new, modern gymnasium, named "Boileau Hall," in memory of Bishop Boileau. Two library–classrooms were added to the high school building in 1960.

Throughout their long history, the Catholic schools of Fairbanks have been singularly blessed, and in countless ways. All along they have enjoyed the good will and support not only of the Catholic Community of Fairbanks, but also that of the Fairbanks community in general. A significant number of the students attending the Catholic schools are not of the Catholic Faith, but all acknowledge the schools to be "a community of Faith," true to its stated philosophy. The Mission Statement of the Catholic schools reads in part:

Within the mission of the diocese, the schools' role is to create an environment of academic excellence and a compassionate Catholic Community to achieve academic excellence through a challenging core curriculum; to prepare students, through education, to proclaim the Gospel of Jesus Christ in word, worship and service; and to prepare students for the vocation of leadership and service in the Church and in society.

To underscore the schools' affirmation of "the centrality of Christian values in all aspects of life," a new chapel, dedicated to the Holy Family, was built in the center of the Catholic schools complex. This was solemnly dedicated on April 14, 2000, by Michael J. **Kaniecki**, S.J., Bishop of Fairbanks at the time.

August 8, 1962, is a date of major significance for the whole of Alaska, but especially for Fairbanks. On that day the Diocese of Fairbanks was officially established. Being directly under Rome's Sacred Congregation for the Propagation of Faith, it is a "missionary diocese." Francis D. **Gleeson**, S.J., Vicar Apostolic of Alaska prior to that date, became the first Ordinary of the Diocese of Fairbanks. Spatially, the Diocese of Fairbanks comprises 409, 849 square miles. This includes all the area of the State of Alaska north of the Alaska Range from the Canadian border on the east to the Bering and Chukchi Seas on the west. Out of a total population of around 155,224, the diocese was, in the year 2002, serving almost 20,000 people, distributed throughout 49 Catholic communities of varying sizes. Only nine of these were accessible by road. Forty to 45 percent of the membership of the Diocese of Fairbanks was Alaska Native groups, either Eskimo or Indian, with Eskimos in the majority. The people in the western part of the diocese were served also by the diocese-owned radio station, **KNOM**, and by the diocesan Native Ministry Training Program located at St. Mary's Mission on the **Andreafsky** River. The communities along the middle Yukon River began to be served by the Kateri Tekakwitha Center, located at **Galena**, as of the year 2003.

Succeeding Bishop Gleeson as Ordinary of the Diocese of Fairbanks have been Bishops Robert L. **Whelan**, S.J., November 30, 1968, to July 28, 1985; Michael J. Kaniecki, July 28, 1985, to the day

of his death, August 6, 2000; and Donald J. **Kettler**, August 22, 2002, to the present (2004). With Sister Eileen Brown, S.N.J.M., as Diocesan Chancellor, from 1985–1992, the Diocese of Fairbanks was one of the very first dioceses in the country to have a woman Chancellor.

The Mission Statement of the Diocese of Fairbanks reads:

We are people of God in the Roman Catholic Diocese of Fairbanks. Blessed with a rich variety of backgrounds and talents, we strive to be a living reflection of the Universal Church. Through our baptism we continue Christ's mission to further the kingdom of God through the human family. We share our living faith by proclaiming the Gospel in word and example. Together we celebrate Christ's presence in worship and sacraments. In a spirit of justice, mercy and love, we dedicate ourselves not only to minister to the people in the urban and rural areas of our Diocese, but also to minister to the world community.

Though Fairbanks was a See city as of August 8, 1962, it had no cathedral church. Till such was built, Immaculate Conception Church—often, and fondly, referred to as "the little church"—had to serve as the pro-cathedral of the Fairbanks diocese. In it a history-making event took place on April 24, 1965. On that day, Angus R. **McDonald** was ordained a priest in it. He was the only man ever to be ordained a priest in "the Immaculate." He was also the first man to be ordained for the Diocese of Fairbanks. The event was history-making also, inasmuch as Father McDonald was the first priest in the United States to be ordained with the liturgy in English rather than in the traditional Latin.

In 1954, Immaculate Conception parish, still the only Catholic parish in the Fairbanks area, celebrated the 50th anniversary of its founding. By then, its church had already become much too small for the number of its parishioners. As many as eight Masses a weekend had to be offered in it to accommodate them. Eight years later, as mentioned, the Diocese of Fairbanks was established, bringing with it the need for a cathedral worthy of the name. Both of these considerations made the construction of a new church building urgent.

Official ground breaking ceremonies for the new church edifice, "the Farthest North Cathedral," took place in May 1962 at the corner of Airport Way and Peger Road. The building took shape slowly, according to available finances and the supply of volunteer labor. Father James C. **Spils**, S.J., was the designer of the 55 × 170′ building and the construction superintendent. To help him with the project, he brought with him some of the work crew that had assisted him so ably when he built **Copper Valley School**. While the building did take shape slowly, it did reach the stage, where it was ready for the Palm Sunday Mass on April 3, 1966. The Cathedral of the Sacred Heart was formally dedicated by Bishop Gleeson on the feast of the Solemnity of the Sacred Heart, June 17, 1966. It was dedicated to the Sacred Heart, in keeping with the wishes of Bishop Gleeson.

During the summer of 1994, the cathedral received a new roof; and, in October, a steeple. New entry ways were built onto it at the east and south entrances in 1999.

Father Anable was the first Rector of the Cathedral parish, 1966–67. At this time, there was still only one parish in Fairbanks, but now with two churches, Immaculate Conception Church and Sacred Heart Cathedral. During the year 1967–68, Father John E. **Gurr**, S.J., served as Rector of the Cathedral, and Father John P. McBride, S.J., as pastor of Immaculate Conception. During the latter part of 1968, Bishop Whelan, Coadjutor Bishop of Fairbanks at the time, served as pastor of Immaculate Conception parish and as Rector of the Cathedral. On January 1, 1969, the Fairbanks parish was canonically divided into Immaculate Conception and Sacred Heart Cathedral parishes. Father **Francis E. Mueller**, S.J., was appointed administrator of the latter parish, until August 1969, when Father Francis W. **McGuigan**, S.J., became its Rector.

Jesuit priests served the Cathedral parish for a little longer than the first decade of its existence as such. They were Fathers: McGuigan, 1969–71; Joseph E. Grady, 1971–73; **Cornelius K. Murphy**, 1973–74; William C. **Dibb**, 1974–79; and Eugene P. **Delmore**, 1979–82.

Diocesan priests next served as pastors of the Sacred Heart Cathedral parish. They were Fathers: J. Albert **Levitre** and David M. **Fitz-Patrick**, co-pastors, 1982–83; Fitz-Patrick, 1983–88; Levitre, 1988–95; Patrick D. **Bergquist**, 1995–97; and

Edward J. **Hartmann**, 1997 to the present (2004). At various times, the parish was served also by priests in the role of associate pastors. They were: Father Angus R. McDonald, Steven C. Moore, Levitre, James R. Miller, Michael J. Murray, Gerhard J. Wallner, and Don M. **Balquin**. Jesuit Fathers Richard L. **McCaffrey**, **George E. Carroll**, and Delmore also were associate pastors at Sacred Heart.

Deacons, too, have been part of the Cathedral ministerial staff: Paul V. **Perreault**, 1986–99; Alvin K. Mazonna, 1999 to 2003; and William G. Dourte, III, 1999 to the present (2004).

The Sacred Heart Parish Mission Statement reads:

As a community of Christian faithful established within the Diocese of Fairbanks, Sacred Heart Cathedral parish exists to carry forward the work of the Catholic Church which is the mission of Jesus Christ. In order to do the work of the Church, and to support the spiritual growth of its members, the parish will continue to direct its spiritual and personal resources, its various God-given gifts, toward the following broad goals: worship of God and proclamation of the Word; building community among and beyond its members; serving all of God's people; and creating and maintaining a place of worship, spiritual growth, and social fellowship.

In conjunction with Sacred Heart Cathedral, should be mentioned also the Diocese of Fairbanks Chancery building. This stands on the same grounds as the Cathedral. It was built in 1968–69 by a crew consisting mostly of Jesuit Lay Brothers. Likewise, in conjunction with the Cathedral, should be mentioned also the 1127 Koyukuk Street residence. This was acquired in the fall of 1973. The first priests to serve at Sacred Heart Cathedral, Fathers Murphy, Carroll, and McCaffrey, were the first priests to reside there. Father Levitre was the last. In 1992, he and Bishop Kaniecki exchanged residences. Father Levitre moved into the mobile home, in the woods near the Cathedral, in which the bishop had been living since 1986, and the bishop moved into the Koyukuk residence. This latter subsequently served as the Episcopal residence.

What began as a simple little frame church on the banks of the Chena River, in the summer of 1904, eventually took on an aura of history, became an historic building. On April 3, 1976, Immaculate Conception Church was officially listed on the

(*above*) Jesuit House ("Kobuk Center" since 2003), Fairbanks—built by Father Richard L. McCaffrey, S.J., during the years 1985–87—as it appeared on June 25, 1994. *Photo by Brian Partridge/LRC.*

(*right*) St. Raphael the Archangel Church, Fairbanks. *Photo by Madeleine Betz.*

National Register of Historic Sites. And, three years later, Immaculate Conception parish celebrated the 75th anniversary of its founding. On December 9, 1979, Bishop Whelan was the principal celebrant at a Mass of Thanksgiving for 75 years of parochial blessings. With him at the altar, along with other clergy, was Bishop Gleeson, who, 25 years earlier, on July 11, 1954, had celebrated the golden jubilee of the parish with a Solemn Pontifical Mass.

At first, priests stationed at Immaculate Conception parish visited the University of Alaska–Fairbanks to offer Sunday Mass there. After the founding of Monroe Catholic High School, it was priests on the faculty of Monroe that began to serve, as "Newman Club chaplains," the faculty and students on campus. This was a low key ministry, consisting of little more than the offering of Sunday morning Mass and the holding of an occasional Monday evening meeting. As the number of people connected with the university community grew, so, correspondingly, did the number of Catholics on and off campus grow, and the need for more pastoral care for them. Accordingly, in 1977, Bishop Whelan formally established the extra-territorial parish of St. Mark's University Parish. This full-service parish billed itself as "the Catholic community at the University of Alaska–Fairbanks." The parish never had a church building. Masses on campus were offered for many years in the Lola Tilly Commons. Thereafter, they were offered in Schaible Auditorium. St. Mark's founding and first pastor was Father James M. **Kolb**, C.S.P. His tenure there lasted twenty years, from 1977 to 1997. Beginning in 1997, and as of the year 2004, Father Gerald S. **Ornowski**, M.I.C., was pastor of St. Mark's.

In connection with St. Mark's, it should be mentioned that at one time there were as many as four priests serving at the University of Alaska–Fairbanks, not directly in a priestly capacity, but as regular faculty members. Father Louis L. **Renner**, S.J., taught German, 1965–80; Father William J. **Loyens**, S.J., Anthropology, 1966–74; Father Wallace M. Olson, Anthropology, 1968–71; and Father Patrick S. Duffy, Education, for several years, in the latter 1960s.

A little to the west of Sacred Heart Cathedral, but on the same grounds, stands the House of Prayer.

This "spiritual fitness center for the Diocese of Fairbanks," originally served as a military barracks on another site, then a variety of other purposes on its present site. Dedicated to St. Therese of Lisieux, the House of Prayer was formally opened on April 20, 1986. Retired Bishop Whelan was its first director. When he left Alaska in 1995, Father Normand A. **Pepin**, S.J., became its director. Bishop Whelan was ably assisted by Sister Marie Teresa **Boulet**, O.P. She assisted also Father Pepin, until the year 2000. As of that year, Sister Ann Sabol, C.S.J., began to be his assistant.

On the same "campus" as the House of Prayer, through the woods to the west of it, stands what was called from 1987, the year it was ready for occupancy, till the year 2002, the year it was vacated, "Jesuit House." (It was subsequently referred to as "Kobuk Center," after the street on which it is located.) It was built by Father McCaffrey. During those 15 years, this large building served as a residence for the Fairbanks area Jesuits, including those serving at Immaculate Conception parish. Many out-of-town guests of all kinds found hospitality at Jesuit House.

On Sunday, May 12, 1991, the new church of St. Raphael the Archangel parish, located a little beyond the northern outskirts of Fairbanks, was solemnly dedicated by Bishop Kaniecki. Almost 15 years earlier, this, Fairbanks' newest Catholic Faith community, began as a small prayer group. Soon the group, steadily growing, began to meet for home Masses. In November 1979, Father Dibb was assigned to serve full-time what was then already designated "St. Raphael's Catholic Community." Masses were first offered in the Fox school gymnasium. By 1981, the group had land for a church. Father Dibb was assigned elsewhere. Father Timothy L. **Sander**, O.S.B., became the ever-growing group's temporary Sacramental Minister. The steady drive toward parish status gained major momentum and formal leadership in 1985, when Bishop Kaniecki appointed Mrs. Betty Johnson Pastoral Administrator of what was evolving into St. Raphael's parish. By 1999, the new church was more or less finished. Father Sander retired as Sacramental Minister in 1995. Father Kolb succeeded him. Father Bergquist began as pastor of St.

Raphael's in 1999, and was its pastor still as of the year 2004.

In the early 1990s, an atmosphere bordering on crisis pervaded much of the Immaculate Conception parish community. At the root of it all was the size of the church. It was too small, as it had been for decades, to meet the needs of the parish. When Father Andrew L. Maddock, S.J., became pastor of the parish in August 1993, he found himself in the midst of a controversy created, when it was announced that the Diocese of Fairbanks was again considering closing Immaculate Conception Church and merging the parish with that of Sacred Heart Cathedral. Brought in to give a two-year lead time to work out the details of this possible merger, Father Maddock asked to hear from the people. He found that many of the parishioners had a strong desire to keep their parish alive, and in the downtown area. Through a process of informational meetings, letters and voting, the majority of the voting parishioners opted to buy available land adjacent to the church's present site and to build a new church, preserving the little church as a downtown chapel. But, there were serious concerns on the part of some about the prudence of building a new church so relatively close to Sacred Heart Cathedral. Others feared that the close community feeling would be lost in a new structure. To the relief of many, when all was said, nothing was done. The status quo of the parish has remained what it was to the present day (2004). To ease somewhat the space problem, Masses on bigger feast days continued to be offered in the Catholic schools' gymnasium. Since the completion of the Holy Family Chapel at the Catholic schools complex, in the year 2000, such Masses have been offered there.

Catholic Church history in Fairbanks began with Father Monroe in 1904, when he founded Immaculate Conception parish. A century later, it was still a flourishing parish. Father McCaffrey became its pastor in October 1998 and was still such as of the year 2004. In addition to the pastors mentioned above, other priests, all Jesuits, have served the parish in that capacity. From 1968–84, Fathers Lawrence A. **Nevue** and Murphy alternated as pastors. From 1984–87, Father **Joseph E. Laudwein** was pastor. He was followed by Father Kevin T.

Clarke, 1987–90; who was followed by Father Loyens, 1990–93; who was, in turn, followed by Father Maddock, 1993–98. Over the years, other priests have served as assistants or associates in the parish, sometimes only for a year: Julius **Jetté**, Philibert **Turnell**, William **McMillan**, James U. **Conwell**, William H. **Babb**, Henry G. **Hargreaves**, Segundo **Llorente**, **Joseph L. Hebert**, Robert F. **Corrigal**, J. Herbert Mead, Arthur **Lopilato**, and Theodore N. Fortier.

As of the year 2004, Immaculate Conception parish was being served also by deacons: Rev. Mr. Robert Mantei, since 1986; and Rev. Mr. Sean Stack, since 1999.

In addition to Brothers Coté and Callahan, mentioned above, three other Jesuit Lay Brothers served at Immaculate Conception parish: Joseph V. O'Hare, 1906–08; Peter P. **Wilhalm**, 1916–20; and Carl F. **Wickart**, 1951–78.

Throughout its history, many lay people, too, have served, competently and generously, the Immaculate Conception parish and its programs. The same is true also of the other Fairbanks area Catholic parishes and schools. For several decades, the schools, in particular, benefited from the services of many members of the **Jesuit Volunteer Corps**, who taught in them.

Ultimately, it is the people of God that serve and are served, in and through a parish, in and through a diocese, in and through the Church.

2, 16, 25, 40, 52, 80, 130, 155, 158

FALLERT, Father Francis J., S.J.

"A Great Man to Remember" is the title the people of **Toksook Bay** gave to the 38-page booklet—a compilation of written tributes and simple drawings by young and old—they produced at the time of the death of Father Francis J. Fallert, S.J.

Father Fallert's life's journey, which ended where the Bering Sea pounds the western shore of Nelson Island in northwestern **Alaska**, began in Harrington, Washington, where he was born on May 6, 1919, the youngest of ten children. Francis received his elementary and secondary schooling at the Harrington grade and high schools. From his earliest years on, he was always of a cheerful and witty disposition. He loved fishing and hunting, and basketball, at which he excelled.

After attending Gonzaga University in Spokane, Washington, for three years, Francis entered the Jesuit novitiate at Sheridan, Oregon, on August 14, 1940. At Sheridan, upon completing his two-year noviceship and taking the vows of poverty, chastity and obedience, he spent an additional two years studying the classics and humanities. From 1944–47, he made his philosophical studies at Mount St. Michael's in Spokane. His two-year "regency" period—generally years devoted to classroom teaching—he spent at **Holy Cross Mission** in Alaska. At that time, Jesuits in training normally had a three-year regency period. Those who went to Holy Cross, however, had only a two-year one. He devoted the years 1949–53 to theological studies at Alma College, Los Gatos, California. In Spokane's St. Aloysius Church, he was ordained a priest, on June 21, 1952. His tertianship he made at Port Townsend, Washington, 1953–54.

Father Fallert spent all his priestly years in Alaska. He served by turns at **St. Michael** and **Stebbins**, at **Kaltag**, **Unalakleet**, and in **Anchorage**. He held station also at **Mountain Village**, **Toksook Bay**, **Newtok**, and **Tununak**. As General Superior of Jesuits in Alaska, from 1976–82, he resided in **Fairbanks**.

From 1956–65, Father Fallert was stationed at **Copper Valley School**, near **Glennallen**. For most of his time there, he was Superior and principal. This boarding school in the wilderness was described as "one of those impossible Alaskan pioneer ventures." During its early years, however, under Father Fallert's competent and dedicated leadership, it became a genuine, successful college preparatory school. Its student body, purposely limited to mainly Alaskan Natives, received a solid education, despite primitive conditions and crowded facilities. Father Fallert, as Superior and principal at the school, insisted on high standards of teaching and learning. At the same time, he fostered an intense community spirit, a family spirit that was remarkable. Students and teachers were united as friends and co-workers. One of his co-workers at the school remembered him many years later as "a man of God

and deeply spiritual, who was able to balance his spirituality with a good sense of humor."

In addition to his more specifically priestly ministrations, Father Fallert had much else to occupy him throughout his years in Alaska. During his first summer there as a priest, that of 1954, he took down the old St. Michael's Church at St. Michael and the one-time convent of the **Ursuline** Sisters there. The salvaged lumber he then barged to Stebbins for the construction of a "new" church and residence. In 1966, he built the residence and the church in the recently established village of Toksook Bay on Nelson Island. Always open to new ideas, he saw to the starting of a Montessori School in Tununak, in 1972. He remodeled the old church to serve as a classroom.

Father Fallert, besides being first and foremost a priest and educator, was also a very practical man, competent in maintaining buildings and machines. He was a ham radio operator. As such, he communicated on a regular schedule with fellow Jesuits in Alaska, sometimes in Latin, when a certain privacy was called for. Early on in Alaska, he learned to bake top quality bread, an appreciated treat to the many, when "pilot bread" was a staple. He was a first-rate cribbage player, using the game to relax, to socialize, to communicate. Acquiring a working knowledge of the Central Yup'ik Eskimo language, however, presented him with a formidable challenge. Less than three years before his death he spent a semester at the University of Alaska–Fairbanks studying that language. For the most part, however, Eskimo eluded him. But, by that time, he had long since found ways of communicating with his people by means other than words. Heart spoke to heart.

"Kenkamken!" That Eskimo equivalent of "I love you!" Father Fallert did master. He had heard and used it often in daily life, but especially during Marriage Encounter sessions. To no ministry did he bring enthusiasm greater than that which he brought to the Marriage Encounter movement. He first became acquainted with it during the 1975–76 sabbatical year he took in Toronto, Ontario, Canada. It was he who introduced the movement to his area of Alaska in 1978. The movement flourished under his guidance. For his burial Mass, many Marriage

Encounter symbols were placed prominently throughout the church.

Father Fallert was on the threshold of his 50th anniversary as a Jesuit, when he died—rather unexpectedly, but peacefully—in his sleep in the Fairbanks Jesuit House on June 2, 1990. Less than two months earlier, his illness had been diagnosed as leukemia. While not afraid of dying, and quite resigned to God's will for him in the matter, he, always a man vibrant and full of life, did, nevertheless, send out shortly before his death an optimistic letter describing his condition and expressing the hope that a planned medical procedure would put his illness into remission and so allow him a few more years of active ministry among his people. That made the news of his death all the more startling.

After rosary services on Monday June 4th, and a funeral Mass in Sacred Heart Cathedral, Fairbanks, on the 5th, Father Fallert's body was flown from Fairbanks to Nelson Island on Wednesday the 6th for burial at Tununak on the 7th. The plane, a new twin-engine Piper Navajo *Chieftain*— piloted by Father James A. **Sebesta**, General Superior of Jesuits in Alaska, and co-piloted by Bruce Hopkins—with the body on board, along with Father Fallert's two sisters, Eleanor Gooley and Rosella Ackerman, Bishop Michael J. **Kaniecki**, S.J., and Father Louis L. **Renner**, S.J., made a refueling stop in **Bethel**, before continuing on its westward flight. When the plane came over Toksook Bay, it flew low and circled over the village. There a big crowd was standing around the church and waving white flags, their way of saying a final good-bye to their much loved pastor. On the road next to the church, in big, white block letters, was spelled out the one word: FAREWELL! On its third and last pass over the village, the plane tipped its wing in salute. In tear-choked silence, those on board flew the last few miles over to Tununak.

At Tununak, many people were gathered at the airstrip, as the plane landed. After the casket was loaded on a pickup truck, Eskimo deacons spoke a few words, then read passages from the Bible and led the people in Eskimo and English prayers. Slowly then, in procession, all, following the casket-bearing pickup, walked from the airstrip to the church. As they went, people sang hymns in Eskimo, Latin, and English. The sky was heavily overcast; the day foggy, windy, cold.

In the church, the casket was placed center-front, and surrounded with flowers. The whole church was brightly decorated with many artificial flowers and sincere messages of love and esteem from the people Father Fallert had served so long and so faithfully. A rosary was said, then a Mass followed. At regular intervals, five more Masses were celebrated, all well attended. At 2:15 on the afternoon of Thursday, June 7, 1990, Bishop Kaniecki and six priests concelebrated the Mass of Christian Burial. The church was crowded to overflowing. Some talks followed the liturgical services. Then the body of Father Fallert was carried to the nearby cemetery, and, with all the appropriate ceremonies, laid to final rest in the land and among the people that had become so much a part of him. With his burial in the Central Yup'ik Eskimo village of Tununak, his last request, "I want to be with my people," was honored. A potlatch followed.

135

FALSEY, Father James E.

James E. Falsey was born on February 13, 1945, in Midland, Michigan, the second child of five born to William P. Falsey and L. Marjorie Homes Falsey. After attending a Midland public school for four years, he attended the newly established Blessed Sacrament Parochial School in Midland for the remaining four grades. It was while attending the Catholic grade school that he first thought about becoming a priest.

During the year 1959–60, James attended St. Lawrence Seminary, Mount Calvary, Wisconsin, a minor seminary staffed by the Capuchins. From there he went on to attend St. Paul's Seminary in Saginaw, Michigan, from 1960–65. He graduated from high school in 1963. From 1965–67, he was at Mount St. Mary's Seminary and College in Emmitsburg, Maryland, from which he graduated in the spring of 1969 with a B.A. degree in Philosophy. He next spent the years 1969–71 at St. John's Provincial Seminary, ending his studies there with an M.A. degree in Sacred Theology, conferred through the University of Detroit. He was ordained to the diaconate on May 2, 1970, and to the priesthood, for the Diocese of Saginaw, on February 19, 1972.

From 1972–90, Father Falsey held a variety of positions in various parishes in his home diocese. During the earlier part of those years, he took a number of classes in art, counseling, and accounting at Central Michigan University for personal enrichment. In 1984, he received an M.A. degree in Counseling from C.M.U. About this same time, he began sky diving—for sport and relaxation, he rationalized. "Free falling takes your mind off your problems. If it does not, that will be the last time you have problems." While still a child, he came to feel at home in the air, as he, sitting in the jump seat just behind the pilot, traveled with his father in the company plane, a DC-3, on business trips. In 1989, he earned his private pilot's license.

Being an avid outdoorsman, Father Falsey routinely spent his annual vacation backpacking or canoeing in the wilderness for several weeks with a priest friend. On one of their hikes, his friend suggested that some year they should backpack in **Alaska**. To Father Falsey two weeks seemed like "an awfully short time" to experience Alaska. "Maybe," he thought to himself, "if I lived there for a year or two, or five, and vacationed there, I could really experience Alaska." Accordingly, he approached his bishop, Kenneth E. Untener, about the possibility of his serving in the Missionary Diocese of **Fairbanks** for a time. To his pleasant surprise, Bishop Untener saw no difficulty with that.

In the summer of 1990, Father Falsey found himself in **Nome**. For the next four years, in conjunction with Father Jack **de Verteuil**, he served the Catholic communities of Nome, **Unalakleet**, **Teller**, and **Little Diomede**, making his headquarters now at one, now at another. On March 19, 1994, he had the joy of seeing the new St. Joseph's Church in Nome dedicated. Making Teller his headquarters, he spent the year 1994–95 as pastor of it and of Unalakleet, and as visiting priest to **Stebbins** and **St. Michael**.

When Father Falsey first arrived in Nome, he learned that there were no planes in Nome to rent.

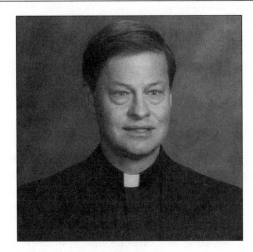

Father James E. Falsey.
Courtesy of Fr. Falsey.

He was faced with the choice: give up flying, or buy his own plane. He bought his own, a Cessna 172. This enabled him to make the rounds of his different stations far more conveniently than commercial travel would have allowed.

In 1995, Father Falsey left the coastal towns and villages to take up station in **Nulato** on the middle Yukon River. For the next three years, he served as pastor of Our Lady of the Snows parish in Nulato and as visiting priest to St. Patrick's parish in **Koyukuk**. In 1998, he left Alaska to resume parish work in his home diocese, the Diocese of Saginaw. Though out of Alaska now, he did not lose interest in it, nor in the work of the Church in northern Alaska. When his parents were killed in a tragic auto accident, he made a substantial donation in their memory to help finance the construction of the new church in **Ruby**.

FELTES, Brother George J., S.J.

He was the first Jesuit to fly an airplane. He met and spoke with Charles A. Lindbergh and Wiley Post. He was described as "a mechanical wizard." He was said to have been "very articulate, might easily have become a priest." He was one of the first two Jesuits to travel from the Northwest to **Alaska** by land. He was an Alaskan for over 50 years, a

Jesuit for over 75. He was a ham radio operator to his dying hour. His last Jesuit Superior said of him, "He was a page out of history."

George J. Feltes was born in San Francisco on October 6, 1898. On March 6, 1916, he entered the California Province of the Society of Jesus at Los Gatos, California, to become a Lay Brother. He remained at Los Gatos for eight years.

When the Los Gatos Jesuits bought their first truck, only Brother Feltes was qualified to drive it. From 1924–26, he served as power plant engineer at Mount St. Michael's, Spokane, Washington. Next he was assigned to the University of San Francisco. He took his final vows on February 2, 1929.

In the summer of 1929, his Father Provincial, Joseph M. Piet, asked Brother Feltes if he would like to learn to fly, to get an airplane and to go to Alaska to fly there for the missions. "I thought he was kidding me," Brother Feltes recalled years later. "It sounded too good to be true." But, Father Piet was not kidding. He went on to tell Brother Feltes how Joseph R. **Crimont**, S. J., Vicar Apostolic of Alaska at the time, and Father Philip I. **Delon**, S.J., General Superior of the Alaska Mission at the time, wanted a plane and someone to fly it for the Alaska missions. Brother Feltes "jumped at the chance." On July 16th of that same summer, he began flight training at the flying school in Alameda, California. He was a fast learner. On August 5, 1929, he made his first solo flight—and a bit of aviation history. This was the first time a Jesuit flew an airplane. By October 31st, he had both his private pilot's license and his limited commercial pilot's license.

In January 1930, Brother Feltes went to New York in search of a plane suitable for mission purposes. A Bellanca Pacemaker powered by a Packard Diesel engine was decided upon. In June 1930, the plane, named the *Marquette Missionary*, as a show of gratitude to the Marquette League of New York which financed it, was ready. It was flown leisurely to the west coast. On August 30th, in Seattle, it was put on the *S.S. Aleutian*, and with it sailed for Alaska Brother Feltes and Father Delon. By September 12th, the plane was in **Fairbanks** and ready for its first flight in the Alaskan sky. From Fairbanks, Brother Feltes and a layman co-pilot, Ralph Wien,

Brother George J. Feltes, S.J. *JOPA-981.17a.*

flew it to **Holy Cross**, and from there on to **Nome**, to the **Pilgrim Hot Springs** Mission, and to **Kotzebue**. There, on October 12, 1930, its short existence ended in a fatal crash killing two priests, Fathers Delon and William F. Walsh, and pilot Ralph Wien. With that tragic crash, Brother Feltes—on the ground at the time, and witnessing the crash—saw shattered, too, his dream of being a missionary–aviator in Alaska. Heart-broken, he accompanied the bodies of the two priests south for burial.

However, one year later, Brother Feltes was again back in Alaska with another plane. This he had flown across the U.S. to Alameda, where he met Brother Martial O. **Lapeyre**, S.J., a member of the New Orleans Province, who had just earned his private pilot's license at Alameda. It was Brother Lapeyre's sister who had paid for the new plane. The two flew the plane to Seattle, saw it put on the *S.S. Alaska*, and with it sailed for **Seward**, Alaska. There they outfitted it with pontoons, and flew it to **Anchorage**. It was now getting late in the year, so they replaced the pontoons with skis. After some delays in Anchorage, they took off for Holy Cross. In a letter, dated Los Gatos, CA., October 14, 1992, to Father Louis L. **Renner**, S.J., Brother Feltes gives some details concerning the fate of that second plane: "A small problem developed in the engine and I landed The Alaska Missionary at Crater Mountain. The snow was very deep, and we were stuck [for 11 days]. After some time I flew the plane to **McGrath**. There Father [Francis M., S.J.]

Ménager told me he sold the plane to Art Woodley, *without* permission of the Bishop. My flying days were over and Bro. Lapeyre returned to New Orleans. There was much unhappiness at this time."

Brother Feltes' primary reason for being in Alaska in the first place was now no longer valid. But, already he had fallen in love with the North and wanted to stay on. He was granted permission to do so—and on and on he stayed, for over 50 years. Once, in the course of those years, a California Province Provincial considered recalling him. Brother Feltes asked him to check his files for a note laying down the conditions for his staying in Alaska. The Provincial found the note. It read: "Brother Feltes is on loan as long has he behaves himself and does some work occasionally." He did behave himself, and he did some work, more than just occasionally. He was allowed to stay on in Alaska.

Brother Feltes spent the years 1931–38 at Holy Cross, prefecting the boys and teaching mechanics. He found the Native boys he trained in his shop "very mechanically inclined." To give them theo-retical training, he had them study manuals; to give them practical training, he had them, under his watchful eye, take apart and put back together again different machines and motors, "everything from wristwatches to aircraft." Most all the boys he trained went on to become competent, responsible craftsmen, and lifelong personal friends. One of his trainees, Ignatius J. **Jakes**, went on to become a Jesuit Brother. When Brother Feltes left Alaska many years later, another of them, Harold **Esmail-ka**, gave him a most substantial monetary gift to show his appreciation for what he had done for him. To his "boys"—now grown men, fathers and grandfathers—he always remained a kind of folk hero.

In 1939, after spending some months at Alma College, California, Brother Feltes was assigned to St. Mary's Mission, **Akulurak**. The St. Mary's Mission diarist noted the arrival of "a mechanical genius." The first order given Brother Feltes was, "Get a shop built!" With enthusiasm he set about putting up and outfitting a combined carpenter and machine shop. Things mechanical had fascinated him all his life. As a young man he was a blacksmith. While at Akulurak, he helped Father Edmund A. **Anable**, S.J., build a mission boat, the *Sifton*. All the metal work and the engine were his responsibility. He spent four years at Akulurak. While there, he obtained his ham radio operator's license, KL7EN.

In 1943, Brother Feltes returned to Holy Cross for another decade of fixing things and training the older boys in his shop. In the spring of 1948, he and Brother Aloysius B. **Laird**, S. J., made a bit of history. They were the first Catholic Alaskan missionaries to travel to Alaska by land. Leaving Spokane in an army-surplus truck crammed with freight, on May 11, 1948, they drove what was then still called the Alcan Highway to Fairbanks, arriving there on June 2nd.

Brother George J. Feltes, S.J., and Charles A. Lindbergh on Long Island, New York, 1932. *JOPA-536.2.11.*

The year before, 1947, a piece of metal had pierced Brother Feltes' eyeball in a welding accident. The eye healed enough to enable him to make the drive north. However, he needed a cornea transplant. This he received during the early part of 1949. The donor was a Scandinavian. Back at Holy Cross, a grateful Brother Feltes rejoiced: "I see with my Swede eye!" Sister Margaret Cantwell, S.S.A., who was with Brother Feltes at Holy Cross for nine years, wrote:

> That seems typical of Brother Feltes. He saw all people as part of the Great Body of Christ, the Great Body of the Church. His international vision was not just physical, but was also a vision of brotherhood, of spiritual insight into the value of every person. With his eye, donated by a Swedish person, Brother Feltes seemed to have insights that added even more to his own 20/20 vision. He could see that miniscule offerings—work, interaction, thoughtfulness, politeness—were treasures sometimes overlooked as inconsequential. But, whenever I recall Brother proudly commenting about his eye, a gift from a Swede, I hear also his expression of gratitude for the vision that made him the unique gentleman and man of prayer that he was.

As an old man, Brother Feltes described his years at Holy Cross as "the happiest years of my life." He found that "it was the children there. They made the difference." He had the highest esteem for the Sisters of St. **Ann** serving at Holy Cross. It was with a heavy heart, then, that he left Holy Cross in 1955 to go to help build the new **Copper Valley School**. From 1955–59, he was in Anchorage, gathering and shipping building materials to the school site. Brother Thomas A. Marshall, S.J., California Province archivist, who knew him well, described him as "a born acquisitions man, a shrewd buyer and salvager."

The longest chapter in the life of Brother Feltes, both as a Jesuit and as an Alaskan missionary, began in 1959, when he was assigned to Fairbanks, there to do what he did best: to run a supply depot and a machine and repair shop to take care of the many needs of the bush missions in northern Alaska. In the woods behind the Diocese of Fairbanks chancery building, he assembled a row of rebuilt Army surplus Quonset huts and sheds, his "shop." In one of these sheds, he had his ham "radio shack." As KL7EN, he spent most of his evenings there,

talking with friends worldwide, but especially with the different mission stations to find out their needs, what he might ship to them, repair for them, do for them. In his shop, he had literally hundreds of thousands of hardware items, everything from giant tractors down to the tiniest washers. There was also household furniture. Most of it was military surplus. What he did not have in store, he knew where to find, or how to coax it out of someone who had it. As a last resort, he would make what was not otherwise available. He was a master of metal, an artist on the lathe. And it was all one grand labor of love. "Repairing things," he admitted to Father Renner during an interview, "getting things to work, gives me a lot of pleasure." More a mechanic than a mystic, he was happy in his work. Still, when questioned, he admitted, too, that he prayed frequently in his shop, "talking with Our Lord, or with St. Joseph, just like I'm talking to you now." Occasionally, one could hear strains of classical music come out of his shop. He had tapes, was fond especially of Italian opera. *Cavalleria Rusticana* and *Lucia di Lammermoor* were several of his favorites.

In 1974, Robert L. **Whelan**, S.J., Bishop of Fairbanks, invited Brother Feltes to accompany him on a trip to Rome. "Elated at the opportunity to go to Rome," he immediately began to study Italian. He spent close to a month in Rome, sightseeing and visiting, by his own count, over 40 churches. In the Sistine Chapel he attended a Mass celebrated by Pope Paul VI. Though 76 years old at the time, he walked a great deal. When asked if this was not rather tiring, he answered, "Oh no! I was all pepped up." On that same trip, he visited also other major European cities, as well as Luxembourg, the country of his father's birth.

During the early 1980s, a more or less typical day in the life of Brother Feltes began at 5:30 A.M., when his alarm sounded. Promptly at 5:40, his measured but unfaltering steps could be heard, as he came down the corridor toward the chapel to serve Father Renner's Mass. Invariably, he would pray at every Mass "for many true and holy vocations to the priesthood, the Sisterhoods, and our Society." His firm handclasp as a sign of peace reminded one that he had been a blacksmith.

By the time Father Renner got down to the kitchen

after Mass, Brother Feltes was already there preparing himself breakfast. This always consisted of a bowl of well-cooked oatmeal, one little sizzler, and half a glass of orange juice. "Good morning, Brother! How are you today?" His predictable answer, "Just barely alive." But, immediately after the grace following what he called his "30-cent breakfast," he would sigh deeply, "I feel better already." And then, with a vigorous "I'll see you anon—the good Lord willing," he would be off to his room for morning meditation. This made, he headed over to his shop. Promptly at 11:20, when that "just barely alive" feeling again came over him, he could be found in the kitchen preparing himself lunch. This was followed by a visit to the chapel and a short nap. Then it was off to the shop again until the late afternoon.

Dinner at 5:30 was always a high point in his day. He enjoyed the well-cooked meals, but more so the company of his fellow Jesuits and the easy exchange of ideas, views, and small talk. Often it was he who dropped the hint that a bottle of wine—*California* wine, of course—would be in order to celebrate some occasion or other, however insignificant. Though he spent over five decades in Alaska, a mission of the Oregon Province, he always remained a member of the California Province. His loyalty to California and to all things Californian, was total and absolute. After dinner, he returned to his shop, knowing that friends and bush missionaries near and far would be waiting to hear KL7EN on the air. With his radio set, he rendered much useful service, but he found in it also "a tremendous recreational value." During summer evenings, or when something urgently needed fixing or packing up, he could be found in the shop till as late as 11 o'clock. The last wakeful hour of his day he spent in the easy chair in his room, reading. As might be expected, he preferred to read books and magazines dealing with mechanics, aviation, and "old times in Alaska." He enjoyed also reading about travel and studying maps. "I love maps," he said. He had quite a collection of them. Often, while still in his chair, before the last word was read or the last prayer said, his venerable head, heavy with the snows of 50 Alaskan winters upon it, would sink to his chest, and he would nod off in peaceful sleep. Many a

night, that chair served him also as a bed. His alarm was already set for the next day.

In Anchorage, on February 26, 1981, feeling truly privileged, Brother Feltes received Holy Communion from Pope John Paul II at a Mass he offered during his stopover there.

On July 19, 1983, after many tearful farewells, Brother Feltes left his beloved Alaska for his equally beloved California, there to enjoy full retirement at the Los Gatos novitiate. He was by then in his 85th year. He was wholly content at Los Gatos, spending his declining years in praying, reading, taking walks, watching the San Francisco 49ers on TV, and in keeping in touch with his ham radio contacts. In August 1986, he visited Alaska again for several weeks. "The trip," he wrote, "gave me a new lease on life. I was never hugged and kissed so much since I was a baby—many years ago." He was in Alaska again, for the last time, the following year, when the Jesuits celebrated the 100th anniversary of their first arrival there. On October 14, 1992, he wrote, "95 years have slowed me down." Two weeks later he wrote, "My health is gradually deteriorating and I don't expect to be here much longer."

Brother Feltes died in the Sacred Heart Jesuit Center infirmary at Los Gatos, at 6:10 A.M., on Monday, January 11, 1993. Several days before his death, he was on ham radio to inform his friends that the end was near and that he was saying his final good-byes. He was "alert up to the end and went very peacefully."

Brother George J. Feltes, S.J., lies buried in the Jesuit plot in the Santa Clara Mission cemetery.

92, 118

FINK, Father Louis B., S.J.

Louis B. Fink was born in Reading, Pennsylvania, on August 8, 1892. He entered the Jesuit novitiate at Los Gatos, California, on July 9, 1915. After completing his two-year noviceship and two years of classical and humanities studies there, he went to Mount St. Michael's, Spokane, Washington, for three years of philosophical studies. His next assignment was to teach at St. Ignatius High School in San Francisco. During the year 1924–25, he studied the-

Father Louis B. Fink, S.J. *JOPA-1063.01.*

ology in Naples, Italy. For the remaining three years of his theological studies, he was at Woodstock, Maryland. He was ordained a priest on June 23, 1927. His tertianship year, 1929–30, he spent at Port Townsend, Washington.

During his pre-Alaskan years as a priest, Father Fink served first as the "Father Socius," executive secretary, to the Father Provincial. After that he was engaged in high school work, mainly in Yakima, Washington. The last two years before he went to **Alaska**, he was principal of Bellarmine Preparatory in Tacoma, Washington. There, in early 1944, when Louis L. **Renner** applied for admittance into the Society of Jesus with hopes of one day serving in Alaska, Father Fink told him that he himself had always wanted to serve in Alaska, and that he hoped his desire to do so would soon be realized.

Father Fink went to Alaska in 1944 and spent his first year there as pastor of Immaculate Conception parish **Fairbanks**. The following year he was in the **Juneau** parish. There he was so faithful a visitor of the sick in the hospital, that he was accused of "wasting" his time. He strongly defended his visiting.

On June 24, 1946, Father Fink arrived in **Kodiak**, where he was to serve for six years. This turned out to be the longest stay in one place in his priestly life. He soon won the esteem and affection of Catholics and non-Catholics alike. Sister St. Hilary, a member of the **Grey Nuns** of the Sacred Heart heading the hospital in Kodiak at the time, said of

Father Fink, "A more representative Jesuit it would be hard to find." Father Fink had a quiet, gentlemanly manner about him, complemented by a refined sense of humor. Often his parting words to any and all were, "And keep out of jail!"

Bishop Walter J. **Fitzgerald**, S.J., died on July 19, 1947. Father Fink's name was one of three submitted to Rome as a possible candidate to succeed him. On July 21, 1947, Father Paul C. **Deschout**, S.J, General Superior of Jesuits in Alaska, wrote to Leopold J. Robinson, S.J., Provincial of the Oregon Province, "We surely would be tickled to have Fr. Fink for our Bishop." Father Fink was never appointed bishop, but he was clearly held in high regard by people in high positions.

For reasons of failing health, Father Fink left Kodiak on June 6, 1952. The *Kodiak Mirror* took note of his departure: "Father Fink has the love and respect not only of his church members but of the entire community. He will long be remembered in Kodiak."

After leaving Alaska, Father Fink spent a year at Mount St. Michael's attending to his health. He soon grew restless. In 1953, he took over the chaplaincy of Mount St. Mary's Hospital in Bellingham, Washington. There he died on January 20, 1955. He lies buried in the Jesuit cemetery at Mount St. Michael's.

FITZGERALD, Bishop Walter J., S.J.

The Eskimos of northwestern **Alaska** called him "the big priest." He was tall and dignified, but also a bishop. One historian called him a "beggar bishop, most genial of disposition." He described himself, aptly, as "a peripatetic mendicant missionary." He spent most of his eight and a half years as a bishop in Alaska traveling and begging funds for the missions of Alaska.

Walter James Fitzgerald was born on a farm near Peola, Washington Territory, on November 17, 1883, of farmer parents. His schooling, from age six to fourteen, took place in a one-room country grade school. In the summer of 1898, he was enrolled as a boarding student in Gonzaga College, Spokane. There he spent four years, during which he distinguished himself with "highest honors." On

July 30, 1902, he entered the Jesuit novitiate at Los Gatos, California, where he made his two-year noviceship, and then studied the classics and humanities for two years. From 1906–09, he taught Latin, Greek and English at Seattle College. He next spent three years studying philosophy at Gonzaga, before going back to teaching again, this time at Gonzaga. For three years he taught the humanities and rhetoric, and prefected boarding students.

In late summer 1915, Walter Fitzgerald left Spokane for theological studies in Montreal. He was ordained a priest on May 16, 1918. After another year of theology in Montreal, he taught a year at Gonzaga, then went on to make his tertianship at Los Gatos. After this last year of formal training as a Jesuit, he began a six-year term as Rector/President of Gonzaga University, 1921–27. He was the first native son to become President of his alma mater. In both appearance and manner, he was the executive type; but, lacking imagination, foresight, and boldness, he was merely "a good President."

When, in 1927, Manresa Hall, in Port Townsend, Washington, opened as a tertianship house, Father Fitzgerald was named its first Rector. Two years later, he found himself Rector of Seattle College. On December 25, 1931, he was appointed Vice-Provincial of the newly erected Rocky Mountain Vice-Province. As Vice-Provincial, he made his headquarters in Spokane. Thanks to his able and energetic organizing of affairs, the Vice-Province soon achieved full status as a Province. On February 2, 1932, the Oregon Province of the Society of Jesus was officially established by the Father General in Rome, and Father Fitzgerald was appointed its first Provincial.

In 1938, Father Fitzgerald went to Rome to attend the 28th General Congregation of the Jesuit Order. On this occasion, all the assembled Fathers met Pope Pius XI. "We stood in a group," Father Fitzgerald related, "and the Holy Father looked us all over, then, suddenly, his eyes stopped moving and they looked squarely at me. I felt so strange, with the Vicar of Christ's eyes looking at *me*."

In the autumn of 1938, Father Fitzgerald's term as Provincial was nearing its end. One of the Fathers, who had successively been pastor of many debt-ridden parishes, jokingly appealed to him for a new assignment. "As a last favor," he said. "Not much, just a *little* parish with nothing to build and no debt." Father Fitzgerald's answer: "If I knew of a place like that, I'd take it myself." Instead, he got Alaska.

By this time, Bishop Joseph R. **Crimont**, S.J., Vicar Apostolic of Alaska, was feeling the weight of his 80 years. He appealed to Rome for a Coadjutor with the right of succession. On December 14, 1938, Rome chose Father Fitzgerald to succeed him. On February 24, 1939, in St. Aloysius Church, Spokane, he was consecrated Coadjutor Vicar Apostolic of Alaska by Bishop Crimont. For his motto he chose the Jesuit motto: *Ad Majorem Dei Gloriam* ("For the Greater Glory of God"). It is the well-founded belief of Jesuit historian Wilfred P. Schoenberg, S.J., that Bishop Crimont would have been much happier consecrating a man of Euro-French origins as his successor. Bishop Fitzgerald was the first native son of the State of Washington to become a bishop—and he was, as well, the son of Irish immigrant parents.

According to Father Schoenberg, "Crimont, totally out of character, received his coadjutor coldly, gave him directions that appear to have been harsh. He could not bring himself to accept Fitzgerald graciously at **Juneau**." It was a case of the older, European mentality meeting up with a more modern, American mentality. Naturally, Bishop Fitzgerald found this low-key conflict of mentalities rather painful. "It is to Fitzgerald's everlasting credit," wrote Father Schoenberg, "that he kept all this to himself, though he was profoundly hurt." In Bishop Crimont's defense, Father Schoenberg wrote, relative to the bishop's attitude toward Americans:

With all his grace and charm, he never came to fully appreciate the American personality. A European to the core, he retained certain unpleasant reservations regarding Americans, prejudices he would have been shocked to discover in himself. He never realized they were there. Because of his native sweetness of disposition, they seldom came to the surface.

Virtually exiled to **Fairbanks**, Bishop Fitzgerald made it his headquarters, and began immediately to familiarize himself with Alaska's northern regions. During his first year as bishop, he traveled by plane, boat, and dogsled, thousands of miles, to visit and confirm in dozens of villages many hundreds of people. On June 21, 1944, he confirmed 17 "youngsters" on **King Island**. Everywhere he found "the Eskimos are wonderfully fine people, patient, with great faith and devotion." On his many begging tours, he spoke mainly about the Eskimos.

Once, while regaling the Jesuit seminarians at Mount St. Michael's, Spokane, he spoke about them and their way of kissing by rubbing noses. Calmly puffing on a big black cigar, pausing now and then to survey the ash on the end of it, he narrated: "I told the Eskimos that special indulgences were granted for kissing my bishop's ring. So they came up, one by one, and rubbed their noses on it. Now," he asked with a big Irish grin, "do you suppose they got the indulgences?"

When asked whether he found life on the trail hard, he responded, "Remember when you were boys? No matter how hard it was, you enjoyed camping trips. Well, I just pretend I'm on a camping trip, and the hardships are not so hard." Then, without realizing that he was paying himself a tribute, he would say, "Those men up there, they are the real heroes in that bleak and desolate land. They are spiritual giants and I feel very small, when I meet them." It is known that Bishop Fitzgerald did, in fact, find life on the trail hard. On one occasion, he broke his breastbone and several ribs in a sledding accident. On one of his dogsled tours among the Eskimos on the tundra of northwestern Alaska, he lost 26 pounds.

Bishop Fitzgerald met up also with other adventures on his travels. On one of his Confirmation tours, while en route to a remote Eskimo village, he and the pilot were guided to safety, literally, by a huge wolf. The pilot admitted to the bishop that he had lost his bearings. As they circled about looking for some sign of habitation, the pilot spotted a wolf. "We'll follow that wolf," he shouted. "He may lead us to a reindeer herd near the village." This is exactly what happened.

During the World War II years, Bishop Fitzgerald traveled extensively, visiting widely-scattered military bases, to administer the Sacrament of Confirmation and to keep in touch with the men and their chaplains.

When not on missionary journeys in the Alaskan bush, Bishop Fitzgerald often traveled from coast to coast on begging tours in the big cities of the United States. It was Bishop Crimont, according to

Bishop Walter J. Fitzgerald, S.J. *DFA.*

Father Schoenberg, who had assigned him "the unpleasant task of begging to dig the Vicariate out of debt." While Bishop Fitzgerald did not take to begging naturally, he did it conscientiously. He talked and preached from any platform respectable enough for a bishop. In the summer of 1940, he could write, "by this time I feel as though I could hold up a policeman and take his money." But, his life as a self-described "peripatetic mendicant missionary" drained his energies severely. By the time he got to St. Paul, Minnesota, in September, he was ready to drop from exhaustion. Nevertheless, he wrote, "I spoke in St. Paul cathedral six times to nearly ten thousand people who attended Mass on that Sunday, and got a fine honorarium. That quickly restored my strength."

Upon the death of Bishop Crimont, on May 20, 1945, Bishop Fitzgerald automatically became Vicar Apostolic of Alaska. He moved his headquarters from Fairbanks to Juneau.

One of Bishop Fitzgerald's first official acts as Vicar Apostolic was to suppress the Congregation of the Sisters of Our Lady of the **Snows**. The words of suppression are rather informal and oblique. They are at the beginning of what seems little more than a routine letter. It is dated Juneau, Alaska, August 5, 1945. It begins:

Dear Father Fox, Today, the feast day of Our Lady ad Nives [of the Snows], you and the former Sisters of the Snow have been in my prayers that you may sustain the blow of dissolution of the pious association to which you have been so devoted. I trust that it was the guidance of the Holy Spirit that directed the action, and I add sincere wishes that you and all will take it as coming from the Will of God.

For Father **John P. Fox**, S.J., founder of "the pious association" 13 years earlier, on the Feast of Our Lady of the Snows, "the blow," coming, as it did, on the feast day of the patroness of the Congregation, was an exceptionally hard one to take. Father Fox decried people who were "too prudent," who did not have enough trust in Divine Providence to take risks, even in the case of worthwhile causes. In this instance, he found Bishop Fitzgerald too prudent.

When Bishop Fitzgerald took over as Vicar Apostolic, he was still a relatively young man, only in his early 60s. However, by then he was a worn out, ailing man. He first showed signs of being seriously ill, when he returned from Washington in the late autumn of 1945. The tension between him and Bishop Crimont, the arduous travels by dogsled, the endless begging tours had taken their toll. When he reached Juneau, on December 11th, he had a cold; asthma was bothering him; and he was generally miserable. A medical check up showed that his blood pressure was abnormally high. During the years 1946 and 1947, he was in and out of hospitals. He died in Seattle, on July 17, 1947.

When Bishop Fitzgerald died, he left behind a host of friends. He had a rather exceptional gift for making friends, whether as priest, rector, provincial, or bishop. This was attributed to the natural simplicity of the man, to his unfailing thoughtfulness for others, and to his abundant good humor.

Bishop Walter J. Fitzgerald, S.J., lies buried in the Jesuit cemetery at Mount St. Michael's, Spokane.

176

FITZ-PATRICK, Father David M.

David Matthew Fitz-Patrick was born on April 13, 1949, in New London, Connecticut, the middle son of Joseph P. and Eleonore (Olsen) Fitz-Patrick. David's father graduated from the U.S. Naval Academy and served for over 20 years, through World War II and the Korean War, as captain of several submarines and submarine tenders. The year after

Father David Fitz-Patrick with his older brother William. *Photo courtesy of Fr. Fitz-Patrick.*

his retirement, when David was 12, his father died in an automobile accident.

David, his mother and two brothers lived in suburban Washington, D.C., in Chevy Chase, Maryland. There he attended Blessed Sacrament Grade School and Cathedral Latin High School. He graduated from La Salle University, Philadelphia, with a B.A. degree in 1971, having done his junior year of studies at the University of Fribourg, Switzerland. After his collegiate studies, he began seminary studies for the Archdiocese of Washington, and spent two years at the North American College in Rome. Taking a leave of absence from the seminary, he returned to Washington, where he worked for the Interstate Commerce Commission for three years. During this time, he attended Georgetown University and completed a Master of Library Science degree there in 1976.

In the winter of 1975, David happened to receive a piece of "junk mail" from the Catholic Bishop of Northern **Alaska**, an appeal for donations to support what he saw as "the wonderful work" being done by the priests, Religious, and volunteers in the missions in northern Alaska. David was captivated by the idea of such work, and especially so by the logo: "Some give by going to the Missions. Some go by giving to the Missions. Without both there are no Missions." He wrote a letter to Robert L. **Whelan**, S.J., Bishop of **Fairbanks**, saying that he had no money to send, but perhaps could give some time. Bishop Whelan personally telephoned him shortly thereafter. Before long, plans were in place for David to join the **Jesuit Volunteer Corps** and, as a member thereof, to teach at Monroe Catholic High School in Fairbanks.

In August 1976, David arrived in Fairbanks, to teach Religion, sociology, and typing for two years at Monroe. In the course of those two years, "an incredible adventure" in his words, he felt himself called to ministry among the people of the Diocese of Fairbanks as a priest. Accordingly, with the blessing of Bishop Whelan, he returned to Rome, to resume studies for the priesthood at the Pontifical University of St. Thomas, the Angelicum. By the end of 1978, he had his Bachelor of Sacred Theology degree from the Angelicum, and, in 1980, the Licentiate of Sacred Theology degree in Spirituality. This latter degree he earned *summa cum laude*.

David was ordained a deacon by Bishop Whelan in Sacred Heart Cathedral, Fairbanks, on June 29, 1979. That summer, he worked primarily with Father **George E. Carroll**, S.J., in ministry to the hospitalized and homebound, and with Father William C. **Dibb**, S.J., in the Cathedral parish. Later that same year, on December 29th, in his home parish, Shrine of the Most Blessed Sacrament in Washington, D.C., he was ordained to the priesthood, likewise by Bishop Whelan.

During his first summer as a priest, Father Fitz-Patrick lived in **Nulato**, working with Sister Jeannette LaRose, S.S.A. "That summer," he wrote years later, "I fell in love with village life and the simple lifestyle one could enjoy in the bush."

In the spring of 1981, with his studies completed, Father Fitz-Patrick returned to Fairbanks, where he served as associate pastor to Father **Cornelius K. Murphy**, S.J., at Immaculate Conception parish, and taught Religion at Monroe. From Father Murphy he learned how to be a pastor, not only to the laity, but also to brother priests.

In the late summer of 1981, Father Fitz-Patrick was appointed pastor of St. Michael's parish in **McGrath**. There he worked in "team ministry" with Father James A. **Sebesta**, S.J., and Sister Dolores Pardini, S.N.D. The three got together often, now in McGrath, now in **Kaltag**, to share success and hardship stories and lessons learned. "It was an incredible year of discovery," Father Fitz-Patrick recalled, "of the beauties of the bush, especially its people and their deeply spiritual lives." Among his fondest memories of life in McGrath were:

> living less than 25 feet away from the Iditarod Trail, in a small log cabin without running water, experiencing the coldest temperature in my life (–62), watching the northern lights dance across the sky, catching salmon in my own net, and having it for dinner that same night, and becoming so closely involved in the lives of the families who made up the Church of McGrath.

In the summer of 1982, Father Fitz-Patrick and Father J. Albert **Levitre** were appointed co-pastors of Sacred Heart Cathedral parish. In 1984, he was named pastor. A reporter interviewing him in 1987, found him to be "tall and clean-cut, like an aging altar boy as he jokes and laughs with his congregation." As pastor of the Cathedral parish, he, not surprisingly, encountered problems, but he also found solutions for them, in "prayer, faith, hope, compassion, devotion to people—and a sense of humor." And he had the support and pastoral assistance of Bishop Whelan and that of his successor, Bishop Michael J. **Kaniecki**, S.J., as well as that of fellow priests stationed in Fairbanks at the time. In addition, he was also very much helped by lay people, foremost among them Susan Timoney, later Dr. Susan Timoney of Trinity College, Washington, D.C. All this support and assistance he gratefully acknowledged.

In 1988, Father Fitz-Patrick began studies for a Master's degree in social work at the Catholic University of America in Washington, D.C. During his first year there, he did case-management at St. Elizabeth Hospital with the chronically mentally ill. During his second year, he did a residency at the National Institutes of Health, in the Allergy and Infectious Disease Institute, working, in large part, with HIV-AIDS patients and their families.

In the earlier part of 1990, Father Fitz-Patrick was incardinated into the Archdiocese of Washington; and, in June of that year, he was endorsed by that archdiocese to join the Air Force Chaplain Service. His assignments were to include: McClellan AFB, Sacramento, California, 1990–92; Dharhan AB, Saudi Arabia, 1991 and 1995; RAF Chickands, England, 1992–95; MacDill AFB, Tampa, Florida, 1995–97; AF Institute of Technology, a year of study and research in Marriage and Family issues, at the University of Nebraska, Lincoln, 1997–98; Faculty Member, Chaplain Service Institute, (Chaplain School), Montgomery, Alabama, 1998–2001; and Air Command and Staff College in residence, also at Montgomery, 2001–02, where he was awarded a Master's degree in Aerospace Science.

Chaplain Fitz-Patrick was promoted to the rank of Major effective November 1, 1999. In the course of his years in the Air Force, he was awarded numerous medals, commendations, and ribbons in recognition of his meritorious service.

On March 5, 2001, Father Fitz-Patrick, ever the pastoral priest, was able to write to Father Louis L. **Renner**, S.J.:

> Life as a military chaplain continues to go well. I was selected to attend Air Command and Staff College, which means I get to stay in Montgomery for another year. It's not at the top of the list of places I'd choose to live, but I am quite involved in one of the local parishes on weekends, and the people are great. I keep reminding them that they are my salvation. If my whole existence were based on this "office job," I'd go crazy!

Father Fitz-Patrick clearly knew how to distinguish job from vocation. During the earlier part of the year 2003, he served in the Middle East.

FORHAN, Father John, S.J.

John Forhan was born in Brooklyn, New York, on June 24, 1854. He entered the Society of Jesus at Sault-au-Récollet, near Montreal, Canada, on September 8, 1879. He was ordained a priest in Montreal in 1892. After teaching for years at St. Ignatius High School in San Francisco, he took ship

In Nome, ca. 1910, Jesuit Brother Alphonsus Lemire and a shaggy dog pose with Jesuit Fathers John Forhan (glasses) and Bellarmine Lafortune. *JOPA-512.C51.*

for **Alaska**, arriving in **Nome** on September 28, 1908. He was at this time a member of the Canadian Province. In 1912, he was transferred to the California Province.

Father Forhan had the reputation of being "extraordinarily gifted as a preacher." Reportedly, people in Nome waited all week to hear his Sunday sermons. The house diary he kept while in Nome "stands," according to Father Segundo **Llorente**, S.J., "as a record of flawless English, a mixture of humor and satire, and a monument to the *mores* of a decaying gold mining town."

And yet, for all that, Father Forhan was not a good choice for Nome. He reacted negatively to almost everything: the climate, the town, the people, and even his Catholic congregation. He had no tolerance for anything or anybody not one hundred percent Holy Roman Catholic. Father Bellarmine **Lafortune**, S.J., found him "too brusque, too impatient with the class of sinners" found in Nome. To his Father Provincial, Father Lafortune wrote, "Rev. Fr. Forhan is hated by many on account of his excessive severity." In the Nome diary, Father Forhan wrote, "Nome is not a locality in which the exercise of the ministry gives any very great consolation."

After being pastor of the Nome parish for six years, Father Forhan left Nome, on September 8, 1914, in poor health to return to the American west coast. He spent the year 1914–15 at Seattle College. He died in San Francisco on August 11, 1916.

FOX, Brother Francis J., S.J.

Francis J. Fox came out of the Fuchs (often renamed, as in his case, Fox) family of Uniontown, Washington. He himself was born in Genesee, Idaho, on February 15, 1918, the son of George and Josephine (Reisenauer) Fox. He attended St. Boniface Grade School in Uniontown for eight years, then St. Boniface High School for three. His sophomore year he spent at St. Martin's High School in Lacey, Washington.

In 1937, Francis tried to enlist in the Army, passed his physical exam, but, because of some oversight, was never sworn in; so, he left Fort Wright, Spokane. On May 14, 1939, he entered the Jesuit novitiate at Sheridan, Oregon, as a Lay Broth-

Brother Francis J. Fox, S.J. *JOPA-1064.23*.

er candidate. While at Sheridan, he baked and helped in the kitchen and on the farm.

By July 4, 1942, Brother Fox was crossing the Gulf of **Alaska**. Onboard that same ship with him were also Jesuit Fathers **John P. Fox**, S.J., his uncle, and Jules M. **Convert**, and Jesuit seminarian, John R. **Buchanan**. They landed in **Seward**, from where they took the train, via **Anchorage**, to **Fairbanks**. After a few days in Fairbanks, Brother Fox and Mr. Buchanan flew on to **Holy Cross**.

Brother Fox was destined for St. Mary's Mission at **Akulurak**, but at Holy Cross the potatoes, recently planted, had not yet been cultivated, so he was asked to stay on to attend to that and to do other work in the garden. Several weeks later, Bishop Walter J. **Fitzgerald**, S.J., phoned and told him to go on down to Akulurak. On the mission boat, the *Sifton*, he arrived there early in the morning of July 31, 1942, the Feast of St. Ignatius. Years later, he recalled in his memoirs, "Father **Llorente** came down to the boat to wake us all for Mass and a welcome breakfast."

"At Akulurak," Brother Fox wrote in his memoirs,

my main job was to prefect the boarding school boys, to supervise the work they did, and their study. As time went on, I had to run a fishing boat, operate the movie projector, operate the radio station for the Air Force weather schedules, the medical schedule, and the commercial station for telegrams and wires coming in from the villages along the river.

While at Akulurak, he also did some substitute teaching, served as a medical aide, and made excursions up the Yukon to gather firewood. For two years, he was a member of the village council. He spent a big part of one of his Akulurak years in bed, recuperating from diphtheria.

From September 1945 to September 1965, Brother Fox was stationed at Holy Cross. There he was in charge of the boats, the fishing, the sawmill, the wood- and fish-camps. "Of course," he recalled many years later, "all this was new to me, but when necessity exists, one soon learns, mostly the hard way. One advantage of learning that way, one almost never forgets." But, it was not all work at Holy Cross. There were also picnics, berry-picking trips, hunting outings, gardening, haying, "and many other interesting jobs." At Holy Cross he was part of "a happy family." Apart from the staff, there were also "a lot of happy children." But life at Holy Cross changed rather radically, in October 1956, when the boarding school closed, and most of the mission staff and a nucleus of students moved to **Copper Valley School**.

Brother Fox spent the next four years of his life in bush Alaska at **Nulato**. There he again had a variety of jobs. He did janitorial and maintenance work, supervised the Alaska Village Electric Cooperative light plant that furnished electricity for the village, trained the altar servers, and directed and sang in the choir. In addition to being an accomplished pianist, he had a fine tenor voice. During his latter years in Alaska, he sang occasionally in the University of Alaska–Fairbanks choir. In 1962, James A. **Kolb**, the future Paulist Father Kolb, passed through Nulato. In an interview many years later he recalled: "In Nulato I met a man named Frank Fox, a Jesuit Brother. He was physically a big man, who had worked at the mission schools for many years. He seemed to really like what he did, liked working in the bush and the people he worked with. He seemed very much at home and in love with what he was doing." Father Kolb's assessment of Brother Fox was accurate. He was a big, lumbering man, whose high-pitched voice came initially as a surprise. His stay at Nulato he himself summarized as "four pleasant years."

In September 1969, Brother Fox was assigned to Fairbanks. In addition to doing some cooking at Loyola Hall, the Jesuit residence where he lived, he was janitor and general maintenance man and caretaker of the demanding coal-fired furnace at the Catholic schools complex. In January 1976, he "wrecked" his back and had to spend a great deal of time in bed. Told that he should take a break from his work, he went to Gonzaga University in Spokane, Washington, to attend the golden jubilee of his uncle's ordination to the priesthood. He then made a retreat "back east" and attended the Eucharistic Congress in Philadelphia. After that he returned to Spokane, where, at Spokane Community College, he took some courses, "tried to catch up on what was going on in the Province, visited relatives, and got a little rest and recreation."

These latter two he needed badly. When, in May 1977, he returned to Fairbanks to continue on at the Catholic schools, he still found "so much to do and so few helpers." He was putting in 12-hour days seven days a week. Finally, in February 1981, Father Francis J. **Fallert**, General Superior of Jesuits in Alaska at the time, in a letter to the Superintendent of the Catholic Schools and the School Board, protested that Brother Fox was working too hard and too long. He asked that Brother be given Saturdays and Sundays off. Father Fallert's demands were graciously met. Some of this new-found freedom Brother Fox spent taking a little drive occasionally, or watching a baseball game, or taking in a movie.

By 1983, Brother Fox had completed 40 years in Alaska. Father Louis L. **Renner**, S.J., recommended that Robert L. **Whelan**, S.J., Bishop of Fairbanks at the time, nominate Brother Fox as a candidate for the Catholic Church Extension Society's 1983 Lumen Christi Award. He did not win the award, but the fact that he was recommended and nominated for it shows the high esteem in which he was held by his fellow Jesuits.

Hard work and advancing age inevitably took their toll on Brother Fox. In 1986, after long years in Fairbanks, years which he summarized as "happy years," he went into retirement at Gonzaga University. Two successive hip surgeries left him semi-crippled. After so long and active a life, it was hard for him to sit idly in his room—or in the coffee shop, smoking like the furnace he had tended so long and faithfully in Fairbanks. But, in retirement, too, he continued to be a happy man, a man at peace with himself. On February 28, 1994, he died in the Oregon Province infirmary at Gonzaga. He lies buried in Mount St. Michael's Cemetery, Spokane.

FOX, Father John P., S.J.

He was considered an "iron man." He himself wrote, "The good Lord knew what He was doing, when He gave me the iron constitution that I have been enjoying for so many years." He was powerful on the trail with sled and dogs. He was an innovator, a man ahead of his times. He decried people who were "too prudent," who did not place their trust in Divine Providence, when risky, but worthwhile, causes were involved. He founded a Congregation of Native Sisters. A noted Alaskan artist painted his portrait. As an octogenarian he helped train an Eskimo man who was preparing for the priesthood. He spent half a century in **Alaska**. A book-length biography of the man begs to be written.

John P. Fox was born in Uniontown, Washington, on June 29, 1892, the son of farmer Paul and Mary (Hagemann) Fuchs. His father was born in Trier, Germany. His mother was born of German immigrants. John was the third of eleven children. He was accused of "betraying his name," when, while at Gonzaga University, in Spokane, Washington, he, upon the advice of one of the Jesuit priests, changed it to "Fox."

John attended St. Boniface School in Uniontown from 1900–07. For a year after that, he was janitor of the parish plant. He lived with the pastor, Father J.A. Faust, who, thinking John had a vocation to the diocesan priesthood, sent him to Gonzaga for high school and two years of college during the years 1908–13.

While at Gonzaga, John made "a particularly sulfuric 'hellfire and damnation' retreat." Influenced by Jesuit Father Herman Goller, who helped out in Uniontown at Christmas and some other times, John reconsidered his vocation, and opted for the Jesuits. On July 21, 1913, he entered the Jesuit novitiate at Los Gatos, California. There he made his two-year noviceship and studied the classics and humanities for three years, before going on to three years of philosophical studies at Mount St. Michael's in Spokane. From 1921–23, he taught at Seattle

Father John P. Fox, S.J., as portrayed by the brush of Muriel Hannah in 1962. *LRC.*

Preparatory, primarily German and history. He next spent four years at Oña, Spain. "At Oña," he said, "you had to speak Spanish or be quiet." He was ordained a priest there on July 29, 1926.

During his years at Mount St. Michael's, Father Fox had been a member of the Mission Stamp Bureau, a group that solicited used stamps to sell to raise money for the missions. As a member of the group, he had become interested in the missions. "Naturally," he wrote, "since Alaska was our mission, I applied for it." At the same time, he had had an interest also in history. "So," he wrote, "I asked our Father Provincial to let me know which to prepare for, to give me some idea of what was in store for me. But I did not know the least thing about my future status till August 15, 1927, when I was called to Portland by Fr. Provincial and told to get ready to go to Alaska as soon as possible." Father Fox arrived at **Akulurak** on the 20th of September.

Father Fox spent his first year in Alaska at Akulurak. Immediately he set about studying the Central Yup'ik Eskimo language. He seems never to have acquired even a passable knowledge of it. Forty years after first arriving in Alaska, he regretted not having brought with him some knowledge of anthropology, of the Native culture. "Looking back now," he wrote, "I see where I missed fabulous opportunities on account of the very primitive area in which I spent most of my 40 years." Realistically, he concluded that, in his case, maybe the best preparation he had for Alaska was "an iron constitution," needed to ward off tuberculosis, so prevalent in his area at that time.

In July 1928, Father Fox became the pastor of the newly founded mission at **Kashunuk**. There he replaced Father Francis M. **Ménager**, S.J., who had very much endeared himself to the people of that village, making him "a hard act to follow." From his first days at Kashunuk, Father Fox, being an historian at heart, meticulously kept a house diary of his doings, of his comings and goings. Throughout his years in Alaska, he was a faithful keeper of diaries and records. He lamented the "slovenliness" with which some of his fellow missionaries kept house diaries and records. At Kashunuk, he had the assistance of a hired Native catechist, Annie Sipary. During all his years as a missionary among the Eskimos, Father Fox relied heavily on the help of Native catechists. He provided them with combinations of lodging and salaries. Out of Kashunuk, he traveled far and wide to various Eskimo villages and camps, including the villages down on Nelson Island.

Father Fox spent the year 1930–31 making his tertianship at Port Townsend, Washington. Back in Alaska again, he reported to Father Ménager, General Superior of the Alaska Mission at the time, who saw in the tall and strong Father Fox, whom he nicknamed "long legs," just the right man for the **Hooper Bay** district, a district Father Fox himself described as "300 miles long and 50 miles wide."

From 1931 until 1946, Father Fox made the Central Yup'ik Eskimo village of Hooper Bay— whose Latinized Eskimo name stretches out to *Napareyaramiutensis*—on the Bering Sea coast his headquarters. As a "roving missionary," virtually the only white man among approximately 1,200 Eskimos, he traveled extensively to tend to his Eskimo flocks in the widely scattered villages of Kashunuk, **Scammon Bay**, Old **Chevak**, **Tununak**, **Keyaluvik**, **Nightmute**, and Kokaklercheraramiut, to mention only the larger ones among them. There were also several dozen smaller villages and camps in his district.

Father Fox was one of the last of the Jesuit missionaries to make the rounds of his missions by dogteam. Generally, he made the big circuit of his stations once or twice per winter, commonly in March–April, when there was more daylight, but the trails were still firm. A given circuit took him three to four weeks. The bigger villages of Old Chevak, Scammon Bay, and Kashunuk, villages closer to Hooper Bay, he visited monthly. When he thought it time to travel, he went, regardless of weather conditions. He knew how to prepare for whatever eventuality he might encounter while on the trail. "As for a guide," he said, "I hardly ever used one." He spent more than one night burrowed in the snow, but never with serious ill effects. "When the weather turned very bad," he wrote, "my Eskimos used to remark, 'Father must be traveling.'" He normally drove a team of 9–13 dogs, never fewer than seven. Reflecting on his years at Hooper Bay, he summarized, "An awful lot of mushing!" In the summer, he visited his missions by boat.

What tried the missionary soul of Father Fox more than the hardships of the trail and the overload of work he, as the lone priest in that vast area, constantly had to live with was the full awareness that he simply could not by himself begin to adequately instruct and serve his people. He used Native catechists extensively and effectively. Outstanding among these were Ivan and Maggie **Sipary**. But, good ones were not always readily found and trained; and equitably compensating them for their work with food, housing, and salaries often taxed his resources to the limit.

Being a forward thinker, an innovator, he, soon upon his arrival at Hooper Bay in 1931, decided to found a Congregation of Native Sisters. On January 25, 1932, he wrote to Mission Procurator, Father Paul P. Sauer, S.J.: "I am starting a native congregation, the members of which I hope will in the near future supply in some way for this terrible lack of priests. I have the first postulants trying out now. They are doing very well, and I will start them on their novitiate in a few months." With the approbation and full support of Joseph R. **Crimont**, S.J., Vicar Apostolic of Alaska at the time, the Congregation of the Sisters of Our Lady of the **Snows** soon became a viable reality, officially as of August 5, 1932.

Father Fox frankly admitted that "one of the motives for a community of Sisters was economy." To this he added, "Another reason for the Sisters was stability. With catechists there was always the problem of having to find a new one to replace one that took sick." The prevalence of tuberculosis in his area at the time was a common cause of sickness. "Besides," he further explained, "for a native family it was very hard to move to another village. A Sister would be much more detached, and so could much more easily be moved from mission to mission." By any standard, the Congregation of the Sisters of Our Lady of the Snows was a successful venture. It was, therefore, with a very heavy heart that Father Fox saw them suppressed on August 5, 1945, by Walter J. **Fitzgerald**, S.J., Vicar Apostolic of Alaska as of May 20, 1945. Speaking of Bishop Fitzgerald's decision to suppress them, Father Fox said in his old age, "To me personally, it was a big blow." He always regarded the decision as a wrong one; but, being an obedient man, he reconciled himself to it. "When these Sisters were gone," wrote historian Father Wilfred P. Schoenberg, S.J, "there was a kind of emptiness in the Alaskan Church, and no one felt it more keenly than Father John Fox." While at Hooper Bay, Father Fox planned to found also a community of Lay Brothers, but "this did not work out, and the plan was quietly dropped."

During his 15 years at Hooper Bay, Father Fox served for some years as an officer in the Alaska Territorial Guard. He was promoted to the rank of Captain on November 6, 1944. In addition to serving as a missionary priest, he was also involved in a multiplicity of other roles, among them: reindeer supervisor, marriage commissioner, village "doctor," and village postmaster. He was also the writer and editor of the mimeographed newsletter, "Hooper Bay Gossip." Routinely, wherever he was stationed, he sent out newsletters to friends and benefactors. He also wrote articles for mission magazines. These were illustrated by photos taken by himself. He was a good photographer. With donations generated by his newsletters and articles, he kept his home-base missions and dependent stations self-supporting. "A certain amount of writing by the missionaries," he wrote in his later years, "was rather important. For me the result has been that I have always been able to support the particular mission at which I happened to be, unless it was a large school."

In 1946, after 19 years among the Eskimos of the Bering Sea coast, Father Fox was transferred to the lower Yukon, to **Mountain Village**. Making this his home base, he served also its dependent stations:

Marshall, **Russian Mission**, **Pilot Station**, Takchak, Pitka's Point, and Chukartulik. During his ten years on the lower Yukon, he relied less on a dogteam of his own. He thought getting and operating a snowmachine of his own too expensive, likewise travel by plane. "So," he wrote, "travel was cut down a great deal; natives too were learning to give an occasional free ride to the missionary." For summer travel, he had an open boat with an outboard motor.

At Mountain Village, too, he served as marriage commissioner. He continued to be an innovator. He introduced electricity to the village. He owned and operated a generator, and sold electricity to the people at cost. There he also started retreats for the people and annual "Conventions" involving the people from the different villages in the area. The Conventions, held in the middle of August, and coming to a grand finale on the 15th, the Feast of Mary's Assumption into heaven, were of both a spiritual and social nature. They were intended, among other things, to bring young people together with a view to finding prospective marriage partners.

In 1953, the Oregon Province Provincial, Father Harold O. Small, S.J., visited the Alaskan missions. In his report afterwards, he noted, "at Mountain Village, Father Fox, a saintly man, provided closed retreats for the Eskimos in the district, still given annually with much fruit."

After ten years among the Eskimos of the lower Yukon, Father Fox, in 1956, moved upriver, to **Holy Cross Mission**. Holy Cross, founded in 1888, was now at the end, and beyond the end, of its heyday. Concerning the physical plant at Holy Cross in the mid-1950s, Father Fox wrote, "Our buildings and much of our equipment was nothing so much as one great junk pile." On October 14, 1956, a number of staff members and 26 students left the Holy Cross Mission Boarding School for the newly opened **Copper Valley School**. "So," wrote Father Fox, "we had empty buildings to be torn down, and a day school to be opened." Concerning the challenge that faced him as the pastor of Holy Cross, he wrote:

Over the years the villagers had gotten accustomed to see the boarders just about fill the church for Mass. So, why should they come? It was a battle to get some of them back to church, even on Sundays. But, gradually, the church filled again. The day-scholars with their teachers, and a scattering of villagers came to Mass daily.

During his Holy Cross years, in 1962, the highly regarded Alaskan artist, Muriel Hannah, painted a portrait in pastels of Father Fox. It was commissioned by Wien Air for a calendar cover. It shows him wearing a fur parka, hood down, a good head of white hair, countenance open and serene. After being rescued at a garage sale by Father Henry G. **Hargreaves**, S.J., the portrait hung for many years in the Birchwood Street Jesuit residence in Anchorage. Around the year 2000, it was transferred to **Bethel**, where it was hung on the vestibule wall of Immaculate Conception Church to serve the Central Yup'ik Eskimo people as a reminder of early-day missionaries. Many postcards were made of the portrait and widely sent around.

Father Fox left Holy Cross in 1963 to spend two years at the new St. Mary's Mission on the **Andreafsky** River. There he did some teaching and tended to nearby villages on weekends. From 1965–68, he was back again at Mountain Village. From there he wrote his opinions, in a letter to Father John E. **Gurr**, S.J., dated February 13, 1967, regarding a topic then current, that of regional high schools for Alaskan Natives:

> I understand a commission of some kind decided that those schools ought to be built at Anchorage or Fairbanks. How stupid. It may cost less, but why drag all the bush natives up there instead of putting the school where they live or near them. Already most of our young people are being uprooted and hauled to other places for high school. Some of our parents are fighting the departure of their children, and from what I hear some of our missionaries are supporting them in that. I myself am badly tempted to do the same. Regional high schools are needed; but let's make them *regional*, not urban.

Again Father Fox showed himself to be a man ahead of his times. In 1976, the settlement of the Molly Hootch case resulted in the passage of a law by the State of Alaska that mandated high schools in the villages. By the late 1970s, over 100 village high schools had been built.

The above quote bears out what some of his fellow Jesuits wrote about Father Fox. "He was a most uncomplicated person," wrote one, "humorless, literal. He said exactly what he thought." Father Segundo **Llorente**, S.J., wrote of him, "He never had an ounce of poetry in his whole system." And

yet, like many large, strong men, he was a gentle soul, childlike in his faith and simplicity. Father Llorente knew Father Fox well. The latter had chosen him as his spiritual director, because he was "the only pious guy in the neighborhood."

In 1968, Father Fox left the bush missions of northern Alaska for **Anchorage**. There he lived in the Birchwood Street Jesuit Community. From 1968 on, his principal assignment was to visit Native peoples in the Alaska Native Hospital. He, in turn, was often visited by them.

On September 3, 1969, Father Fox wrote in a letter to Robert L. **Whelan**, S.J., Bishop of Fairbanks at the time: "Lay Diaconate. The sooner the better. I had asked Bishop **Gleeson** for action along that line four years ago." Here, in the matter of an **Eskimo Deacon Program**, Father Fox yet again showed himself to be a forward-looking man, an innovator, a man of faith ready to take risks. "I don't think," he wrote in that same letter, "we should calculate things too closely, leaving little to Divine Providence."

By the early 1970s, the Eskimo Deacon Program was a flourishing reality. One of the Eskimo deacon candidates, Michael **Nayagak**, was hoping to go beyond the diaconate to the priesthood. The question arose, "Who would train him?" Although Father Fox was by now 81 years old, Bishop Whelan looked to him to do the training. In December 1973, he wrote to him, "You are the only one I can think of who would be able to communicate well enough with him. Would you be willing to undertake this chore?" Willingly Father Fox accepted to be Michael's trainer. He moved to Chevak and, with the help of tapes, translations and interpreters, began to train Michael for the priesthood. Michael was ordained a deacon, but died, very unexpectedly, before he could be ordained a priest. Father Fox returned to Anchorage.

During his last years in Alaska, Father Fox, still in Anchorage, began to be less active, as those "long legs" began to give out. Father René **Astruc**, S.J., who lived with him in Anchorage, recalled how Father Fox would spend hours contemplating "a bloody Christ picture" on the inside of his door. Father Fox was kept alive by breath and prayer. Common parting words of his were "Let's pray for one another. I need your prayers, and mine can't hurt you."

In 1977, Father Fox left Alaska for the last time. He spent a year at Mount St. Michael's, in Spokane; then, when that was closed in 1978, he moved down to Gonzaga University, where he spent his remaining years. At first, he was able to take care of himself, and make it to the dining room for meals with the community. In his latter years, however, he required nursing care. He sat in his room, did but little reading, watched no television, and prayed.

On May 10, 1981, Gonzaga University awarded Father Fox—along with his fellow one-time Alaskan missionary, Father James C. **Spils**, S.J., and two veteran Rocky Mountain missionaries—its DeSmet Medal in recognition of his long years and many achievements as a missionary in Alaska.

Father John P. Fox, S.J., died at Sacred Heart Medical Center, Spokane, on May 6, 1983. He was in his 91st year. He lies buried in the Jesuit cemetery at Mount St. Michael's.

176

FRISTER, Father Jerome A.

Jerome A. "Jerry" Frister, the youngest of four children, two girls and two boys, was born to Andrew Frister and Florence McNamara Frister on December 16, 1931, in Milwaukee, Wisconsin. His father was born in Milwaukee of German ancestry. His mother was born in Chicago of Irish immigrants.

Jerry's boyhood was, by his own admission, "uneventful." In Milwaukee, he attended Sacred Heart Grade School, after which, in September 1945, he entered the Diocesan Minor Seminary of St. Francis de Sales to begin his high school studies. During his high school years, he had many after-school and weekend jobs, among them working in a furniture store. During the summer months, he worked in a pickle factory, a job that gained him some elbowroom. No one would sit next to him in the streetcar, because he smelled like a kosher pickle.

After completing high school in 1949, Jerry continued on with his minor seminary studies for two more years. In 1951, he entered St. Francis Major

Father Jerome A. Frister.
Courtesy of Fr. Frister.

Seminary. After what he called "six arduous years," he was ordained a priest for the Archdiocese of Milwaukee on May 25, 1957, by Archbishop Albert G. Meyer.

During his first ten years as a priest, Father Frister, more commonly known as "Father Jerry," served as an assistant priest in the archdiocese: first, at Sts. Cyril and Methodius parish in Sheboygan, Wisconsin, for one and a half years; then, at St. Augustine's parish on Milwaukee's Southside, for eight and a half years.

While at St. Augustine's, Father Jerry did two things that were to affect the rest of his life. With the county airport near the parish, he learned to fly. He soon had his private pilot's license. Eventually, but before he went to **Alaska**, he earned his commercial pilot's license, with a single-engine land and sea rating. In 1964, he became a military chaplain in the Air Force Reserves.

After three years in the Reserves, Father Jerry asked William E. Cousins, his archbishop at the time, for permission to go on active duty. This was granted. During the next six and a half years, Chaplain Frister saw a variety of tours of duty. He was successively stationed in Arkansas; at Eielson Air Force Base, near **Fairbanks**, Alaska; at Loring AFB in northern Maine; in Danang, Vietnam; at Tahkli AFB in Thailand; and at McCord AFB, near Tacoma, Washington. It was while he was serving in Vietnam that he first began to think seriously about Alaska and its rather severe priest shortage. Accordingly, when he returned stateside, he asked Archbishop Cousins for permission to be separated from active duty, while remaining in the Reserves, and to volunteer to work in Alaska for two years, from 1973–75. This permission, too, was granted.

Francis T. **Hurley** was Bishop of **Juneau** at the time. The Juneau diocese, comprising Southeastern Alaska, is, geographically speaking, made up entirely of many islands and coastal regions. Virtually all of its cities, towns, Indian villages, canneries, logging camps, and the like are located on salt water. Father Jerry—duly licensed and skilled, when it came to piloting a plane off land or water—was "a natural," when there was question of bringing the Mass and Sacraments to the Catholic communities of Alaska's archipelagic Southeast.

Father Jerry's first Alaskan assignment based him at Holy Name parish in **Ketchikan**. Out of there, flying one of the two planes owned by the diocese, he served for three years, from 1973–76, as the fly-in priest in charge of the southern part of the diocese. Bishop Hurley, likewise a skilled land–water pilot, took care of the northern part.

Father Jerry found "life in 'bush' Alaska very simple." Once a month, he would fly to each of the seven villages assigned to him. Upon his arrival, a child would go from house to house to announce that he was there, and that Mass would be celebrated at the house of so-and-so at 7 P.M. Attendance varied, anywhere from as few as ten to as many as fifty, depending on the size of the given community. After Mass, Father Jerry, a gifted storyteller, would tell the children stories. He entertained them also with puppets, and by drawing cartoons for them.

It was not long before Father Jerry came under the spell of Alaska. In 1975, with the permission of Archbishop Cousins, he was formally incardinated into the Diocese of Juneau, which, at the time, had a total of only nine priests.

During his three years in Ketchikan, Father Jerry was stationed with Fathers James F. **Miller** and James D. **Cronin**. To newly-ordained Father Cronin, Father Jerry served as a "mentor." In his later years, Father Cronin referred to him as "my very good friend of Ketchikan days."

In 1978, Father Jerry joined the Alaska Army National Guard as a chaplain. From 1980–83, he was back on active duty with the Army. In 1988, he retired from the Guard, with the rank of Lieutenant Colonel.

From 1976–79, Father Jerry was pastor of St. Rose of Lima parish in **Wrangell**. Part of his duties as such was to continue to minister to the logging camps and fishing villages in that general area. On May 3, 1979, he was back in Wrangell to host the centennial celebrations of the establishment of Alaska's first Catholic parish.

In addition to serving in Ketchikan and Wrangell, Father Jerry ministered also in **Haines**. He was pastor of St. Peter's parish in **Douglas** from 1983–85. From 1985–92, he was pastor of St. Gregory Nazianzen parish in **Sitka**. While in Sitka, he earned his amateur radio operator's license. From 1992 until his retirement, he was "Northern Mission circuit rider priest," spending time each month in Juneau, **Skagway**, and **Yakutat**.

After being "part of Southeast life" for nearly a quarter of a century, Father Jerry, in September 1997, retired to Oceanside, California. Though in retirement, he kept active, helping out with Masses and other services at the nearby Franciscan Mission of San Luis Rey and at the U.S. Naval Hospital at the Camp Pendleton Marine Base.

"In Southeast Alaska," his friend, Father Peter F. **Gorges**, wrote assuringly, "Father Jerry's quick wit, lovely tenor voice, and clever drawings will not soon be forgotten."

GALENA

Galena, now a predominately Koyukon Athabaskan Indian community on the right bank of the middle Yukon River in **Alaska**'s Great Interior, 35 miles east of **Nulato**, was established about 1920 as a supply point for the galena (lead ore) discovered in the area south of the Yukon. It is the site of the former Indian village of Notaraliten. The U.S. Army built a Lend-Lease airstrip at Galena in 1940. This helped make Galena a commercial and transportation center for surrounding villages. In 1930, Galena had 67 inhabitants; in 1940, 44; in 1950, 76; in 1992, 833; and in the year 2000, 675. A Galena post office was established in 1932.

The name Galena first appears in Catholic Church records in 1921. On January 17th of that year, Father Crispin S. **Rossi**, S.J., performed three baptisms in Galena. However, Catholic baptisms had been performed in that area already during the latter half of the 1800s by Catholic missionaries—first by Missionary **Oblates of Mary Immaculate**, then by Jesuits—traveling along the Yukon.

Galena's first church was a saloon building barged down from **Ruby** in 1921 and transformed into a church, with priest's quarters added by 1923. The church was named "St. John's Catholic Church," in honor of St. John Berchmans. At first, Galena was a dependent station of Nulato. In 1952, it became an independent parish. The "saloon" church was badly damaged by the 1972 flood. In 1984, a new, octagonal church was begun at the Alexander Lake town site, commonly referred to as "new site," while Father Charles A. **Bartles**, S.J., was pastor of the Galena parish. This new St. John Berchmans Church, with a residence constructed out of logs built on to it, was formally dedicated on May 22,

1988, by Michael J. **Kaniecki**, S.J., Bishop of **Fairbanks** at the time.

For several decades, the Galena Catholic community was served by priests stationed at Nulato. From 1942–47, however, Father Joseph F. **McElmeel**, S.J., was stationed in Galena. He was followed there by the following Jesuit Fathers: James C. **Spils**, S.J., 1947–54; James W. **Plamondon**, 1954–62; René **Astruc**, 1962–63; **George E. Carroll**, 1963–69. From 1969–73, Father Charles A. **Saalfeld**, S.J., served it out of **Tanana**. Father Bernard F. **McMeel**, S.J., was stationed in Galena from 1973–76. Father Ronald K. **Dunfey**, a priest of the Diocese of **Juneau**, served it out of Tanana, from 1976–77. Father William Brunner, S.S.C., was in residence, 1977–81; as was Father Thomas W. Fisk, S.J., 1981–82; and Father Bartles, 1982–85. Galena was without a listed priest for the year 1985–86.

Franciscan Fathers Andre Schludecker and Jeffery Salwach were in Galena during the years 1986–88. They were followed by fellow Franciscan, Father Joseph **Hemmer**, in Galena from 1988–94. During the years 1992–95, Galena saw the services, in addition to those of Father Hemmer, also those of Franciscan Fathers Edmund Mundwiller and Walter Dolan.

Father Edward J. **Hartmann** was in Galena from 1995–97, and Father Patrick D. **Bergquist** during the year 1997–98. Father Andrzej Maslanka, a priest from Poland, was there from 1998–2002. He was followed by Father J. Albert **Levitre**, priest of the Diocese of Fairbanks, in Galena from the summer of 2002 to the summer of 2003. Father Richard D. **Case**, S.J., undertook the pastoral care of Galena on December 1, 2004.

St. John Berchmans Church, Galena. *LR.*

In the log residence at St. John Berchmans Church, Galena, on November 7, 1990, ministers to villages along the middle Yukon River pose, after a series of meetings, for a group photo. They are, left to right: Sister Monique Vaernewyck, O.S.U.; William E. Cardy, O.F.M.; Brother Kirby Boone, C.F.X.; Sister Ann Waters, S.N.J.M.; Sister Kateri Mitchell, S.S.A.; Father Louis L. Renner, S.J.; Father Joseph Hemmer, O.F.M.; Sister Maria Clarys, O.S.U.; and Brother Robert Ruzicka, O.F.M. *MK.*

Brother Robert **Ruzicka**, O.F.M., was home-based in Galena from 1986–2000, as Pastoral Minister. He spent the year 1991–92 at **Huslia**. Brother Kirby **Boone**, C.F.X., was in residence in Galena from 1991–92, likewise as Pastoral Minister. In the year 2000, Brother R. Justin Huber, O.F.M., began serving as Pastoral Minister in Galena and Huslia, and doing construction and maintenance work in different villages along the middle Yukon.

The following Sisters, too, have served in Galena: Jeannette LaRose, S.S.A., 1981–82; Patricia Ann Miller, O.P., 1983–89; Peggy Glynn, O.P., 1984–89; and Margaret Usuka, S.N.D., 1989–90. Sisters of **Providence** stationed in Fairbanks taught catechism classes in Galena during the summers of 1970–72.

In the fall of the year 2002, Sisters Marilyn Marx, S.N.J.M., and Marita Soucy, C.S.J., took up residency in Galena, there to start and staff a Native Interior Ministry Study Center. This, the Kateri Tekakwitha Center, was dedicated on August 31, 2003.

38, 68, 120

GALLAGHER, Father Thomas N., S.J.

Thomas Neal Gallagher was born in Tacoma, Washington, on August 21, 1928, the third child of John and Bertha Gallagher. He had two older brothers, a younger brother and a younger sister. He grew up in the small community of Dash Point, on the shores of Puget Sound, just north of Tacoma. At Dash Point, he attended a two-room elementary public school. For his intermediate and secondary schooling, he was at Jason Lee Junior High School and Stadium High School, both in Tacoma. From 1946–49, he attended Santa Clara University at Santa Clara, California. During some of his high school summers, he worked on cannery tenders in Southeastern **Alaska**. This awakened in him the desire to work in Alaska some day.

Thomas Gallagher entered St. Francis Xavier Novitiate—the novitiate of the Oregon Province of the Society of Jesus at Sheridan, Oregon—on August 14, 1949. After completing his two-year noviceship and taking his simple vows, he spent two

Father Thomas N. Gallagher, S.J. *BR-897714.*

additional years at Sheridan studying the classics and humanities. His philosophical studies he made at Mount St. Michael's, Spokane, Washington, from 1953–56, ending them with an M.A. degree in philosophy, and a Secondary School Teaching Certificate from the Territory of Alaska.

In the late summer of 1956, "Mister Gallagher" was sent to the **Holy Cross Mission** boarding School, Alaska, to help 26 young boys and girls pack up and get ready for the move to the new **Copper Valley School** near **Glennallen**, Alaska. On October 14th of that year, he was part of "Operation Snowbird." Along with Brother John **Hess**, S.J., and two Sisters of St. **Ann**, Sister M. Edward and Sister M. Alice Therese, he accompanied the 26 children that were flown on that day from Holy Cross, via **Aniak**, to Gulkana, and then bused to the new school. He spent the years 1956–58 at Copper Valley School, prefecting the boys, teaching algebra, hunting meat for the table, and hauling water for the school's kitchen.

From 1958–62, Mr. Gallagher made his theological studies at Innsbruck, Austria. He was ordained a priest there on July 26, 1961. During the year 1962–63, he taught at Monroe Catholic High School in **Fairbanks**, Alaska. The following year, he made his tertianship at Port Townsend, Washington. Then it was back to Alaska again, where, in his words, "my trail took me into classrooms and up and down halls of high school life."

Father Gallagher was principal of Copper Valley School during the years 1964–66, and Superior at the school and pastor of Glennallen during the year 1966–67. The following year he was among the Central Yup'ik Eskimos as pastor of the villages of **St. Michael** and **Stebbins**. He then returned to school work, to Monroe Catholic High, to serve there as principal from 1968–70. After that, for the years 1970–72, he was on the staff—salaried and under contract—of Mt. Edgecumbe, the Bureau of Indian Affairs boarding school in **Sitka**, as a counselor. One of the students attending the school at the time remembered him years later especially for his "gentle and patient ways." During those two years, he was also assistant pastor at Sitka's St. Gregory Nazianzen parish.

From Sitka, Father Gallagher moved to **Bethel** in 1972 to serve there as a counselor—again salaried and under contract—in the newly established Bethel Regional High School. He was among those who helped get the school ready for its opening. During his Bethel years, 1972–78, he also assisted regularly at Bethel's Immaculate Conception parish.

After spending a sabbatical year, 1978–79, updating his theology at the Weston Jesuit School of Theology in Cambridge, Massachusetts, Father Gallagher spent the following year in **Anchorage** ministering to Alaskan Natives. The year after that he was in Portland, Oregon, as Spiritual Director of the **Jesuit Volunteer Corps**. The year 1981–82 found him again in Fairbanks, at the Center for Theological Studies, where he helped prepare Alaskan Natives for the ministry. Then he was back once more at St. Michael and Stebbins for a year.

From 1983–86, Father Gallagher was stationed at St. Mary's Mission boarding school on the **Andreafsky** River. There he served as a counselor and chaplain for the students and the lay staff. For a number of his years at St. Mary's, he was also the Superior of the local Jesuits, and the pastor of St. Marys parish. The 1984–85 St. Mary's Yearbook was dedicated to him by the school's senior class. Though a busy man at St. Mary's Mission, he still found time to indulge in one of his favorite pastimes, that of taking long walks.

During the latter part of the year 1986, Father Gallagher served as the pastor of the **Kotzebue** parish.

For the years 1987–89, he was back in Bethel again, as assistant pastor. Following that, from 1989–91, he was visiting priest to **Alakanuk**, **Nunam Iqua**, **Marshall**, and **Russian Mission**.

At some point, while attending to those Central Yup'ik Eskimo villages in the Yukon-Kuskokwim Delta, Father Gallagher contracted a sickness, which was diagnosed as "Epstein-Barr." In January 1991, he found himself living with the Jesuit community at Bellarmine Preparatory in Tacoma. From there, he wrote to Father Louis L. **Renner**, S.J.:

> I am still progressing along this zigzag trail in "chronic-fatigue-syndrome" country. This has its own weather system, and is humbling and relentless in bringing one to recognize that good health is a pure gift. Also, that our "call" is precisely that, and I'm glad I was struck down in good front-line country among the Yup'ik people in the Deltas.

On August 15, 1999, Father Gallagher celebrated his golden jubilee as a Jesuit. On that occasion, the members of the Twenty-First Alaska State Legislature saw fit to recognize and honor him, and to express their "appreciation to Father Gallagher for his many years of dedication and service to urban and rural Alaskans."

After his recovery from his debilitating malady, Father Gallagher returned to Alaska, to Anchorage. During the years 1991–94, with Anchorage as his home base, he ministered as a member of the Archdiocesan Pastoral Visitation Team. As such, he traveled to various outlying cities, towns, and communities for weekend Masses. During his four years as "a circuit rider," he brought the Mass and Sacraments to places such as **Valdez**, **Cordova**, **Talkeetna**, **Homer**, **Soldotna**, **Kenai**, **Unalaska**, **Trapper Creek**, and Glennallen.

From 1994–97, Father Gallagher served as a voluntary chaplain, a pastoral minister, at Anchorage's old Alaska Native Hospital; and, from 1997–2002, in that same capacity, at Anchorage's new Alaska Native Medical Center. In the course of his long years in Alaska's Native schools and villages, he had come to know literally many hundreds of Alaskan Natives. As a chaplain in the Anchorage hospitals, he had occasion to meet, visit with, and minister to a great number of these, bringing them his gentle presence, the Mass, the Sacraments, the consolations of the Church. He prepared many for death, assisted at over 200 funerals, consoled many bereaved. He also spent much time with those coming to the hospital to visit the sick and dying there. "I do half of my work in the hallways," he told an interviewer. In addition to his hospital ministry, he also did, according to Father Theodore E. **Kestler**, S.J, General Superior of Jesus in Alaska at the time, "a very fine job in his outreach ministry to urban Natives." For a time, during the year 1995–96, Father Gallagher cared also for St. Michael's parish in **McGrath**.

Father Gallagher ended his ministry to Alaska Natives in the year 2002, when, under a new archbishop, a Director of Native Apostolates was appointed for the Archdiocese of Anchorage. That year, he moved to Fairbanks, there to have ready access to the archives of the Diocese of Fairbanks with a view to possibly doing some writing.

A mosaic of various quotes from some of Father Gallagher's writings reveals something about his spiritual, inner life and outlook: "Journey of Faith . . . this zigzag trail . . . we encounter merely one day at a time . . . a gradual sort of revelation, like lifting fog . . . darkness turns into light . . . the presence of God's loving Providence."

GALLANT, Monsignor G.(eorge) Edgar

He was the first man to be ordained to the Catholic priesthood in **Alaska**. He was the first Vicar General of the Diocese of **Juneau**. He was the first priest serving in Alaska to become a Domestic Prelate, a Monsignor. No priest in Alaska ever held station in one locale as long as he. At a height of 6′ 5″, he was a physically imposing man. The clopping of his big feet reverberated throughout the mission boarding school he founded and to which he devoted most of his priestly years. When he died, he was buried at the place of his origins, thousands of miles from his beloved Alaska.

George Edgar Gallant was born on March 17, 1894, on Prince Edward Island, Canada. As a young man searching for his vocation in life, he left his native land, crossed the American continent, and found what he was looking for when he reached the West Coast. At Mount Angel, Oregon, he was admitted into the Benedictine seminary. While

Msgr. G. Edgar Gallant, P.A. *LRC.*

studying there, for the Montana diocese, he spent several summers near **Haines**, Alaska, as time- and book-keeper at a fish cannery. There he heard an old Indian man singing Benediction hymns. Asked where he had learned the hymns, the man told Edgar that he had been taught them by one of the early priests in his area, but that no priest had come to his village for many years. Then and there, Edgar resolved to become a priest and to spend his life among the Native peoples of Alaska.

When Bishop Joseph R. **Crimont**, S.J., shortly after becoming Vicar Apostolic of Alaska in 1917, visited Mount Angel to interest seminarians in Alaska, Edgar volunteered and was accepted. On the successful completion of most of his studies, he was ordained a priest by Bishop Crimont in Juneau on Holy Saturday, March 30, 1918, at the age of only 24 years. This was the first ordination of a man to the Catholic priesthood in Alaska. Problems brought about by World War I and the possibility of Edgar's being drafted into the Canadian Army led to his being ordained somewhat earlier than would otherwise have been the case. He became a naturalized U.S. citizen in 1921.

After completing his studies, Father Gallant was entrusted with St. Mark's parish in **Skagway**. The tall, thin, young priest, at home with culture and expensive tastes, brought promise to the vicariate. His liking for the best in liturgy, music, and craftsmanship of every kind gradually endowed St.

Mark's Church and the school he founded with a distinctive touch of style and grace.

Ever interested in education, Father Gallant, soon after his arrival in Skagway, began to lay plans for a boarding school, in which especially the Native children of Southeastern Alaska would be educated. Resources for such a school were virtually non-existent, but Bishop Crimont did not hesitate to encourage him in his endeavor. "I have very much at heart the erection of a boarding school for Indian children of Southeastern Alaska," wrote Bishop Crimont to Father Gallant. "I commend your zeal. I pray that God may be with you in the great task of gathering funds to put up the building."

In 1930, when Bishop Crimont went to Rome for his *ad limina* visit, Father Gallant again accompanied him. He had accompanied him in 1925, when the bishop went to Rome for the canonization of St. Therese of Lisieux and on a pilgrimage to Lisieux. One evening on that 1930 trip, Father Gallant came into the lounge of the hotel where he was staying. A group of American tourists were at the moment looking for a fourth for a game of bridge and invited him to join them. After introductions, the game got underway. Father Gallant was asked where he was from and what he did there. He stressed his hope for a school for Native children of Alaska. Before the evening ended, one of the players, a certain Mr. John F. O'Dea of Canton, Ohio, drew Father Gallant aside and offered to donate $30,000 for the building of the school, on the condition that it be named for Pope Pius X in gratitude for business favors he had obtained through that saintly Pope's intercession. On August 30, 1931, the cornerstone of Pius X Mission in Skagway was blessed and laid. By December, the first unit, Crimont Hall, was furnished and ready for use. Father Gallant had a special gift for acquiring the necessary means to make good things happen. The school, staffed by the Sisters of St. **Ann**, began classes in the fall of 1932.

Given the man that Father Gallant was, and the key role he played in the school's coming into being, it was to be expected that the school and its programs would reflect his views and tastes. Music, liturgical and other, flourished at the school. He himself taught some music courses, and, at times, directed the school's orchestra and band. He was attracted to the art of weaving and installed looms at the mission. On these both he and the children wove items to sell to tourists visiting the mission. His artistry in creating and weaving liturgical vestments became well known. Much of his tastes and skills he owed to the Benedictines at Mount Angel.

Father Gallant was "the light and the heart" of Pius X Mission, though he was often absent on fund-raising trips. In 1944, he was away for an extended period of time, when he played a key role in getting the **Grey Nuns** of the Sacred Heart, whom he had contacted on a fund-raising tour, to go to **Kodiak** to operate Griffin Memorial Hospital there. He spent several months in Kodiak helping them get established.

Father Gallant's frequent, and sometimes prolonged, absences from Skagway caused misunderstandings and difficulties at times, especially for the mission staff. Had he directed the whole program with a less firm hand and given mission personnel a larger decision-making role, the occasional tensions would have been eased. Still, when he did return to the mission, he was hailed with delight by all. He made a point of being in Skagway every year for his birthday, turning March 17th into a festive occasion. He himself led the singing of "Oh, Danny Boy!" One of the Sisters found him a wonderful, generous priest, who "practically worked miracles" to keep the mission going.

On November 16, 1945, Pius X Mission suffered a great set-back, when fire destroyed Crimont Hall. No lives were lost, but Father Gallant had once again to embark on a major fund-raising and rebuilding phase. By March 19, 1946, a temporary chapel was ready enough for a Mass of Thanksgiving.

In 1951, Father Gallant became Vicar General of the newly created Diocese of Juneau. He continued, however, to be in charge of Pius X Mission and to reside in Skagway. The rural setting of Skagway enabled him to indulge his hobby of collecting ducks and geese to mount. Once he traveled to **Holy Cross Mission** to collect specimens he lacked. The varieties he gradually assembled became tourist attractions.

In 1956, to celebrate the 25th anniversary of the founding of Pius X Mission, and the upcoming 40th of his ordination to the priesthood, Father Gallant traveled to Europe to visit the most famous of the many religious shrines there. As a traveling companion he had with him Francis A. **Cowgill**, his competent and faithful assistant in Skagway during the 1950s. The two spent seven years together in Skagway.

In March 1958, Father Gallant became "Monsignor Gallant," having received the title of Domestic Prelate. Dermot **O'Flanagan**, Bishop of Juneau since July 9, 1951, obtained this honor for him in recognition of his achievements in Skagway and of the services rendered by him as Vicar General of the Juneau diocese. The following year, 1959, saw the end of Monsignor Gallant's long tenure in Skagway. In the late summer of that year he was appointed pastor of Holy Family parish in **Anchorage**.

Looking back years later upon the Father Gallant of Pius X Mission, some of those who then knew him paint the following portrait of him. "He welcomed all who were needy," according to Father Cowgill. "He could take a look at a child and see nothing wrong. There were tears in the eyes of children, when they called him 'Father.' He really was a father to so many children who knew no father." In the 1930s, when the mission boys were not admitted into the scout troop in town, he started the mission's own. One alumnus of the mission remembered him as one who "had a strong ruling, and you lived by the way he ruled, but he was honest and fair." Another one, Byron Mallot, who went on to become a prominent leader in Alaskan Native affairs, said of him: "Father Gallant was a personal inspiration figure to me. He gave me a sense that an individual can make a difference."

Monsignor Gallant served as pastor of Holy Family parish up until January 7, 1967. After that he was in residency there till almost the time of his death. He continued to serve as the Vicar General of the Diocese of Juneau until 1966, the year the Archdiocese of Anchorage was created. He was Vicar General of this latter diocese until 1970. In 1974, he retired to a nursing home in Beaverton, Oregon. On August 4, 1975, he died at the place where he had been born 81 years previously, Prince Edward Island, Canada, while on a final visit "home." The inscription on his gravestone reads: "Pioneer Priest of Alaska."

15, 16

Brother Carmelo Giordano, S.J. *JOPA-962.02.*

GIORDANO, Brother Carmelo, S.J.

He was the first Jesuit Lay Brother to set foot in **Alaska**. One historian described him as an "unusual personality, especially colorful." A fellow Jesuit missionary said of him, "He has become a regular and true Indian in his ways." He could neither read nor write his mother tongue; and yet, in the course of spending a little over two decades on the middle Yukon River, he became a fluent speaker of the Koyukon Athabaskan Indian language. In terms of acculturation, he was a man ahead of his time. His devotion to Mary the Mother of God found concrete expression in the form of a semi-ridiculous shrine he built in her honor.

Carmelo Giordano was born on November 1, 1860 in Sant' Anastasia near Naples, Italy. He entered the Society of Jesus on July 22, 1884, to become a Lay Brother. Two years later, he volunteered to serve on the missions in the American West—this in response to an appeal for missionaries made by Joseph M. **Cataldo**, S.J., Superior of the Rocky Mountain Mission, while on a recruitment tour in Europe. Brother Giordano's first American assignment, a short one, was to the mission at DeSmet, Idaho. On August 21, 1887, having entered Alaska, along with Jesuit Fathers Paschal **Tosi** and Aloysius A. **Ragaru**, by way of the Chilkoot Pass and the Yukon River, he arrived at Nuklukayet, today's **Tanana**. There he met Father Aloysius J. **Robaut**, S.J. The two spent most of the winter

1887–88 at Anvik. In February 1888, he accompanied Father Robaut downriver to Koserefsky, where he helped him establish **Holy Cross Mission**.

Brother Giordano remained in Alaska until 1909. Except for two years spent at Holy Cross, he spent all his Alaskan years at **Nulato**. There he served in many different capacities. His short, stocky, powerful body served him well as a general handyman, a jack-of-all-trades. He did the cooking, the baking, the gardening. He provided firewood for the mission stoves and fish and game for the table. He was said to be "a first class baker, also a great hunter." His first year at Nulato he helped Father Tosi put up a log church there.

After leaving Alaska, in 1909, Brother Giordano lived another 39 years in the Pacific Northwest. His declining years he spent in Port Townsend, Washington, living there in Manresa Hall, the Jesuit tertianship. In the course of those years, "manifesting a brilliant, retentive memory and an agile mind," he dictated his *"Memoirs of the Alaskan Mission,"* a lengthy, colorful account of his early years in Alaska. During those years, too, he built "a massive and ugly stone shrine" to the Mother of God. He collected crutches to hang above it as proof of miracles wrought there.

In 1969, Father Segundo **Llorente**, S.J., wrote, concerning Brother Giordano: "He was sent to the States in the hope that he would become 'white' again; for he had assimilated the native culture to the point that it was hard to tell him from the natives. Today that is the ideal; then it was considered less proper."

Brother Giordano died at the age of 88 years, in Port Townsend, on May 1, 1948. It is said that up to his last days he kept saying his prayers in Koyukon. He lies buried in the Jesuit cemetery at Mount St. Michael's, Spokane.

176

GLEESON, Bishop Francis D., S.J.

He was the last Vicar Apostolic of all **Alaska**. He was the first Ordinary of the Diocese of **Fairbanks**. Catholic schools were a major concern of his, as was the rebuilding and the replacing of rundown mission structures. During his episcopate, the Church

Bishop Francis D. Gleeson, S.J. *DFA.*

in Alaska moved from being primarily a mission territory into being a mature Church consisting of an archdiocese and two dioceses. His death, at the venerable age of eighty-eight years, prompted the Cardinal Prefect of the Propagation of the Faith in Rome to write concerning him, "We have an especially happy memory of the great missionary accomplishments of this excellent bishop." The 13th Alaska State Legislature described him as "a recognized leader and builder of the Catholic Faith in Alaska." In the annals of the North, he has merited an honorable place.

Francis Doyle Gleeson was born in Carrollton, Missouri, on January 17, 1895. While he was still a little boy, the family moved to Yakima, Washington, where he attended St. Joseph's Academy, taught by the Sisters of Providence, and the Jesuit-staffed high school named, rather grandiloquently, Marquette College. After attending Gonzaga High School in Spokane, Washington, during the year 1911–12, he entered Sacred Heart Novitiate, the novitiate of the California Province of the Society of Jesus at Los Gatos, California, on July 15, 1912. His two-year noviceship completed, he took the three simple vows of poverty, chastity and obedience, and then spent three additional years at Los Gatos studying the classics and humanities. In 1917, he went on to Mount St. Michael's in Spokane for three years of philosophical studies. While at Mount St. Michael's, he frequently helped with the cooking. For a time, too, he was one of the engravers of headstones marking the burial sites of deceased Jesuits in Mount St. Michael's Cemetery.

From 1920–23, Gleeson taught Latin, mathematics, and Religion at Seattle Preparatory in Seattle, Washington. He also directed the school's orchestra. He himself sang well. He loved classroom teaching and related well to his young charges.

For his four years of theological studies, Gleeson was sent to Oña, Spain. He was ordained a priest there on July 29, 1926. After making his tertianship at Port Townsend, Washington, during the year 1927–28, Father Gleeson was assigned to the newly opened Bellarmine Preparatory in Tacoma, Washington. There he was a teacher and, from 1933–39, the Father Rector of the Jesuit community. As Father Rector, he was a real father to a community almost totally without resources. To help support it, he procured cows and helped with the milking. He routinely prepared breakfast, and cooked Italian dinners on Sundays. As a cook he was known for his cream puffs—and for "dirtying every pot and pan in the house." He cooked throughout his long life, finding in the kitchen—as well as at the pinochle table—temporary relief from the serious responsibilities his various offices placed upon him. In June 1977, Bellarmine Preparatory bestowed on Father Gleeson, by that time Bishop Gleeson, its St. Robert Bellarmine Award "for his pioneer work as a teacher and Rector at Bellarmine from 1928–1939." The citation recognized also his "untiring zeal on the missions in Alaska, where he begged and borrowed money and built a mission school system throughout Alaska."

On January 27, 1939, Father Gleeson became Rector of St. Francis Xavier Novitiate at Sheridan, Oregon. There, it is said, "he ran a peaceful ship, taught the classics and specialized in Shakespeare." From Sheridan, Father Gleeson went on to serve as pastor of St. Stanislaus parish in Lewiston, Idaho, from 1942–47, and as Superior of St. Mary's Mission, Omak, Washington, from 1947–48. While at Omak, without his knowing it at the time, he was appointed, on January 8, 1948, to replace Bishop Walter J. **Fitzgerald**, S.J., as Vicar Apostolic of Alaska. On February 8, 1948, he sent the following telegram to Father Hugh J. Geary, S.J., the Father Socius of the Oregon Province: "Received telegram from Denver Register congratulating on appointment and asking for biographical data. Is this a joke or should I take it seriously? F. Gleeson." It was no joke. On April 5, 1948, in St. Aloysius Church, Spokane, Francis Doyle Gleeson was consecrated a bishop; and, on May 30, 1948, in **Juneau**, installed as the third Vicar Apostolic of Alaska. On his coat of arms, he had for his motto: *Adveniat Regnum Tuum* ("Thy Kingdom Come").

As Vicar Apostolic of Alaska, Bishop Gleeson made Juneau his headquarters, until 1951, when, upon the establishment of the Diocese of Juneau, on June 23, 1951, he moved to Fairbanks. In 1962, when the Diocese of Fairbanks was established, on August 8th, he became its first Ordinary. He was installed as such on February 21, 1963. On November 30, 1968, he was succeeded by Bishop Robert L. **Whelan**, S.J., and began what turned out to be a period of 15 years of retirement.

During his retirement years, Bishop Gleeson lived in what was then still generally known as the "Bishop's Residence," and what, as of the year 2004, was serving as the Diocese of Fairbanks chancery building. Never having lost his love for classroom teaching, he, soon after retiring, taught Spanish at Monroe Catholic High for a semester. Routinely he cooked the Sunday meals for the community living at the Bishop's Residence. Until his last years, he was active in local affairs.

Bishop Gleeson died, as he had lived, quietly and peacefully, in Fairbanks Memorial Hospital, on April 30, 1983. He lies buried in the Fairbanks Birch Hill Cemetery.

The legacy of Bishop Gleeson—a man known for his one-liners, for his taciturnity, for being a man "short on words and correspondence, but long on action"—is considerable. It was he who is given credit for bringing back to life in the modern Church, on a national scale, the permanent diaconate, which is now so much a part also of the Diocese of Fairbanks. His concern for Catholic education in northern Alaska was such that, despite formidable difficulties and lack of funds, the two mission boarding schools, St. Mary's on the **Andreafsky** River and **Copper Valley School**, came into being. While he was Bishop of Fairbanks, he had, at one time, four priests on the faculty of the University of Alaska–Fairbanks. He supported the expanded use of airplanes by missionaries as pilots. He gave Father James E. **Poole**, S.J., the green light to proceed with plans to establish the Catholic radio station **KNOM** in **Nome**. He saw to it that many rundown mission buildings were upgraded or replaced, and that Sacred Heart Cathedral and the diocesan chancery building were constructed. During Bishop Gleeson's term in office, the **Jesuit Volunteer Corps** flourished in Alaska. With his full consent, Father Segundo **Llorente**, S.J., served as District Representative in the Alaska State Legislature for two terms; and, likewise with his full consent, priests played a major supportive role, when Alaska Natives working in the Bristol Bay canneries encountered union and labor difficulties. After attending the Sessions of the Second Vatican Council, Bishop Gleeson knew well the meaning of the word *aggiornamento*.

In the year 2004, lstBooks in Bloomington, Indiana, published *Gleeson, The Last Vicar Apostolic of All of Alaska: The First Bishop of Fairbanks*, a biography of Bishop Gleeson written by Sister Carol Louise Hiller, O.P.

42, 176

GLENNALLEN

Glennallen is located at the junction of the Glenn and Richardson Highways, in the Copper River Basin. The name is derived from the combined last names of Capt. Edwin F. Glenn and Lt. Henry T. Allen, both members of the U.S. Army, and both leaders of explorations in the Copper River Region in the late 1800s. By that time, the Russian Orthodox Church had already established itself in that part of **Alaska**, among the Ahtna Athabaskan Indians. A Protestant group, Central Alaska Missions, started to reach out to the people there in 1937. The general area began to take on major importance, when the rough roads, carved out by gold-seekers, traders and homesteaders, were upgraded and linked with the Alcan Highway system during World War II. In 1967, Glennallen's population numbered 169; in the year 2000, 554.

What is today Holy Family parish in Glennallen began as a mission of the Vicariate of Alaska right around 1950. It was founded by Father John R. **Buchanan**, S.J., who, in 1952, built a "highway chapel" along the Richardson Highway, just south of the junction of the Richardson and Glenn High-

Holy Family Church, Glennallen.
Photo by Annemiek J. Brunklaus.

ways. Up to 1955, he visited this mission out of **Tok**. After **Copper Valley School** came into being, in 1956, that chapel soon ceased to be Holy Family Mission's place of worship. Until the school closed, in 1971, Holy Family had as its "church" the chapel at the school, and was served by priests stationed at the school: by Father Buchanan, until 1958; by Father James C. **Spils**, S.J., from 1958–66, and by Father Thomas N. **Gallagher**, S.J., during the year 1966–67.

In 1966, Copper Valley School and the surrounding area were absorbed into the newly erected Archdiocese of **Anchorage**. On September 15, 1967, Holy Family Mission at Glennallen became an outlying parish of the new archdiocese, and Father Harold J. **Greif**, S.J., was appointed its first pastor. As such, he served from 1967–69. He was succeeded by Father Richard B. **Saudis**, pastor of Holy Family for one year. Father **Paul B. Mueller**, S.J., living at the school, was Holy Family's pastor for the year 1970–71, the last year the Holy Family parishioners were cared for in the Copper Valley School chapel.

The year 1971, the year Copper Valley School closed, brought with it various questions related to the sustaining of parish life at Glennallen. Among them: where to hold worship services? A donated mobile home proved to be the temporary answer. This was already in place amid a cluster of homes along the Glenn Highway near the junction, and soon amply furnished with various items from the closed school. It served well enough as a place of worship and parish center for a while. It was subsequently moved to a more prominent location near Glennallen's American Legion Hall and somewhat enlarged and enhanced.

The structure serving as Holy Family Church as of the year 2004 was formerly the Glennallen post office. After a new post office came into being, the old one became the property of Harry Heintz, who donated it to the Catholic Church. In 1972, the building was moved to a new site and, with the help of a generous grant from the Catholic Church Extension Society, transformed into "a church." It was further modified in 1988. About that same year, a building that had served first as a surveyor's office, then as an automotive parts shop, was donated to the Church by Edward McElligot. Relocated next to the church and remodeled, the building became Holy Family's Fellowship Hall and Education Center.

Father Edward J. Stirling, C.S.Sp., was in Glennallen during the year 1971–72. Father Thomas E. Power, a priest from England, was there during the year 1972–73, then served as administrator of the parish from 1974–78. Father Ernest H. **Muellerliele** was administrator during the year 1973–74.

During the early 1970s, Father Eugene P. **Burns**, S.J., visited Holy Family from time to time out of **Valdez**. Sisters of St. **Ann**, Ida Brasseur and Margaret Cantwell, both of whom were known in the Glennallen area because of their years at Copper Valley School, accompanied him on their initial visits to the parish. The Sisters formed the "Rural Ministry" team, organized in 1973 to help serve "priestless parishes" in the Archdiocese of Anchorage. In October 1973, Sister Ida was installed in Glennallen as Extraordinary Minister of the Eucharist.

From 1978–83, Father Urban M. **Bates**, O.P., was Holy Family's administrator; Father Michael Shields the same, from 1983–87; Father **Gerard T. Ryan**, C.S.Sp., for the year 1987–88.

After the year 1988, no priests are listed as either residing in Glennallen or as administrators of its Holy Family parish. For over a decade, it was only visited from time to time by various priests stationed elsewhere, mostly in Anchorage. Father Gerald O. Brunet, O.M.I., began serving Holy Family, out of Anchorage, in the year 2001.

Sister Patricia Oliver, R.S.M., lived in Glennallen and served Holy Family, as "Pastoral Associate," from 1986–90. From 1991–96, Sister Dee Marie Reeder, S.N.J.M., was Holy Family's "Pastoral Administrator," as was Mrs. Tami Jindra, from 1996–2001.

15

GORGES, Father Peter F.

Peter F. Gorges was born in the Bronx, New York City, on August 27, 1935, and raised there, receiving 16 years of Catholic schooling. When he was 23 years old, he was drafted into the U.S. Army. Before being drafted, he was employed as an auditor by the Bowery Savings Bank, in New York City.

Father Peter F. Gorges. *LRC.*

While he was in the Army, he looked forward to the end of his two years in the military, so that he could return to his position at the bank. After his basic training and a stint at the Army Administration School at Fort Dix, New Jersey, in recognition of his long years of Catholic schooling, he was appointed a Catholic Chaplain's Assistant. As such, he arrived in **Anchorage, Alaska,** on July 5, 1959. However, after a short stay at Fort Richardson there, he was sent to Wildwood Station, near **Kenai.**

On weekends, when Father Arnold L. **Custer,** S.J., pastor of **Seward**'s Sacred Heart parish at the time, came to Wildwood Station, PFC Gorges assisted him both at the post and in the civilian community. During the week, he took care of the small Quonset hut chapel building and did secretarial work for the Army Protestant chaplain. He found this tour of duty to be "an interesting challenge." He was impressed by Father Custer and the Catholic worship community.

In February 1960, PFC Gorges was assigned back to Anchorage. There he talked to Dermot **O'Flanagan,** Bishop of **Juneau** at the time, about studying to become a priest in Alaska. On being discharged from the Army, he returned to New York City; and, in September 1961, began seminary studies in Haverhill, Massachusetts. After one year there, he began six years of major seminary studies at St. John's Seminary in Boston.

In June 1967, seminarian Gorges went to Juneau, where he was ordained a deacon by Bishop O'Flanagan for the Diocese of Juneau. That summer, he lived in the St. Peter's parish rectory in **Douglas,** and at the Cathedral rectory in Juneau. He spent a weekend in **Skagway** and two weeks in **Ketchikan.** During his "missionary time" in **Hoonah,** he brought about a stirring up of the local Catholic community and the making of contacts. This effort led eventually to the construction of Sacred Heart Catholic Church in the summer of 1971. Moving around from place to place, as he did, gave him an opportunity "to see the diocese."

After completing a final year of preparation for the priesthood in Boston, Peter Gorges was ordained a priest in Boston's Holy Cross Cathedral, on May 29, 1968, by Richard Cardinal Cushing. When a priest in his Bronx parish asked him why he wanted to become a priest, he told him: "I want to help the people get close to God, and I think I can do that. I had some practice, courtesy of the U.S. Army."

Father Gorges' first assignment as a priest was that of assistant to Father James F. **Miller** at the Cathedral of the Nativity of the Blessed Virgin Mary in Juneau. In Father Miller, he found "a good mentor," and a good friend, who gave him "a lot of good practical experience in being an Alaskan priest." While on the Juneau assignment, Father Gorges got out to Hoonah, Pelican and Gustavus about once a month.

After that first year in Juneau, Father Gorges was appointed pastor of St. Rose of Lima parish, in **Wrangell,** and visiting priest to its dependent mission, St. Catherine of Siena, in **Petersburg.** He made Wrangell his main base. As pastor of its parish, he was also Catholic chaplain to the nearby Wrangell Institute, a Bureau of Indian Affairs school for students not yet ready for high school. Along with several volunteers, he taught catechism one night a week at Wrangell Institute, and offered early Sunday morning Mass there. On Sunday afternoons, he flew over to Petersburg, where he offered Mass, after which he stayed on for meetings, for catechism classes, bookkeeping, and the like, until Monday night, when he took the ferry back to Wrangell.

"I was very content," Father Gorges wrote of his Wrangell-Petersburg years, "enjoying not only the church community, but also the secular community." He found using the brand new parish hall that had just been completed in Wrangell "exciting." He was active in the Wrangell Chamber of Commerce, and even did some Little League umpiring. Meanwhile, he earned his private pilot's license, and bought a 16-foot skiff. He got "quite proficient at running and trailering the skiff during the next 15 years."

In 1972, Father Gorges became the first pastor of the newly erected St. Paul the Apostle parish, located in the Mendenhall Valley near Juneau. A church, built by Father David A. **Melbourne** in 1962, awaited him, as well as a full-time administrator, who had been appointed the year before the church was built. For a decade, the Mendenhall area had been served as a dependent mission of Juneau's Cathedral parish.

Father Gorges found his assignment as pastor of the rapidly growing St. Paul the Apostle parish quite a challenge. "In the course of nine years," he wrote,

> we went from two weekend Masses to four. We built a parish hall; we exchanged the mobile-home rectory for a nice new home, paved the parking lot, put in some landscaping, got the valley senior center in, and went on city water. The valley grew up around us, with the brand new Nugget Mall, and the building of Mendenhall Mall, and lots of houses. The parish community was great.

While pastor of St. Paul's, Father Gorges was active in the Charismatic Prayer Group, prison ministry, ecumenical activities, catechetical work, "Kid's Day" activities at the **Shrine** of St. Therese, and hospital ministry. In 1979, he was part of a group from Juneau that went to Rome to attend the Pontifical Mass in St. Peter's Basilica during which Pope John Paul II ordained Michael H. **Kenny**, among others, a bishop. It was while on that trip that Father Gorges "caught the international travel bug."

In February 1981, Father Gorges, having been replaced as pastor of St. Paul's by Msgr. Charles A. **Kekumano**, went to Rome to do the Vatican II Update course at the North American College. "It was a delightful spring," he recalled years later. Highlights of that trip abroad for him were the visit he and his classmates had with the pope in his apartment, a class 10-day trip to the Holy Land, and some overnight visits to Venice and Assisi.

Upon his return to Alaska, Father Gorges was reassigned to the parishes in Wrangell and Petersburg. By this time, St. Catherine of Siena in Petersburg, too, was a full-fledged parish. Accordingly, he divided his time equally between the two, spending two weeks in the one, then two weeks in the other. He also routinely made overnight visits to the dependent mission stations of Kake and the Rowan Bay Logging Camp to offer Mass there.

Being a promoter of Catholic Charismatic Prayer groups, Father Gorges was happy to find such a group, small, but strong, in Wrangell. He encouraged such groups in whatever parish he found himself. From 1975 through 1984, he attended the annual Catholic Charismatic Priests' Retreats in Steubenville, Ohio. From 1975 until his retirement, he was liaison for the bishop of Juneau to the National Catholic Charismatic Renewal. One summer, he spent his vacation traveling around the Pacific Northwest with a Catholic evangelist doing Healing Masses.

In Petersburg, Father Gorges was able, for the first time, to get involved with the Petersburg community at large. Among other things, he became a member of the Ecumenical Pastors Association. As such, he was part of its music group. He also attended the weekly men's prayer breakfast. Every summer, he took part in Petersburg's Ecumenical Summer Vacation Bible School. Yet, preoccupied as he was with all his priestly duties and related commitments, he found time to relax, time to go fishing. How could he not?—with "some of the best fishing in Southeast Alaska only a short skiff ride from the Petersburg boat launching lot."

In January 1986, Father Gorges became pastor of Holy Name parish in Ketchikan, and visiting priest, once a month, to Metlakatla. For most of the next two years he was alone in Ketchikan. There he found having a Catholic school and a brand new church "a delight." He happily spent time each week with the children in their classrooms. He was again part of "a great ecumenical pastors' group." He enjoyed hiking Ketchikan's trails and driving its roads. A highlight for him during his years in Ketchikan occurred in the spring of 1987, when the Ketchikan Catholic Charismatic Prayer group hosted the 13th Alaska State Charismatic Conference.

In October 1988, Father Gorges was appointed Rector of Juneau's Cathedral parish. It took him a while "to fit into the on-going operation of the diocese and parish." But, having been endowed with a nature wholly positive and ever optimistic in outlook, fit in he did. In Juneau, too, he was in his element. Salt water, teeming with all kinds of fish, was just out the front door. He upgraded his fishing outfit, replacing his little skiff with an 18-foot fiberglass C-Dory. And, in Juneau, he had the support of an active Charismatic Prayer group and of an active ecumenical pastors' group. Monthly trips to Pelican allowed him to keep a foot in rural Alaska. "Every priest in a big city parish," he felt, "should have some tiny Catholic community somewhere to know and love."

During his years as Rector of the Cathedral parish, Father Gorges saw the old St. Ann's School building come down and the new St. Ann's Parish Center, with its large hall, meeting rooms, storerooms, and a Director of Religious Education office, go up. This, completed in 1994, was subsequently called Cathedral Parish Hall. By the time his tenure in Juneau was at an end, he had everything at the Cathedral parish "running smoothly," and the St. Ann's Center debt paid off.

By May, 1997, Father Gorges was beginning to experience the "grandfather priest syndrome," as he officiated at the weddings of those whom he had baptized, and celebrated the 25th anniversaries of people whose weddings he had performed. He was by now 62 years old, ready for his last assignment as a full-time active parish priest.

On July 1, 1999, Father Gorges became pastor of St. Gregory Nazianzen parish in **Sitka**. Two years later, in 2001, he retired. "Retirement" meant for him: filling in for priests, when his calendar was empty; leading tours once or twice a year; visiting friends and relatives; and getting around to places and events that he could not squeeze into his schedule, when he was a pastor. The filling in for priests he did gratis, asking only for the round trip ticket. His one formally assigned position in the diocese remained that of Director of the Deacon Formation Program.

As of the year 2004, Father Gorges—"with the blessing of the bishop, and by the grace of the resident pastor"—was making an apartment in the Sitka rectory his home. By then, he had hiked the Chilkoot Trail, and joined the "Pioneers of Alaska." He continued his habit of taking a daily walk and going on wilderness backpacking trips. He continued to enjoy boating and fishing as much as ever. He ended his short autobiographical sketch with, "Life is good!"

GREIF, Father Harold J., S.J.

"Were we to seek apt symbols for Father Greif," begins the obituary by Father Neill R. Meany, S.J., "we might come up with a cross, a happy face, and a treble clef." Father Meany then goes on to talk about "this grand old man of faith, with an affable manner, a wide smile, and a soul full of music and joy."

Harold J. Greif was born in Walla Walla, Washington, on February 18, 1900. He attended grade schools in Uniontown, Washington, and Jesuit high schools in Missoula, Montana, and Spokane, Washington, before going on to collegiate studies at Creighton in Omaha, Nebraska; Loyola in Chicago; and St. Benedict's in Atchison, Kansas.

Born into a music-oriented family (his father insisted that all the children play some musical instrument), Harold chose the piano. Throughout his high school and college days, he played in combos and dance bands. He went on to become an accomplished professional musician, playing in some of the foremost theaters in Spokane, Seattle, and, finally in Chicago. At times, he played background music on the piano and organ for silent movies.

Finding the world of the professional musician too fraught with temptation, Harold entered the Jesuit novitiate at Los Gatos, California, on September 2, 1928. During his years of Jesuit training, he did some teaching at Seattle Preparatory School. He was ordained a priest in San Francisco on June 27, 1940. For the rest of his life, he was known to one and all simply as "Father Greif"; and, for the rest of his life, he was rarely seen not wearing the Roman collar.

Father Greif spent the year 1941–42 at Port Townsend, Washington, making his tertianship. Soon thereafter, he was appointed a chaplain in the U.S. Army. For several years he, and his accordion, served in the South Pacific. Whenever possible, he kept a light bulb burning in the accordion case to protect the instrument against the extreme humidity of the South Pacific. After leaving the Army in 1946, he taught for two years at Bellarmine Preparatory School in Tacoma, Washington.

Father Greif's missionary career in **Alaska** began in 1948. He was to devote the remaining 35 fully active years of his life to the Alaskan missions. He was stationed successively at Holy Cross, 1948–52;

Dillingham, 1952–67; Copper Valley School, 1967–69; and Nome, 1969–83. In all of these places he ministered enthusiastically and untiringly to all in his care, whether they were Native or white, old or young, well or poorly educated. To enable him to reach more readily people belonging to the Russian Orthodox Church in the Dillingham area, he spent several months at Fordham University's Eastern Rite Center to learn how to celebrate the Eastern Liturgy. It can be said of him without reservation that he was wholly "a people's priest." When criticized sometimes for having an occasional beer in the village tavern with some of the men, he asked how else might he meet and get to know certain members of his flock.

For most of Father Greif's years in Alaska, first Dillingham, then Nome, became the scene and home base for his priestly ministrations. He did much work in these two towns, but he also spent a great deal of time on the move as an itinerant missionary to outlying villages, military posts, canneries, and settlements. Living out of a suitcase, he always found a ready welcome and lodging in private homes, at military barracks, in canneries, and roadhouses. Places such as these served him also as impromptu "chapels" or "churches." In the portable Mass kit he always had with him, he carried everything needed for divine services or priestly ministries.

Father Greif spent 16 years in the Dillingham–Bristol Bay area. The impression he made on people was lasting. In 1982, the people there arranged for him to "ta-ke a sen-ti-men-tal jour-ney" to his old mission country. He touched down at various towns and villages, where friends and one-time parishioners put on receptions for their much-loved former pastor. The biggest reception was held at the Senior Citizens Center in Dillingham. Over 150 attended a potluck dinner put on in his honor. With his famous "squeeze box," his accordion, and a turn at the piano keyboard, he was a big hit.

In 1969, after two years at Copper Valley School, where he served as Spiritual Father and student counselor, Father Greif was appointed assistant pastor of St. Joseph's parish in Nome. However, just as Dillingham, so Nome, too, was not only the scene of his pastoral ministry, but also the hub out of which he "spoked" to various Seward Peninsula–Bering

On the steps of his Nome bungalow residence, Father Harold J. Greif, S.J., with suitcase and Mass kit, and dressed for whatever extreme cold he might encounter, is ready to fly off to visit some of his remote mission stations. *DFA.*

Strait area villages. Out of Nome he visited such far-flung places as Gambell and Savoonga on St. Lawrence Island, Teller, Wales, Port Clarence, Shishmaref, and Ignaluk on Little Diomede Island.

When Father Greif first started to visit the Little Diomede Inupiat Eskimos—people with names like Oomiak, Ahkinga, Kaputuk, Okpealuk, Iyapana, Ahkvaluk—some of them still lived in the traditional semi-subterranean houses built into the boulder-strewn slope and entered through a hole in the floor after one had crawled through a long, narrow tunnel. Those houses were heated with seal oil burned in stone or metal shallow, tray-like lamps. By the mid-1970s, most of the people were living in frame houses built above ground—rather above the rocky surface, for there is no ground at the Little Diomede village site. These newer houses had electricity and were heated with conventional oil stoves. Whale, walrus, seal meat were, and continue to be, staples in the Diomeder's diet. Concerning his personal taste for Diomede fare, Father Greif wrote shortly after he began visiting the island: "Christina Kunayak sent over to my little house a dish of diced walrus flipper in a heavy gravy, and it was delicious. The meat, however, has a fishy taste, and while there have been times I was glad to get it, I really wouldn't order it in a restaurant."

Father Louis L. **Renner**, S.J., was on Little Diomede for a month in the summer of 1975. He found Father Greif a hard act to follow. One of the small Diomede boys said to him, "Wish you Father Greif. Father Greif a lot funner [*sic*]."

When in Nome, Father Greif was busy carrying out the routine duties assigned an assistant pastor. He also spent much time visiting the sick in the hospital and the people in their homes. His cheerful smile and consoling, reassuring words brightened the lives of many and endeared him to all.

By 1983, the 83-year-old Father Greif had spent 14 years in Nome and that general area of Alaska. It seemed both to him and to his Superiors that the time had come for him to retire from so demanding an active ministry. He was assigned to Spokane, there, in keeping with his years and strength, to continue a ministry to the sick and elderly. "I'm not retiring," he told a Nome reporter interviewing him. "I'm just going on to an easier job where I won't have to work too hard. I don't want to get to the point, where I can't dance any more."

In that same interview, Father Greif expressed some personal views:

> The style of life I have is based on the Ten Commandments and the law of love. God loves everyone until you conk out, so you try to fit into God's plan for humanity. In my work, wherever there are people, that's where I belong. I don't care whether people belong to the Church or not. My business is to be with them. I have hardly ever been repelled. The attention you give people comes back to you. People are lonely. I'm lonely too. So you visit them—up to the last breath.

Of Nome, his last station in Alaska, Father Greif said: "I've been here 14 years. It's good to have come up here last; it's a good place to leave. It leaves good impressions. This is a very friendly place."

Before Father Greif left Nome, after a 35-year love affair with Alaska and its people, the Bering Sea Lions Club sponsored a farewell party in the Nome Armory for him. They cooked up a banquet of chicken, potato salad, and all the trimmings. Just about all in town turned out for the occasion. They had quite a laugh as they watched him pretend to hobble to the fancy rocking chair set out for him in the middle of the floor.

For his long years of service to the Church, and to the State of Alaska and its people, Father Greif received many expressions of gratitude. From national, state, and city officials came messages thanking him. "Father Greif," read the message from Ronald Reagan, "Nancy and I are delighted to send our heartfelt congratulations on your retirement. Throughout a lifetime of dedication to God, country and your fellow man, you have served the people of Alaska with all your heart. May the years ahead be happy ones. God bless and keep you."

After Father Greif retired to Spokane, "he was missed very much by the people of Nome and the surrounding villages," in the words of Alaska State Representative from Nome Richard Foster. Foster, owner of Nome-based Foster Aviation, considered it an honor and a privilege to fly "a very dear friend," Father Greif—gratis, of course—to his remote mission stations. Along with the people of Nome and the outlying villages, Foster was deeply saddened, when word of the death of Father Greif, "this gentle, caring person," reached him. Father Greif had died quietly in the Jesuit Infirmary at Gonzaga University on October 28, 1991.

In March 1992, the Seventeenth Alaska Legislature issued an *In Memoriam* citation in memory of Father Greif. The citation bears the seals of the State of Alaska and of the State Legislature. It is signed by the Speaker of the House and the President of the Senate. It was requested by nine Senators and nine Representatives. Representative Foster was the prime mover behind the citation, which ends:

> The memory of his smile, his music and his teachings lives on. Those who knew him remember Father Greif's passion for spinning a tale, sitting down to a game of cribbage, or just visiting friends. For Father Greif there were many friends and all of them will miss him dearly. The Seventeenth Alaska Legislature honors the memory of this fine gentleman. Father Harold Greif will always be remembered for his enormous contributions to others. May he rest in peace.

Father Greif lies buried in the Jesuit cemetery at Mount St. Michael's, Spokane.

GREY NUNS

In the fall of 1944, the **Kodiak** City Council contacted Joseph R. **Crimont**, S.J., Vicar Apostolic of **Alaska** at the time, about getting some Sisters to take over Kodiak's Griffin Memorial Hospital, since the city fathers were having considerable trouble running it. Father G. Edgar **Gallant** was delegated by Bishop Crimont to try to find some Sisters for Kodiak. He succeeded in securing the hearty cooperation of the Grey Nuns of the Sacred Heart from Philadelphia, Pennsylvania. On November 6, 1944, Father Gallant and five Nuns arrived at Kodiak. The first five were: Sister Mary Monica (Superioress), Sister St. Hilary (Assistant), Sister Mary Madeleine of the Sacred Heart, Sister Mary Leo, and Sister John Berchmans. On September 3, 1945, Sister Mary Madeleine was replaced by Sister Mary of Lourdes. The Nuns officially took possession of Griffin Memorial Hospital at midnight November 10–11, 1944. Sister St. Hilary was in Kodiak till 1969.

On May 24, 1946, Father Louis B. **Fink**, S. J., arrived in Kodiak. He gave "great credit" to Father Gallant "for his zealous labors in getting the good Nuns established." Regarding them, he wrote,

At first there was considerable feeling against the Catholic resurgence on Kodiak, but the traditional charity, zeal, and discretion of the Nuns have practically eliminated such prejudice or hostility. The work of the Nuns has effected wonders in aiding the efforts of the respective pastors. Nor were the Nuns without their trials and crosses from the very beginning: leaks in roof, broken water pipes, defective equipment— enough to make even stout hearts falter!

But the Nuns did not falter. With professional competency and religious dedication they ran the hospital; and, by June 1946, they had "organized and conducted Catechism classes for the local children, grouped according to age, with some twenty under instruction." The classes were conducted three times a week in the Nuns' quarters in the hospital. By 1948, there were between 20 and 30 children attending these classes every week.

By August 1953, the Kodiak parish, now under the pastoral care of Father Raymond L. **Talbott**, S.J., had a newly remodeled building that, in addition to giving it more worship space, gave it also classroom space. Accordingly, with permission given by Der-

1944 PHOTO OF THE FIRST GREY NUNS IN KODIAK
Sr. Mary Leo, Sr. St. Hillary, Sr. John Berchmans
Sr. Mary Monica and Sr. Madeline of the S. H.
Courtesy of Sister Diane Bardol, G.N.S.H.

mot **O'Flanagan**, Bishop of **Juneau**, in a letter dated August 10, 1954, the parish opened a parochial school in September of that year. A Grey Nun taught the first grade and Father Talbott the second and third.

Teachers for the school year 1961–62 were Sisters St. Ambrose, Mary Carmel, and Paula Marie; and for the year 1964–65 Sisters Mary Marcella, Mary Jude, St. Louis, and Joan Patricia.

During the school year 1966–67, the following Grey Nuns were teaching in the school: Sister M. Marcella, principal and third and fourth grades teacher; Sister Joan Patricia, seventh and eighth grades teacher; Sister Margaret Ann, fifth and sixth grades teacher; and Sister St. Louis, first and second grades teacher. Regarding Sister St. Louis, Father Talbott wrote to Bishop O'Flanagan, "Sister St. Louis is marvelous with the first and second graders."

On May 7, 1968, a milestone in the history of the

Kodiak parish was reached, when, on that day, its school's new four-classroom and gym addition was dedicated and blessed. Sister Diane Bardol's involvement with the school began in 1970. For almost 22 years, she was its principal. Still active in Kodiak as Director of Religious Education in the year 2003, she wrote, in a letter to Father Louis L. **Renner**, S.J., dated May 19, 2003, regarding the new addition:

> An interesting fact is that the bulk of the money needed for the four-room addition came from Margaret Von Scheele's estate. The interesting feature is that Mrs. Von Scheele was the leader of the opposition to the Sisters' taking the hospital. Obviously there was a conversion. She came into the Church and remained a faithful friend, leaving her estate to the Grey Nuns.

After 1965, the Nuns teaching at the school no longer lived at the hospital. Instead, they lived in a mobile home set up in the lot next to the hospital. This gave them a greater sense of community as a teaching body.

In April 1969, the Grey Nuns moved from the old to the new hospital, now named Kodiak Island Hospital. On May 15, 1978, having no longer sufficient personnel to staff it, they left the hospital to the care of the Lutheran Hospitals and Homes Society of America. The Grey Nuns never actually owned the hospital as their property.

The 40th anniversary of the Grey Nuns' arrival in Kodiak and the 30th anniversary of the opening of St. Mary's grammar school were celebrated in 1984. Three of the Nuns still in Kodiak were schoolteachers: Sisters Diane Bardol, Ann McKee, and Margaret Ann Silvey. Sister Margaret Ann spent a total of 29 years in Kodiak. In January 2001, two Grey Nuns came to Kodiak to do work other than in the school. Sister Barbara Harrington came to work with the Hispanic and immigrant communities, and Sister Carol Bartol came to do parish ministry. As of the year 2004, Sisters Diane and Carol were the two Grey Nuns still in Kodiak.

15

GURR, Father John E., S.J.

He was a Doctor of Philosophy, and a professor of philosophy. He taught Jesuit seminarians and university lay students metaphysics. He taught Inupi-

Father John E. Gurr, S.J.
JOPA-1065.05.

at and Central Yup'ik Eskimo children the rudiments of the Catholic Faith. A cheerful, open, sociable priest, he addressed all as "friend." "You couldn't match him," said one of them, "as a person, an educator, and a gentleman." He loved to travel **Alaska**'s highways and byways. Consequently, he knew Alaska from its southern Panhandle to its arctic coast. Setting out to write a history of the Catholic Church in Alaska, he spent the last years of his life under "a cloud of unknowing."

John E. Gurr was born in Yakima, Washington, on February 12, 1913, the son of Alfred and Lena Sample Gurr. About a year after John's birth, his father was offered a job in a bank in **Douglas**, Alaska. John's early education was that of a nomad. He received it successively in Douglas, **Juneau**, and **Wrangell**, Alaska, as well as a little of it in Prince Rupert, B.C, Canada. For two years he attended Gonzaga High School in Spokane, Washington, from which he graduated in 1930. After high school, he worked in Oregon as a salesman for the Swift meat packing company.

On September 30, 1937, John entered the Jesuit novitiate at Sheridan, Oregon. After completing the two-year noviceship and taking his vows, he spent two additional years there in classical and humanities studies. From 1941–44, he was at Mount St. Michael's, Spokane, studying philosophy. Next he taught philosophy for a year at Gonzaga University. He made his theology at Weston College, Weston, Massachusetts, 1945–49, and was ordained there on June 19, 1948. His tertianship was made at Port Townsend, Washington, 1949–50. After teaching philosophy for a year at Seattle University, he spent the years 1951–55 earning a doctorate in philosophy at St. Louis University. For the next ten years, he was a happy teacher of philosophy, both at Seattle University and at Gonzaga University.

"But, then," Father Gurr wrote in a letter, dated **Kotzebue**, Alaska, January 25, 1978, to Father Louis L. **Renner**, S.J., who had asked him for an autobiographical sketch, "it began to look as though the ever-present need for administrators was going to separate me from the classroom. So, after counsel and advice, I took advantage of an option the Society of Jesus often gives its members, and volunteered for the Alaska missions sometime in late 1964. I was accepted and assigned to **Fairbanks**."

From 1965–68, Father Gurr served in Fairbanks as Superintendent of Catholic Schools and as Vicar General to Francis D. **Gleeson**, S.J., Bishop of Fairbanks at the time, who regarded his services highly. Father Gurr proved himself to be generous and hard-working. He threw himself into everything with the utmost orderliness and efficiency. He expected others to do likewise. This, at times, put considerable strain on those less equipped to meet his standards.

Soon after his arrival in Fairbanks, Father Gurr undertook to write a history of the Catholic Church in Alaska, but time ran out. It never got beyond the copious-notes stage. During his three years in Fairbanks, in addition to attending to his primary duties, he also, at every opportunity, traveled to bush villages and highway communities to offer Mass there in the absence of a priest. He was a zealous priest, but he traveled to the bush also to determine whether or not he had a calling to bush ministry. He traveled also for its own sake. He enjoyed driving the highways and byways out of Fairbanks. No road was too long or too dusty for him. His trips to the bush confirmed him in his desire to serve there. In 1968, he became pastor of **Bethel**. He tended the parish, while Father Robert F. **Corrigal**, S.J., stationed in Bethel with him, flew in the mission-owned Piper Super Cub to visit Bethel's dependent mission stations.

During the year 1974–75, Father Gurr served for 15 months as full-time Catholic Chaplain on the Alyeska Pipe Line. As such, he was responsible for the 16 camps and pump stations stretching north for 400 miles, from the Yukon River all the way to the arctic coast. It was an assignment he, a natural-born traveler, found made to order for him. He estimated that, as pipe line chaplain, serving his "unique 'parish' 400 miles long and about 10 miles wide," he traveled about 40,000 miles. When he learned that he was being reassigned, this time to Kotzebue, he wrote to his friends, "I shall miss my 'Pipeline Parish' and the wonderful people there."

But, from Kotzebue, where he took up station in October 1975, Father Gurr was able write to the same friends, "I am happy to be in the service of the Eskimo people again." He was pastor of Kotzebue till 1980, when he moved to Bethel. There his health began to fail perceptibly. Even before that, a faint confusion in his thought patterns became discernible. In 1983, he was sent to Portland, Oregon, for medical help; then, in 1986, to the Regis Community at Gonzaga University. Meanwhile the light in his once keen mind progressively dimmed, and, before long, went out. He was conscious only of each fleeting second at a time. He spent the last five years of his life in the care of the Sisters of Providence in Spokane. After suffering for eight years from Alzheimer's disease, he died at St. Joseph Care Center, Spokane, on February 25, 1994.

He lies buried in the Jesuit Cemetery at Mount St. Michael's, Spokane.

HAFFIE, Father Lawrence N., S.J.

Lawrence N. Haffie was born in Edmonton, Alberta, Canada, on August 26, 1914, the oldest of four children. His mother, Agnes McAleer Haffie was from Scotland. His father, Nicholson Haffie, was an English farmer before he came to America, where he became a boilermaker and a worker as a "tinner" in Seattle's Boeing plant. The boy Lawrence first attended a Winnipeg public school, 1920–21; then St. Mary's, Paisley, Scotland, 1921–22; then St. John's in Seattle, 1923–30. After attending Ballard High School in Seattle, 1931–32, he went on to attend Seattle Preparatory, 1932–34, and Seattle College, 1934–36, and the University of Washington, 1936–37.

On August 14, 1938, Lawrence Haffie entered the Jesuit novitiate at Sheridan, Oregon. After completing his two-year noviceship, he spent an additional two years there studying the classics and the humanities. His philosophical studies he made at Mount St. Michael's, Spokane, Washington, from 1942–45. He was at **Holy Cross Mission**, **Alaska**, for the year 1945–46, after which he went on to Alma College, Los Gatos, California, for four years of theological studies. He was ordained a priest in San Francisco on June 4, 1949. He made his tertianship at Port Townsend, Washington, 1950–51. Having had training in journalism, and being an accomplished photographer, Father Haffie spent the next two years, 1951–53, in New York City as Associate Editor of the magazine *Jesuit Missions*.

In 1953, Father Haffie returned to Alaska. There he was stationed at **Bethel** as assistant pastor and as visiting priest to villages along the Kuskokwim River, among them **Kalskag**, **Aniak**, and **McGrath**. Having a personal problem with alcohol, he left Alaska in 1956. He spent the year 1956–57 as chaplain of Providence Hospital, Seattle, and the following year, still in Seattle, as Alaska Mission Procurator. In 1958, he again returned to Alaska, to serve for three years at St. Mary's Mission, **Andreafsky**. In 1961, he left Alaska for good.

Back in the Northwest, Father Haffie taught at Gonzaga Preparatory from 1961–67. Then, for the next twenty years, he served as a hospital chaplain: Providence, Seattle, 1956–57; Sacred Heart, Spokane, 1969–80; Mount St. Joseph, Spokane, 1980–81. He then spent the year 1981–82 at the B&H Ranch at Bachly, Oregon, as chaplain and counselor, and the years 1982–87 at St. Mary's parish, Eugene, Oregon, as assistant pastor.

During the last three years of his life, Father Haffie was in the Jesuit House Infirmary at Gonzaga University, Spokane. There, according to the nurse who tended him toward the end of his life, he was "the most patient and uncomplaining person" she had ever seen. On January 2, 1990, he died, of heart and lung problems, at Sacred Heart Hospital, Spokane. He had almost died in 1965 before undergoing heart surgery. He lies buried in the Jesuit cemetery at Mount St. Michael's, Spokane.

HAINES

Haines, on Portage Cove in Chilkoot Inlet, is located 16 miles southwest of **Skagway**. Originally a Tlingit Indian village with a name meaning "end of the trail," it was a trading post for both the Chilkat and Interior Indians. In 1884, Haines P. O. was established there, although the place was locally known as Chilcoot. The town became an important outlet for the Porcupine mining district and marked the beginning of the Dalton Trail. In 1967, Haines had a population of 392; in the year 2000, 1,811.

From its earliest years, the Catholic community in Haines was served by priests stationed in Skagway. The first documented Catholic baptism in the Haines area took place at Fort William H. Seward on April 9, 1905. It was performed by Father Philibert **Turnell**, S.J., pastor of St. Mark's parish in Skagway. By 1914, priests stationed in Skagway were making monthly visits to Haines to administer the Sacraments and conduct services. The need for a church in Haines increased steadily; and, in 1920, a 1902 chapel building from Fort Seward was moved to downtown Haines and remodeled into a small T-shaped church, dedicated to the Sacred Heart of Jesus. The longer, narrow section was the church; the tiny cross section was the rectory. In 1972, an addition was built on in the rear. In 1981, during the pastorate of Father **James P. Ryan**, 1978–86, a new church was built next to the old one.

Sacred Heart in Haines is first listed in the 1925 issue of the Official Catholic Directory as a mission cared for by priests out of Skagway. Notable among them was Father G. Edgar **Gallant**, in Skagway from 1918–59. In the course of those years, his successive assistant priests—Fathers Harley A. **Baker**, Raymond W. **Mosey**, and Francis A. **Cowgill**—also ministered at the Haines mission. After the Gallant years, it was served, out of Skagway, by Fathers Francis W. Nugent, James F. **Miller**, Georges E. Bourque, O.P., and David A. **Melbourne**.

By way of an historical footnote: On December 9, 1956, Father George A. Zelenak, S.J., temporarily in Haines, died there of asphyxiation in a trailer fire.

Sacred Heart parish's first resident pastor was Father Edward T. McHugh, O.M.I., in Haines during the years 1975–77. Father Ryan, as mentioned above, was resident pastor from 1978–86. He was followed by Fathers Javier Guttierez, in Haines from 1986–88, and Earl Barcome, there the following year. Sister Kathleen **Radich**, O.S.F., in the absence of a resident priest, served as Parish Administrator from 1989–91. Father Michael Hayden was in residence from 1990–94, and Father Miller from 1994–98. From 1995–98, Sister Judith Gomila, M.S.C., was his Pastoral Associate. During the year 1998–99, Father Jerome A. **Frister** was in Haines. Father Edward Boucher, retired Navy chap-

Sacred Heart Church, Haines.
Courtesy of Father James P. Ryan.

lain, resided in Haines during the year 1999–2000. From July 2000 to early 2004, Father James Blaney, O.M.I., did likewise. By the end of 2001, he had "a very nice new rectory" completed in Haines. Sister Jelaine (Jill) Jaeb, O.S.U., too, provided pastoral care for Sacred Heart parish at this time. In July 2004, Father Edmund J. Penisten became pastor Sacred Heart parish.

HAMILTON

Hamilton—also referred to as "Old" Hamilton, to distinguish it from New Fort Hamilton, which is about ten miles distant from Hamilton—is located on the right bank of the Apoon Pass near the north mouth of the Yukon River. A trading post was established there in 1897. During the early 1900s, Hamilton was an important mail center and transfer point for travelers. The site had been for many generations a Central Yup'ik Eskimo settlement. By the later 1900s, the place was completely abandoned, its people having relocated to **Kotlik**.

Hamilton first appears in Catholic Church records in 1907, when Father Anthony M. **Keyes**, S.J., performed some baptisms there. A church was built that same year. Hamilton was served out of **Akulurak** until 1931, then out of **St. Michael** until 1954. Father Paul H. **Linssen**, S.J., made Hamilton his headquarters for the year 1954–55. It is listed in the Oregon Province catalog for that year as "St. Marjorie's Mission." The following year, he visited it out of **Chaneliak**. From 1956–69, Hamilton was again served out of St. Michael, and, from 1969–75, out of Kotlik. After that, it is no longer mentioned in the catalogs.

HANSEN, John F., S.J.

John F. Hansen was born in Marienburg, Poland, on February 8, 1881. He left **Nome**, **Alaska**, in June 1916, to join the Society of Jesus. On September 14th of that year, he entered the Jesuit novitiate at Los Gatos, California, as a Lay Brother candidate. After spending three years there, he returned to Alaska, arriving in Nome on August 11, 1919, and at the **Pilgrim Hot Springs** Mission four days later.

He spent the rest of his life there: as prefect of the boys, as caretaker of the livestock, as "fisherman," and as a general handyman. He was reputed to be a good hunter.

Brother Hansen was a member of the search party that found the frozen body of Father Frederick A. **Ruppert**, S.J. It was also he who found Father Ruppert's long-lost sled.

On the afternoon of January 26, 1938, Brother Hansen arrived in Nome to see the doctor. On the 29th, in the late evening, he died unexpectedly, for shortly before his death, according to the keeper of the Nome house diary, "he had been feeling quite well." His body was flown to the Hot Springs mission on the 30th, and buried there on February 1st.

HARGREAVES, Father Henry G., S.J.

He spent over 50 years on the **Alaska** missions, mainly as a missionary to the Central Yup'ik Eskimos of northwestern Alaska. He was among the last of the one-time "mushing missionaries." Soon after

St. Marjorie's Mission, Hamilton. This was taken down in 1961.
JOPA-172.1.11.

his arrival on the Bering Sea coast, his local Superior wrote of him, "People like him tremendously." With his ready smile and infectious laugh, he quickly put people at ease in his presence. For over six years he was General Superior of Jesuits in Alaska. He was the last of that generation of Jesuit Alaskan missionaries to wear, for all occasions, the "Alaska tuxedo," the greenish Filson whipcord jacket so popular in early-day Alaska. He played the violin competently, sang well in a rich baritone voice, danced convincingly the traditional Eskimo dances—and played a formidable game of chess.

Henry G. Hargreaves was born, on May 28, 1914, in Seattle, Washington. His father, George Hargreaves, whose parents had come to the United States from England, was married to Marcelline Carrere, who had come from France. Henry attended John Muir Grade School for four years, then St. Mary's for four. After graduating from Seattle Preparatory, he attended Gonzaga University in Spokane, Washington, for three years. In the course of those seven years of Jesuit schooling, he came to know well the Jesuits and their kinds of ministries. He heard about their missionary work in Alaska. He heard about Alaska also from his father, who, though not a Catholic, sent money from time to time to Jesuit Alaskan missionaries Fathers **John P. Fox** and Paul C. **O'Connor**. Gently, but unmistakably, he felt himself drawn to the Society of Jesus. "It was the variety of apostolates," he wrote, "that attracted me to the Jesuit Order."

Henry entered the Jesuit novitiate at Sheridan, Oregon, on September 25, 1935. After completing the two-year noviceship and a year of classical and humanities studies at Sheridan, he went to Mount St. Michael's, Spokane, for three years of philosophical studies, 1938–41. He next spent three years teaching, mainly Religion, Latin and French, at Marquette High School in Yakima, Washington, 1941–44. His theological studies he made at Alma College, Los Gatos, California, 1944–48. He was ordained a priest in San Francisco, on June 16, 1947. His formal training as a Jesuit he rounded out with the making of his tertianship at Port Townsend, Washington, 1948–49.

During the course of his studies, Father Hargreaves kept hearing a call to serve on the Alaska Mission. He volunteered. By late summer 1949, he found himself in "the kingdom of the seal," at **Hooper Bay**. Years later, he recalled how and under what circumstances he had arrived there:

> I traveled from **Anchorage** to **Bethel** on a DC-3. Then hopped a small water-ski plane, known as a Widgeon, and landed on the shores of Hooper Bay. I remember stepping out on the mucky sands of the bay, desperately trying to keep my shoes on, as we headed for dry land. And there was Father O'Connor, waiting—to greet me, I thought—with keys in hand. "Here, take over. If you need anything, ask anyone," he commented, as he boarded the plane. He was on the State Housing Commission, and was going to Anchorage to attend a meeting there.

While Father Hargreaves' introduction to missionary life among the Eskimos was rather unceremonious, Hooper Bay was a good place to begin it. "Hooper is a splendid place for a person to gain a good knowledge of mission work," wrote Father O'Connor to Father James U. **Conwell**, S.J., shortly before Father Hargreaves arrived there. From the outset of his stay at Hooper Bay, Father Hargreaves found the people "most affable." He gave himself wholeheartedly to mission work. On March 22, 1950, Father O'Connor could write to Francis D. **Gleeson**, S.J., Vicar Apostolic of Alaska at the time, "Father Hargreaves is doing extremely well. Thanks ever so much for sending such a high caliber assistant to me."

In addition to ministering to the people at Hooper Bay itself, Father Hargreaves traveled also to the outlying villages of **Keyaluvik**, **Kashunuk**, and Old **Chevak**. Not having a dogteam of his own at first, he relied on Native men to take him on his rounds in winter. In summer, he traveled in a wooden skiff pushed along by a 7-horse outboard motor.

From the day Father Hargreaves arrived at Hooper Bay, he set about learning the Native language, Central Yup'ik Eskimo. He found considerable difficulty in his attempt to make "some headway" in that "language of gutturals, hard breathings and queer sounding words." He never did get a good command of the Native language, but he did have the good judgment to use competent Native interpreters, and so was not greatly hindered in his missionary work.

With Ivan **Sipary** as foreman and many helping hands, Father Hargreaves built a church in present-day Chevak in 1950. When the Chevak post office opened in 1951, he became Chevak's first postmaster. While continuing to make Hooper Bay his headquarters, he served the Chevak mission until 1952.

Father Hargreaves spent the year 1952–53 as an assistant pastor at Immaculate Conception parish in **Fairbanks**. From 1953–57, he was again back at Hooper Bay, taking care of the pastoral needs of that village, along with those of its dependent station, **Scammon Bay**.

From November 28, 1956, to February 4, 1963, Father Hargreaves was General Superior of the Jesuits in Alaska. As such, he made **Bethel** his headquarters. He spent also the year 1963–64 in Bethel. During his Bethel years, he visited its dependent missions up and down the Kuskokwim River, **Kalskag**, **Aniak**, and **McGrath**, among them. After being on the move so much as mission Superior and priest in Bethel, he was happy to stay put, for the year 1964–65, as once again assistant pastor in Fairbanks.

The year 1965–66 found Father Hargreaves again spending much time on the trail. He made **St. Michael** his home base; but, tending to its dependent mission stations, **Stebbins**, **Unalakleet**, **Hamilton**, and **Chaneliak** necessitated much travel. By now, however, he was traveling the trails not by dogteam, but by "the iron dog," the snowmachine. His first such machine was a Ski-Doo Olympic with a Kohler motor. To start it on a cold day, he needed to drain the oil the night before and heat it on the stove.

After spending 15 years among the Eskimos along the Bering Sea coast in western Alaska, Father Hargreaves found himself among the Koyukon Athabaskan Indians along the middle Yukon River in Alaska's great interior. From 1966–69, he was pastor of **Nulato** and its dependent mission, **Koyukuk**. With a degree of smug satisfaction, he related how one day, while he was at Nulato, he and William Ambrose, an experienced Native hunter, went out to get meat for themselves and the Sisters of St. **Ann** who were running the Catholic day school at Nulato at the time. As luck would have it, it was Father Hargreaves who dropped the moose they bagged that day. While William, being faster on snowshoes, was checking out fresh moose tracks they had come upon, Father Hargreaves circled back to the parked snowmachines. Unexpectedly he saw a moose just across

the river. Several shots, and there was fresh meat in abundance. When William heard the shots, he came back, wide-eyed. Together they dressed and divided up the kill.

After many years in the bush, except for the two years in Fairbanks, it was the big city for Father Hargreaves. From 1969–72, while living in the Jesuit residence on Birchwood Street, he ministered to the "social and apostolic" needs of Native peoples living in, or coming and going through, Anchorage.

In his September 1972, *Newsletter*, Father Fox wrote: "Father Hargreaves is just back for packing up his belongings to move them to **Kotlik** and **Emmonak**. He had an enjoyable tour of France and the lower 48 with his mother and brother, by way of a vacation, and is all set for 'the bush.' So, we will learn to get along without him here."

From 1972–80, except for the year 1975–76, when he was on sabbatical leave at the Jesuit School of Theology in Berkeley, California, Kotlik was Father Hargreaves' home base. Out of Kotlik, he visited its dependent missions, Emmonak and Hamilton. During his early years in Alaska, when telephones were non-existent in the villages, or only one per village, Father Hargreaves kept in touch with his Superiors and fellow missionaries through ham radio. While at Kotlik, being an experienced ham radio operator, he had occasion to perform a great service. The father of the school's principal was dying. The family in the lower 48 had no way of keeping in touch with the principal. Father Hargreaves made a radio contact, set up a phone patch, and enabled the family to communicate.

While Father Hargreaves was stationed at Kotlik, the village had the custom of putting on a special program every Christmas. Skits were part of it. One year, David Prince, with his guitar, and Father Hargreaves, with his violin, put on a skit. Father Hargreaves, having always liked the sound of the name *Weecheemal'rea* ("open eyes"), took that as his name. David picked another name that made people laugh. Dressed in hobo clothes, the two pretended to find their instruments in a garbage can, then pretended to wonder how to play them, while screeching and plucking away. Then the Spirit of Christmas, in the form of a child, came on the stage, touched the instruments, and the two played a beautiful song together. The name Weecheemal'rea stuck. Often thereafter, people, smiling, called Father Hargreaves that.

After his years at Kotlik, Father Hargreaves was back in Bethel again for the years 1980–87.

During this stay in Bethel, he visited the villages of **Marshall** and **Russian Mission**. The year 1987–88 found him at **Toksook Bay**, taking care of it and its dependent missions, **Tununak** and **Newtok**. From 1988–94, he made Emmonak his headquarters, out of which he visited also its dependent missions, **Alakanuk** and **Nunam Iqua**.

During his year at Toksook Bay, he received a special gift. "David and Julia Bill," he related during an interview,

> noticed that my Eddie Bauer parka was torn in places, and offered to fix it. David said they had extra cloth to replace the torn covering. Julia, his wife, would repair it. She came later to say that the down insulation needed replacing. She replaced it with musk ox fur. Then she said the wolf ruff on the parka hood was old and they had a ruff to replace it. The day came, when they invited me to their home and had me try on the bright red, all-new parka. The only thing that remained of the original parka was the measurement!

During his Emmonak years, Father Hargreaves had a more modern snowmachine, a Ski-Doo with a rotax engine. One spring day, this gave him a rather adventurous ride. He was on his way from Alakanuk to Emmonak. "Heading back to Emmonak," he recalled years later,

> I asked a man which was the best slough to take to get back to the Yukon. He told me "the one on the right," but he didn't say to stay off the ice. After a mile down the slough, I found myself going fast—straight down, to Davey Jones' locker. I had insulated, buoyant clothes on and managed to paddle over to some ice, where I lay down for 45 minutes, until someone came along. I couldn't move, because there was water on both sides, and I wasn't interested in doing any more swimming. Finally, two hunters came along, and I told them to call John Hanson to bring a boat. Later Hanson arrived, hauling a boat behind his snowmachine. He brought me back to Alakanuk, where I got thawed out. With a hook he fished up the snowmachine and hauled it back to Alakanuk. After he cleaned out the gas tank and the carburetor, the machine started right up. I drove back to Emmonak that same afternoon.

If people always came to Father Hargreaves' rescue, he, in turn, always came to theirs, especially in times of their spiritual need. Night or day, whether convenient or not, he was always ready to sacrifice his needs, his plans, when called upon to minister in whatever way needed. "In his quiet, unassuming way," according to Sister Mary Beck, S.S.N.D., who worked with him and knew him well, "he was always there for others. And the people knew it!"

After his Emmonak years, Father Hargreaves was back once more on Nelson Island. From 1994–97, he again made Toksook Bay his headquarters. Out of it, he took care also of its dependent missions, Tununak and **Nightmute**. During the year 1997–98, he lived at Tununak, out of which he visited Nightmute.

In 1996, during its spring Commencement Ceremonies, Gonzaga University conferred on Father Hargreaves, in recognition of his long years of service on the Alaska Mission, its prestigious DeSmet Medal. This medal—named for Father Peter John DeSmet, founder of the Indian missions in America's Northwest—honors those who have carried on the tradition of apostolic ministry to America's Native peoples. In a noble, selfless gesture, Father Hargreaves made it known that he was receiving the medal as being conferred not only upon himself, but as being conferred also upon his equally deserving fellow Alaskan Jesuit missionaries.

In 1998, Father Hargreaves began serving the Bethel parish as assistant pastor. As such, he occasionally visited the villages of Marshall and Russian Mission on the Yukon. He visited the people in the Bethel hospital. He continued to play the violin and sing at various gatherings. He wrote poetry. He still enjoyed hitting the trail on the parish's snowmachine. His yearly highlight was making his annual eight-day retreat with his fellow Alaskan Jesuits at **Holy Spirit Center** in Anchorage. Though the "Dean of Alaskan Missionaries," and nearing his 90th birthday, he continued to be the zealous, active, joyous priest that he had always been. In April 2003, he joined the Jesuit Community in Portland, Oregon; and, five months later, in mid-September, the Regis Community in Spokane, out of which he began to serve as a pastoral minister to Indian communities in northeastern Washington.

Father Edward J. Hartmann.
Courtesy of Fr. Hartmann.

HARTMANN, Father Edward J.

Edward J. Hartmann was born to Edward J. and Wanda M. Janicki Hartmann on December 25, 1946, in Brooklyn, New York. He received his elementary education at St. Thomas the Apostle Grade School in Woodhaven, Queens, New York, and his secondary at St. John's Prep in Brooklyn, New York. In 1969, he gradated from Don Bosco College in Newton, New Jersey, with a B.A. degree in philosophy. On June 2nd of that year, he joined the U.S. Army. He received his Basic Training at Fort Leonard Wood, Missouri, and his Advance Infantry Training at Fort Polk, Louisiana. After attending Field Artillery Officers Candidate School at Fort Sill, Oklahoma, Lieutenant Hartmann went on to fight in the war in Vietnam with the 5th Battalion, 42nd Field Artillery.

Once back again in civilian life after having been honorably discharged from the Army, Edward, in September 1972, enrolled in St. Joseph's Seminary in Yonkers, New York. He was ordained a priest on December 11, 1976, by Terence Cardinal Cook for the Archdiocese of New York. He had first begun thinking about becoming a priest, when he was a Mass server in grade school. For his first assignment as a priest, he was named to St. Aedan's parish, Pearl River, New York. After three years there, he asked Cardinal Cook for permission to serve in the U.S. Army as a chaplain. Permission was granted, and Chaplain Hartmann went on to see service in the Academy of Health Sciences at Fort Sam Houston, San Antonio, Texas.

At this time, Chaplain Hartmann's widowed mother chose to live with him. Together they lived successively in Babenhausen and Frankfurt, Germany, and in Leavenworth, Kansas. When he was assigned to Fort Greely, **Alaska**, she remained behind in Leavenworth. While in Alaska, Chaplain Hartmann met Michael J. **Kaniecki**, S.J., Bishop of **Fairbanks**. He asked him about the possibilities of his ministering in the Diocese of Fairbanks. Bishop Kaniecki's reaction was favorable.

In 1992, Chaplain Hartmann was transferred to Fort Drum, New York, for his last assignment in the military. During this time, as a member of the 10th Mountain Division, he assisted the victims of Hurricane Andrew in southern Florida, and saw service in Somalia and Haiti. Upon returning from Haiti, he asked his Ordinary, John Cardinal O'Connor, for permission to be assigned to the Diocese of Fairbanks after his retirement from the U.S. Army. Permission was granted.

Father Hartmann's first assignment in the Diocese of Fairbanks was that of pastor of St. John Berchmans parish in **Galena** and visiting priest to St. Francis Regis mission in **Huslia**. He served in that capacity from 1995–97. He found working with the Koyukon Athabaskan Indian people a rewarding, learning experience, and was soon at home with their customs and way of life. Having strong ties with the men of the village, he learned how to hunt, fish, and trap.

In the summer of 1997, Father Hartmann was appointed Rector of Sacred Heart Cathedral in Fairbanks. Shortly thereafter, he was named to serve also as Vicar General of the Diocese of Fairbanks. As of the year 2004, he was no longer Vicar General, but was still Rector of the Cathedral. And, as of that same year, he was still a member of the Archdiocese of New York, but on indefinite loan to the Diocese of Fairbanks.

Among his hobbies, Father Hartmann listed: "hunting, fishing, woodworking, building, plumbing, electricity, gardening, etc." Among his special devotions: "Immaculate Conception, Blessed Sacrament, and the Pope."

HATREL, Thomas J., S.J.

Thomas J. Hatrel was born in New Orleans, Louisiana, on May 21, 1922. There he attended Holy Names Grade School and Jesuit High School. While in high school, he played on the football team and ran the high hurdles as a member of the track team. A Jesuit classmate of his described him as "a tough competitor." On August 14, 1939, he entered the Jesuit novitiate at Grand Coteau, Louisiana. After completing his two-year noviceship, he studied the classics and humanities for two years, then philosophy for three. He next taught for three years at Jesuit High in New Orleans, after which, in 1949, he began his theological studies at St. Mary's Kansas. He was ordained to the priesthood there on June 19, 1952. After completing a fourth year of theology and his tertianship, he spent 20 years teaching at several of the high schools of the New Orleans Province, namely, at Jesuit High in New Orleans and at Jesuit High in Tampa, Florida. From 1974–79, he worked with Tampa High students as director of a community services program. As such, he and "his boys" reached out to the poor, the aged, the addicted, the delinquents—"the underdogs of God's world." After five years in that ministry, he asked to be sent to **Alaska**.

In letters recommending Father Hatrel for a teaching position at Immaculate Conception Grade School in **Fairbanks**, he is variously described as "a very compassionate man who is especially sensitive to the feelings and needs of the poor and disadvantaged. He's simply great with children, probably because he is so simple a person himself." He is praised for being "a fine priest, very close to the Sacred Heart of our Lord."

From 1979–83, Father Hatrel taught mathematics at Immaculate Conception Grade School and served as chaplain to the children there. During his years in Fairbanks, when not at the school, he enjoyed walks in the nearby woods with his faithful companion, Jerry—a black Labrador retriever—adding, as he did so, to his list of new bird sightings. He was interested in birds long before he came to Alaska.

In 1983, St. Ignatius parish at **Alakanuk** found itself without a pastor. Father Hatrel volunteered to go there as pastor of Alakanuk and of its dependent station Sheldon Point, now known as **Nunam Iqua**. While he was still on the staff of Immaculate Conception Grade School, the principal of the school, referring to him, said to Father Bert Mead, S.J., a member of the New Orleans Province stationed in Fairbanks at the time, "We've never had a man like this." The principal hated to see him leave.

Around the mid-1980s, Father Hatrel was back in New Orleans for a visit and a family reunion. At the end of the reunion party, in confidence, he told a fellow Jesuit and former classmate of his that he was having some serious physical problems that had him worried. "I don't want ever to reach the point," he said, "where I can't stay and work in Alaska. Don't tell anybody about this. Just pray for me."

In the spring of 1988, Father Hatrel was faced with heart surgery in **Anchorage**. The only other option he had was to seek a second opinion. This would have meant leaving Alaska. He elected to stay. He died, somewhat unexpectedly, in Anchorage on May 5, 1988. In keeping with his expressed wishes, he lies buried in the cemetery at Alakanuk.

HEALY

Today's Holy Mary of Guadalupe parish in Healy has its roots in Suntrana, a one-time mining camp on the right bank of the Healy River, 3.5 miles east of Healy. In 1930, Suntrana had a population of 61; in 1939, of 78; in 1950, of 130; and in 1967, of 81. Today the site is generally referred to as the Usibelli Coal Mine. Healy itself—on the left bank of the Healy River, and on the Parks Highway some 10 miles north of Denali National Park and Preserve, and at mile 358.1 on the Alaska Railroad—has been on the maps since about 1905, when it came into being as a mining camp. The Healy Fork post office was established in 1921. In 1930, Healy had a population of 36; in 1967, of 77; and in the year 2000, of exactly 1,000.

The story of the Catholic Church in the Suntrana–Healy area begins in 1950, when Father John R. **Buchanan**, S.J., began to make infrequent visits to that area. During the early 1950s, Bishop Francis D. **Gleeson**, S.J., visited Suntrana out of Fairbanks twice a month, traveling there by train or plane. Beginning in 1954, Father Lawrence A.

Nevue, S.J., did likewise. During the latter 1950s, teachers at Monroe Catholic High School, **Fairbanks**, Jesuit Fathers Bernard F. **McMeel** and Charles A. **Saalfeld**, traveled to Suntrana for occasional weekend Masses. Generally they stayed in the mining camp bunkhouse and offered Mass in the recreation hall. At times, the priests stayed also in the Healy hotel and offered Mass there for the Catholic families of railroad workers. In 1957, a church building was put up in Suntrana. The interior was still not finished in 1959, when Father Louis L. **Renner**, S.J., celebrated the Easter Mass there. This church was named "St. Mary's."

In 1964, a road was "punched through" from **Nenana** to Healy. It was "more of a tundra trail upon which cars would often get stuck." However, with the advent of that road, the Suntrana–Healy community began to be cared for by priests stationed in Nenana: Fathers Francis P. Ready 1965–66, Robert F. Dunn 1966–70, and William C. **Dibb**, S.J., 1970–72. No priest was assigned to Nenana during the years 1972–74. It was visited at different times by one or other of the following three: Fathers Donald E. Henkes, Michael P. Murphy, and William A. Zorichak. Father Nevue was stationed in Nenana from 1974–76. That 1964 road brought growth to Nenana, as well as to the Healy area. Roughly ten years later, around the mid-1970s, people began to move from Suntrana to what is now Healy. A bigger church was then needed, and needed in Healy.

When Father **Paul B. Mueller**, S.J., became pastor of Nenana in 1976, he became responsible also for the Catholic community in Healy. It was he who rallied the people of Healy, organized personnel, and drummed up resources to bring about what is now Holy Mary of Guadalupe Church in Healy.

Mr. Ronald Kunkel, a one-time member of the **Jesuit Volunteer Corps**, volunteered his services to design the new church. Mr. Michael Murphy, though not a member of the Healy Catholic community, volunteered to take on, at half salary, the foremanship of the building crew. This consisted primarily of Father Mueller's nephews, Anthony and Paul Mueller, two semi-professional construc-

Holy Mary of Guadalupe Church, Healy. *DFA.*

tion workers in their early twenties from Waldport, Oregon. Father Renner spent six weeks at the building site as a fourth crew member. Many services were rendered also by military personnel in the area and "parishioners."

The slab for the new church was poured on August 5, 1980. By late September of that year, the building was closed in and the roof on. During the year 1981, the new church was finished, inside and out. It was formally dedicated by Robert L. **Whelan**, S.J., Bishop of Fairbanks at the time, on May 30, 1982, under the title of "Holy Mary of Guadalupe." This name was given the parish and the church in keeping with the wishes of Father Mueller, who had made a promise at the Shrine to Holy Mary of Guadalupe in Guadalajara, Mexico, that he would build a church in her honor. Before this title was formally bestowed, the church was referred to informally in an article written about it by Father Renner as "Our Lady of the Mountain." The title "St. Mary's" ceased, when the old St. Mary's Church in Suntrana was sold. This church was moved to Healy, where it was converted into a private home. It was not until October 28, 1984, that the new parish of Holy Mary of Guadalupe was formally established by Bishop Whelan.

In early November 2000, a new rectory, a self-standing wooden frame building with an indoor garage, built next to the church, was ready for occupancy. Most of the labor was donated by parishioners and Healy people. Tim Russell volunteered to be the contractor and designer of the building. Kim Graham and Sherry Baysinger, as members of the building committee, spent countless hours on the project.

Father Jack **de Verteuil**, priest in charge of the Healy parish as of 1994, began to make Healy his headquarters in 1996. He was still doing so as of the year 2004. After Father Mueller, in addition to Father de Verteuil, the following also served the Healy Catholic community: Father J. Albert **Levitre**, 1984–88; Father William T. **Burke**, S.J., out of Fairbanks, 1988–89; Father Gerhard J. Wallner, 1989–91; and Father John A. **Hinsvark**, 1991–94.

During the years 1989–91, Sister Patricia Ann Miller, O.P., was Pastoral Administrator of the Healy parish. For over two decades, and as of the year 2004, Barbara Walters served her parish, ably and faithfully, as Eucharistic Minister, Parish Minister, and Parish Administrator.

Two Sisters of **Providence** stationed in Fairbanks taught catechism at Suntrana during the summers of 1956 and 1957. Sister Joan Marie Reedy and Sister Mary Claire McLaughlin, Sisters of St. Joseph of Carondolet, spent many summers providing religious education for children in Nenana, Anderson, Cantwell and Healy. According to Barbara Walters, "They were beloved by all and encouraged the parents to continue religious training the rest of the year."

61, 100, 205

HEBERT, Father Daniel J.

Daniel J. "Dan" Hebert was born the oldest of five children, three girls and two boys, to Joseph and Reva Hebert in Kankakee, Illinois, on February 20, 1950. Both of his parents were in the medical field. His father was a pharmacist, his mother a nurse. They were devout parents. It was a matter of con-

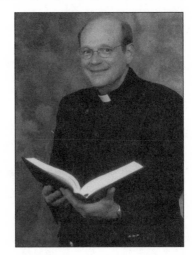

Father Daniel J. Hebert.
Courtesy of Fr. Hebert.

siderable importance to them that the family meet every evening for night prayers and/or the rosary.

For his elementary education, Dan attended Maternity of the Blessed Virgin Mary Grade School, in Kankakee, from which he graduated in 1964; and, for his secondary education, Bishop McNamara High School, also in Kankakee, from which he graduated in 1968. While only in the 9th grade, he started to work at the drug store. His father insisted that work of that kind should be part of his education. At the end of his junior year, he branched out on his own and got a job at Riverside Hospital.

Throughout his elementary and secondary schooling, Dan was surrounded by priests and Sisters. He found that just being around them filled him with excitement. While still in the fifth grade, he began already to dream about becoming a Religious or a priest. He attributes his eventual vocation to the priesthood in large part to watching the priests and Sisters and the joy they showed in their call. But there was also a distinct "faith experience." Before going on to the sixth grade, he had to study during the summer months, then take a test. "The morning of the test," he wrote, "I went to Mass and afterwards stopped, looked at the tabernacle and said, 'If you are in there, you better come with me.' After passing the test and while walking home, I stopped in my tracks and remembered what I had said. At that moment, God became very real to me."

Though Dan did, from the fifth grade on and

throughout his high school years, see the priesthood as "in the cards" for him, he did, nevertheless, consider also the possibilities of his becoming a nurse, or a school teacher—and marriage. All the while, he kept asking himself, "What does God want of me?"

After graduating from high school, Dan attended nearby Kankakee Community College, because he was still not sure what his true calling in life was, even though the call to priesthood remained "very strong." It was during that year of college that he became interested in becoming a Religious Brother. At the end of it, he entered the Brothers of Charity of Immaculate Heart of Mary headquartered in Banning, California. For two years—as "Brother Joseph," his name as a Religious—he taught at schools staffed by the Brothers: Boys Town of the Desert in Banning, California, 1969–70, and Notre Dame High School in Riverside, California, 1970–71. He made his profession of vows as a Brother of Charity on February 20, 1971.

Brother Joseph was happy as a teaching Brother; still, as he recalled years later, "Inside of me there was that very strong feeling of being a priest. However, how do I go about becoming one?"

It was the Brothers of Charity that showed Brother Joseph the way. His Superior, Brother Paul Drew, asked him if he would go with two other Brothers to **Anchorage**, **Alaska**, and work there in the Archdiocese of Anchorage. At first, he thought it might not be God's will for him. However, after much prayer and discerning on his part, he concluded that he was being called to serve God in Alaska.

Brother Joseph arrived in Anchorage on January 22, 1972. During the one and a half years he spent there, he worked in many of the parishes, setting up religious education programs. Meanwhile, he went to school himself. In the course of that year and a half, the priesthood became for him a reality. **Joseph T. Ryan**, Archbishop of Anchorage at the time, saw how he was working, and invited him to become a priest for the archdiocese.

In 1973, Dan Hebert began studies for the priesthood at Holy Trinity Seminary in Dallas, Texas. From the University of Dallas, he received a B.A. degree in philosophy and a Master of Divinity degree. He was ordained a priest by Francis T. Hur-

ley, then Archbishop of Anchorage, on May 5, 1979. At the time of his ordination, he took as his personal motto *Totus Tuus* ("Totally Yours").

From 1979–81, Father Hebert, the one-time altar and choir boy, now priest, served as assistant at Our Lady of Guadalupe parish; and, from 1981–84, as assistant at St. Patrick's parish—both in Anchorage. He was pastor of St. Joseph's parish in **Cordova** during the year 1984–85.

During the years 1985–90, Father Hebert served in the archdiocesan Youth Ministry Office in Anchorage as a Youth Minister. This was a full-time ministry, a ministry he found "very rewarding." Having "a very out-going personality and being drawn to help people," by his own admission, he found "working directly with people" to be his most satisfying ministry. He saw himself as primarily "a sacramental priest." He found administrating a parish more of a challenge and tended to delegate this to others. In two of the parishes he headed, he hired a parish administrator.

In 1988, God allowed Father Hebert to have "a deeper, personal spiritual experience." In his own words:

> On November 17th, I was told that I had cancer, Hodgkin's Disease. I remember the dark nights I went through and the possibility of death. After weeks of depression, prayer, spiritual direction, I said in my heart, "God, I accept this, but if you can use this for anybody else to come to know you, please do." This was a spiritual experience for me. I really found God and the Holy Spirit on a deeper level. For the next year and a half, I had three surgeries and radiation treatments. It was here I learned to be sick and to trust God and, in keeping with my motto, to put my life in His hands.

After leaving the Youth Ministry Office, in 1990, Father Hebert, once again in good health, went on to serve as pastor of St. Elizabeth Ann Seton parish, from 1990–97; and of Our Lady of Guadalupe parish, from 1997–2001. In the year 2001, he became pastor of Holy Cross parish. These parishes are all in Anchorage. In July 2004, he began a six-month sabbatical—in his words, "to continue listening to God by letting go and seeing what God has planned for me."

HEBERT, Father Joseph L., S.J.

Joseph L. Hebert was born on July 28, 1916, in Denver, Colorado. There he attended Catholic grade and high schools. He entered the Missouri Province of the Society of Jesus on August 8, 1934. Before going on to theological studies and ordination to the priesthood, he spent several years at St. Francis Mission, among the Sioux Indians, in South Dakota. From the outset of his Jesuit life, he had hoped to serve as a missionary. He was ordained a priest on June 18, 1947.

Father Hebert, though he had hoped to spend his priestly years as a missionary in the Arctic, spent 22 of them as a traveling missionary in the tropics, in Honduras. At one time he was responsible for as many as 64 villages. He traveled on horseback. "Everything," he wrote, "was primitive—no roads, no phone, no electricity."

In 1971, he returned to the United States for a vacation, not knowing where he would serve after that. He knew only that he "wanted to be led by God." While in the Pacific Northwest for a workshop, he met Father **James R. Laudwein**, S.J., who told him, "There is lots of room in **Alaska**!" When Father Hebert heard those words, he was "filled with a great desire to go to Alaska." By this time, he had been drawn to Catholic Charismatics.

Father Hebert arrived in **Fairbanks**, Alaska, on October 12, 1973, and began to serve as assistant pastor at Immaculate Conception parish. He "discovered a half dozen Catholic women, who had been praying and fasting each Monday, asking that God would send a priest, who could start a Catholic Charismatic group." Under him the Charismatic group prospered. While in Fairbanks, he had two heart attacks, from which he recovered.

In June 1976, Father Hebert became pastor of the **Delta Junction** and **Tok** parishes, residing in Tok. During his three years as pastor of Tok, he had one baptism, one marriage, one convert, and one funeral. Father Hebert returned to his home province, Missouri, in 1979, where he continued to serve as a pastoral minister, mainly in Colorado.

HEMMER, Father Joseph, O.F.M.

Joseph Hemmer was born in Cornlea, Nebraska, on December 23, 1927, the second son of nine children, five girls and four boys. His parents, Albert and Antonetta, were farmers. "Church" was a very important part of family life. Two of his maternal aunts and a cousin were Sisters. For his elementary schooling, Joseph attended the local parish school, Sacred Heart, in Cornlea, from 1933–41. This was two miles from the family farm, so the Hemmer school children, after doing morning chores, commuted to it daily by horse and buggy. The school had a good reputation, because its graduates always did well in the State High School entrance exams.

One day, Joseph's 8th grade teacher spotted him studying a picture of a young man being especially cared for by a loving, gentle Christ. She asked him, "Would you like to be a priest?" Her question led to Joseph's entering Saint Joseph Seminary, in Westmont, Illinois, for his high school studies. This seminary, a boarding school, was staffed by Franciscans of the Sacred Heart Province, headquartered in St. Louis, Missouri.

On July 3, 1946, Joseph entered the Franciscan novitiate of St. Francis in Teutopolis, Illinois. On July 4, 1947, he made his profession of simple vows. He then went on to three years of philosophical studies at Our Lady of Angels Seminary in Cleveland, Ohio. He took his solemn vows on July 4, 1950. From 1950–54, he made his theological studies at St. Joseph's in Teutopolis. He was ordained a priest in Teutopolis on June 24, 1954.

Father Hemmer, along with the rest of his ordination class, spent his first year as a priest at Quincy University, in Quincy, Illinois, taking courses, working in parishes on weekends, and teaching religion classes in local grade and high schools. During the year 1955–56, he took courses in the Industrial Arts at the University of Nebraska, after which, from 1956–79, he was at Corpus Christi/Hales Franciscan High School in the heart of Chicago's black community. At Corpus Christi, he served both as a teacher and as its principal—"always deeply involved," in his words.

In the mid-1970s, while still at Corpus Christi, Father Hemmer worked at Mercy Hospital during odd hours getting training as a hospital chaplain and earning his accreditation with the National Association of Catholic Chaplains. During those same years, he devoted his summers to doing "supply work" at two different parishes in Portland, Oregon.

In 1979, Father Hemmer celebrated his silver jubilee as a priest. He spent part of that year on a trip to South America. In Brazil, after he visited Manaus and Santarem on the Amazon, he flew south from Belem with a fellow Franciscan to Brasilia, Rio, and Sao Paulo.

During the years 1979–86, Father Hemmer was pastor of St. Jude's parish, a needy, struggling parish shifting from white to black, in Warrensville, Ohio. The year 1986–87 was for him a sabbatical year, during which he updated his theology by spending a semester at Catholic Theological Union in Chicago and a semester at the University of Notre Dame. He next spent a year, 1987–88, in chaplain ministry at Quincy University.

While still in the seminary, studying theology and, at the same time, editing an in-house mission magazine, Father Hemmer became interested in "the Church in faraway places." When, in 1985, the call went out to members of the Sacred Heart Province for volunteers to serve among the Athabaskan Indians of northern **Alaska**, he found himself drawn to that ministry. However, at the time he was still committed to St. Jude's parish. When his pastorate at St. Jude's was up, the need for a volunteer priest to serve in Alaska was still there. Thinking that ministry in Alaska would be "a great way to apply the skills developed down through the years," he gladly volunteered, and was accepted, and told by his Father Provincial to buy a one-way ticket. That was in 1988.

By the time Father Hemmer arrived in **Galena**, an Athabaskan Indian village on the middle Yukon River, in the summer of 1988, the Franciscans were no longer being referred to, mistakenly, as the San-friscans, as they had been when they first arrived on the Yukon two years earlier. Upon his arrival in Galena, the people, who had seen a considerable number of teachers, State Troopers, Public Health employees—not to mention several Franciscan priests—come and go during the years immediately preceding, wondered out loud how long he would survive Alaska. He assured them that he intended to stay on the middle Yukon for at least ten years. His answer met with a lot of skepticism. They doubted that this priest from the big cities would survive long in "bush" Alaska, with its different culture, dusty gravel roads, mosquitoes, and long, dark, cold wintry nights.

For his first term in Alaska, Father Hemmer was stationed at Galena, from the summer of 1988 to the summer of 1994. Out of Galena, he served also as visiting priest to its dependent missions, the Athabaskan Indian villages of **Ruby** and **Huslia**. During his first winter in Galena, he lived through what has gone down in Alaskan history as "the Great Cold of January 1989." In Galena, that January, an official low of minus 86 degrees was recorded.

The church–rectory structure in Galena, though virtually new when Father Hemmer arrived, had many flaws and shortcomings, and needed his constant attention. Calling on the practical skills he had acquired on the family farm, and while taking Industrial Arts courses, he was now himself able to make many badly needed improvements.

In the summer of 1994, Father Hemmer took up station in **Kaltag**, but continued to be visiting priest to Ruby. The Kaltag church, being relatively old, too, needed much repair work and upgrading. In the summer of 2002, in Kaltag, to replace the three tin caches there, he put up a new $30 \times 40'$ storage shed, with a $14 \times 18'$ heated workshop. In Ruby, he was part of the team that saw to the replacing of the 50-year-old church with a new one. It took a number of years, before the old church was repositioned to serve as an all-purpose building, and the new church virtually ready for dedication in the year 2004.

In the course of his many years on the middle Yukon, Father Hemmer, always responsible for more than one village, did more than his share of inter-village traveling. None of the villages in interior Alaska are connected by roads. During his earlier years on the Yukon, he traveled by open boat, when the river was ice-free. In the winter, when the river was frozen over, or the trails paved with snow, he traveled by snowmachine. "By contrast," he wrote, after twelve years in Alaska, "flying in one of the bush planes borders on luxury. Nevertheless, travel of any kind in these parts, if it teaches a man nothing else, it does teach him patience. Much of our travel is conditioned: 'God willing, and weather permitting.'"

Father Hemmer, unquestionably, did a great deal of traveling and great amount of manual labor improving and maintaining buildings. That, however, was not his primary purpose for coming to and staying on in Alaska. In his own words:

I did not come north simply to survive the rigors of travel and to attend to material church-related needs, no matter how important. Nor did I come north simply to learn patience. I came north in response to a challenging call to mission, in the best Franciscan tradition.

He saw himself "as one engaged in what was essentially a spiritual enterprise, as one called and sent by the Lord Himself."

As of the year 2004, Father Hemmer was still pastor of Kaltag–Ruby.

38

HESS, Brother John, S.J.

John Hess was born on June 22, 1883, in Bavaria, Germany. He was hired out as a child-laborer in a coal mine, when he was eight years old. During his long years in **Alaska**, he was on the lookout for coal. When he was twenty, he was drafted into the highly trained army of Kaiser Wilhelm. The military training stayed with him all his life. In later life, he was still an expert marksman.

In the summer of 1905, John Hess sailed for the United States at the invitation of some friends, who had left Germany and settled in Yakima, Washington. Shortly after his arrival in the Northwest, he bought and tilled a tract of land in what is now downtown Yakima.

John Hess entered the Jesuit novitiate at Los Gatos, California, on January 24, 1910, to become a Lay Brother. After his novitiate, he spent two years in Lewiston, Idaho, before sailing for Alaska in September 1914. His first assignment, **Holy Cross Mission**, was to last 42 years.

At Holy Cross, Brother Hess served as a general handyman, maintaining and fixing motors, stoves, buildings, wells. He was responsible for the drilling of many wells. In the summer of 1927, he led a construction crew that put up a mission building at **Kashunuk**. The following year, he led a crew that did the same at **Hooper Bay**. "Everything was left in the hands of Bro. Hess," wrote Father Philip I. **Delon**, S.J., General Superior of the Alaska Mission at the time, to Father Provincial Joseph M. Piet, S.J. In June–July 1931, Brother Hess was at **Nightmute** to build a church there.

Brother Hess was noted, above all, for his skills as a gardener and farmer. For many of his years at Holy Cross, he faithfully kept journals and diaries, in which he logged daily temperatures and a great variety of information dealing with the farm and the gardens. His "Farm Diary," written with more than a hint of a German accent, is a detailed record of four decades of farming at the mission. From it we learn, for example, what vegetables, what forage and grain crops did well, and which ones did poorly. We learn that apple trees were planted, but without favorable results; and that sugar cane was tried, "which was a complete failure, for it never came up." Corn did poorly. On April 2, 1917, he "cooked some hay tea just as you cook ordinary tea." He "took some timothy and marsh hay and it seems the cows like it very well." In his diaries he commented on greenhouses, angora goats, milk and beef cows, horses, pigs, and chickens. The diary also reflects the steady correspondence he carried on with the heads of the agricultural experiment stations at **Fairbanks**, Rampart, and **Sitka**.

Brother Hess was clearly a man always open to new information and suggestions concerning vegetables and grain varieties, fertilizers, farming methods, vegetable and animal diseases, and farming in general. He was always ready to try something new, but he did not proceed in a haphazard manner. His experiments in the field of mixed agriculture were genuine scientific experiments. His findings were carefully recorded and communicated to the various station directors. His "Farm Diary" is a fairly complete record of subarctic agriculture on the lower Yukon River.

Brother Hess was diabetic. With the same meticulous care that he kept records of his farming and gardening activities, he kept a log of his medical condition. He was able to diagnose his health problems correctly, and to determine what lifestyle best enabled him to lead a more or less normal life for decades, despite his diabetic condition. Members of the medical profession marveled at the accuracy of his self-diagnosis and at the correctness of the diet he prescribed for himself.

Lacking a typical file cabinet, Brother Hess "filed" his records, notes, observations, and reminders on numerous nails driven into the walls of his room.

In December 1954, Brother Hess was in Fair-

Brother John Hess, S.J.
JOPA-964.23.

banks. It was a memorable month for him. On the 6th, he was received into the Alaskan Pioneers. On the 10th, the following entry was made in the Immaculate Conception Church diary:

> Bro. John Hess reached a goal toward which he had been striving for nearly 50 years, when he was granted citizenship today. Judge Forbes held a special session of court to swear him in. The usual 30-day waiting period after examination was waived through special permission of the Attorney General of the United States in Washington.

In a letter, written the following day to Father **John J. Wood**, S.J., Father James U. **Conwell**, S.J., commented on Brother Hess' reaction to the two honors, "So, he's walking on air."

On October 14, 1956, the 73-year-old Brother Hess was one of the thirty people flown that day from Holy Cross to the new **Copper Valley School**. Despite his years and diabetic condition, he made the move to do "domestic work." Dressed in his faded dungarees and pushing his much-used wheelbarrow, often loaded with bricks, he continued to do much physical work at the school. Summers found him in the garden. He repaired shoes. With his ready smile and buoyant, happy disposition, and with his genuine humility and prayerfulness, and especially with his kindness, he impressed and edified all at the school.

In 1960, Brother Hess—"the old-timer's favorite Brother"—celebrated his golden jubilee as a Jesuit. The following year, his uninterrupted stay in Alaska came to an end. Failing health necessitated his complete retirement, to the novitiate at Sheridan, Oregon. There, bed-ridden during his last days, he accepted his condition with dignity, peace and good humor, as he prepared for his final journey. He kept asking his attendants, every few days, "Is this the Feast of St. Joseph?" only to receive the answer, "No, not yet; but it is coming." Shortly after midnight, on March 19, he woke up, and the attendant with him at the moment said, "Brother, do you know that today is the Feast of St. Joseph?" At that, Brother Hess smiled, closed his eyes, seemed to drift off in sleep. Within the half hour, he died, departed quietly, peacefully. Brother Hess died, as befits a man who had led a hidden life of manual labor, on the feast of St. Joseph, March 19, 1963.

An *In Memoriam* item in the Copper Valley School yearbook reads:

> We felt mostly, I guess, a sympathetic happiness with Brother, who had finally completed his patient, laborious, well-spent life—80 years of it, 48 in Alaska, 52 a Jesuit. No one was better loved by more people than Brother Hess. His example was not lost on our students. One would think they never noticed him, but they did. May we all serve God and man as faithfully and as cheerfully as did Brother Hess.

Brother John Hess, S.J., lies buried in the Jesuit cemetery at Mount St. Michael's, Spokane.

HEYNEN, Father William L.

William (Willem) Lambert Heynen was born on September 16, 1856, in Roermond, Province of Limburg, Netherlands. Ordained a priest on May 22, 1880, in Malines, Belgium, he arrived in Victoria, British Columbia, Canada, that same year. In 1885, he was assigned to **Sitka**, **Alaska**, arriving there in November. In an interview, he recalled: "I said my first Mass in Sitka in an old saloon on a Sunday and I suppose I had about 25 people, Indians and Whites and a few Marines, present." Before long, he converted an old carriage barn into a permanent church. On December 13, 1885, he offered Mass in it for the first time. "On Christmas day," we read in that same interview, "the roof commenced to leak right above

Father
William L.
Heynen. *LRC.*

the altar. That caused a break in the service until I had moved the altar into the corner."

While in Sitka, Father Heynen had occasion to go to the jail to visit Francis Fuller, the man who had killed Archbishop Charles J. **Seghers**. He found Fuller "a fine-looking man," who treated him "very kindly." But, when Father Heynen made an attempt to broach the subject of murder, Fuller "kept silent."

Father Heynen was recalled from Sitka in 1889, and sent to Clayoquet on the west coast of Vancouver Island. He was never to see Alaska again. In 1895, he was sent home to his native Belgium for three months of sick-leave. After this, he—"a good, holy priest"—returned to Vancouver Island to spend the rest of his long life "without respite, in working and suffering for his beloved missions."

Father Heynen died on October 18, 1939. Of him, and of Father John J. **Althoff**, Joseph R. **Crimont**, Vicar Apostolic of Alaska, said: "These two men were pioneers of the Church in Southeastern Alaska."

HINSVARK, Father John A.

At his birth, premature by three months, the attending physician said simply, "He is going to die." He was the second priest to be ordained for the Diocese of **Fairbanks**. He is numbered among the "ice missionaries" of **Alaska**. For a time he had to live down his nickname, that of "Father Crash." Upon his retirement, after serving for 24 years as

a chaplain in the Alaska Army National Guard, he was honored with the rarely conferred Minuteman Award for "outstanding leadership as the STARC Chaplain for the State of Alaska." By the time the third millennium dawned, he was the dean of diocesan priests in northern Alaska.

The oldest of 12 children, John Arthur Hinsvark was born to Arthur Norris Hinsvark and Jolenta Agnes Keimig on May 20, 1940, in the town of Gary, South Dakota. When he was four years old, the family moved to Alameda, California. After attending an Alameda public pre-school for two and one half years, John entered the first grade at St. Joseph's parochial school in Alameda for the rest of the grades, from 1947–54. For high school and two years of college, he attended St. Joseph's Minor Seminary in Mountain View, California, from 1954–60. He made his philosophical studies at St. Patrick's Major Seminary, Menlo Park, California, from 1960–62. By his own admission, he experienced homesickness, even unto tears, during his earliest seminary years. At the same time, he was heartened as he recalled the words his father had spoken to him when he asked to take the entrance examination for the seminary: "Son, remember, your mother and I will support you in whatever you decide to do in your life."

In the fall of 1962, John began his theological studies at Mount Angel Seminary, St. Benedict, Oregon. Having received excellent training in catechetics while still at St. Patrick's Major Seminary, he was chosen to teach catechism to the high school students of Chemawa Indian School just north of Salem, Oregon. This was regarded as "the most difficult assignment" any of the seminarians might receive. The student body at Chemawa consisted of Native American teenagers from reservations in the American Southwest and Alaska. During his second year of theology, John discerned his call to ministry in northern Alaska.

In April 1965, John was accepted as a candidate for the Diocese of Fairbanks by Francis D. **Gleeson**, S.J., Bishop of Fairbanks at the time. That summer he received his first full introduction to Alaska, when, along with seven seminarians from the Josephinum Theologate in Columbus, Ohio, he worked on the construction of Sacred Heart Cathedral in Fairbanks. In early August of that year, he "learned a little bit about the diocese in the area called 'bush Alaska.'"

On August 14, 1965, in **Bethel**, John received the Tonsure and Minor Orders at the hands of Bishop Gleeson. The following day, on the Feast of the Assumption, at St. Mary's Mission, **Andreafsky**, he was ordained to the sub-diaconate by Bishop Gleeson. By the time he left Alaska that summer, he had had a well-rounded introduction to the diocese, in which he would minister as a priest.

Nine months later, on April 22, 1966, having been found to have "priestly qualities," John was ordained a priest, likewise by Bishop Gleeson, in St. Mary's parish church, in Mount Angel, Oregon. Two months after his ordination to the priesthood, on June 28th, he arrived in Fairbanks. During a meeting there with Bishop Gleeson, Father Hinsvark learned that his deepest desire, that he be assigned to the "bush," would be met immediately.

Father Hinsvark was the first diocesan priest to serve among the Central Yup'ik Eskimos of the Yukon-Kuskokwim Delta. From July 10, 1966, to July 1974, he had the pastoral care of St. Catherine of Siena mission at **Chefornak**, and of Our Lady of Perpetual Help mission at **Nightmute**.

In 1967, Father Hinsvark invited three of his Chefornak parishioners to translate the Mass into their vernacular, the Central Yup'ik Eskimo language. They were Adeline Panruk, Mary Tunuchuk and Agnes Kairaiuak. Their translation was presented to translators in neighboring villages acknowledged to be better translators than they. The trio's translation was found to be virtually flawless.

In 1969, Father Hinsvark saw to the building of the new church at **Umkumiut**. On April 28, 1970, he began his 24-year ministry as a chaplain in the Alaska Army National Guard. From 1973–80, he was a Consultor to Robert L. **Whelan**, S.J., the Bishop of Fairbanks at the time. Before he left his Chefornak–Nightmute assignment, he built a new residence at Nightmute. He also supervised the construction of a new parish/community center and rectory at Chefornak to replace the church that had burned to the ground on March 4, 1972.

From August 1974 to August 1980, Father Hinsvark was pastor of Immaculate Conception parish in Bethel, and visiting priest to its two dependent missions on the Yukon, Immaculate

Father John A. Hinsvark.
Courtesy of Dr. Thomas A. Busch.

Heart of Mary at **Marshall** and Our Lady of Guadalupe at **Russian Mission**. During this time, he served also as a member of the Diocesan Liturgical Commission and as a member of the **Eskimo Deacon Program**. From 1973–74, he was Codirector of the program, and, from 1974–75, its Director. During the year 1975–76, he had the joy of having his parents, with their able and willing hands, living and working with him in Bethel.

In 1977, Father Hinsvark earned his pilot's license. In July 1978, while flying into **Newtok**, in an orange Super Cub, a Piper PA-18, to attend the ordination to the permanent diaconate of Nicholas Tommy, he landed too fast, lost control of the plane on the ground, and wound up in the tundra between two ponds with the plane's wheels pointing to the sky. He was not hurt, but he was rather embarrassed. On hand to witness the mishap happened to be Bishop Whelan, a number of priests—among them Jesuit Fathers Michael J. **Kaniecki** and James A. **Sebesta**, both skilled pilots—and Eskimo deacon candidates. It was mainly Father Hinsvark's pride as a pilot and the airplane that suffered damage in the accident. For this ill-fated landing, he was nicknamed "Father Crash" in Bethel, and referred to as the *Bruchpilot* ("crash-pilot") in an article published in Germany a few years after the event. The Super-

Cub was retrieved, repaired, and sold. He then purchased a PA-20, a larger Super-Cub capable of carrying four passengers. This he flew for two years, and then sold, when his Bethel assignment was up.

Father Hinsvark readily admitted to being "accident prone." Before he was out of grade school, he had succeeded in breaking bones in his arms and legs on at least six different occasions.

The year 1980–81 was for Father Hinsvark a sabbatical year, during which he attended a three-month Continuing Theological Up-Date in Rome and Israel.

From August 1981 to August 1990, Father Hinsvark was pastor of Little Flower of Jesus parish in **Hooper Bay** and of Blessed Sacrament parish in **Scammon Bay**. From February 1983 to July 1985, he also provided priestly ministry to the Chefornak parish; and from July 1985 to August 1990, he had the pastoral care also of Sacred Heart parish in **Chevak**. As all of those parishes had their own Armory, he was able to attend to routine National Guard demands wherever he was. By the time he left this nine-year assignment, he had almost finished the remodeling—begun by his predecessor, Father Richard L. **McCaffrey**, S.J.—of the old church–convent building at Hooper Bay, replaced the foundation under the Scammon Bay church, and had added some rooms to the church in Chevak to provide a better worship environment. His final year in ministry to those three parishes was made difficult with his being accused of "burn out" and "serious interpersonal relationship problems." He took another sabbatical, which stretched out to 15 months.

In September 1991, Father Hinsvark became the founding pastor of the parish of St. John Vianney in Anderson, a small town near Clear Air Force Radar Station some 20 miles south of **Nenana**. Until his departure, in July 1994, he helped solidify a new style of ministry in the communities of Anderson, Nenana, Clear, **Healy**, Cantwell, and Denali National Park. He worked with the newly appointed Pastoral Administrators. He tended to the Sacramental and some spiritual needs of the various communities, while the Pastoral Administrators in Nenana and Healy "ran" those parishes. After three years, he was well acquainted with the developing style of ministry in the Fairbanks diocese to meet the needs of parishes not having a resident or assigned pastor.

In March 1993, Father Hinsvark was appointed Vocation Director for the Diocese of Fairbanks. In August 1994, he was appointed pastor of St. Joseph's parish in **Nome**. As such, beginning in July 1995, he was responsible also for its dependent missions of **Teller** and **Little Diomede**. In July 2002, he became the sole priest in the Seward Peninsula area, responsible now also for St. Francis Xavier parish in **Kotzebue**. As of the year 2004, he was still the sole priest in that area.

In 1994, having attained the rank of Lieutenant Colonel, and having served for seven years as the State Area Command Chaplain, Father Hinsvark retired from the Alaska Army National Guard.

For many years, Father Hinsvark had served also on the Diocesan Liturgical Commission and as a Consultor to the bishop. On August 10, 2000, four days after Bishop Kaniecki died suddenly, it was Father Hinsvark who convened the Diocesan Board of Consultors to elect an interim Diocesan Administrator.

HOCH, Father Matthew E.

Matthew Hoch, the sixth of twelve children, was born in the Diocese of Sioux Falls, South Dakota, on October 5, 1906. When he was about 14, the family moved to Madison, Minnesota. His background on a farm gave him a facility with tools and a familiarity with hard work.

Matthew began studies for the priesthood at St. Thomas' Seminary in Denver, where he studied from 1932–36. He then took a break from studies, for personal reasons, and worked at St. Mary's Institute in Huber, Oregon, and taught at St. Ann's School in **Juneau**. On August 2, 1937, he was incardinated into the Vicariate of **Alaska** by Joseph R. **Crimont**, S.J., Vicar Apostolic of Alaska at the time. He was ordained to the diaconate by Walter J. **Fitzgerald**, S.J., then Coadjutor Vicar Apostolic of Alaska. On May 22, 1941, he was ordained to the priesthood by Edward D. Howard, Archbishop of Portland, Oregon.

Father Hoch served in **Wrangell** and **Petersburg** from 1942–59; then as chaplain of St. Ann's Hospital in Juneau, from 1959–60. When he was reassigned, to **Kodiak**, for the year 1960–61, his friends commented, "Juneau's loss is Kodiak's gain."

Father Matthew E. Hoch.
JOPA-414.09.

Father Hoch was noted for his gentle caring. Next he was chaplain at the **Ketchikan** hospital for a time. Sometime before the mid-1960s, he was back in Juneau, to serve there as assistant pastor at the Cathedral of the Nativity of the Blessed Virgin Mary parish and as chaplain at St. Ann's Hospital. Father Louis L. **Renner**, S.J., who spent the month of July 1966 tending the Cathedral parish, so that its regular pastor, Father David A. **Melbourne**, could take a much needed vacation, long remembered with gratitude the great kindness shown him by Father Hoch.

In May 1972, Father Hoch, upon his retirement from a full-time ministry, moved to the Diocese of Santa Rosa, California. There he again served as a hospital chaplain. A stroke suffered in 1981, crippled him and necessitated his spending his last days in a nursing home. He died on December 28, 1983, in California. He lies buried in Holy Cross Cemetery, Los Angeles.

208

HOELSKEN, Father Mark A., S.J.

Mark A. Hoelsken, the second of eight children, four boy and four girls, was born on August 11, 1951, in Denver, Colorado, to Francis A. Hoelsken of Denver and Lucie Briegel Hoelsken of Davenport, Iowa. In Denver, Mark received his elementary and secondary education at Holy Family parochial grade and high schools. After graduating from high school in 1969, he learned to be an electronics technician by attending a trade school for two years, 1969–71. For the next three years he worked as a technician in Colorado Springs.

In 1974, Mark joined the **Jesuit Volunteer Corps** and began to serve at radio station **KNOM** in **Nome, Alaska**, as a newscaster and Chief Engineer. After serving at KNOM during the years 1974–76 and 1977–78—a time he described as "three years of enjoyable radio work"—he entered the Jesuit Novitiate of St. Francis Xavier in Portland, Oregon, on August 26, 1978. His two-year noviceship completed, he studied the classics, the humanities, and philosophy at Gonzaga University in Spokane, Washington, from 1980–84. During the year 1984–85, he taught at Bellarmine Preparatory in Tacoma, Washington, before going on to spend the years 1985–87 at St. Joseph's Church, Seattle, Washington, as a pastoral minister. From 1987–91, he made his theological studies at Regis College in Toronto, Ontario, Canada. On June 15, 1991, in St. Joseph's Church, Seattle, he was ordained a priest by Robert L. **Whelan**, S.J., Bishop of **Fairbanks** at the time.

It was his three years at KNOM that had sparked in Father Hoelsken the desire to enter the Society of Jesus. "I felt a strong desire," he wrote,

> to eventually return to Alaska as a Jesuit priest. I enjoyed the kind of life I'd discovered in the JVC, a life of service to others, and to God. And I was interested in the kind of life I witnessed in Jesuits I met during those years. I hoped to return to Alaska and work by their sides among the Native people of Alaska.

During the first several years of Father Hoelsken's Jesuit training, this hope remained dominant, whenever he thought about future ministry as a priest. Then, however, he began to reproach himself, fearing that he had closed his mind as to what God might be calling him. He dropped the notion of returning to Alaska and, for some years, "struggled a great deal with vocation questions."

In the course of his theological studies, Father Hoelsken had had occasion to work at the Center of Native Spirituality at Anishinable, outside

Father Mark A. Hoelsken, S.J.
BR-CD 0308-A3-15.

Espanola, Ontario, on the north shore of Lake Huron. That work, and the inspiring example of fellow Jesuits he met there, gave him a vision of priesthood that interested and excited him. "I had come," he wrote, "to discern a place for myself as a priest in some dimension of Native ministry."

To his great consolation and reassurance that he was, unquestionably, being called to return to Alaska as a priest to serve its Native people, Father Hoelsken—around the time he was ordained to the transitional diaconate in 1990—received a letter from Theodore E. **Kestler**, S.J., General Superior of Jesuits in Alaska at the time, inviting him to consider coming to Alaska and joining the Jesuits serving the Central Yup'ik Eskimos in the Yukon-Kuskokwim Delta. To this invitation he responded "immediately and with delight and new hope, and with a profoundly consoling conviction that those earlier desires to serve Native peoples in Alaska had their origin in the Spirit of God."

In the summer of 1991, Father Hoelsken returned to Alaska to take on his first assignment there as a priest, that of providing pastoral care for the three Bering Sea coast villages of **Hooper Bay**, **Chevak**, and **Scammon Bay**. On his initial visit to those villages, he was accompanied by Father Charles J. **Peterson**, S.J., who introduced him to local circumstances and to as many people as the two could meet in a short time. Father Hoelsken found himself "quickly and remarkably at home." Whenever

he returned to any one of his villages, the people there greeted him with a spontaneous and warm "Welcome home!" For the next five years, the three villages were indeed home, and "school," to him. "The fact is," he wrote, "that I learned in large part from the people of Hooper Bay, Chevak, and Scammon Bay what it is, and how, to be a priest."

Early on during that first Alaskan assignment, Father Hoelsken learned also how to enjoy the use of a snowmachine as a means of traveling between his villages. With his mechanical skills, he had no trouble keeping the one salvaged for him running, even though it was a rather ancient model. "I love winter and snow, and I love to ski," he wrote. He took advantage of every opportunity to do some cross-country skiing. He found himself eminently suited to the life he was now leading.

At the end of his first year as visiting priest to the three villages, Father Hoelsken wrote, "I look forward to being here indefinitely." However, by the fall of 1996, he found himself far from the Eskimos and snows of western Alaska. During the year 1996–97, he was in Manila, Philippines, making his tertianship. The program there emphasized solidarity with the poor. To this principle of apostolic ministry he could relate wholeheartedly. He happily spent time with the aboriginal people living in the mountains of the Philippines. All the while, however, he was consoled by the deep conviction that his true "home" and calling was waiting for him in Alaska, and that it was in Alaska where he belonged. In spite of health problems that he endured throughout his months in the Philippines, he found the whole tertianship experience entirely reconfirming of his vocation to the Society of Jesus, to the priesthood, and to ministry in Alaska.

While Father Hoelsken was in the Philippines, Father **Gregg D. Wood**, S.J., replaced him in the three villages of Hooper Bay, Chevak, and Scammon Bay. After one year there, Father Wood opted to continue on as visiting priest to them. Accordingly, upon his return from the Philippines in 1997, Father Hoelsken was assigned visiting priest to the Nelson Island villages of **Newtok**, **Chefornak**, and **Toksook Bay**. Around Easter 1998, he was replaced at Toksook Bay by Father David J. **Anderson**, S.J., leaving him, for some months, the care only of Newtok and Chefornak. In the summer of 1998, however, Father Hoelsken assumed responsibility also for the village of **Nightmute**.

By this time, Father Hoelsken was making visits also to radio KNOM, in Nome, where his whole love affair with Alaska had first begun. In February 1998, he was appointed the station's Spiritual Director by Michael J. **Kaniecki**, S.J., Bishop of Fairbanks at the time. Thereafter, he visited the station from time to time to conduct annual spiritual retreats for the KNOM volunteer crew, to record "spots," and to meet and socialize with the radio staff.

On July 31, 1999, Father Hoelsken, while continuing on as visiting priest to the villages of Chefornak and Newtok, became Superior of the Brother Joe **Prince** Community, a community composed of the Jesuits serving in western Alaska. At regular intervals, they gathered at the St. Mary's Mission complex on the **Andreafsky** River for spiritual renewal, Jesuit companionship, and relaxation. At the same time he became Superior of the Brother Joe Prince Community, he became also Provincial Assistant for Alaska. In the year 2001, he was assigned the additional responsibility of Director of the **Eskimo Deacon Program**.

In carrying out his multiple responsibilities, Father Hoelsken was sustained by a deep personal spirituality, a firm sense of apostolic commitment, and a genuine feeling of solidarity with the people he served and with his brother Jesuits. He was sustained, too, by his ability to see also the lighter side of life. While people appreciated him for his compassionate understanding, they appreciated him also for his sense of humor and for his hearty, reverberating laugh.

116

HOLY CROSS MISSION

The village of Holy Cross, **Alaska**, grew up around a mission located on the right bank of the Yukon River 279 miles upstream from the Bering Sea. The mission was across the river and a little down from the Indian village of Koserefsky.

Before Holy Cross Mission was established in 1888, the site was, according to the mission's founder, Father Aloysius J. **Robaut**, S.J., "a perfect wilderness." Wrote Father Robaut: "There was not, nor seemed to have ever been, any Indian or White settlement in that place, it being nothing but a perfect wilderness, not a soul living there, nor the least sign of any one having ever lived there." He wrote that in 1909, in a moment of enlightened self-interest, one suspects, in a statement dealing with the land on which the mission was located. If the one-time Native village of Anilukhtakpak was not located on the actual mission site, it was located very near it.

When a post office was established at Holy Cross Mission in 1899, the mission complex was named Koserefsky after the Native village. In 1912, the name was changed to Holy Cross. The village of Koserefsky ceased to be around 1915. By then most of the people from there had moved over to Holy Cross. At Holy Cross the Athabaskan Indians of the interior meet the Central Yup'ik Eskimos of the Yukon-Kuskokwim Delta. According to official census reports, Holy Cross had a population of 131 in 1890, 277 in 1990, and again 277 in 2000.

Holy Cross was located on a main channel of the Yukon until the 1930s, when the channel began to change. By the mid-1940s, Ghost (Gost) Creek Slough, also called Walker Slough, on which the community is now located, had formed. Today one could drift down the Yukon, past Holy Cross, without even suspecting that it is there.

The name "Holy Cross" was given the mission by Father Robaut in compliance with the express wishes of Louis A. Lootens, one-time bishop of Idaho, then retired in Victoria, who had given the Archbishop Charles J. **Seghers** party, before it left Victoria for Alaska, his pectoral cross containing a relic of the true cross with the desire that the first mission to be founded in northern Alaska be given the name "Mission of the Holy Cross." Holy Cross was actually the second mission founded in northern Alaska. The **Nulato** mission was founded the year before.

In June 1888, Father Robaut and Brother Carmelo **Giordano**, S.J., moved to the Holy Cross site and began to put up a log mission building. Sometime later that summer, they were joined by Brother John

(*right*) A 1982 aerial view of Holy Cross. When Holy Cross Mission was established in 1888, and for over half a century thereafter, the Yukon River came to its doorstep. Around 1950, however, the river began to shift its course away from the village, until only a small slough made Holy Cross accessible by water. *LR.*

(*opposite, top*) Holy Family Church, Holy Cross. *MK.*

(*opposite, bottom*) Holy Cross Mission as it appeared in 1931. It is springtime. The Yukon River is still frozen over, but piles of manure to fertilize the ground dot the gardens and fields. *BH/JOPA-549.6.08.*

B. **Rosati**, S.J., newly arrived in Alaska. Before the building was up, three Sisters of St. **Ann**—Mary Stephen Leahy, Mary Pauline Brault, and Mary Joseph Calasanctius De Ruyter—arrived, unexpectedly, on September 4, 1888. They brought with them three-year-old Anutka Neumann, daughter of Henry Neumann, the agent of the Alaska Commercial Company at **St. Michael**. Anutka had the distinction of being Holy Cross Mission's first pupil.

On September 8th, the Sisters moved into the first log cabin built at Holy Cross. This had been intended for the Jesuits, but was hastily finished and given to the Sisters for temporary use. Five inches of snow fell on the 17th. On October 8th, the Sisters were able to move into their two-story log-cabin convent–school. This had a small chapel on the first floor.

By January 9, 1889, the Holy Cross Mission school had 31 pupils, day scholars and boarders. Emphasis was from the outset on boarders, and their number grew steadily. Before the end of September 1889, a much needed new schoolhouse was ready. Boarders came from various villages up and down the Yukon and from the Yukon-Kuskokwim

Delta. Father William H. **Judge**, S.J., at Holy Cross from 1890–92, voiced a general belief when he noted that "these children are our greatest hope for the future. As they are taken from all parts, we hope that when they return to their homes they will sow the good seed everywhere."

In 1902, under the direction of six Sisters, five Jesuit Brothers, and two Jesuit priests, there were 42 boys and 46 girls from many different villages and communities in the boarding school, each group divided into two classes. In the first class were older students who had already made progress in the "ordinary branches of an elementary English education." English was taught for its own sake, but also to provide a common language for students coming from different ethnic backgrounds, chief among them: Koyukon Athabaskan Indian, Central Yup'ik Eskimo, and Inupiat Eskimo. The older boys received, for the most part, manual training in mechanics, carpentry, shoemaking, farming, and gardening. During the 1930s and 1940s, Brother George J. **Feltes**, S.J., ran a machine shop that trained skilled mechanics. These were much in demand up and down the Yukon to maintain and operate steamboats and airplanes. The older girls, too, were taught practical skills such as home-making, sewing, and gardening. All at the mission were also encouraged to develop their talents in arts and crafts. Furthermore, all were thoroughly grounded in the basics of the Catholic Faith and its devotional life.

From their earliest days at Holy Cross, the Sisters and priests filled the roles of "doctors" and nurses, dispensing medicines and first aid and assisting the sick and injured. When a major epidemic—variously identified as cholera, typhoid fever, influenza— struck Holy Cross and the surrounding area in 1900, they and the Lay Brothers worked heroically to help the sick and dying. Father John L. **Lucchesi**, S.J., and Brother Joseph V. O'Hare, S.J., buried literally scores of its victims. Among them was Sister Mary Seraphine of the Sacred Heart, the Sister Superior of Holy Cross at the time. Lieut. J. C. Cantwell, an officer in the Revenue-Cutter Service and Commander of the U.S. Revenue Steamer *Nunivak*, on the Yukon River during the year 1899–1900, wrote in his 1902 Report:

> At Holy Cross we found the sick people had been taken care of by the priests and sisters of the mission with a tenderness and devotion which no words can adequately describe. Besides those directly under the care of the mission, the fathers had visited and attended to the wants of the natives at various settlements along the river within reach by boat, and their work had been constant, arduous, and self-sacrificing almost to the limit of human endurance. There was not one of the little community of Christian men and women who did not show the evidence of long days of weary watching and constant attention to the wants of their stricken fold. And yet on all their faces there was such an expression of patient cheerfulness that the heart must be made of stone that could remain unmoved in the presence of such absolute and unostentatious devotion to duty.

Around 1915, a small one-time private dwelling was converted into an infirmary. In 1930, this was rebuilt to serve as a kind of "hospital." It had eight small rooms and two solariums. These latter were meant to help especially victims of tuberculosis. Lacking running water and indoor plumbing, the hospital was still little more than an infirmary. Nevertheless, it was an indispensable part of the mission complex. In it, professional doctors, dentists, and nurses, making the rounds in northern Alaska, treated numerous patients. Father Robaut

spent the last days of his life in that hospital, and died in it on December 18, 1930.

Throughout its existence, the Holy Cross Mission also did much "good Samaritan" work. The winter of 1901–02 was a particularly cold one with a recorded low of minus 62 degrees at the mission in January. Mission records report that some miners perished from the cold that winter, while others arrived at the mission suffering from frostbite and malnutrition. Obviously, these needy individuals could not be turned away, and there is no record that any ever were.

Throughout its history, till the closing of its boarding school in 1956, Holy Cross Mission was expected to be, and was forced by circumstances to be, as self-reliant, as self-supporting as possible, no matter what its needs. This was especially true when it was a matter of obtaining or producing enough food to feed as many as 300 people. Much of the food consumed at the mission was native food: wild game, fowl, berries, and fish and eels from the river. But a great deal of what appeared on the mission tables was grown right at the mission in its extensive gardens. In the spring of 1889, the Sisters had already a primitive kind of garden. Soon highly productive gardens and successful livestock farming were part of the Holy Cross scene. In 1909, 20 years after subsistence farming at Holy Cross, the "garden spot of the Yukon," began, Major Adolphus W. Greely wrote:

> Despite predictions of failure as to agriculture and stock-farming, this mission is a striking evidence of what zeal, intelligence, and labor can do in an unfavorable environment. Some forty acres of land are under high cultivation, yielding such wealth of vegetables, forage, and flowers as must be seen to be fully appreciated.

Throughout most of the first four decades of the 20th century, the mission had also a reindeer herd to provide meat and skins for the mission's needs.

During its long history, Holy Cross saw a great number and variety of structures go up and come down. The focal point of the whole mission was, of course, the church. This was begun in 1904 and ready for the 1906 Christmas Mass. It was built out of dressed lumber. By the end of the 1800s, the mission had its own sawmill. Many mission buildings downriver and in the Yukon-Kuskokwim Delta

Standing in front of the Brothers/Boys house at Holy Cross Mission ca. 1907 are: 1) Brother René-Maurice Allory, F.I.C.; 2) Brother Bartholomew Marchisio, S.J.; 3) Brother Eugene Lefebvre, S.J.; 4) Father Joseph Perron, S.J.; 5) Father John L. Lucchesi, S.J., Superior of Holy Cross Mission; 6) Father Aloysius J. Robaut, S.J., Founder of Holy Cross Mission in 1888; 7) Brother Edward J. Horwedel, S.J.; 8) Brother Constantine-Marie Roulin, F.I.C.; 9) Brother Aloysius Markham, S.J. *JOPA-136.2.01.*

During the year 1942–43, in his machine shop at Holy Cross Mission, Brother George J. Feltes, S.J., gives "his boys" a demonstration on the use of certain tools. Future Jesuit Brother Ignatius J. Jakes is the young man wearing the cap with the upturned visor. *JOPA-536.1.03.*

were built with lumber produced at this sawmill. Proudly the Holy Cross church stood for over 63 years, until it was taken down by Father Andrew Eördögh, S.J., in 1969, very much to the dismay of the Holy Cross people. He believed it to be no longer safe for use. On May 17, 1989, a new church, built along lines similar to those of the old one, was dedicated. This, too, was dedicated under the patronage of the Holy Family, as had been the old one, ever since 1929.

In 1938, Holy Cross celebrated its Golden Jubilee. In a booklet produced on that occasion, the following statistics are given: number of pupils admitted, 983; number of Baptisms performed, 1439; number of First Communicants, 1187; number of Confirmations, 937; number of deaths among mission children, 106.

The first high school to open along the whole length of the Yukon was at Holy Cross. Sister M. Anne Rita, S.S.A., and Jesuit seminarian William J. **Loyens** were its core faculty, teaching basic high school courses. The primary purpose of the school was "to train leaders among the aborigines." In the "Holy Cross Chronicles" kept by the Sisters of St. Ann, under date of September 8, 1953, there is the following entry:

> A new school year begins with an enrollment of over 150 pupils in Grade School and in High School. Our High School is the great topic of conversation, the important event of 1953 that seems to make so many people happy; since this is a very effective way to make our students better men and women who will, we hope, be stauncher Catholics and more convincing leaders among their own.

On October 13, 1953, Sister M. George **Edmond**, S.S.A., was able to write to Father James U. **Conwell**, S.J., "Our High School is going along very satisfactorily. The nine students are all enthusiasm and work like Trojans to get all their assignments in on time."

By the early 1950s, the traditional Holy Cross Mission was on a threshold. One era was about to end, another about to begin. Various factors contributed to the major changes that were then about to take place at the mission, once described by Father Joseph R. **Crimont**, S.J., who was to become Alaska's first bishop, as "the smile of the Yukon."

Concerning the condition of the physical plant at Holy Cross at the mid-1950s, Father **John P. Fox**, S.J., wrote, "Our buildings and much of our equipment was nothing so much as one great junk pile." This reality, and new thinking regarding the kind of education that should be offered to Alaska's young Natives, led to the closing of the Holy Cross boarding school, or, rather, to its being "moved" to **Copper Valley School** in 1956. The move marked the end of 68 years of harmonious collaboration between the Sisters of St. Ann and the Jesuits to bring education to the Alaska Natives congregated at Holy Cross Mission. It should be mentioned here that in its early years, the mission was served also by two Brothers of Christian Instruction (**F.I.C.**). During the years 1904–09, Brothers Constantin-Marie Roulin and René-Maurice Allory were members of the mission staff.

In her book, *Fishcamp*, Dorothy Savage Joseph, one of the last to attend the mission school at Holy Cross, wrote:

> But the missionaries, despite some of their strictness, did do a lot of good for the people. They were sort of our guardian angels making sure people had a minimum of health care, food, clothes, education and religion. Even though the nuns were strict, they taught us a lot about self respect and respect for others. Caring for people was their daily chore. I think they sort of raised all the village people, some as small children who lived in the mission until growing up and marrying and moving to their own homes in the village.

The Holy Cross Mission boarding school was officially closed on the Feast of the Exaltation of the Holy Cross, September 14, 1956. By then the mission and its school, opened in 1888, had seen the service of 95 different Jesuits—28 Brothers, 42 priests, and 25 seminarians—for a total of 503 years; and of 58 different Sisters of St. Ann for a total of 557 years. A total of 1,457 children—727 boys and 730 girls—had been cared for at the mission. It should be noted that the priests stationed at Holy Cross ministered not only to people at the mission, but also to the Holy Cross villagers, and that they routinely made excursions, sometimes quite lengthy ones, both as to time and to distance, to mission stations dependent on Holy Cross.

Buried in the mission cemetery on the hill behind

the mission are four Sisters of St. Ann: Sisters M. Angilbert, Seraphine of the Sacred Heart, M. Perpetual Help, and M. Pius. Also buried there are Jesuit Brothers Patrick S. Heaney, Hugo Horan, Eugene Lefebvre, and Jeremiah McSweeney, and Jesuit Fathers Anthony M. **Keyes**, Lucchesi, Robaut, and Crispin S. **Rossi**.

After the boarding school closed, Sisters of St. Ann staffed a Holy Cross day school for a few years, then the Church ceased to be in charge of what became a conventional village school. Jesuit priests, however, continued to reside in Holy Cross and serve Holy Family parish until1984. That year, Michael J. **Kaniecki**, S.J., Holy Family's last Jesuit pastor, became Coadjutor Bishop of **Fairbanks**, and Father Andrew P. **D'Arco**, a diocesan priest residing in **Aniak**, became visiting priest to Holy Cross, until his tragic death on May 27, 1992, at Aniak.

After Father D'Arco, Father William E. **Cardy**, O.F.M., visited Holy Cross, likewise out of Aniak, from 1992–2000. For a year, there was no assigned priest for Holy Cross. Beginning in 2001, and as of the year 2004, Father Maciej Napieralski, residing in Aniak, had the care of Holy Family parish.

Sisters, too, continued to serve in Holy Cross. Sister Marie Teresa **Boulet**, O.P., was there, 1978–83; Sister Judy Tralnes, C.S.J.P., 1978–84; Sister Mary Faith Lautz, B.V.M., 1983–86; Sisters of St. Ann, Margaret Cantwell and Anne Eveline Paquette, 1987–93; Sister Maureen Freeman, C.S.J., and Sister Paul Bernadette Bounk, C.S.J., 1993–96; and Sister Frances McCarron, I.B.V.M., and Sister Anne Hogan, S.S.J., 1996–98. These Sisters served in a variety of capacities, including as teachers in the village school.

During the years 1998–2000, a lay couple, Jim and Mary Jean Smith, served Holy Family parish as Co-Pastoral Administrators.

16, 30, 32, 43, 48, 64, 99, 113, 174

HOLY SPIRIT CENTER

In February 1967, after prior consultation with Archbishop **Joseph T. Ryan**, three Sisters Adorers of the Precious Blood from Portland, Oregon, visited **Anchorage** with a view to establishing a monastery there. The plan was for them to live temporarily at a "Retreat House" at Fire Lake, about 12 miles out of Anchorage. During the earlier part of 1970, the Sisters were able to move into what was then still known as Christian Family Center, located on a 22-acre tract of land at the intersection of Hillside Drive and O'Malley Road.

In August 1971, Father Vincent P. **Kelliher**, S.J., arrived in Anchorage. He changed the name from Christian Family Center to Holy Spirit Retreat House. He came to Anchorage with a two-fold assignment: fund-raising for the Archdiocese, and chaplain to the Sisters who were staffing the retreat house. In the summer of 1972, the Sisters Adorers of the Precious Blood officially withdrew from **Alaska**. For a year or so, Archbishop Ryan, Father Richard B. **Saudis**, his Chancellor, along with Father Kelliher, made their home and headquarters at the retreat house. Sister Margaret Cantwell, S.S.A., did likewise, during the years 1971–73.

Frustrated in his several attempts to have members of other Religious Orders replace the Sisters, Archbishop Ryan asked Father Kelliher to take over the administration of the place. This involved not only encouraging greater utilization of the facility as a spiritual center, but also the raising of funds for its operation, improvement and expansion.

In the early 1970s, two modular units, measuring 24 × 52′, were put up near the retreat house to accommodate more retreatants and to provide more space for retreat activities. The "upper" modular was above a conference room, equipped for lectures and film presentations. The "lower" modular was above a lounge, suitable for social activities. For a time, the Brothers of Charity of Immaculate Heart of Mary, headquartered in Banning, California, were housed at the retreat house. At first, Charles "Chuck" Reddick, a talented young maintenance man, lived in a mobile home unit on the property. He later moved off site into his own home.

Under Father Kelliher, the retreat house soon became a developing spiritual undertaking, and was declared a major ministerial work of the Society of Jesus in Alaska.

In May 1978, Father James R. Conyard, S.J., visited the retreat house. There, in addition to meeting Father Kelliher and Sister Kathleen O'Hara,

(*left*) Resurrection Chapel at Holy Spirit Center, Anchorage. *LR.*

(*below*) The main building of Holy Spirit Center, Anchorage, as it appeared on July 26, 1986. *LR.*

R.S.M., who gave him "a scope of Catholic life and activities in the Archdiocese," he met also Archbishop Francis T. **Hurley**, who, at the time, was using the retreat house for his chancery offices. Father Conyard liked what he saw. He returned in September. By then, Archbishop Hurley had moved to his downtown offices.

When Father Conyard started at the retreat house, Father Kelliher was, in addition to doing retreat work, also putting out, on behalf of the retreat house and the Archdiocese of Anchorage, a newsletter, *The Anchor.* Father Conyard, recognizing that the retreat house often stood idle, undertook to bring more spiritual activity there, to make it a center of spiritual growth for the archdiocese. In this he had the encouragement of Archbishop Hurley, whom he found to be "always hopeful, pleasant and encouraging."

With things rather slow at Holy Spirit, Father Conyard explored the possibility of making it the meeting place for the Marriage Encounter movement in the archdiocese. "This idea was a little bit of a risk," he recalled years later, "but Father Kelliher agreed to try it, and eventually it really paid off." Soon the Engaged Encounter movement, too,

made the retreat house its meeting place. It was not long before both groups felt that they needed some kind of spiritual follow-up to their meetings. To provide this, Father Conyard started the "Couples Retreats."

Under Father Kelliher's direction, "things hummed along very well," according to Father Conyard. It should be added that, during his latter years at the retreat house, Father Kelliher was ably assisted by Mrs. Mae Ferrari, who ran the office and put out the retreat house calendar.

From 1982–85, Father Eugene P. **Delmore**, S.J., was at Holy Spirit "doing retreats and lots of pastoral ministry to surrounding parishes." Father **Paul B. Mueller**, S.J., was on the retreat house staff during the years 1985–88. By the mid-1980s, "an era of retreat house history was about to end," wrote Father Kelliher. In 1986, at the request of the Father Provincial of the New England Province, he returned to Boston. After ten years at Holy Spirit, Father Conyard, "filled with happy memories," likewise left Alaska.

In 1986, Father Vincent J. **Beuzer**, S.J., succeeded Father Kelliher as Executive Director of the retreat house. Upon his arrival there, he found "the challenges were many: personnel, financial, buildings and maintenance, and spiritual ministry." Accordingly, the Father Beuzer era, too, brought significant improvements and changes to Holy Spirit Retreat House and its operation.

Most notable among the changes wrought at Holy Spirit during Father Beuzer's time was the building of Resurrection Chapel on the retreat house grounds in 1991. A plaque on the chapel wall reads: "Dedicated on April 7, 1991, as a gift to honor the Archdiocese of Anchorage and Archbishop Francis T. Hurley from Ben and Dawn Tisdale." The first Mass in Resurrection Chapel was offered on December 24, 1990. Thereafter, every Sunday, an alive and dynamic Catholic community began to worship in Resurrection Chapel, a chapel described as "one of the most beautiful chapels in all of Alaska, overlooking the city, Cook Inlet, the Alaska Range to the west and the Chugach Mountains to the East."

During Father Beuzer's time at Holy Spirit, the first "Five Year Agreement" concerning it was worked out by him, the Archdiocese of Anchorage, and the Society of Jesus. Several months after Resurrection Chapel was finished, the archdiocese gave him a capital building needs assessment list totaling $170,000. In his own words:

> The three-year capital improvement drive organized by Dave Belanger, Jack Van Alstine, and Joe Murdy, with Chuck Reddick from the Retreat House, and supported by a three-year fund-raising drive by Elizabeth Kellard, was our response. New sleeping quarters, new dining facilities, new rugs throughout, new interior and exterior painting, new roofing and new sheet rocking as needed, new leach fields and new septic tanks and extensive landfill resulted. The leadership for the interior renovation of some twelve rooms was successfully provided by Priscilla Belanger. The Belangers' and the Tisdales' involvement had remodeled Holy Spirit Retreat House buildings and property.

In addition to overseeing those physical plant improvements, Father Beuzer saw to it, too, that the retreat house was adequately staffed and the operational budget balanced. Meanwhile, on the more spiritual side, he and Kathryn Gallagher, Director of Ministry, inaugurated the "19th Annotation Retreat in Everyday Life" program. Numerous "Challenge Groups," with adult lay ministry associates serving as facilitators, were formed. About this same time, a Saturday Men's Group, involving some 20-plus men, began to meet bi-weekly from 7 A.M. to 9 A.M. for Mass, continental breakfast, and an hour of faith-sharing. As the third millennium dawned, this group was still in full vigor. Along with those programs, there was a sudden surge in demands for individual spiritual direction. To meet the demand, a two-year program for the formation of Spiritual Directors, "Seeking the Spirit I," was started in 2000. Father Beuzer, though no longer Executive Director of Holy Spirit by that time, served as the program's coordinator.

Father Beuzer, after having served as Executive Director of Holy Spirit for 12 years, resigned that post in 1998. Father Paul B. **Macke**, S.J., who had been a spiritual director and pastoral counselor at Holy Spirit since 1996, became its Executive Director in June 1998. It was he who, in 1999, changed the name of Holy Spirit Retreat House to Holy Spirit Center. The change in name was made to highlight the fact that the Center does so much more than just serve as a retreat house. In the year 2001, he wrote, "we continue to focus on adult faith formation and Ignatian Spirituality. We strive to be a Center of Spirituality for all of Alaska."

It was Father Macke who began an extensive program of development to get the Center out of debt and also reached out to all the parishes of the Archdiocese of Anchorage with programs of lay leadership development and parish mission type retreats. Mrs. Maureen Cowles, Director of Development, combined fund-raising with spiritual ministry by commissioning Father William H. McNichols, S.J., to create two new icons for Holy Spirit Center. Sister Mary Noel, O.P., the new Coordinator of Ministry, greatly expanded the 36-week Ignatian programs, so that during the year 2002–03 over 120 people were involved with 18 facilitators. Mrs. Noreen Weishaar, Business Manager, used her friendliness and skill with detail to develop the Center into an attractive conference facility. With a new computer network and telephone system, Father Macke brought the Center into the 21st century. Under his directorship, numerous deferred maintenance projects were successfully completed. The kitchen problems related to personnel and money loss were greatly remedied by the hiring of S&S Management as the food service for Holy Spirit.

Father Robert H. Fitzgerald, S.J., on the staff of Holy Spirit Center from 1998–2002, added programs concerned with spirituality and addictions. In the year 2001, Father Joseph J. Schad, S.J., was hired to bring new dimensions to the Center, especially to explore the possible use of the media.

Throughout all those years and changes, and up to and well into the third millennium, Chuck Reddick continued to serve faithfully and competently as Director of Maintenance. From the outset, and up to the year 2004, the Center's core professional staff was singularly blessed in having the generous, voluntary help and support of numerous Sisters and lay people in maintaining and running the Center. To no one's surprise, it began to enjoy, since the day he first took office, on March 3, 2001, also the wholehearted support of Roger L. **Schwietz**, O.M.I., Archbishop of Anchorage.

As of the year 2004, over three decades after its founding, things at Holy Spirit Center—thanks to the strong direction of the Holy Spirit, as well as to the financial, lend-a-hand, and moral support of

countless people—were continuing to "hum along very well."

The Mission Statement for Holy Spirit Center reads:

Holy Spirit Center, incorporated as Catholic Retreat House Ministries, Inc., is a center of the Archdiocese of Anchorage for the spiritual development, faith-justice leadership formation, and renewal of God's people in the Church. The Archbishop of Anchorage entrusts its operation to the Oregon Province of the Society of Jesus. As a center for spiritual growth in the Jesuit tradition and drawing upon the formative power of the Spiritual Exercises of St. Ignatius, the Center provides opportunities for a variety of retreats and professional services that enhance spiritual discernment, such as spiritual direction and other programs of Christian spirituality. Additionally, the Center offers the hospitality of its facilities and professional staff to parishes, groups and agencies of the Archdiocese and Dioceses of Alaska, as well as groups whose purposes are compatible with the mission and ministry of Holy Spirit Center.

15

HOMER

The town of Homer, located on the Kenai Peninsula, on the north shore of Kachemak Bay, Cook Inlet, is named for Homer Pennock, a prospector in the Cook Inlet area. The Homer post office was established in 1896. In 1967, Homer's population numbered 1,247; in the year 2000, 3,946.

When, in the fall of 1950, the road from **Seward**

St. John the Baptist Church, Home
Photo by Annemiek J. Brunklaus.

to Homer was opened, Father Martin G. Borbeck, S.J., stationed in Seward at the time, began to make monthly visits to Homer, **Ninilchik**, and **Soldotna**, offering Mass for the people in private homes. Father Arnold L. **Custer**, S.J., stationed in Seward from 1952–61, continued Father Borbeck's practice of monthly visits to those communities.

In 1961, Redemptorist Fathers from the Oakland Province began to serve the Catholic communities on the Kenai Peninsula. The first three, all headquartered in Seward to begin with, were Fathers Edward C. **O'Neill**, pastor of the Seward parish, James Van Hoomissen, and Robert L. Woodruff. Out of Seward they began to care for the Kenai missions of Homer, **Kenai**, Ninilchik, **Seldovia**, and Soldotna. In the course of the years, others joined or replaced them. Father Richard G. **Strass** was responsible for the Homer mission from 1974–79. On June 21, 1975, he witnessed the blessing of the new log church, dedicated to St. John the Baptist, by **Joseph T. Ryan**, Archbishop of **Anchorage**. The log church was subsequently replaced by the present church.

The Redemptorists cared for the Homer parish up until 1992. By that time, a total of nine different ones had served it. Father Strass, there again from 1988–92, was the last one to do so. After him Father Charles B. Crouse, a diocesan priest, held station in Homer for several years. During the year 2001–02, Father Balaswamy Gangarapu, a priest on loan from India, was pastor of Homer. As of the year 2004, "circuit rider" priests out of Anchorage, along with local lay people serving as Pastoral Administrators, tended to Homer's Catholic community. Annemiek J. Brunklaus was its Pastoral Administrator as of the year 2003; and Sister Carol Ann Aldrich, R.S.M., its Parish Director as of the year 2004.

15

HOONAH

The village of Hoonah is located on the east shore of Port Frederick on Icy Strait, 40 miles southwest of **Juneau**. It is the principal village of the Huna (Hoonah), a Tlingit Indian tribe. Its population numbered 800 in 1880, 447 in 1900, 402 in 1920,

A "crucifix," painted after the manner of a Tlingit Indian totem/icon, adorns the wall behind the altar in Sacred Heart Church, Hoonah. *Courtesy of Sacred Heart parish, Hoonah.*

514 in 1930, 563 in 1950, 686 in 1967, and 860 in the year 2000. The Hoonah post office was established in 1901, giving the village its present name.

Sunday, July 25, 1971, was a memorable day for the Catholic community of Hoonah. On that day, Francis T. **Hurley**, Bishop of Juneau, offered the first Mass in Hoonah's new Sacred Heart Church. This, Hoonah's first Catholic church, was built on land donated by Mrs. Louise Kane, and constructed by a Christian Brothers summer volunteer team. A crucifix, painted after the manner of a Tlingit totem/icon, adorns the wall behind the altar. Done by Claudia McConnell in black and rust red colors, it shows the Sacred Heart under the face of Christ. Coming from the heart are three flames intertwined symbolizing the Holy Trinity. Two hands, palms out-turned, extend on either side of the Heart and speak of Christ's universal love. The new church, according to Father Peter F. **Gorges**, "was Bishop Hurley's pride and joy, and showplace for visiting Church dignitaries."

(*right*) Little Flower of Jesus Church, Hooper Bay. *LR*.

(*opposite*) This is the building at Hooper Bay that, at one time, housed the Sisters of Our Lady of the Snows and the church on the second floor and the priest and meeting rooms on the first floor. *JOPA-105.02*.

The Hoonah parish was, for the most part, served by priests stationed elsewhere. In July 2004, Father James Blaney, O.M.I., replaced Father Perry M. Kenaston, pastor of the Hoonah parish at that time.

HOOPER BAY

The Community of Hooper Bay is located on Hooper Bay, on the Bering Sea coast of western **Alaska**, 20 miles south of Cape Romanzof, and approximately 25 miles south of **Scammon Bay**, in the Yukon-Kuskokwim Delta. The village is separated into two sections. The old, heavily built-up section sits on two gently rolling hills, one referred to as "the Covenant Hill," the other as "the Catholic Hill." The newer section, which started to build up in the mid-1980s, is located on lower lands a half mile southwest of the older section and toward the airport. The Eskimo name for the older part of the village was *Askinuk*. The Hooper Bay village site has been occupied by Central Yup'ik Eskimos for many generations. The present-day Eskimo name for the village is *Naparagamiut*, meaning "the stake village people." Just what "stakes" are referred to is not known. The name, "Hooper Bay," came into common usage after a post office with the same name was established there in 1934. The population of Hooper Bay grew rapidly: from 138 in 1890,

to 297 in 1939, to 307 in 1950, to 460 in 1960, to 490 in 1970, to 1,014 in the year 2002.

Hooper Bay was first visited by Catholic missionaries beginning around 1890. The U.S. government, early in the 1900s, opened a school there staffed by Lutheran (Swedish Covenant) teachers. They allegedly used their position to spread their religion, much to the dismay of the Jesuit missionaries. For many years, therefore, the Jesuit missionaries urged that a Catholic mission, with a school, be established in Hooper Bay. The mission was finally established, in 1928. Father **John P. Fox**, S.J., left details concerning its establishment. Father Anthony M. **Keyes**, S.J., and Brother John **Hess**, S.J., along with a group of "big boys," came down from **Holy Cross Mission** on the mission boat, the *Little Flower*, which was loaded with building materials. Brother Aloysius B. **Laird**, S.J., operated the boat. When the building was about three-fourths finished, Jimmy Droane, one of the "big boys" from Holy Cross, was left behind to finish it. Soon thereafter, in September 1928, Father Francis M. **Ménager**, S.J., took charge of the new mission, named "Little Flower of Jesus Mission." The dream of having a Catholic school in Hooper Bay remained just that, except for the three years, when the Sisters of Our Lady of the **Snows** conducted a kind of "school" there.

No name is more closely associated with the Hooper Bay mission than that of Father Fox. He was stationed there from 1931–46, longer than any other priest before or after. In many respects, he is the one who set the tone of the mission. In 1932, he founded the Sisters of Our Lady of the Snows, who had their motherhouse in Hooper Bay. He built a convent for them in 1938. He was Hooper Bay's first postmaster. He was the radio operator in Hooper Bay. He saw a reindeer herd given to the Hooper Bay mission, in 1933, "as trust property to manage for the people's benefits." In general, he strove to improve the lives of the Hooper Bay people, and he did so with notable success. As a captain in the Alaska Territorial Guard, he was head of the Hooper Bay company during World War II.

Throughout its history, Little Flower of Jesus Mission in Hooper Bay virtually always had a resident priest, though generally he was responsible also for outlying stations, and so was away from time to time. Some years, two priests were stationed there. The principal pastors of the Hooper Bay parish have been Jesuit Fathers: Ménager, 1928–30; Fox, 1931–46; Paul C. **O'Connor** (who found Hooper Bay "a mud-hole during the summer and a wind-swept tundra during the winter," and who, as a member of the Alaska Housing Authority, brought new housing to Hooper Bay),1946–53; Henry G. **Hargreaves** (who found the people of Hooper Bay "most affable"), 1953–57; Norman E. **Donohue**, 1957–64; George S. **Endal**, 1964–68; **James R. Laudwein**, 1968–69; James E. **Jacobson**, 1969–76; Bernard F. **McMeel** (who oversaw the building of the new church in 1977), 1976–77; Daniel J. **Tainter**, 1977–78; Charles J. **Peterson**, 1978–79; and Richard L. **McCaffrey**, 1979–81. He was followed by Father John A. **Hinsvark**, priest of the Diocese of Fairbanks, 1981–90. Jesuit priests from St. Mary's Mission, **Andreafsky**, visited Hooper Bay during the year 1990–91. Jesuit Fathers Mark A. **Hoelsken** was at Hooper Bay from 1991–96, and **Gregg D. Wood** beginning in 1996 and as of the year 2004.

Eskimo Deacons, too, have served and continue to serve their Hooper Bay parish: Joseph Lake (deceased) and James Gump.

Hooper Bay saw also the services of different Sisters. Foremost among them were the Sisters of Our Lady of the Snows, 1932–45. During the years 1942–45, **Ursuline** Sisters Mother Mary of the Blessed Sacrament Hardegon and Mother Scholastica **Lohagen** were at Hooper Bay to help with the formation of the Sisters of Our Lady of the Snows. During the early 1980s, Sister Mary Schrader, C.S.J., ministered at the Hooper Bay parish. From 1989–94, Sister Julie Marie Thorpe, S.N.D. de N., and Sister Angela Fortier, C.S.J., did likewise.

Buried at Hooper Bay are Father John B. **Sifton**, S.J., who died unexpectedly at Hooper Bay on October 20, 1940, and Deacon Joseph Lake. Also buried at Hooper Bay are two Sisters of Our Lady of the Snows: Clotilda Leo Chakatar and Mary John Baptist.

72, 138, 192, 207

Brother Edward J. Horwedel, S.J. *JOPA-891.02.*

HORWEDEL, Brother Edward J., S.J.

He spent 34 years on the banks of the Yukon River. Though he was small in size, he was "a giant in character and intelligence, and he carried authority in his very presence." His Superior at **Nulato**, Father Joseph F. **McElmeel**, S.J., when asked about Jesuit Lay Brothers at Nulato, wrote in 1933: "Brothers. One only, but worth a dozen other men. Brother Horwedel, S.J. He is almost seventy years of age, and yet he can cut his cord of wood a day without effort. He is a man of all work, a true 'sourdough' mechanic in that he can make use of odds and ends of things to make what we need here. He can build a steamboat, run a sawmill, care for a dog team without swearing." Brother Horwedel's life was such that he became "renowned as an exceptionally holy missionary."

Edward J. Horwedel was born in Conewaga, Pennsylvania, on October 19, 1864. In 1894, he went west to enter the Jesuit novitiate at DeSmet, Idaho, as a Lay Brother candidate. After completing his two-year noviceship and taking his vows of poverty, chastity and obedience, he was assigned to St. Ignatius Mission, Montana, where he spent the years 1896–99. While at St. Ignatius, he thought that perhaps he should study for the priesthood. On the advice of his Superior and spiritual director, he decided to make a novena to beg light from God on the matter. Before the end of the novena, he received his answer. While working in the mission sawmill, of which he was in charge, he lost two of his fingers in an accident. One of these was an index finger, a "canonical" finger. The loss of that finger was, at the time, an impediment to the priesthood. This seeming misfortune he willingly accepted as a sign from God that he should continue on as a Lay Brother.

Brother Horwedel spent the years 1899 to 1902 at Gonzaga College, Spokane, Washington. There he served as carpenter and operator of the heating plant. His next assignment took him to **Alaska**. On July 14, 1902, he arrived in **Nome**, on his way to **Holy Cross Mission**, where he was to spend a total of 27 years.

Brother Horwedel was a master of several trades—carpenter, blacksmith, mechanic—and a licensed engineer. At Holy Cross, he plied these trades, as well as maintained and operated the mission steamers. Occasionally, he was away from Holy Cross for a time, at some mission to help put up a church or some other building. During his Holy Cross years, he made a name for himself also as prefect of the older boys. Though some were taller than he, he had the respect of all and was able to keep perfect order. At times, he was away with some of them at a wood-camp to provide firewood for the mission's many stoves.

Brother Horwedel's Holy Cross years were interrupted for three years, 1909–12, when he was back at St. Ignatius, Montana, to run the sawmill and work on the mission farm. In 1912, he returned to Holy Cross to resume his former duties—and to cultivate an intense spiritual life of prayer and of seeking to find and do the will of God for him. This he discerned to consist, as it had all along, in the humble service of God and neighbor.

Brother Horwedel's second stay at Holy Cross stretched out to two decades. In 1932, he was named to Nulato, where he spent the last seven years of his life. During those years, he helped put up two large buildings, ran the mission boat, did maintenance work, and kept the mission stoves going.

On November 8, 1939, Father John B. **Baud**, S.J., Superior at Nulato, visited Brother Horwedel in his wood-camp. In the Nulato House Diary he wrote, "Had lunch together, enjoyed the visit very much." On the 30th, he and Brother Horwedel began their annual 8-day retreat. On December 5th: "Brother is pretty sick, two abscesses on account of his teeth. He should have all his teeth pulled." Their retreat ended on the 8th. Father Baud wanted Brother to go to **Fairbanks** to have his teeth attended to. After some hesitation, he assented to the trip. The marshal in Nulato and two other admirers of Brother Horwedel volunteered to pay his plane fare. However, Father McElmeel, now General Superior of Jesuits in Alaska, had already arranged for the flight to Fairbanks. The three men then decided to pay for the set of dentures Brother was expected to need. They and two other of Brother Horwedel's Nulato friends all chipped in to provide him with spending money. "We are all astonished," wrote Father Baud in the diary, "over such kindness, but happy that Brother is the one to receive it." By mid-December, Brother Horwedel was in Fairbanks.

On December 19th, Father Baud wrote in the diary, "A very sad telegram reached us today."

Father S. Aloysius **Eline**, S.J., pastor of the parish in Fairbanks at the time, had wired: "Horwedel fell yesterday on stairs. Concussion followed, patient still unconscious. Doctors state outcome unfavorable." In Nulato, all the people were very much affected by the sad news. The next day, Father Eline wired: "Patient remains unconscious; sinking spell after midnight seemed to indicate the end, but rallied some later." The following day, however: "Still unconscious and weaker. Hope abandoned. May last several days." At 8 A.M., on December 24, 1939, Brother Horwedel died, but not without first having regained consciousness. Father Baud noted in the diary, "He just went to Heaven to celebrate Christmas at home. We lose a most valuable Brother and above all a saintly one." On the 27th, a Requiem Mass was held for Brother Horwedel at Nulato. It was well attended, for "the people loved Brother very much." That same day, in Fairbanks, a funeral Mass was held for him, and then he was buried in the Clay Street Cemetery in downtown Fairbanks.

HUBBARD, Father Bernard R., S.J.

When he died, the *New York Herald Tribune* hailed him as the "Renowned 'Glacier Priest' of **Alaska**." In recent times, when Alaska's advancing Hubbard Glacier threatened the lives of seals and whales, many older people immediately thought of the "Glacier Priest." (Truth be told: Hubbard Glacier was named, in 1890, for Gardiner G. Hubbard, first president of the National Geographic Society.) For decades after his death, people kept asking, "Whatever happened to Father Hubbard?" Alaskan missionaries never considered him to be one of their number, nor did he ever claim to be such. Nevertheless, the names "Father Hubbard" and "Alaska" are so closely connected that he deserves an honorable place in any history of Catholic Alaska.

Bernard Rosecrans Hubbard was born in San Francisco on November 24, 1888. When he was ten, his father bought 200 acres of property south of San Francisco in redwood country. There, with dog, gun and camera, the boy spent much time exploring woods and high country, climbing seashore cliffs, and developing habits of acute observation. There, too, he acquired a robust constitution and a taste for outdoor life.

By 1908, Bernard had completed high school in San Francisco and two years of college at Santa Clara. On September 7th, he entered the Jesuit novitiate at Los Gatos, California. After completing his two-year noviceship and three years of classical and humanities studies there, he went on to spend the years 1913–18 at Loyola High School in Los Angeles, where he taught mathematics, history, Greek and Latin. He also directed the school's football and baseball programs. Frequently he led student groups on hikes along the beach or in the high country. They also visited the Mt. Wilson observatory. Wherever he went, he collected rock specimens and fossils. His students dubbed him "fossil Hubbard." He seems never to have had trouble getting permission from his Jesuit Superiors for an outing. One of his fellow Jesuits wrote of him, "In some respects, he was like a little boy. He had a charm and an uncanny way of wresting permissions from his Religious Superiors."

The years 1918–21 found Bernard Hubbard at Mount St. Michael's House of Philosophy, Spokane, Washington. As the protégé of Father Paul F. Galtes, S.J., a careful scientist, in addition to studying philosophy, Bernard Hubbard made many field trips to geologically interesting areas in the Northwest.

In 1921, Bernard Hubbard began his theological studies for the priesthood in Innsbruck, Austria. There he found himself in the very heart of the Tyrolese Alps, a mountaineer's paradise. He spent his vacations exploring mountains and glaciers. After his successful climbs of Tyrol's major peaks, his guides gave him the name "*Der Gletscherpfarrer*" (The Glacier Priest), and conferred on him their highest award, the Double Edelweiss.

Bernard Hubbard was ordained a priest on July 29, 1923. After two more years in Innsbruck and one at St. Andrew-on-Hudson, New York, where he made his tertianship, he returned to Santa Clara to teach German, Greek, geology and mineralogy.

Father Hubbard's life-long love affair with Alaska came about through a kind of fluke. A man was needed, in the summer of 1927, to give a retreat in **Juneau**, Alaska. "If Father Hubbard took the assignment," his Superior speculated, "perhaps he would find something up there to add to his collection."

For the next 30 years, Father Hubbard kept finding things in Alaska to add to his collection. That same summer, while on his first trip to Alaska, he and two companions crossed the awesome Mendenhall Glacier. They were the first to do so. The following year, he and two companions attempted to cross the 100-mile neck of the Alaska Peninsula through the Valley of Ten Thousand Smokes. Knee-deep volcanic ash and quicksand proved to be too much for them. However, accompanied by students from Santa Clara, Father Hubbard returned to the area and succeeded in scaling and exploring some of the world's largest active volcanoes. Much of what the party saw on those expeditions he recorded on movie film and in countless still pictures. His photos of the Alaska Peninsula's volcanoes are of such quality and detail that they are studied by volcanologists and earthquake specialists to this day. His two books, *Cradle of the Storms* and *Mush, You Malemutes!*, contain accounts of his glacier crossing and of his explorations of Alaska's volcanoes. The latter book also recounts the 1,600-mile dogsled trip along the Bering Sea coast and the Yukon River he made in 1931.

So productive were Father Hubbard's early Alaskan sojourns, that he was freed from teaching to devote full time to explorations in Alaska, and to writing and lecturing. Besides books, he also published, over the years, many articles and press releases. In addition, he produced a dozen travelogues for Fox Movietone.

From the outset, Father Hubbard proved to be an articulate, spell-binding lecturer. He was said to be gifted with a "larger than life public persona." One who heard his lectures, described him as "a marvelous raconteur, who knew how to *spark* the imagination." During his peak years, hundreds of thousands annually heard his talks and saw his films. Once, within a five-month period, he delivered 275 lectures across the nation. For three decades, he followed basically the same pattern, spending his summers in Alaska and his winters lecturing. Truly, as veteran Alaskan missionary Brother Peter P. **Wilhalm**, S.J., observed: "That Father Hubbard, he said many things—besides his prayers."

There was, however, one winter, a most memorable one, which Father Hubbard did spend in Alaska. In June 1937, with three assistants, he landed

Father Bernard R. Hubbard, S.J.
JOPA-1025.70.

on **King Island**, home of several hundred Inupiat Eskimos and their veteran pastor, Father Bellarmine **Lafortune**, S.J. Father Hubbard's intention was to study in detail those cliff-dwelling Eskimos. To do this he allowed himself a whole year with them. His 1937–38 King Island expedition was, by all accounts, the most ambitious undertaking of his life.

Father Hubbard deserves above all to be remembered as a superb photographer. Nowhere else did he shine as such more than on King Island, where he took literally thousands of still pictures and shot 286,000 feet of movie film showing every aspect of King Island life. Father Lafortune wrote in the King Island diary, "One can hear the click of the camera at any hour. What is commonplace to me is wonderful to Father Hubbard." Anthropologists have described his King Island pictures as "of enormous ethnographic and historical significance."

The King Islanders did not in any way look upon Father Hubbard and his cameras as an unwanted intrusion into their lives. The people welcomed him to their island and posed willingly for him and his cameras. Many years after his stay on the island, some of them "took pains" to visit him at Santa Clara. His photos were treasured by them. Many of them hung on the walls of their homes and cabins.

They continued to be excited, thrilled to see themselves in films he made.

Father Hubbard used the best photographic equipment available. In makeshift darkrooms, he also printed his pictures where he took them, and so he was able to control their quality as he went.

Father Hubbard's highpoint on King Island was the last day of October 1937, when he, in a solemn ceremony, blessed the life-size bronze statue of Christ the King standing atop the island. He himself had brought the statue to the island. Father Lafortune and almost all the villagers were present for the occasion. As an old man, Father Hubbard remembered that day as one of the two happiest of his life—the other being the day he presented to Pope Pius XII a replica of the statue carved out of walrus ivory by one of the King Island men.

In June 1938, Father Hubbard and his assistants left King Island in an *umiaq*, a Native-built skinboat, manned by nine King Island men. They spent five weeks voyaging around 2,000 miles along the arctic coast and visiting Eskimo villages. By comparing the dialect spoken in one village with that spoken in another, he was able to satisfy himself that the northern Bering Sea and the arctic coast Eskimos all belonged to the same ethnic group.

During World War II, Father Hubbard advised the Army on cold-weather clothing and equipment, and taught courses in arctic survival. For a short time, he served as chaplain to Seabees on the island of Attu. At war's end, he gave lectures to Armed Forces units in Europe. There he met General George S. Patton, who was so impressed with Father Hubbard's talks, that he wrote, "I will be glad to have him in any unit I may command."

Over the years, Father Hubbard befriended many famous and powerful people, among them Generals Douglas MacArthur and Albert C. Wedemeyer, Richard Cardinal Cushing, Ex-Empress Zita of Austria, Walt Disney, and the heads of various corporations such as RCA, Johnson Outboard Motors, Libby's, Lockheed, and Agfa-Ansco. These corporations provided him with equipment; he, in turn, publicized their products.

Was Father Hubbard a missionary? Veteran Alaskan missionary Father Segundo **Llorente**, S.J., who knew him well, wrote, in answer to the question, "The answer pure and simple is that he was not. He came to Alaska as a scieniitist, an explorer, anything but a pastor of souls." Was Hubbard the priest overshadowed by Hubbard the adventurer? Not really. Father Llorente wrote also, "Father Hubbard was a very pious and religious man." It is well documented that he was always, first and foremost, a priest.

An outstanding feature of his religious life was the importance he attached to daily Mass. His appreciation of it was such that he offered it daily, even in the wilds of Alaska. Later, when a series of severe strokes seriously handicapped him, he still struggled to the altar in the Santa Clara infirmary to offer Mass. He himself wrote toward the end of his life, "Daily Mass and breviary meant everything to me all my life, and in all my traveling the schedules had to be made out so that neither the privilege nor the obligation would be endangered."

Once the National Geographic Society had scheduled Father Hubbard to lecture in New York. Their representative came to him just before the curtain was to open before 5,000 people. He said to Father Hubbard, "We omitted the scene of the Mass in the volcano, because of the sentiments of so many in your audience." Father Hubbard ordered, "Put that Mass scene back in, or there will be no lecture tonight." The scene was put back in.

In December 1955, Father Hubbard was scheduled to lecture in the East. En route, he stopped off in Chicago for a physical checkup. He was found to be in good condition. He took the train on to Newark, New Jersey, to see friends and to offer Mass at a Sisters school. There, as he was vesting, his head began to buzz. Soon the full force of the stroke hit him. He asked for a priest and a doctor. He went to confession and was anointed. The doctor, finding his blood pressure over 300, said, "He won't be here in the morning." Faintly, Father Hubbard muttered, "Oh, yes, Doc, I will!" Back at Santa Clara, he made a slow, but steady, recovery.

By 1958, Father Hubbard's physical condition was again nearly back to normal. There remained only a slight drag of his right foot and an incomplete use of his right hand. Again he went to Alaska, climbed in and out of boats, held his motion picture camera with his limp right, and operated it with his left.

Father Hubbard spent the next several years editing his films, conducting visitors through the Hubbard Photo Gallery at Santa Clara, and giving an occasional lecture. Then, on December 27, 1961, he suffered another stroke. With therapy and determination on his part, he was able to resume daily Mass in May 1962. Soon he again accepted lecture engagements. He planned a summer trip to Alaska, where, he felt, the quiet and beauty of a cabin in Taku Harbor would benefit him. His doctor approved the plan, reasoning that Alaska would be better therapy than the realization that he was permanently "on the shelf." It was not meant to be.

On May 28, 1962, as he was vesting for Mass, he suddenly said to the nurse helping him, "I can't make it. I will have to lie down." A priest came and administered the last rites. Fifteen minutes later Father Bernard Rosecrans Hubbard, S.J., the famous Glacier Priest, was dead. He was laid to rest in the Santa Clara Mission Cemetery, far from the glaciers of Tyrol and Alaska that had so stamped his personality. His memory, however, and his priceless legacy of books, films and photographs—along with the example of his priestly life and ministrations—live on and continue to enrich the lives of many.

9, 44, 45, 83, 127, 175

HUCK, Brother John, S.J.

John Huck was born in Yakima, Washington, on March 20, 1938. With the intention of becoming a Jesuit Lay Brother for the Oregon Province of the Society of Jesus, he entered the Jesuit novitiate at Florissant, Missouri, on March 8, 1958. After completing his two-year noviceship, he was stationed for a year at Mount St. Michael's, Spokane, Washington. Then, for several years, his home base was the novitiate at Sheridan, Oregon. He was generally away, however. During his pre-Alaskan years, while serving as a member of the "Jesuit Brothers Construction Crew," a group of skilled Jesuit Lay Brothers who built various facilities in Oregon and Washington, he moved from construction site to construction site.

Brother Huck first went to **Alaska** in 1965 to serve as a roving maintenance and construction man. He spent his first year in Alaska working out of **Fair-**

banks. In October 1965, he was working in **Kalt-ag**. During the summer of 1967, he and Thomas V. Karlin, a former Trappist Brother and expert cabinetmaker, built the new Sacred Heart Church in **Emmonak**. After the great flood of August 1967, which devastated Fairbanks, he helped clean up and, among other things, dry out and relay the school gymnasium floor. During the summer of 1968, he was in **Nome**—"doing a great job," according to Father James E. **Poole**, S.J.—remodeling old facilities to ready them to house the projected radio station, **KNOM**, and the staff members operating it. From time to time, he left Nome to attend to more pressing needs elsewhere. He was in Nome, however, on July 14, 1971, to witness the station's official going on the air for the first time.

During the summer of 1971, Brother Huck "did something unique," in the words of Father Richard L. **McCaffrey**, S.J., who was with him. At **Sheldon Point** (now known as **Nunam Iqua**), with the help of Father McCaffrey, he built a new rectory. This he himself designed in such a way that it had a "sub-floor" under the main floor to create a heat chamber. The furnace, firing hot air into this insulated chamber, always kept the main floor warm.

That same summer, Brother Huck worked also on a very similar rectory at **Marshall**. He chose to work at Marshall at that time, because he wanted to be in that area for the moose hunting season. This turned out to be the last project he worked on. By this time, the shell of the dormitory for members of the **Jesuit Volunteer Corps** at St. Mary's Mission on the **Andreafsky** River, which he had overseen, was completed. This was named for him "Huck Hall." It was his eagerness to move ahead with this latter project that caused him and Jim Churbuck, along with Alaskan Natives George Tyson and George Taller, to lose their lives. In a boating accident, while they were going from Marshall to St. Mary's Mission, they drowned in the icy waters of the Yukon near its confluence with the Andreafsky, on October 8, 1971. Only one body was ever found. The students of St. Mary's Mission boarding school dedicated their 1972 yearbook to him, "for all that he has given us, not only in building and repair work, but of himself, his deeply Christian life, and his warm friendship."

Brother John Huck, S.J. *LRC.*

According to the account of the accident published in the Oregon Province's newsletter:

> The four had been at Marshall and **Pilot Station** for several days, and were anxious to return to St. Mary's. They set out, but the water became so rough that they put to shore on an island, where two other men had already sought refuge from the cold, wet weather. These tried to persuade John and his companions to stay, but the urge to go home was too strong. The St. Mary's crew launched out into the river and was gone. About an hour later the two men on the island judged that it would be safe to leave their haven. Downriver they found the overturned, drifting boat and the body of George Taller. The heavy news reached the mission and was flashed to the lower forty-eight; and the Province waited in sorrow and shock for several days, while all attempts to recover the other bodies failed.

Brother Huck was only 33 years old, when he died. His death was a great loss to the Alaska Mission. Though his body was never found, a gravestone in the Jesuit cemetery at Mount St. Michael's commemorates his death.

HURLEY, Archbishop Francis T.

Francis T. Hurley was born on January 12, 1927, in San Francisco, California. He received his elementary education at St. Agnes Grammar School, after which he attended St. Joseph's College in Mountain View and St. Patrick's Seminary in Menlo

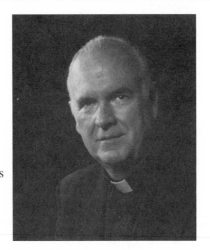

Archbishop Francis T. Hurley. *LRC.*

Park, California. He was ordained a priest on June 16, 1951. His first assignment as a priest was that of assistant pastor at Holy Name's parish in San Francisco. He then taught for a number of years at Serra High School for Boys in San Mateo, California, before going on to post-graduate studies in sociology at the Catholic University of America in Washington, D.C., and the University of California, Berkeley.

In June 1957, Father Hurley was assigned to Washington, D.C., to the National Catholic Welfare Conference, the national coordinating office for the Catholic Bishops of the United States—later known as the National Conference of Catholic Bishops (NCCB)—a research and coordinating agency for the Bishops of the United States in matters relating to Church practices and for national public policy affecting relations between Church and State. During the year 1957, he served in the Department of Education. From 1958–70, he was Associate General Secretary.

On February 4, 1970, Father Hurley was appointed Auxiliary Bishop of the Diocese of **Juneau**. He was ordained a bishop on March 19, 1970, by his older brother, Mark Hurley, Bishop of Santa Rosa, California. This was the first time in the United States that a brother ordained his brother a bishop. The following day, on March 20, 1970, Bishop Francis T. Hurley took up residency in Juneau. On July 20, 1971, he was appointed Ordinary of the Diocese of Juneau. He was installed as such on September 8, 1971.

Soon after beginning to serve as Bishop of Juneau, Bishop Hurley earned his pilot's license. Flying his own plane gave him more mobility, enabled him to visit more readily the smaller and more remote communities of his diocese, and thus greatly expand Catholic ministry. "To serve the needs of the people" was his guiding principle throughout his years as a bishop. This was very much in keeping with his motto *Populo Dei* ("for the people of God"). Being a pilot helped him significantly to live up to that principle. However, to expand Catholic ministry and better serve the needs of the people, he relied not only on himself and his airplane, but also on his priests. As he implemented the reforms mandated by Vatican II, he promoted more active roles for lay people in the life of the Church.

During his years in Juneau, Bishop Hurley was co-founder of Alaska Housing Development Corporation, and of Catholic Community Services, the Catholic social service agency of the Juneau diocese. Under this latter agency, he initiated the "Trays on Sleighs" (the Alaskan version of Meals on Wheels) food program for senior citizens in six villages located in Southeastern Alaska. In 1977, he established St. Ann's Nursing Home in Juneau. Under his direction, five Catholic churches were built in the Diocese of Juneau. In 1970, he started the diocesan paper, *The Inside Passage*, to give a greater sense of unity, of family, to the widely-scattered Catholic communities in the diocese. No community was too small in his eyes. "We don't play the numbers game here," he often said, refusing to allow small numbers to discourage him from offering the services of the Church.

As Bishop Hurley flew the rounds of his vast diocese, visiting his small flocks living on remote islands, he—essentially a shepherd at heart, always accessible and sensitive to basic human needs—came to see how difficult it was for some of the people to go to confession to the priest assigned to minister to them, and so close to them. In larger cities, people have options, when it comes to choosing a confessor; not so, in much of the Juneau diocese. To protect the anonymity of penitents, with a delicate pastoral touch and while still encouraging private confession, he allowed for communal penance liturgies with general absolution, limiting them to four times a year. This made it easier for people, who might otherwise not have done so, to come back to the Church.

After Vatican II, there was a tendency in the Church to merge small dioceses with neighboring ones. The Diocese of Juneau was one such diocese under consideration for a possible merger. Bishop Hurley, however, recommended that it be allowed to continue to exist as an independent diocese. "In the case of Juneau," he explained, "numbers, about 4,000 Catholics, would not seem to warrant a separate diocese. It is, however, the capital of the State of Alaska, and its territorial size and its distance from other dioceses present special conditions." His recommendation was looked upon favorably by Rome.

On May 4, 1976, Bishop Hurley was appointed Archbishop of **Anchorage**, as successor to Archbishop **Joseph T. Ryan**. He was installed on July 8, 1976. Until June 15, 1979, when Michael H. **Kenny** was installed as Bishop of Juneau, Archbishop Hurley was also the Apostolic Administrator of the Juneau diocese.

As Archbishop of Anchorage, Archbishop Hurley continued to serve the needs of the people, especially those of the poor and the needy. Through Catholic Social Services of the Archdiocese of Anchorage, he was instrumental in the establishment of a daycare center for the handicapped; the Brother Francis Shelter for homeless street people; Clare House, temporary housing for women and children; McAuley Manor for young women; and Covenant House, part of Covenant House International for homeless youth. During his years as archbishop, seven Catholic churches were built in the archdiocese.

Along with promoting social ministries, and healthy family life, which he regarded as "central to society and to the Church," Archbishop Hurley promoted also, even if only indirectly, the more purely spiritual ministries. According to Father James R. Conyard, S.J., speaking of Anchorage's **Holy Spirit Center**, "The archbishop paid most of the bills. He was always hopeful, pleasant and encouraging. He felt that having a retreat center was a good thing."

As it had served Bishop Hurley well, while he was Bishop of Juneau, so the airplane continued to serve him well as Archbishop of Anchorage. This "local mode of transportation," as he termed it, helped him shrink his sprawling archdiocese down to size. By the time he retired as Archbishop of Anchorage, he had flown many thousands of miles in the Alaskan skies. He began his career as a pilot flying a Cessna 180 on floats. While in Anchorage, he flew a Cessna 182 and a Mooney. As a general rule, he preferred to fly by instruments. Though he admitted to having done some "foolish" things as a pilot, he never had a major mishap. He admitted also to enjoying his work as bishop and pilot, "because it is centered around people in their quest for the spiritual aspects of their lives. And, in **Alaska**, that would be much more difficult without one very important tool—the airplane." Beginning in 1978, he was a member of the Alaskan Air Command Civilian Advisory Board. As a private pilot, he was also a member of the Anchorage Civil Air Patrol.

Not surprisingly, during the course of his 25 years as Archbishop of Anchorage, various highlights marked also Archbishop Hurleys's life. On February 26, 1981, along with the whole archdiocese, he had the privilege and joy of hosting Pope John Paul II during his visit to Anchorage. About 65,000 attended the Mass offered by the pope on the Delaney Park Strip. This was the largest group of Alaskans ever gathered in one place.

In December 1990, as policies of openness and liberalization were changing the face of the Soviet Union, Archbishop Hurley and Father Michael Shields went to the city of Magadan, in Siberian Russia, to offer the Christmas Mass. Around 300 people jammed the theater for the first public Mass celebrated in that city. After that Christmas Mass, the archbishop's return flight to Anchorage was canceled, forcing him to remain in Magadan for three more weeks. During that time, he was able to gather the 12 signatures needed to officially register a new church. The new parish was registered on January 4, 1991, the date that marks the founding of the parish of the Nativity of Jesus in Magadan, Russia. Archbishop Hurley had made the first of his nine trips to Magadan in July 1989. On January 14, 2001, he was there to celebrate a dramatic 10th Anniversary Mass.

In 1997, Archbishop Hurley was named "Alaskan of the Year." He was the first religious leader to be selected for this honor. He was also named to the "Top 25 Alaskans" list a number of times.

On August 6th, during the Great and Sacred Jubilee of the Year of Our Lord 2000, Michael J. **Kaniecki**, S.J., Bishop of **Fairbanks**, died suddenly at **Emmonak** an hour before the noon Mass, at which he was scheduled to confirm 25. With eager anticipation, the Diocese of Fairbanks was looking forward to celebrating the Great Jubilee, on August 27th, with a solemn Mass, at which many were to be confirmed. The sudden death of Bishop Kaniecki left many, understandably, deeply saddened and wondering about the confirmations that had been scheduled for Emmonak and the jubilee celebrations that had been scheduled for Fairbanks.

With great generosity of heart, it was Archbishop Hurley who stepped in. On Saturday, August 12th, he was in Fairbanks to be the principal celebrant at the Mass of the Resurrection offered for Bishop Kaniecki. On August 19th, he was at Emmonak to offer Mass and to confirm the 25 awaiting Confirmation. "It was my great fortune," he wrote, "to go to Emmonak to pick up where Bishop Kaniecki left off, to offer Mass for the people and to confirm those who had been waiting for the imposition of Bishop Kaniecki's hands." After the services in the church, the archbishop took part in the potluck dinner and the Native dancing that followed them. "They invited me into the dance," he recalled with obvious delight, "and clapped at my effort to get synchronized with the leaders. The elders welcomed me as an elder." His presence and active participation in the dinner and dancing did much to lift the spirits of the people. One year later, he was again in Emmonak, to offer an anniversary Mass at the place where Bishop Kaniecki had died.

On August 27th, in Fairbanks' crowded Carlson Center, it was Archbishop Hurley who offered the Great Jubilee Mass and conferred the Sacrament of Confirmation on many. The positive, upbeat tone of his presence and homily that day did much to brighten the occasion for the many who had come from all over the Diocese of Fairbanks.

With his 75th birthday rapidly approaching, Archbishop Hurley, in July 1999, asked Pope John Paul II for a Coadjutor. His request was granted, in January 2000, with the appointment of Archbishop Roger L. **Schwietz**, a member of the Missionary **Oblates of Mary Immaculate**. In a letter dated January 8, 2001, Archbishop Hurley, having "no intention of being a lame duck bishop," offered his resignation as Archbishop of Anchorage to the Holy Father, who accepted it. "My message to the Holy Father," he said, "was simply, 'It is time.'" By then, he was about to celebrate his 50th anniversary as a priest, and had been a bishop in Alaska for over 30 years, and Archbishop of Anchorage since 1976. Officially, as of March 3, 2001, he was succeeded as Archbishop of Anchorage by Archbishop Schwietz. The passing of archiepiscopal power from the one archbishop to the other took on visible form the following day with a ceremonial "passing of the crosier."

As of the year 2004, Francis T. Hurley, Archbishop Emeritus of Anchorage, was in retirement in Anchorage.

HUSLIA

The Koyukon Athabaskan Indian village of Huslia, located on the left bank of the Koyukuk River some 70 miles north of **Galena**, came into being in the late 1940s and early 1950s, when the people of a settlement called Cutoff moved to this new location four miles to the south. The name was changed to Huslia in 1952 after the Huslia River, which enters the Koyukuk near the village. In 1947, a post office was established at Cutoff. In 1952, the name was changed to Huslia, when the post office was moved to a new location on higher ground. In 1992, Huslia had a population of 224; and in the year 2000, of 293.

The Huslia mission is dedicated to St. Francis Regis. In 1954, there were 25 Catholics in Huslia. Some of the people of Huslia have moved back and forth between the Catholic and Episcopal Churches. The village has never had a Catholic priest in residence, and at times was visited very infrequently. However, Catholic baptisms in the area took place already during the early part of the 1900s. They were performed by priests traveling out of **Nulato**, or when people of the Cutoff–Huslia area traveled to Nulato.

Huslia began to be visited on a more or less regular basis by a priest in 1955, when Father James W. **Plamondon**, S.J., started to visit it out of Galena. This he did until 1962. It was he who, with the help of some of the men of the village, built Huslia's present church, around 1955. The following Jesuit Fathers also visited Huslia: Jules M. **Convert**, out of **Kaltag**, 1962–66; Charles A. **Saalfeld**, out of **Tanana**, 1966–73; Bernard F. **McMeel**, out of Galena, 1973–76; Saalfeld, out of Nulato, 1976–78; James A. **Sebesta**, out of Kaltag, 1978–82; Charles A. **Bartles**, out of Galena, 1982–85. No priest is listed as serving the Huslia parish for the year 1985–86.

Franciscan priests stationed in Galena visited Huslia during the years 1986–95. Diocesan priests, likewise stationed in Galena, followed them: Father Edward J. **Hartmann**, 1995–97; Father Patrick D. **Bergquist**, 1997–98; Father Andrzej Maslanka, 1998–2002; and Father J. Albert **Levitre**, 2002–03. In December 2004, Father Richard D. **Case**, S.J., began to visit Huslia out of Galena.

Brother Robert **Ruzicka**, O.F.M., was in residence in Huslia, part time, during the years 1986–94, serving as Pastoral Administrator. Beginning in 2000, and as of the year 2004, Brother R. Justin Huber, O.F.M., both visited and resided in Huslia as Pastoral Minister.

Sister Patricia Wauters, S.F.C.C., was in residence in Huslia, as a Pastoral Minister, from 1983–86.

Harry and Rose Ambrose took care of the Huslia parish facilities and served as faithful, powerful prayer leaders of Huslia's Catholic Community for decades. Harry died in 2003.

151

St. Francis Regis Church, Huslia. *MK.*

IDITAROD

The town of Iditarod, located on the left bank of the Iditarod River and some 80 miles northeast of **Holy Cross**, was established in June 1910 as a supply and commercial center for the district after the rush to the Iditarod gold mining region began in 1909. During the summer of 1910, there were approximately 2,500 people in the Iditarod region. In 1911, it had a population of 600 to 700 persons. A post office was maintained there from 1910–29. In 1920, its population was 50; in 1930, 8; and in 1940, 1. Today Iditarod is a ghost town, except for several weeks during March of odd years when the Iditarod Trail Sled Dog Race goes through it.

In the annals of Catholic Alaskan history, Iditarod does not loom large. Father Francis M. **Monroe**, S.J., built a chapel there around 1910. He visited it at irregular intervals out of **Fairbanks**. In 1916, he performed a baptism there. For some years, it was visited from time to time out of Holy Cross. Father Philip I. **Delon**, S.J., stopped at Iditarod in December 1923.

JACOBSON, Father James E., S.J.

James Edward "Jim" Jacobson, the seventh of eight children, was born to Henry Jacobson and Lela Irene Philips Jacobson in Seattle, Washington, on December 14, 1923. His father worked for the Union Pacific Railroad, so Jim's early years were spent in Georgetown, a suburb of Seattle. He received his elementary and secondary education in public schools in and near Seattle. As a student at Foster High School, he was a member of the student council, a player on the football team, and the head cheerleader at basketball games. To earn money for school clothes, he worked in Seattle, as well as in country fields picking beans and berries. He also caddied at a local golf course.

Jim was in his senior year at Foster, when the bombing of Pearl Harbor took place, leading to the beginning of World War II. He was ready to go into the military, but was counseled to stay in school and graduate. He graduated in June 1942, and immediately went to work in a shipyard as an apprentice pipe fitter's helper. He quit that job in September to begin studies at the University of Washington, and to await the draft.

In February 1943, Jim was drafted into the U.S. Army. In March, he reported to Fort Lewis, Washington, where he took tests to determine what kind of duty he was best suited for. During one of his high school summers, he had learned how to use dynamite when he helped a man dynamite tree stumps. Because of that experience, he was sent to Camp Hood, Texas, to be a demolition man in a tank destroyer battalion. After several months of training, he was sent to DePaul University in Chicago for courses in engineering. After attending classes there through December 1943, he was called to

Camp Carson, Colorado, to join the 71st Mountain Division (Mule Pack) as a combat engineer. Training took him from the mountains of Colorado to the coastal range of California, and from there to Fort Benning, Georgia. After still further training, he went to Europe, in the spring of 1945, as a combat engineer. There, for six months, he repaired roads and bridges. He spent the last six months of his Army career in the 6th Finance Division.

While Jim was overseas with the Army, he met young men from a number of different religions, went to a number of different Churches, but belonged to none of them. In reality, he did not want to belong to any of them. He was negatively impressed by all the squabbling and the violent history of Christianity. However, while he was still overseas, one of his sisters became a Catholic and urged him and his two brothers to enroll at Seattle University after they were discharged from the service.

Jim began his education at Seattle University with the spring quarter of 1946. He became a Catholic in the spring of 1947, and applied to join the Oregon Province of the Society of Jesus that same year. He was told, however, that, in his case, there would have to be a three-year wait before he could apply. Accordingly, he continued on with his studies at Seattle University, ending them in 1949 with a B.A. degree in philosophy. During those years at Seattle University, he received his first formal education in all aspects of religion and philosophy.

On August 13, 1949, after only two years of waiting, Jim was allowed to enter the Jesuit Novitiate of St. Francis Xavier at Sheridan, Oregon. After completing his two-year noviceship and taking his simple vows of poverty, chastity and obedience, he

Father James E. Jacobson, S.J. *LRC.*

spent an additional year there studying the classics and humanities. From 1952–55, he made his philosophical studies at Mount St. Michael's in Spokane, Washington.

During his three years at Sheridan, Jim had kept volunteering to serve on any mission where he might be needed. In 1955, he was needed in **Alaska**. From August 1955 to July 1956, he was stationed at **Holy Cross Mission** as a teacher of English, mathematics, biology, and history, and as prefect of the "big boys." He found joy in spending time with them cutting stove wood, emptying nets of big salmon, picking berries, and being with them on various other outings. Years later, he recalled his year at Holy Cross as "a very happy year."

In the fall of 1956, Jim began his theological studies at Alma College, near Los Gatos, California. Always interested in ideas, he found himself, while at Alma College, wishing that he could stay in school forever. But, it was not only the study of theology that made his Alma College years "the happiest four years," up to that time, of his life. On Saturdays, along with other Alma College seminarians, he went to Our Lady of Guadalupe Church in San Jose to teach catechism to boys preparing for their first Holy Communion. By his own admission, he had to stifle the temptation to learn Spanish and spend the rest of his life working with Mexican-Americans in California.

Jim was ordained a priest in St. Aloysius Church, Spokane, on June 13, 1959. After finishing his fourth year of theology at Alma College, he made his tertianship at Port Townsend, Washington. In August 1961, he drove up the Alaska Highway to begin his Alaskan ministries as a priest. From August 1961 to December 1961, he was the pastor of the Central Yup'ik Eskimo villages of **Chefornak** and **Nightmute**. In January 1962, when Father Paul C. **Deschout**, S.J., left **Tununak**, he assumed the pastoral care of that village also.

In the summer of 1962, Father Jacobson and Maxie Altsik—eventually to be ordained to the permanent diaconate as one of the **Eskimo Deacons**—went to Bristol Bay to get a 32-foot Columbia River fishing boat. After much work to make it seaworthy, they sailed up the coast. Stormy weather kept them from rounding Cape Newenham for six days. They spent the time on Hagemeister Island fishing, beachcombing, and working on the boat. Once they got the boat to Nelson Island, it was used as a supply boat, making trips to **Bethel** for oil, gas, and other necessities.

In 1964, Father Jacobson witnessed the founding of the village of **Toksook Bay**. He ordered lumber and furnishings for a new church there. The material arrived in the summer of 1965. At the same time, lumber and furnishings arrived for the school which was to be built there. In Father Jacobson's absence, the workmen made the mistake of thinking that the heavy timbers ordered for the foundation of the church were ordered for the school and cut them up and used them. The church was built in 1966.

From September 1966 to July 1967, Father Jacobson was pastor of **St. Michael** and of its dependent stations, **Stebbins** and **Unalakleet**. During that year he served also as an Air Force auxiliary chaplain at the DEWline (Distant Early Warning) station at Unalakleet .

From July 1967 to August 1970, he was Jesuit Superior and Principal of **Copper Valley School**. He was the last Jesuit to serve there in that dual capacity. The school was closed in 1971.

In August 1970, Father Jacobson began to serve as pastor of **Hooper Bay**, **Scammon Bay**, and

Chevak. In the spring of 1971, he became an Air Force auxiliary chaplain. As such, he spent three days a month at the Cape Romanzof DEWline station. On October 6, 1975, he was in Chevak to concelebrate at the Mass of Christian Burial for Eskimo Deacon Michael **Nayagak**.

In June 1976, Father Jacobson began a year of sabbatical leave in Berkeley, California. While there, he heard something about a community organizing program. Hoping that it would help him learn who the true leaders were in Eskimo villages and how to train them, he asked to spend the summer of 1977 working in Oakland. He wound up spending the next two years there getting on-the-job training in community organization. In 1979, he returned to Alaska to begin community organizing in western Alaska. His Superior, however, wanted him to do other work, either in **Fairbanks** or in **Anchorage**. Several months later, he was called to serve as Catholic Chaplain at the Oregon State Penitentiary at Salem, Oregon. That assignment was intended to last two or three years. However, it became the major assignment of his priestly life. For a time he served as the President of the National American Correctional Chaplains' Association. Of his prison ministry work, he wrote, on February 17, 2001—while at the same time admitting that Alaska was "still a great drawing card" on his heart and thoughts—"It has been a wonderful experience and a true vocation for me. I never even thought of prison ministry as a vocation, but that is what it has turned out to be." As of the year 2004, he was still happily engaged in that Salem, Oregon, prison ministry.

JACQUET, Father Aloysius, S.J.

Aloysius Jacquet, a Walloon, was born in Bruges, Belgium, on January 18, 1854. He entered the Jesuit Order on March 19, 1872, arriving in Spokane, Washington, on April 21, 1883. His pre-Alaskan years he spent in the Pacific Northwest and in California. Fellow Jesuits described him as "brilliant, magnetic," and as "adept at gathering other people's money for good causes." On July 4, 1901, he arrived in **Nome, Alaska**, where he established St. Joseph's parish. By September 17th, he had

Father Aloysius Jacquet, S.J.
JOPA-1066.01a.

already completed the rectory; and, one month later, the church. Fund-raising and the speedy erection of those buildings, however, had put him under such great stress that he lost his sanity. He was declared legally insane on November 6th. On the 22nd, he left Nome under the care of Dr. Samuel J. Call, who had volunteered to take him by dogteam to **Holy Cross Mission** for treatment and safe-keeping. The staff at Holy Cross, where the party arrived on December 18th, was unable to take care of him. Five days later, he was sent to **St. Michael**, where he spent the winter. From there, he returned to California. After spending several years recovering his sanity, he taught for a number of years at Santa Clara University and at St Ignatius High School in San Francisco. He died in Montreal, Canada, on March 27, 1922.

97

Jakes, Brother Ignatius J., S.J.

He was a member of that great Inupiat Eskimo race that extends from Siberia through northern **Alaska** and northern Canada all the way to Greenland—and for over 55 years he was also a member of the Society of Jesus, the only Inupiat Eskimo ever

Brother Ignatius J. Jakes, S.J. *LRC.*

to serve in that Society. Throughout those years he was, by his own admission, strengthened and sustained, in large part, by his singular devotion to Mary, the Mother of the Lord. "Strength," both physical and spiritual, was, according to one of his Jesuit co-missionaries, the one word that best summarized his personality.

Ignatius Joseph Jakes was born on November 24, 1924, at Shelton, a settlement on the right bank of the Kuzitrin River 53 miles northeast of **Nome**. His father, Louie A. Jake [*sic*], was a reindeer herder. From 1932 to 1941, Ignatius attended school at the nearby **Pilgrim Hot Springs** Mission, boarding there during the school year, spending the summers at home. The mission was staffed by **Ursuline** Sisters and Jesuit priests and Brothers. When Ignatius first started school, he could speak only his Native Inupiaq Eskimo, no English. However, he "picked it up fairly soon enough," and before long was able to read and write it.

When the Pilgrim Springs mission was closed in the summer of 1941, many of the children, along with members of the mission staff, moved to St. Mary's Mission at **Akulurak**. Ignatius was among them. He had no trouble adjusting to his new surroundings, though he was now in the heart of Central Yup'ik Eskimo country. After he was there a few

months, the boys elected him prefect of their Sodality. Father Segundo **Llorente**, S.J., Superior of St. Mary's at the time, saw in him "a conscientious and persevering student. His aptitudes were along practical lines, and he soon proved himself to be the most handy boy around the school. He also seemed to be sincerely religious." Father Llorente, therefore, asked Ignatius if he had ever thought that he would like to be a Brother. "His face beamed," recalled Father Llorente. "No, he had not thought about it, but he believed he would like it." By this time, Ignatius had come to know well the Brothers stationed at Pilgrim Springs and St. Mary's.

Ignatius was given plenty of time to think the matter over. After doing so, the idea still appealed to him. Accordingly, in September 1942, he was sent to **Holy Cross Mission**, as a test, to work in the machine shop there under Brother George J. **Feltes**, S.J., an expert mechanic. Ignatius gave a good account of himself during his year at Holy Cross. After being officially "examined," and found to be a suitable candidate for the Jesuit Brotherhood, he was accepted for the Jesuit novitiate at Sheridan, Oregon, the novitiate of the Oregon Province, to whose care the Alaska Mission was entrusted. By the time he arrived at Sheridan, he had read St. Alphonsus Liguori's *The Glories of Mary* four times.

Under date of September 4, 1943, the novitiate diarist recorded: "This afternoon Br. Ignatius Jakes, an Eskimo boy from Alaska, entered our novitiate as a coadjutor postulant." During an interview held exactly 50 years later, Brother Jakes described his decision to enter the Jesuits as "like jumping off a cliff." He never regretted that leap of faith. "When I got to Sheridan," he said, "I saw it was just what I wanted."

After completing his six-month postulancy, Ignatius began his canonical two-year noviceship on March 4, 1944. This date formally marked the beginning of his life in the Society of Jesus. On March 12, 1946, the anniversary of the canonization of Sts. Ignatius and Francis Xavier, Ignatius pronounced the three canonical vows of poverty, chastity and obedience. This made him a full-fledged Temporal Coadjutor of the Society of Jesus.

The young Brother Jakes was described at this time by one of his co-novices as: "quick and energetic in his movements, of medium height, with a husky build, and straight, jet-black hair. His fingers are short and powerful, and look as though they have been accustomed to hard work."

Hard work it was that characterized most of Brother Jakes' 55 years as a Jesuit Brother. At Sheridan, working on the novitiate farm, among other things, he milked cows and kept machinery operational. In 1947, he was assigned to Port Townsend, Washington, where he spent a year tending the furnace, and working in the laundry and linen closet. He spent the years 1948–51 at Mount St. Michael's on the outskirts of Spokane, Washington. Driving a four-cord dump truck hauling sawdust from the city up to "the Mount" for the heating plant was his chief duty during those three years. One autumn, an unusually early snowfall deposited a deep layer of wet, slippery snow on the two-track ramp leading up to the sawdust bin. Instead of resorting to tedious shoveling, Brother Jakes simply made a snowball at the top of each track. These he rolled down the tracks, clearing them with hardly an effort.

By now Brother Jakes had been out of his "native element" for close to a decade. Great, then, was his joy when he learned that he was being reassigned. "I got to go back to Holy Cross in 1951," he exuberantly recalled many years later. During his 11-year stint at Holy Cross, he worked in the laundry, tended the furnace, did carpentry, and served as a general handyman. And again he found himself in the machine shop with Brother Feltes, whom he very much admired and from whom he learned a great deal about machines and tools.

The two Brothers were together again for the years 1962–66, in **Fairbanks**, where they gathered military surplus supplies of every kind and whatever else was useful to, or needed by, the various schools and missions in northern Alaska. In the course of those four years, the Brothers collected, repaired, packaged and shipped great quantities and varieties of materials and supplies to places like **Copper Valley School**, Holy Cross, and St. Mary's Mission, **Andreafsky**.

Twenty years after Brother Jakes pronounced his vows at Sheridan, he was back there again, for a two-year stay, 1966–68, before going on to Jesuit High School in Portland, Oregon. He was to spend four years there, as a grounds-keeper. As such he

waged a constant battle with the gophers digging up the athletic fields. At the same time, he waged also a "battle with the bottle." He won both battles. (It was because of a growing problem with alcohol that he had been assigned outside Alaska.) Concerning Brother Jakes, his Superior at Jesuit High School wrote to Father Jules M. **Convert**, S.J., General Superior of the Jesuits in Alaska at the time: "Although he has found it difficult to work on our grounds, he has done a good job. He is a hard worker. We will miss Br. Jakes, but I am happy he is returning to his beloved Alaska."

Brother Jakes returned to Alaska in 1972. There St. Mary's was his home base for the next 23 years. At St. Mary's itself, he served in various capacities, but mainly as maintenance man and as driver to and from the airport. With the airport eight miles out of town, he logged countless miles over the narrow, rocky road under every imaginable weather condi-

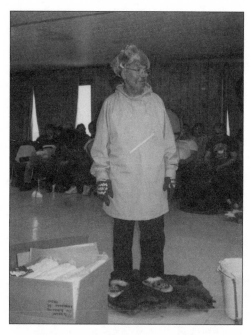

Brother Ignatius J. Jakes, S.J., wearing newly-made Native clothes and standing on a beaver pelt, presides as gifts are distributed in his name to guests attending the potlatch held in his honor at St. Marys on the occasion of his golden jubilee as a Jesuit. Brother became a Jesuit on March 4, 1944. The potlatch took place on April 22, 1994. *LR.*

tion. He had the reputation of being able to keep the road under the wheels, even during blizzards and whiteouts, when others often found themselves off the road and out on the tundra.

One was well advised, in any given year, not to expect Brother Jakes to be at St. Mary's during September. September is moose hunting season in that part of Alaska, and he was sure to be out in the wilds, hunting. Seldom did he return home without "meat for the pot." He was a natural-born hunter.

During his roughly two decades at St. Mary's, Brother Jakes was often away to do needed maintenance work at various missions: here fixing a leaky roof, there leveling a village church that had begun to settle into the tundra, elsewhere replacing rotten foundation logs. He more or less single-handedly laid the foundation for the new **Chevak** church, lifting and carrying the heavy planks and beams by himself. Single-handedly, too, at **Kaltag**, he lifted logs generally considered two-man logs onto the cordwood saw. His physical strength was prodigious, legendary.

When asked which of the many projects he had worked on had given him particular satisfaction, Brother Jakes said it was helping build, in 1978, the new church on **Little Diomede** Island. He found constructing the foundation on the steep, rocky slope of the island a special challenge. While on Little Diomede, he was working for the first, and only, time in his 55-year Jesuit life in his own Inupiaq territory. Brother Jakes never complained about any of his assignments; in fact, he never complained about anything. He was content to lead a hidden life of humble service, serving the Lord with his hands, and with all his heart, wherever obedience called him.

Brother Jakes was a quiet man, more a doer than a talker. During the latter part of his life especially, he became noticeably taciturn. An affirmative grunt from him in response to a question put to him bordered on loquacity. This does not mean that he was anti-social. He was, in fact, quite sociable—in his Eskimo way. He routinely took part in Jesuit community doings. He was always with his fellow Alaskan Jesuits for the annual retreat. He visited and ate with the people of whatever village he happened to be in. He took steam baths with the men, hunted with them. He was always ready for a game of pinochle. He was a formidable chess player.

Details about Brother Jakes' life and stories about him had to come mostly from others who knew him. In one of the villages, a family was celebrating an anniversary. The Jesuit Father attended, but Brother Jakes had not come along. He was then specifically asked for. A member of the family related: "We will always remember Brother Jakes. When we were little kids and did not have food, someone would leave fish and birds outside our door. We watched to see who it was. It was Brother Jakes. We were hungry, and he knew it, and he brought food to us without embarrassing us. We will always remember that." Brother Jakes had the reputation of being a man who knew who needed what and where hard-to-find items might be found and how to get them to the needy without causing them embarrassment.

Brother Jakes also had the reputation of being a holy man. One day he was a member of a party out to gather firewood along the riverbank. When they had come to a good site and set up camp, he sat down and watched the others work. The caretaker of the St. Mary's mission buildings asked him to help. One of the Eskimo men spoke up: "Don't bother him. Brother Jakes doesn't have to work. We just want him in camp to pray for us. His job is to be holy for us."

On the occasion of Brother Jakes' golden jubilee as a Jesuit, big celebration doings were held in his honor at St. Mary's on Friday, April 22, 1994. There was a concelebrated Mass at 11 A.M. in the old mission chapel, with Michael J. **Kaniecki**, S.J., Bishop of Fairbanks, as principal celebrant and many priests as concelebrants. This was followed by lunch, leisurely visiting, walks, and dinner at 5:30. The Eskimo potlatch honoring Brother Jakes began at 7:30 that evening in the St. Mary's city hall. This was soon filled with guests from near and far. Among them were also two very special, surprise guests from beyond the Arctic Circle: Helen Schaeffer and Lucy Stalker from **Kotzebue**. Over 50 years earlier, at the Pilgrim Springs mission boarding school, they and Brother Jakes had been classmates. They and members of his immediate family were honored guests at the whole affair.

The evening's ceremonies began with an opening prayer, followed by words of welcome and introductions of honored guests. Eskimo drumming and dancing came next. After several hours of this, gifts to be distributed were brought in. Then in walked

Brother Jakes, wearing, in part, new, specially made Native clothes: an Eskimo parka, a fur hat, beaded sealskin mukluks on his feet, and beaded moosehide gloves on his hands. Standing in the middle of the hall on a beaver pelt, he presided as gifts were distributed to the assembled crowd in his name. After the distribution of gifts, which constitutes the heart of a potlatch, more drumming and dancing followed. It was near midnight, before the last echo of the last drumbeat died out.

The Golden Jubilee Mass, a Mass of thanksgiving, was celebrated the following day, on April 23rd, in the city hall. Bishop Kaniecki was again principal celebrant; 14 priests concelebrated. After the Lord's Prayer, recited in Eskimo, Brother Jakes, kneeling before the Sacred Host and chalice, renewed his vows as a Jesuit Brother. After the renewal, he was formally received into the Central Yup'ik Eskimo community by being given a new name translating into English as "Our Brother." After Mass, Brother Jakes received some special gifts from members of his immediate family—and, from the St. Mary's parish, as a token of special esteem, a fishing rod and reel. The whole potlatch celebration ended with a grand smorgasbord-type of dinner.

A year after the golden jubilee celebrations, the active life of Brother Jakes came to an abrupt end. A severe stroke in May 1995 paralyzed him on his right side and forced him to spend the next four years either in bed or in a wheelchair. During those years he lived with the Jesuit community in Fairbanks. There he received the best of care. As he had never in his previous life complained about his assignments, so now, too, he accepted this "assignment," much as he would have liked to return to a more active life at St. Mary's, without complaint, and as coming from the hand of God.

But, Brother Jakes did get to return once more to St. Mary's, in July 1997, accompanied by his nurse, for a week-long stay. Though confined to his wheelchair, he still managed, with help, to move about the village for farewell visits and final good-byes. At the end of the week, he was ready to return to Fairbanks. Not long after his return to Fairbanks, he told his nurse, "I want to go home." "But, Brother Jakes," she said to him, "you are home!" "No," he answered, "I want to go to heaven."

Brother Jakes did not have to wait long to go to heaven. On June 16, 1999, he was taken to Spokane, there, in the Jesuit Infirmary at Gonzaga University, to spend his last days. Death came to him a little over two months later, on August 23rd. It was described as "a very peaceful passing."

People who knew how difficult it is for a person to live in and, at the same time, to be at home in two cultures as diverse as the Eskimo and white-man cultures had nothing but admiration for the way Brother Jakes had in his own life resolved what in similar cases often brought about a personal culture conflict or a self-identity crisis. By strength of character, and by God's grace, he was equally at home in the Eskimo and in the white culture. He drew strength by sharing the lives of both races.

Brother Ignatius Joseph Jakes, S.J., a credit to his Inupiaq Eskimo race and to the Society of Jesus, lies buried in Mount St. Michael's Cemetery, Spokane, far from the land of his origins.

146

JESUIT VOLUNTEER CORPS

What has become, in the course of roughly half a century, a loosely-knit national and international organization and has, for decades, been known as the "Jesuit Volunteer Corps" has its humble roots in the wilds of **Alaska**.

In 1955, Sister M. George **Edmond**, S.S.A., who had been at **Holy Cross Mission**, Alaska, since 1946, left Alaska to spend the year 1955–56 in Massachusetts preparing herself to be the Sister Superior of **Copper Valley School**. This was scheduled to open in 1956. While in the East, she had occasion to lecture at Regis College in Weston, Massachusetts, about the Alaska missions. Two young women, after hearing her speak, offered to serve as lay volunteers at the new school about to open near **Glennallen**. They were Marge Mannix and Ann Kent, due to graduate in the spring of 1956.

Sister M. George wrote to Francis D. **Gleeson**, S.J., Vicar Apostolic of Alaska at the time, asking his views about introducing lay helpers at the Copper Valley School project. He took the question to his Consultors. Some of them had misgivings about such a new move. He, however, seeing the positive advantages of such an innovation, gave Sister M.

George the green light. At Anna Maria College, a college run by the Sisters of St. **Ann** in Paxton, Massachusetts, she did further recruiting. Before long, she had an additional four volunteers: Rosemary Bobka, Jacqueline Langlois, Jeannette Rageotte, and Shirley Richards. That group of six marked the beginning of the lay volunteer program in Alaska and served as a forerunner of the Jesuit Volunteer Corps. "Thus, unbeknownst to me," said Sister M. George in an April 5, 1987, interview, "I was planting the first seed for the Volunteer Movement, now known as the JVC."

Before "Jesuit Volunteer Corps" became the lay volunteer movement's standardized name in 1967, the movement was variously referred to as "Lay Apostle Volunteers," "Alaska Lay Volunteers," "Jesuit Lay Volunteer Program," "the Volunteer Movement," "Lay Volunteer Corps," and the like. For the school year 1957–58, eight students from Gonzaga University in Spokane, Washington, went to Copper Valley School to join the first group from the East. Together the two groups, in 1959, formed the nucleus of a volunteer alumni association: the L.A.M.B., the Lay Apostolic Mission Board. The L.A.M.B.s, who had a great deal to do with establishing what came to be the JVC spirit, were organized by Mickey Byrnes, who had been among the first group of volunteers from Gonzaga. For the time being, Gonzaga was a major supplier of volunteers for Copper Valley School. Soon, however, volunteers, with a great variety of skills, in generous numbers, not only from Gonzaga, but also from other Catholic universities and colleges, went north to serve at Copper Valley School, or at other places in Alaska. Among the first to avail themselves of the services of volunteers, in addition to Copper Valley School, were Holy Cross, **Fairbanks**, and **Dillingham**.

During the first ten years of its existence, this lay volunteer movement was little else than a more or less felicitous happening, "a happening of the Holy Spirit," in the words of Father John J. Morris, S.J., the man often credited with founding the whole volunteer program, an honor which he never ceased to disclaim. In a letter to Father Louis L. **Renner**, S.J., he wrote, regarding the founding of the Corps, "My point of view is that it was a happening of the Holy Spirit, something none of us planned. For the first ten years, there was no Corps, as it were, but rather a loosely, unorganized procession of volunteers coming to our missions. Bishop Gleeson was handling (many would contend 'mishandling') the thing." While neither would take credit for "founding" what has become known at the Jesuit Volunteer Corps, history does well to recognize Sister M. George Edmond and Father Morris as the "cofounders" of the Corps.

John Morris, then still a Jesuit seminarian, first arrived in Alaska in 1957, to spend the years 1957–59 at Copper Valley School. As a priest, he spent the years 1963–65 teaching at Monroe Catholic High School in Fairbanks. During those latter two years, he—along with Father George T. **Boileau**, S.J., pastor of Fairbanks' Immaculate Conception parish at the time—found himself involved, not without a considerable amount of frustration, with the volunteer program. The two saw the many merits of the program, but also its shortcomings in the haphazard way in which it was handled. Mostly it needed to be better organized, better structured, and better supported both at the recruiting end and in the field. Father Boileau was a clear-headed, persuasive man, and he had the respect of Bishop Gleeson. From him he obtained permission for himself and Father Morris to take over the program. That was in the early spring of 1964. Father Boileau was ordained bishop on July 31, 1964, but died suddenly seven months later, on February 25, 1965, leaving Father Morris now the sole man in charge of the volunteer program.

Father Morris made his tertianship during the year 1965–66. At the end of that year, he was still in charge of the volunteer program, ten years after it first came into being. Seeing that "it didn't make much sense trying to run it from Alaska—to recruit, to screen, telephone, coordinate, etc.," he decided not to return to Alaska, but, instead, to make Portland, Oregon, his headquarters. For "one who loved his time in Alaska," as he wrote of himself, "that was a hard move." It was during his first year in Portland that the title "Jesuit Volunteer Corps" became the official name of the program, trumpeted as "Twice as old as the peace corps, twice as tough, and ten times more rewarding!" In the homily he gave at the celebration marking the 30th anniversary of the founding of the JVC, he said, "I gave it a name, an office, and a shape."

By 1970, Father Morris had been closely involved with the volunteer movement for a total of seven years. He had not had a vacation of any kind during those years and was, by his own admission, "exhausted." He saw, too, "the need to do new things with the Corps." Up to around 1970, the JVC was still supplying volunteers only for Alaska and for several Indian Reservations in the Pacific Northwest. He, therefore, felt it was time for him to turn the directorship of the Corps over to someone else. By that time, there were some 150–175 volunteers in the field each year, most all of them in Alaska, serving in a great variety of capacities at places such as **Anchorage**, **Bethel**, Copper Valley School, Dillingham, Fairbanks, Holy Cross, **Kaltag**, **Kotzebue**, **Nome** (at radio station **KNOM**), and at St. Mary's Mission on the **Andreafsky** River.

It was especially during roughly the first three decades of the volunteer program's existence that lay volunteers played a truly major, critical role in Alaska, particularly in the Catholic schools there. In the words of Father Morris, they—as the numbers of men and women Religious continued to decline—were a "third force." The very existence of schools such as the two in Fairbanks, the ones at Copper Valley, Holy Cross, Dillingham, and St. Mary's Mission School depended on lay volunteers. Radio KNOM, too, would not have been possible without the services of the volunteers.

The last school in Alaska to rely heavily on lay volunteers was St. Mary's. In 1983, in recognition of its "exemplary volunteer achievements," the St. Mary's volunteer staff was named one of the "Citationists" for the 1983 President Ronald Reagan Volunteer Action Award. The letter accompanying the Citation read in part: "Your volunteer achievements are so outstanding that you were one of the 60 finalists—out of more than 2000 nominations—in the awards judging process. Your significant private sector initiative contribution is deserving of special recognition."

When, in 1970, Father Morris resigned as Director of the Jesuit Volunteer Corps, that role was assumed by Father William J. Davis, S.J. "Really, in all honesty," wrote Father Morris, "he reinvented the Corps, and did a fantastic job in just three years." After Father Davis came a succession of other competent, dedicated Jesuits. They, in turn, were followed by equally competent and dedicated lay men and women. Under their directorship, the Corps continued to become still more efficiently organized, to grow, and to become the national and international organization that it was as it sailed smoothly into the third millennium and on to the 50th anniversary of its founding.

As a tree is known by its fruits, so, too, the lay volunteer movement here under discussion. But, no human power can even begin to assess these adequately. The services that the lay volunteers have rendered over the decades are beyond calculation. So are the personal benefits that they have reaped from their time in the Corps. In their giving, they have received. Many owe their life's career, their life's vocation, to the time they spent serving in the Corps. Many found their spouses in the Corps. A significant number found their calling to the priesthood, to Religious life, or to a life of service to the Church as devout lay persons in the Corps. The following, to mention but some, all served as volunteers in Alaska before becoming priests: Fathers Thomas F. **Carlin**, S.J., Andrew P. **D'Arco**, David M. **Fitz-Patrick**, Mark A. **Hoelsken**, S.J., James M. **Kolb**, C.S.P., J. Albert **Levitre**, Steven C. Moore, Ross A. **Tozzi**, and John D. Whitney, S.J., Provincial of the Oregon Province as of July 31, 2002. Outstanding among former lay volunteers are: Mary Therese **Burik**, Thomas A. **Busch**, and Patrick C.W. **Tam**.

39, 177

JESUITS in Alaska

The first Jesuit to set foot in Alaska, but not as a missionary, was Father Patrick F. Healy. As a guest of his brother Michael Healy, captain of the U.S. Revenue Cutter *Corwin*, he visited the west coast of northern **Alaska** in the summer of 1883. Four years later, in the spring of 1887, Jesuit missionaries Fathers Paschal **Tosi** and Aloysius J. **Robaut** entered Alaska. Jesuit missionaries have, without interruption, been in Alaska ever since. By the year 2000, around 300 different Jesuit priests and Lay Brothers had—at one time or another, for many years or few—served on the Alaska Mission.

Fathers Tosi and Robaut came to Alaska as members of the Rocky Mountain Mission, a mission of

(*left*) Father Patrick J. Healy, S.J., President of Georgetown University 1874–82, needing a vacation, sailed to Alaska in 1883 on the U.S. Revenue Cutter *Corwin* captained by his brother Michael A. Healy. Father Healy was the first Jesuit to set foot in Alaska, though not as a missionary. *Photo by Julius Ulke/Georgetown University Archives.*

(*below*) Father Julius Jetté, S.J. *JOPA-824.27.*

the Turin Province of the Society of Jesus. From 1886 to 1907, all Alaska was under the Turin Province. On August 15, 1907, the missions of northern Alaska were entrusted to the French-Canadian Province. From 1907 to 1910, Turin kept only the missions of southern Alaska. From 1911 to 1912, southern Alaska was turned over to the California Province; and, from 1912 to 1932, all Alaska was entrusted to the California Province. In 1932, the Oregon Province came into being; and, after that, all Alaska was under it as a dependent mission.

This whole matter is further complicated by the facts that, from 1900 to 1902, the General Superior of the Rocky Mountain Mission was also the Superior of southern Alaska, and that, from 1903 to 1907, one and the same man was General Superior of both the Rocky Mountain Mission and of all Alaska. For nearly four decades, the Superiors of northern Alaska kept their hands off southern Alaska, leaving that part of Alaska in the care of the Oregon Province Provincials. In late 1967, the Father General of the Jesuits, Father Pedro Arrupe, saw fit to change this state of affairs. By a decree given in Rome on October 10, 1967, all Alaska, from **Ketchikan** to **Barrow**, was placed under the General Superior of the Alaska Mission. This remained the reality, until July 31, 1999, when, owing to diminishing numbers and improved modern means

of communication, all Alaska became an integral part of the Oregon Province.

GENERAL SUPERIORS OF JESUITS IN ALASKA:

Paschal Tosi	1886–1897
John B. **René**	1897–1902
George de la Motte	1902–1907
Joseph **Perron** (Vice-Superior)	1907–1909
John L. **Lucchesi**	1909–1913
John B. **Sifton**	1913–1923
Philip I. **Delon**	1923–1930
John L. Lucchesi	1930–1931
Francis M. **Ménager**	1931–1933
John B. Sifton	1933–1936
Francis B. **Prange**	1936–1937
Joseph F. **McElmeel**	1937–1944
Paul C. **Deschout**	1944–1950
Norman E. **Donohue**	1950–1956
Henry G. **Hargreaves**	1956–1963
George T. **Boileau**	1963–1964
Jules M. **Convert**	1964–1968
Bernard F. **McMeel**	1968–1973
William J. **Loyens**	1973–1976
Francis J. **Fallert**	1976–1982
Michael J. **Kaniecki**	1982–1984
Francis E. Mueller	May 1–May 22, 1984
James A. **Sebesta**	1984–1990
Theodore E. **Kestler**	1990–1999

63

JETTÉ, Father Julius, S.J.

His life's trail ended on the bleak, frozen tundra of western Alaska, near the Bering Sea, far from the land of his birth. He was not an old man at the time of his death—only 63—but the 27 years he had spent on the **Alaska** Mission had taken their toll.

Thirteen years before his death, he was already hailed as "the most distinguished scholar in Alaska, the chief authority on the native language, and manners and customs, beliefs and traditions of the middle Yukon," and, shortly before it, as the "bright star of the Tennah." Neither as scholar nor as missionary had he labored, at times heroically, and spent his life for human applause, yet this does not dispense those who know of his noble life and extraordinary achievements from keeping alive for posterity the memory of them.

Joseph Jules Jetté—known to the French world as Jules, to the English as Julius—was born in Montreal, Canada, on September 30, 1864, of aristocratic parentage. His father, the Honorable Louis-Amable Jetté, was to become Lieutenant Governor of the Province of Quebec. His saintly mother, Berthe Laflamme, came from a rich Montreal family of long standing. A highly gifted, precocious student, the young Jetté was educated at the Collège de Montréal and at the Collège Sainte-Marie. In 1882, he entered the Jesuit novitiate at Sault-au-Récollet to begin 14 years of training and studies that led to his ordination to the priesthood on May 26, 1896. During the 12 years following his novitiate, he took the customary courses in the classics, the humanities, the natural sciences, and in philosophy and theology. He also spent three years teaching and two in France studying. On October 24, 1888, the Paris Academy of Sciences conferred on him the Bachelor of Science degree; and, in 1890, he received the Licentiate degree in higher mathematics from the University of Angers. One of Jetté's classmates, who had spent many years with him, attested to his extraordinary memory and intellectual gifts. He wrote of him, "The more difficult a problem was, the more determined he was to solve it."

After his ordination to the priesthood in 1896, and two years at Sault-au-Récollet, Father Jetté left Montreal on May 25, 1898, for San Francisco to take ship to Alaska. Only on the 10th had he received word from the Jesuit Father General in Rome informing him that his request to be assigned to the Alaska Mission was granted. As far as can be determined, Father Jetté, despite his intellectual accomplishments and his success as a teacher, was allowed to go to Alaska—"at least for a time, as an experiment, to see whether his health is able to bear the rigors of that region"—because, throughout the course of his studies, he had suffered from headaches. What motivated him to volunteer for Alaska in the first place is not known. When Jesuit colleagues of his, who knew him well, learned of his being assigned to Alaska, they said among themselves, "What a loss, to bury such a talent in the snow!"

On June 10, 1898, on the Alaska Commercial Company's ship, the new *St. Paul*, Father Jetté left San Francisco for Alaska. On the 25th, he arrived at **St. Michael**, where he spent the summer months. As captain of the mission boat, the steamer *St. Joseph*, in company of other Jesuit missionaries, he left St. Michael on September 24th and arrived at **Nulato** on October 11th. He was to spend only eight of his 27 years in Alaska at Nulato. Nevertheless, it and its people enjoyed ever after "the right of the first born" in his heart.

Immediately upon his arrival at Nulato, Father Jetté set about learning the language of the area, Koyukon Athabaskan. He was to understand the Koyukon and master their language as no other white man before or after him ever did. His early and thorough mastery of the language was greatly facilitated by his having an excellent memory and a natural gift for languages, and by the fact that from his first days among the Koyukon a bond of mutual respect and affection was established. To his Superior he wrote on July 5, 1902: "I am indeed very much like a native on the point of sensitiveness, and this gives me a wonderful facility to understand them and get along with them, for I have only to treat them as I would be treated." In another letter he wrote, "I was paid the compliment that I was really a born Ten'a, and the Father of the people. In their delight they began to give me geographical information, of which they know I am very fond." By 1902, the London *Tablet* recognized Father Jetté as one who had acquired "a thorough mastery of the Nulato language."

What enabled Father Jetté to accomplish so much both as a missionary and as a scientist was the fact that these two capacities coincided in him. Whenever and in whatever capacity he dealt with his people, he was always ministering to them, observing them, and learning from them. A missionary excursion, or a visit to a hunting or fishing camp, was for him at the same time also a scientific field trip. Little notebooks accompanied him wherever he went, whether in his boat, by dogsled, or on snowshoes. In these he faithfully and carefully noted new words, grammatical details, geographic data, Koyukon behavior, as well as baptisms performed, marriages blessed, last rites administered, burials conducted. Later the contents of these notebooks were meticulously edited and properly recorded in scientific manuscripts and in parish registers.

No ceremonial is more sacred to the Nulato Koyukon than that of the *hi'o*, the "stickdance," or "Feast for the Dead." While some of the subsequent missionaries at Nulato would have nothing to do with this traditional cultural ceremonial and condemned it outright, Father Jetté understood its social implications, and did the people the courtesy of attending it and learning what it was all about. It was in large part because of his attitude toward the people and their culture, coupled with his keen scientific mind, that he achieved pre-eminence as

a scholar and anthropologist. One expert in the field of Alaskan anthropology wrote of him: "Leaving some ethnocentric indiscretions aside, the depth, insight, and magnitude of his work are unequalled in all of Alaskan anthropology." Another wrote: "No bibliography of Alaskan ethnology would be complete without the publications of Father Jetté, for they possess the rare combination of scholarship plus sympathetic understanding of the native."

By the summer of 1903, Father Jetté had spent five fruitful happy years in Alaska. Suddenly, that summer, he was asked to leave "this blessed soil," as he described Alaska, and to return to Canada. He was perplexed by the summons, all the more so as his health was excellent. Obediently, but reluctantly, he left Nulato, on July 13, 1903, for the Jesuit college of St. Boniface in Winnipeg, where he had taught before his ordination to the priesthood. Here, as a professor of mathematics, he caused a mild sensation by wearing Indian moccasins and smoking his pipe in class. As time allowed, he readied for

Father Julius Jetté, S.J., in Nulato with camera, 1914. *JOPA-824.03.*

the press his first work to be published. In the spring of 1904, his modest booklet of prayers and hymns in Koyukon, "Yoyit Rokanaga" (Heavenly Words), was published. While he was "in the land of exile," as he put it, he also began to compile a short Koyukon grammar.

Back in Alaska again in 1904, Father Jetté accompanied his dear Koyukon on their fall hunt. Normally he stayed at home in autumn, when the people were scattered far and wide along the rivers, sloughs and ponds across the Yukon from Nulato. Later he wrote why he deviated that year from his general rule:

> As I arrived in Nulato after a full year's absence from my flock, having lost one-half of my Indian language, and my muscles softened by quiet college life, I felt bound to plunge into Indian life again, renew old acquaintances, pick up some strength of limb and some fluency of speech, and above all keep company with the natives and remind them that there is a God to serve and a religion to practice. I therefore made up my mind to take a trip through Kayar, the Indians being just on the start of their fall outing.

By 1905, Father Jetté had produced in rough form a small grammar and a dictionary of Koyukon roots, each root accompanied by all the derivatives he could find.

On March 25, 1906, Episcopal Archdeacon Hudson Stuck arrived in Nulato just as Father Jetté was about to begin Sunday Mass. Later he wrote of Father Jetté's preaching: "Here for the first and only time I listened to a white man so fluent and vigorous in the native tongue that he gave one the impression of eloquence." Reverend Stuck admired Father Jetté, too, for being "a man of wide general culture," and for his "broad-minded tolerance and the charm of his courtesy."

In the summer of 1906, Father Jetté served for short periods of time first in **Tanana**, then in **Fairbanks**. In a letter, he wrote that, while on a trip up the Tanana River, because of his "shabby clothes and siwash manners," he was "dubbed a 'bum-priest.'" One senses that he felt rather honored to be so dubbed.

By October 1906, Father Jetté was back in Tanana. From a letter he wrote there on November 26th, it is apparent that the life of the scholar on the cold, subarctic frontier of Alaska was not always an easy one. He had to write away for foolscap. He commented on the weather: "It is very cold. My water-hole showed a thickness of ice of 2 ft. 5 inches by actual measurement, and my sourdough was frozen hard on Saturday morning. Just now I hear—and feel—the wind beginning to blow in a storm-fashion that promises a cold night." Another time he wrote, "I should have answered your letter then and there, but my ink had been frozen and had become so pale." And on a November day, "The days are getting so short that I cannot find time to do much by daylight, and I work much more slowly by lamp light."

Toward the end of 1906, Father Jetté was invited to attend an anthropological society meeting in Quebec, or at least to submit a paper. He did not attend, but he did submit an article written in English. It bore the title, "On the Social Condition of the Ten'a." This was translated into French and read for him at one of the sessions by a fellow Jesuit. It was published in 1907.

In April 1907, the first part of Father Jetté's grammar was published in *Man*. What makes this article especially significant is that in its first two paragraphs he stakes out most admirably the geographical habitat of the Koyukon people.

On May 14, 1907, Father Jetté became a member of The National Geographic Society. By early 1908, he, an expert cartographer, had ready for publication a manuscript entitled "Geographic Names." One of his maps covers the entire field of his labors. Over 30 smaller ones deal with more limited areas.

In 1908 and 1909, the Royal Anthropological Institute of Great Britain and Ireland published his 85-page article, "On Ten'a Folk-Lore." This consists of a series of Koyukon tales and legends—some still remembered only by the older Koyukon—which he himself heard from people and wrote down. Included among these are tales derived from facts acknowledged as having actually happened. "These," he wrote,

> present the mythology of the Ten'a and are intimately connected with what may be considered as their historical records. They are especially difficult to obtain, and the natives are very reluctant to let them be taken down in writing. Story-telling is resorted to as an entertainment to pass the long winter evenings. The narrator winds up his tale by stating that he has "shortened the winter."

On February 25, 1910, Father Jetté wrote:

My sheep are now scattering towards the hunting grounds, not for any reasonable purpose, for they have no hopes of getting martens, and they have here all the meat they can want, but driven by a blind impulse, irrational and inborn, which makes them crave for the wilds. This instinct is, I believe, irrepressible.

Something similar may well be said of Father Jetté himself, who, as scholar and scientist, engaged as naturally and instinctively in linguistic and ethnographic research as the Koyukon flock he tended engaged in hunting, fishing, trapping and gathering.

In 1911, Father Jetté's first of two articles in *Anthropos* appeared. It bears the title, "On the Superstitions of the Ten'a Indians." His second article in *Anthropos* was the 43-page contribution, "Riddles of the Ten'a Indians." This is illustrated by seven sketches drawn by himself.

Around this same time, Father Jetté had several other manuscripts almost ready for publication. One, 29 pages long, dated March 25, 1909, is titled, "On the Time-Reckoning of the Ten'a." It treats the whole broad subject of time as understood by the Koyukon. Their calendar divides the year into 16 months. To illustrate the workings of this calendar, he quoted the proclamations of the Church festivals as he made them to his **Kokrines** congregation for the year 1909. Here, in translation, is an example:

On the Sunday following, the seventh day after the moon of the geese has become full, the day on which Christ, who rules over us, rose again, with joy we shall celebrate a great day, that is Easter Sunday (April 11). And then on the second day after the month of the launching of canoes shall have begun (May 20), the day when he ascended back to heaven we shall celebrate.

The legacy of Father Jetté includes also works in the Koyukon language dealing with religious matters: a Bible history, a life of Christ, a hymnal, a Church calendar. His translations include: the epistles and gospels for all Sundays of the year, a large part of St. Matthew's gospel, and both the Baltimore and Deharbe Catechisms.

Unquestionably, the crowning achievement of all of Father Jetté's scholarly endeavors is his dictionary of the Koyukon language. It is a masterpiece of its kind, a work of lexicographical art. As a manuscript it comprised seven volumes, semi-bound in covers made by Father Jetté himself, and contained 2344 pages. The dictionary is, in reality, and at the same time, an encyclopedia embracing the whole of Koyukon culture. It contains many drawings made by himself to illustrate what words cannot adequately describe. It is utterly thorough, exhaustive. Words beginning with the letter 't' alone cover 731 manuscript pages. He devotes 600 words to the *hi'o*, the "stickdance."

As early as 1905, Father Jetté felt that, given a little leisure, he could have his dictionary manuscript ready for publication. On December 3, 1914, he wrote, "I am doing a little work on the Dictionary, re-writing the beginning of it, because I wrote that part before I learnt how to write a Dictionary." The following year, on July 10, 1915, he wrote, "I have a Ten'a Dictionary completely written, from a to z, and profusely supplied with genuine native phrases and expressions." He mentions his dictionary for the last time in 1919. At the time of his death, in 1927, his dictionary, his *opus magnum*, was still in manuscript form.

Various reasons can be given to account for the dictionary's not being published during Father Jetté's lifetime. There were time constraints. He was first and foremost a totally committed missionary priest. Furthermore, he was in all of his scholarly pursuits ever the perfectionist, not easily persuaded in his own mind that a manuscript was finally ready for publication. This was especially true in the case of his dictionary. Specifically, it was problems concerning matters of transcription, of orthography, to which, in his eyes, there was no satisfactory solution, that kept him, therefore, from advancing the dictionary manuscript for publication.

But the dictionary manuscript was not destined to remain forever merely an unpublished manuscript. In the year 2000, the 1118-page *Koyukon Athabaskan Dictionary*, with authorship ascribed equally to Jules Jetté and Eliza **Jones**, was published by the Alaskan Native Language Center, University of Alaska–Fairbanks.

In 1906, as mentioned above, Father Jetté left Nulato to serve at Tanana, then in Fairbanks, then again at Tanana. In 1907, he began what was to be a six-year stay at Kokrines. After Tanana, he was more than happy to be there. From Kokrines he wrote that there he felt "ten thousand times better than at Tanana. Kokrines is a little paradise compared with Tanana." He found the Kokrines people, around 65, "very well disposed," faithful in attending Church services and catechism classes. There being neither a school nor a teacher at Kokrines in 1906, he himself, in his cabin, taught school. The following year a school was built, and he was hired to be the teacher, a post he held throughout his years at Kokrines. From time to time, he made trips to nearby encampments, to Tanana, and to **Ruby**, after gold was discovered in that area in 1907. When the people were off in their hunting camps, he, alone in his cabin, worked on his manuscripts.

In 1908, Father Jetté bought the Episcopal church at Kokrines and converted it into a Catholic church and residence. There is a well-authenticated story that one day, when the Episcopal bishop was visiting Tanana, an officer from the Army base there approached him and, without ceremony, asked him, "Why don't you give us a man like Father Jetté?" In answer, likewise without ceremony, the honest bishop answered, "Men like Father Jetté don't grow on every bush."

[Note to the reader: for further information concerning Father Jetté's stay at Kokrines and the "Kokrines Curse," see **Kokrines!**]

On March 17, 1913, Father Jetté left Kokrines for Nulato, where, as he wrote his mother, he was received with "universal rejoicing." After spending the year 1913–14 at Nulato, he took up station at Tanana, where he was to spend nearly ten years. Here, too, he continued to occupy his free time in scholarly pursuits. As he had done at Kokrines, so at Tanana he did a considerable amount of carpentry work, grew his own fine gardens, chopped his own firewood, carried his own water, did his own housekeeping. He continued to get excellent results with his camera. On November 5, 1914, he wrote, "I am on very good terms with the natives, thanks to my camera." He was an accomplished photographer, did all his own developing and printing. Generously, he gave prints to his subjects. He left an outstanding record of Koyukon life in photographs. His archive file contains 12 albums of photographs he either took or collected.

During his Tanana years, Father Jetté became a naturalized U.S. citizen, at Ruby, on July 18, 1916. In 1913, he had become a member of the California Province of the Society of Jesus, when the missions of northern Alaska were transferred from the Canadian Province to that Province. He had expressed the ardent wish to be ascribed to the California Province, so that he might be allowed to stay on in Alaska. It is known from a letter he wrote on August 25, 1912, to his Father Provincial that he had already in 1907, with the permission of his Alaska Superior to do so, pledged himself "by vow to remain in the Alaska Mission until death." Also, that same year, on December 27, 1916, he became a member of the American Anthropological Association.

On October 19, 1922, the 59-year-old Father Jetté "lifted some very large log he wished to saw." In doing so, he ruptured himself. It was freeze-up time, when the rivers were running ice, the lakes barely frozen over, the trails still almost without snow. Travel of any kind was nearly impossible. It was eleven days before his friends in Tanana were able to bring him by boat and dogsled to a doctor in Nenana. On his way there, he was met by Father Francis M. **Monroe**, S.J., who administered him the Last Rites. Father Jetté was near death upon his arrival in Nenana. An immediate operation revealed a strangulated hernia already gangrenous. After spending almost a year in St. Joseph's Hospital in Fairbanks, he was taken to Seattle for another operation. Father Monroe accompanied him from Fairbanks to **Seward**, and Bishop Joseph R. **Crimont**, S.J., from there to Seattle.

In the fall of 1924, Father Jetté went to recuperate at Seattle College. While there, he taught French in the high school and was Spiritual Father to the Jesuit community. At this time, too, he began to gather materials for what was to be his last major undertaking, a projected "History of the Alaska Mission." He had been assigned to produce such a history by his Father Provincial. Of this he was to complete only the first three chapters. The manuscript, titled "Jottings of an Alaskan Missionary," consists of 23,000 words and covers the history of Alaska from 1741 to 1877. This painstaking, meticulous study of historical events, done with all the precision of his mathematical mind, he called "Jottings," because "it is not meant to be 'sophisticated.'"

No account of Father Jetté's vast written legacy would be complete without mention of the innumerable letters he wrote to people of all walks of life. Some of the letters are quite lengthy. Many are studded with gems of wit, urbanity, erudition, human warmth. Those in English are written in clear, beautiful, flawless English, though this was not his native tongue. And all are penned in a handwriting absolutely perfect.

In the summer of 1925, Father Jetté returned to Alaska. For a year, he served as an assistant in the Fairbanks parish and as hospital chaplain. In May of 1926, on the *Matanuska*, he left Fairbanks for **Holy Cross Mission**, where he arrived on the 23rd. There, on July 1st, he was host to Aleš Hrdlička, eminent anthropologist from the Smithsonian Institution, on a field trip along the Yukon. Hrdlička found Father Jetté to be "a fine old Frenchman and scholar, whose meritorious work deserves to be known and published." On the 15th, Father Jetté left Holy Cross on the mission boat, the *Tosi*, for St. Mary's Mission, **Akulurak**, where he arrived on the 17th.

Father Martin J. **Lonneux**, S.J., began the Foreword to his "Complete Graded Baltimore Catechism in Innuit" with "Father Jetté came to **Akulurak** to learn the Innuit Language. This knowledge was necessary for some special work he was doing." In a letter Father Lonneux wrote to Bishop **Crimont** on February 4, 1927, the day Father Jetté died, he gave a more precise reason why Father Jetté came to Akulurak: "He came to pay us a short visit, in order to gather datas [*sic*] for the History he was intending to write." Father Jetté, seeing the Akulurak mission very much in need of additional priestly help, asked Superiors to be allowed to prolong his stay there, and was allowed to do so.

On August 17, 1926, he wrote to his Father Provincial:

> I came here just a month ago and, finding Fr. Lonneux alone, overworked, seriously handicapped by lack of support and cooperation from our Alaskan Superiors, decided to remain as long as possible, instead of paying only a flying visit as was first intended. Even more, I have applied, with Fr. L's full approval, to be stationed here for the winter, to give him at least the advantage of congenial companionship, which may in some degree make up for the incapacity resulting from my battered condition. The others, it seems, cannot put up with his outspoken language, or his progressive methods. The latter I approve, and the former I rather enjoy. I cannot understand why older people (of whose number I am) should be so attached to our old methods,

which have not yielded extra bright results after all, as to reject *a priori* and without trial any change or improvement proposed by the younger men. This seems very unreasonable, and after we have begged for years to have some young men sent to this country, we ought to welcome them, and their ways too, with an open heart and an accommodating mind.

It was of this man, and at this time, that Father John L. **Lucchesi**, fellow Jesuit and veteran Alaskan missionary, wrote, "Fr. Jetté, the bright star of the Tennah, is in his old age, studying another language, and out of his native district." Perhaps "in his old age," but surely not old in mind and outlook, nor in scholarly plans. One could wish that he had been spared another decade or two, but this was not the case.

In the Akulurak mission diary, Father Lonneux recorded the gradual setting of "the bright star of the Tennah."

> Dec. 30: Fr. Jetté not feeling well. Jan. 12: Fr. Jetté's condition is not improving—on the contrary. Jan. 29: The health of Fr. Jetté gives great worry. He could scarcely move to his table for meals. His strength is giving way gradually. Jan. 31: Father still going down; scarcely eats. Feb. 3: Father Lonneux spent again the night with Fr. Jetté. He suffers very much. At 8 A.M. Fr. Lonneux gives him the last sacraments. Fr. Jetté answered all the prayers. After that he suffered so much that he was quite unconscious. He came back to himself for a very short while at 2 P.M. At 6:30 P.M. he told Fr. Lonneux he did not want anything but sleep. Feb. 4: Fr. Lonneux passes night with Father. At 11:40 A.M. Father noticed that Fr. Jetté's breathing became less regular, and, at 12:40, quickly, peacefully he rendered his soul to God. At once he was prepared and at 4:30 was placed in the church. Although only six full months here, his sound judgment, his great activity, his clear understanding of native ways and his straightforwardness did an immense good for the Mission. He was regretted by all, but especially the boys and above all by the Brothers. Feb. 5: The house seems dead. Feb. 6: Children visit Fr. Jetté in church. Feb. 7: High Requiem Mass for Fr. Jetté in Sisters' chapel as church was too cold.

On that same February 7, 1927, the Sister diarist wrote in the **Ursuline** *Annals* of St. Mary's Mission, Akulurak: "Fr. Jetté radiated sanctity and sunshine."

The body of this great missionary and scholar—who 29 years earlier was granted permission to go to Alaska, "at least for a time, as an experiment, to see whether his health is able to bear the rigors of that region"—was laid to rest in the mission cemetery, where it lies buried in the frozen tundra to this day. The written legacy and the memory of the man, however, live on. His published works and his manuscripts still receive much attention, and older people along the Yukon still remember well and speak fondly of Julius Jetté, known to them as "Father Jetty."

29, 33, 47, 90, 174, 187

Dr. Eliza Jones. *LR.*

JONES, Dr. Eliza

She was described as "a Native elder, an intellectual within her own tradition and an academic scholar . . . the most expert writer of her Koyukon Athabaskan Indian language there has ever been . . . a distinguished linguist and guardian of culture." For her scholarly achievements, she was awarded an honorary Ph.D. For years she served her parish, St. Patrick's in **Koyukuk**, as Parish Administrator, Eucharistic Minister, and a prayer leader in the absence of a priest. Brother Robert **Ruzicka**, O.F.M., who knew her well, wrote of her as the third millennium dawned: "She has a very healthy balance of Native spirituality and a strong belief in Jesus Christ and His presence in the Eucharist."

Eliza Jones grew up during a period of rapid transition in Koyukon society from the traditional subsistence-based lifestyle to modern systems of economics, education, health-care, and politics. Born on February 28, 1938, in a winter camp near the site of Cutoff, now abandoned, four miles above present-day **Huslia**, she was the fifth of Little Peter and Josie Peter's seven children. Her Koyukon name *Neelteloyeeneelno* ("she has versatile talent") was given her by her grandmother, Cecilia Happy—a skilled seamstress, hunter, fish cutter—as a way of recording her own story and passing on her talents.

The family followed a yearly round of activities based on the seasonal availability of resources. In April, they left winter camp and traveled to a spring camp, where the women made fish nets, while the men worked on paddles, boats, and fish traps. In June, they moved to Cutoff for a few weeks, before setting up fish camp for the rest of the summer. In fish camp each member of the family had his or her chores. The main activity was putting up fish, but

the children picked berries and the women worked on tanning moose and caribou hides to make into winter clothes. The men hunted ducks and geese in late summer and moose in the fall. Back at winter camp, adults hunted and trapped, and the children ran snare lines for rabbits and ptarmigan.

Cutoff had no school, but Eliza's mother had attended St. John's-in-the-Wilderness, the Episcopal mission school at Allakaket, and she was able to teach her children some reading and writing skills in English. In the early 1950s, Cutoff village was moved to its present location and renamed Huslia. There Eliza, beginning at about age twelve, received three years of formal education in a school run by the territorial school system.

Eliza married Benedict Jones in 1959, and the couple moved to his home village of Koyukuk. Benedict hunted and fished and took seasonal jobs in mining camps, while he and Eliza together raised eight children. Eliza worked for ten years as a volunteer village health aide and continued to take her children to fish camp every summer. In those days, before snowmachines became widely used, the family always had at least twelve dogs for use on the trap-line and for hauling wood and ice. The children had the job of caring for the dogs all summer at fish camp. In 1966, Benedict bought his first snowmachine, an event Eliza recalled as "a big relief for me."

Eliza's first opportunity to work with the

Koyukon language came in 1963, when Wycliffe Bible translators David and Kay Henry arrived in Koyukuk and asked for her help as a language consultant. They sought her out, in particular, because of her excellent skills in both Koyukon and English. Nevertheless, she felt frustrated because, even though she was a Native speaker of Koyukon, she had no experience in reading and writing the language, nor knowledge of the orthography being used in the Bible translation. It was during the 1970s, with the rise of bilingual education and the growth of Native language learning opportunities, that she acquired and polished her linguistic skills.

Eliza and Benedict moved their family to **Fairbanks** in 1970, when Benedict took a job with the Alaska Department of Transportation. In 1972, Eliza attended her first Summer Institute of Linguistics workshop. This was sponsored by the Wycliffe Bible translators and conducted by David Henry in Fairbanks for the purpose of training people in Koyukon literacy. For her first assignment, Eliza wrote down in Koyukon a story she had learned as a child. Later that year, after the passage of a state law providing for bilingual education in Alaska's public schools, she worked with David Henry on a grant to develop classroom materials for teachers of Koyukon students. By the end of that same year, she had earned a General Education Diploma, worked as a teacher's aide in the Fairbanks Head Start Program, and taught introductory Koyukon at Monroe Catholic and Lathrop, two high schools in Fairbanks.

It was at one of the Summer Institute of Linguistics workshops that Eliza first met Dr. Michael E. Krauss, the director of the Alaska Native Language Center at the University of Alaska–Fairbanks. He was at the workshop to speak to the class about Athabaskan grammar. "He made such an impression on me!" Eliza said, recalling that first contact. "I remember thinking, 'This is the guy I want to work with!' Then I started to come in to talk to him, because I was so fascinated. That's when he introduced me to Father Julius **Jetté**'s Koyukon dictionary manuscript. The next thing I knew, I had a job there."

Eliza began at the ANLC in 1973 by re-transcribing Father Jetté's Koyukon words into the modern orthography. She relied on elder Native speakers to help her with words she did not know. She also corrected Father Jetté's confusion about the sounds of certain Koyukon consonants, as well as his misspellings and inexact alphabetization. For the rest, she found his "information was good." While reading the dictionary material, she found that "it was just like listening to the elders talking to me from long ago."

Eliza was especially captivated by Father Jetté's descriptions of Native customs he had observed during his missionary activity along the middle Yukon River from 1898 to 1922. She found that he wrote detailed accounts of Koyukon activities no longer engaged in by the 1940s, when she was growing up. "The ethnographic material," she found,

> is just beautiful. He wrote a detailed description of a firedrill [bow and spindle used to start a fire] and how it works, and that was something I had never seen. Another description of tanning hides struck me by how thorough it was. He stood and watched the women and counted the number of times they scraped the skin with a rock to dry it.

"By the time I got through the entire dictionary manuscript," Eliza said at an interview,

> I felt like I knew him and he was a friend telling me stories. Sometimes he seemed just like us. He became fluent in the language and thought like us and talked about the language as "our language." But he was also a Catholic priest, and sometimes he would step back and write like an observer of a more primitive culture.

Work on Father Jetté's dictionary, however, was only a part of Eliza's activities at the ANLC. She began to teach Koyukon language classes, and to conduct workshops on cross-cultural communication. At these she taught doctors, nurses, teachers and other professionals about the different ways in which various ethnic groups communicate verbally and non-verbally with one another. She also carried out research on Native place names and genealogies, and collaborated with researchers in anthropology collecting Native oral histories. All the while, however, she never stopped working on the dictionary.

Eliza remained on the staff of the ANLC as a Koyukon language specialist, writer, and instructor until her retirement from the University of Alaska–Fairbanks in 1990. After her retirement, she and Benedict returned to Koyukuk, where she taught the

Koyukon language in the local school, as well as by audio conferences and correspondence through the UA–F Center for Distance Education. She also served on a variety of committees and advisory boards, and as a consultant and translator for several federal and state agencies, including the National Park Service, the U.S. Census Bureau, and the Smithsonian Institution.

The list of Eliza's published works is a lengthy one, and the honors conferred upon her are as numerous as they are justly deserved. In 1990, in recognition of her accomplishments and years of service not only to the UA–F, but also to her language, her people, and her community, Eliza, as noted above, was awarded an honorary Ph.D. by the University of Alaska–Fairbanks. The Festival of Native Arts, in dedicating its annual celebration to Eliza that same year, referred to her as "a bridge between cultures and generations, a valued teacher, elder, friend, and family member." In 1993, the Alaska Association for Bilingual Education named Eliza its statewide "Outstanding Bilingual Educator of the Year."

As for Father Jetté's dictionary manuscript, to which Eliza had devoted so much time and effort, and upon which she had lavished so much affection: in the Year of Our Lord 2000, the Alaska Native Language Center at the University of Alaska Fairbanks published the *Koyukon Athabaskan Dictionary*. Listed as its co-authors are Father Julius Jetté, S.J., and Dr. Eliza Jones.

47

JUDGE, Father William H., S.J.

For over a century, he has been hailed as "The Saint of Dawson." Toward the end of the second millennium, a movement was afoot to have his "Cause" introduced and to have him declared the "Patron Saint of Miners." On August 17, 1991, the Historic Sites and Monuments Board of Canada commemorated him as a man of national historic significance by erecting a monument to him on the banks of the Yukon River at Dawson City, Y.T., Canada. To grandnieces and grandnephews and their children, he continues to be simply "Uncle Will."

Father William H. Judge, S.J. *JOPA-809.01.*

William Henry Judge was born in Baltimore, Maryland, on April 28, 1850. Poor health forced him to leave school in 1865, and for ten years he worked as a clerk in a wood-planing mill. Skills he acquired while so employed stood him in good stead later on in life, when he had to put up buildings and construct altars. He entered the Jesuit Order in 1875, and was ordained a priest on August 28, 1886. After his ordination, he served for two years as Father Minister of the Jesuit community at Woodstock, Maryland. Though he was content with his position of humble service, he felt himself drawn to the Rocky Mountain Mission and asked to be sent there. In the fall of 1889, he arrived at DeSmet, Idaho, to make his tertianship, the final year of his training as a Jesuit. While there, he learned that volunteers were needed for the newly founded **Alaska** Mission. He offered himself and was accepted.

On June 10, 1890, Father Judge, along with Brother **Bernard I. Cunningham**, S.J., left San Francisco on the *St. Paul*, bound for **St. Michael**, Alaska. Two days before sailing, he had written to his Superior: "My health is good, and I was never happier in my life. May God grant me grace and strength to do and suffer something for His glory." The grace to suffer something for God's glory was promptly granted him. The *St. Paul*, being "not over-steady," he was "quite sea-sick" the first two days of the voyage. But, apart from those two days, he found the time passed very pleasantly. To his sister he wrote, "I brought with me a flute and some music, which, with my office and the reading of some books, have made the days seem short."

While Father Judge was on his way to Alaska, his former Superior at DeSmet wrote to the Alaska Mission Superior, referring to Father Judge: "A holy missionary will come to Alaska."

The *St. Paul* arrived at St. Michael on July 13th. At once, Father Paschal **Tosi**, S.J, Superior of the Alaska Mission, assigned Father Judge to look after the provisions for the various missions. When not busy with the mission supplies, he observed the Native people, and soon concluded that they were "fond of work, anxious to learn, and very good-natured." After a delay longer than he had anticipated, he finally found himself steaming up the Yukon on his way to **Holy Cross Mission**, which he reached on September 16th.

"The highlight of the summer of 1890," wrote Sister Mary Joseph Calasanctius, a member of the Sisters of St. **Ann**, in her book, *The Voice of Alaska*, "was the arrival of Father Judge. As he was stationed at Holy Cross during the following two years, we had time to learn and appreciate the sterling worth of the priest, the man, the missionary."

For all his seeming frailty and asceticism, Father Judge was as practical as he was saintly.

One of the many improvements he made at Holy Cross was to attach a boiler to the kitchen stove so that hot water was always available. He also constructed a bake-oven and appointed himself baker for the whole mission. He invented a system of Turkish baths to help the children overcome stiffness brought on by scurvy.

Father Judge's first autumn in Alaska was an unusually busy one. In addition to helping with the building of a new dwelling for the Fathers and the boys, he also studied the Koyukon Athabaskan Indian language, taught catechism to the 51 children boarding at the mission, led the people in singing, played the flute for them, made violins out of birch wood, and kept the mission diary, as well as carried out the normal priestly functions.

On February 10, 1891, he set out with sled and dogs to visit the villages on the **Shageluk** River. He soon learned to drive dogs "like an Indian." He was well received at the first village, but was unable to do much with the adults, for they had their spirit sticks up and refused to break them. He visited three more villages, before returning to Holy Cross on March 6th. On this missionary excursion, he gave instructions, baptized 29, officiated at one marriage.

Father Judge had little free time during his first years in Alaska. On June 19, 1891, he wrote to his Superior: "I can truly say I have not had five minutes to spare since I arrived here last year. There is always so much to do and so little time to do it in, although I make my days as long as possible, often from 5 A.M. to 12 P.M."

The better part of the summer of 1891 Father Judge again spent at St. Michael handling the supplies for the various missions. On August 6th, while on his way to Holy Cross on the mission steamer, the *St. Michael*, he wrote to his brother, Father Charles Judge, a priest of St. Sulpice: "I am in excellent health and spirits, and could hardly be happier in this world." On October 5th, he left Holy Cross "with an Indian in a covered skinboat which we call a *bidarky*. It is all closed except three holes where the men sit." He found that "it is very pleasant to travel in these boats; they are fast, safe, and comfortable."

In November 1891, Father Judge again visited the Indian villages on the Shageluk. On this trip, he tried out his latest invention. To his Superior he wrote:

> Fixed our supper of fried fish, tea, and hot steam bread made in my patent oven which I used for the first time on this trip and found to be a great success. It consists of a sheet-iron camp kettle about 10 inches high, in which I have put some pieces of iron so as to support two round tin pans, one over the other. When I want to bake, I fill the pot with water up to the first iron, mix my soda bread, put it in pans, cover the kettle and hang it over the fire. The steam cooks the bread very nicely, and you have no trouble with it, as it cannot burn; and as the fire around the kettle keeps it hot, there is no distillation; and, therefore, the bread comes out dry and nice. One hour will cook a large loaf.

During this missionary excursion, Father Judge followed his customary routine of offering Mass, teaching hymns, prayers, and the catechism, and baptizing. By now the Indians on the Shageluk had become fond of him and referred to him as *Menalekaken*, "the American priest." He was the second American-born priest to serve in Alaska. Father Francis A. **Barnum**, S.J., was the first.

On December 14th, on his return trip to Holy Cross, Father Judge stopped off at Anvik, where a potlatch was just in progress. Finding it "harmless," he joined in the feast and exchange of gifts, giving eight red handkerchiefs and receiving two mink skins in return. He arrived at Holy Cross for "a very happy Christmas."

"I write this in a tent on the bank of the Shageluk River," Father Judge wrote to his brother on August 3, 1892, "about 75 miles northeast of Holy Cross. I came here ten days ago to build a log-house, which is to serve as a church and residence. It will be 40 by 24 inside and two stories high. I believe Father Superior intends to put a priest here."

But, although eager to establish a permanent mission on the Shageluk and to reside there, Father Judge could not be spared for that work. When the walls were only seven feet high, he was reassigned, to **Nulato**, where he arrived in October 1892. At Nulato, he again put to use his practical skills as a worker in wood. He built the main altar, carving the decorations for it with a penknife.

Life at Nulato was quiet compared to life at Holy Cross. At Nulato, he spent most of his time, when not on the trail to nearby villages, teaching the children their prayers in their own language, as well as a little English. He also tried to learn their language. "The first task," he wrote, "I like very much, for I am fond of children, and have no trouble to make friends of them; but the second is very much like hard work, and my genius does not run that way." Father Judge never became fluent in the Native language, but he did compile a Koyukon-English dictionary of some merit.

Father Judge spent only two years at Nulato, but when Father Joseph F. **McElmeel**, S.J., was stationed there in 1924, he met many Indians who had known Father Judge. "They spoke of him," according to Father McElmeel, "but not of many others who were there in the intervening years. According to the Indians he was a very holy man. When Indians remember a man for more than 30 years, you may be assured that he had outstanding qualities."

In the summer of 1894, Father Judge received orders to go to Fortymile, a new mining camp downstream from Dawson. From the steamer *Arctic*, he wrote on August 27th:

I have been taken from my good Indians at Nulato, where I was so happy, and sent here. I had no notice of the change until the steamer, which was to take me away, came; so I had to take hurriedly what I could, and leave, without time to say "good-bye." But I assure you, I have never felt happier or more like a Jesuit than I do now; and I am sure it will not be long before I am as much attached to this new mission as I was to the other. Of course, miners, as a rule, "ain't no saints"; but I am not afraid, and, in fact, I rather like to deal with such men.

However, human carelessness and low water in the Yukon caused Father Judge to spend the winter 1894–95 at Shageluk rather than at Fortymile. The captain of the *Arctic*, to whom Father Judge's demijohn of Mass wine had been entrusted at Holy Cross for safekeeping, broke it. Thereupon, Father Judge returned to Holy Cross for the necessary wine, hoping to ascend to Fortymile again, when the steamer made her next up-river trip. But, by then, the river was too low and the steamer could not get beyond Fort Yukon. He returned to Holy Cross.

As he had done in previous years, Father Judge spent the summer of 1895 at St. Michael attending to new shipments of mission supplies. On August 29th, he left Holy Cross on the brand new steamer *Alice* for Fortymile, where he arrived on September 13th. Going to Fortymile, "that new and undesirable mission," as he described it in his diary, entailed a great sacrifice for him, for it meant leaving behind the "much beloved Indians."

At Fortymile, Father Judge had "two log-cabins under one roof: one for our Lord, the other for his poor servant." From this home base, with his sled and "only one dog, for dogs are scarce here and sell for 50 to 75 dollars apiece," he traveled out in various directions as far as 100 miles to the miners scattered on the different creeks to bring them the Mass and Sacraments in their cabins and tents.

On one such trip, on January 16, 1896, he broke through the ice, got soaked up to the knees, and froze one foot, "hard as a stone." Having doctored others, he knew how to treat the foot, and suffered no damage.

On May 31, 1896, Father Judge left Fortymile for St. Michael, where he again spent the summer. By September 30th, he was back upriver, at Circle City, where he was assigned to spend the winter 1896–97, and where he had shipped all his supplies for the year, including an organ and church-bell, The next day, however, he left Circle City to go upriver to Fortymile to pick up some items he had left there. After battling ice and mechanical breakdowns for several days, the steamer was completely stopped by a major ice jam some distance from Fortymile. He, and nearly all the passengers, left the steamer to walk to Fortymile. The trail was very bad, being along the slanting bank of the river, which for the most part was stony and covered with six inches of snow. But the worst part was crossing the mountain at Cudahy. It took him three hours. He was "more dead than alive," when he arrived at Fortymile.

By now, ice had made further river navigation impossible. Father Judge found himself stranded at Fortymile for the winter. However, it was not long before he saw the unusually early closing of the river as "very providential." The stampede to the Klondike, where gold had been discovered several months earlier, was already on. Dawson was mushrooming into a large, new mining camp.

On December 27, 1896, Father Judge, although he had not yet been to the "new diggings," wrote to his brother: "Lots there 50×100 feet are selling for as high as a thousand dollars already. I have secured three acres as a site for a church and a hospital, and I expect Sisters to come up next spring to take charge of the latter. The new settlement will be by far the largest place on the Yukon."

On January 21, 1897, Father Judge bought 5,000 feet of lumber from the North American Trading and Transportation Company and arranged to have logs cut for building in Dawson. Two months later he wrote in his diary: "Started at 8 A.M. with Mr. Young and John, my boy, for Dawson City. Mr. Young will cut logs for me." The three traveled with Father Judge's sled and lone dog. On March 25th, he saw for the first time the scene of his last labors on earth. He spent three weeks in Dawson, visiting the miners and making preparations for the building of a church and hospital. "Last night," he wrote in his diary under date of March 31st, "the kindling near the stove took fire and burnt a large hole in the side of the tent, but I awoke in time to save it." By April 13th, he was back in Fortymile—now all but deserted—and, by June 3rd, back in Dawson again,

already a city of over 4,000. His freight from Circle City arrived the following day and his logs on the 5th. However, because the current was too strong, it was impossible to land the two rafts of logs and both were lost. For one raft alone he had paid $180.

The loss of the logs was great, but he had to have logs to build, so he bought a raft for $1,000. Nine men began work on the hospital immediately. Father Judge cooked for them in his tent. The sack of flour he dipped into had cost him almost $100. Supplies were scarce and expensive. A mug of milk in the Aurora Saloon cost $5.00, five times the price of whiskey. In his tent, "the old man," as he was sometimes called, although he was only 47, was already nursing five typhoid cases. Almost daily, deaths from typhoid, cholera, scurvy, and the usual accidents made the urgent need for a hospital clear to all. Contributions came in, and, by August 5th, the 50 by 20-foot, two-story hospital was ready for the roof. The first patient was admitted on the 20th. By the end of August 1897, Saint Mary's Hospital was finished. It was filled as soon as it was opened, and continued to be filled thereafter. Men of all faiths, and of none, whether able to pay or not, were admitted to the hospital. In the eyes of Father Judge, they were all God's children deserving of his ministry and care.

For a time, the Reverend Dr. S. Hall Young, a Presbyterian minister, was also in Dawson. "The very first day I was in the camp," he wrote in his autobiography,

> I was called to see some Protestant patients, and thereafter, as long as I was in Dawson, I was almost a daily visitor, finding plenty to do for the poor stricken fellows. Father Judge and I were always great friends, although he was fond of theological controversy and good-natured arguments took place daily. I found him an eager chess player, and the relaxation of the game was good for both of us.

Mass was offered for the first time in the new St. Mary's Church on September 26, 1897. Father Judge, as he had at Nulato, made the altar himself, doing the ornamental work with his penknife. At first, there being no glass for the windows, heavy white muslin was tacked to the frames. Even at temperatures of 60 degrees below zero, two large stoves kept the church warm. It was never locked. As for his own quarters, Father Judge wrote: "My own house adjoining the church is also closed in and is used for a carpenter-shop, laundry, and quarters for all those employed around the hospital."

Father Judge faced his first winter in Dawson, that of 1897–98, with anxiety and apprehension. In mid-October he noted: "Provisions very short." One month later: "Many are paying as much as $100 for a sack of flour, and it is hard to get it even at that exorbitant price. There is only one thing spoken of here, and that is grub."

During that winter, help was short, money was short, food was very short, while work and cares were overwhelming. Slowly but steadily, Father Judge's health was being undermined. He informed his Superior:

> Of late my own health has not been as good at times, as it might be, but I cannot complain. I had a slight attack of chills a few weeks ago, but I was not laid up at all. I have not missed Mass a single day, nor have I been prevented from attending to my duties. However, the work is too much for one priest.

The hospital was so crowded with the sick and the frozen from the time it opened its doors, that Father Judge often gave up his "bed," the couch he slept on in his office, to a new patient and slept on a cot in some still vacant corner. He had a standing order with nurses that he was to be called at any hour, day or night, if a patient wanted to see him for any reason whatever. When nurses pleaded with him to get some rest, he merely assured them that he would have plenty of time to rest once his work was finished.

After his death, the *Klondike Nugget*, referring to Father Judge and his hospital work during the winter of 1897–98, commented:

> The Father's charity was broad as the earth, and none of the hundreds of applicants were even asked their religious preferences. By the side of the dead and dying, burying them when none others appeared on the scene for that duty, superintending and personally directing even the minutest detail of the rapidly increasing hospital, cheering the sad, joking with the convalescent, devising means of comfort for the irritable sick, coaxing the obstinate, praying with and for the religiously inclined, planning appetizing morsels from an almost empty larder, cheering and encouraging the downhearted and sad—thus we find the good man spending his time until he is himself laid low.

In an April 25, 1898, letter, Father Judge, after that first winter in Dawson, assured one of his sisters that he was "well and happy, and not starved," as she had feared.

On June 5, 1898, Trinity Sunday, Father Judge made the following entry in his diary:

> Last night at 11:45 the church took fire from a candle left before the Blessed Sacrament and was burned to the ground with all the vestments, altar trimmings and everything necessary for Mass and Benediction. The hospital was in great danger, but was saved by the hard work of about 500 willing hands who came to its rescue.

What must have made the loss of the church doubly painful for Father Judge was the fact that he himself was the innocent cause of the misfortune. As he was accustomed to do, he had gone into the church late Saturday night to pray the Divine Office. For light, he had a candle fixed on a wooden hold-

"Here is buried the body of Fr. Wil. H. Judge, S.J., a man full of charity, who, with the cooperation of all, first erected in the city of Dawson a house for the sick and a temple to God; and who, being mourned by all, died piously in the Lord, the 16th day of Jan. 1899." *JOPA-809.03.*

er. While he was engaged in prayer, someone came to call him to the aid of a very sick patient in the hospital. Without hesitation, Father Judge went to the aid of the sufferer. Before he returned, the candle burned down, set the wooden holder on fire, which, in turn, set the church on fire.

Without delay a collection was started to build a new church. People of all faiths contributed generously; but, before the collecting was finished, one able and exceptionally generous man, Alexander McDonald, offered to assume the whole expense. His offer was accepted. Two months later, a much bigger and finer church stood upon the site of the old one. Money and "dust" collected for it was donated to the hospital. Father Judge blessed the new church and said the first Mass in it on August 21st, then turned it over to the Missionary **Oblates of Mary Immaculate** in the person of Father Edmond Gendreau, who had arrived the previous month, on July 3rd. Father Judge received additional much needed help that summer. Two days after Father Gendreau's arrival, the three eagerly awaited Sisters of St. Ann arrived to work in the hospital. With them came also Brother Cunningham. Father Judge was allowed by his Superior to stay on in Dawson for some time longer, to help the Oblate Fathers get established and to run the hospital until the spring of 1899, at which time he was to turn it over to the Sisters, and then return to the American side, to **Eagle**, to start a new mission there.

On Christmas Day, 1898, Father Judge celebrated a Solemn High Mass in the new church. The subject of his sermon: "The love we owe to God, and our loved ones at home." This turned out to be his last sermon.

A letter he wrote to his Superior two days after Christmas gives no indication that he was anything other than well. Nor did anyone suspect that he, who never spared himself when others needed help, was already in the final weeks of his life. People had gotten used to the rather emaciated, gaunt look of this ascetic man of God—"wearing hobnail boots, glasses tied on with a string, clothes seedy, but clean."

On January 7, 1899, Father Judge vested and went to the altar to offer Mass, but then he felt too ill to do so. Sick with pneumonia, he took to his board bed. Knowing that his death was near, he wrote his last will and testament on the 11th. In part this read: "I, William H. Judge, being strong of mind but physically weak, declare this to be my last will and testament. Firstly and principally, I most willingly resign my soul into the hands of Almighty God."

His last will made, and having received the Last Rites of the Church, Father Judge expressed himself fully reconciled and resigned. He remarked, "If our dear Lord is about to call me to my reward, I am prepared." In spite of great suffering, he remained alert throughout his last days.

There are indications that Father Judge had a clear premonition of his approaching death. Several days before it, he told those at his bedside that he would die on Monday the 16th. When the Sister who tended him protested: "Oh no, Father! You are not going to die. We shall pray hard, and you will not die," he answered with cheerful confidence, "You may do as you please, but I am going to die." At 1:50 P.M., on Monday, January 16, 1899, surrounded by the Sisters of St. Ann., Oblate Father Alphonse Desmarais, and Brother Cunningham, and conscious to the end, Father Judge died as the saints die, peacefully and joyfully in the Lord.

The death of "good Father Judge"—who "rarely smiled, and yet his face was radiant, beaming with an indescribable light," from whose eyes "a mysterious and attractive light seemed to issue," and whose "very glance was a blessing"—plunged all of Dawson into heartfelt grief and mourning. Many owed their lives to him and his hospital. All lost in him "a devoted friend, whose heart and ears were always open, his door never closed."

The miners of Dawson insisted that Father Judge be buried under the church he had founded. Accordingly, a grave was dug out of the frozen earth under the gospel side of the altar, and, on Friday, January 20th, at 11:00 A.M.—with flags flying at half-mast and stores closed, in the presence of a great throng representing every strata of Dawson society—a Solemn Requiem Mass was celebrated, and what was mortal of Father William Henry Judge was laid to rest "in the earth he made less harsh by reason of his brief sojourn there."

In dying, as in living, Father Judge lived up to his advance billing: "A holy missionary will come to Alaska."

49, 109, 132

JUNEAU

On October 3, 1880, **Alaska**'s first major gold strike took place, when Richard H. Harris and Joseph Juneau found plentiful gold on Gold Creek near what is today the city of Juneau. For a brief time, the mining camp had various names, among them that of Harrisburg. In 1881, a gathering of miners agreed to call it Juneau officially. The Juneau post office was established in 1882. The Alaska Civil Code of 1900 allowed Juneau to incorporate, and named it the "temporary seat of government" once adequate buildings were provided. Since 1900, Juneau has been the capital of Alaska. The population of Juneau was 1,644 in 1910; 3,058 in 1920; 4,043 in 1930; 5,729 in 1939, 5,956 in 1950; and 13,556 in 1970. In 1992, Juneau city and borough had a population of 28,965; and in the year 2000, one of 30,711.

Official Catholicism came to Juneau in 1882. On July 17th of that year, Father John J. **Althoff** offered the first Mass and recorded the first baptism performed there, that of the infant Victor Lachert. In 1885, Father Althoff, Juneau's first pastor, began a ten-year residency in Juneau. He held services in an interdenominational building that was long known as "the Log Cabin Church." On July 9, 1889, Bishop John N. Lemmens of Victoria, assisted by Father Althoff, blessed a new parish church, dedicated under the title of Nativity of the Blessed Virgin Mary. This was replaced by the church built in 1910. In 1951, when the Diocese of Juneau was established, this church began to serve as the diocesan cathedral.

On September 11, 1886, through the zealous efforts of Father Althoff, three Sisters of St. **Ann**— Sister Mary Zenon (Superior), and Sisters Mary Bonsecours and Mary Victor—arrived in Juneau to open St. Ann's Hospital in September, and St. Ann's School in November. The first school year, the church was used as a classroom. In 1887, the Sisters started a boarding school. That same year, too, they were able to move into a new two-story hospital. A new boarding school building was put up in 1896. The hospital facilities were greatly expanded in 1914, when an additional hospital structure, 40 × 110', was built on Sixth Street. A new wing was added in 1916. In 1915, St. Ann's School became a parochial school. A new parochial school building was erected in 1918, and dedicat-

Cathedral of the Nativity of the Blessed Virgin Mary, Juneau. *JOPA-419.1.13.*

ed in 1919. That same year, the boarding school closed. In 1968, the Sisters of St. Ann withdrew from both the hospital and the school in Juneau. The Diocese of Juneau took over the empty hospital building in 1971. In 1977, St. Ann's Nursing Home opened in Juneau, under diocesan sponsorship.

On September 14, 1895, Father John B. **René**, S.J., succeeded Father Althoff as pastor of the Juneau parish and visiting priest to outlying towns. He is given credit for having "organized" the Juneau parish. After he was appointed successor to Father Paschal **Tosi**, S.J., as Prefect Apostolic of Alaska, effective as of March 16, 1897—and, at the same time, General Superior of all Jesuits in Alaska—he traveled widely throughout Alaska, but he continued to make Juneau his headquarters. (In passing, it should be mentioned that Father Tosi died in Juneau, on January 14, 1898, and lies buried there. He was the first Catholic priest to die and be buried in Alaska.)

Father Joseph M. **Tréca**, S.J., was in Juneau from 1897–99. In 1904, Father Joseph R. **Crimont**, S.J., succeeded Father René as Prefect Apostolic. He, too, made Juneau his headquarters, and helped with

pastoral needs as his time allowed. Father Edward H. **Brown**, S.J., arrived in Juneau on August 12, 1904, to serve as its pastor until 1913. He saw to the building of the new church in 1910, and to the laying of the foundation for a new rectory on April 7, 1912. During the year 1913–14, Father Anthony Drathman, S.J., was in Juneau. In 1914, both Fathers James A. Kennelly, S.J., and George M. Bailey, S.J., arrived. Father Bailey left after one year; Father Kennelly after two.

On October 3, 1915, Father Aloysius J. **Roccati**, S.J., began his ten-year pastorate in Juneau. As pastor, according to historian Gerard G. Steckler, S.J., he

> cemented the unity of the group of buildings on the Catholic block by the erection of a parish school, dedicated in the autumn of 1919 as a monument to the zeal of Father Roccati, the pastor, and to the devoted cooperation of the Sisters of St. Ann. It serves as a school, a parish house and a social and recreational center.

After the Vicariate of Alaska was established in 1916, and Father Crimont consecrated Vicar Apostolic in 1917, Father Roccati served also as Chancellor of the Vicariate, until he left Juneau in 1925.

The Log Cabin Church, in which the first Mass offered in Juneau was celebrated, on July 17, 1882, by Father John J. Althoff. *JOPA-419.1.02.*

Father John F. Hayes, S.J., was pastor of the Juneau parish from 1925–28. For a time, in early 1927, he was sick, and was, therefore, replaced by Father Gabriel Ménager, S.J. Father Ménager was pastor from 1928–30. He, in turn, was followed by Father William G. **Levasseur**, S.J., who was pastor of the Juneau parish longer than any other priest, from 1930–45. It was Father Levasseur who brought into being the **Shrine** of St. Therese 23 miles north of Juneau.

During the years 1945–57, the following Jesuit priests, too, staffed the Juneau parish, either as pastors or assistant pastors: Louis B. **Fink**, William T. **McIntyre**, Edward A. McNamara, James U. **Conwell**, Joseph F. **McElmeel**, Alfred T. Brady, and Robert L. **Whelan**. Father Clifford F. Allbutt, who later left the Jesuit Order, was pastor during the year 1946–47. Most served for only a year. There were two notable exceptions: Father Whelan, pastor from 1946–57; and Father McElmeel, pastor during the years 1947–48 and 1952–57. Jesuit Brother Carl F. **Wickart** served the parish as a general handyman from 1945–51.

From 1945–47, Walter J. **Fitzgerald**, S.J., Vicar Apostolic of Alaska at the time, made Juneau his headquarters, as did Bishop Francis D. **Gleeson**, S.J., from 1948, the year he became Vicar Apostolic of Alaska, to 1951.

The Diocese of Juneau—carved out of the 591,004-square-mile Vicariate of Alaska, which, at the time, was coterminous with the Territory of Alaska—was formally established as of June 23, 1951, as a suffragan of the newly created Archdiocese of Seattle. At the time of its establishment, the Diocese of Juneau comprised 70,800 square miles, taking in the southeastern and southcentral parts of what was then still the Territory of Alaska. "The Diocese of Juneau," read the official notice, "will be bounded on the south by the Pacific Ocean. On the west it will be bounded by an imaginary line drawn from the intersection of the 156th meridian and the 56th parallel to the north through Shelikof Strait, Cook Inlet and up the Susitna River to a point five kilometers above the city of **Talkeetna**. On the northeast it will be bounded by an imaginary line from a point on the Susitna River five kilometers north of Talkeetna drawn in a southeasterly direc-

tion, passing five kilometers northeast of the cities of Chickaloon and Ptarmigan, and touching the summits of Mount Miller and Mount Saint Elias, and continuing in a southeasterly direction along the Canadian border past the Portland Canal and the Dixon Entrance to the Pacific Ocean."

Father Dermot **O'Flanagan** was appointed the first Ordinary of the Juneau diocese, on July 9, 1951. He was consecrated a bishop in **Anchorage** on October 3, 1951, by Bishop Gleeson, and formally installed as the first Bishop of Juneau on October 7, 1951, in Juneau's Church of the Nativity of the Blessed Virgin Mary, now raised to the rank of a Cathedral. Seating around 150, it has the distinction of being the world's smallest cathedral.

In 1963, the Juneau diocese numbered some 20,000 Catholics. They were organized into 11 parishes and 12 missions, served by 26 priests. There were two high schools, one elementary school, and four general hospitals under Catholic auspices.

When the Archdiocese of Anchorage was established on February 9, 1966, the Juneau diocese shrank down to an area comprising only 37,566 square miles. At the same time, it became a suffragan of the Anchorage archdiocese.

For reasons of declining health, Bishop O'Flanagan resigned as Bishop of Juneau on June 19, 1968. For several years, the Juneau diocese was administered by Archbishop **Joseph T. Ryan** out of Anchorage. On March 19, 1970, Francis T. **Hurley** was ordained Auxiliary Bishop of the Diocese of Juneau. On July 20, 1971, he became its Ordinary.

After Vatican II, there was a tendency in the Church to merge small dioceses with neighboring ones. The Diocese of Juneau was one such diocese under consideration for a possible merger. Bishop Hurley, however, urged that it be allowed to continue to exist as a separate diocese. "In the case of Juneau," he explained, "numbers—about 4,000 Catholics—would not seem to warrant a separate diocese. It is, however, the capital of the State of Alaska, and its territorial size and its distance from other dioceses present special conditions."

Bishop Hurley was appointed Archbishop of Anchorage on May 4, 1976. For his first three years as such, he was also Apostolic Administrator of the Diocese of Juneau. On March 20, 1979, Michael

H. **Kenny** was appointed Bishop of Juneau. He was ordained a bishop on May 27, 1979, and installed on June 15, 1979. After the unexpected death of Bishop Kenny on February 19, 1995, Father Michael Nash became Administrator of the Juneau diocese. Michael W. **Warfel** was appointed Bishop of Juneau on November 19, 1996. He was ordained a bishop on December 17, 1996, and, that same day, installed as the fourth Bishop of Juneau.

Beginning in 1957, when the last of the Jesuit Fathers left Juneau's Cathedral parish, the following diocesan priests served as pastors or Rectors: Raymond W. **Mosey**, 1957–59; David A. **Melbourne**, 1959–67; James F. **Miller**, 1967–70; Robert Mihelyi, 1970–73; Joseph Saba, 1973–76; Miller, 1976–78; James D. **Cronin**, 1977–85; Bernard A. **Konda**, 1985–87; Bishop Michael H. Kenny, 1987–88; Peter F. **Gorges**, 1988–99; and Michael Nash, 1999–2003. He was followed by Bishop Michael W. **Warfel**.

Over the years, since 1957, a considerable number of other priests, too, served, in one capacity or another, at the Cathedral, or resided there: Fathers John A. **Lunney**; Harley A. **Baker**; John E. McGarity, C.S.P.; Ronald K. **Dunfey**; James J. **Manske**; John M. Jensen; J. William Garvey, S.J.; Charles B. Casale; Kevin O'Conor [*sic*], O.M.I.; Edward T. McHugh, O.M.I.; Edward Cunningham, O.M.I.; John Sewell; Dennis O'Neil; Patrick T. Dahlquist, O.S.B.; Javier Gutierrez; Patrick Hurley, O.S.B.; and Victor Capriolo. Father Matthew E. **Hoch** was at the Cathedral during most of the years 1959–67. Father Everett Trebtoske was there from 1976–81.

Sister Carol J. Crater, S.H.F., served at the Cathedral as Pastoral Associate from 1994–98. The Cathedral parish has seen the services also of Permanent Deacons J. Anthony Duvernay and Charles Seslar.

For eighty years, it was solely the Nativity of the Blessed Virgin Mary parish that served the spiritual needs of Juneau's Catholic community. It was not until 1962 that what is now Juneau's second parish, that of St. Paul the Apostle, located in the Mendenhall Valley, came into being. It began as a mission of the Cathedral parish. The first St. Paul the Apostle Church was built in 1962, under the direction of Bishop O'Flanagan and Father Melbourne. As a mis-

sion, it was cared for by priests from the Cathedral. The steady population growth in the Mendenhall Valley, Auke Bay area, and beyond prompted Bishop O'Flanagan to declare St. Paul the Apostle an independent mission as of June 1968. Father Hoch was named its first priest-in-charge. On January 25, 1972, in response to the express wishes of the people, Bishop Hurley raised St. Paul's to the status of a parish, with Father Leo McCaffrey as its administrator. His tenure was short. Father Peter Gorges was named the first pastor of the new parish in October 1972. He served as St. Paul's pastor until 1981. During the year 1979–80, he had with him Deacon Michael Nash, who—with some back and forth to Mount Angel Seminary at St. Benedict, Oregon—was at St. Paul's for some on-the-job training. After being ordained, Father Nash returned to St. Paul's as associate to Father Gorges. Father Gorges left St. Paul's in February 1981, to take the Vatican II Update Course at the North American College in Rome.

From 1981–84, Msgr. Charles A. **Kekumano**, with Father Nash as his associate, was pastor of St. Paul's. At the same time, Father Nash was doing fly-in mission work to the "Northern Missions." Father William Finn, with Father Konda as his associate, was at St. Paul's until 1986. From 1986–94, Father Miller, now Msgr. Miller, was pastor. Father Victor Capriolo served as associate from 1988–91. In 1994, Father Michael Hayden became pastor, with Father Patrick J. **Travers** as associate. That year, a Spanish Mass was added. During this time, too, Sister Carol Crater, S.H.F., began her ministry at St. Paul's. In 1995, Father Travers was named administrator of St. Paul's, with Father Jef [*sic*] Johnson, O.M.I., as priest-in-residence. In late 1995, Father Johnson was named administrator of St. Paul's; and, in the spring of 1996, its pastor. Father Anthony Dummer, O.M.I., began serving as pastor of St. Paul's in the summer of 1998. It was he who saw to the building of the new St. Paul the Apostle Church. This was dedicated on June 2, 2002. Father Dummer had Father Thomas J. Weise as his associate. As of the year 2004, Father Dummer was still pastor of St. Paul's.

Since 1974, a number of deacons have served, and were serving as of the year 2004, the St. Paul's parish in various capacities: George Michaud, Jerrod Jones, Pasquale Benigno, Gary Horton, and Paul Paradis.

July 1, 1987, was a memorable day for the Catholic people of Juneau and **Douglas**. On that day the Cathedral of the Nativity of the Blessed Virgin Mary parish in Juneau and St. Peter's parish in Douglas were merged to form one parish.

During his years as Rector of the Cathedral parish, Father Gorges saw the old St. Ann's School building come down and the new St. Ann's Parish Center—with its large hall, meeting rooms, storerooms, and a Director of Religious Education office—go up. This, completed in 1994, was subsequently called Cathedral Parish Hall. By the time his tenure in Juneau was at an end, he had everything at the Cathedral parish "running smoothly," and the St. Ann's Center debt paid off.

The Mission Statement of the Diocese of Juneau reads:

God of everlasting love and power, you call each of us by name and bring us together as your holy people. Led by the Holy Spirit, formed as disciples and sent as apostles, we the Catholic Church of Southeast Alaska embrace the call of Jesus, "to put out into the deep for a catch": Duc in altum! (Lk. 5:4). Rooted in prayer, we respond to your call to holiness by reaching out to our sisters and brothers of diverse cultures, scattered across the vast land and waters we call home. Transformed by your ever-present grace, as stewards of your gifts, we proclaim your Gospel, celebrate the sacraments, serve those in need, and invite all to know, love and follow Jesus Christ. And to this we say, "Amen!"

16, 41, 182

The new St. Paul's Church, Juneau.
Courtesy of St. Paul's parish.

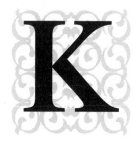

KALLAND, Mr. Edgar

His long life was, at both ends, not without the presence of a Jesuit priest. He was both a licensed riverboat engineer and a licensed riverboat pilot. He was a respected storekeeper. He was a trusted mail carrier. For long decades he lived, with his wife, in a rambling log cabin in a small Koyukon Athabaskan Indian village on the middle Yukon. He was awarded a medal for running a relay in the 1925 **Nenana** to **Nome** serum race. After his death, his wife of over 50 years told Father Louis L. **Renner**, S.J.: "You know, Father, the day he died, I just felt like the Blessed Virgin came down and took him up. I still feel so." When he died, he took his family name with him to the grave. The memory of the man, however, deserves to live on.

Edgar Kalland was born at "Fairiland," near Kallands on the middle Yukon, on October 18, 1904, and baptized two months later, on December 11th, by pioneer missionary Father Aloysius A. **Ragaru**, S.J. His father, a Catholic of French-Irish descent, was from St. John's, Newfoundland, Canada; his mother, also a Catholic, was an Indian woman from near **Nulato**. Their home was a place called "Kallands," and they ran a roadhouse and cut firewood for steamboats plying the Yukon.

As a boy, Edgar learned to hunt, trap, fish, cut wood, mush dogs. While still in his teens, he began hauling mail by dogteam. During the summers, he worked on riverboats. His skill as a dog musher was to win him a permanent place in Alaskan history, and river-boating was to make him known and esteemed up and down the whole Yukon.

In January 1925, a diphtheria epidemic broke out in Nome. Getting antitoxin to immunize the susceptible to that outpost of civilization during the dead of the subarctic winter presented a formidable challenge. Serum found in **Anchorage** was brought to Nenana by train. From there, dog mushers, in a series of forced runs, relayed it to Nome. Edgar Kalland, on January 28th, ran the second link in that chain of mercy, taking the 20-pound serum package 31 winding miles, from Tolovana to **Manley Hot Springs**.

In 1979, 54 years after the event, Edgar still recalled his role in that historic drama. "During the serum run," he reminisced,

> I was just over 20. Time stands still at that time, the prime of life. It was just an everyday occurrence, as far as we were concerned. I was working for the Northern Commercial Company as an extra driver. I didn't have my own dogs, but used the company's. Johnny Palmer told me to take the mail up to Nenana for the NC people. The horse teams were tied up. They couldn't take them out in 50 degrees. It froze their lungs. I got into Minto and got a phone call from T.A. Parsons. He told me he wanted me back in Tolovana. I had to backtrack 20 miles, so I could pick up the serum from Bill Shannon at about 1:30 P.M. Bill Shannon was the NC manager in Nenana. I took it from Bill at Tolovana to Manley Hot Springs.

For his part in that race against death, Edgar received a medal for "heroic service" and saw his name appear in the *Congressional Record*.

In 1928, Edgar, living in **Tanana** at the time, was working on a riverboat. In June, that boat put in at **Marshall** on the lower Yukon. During its six-hour stay there, Virginia Kozevnikoff—born at **St. Michael** of an Eskimo mother and a Russian father, raised at **Kotlik**, and schooled at White Mountain— caught Edgar's eye, and he caught hers. Several months later the two met again for a few hours. The following November, when the boat returned again, on the 7th, the two were married in a "mixed Marriage." Shortly after the wedding, Virginia converted from Russian Orthodoxy to Roman Catholicism.

The Kallands moved from Tanana to **Kaltag** in

the fall of 1935. There they opened a family-oper-
ated store. It continued in business for over half a
century. During the shipping season, when Edgar
was on the river, Virginia minded the store. At the
same time, she served as postmistress, a position
she held for many decades.

Throughout most of his active years, Edgar's chief
occupation was river-boating. Beginning as a deckhand, he rapidly worked his way up. Soon he had
his engineer's license, and not long thereafter his
pilot's. From 1947 to 1963, he piloted the Northern Commercial Company's *Mildred* on her St.
Michael–Marshall run.

Life on the boats under Edgar's captaincy was
noted for crew harmony and contentment. This he
attributed mainly to the fact that there was no drinking among his crew members. "I told them: 'Boys,
leave the drinking to me.' And there was no drinking. There were few accidents. We had a happy crew."

Heart trouble afflicted Edgar during the latter part
of his life. Four times this put him in the hospital.
Doctors told him, "Take your time; slow down!" But
they were asking too much of him. Less than two
years before his death, he was still fully active. "I
couldn't just lay around," he said. "I never laid up
no time."

The honorary No.1 spot in the 1981 **Iditarod**
Trail Sled Dog Race from Anchorage to Nome was
reserved for Edgar Kalland. Two months later the
veteran dog musher, riverboat skipper, storekeeper, devoted husband, raconteur—fortified by the
Sacraments of the Church—was dead.

Edgar was alert to the very end. In a "Twin
Bonanza"—a mission plane stationed at Kaltag
and piloted by Father James A. **Sebesta**, S.J.—that
noble Kalland heart beat its last on May 2, 1981.
He had been placed in the plane not with the intention that he be flown to the hospital in Anchorage,
as press reports mistakenly claimed, but simply to
ease his breathing. The "Twin" had oxygen. His last
prayer was answered. He had dreaded the thought
of yet another spell in the hospital.

In life, Edgar Kalland had walked tall along the
Yukon and in the village of Kaltag. In death, his fellow villagers honored him by fashioning for him
an unusually splendid casket. They laid him to rest
among the birches and spruce trees of the upriver

Mr. Edgar Kalland.
Photo by Fr. Donald A.
Doll, S.J./LRC.

cemetery, not far from where the mighty Yukon, that
had been so very much a part of his life, flows silently, majestically, timelessly by.

His passing was mourned by Virginia, his wife
of 52 years, by his one surviving daughter, Anna
Madros, and by ten grand- and 16 great-grandchil-
dren. He had no sons. Virginia and the map of Alaska alone were left to carry on the name of Kalland.

Father Segundo **Llorente**, S.J., who during his
years at **Alakanuk** came to know Edgar well, wrote
of him: "I never heard him utter one bad word. His
kindness towards his deckhands was well known.
His calm and composure in the face of bad weather was reassuring. He gave the impression of a tower
of strength."

Edgar Kalland was a strong man, a self-assured
man. And yet, there was another side to him, a tender side. "I had to be careful what stories I told Ed,"
wrote Father Llorente. "If I told him a sad story
about anything, he would invariably break down in
front of me. He admitted he simply could not stand
hearing sad stories about anyone. There was such
an amount of compassion in his heart."

In the annals of the North, the name of Edgar
Kalland has merited an honored place. According
to Father Llorente, "Ed Kalland was made of a superior fabric."

50, 107, 142

KALSKAG

Upper Kalskag, a Central Yup'ik Eskimo village, is located on the north bank of the Kuskokwim River, some 30 river miles west of **Aniak**, in the Yukon-Kuskokwim Delta. Baptisms were performed in the Kalskag area as early as in the 1890s. In the fall of 1939, the Nick Kameroff family relocated from what is now known as Lower Kalskag to what is now known as Upper Kalskag. The two are only a short distance apart. Around the mid-1950s, some of the people who had been living at **Ohagamiut** and **Paimiut**, villages on the lower Kuskokwim and Yukon Rivers respectively, moved to Upper Kalskag. They had been baptized in their original villages by Jesuit missionaries traveling out of **Holy Cross Mission**. In 1992, Upper Kalskag had 127 inhabitants; in the year 2000, 230.

In the earlier 1900s, Jesuit priests stationed at Holy Cross, among them Fathers Aloysius J. **Robaut**, Philip I. **Delon**, and **Edward J. Cunningham**, visited Upper Kalskag. Father Delon built a church there in 1926. A new church was built in 1965, in large part by Father **Paul B. Mueller**, S.J., then pastor of **Bethel**.

As late as 1954, the Upper Kalskag parish was still dedicated to the Sacred Heart of Jesus. By 1981, it was dedicated to the Immaculate Conception.

In addition to Father Mueller, the following Jesuit Fathers also cared for the Upper Kalskag parish out of Bethel: Francis M. **Ménager**, 1943–48; Segundo **Llorente**, 1948–50; Norman E. **Donohue**, 1950–53; Lawrence N. **Haffie**, 1953–56; Pasquale M. Spoletini, 1956–57 and 1958–59; Henry G. **Hargreaves**, 1957–58; and **John J. Wood**, 1959–60.

After 1960, Upper Kalskag began to be served, still by Jesuit Fathers, but not always out of Bethel, as follows: Wood, out of **McGrath**, 1960–62; William T. **McIntyre**, out of McGrath, 1962–63; Robert F. **Corrigal**, out of Bethel, 1963–65; **Cornelius K. Murphy**, out of Bethel, 1965–66; Corrigal, out of McGrath, 1966–67; Corrigal, in residence, 1967–70; various priests out of Bethel, 1970–75; Michael J. **Kaniecki**, out of Holy Cross, 1975–84.

Father Andrew P. **D'Arco**, priest of the Diocese of **Fairbanks**, visited Upper Kalskag out of **Aniak**, from 1984–92; and Father William E. **Cardy**, O.F.M., likewise out of Aniak, from 1992–2000. In the year 2001, Father Maciej Napieralski, a priest from Poland serving in the Diocese of Fairbanks, making Aniak his headquarters, began to visit the Upper Kalskag parish on a regular basis. He was still doing so as of the year 2004.

The following Sisters have been in residence in Upper Kalskag: Susan Michelle Dubec, S.S.N.D., Pastoral Administrator, 1990–93; Linda Hogan, C.S.J., Pastoral Administrator, 1993–95; and Paul Bernadette Bounk, C.S.J., Pastoral Minister, 1995–96. Sister Anne Hogan, S.S.J., was "Visiting Sister" to Upper Kalskag out of Holy Cross from 1996–98. From 1998 to the year 2003, the year she left Alaska, she was in residence in Upper Kalskag, serving as Pastoral Minister and Pastoral Administrator.

Immaculate Conception Church, Kalskag. *MK.*

(*left*) The eleventh station of the Way of the Cross lining the walls of St. Teresa's Church, Kaltag. The multi-colored painting is executed on birch bark and framed with split birch limbs. *LR.*

(*opposite*) St. Teresa's Church, Kaltag. *Photo by John D. Lyle/DFA.*

KALTAG

The Koyukon Athabaskan Indian village of Kaltag is located on the right bank of the middle Yukon River, 33 miles southwest of **Nulato**. Kaltag and Nulato are the two villages at which the Koyukon "Feast for the Dead," the "stickdance," takes place. Situated, as it is, at the Yukon River end of the **Unalakleet**–Kaltag portage, it occupies an unusually important site and has a long history. The Kaltag post office was established in 1903. Kaltag had a population of 141 in 1910, 89 in 1920, 137 in 1930, 140 in 1940, 121 in 1950, 240 in 1992, and 230 in the year 2000.

Catholic baptisms by Jesuit missionaries took place at Kaltag already in the 1890s. For most of its history, the Kaltag mission, St. Teresa ("the Little Flower"), has been cared for out of Nulato. The present church was built in 1965–66, to replace the one built in 1931–32. In 1935, Brother Edward J. **Horwedel**, S.J., built a new mission house at Kaltag, which Father John B. **Baud**, S.J., found "very nice and comfortable."

The following Jesuit Fathers, all out of Nulato, unless otherwise noted, served at Kaltag: Julius **Jetté**, 1901–03; Crispin S. **Rossi**, 1903–04; Jetté 1904–06; Rossi, 1906–10; Rossi and Joseph-Alphonse **Desjardins**, 1910–12; Rossi, 1912–13; Jetté, 1913–14; Rossi, 1914–16; Joseph **Perron**, 1916–19; Rossi, 1916–27; Joseph F. **McElmeel**,

1927–28; Francis B. **Prange**, 1928–31; McElmeel, 1931–36; Baud, 1936–47; **Cornelius K. Murphy**, 1947–48; James C. **Spils**, out of **Galena**, 1948–50; Baud, 1950–52; Spils, out of Galena, 1952–53; James W. **Plamondon**, 1953–54; Plamondon, out of Galena, 1954–55; Francis J. **Fallert**, out of **St. Michael**, 1955–56; Jules M. **Convert**, in residence, 1956–67; Norman E. **Donohue**, in residence, 1967–69; Donohue, 1969–72; James A. **Sebesta**, in residence, 1972–82; and Theodore E. **Kestler**, in residence half time, 1982–85. During the year 1985–86, Kaltag was visited by Father **Paul B. Mueller**, S.J., out of **Anchorage**; Father Sebesta, out of St. Marys; and Father Fallert, out of **Mountain Village**.

Franciscan and diocesan priests followed the Jesuits as tenders of the Kaltag flock. Father William E. **Cardy**, O.F.M., was in residence at Kaltag half time from 1986–92. Father Vernon Uhran, Diocese of Orlando, was at Kaltag from August to October 1992. From December 1992, Father John B. **Martinek**, priest of the Diocese of **Fairbanks**, visited Kaltag out of Nulato until 1994. From 1994 to the present (2004), Father Joseph **Hemmer**, O.F.M., has been in residence at Kaltag.

The following Sisters, too, have served the Kaltag parish: Dolores Marie Pardini, S.N.D., 1979–84; Irene Wytmans, S.N.D., 1984–85; Dolores Steiner, S.N.D., 1985–86; Ann Waters, S.N.J.M.,

1989–92; Ann Brantmeier, 1992–94; Rose Beck, S.S.N.D., 2001 to the present (2004).

Lay volunteer Margaret Graue served the Kaltag parish from 1968–74.

Since 1973, the **Iditarod** Trail Sled Dog Race has been run through Kaltag, putting it on the international map. The race commemorates the 1925 **Nenana** to **Nome** serum run. One of the participants in that race against time was Edgar **Kalland**, long-time Kaltag resident, and buried at Kaltag.

Unlike the Iditarod Trail Sled Dog Race, the seasonal drumming festivals that take place in Kaltag have not put it on the international map. In no travel guide listing the world's great meccas of music does one come across the name of Kaltag, **Alaska**. And yet, Kaltag, with its year-round Drum Festival, or, more precisely, "Serenade of the Drums," offers the connoisseur of avant-garde music a unique classico-rustico musical experience.

A more magnificent natural setting for the Kaltag Drum Festival would be hard to imagine. Behind and on the sides of this Koyukon Athabaskan Indian village, rises a semicircle of low mountains and high, rolling hills. Streaming past the face of the village, the mighty Yukon flows silently, majestical-

ly, timelessly to complete this natural amphitheater. Above, by day, the village is domed over by the immaculate purity of a fathomless azure sky; and, by night, by an immense slate-black canopy studded with myriads of trembling stars. On especially gala occasions, flaming, rushing curtains of brilliant celestial light create a nocturnal spectacle that reduces its viewers to utter, awestruck silence. Kaltag's canine chorus alone is emboldened by this display of auroral splendor to raise its voice in howling song. Softly, somewhere, one sounds the opening note. Gradually, others join in with their long-drawn, haunting howls, until all the dogs in the village are vocalizing in fractured harmonies.

"Serenade of the Drums" performances can be heard not only at any hour of the day or night, but also on any given day of the year. To those, however, who wish to experience these performances at their splendid best, two times of the year and two times of the day are especially recommended. The most sparkling performances of all are those semi-annual productions that take place around the time of the vernal and autumnal equinoxes, when the sun's rays are intense enough to warm the days, but the nights are cold. And the choicest hours of any given day are those of dawn and dusk, when temperature variations are likely to be the greatest. However, since not only the sun, but also clouds and breezes affect the quality of the concerts, memorable, exciting drumming may be heard at even the oddest, most unexpected times.

The performers at the Kaltag Drum Festivals are the sun, the breezes, and the clouds. The musical instruments, the timpani, on which they perform those impromptu serenades, are the empty oil drums stacked up next to the cache at the Catholic mission. Changing temperatures cause the gases in the drained drums to expand and contract. This, in turn, causes the metal drums to stretch and shrink, giving rise to a series of unusual sounds: vroom! click! boink! pwhamm! thunk! bwong! ping! These metallic, yet melodious, sounds are what make up Kaltag's "Serenade of the Drums."

38, 65, 102, 106, 142

KANIECKI, Bishop Michael J., S.J.

The day after he was ordained a bishop, he stood next to Pope John Paul II and President Ronald Reagan at the **Fairbanks** International Airport. He was a pilot for over 35 years. His coat of arms carried an airplane propeller and the motto: "TO LOVE AND TO SERVE." As Bishop of Fairbanks, on wing and on wheel, he traveled far and wide throughout his 409,849-square-mile missionary diocese, conferring the Sacrament of Holy Orders on men, both Native and white, and the Sacrament of Confirmation on countless young and old, blessing new churches, meeting and greeting, loving and serving the widely scattered flocks—20,000 souls in 48 parishes—entrusted to his pastoral care. It was while loving and serving one of his remote flocks in bush Alaska that the Lord he loved and served above all called him out of this life. Taking the measure of the man fallen, Bernard Cardinal Law, Archbishop of Boston, wrote of him: "He was indeed, an exemplary bishop and served the Church as a good and faithful shepherd."

At 9:00 in the morning, on Sunday, August 6, 2000, Bishop Michael J. Kaniecki, S.J.—with diocesan seminarian Sean Thomson on board in the Cessna 207, the airplane he flew for the Diocese of Fairbanks—made his final approach and landing, at **Emmonak**, a Central Yup'ik Eskimo village near the mouth of the Yukon River in western **Alaska**. The two had spent the night in nearby **Alakanuk**, likewise an Eskimo village, where, on Saturday, Bishop Kaniecki had celebrated Mass and administered the Sacrament of Confirmation. On the last evening of his life, along with Sean—after he had given Sean a haircut (Bishop Kaniecki was a skilled barber)—he watched a video life of St. Therese, "the Little Flower," the patroness of the Missionary Diocese of Fairbanks.

After securing the plane, Bishop Kaniecki arrived at Emmonak's Sacred Heart Church at 9:30. Inside it, he hung up the Jubilee 2000 Quilt of Unity, a big quilt created in celebration of Jubilee 2000 containing a block from every parish in the Diocese of Fairbanks that Bishop Kaniecki had with him, as he visited the various parishes on his Confirmation tours. He then helped prepare things for the Mass scheduled for noon, a Mass at which 25 people were to be confirmed. When everything was set up for Mass, he went to the rectory to relax with a cup of coffee and to attend to some parish business matters. There, feeling pain in his upper body, he asked for an aspirin. No aspirin was available. A neighbor, however, was able to provide a Tylenol, which Bishop Kaniecki took. Then, with Sean as his companion, he went for a walk. After a walk of about a quarter of a mile, and when about 100 yards from the church, though still looking "quite vigorous," Bishop Kaniecki, rather suddenly, experienced extreme dizziness and discomfort, and at once had to lie down. Almost immediately, Father Thomas G. **Provinsal**, S.J., pastor of Emmonak, was there to administer the Last Rites. Bishop Kaniecki was alert enough during these to pray along with Father Provinsal. An elderly Eskimo woman, Virginia Kassock, took off her coat, folded it and placed it under Bishop Kaniecki's head to keep it out of the mud. Personnel from the Health Clinic and the village police officer were also soon there. They did all they could to keep Bishop Kaniecki alive—but, in vain. His hour had come. In bush Alaska, among his beloved Eskimos, while he was lying on his back and facing the Alaskan skies he had so often, and

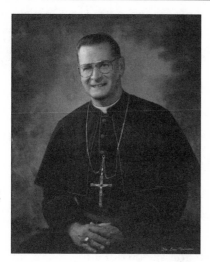

Bishop Michael J.
Kaniecki, S.J.
*The Lens Unlimited,
Fairbanks/DFA.*

so recently, flown, and while he was doing what so very much befits a bishop, a massive heart attack put an abrupt end to his earthly life. It was the Feast of Our Lord's Transfiguration.

Via **Bethel** and **Anchorage**, Bishop Kaniecki's body was flown to Fairbanks on Wednesday, August 9th. For several days it lay in state in Sacred Heart Cathedral, where people gathered for evening rosaries. On Friday, there was a major wake service in the Catholic Schools' Holy Family Chapel, a chapel which Bishop Kaniecki had dedicated the previous April 14th and the bringing about of which he had considered one of his crowning achievements as bishop. On Saturday, August 12th, at 11:00 A.M., in Sacred Heart Cathedral, in the presence of five other members of the hierarchy and that of numerous priests and an overflow crowd of faithful—among them members of various Christian denominations and races, especially members of the Indian and Eskimo peoples—the Mass of Christian Burial was solemnly celebrated by Francis T. **Hurley**, Archbishop of Anchorage.

Burial followed in Fairbanks' Birch Hill Cemetery. The day Bishop Kaniecki was laid to rest was a very rainy day. However, to the wonderment of many, "the Lord of snow and rain" saw fit to let fall neither snow nor rain the whole while the graveside ceremonies took place. At graveside, as at the

Mass, there were readings and songs both in the Central Yup'ik Eskimo and in the Koyukon Indian languages, as well as in English.

Bishop Kaniecki was buried in a manner similar to that in which Alaskan Natives are buried. Most all the rites surrounding his death—mourning, funeral and burial—resembled those that take place, when one of the Catholic Alaskan Natives dies. For example, at the beginning and at end of the funeral Mass in the cathedral, the body was incensed, but not in the traditional manner. Instead, Athapaskan Indian women and Central Yup'ik Eskimo deacons—the former using spruce twigs and the latter feathers—fanned *ayuq* smoke over and around the casket. Eskimo artifacts, a homemade miniature spear and a simple cross woven out of tundra grass, were placed in the casket and buried with the body. Indian-made beaded moccasins of tanned moose hide adorned his feet. Bishop Kaniecki, true to the spirit of Vatican II, was all for inculturation.

Random quotes from the many who mourned the passing of Bishop Kaniecki—quotes from personages at home in palaces and purple, as well as quotes from people at home on tundra and taiga—create a fitting epitaph for the bishop, the priest, the man that was Michael J. Kaniecki:

He was a wonderful man, faithful and holy, and beloved by all who knew him . . . it was always a joy to be associated with Bishop Kaniecki . . . he exhibited such a good and kind spirit . . . a real man of God . . . he had a quality of caring about each person he met . . . he was a most admirable priest and bishop . . . a good and caring shepherd . . . that humble Pole, who took it upon himself to empty the honey bucket . . . this priest who gave so selflessly in living the challenge of the Gospel message . . . I think we all feel like he was our own personal bishop . . . he was a teacher in his homilies . . . he always had the knack of popping in at the right time . . . he was so unpretentious, so easy to talk to . . . he teach us how to run the church . . . in his homilies he touched the deepest part of us . . . the best seat-of-the pants pilot among us . . . I have tears in my heart . . . a vibrant presence . . . At six feet two inches, Kaniecki was equally imposing, whether in his red-trimmed bishop's cassock or dressed in Levis and a flannel shirt . . . he was very demanding of himself and everyone who worked for him . . . there was a side of him that liked to be in control . . . there was also a light, gentle side to him, telling jokes and singing songs . . . he touched Alaskans of all religions . . . his was a generous, loving missionary heart.

Michael Joseph Kaniecki was born in Detroit, Michigan, on April 13, 1935. Already as a young boy, he felt called to the priesthood. He was, however, at the same time, drawn also to an outdoor, wilderness, type of life, having spent a good part of his youth in northern Michigan and in northern Canada hunting, fishing and trapping. (During his latter years, he hunted only with a camera. In fact, the Tuesday before his death, while on a fishing outing on the Andreafsky River with Sean Thomson, he took numerous photos of a grizzly bear that came very near them. With boyish enthusiasm he phoned several friends to tell them about the encounter and the close-up photos he was able to get.)

As Michael neared the end of his high school years, he found himself facing a kind of dilemma: to lead the life of a priest? or a more outdoor type of life? Then he was granted a scholarship to the Naval Academy in Annapolis. However, he failed to pass the physical. He had a sports-related knee problem, needed to have surgery, and had to wait a year. During that year he learned about **Alaska** and its challenges, and saw that in Alaska lay the answer to his dilemma. There he could serve as a priest and, at the same time, live in an environment so very much in keeping with his natural inclinations.

Michael entered the Chicago Province of the Society of Jesus on August 8, 1953, at Milford, Ohio, having made it known at the time that he had every hope of one day serving in Alaska. In 1957, he transferred to the Oregon Province, which had sent men to Alaska for almost seventy years. After studying philosophy in Spokane for three years and serving on the staff of **Copper Valley School** for two years, he began theological studies in 1962, at Regis College, Willowdale, Ontario. He was ordained a priest on June 5, 1965.

By the summer of 1966, Father Kaniecki was back in Alaska, at **Holy Cross Mission**, out of which he served also **Kalskag**, **Aniak**, and **McGrath**. In November of that year, he was assigned to teach at St. Mary's Mission School on the **Andreafsky** River and to prefect the boys there, as well as to tend to the **Marshall** parish. During the summer of 1967, he added **Mountain Village** and **Pilot Station** to his circuit.

In August 1967, Father Kaniecki was assigned to **Kotzebue** and surrounding villages. At the same time, he was Auxiliary Chaplain to the Air Force Site at Kotzebue. While at Kotzebue, he completed the unfinished rectory and social hall and remodeled the old church. He was described as one who knew "how to fix anything and everything."

In August 1975, Father Kaniecki again took up station at Holy Cross, out of which he cared also for Kalskag, Aniak, and various small places—among them the mining camp of Nyac—as need arose.

Father Kaniecki was appointed Religious Superior of Jesuits in Alaska in 1982. He continued, however, to make Holy Cross his headquarters until 1984, when, on March 8th, he was appointed Coadjutor Bishop of Fairbanks. In Sacred Heart Cathedral, Fairbanks, on May 1, 1984, Father Kaniecki was ordained Coadjutor Bishop of Fairbanks, with right of succession, by Bishop Robert L. **Whelan**, S.J. He was installed as Ordinary of the Diocese of Fairbanks on July 28, 1985.

As Bishop of Fairbanks, Bishop Kaniecki proved to be much more than a mere paper-pushing administrator. Not that his desk work got short shrift, but he felt himself most a bishop, most a shepherd, when he was out among the people, especially those in bush Alaska. It gave him special satisfaction to see the **Eskimo Deacon Program** continue to flourish. In 1990, the National Association of Permanent Diaconate Directors presented its award to Bishop Kaniecki "in recognition of the outstanding service rendered in developing indigenous leadership within the Diaconate Movement of the United States." It gave him special satisfaction, too, to see the diocesan Catholic radio station, **KNOM** in **Nome**, continue to receive top awards year after year, and the Catholic Schools in Fairbanks to strive so earnestly, and successfully, to be truly Catholic schools and, at the same time, schools achieving academic excellence. He was gratified to see the diocese gain a more solid financial footing and, more importantly, blessed with a nucleus of diocesan priests, and so, while still officially remaining a missionary diocese, gradually become a diocese of age.

There were many highlights, many joys, many happy memories, too numerous to mention, in the life of Bishop Kaniecki as Bishop of Fairbanks. Among his fondest memories, however, were those of his various meetings and private audiences with His Holiness, Pope John Paul II, to whom, and to the *Magisterium*, he was fiercely loyal. The two were mutual personal friends.

Addressing the benefactors of the Missionary Diocese of Fairbanks in *The Alaskan Shepherd* calendar 2000, Bishop Kaniecki, little realizing that this would be the last year of his life, wrote:

> The Year of Our Lord 2000 is also for me personally a year of some round numbers, of some personal anniversaries: 65 years of life, 40 years since I first set foot in Alaska, 35 years of priesthood, 15 years as Ordinary of this Missionary Diocese of Fairbanks. They have been good years for me. Throughout them all God has blessed me in countless ways. I am sincerely grateful to Him for every one of them.

In 1992, Bishop Kaniecki, as were all the Jesuits of the Oregon Province, was asked to answer the question: "Where do you see yourself in the year 2000, and what do you see yourself doing?" He concluded his answer to the question with the words: "My daily prayer continues to be the same, and I hope that in the year 2000 it will still be, 'Lord, teach me to live my motto: TO LOVE AND TO SERVE.'"

51, 52, 53, 54, 114, 142, 160

KASHUNUK

Kashunuk, a former Central Yup'ik Eskimo village, was situated on a large man-made knoll on a tributary of the Kashunuk River 1.5 miles inland from the Bering Sea. It was 10 miles south of present-day **Chevak**. Its Eskimo name was *Qissunaq*, hence its inhabitants were the *Qissunamiut*. During its day, it was one of the major Native settlements in the Yukon-Kuskokwim Delta. According to the 1890 census, it had 232 inhabitants. In 1947, because of frequent flooding of the area, and difficulty of access, it was almost totally abandoned in

Sacred Heart Mission, Kashunuk. *JOPA-504.2.01.*

favor of a nearby place then called "Old Chevak." The Kashunuk people were primarily seal hunters. Eskimo deacon Michael **Nayagak** was originally from the Kashunuk area. Sister Josephine Theresa **Aloralrea**, O.S.U., was born in Kashunuk.

Catholic missionaries visited Kashunuk as early as 1889, when Father Paschal **Tosi**, S.J., baptized some children there. From that year on, up to 1927, it was regularly visited by priests serving at **Tununak**, at **Akulurak**, and at **Hooper Bay**. Father Joseph M. **Tréca**, S.J., baptized several generations of Kashunuk people. Father Philip I. **Delon**, S.J., deserves credit for founding Sacred Heart Mission at Kashunuk, in 1927. Father John L. **Lucchesi**, S.J., and Father Charles **O'Brien**, S.J., too, were missionaries to the Kashunuk people.

Father Francis M. **Ménager**, S.J., was the first priest to reside at Kashunuk. He arrived on September 27, 1927, and left the following March. The summer before his arrival, a construction crew from **Holy Cross Mission**, led by Brother John **Hess**, S.J., put up a mission structure at Kashunuk. Father **John P. Fox**, S.J., was stationed there from August 1928 to the summer of 1930. During the year 1930–31, when Father Fox was at Port Townsend, Washington, making his tertianship, Father Ménager visited Kashunuk out of Hooper Bay. During the years 1931–43, it was visited out of Hooper Bay by Father Fox. In 1943, Father Jules M. **Convert**, S.J., became resident missionary at Kashunuk. The following year, he put up the "igloo church." This was constructed out of drift logs placed vertically. The whole structure, including the roof, was covered with sod. The igloo church replaced the "Hess church," which Father Fox took down in 1936 to get lumber to build at Old Chevak. In 1947, the igloo church, too, was taken down and reassembled at Old Chevak. After 1947, Kashunuk was visited for a short time, until it was totally abandoned.

24, 72

KEKUMANO, Msgr. Charles A.

Charles Kekumano was born in Kona, Hawaii, on May 12, 1919, and raised in Honolulu in the old hanai tradition by his grandparents. After graduating from Honolulu's St. Louis School, he went on to earn a doctorate in Canon Law at the Catholic University of America in Washington, D.C. He was the first priest of the Honolulu diocese to earn that degree. He was ordained a priest in 1949 in Our Lady of Peace Cathedral in Honolulu, after which he was stationed successively at St. Joseph's parish in Hilo and Holy Rosary parish on Maui. As Chancellor of the diocese from 1954–68, he oversaw some 60 parishes in the State of Hawaii and served as secretary to Bishop James Sweeney. In 1961, Pope John XXIII made him a monsignor. This was only the second time the Vatican honored an island priest with the title.

In 1976, Msgr. Kekumano, after being pastor of Our Lady of Peace Cathedral and of St. Anthony's parish on Maui, volunteered to serve in the Diocese of **Juneau, Alaska**. From 1976–81, he was pastor of St. Catherine of Siena parish in **Petersburg**; and, from 1981–84, pastor of St. Paul's parish in Juneau.

In 1984, Msgr. Kekumano returned to his native Hawaii and retired from active parish ministry. In 1986, he was appointed one of the three trustees of the Queen Lili'uokalani Trust. As such, he was esteemed for his "strong sense of the value of family and community, his courage, his down-to-earth and accessible nature, and his ever present humor." Until near the end of his life, he was involved in community work. He served as a member of the University of Hawaii Board of Regents, as Chairman of the Maui County Charter Review Commission, as a member of the Chaminade University Board of Regents, and as a member of the Hawaii Commission on Children & Youth. He was president of the Association of Hawaiian Civic Clubs. For 15 years, he was a board member, fund-raiser and volunteer for the American Cancer Society.

It was of cancer that Msgr. Kekumano, at St. Francis Hospice and surrounded by friends, died, on January 19, 1998.

KELLEY, Father James F.

James F. Kelley was born on February 25, 1929, in New Bedford, Massachusetts. After finishing high school, he served in the U.S. Navy for four years, from 1947–51. During this time, he discerned his vocation to the priesthood. Back in civilian life, he entered St. John's Seminary in Boston.

Father James F. Kelley at Dutch Harbor/ Unalaska servicing the Seneca, the plane he flew while ministering to the many Aleutian Island missions. *Photo by Annemiek J. Brunklaus.*

On February 2, 1961, he was ordained a priest for the Diocese of Fall River.

As a young priest, Father Kelley began taking flying lessons, more for recreation than for ministry. In 1968, during the Vietnam War, he volunteered to serve as a chaplain in the Navy. As such, for the next 23 years, he sailed the seven seas. Once, while assigned to Kagnew Naval Station in Ethiopia, he volunteered to fly food and medicine to Ethiopian villages. Years later, he recalled this as "the most fulfilling year" of his life.

After completing a distinguished career in the Navy in 1991, Father Kelley went to **Alaska**, to serve in the Archdiocese of **Anchorage**. He soon found himself home-based in **Dillingham**, but flying his own plane out of there to bring the Mass and Sacraments to 22 more or less remote communities of various sizes, even to isolated individuals, scattered over more than 33,000 square miles of Alaska's mainland and islands stretching out the Aleutian Island chain all the way to **Unalaska**. This great area he designated as his "St. Paul Mission."

For a little over a decade, Father Kelley was a very happy man, doing the two things he loved best: bringing the Mass and Sacraments to people, and flying an airplane. He found his vocation and avocation harmoniously blended, in spite of the fact that his ministry and flying took place in an area known for its rough terrain and for its often notoriously bad flying weather. It was this combination of both hostile terrain and bad flying weather that put an end to his ministry, to his flying, and to his life on this earth.

On Saturday afternoon, March 23, 2002, Father Kelley, alone in his single-engine Piper Cherokee 140, left Dillingham headed for the Central Yup'ik Eskimo village of Togiak, some 80 air miles west of Dillingham, to celebrate Palm Sunday Masses in that area. Before the day was out, he was dead, having crashed into Tuklung Mountain about 30 miles west of Dillingham in a snowstorm. Poor visibility and high winds in the area delayed the rescue of his body for several days. Father Kelley lies buried in New Bedford, next to his parents.

It was said of Father Kelley that he was "one of those guys who instantly put people at ease," that "no one was a stranger to him, whether Catholic or non-Catholic," that "he had a remarkable gift for making people feel close to him." He knew most of his flock by name. People delighted in giving him photos of themselves. Roger L. **Schwietz**, O.M.I., Archbishop of Anchorage, referring to Father Kelley, summarized simply: "He was one of the finest priests we had."

KELLIHER, Father Vincent P., S.J.

Vincent P. Kelliher was born on July 18, 1922, in Malden, Massachusetts. He attended grammar school in nearby Melrose, to where his family had moved. From 1936–40, he attended and graduated from Boston Trade School. He then worked briefly in the printing trade. Feeling called to the priesthood, but recognizing his deficiency in Latin, he enrolled in St. Philip Neri Preparatory School in Boston for a short time and Boston College for a year to make good the deficiency. Along came World War II to disrupt his plans.

Not yet convinced of the authenticity of his priestly vocation, and even apprehensive that, in his circumstances, his following of such a vocation might be just a welcome alternative to military service, Vincent enlisted in what was then the U.S. Army Air Corps. Placed on active duty at the end of his freshman year at Boston College, he served for three years in Florida, Alabama, Utah, New Mexico, South Dakota, and Iowa. He also spent 18 months with the 8th Air Force in Europe.

Soon after the German surrender, Vincent returned to the U.S. in June 1945. Convinced now of his being called to the priesthood, and having received an honorable discharge from the military, he entered the Shadowbrook novitiate of the New England Province of the Society of Jesus at Lenox, Massachusetts, on February 1, 1946. After his years at Shadowbrook, he studied philosophy at Weston College, Massachusetts, then he taught at Boston College High School during the year 1951–52. He next spent four years at Weston College in theological studies. He was ordained a priest by Cardinal Richard Cushing on June 18, 1955.

After completing his final year of Jesuit training, his tertianship, at Pomfret, Connecticut, Father Kelliher was assigned to the Shadowbrook Fund office in Boston. The Fund was to provide monies to rebuild the novitiate after the tragic fire that destroyed the place in 1956, taking the lives of four Jesuits. Father Kelliher proved to be a competent fund-raiser, and spent the next 15 years in that work. From 1967–71, he directed the Jesuit Missions Office.

In 1970, Father Kelliher asked his Father Provincial for a mission assignment, one where it was not hot and where no language other than English was

Father Vincent P. Kelliher, S.J. *LRC.*

required. On Christmas Eve 1970, his Provincial telephoned him Christmas greetings and the permission: "You can go and try **Alaska** for a year, if you want." During his many Alaskan years, Father Kelliher often remarked, "I never heard from him again, and he never heard from me."

Father Kelliher arrived in **Anchorage** in August 1971 with a two-fold assignment from **Joseph T. Ryan**, Archbishop of Anchorage at the time. The two had previously met in Boston and talked about Alaska. Father Kelliher was to raise funds for the Archdiocese, and to serve as chaplain to the Sisters Adorers of the Precious Blood, who were staffing the Holy Spirit Retreat House. When the Sisters withdrew from Anchorage, he was asked to take over the administration of the retreat house. This involved not only encouraging greater utilization of the facility, but also the raising of funds for its operation. Under his administration, the retreat house soon became a financially self-sustaining enterprise; but, more importantly, it became a true spiritual center. He himself, in his quiet way, proved to be an excellent personal spiritual director. Given Father Kelliher's all-around success at the retreat house— renamed **Holy Spirit Center** in 1999—it was not long before the staffing and operating of it was espoused as a major work of the Jesuits in Alaska.

Father Kelliher's happy, 15-year sojourn in Alaska came to an end in 1986, when his Provincial asked him to return to Boston to do fund-raising there. But, longing all the while to return to Alas-

Our Lady of the Angels Church, Kenai. *Courtesy of Sr. Joyce A. Ross, R.S.M.*

ka, he was given permission by his new Provincial to do just that. His eagerness to return to Alaska was such that, in the summer of 1989, he drove solo all the way from Boston to Anchorage in a little more than four days, from June 29th to July 3rd.

Father Kelliher's new Alaskan assignment, however, was not in Anchorage, but in **Fairbanks**. There, from 1989–94, despite serious diabetes-related complications, he served as hospital chaplain. As such, in his quiet way and with his subtle sense of humor, he brought consolation and cheer into the lives of a great many. From 1994 until his return, for health reasons, to his home Province of New England on October 27, 1997, he lived in Jesuit House, Fairbanks, spending long hours in the chapel praying, and at his computer carrying on a true "apostolate of the pen." Countless letters of consolation, of congratulations, of advice were meticulously composed and sent by him. They were but the bubbling up of his own vast and deep personal spirituality. When he sensed death was near, he announced, quietly, that he was ready—when God was. He died in Weston, on January 7, 1998. His death left a void in the lives of many. Two years before Father Kelliher's death, Archbishop Ryan, in a personal letter to him, addressed him as "a great priest and a wonderful Jesuit." Such he was.

KENAI

The town of Kenai is located at the mouth of the Kenai River, on the east shore of Cook Inlet and 65 miles southwest of **Anchorage**. In 1869, a U.S. Military Post, named "Fort Kenai" for the Indians living in the area, was established. In 1899, the Kenai post office was authorized. In 1890, Kenai had a population of 263; in 1910, 250; in 1920, 332; in 1930, 286; in 1967, 778; and in the year 2000, 6,942.

The first Catholic services in Kenai were held in the old Territorial School, at Fred Miller's Bar, and at Louisa Miller's Café. With local help and volunteers from Wildwood Army Base, a log church, named Our Lady of the Angels, was built in 1953 on what is now Willow Street. This was served by Army chaplains and by Father Arnold L. **Custer**, S.J., out of **Seward**, who made the rounds of the Kenai Peninsula once a month. One of the Army chaplains, Father Mark C. Thompson, offered the first Mass in the log church. This was later sold and moved to Forest Drive, when the present church was built on Spruce Street during the year 1967–68. The new church was dedicated on May 25, 1968. In 2002, the old church was bought back and returned to the Catholic Church grounds to serve as a youth center.

In 1961, Redemptorist Fathers from the Oakland Province, California, began ministry on the Kenai Peninsula. In 1963, Father Thaddeus Dean began

The first Our Lady of the Angels Church, Kenai. *Courtesy of Redemptorists Denver Province.*

to serve as the first pastor of Our Lady of the Angels parish. He was followed by Fathers Robert L. Woodruff, 1965–68; Daniel J. Buckley, 1968–69; Edward C. **O'Neill**, 1969–72; William M. Cleary, 1972–73; and Robert J. Wells, 1973–89. On October 9, 1970, Our Lady of the Angels was raised to the status of a parish.

In 1979, two Sisters arrived to assist with ministry in Our Lady of the Angels parish: Sister Joyce A. Ross, R.S.M., and Sister Joan Barina, S.C.M.M. When Father Wells was transferred to Seward in 1989, Sister Joyce was appointed Parish Administrator, and Sister Joan her Pastoral Associate. As of the year 2004, the two Sisters were still serving the Kenai parish in those two capacities.

The first Kenai rectory was a trailer adjacent to the church. In 1977, a new rectory was built. In 1992, an arctic-handicapped entrance was built onto the church. For over two decades, Sisters serving in Kenai lived in a "convent" in Woodland Subdivision. As of the year 2004, they were still living there.

KENNY, Bishop Michael H.

Michael Hughes Kenny was born on June 26, 1937, in Hollywood, California, the son of Arthur H. and Esther E. Kenny. "I was very pious as a little kid," he recalled in later life. His mother died of tuberculosis, when he was eight. When he finished the eighth grade, he insisted on enrolling in a San Francisco seminary. His father, a Chevrolet dealer, wanted him to wait a few years before deciding to be a priest. But, Michael persisted. He went on to attend St. Joseph's College in Mountain View, California, and St. Patrick's Seminary in Menlo Park, California. He was ordained to the priesthood for the Diocese of Santa Rosa on March 30, 1963, by Bishop Leo T. Maher. After his ordination, he served for two years at the Cathedral of St. Eugene parish in Santa Rosa. He then taught for seven years at St. Bernard's High School in Eureka, California. As a bishop, he returned often to Eureka to preside at weddings and baptisms of former students and their children.

In 1972, Father Kenny was named Chancellor of the Diocese of Santa Rosa, headed by Bishop Mark J. Hurley, the brother of Francis T. **Hurley**, who served in **Alaska** both as the second bishop of the Diocese of **Juneau**, and as the second archbishop of the Archdiocese of **Anchorage**. Father Kenny became Monsignor Kenny in 1977. On March 27, 1979, he was named the third bishop of the Diocese of Juneau. As such, he succeeded Archbishop Hurley, who had been serving as Apostolic Administrator of the Juneau diocese since his appointment in 1976 as Archbishop of Anchorage.

On May 27, 1979, as Msgr. Kenny's 25 co-ordinands were processing solemnly alongside him down the aisle in Rome's St. Peter's Basilica,

Bishop Michael H. Kenny. *LRC.*

> with heads bowed and hands folded in prayer, looking like they were going to a funeral, there was Kenny, with unpriestlike ebullience and joy of life, that he always did his best to share, striding down the aisle with arms and hands waving, blowing kisses to his relatives, friends and strangers in the crowd. Never mind that he was about to be elevated to the rank of bishop by Pope John Paul II himself.

Pilgrims from both Alaska and California attended the ordination ceremonies. For his motto, Bishop Kenny chose: "Receive the Holy Spirit."

The day after his ordination, in a homily, Bishop Kenny told his assembled relatives and friends: "If I, as a bishop, am true to my vocation, I'm never going to be far from the cross." On June 15, 1979, with crosier in hand, he was officially installed as the third Bishop of Juneau. Under his inspirational leadership—even if this did not seem in the eyes of all to be always in keeping with conventional orthodoxy—the Church of Southeastern Alaska continued to grow and flourish.

It did not take Bishop Kenny long to set the tone of the nature of his leadership and service. Almost from the outset of his episcopacy, he frequently wrote and spoke out about social justice issues. In the diocesan newspaper, *The Inside Passage*, he wrote, on July 27, 1979, about the death penalty: "My own view? Violence begets violence. Correction takes preference over punishment. And when it comes to judgment—particularly my final judgment—I hope that the decision will be based more on mercy than on justice." Continuing his reflections on capital punishment, he later wrote: "If I live in a society, then what that society does in my name, I do. It is not the hangman or the warden or the electrician who executes. It is I. As a follower of Jesus, I cannot do this thing."

When Bishop Kenny ate a meal at a parish or mis-

sion potluck, he did so with gusto. When he jogged, as he routinely did, he did so with the sprint of a young athlete. Whatever he did in life he put the convictions of his head and heart into it. One columnist described him as "a man cut from different cloth. Young, gregarious, unorthodox, he is one of a new breed of U.S. Catholic bishops willing to speak out on politics, social causes and controversies within the Church." He was one of about 80 bishops in Pax Christi, a national Catholic group opposed to nuclear weapons. He supported a controversial draft of a pastoral letter from U.S. Bishops that denounced the "massive and ugly" failures of the U.S. economy to help the poor. He said he would "come out with both barrels" against any effort to institute the death penalty in Alaska. He was, predictably, adamantly opposed to any bill favoring abortion in any way. In a word, Bishop Kenny was, unconditionally, for life at all its various stages. He was opposed to anything whatever that was hostile to the sacredness of life.

Bishop Kenny conceded that his political views probably did not reflect the mainstream, more conservative views of the Catholics in his diocese. "My concern," he said in a 1985 interview, "is that my views fit the teachings of Christ and the teachings of the Church. I don't want people to just go along with what I say. I want people to think for themselves within the teachings of Christ." One of Bishop Kenny's friends conceded that some of the older members of the Juneau diocese might have been "a little turned off by his hip style." He went on to add that, at the same time, Bishop Kenny was, nevertheless, "loved and respected by the vast majority of Catholics in Juneau and Southeastern Alaska."

Bishop Kenny was seen throughout his diocese as a shepherd who knew his people by name, both in the See city of Juneau and in the small parishes and missions. He reached out to the Native American and the Spanish-speaking communities. He was highly esteemed especially by his priests, for whom he always showed special concern.

Bishop Kenny was not bound by other people's ideas of how a cleric should act. There were no airs about him. He was always his natural self. In Juneau and elsewhere, and as bishop, he lived his own life, and lived it to the full, and with contagious pleasure and joyousness. He played tennis, jogged daily, and skied downhill—often singing at the top of his voice. On almost any occasion, and needing little persuasion, he sang out with a beautiful, powerful tenor voice. He loved drama and was an enthusiastic supporter of the theater. He was recognized as a gourmet cook, and as ever a most gracious host to any and all who came to his table or to his home. Routinely he led groups on pilgrimages. He had a knack for turning pilgrimages into trips, and trips into pilgrimages.

In the autumn of 1989, Bishop Kenny was injured in a bicycling accident. On October 6th, he wrote:

> How fragile our lives are. One minute I was basking in the glory of the day's ride. The next second, I was lying helpless on the road. This, in turn, makes me appreciate in a profound way two simple truths: we need one another; and, ultimately, our lives are in the hands of God. He has given His angels charge over us, and they will bear us up. Whatever happens in life or death, we can count on God. We are His beloved children, and our rest is in him.

From October 17th to November 5, 1990, Bishop Kenny participated in a trip to Iraq under the auspices of the Fellowship of Reconciliation. Five years later, he made another trip to the Middle East. It was on that trip, that he experienced fully, and with finality, how really fragile our lives are, and how, ultimately, they truly are in the hands of God. On February 19, 1995, while visiting ancient Roman ruins in Jerash, Jordan, about an hour's drive from Amman, he became nauseous, lost color and collapsed. He died immediately, of a brain aneurysm. Father William Corcoran, an American priest from Vermont, who, at the time, headed the Pontifical Commission for Palestine, was with him. He it was who notified the Diocese of Juneau.

At 11:00 A.M., on Saturday, March 4, 1995, at Juneau's Dzantik'i Heeni Middle School, an estimated 1600 friends and family members attended the funeral services for Bishop Kenny. While many tears were shed during the services, the overall atmosphere was more one of celebration of a life well lived than one of mourning. Presiding at the "Mass of Christian Resurrection" was Cardinal Roger Mahony of Los Angeles. The principal celebrant was Archbishop Hurley, assisted by Bishop Michael J. **Kaniecki**, S.J., and retired Bishop Robert L. **Whelan**, S.J., both of **Fairbanks**. Music was provided by a 65-member ecumenical choir. That same afternoon, the body of Bishop Michael Hughes Kenny, in keeping with his wishes, was laid to rest in the crypt of the **Shrine** of St. Therese.

KEOGH, Brother Bartholomew, S.J.

He spent 40 consecutive years in **Alaska**. He was the last of the early-day Italian missionaries in Alaska. He served as a woodchopper, a dog-boy, a mechanic, a general factotum. He was described as "the dandiest and dirtiest cook," as "a cook who had no equal," as "a master chef." He was adept at making different kinds of fishnets and fishtraps. He was a violinist, a painter, a cabinetmaker. Many of the altars in the earlier missions up and down the Yukon were carved and painted by him. His masterpiece, however, was the new church at **Akulurak**, which he designed and built in 1933. After his death, a mission barge, the *Kio*, was named for him.

The Eskimos called him "the big brother." He was no longer the "narrow-back" that he had been, when he first came to Alaska. Tipping the scales at around 250 pounds, he was so stout, that he could not tie his shoes, so he wore short skin boots that needed only to be slipped on. He shaved but once a week. Upon being asked, he could not recall ever having swept his room. He had no sheets on his bed, just layers of blankets. Depending on how cold it was, he would sleep under whatever number were needed to keep him warm. For all his unkempt external ways, he had a big, tender heart. Father Paul C. O'Connor, S.J., his Superior for six years, wrote of him: "He had sincere affection for tiny Eskimo babies, as well as for tottering old Eskimo grannies. Brother won the hearts of the Eskimo far and wide around Akulurak by being ever alive to the wants of the poor and ever ready to console." The Natives loved him as one of their own. He was a man without guile.

Brother Keogh was born as Bartolomeo Chiaudano in Turin, Italy, on April 17, 1871. He entered the Turin Province of the Society of Jesus at Chieri, Italy, on November 13, 1890. There he spent all his early Jesuit years, except the year 1896–97, which he spent in Turin. In 1899, he came to the United States. After a year at Gonzaga College in Spokane, Washington, he went to Alaska.

During the year 1900–01, Brother Keogh was stationed at **Holy Cross Mission**. For four months of that year, he lived and worked with Father Aloysius J. **Robaut**, S.J., at **Ohagamiut**. During his 40 years in Alaska, he was to be stationed, at various times and for durations varying from a few months to a number of years, also at **St. Michael**, **Nome**, **Nulato**, **Mountain Village**, and **Pilot Station**. But, no other place in Alaska was more closely associated with Brother Keogh than St. Mary's Mission, Akulurak. He spent well over two decades there, serving mainly as cook, but also as a general handyman.

In his biographical sketch of Brother Keogh, written shortly after his death, Father O'Connor wrote:

> A deep spirituality that was hidden behind an easy and joking exterior came prominently to the fore during his last illness. These thin walls of our rickety mission building do not yield much privacy. For hours at a time, I would hear him repeat unceasingly with every respiration, "Jesus, mercy. Jesus, come. Come, Jesus, come." I marveled how he could keep it up.

On May 27, 1940, Brother Keogh died, "very quietly, in a coma." On that day, Father Edmund A. **Anable**, S.J., wrote in the mission house diary: "So goes to his reward the last of the old timers from

Brother Bartholomew Keogh, S.J., and Joe Afcan at Akulurak.
JOPA-510.40.

Italy after 40 years in the country." Brother Keogh was buried the following day in the mission cemetery at Akulurak.

KESTLER, Father Theodore E., S.J.

Theodore E. "Ted" Kestler was born in Tacoma, Washington, on December 18, 1943, along with his twin sister, Mary Ann. In Tacoma, he attended Franklin Public Grade School and, as a member of St. Leo's parish, St. Leo's Parochial School. After his father died in 1955, the family moved to Spanaway, a small town a little south of Tacoma, to live on a farm next to his uncle and aunt. Ted graduated from Clover Creek Elementary School in 1958, and from Bethel Senior High School in 1962. He then went on to attend Central Washington State College in Ellensburg, and Gonzaga University in Spokane, Washington.

On September 7, 1964, Ted entered the Jesuit novitiate at Sheridan, Oregon. After completing his two-year noviceship, he spent the years 1966–69 at Mount St. Michael's, Spokane, studying the classics and humanities, and philosophy. From 1969–72, he taught geometry and mathematics at Gonzaga Preparatory in Spokane. By the time he finished his three years of teaching, he had earned a B.A. in classical studies and a B.S. in chemistry from Gonzaga University, and an M.A. in mathematics from Bowdoin College in Brunswick, Maine. He found his three years of teaching at Gonzaga Preparatory so satisfying that, at the end of them, he hoped to return to secondary education after completing his theological studies and being ordained a priest.

Ted made his theological studies at the Jesuit School of Theology at Berkeley, California, during the years in 1972–75. He ended them with a Master of Divinity degree in Theology. In Spokane, on June 14, 1975, he was ordained a priest.

In the course of his theological studies, Father Kestler became vitally interested in Sacred Scripture in general and in "the historical Jesus question" in particular. He took all the courses offered in Scripture, and began a life-long habit of keeping up to date on matters related to Scripture and theology by reading the latest publications in those fields. This reading habit laid the foundation of his personal spiritual life. At the same time, it made him

Father Theodore E. Kestler, S.J. *BR-CD 0308-A364.*

the much-in-demand lecturer, spiritual director, and retreat master that he eventually became. In addition to being highly respected for his expertise in the areas of Scripture and theology, he, quite early on, became a recognized authority also on the Constitutions of the Society of Jesus and on the Spiritual Exercises of St. Ignatius Loyola.

Father Kestler's first assignment as a priest was to Bellarmine Preparatory in Tacoma, where, from 1975–80, he taught in the mathematics and theology departments. From 1980–81, he made his tertianship in Spokane. It was during his tertianship year that his "interest in **Alaska** was sparked."

Father Kestler left an account of how he first happened to go to Alaska:

> As part of the program, each tertian had to undergo an apostolic experiment in an area he was not familiar with. One day I came down to breakfast, and there was a map of Alaska on the refrigerator with a note that Bishop **Whelan** needed a priest in **Alakanuk**. My first response was, "It's cold there! It's not for me!" But then I bumped into Father Jake Morton, who had done his regency [teaching as a seminarian] in Alaska. I told him about the need for a priest in some village in Alaska, and that I had considered going. In his gentle manner, he told me, "You should go there. The people are wonderful, and you will get a sense of a different culture." I thought it over, and decided to volunteer. I went into the tertian instructor's office that evening to say that I would volunteer—only to learn that two others had beaten me to it. The next day, however, I was informed that Bishop Whelan could use all three of us. I was chosen

for **Kaltag**, to replace, temporarily, Father James A. **Sebesta**, S.J., who needed to get away for his annual retreat and some rest. That was in early October, 1980.

While at Kaltag, Father Kestler met Eskimo Brother Ignatius J. **Jakes**, S.J., at Kaltag to do some maintenance work, and Father Louis L. **Renner**, S.J., who had come there to help Father Sebesta lay in a winter's supply of stove wood. Together the four sawed, split and stacked wood. All in all, Father Kestler found that, and the whole of his Kaltag stay, a rather agreeable experience, so much so that, after some prayer, he asked Father Thomas R. Royce, S.J., Provincial of the Oregon Province at the time, to be sent to serve on the Alaska missions. Father Royce, however, thinking that Father Kestler was acting merely out of initial enthusiasm, assigned him to Gonzaga Preparatory, telling him that if, after a few years, he still wanted to serve in Alaska, he, Father Royce, would consider it. While teaching at Gonzaga, Father Kestler, whenever he saw Father Royce, told him that his desire to return to Alaska remained strong.

After taking his final vows, on September 7, 1982, Father Kestler found himself, happily, assigned to Alaska. Attractive as Kaltag was to him, he had little hope of being stationed there. Great, then, and very pleasant, was his surprise, when he received a letter from Michael J. **Kaniecki**, S.J., General Superior of Jesuits in Alaska at the time, informing him that he was to be pastor of the Kaltag–**Nulato** missions. For a little over three years, from 1982–85, he divided his time, more or less equally, between the two villages, commuting between them by boat, when the Yukon River was open, and by snowmachine, when it was paved over with ice and snow. Contrary to what some of his classmates anticipated, he, in his own words, "loved every moment of it."

But, it was an assignment too good to last. Father Kestler now had to pay a price for being the acknowledged Scripture scholar, theologian, spiritual director, and specialist in the Jesuit Constitutions and in Ignatian spirituality that he was. As of August 15, 1985, he was appointed Rector and President of St. Michael's Institute, a philosophate affiliated with and on the campus of Gonzaga University. All the while, however, his desire to return to Alaska continued undiminished.

Again, a big and pleasant surprise awaited him.

A year before he was to leave his Spokane assignment, his Provincial informed him that his name was on the list of candidates for the post of General Superior of Jesuits in Alaska. He was chosen, and, for nine years, beginning on July 31, 1990, served as such. From November 6–18, 1991, he was in Rome to attend "Superior School" for Father Provincials and Regional Superiors. For the first several years as General Superior, he made his headquarters in **Fairbanks**, out of which he traveled far and wide to visit his fellow Jesuits in the places of their ministries. Beginning in 1993, he made his headquarters at St. Mary's Mission, on the **Andreafsky** River. Out of there, he continued his visitations, but he also began serving as the director of the tertianship he had established at St. Mary's. While the number of tertians began and remained low, being their director, nevertheless, made further demands on him.

From January 5 to March 22, 1995, Father Kestler was again in Rome, this time as one of two elected delegates to the 34th General Congregation of the Society of Jesus. On October 1, 1997, he became Superior also of the St. Mary's Jesuit community. This consisted of around ten priests serving in western Alaska. In addition to serving now as a Superior on two levels, he was also a pastoral minister and an instructor in the Native Ministry Training Program.

The NMTP was, from its inception in 1990, a program very dear Father Kestler's heart. He was a firm and vocal believer that Alaska's Native people, in this case the Central Yup'ik Eskimo, can be and must become, by design of Divine Providence, ever more truly Catholic, while, at the same time, remaining ever more truly Yup'ik. The more they are the one, the more they are the other, he reasoned. "I am profoundly convinced," he wrote, "that 'seeds of the word,' as the early Church Fathers and the Second Vatican referred to them, were already present in the life and customs of all indigenous peoples before missionaries actually arrived."

As time went on, it became more and more clear to Father Kestler that, because of falling numbers in Jesuit personnel, Alaska was never going to become an independent Province, and that its juridical structure needed evaluation. After prayer and consultation, and on-going discussions with the then

Provincial, Father Stephen V. Sundborg, S.J., both he and Father Sundborg thought the time had come for them to ask the Father General in Rome to suppress the Dependent Region of Alaska and make its personnel directly a part of the Oregon Province. On July 31, 1999, the Feast of St. Ignatius, at the end of the 8-day retreat made by the Alaskan Jesuits at **Holy Spirit Center**, **Anchorage**, Alaska, the official Decree of Suppression was read. With that reading, the Dependent Region of Alaska ceased to be, and Father Kestler's terms, both as General Superior and local Superior, came to an end. He continued, however, to reside at St. Mary's Mission, and to serve as tertian director, as an instructor in the Native Ministry Training Program, as visiting priest to the St. Marys parish, and as "sacramental priest" to **Pilot Station** and **Mountain Village**.

In the course of his years in Alaska, Father Kestler's interest in Scripture and theology continued unabated. The same can be said for his interest in giving spiritual direction and doing retreat work. More than once he directed his fellow Alaskan Jesuits, as a group and as individuals, during their annual retreats. In October 1994, he led the priests of the Diocese of Boise in two separate, week-long retreats. About 60 priests participated in the retreats. Among other virtues, he stressed the virtue of hope, a key virtue in his personal spiritual life.

Earlier in the year 1994, in April, when Brother Jakes celebrated his golden jubilee as a Jesuit, Father Kestler saw to it that no expense, no effort was spared to make the event one of major importance not only in the life of Brother Jakes, but also in the lives of the Eskimo people of western Alaska. In July 1995, Brother Jakes suffered an incapacitating stroke. From that time on, until he left Alaska on June 16, 1999, the concern shown for him by Father Kestler can be described only as "maternal." Father Kestler was the last General Superior of the Jesuits in Alaska, and they never had a finer one.

As of the year 2004, Father Kestler was still stationed at St. Marys, serving as pastoral minister to St. Marys' Church of the Nativity parish, as sacramental minister to Pilot Station and Mountain Village, and as a staff member of the Native Ministry Training Program.

KETCHIKAN

Ketchikan, located on the southwest coast of Revillagigedo Island near the southern extremity of Southeastern **Alaska** and port of entry to Alaska, was established as a fishing town, when a cannery was built there in 1887. The town became a supply center during the gold rush period in the late 1890s. Its population was 40 in 1890; 800 in 1900; 1,613 in 1910; 2,458 in 1920; 4,695 in 1939; 5,305 in 1950; 6,483 in 1967; and 7,922 in the year 2000. The Ketchikan post office was established in 1892.

An official Catholic presence in Ketchikan first began to make itself felt at the beginning of the 20th century, when it was visited several times a year by a priest stationed in **Juneau** or in **Douglas**. Masses were first offered in the Red Men's Hall, or in the public library, or in the home of a certain Manuel Diaz by Father Peter C. **Bougis**, S.J. In 1904, the old schoolhouse was purchased and converted into a church. Father Adrian Sweere, S.J., was the first resident pastor of Ketchikan's Holy Name parish, serving in that capacity from the summer of 1907–1912. It was he who built a rectory next to the church. In the course of those years, as he "endeared himself to the people," he also visited **Wrangell** from time to time.

Father William A. **Shepherd**, S.J., was pastor of Holy Name, 1912–13 and 1919–20; Father Patrick J. Mahoney, briefly in 1913; Father John F. Hayes, S.J., 1913–14, and Father Paul Kern, S.J., 1914–19.

From 1920–24, Father John B. **Van der Pol**, S.J., was pastor of Holy Name. In the fall of 1920, he oversaw the construction of a parish hall. That same year, plans were laid for a hospital. Work on it began in 1922, with Father Francis M. **Monroe**, S.J., directing the procedure. The hospital was blessed by Bishop Joseph R. **Crimont**, S.J., on February 22, 1923. Three Sisters of St. Joseph of Peace-Newark—Sister Mary Antonius (administrator), and Sisters M. Benedict and M. Germaine— came from Bellingham, Washington, to staff the hospital. Because the original hospital had accommodations for only 30 patients, Father Monroe doubled the bed capacity by enlarging and remodeling the hospital in 1928. The Sisters took over full control of the hospital from the bishop in 1941, and, three years later, added another wing. Ketchikan

Holy Name Church, Ketchikan. *Courtesy of Holy Name parish.*

General Hospital, as it is known—though its official title has from the beginning been "Little Flower Hospital"—for many years enjoyed the reputation of being a quality hospital. By 1959, however, it had become obsolete, could no longer be modified to meet the requirements for state licensing. It was closed. The Sisters turned to the people of Ketchikan for help with a new hospital. As a result, the City of Ketchikan approved a bond issue to finance the construction of a new 65-bed hospital. This was built and leased to the Sisters, who opened it in 1963, and continued to operate it thereafter. In the fall of 1946, the Sisters began to staff also Holy Name Grade School. This was closed in 1960 due to the inadequacy of the building.

After Father Van der Pol, the following Jesuit Fathers served as pastors of Holy Name parish: Joseph F. **McElmeel**, briefly; John J. Bolster, 1925–26; Joseph A. Farrell, 1926–28; Edward C. Budde, 1928–31; Joseph **Tomkin**, 1931–32; Harold J. Buckley, 1932–36; Augustine A. Dinand, 1936–38; and Auguste J. Coudeyre, 1938–39. Soon after Father Coudeyre was appointed pastor of Holy Name, on July 18, 1938, he remodeled the old schoolhouse that had served as a church since the early 1900s. The newly remodeled church was dedicated on Thanksgiving Day, November 24, 1938.

After Father Coudeyre, the following Jesuit Fathers served as pastors of Holy Name parish: Natale J. Maruca, 1939–42; Anthony J. Baffaro, 1942–48. It was he who, in 1946, started the Catholic school in Ketchikan. He was followed by Jesuit Fathers Gerard A. Morin, 1948–51; John A. **Concannon**, 1951–60; and Robert M. Bickford, 1960–64.

Father Harold J. Free, pastor of Holy Name parish from August 17, 1964, to July 31, 1968, was the last Jesuit so to serve there. On April 11, 1965, he witnessed the ground-breaking ceremony for the new Holy Name Grade School. On September 7, 1965, classes began to be held for the first and second grades in the parish hall. Sisters of St. Joseph of Peace-Newark Alice Kennard and Sylvia Hammond were the teachers. In January 1966, classes began to be held in the new school. Until 1979, the school was administered and partially staffed by the Sisters of St. Joseph of Peace-Newark. This is the only Catholic school in the Diocese of Juneau.

In addition to the above mentioned priests who served as pastors of Holy Name, the following Jesuit Fathers, in the course of the years, also served in Ketchikan as assistant pastors and hospital chaplains: Philibert **Turnell**, Edward A. McNamara, Alexander D. Tourigny, Frederick E. Simoneau, William G. Elliott, Maurice F. Corrigan, and Francis B. **Prange**.

Father Andrew W. Vachon, S.J., was assistant pastor and hospital chaplain in Ketchikan during the

S-326 Ketchikan, Alaska's Catholic Church

(*above*) An earlier Holy Name Church, Ketchikan. The parish hall and school of 1946–60 are next to it. *JOPA-414.12a.*

(*left*) Holy Name Church, Ketchikan, around 1910. The building served first as the town's schoolhouse. *JOPA-414.02.*

(*opposite*) In the early 1940s, Sisters of St. Joseph of Peace of Newark, the staff of Ketchikan General Hospital, pose with Father Matthew E. Hoch, Bishop Joseph R. Crimont, S.J., and Jesuit Fathers Anthony J. Baffaro and Edward A. McNamara. The Sisters are: 1) M. Borromeo, 2) M. Helena, 3) M. Stanislaus, 4) M. Pauline, 5) M. Lelia, 6) M. Rita, 7) M. Evangelista, 8) M. Edgar, 9) M. Annunciata. *JOPA-414.09.*

years 1958–60. However, being the artist that he was, he devoted most of his time to sketching and drawing objects and scenes in and around Ketchikan. This resulted in two books of black and white sketches and drawings: *Ketchikan Alaskan Sketches*—dedicated to Father Bernard R. **Hubbard**, S.J.—published in 1959; and *Fish without Chips*, published in 1960.

Father John H. Smyth, C.M., followed Father Free as pastor of Holy Name parish. He was followed in turn by Msgr. James F. **Miller**, 1970–76; and Father Joseph Saba. Father Saba, in Ketchikan from 1976–86, deserves much of the credit for bringing about the new Holy Family Church, solemnly blessed and dedicated on October 20, 1985, by Michael H. **Kenny**, Bishop of Juneau at the time. Ground for this church was broken one year earlier, on October 21st. By that time, the cornerstone, a piece of marble obtained at nearby Marble Island, had already been blessed—by Pope John Paul II, on May 2, 1984, during his brief stop-over in **Fairbanks**.

Father Peter F. **Gorges**, following Father Saba, was in Ketchikan from 1986–88. He was followed by Fathers Owen Hope, O.M.I., 1988–93; Jef [*sic*] Johnson, O.M.I., 1994–95; and Father Bernard A. **Konda**, 1995–99. Many projects were accomplished during Father Konda's years in Ketchikan: a parish hall was constructed; the parking lot was black-topped; the rectory, the school, and the annex, in which the Director of Religious Education and her family lived, were renovated.

Father Konda was succeeded in 1999 by Father Patrick J. **Travers**, pastor of Holy Name until the early part of 2004, when Father Edmund J. Penisten succeeded him.

During some years other priests, too, served the Ketchikan parish. To mention but a few: Father Raymond Churchill was assistant at Holy Name from 1971–76; Father Jerome A. **Frister** was in residence at Holy Name during the years 1973–76, serving there and in the outlying areas; Father James D. **Cronin** assisted at Holy Name, 1974–76. Oblate Father Gerald Brunet was at Holy Name for two and a half years, 1977–79; and Father Michael G. Schwarte from 1995–99.

6, 195, 196

KETTLER, Bishop Donald Joseph

On August 6, 2000, Michael J. **Kaniecki**, S.J., Bishop of **Fairbanks**, died suddenly of a massive heart attack at **Emmonak**, **Alaska**. The Diocese of Fairbanks was now without a bishop, and was to remain so for nearly two years. On June 7, 2002, Pope John Paul II announced the appointment of Msgr. Donald J. Kettler as the fourth Bishop of the Diocese of Fairbanks.

Donald Joseph Kettler, one of four children, two boys and two girls, was born to Norbert and Marguerite Kettler on November 26, 1944, in Minneapolis, Minnesota. He was baptized on December 10, 1944, in Our Lady of Lourdes Church in Minneapolis. At an early age, he moved with his family to Sioux Falls, South Dakota. His father, a federal meat inspector, died in 1998. Donald attended St. Joseph Cathedral Grade School in Sioux Falls; then, for his secondary education, Trinity Prep School in Sioux City, Iowa. He went on to earn college degrees at Crosier Seminary, Onamia, Minnesota, and St. John's University, Collegeville, Minnesota. He spent the summers of his seminary days working in parishes in Chicago, in impoverished neighborhoods, and at missions in South Dakota working among Native American Indian people. As a deacon, he served at St. Joseph Cathedral. He was ordained a priest in St. Joseph Cathedral, Sioux Falls, on May 29, 1970, by Bishop Lambert A. Hoch.

Father Kettler was associate pastor at Sacred Heart parish, Aberdeen, South Dakota, from 1973–76 and from 1977–79. He spent the year 1976–77 as associate pastor at St. Therese's parish in Sioux Falls. From 1979–81, he was Director of the Diocesan Catholic Pastoral Center and a member of the Diocesan Marriage Tribunal. During the years 1981–83, he earned a degree in Canon Law at the Catholic University of America in Washington, D.C. In 1983, he was Officialis on the Marriage Tribunal. The year 1983–84 saw him serving as pastor of St. Joseph's parish, Huntimer, South Dakota, and offering Mass at the State Penitentiary.

In 1984, Father Kettler became part of the Sioux Falls Diocese's innovative television ministry to shut-ins. Offering Mass every Sunday morning for television viewers estimated to number between 12,000 and 15,000, he soon became known all

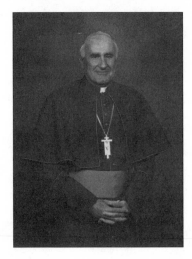

Bishop Donald J. Kettler. *DFA*.

over South Dakota as "the TV Mass priest." In 1995, Father Kettler became Monsignor Kettler. Much of the TV program's success was attributed in large part to Msgr. Kettler's "really fine" preaching. He offered the TV Mass from 1984 to the year 2002. During those same years, being the diocese's top canon lawyer, he served also as its Judicial Vicar. By the time he headed north to his future in Alaska, in the year 2002, he had served his diocese also as a member of its Finance Council and Stewardship Committee, and had sat on its boards of Catholic Family Services, of Sioux Falls Catholic School System, and of the Association of Christian Churches of South Dakota.

During the years 1987–1995, Msgr. Kettler was pastor of St. Joseph Cathedral; and, during the years 1995 to 2000, of St. Lambert's parish, Sioux Falls. He spent his final two years in the Sioux Falls Diocese serving as pastor of Christ the King parish, Sioux Falls.

When, in late April 2002, the Apostolic Nuncio to the United Stats of America, Gabriel Montalvo, called Msgr. Kettler to ask if he was willing to be appointed the new bishop of the Diocese of Fairbanks, Msgr. Kettler instantly had two thoughts that enabled him to swallow his fears. He recalled visiting Fairbanks on a camping trip ten years previously and, on that occasion, going to Mass in the historic Immaculate Conception Church. He was so taken with that experience that he signed up to receive *The Alaskan Shepherd*, which he continued to read from that time on. His second thought was that maybe it wasn't just a coincidence that he'd decided a few years back to begin learning to fly a small airplane. These two thoughts prompted him to see a kindly Providence at work in his personal life and that of the Missionary Diocese of Fairbanks. He was given six hours to think the matter over, to accept or decline the appointment. "It was a shock. I didn't expect it," he said of his conditional appointment. By his own admission, during the six hours allowed him to come to a decision, he "experienced a wide range of emotions, from reluctance to thinking about the challenges of the office—and did a lot of praying." Reassured by the reflections that "when you get called to this type of position, God says He is going to help you," and that the whole turn of events was more than a mere coincidence, Msgr. Kettler consented to being appointed Bishop of Fairbanks.

On June 7, 2002, the news of Msgr. Kettler's appointment became public in Alaska and nationally. On that day, he was introduced to the chancery staff of the Diocese of Fairbanks and held a press conference. All felt immediately at ease with him, in spite of his imposing 6′3″, square-jawed presence. He smiled, laughed, joked, listened. The following day, he held a press conference in **Anchorage**. The next day, Sunday, June 9th, he offered his first Mass in Fairbanks, in Sacred Heart Cathedral. After waiting for 22 months for a new bishop, the people of the Diocese of Fairbanks greeted the news of his appointment with much joy and gratitude. The people of the Sioux Falls Diocese were proud that one of their highly esteemed priests was so honored, while at the same time they were somewhat reluctant to "lose" him. Bishop Robert J. Carlson of the Sioux Falls Diocese stated, "The Diocese of Fairbanks is receiving a wonderful shepherd. It is a great appointment. He has a missionary spirit, a missionary heart." He praised Bishop-elect Kettler for "his ability to listen and work with people." Jerry Klein, his Chancellor, praised him for his "good balance of administrative prowess and pastoral sense." Bishop-elect Kettler, for his part, admitted that "leaving family, friends and co-workers will not be easy. Switching parishes was hard; this is tougher." He showed special concern for his 89-year-old mother, who, he said, was "not terribly excited"

about his pending departure for Alaska. The two, by then, had lived in the same city for 25 years.

Ordination-related activities began on Wednesday, August 21, 2002, in Sacred Heart Cathedral with a service consisting of evening prayer and the blessing of the Pontifical Insignia by Michael W. **Warfel**, Bishop of **Juneau** and, at the time, still Apostolic Administrator of the Diocese of Fairbanks. The following day, in Fairbanks' large Carlson Center, before a huge crowd of faithful and dignitaries, Donald Joseph Kettler was ordained a bishop by Roger L. **Schwietz**, O.M.I., Archbishop of Anchorage, and installed as the fourth Bishop of the Diocese of Fairbanks. Archbishop Schwietz was assisted by Bishops Warfel and Carlson. Apostolic Nuncio Gabriel Montalvo was present and read the mandate from the Holy See appointing Bishop Kettler Bishop of Fairbanks.

For his motto, Bishop Kettler had chosen "Faith, Hope, and Love"—admitting, with a smile, that the wording was not really all that original. In his short talk at the end of the ordination service, he explained why he had chosen that motto: "Faith and trust in the Lord; Hope of doing something new and challenging; and Love—God loves us so much, we can share it with other people." He assured the people, "I'll be there with you. I will pray with you, and I will suffer with you." On Friday, the day after the ordination, joyous, informal, lighthearted "Meet the Bishop" festivities were held in Fairbanks' River's Edge Convention Center.

Even before he was ordained a bishop, Bishop Kettler, described as "a roll-up-your-sleeves-type of man," made it known that one of the first things he wanted to do as a bishop was to get in a plane and start visiting the villages in his diocese. "I cannot shepherd," he said, "where I have not been." Accordingly, only three days after his ordination, he was airborne—in the diocesan Cessna 207, with his Chancellor, Father Richard D. **Case**, S.J., at the controls, and Patricia Walter, editor of *The Alaskan Shepherd* on board as a passenger—on a trip that was to last eight days and take him to nine villages in western Alaska. Bishop Kettler stated his intentions: "I want first to listen, to see what the people are doing, and then maybe give my own vision as we go on. My primary concern as bishop is to be a pastoral bishop, not just an administrator."

On the second night of his trip, Bishop Kettler found himself in **Bethel**. His host there, Father Eugene P. **Delmore**, S.J., described him as "moving into his ministry with grace, wit and lots of questions." By the time Bishop Kettler returned to Fairbanks, he had met many of his flock, had taken part in Eskimo dancing and drumming, had taken an Eskimo steam bath, had eaten Eskimo ice cream, had gassed up the Cessna 207 a number of times, had spent many hours at its controls as co-pilot—and had some answers to some of his many questions.

In village after village, at the Masses he offered, he conveyed the same sincere message to the people: "I am here to do what St. Paul did 2000 years ago. I am here to help you. I am here to support you, and to continue doing with you the work that is already in progress in your parish. Thank you for being here with me today."

Before the year 2002 was out, Bishop Kettler had dedicated the new church at **Stebbins** and ordained two Eskimo men to the permanent diaconate. Weather and other complications made the ordinations less than routine. However, according to Father Delmore, "Bishop Donald was calm, good humored about the glitches that are part of something new, and spoke directly and simply to the deacon candidates and their wives about their ministry of service to their people."

Bishop Kettler, in imitation of Jesus, the Good Shepherd, Who knows the sheep of His flock, made it a point from the time he first began to shepherd the flock of the Missionary Diocese of Fairbanks to know the people he was called to serve. In an interview held shortly before he was ordained a bishop, he said:

> My approach has to be very pastoral, because that's something I know. I plan to spend as much time with people as possible. I don't need to be with people only with my agenda, but just to spend time with people where they are. I like doing things. I like going to basketball games, to watch the hockey team play. I like to go to ecumenical events.

Among his hobbies he listed golf, downhill skiing and hiking.

202, 203, 204

KEYALUVIK

The Central Yup'ik Eskimo village of Keyaluvik, a one-time sod-house village, was located on the Kealavik River ten air miles from the present-day **Newtok**, just north of Nelson Island in the Yukon-Kuskokwim Delta. At one time, it was populous enough to support two traditional men's houses, indicating that there must have been from 180 to 200 people living there.

Keyaluvik never had a resident priest. It was visited as early as around 1895 by priests stationed at **Akulurak**, principally Father Joseph M. **Tréca**, S.J. During the earlier half of the 1930s, it was visited out of **Hooper Bay** by Father **John P. Fox**, S.J., then for a short time by Father Paul C. **Deschout**, S.J., out of **Tununak**. It was he who hired and directed George Aluska of Tununak to build the Holy Angels mission church at Keyaluvik, in the summer of 1938. Concerning the Keyaluvik people, Father Deschout wrote, "The Keyaluvik district is no mean source of consolation. I don't think I ever met a bunch more hungry for the Sacraments."

Beginning in 1939, Father Fox again served that mission until 1945. It was then tended out of **Kashunuk** for the next two years by Father Jules M. **Convert**, S.J. From 1947–50, it was a mission of Old **Chevak**. Thereafter, it was cared for out of New Chevak. The major move away from Keyaluvik, to escape the seasonal flooding, began in 1949. The last priest to visit Keyaluvik was Father Henry G. **Hargreaves**, S.J. On February 22, 1951, he wrote, "The last two weeks I've spent at Keyaluvik, a little mound in the tundra. Some 50 people live there." By the end of 1951, most of the people had relocated to form the new village of Newtok. During the winter of 1951–52, the small church Father Deschout had built, "was dragged by sled dogs and human backs" five miles across snow and ice to Newtok. In 1951, Father **John J. Wood**, S.J., built a new church at Newtok.

KEYES, Father Anthony M., S.J.

He was described as "a notoriously pious priest," and as "a very fine musician." Humorously he referred to himself as "the choirmaster." He had a functional command of the Central Yup'ik Eskimo language. For close to 30 years, he worked among the Eskimos of the lower Yukon region.

Anthony Keyes was born Antonio Chiavassa in Turin, Italy, on June 15, 1866. His father died soon after Antonio was born. The boy was schooled in the "Little House of Divine Providence," an institution founded by St. Joseph Cottolengo. There he acquired the spirit of simple piety, charity, humility, and spiritual joy. This spirit of joy stayed with him throughout his life. It radiated out to those around him, and endeared him to them.

On September 22, 1882, Antonio entered the Jesuit novitiate of the Turin Province at Chieri, Italy. It was soon discovered that he had an extraordinary gift for preaching. Even before he was ordained a priest, he preached in the churches of Chieri, drawing over-flowing crowds.

After his ordination, Father Keyes requested to be sent to **Alaska**. He came to the United States in 1899. He devoted the year 1899–1900 to the study of English at the Colville Indian mission in Washington Territory. His first year in Alaska, 1900–01, he spent at **Holy Cross Mission**; his second at **St. Michael**. From 1902–07, he was stationed at St. Mary's Mission, **Akulurak**. Then he was back at St. Michael again for the years 1907–10; and then back to Akulurak again for the years 1910–14. In 1917, Father Aloysius J. **Robaut**, S.J, visited Akulurak. From there, he reported his findings of the conditions at that mission to the Father Provincial. Among Akulurak's other shortcomings, he found that the people were spoiled, and for that he blamed Father Keyes. "They could," he wrote, "always get from Father Keyes all they wanted."

Father Keyes made **Pilot Station** his headquarters from 1914–21. During those years, he regularly visited **Mountain Village** and **Marshall**. From 1921–28, he made Mountain Village his headquarters, with Pilot Station and Marshall as dependent stations. For a short time, in 1926, he was in the Pacific Northwest for medical treatment. In the latter part of August of that year, he suffered "a slight stroke," resulting in "temporary loss of speech, memory, and use of his hands." In 1928, he helped establish the mission at **Hooper Bay**.

For the last several weeks of his life, Father Keyes was at Holy Cross. Sensing that his death was

Father Anthony M. Keyes, S.J.
JOPA-879.02.

not far off, he prayed to die on October 1st, the feast of St. Therese, patroness of the Alaska Mission. Very early in the morning of that day in 1928, fully conscious to the end, he died peacefully, his prayer answered. The following day he was laid to rest in the Holy Cross cemetery.

Father Philip I. **Delon**, S.J., General Superior of the Alaska Mission at the time, who was at Holy Cross during Father Keyes' last days, wrote to the Father Provincial:

> The death of Fr. Keyes was most edifying. He longed for death, and was thrilled with joy at the thought of going to heaven. For 17 days, from Sept. 13 to Oct. 1, his life was one continual prayer. The sweetest and most touching, childlike aspirations to Jesus and Mary and St. Ignatius, etc., were constantly on his lips.

Father John L. **Lucchesi**, S.J., who knew Father Keyes well, wrote of him: "Gifted with a cheerful disposition and optimism, he was charitable, obliging and warmed all the hearts that approached him by his simple piety and lively faith." In the Mountain Village diary, he wrote, "The news [of his death] impressed all here very much, as they liked him very much, who was the first to teach them."

"The death of Father Keyes," summarized Father Delon, "is a very great loss to the mission. He was a valiant missionary, who died the death of a saint."

KING ISLAND

King Island, some 90 miles northwest of **Nome** and 35 miles off the Seward Peninsula, was officially "discovered" in 1778 by Captain James Cook of the English Royal Navy, who named it after his executive officer, Lieutenant James King. Its Inupiat Eskimo inhabitants, however, called it, and their village on it, *ugiuvuk* (Ukivok on present-day maps), meaning "big winter" or "winter home." This name reflects the traditional yearly cycle of the Bering Strait Islanders who spent the winter months on their isolated island and the summers traveling along the mainland coasts.

King Island—only two and a half miles long, a mile and a half wide, and from 700 to 1,200 feet high—rises abruptly out of the dark, blue-green waters of the Bering Sea. The longer axis is oriented east and west, and sheer cliffs ring the island except for slight embayments in the southern and northern shorelines, where the slopes are somewhat less steep. The island has no beaches, and granite boulders rounded off by the waves provide landing spots in only three places. The village, now abandoned, clings to the south side of the island on a rock slide 200 feet wide, with a pitch of about 40 degrees to the sea. The King Islanders, the *Ugiuvangmiut*, were true cliff dwellers. Earlier generations of King Islanders lived in semi-subterranean dugouts with a short tunnel. Sometime during the second half of the 19th century, they began living in cube-like dwellings built on platforms supported by long driftwood poles. The walls and roofs of these dwellings were made out of walrus hides between which dry moss or grass was packed. Around 1920, a third kind of dwelling, a small one-room house of dressed lumber, began to replace the old dugouts and cube-like structures on platforms.

White people who visited King Island described it in the austerest of terms:

> a high, rocky mass with steep cliffs on all sides . . . a most inhospitable place, in calm weather usually swathed in mist, in clear weather windy . . . a melancholy granite rock . . . a more forsaken, wildly-desolate, oppressingly-isolated isle, wrapped in cold deathliness, cannot be imagined . . . the paradise of the birds and the storms.

Why would countless generations choose such a place for a home? Father Bellarmine **Lafortune**, S.J., the "Apostle of King Island," saw the island as "a true paradise. Wherever you look [in spring] you see nature, immense, wild, without a trace of human efforts to improve it, and the whole covered with a vegetation that God alone controls. Above your head you see thousands of sea birds circling

King Island, two and a half miles long, a mile and a half wide, rises abruptly out of
the dark blue-green waters of the Bering Sea to a height of 1196 feet. It is located
92 miles northwest of Nome and 35 miles off the coast of the Seward Peninsula.
The village of Ukivok hangs center front near the water. *LRC.*

in all directions." Gardening on the island was impossible, but the vegetation on the island provided various edible greens which were picked and preserved in seal oil. Birds—mainly murres, auklets and puffins—and their eggs were a staple during the spring and summer months. The waters around the island, which lies in the direct route of the annual spring and fall walrus migrations, abounded in sea-mammal life that provided meat, skins, bone, and ivory for basic needs. Besides walrus, the King Islanders harvested annually also a variety of seals, an occasional whale, and in some years a number of polar bears. In the winter, they caught bullheads, cod, crab, and shrimp through holes in the ice. The King Islanders were seldom faced with starvation, because they could store great quantities of food in a large cave, a natural, year-round deepfreeze, just east of the village. About 50 yards east of the village, there was a small stream, which drained most of the upland surface. This provided clean, fresh water during the summer and fall; snow was melted during the rest of the year.

King Island was first visited by a Catholic Missionary in 1916, when Father Lafortune was there from June 15–22. Several years previous, the Natives had put up a "church" for him. This he described as "the old shack." By 1916, a good number of the King Islanders were already Catholic, having been brought into the Church by Father Lafortune during their summers in Nome. He made his first contact with them in 1903, the year he arrived in Alaska. For over two decades, he kept agitating for a permanent mission on the island. By 1929, there were over 200 King Island Catholics, but still no mission on the island. What finally convinced his Superiors to give him permission to move to the island was the threat of either a government school, "a godless institution," or a "protestant bible school supported by the government." As it turned out, in the summer of 1929, both the Church and the government, in the form of a school, established themselves on King Island.

After Father Lafortune had been on the island for a month, he was able to write to his Father Provincial:

I wish you could find time to visit this place; you would see the wildest country in the world. Every inch of it is wild. It is nature untouched, unrefined, superb, majestic in its roughness. Steep, abrupt, craggy, the island rises nine hundred [1,196] feet above sea level. The top is bristling with huge peaks like steeples of some fairy temple. Here I am just one month building a church to Christ the King, and I am amazed at the amount of work we have done.

The church Father Lafortune began to build in 1929 was not finished and formally dedicated until October 25, 1931. A shortage of lumber and the fatal crash of the *Marquette Missionary* airplane on October 12, 1930, at **Kotzebue**—which necessitated his presence there from October 1930 to June 1931—had prevented the completion of the church until that time.

Father Bernard R. **Hubbard**, S.J., and his crew spent the winter 1937–38 on King Island. With them they brought a life-size bronze statue of Christ the King. This was man-hauled up to a bluff 700 feet above the village on October 17th, and, on the 31st, the Feast of Christ the King, in the presence of Father Lafortune and most of the villagers, solemnly blessed by Father Hubbard.

From 1929 to 1947, Father Lafortune spent all but three winters on King Island. He was replaced as pastor of King Island by Father **Thomas P. Cunningham**, S.J., who was resident missionary there from 1947–50. On March 17, 1949, a bit of aviation history was made, when Tex Ziegler landed a plane on top of King Island. That was the first, and last, such landing. Father **George E. Carroll**, S.J., replacing Father Cunningham, was on the island from 1951 to April 1960, the year the mission on the island was closed. The school was closed the previous year. During the 1950s, more and more King Islanders had begun to make King Island Village, a short distance east of Nome, their year-round home. It was the gradual exodus from the island that brought about the closure of both the school and the mission. Since 1966, except for summer excursions, the island has been completely abandoned. The last priest to set foot on the island was Father Louis L. **Renner**, S.J., who spent eight days there during the latter half of June 1974. On the 23rd, in the church built 45 years earlier by Father Lafortune, he celebrated the last Mass offered on the island. About 1985, the church, having become unstable by then, was taken down by King Island men.

In November 1974, a devastating autumnal storm leveled the Nome King Island Village. The people moved into Nome proper. Some of them were, by then, already living elsewhere. Paul **Tiulana**, for example, had moved to **Anchorage** in 1967. The "old chief," John Charles **Oalaranna**, had died ten years earlier. Whether living in Nome, or elsewhere, the King Islanders have continued to identify themselves as King Islanders and have, for the most part, remained staunch Catholics.

During their years on King Island, Fathers Lafortune, Cunningham and Carroll, each in turn, faithfully kept the mission diary. A chronological sequence of discontinuous entries made by them in the diary weaves a rich and colorful tapestry of day-to-day life on King Island.

Father Lafortune's first entry was made on August 19, 1929:

On the Feast of the Most Pure Heart of Mary we anchor below the village in the smoothest water I ever saw. By evening we had unloaded all the lumber of the church, 10 tons of coal and about one ton of provisions. To say we were tired is to put it mild. But that did not prevent us to take a good round supper à la Eskimo: bullhead fish dry and cooked with seasoning of seal oil . . . Five youngsters are getting ready for first Holy Communion . . . The few hunters that are here gather over 1000 lbs. of grub, 9 seals and one oogruk . . . During Advent the natives prepared themselves for Christmas in a very edifying way . . . At 12 o'clock, midnight Mass. A surprise was in store. After the gospel was heard the rattle of money in a collection box which the natives made on the sly . . . Mountains of snow fell during the night . . . A child is prematurely born to Atkritoac. It was baptized, confirmed and buried the same day . . . A deep gloom falls over the village. One of the strongest hunters was drowned . . . In spite of dense fog, the hunting is on for good. We hear the roar of the guns of 45 hunters. The hunting brings 45 large walrus, 11 small ones and a few seals . . . the *Northland* is sighted. She comes with the saddest news it has been my lot to hear so far . . . The message contained the news of the tragic death of Fr. **Delon**, Fr. Walsh and Ralph Wien when our plane "The Marquette" crashed at Kotzebue two days ago . . . Nature seems to share our sorrows . . . The child of Kunnuk dies and is buried in the new graveyard. In the evening Killarzoac is married to Kattac . . . A roar is heard from the sky . . . the big bird landed gracefully and without mishap. The distinguished visitors were our Rev. Fr. Superior, Father **Ménager**, piloted by a good Catholic aviator, Mr. Woodley . . . Heavy fog. At a distance we hear the mighty roar of an immense herd of walrus . . . Lots of ivory and meat . . . Mayac and Kunnuk come back with a polar bear each . . . My trip from K.I. to Nome was novel. We had to camp 3 days on account of contrary winds . . . During Dec. the natives got over 500 seals . . . I am buying all the blubber I can to save coal . . . The eggs and the birds and the greens are plentiful . . . Christmas: Fr. Hubbard said the midnight Mass . . . Toward the end of January 10

polar bears are killed . . . Fr. Hubbard is more than busy taking pictures . . . Two seal pups were brought alive . . . we begin to install the windcharger . . . I bless the house of Peter Mayac . . . A howling blizzard visits us . . . The natives are apprehensive. Everything is so unusual this winter. Never before was so much snow seen on the island, never so much northwind, never so much accord between the winds and the current . . . The kayak races and oomiaks were spectacular . . . They know now how foolish it is to go hunting alone . . . Without warning a plane came today and dropped 1st and 2nd class mail. That is very welcome . . . Easter is beautiful in every way . . . One of our most husky boys, Paul Tiulana, while working in Nome met with a very bad accident that makes us fear for his life . . . The year 1943 was opened with a salvo of I don't know how many guns . . . Rita Kunnuk goes to her reward.

Her death was as peaceful as her life . . . A rock weighing about 100 lbs. fell from the very top of the island and punched a hole in the wall of the church. Let us hope that Christ the King will protect His church from further damage . . . Anguac catches a good size flounder (23 pounds) . . . the natives found a whale in perfect condition. They are taking it apart now and will have quantities of moctac and oil . . . June 18, 1944: The Lomen's tugboat came for longshoremen and she brought with her the Right Rev. W. **Fitzgerald**, the first bishop to put his foot on this island . . . Seventeen youngsters receive the sacrament of Confirmation . . . Four of our men have a very narrow escape . . . They were hunting and were carried away by the ice . . . They passed the whole night on the ice . . . The new year 1946 is ushered in by a windstorm. However, the services were perfectly attended . . . A little excitement was

Christ the King Church on King Island. *BH/JOPA-171.2.02.*

(*opposite*) A profile of the King Island village of Ukivok, ca. 1955. Christ the King Church and the house Father Bellarmine Lafortune, S.J., lived in are at top left, the school at bottom right. *Photo by Fr. George E. Carroll, S.J./JOPA-540.2.89.*

caused by two mad white foxes . . . June 13, 1947: I will now get ready for Nome. That is not pleasant, but it is God's will. My glasses need to be changed . . . The *Bozo* comes for longshoremen. Quite a few went, but the real tough ones want to finish work here. Some don't seem to be in a hurry to do that work. It may be too hard for them.

This was Father Lafortune's last entry in the King Island diary.

Father Cunningham's first entry in the diary was made on October 14, 1947:

The *Bozo* came today with 17 longshoremen and Fr. T. Cunningham who replaces Fr. Lafortune . . . Heard general confession of Romeo. He seems to have lost his mind . . . Gave Romeo last sacraments. He is definitely of unsound mind . . . Romeo committed suicide this morning. Shot himself . . . Baptized one baby . . . the men are getting a few seals every day . . . Rather heavy storm raging. The waves seem to be about 100 feet up on the rocks . . . Blessed one house! . . . Freezing rain makes all the stairs dangerous . . . A snowslide on the creek today nearly ended the life of Xavier Siloak. He was down at sea level, when the snow slid down and took him over the rocks and into the water, but he kept his head and wormed his way up through the snow . . . Gave last sacraments to Kasignac . . . Oalaranna brought me a large chunk of walrus meat . . . The snow is mountainous . . . gale of hurricane proportions. Consequently, the church was so cold the wine crystallized in the chalice. In spite of all this, the crowd were all there . . . Two oogruks were taken today . . . There is a clear sweep of snow from the store to the ice, covering all the houses . . . Two polar bears killed today . . . For the first time this season the church couldn't be used. There's a terrific north wind and the draft

Atop King Island stands the life-size, 900-pound bronze statue of Christ the King. It was brought to the island by Father Bernard R. Hubbard, S.J., and put in place and blessed in October 1937. *LR.*

Helen Aayüq-Mizana at the entrance of one of the semi-subterranean community houses on King Island. A whale jawbone frames the entrance. *BH/JOPA-548.5681.12.146.*

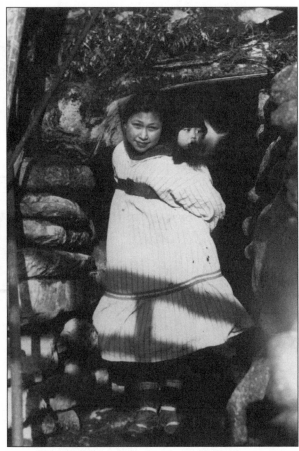

forces the smoke down, puts out the fire, and then the fire re-ignites with a mild explosion. The building is soon filled with gas . . . The people are not pleased with the idea of the priest leaving. They are praying for bad weather, or anything that will put off the plane . . . Anaruk had a narrow escape yesterday. The chunk of ice he was riding turned turtle. He lost his rifle, bag, and Aalic's kayak . . . Thank God there has been very little sickness this year . . . Pullach got the first white whale of the season today . . . Great excitement today. A plane came over and without any preliminary circling landed on smooth, slowly moving ice . . . When they took off, their field was already beginning to break up . . . All last night and today the ice is roaring louder than usual. It resembles in sound a lot of freight cars moving slowly . . . Easter Sunday. The weather rejoiced with Our Lord's Resurrection . . . The store is out of coffee, tea, lard; short on sugar and no baking powder or soda . . . Mayac and Kokuluk finished their boat today and had it blessed . . . Two men had a narrow squeak on the ice today. They went rather far out and the moving ice started to break up. After dark they lighted matches and we could see where they were. We helped out on shore with lantern, rifle shots and much shouting. It was 3 A.M. before they were really safe . . . Bad news today. Three of our young men floated away northward on the ice . . . Great day. Feast of Christ the King. In the evening, though very stormy, most of the men went up to visit the statue . . . the cold storage meat is very good . . . June 30, 1950: Today the sea is good and we are loading to go to Nome. There are three boats going together. Oalaranna's, Kunnnuk's and mine. The rest of the people will remain for a few days yet. Mayac's wife is a little too weak to travel.

This was Father Cunningham's last entry in the King Island diary.

Father Carroll's first entry in the diary was made on October 20, 1951:

~

King Island has been without a priest since the above departure of Father Tom Cunningham . . . Baptized Seegana baby, "Stella." . . . walrus hunting very poor . . . All the boats left around midnight. I went with Paul Tiulana . . . First slush ice on the south side of island . . . population of the island about 130 . . . lots of crabs being caught . . . Three more polar bears! . . . no hunting except for eggs and greens . . . About 30 walrus killed . . . The hunters divided the ivory this evening. The general average was about 12 tusks per man . . . Our native population this year is down to 99 . . . Eclipse of the sun at 12.02 P.M. . . . Finally leave—or try to!! We go about 10 miles on the way when it is discovered that the skin boat is leaking!! We turn back and unload all the baggage and pull boat upon the rocks

. . . December 25, 1959: Due to our small numbers I did not use the big church but fixed up the crib in the small chapel attached to my quarters. One Mass at midnight with practically everybody in attendance. Everybody also at the two morning Masses.

This was Father Carroll's last entry in the King Island diary.

8, 9, 36, 55, 56, 75, 88, 89, 97, 115, 170, 171, 179

KLAWOCK

The town of Klawock is located on the west coast of Prince of Wales Island in Alaska's Southern Panhandle. It is the second largest town, after **Craig**, on that island. It was originally a Tlingit Indian village. Today about half the residents are Native, mostly Tlingit. In 1878, a cannery was established at Klawock, making it the birthplace of the **Alaska** salmon industry. After cannery operations came to an end in the 1980s, logging became Klawock's main industry. Klawock's population numbered 261 in 1890, 131 in 1900, 455 in 1939, 404 in 1950, 251 in 1967, and 854 in the year 2000. The Klawock post office was established in 1882.

As early as July 1913, Father William A. **Shepherd**, S.J., had alerted his Superiors that there were Catholics in the villages of Klawock and Craig needing pastoral care. In 1925, Bishop Joseph R. **Crimont**, S.J., designated northern Prince of Wales Island as a mission of St. Rose of Lima parish in **Wrangell**. However, it was not until two decades later that priests from there began to visit Klawock and Craig with any kind of regularity. In 1946, after being informed that there were 28 Catholics in Klawock, Father Matthew E. **Hoch**, pastor in Wrangell from 1942–59, began to make intermittent visits to Klawock. When he had accepted it as a dependent mission of the Wrangell parish, little did he realize that in doing so he was opening up an entirely new and vast mission territory taking in the logging and fishing camps on Prince of Wales Island. Father Hoch is rightly regarded as the founder of the Klawock mission, St. John by the Sea.

After Father Hoch, priests stationed in Wrangell and **Petersburg** continued to visit Klawock from time to time. From 1973–76, Father Jerome A. **Frister** visited it as fly-in priest out of **Ketchikan**; then,

St. John by the Sea Church, Klawock. *DJA.*

from 1976–79, out of Wrangell. While, as of the year 2004, Klawock never had a resident pastor, it did begin to be visited with some regularity after Michael H. **Kenny**, Bishop of **Juneau** at the time, assigned full-time ministers to Prince of Wales Island.

In 1974, Sister Marguerite Gravel, C.S.C., began pastoral ministry at Klawock and at other communities on Prince of Wales Island. This she continued to do for roughly a decade. She was followed by Sister Nadine Grogan, S.N.J.M. She and Father Michael Nash "began the real history" of the Catholic community at Klawock. Father Nash was the first priest assigned, on September 1, 1983, to serve the Catholic communities on Prince of Wales Island and on the surrounding islands. Flying his own plane out of Thorne Bay, "he made pastoral outreach a reality in that area." He left the area in 1988. St. John by the Sea became a parish in the late 1980s. All the Catholic communities on Prince of Wales Island are part of the one St. John by the Sea parish.

Sister Laetitia Lariviere, I.H.M., arrived on Prince of Wales Island in 1987, and Father James Blaney, O.M.I., less than a year later. The need for a church in Klawock was obvious to all. Many talents and many hands working together soon created a center for the Catholic community, "a place for worship and education, for hospitality and sharing." The new church was blessed and dedicated by Bishop Kenny on April 28, 1992. The Native designs incorporated into the church reflect the desires of Bishop Kenny to reach out to all the peoples of Southeastern Alaska, whether Catholic or not.

Father Blaney left the area in 1999, and Sister Laetitia a year later. Father Edward Matthews, O.M.I., was there for the year 1999–2000. Father Jean-Paulin Engbanda Lockulu and Sister Zita Simon, O.P., began ministry in Klawock in the year 2000. In June 2003, Father Lockulu was transferred to **Sitka**. As of the summer of 2003, Michael W. **Warfel**, Bishop of Juneau, was pastor; Father Edmund J. Penisten Parochial Vicar; and Sister Zita Parish Administrator. In early 2004, Father Perry M. Kenaston became pastor of the Klawock parish.

KNOM

By mid-July 1971, what had once been called "an idle pipe dream" was a reality, a humming 780-kilocycle AM radio station with a 10,000-watt Collins 820F-1 transmitter located on the tundra about three miles east of **Nome, Alaska**. "Announcing the world's newest radio station! This is KNOM, Nome, Alaska!" With those brief sign-on words, the radio station KNOM (pronounced Kay-Nome) proudly proclaimed its birth. The exact date was July 14, 1971; the exact time, 5:00 P.M. The man with the drive behind that anything but "an idle pipe dream" was Father James E. **Poole**, S.J.

Father Poole first had the idea for a radio station in western Alaska some ten years earlier, around 1961, while he was at St. Mary's Mission on the **Andreafsky** River installing a village-wide public address system. The early 1960s found him contacting lawyers, engineers, and the various Federal agencies necessary to begin application for permission to build a station. At the same time, recognizing that he himself was totally lacking in knowledge and skills when it came to electronics and technical matters related to radio, he was contacting also people with radio-related talent, and soliciting funds for a venture that he hoped would reach daily some 30,000 people living in around 90 different Eskimo and Indian villages in western Alaska. One of the primary stated intents of the proposed station was "to help the Alaska Native people to adapt to modern society, while, at the same time, to help them to maintain pride in themselves and in their traditional culture."

From the outset, Father Poole was singularly blessed in having highly skilled and totally dedicated volunteer men and women to help him get KNOM on the air and to keep it there. They are too many to mention all by name, but two stand out and must be mentioned by name. To no one person, after Father Poole, is KNOM more indebted for its coming into being and its going on to become a multi-award–winning station than to Thomas A. "Tom" **Busch**: with KNOM, except for the years 1973–75, from February 8, 1970 to the present (2004). Without his all-around versatility in matters radio and his exceptional managerial skills, the station would simply never have become what it was as of the year 2004. Mentioned by name, too, must be Mary Therese "Tweet" **Burik**, who first went to KNOM in 1967. She left after one year; but returned in 1971, to spend another 14 years there. During those early, critical years of the station's existence, when finances were a constant, major concern, it was she who, with her sharp business sense and careful budgeting, kept KNOM financially solvent. It was Tweet who, by staying on, and thereby giving some stability to the ever rotating staff, did much to keep also the domestic side of the whole KNOM opera-

tion in good order. Deserving of special mention, too, is Mrs. Luella Poole, "Ma Poole," mother of KNOM's founder, Father Poole, who, from 1966–79, was a cook at KNOM and a mother to many of the volunteers on the KNOM staff.

Throughout its history, KNOM has existed, and flourished, only because of donated volunteer labor and freely donated funds. Hundreds of volunteers have served at KNOM. At first they were mostly members of the **Jesuit Volunteer Corps**. In more recent years, they have been members of the KNOM Volunteers. Members of the Congregation of the Brothers of Christian Instruction (**F.I.C.**), too, donated many years of dedicated, competent service to the cause of KNOM. Up until 1994, registered nurses, rooming and boarding at KNOM, but working full-time at the Nome hospital, donated their salaries to help finance the station. In addition, the station, throughout its history, has solicited funds from friends and benefactors local and national. This it has done through its monthly newsletter, "*Nome Static.*" While radio KNOM is, as of the year 2004, a ministry of the Missionary Diocese of **Fairbanks**, it has, all along, been expected to be self-supporting.

KNOM's Mission Statement reads:

KNOM is on the air to inspire, to inform and to uplift listeners in villages throughout 100,000 rugged square miles of western Alaska, to provide Catholic programming to remote listeners, to bring spiritual consolation and education to the needy, the hurting, the poor and the unchurched.

Although this Mission Statement was formulated only years after the station first went on the air, the aims of the station were, from the outset, those listed in the Statement.

KNOM has, for over 30 years, sought to carry out its stated mission by using what, in radio parlance, are called "spots." These are short—less than a minute long—to the point, never preachy, nondenominational messages geared to inform and to inspire its listeners. Many of the spots are styled in an easy-to-take dramatic form. Sometimes the voices used in making them are those of local Eskimos.

KNOM spots fall into various categories: purely spiritual, health and child care, social and economic problems, character formation, general education, and the like. The spots punctuate the regular pro-

Radio station KNOM,
Nome. *MK.*

gramming at regular intervals. At first, on any one day, 64 different spots were alternating on the air. In more recent years, the number of spots in rotation on any one day has varied from about 80 to 100. As many as 200 spots may be aired on a given day. A certain percentage of these are changed every week. For its inspirational spots, KNOM was awarded a Gabriel statuette in 1984.

A radio station is, obviously, only as viable and good as its programming. Much of KNOM's programming has been, and continues to be, "easy listening" music, both contemporary and "oldies." From the day he first began planning the station, Father Poole was firmly persuaded that to attract and hold listeners, and, at the same time, to "inspire" and "educate" them, he would have to mix the useful with the pleasant. In addition to music, plus inspirational and educational spots, KNOM broadcasts news on the hour, with several 15-minute summaries daily. Broadcasting vitally important, updated weather, marine, tide, ice reports and advisories is one of the station's top priorities. There are people who owe their very lives to some of these timely, accurate reports and advisories. The station broadcasts also public service announcements, air travel information, regional meetings, interviews with dignitaries, and the like. Another popular feature is a daily "hotline" program, a kind of bulletin board of the air.

Since its beginning in 1973, the annual Iditarod Trail Sled Dog Race has been faithfully and thoroughly covered and broadcast by KNOM, winning the station numerous citations and awards. KNOM was the first station to broadcast the Iditarod world-wide, through the American Forces Network.

However, KNOM has never lost sight of the fact that it is essentially a Church-related, apostolic enterprise, a radio, a microphone mission. Religious programs have always been among its regular features. Principal among these is, of course, the 10-o'clock Sunday morning Mass. Daily, the station brings its listeners the recitation of the Rosary, a solace to many. From 1990–97, a series of programs entitled "The Lord Be With You!"—written and taped by Father Charles J. **Peterson**, S.J.—was broadcast by KNOM. It is estimated that he produced over 700 individual programs of this feature. Patrick C.W. **Tam** produced the show from August 1998 to the summer of 2000. Since then, and as of the year 2004, it has been produced by Father Paul M. **Cochran**, S.J.

Over the years, KNOM has broadcast also seasonal plays and dramas, especially at Christmas time. Its programming has included traditional Eskimo music and a show on Eskimo stories and legends. There have been readings from different books, including *Nulato: An Indian Life on the Yukon*, by Poldine **Carlo**; *People of Kauwerak*, by

William A. Oquilluk; and *Pioneer Missionary to the Bering Strait Eskimos: Bellarmine Lafortune, S.J.*, by Father Louis L. **Renner**, S.J., in collaboration with Dr. Dorothy Jean Ray.

In 1968, while talking with radio people in **Anchorage**, Father Poole was told that, after one year on the air, his program format would change beyond recognition. This he himself believed at the time. However, while KNOM has grown and changed with the times, its basic format and programming philosophy have remained remarkably constant over the three decades-plus of the station's existence. Neither Father Poole nor Tom Busch ever saw compelling reasons for changing the station's basic format and programming. The initial vision as to what KNOM should be all about proved to be the correct one.

By the end of the year 2004, KNOM had received an extraordinary number of state and national awards. Among them, to mention only the major ones: 12 Gabriel "Radio Station of the Year" statuettes and three National Association of Broadcasters "Crystal Award for Excellence in Community Service." In 2003, it won the NAB Marconi Radio Award as the best Religious Station of the Year. By the end of that same year, the station had received also the Alaska Broadcasters Association's highest Goldie Award, for "Best Service to the Community," a total of five times. For what he has been at KNOM, and done at and for the station, Tom Busch personally has received much recognition and numerous awards, including more than once the "Broadcaster of the Year" award, presented to him by the Alaska Broadcasters Association.

Even when KNOM was only a 10,000-watt station by day and a 5,000-watt station by night, and on the air for only 16 hours a day, many a lonely berry-picker, or fisherman tending his net during the long, cold subarctic night, found in it a welcome, quasi-human companion. In August 1974, KNOM began broadcasting 18 hours a day, from 6 in the morning to midnight. On January 9, 1996, the station began broadcasting 24 hours a day, still at 10 kW. February 5, 1998, was KNOM's first 25,000 Watt day. KNOM has been an AM–FM station since 5:53 A.M., May 17, 1993, the same year it began operating from the newly built Keller Broadcasting Center.

Father Poole left KNOM in 1988. Tom Busch, the first person to be hired on at KNOM, in June 1975, at a small salary, as KNOM's General Manager, was, as such, beginning in 1988, the number one man responsible for the whole KNOM operation. Under his leadership, this Alaska Radio Mission— for some years now, the oldest Catholic radio station in the United States— continued to be blessed and to flourish beyond all human dreams and expectations. In July 2004, Tom, with his wife, Florence, anticipated moving to Anchorage "in early 2005," there to continue to serve the station as its principal fund-raiser. Norman Eric "Ric" Schmidt was to succeed Tom as KNOM's General Manager.

The hundreds of volunteers who have provided generous and indispensable contributions at KNOM are far too numerous to mention all by name. In a general way, however, their generous and indispensable contribution to the station's very existence and success, too, must be acknowledged. Mentioned by name, however, must be KNOM's first support nurse, Betty Connors, who arrived in September 1968, and its last, Anne Irsfeld, who departed in August 1994. They were among 71 nurses and four doctors who, in the course of those 26 years, worked in the Nome hospital and donated their salaries to the station. From afar, literally tens of thousands of individuals have, over the years, and up to the present (2004), with their prayers supported the station's mission and with their contributions made it possible for the station to pay its bills.

For the first spot to appear in KNOM's newsletter, *"Nome Static,"* Father Poole chose: "When we see the lilies of the field spinning in distress, worried how to create beauty; when we see the birds of the air building barns to store food for the future, then it will be time to worry. Until then—trust Him!"

14, 86, 116, 134

KODIAK

The town of Kodiak, **Alaska**, located on the northeast coast of Kodiak Island, is an old town, having been founded by Alexander Baranov in 1792. A post office was established there in 1869. This was discontinued in 1875, but reestablished in 1888. According to official census reports, Kodiak, in 1990, had a population of 6,335, and, ten years later, one of 6,334.

The Catholic Church established itself in Kodiak in November 1944. Prior to that, Masses had been offered there at various times only by priests who happened to be passing through, or by military chaplains stationed in the area. On November 6, 1944, accompanied by Father G. Edgar **Gallant**, who had drawn their Congregation's attention to Kodiak's needs, five **Grey Nuns** of the Sacred Heart arrived in Kodiak. They were Sisters Mary Monica (Superior), Saint Hilary, Madeleine of the Sacred Heart, John Berchmans, and Mary Leo. Father Gallant offered Mass for them that same day. On the 11th, the Nuns officially took over the management of Griffin Memorial Hospital. On the 14th, Father Joseph T. Walsh arrived from **Anchorage** to serve as "temporary pastor" in Kodiak. On the 19th, in the Orpheum Theatre, he offered the first "parochial" Mass celebrated in Kodiak. On December 11, 1944, he was recalled to Anchorage. Father Gallant, who had left Kodiak on business, was back in time to celebrate the Christmas midnight Mass, the first such Mass celebrated on the island.

A one-story frame building across the corner from the hospital and known as "The Wayfarers' Club," or the "Masonic Hall," was leased by Father Gallant from the Erskine Company on January 7, 1945, for $20.00 a month, a rental fee that was raised to $50.00 after one year. This building became St. Mary's Church and rectory. On that same January 7th, Father Gallant offered the first Mass to be celebrated in it.

On June 13, 1945, Father Vincent Edge, Society of Atonement, arrived in Kodiak to serve as pastor and hospital chaplain. He was, however, soon disenchanted with the "uncanonical" conditions and the "irregularities" he found in that frontier town, and left it in May 1946. On May 24, 1946, Father Louis B. **Fink**, S.J., came to replace him.

It was Father Fink who obtained a decision from Walter J. **Fitzgerald**, S.J., Vicar Apostolic of Alaska at the time, regarding the name of the parish. During its first year, it bore the name of "Notre Dame de Kodiak" in deference to the wishes of a generous prospective benefactor. Bishop Fitzgerald, however, determined that the name should be "St. Mary's."

Under Father Fink, St. Mary's parish was soon very much alive. The Grey Nuns, shortly after their arrival in Kodiak, began to teach catechism on a regular basis in their quarters in the hospital. Francis D. **Gleeson**, S.J., newly appointed Vicar Apostolic of Alaska, on his first visit to Kodiak, at the end of July 1948, found waiting for him a class of 13 ready to be confirmed. The following March, he confirmed a class of 20. After serving competently in Kodiak for six years, Father Fink left in 1952. He was followed by Father Thomas F. Maher, S.J., who, for health reasons, left Kodiak after only one year there.

In 1947, the Kodiak parish purchased for $5,000 the Masonic Hall that it had been leasing. Some modifications were made, but it continued to be much too small for the needs of the Catholic community. People kept planning for a new, larger church, but never got beyond the planning stage. When Father Raymond L. **Talbott**, S.J., who succeeded Father Maher in the summer of 1953, arrived in Kodiak, he found neither a "decent" church nor any kind of school building. He immediately set about providing both. His arrival brought about renewed interest in the possibilities of an adequate parish plant. A wholly new church, however, was ruled out by Dermot **O'Flanagan**, Bishop of **Juneau**, under whose jurisdiction Kodiak fell as of October 3, 1951. Instead, the decision was reached to double the width of the present building and to add to its length. By August 30th, the enlarged, renovated structure was ready for use. The parish now had a two-story building with plenty of room for priest's quarters on the second floor and for classrooms on the main floor.

With classroom space available, Father Talbott asked himself, "Why not a parochial school?" Under adverse circumstances, the first three grades opened in September 1954. Sister Saint Hilary taught the first grade and Father Talbott the second and third grades. The school was on its way. A new school was dedicated and blessed on May 7, 1968. In 1984, St. Mary's parish celebrated the 40th anniversary of it founding and the 30th anniversary of the founding of St. Mary's grammar school.

As regards the hospital, the Grey Nuns operated it until 1978. In April 1969, they moved from the old to the new hospital, now called Kodiak Island Hospital. Lack of enough personnel to staff it forced them to leave it in the care of the Lutheran Hospi-

(*above*) St. Mary's Church, with the school to the left, Kodiak. *Photo by Father Fernando T. Bugarin.*

(*left*) View of Kodiak from Pillar Mountain. *Photo by Sr. Carol Bartol, G.N.S.H.*

tals and Homes Society of America on May 15, 1978. The Nuns never did have ownership of the hospital.

In 1958, St. Mary's parish bought 15 and two-thirds acres of woodland bordering on the city limits for $5,000. Part of this was to be used for a parish cemetery; the rest for a church, rectory, school, and convent. Misunderstandings between Father Talbott and his parishioners allowed only the cemetery to become a reality. Burdened as he was by the constant problems he faced during his years in Kodiak, he was relieved, when, in the summer of 1960, his Superiors assigned him elsewhere. "My labors

on Kodiak," he wrote, "were terminated, by the grace of God, in June of 1960."

During the year 1960–61, Father Matthew E. **Hoch** served the Kodiak parish. On June 1, 1961, Father John J. **Marx** was named administrator at St. Mary's and began his three-year stay on the island. With the aid of parish and military volunteers, he painted the interior of the school and the exterior trim of the church, as well as made other improvements. On Kodiak Island during the Good Friday earthquake of March 27, 1964, he witnessed much of the destruction that it caused.

In the summer after the earthquake, Father Francis A. **Cowgill** became pastor of the Kodiak parish. He had the distinction of being the only certified bowler on the island. As such, he gave bowling lessons to the island's young people. That same year, 1964, Father Peter Houck, O.S.B., too, was named to serve in Kodiak. The vitality of the parish is evidenced by the fact that in 1965 it registered 19 baptisms—three of them adult—26 confirmations, five marriages, two burials, and three converts received into the Church. Both Fathers Cowgill and Houck served in Kodiak until 1966, when they were replaced by Father Francis A. Murphy.

Father John B. **Baud**, S.J., was hospital chaplain in Kodiak for the years 1966–68. In 1967, a residence for priests was purchased on Mill Bay Road. For a time Father Ronald Holdorf, C.Ss.R, assisted Father Murphy in Kodiak. Father Francis J. Fish, C.M., replaced Father Murphy in 1967. He was, in turn, replaced, in 1968, by Redemptorist Fathers Edward C. **O'Neill** and William M. Cleary. Father J. Thomas Connery replaced them in 1969. Father Sean O'Donoghue, C.S.Sp., who had substituted for Father Connery during September–October 1970, succeeded him in February, 1971. He held station in Kodiak until 1977. Under him, in the summer of 1975, an addition was built to St. Mary's school. Father O'Donoghue was replaced by Father Urban **Bates**, O.P., in 1977; and he, in turn, by Father Richard D. **Tero**, in 1978. To build up funds for the new projected church, Father Tero developed part of the parish land for a subdivision. He left Kodiak in 1984. Father Leo C. **Desso** replaced him, and was himself replaced, in 1989, by Father Michael W. **Warfel**. It was while Father Warfel was in Kodiak that the new St. Mary's Church was completed and dedicated, on March 10, 1991. He left Kodiak in 1995. Father Gerald Brunet, O.M.I., spent four and a half months in Kodiak in 1992. During the year 1995–96, Father Raymond C. Cotter was in Kodiak. He was replaced by Father Fred T. **Bugarin**, in Kodiak from 1996 to 2003. As of the year 2004, Father Robert C. Bester was pastor of St. Mary's.

Likewise as of the year 2004, Sisters Diane Bardol and Carol Bartol, Grey Nuns of the Sacred Heart, were serving the Kodiak parish as Director of Religious Education and Pastoral Associate respectively.

KOKRINES

Kokrines, a one-time Koyukon Athabaskan Indian village on the right bank of the Yukon River, 96 miles downriver from **Tanana** and 27 miles upriver from **Ruby**, has for many long years been a wholly abandoned site. Even though the name still appears large on maps of **Alaska**, only the cemetery and some cabin ruins remain of what was once a village of around 100 inhabitants. Its name derives from a certain Russian, Gregory Hakara, from Kuopio, Finland, who, given the option of going into exile either in Siberia or in Russian America, opted for the latter. After the purchase of Alaska from Russia by the United States in 1867, Hakara, in 1869, opened a trading post first at 14 miles above the present Kokrines site, then at the site that now bears his name, albeit in a transmuted form. The name Kokrines became official, when a post office was opened in the village in 1907. As Ruby came more and more into prominence, Kokrines eventually became totally deserted.

The people in the Kokrines area were first visited by Catholic missionaries in the spring of 1873, when **Oblate** Bishop Isidore Clut and future Oblate Father Auguste Lecorre arrived, spent some days instructing the people, and baptized 14 children. They were visited again in 1878 and 1886 by Archbishop Charles J. **Seghers**. After the mission at **Nulato** was established in 1887, missionaries from there visited Kokrines.

In 1904, Father Aloysius A. **Ragaru**, S.J., established a mission at Kokrines. This was first dedicated under the title of St. Stanislaus, but, soon thereafter, under that of St. Paul the Apostle.

Father Ragaru was the first missionary to reside at Kokrines, in a cabin he himself built. To this he added a small room to serve as a chapel. He tended the Kokrines mission for several years. From October 1905 to February 1906, he had with him Brother René-Maurice Allory, F.I.C., who taught school there.

In February 1907, Father Julius **Jetté**, S.J., began his six-year stay among the Kokrines people. The following year, he bought the Episcopal church at Kokrines and converted it into a Catholic church and residence. During the years 1907–13, Father Jetté, too, taught school at Kokrines. At times, he was helped by Brother Joseph V. O'Hare, S.J. After Father Jetté left, Father Joseph-Alphonse **Des-**

jardins, S.J., spent the years 1913–15 at the Kokrines mission. After 1915, it was visited periodically by priests from downriver, but more often by the priest stationed at Tanana.

At the end of the second millennium, the name Kokrines was kept alive, not only by people who bore the name, but also by people living in Ruby, who kept referring to the "Kokrines Curse." Father Louis L. **Renner**, S.J., visiting priest to Ruby during the 1980s and 1990s, still heard people refer matter-of-factly to the "Kokrines Curse," whenever tragedy struck a former Kokrines villager or a member of a former Kokrines family. No matter whether a Kokrinian met death through drowning, freezing, fire, gunshot, or the like, non-Kokrinian Rubyites routinely attributed the misfortune to the "Kokrines Curse." The unquestioned belief was that it was Father Jetté who had called the curse down upon Kokrines and its people.

During Father Jetté's first years at Kokrines, he enjoyed much success and much consolation. By his kindness and concern for the people, he gradually won most of them over to the Catholic Faith. The people came to love him as children love their father. But, it was too good to last.

After the discovery of gold in the Ruby area in 1907, miners flocked there, and with them the whiskey peddlers. Soon "the hooch" had its deleterious effects also on the Kokrines people. From the pulpit Father Jetté spoke out forcefully against alcohol abuse. The "deluge of whiskey" was ruining his people. He tried to reason with them, pointed out to them the devastating effects it was having on them, their families, their village. All to no avail. Knowing how much the Christmas midnight Mass meant to them, he decided to force them to choose between his ministrations and alcohol. "Unless the drinking stops," he told them, "there will be no Christmas midnight Mass." The drinking did not stop. On Christmas Eve 1911, he informed his people that there would be no midnight Mass. Their reaction was not what he had expected. They took the news stoically, said nothing. However, his Kokrinian flock had a long memory.

Toward the end of 1912, Father Jetté made all-out efforts to prepare Christmas solemnities such as his people had never before witnessed. As Christmas approached, the people gave the impression that they were most eager to take part in the liturgical celebrations. However, when time came for mid-

St. Paul the Apostle Church, Kokrines. *JOPA-510.34.*

night Mass, not a soul showed up. In a neighboring village, his Kokrines people were dancing and drinking to the health of their heart-broken pastor. That Christmas of 1912, as events would have it, was Father Jetté's last in Kokrines.

According to people living in Ruby, Father Jetté, because of the Christmas incident, and the continued abuse of alcohol, cursed the people and the village of Kokrines, and prophesied that dire misfortunes would befall the people, and that soon their village would cease to exist as such, and that only tall grass would grow where people once lived and cabins once stood. What confirmed the people's belief in the authenticity of the supposed curse and the prophecies is the fact that many Kokrines people did, in reality, soon meet violent deaths, and did, in the course of the years, continue to meet up with more than their share of tragedies, and that the village did soon begin to be abandoned, until it was totally abandoned. Many of its inhabitants moved downriver to Ruby.

The "Kokrines Curse": historical fact, or mere folklore? Because so many people in Ruby believed in it, attached so much importance to it, and lived in fear of it, Father Renner made a careful investigation of it, both in the field and in the written records. People interviewed gave somewhat varying versions of it. For the most part, however, there was general agreement as to its nature and as to why it was supposedly uttered. A thorough and careful examination of all potentially relevant materials in Father Jetté's archival file turned up nothing specific regarding the alleged curse.

Two letters, however, written by Father Jetté seven months before he left Kokrines reveal that he was already at that time deeply disenchanted with his Kokrines flock. On August 18, 1912, he wrote to his Superior at Nulato, Father Crispin S. **Rossi**, S.J.:

> The time seems to have finally come to abandon the place altogether. I have lost all hopes of ever making Christians out of these people. This morning I invited them quite earnestly "not to visit me, because, as I can do them no good, all the time I spend talking with them is time lost," and further, "not to give me any presents, because we do not receive presents except from friends, and they are not my friends."

A week later, on the 25th, he again wrote to Father Rossi: "This place deserves to be utterly abandoned and drowned in a flood of hooch."

Given these sentiments on the part of Father Jetté already before the 1912 Christmas incident, it is easy to see why people could readily believe that, in a fit of anger, he had, indeed, called a curse down upon them and their village, resolved to leave it and never to set foot in it again. That he should, de facto, have cursed the people in whom, and the village in which, he had invested so much time and labor, is scarcely thinkable, and would seem to be totally out of character for him, both as the kindly man that he was and as the dedicated missionary priest that he was. What is thinkable is that, in his role as their spiritual leader, he felt himself called upon to forewarn them, and to point out to them the inevitable consequences of continued alcohol abuse on their part.

It is true that Father Jetté did leave Kokrines relatively soon after the 1912 Christmas incident. There is no evidence, however, to support the belief that he left it in a fit of anger, resolved never to set foot in it again. From the written record we learn the circumstances of his leaving Kokrines on March 17, 1913. Down in Nulato, Father Rossi had fallen seriously ill. Father Jetté received a telegram telling him to go to Nulato to replace him. When Father Jetté left Kokrines, he expected to return. As it turned out, he was never stationed there again. He did, however, visit it on a regular basis during his subsequent years in Tanana, several times covering the 96-mile trail on snowshoes. Regarding the people of Kokrines, he wrote, as late as July 13, 1921, that he still had for them "a tender spot" in his heart.

KOLB, Father James M. C.S.P.

Artists in both water colors and paint made him the subject of their brushes. He was described as "boisterous," as having a "booming rattle-the-roof voice." Standing well over six feet tall, and weighing "a tad more than the 230 pounds reported on his driver's license," he was easily seen as "larger than life, as inconspicuous as an earthquake." Owing to his wild, disheveled hair, to his full beard, and to the casual clothes he commonly wore—and the "barbarian" coffee he brewed—he resembled more a lumberjack than the man of the cloth that he was.

James M. "Jim" Kolb was born, of German heritage, in Philadelphia, Pennsylvania, on July 9, 1940. There he attended St. Ambrose grade school from 1946–54, and La Salle high school, graduat-

Father James M. Kolb, C.S.P.
Courtesy of Fr. Kolb.

ing from the latter in 1958. He went on to take courses at La Salle University. By 1965, he had a B.A.
degree in sociology from LaSalle. His childhood
and school years he described as "very happy ones."

As a young man, Jim increasingly felt himself
called to be a minister, a priest. He tried St. Charles
Seminary in Philadelphia, but soon became discouraged by the "very conservative atmosphere"
there. He left the seminary, and spent several years
in construction.

About this time, Jim heard about the **Jesuit Volunteer Corps**. He inquired, applied, and was accepted as a member of it. As such, he made known his
wishes to serve in **Alaska**. He was assigned to **Holy
Cross**, arriving there in August 1968. Soon, however, he discovered that he and the pastor, Father
Andrew Eördögh, S.J., were "less than compatible
personalities." He asked for a change. This was
granted. He became a member of "The Bishop's
Construction Gang," led by Brother John **Huck**, S.J.
The construction/maintenance crew spent that fall
in **Aniak**, building a priest's house and rebuilding
the church. Late in November, the crew moved to
Bethel to do some remodeling work there. From
January to June of 1969, Jim found himself "wad-
ing through plaster dust and sawdust," as he helped

with the interior finishing work on the Bishop's Residence–Chancery Building in **Fairbanks**.

Still feeling himself called to some kind of priestly life, but not to Jesuit life, in September 1971, Jim
entered the novitiate of the Missionary Society of
St. Paul the Apostle, more commonly known as the
"Paulists," in Oak Ridge, New Jersey. On August
26, 1972, he made his "first profession." From
1972–75, he studied theology at Washington Theological Union in Silver Spring, Maryland. He took
his "final promises" on August 24, 1975. Though
not yet ordained, he spent the year 1975–76 at St.
Nicholas parish in **North Pole** as "associate pastor"
to Father Louis F. McKernan, C.S.P. That fall, he
also served as Religion teacher at Monroe Catholic
High School in Fairbanks. On October 24, 1975, in
Fairbanks' Sacred Heart Cathedral, he was ordained
a deacon by Robert L. **Whelan**, S.J., Bishop of Fairbanks. (Over 25 years after that event, Father Jim
Kolb, referring to Bishop Whelan, who had in the
course of the years become a very close friend of
his, wrote, "He formed me as a priest.")

While Jim was working as a volunteer in Bethel,
he developed a long-lasting friendship with Father
John E. **Gurr**, S.J., pastor of the Bethel parish.
Father Gurr deserves the credit for bringing it about
that Paulists served in Alaska. When Jim was in theological studies, Father Gurr asked, "Why don't we
have any Paulists in Alaska?" The response was
wholly positive. During the 1970s, Paulist seminarians spent summers in Alaska at places such as
Bethel and **Nome**. For 20 years, Paulist Fathers
staffed the parish in North Pole. And for over 20
years, a Paulist, namely Father Jim Kolb, served at
the University of Alaska–Fairbanks.

In February 1976, Bishop Whelan and the Paulists
began negotiations regarding the feasibility of
Paulists taking over the Catholic campus ministry
at the University of Alaska–Fairbanks. The two parties agreed that Paulists, in keeping with their tradition of ministering on non-Catholic university
campuses, should assume responsibility for ministry
to Catholics at the University. Accordingly, at the
end of April, "the little white house" on Deborah
Street, near the University, was purchased to serve
as a "University Catholic Center." Paulist Jim Kolb,
due to be ordained a priest on May 15, 1976, in New
York, by Terence Cardinal Cooke, and soon to

have, by the spring of 1976, from La Salle University, a Master of Religious Education degree, and being, furthermore, a man who knew and loved Alaska, was the obvious choice for the campus ministry post.

So, on July 11, 1976, on the University of Alaska–Fairbanks campus: enter Father James M. "Father Jim" Kolb, C.S.P., tall, husky, a full head of black curly hair, luxurious beard, rich baritone voice! Being by nature out-going, personable, ecumenically inclined, always ready to meet and greet any and all, whether new arrivals on campus or campus veterans, he was soon a well-known, respected figure on campus, an active participant of much of campus life.

In September 1976, Father Jim talked to Bishop Whelan about making the University ministry a "University Parish." It was an idea whose time had come. On March 3, 1977, the campus ministry was made an extra-territorial parish under the name of "St. Mark's University Parish." At the same time, Father Jim was officially appointed its pastor. During his first year as pastor of St. Mark's, 1976–77, he continued to live in North Pole and commuted to the University, a round-trip of 38 miles. At the end of that year, he moved into the Deborah Street house. It was a great step forward for Father Jim, when that little white parish house—amidst spruce, birch, aspen, cottonwood trees and a profusion of wildflowers during the summer—became also his home. Much as he enjoyed moving about, he was, by his own admission, "a nester." His new home ideally suited his nesting instincts. It was simply furnished; but, with loaded bookshelves, rocking chairs, braided rugs, a wood-burning stove, it was a warm, cozy place. Among his hobbies, he listed "the daily care and 'feeding' of a wood stove."

As pastor of St. Mark's, Father Jim continued to bring new ideas and a new, more relaxed, informal style to the parish. To help build a family spirit among Mass attendants, Sunday Masses were often followed by picnics or potlucks. Earlier members of St. Mark's—students, faculty and campus staff members, along with "townies," people not associated with the University, but still attracted to the budding parish—remembered years later in particular "the feeling of being part of a family," something they had not experienced in other parishes.

It was one of Father Jim's principles to involve as many people as possible in the various aspects and needs of the parish. All were expected to help in some way, to make some kind of a contribution, to be an active ingredient in parish life. The parish was meant to be self-supporting. He never preached money. Parishioners unable to help financially were invited to render various kinds of volunteer service: house maintenance, stove-wood gathering, leaf raking, snow shoveling, Sunday school teaching, bulletin production, setting up for the liturgies, phone answering, and the like. Rendering services of this nature not only took care of basic needs, but also helped bring the people closer together, helped create a feeling of belonging to a worshiping family. St. Mark's had no paid staff positions. Father Jim was his own secretary, gardener, cook and housekeeper. He soon became well known for his soups-from-scratch and one-pot meals featuring homemade sauerkraut.

Regarding setting up for liturgies: There was a small chapel in Father Jim's home, which continued to serve, at the same time, also as the parish house. On a small scale, Masses were celebrated in that chapel. The parish, as such, had no church. All parish liturgies were held on campus, in the Lola Tilly Dining Commons. Everything necessary for a given liturgy had each time to be set up anew and taken down again. St. Mark's was strictly "a portable church." Inconvenient as this arrangement was, it did make the Church accessible to students and campus staff in a way an off-campus building never could have.

Though St. Mark's, at the outset, defined itself as a "Christian community rooted in the Catholic tradition," Father Jim's liturgies, homilies and sermons seemed, in the eyes of some, to be, at times, too informal, too laid-back, even "somewhat unorthodox." His liturgies, his homilies and sermons, however, because they were non-traditional and avoided being stylized, staid, or perfunctory, were, by and large, very positively received. People liked them precisely because they were down-to-earth, all-welcoming, straight from a compassionate, non-judgmental heart. They put people at their ease, were "people friendly." Said Father Jim, "I deal with people as people." The first time his mother visited him in Fairbanks and attended his Mass, she said to a female parishioner after the Mass, "He's not very pious." The woman, not knowing that she was speaking to Father Jim's mother, snapped back, "That's why we like him!"

During his years as pastor of St. Mark's, Father Jim also filled numerous other roles. He was a member of the Alaska Christian Conference, of the National Catholic Campus Ministry Association, and of the Social Justice Lobbying Group. He served on various University of Alaska–Fairbanks committees. He was active in the Boy Scouts of America, and involved with the Fairbanks Counseling and Adoption Agency. He served the Diocese of Fairbanks as director of its Respect for Life program, and as director of its Ecumenical Affairs program. Throughout his priestly years in Alaska, he happily served, from Memorial Day to Labor Day, as "pastor" of St. Mary's of the Lake "parish," a "summer church" for vacationers at Harding Lake, 44 miles southeast of Fairbanks. An old Quonset hut served as the church building. Standing outside this, greeting people after Mass, Father Jim, fully vested, was, in 1993, "immortalized" in a charming, light-hearted, but well executed, drawing by noted Alaskan watercolorist, Barbara Lavallee.

In the course of the years, Father Jim and St. Mark's matured together. Though there was a steady turnover of students and faculty, the parish continued to flourish, to be truly a close-knit family-style parish. He became a "father figure" to literally thousands. His beard, now quite grizzled, earned him the nicknames of "Father Bear" and "Father Scruff." No offense was intended, none taken. Right up to the end of his tenure at St. Mark's, he continued to meet people "on their own turf." He rejoiced with the rejoicing, sorrowed with the sorrowing. Many did he marry, and many did he bury. He was a good shepherd to his diverse flock, to people of all faiths—and of none.

Toward the end of the last millennium, there arose—as is all too often the case, when men of powerful personalities and strongly held personal views no longer see eye to eye on important issues involving both—irreconcilable misunderstandings between Father Jim and Michael J. **Kaniecki**, S.J., Bishop of Fairbanks at the time. In 1998, Father Jim's long and satisfying tenure as pastor of St. Mark's and priest at the University of Alaska–Fair-

banks came to a sad, unfortunate end. Before he left those two posts, the University honored him with a plaque, and acknowledged his "huge impact on campus life." The Catholic community of St. Mark's, in recognition of all he had done for it in the course of over two decades, put on a well-attended farewell picnic party for him. That was on August 23, 1998. Soon thereafter, Father Jim left Alaska, but not without leaving a big part of his heart behind. In subsequent years, he revisited Alaska any number of times: to attend the anniversary celebrations marking the founding of the parishes in North Pole and at the University, to be present at the funerals of close friends, and simply to be, even if for only a short time, once again in Alaska.

His first year out of Alaska, Father Jim spent on a kind of sabbatical leave. Among other things, he did some traveling, and he saw to it that a troublesome knee finally received the medical attention it needed. (The knee trouble he blamed on "wear and tear from too much genuflecting.") He spent the year 1999–2000 at St. John's University, Collegeville, Minnesota, taking advanced courses in theology. The following year, he was engaged in "pastoral supply" work in various parishes in Minnesota and Florida. On November 1, 2001, he became of pastor of St. Elizabeth of Hungary parish in Portland, Oregon. Six months after taking that assignment, he could write, "After four very discouraging years, it is good to be settled again in a very nice parish. The ministry here is good—but I will always miss Alaska and the University of Alaska." As of the year 2004, he was still pastor of St. Elizabeth's.

80

KONDA, Father Bernard A.

Bernard A. "Ben" Konda was born on July 10, 1939, in a small town near Dodge City, Kansas. He was raised on a farm-ranch, and received 14 years of Catholic schooling in that immediate area. He ended his pre-seminary education at the University of Kansas. Having throughout his early years of grade and high school considered being a priest, he arrived, at this time, at the decision to begin seminary studies for the Diocese of Dodge City, Kansas.

From 1961–63, Ben received his training in philosophy at the Benedictine Conception Seminary, Conception, Missouri. When he began his theological studies in 1963, two of his brothers were already priests in the Diocese of Dodge City. To avoid "over saturating" that small diocese with three Konda priests, he decided to seek admission into the Diocese of Tucson, Arizona. From Marion F. Forst, Bishop of Dodge City, he received permission to make the change. Francis J. Green, Bishop of the Diocese of Tucson at the time, accepted him and assumed financial responsibility for his theological training. From 1963–67, Ben studied theology at St. Thomas Seminary in Denver, Colorado. During those years, he earned a Master's degree in Religious Education. On May 27, 1967, in the chapel of St. Mary of the Plains College, in Dodge City, he was ordained a priest by Bishop Forst for the Diocese of Tucson.

During his first year as a priest, Father Konda was an assistant pastor at Sts. Peter and Paul, a large parish near the University of Arizona. He was then selected by Bishop Green to attend the Catholic University of America in Washington, D.C., to do post-graduate work and to obtain a Doctoral degree in Canon Law. By June 1971, he had earned that degree.

Upon returning to the Diocese of Tucson, he served in various capacities, among them as Officialis of the Marriage Tribunal, Vice-Chancellor of the Curia, the first Director of the Permanent Deacon Program, a Diocesan Consultor, and a Staff Member at the Diocesan Minor Seminary. While serving in those capacities, he resided at St. Augustine's Cathedral as an "assisting priest."

After having survived a battle with cancer in November 1972, and after having undergone the pain experienced at the death of one of his priest-brothers, and after having endured other complications, Father Konda received permission in 1976 from Bishop Green to become an "inactive" priest. During the next eight years, he rose to an executive position in a well-known health organization, and was selected by the president of the organization to obtain a Master of Business Administration degree from Pepperdine University in Malibu, California. He and a physician then formed their own health organization, of which Father Konda, co-owner of the partnership, served as President and Chief Executive Officer.

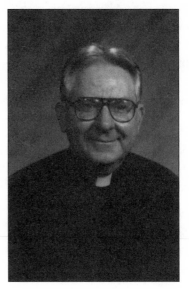

Father Bernard A. Konda
Courtesy of Fr. Konda.

Throughout those eight years, his love for the priesthood never left Father Konda. In 1984, he made the decision to return to the "active" priesthood. Always having had a desire to serve in the mission areas of the Church, he requested to be released from the Diocese of Tucson, so that he might serve in the Diocese of **Juneau, Alaska**. His request was granted. Shortly after his arrival in Alaska, on July 8, 1984, he was incardinated into the Diocese of Juneau by Michael H. **Kenny**, Bishop of Juneau at the time.

Father Konda's first assignments from Bishop Kenny included that of Judicial Vicar for the Marriage Tribunal, which Father Konda revised and updated in keeping with directives initiated by the Second Vatican Council. He was assigned also the role of Episcopal Vicar of Administration of Canonical Affairs. In addition, given his fiscal talents, he was instrumental in guiding the diocese through the turbulent "post-oil-boom days," when overall finances were in decline. While filling the above roles, Father Konda served also as Parochial Vicar of Juneau's St. Paul's parish.

In 1985, Father Konda was assigned Rector of Juneau's Cathedral of the Nativity of the Blessed Virgin Mary parish and pastor of St. Peter's parish in **Douglas**. As Rector of the Cathedral, he contracted for the complete renovation of the Cathedral, which included the installation of new stained glass windows. He saw also to the restoration of the Cathedral rectory to a state similar to that in which it was, when the Jesuit Vicars Apostolic had resided there.

It was Father Konda who oversaw the merger of the Cathedral and St. Peter's parishes, on July 1, 1987, into one parish, with the resulting closure of the latter. He was the last priest to celebrate Mass in St. Peter's Church in Douglas. While Rector of the Cathedral parish, he was instrumental also in bringing about a better utilization of the **Shrine** of St. Therese.

In 1988, Bishop Kenny granted Father Konda sabbatical leave from the diocese to assist the newly formed Diocese of Victoria in Texas [*sic*], in Victoria Texas. For ten months, he served there as Adjutant Judicial Vicar of the Marriage Tribunal. After completing that assignment, he was asked by the Archdiocese of Seattle to assist them with the total revision of their Marriage Tribunal. From 1989 through 1991, he worked first with Archbishop Raymond G. Hunthausen, then with his successor, Archbishop Thomas J. Murphy. His duties included being a Judge on the Regional XII Court of Appeals for marriage cases. During that period, he continued to serve, simultaneously, as Judicial Vicar of his home Diocese of Juneau, as well as Canonical Advisor to its bishop. While on his Seattle assignment, as his time allowed, he also assisted sacramentally at one of Seattle's larger parishes.

In 1992, Father Konda returned to Alaska. By mutual agreement between Bishop Kenny and Francis T. **Hurley**, Archbishop of Anchorage at the time, Father Konda, living all the while at Anchorage's **Holy Spirit Center**, served for six months in the Archdiocese of Anchorage as a member of a team of "sacramental priests" who traveled near and far to bring the Mass and Sacraments to parishes and missions not having a resident priest. Each weekend found him at a different parish or mission, from **Cordova** to far away missions in the Aleutian Islands.

Upon his return to the Diocese of Juneau in mid-1992, Father Konda was given a similar assignment by Bishop Kenny. He was to "sacramentally assist" at the various parishes and missions in the diocese that had no resident priest.

From 1992 to the summer of 1995, Father Konda served as pastor of St. Gregory Nazianzen parish in **Sitka**. In addition to attending to his normal pastoral duties, he was instrumental in the renovation of the church and rectory. The first move toward the restoration of "the old church" was made as this time. During his years in Sitka, he was active in the Ecumenical Alliance and served a term as its president.

Father Konda was with Bishop Kenny the evening before the latter left for Jordan, where he unexpectedly died. In the bishop's residence, the two reminisced about the past and watched a movie. By this time, Bishop Kenny had already assigned Father Konda to become pastor of Holy Name parish in **Ketchikan** and visiting priest to its dependent mission at Metlakatla, assignment to be effective as of August 1995. At Holy Name, Father Konda was joined by newly ordained Father Michael Schwarte. Many projects were accomplished at this time: a parish hall was constructed; the parking lot black-topped; the rectory, school and Annex (where the Director of Religious Education lived) renovated. Father Schwarte's presence in Ketchikan made it possible for Father Konda, in 1997, to attend the "Continuing Theological Education Session" at the North American College in Rome.

Back from Rome, Father Konda resumed his normal pastoral duties in Ketchikan. However, in 1998, he suffered an injury related to icy conditions. This quickly brought on a severe arthritic condition, which was greatly aggravated by the cold, rainy climate of Southeastern Alaska. His personal physician advised him to seek relief in a hot, dry climate. Michael W. **Warfel**, who succeeded Bishop Kenny as Bishop of Juneau, gave Father Konda permission to spend his last five years before retirement in his original Diocese of Tucson with the status of "working outside the Diocese of Juneau."

In July 1999, Father Konda arrived in the Diocese of Tucson and was appointed Chancellor of the Diocese. Three months later, he was named Episcopal Vicar for Administration and Canonical Affairs. During this time, he also served at various missions in the diocese. In December 2000, he was asked to assume the role of Administrator of St. George Catholic Community in Apache Junction, Arizona. In March 2002, he was named its pastor.

In April 2003, Father Konda suffered yet another setback, due to cancer. Upon the recommendation of physicians, he was, as of that date, scheduled to retire in July 2004. By that time, he had rendered 15 years of service in the Diocese of Juneau and 15 in the Diocese of Tucson.

While Father Konda may not, by his own admission, have achieved all of his life's goals, he had, at the time of his retirement, the consolation of knowing his priesthood had been centered all along on being a good pastor. Confidently, and with satisfaction, he could quote the words found in the Second Vatican Council's *Dogmatic Constitution on the Church*: "Let their heroes be those priests who have lived during the course of the centuries often in lowly and hidden service, and have left behind them a bright pattern of holiness."

KOTLIK

Kotlik, today a major village, located on the east bank of the Kotlik River and on the northern mouth of the Yukon River, has long been a Central Yup'ik Eskimo settlement. The word "kotlik," in Eskimo, means "pants," as the river in front of the village with two branches is shaped like a pair of pants. Prior to the mid-1960s, Kotlik was a small settlement of only a few families. About that time, the channel from Norton Sound to **Chaneliak**, a small village nearby, became too shallow for barge traffic. After Chaneliak became inaccessible to the oil

and freight barges serving the delta, the 30 residents of Chaneliak moved to Kotlik.

Residents of the nearby villages of **Hamilton**, Bill Moore's Slough and Pastoliak also moved to Kotlik, in the early 1960s, after the Bureau of Indian Affairs constructed a school at Kotlik. By 1965, Kotlik had emerged as one of the larger ports and commercial centers of the lower Yukon. The population of Kotlik fluctuated between 10 and 83 from 1880 to 1960. The consolidation of Kotlik, Chaneliak, Bill Moore's Slough, Hamilton and Pastoliak resulted in a 300% increase in population from 1960 to 1970, when the census recorded 228 residents in the community. By 1979, Kotlik had 305 residents; by 1990, 499; and by the year 2000, 591.

The Kotlik mission, dedicated to St. Joseph, was first served by Father Martin J. **Lonneux**, S.J., out of **St. Michael**, from 1931–52. He was followed by Jesuit Fathers: Jules. M. **Convert**, out of St. Michael, 1952–54; Paul H. **Linssen**, out of Hamilton, 1954–55, and out of Chaneliak, 1955–56; René **Astruc** (who celebrated the first Christmas Mass offered in Kotlik, in 1962), out of St. Michael, 1956–63; James W. **Plamondon**, out of St. Michael, 1963–65. Sometime in the fall of 1965, or winter of 1965–66, he moved the church building at Chaneliak to Kotlik. From 1965–72, he resided at Kotlik—where he found the people "quite fervent and devoted."

The following Jesuit Fathers likewise resided at Kotlik: Henry G. **Hargreaves**, 1972–75 and 1976–80; Joseph J. Henninger, 1975–76; Astruc, 1980–82. Father James J. Strzok, S.J., served Kotlik out of **Emmonak**, 1982–83. During the next two decades, the Kotlik parish was cared for by the following, either living there or visiting it: Jesuit Fathers Astruc,

St. Joseph's Church, Kotlik. *DFA.*

Hargreaves, Robert V. Paskey, Eugene P. **Delmore**, and Thomas G. **Provinsal**, as of the year 2004.

Eskimo Deacons, too, served and, as of the year 2004, were serving their Kotlik parish: Larry Chiklak, Henry Teeluk, Aloysius Wasuli, David Mike, Joe Sinka, and Raymond Teeluk.

School Sisters of Notre Dame, Sisters Mary Beck and Jane Resop, also engaged in ministry at Kotlik; as did Sister Cecilia Huber, O.S.U.

In connection with Kotlik, mention must be made also of long-time Kotlik resident, Margaret Koka Hunt (Mrs. Margaret K. Andrews), who during the late 1930s and the 1940s collaborated with Father Lonneux in what was truly a monumental achievement: the production of idiomatic translations into Central Yup'ik Eskimo of the Baltimore Catechism and of hymns, as well as of texts of Sacred Scripture, the Mass and Sacraments.

Kotlik, it should be noted, was the birthplace of Maggie Kamkoff **Sipary**, long-time catechist and translator for many missionaries, both in the Yukon-Kuskokwim Delta region and elsewhere.

KOTZEBUE

Kotzebue, an Inupiat Eskimo town about 25 miles above the Arctic Circle on the northwest shore of the Baldwin Peninsula in Kotzebue Sound, became a permanent settlement in 1897, when a reindeer station was located there. Before that, the site had been used by Eskimos as a summer fish camp. The Kotzebue post office was established in 1899. That same year the Society of Friends (Quakers) founded a mission at Kotzebue. Father Paschal **Tosi**, S.J., had already visited Kotzebue Sound in March 1895 with a view to establishing a mission there at first opportunity. In 1930, the

Kotzebue population numbered 291; in 1992, 3,075; and in 2000, 3,082.

Kotzebue, the largest town in northwest **Alaska**, serves as a trade and supply center and a transportation hub to around a dozen villages in that general area. The airfield is named for Ralph Wien, who died while at the controls of the *Marquette Missionary* when it crashed at Kotzebue on October 12, 1930.

On May 9, 1931, Father Bellarmine **Lafortune**, S.J., made the first entry in the Kotzebue house diary: "For many years past we had our eyes on this place, but the lack of men prevented us from entering the field." During the first half of 1929, Father Philip I. **Delon**, S.J., flew to Kotzebue "at the request of all the whites there, with the exception of one," to look into the feasibility of the Catholic Church's establishing a mission there, something Kotzebue's white people had urgently requested for many years. Catholics wanted not only pastoral care for themselves and their families, but, along with virtually all of Kotzebue's white population, they hoped that a Catholic mission would help counteract to some degree what they considered to be the negative impact the Society of Friends was having on Kotzebue's Native people and the community in general. Father Delon moved quickly. He wired for building materials, and had Father William F. Walsh—a 29-year-old volunteer priest ordained for the Archdiocese of San Francisco on June 11, 1926—come to Kotzebue to be in charge of the building project and

In Kotlik's St. Joseph's Church, on April 23, 1994, the newly confirmed— distracted by a little intruder—pose with Bishop Michael J. Kaniecki, S.J. *LR.*

to serve as Kotzebue's first priest. Father Walsh—described by Father Segundo **Llorente**, S.J., as "the soul of kindness and generosity. Everyone loved him."—arrived in Kotzebue on July 28, 1929, and put up the church-residence.

Father Walsh's ministry among the Eskimos, while not a great success, since Kotzebue was a Quaker stronghold, was, nevertheless, not wholly fruitless. By his cheerfulness and concern for the sick, as well as by the entertainments he hosted in the church hall, he was able to break down prejudices and attract a number of Eskimos to the Church. His first year in Kotzebue proved also to be his last. He died in the fatal crash of the *Marquette Missionary*.

On October 20th, Father Lafortune arrived in Kotzebue. The people there had asked Bishop Joseph R. **Crimont**, S.J., for him specifically. The church and living quarters he found were, according to him, the coldest he had ever lived in. "There is not an Eskimo shack as cold." He spent two weeks after his arrival caulking the entire building, which was made of 6 by 6-inch timbers spiked together. "Without being bad," he commented in the Kotzebue house diary, which he originated, "the idea is not very good. The lumber, being green, contracted in drying and left an opening between the timbers and gave free access to the cold, the wind and the rain." He found also that the stoves were too small. "Undoubtedly, though he did not complain," concluded Father Lafortune, "Father Walsh suffered a good deal from the cold."

In Kotzebue, Father Lafortune found "a peculiar crowd." Nevertheless, in addition to turning his quarters into a habitable residence and a fitting church, he carried out faithfully the usual round of priestly duties.

Everyday throughout his eight-month stay in Kotzebue, Father Lafortune had to face the grim reminder of why he was there in the first place and not on King Island, where his heart was. Behind the church sat the mangled *Marquette Missionary*. Toward the end of May, helped by several men, he dismantled the wreckage and was "amazed how carefully it was put together."

On June 17, 1931, Father **Hubert A. Post**, S.J. arrived in Kotzebue to replace Father Lafortune. On September 5th of that same year, Father Post was transferred. His replacement was Father Peter L. **Baltussen**, S.J., who found his year in Kotzebue anything but pleasant. On March 14, 1932, he wrote to Father Paul P. **Sauer**, S.J., the man in Spokane responsible for getting supplies to the Alaska missions: "This house is in an awful shape. I will not live in this place another winter. God alone knows what I have gone through this last winter. I have had enough of this hell. I have not undressed to go to bed since Thanksgiving. Many a night I did not even dare to go to bed for fear that I might freeze."

A new assignment for Father Baltussen brought Father John A. **Concannon**, S.J., to Kotzebue on August 23, 1932. He was followed by Father Aloysius G. **Willebrand**, S.J., who took over in July 1933. An entry penned by him in the house diary about his predecessor reads: "He seemed to be well liked here. The people hated to see him go." Father Willebrand spent only two months in Kotzebue. On September 28, 1933, Father Francis M. **Ménager**, S.J., began a five-year term as pastor of the Kotzebue mission, a mission dedicated under the patronage of St. Francis Xavier. Soon after his arrival, Father Ménager, a gifted musician, organized the "Kotzebue Catholic Artists," a musical society open to all. Through this, he hoped to have a community-wide influence.

Father Llorente was the next priest to hold station in Kotzebue, from July 1938 to July 1941. As did priests before him, so he, too, found his Kotzebue stay a very difficult one. It was not the weather, nor the isolation that some of the priests found so trying. It was rather the general mores of the town and the lack of constancy on the part of their mostly all-white Catholic flock that tried their patience and pastoral zeal to such a great degree. House diary entries made by different priests create a rather interesting chiaroscuro mosaic: "The village is the most rotten I know in Alaska . . . our little flock are in the main faithful . . . this pagan town . . . there is much good will on the part of the whites . . . Sometimes I think we made a big mistake in coming here . . . very good attendance . . . Kotzebue has been a sort of a trial . . . church packed." Summarizing his three-year tenure in Kotzebue, Father Llorente wrote in the house diary—not without a touch of humor on his part: "After three years of failure, I leave Kotzebue. Three things kept me from going insane: the tabernacle, the typewriter, and the cat-

(*above*) St. Francis Xavier's Church, Kotzebue. *JOPA-174.1.01.*

(*right*) Father William F. Walsh, founder of St. Francis Xavier's Mission at Kotzebue in 1929. He died in the crash of the *Marquette Missionary* on October 12, 1930. *DFA.*

echism children. Thanks to these three I live happy and busy. The town is such as to freeze the ardor of St. Paul." His final entry in the diary reads: "The priest who keeps his smile in this town and goes on with zeal and courage deserves to be canonized at once without any other miracles bearing evidence on the matter."

On September 24, 1941, Father Paul C. **O'Connor**, S.J., began his five-year term in Kotzebue. Being an athletic type, he organized baseball and hockey games, skiing and skating parties for the youngsters of Kotzebue. He himself enjoyed cross-country skiing and ice skating on Kotzebue Sound, "using a sail unto advantage." While in Kotzebue, he took an active interest in the legal system, doing what he could to bring about fair trials, especially in cases involving Natives.

During the Holy Week of 1946, Father **George E. Carroll**, S.J., arrived in Kotzebue to replace

Father O'Connor, who left at that rather odd time of year to go to Portland, Oregon, for needed medical attention. Immediately upon his arrival in Kotzebue, Father Carroll did much remodeling of the interior of the church. In 1951, he left Kotzebue to go to **King Island**. For a year, the Kotzebue mission was without a priest.

In early February 1936, Father **Thomas P. Cunningham**, S.J. spent a week in Kotzebue visiting Father Ménager. "The more I saw of Kotzebue," he

(*left*) St. Patrick's Church, Koyukuk. *MK.*

(*opposite*) The second St. Patrick's Church, Koyukuk, as it appeared on October 4, 1980. It was built during the years 1958–62 by Father James W. Plamondon, S.J., and Robert Betz. *LR.*

wrote to Bishop Crimont on the 26th, "the more I felt disappointed at having my status changed." Father Cunningham had felt himself drawn to missionary work in the Arctic ever since he first came to Alaska as a priest in 1935. His long-cherished hope of one day serving in the Arctic was realized, when, on November 5, 1952, he landed in Kotzebue, where he made his headquarters until March 1954. During his 17-month stay in Kotzebue, however, he was away much of the time. He made trips to **Nome**, **Little Diomede**, and **Barrow**. As auxiliary military chaplain, he traveled to military posts and bases scattered far and wide throughout Alaska.

From March 4, 1954, to July 12, 1959, Father William T. **McIntyre**, S.J., was pastor in Kotzebue. In a witty, but informative, newsletter, *The McKotzebugle*, he chronicled his years there. He was succeeded in Kotzebue by Father Pasquale M. Spoletini, S.J., who had left his native Italy to be a volunteer missionary in Alaska. He held station in Kotzebue from 1959 to 1967. It was he who made a major addition to the parish complex in the form of a whole new building. As he described it: "It is 60 × 32 ft. in size. It has two classrooms, a library, teachers room and living quarters for me all on the first floor. There is a full basement. And there will be running water and flush toilets!" Father Spoletini was the first priest in Kotzebue to have the assistance of lay volunteers, members of the **Jesuit Volunteer Corps**.

In August 1967, Father Michael J. **Kaniecki**, S.J.—future Bishop of **Fairbanks**—replaced Father Spoletini as pastor of Kotzebue. He finished the new building. Being a pilot with a plane at his disposal, he did a fair amount of flying in the area, both for pastoral purposes and for hunting. From 1975 to 1980, Father John E. **Gurr**, S.J., served as pastor of Kotzebue, where he found "a wonderful cross section of parishioners and friends." After him came, for a short time only, Father James R. Miller. He, in turn, was followed by Father Arthur **Lopilato**, S.J., who was in Kotzebue from 1982 to 1985. Father Thomas N. **Gallagher**, S.J., tended the Kotzebue flock during part of 1986. He was succeeded by Father Thomas F. **Carlin**, S.J., who brought some stability to the Kotzebue mission by remaining from 1987 to 1995. He was succeeded in 1995 by Father John B. **Martinek**, pastor until 2002. He was Kotzebue's last resident pastor. In the year 2002, the Kotzebue parish began to be served out of **Nome** by Father John A. **Hinsvark**. While still in Kotzebue, Father Martinek wrote: "As I loved priestly ministry on the middle Yukon, I now love and find joy in priestly ministry here in Kotzebue."

During the summers of 1960–65 and that of 1969, Sisters of **Providence** stationed in Fairbanks taught catechism classes in Kotzebue.

37, 64, 67, 76, 92

KOYUKUK

Koyukuk is a Koyukon Athabaskan Indian village at the confluence of the Yukon and Koyukuk Rivers, 16 miles northeast of **Nulato**. A post office was established at Koyukuk in 1898. This was discontinued in 1900, but re-opened in 1933. Koyukuk had 121 inhabitants in 1910, 124 in 1920, 143 in 1930, 106 in 1940, 79 in 1950, 126 in 1992, and 101 in the year 2000.

Catholic baptisms by **Oblate** and Jesuit missionaries took place in the Koyukuk area as early as the latter 1800s. Nevertheless, the Koyukuk parish, under the patronage of St. Patrick, has never had a resident priest.

During the year 1987–88, Koyukuk's old generator building was transformed into what is presently Koyukuk's St. Patrick's Church. This replaced an earlier one built during the years 1958–62 by Father James W. **Plamondon**, S.J., and Mr. Robert Betz.

From 1901–86, the Koyukuk Catholic community was served by Jesuit priests stationed, with a few exceptions, at Nulato. It was served out of **Galena** from 1954–63 and from 1982–86, and out of **Tanana** from 1970–73.

During the year 1986–87, priests stationed in Galena visited the Koyukuk flock. Then, from 1987–98, it was visited by priests stationed at Nulato. Since 1998, it has been visited by priests stationed in Galena.

During the years 1989 to 2002, Brother Robert **Ruzicka**, O.F.M., served as Pastoral Administrator of the Koyukuk parish. As of the year 2004, Dr. Eliza **Jones** was serving her Koyukuk parish as Parish Administrator.

Sister Margaret Usuka, S.N.D., resided in Koyukuk and served that community pastorally from 1984–89. During the early years of the third millennium, Sister Rose Beck, S.S.N.D., visited Koyukuk out of **Kaltag**, likewise as a Pastoral Minister.

101, 194

LAFORTUNE, Father Bellarmine, S.J.

I should like to be able to convey to Your Paternity my impression of Father Lafortune. For many years I had heard many things about the "Little Father of the Eskimos." The fame of his virtue, his courage, his devotion to his work, had come to me from many and worthwhile sources. I was not quite prepared, though, for the actual Father Lafortune I met in **Nome**. He stands about five feet five inches high and, though seventy years, is more vigorous than most young men of thirty. He speaks the Eskimo language fluently, and ten times faster than any Eskimo. For more than twenty-five years he has worked among the Eskimos of Nome and **King Island** and has not lost one bit of enthusiasm for his work.

This testimonial is of singular significance, for it was written by no one less than the General Superior of the **Alaska** Mission, Father Joseph F. **McElmeel**, S.J., to no one less than the Jesuit Father General in Rome, Wlodimir Ledochowski. It was written in 1938, thirty-five years after Father Lafortune was side-tracked in Nome to take "the charge of the Eskimos," as he put it. When he landed in Nome, on July 16, 1903, one year after his ordination to the priesthood, he was actually on his way to **Holy Cross Mission** on the Yukon River. But the need for a priest to minister to the Eskimos in and around Nome, and to those of the Bering Strait islands, was so great, that Superiors decided he should stay on in Nome.

Bellarmine Lafortune was born in Saint-Roch-de-l'Achigan, a small town about 40 miles north of Montreal, on December 11, 1869. He was one of eleven children and spent his early years on a farm. In 1882, he was placed in the Jesuit Collège de l'Assomption, where he learned with "good success and awards." On July 30, 1890, he entered the Jesuit novitiate at Sault-au-Récollet near Montreal. In keeping with the French-Canadian attitude of those times, his training as a Jesuit was rather rigid, conservative, and voluntaristic. In spite of that, his intellectual life was not neglected; and, in keeping with the broader French tradition, his training encouraged individual initiative and personal responsibility.

After completing the two-year noviceship, and devoting four years to the study of the classics and humanities, and the sciences and philosophy, Bellarmine Lafortune was assigned to teach physics and chemistry at the Collège de Saint-Boniface in Winnipeg for two years. He was such a success as a teacher of those two disciplines, that he was sent to Paris in 1898 to study mathematics for a year. After the year in Paris, he spent three years studying theology. He was ordained a priest on July 27, 1902. Soon after his ordination, he made his tertianship at Poughkeepsie, New York. From there he wrote to a niece, "Where will I be sent? That I don't know yet, but I am just about certain that it will be Alaska."

When Father Lafortune took leave of his family and native Quebec in the late spring of 1903, it was a final leave-taking. He never saw any of his relatives or his native land again. He became a U.S. citizen on September 11, 1918.

Father Lafortune's first year in Nome was devoted mostly to the routine duties of an assistant parish priest. In December 1903, he preached their annual retreat to the Sisters of **Providence**, something he was to do many times during the following years. He taught catechism to the white children. And he began his work with the Inupiat Eskimo people. He lamented the fact that he had so "very little time to consecrate to that work." He catechized and baptized his first converts while trying, at the same time, to learn their language, Inupiaq, without books of

Father Bellarmine Lafortune, S.J. *JOPA-948.05.*

sensitive white noses, but to meet the more specific needs of the Eskimo people. The bond between Father Lafortune and the Eskimo people was strong from the time of his first contact with them. His dedication to them and their welfare, both temporal and spiritual, was total. It was said of him that "he was wedded to the Eskimos." Soon he was to them *ataatazuuraq*, "the little Father." This referred to his short stature, but it also carried overtones of appreciation and affection.

Father Lafortune's work as itinerant missionary became easier for him on January 31, 1907, when he dispensed with hired dogteams and drivers and bought a team of his own. This gave him greater freedom and mobility. He soon became an expert musher. Apart from being physically tough, he was resourceful and planned his trips carefully, anticipating all the hazards that could befall him on the trail. He had good judgment about even the most "elementary things: how to gauge the strength of your dogs and your own, how to camp, and when and where." Often on trips, he avoided the road-houses, preferring to sleep in a snowbank along the way, because "it costs too much to pass a night in those miserable huts."

As the practical man that he was, Father Lafortune was constantly experimenting, inventing, improvising, and trying to improve the living conditions of those around him. He helped Eskimos build better sleds, boats, make better fishing nets. He made soap from seal oil. He built coffins. He devised a folding bed that lifted up and fit into the wall. He found a way of burning crude oil in the parish-house stove without leaving ashes. He tried printing and bookbinding. He even learned how to knit, so that he could show the Eskimos how to do it.

On September 30, 1912, his Father Provincial wrote: "Rev Fr. Lafortune is a man of rare merit, the best and most efficient missioner at present in Alaska."

One of Father Lafortune's favorite projects was the Eskimo workshop. Father Michael M. O'Malley, S.J., who was his assistant for the year 1912–13, wrote:

> Fr. Lafortune lived for the Eskimos. He was their pastor, doctor, adviser, supervisor and provider of work. They made better and more attractive sleds than did the white men in the workshop, which was an exten-

any kind. Soon, however, he gained such a mastery of that language that the Eskimos themselves said that he spoke it like one of them.

Father Lafortune exercised much of his ministry to the Eskimos of the Seward Peninsula area without ever having to leave Nome, for the Eskimos came there during the summers to trade and to work, mainly as longshoremen. They came from places such as **Marys Igloo**, **Teller**, and Wales. In their great skinboats they came also from **Little Diomede** Island and King Island. When they returned home to their villages in the fall, they took back with them also something less tangible than store-bought goods and white man's food. They took back with them "the Christianity" imparted to them by Father Lafortune. Entries in the Nome baptismal record for the years 1904 and following show that many Eskimos were brought into the Church during those years by Father Lafortune.

With more and more Eskimos beginning to attend Nome's St. Joseph's Church, white people began to complain about the odor of seal oil in the church. In a loud voice, Father Lafortune made known his feeling about the matter: "There's a door back there. There's a door up front here. If you don't like the smell in here, you can go out that back door. And," shaking his finger, "you can go out this front door!"

In early October 1905, one of Father Lafortune's dreams came true, when the workshop–chapel building of the Holy Angels Mission was opened for the Eskimos. It was built, not in deference to sion of their chapel. Every evening, winter and summer, men, women and children gathered in the workshop for conversation and recreation. From time to time Fr. Lafortune, always smiling, would appear opening the folding door and calling a group out into the chapel for instruction in religion, in Eskimo, sending a group back into the workshop. On Sundays about one hundred men, women and children would attend Mass in the chapel and sing with gusto. The Eskimos sang in English, Latin and Eskimo, and were eager to sing. A few played the organ well enough. There was always an air of friendliness, piety and subdued hilarity in the place.

During his 44-year apostolate in Alaska, Father Lafortune was many things to the Eskimos, but above all he was their teacher, their catechist. Whenever his schedule and that of the people allowed, he maintained an almost unvarying catechism routine. He divided the people into four classes. "To the 1st class," he wrote, "I teach the prayers and the easiest part of the catechism of Baltimore. To the 2nd class, the whole catechism. To the 3rd class, the history of the Bible and the recapitulation of the catechism. To the 4th class, I teach the history of the Church with maps of my own make." As teaching aids he used large colored charts. "When a pupil can give a good account of every one of those pictures," he wrote, "he knows his catechism thoroughly and a good deal of the Bible."

Father Lafortune closed the catechism season with ceremony and celebration. He read the results of the classes—amount of material learned, attendance, behavior, and the like—for "that always makes quite an impression." The deserving received prizes. Then followed a party with food and punch prepared by himself. Classes ended in early June, when spring hunting began. "In the spring of the year," he wrote, "nothing but absolute compulsion can hold the children and that should not be resorted to, unless one wants to make religion odious to the people."

Father Lafortune spent the year 1915–16 at Marys Igloo. While at "the Igloo," he had almost more to do than he could handle: the spiritual ministry itself, housekeeping, woodcutting, water carrying, dog-keeping. There were dogteam excursions to converts scattered widely all over the Seward Peninsula. "If the good Lord had not given me a constitution of steel," he wrote, "I could not hold out for two weeks."

In 1917, Father Lafortune was given the **Pilgrim Hot Springs** property, and the following year, in April, he moved there to turn it into a new center for missionary activity and a boarding school-orphanage. In October 1918, the influenza epidemic struck the Seward Peninsula in full force. He did not fall victim to it, but it preoccupied him as nothing before or after ever did. In Nome, where, in his words, "the natives were simply mowed down," he and two others were asked by the mayor to care for the Eskimos. From entries made in the Nome house diary by Father Frederick A. **Ruppert**, S.J., we learn that: "Fr. Lafortune gives last sacraments and brings relief to the natives all day . . . works on coffins . . . evokes universal admiration . . . working hard to help natives . . . slaves to help natives from morning to night as usual."

Except for missionary excursions to outlying villages, Father Lafortune spent all but the last four and a half months of the 1920s in Nome. On December 23, 1923, he and all of Nome were shocked, when they learned that Father Ruppert had frozen to death on the 15th. "It is an awful day for the missions," he wrote in the Nome diary, "the most gloomy Christmas I have ever had." On June 1, 1926, he met Roald Amundsen, the Norwegian polar explorer, Lincoln Ellsworth, financier, and Umberto Nobile, the Italian designer and pilot of the dirigible *Norge*, which had brought them over the pole to Teller. The following month, Aleš Hrdlička, a physical anthropologist from the Smithsonian Institution came to Nome. Before he left on July 23rd, he had long visits with Father Lafortune, whom he found "a sturdy but lively Frenchman (by origin) of about 50. Speaks the Eskimo language. He is a matter-of-fact, always ready to help, natural he-man, rather than a priest or a teacher, and a great practical helper to the natives, all of whom are his devoted friends; worth, in these parts of the world, ten in a pulpit."

In July 1928, an epidemic of smallpox broke out among the Eskimos and Father Lafortune was kept busy visiting them, dispensing remedies, acting as interpreter for the doctor. "The summer is past," he wrote to his niece in October, "and I am not sorry. I have never run so much. All the Eskimos were sick. In the end my legs refused to move, but that did not last long. I am now ready again to make forty miles a day."

On July 16, 1929, Father Lafortune—in recognition and appreciation of "his tireless labors and devotedness, and for the results that he has obtained," and for his "expertise in the native language"—was admitted into the ranks of the Solemnly Professed Fathers of the Society of Jesus. This is an honor rarely conferred on a Jesuit who has taken final vows as a Spiritual Coadjutor, as had Father Lafortune. On July 24th of that year, he wrote to his Father Provincial:

> Your Reverence granted me a very unexpected and unmerited favor by admitting me to the four vows of the Professed of the Society. Had my consent been asked, I would have refused, not because I don't value those vows, but because the Society expects from its professed a service that in many instances I cannot render. I will do the best I can; that is all what I can possibly promise.

The name of Father Lafortune and that of the King Islanders are inseparably linked. For over four decades they were in close contact with one another. As early as 1906, he was already writing Superiors about his hopes of establishing a mission on their island and spending the winters with them. He knew it was "a hard country," but he declared himself "ready to go in that exile." For eight days, in June 1916, he was able to visit the island for the first time.

By the late 1920s, Father Lafortune had almost despaired of ever seeing a mission on King Island. However, because of the imminent threat of a government school on the island, he was finally given the oft-requested permission to establish a mission there. This he did in 1929, when he founded the Mission of Christ the King on the island. As it turned out, his race with the government to be first on the island ended in a draw. That same year the government built a school on the island. From 1929 on, till 1947, the year of his death, he spent all but three winters on the island.

The winter of 1930–31 Father Lafortune spent in **Kotzebue**, replacing Father William F. Walsh, who had been killed in the crash of the mission plane, the *Marquette Missionary*. The people of Kotzebue had asked the bishop to send them Father Lafortune specifically. In Kotzebue, in addition to doing the routine work of a parish priest, he also did much caulking and remodeling to make the church–residence building habitable. This he had found upon his arrival to be the coldest building he had ever lived in. "There is not an Eskimo shack as cold," he wrote of it. During the latter part of June, before he left Kotzebue, he, with some help from others, dismantled the *Marquette Missionary*.

Upon his return to King Island in September 1931, Father Lafortune found the new church completed. During the summer of 1932, he was able to spend enough time on Little Diomede Island to establish that mission, something he had been hoping to do for many years. He had first visited the island in June 1913, when he spent a short time there.

During the winter 1934–35, Father Lafortune was in Nome, being the only priest available for that post. After the King Islanders spent that winter without a priest, the King Island men, led by their "chief," Charles **Oalaranna**, pleaded with Father John B. **Sifton**, S.J., General Superior of the Alaska Mission at the time, not to be left without a priest again during winter. They made their case. Thereafter, Father Lafortune was with them every winter, except for that of 1936–37, till the end of his life.

The winter 1937–38 proved to be the most exciting one Father Lafortune and the King Island people ever lived through. That was the winter Father Bernard R. **Hubbard**, S.J., and his party were on the island. They made many improvements and recorded on film almost every aspect of King Island life. "One can hear the click of the camera at any hour," wrote Father Lafortune. "What is commonplace to me, is wonderful to Father Hubbard." It was Father Hubbard who brought the life-size, 900-pound bronze statue of Christ the King to the island. This, on October 17, 1937, was hauled up to the top of a 700-foot bluff overlooking the village, and solemnly blessed by him on the last day of October, Sunday, the Feast of Christ the King. It became a place of pilgrimage for the King Islanders. At its base, Father Lafortune planted "every kind of plant and flower that grows on the island."

In 1931, Father Lafortune, who as a Jesuit seminarian was officially described as "*robuste*," now 62 years old, wrote to his niece, "God gives me health of iron. May I use it solely for his greater glory!" In 1940, he wrote, "Before long I will need a successor. I cannot live forever. Old age is coming slowly but surely, and old age means proximity of death." In September 1946, he informed his niece that his health was "perfect, but I cannot keep myself from getting older."

Letters written during the winter of 1946–47 by Father Lafortune, who had never needed a doctor, continued to dwell on the difficulties of getting old. "Climbing up and down [the rocky slope of King Island] kills me." On June 19, 1947, he wrote to Bishop Walter J. **Fitzgerald**, S.J.: "A great change came over me this last winter. I have lost at least the half of my strength. I am not sick, but I am weak. My steps are faltering, easy exhausted. I cannot account for that change except my age." Two days later, just before stepping into a skinboat for his last crossing to Nome, in the last letter he wrote on the island, he wrote to Louis L. **Renner**, S.J., "I don't hope to see you in the mission. I have not long to live; I will be 79 in a few months. Kindly pray God to grant me a happy death."

Around the middle of July, while in Nome, Father Lafortune collapsed at the altar, as he was offering Mass. He was immediately taken to the Nome hospital. But, on July 29th, because he had expressed a strong desire to be in a Catholic hospital, accompanied by Jesuit Fathers Edmund A. **Anable** and **Thomas P. Cunningham**, he was brought to St. Joseph's Hospital, staffed by the Sisters of Providence, in **Fairbanks**. There, on October 22, 1947, fortified by the Sacraments of the Church, and surrounded by hospital chaplain Father John W. Laux, S.J., and the Sisters, God granted him the happy death he had desired. On the 28th, he was buried in the Fairbanks Clay Street Cemetery, far from the land of his origins, and far from the Eskimos who had been so much a part of his priestly life.

At the time of Father Lafortune's death, Father Cunningham, who replaced him on King Island, summarized in the King Island diary concerning him, "He was a good man to have in this world." Father Segundo Llorente, S.J., who was with Father Lafortune in Nome, during the year 1939–40, wrote: "With the death of Father Lafortune one may say that an era came to an end. It was the era of the giants. When he died, everybody knew there was a new saint in heaven."

87, 97, 115, 174

Brother Aloysius B. Laird, S.J. *LRC.*

LAIRD, Brother Aloysius B., S.J.

Aloysius B. Laird was born in Graceville, Minnesota, on May 15, 1899. He entered the Jesuit novitiate at Los Gatos, California, on July 30, 1922. After finishing his two-year noviceship and taking his vows, he spent a year at Mount St. Michael's in Spokane, Washington, before going to **Alaska**. He spent the years 1925–30 at **Holy Cross Mission**, where he was to spend most of his Alaskan years. At Holy Cross he served in a considerable variety of capacities: prefect of the boys, mechanic, blacksmith, carpenter, manager of the livestock and farm, furnace man, and operator of the mission sawmill. He made a name for himself as "our fish-trap expert." He was also the operator of the mission boat, the *Little Flower*, in 1928, when it was used to freight building supplies to **Hooper Bay** for the new mission being built there.

Throughout most of the 1930s, Brother Laird was back in the Northwest: at Seattle College, at Gonzaga University in Spokane, at the novitiate at Sheridan, Oregon, and at Mount St. Michael's. At those places he generally served as tailor and as furnace maintenance man.

He returned to Holy Cross in 1938, and was there until 1945, when, in need of a change, he was assigned to St. Mary's Mission, **Akulurak**, for the years 1945–48. There he again served as prefect of the boys, and also as infirmarian. He was not a good prefect, too severe.

In the spring of 1948, Brother Laird, along with

Brother George J. **Feltes**, S.J., made a bit of history. They were the first Catholic Alaskan missionaries to travel to Alaska by land. Leaving Spokane in an army-surplus truck crammed with freight, most of it army-surplus materials, on May 11, 1948, they drove over what was then still known as the Alcan Highway, or the Alaska Military Road, to **Fairbanks**. Some of the bridges along the way were in such poor condition that they crossed them, in the words of Brother Laird, "only with the help of our guardian angels and the Providence of God." The two arrived safely, but exhausted, in Fairbanks on June 2nd.

After spending the years 1948–56 at Holy Cross, Brother Laird was transferred to Fairbanks. There, until, 1964, he served as furnace maintenance man and as custodian at both the Jesuit residence and at the Catholic schools. During the years 1958–60, he routinely drove Father Louis L. **Renner**, S.J., to the University of Alaska for Sunday Mass and back. Occasionally, he went moose hunting. He played many winning games of chess. A special ministry of his was visiting Alaska Native people, shut-ins, and the sick. As often as he could, he arranged to have priests accompany him to hear their confessions and bring them Holy Communion. A faithful stoker of his pipe, Brother Laird was a big, rugged man, but he was tender-hearted, and a man of a deep personal spirituality, with a special devotion to St. Therese of Lisieux, patroness of the Alaska missions. He had a habit of making the Sign of the Cross before drinking a glass of water.

Failing health necessitated his leaving Alaska. In 1964, he returned to Gonzaga University, where, in semi-retirement, he was given charge of the chapels and rendered such services as he was able. He died on January 19, 1968, and lies buried in the Jesuit cemetery at Mount St. Michael's.

LAPEYRE, Brother Martial O., S.J.

Martial O. Lapeyre was the eighth of ten children born to James Martial and Louise Minor Lapeyre, a socially prominent New Orleans family. Four of the children entered Religious life. Martial, born on September 16, 1908, entered the novitiate of the New Orleans Province of the Society of Jesus at Grand Coteau, Louisiana, in August 1926, as a candidate for the priesthood, but he then decided to become a Jesuit Lay Brother. He pronounced first vows as a Brother in 1930. Besides a pious spirit, he brought to the Society of Jesus a knack for making, repairing, and operating all types of mechanical and electrical equipment.

Even before he entered the novitiate, Brother Lapeyre had wanted to be a missionary. Shortly after taking his vows, he heard about Brother George J. **Feltes**, S.J., who was going to fly the **Alaska** Mission Superior from mission to mission in the *Marquette Missionary*, a newly acquired and specially designed airplane. Here Brother Lapeyre saw his opportunity to be both a missionary and a pilot. With permission of his Superiors, he took a correspondence course in aviation, and then flying lessons at the Alameda airport in California.

The *Marquette Missionary* crashed at **Kotzebue** on October 12, 1930. The following year, a replacement plane was obtained. Brother Lapeyre's sister contributed $8,000.00 toward its purchase price. From California, Brothers Feltes and Lapeyre flew this new plane to Seattle, where they put it on a ship sailing for **Seward**. From Seward, the two flew the plane to **Anchorage**. After waiting there for some weeks for favorable flying weather, they took off for **Holy Cross Mission**. En route, at Gaines Creek near Crater Mountain west of **McGrath**, they encountered engine trouble, and were forced to land. It was eight days before they were located, and several more days before they were rescued and taken to McGrath. From there, by commercial plane, they flew on to Holy Cross, arriving there just in time for Christmas. After Christmas, they returned to the crash site and repaired the plane. Brother Feltes flew it to a nearby river, where Brother Lapeyre joined him for the flight to McGrath. Meanwhile Father Francis M. **Ménager**, S.J., General Superior of the Alaska Mission at the time, had sold the plane. The two went on to Holy Cross, where Brother Lapeyre ended his dream of being a missionary and a pilot by serving, for half a year, as prefect of the dormitory for the younger boys.

In the summer of 1932, Brother Lapeyre returned to his home Province, to serve there in various capacities and in various places. It was written of him that "there probably was not any Jesuit in the Province more in demand than Lap. It was easy to

(above, left) Jesuit Brothers George J. Feltes and Martial O. Lapeyre, the first Jesuit pilots in Alaska, at a meeting in Mobile, Alabama, ca. 1985. *LRC.*

(above) Father James R. Laudwein, S.J. *LRC.*

see why. He was a hard worker, who could do anything. He lived poorly, never complained, and got along with everyone."

Brother Feltes closed his account of his Alaskan adventures with Brother Lapeyre: "Brother Lapeyre went back to his Province. Over the years he has made a great reputation as a holy and very talented Brother. He is on his way to Heaven via the Southern route, and I am trying to make it via the Northern one. God is still watching over us."

Brother Lapeyre died in New Orleans, on April 18, 1989.

LAUDWEIN, Father James R., S.J.

James R. "Jim" Laudwein was born on April 28, 1930, in Spokane, Washington, the son of Jacob and Irene Laudwein. His brother **Joseph E. "Joe" Laudwein** followed him into this world by about fifteen minutes. In 1934, their father, an employee of the Great Northern Railway, was transferred to Great Falls, Montana. It was there that Jim and Joe and their two younger sisters, Patricia and Elizabeth, spent most of their childhood years. The boys attended Emerson Public School for the first three grades; then, for the rest of their elementary and for the first three years of their secondary education, St. Mary's Grade and High School, staffed by the Sisters of the Humility of Mary. Following that, the family moved back to Spokane, where the boys

attended Gonzaga Preparatory for their senior year, and from which they graduated in May 1948. They then attended Gonzaga University for a year, after which the two entered the Jesuit Novitiate of St. Francis Xavier at Sheridan, Oregon, on September 7, 1949. Independently of one another, after much prayer and thought, both concluded that they had a vocation to the priesthood in the Society of Jesus.

After completing the customary two-year novice-ship, the Laudwein brothers spent another two years at Sheridan studying the classics and humanities. From 1953–56, they were at Mount St. Michael's in Spokane for philosophical studies. Jim spent the years 1956–59 teaching English, Latin and Religion at Marquette High School in Yakima, Washington. At the same time, he was also involved with the school's athletic program.

Jim and Joe made their theological studies at Regis College in Toronto, Ontario, Canada, from 1959–63. In Spokane's St. Aloysius church, on June 16, 1962, they were ordained priests by Bishop Bernard J. Topel. By the time they left Regis, each had earned an M.A. degree in Sacred Theology. Jim subsequently earned an M.A. degree also in Education Administration, from the University of Alaska–**Fairbanks**, in 1969; and an M.A degree in Religious Education, from Seattle University, in 1972.

Father Jim made his tertianship at St. Stanislaus Novitiate in Cleveland, Ohio, during the year 1963–64. Then, having volunteered for **Alaska**, he began his decades-long ministry there. From 1964–66, he was on the faculty of Monroe Catholic High School, Fairbanks, as a teacher and student counselor. He was its principal from 1966–68. As such, he worked closely with and had excellent rapport with the Sisters of **Providence** and the members of the **Jesuit Volunteer Corps** staffing the school. During his years at Monroe, he served also as the chaplain of the Newman Student Federation at the University of Alaska–Fairbanks. In the spring of 1967, Father Jim, the athletic half of the Laudwein twins, made headlines in the *Fairbanks Daily News-Miner* by taking first prize in the principals' division of the Equinox Marathon sponsored by the UA–F.

After his four years at Monroe, Father Jim served for over a year as pastor of Little Flower of Jesus Mission in **Hooper Bay**. On June 10, 1970, he became Superior of the Jesuits at St. Mary's Mission, **Andreafsky**, and Administrator of the mission school. Given his youthful disposition and his interest in not only academics but also in athletics and sports (he was an enthusiastic swimmer, cross-country skier, volley- and basketball player) he was very much the right man for the St. Mary's Mission of the time. One of the first things he did as Administrator was to turn the first six grades of the mission school over to the Public School District of the City of St. Marys. In 1974, he turned over also the seventh and eighth grades. His aim was to make of St. Mary's Mission High School a school that would provide the best secondary program for students in the area, "an alternate educational program," in his words, "that is Catholic, that is quality, that is marked by our rich spiritual and academic tradition." Predicting a "bright and promising" future for the school, and acknowledging that it was time "for a change, transition and new vision," he left St. Mary's for a sabbatical year at the Jesuit School of Theology at Berkeley, California, "to study new concepts in moral theology and communication skills."

In 1982, Father Jim began his multifold, 12-year ministry in **Anchorage**. From the outset, he ministered to Alaskan Native people living or hospitalized in Anchorage and served in a "low profile" way as a campus minister at the University of Alaska–Anchorage and at several other centers of higher learning in Anchorage. From the outset, too, of his years in Anchorage, he served as a member of the "Archdiocesan Pastoral Visitation Team." As such, he traveled far and wide throughout the archdiocese on weekends to bring the Mass and Sacraments to parishes and missions without a priest. For all the physical work he put into readying the foundation for a modular home at **Unalaska**, he was hailed as "a real hero."

On September 18, 1986, Father Jim was appointed Superior of the Anchorage Jesuit community, a position he held for the next eight years. In 1987, he added to the above mentioned responsibilities that of "Advisor to Jesuit Volunteers in Alaska." The following year, he was given the added responsibility of caring for Anchorage's Catholic Filipino community. On top of all these ministries, he undertook, in 1992, to serve as chaplain of Anchorage's Brother Francis Shelter and its Covenant House, Alaska. The word "no," when he was asked to take on a new or an additional ministry, was not in Father Jim's vocabulary. Interviewed, in 1993, concerning his many ministries in and out of Anchorage, he said simply, "The more I give of myself, the more Our Lord gives back to me."

At the end of December 1993, after almost three decades in Alaska, Father Jim left it for similar ministries in Portland, Oregon. On July 31, 1995, he began his six-year term as Superior of the Colombière Community. During the course of those years, and continuing on, as of the year 2004, he engaged in pastoral ministry to "street people" and to Native Americans, and helped out in various parishes. For a number of years, he also worked in the Portland Development Office. In 2001, he became the Father Minister of the Jesuit Novitiate of St. Francis Xavier in Portland.

LAUDWEIN, Father Joseph E., S.J.

Joseph E. "Joe" Laudwein was born on April 28, 1930, in Spokane, Washington, the son of Jacob and Irene Laudwein. His brother **James R. "Jim"**

Laudwein preceded him into this world by about fifteen minutes. In 1934, their father, an employee of the Great Northern Railway, was transferred to Great Falls, Montana. It was there that Joe and Jim, and their two younger sisters, Patricia and Elizabeth, spent most of their childhood years. The boys attended Emerson Public School for the first three grades, then, for the rest of their elementary and for the first three years of their secondary education, St. Mary's Grade and High School, staffed by the Sisters of the Humility of Mary. After that, the family moved back to Spokane, where the boys attended Gonzaga Preparatory for their senior year, and from which they graduated in May 1948. They then attended Gonzaga University for a year, after which the two entered the Jesuit Novitiate of St. Francis Xavier at Sheridan, Oregon, on September 7, 1949. Independently of one another, after much prayer and thought, both concluded that they had a vocation to the priesthood in the Society of Jesus.

After completing the customary two-year noviceship, the Laudwein brothers spent an additional two years at Sheridan studying the classics and humanities. From 1953–56, they were at Mount St. Michael's in Spokane for philosophical studies. Joe spent the next three years at Gonzaga Preparatory, Spokane, teaching mainly mathematics, his specialty. "Trying to teach algebra to 44 not-so-eager young minds in the freshman 'F' class," he recalled many years later, "was an experience I did not soon forget." But, he found that those years at Gonzaga Prep, challenging as they were, engendered in him an interest in teaching high school mathematics.

From 1959–63, Joe made his theological studies at Regis College in Toronto, Ontario, Canada, finishing them with a Master's degree in Sacred Theology. On June 16, 1962, in St. Aloysius church, Spokane, he was ordained a priest. During the year 1963–64, he made his tertianship at Port Townsend, Washington.

During the year 1964–65, Father Joe taught mathematics at Jesuit High School in Portland, Oregon. In the course of that year, word came to him that there was an opening for a math teacher at Monroe Catholic High School in **Fairbanks, Alaska**. Was he interested? He wasn't sure. He knew Fairbanks to be a cold place, and he did not take well to cold. His brother, Father Jim, was already in Fairbanks.

Father Joseph E. Laudwein, S.J. *BR-897955.*

Father Joe called him and asked his opinion. "Come," he was told, "you'll love it!" In September 1965, Father Joe found himself in Fairbanks, teaching math and Religion at Monroe High.

Teaching at Monroe was for Father Joe "a rewarding experience, not just because of the receptiveness of the students, but also because of the opportunity to work closely with members of the **Jesuit Volunteer Corps**." He found their generosity, enthusiasm, and dedication "an inspiration."

During his first four years at Monroe, Father Joe continued his study of mathematics by enrolling in a summer program, sponsored by the National Science Foundation, at Seattle University in Seattle, Washington. At the end of his fourth summer in the program, he had his Master's degree in mathematics.

After 15 years at Monroe—"good, rewarding years," in his words, "even the few spent in administration"—Father Joe decided it was time for him "to look in other directions." He was given a sabbatical year at the Jesuit School of Theology in Berkeley, California, to help him discern future ministry.

As of August 15, 1981, Father Joe found himself Superior of St. Mary's Mission, **Andreafsky**, and teacher of mathematics. In July 1982, he became pastor of Immaculate Conception parish in Fairbanks, a post he held until July 1987. At the end of his tenure as pastor of Immaculate Conception, he was praised by his General Superior, Father James

A. **Sebesta**, S.J., for maintaining, in spite of difficulties and frustrations arising from problems in the parish, "a constant, responsible, and thoughtfully pastoral presence in the parish."

In July 1987, Father Joe was appointed pastor of Our Lady of Sorrows parish in **Delta Junction** and of Holy Rosary parish in **Tok**. As such, he ministered also to the people of **Eagle**. With joy, on September 17, 1989, he witnessed the dedication of the new church in Delta Junction.

In 1994, after logging countless miles on Alaska's highways, Father Joe was assigned back to Fairbanks, there to serve as Catholic chaplain at Fairbanks Memorial Hospital and as a minister to inmates in the Fairbanks Correctional Center. Given his kindly and gentle nature, and the "easy and sensitive way he deals with individuals," he was ideally suited for those ministries. That same year, 1994, he began to serve also as visiting priest to **Tanana**.

For years, Father Joe was a Consultor to a succession of General Superiors of the Jesuits in Alaska. In 1987, he became a member of the Diocesan Marriage Tribunal as a Defender of the Bond. On November 11, 1999, he was appointed Superior of the Fairbanks Jesuit community.

In contrast to his twin brother, Father Jim—an outgoing, athletic type—Father Joe was a quiet, stay-at-home type of man, happy in his room, relaxing occasionally by playing a game of solitaire. But, at any hour of day or night, he was ready for any emergency.

As of the year 2004, Father Joe was still serving as visiting priest to Tanana, as Catholic chaplain at Fairbanks Memorial Hospital, as a minister to the Fairbanks Correctional Center, as Superior of the Fairbanks Jesuit community, and as a member of the Diocesan Marriage Tribunal.

LEMIRE, Brother Alphonsus, S.J.

Little is known of Alphonsus Lemire's early life. He was born on September 28, 1858, and entered the French-Canadian Province of the Society of Jesus on July 30, 1883. On August 9, 1908, he landed in **Nome**, where he was to spend all his Alaskan years. He made several trips up to **Marys Igloo** to help Father Joseph **Bernard**, S.J., with building projects. Father Bernard described him as "a first class carpenter." Brother Lemire was also musically gifted. According to the Nome diarist, he was the "director and mainstay of the singing." On May 10, 1913, Brother Lemire was operated on in the Nome hospital. "A case of tuberculosis" was the finding. The operation was termed "successful." He sang again in the choir two weeks later. However, his health problems were not at an end. In mid-August of that year, he sailed for Seattle. There, in Providence Hospital, he died on September 27, 1913. He lies buried in the Jesuit cemetery at Mount St. Michael's, Spokane, Washington.

LEVASSEUR, Father William G., S.J.

William G. Levasseur was born in Quebec, Canada, on August 12, 1876. He entered the Jesuit novitiate at Los Gatos, California, on July 28, 1904. After completing his two-year noviceship, he spent two more years at Los Gatos studying the classics and humanities. He made his philosophical studies at Gonzaga College, Spokane, Washington, from 1908–11. During the years 1911–14, he taught at Los Angeles College, Los Angeles, California. From 1914–18, he studied theology in Montreal, Canada. He was ordained a priest on July 25, 1917. His tertianship he made at Los Gatos, 1918–19.

After spending a year at St. Leo's parish in Tacoma, Washington, Father Levasseur served as the Father Minister at the Los Gatos novitiate from 1920–24. The years 1924–31 saw him ministering among the Indian people of Montana. From 1931–45, he was stationed in **Juneau**, **Alaska**, where he was pastor of the parish and Chancellor of the Vicariate of Alaska. While in Juneau, he routinely gave talks over radio station KINY. He became a U.S. citizen in Juneau on April 11, 1934.

It was Father Levasseur—described by historian Wilfred P. Schoenberg, S.J., as "a pious dreamer, but *French*"—who conceived what Father Leo J. Robinson, Provincial of the Oregon Province from 1942–48, called "the fantastic idea of erecting a national **Shrine** to St. Teresa on an island some twenty-three miles distant from Juneau by car." It took ten years, before Father Levasseur saw his dream realized. Shortly after his arrival in Juneau in 1930, he filed for five acres of land at the shrine site. The new chapel at the shrine complex was ded-

Father William G. Levasseur, S.J.
JOPA-1067.01.

icated on October 26, 1941. From 1938–45, there was a "St. Terese, Alaska" post office at the shrine. Father Levasseur was its first postmaster.

After Father Levasseur left Juneau in 1945, he served on the Indian missions in Montana. Then, in poor health, he spent the last three years of his life at Mount St. Michael's, Spokane, where he died on October 6, 1957. He lies buried in the Jesuit cemetery at Mount St. Michael's.

LEVITRE, Father J. Albert

J. Albert "Al" Levitre was born on December 13, 1949, to J. Albert Levitre, Sr., and Joan Gorlaski Levitre, in Woonsocket, Rhode Island. There he attended public schools from kindergarten through high school. He graduated from high school in June 1968. From July 1968 to June 1971, he served in the U.S. Army as a clarinetist in Army bands stationed at Fort Devens, Massachusetts, and Fort Richardson, **Alaska**. With hopes of making a career of music, he entered the Army band program. The two years at Fort Richardson gave him his first exposure to Alaska. "I really found myself attracted to the state then," he wrote years later.

While in the Army, Al began to think, for the first time in his life, about becoming a priest. Accordingly, after leaving the Army, he began studies at St. John's College Seminary in Camarillo, Califor-

nia, for the priesthood in the Diocese of Phoenix, all the while aware that he would eventually change to another diocese. After three semesters at St. John's, from September 1971 to December 1972, he decided to leave, "NOT," as he wrote, "because I no longer felt called to the priesthood, but because of politics. Another seminarian and I got actively involved in the George McGovern presidential campaign on campus, which didn't sit well with most of our classmates. The atmosphere that this engendered was anything but healthy toward this seminarian and me, even after the election was over. For this reason I decided to leave, assured that at some future time I would resume seminary studies and eventually be ordained a priest."

In the summer of 1973, Al began attending Northern Arizona University in Flagstaff, graduating from there in May 1975 with an undergraduate degree in secondary education. At this time, recalling his love affair with Alaska during his two-year stint at Fort Richardson, he still had his sights set on Alaska, hoping now to go there as a teacher, even as a volunteer teacher, preferably in a Catholic high school. Monroe Catholic High School in **Fairbanks** turned out to be the one school that offered him the opportunity for which he was looking. After being screened through the **Jesuit Volunteer Corps** and becoming a member thereof, he taught at Monroe during the school years of 1975–76 and 1976–77.

While Al was at Monroe, his interest in resuming studies for the priesthood "rekindled." During his second year, after reading materials from many different Orders, Congregations, and Societies, he decided to apply to enter the California Franciscans. However, "Just as I was about to fill out the application form," he wrote, "I found myself facing an important question: 'How important is it for me to be in Alaska?' It didn't take me long to realize that my love for northern Alaska and its people had grown to the point where this was now home." For him to serve in northern Alaska meant, in those days, doing so either as a Jesuit or as a diocesan priest. Seeing that, at the time, there was still only one incardinated diocesan priest in the Diocese of Fairbanks, the challenge to help establish a strong diocesan presbyterate there had great appeal for him. He approached Robert L. **Whelan**, S.J., Bishop of Fairbanks at the time, about being accepted as a priest candidate for the Fairbanks diocese. He was accepted. In the fall of 1977, he began a three-year program of theological studies at Weston School of Theology in Cambridge, Massachusetts.

During the summers of 1978 and '79, seminarian Al did volunteer work at radio station **KNOM**, in **Nome**, where he was "a tremendous help in radio and in the parish." During the summer of 1979, he was ordained to the diaconate, "right in Nome, the first Catholic deacon ever to be ordained there." On May 31, 1980, J. Albert Levitre, having successfully completed his preparation for the priesthood, and having received his Master of Divinity degree, was ordained a priest at Most Holy Trinity parish in Phoenix, Arizona, by Bishop Whelan. Within a month after his ordination, now known as "Father Al," he found himself at Sacred Heart Cathedral parish, Fairbanks, to begin two years of priestly ministry as associate pastor.

On September 9, 1982, Bishop Whelan officially appointed Father Al and Father David M. **Fitz-Patrick** co-pastors of Sacred Heart Cathedral parish. They were formally installed by him as such on October 3rd. This marked the first time that diocesan priests alone were in full charge of that parish. The two served as co-pastors for two years.

In 1984, Father Al was assigned pastor of the "Railbelt"—the communities strung out for 110 miles along the Parks Highway and the Alaska Railroad from **Nenana** all the way to Cantwell. Making Nenana his home base, he spent much time on the road, bringing the Mass and Sacraments to Catholic in the various communities. In addition to tending to the people of Nenana, he provided pastoral ministry also for those at Clear Air Force Station, at **Healy**, at Denali National Park, and at Cantwell. As a "circuit-riding, railbelt missionary," he logged roughly 25,000 miles annually.

As of July 1, 1988, Father Al found himself back at Sacred Heart Cathedral parish, this time as Rector thereof. For his first four years as Rector, he lived in a one-time family home on nearby Koyukuk Street, while Michael J. **Kaniecki**, S.J., Bishop of Fairbanks at the time, lived in a mobile home located in the woods a short walk from the Cathedral. In 1992, the two traded residences. In his secluded new home, Father Al had the company of his pet

bird to make cheerful noise. The clarinet of his younger days he had long since put aside. For years, birds were part of his hobbies. As a man inclined by nature to be prone to stress, he found relaxation in playing racquetball, in watching baseball games on television (especially the Boston Red Sox), in wilderness hiking, and in jogging. He ran Fairbanks' grueling Equinox Marathon a number of times, running it once well under five hours. But, his main "hobby," he made it known, was, of course, his priestly ministry.

On September 1, 1995, Father Al arrived in **North Pole**, to begin a seven-year term there as pastor of St. Nicholas parish. Before him, the Paulist Fathers had cared for that parish. "This is a new page in the history of the parish," he stated in an interview held shortly after he came to North Pole. As pastor, he hoped to enable the lay people to "take responsibility for what the Church means to them." Ever ecumenically minded, from the outset of his North Pole pastorate, he fostered good relations with other local pastors. For a time, he was President of the Tanana Valley Conference of Churches.

When Father Al began his stay at North Pole, he expressed the hope that it would be a long one. It lasted seven years. Near the end of it, he could write, "My 22 years of priesthood have been immensely blessed by the good Lord, everywhere I have served."

Up to this time, all Father Al's priestly ministry had been in the cities of Fairbanks and North Pole, and along the Railbelt. In addition to the normal duties incumbent upon him as a parish priest in an urban setting, he had been involved, in the course of over two decades, also in prison ministry, Stephen ministry, Retrouvaille ministry, and Cursillo. "All of this," he wrote, "has incredibly enriched my priesthood." However, his life of urban ministry was about to come to an end.

In the summer of 2002, Father Al was assigned to what for him was almost a radically new type of ministry, a ministry that he anticipated would take him out of his "comfort zone." "But," he wrote, "I welcome that, hoping for continued growth personally and in my priesthood." He was assigned to **Galena** and to its dependent missions of **Koyukuk**, **Nulato**, and **Huslia**. He was now away from road systems. Travel between villages would be by bush plane; by open skiff with outboard motor, when the Yukon was open; and by snowmachine in winter.

It should come as no surprise to anyone acquainted with Father Al, that it did not take him long to make the transition from urban, white ministry to village, Native ministry; and to adjust to a new culture and to a new lifestyle. On February 4, 2003, he wrote to Father Louis L. **Renner**, S.J.,

> Greetings from Galena on the middle Yukon River! Just returned here yesterday after spending a week in Huslia. All in all, this assignment is agreeing with me. I actually had my first snow-go trip on the Yukon a few weeks ago, with Brother Justin [Huber, O.F.M.], downriver 50 miles to Nulato, then returning solo a few days later. A wonderful experience!

In August 2003, Father Levitre asked to be freed of the Galena assignment. In September, 2003, he became a member of the St. Michael's Community in St. Louis, Missouri, "to deal with some personal health issues." He left the active ministry as a priest late in the year 2004.

61

LINSSEN, Father Paul H., S.J.

Paul H. Linssen was born in Maastricht, Netherlands, on October 6, 1919. On September 7, 1939, he entered the novitiate of the Netherlands Province of the Society of Jesus at Mariendaal, Grave, Netherlands—but, because he hoped to serve in **Alaska** one day, as a member applied to the Oregon Province. He made his philosophical studies in Nijmegen, where he also taught school at Canisius College for two years, 1945–47. He arrived in the United States in 1947. From 1947–51, he made his theological studies at Alma College, Los Gatos, California. He was ordained a priest on June 17, 1950, in San Francisco. After making his tertianship at Drongen (Tronchiennes), Belgium, 1951–52, he went to Alaska. For his first two years in the North, he was stationed at **Holy Cross Mission**. During his second year, he visited **Paimiut** and **Shageluk**. He had a new church at this latter village well underway by the summer of 1954, before he was assigned to the lower Yukon. He made **Hamilton** his headquarters for the year 1954–55, and **Chaneliak** for

Father Paul H. Linssen, S.J. *JOPA-1068.02.*

the following year. Out of these two stations he visited other missions dependent on them.

In 1956, Father Linssen joined Father Paul C. **Deschout**, S.J., at **Tununak** on Nelson Island. In addition to carrying out the routine duties of a priest at Tununak and its dependent stations, **Nightmute** and **Chefornak**, he studied the Central Yup'ik Eskimo language. A first-rate photographer, he also continued to take very fine photographs of the people and places he served. He was now in the prime of life as a missionary priest, and there was every reason to believe that he would continue on to a highly successful career as such in the Nelson Island area.

"On September 16th," begins the letter Father Henry G. **Hargreaves**, S.J., wrote to Bishop Francis D. **Gleeson**, S.J., Vicar Apostolic of Northern Alaska at the time, in October 1960,

> in the morning, Fr. Linssen and a pilot Bernard Nevak, of Chefornak, left **Bethel** for downriver. It was a calm, clear day, and the weather remained the same for several days. His boat, the *Klutch*, was loaded heavily with stove oil plus some drums of kerosene and gas, intended for Fr. Deschout at Tununak. On top of the drums was a load of lumber.
>
> Some men who came upriver the next day or two mentioned seeing the *Klutch* on sandbars. Other than that the boat appeared in good shape. They should have reached Kwigillingok one or two days after leaving Bethel. On the 20th and 21st, heavy winds, with gusts up to 40 and 50 miles per hour, hit the coast, and for the next two weeks the weather was very unsteady.

Pilots were asked to check on the *Klutch*. On the 23rd, Don Murphy, flying a Cessna 180, sighted it.

The boat was abandoned, on a sandbar in the open water at the mouth of the Kuskokwim River. The sandbar is ten miles from Kwigillingok, toward Bethel, and about four miles from shore. The boat, empty even of freight, had anchors off the bow and stern. The water from the tides could fill and empty the boat through the open seams. Murphy landed near it, found nothing. Another plane also landed. This time a monstrance was found in the bottom of the boat, still in good shape, and some Stations of the Cross, all intended for Tununak.

During the next three days, planes searched the coast and bay, but found no trace of persons or debris. Stormy weather prevented searchings at various intervals. On October 3rd, the teacher at Platinum, while walking along the beach, spotted a body floating near the shore. It was recognized, but with difficulty, due to immersion and stone bruises, as that of Fr. Linssen. The men at Platinum made a coffin. Next day the body was shipped to Bethel. Requiem Mass was offered on October 5th in a packed church. Father was buried in the Catholic cemetery in Bethel. R.I.P.

LITTLE DIOMEDE

Some 50 miles below the Arctic Circle, and exactly in the middle of Bering Strait, a 57-mile wide band of water that separates the two continents of North America and Asia, lie two immense crags of granite rock, Big Diomede and Little Diomede Islands. Big Diomede was "discovered" by Vitus Bering in 1728, and named for St. Diomede, a Russian Orthodox saint, whose feast day it was. Separated by the International Date Line, Big Diomede belongs to Russia, Little Diomede to the United States. For countless generations the two islands, less than three miles apart, served as steppingstones between Siberia and Alaska for the Inupiat Eskimos living on them and acting as middlemen for the trade that flowed freely between the two continents. During the post-World War II "cold war," beginning in 1947, an invisible, impenetrable iron curtain hung between the two islands. This came down around 1970 with the easing of tensions between the Soviet Union and the United States, the "détente." Since then, people have again moved rather freely between the two islands and the two continents.

Little Diomede Island—bleak, lashed almost year-round by wind and wave, remote to western civilization—rises abruptly out of the icy blue-green waters of Bering Strait to a plateau 1308 feet above sea level. The flanks of the island are near perpendicular cliffs on all sides except the southwest side, where a massive rock slide created a more gentle slope. It is on this slope that the Eskimo village, noted on maps as "Ignaluk," but referred to generally simply as "Little Diomede," is located. Below the village, there is a narrow, 300-yard long "beach" of wave-worn boulders that serves as a boat-landing place. Even this is covered by breakers in stormy weather. The village, though threatened by boulders from above and the sea from below, has stood on its present site since pre-historic times. Earlier generations of Little Diomeders lived in semi-subterranean dugouts. During the twentieth century, frame houses gradually became the norm. In the year 2000, there were 146 people living on Little Diomede. Until the advent of the helicopter, the island was inaccessible during times of the fall freeze-up and the spring breakup. For days and days, adverse weather conditions still often strand people hoping to get to or off the island.

The mainland Eskimos call the Diomeders "the people of the open water," the "open water" being the ever-shifting leads in the ever-moving pack ice (the "ice that never sleeps") that chokes Bering Strait from October to July. It is in this open water, in these leads, and on these ice fields that great herds of migrating walrus abound. From these marine mammals come the meat, oil, skins, and ivory so basic to the Diomede way of life. It is these readily available walrus, along with the seal and the ugruk, that have kept the Diomeders on their seemingly inhospitable island up to the present day.

In addition to the riches of the sea, the island itself is a source of substantial quantities of food, despite its apparent bareness. On the island proper, the people gather the "Eskimo potato," an edible tuber, and various greens, which are eaten fresh or preserved in seal oil or water to supplement seal and walrus meat during the winter. In summer, birds and their eggs are also taken in great quantities. Crab, tomcod, and bullheads are caught through holes in the ice in winter.

Little Diomede Island was first visited by a Catholic missionary in 1913, when Father Bellarmine **Lafortune**, S.J., spent a very short time

(*left*) St. Jude's Church, Little Diomede Island. *MK.*

(*below*) Ignaluk, the Inupiat Eskimo village on Little Diomede Island. St. Jude's Church is the building at top center. *MK.*

there in June. In August 1916, Father **Hubert A. Post**, S.J., visited the island briefly. By this time a fair number of Little Diomeders were already Catholic, having been brought into the Church by Father Lafortune during their annual summers in **Nome**. In the summer of 1932, he was on the island from July 12th to August 28th. He spent that time instructing the people and converting an old house owned by the Church into a chapel and living quarters. Conditions on Little Diomede he found "simply dismal. The sight of our house made my heart go into my boots. Built long ago [by some-

one else for other purposes], it had never been occupied. The windows were covered with gunny sacks, the original windows having been broken by the snow and the youngsters. The inside was uncovered and black. No stairway of any kind led to the door, which is about 4 feet from the ground. Entering the house was a good gymnastic."

Father **Thomas P. Cunningham**, S.J., went to the island in October 1936. It was he who finished the church, dedicated to St. Jude, and the living quarters begun over a year earlier by the Eskimos using lumber given them for that purpose by the priests

A final resting place among the rocks above Ignaluk, the Inupiaq Eskimo village on Little Diomede Island. *LR.*

in Nome. Father Cunningham was the first resident priest on the island. Between 1936 and 1947, he spent a total of eight years there. After that, he visited the island at irregular intervals until 1955, the year Father Vsevolod **Roshko**, a priest of the Eastern Rite, began to reside there for three years. During the following 20 years, priests from either Nome or **Kotzebue** visited Little Diomede at more or less regular intervals. Among the more notable and most popular of these was Father Harold J. **Greif**, S.J., who visited the island out of Nome during most of the 1970s.

On May 2, 1954, Bishop Francis D. **Gleeson**, S.J., visited Little Diomede. He was the first Major Superior to do so. The **Little Sisters of Jesus** had a fraternity on the island from the mid-1950s to the mid-1990s.

In the summer of 1975, Sister Marie Teresa **Boulet**, O.P., Sister Judy Tralnes, C.S.J.P., and Father Louis L. **Renner**, S.J., were on the island. Father Renner spent three weeks, attending to pastoral needs and doing field work for his projected biography of Father Cunningham. The Sisters, as catechists, remained five weeks. The three were warmly received by the Diomeders, thanks to the great, and well-deserved, popularity enjoyed on the island by Father Greif and the Little Sisters of Jesus.

In the summer of 1978, Father Thomas F. **Carlin**, S.J., began a five-year stay on Little Diomede. That summer, he and Jesuit Lay Brothers Ignatius J. **Jakes** and James J. Lee built a new church–residence. After Father Carlin left the island in 1983, it was visited by priests out of Nome. Except for the year 1990–91, when Father Joseph G. **Stolz** resided on the island, this continued to be the case, as of up to the year 2004.

Ursuline Sister Cecilia Huber arrived on Little Diomede on March 19, 1990. She spent four weeks there teaching catechism and preparing First Communicants.

A chronological sequence of discontinuous entries made by various hands in the Little Diomede diary from October 1936 to 1985 weaves the following rich and colorful tapestry of day-to-day life at that island mission:

~

In October 1936 the first priest to winter on Little Diomede Island arrived with most of the Natives on the *North Star*. Unloading began on Sunday Oct. 16th . . . The natives were waiting for some good weather to go and do some trading on Big Diomede Island . . . the children surely need instruction—and it must be in Eskimo . . . two boats finally got away to Big Diomede. I bought a few yards of dark cloth for a curtain before the altar . . . almost a continuous seven-day blizzard . . . Three adult and two infant baptisms today

... Straits choked full of ice and everyone hunting with good results ... Some Siberians wintering on Big Diomede came here. All visited me ... This diary is not any ways bulging out with news, but nothing of great importance has happened beyond catching a whale and the visit of Fr. **Ménager** and Jack Herman via aeroplane ... About Nov. 14 we had terrific blizzard storm which endangered the first row of houses. None of the old natives could remember a storm quite as bad ... Quite a few walrus and a polar bear have been caught to date ... Four boats made trips to East Cape and Uelen, Siberia. The people were well treated by the natives and the Russian Officials ... I have arranged to teach school for three hours a day. I live in the schoolhouse ... The whale hunting is more or less of a gesture they go through every spring ... the children do not differentiate between day and night and it is difficult to get them for catechism ... in the spring of 1951 Fr. [George E.] **Carroll**, S.J., of **Kotzebue** spent some time here and did excellently instructing the people ... May 2, 1954, the Bishop came this morning around 11 A.M. and remained until 4 P.M. This is the first time any major superior of any kind has visited Diomede ... The French nuns left today. They made an excellent impression here ... the landing was hard, and not all the baggage was unloaded ... I live in the kitchen, and made of the main room a winter chapel ... I went to visit the houses and was very much impressed by the way they keep them clean ... Old man Ayapana came up and gave me a big crab ... since the surface is everywhere 2 inches of ice, walking is very risky ... Had a grand time with the catechism children. Such lovely creatures! ... an inner irresistible compulsion drives them to follow the oogruk and walrus ... a killing beastly north wind ... walrus hunting takes the older boys and the birds take the little ones ... people are most friendly when you visit them ... They eat clams out of walrus stomachs ... There was a very lively Eskimo Dance in the community hall.

8, 46, 72, 91, 97, 115

LITTLE SISTERS of Jesus of Brother Charles of Jesus

Under date of August 8, 1952, Father **Cornelius K. Murphy**, S.J., wrote in the **Nome** house diary: "A French priest and two French Sisters of the Congregation of the Little Brothers [*sic*] of Jesus arrived in Nome to look over the prospects of beginning a convent here." The French priest was Father Voillaume, the founder of the Congregation of the Little Brothers of Jesus. The two Sisters were Little Sister Magdeleine and Little Sister Jeanne. They belonged to the Congregation of the Little Sisters of Jesus of Brother Charles of Jesus, a group founded in 1939 at Touggourt in the Sahara in Algeria. On August 25th, Father Murphy wrote: "Little Sister Yvonne Marie of Jesus, Little Sister Georgette and Little Sister Andrée Binit arrive in Nome from **Fairbanks** to take up residence in Nome." According to historical records, it is Little Sisters Georgette and Yvonne Marie who should be recognized as the first members of the Nome Fraternity, as Andrée Binit left Nome the following January to finish her novitiate.

On December 2, 1952, Father Murphy, in a letter to Bishop Francis D. **Gleeson**, S.J., who was "very happy to have the Little Sisters in Nome," wrote: "To my mind these Little Sisters are grand and not afraid of any situation. They are liked very much universally throughout the town."

Father Jules M. **Convert**, S.J., born in France and missionary priest in **Alaska**, is given credit for bringing about the presence of the Little Sisters in Alaska. For some years he had been corresponding with Little Sister Georgette, a former classmate of his who had become a member of the Congregation of the Little Sisters. In light of this correspondence, the foundress of the Congregation, Sister Magdeleine of Jesus, was inspired to establish a community among the Eskimo people of Alaska.

In keeping with the spirit of the Congregation of sharing the living conditions of poor minority groups, the Little Sisters, in 1954, built themselves a simple little tarpaper-covered frame house, with a chapel, among the King Islanders living in **King Island** Village about a mile east of Nome. They shared, to a large extent, the subsistence lifestyle of the people, so much so that soon the Nome and King Island Eskimos adopted them and told them "You are one of us." But, also in keeping with the norms of their Congregation, namely, that the Little Sisters be self-supporting by doing salaried manual work in a milieu of ordinary workers, one or two of them generally worked for a salary. As the years went by, and replacement Little Sisters came, they took on different types of work. One worked as a nurse's aide, another in a dry-cleaning business and Laundromat. Some did house cleaning, or were employed in stores, or as caregivers. Another did some clerical work. In keeping with a basic charisma of the

(*left*) Little Sisters of Jesus Damiene and Nobuko making a crabbing hole i the ice near Little Diomede Island. Bi Diomede Island is in the background. *Courtesy of the Little Sisters of Jesus.*

(*opposite*) In King Island village—a short distance east of Nome—in 1961 Little Sisters of Jesus Solange Mae of Jesus (in back) and Yvonne Mary of Jesus pose with King Island women and children in front of the home of the Little Sisters. *JOPA-408.4.01.*

Congregation, a ministry of prayerful presence and friendship in Christ poor, the Little Sisters, though an integral part of the Nome parish, never formally served as parish staff members.

In November 1974, a violent storm quite literally destroyed the whole of Nome's King Island Village, the house of the Little Sisters along with it. The people, including the Little Sisters, moved into somewhat scattered houses in Nome proper. This meant, to the regret of the Little Sisters, that they no longer had the close physical contact with the people that they had had, when all were still living together in King Island Village. However, in the summer of 1979, they began to join the King Islanders at Woolley Lagoon, 37 miles northwest of Nome, where the King Islanders had their spring and summer hunting and fish camp. Little Sisters Alice Ann and Monique Jeanne were the first Little Sisters at Woolley Lagoon. There they built a tent frame and set up a tent to live in. Little Sister Alice Ann spent several summers at the camp, along with one or other of the Little Sisters living in Nome at the time. The Little Sisters also put up a second tent to serve as a small chapel, where they could keep the Blessed Sacrament. Then, in the early 1990s, as more cabins were replacing the tents, they them-

selves built a small wooden cabin. At Woolley Lagoon they shared the Eskimo lifestyle. They fished and gathered greens, and shared the fruits of the men's hunts. Occasionally, priests came from Nome to offer Mass in the tent chapel or in some other tent or cabin, as well as in the community hall.

In the course of the Congregation's half century in Nome, a considerable number of Little Sisters served at various times as members of that Fraternity. Little Sister Odette of Jesus first arrived in Nome in 1956, and Little Sister Damiene Josephe of Jesus in 1958. Though having been stationed elsewhere at times, they were the ones to have the good fortune to be stationed in Nome in the year 2002, when the Little Sisters celebrated the Golden Jubilee of their Congregation's first coming to Alaska, to Nome.

Under date of April 9, 1954, Father **Thomas P. Cunningham**, S.J., wrote in the **Little Diomede** Island house diary: "Two Sisters of the *Petites Soeurs de Jésus* came over for a few days' visit with hopes of being here permanently. At their own insistence they are living in an Eskimo house in the village and are doing very well. They adapted themselves immediately to Eskimo life and all the people are fond of them and help them." On the 15th, in a letter to Father James U. **Conwell**, S.J., he wrote:

The nuns are here, two of them. On their arrival, I offered them my house which they naturally refused, so I rigged up an Eskimo house in the village, complete with seal-oil lamp, skylight, and I even contemplated training a couple of dogs to lie in the tunnel entrance. The nuns have made a great hit with the people and mixed in with Eskimo life very well. They are seriously thinking of making a permanent home here, and I have begun negotiations for a large Eskimo-type house with partitions spacing off chapel–dormitory. The more I see of these nuns, the more I am in favor of them.

In 1954, the Little Sisters established a permanent Fraternity on Little Diomede Island. In 1955, they bought an old semi-subterranean Eskimo type of house. This kind of house needed to be rebuilt periodically. In 1958, they demolished the old house and began to build themselves a small frame house. It took them three short summers to complete this. By that time, more and more of the Natives were building and moving into above-ground frame houses. The first two Little Sisters on Diomede were Little Sisters Yvonne Mary and Solange Mae (Marie). The Little Sisters who spent the most time on the island afterwards were: Josephe Alice, Monique Jeanne, Damiene Josephe, and Clara Nobuko. Others were there also, but for short stays only.

On Little Diomede, too, as at Woolley Lagoon, the Little Sisters shared in the Eskimo subsistence lifestyle. They accepted gifts of walrus and seal meat offered them after the men had had a successful hunt. They themselves fished through holes in the ice for various kinds of fish and crabs. With the women, they gathered greens growing on the island. Wild birds and their eggs also were part of their diet. From the women, they learned the art of skinning a seal, and how to care for the meat and skin. They also learned how to sew skins and do beadwork. In the spring and fall, they were busy sewing white covers for the men's hunting parkas, and replacing zippers. After it became a law that only Native people could sell objects made from skins, the Little Sisters earned a little money by knitting socks and mittens, and making nets to catch birds. While on the island, the Little Sisters also helped women prepare children for their first Holy Communion.

When the Little Sisters first went to Little Diomede, an invisible, but impenetrable, "iron curtain" separated not only the Soviet Union from the United States, but also Little Diomede Island from Soviet Big Diomede Island less than five miles across the waters of Bering Strait. The curtain dropped in 1947, separating East from West, and, in some cases, family from family. Out of the window of their new frame home, the Little Sisters could look over to Big Diomede, to the Soviet Union, to Asia, and into tomorrow. For almost a quarter of a century, there was no contact between the two worlds. For a short time, in 1971, a kind of détente between the USSR and the USA made itself felt also on the Diomede Islands. Between the two islands, on the ice, contact was again established between hunters living on Little Diomede and Siberian hunters living temporarily on Big Diomede. During the following years, contact between East and West became more frequent, and more friendly, to the extent that gifts were exchanged. Little Sisters Josephe Alice and Clara Nobuko were privileged to witness this easing of tensions, and to be recipients of gifts from their Siberian neighbors. "It was a moving experience for us to get something from Siberia." wrote Little Sister Josephe Alice. The Sisters received "ten clothes pins, two red ones and eight orange ones." When Father Louis L. **Renner**, S.J., was on Little Diomede in the summer of 1975, he saw the clothes pins clipped in an honored place above the window facing Big Diomede. In 1989, an official détente between the USSR and the USA became a political reality, and thereafter any visitors from Siberia or the Chukchi Peninsula were warmly welcomed, even if for only a short stay, into Little Diomede homes.

After the winter of 1993–94, the Little Sisters ended their year-round presence on Little Diomede Island, but their ministry did not stop there. They continued to spend a few months on the island whenever possible. As of the year 2004, that was still their practice. The Little Sisters, especially Little Sister Damiene Josephe, who spent 12 years on the island, continued to stay in touch with Little Diomede people visiting or moving to Nome.

In 1960, Little Sister Jacqueline, responsible for the region of Alaska at the time, opened a third Alaskan Fraternity, in Fairbanks, with Little Sisters Yvonne-Mary (Yvonne-Marie) and Solange Mae. At various times, different members of the Fairbanks Fraternity, braving the elements on bicycles, worked in the hospital, in a printing plant, and in a dry-cleaning business. For a short while, one of them was the secretary of a University of Alaska–Fairbanks professor. At the time, Fairbanks was Alaska's second most important population and transportation center. As such, it seemed the logical place for a Fraternity, since it would serve well both as a central gathering house for the Little Sisters in Alaska and as a place where they could fulfill their hopes of establishing relationships with other Alaska Native groups. These hopes, it turned out, were not meant to be realized.

However, after the Alaska pipeline was built, in the 1970s, **Anchorage** took on new importance as Alaska's number one city and transportation center. A large state of the art hospital for Alaska Native people was built there. In 1988, the Little Sisters decided to relocate from Fairbanks to Anchorage, in order more readily to keep in touch with Alaska Native friends from King Island and Little Diomede coming to Anchorage for medical care, or simply to make their homes in Anchorage. In Anchorage, too, the Little Sisters would meet Native peoples coming also from other parts of Alaska. Anchorage had the additional advantage of being more central for travel both within Alaska and travel to and from Alaska, making it easier for the Little Sisters in Alaska to get together for meetings, retreats, and the like.

Little Sisters Josephe Alice, Odette, and Yoshie started the Anchorage Fraternity. In Anchorage, as elsewhere, the Little Sisters took on full- or part-time jobs to earn a living. Serving in Anchorage, in the year 2002, when the Little Sisters celebrated the 50th anniversary of their presence in Alaska, were Little Sisters Monique Jeanne, Josephe Alice, Clara Nobuko, Alice Ann, Nirmala, Yoshie, and Solange Mae.

In 1959, Little Sister Yvonne-Mary became an American citizen, in Nome. In 1980, Little Sisters Damiene Josephe and Odette, too, became American citizens, in Fairbanks. Some years later, Little Sister Solange Mae did the same, in Anchorage.

As of the year 2004, six of the first Little Sisters to serve in Alaska were retired from salaried work. They continued, however, to live their lives of presence, friendship and prayer among the people, believing that such lives can be signs of hope and healing in a broken world. In their communities, the Little Sisters are often from different races, nationalities and backgrounds, a sign of their desire to bring unity and harmony among people and a witness to the unity for which Jesus prayed.

The village of Nazareth in the Holy Land is far removed from Alaskan places such as Nome, Little Diomede, Fairbanks, and Anchorage. For over half a century, however, the hidden life Jesus lived in Nazareth over 2000 years ago was brought into the lives of people living in these four Alaskan places by the Little Sisters of Jesus, inasmuch as they, in their daily lives, lived that hidden life of Jesus in Nazareth

LLORENTE, Father Segundo, S.J.

He was the only Spanish Jesuit ever to serve in **Alaska**. He was described in *Time* Magazine as "one of the most exciting things that ever hit the tundra." As a writer for the **Fairbanks** *Daily News-Miner*, he was described by its managing editor as "the best stringer we've got." He wrote voluminously about the Alaskan missions, was widely read throughout the Spanish-speaking world, yet none of his readers and admirers ever came forward to emulate him. He mastered the writings of the Spanish mystics, and was himself described as "an exuberant, joyous, modern-day card-carrying mystic." He was the first Roman Catholic priest to hold elected legislative office in a U.S. state. He served two terms in the Alaska State Legislature, and was honored by the Sixteenth Alaska Legislature with a special *In Memoriam* document. Renowned Trappist monk Thomas Merton described him as "a remarkable person, a sort of legend" in Alaska.

Segundo Llorente was born near León, Spain, on November 18, 1906, the oldest of nine children, seven boys and two girls. (Amando, one of his brothers, too, became a Jesuit.) During the years 1919–23, he attended the seminary of the Diocese of León. On June 16, 1923, he entered the Jesuit novitiate at Carrión de los Condes in Castile. He took his vows as a Jesuit on June 19, 1925. He spent another year at Carrión studying the classics before going to Salamanca for an additional year of classical studies. From 1927–30, he studied philosophy and sciences at Granada. On October 1, 1930, he arrived at Gonzaga University, Spokane, Washington, to learn English. He made his theological studies at St. Mary's, Kansas, from 1931–34. On June

24, 1934, he was ordained a priest. After another year of theological studies, at Alma College, Los Gatos, California, he—"a very cheerful, pleasant person," according to the **Akulurak** diarist—arrived at Akulurak, Alaska, on October 6, 1935.

St. Mary's Mission, Akulurak, was Father Llorente's first Alaskan assignment. He had volunteered for the Alaska Mission back in 1926. He spent two years at St. Mary's. During the year 1937–38, he made his tertianship at Port Townsend, Washington. From August 1938 to August 1941, he was stationed at **Kotzebue**. While there, from time to time, as airplane rides were offered him, he visited Candle and Deering. During the summer of 1939, he spent several months in **Nome** as substitute pastor. Along with his priestly work, he did much housecleaning and scrubbing down of walls. "I could hear every board," he wrote in the Nome house diary, "thank me for it." While in Nome, he had occasion to loan Father **Thomas P. Cunningham**, S.J.—just in from **Little Diomede** Island and penniless—"$50, to be paid back within the next 99 years."

As did other priests before and after him, so Father Llorente, too, found his Kotzebue years, despite the fact that he had there "a core of very loyal faithful," in many respects difficult ones. At the end of his stay in Kotzebue, he wrote in the Kotzebue house diary: "After three years of failure, I leave Kotzebue. Three things kept me from going insane: the tabernacle, the typewriter, and the catechism children. Thanks to these three I live happy and busy. The town is such as to freeze the ardor of St. Paul." His very last entry in the diary reads: "The priest who keeps his smile in this town and goes on with zeal and courage deserves to be canonized at once without any other miracles bearing evidence on the matter."

In reality, Father Llorente had good rapport, good social contact with the people of Kotzebue. He made it a point to visit every Catholic home at least twice a week. Adults came every Wednesday for instructions. Children came daily after school for catechism. As Kotzebue had no barber shop, he "learned to cut hair, after a fashion." He never charged for services, but he let it be known that, if a man was married, "one loaf of bread would be more than welcomed." If a man had no wife, "it was all on the house."

Especially during his earlier years in Alaska, Father Llorente, without his typewriter, by his own admission, would have "been lost, gone insane." He told Father Louis L. **Renner**, S.J., "If you are a writer, there is always something to write about." He had no sooner set foot in Alaska, than he began to write a steady stream of articles for the Spanish mission magazine *El Siglo de las Misiones* about everyday life as he experienced it. The articles, appearing in the course of over 30 years, were later reprinted in a series of books. These were never translated into English.

Around 1980, Dr. Theodore Mala—born in Kotzebue of a Russian father and an Eskimo mother, and having earned his M.D. in Mexico—hoped to translate one or other of the books. He translated a chapter from one of them and submitted it to Father Llorente as a sample of what he could do. Father Llorente, in turn, submitted it to Father Francis J. **Fallert**, S.J., General Superior at the time of Jesuits in Alaska. "Well, frankly, Segundo," wrote Father Fallert, on February 2, 1982, after reading it, "I was appalled by what you have written. I feel it is a real caricature of the Eskimos. It is so completely different from the Eskimos as I have known them." Father Fallert then grants that the Eskimo people did undergo rapid cultural change. "My real concern," he continued in his letter, "is that this kind of writing translated into English where our young Eskimos will read it will only result in harm to your own reputation, and you'll be held up to ridicule." Father William J. **Loyens**, S.J., professional anthropologist, to whom Father Fallert had submitted the chapter in question for his opinion, found Father Llorente's writing "ethnocentric, culturally demeaning, inaccurate, generalizing." Father Fallert urged Father Llorente to put an immediate end to the whole translation project.

Four days after Father Llorente received the above letter, he responded: "I thank you heartily for your letter. I appreciate your concern and your brotherly advice." He then went on to put the whole matter into context: "I arrived in the summer of 1935 and I began to write immediately. I was then 28, quite impressionable. I was told that if I did not write immediately, the novelty would soon wear out and I would find nothing interesting to say. Perhaps that

was an imprudent decision. I cannot tell." His earlier writing, he adds, "carried with it nuances of humor and compassion. Readers laughed and wept." However, both as an observer and a writer he gradually underwent a change.

> As the years went by, my experience became richer; so I modified a good many of my previous observations. Finally I arrived at the day when I was sort of scared of much of what I had written and wished that I had never written it. Then and there I decided that my Spanish writings would NEVER be translated into English, at least while I lived.

Father Llorente's writings continued to remain in their original Spanish. He had been "very much upset" at the prospect of their being translated into English. He concludes: "So I was at peace with myself, knowing that my writings would never be translated, not because what I wrote was false, but because it would be imprudent to print them *now*."

When fellow Jesuits, who knew of Father Llorente's earlier articles in Spanish, heard that he had written a book of his memoirs, they had misgivings, sincerely hoped that the memoirs would not resemble the articles. Very pleasant, then, was their surprise, when they read *Memoirs of a Yukon Priest*, published by Georgetown U. Press in 1990, the year after his death. The humor and compassion are there. Historical accuracy is there. There is nothing that could possibly give offense to anyone.

How *Memoirs* came about is rather interesting. Around 1980, Father Llorente was encouraged by Father Renner, and by Fathers Clifford A. Carroll, S.J., and Richard J. Sisk, S.J.—Oregon Province archivists at the time—to write his life's story. In spite of his reluctance to do so, he, did, nevertheless, yield to their wishes. "I typed," he wrote in a June 1981 letter to Father Renner, "what I saw and what I heard in my many years in Alaska. I have no idea of what may become of said manuscript." The manuscript was a considerable disappointment to the three. It was flat, uninspired, uninspiring. It lacked the colorful, witty, sparkling, yet broad and deep, personality that was Father Llorente. The manuscript was filed in the Oregon Province Archives at Gonzaga University and forgotten. "Great, then," wrote Father Renner in his Foreword to *Memoirs*, was my surprise when in October 1989 John B. Breslin, S.J., of Georgetown University Press asked me if I would consider writing a Foreword to *Memoirs*. I was not sure what we were talking about and asked to see a copy of said *Memoirs*. Great again—and very pleasant—was my surprise, when I read what was a wholly new manuscript, written in the genuine, inimitable Llorente style: an outpour, a torrent of words rich in vivid concrete detail, saturated with personal opinions, reflections, observations.

From Father John J. Morse, S.J., Father Llorente's Religious Superior in Lewiston, Idaho, where Father Llorente was stationed at the time, it was learned that he spent long hours at the typewriter during the final months of his life. Who inspired him, what inspired him, drove him to produce a wholly new, a lengthy account of his forty years in Alaska, will never be known. His own brother, Father Amando Llorente, S.J., to whom he handed the finished manuscript in the summer of 1988, did not know. No secretaries, no re-writers, no proofreaders were involved. The manuscript was published as written. The book was very well received, so much so that it went through several re-printings. One reader of *Memoirs* was so "truly impressed with the simple sincerity of [Father Llorente's] manner and the life of self-sacrifice he led," that he made a donation of $25,000 to the Missionary Diocese of Fairbanks.

In his Preface to *Memoirs*, Father Llorente wrote: "I was encouraged by my friends to write these memories (and to tell it as it was). This book is written by memory. Here I tell what I saw and what I heard and what I did and what I read about the Land of the Midnight sun on those long winter nights when a book can save a man from going temporarily insane."

After his years at Kotzebue, Father Llorente was back again at Akulurak, from 1941–48, now as Superior. As he had done during his earlier two years at Akulurak, he continued to travel out of there to visit other villages in that district, among them **Hooper Bay** and **New Knock Hock**. He was not much of a dog driver, nor was he at all fluent in the Central Yup'ik Eskimo language. He, therefore, relied on Eskimo guides and interpreters. During his Akulurak years, he served also as spiritual director to Father **John P. Fox**, S.J., who chose him as such, because he was "the only pious guy in the neighborhood."

While at Akulurak, Father Llorente routinely regaled the boarding school boys and girls with stories. He was an excellent storyteller, dramatizing his stories with assumed voices and wild gestures. With his ghost stories, told with lights out, he evoked many a scream.

It was not Father Llorente the story-teller that visited the **Ursuline** Sisters in their community room at Akulurak. It was the medieval mystic. One of the Sisters, Lucy Daly, O.S.U., wrote to Father Renner: "I think the enthusiasm for reading Saint Theresa and Saint John of the Cross was more Father's enthusiasm, although we did enjoy his visits to our community room with the large volume of the Autobiography of Saint Theresa under his arm."

In the course of many years, many an Ursuline Sister received many a letter from Father Llorente. One of them said of them: "His letters are unique. He writes in a humorous way, but ticks off some very spiritual messages."

Father Llorente knew, too, how to entertain his fellow Alaskan Jesuits, not only with congenial conversation, but also with humorous stories and anecdotes. To Father Renner he described how he once had Father Paul C. **Deschout**, S.J., laughing so hard that the latter was down on all fours pounding the floor with his hands and with streams of tears flowing from his eyes.

From 1948–50, Father Llorente served on the Kuskokwim River, working in and out of **Bethel**. He found Bethel "quite agreeable." While there, he routinely visited the sick in the hospital. Eskimos from the Catholic villages were especially delighted to see him. If they died in Bethel, he would take care of the coffin and burial.

For the year 1950–51, Father Llorente was back once more at Akulurak. When St. Mary's Mission was moved from Akulurak to its new site on the **Andreafsky** River, on August 3, 1951, he moved to **Alakanuk**, where he held station until 1963. Out of Alakanuk, he visited also its dependent stations, among them: Akulurak, **Emmonak**, **Sheldon Point (Nunam Iqua)**, New Nock Hock, Kwiguk, and Fish Village. For winter travel, he again hired dogteams and drivers; for summer travel, he had his own skiff with a "15 hp kicker."

While stationed at Alakanuk, Father Llorente, in 1952, went to Mexico as a delegate from the Polar

Regions to a Congress in Monterrey. From there, he went to Mexico City for two months. His stay at Alakanuk proved to be his longest in one place of all his years in Alaska.

Father Llorente's Alakanuk years did not get off to auspicious beginnings. "The Yukon ice," he wrote in *Memoirs*, "had jammed just below the town of Alakanuk. The town had flooded. The current had cut a channel between the Catholic church and the rectory. The ice had pushed both buildings into the lake and both had disappeared. Where the church and rectory had stood, there was now nothing but mud." It was the spring flood of 1952 that carried off those buildings. Nevertheless, in spite of such inauspicious beginnings, he could, in later years, describe his Alakanuk years as "perhaps the happiest of my life."

In November 1960, Father Llorente made headlines across the nation—and history—when he was unanimously elected, without campaigning, by a write-in vote to serve in Alaska's newly formed House of Representatives. *Time* magazine immediately sent a reporter to Alakanuk to interview him. To the reporter, Father Llorente said: "It's a great testimony to the strength of American culture, when a Spaniard who is a Catholic priest is elected to the legislature by Eskimos." He had become a U.S. citizen in Nome on May 4, 1956, because he was "tired of being a foreigner." On May 20, 1981, at his request, he was officially transcribed to the Oregon Province.

Father Llorente had the somewhat reluctant "go ahead" to accept the verdict of his constituents from both the Father General in Rome and from his bishop, Francis D. **Gleeson**, S.J. Dermot **O'Flanagan**, Bishop of **Juneau** at the time, however, was opposed to having a priest in his diocese serving in public office. He forbade Father Llorente to serve as a priest in any public capacity. He did permit him to offer Mass, but only privately, and only early in the morning, in the Sisters' chapel in the hospital. But Bishop O'Flanagan was not a small, narrow-minded man. On March 6, 1961, in a letter to Bishop Gleeson, he wrote: "Father Segundo Llorente appears to be doing well. He is highly spoken of in town, is conducting himself in an excellent and priestly manner and it looks as proof that my fears about his coming to the Legislature were not too solidly founded. I am most happy to know that I was mistaken."

Father Llorente was the first Roman Catholic priest in the United States to hold elected office of that rank. He served two terms in the state legislature in Juneau, 1961–64. The people of his district wanted him to run for a third term, but he would not hear of it.

In 1963, Father Llorente made his first visit to his homeland since he had left it over 30 years earlier. There, by his own count, he "gave 600 talks and slept in 107 beds all over Spain."

Back in Alaska, he was substitute pastor of the Nome parish from September 1964 to November 1965, when he became assistant pastor of Immaculate Conception parish in **Fairbanks** for two years. He next spent three years as pastor in **Cordova**, from October 1967 to October 1970. In 1970, the Alaska Press Club voted him one of the 49 "Outstanding Citizen in Alaska." From 1970–76, he served in **Anchorage**'s Holy Family Cathedral and St. Benedict's parishes. In 1976, he left Alaska to begin five years of ministry in Moses Lake, Washington, principally among the Hispanic people. In 1982, he began a two-year stay as assistant pastor of St. Joseph's parish in Pocatello, Idaho. From 1984–89, he was hospital chaplain in Lewiston, Idaho.

In 1973, Father Llorente underwent a serious operation. A cyst "the size of a grapefruit," in his words, was removed from one of his kidneys. He survived that ordeal with no further complications. In 1979, he wrote to Father Renner:

In the meantime we grow older and come closer to the Pearly Gates where Saint Peter will turn his magnifying glass on our poor trembling souls. But it won't be that old renegade Pete who will judge us, but Our Lord Himself in person aided by our blessed Mother who will stand there also to put in a good word for us, priests of her Son the High Priest. And the Lord will be kind to us and will take us to himself and bury us in His divine Heart. May you and I enter that place and be immersed in God to live his divine life forever. Amen.

Six years later, in 1985, he wrote: "I have begun my 51st year as a priest and my 62nd in the Society. How much longer? It can't be far away now. May our dear Lord temper His justice with mercy. Amen."

In mid-November 1988, in Lewiston, Idaho, where Father Llorente was still active as chaplain at St. Joseph's Hospital, he collapsed after struggling through Mass. He was found to have cancer of the lymph glands. Told that it was treatable, he said: "No. I'm 83 years old. I want to meet St. Ignatius and his first companions." It would have been a surprise to those who knew him, if he had opted for treatment. Two months later, on January 26, 1989, in the Jesuit House Infirmary at Gonzaga University, he died. He lies buried among the Indian people of the Pacific Northwest, in the mission cemetery at DeSmet, Idaho.

The passing of this exuberant, joyous, modern-day mystic from sunny Spain was noted in high places. In Alaska's capital, Juneau, where he had served two terms in the state legislature, he was honored by the Sixteenth Alaska Legislature with a special *In Memoriam* document. This states that "he served with distinction and was loved by all who worked with him." He is cited, too, for having been "a perceptive and knowledgeable legislator who gave outstanding service in his term."

In the nation's capital, Father Llorente's close friend and admirer, Senator Ernest Gruening, after pointing out that Father Llorente had made history, inasmuch as he was the first Roman Catholic priest to hold elected office in a U.S. state, asked that the lengthy article that appeared in *Time*, when Father Llorente was elected unanimously to the House of Representatives of Alaska as a write-in candidate, be printed in the *Congressional Record*. There being no objections, the article was ordered to be printed in the *Record*.

63, 64

LOHAGEN, Sister Scholastica, O.S.U.

"She materialized," wrote a reporter visiting St. Mary's Mission, **Andreafsky**, for the first time, "from one of the hallways. She was a tiny, stooped, ancient woman with gleaming, steel-rimmed glasses. She wore a nun's black habit, and a huge pair of tennis shoes because, as we learned later, tight leather shoes hurt her feet. A big clutch of keys dangled from her waist on a string." The keys she needed, when she made her nightly rounds to make sure all the mission doors were locked, and all the lights and faucets turned off. In a thick German accent the reporter was told that, yes, he could talk with her

Sister Scholastica Lohagen, O.S.U., at St. Mary's Mission, Andreafsky, 1980. *Photo by Eric Muehling/with permission from the* Fairbanks Daily News-Miner.

and take some pictures. "Nine o'clock tomorrow you come to the laundry." It was not long before one got the impression that people generally did what she said.

Sister Scholastica (née Maria Lohagen) was born, the third of 13 children, on September 23, 1897, in Germany's Rhineland, in Elberfeld, 30 miles east of Cologne. Her father was from a very poor family; her mother from a well-to-do middle class family. Her childhood she described, in an autobiographical sketch written in October 1969, as "uneventful, but happy." Very early in life she learned how to sew, crochet and knit. She was a fast learner in school, and throughout her school years she was always number one in her class. She did not attend a school staffed by Sisters; but, during her last four years in grade school, she had "a very holy man" for a teacher, whose words and example made "a lasting impression" on her.

Sister Scholastica made her first Holy Communion, when she was 13 years old. Recalling that day many years later, she wrote:

That day brought a change in my life, though I was not aware of it at the time. Only some years later I saw it all. I still remember the day, that Sunday after Easter. I had come back from the altar with my God in my heart. The sodality choir was singing, and I was silently praying, when, all of a sudden, the church seemed full of a strange light. Then I heard—how, I don't know—the words, "Follow me!" I did not think of becoming a Religious. I had never spoken to a Sister in my life. But the words "Follow me!" kept haunting me. So I procured *The Following of Christ* and the *Philothea* of St. Francis de Sales, and tried to follow Christ according to those books.

In part, her following of Christ consisted in attending Mass and receiving Communion daily.

During World War I, she served as a volunteer in a hospital. There for the first time she had contact with Sisters, and came to realize what God wanted of her, when He said, "Follow me!" She felt called to be "a Sister in a far-off place." However, both her confessor and mother thinking her still too young for Religious life, told her to wait a year or two. It turned out that, because of family poverty and the need, therefore, for her to work to support brothers and sisters, she had to wait nine full years, before she was able to realize her call to Religious life and, in her case, specifically, a call to be a missionary Sister. "God Himself," she recorded,

showed me the way. A missionary magazine fell into my hands, and I read it from cover to cover. On the last page there was a small ad which said, "The Sisters of St. **Ann** and the **Ursulines** are working with the **Jesuits** in the Ice Missions in **Alaska**. Any girl interested please contact Father," (I forget his name), "who is presently in Bonn." I read it twice, and it flashed through my mind, "This is the place!" I cut out the ad and waited, and prayed, and trusted in God.

In January 1926, Sister Scholastica wrote to the address in Bonn. When she received no answer, she wrote a second time. This time she did receive an answer, to the effect that the priest who had placed the ad had gone back to Alaska, and that she should write to the Ursuline Novice Mistress in Seattle, Washington. She wrote. After a wait of about six weeks, she received a letter from Mother Angela Lincoln in St. Ignatius, Montana, telling her that she was accepted as a candidate for the Ursulines and that she should get her papers, passport and visa lined up.

On February 2, 1927, Sister Scholastica sailed from Hamburg, Germany, never to see her native

Ursuline Sisters Scholastica Lohagen (left) and Mother Mary of the Blessed Sacrament en route from Akulurak to Hooper Bay in October 1942. *JOPA-153.1.06.*

land again. Relatives and friends, even her confessor, had tried to dissuade her from following her hopes and dreams by painting in the darkest colors the difficulties and dangers that lay ahead of her in parts unknown. "But," she wrote, "I had no fears. I was so sure that this was God's call and God's will for me, and that His grace would help me."

She landed in New York on February 16th, then took the train to Chicago, where she met Mother Perpetua, who took her to the Ursuline novitiate at Mukilteo, Washington. While not everything about novitiate life was easy for her, and she did suffer from homesickness, she could, nevertheless, summarize, "I loved the novitiate and everything in it. The time passed too quickly." Her command of English was soon such that she was put on the list of refectory readers.

After completing her noviceship, Sister Scholastica was assigned to St. Ignatius Mission, Montana, where she was put in charge of the kitchen. She knew well how to cook and bake; but, being practically alone, found cooking for almost 200 people a formidable challenge. She admitted that she wished she had had more contact with the children; but, having told the Lord that He could put her any place He wanted, she willingly accepted her assigned role.

On July 11, 1934, after having served at several other missions in Montana and Idaho in various capacities, such as cook, laundress, and mistress of children, Sister Scholastica sailed for Alaska, with St. Mary's Mission, **Akulurak**, as her destination. She was never to leave Alaska again.

Sister Scholastica spent the years 1934–42 at Akulurak. Despite the difficulties of life at Akulurak, she was happy there. In October 1942, she moved to **Hooper Bay** to assist Mother Mary of the Blessed Sacrament with the training of the Sisters of Our Lady of the **Snows**. This assignment ended in 1945, and she returned to Akulurak, where she continued to serve, until she, along with the whole mission, moved to the new St. Mary's on the Andreafsky River in 1951. In 1969, she could write, referring to the new St. Mary's, "I have been here ever since. How long will I be here? That's in God's hands. In Him I trust, and there is only one wish left. That is that I may always be ready and willing to do His Holy Will."

Sister Scholastica was to spend the remaining 16 years of her life at St. Mary's. For the most part she did what she had done most of her life: cook and bake, wash and iron, and mend clothes. She put in long days at these, from six in the morning till eleven at night. It was a key principle of her spiritual life never to waste a moment of God's precious time. In 1979, she received from Rome the Award of the Holy Cross: *Pro Ecclesia et Pontifice*.

In a 1984 interview, Sister Scholastica was asked how much longer she would be staying at St. Mary's. Her answer: "Until the Lord calls me. And I don't think that will be too long." It was not too long. On Monday, April 29, 1985, at St. Mary's Mission, at the age of 87 years, Sister Scholastica died "of natural causes." In keeping with her wishes, she died in her own bed, rather than in a hospital. On Wednesday, two days after her peaceful death, after a Mass was concelebrated by Jesuit Bishops Robert L. **Whelan** and Michael J. **Kaniecki**, she was laid to rest in the mission cemetery, among the Eskimo people she had so unstintingly served for over half a century.

Sister Scholastica is one of only two Ursulines buried in Alaska. Sister Irene Arvin, buried at the **Pilgrim Hot Springs** Mission, is the other.

Sister Scholastica's long life was, for the most part, and to all outward appearances, a mundane, monotonous life. Yet, in reality, it was anything but that. Hers was a truly saintly life, a life of unsung, hidden heroism, lived out, as it was, in a constant whole-hearted effort on her part to conform in all things to God's will for her as she discerned it. Her long life in Alaska was her generous, beautiful answer to the call to serve as a missionary Sister in a far-off place.

LONNEUX, Father Martin J., S.J.

On June 12, 1924, Father Bellarmine **Lafortune**, S.J., wrote in the **Nome** house diary: "The *Victoria*, after a good deal of struggle with the heavy ice, drops anchor. Aboard she had Father Lonneux. He comes to give a missionary help and I hope to stay for many years." Father Lonneux did stay for many years in **Alaska**, almost three decades. These he spent among the Central Yup'ik Eskimos at, or near, the mouth of the Yukon River. He gained a working knowledge of their language, and produced various works in it. He was said to have been "many things: a carpenter, a cook, an actor, a mimic, a benevolent dictator, a thorough monopolizer of every conversation." But, above all, he was regarded as "a first class missionary."

Martin Joseph Lonneux was born on February 2, 1890, in Hodimont-Verviers, Belgium. After three years in a public school, he attended the Jesuit school in Verviers, 1899–1903, then the school of the Christian Brothers in Verviers, 1903–05. He next attended the University in Liège, 1905–07, and the Apostolic School in Turnhout, 1907–12.

On September 2, 1912, Martin Lonneux entered the Jesuit novitiate of the Canadian Province at Sault-au-Récollet. With a view to serving on the Alaska Mission, he transferred to Los Gatos, California, for his second year of novitiate. After completing the two-year noviceship, he studied the humanities and classics, 1914–15, before going on to Gonzaga College in Spokane, Washington, for his first year of philosophical studies. The other two years of these, 1916–18, he made at Mount St. Michael's near Spokane. From there, he went directly to St. Louis University for theological studies. After two years there, he was ordained a priest, in St. Louis, in June 1920. Two more years of theological studies followed, before he went on to make his tertianship in Cleveland, Ohio, 1922–23. Health problems, however—"nervous trouble"—forced him to leave Cleveland in January 1923. He went to St. Xavier Mission, among the Crow Indians in Montana, where he was until May 31, 1924.

As we saw, Father Lonneux began his years in Alaska in Nome, on June 12, 1924. After three months there, he left, on September 17th, for St. Mary's Mission, **Akulurak**, where he arrived a week later on the *Mudhen*. After his first year at Akulurak, he was named Superior of that mission, an office he held till 1927. According to Father Philip I. **Delon**, S.J., General Superior of the Alaska Mission at the time, when Father Lonneux arrived in Alaska, "he came with an uncommon dose of self-conceit, and with the idea that he was destined to be the liberator of the Mission. He talked that way and he acted that way right from the start, at Akulurak."

Father Lonneux was persuaded that a great deal at Akulurak needed reforming, updating. In his favor it must be said that he was, to a large extent, sup-

ported in his views by no one less than veteran Alaska missionary Father Julius **Jetté**, S.J. Referring to Father Lonneux's "candor and new ways," Father Jetté wrote to the Father Provincial, "The others, it seems, cannot put up with his outspoken language, or his progressive methods. The latter I approve, and the former I rather enjoy."

In Father Lonneux's own mind, there was no ambiguity as to what needed to be done. Being a most orderly and energetic person—as well as a person given to worrying and fretting, a person suffering from "nervous trouble"—he wasted no time getting down to the business of bringing about change at Akulurak. His approach was said to be "heavy-handed"; his manner "dictatorial." Needless to say, this caused much pain, especially to the **Ursuline** Sisters, on whom the very survival of the whole boarding school program in large part depended. However, when the building that housed the Sisters and girls was destroyed by fire on June 12, 1925, he personally took quick action to obtain funds, and expended a great deal of personal energy in the process of putting up a new and better building. Throughout this ordeal of displacement and rebuilding, he showed exceptional solicitude for the well-being of the Sisters and the girls. By December 9, 1926, the Sisters and girls were able to move into their new quarters. Still, unfortunately, the wound of alienation between him and his "new ways" and the Sisters was never healed. To his own relief, and to that of the Sisters, he left, in the summer of 1927, for **Tununak**, where he spent the year 1927–28 studying the language, putting up a chapel, and, according to Father Delon, sowing the "good seed, which was taking root."

Looking back on his Akulurak years, Father Lonneux wrote, on May 2, 1927, to his Father Provincial, Joseph M. Piet, S.J., "My removal from office is a great consolation and satisfaction to me. I am not sorry for what I did; and, if I had to start over, I would do it with a stronger hand, using a little more diplomacy."

A month later, on June 6, 1927, the new Superior at Akulurak, Father John B. **Sifton**, S.J., wrote to the same Father Provincial:

I took charge of Akulurak last April. Fr. Lonneux has been with me ever since, and I have had a good chance to study and observe him, and I am pleased to say the more I see of him the more I admire him. I find him a most willing, helpful and cheerful companion. It is really a pity that he got off on the wrong foot. He blundered, I think, not in trying to change certain things, but in the manner in which he went about it. As an organizer he has not his equal up here, and his energy is amazing. Fr. DeSmet seems to have been a free lance. So is Fr. Lonneux, and I think there is every hope that he will yet do great things for Alaska. Akulurak owes him a debt of lasting gratitude.

According to Father Delon, writing to Father Provincial Piet under date of February 3, 1928, "When Father Lonneux went to Tununak in the summer of 1927, he really selected his own status." Father Delon had intended him for **St. Michael**. Nevertheless, he "willingly let him go," giving as his reasons for doing so, that he "did not want to discourage him, since he was in such good earnest," and that in Tununak "there was a safety-valve needed for that geyser of energy."

Father Lonneux spent most of his years in Alaska, from 1928–52, in the St. Michael–Lower Yukon district. According to his fellow missionary and admirer, Father Joseph F. **McElmeel**, S.J., "Old" **Hamilton**, **Chaneliak**, **Unalakleet**, **Kotlik**, **Stebbins**, St. Michael, and other nameless places inhab-

ited by Eskimos profited from his more than 20 years of "devoted, intelligent, systematic work." During his years in that district, he replaced or improved with his own hands many of the chapel and church buildings, first-generation structures that had seen better days. His chapels were, according to Father McElmeel, "the pride of the Yukon. Nowhere will you find greater cleanliness and orderly arrangements." There was nothing extravagant in what he built, but there was order, convenience, and that amount of comfort necessary for a missionary who intended to stay in a place for a time. "The cleanliness of his place," wrote Father McElmeel, "was so marked that we used to tease him a bit about it." Once, Father Lonneux returned to one of his mission stations to find all the pots, pans and dishes in a pile on the middle of the floor. The note on top of them read: "Not knowing just exactly where all of these items belonged, I thought it better to leave them here for you to put in their proper places." Many Eskimos modeled their houses on Father Lonneux's. His religious instruction of the people, too, was orderly, systematic and thorough. Fellow missionaries referred to "Lonnie's system," and considered it model.

Margaret Koka Hunt, Father Martin J. Lonneux, S.J.—holding a muskrat—and Roy Hunt in a springtime seal and muskrat camp at Point Romanof. Mukluks and muskrat are drying on a pole. It is May, the sun is warm, the mosquitoes not yet out. It is pleasant to be in camp. *JOPA-829.01.*

During the fishing season, Father Lonneux traveled from camp to camp in an open boat propelled by an outboard motor. With him he had a tent big enough to enable him to set up an altar in it. For Mass, the front flaps were tied back, and the people knelt outside on the ground. The tent served him also as his living quarters.

Father Lonneux, however, is best remembered for the work he did in the Central Yup'ik Eskimo language. He was not a great natural linguist, but he was linguist enough to recognize that fact and to know how to help himself, when it came to dealing with the Eskimo language. With the help of two Eskimo women, he put the Mass, hymns, prayers, Scripture texts, and the Baltimore Catechism into Eskimo. The end results were not literal translations, but genuine Eskimo equivalents of the English. What was translated had to be doctrinally accurate and "in a language such as the Natives themselves speak." In the Foreword to his catechism, dated July 2, 1942, he wrote: "I undertook to guide my catechist through this work. All the honor goes to my faithful catechist, Mary [Emmanak]. I did not translate. This is why this work is truly Innuit [Central Yup'ik Eskimo]. I wanted pure native." In 1942, Margaret Koka Andrews was his catechist and helper with his translations into Eskimo. Concerning his knowledge of Eskimo, she recalled many years later that he spoke it "so-so, but he was a little bit dumb for it."

Father Lonneux undertook to produce the translations into Eskimo "to help the new Fathers and for my own people." His work with the language was over and above that of his work as a missionary. "All this work on the language," he wrote, "is extra and often very heavy." He was convinced that Eskimo would continue to be in common use for decades to come, otherwise, as he wrote, "I would never have broken my health in trying to do the heavy work in the language as I did." Time proved him to be right regarding the continued use of Eskimo by subsequent generations. Such was the demand for his hymnal, that it had to be reprinted in the early 1980s.

Around 1950, Father Lonneux's health began to fail. The problem seems to have been his lungs. However, he continued on with his missionary work and with his language works, trying to ready

them for the press. By late December 1951, he was, by his own admission, "in a bad condition." On March 17, 1952, he was operated on in Providence Hospital, Seattle, for what he called "an infected Gland the size of a fist." He spent most of 1952 in the Northwest, in and out of and back again in the hospital.

In mid-July 1952, Father Lonneux received word that his catechism had finally been printed. From Providence Hospital he wrote on July 16th, "Happy to report I am improving fast and walking around. Still expect to return to Chaneliak in September." It was not to be. He spent the last several months of 1952 in the hospital; then, on December 6th, accompanied by Francis D. **Gleeson**, S.J., Vicar Apostolic of Alaska at the time, he returned to Alaska, to **Fairbanks**. He went straight to the hospital there, as he had trouble breathing, needed oxygen. He was able to offer Mass for the last time on January 15, 1953. Death came to him on January 21st. Father James U. **Conwell**, S.J., wrote, "He was a cheery person right down to the very end." In 1950, Father Lonneux had written to him, "I have never been able to become a Citizen." Father Lonneux lies buried in the Clay Street Cemetery in downtown Fairbanks.

After Father Lonneux's death, Father McElmeel left "some notes on the life and tribulations of Father Martin Lonneux—lest the memory of a great man be forgotten." He described him as "a giant among Alaskan missionaries, who served the Lord with distinction." He said of him, "Trials purified Father Lonneux, did not sour him." According to Margaret Koka Andrews, "the Eskimo people *really* loved him. They loved him like the old dad of the whole village."

94

LOPILATO, Father Arthur, S.J.

Arthur Lopilato was born in Boston, Massachusetts, on July 29, 1916. His early life he spent in Our Lady of Mt. Carmel parish in East Boston. His elementary and secondary education he received in Boston public schools. He spent a post-graduate year taking a business course at Boston's Graduate School of Commerce. During the depression years,

Father Arthur Lopilato,
S.J. *JOPA-1069.04.*

he managed to find work, off and on, as a journeyman printer and a shipyard worker on the Boston waterfront. When World War II broke out, he was inducted into the military and assigned to the Army Air Corps. For three of his four years in the military, he was stationed at a British Air Base, and took part in the bombardment of Western Europe, mostly of Germany. During those wartime years, he wondered and prayed at length about what he would do at war's end, assuming he survived the war. Before the war was over, he decided to enter the Jesuit Order as a Lay Brother. On November 1, 1945, shortly after being discharged from the military, he entered the Jesuit novitiate of the New England Province of the Society of Jesus at Lenox, Massachusetts. He took his first vows in 1948 and his final vows in 1956. In becoming a Jesuit, he found "great peace and a measure of security" that helped him feel he "was heading in the right direction in serving the Lord in a life that would lead to eventual eternal peace."

After completing his noviceship, Brother Lopilato was assigned to the Jesuit philosophate-theologate at Weston College in the town of Weston, Massachusetts, on December 16, 1948. He spent twenty years at Weston, serving in various capacities. For 17 of those years, he worked at all-around printing as a compositor, stoneman, and press operator. He was a full journeyman printer. For ten years,

as a state-licensed operator, he ran the movie projector, showing movie films to the seminarians. He himself booked the films. For three years, he was the baker for 300 people.

On June 1, 1968, Brother Lopilato arrived in **Fairbanks, Alaska**. There he helped the "Jesuit Brothers Construction Crew," working out of Portland, Oregon, build the Bishop's Residence-Chancery Building. At the end of the summer, he went back to Weston. However, he wanted to return to Alaska. A month later, he found himself in **Anchorage**, working in a warehouse belonging to the Diocese of Fairbanks. At the same time, he also helped Father Jules M. **Convert**, S.J., in his work at **Nulato**, **Kaltag**, and **Koyukuk**. Alaska was now in his blood. In Fairbanks, after learning all the phases of the diocesan treasurer's job, he took over that position and held it until mid-1976. While still at Weston, Brother Lopilato had been involved in counseling alcoholics. He continued this work in Fairbanks, mostly in the evenings.

By the 1970s, it had become thinkable in the Society of Jesus that a Lay Brother could go on to study for the priesthood and be ordained. The need for more priests in Alaska was growing. Brother Lopilato saw this, as did Robert L. **Whelan**, S.J., Bishop of Fairbanks at the time. So did Father William J. **Loyens**, S.J., then General Superior of Jesuits in Alaska. It was especially the latter who encouraged Brother Lopilato to consider going on to become a priest. After thinking and praying about the matter for several months, Brother Lopilato saw the logic of it all. With permission from the Jesuit Father General in Rome, he entered Pope John XXIII National Seminary in 1976. He chose this seminary, because it was "especially geared to be strong in a pastoral direction." He found the seminary studies quite difficult; but, after he had successfully completed them, he could write in his autobiographical sketch: "Those four years turned out to be the happiest of my life up to that point!" On January 25, 1980, in St. Ignatius Church, Chestnut Hill, Massachusetts, Arthur Lopilato was ordained a priest by Bishop Whelan. At age 63, he was the oldest man from that seminary to be ordained a priest. The year before his ordination, he had himself transcribed from the New England Province to the Oregon Province, under which the Alaska Mission was. As

Oregonian and "Father" Lopilato now, he returned to the Diocese of Fairbanks.

What strongly motivated Father Lopilato to enter the priesthood was his inability as a non-priest to help recovered alcoholics to return to the Church's sacramental life through the Sacrament of Reconciliation. He found it difficult to have to send them to some priest, who would be more or less a stranger to them.

From 1980–82, Father Lopilato served as assistant pastor in Immaculate Conception parish, Fairbanks. From the outset, he found priestly ministry very satisfying and fulfilling. "Needless to say," he wrote, "the shift to the priesthood brought an enormous lift in my existence as a Jesuit." After two years in Fairbanks, he spent the years 1982–86 as pastor of the **Kotzebue** parish. In 1986, he had to travel to Anchorage because of health concerns. It was determined that he should stay there to be "close to the medics." Being, by his own admission, "a city guy," he was happy to be back in a city. In Anchorage, he was assigned to St. Elizabeth Ann Seton parish as assistant priest. At the beginning of July 1989, he was asked to fill a needy spot at Our Lady of Guadalupe parish, also in Anchorage. He served in that parish until 1996. Being an older man, somewhat more conservatively, traditionally inclined, he was popular especially with the elderly. He was an intense man, but with a ready smile. All in all, he was a happy, healthy big city parish priest.

In November 1992, he could still write: "I am 76 years old and in excellent health, mostly through proper diet and daily exercise. I'm going full-time and at a steady pace—knowing there is no other type of life or occupation in which I would rather be engaged!" From his earliest years as a Jesuit, he had played baseball each summer and hockey each winter. Small in size, he was, nevertheless, a ferocious hockey player. At the age of 72, he stopped playing hockey, but continued to skate and play ball till near the end of his life.

During the last two years of his life, Father Lopilato, now semi-retired, served as a hospital chaplain in Anchorage and continued to help out in various parishes. He was an active man right up to the very end of his long life. While on his way to **Soldotna** to celebrate Sunday Mass, riding in the back seat of a car driven by friends, he died very peacefully, of heart failure, on Saturday, March 7, 1998.

Father Arthur Lopilato lies buried in the Catholic plot of Anchorage's Angelus Memorial Park Cemetery.

LOYENS, Father William J., S.J.

His life's accomplishments belied his humble origins. He was a man of three continents. A noted Alaskan artist painted his portrait. Successively, he headed the Department of Anthropology at the University of **Alaska–Fairbanks**, was General Superior of all **Jesuits** in Alaska, was Provincial Superior of all Jesuits in the Pacific Northwest. For some years, he served as pastor of Fairbanks' oldest parish. But, above all, he was a teacher, both by word and by example. Sitting before him as students in the course of the years were not only whites, but also numerous Koyukon Athabaskan Indians, Central Yup'ik and Inupiat Eskimos, as well as Bantu-speaking black Africans.

William John (christened Guillaume Jean by a Francophile priest, hence the Flemish Lom) Loyens, the oldest of ten siblings, was born on December 22, 1926, in Vlijtingen, a small town in the Province of Limburg, Belgium. He was baptized an hour after his birth, an indication, perhaps, that he was considered too frail to await the customary ceremonies. From 1943–47, he attended the Jesuit-staffed St. Joseph's College in Turnhout, Belgium, completing a six-year course in four years. In part, those were World War II years. Recalling the war, he said in an interview, "I was 13 years old, when the war started. As a 13-year-old kid, I found the war much more exciting than scary."

It was while attending St. Joseph's College, an Apostolic School, that Loyens became acquainted with, and drawn to, the Jesuits. He found them "friendly and encouraging." He also sensed them to have "a real esprit de corps." As he got more and more into his studies, he found himself more and more attracted to the Jesuits, not only as a group of intellectuals, but also as "a great group to be part of." During those college years, he also began reading all sorts of travelogues. He was captivated especially by travels in the Arctic, and saw that most of the priests in Alaska were Jesuits. From then on, he began to "scheme" how he could become a Jesuit and go to Alaska.

Father Paul C. **Deschout**, S.J., too, had attended St. Joseph's. On February 2, 1947, Loyens, before he had studied English "like blazes," wrote to the Oregon Province Vocation Director:

> The Rev. Father [Deschout] made me bold enough to write you. As I will make myself a Jesuit and follow the example of Father de Schout, a big difficulty arises. How could I see my vocation realized, if I have to enter the Flemish Province? There is no how to push away this problem. I am ready to leave yet this country. What have I to do, Father?

Loyens, with assurance that he would one day serve in Alaska, was accepted into the Society of Jesus, on September 7, 1947, as a member of the Oregon Province. From 1947–49, he made his noviceship at Drongen (Tronchiennes), Belgium. The following year, he studied tropical medicine and English at the University of Louvain, Belgium. He left Belgium on March 12, 1950, for the novitiate at Sheridan, Oregon. After a few months at Sheridan, he went to Mount St. Michael's on the outskirts of Spokane, Washington, to spend the years 1950–53 in philosophical studies. By the end of the academic year 1953, he had earned B.A. and M.A. degrees, conferred by Spokane's Gonzaga University, as well as a State of Washington Teacher's Certificate.

In early June 1953, Loyens received a letter telling him that he was to go to Alaska, to **Holy Cross Mission** on the lower Yukon River, and there to start a high school. The prime mover behind a high school at Holy Cross was Sister M. George **Edmond**, S.S.A. And start a high school Loyens did! This was the first high school the whole length of the Yukon. He was recognized, in the words of Father William T. **McIntyre**, S.J., Superior of Holy Cross at the time, as its "first teacher and really the spark plug behind the whole deal, along with Sister George Edmond." During its first year, the school had ten students. In addition to teaching school during his two years at Holy Cross, Loyens helped also with the prefecting of the boys, the supplying of firewood for the mission's many stoves, the gardening, hunting and fishing, and "all the other things necessary to keep the place going." He found his two years at Holy Cross "really an exciting time."

Loyens spent the years 1955–59 at Alma College, the Jesuit theologate near Los Gatos, California, in theological studies. He became an American citizen

Father William J. Loyens, S.J. *BR/JOPA-1070.07.*

in 1956. On June 14, 1958, he was ordained a priest in Spokane. While at Alma, he so impressed his professors by his grasp of matters theological that they urged higher Superiors, appealing even to Rome, to have him go on to get a doctorate in theology with a view to his returning to Alma as a member of its faculty. (The faculty at Mount St. Michael's had wanted him to get a doctorate in philosophy with a view to his teaching that subject there.) "His dilemma was simple," wrote one historian, "for he seemed to be a genius at everything he studied." For a time, it looked as though his future would be that of a professor of theology. However, after "a great struggle," and the exchange of many letters, it was determined by his Superiors that Alaska was to be the field of his future work as a Jesuit. After all, had he not left his native land to serve in Alaska?

After his fourth year of theology at Alma College, Father Loyens taught a course in theology at Gonzaga University's Summer School, before going on to make his ten-month tertianship at Drongen, Belgium. He spent the years 1960–62 in Fairbanks, teaching Latin, history and Religion at Monroe Catholic High School, as well as serving as Moderator of the Sodality and as "Spiritual Father" to the faculty and student body. During those same two years, he served also as Newman Club Chaplain to the students at the University of Alaska–Fairbanks. During the summer of 1961, he worked toward an M.A. degree in Education at the University.

About this time, Jesuits in Alaska came to the realization that one or other among them should qualify himself to teach and prepare young Alaskans for a world rapidly changing, especially socially and culturally. "The lot fell on me," said Father Loyens in an interview. Accordingly, he spent the summer of 1962 and the academic year 1962–63 studying anthropology at the University of Alaska–Fairbanks. While doing so, he lived on campus, in Stevens Hall, "taking all the classes and clearing out anything having any remote connection with anthropology." Of his 1960–63 year spell in Fairbanks, Father Loyens said, "it was fun and I thoroughly enjoyed it."

Father Loyens spent the academic years 1963–66 at the University of Wisconsin, Madison, earning a doctorate in cultural anthropology. In 1964, that university granted him an M.A. degree in anthropology. Being not "too keen on once again going through the mickey mouse routine of getting another master's degree," he had simply petitioned for the degree. (He had helped his cause considerably, and above all, by extensive, in-depth reading. It was his opinion that "succeeding well in studies obviously requires a certain amount of talent, but if you can really read, read, read, that's a great help. Reading is the key to a lot of education.") During the years 1964–66 he was a National Science Foundation Fellow. In the summer of 1964, he attended the International Institute of Linguistics at Indiana University, Bloomingdale. He spent four summers doing field work in Yukon River Koyukon Athabaskan Indian communities. His lengthy, scholarly article, "The Koyukon Feast for the Dead," was published in 1964. In 1965, he spent seven months in **Nulato** doing the research needed to produce his doctoral thesis, "The Changing Culture of the Nulato Koyukon Indians." On May 25, 1966, he received his Ph.D. degree (*magna cum laude*), along with the prestigious Bobbs-Merrill Award in Anthropology for being the outstanding graduate student in his class. Dr. Loyens was for many years a member of the American Anthropological Association, as well as of the American Biblical Association and the Biblical Archeological Association.

While Father Loyens was, unquestionably, a highly talented, first-rate research scholar, his natural orientation was more toward the practical application of the fruits of his research and scholarship. He was, before all else, both in and out of the classroom, both formally and informally, a teacher. "As long as I can teach," he said in an interview, "I'm happy." And teach he did, as a tenured Associate Professor of Anthropology at the University of Alaska, from 1966–73. For some of those years he headed the Department of Anthropology. He was a highly popular lecturer. Students packed his classes. In 1967, he received the Outstanding Service to the Students Award, an award conferred by the Governor of the State of Alaska. The respect he enjoyed as a professor earned him a spot in the unofficial Fairbanks Hall of Fame, a series of portraits of 25 people painted in 1984 for the celebration of Alaska's 25 years of statehood.

"Teaching is an important part of my life," said Father Loyens. But it was not just classroom teaching. Soon after he began his career at the University of Alaska–Fairbanks, his influence as a cultural anthropologist was felt well beyond the lecture halls. Early on, for example, he became associated with the Rural School Project, which summer after summer trained 50 teachers new to Alaska. It is he who is credited with having brought about a changed attitude on the part of Jesuit missionaries in Alaska toward the traditional Koyukon Athabaskan "stickdance" or "Feast for the Dead."

In 1973, Father Loyens' career at the University of Alaska came to an end, when he was appointed General Superior of all the Jesuits in Alaska. (In hopes of having him back again as a member of its faculty, the university granted him a leave of absence.) This meant that he had to visit a great number of places throughout northern Alaska to see personally all his fellow Jesuits in the areas of their various ministries. He had meetings to attend, reports to write up, assignments to make. All in all, he found his three years as General Superior "exciting," just as he had been "very excited" eleven years previously about going into the field of cultural anthropology.

On March 8, 1976, the Father General of the Jesuits appointed Father Loyens Provincial Superior of the Oregon Province. This appointment, too, meant that he would have to be on the move most of the time, traveling throughout the states of Oregon, Washington, Idaho, Montana and Alaska, visiting men and places, being concerned about matters both spiritual and temporal, attending meetings both near and far, working in conjunction with the hierarchy in those states, and much else besides. Those were still the turbulent post-Vatican II times, when the men under him needed to be reassured and encouraged to have a positive, upbeat outlook on Jesuit life, and Church life, in general. With enthusiasm, Loyens embraced his new assignment, confident that he could communicate to others his own kind of "joyful Christianity." It was written of him that within a few months he knew all the members of the Province by their first names, and that during his four years in office—described as "golden years"—"he brought much peace and joy to the Province."

Toward the end of 1979, Father Loyens was slowed down by rather serious health problems. He seemed never to have wholly recovered from the "London Flu" he had contracted in 1973. He was troubled by stomach ulcers. On December 7, 1979, he appointed an "acting Provincial," then left for Belgium to breathe his native air in hopes it would cure him. His health, however, remained problematical. After consulting with Father General in Rome, on March 20, 1980, he returned to the Province and informed its members that he, for health reasons, would not be able to continue on as Provincial. He then returned to Belgium for a prolonged period of rest. A new Father Provincial took office in June of that year.

By sometime in 1980, Father Loyens began to feel alive once more after his long illness. He was back in Fairbanks again by December, where, seeing "an incredible need," in the Church at the time to "get the word out," he, always a teacher at heart, committed himself to teaching adults courses in Church history, theology, Sacred Scripture and Christian Spirituality. The courses, begun in September 1981, were well attended. The University of Alaska gave credit to students attending some of them. Tapes of his lectures were made and widely circulated. After devoting ten years to adult education, Father Loyens, in 1990, while continuing to teach "Adult Ed," became pastor of Fairbanks' Immaculate Conception parish, a post he held until 1993.

On June 15, 1993, Father Loyens, lured by a personal calling and a far-away plea for help, left Alaska to take a position at St. Peter's Major Seminary in Zomba, Malawi, Africa. (Here he was relatively near the one-time Belgium Congo, that had moti-

vated him in his younger days to study tropical medicine.) He decided to make the move to Malawi on the principle: "Do what you do best, for those who need it most!" To his seminary teaching in Malawi he brought the same scholarly, yet personable, style he had brought to all of his teaching. The month before he left for Africa, he was, in an official document issued by the mayor of Fairbanks, recognized and honored—on the basis of his being "the epitome of unselfishness," and because of "his commitment and dedication to his fellow man"—as one of Fairbanks' "finest and best," and named as one of Fairbanks' outstanding senior citizens of 1993.

Father Loyens taught theology in the Malawi seminary until 1998, when the leukemia, which had been diagnosed already in 1987, and for which he had undergone chemotherapy treatment, again became cause for serious concern. He returned to Fairbanks, where he spent two years receiving the needed medical care, the while serving as a "pastoral minister." He then went back to Malawi in February 2000, and resumed teaching, until the cancer forced him, in November, to return to the States. At that time, he became a member of the Regis Jesuit Community, housed in Bea House on the campus of Gonzaga University in Spokane. As such, he was listed in the Oregon Province Catalog as "praying for the Church and the Society." In his Bea House room, at 2:37 A.M., on the Feast of the Immaculate Conception, December 8, 2004, he died "very peacefully." Just one week earlier, at a special Mass liturgy concelebrated for and by him, he told the assembled Jesuit priests and Lay Brothers, shortly before he received the Sacrament of the Sick, "I am at peace—at peace with myself, at peace with the world, at peace with God." He lies buried in the Jesuit cemetery at Mount Saint Michael's, Spokane.

Words spoken by Father Loyens in 1985 well summarize his long, interesting, inspiring life: "I've always seen my presence as being basically a kind of instrument in the hands of the Lord to allow others to get to know Him and love Him." Other words spoken by him at the same time could well serve as a fitting epitaph for him: "I think my being a priest and being associated with the Society of Jesus is the greatest thing that ever happened in my life."

65, 66, 142, 176

LUCCHESI, Father John L., S.J.

The General Superior of the **Alaska** Mission described him to the Father Provincial of the California Province as "the meekest and most charitable of men, a prince among men, and easily the most level-headed Father here." One historian wrote of him that he was "one of Alaska's most distinguished missionaries." A fellow missionary said of him that "there was much compassion in him, and a fatherliness and friendliness that endeared him to everyone he met." Another listed him under "the era of the giants."

John (Giovanni, in Italian) L. Lucchesi was born in Genoa, Italy, on October 19, 1858. Renouncing honor and great wealth, he went on to study for the priesthood. At the age of 24, he was ordained a diocesan priest. Prior to entering the Jesuit Order at Chieri, Italy, on July 10, 1891, he was the Superior of the seminary in Genoa. Before coming to the United States in the autumn of 1897, he worked in Genoa, giving the Spiritual Exercises and directing Catholic societies. He next served in Bastia, where he managed the household, was Spiritual Director, and taught Christian Doctrine.

Father Lucchesi spent his first year in America, 1897–98, at Frederick, Maryland, making his tertianship. In 1898, he arrived in Alaska. There he began his long years in the North at **Holy Cross Mission**. Stories about him say that he arrived wearing a top hat and a tail coat. Soon after his arrival, the tall, slim man, with the short beard, which he always wore, set about learning one or other of the native languages. He never gained a working knowledge of any of them.

During the year 1900, Father Lucchesi's third summer in Alaska, a mysterious plague—variously identified as influenza, measles, cholera, typhoid fever—struck much of western Alaska, Holy Cross included. Whole villages were wiped out. Tirelessly he ministered to the sick and dying. With his own hands he dug graves and buried a great number. While doing so, he wore the same cassock. After a night of burying bodies in various stages of corruption, he would give the cassock to be washed and made ready for the next night. The "laundresses," almost as heroic as Father Lucchesi himself, were implored to keep the "odious secret" to

Father John L. Lucchesi, S.J. *JOPA-813.02.*

themselves. Not until many years after, did the story become known.

Except for shorter stays at **Nulato** (1903, 1913–14), **Pilgrim Hot Springs** (1925–26), **Mountain Village** (1926–29), **Paimiut** (1929–30), and **Hooper Bay** (1933–34), Father Lucchesi spent the rest of his 39 years in Alaska at what were at the time its two major missions, Holy Cross Mission and St. Mary's Mission, **Akulurak**. He was at the latter during the years 1907–09, 1914–16, 1917–25, 1927, 1928, 1931–33, and 1934–36. The rest of his Alaskan years he spent at Holy Cross. During some years he spent months now at one, now at the other of these two missions, often troubleshooting, or because of some emergency. Generally he was the local Superior of the given mission. He excelled as a Superior at all levels. Twice he was General Superior of the Alaska Mission, 1909–13 and 1930–31. For many years he was a Consultor to the General Mission Superior. In 1910, he visited the Vatican.

During his younger years, Father Lucchesi was known for his "indefatigability on the trail, forever running ahead of the dogs breaking trail for them." However, during the last years of his long life, he suffered much from hearing loss, hernia, and suffocating asthma. He spent most of his nights sitting upright in a chair. No complaints ever escaped his lips. He had an encouraging word for any and all who came to visit him. Thought to be at death's door, he received the Last Rites at least 20 times. He was able to offer Mass up to the last two weeks before he died. Toward the very end of his life, village women vied with one another to relieve the Sisters of St. **Ann** who cared for him. Even before his death, the villagers of Holy Cross revered him as a saint.

Father John L. Lucchesi, born to Italian nobility 80 years earlier, died on November 29, 1937, at Holy Cross and lies buried in the hillside cemetery there. What he wrote about the dying of his compatriot, Father Anthony M. **Keyes**, S.J., when he died nine years earlier, may well be written of Father Lucchesi's own dying: "He died as he had lived, like a saint."

Msgr. John A. Lunney. *LRC.*

174

LUNNEY, Msgr. John A.

John Albert Lunney, was born in Haverstraw, New York, on March 15, 1924. He attended school in North Adams, Massachusetts. In 1946, after he had served in the Army during World War II, he entered St. Anselm's College in Manchester, New Hampshire, from which he obtained a B.A. degree in 1950. He next spent 18 months with the Benedictine community at Benet Lake in Wisconsin. However, after having come to the realization that his vocation in life was more toward a direct apostolate as a priest, rather than an indirect, monastic one, he left the Benedictines. In Boston, he met Dermot **O'Flanagan**, the recently consecrated Bishop of **Juneau**, who helped him get into a seminary—with the understanding that, as a priest, he would serve in **Alaska**.

When, in 1952, the newly ordained Father Ronald K. **Dunfey** drove to Alaska, he brought with him the future Father Lunney. It was in large part to Father Dunfey that Father Lunney attributed his interest in Alaska and his desire to serve there as a priest.

After completing theological studies at St. Thomas Seminary in Denver, Colorado, John A.

Lunney was ordained a priest on May 26, 1956, in St. Michael's Cathedral in Springfield, Massachusetts, for the Diocese of Juneau. He spent his first year as a priest in **Ketchikan**. Then, after two years in Juneau, 1957–59, he was named pastor of St. Joseph's parish in **Cordova**. As such, he was responsible also for **Valdez** and **Yakutat**.

During his years in the fishing town of Cordova, Father Lunney, to keep the parish in the limelight of town happenings, issued periodic press releases. These gave thanks to parishioners involved with parish activities and singled out faithful altar boys for recognition. This limelighting helped build up his congregation.

But, Father Lunney was eager for further parochial progress. He believed that, by having a better physical plant, the Faith of the people would be stirred up. The old 1908 church was on a hill and, therefore, inaccessible for many parishioners when rain, snow, or wind blasted the buildings and people with gale force. For years, a Quonset hut, in a more accessible area, had served as the parish church. A push for a new church came from within the town itself, when, on May 2, 1963, fire gutted the nearby Cordova business area. Although no church property was involved, the fire made Father Lunney and parishioners aware of how vulnerable to fire the old

1908 church structure was and of how inadequate the low, dark, and damp Quonset was becoming.

On December 1, 1963, parishioners launched a drive to raise funds for the construction of a new church. The destruction caused by the March 27, 1964, earthquake and the consequent tidal waves provided added incentive and urgency to the drive. To raise funds, Father Lunney spent part of the summer of 1964 preaching in the San Francisco Bay area. Through his own efforts, and from various sources, funds were forthcoming. Construction of a new parish plant began in September 1964. Though far from finished, the new St. Joseph's Church was ready for limited use by December 22, 1964. It was formally dedicated on May 1, 1965, by Bishop O'Flanagan. This was the first of the various churches Father Lunney was to build in Southcentral Alaska.

On March 25, 1966, Father Lunney was in Albany, New York, to attend the ceremonies at which **Joseph T. Ryan** was consecrated the first Archbishop of **Anchorage**. Later that same year, Father Lunney was appointed pastor of St. Michael's parish in **Palmer**, and put in charge of the diocesan Liturgical Commission. In October of that year, Father Lunney became Monsignor Lunney. As the year 1966 neared its end, Msgr. Lunney could say: "It has become a busy life since the days of the old Juneau Diocese! But, great progress is being made in Alaska, and I'm very happy to be a part of it."

In 1967, Msgr. Lunney made a trip to Ireland with Archbishop Ryan to recruit priests for the Archdiocese of Anchorage. As a result, three Holy Ghost Fathers came to Alaska. Before the year was out, he found himself pastor of Anchorage's Holy Family Cathedral parish. This pastorate ended in 1970, when he was assigned to establish the new parish of Our Lady of Guadalupe. For the first five years of its existence, this parish, having as yet no church of its own, used the Methodist church on Northern Lights Boulevard, then, for a year, the Turnagain Public School. On Sunday, April 18, 1976, ground was broken for the new Our Lady of Guadalupe parish plant at the Wisconsin Street site. Msgr. Lunney, Archbishop Ryan's Director of the Building Commission, presided at the groundbreaking ceremonies.

The year before construction of the new Our Lady of Guadalupe Church began, Msgr. Lunney went to Europe for what was intended to be a three-month theological update in Rome. However, while in Europe, he developed a disabling leg ailment that necessitated hospitalization, and postponement of the update. He was disappointed in that. The church building project begun in 1976, however, was an unqualified success. In 1977, Father Lunney returned to Rome for the update.

In passing, it should be noted that Msgr. Lunney was a man concerned with much more than just buildings. When Archbishop Ryan was hesitant about having Sisters of St. **Ann** in his archdiocese—after the closing of **Copper Valley School** in 1971—Msgr. Lunney, as Vicar General, spoke forcefully and favorably that this missionary group of many years in Alaska have a house in Anchorage. Later, when the Sisters were established on Stanley Drive, Msgr. Lunney presented them with an outdoor statue of Our Lady of Guadalupe.

In the late 1970s, Msgr. Lunney was already found to be suffering from diabetes. However, he stayed on as pastor of Our Lady of Guadalupe parish, until Francis T. **Hurley**, Archbishop of Anchorage at the time, asked him, for reasons of health, to retire on his 70th birthday, March 15, 1994. After his retirement, he continued to live in the rectory of Our Lady of Guadalupe parish, doing such ministry as his health allowed. "It was not his nature to slow down or to change his habits," said Sister Kathleen O'Hara, R.S.M., a longtime friend of Msgr. Lunney, who, during the last four years of his life—now living in assisted-living quarters—visited him frequently. "He kept his sense of humor right to the end," according to Sister Kathleen. Msgr. Lunney died on March 16, 2001.

Msgr. Lunney's friends and colleagues, who were gathered in Holy Family Cathedral on March 19th for the funeral Mass, described him as a "good-hearted, independent-minded, and sometimes hard-nosed priest, who was beloved in spite of his quirks." In his homily, Archbishop Hurley made special mention of Msgr. Lunney's talent for good liturgies, his promotion of family and community, and the crucial role he played in building churches to accommodate Alaska's growing population.

Msgr. John A. Lunney lies buried in the Catholic plot of Anchorage's Angelus Memorial Park Cemetery.

MACKE, Father Paul B., S.J.

Paul B. Macke was born to Bernard J. and Louise Froelich Macke, in Cincinnati, Ohio, on November 21, 1944. Both his parents were of German ancestry. His father was a pharmacist. As a little boy, Paul, having only one sister, Jane, older than he by almost twelve years, felt "like an only child with two mothers." While he was still a pre-schooler, his father often took him to weekday morning Mass.

From 1951–59, Paul attended St. Catherine of Siena elementary school. In the parish, he served as an altar boy and sang in the choir. He spent many of his leisure hours playing baseball, his favorite sport, in the big field behind his home.

When it came time for Paul to go to high school, his father wanted him to attend his alma mater, the Jesuit-staffed St. Xavier High School in Cincinnati. But, Paul had other ideas. He chose to go to Elder, the diocesan high school, because that is where most of his friends were going. His father, who was strongly pro-Jesuit, having a brother in that Order, must have thought to himself, "Well, so much for having a son in the Jesuits!" His hopes of seeing his son in the Jesuits were further dimmed, when Paul began to date regularly, and to attend meetings of the Third Order of St. Francis.

However, "the Jesuits got their shot at Paul," in his words, during his senior year in high school, when he made a Jesuit-directed retreat. After the retreat, well acquainted with his family's Jesuit connections, he applied to be accepted into the Society of Jesus. He was accepted. On August 8, 1963, he smoked his last Lucky Strike—for a while—said good-bye to his family, and entered the novitiate of the Chicago Province of the Society of Jesus at Milford, Ohio. Having had his own private room for 18 years, he found it somewhat of a shock to have to share a dorm room with five fellow novices. It

was a shock he, nevertheless, absorbed with good grace.

After completing his two-year noviceship, Paul took his first perpetual vows, on August 15, 1965, the Feast of Mary's Assumption into heaven. Having been born on November 21, the Feast of the Presentation of the Blessed Virgin Mary, Paul's favorite color had always been blue, and Mary the object of his special devotion. He considered himself singularly blessed to be taking his vows on another major Marian feast day.

During the years 1965–67, Paul continued to live at the novitiate, but commuted to Xavier University in Cincinnati for studies in the classics and humanities. Having been a top student in his high school years, he had little difficulty with college-level courses.

In August 1967, Paul bade farewell to the novitiate at Milford, and drove off with classmates to North Aurora, Illinois, a western suburb of Chicago, for his philosophical studies. Here, again, he was somewhat shocked, quite pleasantly so, to find he had a room all to himself, with a queen-size bed, four channels of piped in music, a private bath, and a patio leading to an outdoor pool. He and his fellow philosophy students were being housed in a former Hilton resort hotel. The dining room and recreation rooms were the one-time ballrooms of the former hotel.

Paul soon fell in love with philosophy and excelled in it, in spite of the fact that, for two years, he was taking about 22 credit-hours a semester. Meanwhile, he also took courses in theology, and so was able to shorten to two years what normally would have been a four-year theology program for him. During this same time, he was also apostolically involved, giving retreats to high school girls in Joliet, Illinois. At this time, too, he earned his advanced amateur radio license. After his first year

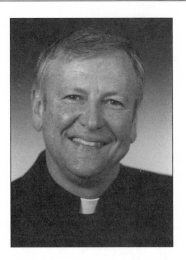

Father Paul B. Macke, S.J.
*Courtesy of Society of
Jesus, Chicago Province.*

of philosophy, he spent the summer studying sociology at Fordham University in New York City. After his second year, he did his student teaching at St. Xavier High School, the school his father had wanted him to attend for his secondary education.

For his teaching years, Paul was sent to a state he would never have chosen, there to teach subjects he was ill prepared to teach. From 1969–71, he taught Religion, English, sociology to all four years at Brebeuf Preparatory in Indianapolis, Indiana. But, this turned out to be an important assignment for him. With over 50% of Brebeuf's students being non-Catholic, he came to know and appreciate ecumenical values. This stood him in good stead later, when he studied pastoral psychotherapy at a Methodist school in Evanston, Illinois. During his teaching years, he spent the summers gaining theoretical knowledge and practical experience as a professional psychotherapist. In 1975, he received his M.A. degree from Loyola University, Chicago.

From 1971–73, Paul made his formal theological studies at the Jesuit School of Theology in the Hyde Park area of Chicago. During those years, as a member of "a small stairwell Jesuit community" living in the south-side of Chicago, he learned to cook for others and was soon quite proficient in producing gourmet-style dinners. During the summer of 1972, he did his eleven-week Clinical Pastoral Education at the University of Southern California Medical Center in Los Angeles. He considered it a privilege to live that summer at the Baptist Seminary of the West in Covina, California.

In February 1973, in Chicago, Paul was ordained a deacon. That same year, in June, he received his Master of Divinity degree. On the 16th, he was ordained a priest in Cincinnati's St. Peter in Chains Church by Archbishop Joseph L. Bernardin. "That ordination experience," he wrote years later, "was so special to me, because it brought together people from all parts of my life and from many geographical places. It was a tremendous experience of joy and unity, along with the awesome sense of God's gift of grace."

Father Macke spent his first summer as a priest giving retreats in South Bend, Indiana, and in Ontario, Canada. He also attended a symposium on the Spiritual Exercises of St. Ignatius in San Francisco. From 1973–79, he was stationed at Loyola University of Chicago's Lakeshore Campus, serving as a Campus Minister. As such, he was heavily involved in liturgies, the University Retreat Program, student housing issues, and the like. In his spare time, he taught counseling psychology as an instructor in the University's psychology department.

In the summer of 1975, Father Macke, loving to travel, took his first trip to Europe. With a fellow Jesuit, he traveled extensively throughout the continent, before he settled down to six weeks of parish work at St. George's Cathedral in London, England. (He was, subsequently, to make four more trips to Europe, as well as one to New Zealand.) The summers of 1976 and '77 he spent making his tertianship. On March 25, 1978, the Feast of the Annunciation, in Loyola University's Madonna Della Strada Chapel, he pronounced his final vows as a Jesuit.

Tertianship brought with it a major turning point in Father Macke's life. A classmate of his suggested that, for his tertianship experiment, he consider parish and radio work in **Nome, Alaska**. Accordingly, in June 1977, he went to Nome to serve as assistant priest in St. Joseph's parish and to do radio work at **KNOM**, the Catholic radio station next to the church. Among his main occupations that summer were producing inspirational "spots" for the station, taking his turn on the air, and visiting parishioners. The summer ended with his taking a five-day camping trip at Wonder Lake in Denali National Park. By trip's end, he was thoroughly "hooked" on Alaska.

In the summer of 1978, Father Macke, at the request of Father James E. **Poole**, S.J., pastor of St.

Joseph's parish and director of KNOM, was back in Nome to help out. He then spent the year 1979–80 as acting pastor and station director, while Father Poole took a sabbatical year in Berkeley, California. While still on his sabbatical, Father Poole asked Father Macke to stay on in Nome. In an official letter, dated February 27, 1980, Robert L. **Whelan**, S.J., Bishop of **Fairbanks** at the time, appointed Father Macke pastor of St. Joseph's parish. As "a popular pastor and an able radio man," he, according to Father Poole, did "a great job." Father Macke's Nome pastorate ended in June 1983.

In the fall of 1983, Father Macke returned to Chicago to become the Father Minister of the Jesuit Community at Loyola University, and to begin doctoral studies in Pastoral Psychotherapy at Garrett Evangelical Theological Seminary in Evanston, Illinois. Under close supervision, and while integrating the best of psychology with the best of spirituality and theology, he did his three-year residency in Pastoral Psychotherapy at Lutheran General Counseling Center in Park Ridge, Illinois. To carry out his doctoral research project on the stress faced by Jesuit priests engaged in cross-cultural ministry in isolated areas like Alaska, he moved to **Anchorage**, Alaska. He received his Doctor of Ministry Degree in Pastoral Psychotherapy from Garrett in May 1987. A most memorable aspect of that occasion was that it was the first graduation ceremony he ever attended for any of his degrees, and that the commencement speaker was Coretta Scott King, wife of the late Dr. Martin Luther King, Jr.

Back in Anchorage, Father Macke took a full-time position as staff pastoral psychotherapist at the Samaritan Counseling Center of Alaska. When asked by his Father Provincial if he wanted to take a special trip on the occasion of getting his doctoral degree, he asked to be allowed, instead, to take flying lessons. Before the year 1987 was out, he had his private pilot's license; and, soon thereafter, his instrument rating. No other pilot at that particular flying school in Anchorage had ever earned his instrument rating in so short a time. As a fledgling pilot, he was given permission by Francis T. **Hurley**, Archbishop of Anchorage at the time, to fly one of the archdiocesan airplanes for weekend ministry in the area—and for pleasure, the condition being that he pay for the gasoline.

From 1981–91, Father Macke was actively involved as a presenting team priest for Worldwide Marriage Encounter. For two years during that decade, he served on the National Executive Board for Marriage Encounter, as well as local executive priest for the Archdioceses of both Chicago and Anchorage. While on the National Board, he was one of the section leaders for Marriage Encounter in Alaska, Idaho, Montana, Oregon, and Washington.

In August 1989, Father Macke was called back to Chicago by his Father Provincial to serve on the Chicago Province staff as Vocation Director and office manager. By now, however, he was thoroughly "Alaskanized," and needed to return. He was given permission to do so. In October 1993, he found himself in rural Alaska, living at St. Mary's Mission, **Andreafsky**, and working at the Native Ministry Training Program there. He soon became the field education director. As such, he regularly visited 18 villages in the Yukon-Kuskokwim Delta. While he found this ministry personally very enriching in a cross-cultural way, he also found the extensive village travel and the lack of opportunity to exercise his skills as a professional psychotherapist difficult. So, in 1996, he applied to be spiritual director and pastoral counselor at Holy Spirit Retreat House in Anchorage, and was accepted. In June 1998, he became the Executive Director of this center for spirituality. In 1999, he changed its name to **Holy Spirit Center**. Under his directorship, the Center began to flourish even more. One of his main joys at the Center turned out to be "the dynamic and alive Sunday community that worshiped at the Center's Resurrection Chapel."

Over the years, Father Macke found Alaska, "the Great Land," to be indeed a great land, a land that he admitted to "deeply loving." He found his various ministries there wholly enjoyable and satisfying. He also found pleasure and relaxation in flying, cross-country skiing, hiking, canoeing its wilds. With three traveling companions, in 1995, he spent 18 days hiking and canoeing in the Arctic National Wildlife Refuge. At the end of almost 25 years in Alaska, he summarized: "I have been very happy in Alaska—and wherever I have been missioned."

As of the year 2004, Father Macke was still Executive Director of Holy Spirit Center.

St. Joseph's Church,
Manley Hot Springs. *MK.*

MANDART, Father Joseph M.

Joseph Marie Mandart, a native of Brittany, became a member of the Diocese of Vancouver Island in 1862. He was the first diocesan priest to visit **Alaska**. On December 23, 1867, the year of the purchase of Alaska from Russia, the Catholics in **Sitka** petitioned Modeste **Demers**, Bishop of Vancouver Island, for a priest to serve them. In February of the next year, Father Mandart sailed for Sitka, where he stayed till July. Nine years later, he accompanied Archbishop Charles J. **Seghers** on his second trip to Alaska. The two left for northern Alaska on June 17, 1877, arriving at **St. Michael** a month later. On July 19th, they set out for interior Alaska via the **Unalakleet–Kaltag** portage. For almost a year, while the archbishop ranged widely throughout Alaska's interior seeking to make converts and looking for possible future mission sites, Father Mandart instructed the people at Nulato. In the spring of 1878, the two visited **Tanana** for two months. They left Alaska on July 14th of that same year, sailing south from St. Michael. Father Mandart, described as "somewhat of an eccentric man," spent 31 years on Vancouver Island. He died on October 16, 1893.

185

MANLEY HOT SPRINGS

The community of Manley Hot Springs is located virtually on the right bank of the Tanana River and roughly halfway between **Nenana** and **Tanana**. In 1907, Frank Manley built a four-story Hot Springs Resort Hotel. The community numbered 101 in 1910, 45 in 1930, 29 in 1950, 72 in 1967, and still 72 in the year 2000. The Hot Springs post office was established in 1907. The name was changed to Manley Hot Springs in 1957.

Manley Hot Springs never had a resident priest. For the most part, the mission there, dedicated to St. Joseph, was served by priests out of **Fairbanks**. From 1963–66, it was served by Father Charles A. **Saalfeld**, S.J., out of Fairbanks; then, until 1973, by him out of Tanana. Thereafter, other priests visited it at very irregular intervals.

Deacon Walter H. Gelinas, stationed at St. Nicholas parish, **North Pole**, began pastoral ministry at St. Joseph's mission in 1991. In addition to holding services there every other Sunday and on Holy Days, he did much to maintain and improve the old log church. He ended his ministry there in the year 2003.

Sometime in the 1990s, the church began to be used also by the Manley Hot Springs Baptist community.

By the year 2003, there were no longer Catholics living in Manley Hot Springs. Accordingly, the mission was closed and the church building transferred to the city for a token fee with the stipulation that it be used for religious purposes only. If used for other purposes, it could be taken back by the Diocese of Fairbanks.

July 3, 1993, was a memorable day for the whole of the Manley Hot Springs community. On that day, at an outdoor Mass celebrated by Father Louis L. **Renner**, S.J., assisted by Deacon Gelinas, Jay DeLima and Ginger **Esmailka** were joined in Holy Matrimony.

MANSKE, Father James J.

Calvin James Manske, known throughout life as James J., was born on May 12, 1924, in Green Bay, Wisconsin. After graduating from high school in Wisconsin, he joined the U.S. Maritime Service. In 1946, he had occasion to visit **Juneau**. After leaving the Maritime Service, he entered Mount Angel Seminary at St. Benedict, Oregon. He was ordained a priest on May 26, 1962, in his hometown of Wabeno, Wisconsin, by Bishop Dermot **O'Flanagan** for the Diocese of Juneau.

Father Manske served as assistant pastor of the Cathedral parish in Juneau, as pastor of St. Peter's parish in **Douglas**, and as pastor of St. Rose of Lima parish in **Wrangell**. For many years, he also held the offices of Chancellor, Vicar General, and Business Manager of the Juneau diocese.

Father Manske retired in February 1985. During his retirement years, he spent much of his time helping others. He made several trips to Russia to bring food, clothing, and money to people he knew there and wanted to help. He made the trips personally to ensure safe delivery of his gifts.

Father Manske died on August 12, 1998, in **Anchorage, Alaska**. He lies buried in Wabeno.

MARKHAM, Bro./Fr. Aloysius J., S.J., Dio. Priest

Aloysius J. Markham was born in Washington, D.C., on May 1, 1867. He entered the Jesuit novitiate at Frederick, Maryland, on August 14, 1886, as a candidate for the priesthood. During the early 1890s, he taught at several of the mission boarding schools in Montana. In 1895, he chose not to proceed with his training for the priesthood, but to become instead a Jesuit Lay Brother.

Brother Markham first went to **Alaska** in 1901. There he served at the **Holy Cross Mission** boarding school as infirmarian, prefect of the boys, and teacher. He left Alaska in 1908. He next spent a year at Santa Clara College, California, then a year at St. Francis Indian Mission in South Dakota, his last assignment before leaving the Jesuit Order.

For a short time, Aloysius Markham attended St. Mary's Seminary in Baltimore, Maryland. On November 27, 1910, he entered St. Thomas Seminary in Denver, Colorado, as a "special student" for the Prefecture Apostolic of Alaska. He was ordained a priest in the new Denver cathedral on May 11, 1913. He was the first diocesan priest ordained for Alaska.

Father Markham returned to Alaska in 1919. During the years 1919–29, he was pastor of Holy Family parish in **Anchorage**. Shortly after his arrival there, he was able to write to Joseph R. **Crimont**, S.J., Vicar Apostolic of Alaska at the time, that he was "pleased at Anchorage," and that he "was making many friends." He showed special concern for the sick at the Alaska Railroad Hospital. For a time, he served as chaplain of the Alaska Pioneers. During his Anchorage years, he also tended the Catholic flock in **Seward**.

Not a healthy man, by 1926, Father Markham found it difficult to walk, and suffered from dizziness and fainting spells. He moved from the parish rectory to the Parson's Hotel, where he was warm and had decent meals. In 1929, he left Alaska for Oregon. His last assignment was that of chaplain at Marylhurst College in Oswego, Oregon, where, on January 7, 1933, he was found dead in bed. He lies buried in Mount Calvary Cemetery in Portland, Oregon.

15

MARQUETTE MISSIONARY

The airplane, the *Marquette Missionary*, so named by way of thanking and honoring the members of the Marquette League of New York, its donors, was the first airplane owned by the Catholic missions of

Alaska. It was a custom-built six-seater Bellanca Pacemaker, powered by a Packard Diesel engine. It was the first diesel-powered plane to fly in Alaska.

The plane, after having been flown from the East Coast to California, and then to the Pacific Northwest, was put on the *S.S. Aleutian* in Seattle, Washington, on August 30, 1930, and from there shipped to **Seward**. On board with it were Father Philip I. **Delon**, S.J., General Superior of Jesuits in Alaska, and Brother George J. **Feltes**, S.J., pilot of the plane. The *S.S. Aleutian* arrived in Seward on September 5th. From Seward the plane was shipped to **Fairbanks** by rail. A week later, on the 12th, it made its first flight in the Alaskan sky. The plane and motor performed perfectly, as they had from the outset. In Fairbanks, Father Delon engaged Ralph Wien, an airplane mechanic and pilot, to serve as co-pilot.

On September 18th, with Brother Feltes as pilot, Ralph Wien as co-pilot, and Father Delon as passenger, the *Marquette Missionary* flew from Fairbanks to **Holy Cross Mission**, its intended home base. On the 24th, Father **Hubert A. Post**, S.J.,

joined the three for the flight to **Nome**. But, just before the plane left Holy Cross, the two pilots took Father Aloysius J. **Robaut**, S.J., up for "a short hop" over the mission he had founded 42 years earlier.

On September 29th, the *Marquette Missionary* left Nome for **Kotzebue**, but was turned back by bad weather. On the way back to Nome, it landed at the **Pilgrim Hot Springs** Mission to drop Father Delon off to attend to some business there. For the next week, the weather was too poor for flying. On October 7th, it did allow Ralph Wien to fly to "the Springs" to pick up Father Delon and fly him back to Nome. All this time, the three were waiting for weather favorable enough to allow them to fly to Kotzebue. This was the case on the 9th. At 4:32 that afternoon, the *Marquette Missionary* landed at Kotzebue, where the three were met by the 31-year-old pastor of Kotzebue, Father William F. Walsh, a volunteer priest ordained for the Archdiocese of San Francisco on June 11, 1926. Understandably, Father Walsh was very happy to see them.

On October 10th, Fathers Delon and Walsh

On June 29, 1930, Bishop Joseph R. Crimont, S.J., blesses the mission plane, the *Marquette Missionary*, on Long Island, New York. Brother George J. Feltes, S.J., pilot, and George Pickenpack, co-pilot, stand to the extreme right. *JOPA-536.2.08.*

attended to the business that occasioned the trip to Kotzebue in the first place. On that day, and on the following day, the weather was too poor for any kind of flying. In his account of events that followed, Brother Feltes wrote, "October 12th: Sunday, Father Delon and Father Walsh finished their last work on earth."

In the afternoon of that fateful Sunday, October 12, 1930, Father Delon wanted to take a trip to Deering to take care of some business, and, at the same time, to show Father Walsh some of his territory from the air. Father Walsh welcomed the opportunity.

The two pilots readied the plane for the flight. Just when everything was ready for takeoff, some snow flurries blew in. By the time the weather had cleared, it was too late for the flight to Deering. But, as the plane was all set to go anyway, Father Delon decided to take Father Walsh up for a short swing over Kotzebue. Ralph Wien was already at the controls, so Brother Feltes told him to take the two up.

In a telegram to his Provincial Superior, Father Joseph M. Piet, S.J., Brother Feltes left an eye-witness account of what followed:

> Ralph took off with the two Fathers. He got into a little snow. Some of it must have got on the windshield and he decided to come in to land. In turning to the left, he made a very sharp nose high turn and stalled the plane at an altitude of about 350 feet. It fell out of control in a wide sweeping turn, very much like a spin. When he had turned back from his first attempt at landing, he had turned on his motor and had shut it down about half before starting his last turn. About 30 feet from the ground he turned it on and went into a straight dive for the ground and struck it head on and the plane stood straight up on its nose with the motor buried in the ground.

The three on board were killed instantly. A Coroner's Jury found that "adverse weather conditions, alone," were responsible for the tragic event. Brother Feltes simply could not agree with that finding, neither at the time nor some 40 years later. In his account of the accident, written shortly after it occurred, he wrote, "The sole cause of the accident was an error of human judgment."

On the 20th day of that October, Father Bellarmine **Lafortune**, S.J., arrived in Kotzebue to replace Father Walsh. As he dismantled the plane, he was "amazed how carefully it was put togeth-

er." The motor was in good enough condition to be sent to the Packard factory in Detroit.

All in all, the *Marquette Missionary* survived the crash remarkably well.

37, 92, 97

MARSHALL (Fortuna Ledge)

The Central Yup'ik Eskimo village of Marshall is located on the east bank of the Poltes Slough, north of Arbor Island on the right bank of the Yukon River in the Yukon-Kuskokwim Delta. The village came into prominence when gold was discovered in July 1913 on nearby Wilson Creek. It was named for Thomas R. Marshall, vice president of the United States under Woodrow Wilson. When a post office was to be established there in 1915, the U.S. Postal Department, fearing that this Marshall could be too easily confused with other communities of the same name in other parts of the United States, declined the name Marshall. Donald Hunter, postmaster at Marshall at the time, submitted as a possible name that of his wife, Fortuna. Fortuna Ledge became the official postal name of the village. The village was incorporated as Fortuna Ledge in 1970. However, it is still commonly referred to as Marshall. In 1939, Marshall had 91 inhabitants; in 1950, 95; in 1960, 166; in 1970, 175; in 1979, 210; in 1990, 294; and in the year 2000, 349.

Under date of May 7, 1950, Father **John P. Fox**, S.J., wrote concerning the history of the Marshall mission:

> On passing through here in 1927, I saw a tiny chapel here about 12′ × 20′. It was very old and the floor was just about rotted through in places. . . . Various missionaries, beginning with Father Anthony **Keyes** in 1914, (when the **Pilot Station** mission was founded, and Marshall and **Mountain Village** were visited about five or six times a year from there) visited Marshall at intervals, as well as the surrounding mining camps. Before that time a priest occasionally passed through.

In 1945, Father Fox wrote, "The chief event of the year 1945: the finishing and blessing, by Bishop [Walter J.] **Fitzgerald**, S.J., of the new chapel of the Mother of God at Marshall." It was Father

Immaculate Heart of Mary Church, Marshall. *Photo by Ms. Mary Therese Burik.*

George S. **Endal**, S.J., who put up that chapel. In 1971, under the foremanship of Brother John **Huck**, S.J., a new rectory was built at Marshall. On December 5, 1997, Marshall's present church, dedicated under the title of Immaculate Heart of Mary, was dedicated and blessed by Michael J. **Kaniecki**, S.J., then Bishop of **Fairbanks**. It was Deacon Paul V. **Perreault**, P.E., Engineer for the Diocese of Fairbanks, who designed and oversaw the construction of the new Immaculate Heart of Mary Church.

In recent decades, the Marshall Catholic community has been visited and served by priests stationed at neighboring villages and at **Bethel**. It had a resident priest during the year 1989–90, when Father Thomas N. **Gallagher**, S.J., resided there.

Church history was made in Marshall on February 8, 1975, when Marshall resident Alvin F. Owletuk, one of the first enrollees in the **Eskimo Deacon Program**, was ordained there to the permanent diaconate by Robert L. **Whelan**, S.J., Bishop of Fairbanks at the time. Deacon Owletuk was the first Eskimo to be ordained to the permanent diaconate. For several years, the Catholic community of Marshall had the services also of Deacon Gabriel Evan.

As of the year 2004, Clara Shorty was ably administering the Marshall parish.

MARTINEK, Father John B.

John B. Martinek, son of Raymond G. and Rose B. Novak Martinek, was born on March 6, 1947, in Edgerton, Wisconsin. In 1952, he moved with his parents back to their hometown of Chicago. There he attended parochial schools for his elementary education. In 1961, he entered Quigley Preparatory Seminary South, the minor seminary of the Archdiocese of Chicago. He was encouraged in his vocation to the priesthood by the example of his parents—very devout and active Catholics—and by that of their pastor, Father Aloysius A. Menarik. After graduating from Quigley in 1965, he continued his studies for the priesthood at Niles College of Loyola University, the archdiocesan major seminary.

John, along with other seminarians, spent the summer of 1966 in Mexico as part of a program coordinated by the Maryknoll Fathers. In the small village of Tlaxco, in the Sierra Madre Mountains southeast of Mexico City, he was involved in community organization and Religious education. It was a difficult summer for him, knowing little Spanish and being afflicted early on with dysentery. As the summer was drawing to a close, he had little intention of returning. On his final night in the village, two of the locals got involved in a gun fight over a card game. One of the men died in John's arms, as he and another seminarian tried to treat his wounds. The people of the village, who had been very kind to and patient with the seminarians, were sure that they would never see these Americans again. However, as the single-engine plane lifted off from the cow pasture "airport," John and fellow seminarians on board vowed that they would return. During the next four summers, he was back in Mexico. His subsequent involvement in Hispanic ministry in inner-city Chicago was traceable back to those five summers in the remote mountains of Mexico.

After graduating from Niles College with a B.A. degree in sociology in 1969, John continued his education toward the priesthood at St. Mary of the Lake Seminary in Mundelein, Illinois. During his years there, he helped out in the Hispanic parishes on Chicago's Westside, working especially with Latino street gangs. He became involved also as a legal aide and interpreter at the Cook County jail and the county criminal court. His final year of preparation for the diaconate saw him at St. Mary of the Lake parish, Chicago. He was ordained a priest on May 9, 1973, by Cardinal John P. Cody, Archbishop of Chicago.

Father Martinek's first assignment as a priest was to St. Jerome's parish, Chicago, where he ministered especially to the Cuban exile community and to the children in the parish school. From 1974–78, he taught Spanish and Religion at the Quigley seminary, meanwhile also ministering, as time allowed, to Hispanic parishioners in the several different parishes in which he resided.

After four years of teaching in the minor seminary, Father Martinek felt a strong call to return to full-time parish ministry. For the next 13 years, from 1978–91, he served in a number of different parishes, now as associate pastor, now as pastor. In 1983, he was named pastor of St. Ann's parish. During his final six years as pastor of that 1500-family parish, he was the only priest there. Most of his ministry continued to be to Hispanic parishioners. Toward the end of his years at St. Ann's, both of his parents became seriously ill. An only child, he gave as much time as his parish responsibilities allowed caring for them. After his mother died in 1989, and his father in 1990, he recognized that his caring for them and his parish ministry had drained him both emotionally and physically, and that he needed to get away for a time to revitalize himself.

In 1991, Cardinal Joseph L. Bernardin of Chicago graciously and generously accepted his resignation as pastor of St. Ann's parish and granted him six months to travel and renew himself. On April 7, 1991, the Sunday after Easter Sunday, Father Martinek began what he called "the great adventure." He loaded a tent, a sleeping bag, and his two dogs in the

Father John B. Martinek.
Photo by Patricia Walter.

back of a Jeep, and began a drive to **Alaska** by way of Nova Scotia and over the back roads of Canada. He arrived in Alaska in June for what he thought was a once-in-a-lifetime visit. "As I experienced the beauty," he wrote, "of mountains and rivers, the wildlife and the wilderness of Canada and Alaska, all opening to me the beauty and love of God, I gradually began to be renewed in body and in spirit." As he was returning to the Lower 48, he became aware of a desire in him to return to Alaska, not just as a visitor, but as a priest. In San Francisco, he abandoned his further planned itinerary, and drove back to Alaska, to talk to Michael J. **Kaniecki**, S.J., Bishop of **Fairbanks** at the time, about the possibilities of ministering in the Diocese of Fairbanks. Bishop Kaniecki's reaction was favorable.

In September 1991, Father Martinek returned to Chicago, as scheduled, and continued on in a program of personal renewal. During this, he discussed with Cardinal Bernardin the possibility of his ministering in Alaska. Rather reluctantly, the Cardinal gave him permission to serve in the Diocese of Fairbanks, "on loan," for three years.

In December 1991, Father Martinek began his Alaskan ministry, among the Koyukon Athabaskan Indians along the middle Yukon River, as pastor of Our Lady of the Snows parish in **Nulato**, and as visiting priest to its two dependent missions, **Koyukuk** and **Kaltag**. Travel by snowmachine and boat was something new to him. However, after being patiently instructed and guided by men of the village, he was soon at ease "traveling the river," whether by snowmachine or boat. Before long, he came to enjoy the wilderness trips and "the peace of being in the beauty of God's creation." While in Nulato, after spending the morning hours in prayer and doing maintenance work around the church/residence building, he generally spent the afternoons doing "the main village activity," visiting homes, where he felt he did his most effective pastoral care work.

After some three years on the middle Yukon—and after Cardinal Bernardin had granted him another, and "final," three years in Alaska—Father Martinek, in 1995, took on the assignment of pastor of St. Francis Xavier's parish in **Kotzebue**. There he found himself in the land of the Inupiat Eskimos. He found himself also in a land not without natural wonders of its own. With the pen of a poet, he wrote: "In December, we get down to less than three hours of 'daylight.' This, in reality, is no more than a twilight, when the sun, barely brushing the southern horizon, paints, in pastel colors, at the same time the sunrise and sunset across the sky, the frozen Sound, and the distant mountains." He was fascinated, too, by the "brilliant displays of northern lights."

After three years of ministry in Kotzebue, Father Martinek could write, "As I loved priestly ministry in the inner-city of Chicago, and loved priestly ministry on the middle Yukon, so I now love and find joy in priestly ministry here in Kotzebue." That was in 1998, the year he celebrated his silver jubilee as a priest. By now, he was convinced that it was in Alaska that he wanted to spend the rest of his active years as a priest. While in Chicago for jubilee celebrations, he asked the new Archbishop of Chicago, Cardinal Francis E. George, O.M.I., for permission to be incardinated into the Diocese of Fairbanks. Permission was granted. On January 1, 2000, Father Martinek officially became a priest of the Missionary Diocese of Fairbanks.

In the year 2002, Father Martinek ended his tenure in Kotzebue, to become pastor both of Our Lady of Sorrows parish in **Delta Junction** and of Holy Rosary parish in **Tok**, as well as visiting priest to the latter's dependent mission, **Eagle**. For the first time, since he came to minister as a priest in Alaska, he was now on the highway system. To his joy, he was still, more than ever, surrounded by the beauties of the Alaskan wilderness, especially by mountains.

During his summers in Mexico as a seminarian, many years earlier, Father Martinek had prayed Psalm 121 every time he looked out the window toward the Sierra Madre Mountains. In Kotzebue, every time he went out the front door of St. Francis Xavier's Church and looked across the waters of Kotzebue Sound to the mountains on the far side, he had prayed it. On his new assignment, too, as he drove between Delta Junction and Tok in the shadow of the Alaska Range, he continued to pray:

> I lift up my eyes toward the mountains:
> whence shall help come to me?
> My help is from the Lord,
> who made heaven and earth.

As of the year 2004, Father Martinek was still happily on the highway system southeast of Fairbanks.

67

MARX, Father John J.

John J. Marx was born in Tacoma, Washington, on June 14, 1925. He was baptized, made his first Holy Communion, and was confirmed in St. Patrick's parish there. In Seattle, he attended St. Edward's Minor Seminary. He graduated from O'Dea High School, also in Seattle. After enlisting in the U.S. Army, on October 5, 1944, he served as a medical technician. In 1951, he graduated, *magna cum laude*, from Seattle University and began a career with the Internal Revenue Service as a deputy collector in **Anchorage**, **Alaska**. On a fishing trip with Dermot **O'Flanagan**, Bishop of **Juneau** at the time, he realized that he wanted to return to his earlier vocation, that of being a priest. In March 1955, he entered the Major Seminary at Mount Angel, Oregon. On March 19, 1960, Bishop O'Flanagan ordained him a priest for the Diocese of Juneau.

Father Marx served communities in both the Archdiocese of Anchorage and the Diocese of Juneau. For his first assignment as a priest, he had St. Mary's parish in **Kodiak**. He began his three-year stay there on June 1, 1961. From the very first, he was well received by his parishioners. He did

Father John J.
Marx. *LRC.*

much to improve the physical condition of the school. He organized the Order of Martha, which encouraged ladies to make altar linens and vestments for home missions.

For the years 1964–66, Father Marx was at Holy Family Cathedral parish in Anchorage. He next served for a year as pastor of St. Joseph's parish in **Cordova** and of St. Francis Xavier's parish in **Valdez**. The year 1968–69 saw him at Holy Rosary parish in **Dillingham**. During the early 1970s, he was pastor in **Douglas**. St. Michael's parish in **Palmer** had his services during the years 1974–77. From 1977–82, he was again in Valdez.

In 1982, Father Marx, as a priest of the Archdiocese of Anchorage, retired to Seattle. There he lived for many years with his sister, Joan Marx, and "pursued his tremendous interest in reading and conversation with his many friends and family." Following a lengthy illness, he died in a Seattle hospital, on June 21, 2001.

15

MARYS IGLOO

Marys Igloo, north of **Nome**, is located on the northwest bank of the Kuzitrin River, two miles northwest of Marys Mountain and 40 miles southeast of **Teller**. This Inupiat Eskimo settlement at the head of steamboat navigation on the Kuzitrin River was properly called "Mary's Igloo" by the gold prospectors in the area. Mary was an Eskimo woman who extended generous hospitality to transient prospectors, trappers, and travelers. A Marys Igloo post office was established in 1901. This was closed in 1952. In 1910, the settlement had a population of 141; in 1930, 113; and in 1950, 64.

Marys Igloo was first visited by a Catholic missionary in 1906, when Father Bellarmine **Lafortune**, S.J., visited it out of Nome. In the fall of 1907, during his second visit, he converted the roadhouse, which he had bought earlier in the year from the Bruce Lloyd family, into a chapel and living quarters for a priest. By this time, there were 35 Catholics at Marys Igloo. They had been converted and baptized by him during their temporary stays in Nome.

On September 29, 1908, Father Joseph **Bernard**, S.J., became the resident missionary at Marys Igloo. He dedicated the mission to Our Lady of Lourdes. In the summer of 1911, with the help of Jesuit Lay Brothers Alexis Dugas and Alphonsus **Lemire**, he put up a new church, a prefabricated building he had purchased the summer before in Seattle from the American Portable House Company.

Father Bernard left Marys Igloo in 1915. He was replaced, for the following year, by Father Lafortune. After 1916, Marys Igloo was down-graded to a station. As such, it was only visited from time to time, out of Nome or out of the **Pilgrim Hot Springs** Mission. The name, "Our Lady of Lourdes," was transferred from Marys Igloo to the Pilgrim Springs mission, when this latter mission was established in 1918. By the early 1950s, Marys Igloo, was, more or less, totally abandoned as a year-round village.

97

McCAFFREY, Father Richard L., S.J.

Richard Leo McCaffrey was born of Scottish/Irish ancestry on March 28, 1943, in Boston, Massachusetts, the youngest of three sons born to Philip F. and Margaret Hendry McCaffrey. His father was a third-generation Irish-American. His mother was born in Glasgow, Scotland, and immigrated to the United States, when she was sixteen years old. Richard grew up in Boston, where, from 1948–56, he attended St. Catherine and St. Raphael grade

(*top*) The first "shack and chapel" at Marys Igloo north of Nome, April 1907. *Photo by Father Joseph Bernard, S.J./JOPA-512.A15.*

(*bottom*) The second church at Marys Igloo. *Photo by Father Joseph Bernard, S.J./JOPA-512.H41.*

(*opposite*) Catholic Eskimos at Marys Igloo, June 1915. *Photo by Father Joseph Bernard, S.J./JOPA-512.B97.*

schools, and Jesuit-staffed Boston College High School, from which he graduated in 1960. He spent the year 1960–61 attending the College of the Holy Cross in Worcester, Massachusetts. As one of his high school teachers he had Normand A. **Pepin**, S.J., to whom he attributes, in part, his vocation to the Society of Jesus.

On July 30, 1961, Richard entered the Jesuit novitiate at Shadowbrook, Lenox, Massachusetts. There, after completing his two-year noviceship, he pronounced the vows of perpetual poverty, chastity and obedience, making him a full-fledged member of the Society of Jesus. He spent one more year at Shadowbrook studying the classics and humanities, before going on to two years of philosophical studies, from 1964–66, at Weston College in Weston,

Massachusetts. He then, for a year, attended Boston College, Chestnut Hill, Massachusetts, to earn an M.A. degree.

Having all along been interested in one day serving "on the missions," Richard, while still a novice, had the good fortune to meet Father Paul C. **O'Connor**, S.J., veteran missionary from **Alaska**, when the latter visited Shadowbrook in 1962 to make his annual retreat. At the close of his retreat, Father O'Connor gave a talk to the novices. This got Richard thinking, dreaming about Alaska. In 1967, his dream became reality, when he was assigned to serve for two years at **Copper Valley School** as a teacher of mathematics, General Science, and economics, as well as Dorm Prefect of the boys.

In 1969, Richard returned to Boston for a year's

work with the Urban Sisters' League, a cooperative enterprise aimed at raising educational levels among inner-city youth. Before leaving Alaska, however, he had visited Father James E. **Poole**, S.J., in **Nome**, who made known to him his need for a volunteer radio engineer to help him get his projected radio station on the air. Checking several commercial stations for a possible engineer, Richard met with no success. But, during a chance visit to the campus radio station at Boston College, he happened to meet Thomas A. "Tom" **Busch**, a Boston College grad, whom he had come to know during his own Boston College days. He informed Tom of Father Poole's need, and gave him his address. As the year 2004 began to unfold, Tom Busch was still at radio **KNOM**, Nome, as its General Manager.

Richard made his theological studies at Weston Jesuit School of Theology from 1970–73, during which time he served also as the Treasurer of the Jesuit Community. He spent the summers of 1970 and 1971 back in Alaska, working with the Upward Bound Program at the University of Alaska–**Fairbanks**. During the latter part of the summer of 1971, he helped Brother John **Huck**, S.J., build a rectory at **Nunam Iqua** (at the time still known as Sheldon Point). Richard was ordained a priest on May 26, 1973, in St. Joseph's Chapel on the campus of the College of the Holy Cross.

Father McCaffrey spent the years 1973–76 in Fairbanks serving on the Diocesan Marriage Tribunal part-time and as associate pastor of Sacred Heart Cathedral parish. In 1977, he was Acting Chancellor of the Diocese of Fairbanks and visiting priest to St. Patrick's parish in **Barrow**.

After making his tertianship in Spokane, Washington, from January to June 1978, Father McCaffrey was pastor for a year of the Central Yup'ik Eskimo villages of **Tununak**, **Toksook Bay**, and **Nightmute** on Nelson Island. He then moved further up the Bering Sea coast, serving as pastor, from 1979–81, of the villages of **Hooper Bay** and **Scammon Bay**.

From 1981–85, Father McCaffrey was Chancellor of the Diocese of Fairbanks, living during those years in the diocesan chancery building. In addition to being Chancellor, he was also pastor of St. Aloysius parish in **Tanana**, commuting there by commercial air every other weekend. Both in Fairbanks and in Tanana, he spent long off-duty hours working as a jack-of-all-trades significantly upgrading the physical plants and facilities. In Tanana, he did extensive remodeling of an old house to make it habitable for the two **Ursuline** Sisters engaged in pastoral ministry in Tanana at the time. In Fairbanks, he saw to it that the whole basement level of the chancery building received a cement floor, properly tiled. During evening hours, he built four guest rooms, a laundry—and a bathroom in one of the basement wings.

Father McCaffrey spent the years 1985–87 absorbed full-time, except for the weekends in Tanana, in a major building project. In Fairbanks, he designed and oversaw the construction of the two-story, with full basement, 15,000 square-foot Jesuit House with accommodations for eleven residents and six guest rooms, plus an eight-car garage.

Bethel, on the lower Kuskokwim River, was the next scene of Father McCaffrey's spiritual and physical labors. From 1987–98, he held station there. He was assigned there in large part because of his building skills. The old Immaculate Conception Church in Bethel badly needed to be replaced. No sooner was he there, than he began to lay plans for a new church. Being, as he was, the sole pastor of the Bethel parish and its two dependent stations, **Russian Mission** and **Marshall** on the lower Yukon River, he had more than enough work for two full-time men. Nevertheless, the new church was up by 1993 and ready for dedication by 1995.

During both his Fairbanks and Bethel years, Father McCaffrey wore many hats. In addition to serving in the capacities already mentioned, he, at various times, served also as a Diocesan Consultor, as well as a Consultor to the General Superior of Jesuits in Alaska. For many years, he was a member of various diocesan boards and committees: Personnel, Liturgical, Financial, Ecumenical, and Construction. It was especially as Chairman of the Construction Committee and as a builder in his own right that he made major and lasting contributions to the Missionary Diocese of Fairbanks. After Father James C. **Spils**, S.J., described as "God's Builder in Alaska"—a man much admired by Father McCaffrey for the priest and builder that he was—

no one else deserves that same title more than Father McCaffrey himself.

While stationed in Bethel, Father McCaffrey made unexpected, unintentional headlines. *The Anchorage Daily News*, under date of April 19, 1990, reported: "Priest in Bethel shoots attacker." In the body of the article we read: "A Bethel priest scared off a wrench-wielding attacker by wounding him with a .357-caliber Magnum revolver." After he was struck on the head and knocked to the floor by an intruder, who had broken into his rectory bedroom through two locked doors at around 3:30 a.m., Father McCaffrey shot and wounded him with the revolver he had purchased for survival during snowmachine travel between remote villages. He himself immediately called the police, who arrived within 15 minutes. Following a trail of blood from the bedroom door to an exit and out into the yard, they found the assailant wounded and lying in the snow. With him he had a pipe wrench. The final ruling was that it was a case of "self-defense."

Up to this time, Father McCaffrey had remained a member of the New England Province of the Society of Jesus. In 1992, however, by then thoroughly at home in Alaska, he opted to become officially a member of the Oregon Province, under whose jurisdiction the missions of northern Alaska had been since 1932.

Father McCaffrey's tenure in Bethel came to an end in January 1998. After a short sabbatical leave, he became pastor of Immaculate Conception parish, Fairbanks, in October 1998. As such, he became known for the wisdom—and the wit—he brought to his homilies. For example, one year, for the series of sermons he preached during the Novena of Grace on the Seven Capital Sins, he chose, as a mnemonic aid for his listeners, the summary acronym GEL-CAPS (Gluttony, Envy, Lust, Covetousness, Avarice, Pride, Sloth). Words came easily to Father McCaffrey. He was a noted conversationalist. Among his hobbies, should be listed two: having a good conversation and having a special interest in Canon Law and ecclesiastical affairs.

As of the year 2004, Father McCaffrey was still pastor of Immaculate Conception parish in Fairbanks.

McDONALD, Father Angus R.

Angus McDonald was born on August 18, 1923, at Grand Forks, North Dakota, to Angus and Amelia Hobert McDonald. He had one brother and two sisters. As a child he lived in East Grand Forks, Minnesota, where his mother owned and operated a theater. From 1937–41, he attended St. Paul Academy High School in St. Paul, Minnesota. He was in the U.S. Army Air Corps for the year 1941–42. He spent the year 1942–43 at St. Louis University; the year 1944–45 at St. John's, Collegeville, Minnesota; the year 1945–46 at St. Thomas College in St. Paul; and the year 1946–47 at the University of Minnesota. According to a notation in the records, he "attended these various colleges on account of father's health."

On August 14, 1948, Angus McDonald entered the novitiate of the Society of Jesus at Los Gatos, California. After finishing the two-year noviceship and taking vows of poverty, chastity and obedience, he stayed on for two years of classical and humanities studies. In 1952, he went to Mount St. Michael's, Spokane, Washington, for philosophical studies. These he ended in 1955 with B.A. and M.A. degrees. On May 4th of that year, he received the Tonsure, constituting him a cleric, and the following day, Minor Orders. He spent the year 1955–56 teaching mathematics at Loyola High School in Los Angeles, and the year 1956–57 teaching mathematics at St. Ignatius High School in San Francisco. He left the Society of Jesus on May 27, 1957.

After leaving the Jesuits, McDonald studied medicine at Ottawa Medical School for two years, briefly joined the Carthusians in Vermont, and taught high school in London, England. He next went on to study theology at the Gregorian University in Rome. There, in 1963, he approached Bishop Francis D. **Gleeson**, S.J., Bishop of **Fairbanks**, about joining that diocese. He was accepted. Two years later, in Fairbanks' Pro-Cathedral of the Immaculate Conception, on April 24, 1965, he was ordained to the priesthood by Bishop Gleeson. It was a history-making event. Father McDonald was the first man to be ordained a priest in and for the Diocese of Fairbanks, the one and only man to be ordained a priest in "the Immaculate," and the first priest in the United States to be ordained with the liturgy in English rather than in the traditional Latin. After his ordination he returned to Rome for a final year of theology.

Father McDonald served as pastor of St. Patrick's parish in **Barrow**, **Alaska**, from June 1966 to April 1972. During his Barrow years, he provided the parish with a new rectory–residence building. From 1966–71, he resided in Barrow. During his last year as pastor of St. Patrick's, he commuted from Fairbanks. From June 1972 to July 1973, he was on loan to the **Anchorage** Archdiocese. He was then on loan to St. Thomas Regional Major Seminary at Kenmore, Washington, for the years 1973–75. In August 1975, he was appointed pastor of St. Francis Xavier's parish in **Kotzebue**. One month later, he was diagnosed as having pulmonary fibrosis. A warmer climate was prescribed for him. For several years he taught at Chaminade College in Honolulu, Hawaii, during which time he also did some pastoral work. After leaving Hawaii, he was engaged in various pastoral ministries in California and Oregon. The time came, when he needed nursing home care. He was received into the Maryville Nursing Home—owned and managed by the Sisters of St. Mary of Oregon—in Beaverton, Oregon, where he died, on December 18, 1988. He was buried ten days later at Calvary Cemetery in Grand Forks, North Dakota. Michael J. **Kaniecki**, S.J. Bishop of Fairbanks, was the officiating clergyman. Father **Francis E. Mueller**, S.J., who succeeded Father McDonald as pastor at Barrow, said of him: "He was a good priest."

Father Joseph F. McElmeel S.J. *JOPA-881.01.*

McELMEEL, Father Joseph F., S.J.

To most all who knew him, he was simply "Father Mac." Though he had a keen interest in Alaskan history, especially in Catholic Alaskan Church history, and collected many documents and made many notes concerning it, he himself never published anything. He considered himself a revisionist historian, maintaining that what could be written about the Alaskan missions would not be interesting, and what would be interesting could not be written. As a missionary new to **Alaska**, he was critical of events, of people, and even of his fellow missionaries to the point, at times, of being harsh in his judgments of them. And yet, for all that, he admired "the founding Fathers," of the Alaska Mission and wanted their story "told to the world." He was regarded as one of the best mushers on the trail. He was a devoted fan of baseball, played the game well himself, and promoted it while at **Nulato**. For six years, he was General Superior of Jesuits in Alaska.

Joseph Francis McElmeel was born on January 17, 1884, in Delhi, Iowa. He attended St. Joseph's parochial school in Earling, Iowa, from 1890–97, then Gonzaga High School and Gonzaga College, in Spokane, Washington. On July 23, 1905, he entered the Jesuit novitiate at Los Gatos, California. After completing his two-year noviceship and two years of classical and humanities studies, he went on to teach at Gonzaga from 1909–12, and at St. Leo's in Tacoma, Washington, for a year. He made his philosophical studies in Spokane, at Gonzaga and at Mount St. Michael's during the years 1913–16. He next spent the years 1916–19 teaching at Santa Clara University. From 1919–23, he made his theological studies at St. Louis University in St. Louis, Missouri. He was ordained a priest in St. Louis on June 26, 1921. In 1924, while making his tertianship at Poughkeepsie, New York, he volunteered for the Alaska Mission. On August 23rd of that year, he arrived at Nulato. Father Crispin S. **Rossi**, S.J., who greeted him, soon found him to be "a very able and efficient father."

Father McElmeel, "Father Mac," spent the majority of his Alaskan years at Nulato. From his earliest years there, he proved to be an energetic, well-adjusted missionary. Out of Nulato, his home base, he traveled extensively up and down the Yukon River, ranging from **Tanana** upstream to **Kaltag** downstream, to visit those villages, along with the in-between villages of **Kokrines**, **Ruby**, **Galena**, and **Koyukuk**. In addition to these major villages, he visited also a number of minor ones and small settlements and camps. To save money, he developed his own dogteams and traveled alone. He took pride in his teams and in his acknowledged mushing stamina and skills. After four years on the Yukon, he was able to write to his Father Provincial, "I know every wrinkle in the trails in my district. There is little danger of getting lost on the Yukon. And, all in all, there is far less danger on the Yukon than on the busy streets of Seattle."

To cover his mission stations and the fish camps scattered along the Yukon during the season of open water, he built himself a chapel houseboat, the *St. Anthony*. Father Mac showed special concern for the sick. In her book, *Nulato: An Indian Life on the Yukon*, Poldine **Carlo** wrote: "If someone was very sick and [someone] came to the village from other villages for the priest, Father always would go, even if he had to walk."

During the long Alaskan summer days, the crack of the baseball bat and the roar of the Nulato crowd could often be heard at the airstrip. Father Mac, in keeping with his own interest in baseball, had organized the "Mosquito League." The people took to baseball with enthusiasm. In her book, Poldine Carlo also wrote: "On Sunday afternoons all the young men and boys used to go to the airfield and have a big baseball game. That used to be so exciting, especially to watch our boy friends in the game. Father Mac used to be the umpire. He was just so good."

In contrast to the long, hot, bright and sunny days of summer on the middle Yukon, there were the short, cold, dark days of winter. Some of the people, including Sisters of St. **Ann** new to Alaska's interior, were prone to suffer from feelings of depression and loneliness during Nulato's long, dark, winter months. Father Mac told one of the Sisters suffering from loneliness brought on by the darkness, "Sister, every missionary has to be her own light." Native storytellers always ended their

stories with the cliché, "I have shortened the winter." To shorten the winters of the Sisters, Father Mac taught them courses in Sacred Scripture.

Father Mac spent the year 1929–30 teaching at Seattle College, and the year 1930–31 at Tanana. During his Tanana year, he routinely visited Kokrines and Ruby. From 1931 to 1941, Nulato was again his home base. For some weeks, during the early part of 1939, he served as substitute pastor of the **Nome** parish.

Fairbanks was the scene of Father Mac's labors for the year 1941–42, then he was back on the Yukon again, "happy to be with his Indians." However, he was now stationed at Galena, where he was to spend the next five years. Of his Galena years he wrote: "In April 1942 I was sent to Galena to look after the Indians who had gathered there to work on the air field, and also to act as chaplain for the soldiers at the Base." He found his Galena years difficult ones, because, in his judgment, "the soldiers and officers at the Base and the white traders and construction workers did their best to ruin the Indians, and with some success."

Father Mac stayed on at Galena until September 1947, when he was transferred to **Juneau** for a year. He found it "a most enjoyable year." In 1948, he was reassigned to Fairbanks, for "one year"—which turned out to be three. Then he was back in Juneau again for the years 1952–57. He spent the years 1957–60 in **Sitka**, before going still further south, to **Ketchikan**, for the final year of his life.

On January 17, 1961, Father Mac suffered a mild stroke, from which he recovered rather quickly, and soon was again his "peppy self," able to walk vigorously two miles a day. He once more took up his duties as hospital chaplain and parish assistant. During the summer, he made trips to Portland to visit his Father Provincial, and to Seattle to make his annual retreat. He returned to Ketchikan on August 11th. On the 13th, while walking back from the parish church to his quarters in the hospital, he was stricken by a heart attack. He was conscious almost to the end. "If God wants it this way, I am happy" were his last words. He died on the 16th. His wish to die in Alaska was granted; his wish to be buried in Alaska was not. He lies buried in the Jesuit cemetery at Mount St. Michael's.

Father Joseph F. McElmeel, S.J., was a man gifted above the average. He served as General Superior of the Alaska Mission from 1937–44, and as a Consultor to the General Superior from 1931–37. He was of a practical bent. He felt strongly, for example, that the **Holy Cross Mission** school should stress the teaching of practical skills that would suit its pupils well when they returned to village life. In a letter he wrote to his cousin Bernard F. **McMeel**, S.J., on December 19, 1953, he defined a missionary as "a man who teaches catechism in season and out of season to the children and grownups of his district." He felt strongly that a priest who did not teach catechism every day, did not belong on the Alaska Mission. "The teaching of CATECHISM," he summarized, "is the real test."

Anthropologically speaking, he was a man of his time, when it came to shamanism and to what he deemed "pagan, superstitious" cultural practices, in particular, the "stickdance," or the "Feast for the Dead," which was held at Nulato and Kaltag. During his years on the Yukon, he spoke out forcefully against those traditional cultural ceremonials, preached against "trying to follow two trails at the same time." He regretted having so relatively few "real Catholics" in his Koyukon flocks. "I mean to say," he informed his Superior, "that all the others are carrying water on both shoulders, mixing shamanism with Catholicism." With the passing of the years, the judgments of that man with "a square-set determination about his shoulders" mellowed. "Father Mac" is still fondly remembered and kindly spoken of along the Yukon.

44, 142

McGRATH

McGrath is located on the left bank of the Kuskokwim River in **Alaska**'s interior, directly across (south) from the Kuskokwim's confluence with the Takotna River. The Kuskokwim makes a horseshoe around the town. A small trading post was established across the river from the present site of McGrath in 1907, when gold was discovered on the Innoko River. A McGrath post office was established in 1913. A major flood in 1933 and riverbank erosion at the original site caused people to start

moving to the present site in the 1930s. By 1940, the new town site was firmly established with a population of 138. Ten years later, McGrath had a population of 175; and in 1992, 528. By the year 2000, however, that number had dropped back to 401. Whites and upper Kuskokwim Athabaskan Indians make up the population of this transportation, communication, and supply hub.

There is nothing to indicate that Catholic missionaries visited the McGrath area before Father Francis M. **Ménager**, S.J., began to visit it out of **Bethel** in the early 1940s. In 1947, he bought a Quonset hut for $700 and had it moved into place, "near Aviation Field," to serve as a church. In July 1955, this Quonset hut church was moved again, by Father Lawrence N. **Haffie**, S.J., serving McGrath out of Bethel. During the year 1959–60, Father **John J. Wood**, S.J., ably assisted by his skilled father, built the present log church. This new church, dedicated to St. Michael, was ready for "the grand opening," in the words of Father Wood, for the 1960 Christmas Mass. He was proud of the church's pews—"appear the best in the Vicariate," he informed Francis D. **Gleeson**, S.J., Vicar Apostolic of Alaska at the time.

The following Jesuit Fathers, traveling out of Bethel, tended the McGrath parish: Ménager, 1944–48; Segundo **Llorente**, 1948–50; Norman E. **Donohue**, 1950–53; Haffie, 1953–56; Pasquale M. Spoletini, 1956–57 and 1958–59; Henry G. **Hargreaves**, 1957–58; and Wood, 1959–60.

Father Wood resided in McGrath, 1960–62; as did Fathers William T. **McIntyre**, S.J., 1962–63, and George T. **Boileau**, S.J., 1963–64. Father Robert F. **Corrigal**, S.J., visited McGrath, out of Bethel, 1964–65; then resided there, 1966–68. Father Wood resided there, 1965–66.

After them, Father Bernard F. **McMeel**, S.J., visited McGrath, first out of **Fairbanks**, 1968–73; then out of **Galena**, 1973–76; then again out of Fairbanks, 1976–78. Father James A. **Sebesta**, S.J., visited McGrath out of **Kaltag**, 1978–81.

Father David M. **Fitz-Patrick**, priest of the Diocese of Fairbanks, resided in McGrath, 1981–82, as did Father Thomas W. Fisk, S.J., 1982–83. Father Michael W. **Warfel**, priest of the Archdiocese of **Anchorage** at the time, later Bishop of **Juneau**, vis-

St. Michael's Church, McGrath. *LR.*

ited McGrath out of Anchorage, 1983–85. Father Sebesta visited it, out of St. Marys, **Andreafsky**, 1985–87 and 1990–91, and out of Fairbanks, 1987–90. Father William C. **Dibb**, S.J., resided in McGrath, 1991–95. During the years 1995–2000, Father Thomas N. **Gallagher**, S.J., either resided in McGrath or visited it out of Anchorage. In the year 2001, Father Gerald S. **Ornowski**, M.I.C., began to visit McGrath out of Fairbanks.

The following Sisters, too, served the McGrath parish: Judy Tralnes, C.S.J.P., 1984–87; Grace DiDomenicantonio, C.S.J.P., 1984–89; Dolores Steiner, S.N.D., 1989–91; and Frances McCarron, I.B.V.M., 1997–98.

In 1999, Brother Kirby **Boone**, C.F.X., began to serve as Pastoral Administrator of the McGrath parish.

64

McGUIGAN, Father Francis, W., S.J.

He was a high school honor student and athlete, a teacher, a coach, a high school principal, a counselor, a fund-raiser, an avid golfer, a parish administrator. But, before all else, he was a self-described "community priest." As such, he served in various capacities, competently and loyally, both the Catholic Church in **Fairbanks** and the Fairbanks

community at large for nearly four decades. This is all the more remarkable to those who knew, what few knew, that his first choice for priestly ministry had been, not **Alaska**, but China. "Alaska," he confided to close friends, "was the last place I wanted to go. It shows you how Divine Providence works."

Francis W. McGuigan was born on December 13, 1919, in Spokane, Washington, to James McGuigan and Elizabeth Quinn. He was the seventh in a family of seven boys and one girl. He was born a stone's throw from the Jesuit complex consisting of St. Aloysius Church, St. Aloysius Grade School, Gonzaga High School, and Gonzaga University. He received his elementary and secondary education at St. Aloysius Grade and Gonzaga High respectively. From his earliest years, he was sports-minded. In sports, he excelled both in football and baseball. As a sophomore in high school, he was voted to the all-city football team as a tight end. He earned four varsity letters in baseball and won all-city honors in that sport.

While athletics were big in the life of young Francis, and came ahead of other extracurricular school actives such as drama, speech, and the school paper, academic studies were given top priority. By his own admission, he was motivated less by ambitions of lofty scholarship than by fear of losing eligibility for sports. He made the honor roll as a sophomore. By the time he graduated from Gonzaga High, he had served as vice-president of the student body and president of his 1939 graduating class, and had earned an Honor Classical diploma.

But, the pre-Jesuit life of Francis McGuigan was not all sports and studies. While still in grade school, he earned spending money for himself and family needs by selling newspapers on downtown street corners and magazines from door to door. From the age of 15 on, his summers were filled with eight-hour workdays: in "the market place," the lumber yard, the State of Washington Department of Highways.

Francis entered the Jesuit novitiate at Sheridan, Oregon, on August 15, 1939. After completing his two-year noviceship and two years of classical and humanities studies, he went to Mount St. Michael's in Spokane for three years of philosophical studies. These he ended in 1946 with a master's degree.

Father Francis W. McGuigan,
S.J. *Courtesy of Monroe
Foundation, Inc./Fairbanks.*

He next went on to spend three years teaching and coaching at Marquette High School in Yakima, Washington. He found his Yakima years "very satisfying." From 1949–53, he was engaged in theological studies at Alma College, Los Gatos, California. He was ordained a priest in Spokane on June 21, 1952.

From 1953–55, Father McGuigan again served at Marquette, this time as vice-principal, teacher, athletic director, and assistant coach in all sports. During the year 1955–56, he made his tertianship, the final year of his formal training as a Jesuit, at Port Townsend, Washington. Before beginning another stay at Marquette, this time as principal, he spent the summer of 1956 soliciting funds for the newly established Jesuit High School in Portland, Oregon. This he did begging from door to door. Little did he suspect at the time that this was to serve him as an apprenticeship for his future fund-raising for education in Fairbanks.

After Marquette closed in the spring of 1959, Father McGuigan went on to become the "Father Minister" at Mount St. Michael's for the next three years. In that capacity, he oversaw several construction projects and the purchase of a new summer villa for Jesuit seminarians on Priest Lake, Idaho.

On June 10, 1962, Father McGuigan received a letter from his Father Provincial directing him to report to Fairbanks to take over as principal of Monroe Catholic High School. There, one of his first major concerns, in addition to the academic program, was seeing to it that the school's makeshift Quonset hut gymnasium be replaced with a full-fledged gym. The new one, named for Bishop George T. **Boileau**, S.J., was completed in 1965.

The year 1966 saw Father McGuigan back in Spokane, now as pastor of St. Aloysius parish, the largest parish in the Spokane diocese at the time. It was in St. Aloysius Church that he had been baptized, received his first Holy Communion, been confirmed, and ordained a priest. During his tenure as pastor of St. Aloysius parish, major renovations of the church building were carried out, and the parish became debt-free for the first time in 75 years.

In August 1969, Father McGuigan was asked by his Father Provincial to return to Fairbanks, to serve as the first pastor of the newly established Sacred Heart Cathedral parish. Robert L. **Whelan**, S.J, Bishop of Fairbanks at the time, had asked for this appointment. Again, trusting in Divine Providence, Father McGuigan rose to the challenge. He worked hard to establish good relationships all around, and to have a parish liturgically alive. He established a strong Parish Council and put the parish on a stable economic basis.

Before long, Father McGuigan was asked by Bishop Whelan to work out an annual program for raising funds for the Catholic schools in Fairbanks. In 1970, the first HIPOW ("Happiness Is Paying Our Way") Charity Auction took place. Year after year, this fund-raiser became an ever greater success.

In 1971, Father McGuigan—who, during his years of training, had chosen a curriculum that specialized in school administration and counseling— was contacted by the Fairbanks Public School System, which was in need of a certified counselor on an emergency basis at Main Junior High School. With Bishop Whelan's approval, he accepted this challenge as part of his pastoral duties. However, in May of that year, he was asked by the Superintendent of Schools to remain on as counselor also for the following school year. With the approval of his Religious Superiors, and in hopes of helping youth to succeed in life, he accepted to stay on as

At the Fairbanks International Airport, on May 2, 1984, flowers are being presented to First Lady Nancy Reagan, while Pope John Paul II and Father Francis W. McGuigan, S.J., look on. Bishop Robert L. Whelan, S.J., is partially visible behind Father McGuigan. *BR-843643.*

a full-time counselor. After having served for five years as a counselor at Main and Tanana, two junior high schools in Fairbanks, he was asked to join the counseling staff at West Valley Senior High in Fairbanks. He was on the staff there for nine years, from 1976–85. Of his years as a student counselor, he said he could not remember having had what he might call "a really bad day."

Given Father McGuigan's skills, when it came to organizing affairs, it is no wonder that it was to him that Bishop Whelan turned, in early 1984, when a coordinator was needed to plan for the upcoming visit to Fairbanks of Pope John Paul II and President Ronald Reagan. The visit took place on May 2, 1984, and, predictably, everything went smoothly.

In 1985, at the request of Bishop Whelan, Father McGuigan became director of the newly created Monroe Foundation, Inc. Henceforth, his main responsibilities were the Monroe Foundation and the annual HIPOW Charity Auction. Ever resourceful, and knowing how to mix the useful with the pleasant when it came to raising money for the support of the Catholic schools of Fairbanks, Father McGuigan resorted to gaming, raffles, and ad hoc auctions. He also arranged golf tournaments. He himself was an avid and successful golfer. He was highly successful as a fund-raiser. People found his appeals, his "pitch," irresistible. And he had a spe-

cial gift, a special "touch," when it came to recruiting volunteer helpers. Those who did not find it in them to refuse his entreaties soon found themselves enthusiastic supporters of his cause. They admitted to having become "McGuiganized."

But, with Father McGuigan, it was not all business and play. Being the self-proclaimed "community priest" that he was, he was always available to help out on weekends in one or other of the parishes or on a military base. He routinely conducted weddings and burials. He was an active counselor of adults. The sick especially were of concern to him, even when he himself was one of them.

And Father McGuigan was actively involved with the Boys Scouts of America. On December 13, 1995, the Midnight Sun Council honored him at its annual Distinguished Citizen Award Banquet. The Fairbanks community at large, too, acknowledged its indebtedness to him. On November 2, 1999, the Greater Fairbanks Chamber of Commerce conferred on him *The Fairbanks Daily News-Miner* Citizen of the Year Award in recognition of his being "a tireless advocate," when it came to furthering education in Fairbanks.

The month before Father McGuigan received this second award, he was diagnosed as having cancer. Treatment followed, and his hopes of surviving the cancer for a few years were high. Alas, it was terminal. Slowly his life of 80 years was coming to an end. But, even during the last months, weeks of it, to the extent that he was able, he remained the active priest that he had always been. He brought Communion to the sick, visited them in the hospital, phoned people to inquire about their health and to wish them well. The focus was on others.

Finally, Father McGuigan himself was totally confined to his bed, in Denali Center, Fairbanks. There, during an interview, he said of his life, "It's been a good career, a happy one, especially working with young people in public and private schools." He died on June 3, 2000. One who had worked closely with him for years and was with him as he died, described his death as "very peaceful." On the tray table next to his bed were his breviary, his rosary, and a bottle of Lourdes water—his silent companions during his last days. On June 8th, after the Mass of Christian Burial in Sacred Heart Cathedral—filled to over-flowing by peoples of all Faiths—he was buried in Birch Hill Cemetery, Fairbanks.

On April 28, 2000, a little over five weeks before Father McGuigan died, the 21st Alaska State Legislature, in a formal document, recognized his long years of commitment and service to the youth of Alaska. It celebrated his "many accomplishments in life," and it commemorated "his exceptional contributions to the many lives he touched throughout Alaska." The final paragraph of the document reads:

> For those of us who have had the extraordinary experience of knowing Father Francis McGuigan, our lives will forever be changed. This is a man who never takes "no" for an answer, and expects only the best from himself and those around him. His gentle ways and Irish wit have taught us to always strive for excellence, for patience and for wisdom. His life has been dedicated to actions benefiting others, a true inspiration to us all. Father McGuigan, "Thank you for all that you do."

McINTYRE, Father William T., S.J.

He was Alaskan and missionary to his Irish core. By the time of his death, Father William T. McIntyre, S.J., had spent 55 years in **Alaska**. But, by having been born in Alaska, he had an advantage no other white Jesuit could claim. Except for the years devoted to studies, and the last two years of his life, he spent the whole of his life in Alaska.

"Father Mac," as all knew him, was born in the old gold-rush town of **Skagway**, on December 10, 1910. Not long after, his father, a mercantile clerk, moved the family to **Douglas** Island. There, and in nearby **Juneau**, where the family moved in 1921, young Willie received his grade school education from the Jesuits and the Sisters of St. **Ann**. As a boy he was so good that, when his mother died, a Jewish family wanted to adopt him. However, he and his brother chose to batch with their father. Their two sisters went to live with relatives in Seattle.

After a year of high school in Juneau, Willie lived with a former Juneau family in Cupertino, California, while he attended Jesuit-staffed Bellarmine College Preparatory in San Jose. Upon graduation from there in 1930, he entered the Jesuit novitiate at Los Gatos, California. He took his vows in 1932, then went to Mount St. Michael's, Spokane, Washington, for a year of classical and humanities studies. He devoted a second year to those studies at the newly opened novitiate at Sheridan, Oregon. Then, it was back to Mount St. Michael's again for three years of philosophy, 1934–37. He found studies difficult, but he had his heart and mind set on being a priest in Alaska and pushed resolutely on toward that goal.

The young Jesuit, "Mister" McIntyre, spent the year 1937–38 prefecting the boys at St. Ignatius Mission, Montana, before going on to do the same at **Holy Cross Mission** on the Yukon River from 1938–40. He next studied theology at Alma College, Los Gatos, California. In San Francisco, on June 12, 1943, he was ordained a priest. After another year of theology, he made his tertianship at Port Townsend, Washington, during the year 1944–45.

Father Mac's first Alaskan assignment as a priest was that of assistant pastor in Juneau. After a year, he moved north to spend almost the whole of his missionary life among the Eskimos. He never had an easy mission. Throughout his missionary years he wrestled with the difficult climate, chronic shortages of funds, excessive demands made upon him as a priest. Through it all, however, his faith was unwavering, his sense of humor sharp—the one nourishing the other. Amused at seeing his status listed in the Oregon Province catalog as "quasi-pas-

Father William T.
McIntyre, S.J. *DFA*.

tor," he entitled the journal he kept "Wrectory Notes of a Kwazy Pastor." He didn't mind being a "Kwazy Pastor," because, whether kwazy or not, his salary was the same: "three zeros preceded by another!" His comment on a lady given to exotic perfume: "Her passing is 'a melody that lingers on'—until we can open both doors and let the wind whistle through."

In 1946, Father Mac was back at Holy Cross, this time as Superior and postmaster. Here, with his support, the first high school on the Yukon was opened, in 1953. Sister Margaret Cantwell, a Sister of St. Ann who was with him at Holy Cross, wrote:

> The children loved him. Wearing a brimmed hat, he would come, at the end of the day, into the "Second Course," sit on one of the long red and black benches that lined the wall, and let the children climb all over him. His hat went from one child to another, and everybody in the Course experienced a little bit of what a father's affection was like. It was beautiful.

In February 1954, Father Mac was, unexpectedly, assigned to **Kotzebue**. "Well," wrote Sister M George **Edmond**, S.S.A., Superior of the Sisters at Holy Cross at the time, to Father James U. **Conwell**, S.J., on February 21, 1954, "we did have a lot of surprises lately, not the least of which is Father McIntyre's transfer to Kotzebue. The children especially are heart-broken. We will always miss his kindness and understanding."

During his five-year stay north of the Arctic Circle, Father Mac chronicled his life there in a witty, but informative, newsletter, *The McKotzebugle*. While at Kotzebue, he also served for some months as chaplain to the DEWline (Distant Early Warning) stations on the arctic coast. He left Kotzebue on July 12, 1959, for **Bethel**, where he was until October. He was then to return to the Dewline, but had to spend the month of November in St. Joseph's Hospital, **Fairbanks**, because of pneumonia and a collapsed lung. He spent the next four months in Fairbanks convalescing.

From 1960–62, Father Mac was back on the Yukon, this time at **Mountain Village**. And from 1962–63, he was on the Kuskokwim River, stationed at **McGrath**, out of which he served also the villages of **Aniak** and **Kalskag**.

Next, Father Mac was assigned to the lower Yukon village of **Alakanuk**, with its dependent stations of **Emmonak** and **Sheldon Point** (called again, since the year 2000, by its original name, **Nunam Iqua**). He was to spend the years 1963–68 there. To those who wondered what that flat, soggy country looked like in the winter, he suggested they take a big white bed sheet with a few wrinkles in it, spread it out, and stare at it for twelve hours. At Alakanuk, as elsewhere, he was a happy, contented man. From there he wrote:

> Each evening the children crowd into my little place. Believe it or not, there are 23 boys and girls of various ages entertaining themselves while I write. Two or three groups are playing jacks; others are reading or playing other games. Comics hold the attention of several. There is no other place in the village for them to go. These children are a delight; the adults are helpful and kind.

From Sheldon Point at the southern mouth of the Yukon he wrote:

> I have a nice little chapel here. The living quarters leave much to be desired—a room of about 8 feet by 15. There is no stove for heating. I use a kerosene two-burner table-top cook stove. A bit smelly, but no more than the odor of seal oil, dogs, fish and other assorted odors in the cabins. Don't know how I will make out at 20 or 30 below, but I guess I'll survive.

It is no secret that Father Mac was a heavy smoker, and that this surely contributed to the emphysema that incapacitated him during the last years of his life. However, that stove, too, was in no small part to blame for the pulmonary problems he had. He himself said that, when the noxious fumes it gave off became simply unbearable, he would shut it off. When the cold then became unbearable, he would have the stove on, until the cold again seemed preferable. So it went throughout much of the time he spent that winter at Sheldon Point.

"Sheldon Point": a name that became indelibly etched in Father Mac's lungs—and feet! "Let me tell you," he wrote, on March 21, 1965, in a letter to Francis D. **Gleeson**, S.J., Bishop of Fairbanks at the time, "how I got into this mess in the first place." The "mess" began on Sunday, March 7, 1965.

Father Mac left Alakanuk, some ten miles upriver from Sheldon Point, at about 12:30 with the intention of offering a third Mass that day at Sheldon Point and of staying there for a while. His account of the misadventure of his life:

> I was on a routine trip to Sheldon Point, when the weather began to close in and I got turned around in a whiteout. It was a fairly warm day. Because of the short distance, I had not taken a sleeping bag, nor any provisions. Anyway, as it was quite late in the afternoon and I couldn't get my bearings, I parked for the night. I couldn't lie down and sleep, as that would mean almost certain freezing. So I walked in a small circle all night. The next morning the weather had closed in. But I could see just a little better, and I started up the Ski-doo. Then I began to run into water flowing over the ice. The tide was coming in, aided by a brisk wind. It also began to rain, a freezing rain. My outer clothing got stiff as a board. I ran up the bank, and decided to stay there until conditions got better. I cut some willows and made a bed by my Ski-doo. I didn't get much rest. The wind had sprung up, and so, to keep my feet from getting cold, I walked considerably, though I was mighty tired. Tuesday morning the weather was down and the wind still blowing. The temperature had dropped, and visibility was almost zero. There were at least two feet of water on the ice, close to the bank. My Ski-doo was frozen—the controls and carburetor iced up. I found out later I was on an island in the Yukon. There were a few stunted willows here and there—impossible to build a fire. So I tried to rig up some kind of shelter out of snow blocks hacked out with the heel of my boot. The night was a little more comfortable. However, I again did considerable walking. On Wednesday I worked on the Ski-doo and finally got it running again. The gas throttle, however, still remained iced up. On Thursday I realized that my feet were freezing. It wasn't extremely cold, but, with the steady wind, the chill factor was pretty low. Thursday brought a lifting of the clouds and fog, and seeing an

opening, I started up the Ski-doo again and headed upstream. Three or four miles up, the fog rolled in again and I couldn't see the bank. Not wanting to spend the night out on the ice, I headed back to my "shelter." Missed that, and did spend the night on the ice alongside my Ski-doo. I did much walking. My feet were becoming quite cold. The next morning, Friday, about noon, I headed back to my shelter. I found that someone had been there recently. The wind was blowing hard and kicking up much snow. I fixed up my shelter. Had just settled down for a rest, when along came three Ski-doos. What a welcome sight!

Father Mac was brought to Sheldon Point, where two nurses from St. Mary's Mission gave him first aid treatment. Soon Dr. Reed of Arctic Health and Research, who just happened to be in Emmonak at the time, arrived. He suggested that Father Mac's feet be soaked in warm water for three to four hours. The next morning, Saturday, he was flown to Bethel, and from there to **Providence** Hospital in **Anchorage**, where Dr. William Mills, the military expert on frostbite, took him under his care.

Father Mac concluded his account of his ordeal: "To him and to the wonderful Sisters of Providence, I owe a world of gratitude, as well as to the fine Eskimo men who spent long hours searching for me, and to all the wonderful people who prayed for my safety. To all of them I am deeply indebted for the fact that I have feet today and can once again walk."

According to Father William C. **Dibb**, S.J., who shared a hospital room with Father Mac, likewise because of frozen feet, "They loved Father Mac. Uncomplaining, always cheerful."

It was at **Chevak**, and at its dependent station, **Scammon Bay**, that Father Mac spent the years 1968–70. Then, after all the moving about, he was content to return to and settle down again, for a solid decade, in Mountain Village, with only **Pilot Station** to visit.

The year 1980 was a milestone year in Father Mac's life. On July 18th, he celebrated his golden jubilee as a Jesuit. It was also the year of his retirement from active missionary work. Long, hard years on the trail, years of adjusting and readjusting to place after place, along with debilitating emphysema, had finally slowed him down. He spent his last Alaskan year in Anchorage.

Father Mac, described as "a true gentleman, extremely sensitive to the feelings of others, most careful to hurt nobody," left Alaska in 1981 for medical care in Seattle. The same deep faith that had sustained him throughout his long years as a missionary in Alaska sustained him during the last two years of his life, years of sickness that he accepted patiently and cheerfully. Father William T. McIntyre, S.J., died in Seattle, on August 27, 1983, and lies buried in the Jesuit cemetery at Mount St. Michael's, Spokane.

123

Father Bernard F. McMeel, S.J. *JOPA-844.05.*

McMEEL, Father Bernard F., S.J.

He was the first principal of Monroe Catholic High School in **Fairbanks, Alaska**. For a term, he was General Superior of Jesuits in Alaska. He was a pilot, and an amateur radio operator. As a priest, he preached "understanding and compassion"—and practiced what he preached. His spiritual life as a priest and Jesuit, he wrote, was sustained in large part by that "great cloud of witnesses," the good example and prayers of his fellow Jesuits, living and departed. He was known to be "a very humble, courteous man, a quiet and gentle man, with a warm, friendly smile." He took people as they were; was totally non-judgmental. By the time of his death, both the Assiniboine and the Gros Ventre Indian nations had recognized and accepted him as one of their own, and as "a true man of God."

Bernard F. "Barney" McMeel was born to Leo and Cora Kennedy McMeel on November 29, 1921, in Great Falls, Montana. He was the fourth in a line of six, with three older sisters and a younger sister and brother. He received his elementary schooling at the **Ursuline** Sisters Academy in Great Falls. During his grade school years, he was occasionally excused from school, so that he could serve Mass for Father Gabriel M. Ménager, S.J., who ministered to a group of landless Indians. He referred to this as the "seed time" of his Jesuit and mission vocation. He was inspired in his dual vocation also by the example of his uncle, Father Joseph F. **McElmeel**, S.J., veteran Alaskan missionary.

Barney attended Great Falls High School. While in high school, he was active in sports, making all-state as a guard on the football team. He was an asso-

ciate editor of the school's yearbook. He graduated from high school in 1939, then was enrolled for a year in the School of Forestry at the University of Montana, in Missoula. It was during that year that he felt himself called irresistibly to become a Jesuit. Having never studied Latin or Greek, he was asked to spend a year at Gonzaga University in Spokane to study them. On June 30, 1941, he entered the Jesuit novitiate at Sheridan, Oregon. Father Neill R. Meany, S.J., who entered the novitiate that same day, wrote of him, "His manliness and maturity made him probably the most looked-up-to among his fellow novices."

After completing his two-year noviceship and two years of classical and humanities studies at Sheridan, Barney moved on to Mount St. Michael's in Spokane for three years of philosophical studies. During those years, he wrote first to Father Provincial Leo J. Robinson, S.J., then to his successor, Harold O. Small, S.J., expressing his hopes that he would be sent to **Holy Cross Mission**, Alaska, for his teaching practicum. Instead, he was assigned to teach at Gonzaga Preparatory for three years. There he taught physics, mathematics, and Religion. He was also manager of the athletic property room. He recalled those three years as "busy, but also very happy years."

From 1951–55, Barney was at Alma College, Los Gatos, California, making his theological studies.

After the hyper-busy three years of high school teaching, he found the quiet routine of the theologate "a bit confining." To break the routine of academic life, he became quite active in ham radio, soon earning his license—with the call letters of KL7BSU. In St. Aloysius Church, in Spokane, on June 19, 1954, he was ordained a priest.

On August 30, 1955, Father McMeel arrived in Fairbanks. He had been expected there sooner, but needed to go to Great Falls for the funeral of his father. On September 2nd, the keeper of the house diary wrote, "Fr. McMeel makes good impression on all he meets." His first formal assignment in Alaska was to serve as principal and a faculty member of the newly opened Monroe Catholic High School in Fairbanks. The school opened with 12 freshmen in the basement of Immaculate Conception Church. The following year, the school, with a total enrollment now of 32 in the freshman and sophomore classes, moved into the new building in Slaterville. During his two years at the high school, Father McMeel, in addition to serving as principal and teacher, and a self-described "general factotum," also made trips to **Nenana** and Suntrana (the coal mine across the Nenana River from present-day **Healy**) to bring the Mass and Sacraments to the people there. One evaluator of Father McMeel as a principal found him to be "too kind-hearted to be a good disciplinarian, especially in the case of the girls."

During the year 1957–58, Father McMeel made his tertianship at Port Townsend. At the end of that he was evaluated by his tertian master as "calm, obedient, zealous, imperturbable, a consolation for Superiors to have around." As to his aptitude for governing, it was rated as good enough "even for high office." Another evaluator, however, had misgivings. He felt Father McMeel was "too self-effacing," and might, therefore, not be assertive enough to be a good Superior.

Father McMeel's first post-tertianship assignment took him to the northern extremities of Alaska. For a year and a half he served as Catholic Chaplain on the DEWline (Distant Early Warning). This meant more or less constant travel, back and forth, between stations strung out along the arctic coast all the way from Cape Lisburne on the northwest coast of Alaska to Tuktoyaktuk, an Eskimo village east of the mouth of the Mackenzie River in Canada's Northwest Territories. Finding the "pin-up art" stretching from one end of the DEWline to the other offensive to "pious eyes," he, along with the Protestant chaplain, protested. It was taken down—at least, while they were at a given station.

From the time Father McMeel first felt himself called to serve on the Alaska mission, it was in rural Alaska, among Alaska's Native peoples, that he hoped to serve. That hope he began to realize in December 1959, when he was assigned as pastor of **Chevak** and its dependent station, **Newtok**, two Central Yup'ik Eskimo villages near the Bering Sea coast. Occasionally, he visited, unofficially, the Air Force station at Cape Romanzof. In the summer of 1963, at the request of Bishop Francis D. **Gleeson**, S.J., he captained the *Cabna* (Catholic Bishop of Northern Alaska), a riverboat owned by the Diocese of Fairbanks, on its trip from Fairbanks downriver to St. Mary's Mission on the **Andreafsky** River.

From April 1964 to February 1968, Father McMeel was pastor of Holy Family parish in Holy Cross. "During this period," he wrote, "the 'face' of Holy Cross was drastically changed." Old mission buildings were taken down, and new school and convent buildings put up. The old church, however, was not disturbed.

During the summer of 1965, Father McMeel "took up flying" with Oswald's Flying Service in Tacoma, Washington. He soon became a skilled "seat-of-the-pants" pilot. During the remainder of his stay at Holy Cross, he made periodic visits to **Shageluk**, **McGrath**, **Marshall**, **Russian Mission**, and Grayling.

Given his aptitude for governing—rated, as mentioned above, good enough "even for high office"—it came as no surprise to anyone, that he was chosen to be General Superior of Jesuits in Alaska, as of February 23, 1968. He himself, being the humble, self-effacing man that he was, was "most flabbergasted" at the confidence his fellow Jesuits and the Father General in Rome placed in him. As General Superior, he made his headquarters in Fairbanks, and flew out of there to visit the men and mission stations scattered throughout northern Alaska.

While Superior, Father McMeel also cared for the

parish in McGrath. On January 16, 1970, in his Cessna 180, he took off from Fairbanks for McGrath. He never arrived there. An account of his mishap appeared in the July 1970 issue of "Air Progress." It reads:

> On a crisp 10-below zero morning in Fairbanks, Alaska, he checked the weather (clear, 70 miles visibility), scraped the snow off the wings and removed the oil-spotted canvas cowl cover and the two 2400-BTU catalytic heaters that had kept the engine toasty warm all night. He stashed the heaters, cover and his canvas flight bag full of clothes into the baggage compartment, started up and took off VFR for McGrath, 275 miles to the southwest.
>
> Cruising at 3,000 feet over the Kuskokwim foothills near Minchumina, the 180 shuddered through some moderate to severe turbulence. A few minutes later, eight miles past Minchumina, the pilot noticed smoke curling out of the baggage compartment. The turbulence had apparently knocked the lid off one of the catalytic heaters and set the chemicals to cooking. The exposed heater was lodged against the flight bag, burning a smoky, smoldering hole in the canvas.
>
> Eyes watering, the pilot managed to extinguish the visible sparks, but radioed Minchumina that he was returning to land because of the acrid smoke in the cockpit. A minute or so after the call, the entire baggage compartment burst into flame. Because of the intense heat, the pilot decided to get the aircraft on the ground immediately. He landed in a forested area, substantially damaging the plane, but managed to escape with only minor injuries. The fire burned itself out, and the pilot was rescued shortly by a track vehicle from Minchumina.

It was during Father McMeel's term as General Superior that the controversial closing of **Copper Valley School** was announced in 1971.

From September 1973 to July 1976, Father McMeel was stationed in **Galena**. Out of there, during those years, he visited McGrath, **Huslia**, and **Manley Hot Springs**. During the year 1973–74, he visited also **Tanana** and **Ruby**. During this same period, he served also as Auxiliary Chaplain to Air Force personnel based at Galena and at the Campion radar site near Galena.

From August 1976 to November 1977, Father McMeel was pastor of **Hooper Bay** and its dependent station, **Scammon Bay**. In the summer and fall of 1977, he oversaw the construction of the new Little Flower of Jesus Church at Hooper Bay. During his stay at Hooper Bay, he served also as Auxiliary Chaplain to Air Force personnel stationed at Cape Romanzof.

In December 1977, Father McMeel began serving as pastor of the Nelson Island villages of **Tununak**, **Toksook Bay**, and **Nightmute**. Here he was again among Central Yup'ik-speaking Eskimos. Regarding that language, he wrote to Father Louis L. **Renner**, S.J, on February 17, 1978, "I regret that I didn't have an opportunity to get a formal start in the language as our young priests now do. The year of language study at the University of Alaska is a very 'enlightened' policy."

Father McMeel's stay on Nelson Island was a short one. He was on sabbatical leave during the year 1978–79. The fall of that year he spent helping out at St. Paul's Mission, Hays, Montana, and the spring attending an Institute for Clergy Education at Notre Dame University. Following this renewal program, he served as administrator at St. Rose of Lima parish in **Wrangell**, Alaska, for six months.

From 1980 on, to the year of his death, Father McMeel was based at Hays, at St. Paul's Mission on the Fort Belknap Reservation in Montana. He cared for it and its several dependent missions. At Hays, he was in "his element." He was working with and ministering to Native Americans; and, in doing so, fulfilling the one and only real desire he ever had throughout his life as a priest. Near Hays, the hunting and fishing were good and appreciated by Father McMeel, who was fond of the outdoors. Nevertheless, during the year 1991–92, he felt the need for another sabbatical.

In 1992, Father McMeel was asked, as were all the members of the Oregon Province, the two-pronged question: "Where do you see yourself in the year 2000, and what do you see yourself doing?" He saw himself "at the ripe old age of 78, and engaged in active ministry, still serving Indian people." He also saw "the laity in the year 2000 playing a major role in the conduct of the local church communities," especially those of Native Americans, and himself as a "support person and enabler."

It was not granted to Father McMeel to see "the ripe old age of 78." It was granted him, however, to continue to be engaged in active ministry to

Native Americans right up to the very end of his life. This came to him, somewhat unexpectedly, after a short illness brought on by several strokes. He died on January 6, 1994, in Northern Montana Hospital, Havre, Montana.

The day after his death, the President of the Fort Belknap Community Council wrote to Father Stephen V. Sundborg, S.J., Provincial of the Oregon Province, "This is to inform you that Fort Belknap Community Council hereby authorizes the burial of Father Bernard "Barney" McMeel on the Fort Belknap Reservation. Father McMeel was a well respected Catholic Priest at St. Paul's Mission, and was considered exceptionally special to our community and to our people." The letter implied that Father McMeel himself had expressed a desire to be buried among his beloved Indians. However, since he left nothing to that effect in writing, and since it was the understanding of his brother and sisters that he wanted to be buried with his brother Jesuits in the cemetery at Mount St. Michael's, Father Sundborg judged it best that he be buried there. A wake service and funeral Mass were held at St. Paul's Mission on January 9th and 10th respectively. Anthony M. Milone, Bishop of Great Falls, was principal celebrant at the Mass. "A large gathering" of priests concelebrated. On January 11th, Father McMeel was laid to rest in the Jesuit cemetery at Mount St. Michael's. A bronze statue of St. Francis and a bronze plaque at St. Paul's Mission commemorate the one-time presence there of Father Bernard F. McMeel, S.J.

McMILLAN, Father William, S.J.

William McMillan was born on September 2, 1864, in Philadelphia, Pennsylvania, where he spent his youth. On November 12, 1888, he entered the Jesuit novitiate at Prairie du Chien, Wisconsin. After completing his novitiate there, and his studies of the classics and humanities at Sacred Heart Mission, DeSmet, Idaho, he taught at Saint Ignatius, Montana. There, too, he made his philosophical and theological studies; and there he was ordained a priest, on May 19, 1899. The following year, he made his tertianship at Frederick, Maryland.

During the first 18 years of his priestly life,

Father William McMillan, S.J. *JOPA-1071.01.*

Father McMillan served mainly at various Indian missions in Montana, Washington, and Wyoming. For a short time he was stationed at Klamath Falls, Oregon. After that he was pastor of St. Jude's parish in Havre, Montana.

In 1918, Father McMillan was assigned to **Seward, Alaska**. It was his misfortune to be in Seward at the time of the formal closing, on June 7, 1919, of Seward General Hospital, staffed by Sisters of St. Joseph of Peace–Newark. He inherited many of the problems connected with the closing, such as caring for the empty building and following up on various plans for its use.

After one year at Seward, Father McMillan became pastor of **Cordova–Valdez**. From 1919–25, he lived in Valdez; and, from 1925–33, in Cordova. His last year in Alaska, 1933–34, he spent as assistant pastor at Immaculate Conception parish in **Fairbanks**. Failing health necessitated his leaving Alaska after that year.

Father McMillan next spent the year 1934–35 at Port Townsend, Washington, and the final year of his life at Mount St. Michael's, Spokane, Washington. He died in Seattle, Washington, on July 15, 1936, after having "edified all, especially during his last illness, by his calm patience, sincere humility, and unfailing gentleness." He lies buried in the Jesuit cemetery at Mount St. Michael's.

15

Father David A. Melbourne.
LRC.

MELBOURNE, Father David A.

David A. Melbourne was born in Seattle, Washington, on April 19, 1903. His schooling completed, he worked in the business world from 1925–32. One job, during the year 1931–32, had him working for the auditing department of the White Pass and Yukon Railway in **Skagway**. While on that job, he lived in the church rectory with Father G. Edgar **Gallant**. It was during this time that he decided to study for the priesthood, for the Vicariate of **Alaska**. From 1932–35, he studied at Mount Angel Seminary in St. Benedict, Oregon. He was ordained a priest in St. James Cathedral, Seattle, on June 3, 1939, by Archbishop Gerald Shaughnessy, S.M.

Father Melbourne's first Alaskan assignment was that of pastor of St. Joseph's parish in **Cordova**. As such, he also cared for its dependent missions, St. Francis Xavier's in **Valdez** and St. Ann's in **Yakutat**. He was to spend 20 years, 1939–59, ministering to the Catholics in those three coastal towns. During World War II, he served also as auxiliary chaplain to the troops quartered near Cordova. From 1959–67, he was stationed at the Cathedral of the Nativity of the Blessed Virgin Mary in **Juneau**. In addition to being pastor of the Cathedral parish, he also directed St. Ann's School and was visiting priest to Juneau's outlying communities. These duties gave him little time for relaxation, much less, time for a vacation. However, during July 1966, he was able to take a month-long vacation, when Father Louis L. **Renner**, S.J., volunteered to

fill in for him. From 1967–74, Father Melbourne was pastor of St. Therese of the Child Jesus parish in Skagway. At the same time, he also cared for its dependent mission, Sacred Heart in **Haines**. He retired in 1975, but returned to Cordova, because there was no priest there.

Father Melbourne, though a priest of the Diocese of Juneau, moved into **Anchorage** in 1983. There he lived in his own apartment until three months before his death. On weekends, he assisted in various parishes in and around Anchorage. For the last ten years of his life, he served as chaplain and priest for the Joy Community, a community made up of families with mentally and physically challenged children.

After 96 years of life and 60 of priesthood, Father Melbourne, after a brief illness, died of natural causes on November 7, 1999, at Providence Alaska Extended Care, Anchorage.

Though Father Melbourne, during his younger days, had a pilot's license and flew a small plane for a time—and even served at times as "the town mortician"—he was, first and foremost, always the priest. Francis T. **Hurley**, Archbishop of Anchorage at the time, said on the occasion of Father Melbourne's death: "Father Melbourne was a priest who could not stop working as a priest. He also came to all priests' gatherings and often went to parish social events. He was known and loved by many people, and took great joy in telling others what it was like in the 'old days.'"

Father David A. Melbourne lies buried in the Catholic plot of Anchorage's Angelus Memorial Park Cemetery.

MÉNAGER, Father Francis M., S.J.

He spent 25 years on the missions of northern **Alaska**. He did pioneer Catholic missionary work along the Kuskokwim River. He acquired a working knowledge of Central Yup'ik Eskimo. He was acknowledged to be a successful practitioner of medicine, having received from his father, who was a doctor, "good books, a plentiful supply of drugs, and a surgical kit." He was musically gifted, sang well with a beautiful tenor voice, composed songs. Some of them were professionally recorded, with him doing the singing and accompanying himself on the piano or organ. He wrote a book, which he himself illustrated. He had many articles published. He had a special devotion to the Sacred Heart of Jesus. For a time, he thought he had been sent to Alaska to become Alaska's second Vicar Apostolic. He hoped to become a full-fledged airplane pilot. He became neither a bishop nor a pilot.

Francis M. Ménager was born in Nantes, Brittany, France, on September 4, 1886, the seventh child of 14 children, eight boys and six girls. Three of the boys became Jesuit priests; two of the girls **Ursuline** Sisters. Their father was a medical doctor. The family moved into Washington State's Yakima valley in 1903; then to Spokane, Washington, in 1905. Francis received all his early schooling in his native city. He had an in-house tutor from 1890–96, then attended the college–seminary Notre Dame des Couets in Nantes from 1896–1902.

On July 2, 1907, Francis entered the Jesuit novitiate at Los Gatos, California. After completing his two-year noviceship, he studied the classics and humanities for a year. Next he spent the years 1910–12 at St. Ignatius Mission, Montana, as prefect of the boys in the boarding school. From 1912–15, he studied philosophy at Gonzaga College in Spokane, Washington, before going on to teach physics and chemistry at Seattle College from 1915–18. While there, he worked also with the Glee Club and the orchestra. He spent the year 1918–19 teaching at Gonzaga. In the fall of 1919, he began theological studies at St. Louis University. He was ordained a priest in St. Louis on June 26, 1921. After two more years of theology at St. Louis, he returned to Spokane to teach cosmology at Mount St. Michael's for two years. While in St. Louis, on December 8, 1922, he became a U.S. citizen. He spent the year 1925–26 making his tertianship in Cleveland, Ohio. This was followed by another year of teaching cosmology at Mount St. Michael's.

"Whilst at Mt. St. Michael's," Father Ménager wrote, "I was asked to collect edifying stories about Alaska, and I got interested. The death of Father **Tréca**, who evangelized the Bering Sea coast and the **Hooper Bay** district, impressed me deeply. Then suddenly came the report of the death of my old science teacher, Father **Ruppert**, frozen on the

trail near **Nome**, so I volunteered for the Alaska Missions."

It was midnight, September 27, 1927, when Father Ménager stepped off the boat and onto the mud-bank at **Kashunuk**, the scene of his first year of missionary work in Alaska. He had come to Alaska the previous month. At Kashunuk, he immediately set about learning the Central Yup'ik Eskimo language. While there, he had frequent occasion to put to good use the limited medical skills he had acquired before coming to Alaska. "Day after day," he wrote, looking back on his days in Alaska, "for many years I treated sores, sprains, stomach-aches, head-aches, wounds of every sort, and cuts more or less severe, always combining medicine and prayer."

Father Philip I. **Delon**, S.J., General Mission Superior of Alaska at the time, was able to report to Father Joseph M. Piet, S.J., Provincial, that Father Ménager at Kashunuk was doing "wonderfully well." The people really took to him. After he had left Kashunuk, and was returning there to pick up his belongings, "People, esp. children," wrote his replacement, Father **John P. Fox**, S.J., in the Kashunuk house diary, "were wild with delight at Father's coming. They noticed him and knew him, when he was still a great way off, and ran out to meet him. Some wept for joy."

The new missionary to Alaska did not find life at Kashunuk all that easy. His fellow Jesuit Alaskan missionary Father Segundo **Llorente** wrote: "Fr. Francis Ménager, a former professor of cosmology and a voracious reader of big books, found himself in Kashunuk in 1927 with only one magazine. I believe it was called *General Mechanix*, a thick pulpy magazine full of tools and engines. He told me that he learned it by heart to keep from 'going bugs.' The winters were long and cold and fuel was hard to get. The buildings were poorly insulated against those abominable blizzards. The winter nights were long, but Blazo gasoline or coal oil for the lamps was scarce and expensive."

From Kashunuk, Father Ménager moved to nearby Hooper Bay, "the kingdom of the seal," where he spent the years 1928–30. After the death of Father Delon in the October 12, 1930, crash of the *Marquette Missionary* at **Kotzebue**, Father Ménager

Father Francis M. Ménager,
S.J. *JOPA-1072.05.*

became General Superior of the Alaska Mission, as of January 6, 1931. As such, he made **Holy Cross Mission** his headquarters for the year 1931–32; then **Nome**, for the year 1932–33. In April 1932, in a plane piloted by Arthur Woodley, he landed at **King Island** to visit Father Bellarmine **Lafortune**, S.J. This was the first time a plane landed at King Island.

By this time, Father Ménager was firmly convinced that the Alaska Mission Superior should have and fly a plane of his own. This conviction first came to him, while he was still at Hooper Bay. In March 1929, he was visited by Father Delon, brought there in a plane piloted by A. A. Bennett. It was airplane-related matters that brought about Father Ménager's removal as Alaska Mission Superior. When a second mission plane was brought to Alaska in 1931 to replace the crashed *Marquette Missionary*, he took it upon himself to sell it to Woodley, a deed for which Joseph R. **Crimont**, S.J., Vicar Apostolic of Alaska at the time, had him removed as Superior. It was also a deed for which Brother George J. **Feltes**, S.J., who was the man primarily responsible for the plane, found it very hard to forgive Father Ménager.

In September 1933, Father Ménager began his five-year stay in Kotzebue. He faithfully kept a diary of daily doings there. The flock he found in Kotzebue left, in his eyes, much to be desired: too many "backsliders," not enough "real Catholics." Yet, judging by his diary entries, the people, by and large, responded well to his ministrations. Frequently he recorded "good crowd," "good attendance" at church services. He was able to consecrate many families and homes to the Sacred Heart of Jesus, one of the principal focuses of his personal devotions. (After his death, Father Llorente wrote, "Because of his great devotion to the Sacred Heart, I always felt that he would have a quiet, happy death.") He wrote minstrel shows that were big hits. Shortly after his arrival in Kotzebue, he organized the Kotzebue Catholic Artists, "a musical society started to keep up interest and to furnish music on every occasion." He found the Kotzebue Eskimos to be "full of music and they enjoy it so very much." While at Kotzebue, on May 9, 1937, he had occasion to visit, by plane, Father **Thomas P. Cunningham**, S.J., on **Little Diomede** Island. Father Ménager left Kotzebue in the spring of 1938.

As of June 4, 1938, Father Ménager was officially local Superior of Holy Cross Mission. However, he did not arrive there until July 7th. During his three years at Holy Cross, he visited also its dependent mission stations: **Paimiut**, **Aniak**, **Bethel**, and **Kalskag**. On August 24, 1941, he was replaced as Superior of Holy Cross by Father James C. **Spils**, S.J.

On September 19, 1941, Father Ménager arrived at St. Mary's Mission, **Akulurak**, to be Father Llorente's assistant. After a little over four months, he was sent to Hooper Bay, where he arrived on January 31, 1942. At Hooper Bay, he regularly gave sermons in the Native language. Out of Hooper Bay, he visited the villages of Kashunuk, **Scammon Bay**, Old **Chevak**, and **Keyaluvik**.

The Hooper Bay diary entry for August 16, 1942, reads: "Father Ménager leaves by plane at 4:30 P.M. for **Bethel** to open a new mission there." By this time, the Kuskokwim River region had been visited on and off by Catholic missionaries for half a century, but Bethel was to become its first permanent mission center.

Father Ménager was well received in Bethel, by the Natives, the whites, and the soldiers across the river. He took up residence in a small cabin next to

"Honey Bucket Lake." In this cabin he offered daily Mass and taught catechism, until Immaculate Conception Church, with priest's quarters, was built, between August 22nd and September 23rd of 1943. Before the church was up, he offered Sunday Masses in the Territorial school hall. Once a week he celebrated Mass in the Bethel hospital. From time to time, he entertained the soldiers by playing his accordion and singing. He was an auxiliary military chaplain from 1943–47. From his earliest years in Bethel, he traveled extensively up and down the Kuskokwim River by boat, dogsled, and plane, visiting, on a fairly regular basis, the various villages and mining camps, among them **Aniak**, **Kalskag**, Sleetmute, Nyac, and **McGrath**. At first, he had only an open skiff. In February 1943, he was able to buy, for $1,000, the *Monitor*, a cabin boat. This he renamed *Tessita*, after St. Therese, "the Little Flower." It proved to be a reliable boat.

In the third week of September 1945, the Father Provincial of the Oregon Province, Father Leopold J. Robinson, S.J., visited Father Ménager. To the Province members he reported, "I cannot speak too highly of this Father."

On February 25, 1948, Father Llorente arrived in Bethel to take over the Kuskokwim district. As of August 23, 1948, Father Ménager was officially assigned to St. Mary's Mission. Before taking over that post, however, he did a considerable amount of traveling. It was not until the last week of November that he was settled in and "reacquainted" with that mission. When St. Mary's was moved, on August 3, 1951, from Akulurak to its new site on the **Andreafsky** River, he made the move with it. On January 8, 1953, he left the New St. Mary's for **Fairbanks**; and, on the 26th, he flew to Seattle, never to see Alaska again. Failing health necessitated the move.

Father Ménager spent his first two years in the Northwest doing pastoral work at St. Leo's parish in Tacoma, Washington. During the years 1955–58, he served as Spiritual Father at the Jesuit novitiate at Sheridan, Oregon. This was followed by pastoral work in Yakima for two years. He spent the years 1961–64 at Bellarmine High School in Tacoma. In 1962, his book, *The Kingdom of the Seal*, was published. The book, copiously illustrated with pen and ink drawings done by himself, is mainly an account of his years at Kashunuk and Hooper Bay. During his years in Tacoma, he also produced a series of biographical sketches of Alaskan missionaries, which he entitled "They Were Giants." Written from memory, they are not always accurate history.

Father Ménager spent most of the last year of his life at Gonzaga University. The Oregon Province Catalog lists him as "writer." At Sheridan, on June 29, 1965, he died "a quiet, happy death." He lies buried in the Jesuit cemetery at Mount St. Michael's, Spokane.

72, 94

MILLER, Msgr. James F.

James Francis Miller was born in Stillwater, Minnesota, on November 13, 1929. He graduated from high school there, and, in 1952, from St. John's University in Collegeville, Minnesota. He served in the U.S. Army from 1952–55. While in the Army, as a corporal, he was stationed at Gambell, **Alaska**, on St. Lawrence Island. After an honorable discharge, he attended St. John's Seminary in Collegeville from 1955–61. In the Cathedral in St. Cloud, Minnesota, he was ordained a priest on June 3, 1961, for the Diocese of **Juneau**. It was during his tour in Alaska with the Army that he had first begun to think about being a priest in Alaska.

In the course of his 38 years of priesthood, Father Miller served in all the parishes in the Juneau diocese. He began his priestly ministries as an assistant pastor at the Cathedral of the Nativity of the Blessed Virgin Mary in Juneau. From 1961–66, he was pastor of St. Therese of the Child Jesus parish in **Skagway**. While there, he made weekly visits to the mission at **Haines**, and frequent visits to the mission at Klukwan. From 1966–67, he was pastor of St. Rose of Lima parish in **Wrangell**, out of which he made weekly visits to **Petersburg**. While at Wrangell, he occasionally visited also the U.S. Coast Guard lighthouse at 5-Finger Light, just north of Petersburg. In 1967, he returned to the Cathedral parish to serve there as pastor until 1970.

While in Juneau, Father Miller encouraged Dixie Belcher to organize a group of folk singers to sing

Msgr. James F. Miller. *LRC.*

for St. Paul's Church in Juneau. An ecumenical group, they enjoyed singing together. Father Miller sang with them. The group of musicians and singers, directed by Dixie Belcher, became known as "The St. Paul's Singers." Before long, they were doing also community concerts, and, during the earliest days of *glasnost*, they went on a tour in Soviet Russia. The group continued long after Father Miller, having been assigned away from Juneau, left it.

From 1970–76, Father Miller was pastor of Holy Name parish in **Ketchikan**. In 1971, he was named Vicar General of the Diocese of Juneau, a position to which he was reappointed in 1974. In 1976, when Bishop Francis T. **Hurley** was named Archbishop of **Anchorage**, and Apostolic Administrator of Juneau, Father Miller was named Chancellor of the Juneau diocese, and once again appointed pastor of Juneau's Cathedral parish. That same year he was made a Monsignor. "With that exalted title," wrote Father Peter F. **Gorges**, "he was the Chancellor 'on location' representative of Archbishop Hurley, who spent most of his time in Anchorage. Msgr. Miller's 'Monsignor robes' consisted of a pair of purple sox."

From 1978–85, Msgr. Miller was pastor of St. Gregory of Nazianzen parish in **Sitka**. In 1986, he was appointed pastor of St. Paul's parish in Juneau. In 1994, he became pastor of Sacred Heart parish in Haines. He retired in 1996, but continued to serve the Haines parish by celebrating Mass there two

Sundays a month. As there was no other priest available to take care of the Haines parish, this was a solution acceptable to Michael H. **Kenny**, Bishop of Juneau at the time, and to the people.

During his Skagway years, 1962–66, Msgr. Miller, then still Father Miller, had been part of a local acting troupe. Now, some 30 years later, he was part of the Haines acting troupe. He also rendered services as a volunteer at the Haines museum.

Father Gorges, who knew Msgr. Miller well, wrote of him:

> He was very creative, thinking of decorating ideas which would never occur to me. At Sitka's St. Gregory's church he had a banana tree growing in the sanctuary, which actually produced a couple of bananas. (Paul Harvey noted the fact on his radio program.) Once he had a full fishing seine net hanging from the ceiling of the Sitka church.

In the words of his long-time and very close friend, Father Jerome A. **Frister**, "Msgr. Miller was a presence of Christ to everybody, whether they belonged to the parish or not. In his own little quiet way he reached everybody. He reflected the presence of Christ in whatever he did."

Msgr. Miller was widely loved and respected. The Tlingit Indian people of **Yakutat**, a mission which he served from 1967–70 while pastor of the Cathedral parish, adopted him into their Eagle clan.

Msgr. Miller, after suffering for three short painful months from pancreatic cancer, died in Stillwater, the city of his birth, on June 2, 1999. He lies buried there in the family plot.

MONROE, Father Francis M., S.J.

He was described variously as "a man of steel," as "a man of indomitable courage." For the extraordinary, arduous labors he endured, and for the daring treks he made throughout the vast wilderness of the upper Yukon River regions during his 46 years in **Alaska**, he was called "the Alaskan Hercules." It was said of him that he, as a dog-musher, "spoke the language of the dogs." He was remembered as "the friend of the struggling miner." As "the man with the big hands," he left behind him a string of churches, hospitals, and chapels stretching from **Eagle** to **Iditarod**, and from **Fairbanks** to

Wrangell. "His death," wrote a witness, "was as beautiful and edifying as his long and useful life." He has gone down in history as one belonging to "the era of giants." In Fairbanks, where he pioneered and ministered as a priest for 20 years, both a street and a high school bear his name. "His is a life," wrote one historian, "that begs to be written."

Francis Monroe was born one of nine children on June 2, 1855, at the Chateau de Chervé, Perreux (Loire), near Lyons, France. His classical studies and two years of philosophy he made successively at St. Clement at Metz, at Notre Dame in Boulogne, and at La Providence in Amiens. At Metz, he had as classmates two future greats: Maréchal Ferdinand Foch, Commander-in-Chief of the allied armies during World War I, and Général Charles Mangin. The latter's brother, Leo Ignatius Mangin, a fellow novice of Monroe's, died a martyr in China during the Boxer persecution. At La Providence, in 1873, Monroe met for the first time the future first bishop of Alaska, Joseph R. **Crimont,** S.J. With that meeting began a 65-year-long friendship between the two.

Francis Monroe entered the Society of Jesus at St. Acheul, Amiens, on November 4, 1874. He spent some time working in several colleges in Belgium. He studied theology at St. Helier on the British Isle of Jersey and in Lyons, where he was ordained a priest on June 24, 1886. Two months later, he landed in New York, with his final destination the Rocky Mountain Mission. After having heard Archbishop Charles J. **Seghers** speak, he had volunteered and been accepted for this, on July 2, 1885. He spent a year at Woodstock, Maryland, then was appointed Father Minister of the Jesuit community at St. Michael's, Spokane Falls, Washington Territory. After that he served on the Indian missions in Montana for some years.

On May 19, 1893, Father Monroe, in company of Father Paschal **Tosi,** S.J., General Superior at the time of Jesuits in Alaska, along with Jesuit Brothers Bartholomew Marchisio, James Sullivan, and James **Twohig,** sailed from San Francisco on the *Bertha*, bound for **St. Michael,** Alaska, where they arrived on June 21st. On July 1st, Father Monroe arrived at **Holy Cross Mission,** where he spent his first Alaskan year. As prefect of the boys there, he undertook to teach his young charges the value and

Father Francis M. Monroe, S.J. *JOPA-1074.01.*

use of money as a means of exchange, instead of barter. To do this, he had some tin coins made. The imagined value of the coins resembled that of American silver coins. They were to be used only at the mission. The children, boys and girls, were paid a given wage for a given service rendered. With the "money" earned, they were free to buy whatever they wished from the Fathers' or Sisters' "stores." Business was always conducted on a cash-and-carry basis, never on credit. Another device introduced by Father Monroe—whom Father Julius **Jetté,** S.J., described as a man "who is very orderly about everything"—was a school bell. This was intended to bring greater regularity and punctuality into daily life of the school children at Holy Cross.

In 1894, Father Monroe moved upriver, to **Nulato,** where he was stationed until 1898. During the summer of 1895, from June 8th to August 12th, he was further upriver, visiting mining camps in the Fortymile–Circle City country. Writing in the third person, he left an account of that excursion. This begins: "In 1895 he traveled more than 500 miles, alone and on foot, in a country where roads and even trails were yet unknown. In his travels he administered for the first time the sacraments to white people in that part of Alaska." On July 2nd, at Miller Creek, some 60 miles from Fortymile Post, he baptized the twin sons of Mr. and Mrs. Hubert Day. Two days later, at Glacier Creek, he offered Mass for three men in the tent of one of the miners. After hiking across another long, hilly stretch of mosquito-infested, uncharted wilderness for some days, he arrived at another mining camp. There he officiated at the marriage of Charles and Bridget Aylward, the first Catholic white couple ever to be married in northern Alaska. From there he went on to visit the miners at Franklin Gulch. Two days later, as he and a party of prospectors and trappers were going down the treacherous Fortymile River, their boat hit some bad riffles and swamped. He considered himself "twice fortunate" to be able to save both his Mass kit and his life. From Fortymile Post, he floated some 225 miles down the Yukon to Circle City. In that area, too, he visited every stream and creek where mining was carried on. During the latter part of his 500-mile tramp through the upper Yukon wilds, he felt his moose-hide boots were getting too dry and brittle. So he put them in a creek to soak. Then he went to rest. Soon he heard the snarling of dogs. He got up to separate them. Poor Father Monroe! The dogs were fighting over his boots. He had nothing but a light pair of moccasins to replace them with. These were soon worn out. Miners offered him their boots, but they were all too large for him. Somehow he made it back to Nulato.

Father Monroe spent a second year at Holy Cross, the year 1898–99. On August 19, 1899, he arrived at his next assignment, Eagle, where he was sent to tend to the miners in that area. In Eagle, he at first rented a cabin for $10 a month. "The water is pouring freely through the roof when the rain is heavy, but this is a very common thing here," he wrote stoically. Before long, a Catholic couple about to leave Eagle offered him a site with two log cabins on it for $300. This he bought. The larger cabin became the chapel of St. Francis Xavier. Since the mission was located on the military reservation, he sought the Army's approval to occupy six more lots to use for gardening. Approval was granted. During his Eagle years, he survived mainly from the yield of his garden. At first, he had little to do in Eagle, but he stayed on, hoping to see the town and country develop. Soon he saw the need for a hospital for non-military patients, so he opened one next to his residence. This he operated for three years. While stationed in Eagle, he also spent a fair amount of time visiting the miners on their creeks.

In 1902, gold was discovered in the Tanana Valley, near what is today **Fairbanks**. Soon the rush was on. Father Monroe was anxious to follow the crowd there, in order to establish the Church in an already rapidly mushrooming town. Even though the place was roughly 300 miles from Eagle, he considered it part of his district. However, when, in the summer of 1903, Father George de la Motte, S.J., General Superior of Jesuits in Alaska at the time, visited him, he told him to stay on at Eagle—this, despite the fact that Father de la Motte found that "the poor father is all alone for more than nine hundred miles, and sees Jesuits only once a year." Father de la Motte described Father Monroe's house and chapel as "exquisitely neat." The following year, when Father Crimont, newly appointed Prefect Apostolic of Alaska, visited Father Monroe in Eagle, he closed the mission. The two left Eagle on June 21, 1904, and arrived in Fairbanks ten days later, on July 1st.

In Fairbanks, Father Monroe, standing alone on the banks of the Chena River, found himself, in the words of one historian, "penniless, landless and forlorn." But, there was no time to waste on self-pity. Immediately he set about raising money and acquiring land suitable for a church site. On the south side of the Chena, he found suitable land. Architectural drawing and carpentry were skills not new to him. In his young days in France, he had shown himself to be an excellent carpenter. His Father Provincial remarked that, "had he not become a missionary, he would have made a fine architect." On the Feast of All Saints, November 1, 1904, Immaculate Conception Church was opened for public service. The year 1904 marks the founding of Immaculate Conception parish, Fairbanks.

In 1906, Father Monroe built St. Joseph's Hospital in Fairbanks. This was located on the north side of the Chena, and a little downstream from the church, where he lived. As the work connected with the church and the hospital increased, he found himself spending too much valuable time on the road between the two. The two structures needed to be side by side. He discussed the matter with his Superior, Father Crimont. "Move the church!" was the latter's directive. That was on the last day of September 1911.

Though not a professional engineer, Father Monroe was resourceful and a man possessed of practical good judgment. He determined that the church could be moved across the river next to the hospital. Townspeople were skeptical, thinking the Herculean task impossible. But, Father Monroe had a plan, as simple as it was ingenious. When the Chena froze solid enough to bear the weight of the church, he drew two parallel lines 30 feet apart on the ice. Holes were cut through the ice at eight-foot intervals along these lines. Upright logs were wedged into these holes and left to freeze in solid. The following day, the tops of these were sawed off two feet above the ice, making strong supports for heavy timbers. On these, the church was rolled diagonally several hundred feet across the frozen river to its present site. That was in late November 1911. In the course of the following years, until he left Fairbanks, in 1924, he continued to make notable improvements on the church.

During his two decades in Fairbanks, Father Monroe, while responsible primarily for the Catholic community there, also made frequent excursions to the surrounding mining camps, and even to places as remote as Eagle and Iditarod. The summer before he moved the Fairbanks church, he built one in Iditarod, and, in 1918, one in **Nenana**.

In late October 1922, Father Monroe again proved to be a man of Herculean proportions. On October 19th of that year, in **Tanana**, Father Jetté, while lifting a heavy log, ruptured himself. It was freeze-up time, when the rivers were running ice, the lakes and sloughs barely frozen over, the trails still almost wholly without snow. Travel of any kind was nearly impossible. But, as his condition rapidly worsened, it was imperative that he be brought to a doctor as soon as possible. By boat and by dogsled, friends made every effort to bring him to a doctor in Nenana. When Father Monroe heard about Father Jetté's condition, he immediately set out to bring him the Last Sacraments, and to join in the rescue effort. At Dugan Creek, about 80 miles from Nenana as the Tanana River winds and bends, he met the seriously sick Father Jetté and his two Good Samaritan rescuers, Andrew Vachon, storekeeper in Tanana, and George Edwine, a young Native man. Shortly after the whole event, Andrew wrote his brother, Peter, an account of it:

> On the third day, October 28, at Dugan Creek, we met Father Monroe, who had mushed or walked from Nenana, to give Father Jetté the Last Sacraments. I was expecting to meet him and a doctor there with a dogteam, but no, the poor Father was walking. Father Monroe had left Tolovana at 9 in the morning, walking in heavy shoe pacs. He was advised to take a pair of snowshoes with him to wear crossing the lakes, as the ice would support him with the snowshoes where it wouldn't without them. So, after packing a large pair under his arm, over the trail he came to a sizeable lake. About seven miles from Dugan Creek, where the ice didn't appear to be very strong, putting on the snowshoes, he made good headway, when suddenly the ice gave way and he plunged into the water over his knees. I will never forget poor Father Monroe, as I saw him coming into the roadhouse with his trousers frozen stiff above the knees, and carry the large snowshoes under his arm. We were over an hour thawing out his trousers so we could get his shoe pacs off. His heals were blistered and bleeding, but he was laughing, and didn't seem to mind. He said he'd had worse blisters than those from walking many a time. After we got him thawed out, he gave Father Jetté the Sacraments. Father Jetté then seemed much happier. He told me he was very thankful to me and George for bringing him to Father Monroe.

After a forced march, the party arrived safely in Nenana, where Father Jetté received emergency medical attention, before being taken by train to Fairbanks. Father Monroe looked upon his icy soakings and blisters as a small price to pay for the survival of his fellow Jesuit and close friend.

On July 24, 1924, Father Monroe left Fairbanks, never to see it again. He went south to spend the remainder of his Alaskan years in Southeastern Alaska. For a time, he served in **Juneau** and in **Ketchikan**. In this latter town, he was involved in enlarging and remodeling a hospital. But his main station in the Panhandle during those last 15 years of his active life was **Wrangell**, with **Petersburg** as a dependent station. In Wrangell, Father Monroe, ever the builder, enlarged the church, placed a full basement under it, and added a rectory building.

Father Monroe's life in Wrangell was frugal. Mass stipends kept him from going hungry. In 1931, he wrote in a letter, "A salary is unknown. I spent last year for my meals and personal expenses about 50 cents a day."

In 1933, in Wrangell, a serious accident almost put an end to Father Monroe's life. His own account of it reads:

> We were building a scaffolding ten feet high to support a platform from which we could work on the ceil-

ing of the church. We had completed one trestle, a timber 25 feet long fitted with 3 ten-foot legs, and had it set up against the wall. My helpers were engaged in constructing a similar set, while I was taking some measurements. Without warning the heavy trestle started to topple on us. Thanks to Divine Providence I perceived the danger in time to warn my companions. With upraised arms I broke somewhat the force of the blow, but the timber grazed my cheek and struck me full upon the chest. The injury to my ribs prevented me doing any of the heavier work afterwards, but now I am feeling much better and expect to recover completely in a short time. I was not knocked unconscious, and I am thankful that my injuries are so slight, as compared to what they might have been.

Father Monroe never again referred to the accident. His friends, however, noticed that, though already bent, he was now almost hunchbacked. It was only when he said Mass that he seemed by an incredible effort to lessen the right-angled position of his body. In 1939, about ten months before his death, he had to go to the hospital in Seattle. There doctors discovered that his back had been broken.

By 1939, Father Monroe was almost 85 years old, and had spent 46 years in the North. His health was failing. He went south to spend the last months of his long life at Mount St. Michael's in Spokane. He remained alert to the end, dictating letters to be sent to his many friends, and especially to members of his family in France, with whom he had always stayed in close contact. He never lost his affection for his homeland and for his relatives and friends there. As he lay dying, he was heard, according to the Father Rector of Mount St. Michael's, who was with him to the last, to pray, somewhat anxiously, "Jesus, have mercy on me! Have mercy on me!" On the afternoon of January 9, 1940, he passed quietly, peacefully away.

In his obituary of Father Monroe, his almost lifelong friend, Bishop Crimont, said of him: "The dominant characteristics of Father Monroe were an uncommon unselfishness and self-devotion throughout his long life; and his courage and fortitude in undertakings which involved enormous difficulties."

Father Francis M. Monroe, S.J., "the Alaskan Hercules," lies buried in the Jesuit cemetery at Mount St. Michael's.

26, 96, 174

Father Raymond W. Mosey. *LRC.*

MOSEY, Fr. Raymond W.

Raymond W. Mosey was born in Portland, Oregon, on July 30, 1920. His parents were Joseph and Theresa Mosey. In St. Andrew's Church, Portland, he was ordained a priest by Francis D. **Gleeson**, S.J, Vicar Apostolic of **Alaska**, on June 25, 1949. From 1949–52, Father Mosey served as pastor in **Skagway** and as principal of Pius X Mission school. Around 1950, the chapel at Pius X Mission, dedicated to St. Therese of the Child Jesus, became the Skagway parish church, replacing the old 1898 St. Mark's Church, which was taken down by Father Mosey. During the years 1952–57, he was an assistant priest at the Cathedral of the Nativity of the Blessed Virgin Mary in **Juneau**, and, from 1957–59, its pastor. Throughout five of his years in Juneau, he served also as Chancellor of the Juneau diocese.

In 1959, Father Mosey became pastor of St. Rose of Lima parish in **Wrangell**. With a grant from the Catholic Church Extension Society he installed a new heating system and applied asbestos shakes to the church and rectory in 1961. Father Mosey was very popular in both Wrangell and its dependent station, **Petersburg**, where a new St. Catherine of Siena Church was built during his time. Wrangell turned out to be the last scene of his priestly labors. There, on February 2, 1964, he died in his sleep.

Father Mosey, described as "an exceptionally zealous priest," lies buried in the city of his birth.

208

444 · Mountain Village

MOUNTAIN VILLAGE

Mountain Village, so called because it lies at the foot of the first "mountain" met as one ascends the Yukon River, is located on the right bank of the Yukon and 87 miles upstream from its mouth. It was a Native fish camp, until the opening of a general store there in 1908 prompted people from nearby settlements to move to the site. A post office was established there in 1923, a salmon saltry in 1956, and a cannery in 1964. During the 1950s, people from the Black River drainage also moved to Mountain Village. It became a regional educational center, after it was selected as headquarters for the Lower Yukon School District in 1976. For many years, this Central Yup'ik Eskimo village had a regional hospital. In 1920, Mountain Village had 136 inhabitants; in 1930, 76; in 1939, 128; in 1950, 221; in 1979, 568; in 1990, 742; and in the year 2000, 755.

Jesuit missionaries stationed at St. Mary's Mission, **Akulurak**, baptized people in the lower Yukon region as early as the 1890s. Mountain Village first appears in the California Province catalog for the year 1914–15, when Father Anthony M. **Keyes**, S.J., visited it out of **Pilot Station**. This he continued to do until 1921. The Mountain Village mission was, for a short time, dedicated to St. Barbara, thereafter to St. Lawrence. From 1921–28, Father Keyes resided at Mountain Village. During the year 1926–27, Father John L. **Lucchesi**, S.J., did likewise, with Father Keyes doing the visiting of dependent stations. During the year 1928–29, Father Lucchesi was alone. After him came Father **Edward J. Cunningham**, S.J., from 1929–31. From 1931–33, Father Paul C. **O'Connor**, S.J., visited Mountain Village out of Pilot Station. Father John B. **Sifton**, S.J., made Mountain Village his headquarters for the years 1933–37; as did Father George S. **Endal**, S.J., for the years 1938–46. Father Endal made efforts to launch a local economy with a sawmill, but had little real success with the venture. While at Mountain Village, Father Endal had, according to his successor there, Father **John P. Fox**, S.J., "the practice of giving absolute priority to the seriously sick, regardless of time or inconveniences involved." In his old age, Father Endal remembered his Mountain Village years as "the happiest of my life."

Father Fox held station at Mountain Village dur-
ing the decade 1946–56. He had a major impact on that village, and on its dependent stations. He brought electric power to them; and, following a precedent set by Father Endal, he held annual, closed, three-day retreats for men and women at both Mountain Village and Pilot Station. Moreover, he organized annual "Conventions," "Congresses," at those two villages. These were held in the middle of August—to coincide with the Feast of the Assumption of the Blessed Virgin Mary—now at one village, now at the other. All the people of that general area were invited to them. The Conventions had a twofold purpose according to Father Fox. They were meant to help the people to know and love Christ and His Church better; and, at the same time, to help the people get to know and love their neighbor better. The program was, accordingly, partly religious, partly social. The Conventions were intended also to enable young men and women to find suitable spouses from outside their own small villages. At Mountain Village, as at his other stations, Father Fox continued to rely heavily on competent Native catechists.

Father James E. **Poole**, S.J., served the Mountain Village parish from 1956–59 as resident priest, and during the following year as visiting priest out of St. Marys. In 1957, he saw the completion of a new church at Mountain Village. This replaced the one Father Keyes had built in the early 1920s.

The following Jesuit Fathers, too, held station at Mountain Village: William T. **McIntyre**, 1960–62, and 1969–80; **Paul B. Mueller**, 1962–64; William C. **Dibb**, 1964–65; Father Fox again, 1965–68; Paul Jordan, 1968–69; J. Herbert Mead, 1980–81; **Joseph E. Laudwein**, out of St. Mary's Mission, 1981–82; Francis J. **Fallert**, 1982–86; Eugene P. **Delmore**, 1986–91, and 1995–97; James A. **Sebesta**, out of St. Mary's Mission, 1991–94; Robert V. Paskey, 1994–95; René **Astruc**, 1997–2002. In 2002, Mountain Village began to be served out of St. Mary's Mission.

While Father Delmore was pastor of Mountain Village, the present church was built. "On Palm Sunday, April 12, 1987," his account reads, "the Catholic population of Mt. Village gathered in the little church that had been used since 1957 and processed over to the new church with palms wav-

St. Lawrence Church, Mountain Village. *PP.*

ing and incense flowing." This new church was built by local people under the foremanship of Jerry Carpluk. Its furnishings—benches, tables, a lectern and altar—were likewise constructed by local volunteers. The new church was dedicated on August 23, 1987, by Michael J. **Kaniecki**, S.J., Bishop of **Fairbanks** at the time.

Eskimo Deacon Elmer Beans served the Mountain Village Parish for many years, and was still doing so as of the year 2004.

Sister of St. **Ann** Jeannette LaRose, spent the year 1991–92 at Mountain Village as Pastoral Minister. Sister Dorothy Giloley, S.S.J., was there as a Pastoral Facilitator as of the year 2004.

Rosalie Elaine L'Ecuyer, a "diocesan volunteer," served the Mountain Village parish as Religious Education Coordinator and Pastoral Minister from 1980 to 1983.

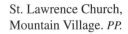

59

MUELLER, Father Francis, E., S.J.

Francis E. Mueller was born on August 9, 1922, in Portland, Oregon, the child of Joseph Mueller and Mary Theresa Gappa. His father immigrated from Germany in 1910; his mother was the child of parents who had immigrated earlier from Germany. Francis was the fifth in a family of six children, four boys and one girl. (His younger brother, **Paul B. Mueller**, too, became a Jesuit.) For his elementary and secondary schooling he attended the parochial school in Milwaukie, Oregon, staffed by the Sisters of St. Mary of Oregon.

After graduating from high school, Francis

entered the Jesuit novitiate at Sheridan, Oregon, on August 14, 1940. Two years later, he made his profession of the vows of poverty, chastity and obedience. Continuing on at Sheridan, he spent the next two years in classical and humanities studies. The next three years, 1944–47, he spent at Mount St. Michael's, Spokane, Washington, engaged primarily in philosophical studies. Having completed these, with an M.A. degree in philosophy, he spent the years 1947–50 teaching mainly Latin, German, and Religion at Seattle Preparatory School. After this teaching practicum, he went on to theological studies at Alma College, Los Gatos, California. He was ordained a priest in St. Aloysius Church, Spokane, on June 20, 1953, by Bishop Charles D. White. Father Mueller completed his basic Jesuit training by doing a fourth year of theology at Alma and then his ten-month tertianship at Port Townsend, Washington.

Father Mueller spent the years 1955–59 in Rome earning the J.C.D. degree in Church law. (During the summer of 1956, he was in the Pacific Northwest helping nine of his fellow Jesuits solicit funds for the new Jesuit High School just then being built in Portland.) From 1959–61, he taught moral theology and canon law at Regis College, Toronto, Ontario, Canada. In September 1961, he returned to Sheridan, this time as Master of Novices. He held this very important and demanding position for seven years. The latter years of his term of office as Novice Master were noticeably affected by the general post-Vatican II turmoil and confusion that reigned throughout the Church at the time. The Society of Jesus and its novitiates were not exempt from these. Referring to Father Mueller's years as Novice Master, one historian summarized tersely, "He had a stormy term of office." It can safely be concluded, then, that it was with a great sigh of relief that he yielded his burden as Novice Master in 1968 and took on a new assignment, in **Alaska**.

On August 1, 1968, Father Mueller landed in **Fairbanks**, Alaska, to assume the position of Chancellor of the Diocese of Fairbanks, a position he was to fill for ten years. At the same time, he became Officialis for the Diocesan Marriage Tribunal. He was to serve as such throughout most of his years in Alaska. During the fall of his first year in Alaska, he ministered also as chaplain to the Newman Club at the University of Alaska–Fairbanks. In January 1969, he was appointed administrator of the newly formed Sacred Heart Cathedral parish. This position he held until the following August.

After Fairbanks, no other city in Alaska was to witness more of Father Mueller's ministrations than **Barrow**. Beginning in 1972, he ministered to the people of St. Patrick's parish in Barrow as their pastor for almost three decades. As of the year 2004, no Catholic priest in Alaska had ever served one and the same flock for a longer period of time than that. On a regular basis, generally every two weeks, he commuted to Barrow, a roundtrip of over a thousand air miles, for stays of varying durations.

Over the years, as the parish grew, the need for a new and more spacious facility for worship and parish activities became ever more urgent. Accordingly, Father Mueller—a man handy with tools and machinery, and who in 1980 had helped with the construction of the new church in **Healy**—took it upon himself to oversee the construction of the new St. Patrick's Church in Barrow. Construction began in 1992. Father Mueller himself spent much time at the site and did much of the actual construction work. The following year, on March 28, 1993, the new church was ready to be formally blessed and dedicated. Michael J. **Kaniecki**, S.J., Bishop of Fairbanks, with Fathers Mueller and Louis L. **Renner**, S.J., concelebrating, did the honors.

Father Francis E. Mueller, S.J. *Photo by Bud Nelson Studio, Fairbanks, and courtesy of Fr. Mueller.*

During his many years of service to the Barrow Catholic community, Father Mueller tried routinely to visit as many of his parishioners as possible. He had an easy manner about him when it came to meeting, greeting and visiting people. During the long winter months, while visiting from house to house, he wore the black quilted parka, with a huge polar bear fur ruff sewn to the hood, that his people had given him. When, in the year 2000, he finally retired as pastor of St. Patrick's, the people gave him a truly royal send-off.

In 1982, Father Mueller was appointed Vicar General of the Fairbanks diocese, a position he left in 1996. During the course of his long years in Alaska, he served in a great number and variety of different capacities. He was generally the Superior of the Jesuit community he lived in. For years he was an officially appointed Consultor both to the Bishop of Fairbanks and to the General Superior of the Jesuits in Alaska. He was involved in ecumenical work, working for a time with the Alaska Christian Conference, a state-wide organization. From 1977–79, he was its president. He spent many a weekend with the Engaged Encounter Group in Fairbanks. For years he was diocesan archivist. As such, being by nature a man of orderly mind and manner, he did much to put in order and preserve official documents and records, especially baptismal, marriage, and burial records.

Father Mueller was blessed with a very level-headed, calm approach to life. As a counterbalance to the demands made upon him by his spiritual ministry and the great load of clerical, indoor, desk and head work, he made a point of regularly spending some time outdoors. Often, after the snows of a winter's night had fallen and were lying deep on the parking lots around the chancery building and Sacred Heart Cathedral, he could be seen during the early morning hours out there on the grader clearing them away. This was demanding, self-sacrificing work. At the same time, however, it served him also as recreation. By way of hobbies, he fished and hunted. For years, a beautifully shaped rack of moose antlers, the trophy of a successful hunt, adorned the top of the bookshelf in his room. In general, he loved the Alaskan wilderness. With fellow Jesuits and priest friends, he floated the Copper and Porcupine Rivers, and with them he hiked the Pinnell and Chilkoot Trails. And he liked simply to spend "time at the wheel," to drive. He would, by his own admission, have been a happy trucker.

But, far more than physical, outdoor activities, it was matters of the spirit that kept the Alaskan life of the seemingly overburdened, one-time Master of Novices sane and on an even keel. Father Mueller was, above all, a man of prayer. Faithfully, year after year, with his fellow Alaskan Jesuits, he made his annual eight-day retreat. At times, he had his own personal director for a given retreat. Father Mueller's spirituality was essentially "Ignatian," based, as it was, on the Spiritual Exercises of St. Ignatius.

In the summer of 2000, Father Mueller left Alaska to become the administrator of St. Michael's parish in Oakridge, Oregon. There, a several-hours drive from where he had spent his childhood, he happily took up a new ministry, a ministry less demanding than any he had had up to that point in his life. At St. Michael's, in the evening of his long, fruitful life, he found peace and contentment. On July 14, 2002, he wrote to Father Renner: "As for myself, I am doing well here at St. Michael's. The setting is magnificent, located, as we are, in the foothills of the Cascades. The people are friendly and caring. In some respects, my ministry is like being a chaplain in an older folks' home. So, I spend a good portion of my time doing the corporal works

of mercy, viz., visiting the sick and burying the dead."

On July 16, 2003, that peaceful life of active pastoral ministry at Oakridge came to an abrupt end. Feeling his left leg going numb, Father Mueller sought medical attention. He was rushed to Sacred Heart Medical Center in Eugene, Oregon. The following day, to save his life, his left leg was amputated above the knee. On July 30th, he was brought to St. Luke's Rehabilitation Institute in Spokane; and, on August 8th, to the Jesuit House infirmary at Gonzaga University. A week later, he moved into Bea House, across the street from Jesuit House, as a member of the Regis Community. As of the early part of the year 2004, he was happily living in Bea House and slowly getting accustomed to walking with a prosthesis.

Interviewed in April 2004, he said: "I don't know why I had to lose my leg, but it comes under the framework of God's divine providence. When I look at it that way, it makes sense. What has happened in my life is unbelievably marvelous. It was God who chose me to do this. I am very content."

126, 139, 169

MUELLER, Father Paul B., S.J.

Paul Bernard Mueller, born on April 23, 1925, in Portland, Oregon, was the youngest of six children born to Joseph Mueller and Mary Theresa Gappa. His father immigrated from Germany in 1910; his mother was the child of parents who had immigrated earlier from Germany. For his elementary schooling, Paul attended St. John's Grade School, 1931–39; for his secondary, St. John's High School, 1939–43. Both schools, in Milwaukie, Oregon, were staffed by the Sisters of St. Mary of Oregon.

On January 26, 1943, following the example of his next older brother, **Francis E. Mueller**, Paul entered the Jesuit novitiate at Sheridan, Oregon. Two years later he pronounced his first vows: poverty, chastity and obedience. After two years of classical and humanities studies at Sheridan, he went on to three years of philosophical studies at Mount St. Michael's, Spokane, Washington. In 1949, he received the A.B. degree from Gonzaga

University, Spokane. He spent the years 1950–52 at **Holy Cross Mission**, **Alaska**, as prefect of the boys and as Religion teacher. From 1952–56, he was at Alma College, Los Gatos, California, studying theology. He was ordained a priest in St. Aloysius Church, Spokane, on June 18, 1955, by Bishop Joseph P. Dougherty. During the summer of 1956, Father Mueller was a member of "the begging team" soliciting funds for the construction of Jesuit High School in Portland. He spent the year 1956–57 at Port Townsend, Washington, making his tertianship at Manresa Hall. He next taught at Seattle Preparatory School for two years, 1957–59. He took his final vows as a Jesuit in the Seattle University chapel on August 15, 1958.

Father Mueller's first Alaskan assignment as a priest was at **Copper Valley School**, near **Glennallen**. During his three years at the school, 1959–62, he served as "Spiritual Father," taught Religion, and offered Sunday and feast day Masses in the nearby communities of **Tok** and **Northway**. The following two years found him back on the Yukon, as pastor of **Mountain Village** and its dependent missions: **Marshall**, **Pilot Station**, and **Russian Mission**. He spent the year 1964–65 in **Bethel** as pastor of the parish and visiting priest to its dependent stations on the Kuskokwim. In large part, it was he who built the new church at **Kalskag** in 1965. The following year he was in **Nome**, as pastor of St. Joseph's parish. In 1966, he supervised the demolition of the old Holy Cross Hospital in Nome.

From 1966–70, Father Mueller was at St. Marys City on the **Andreafsky** River. There he taught in the mission high school, and served as the first official pastor of the Church of the Nativity parish. In addition, he was visiting priest to Pilot Station. After those four years, he was stationed again at Copper Valley School, where he taught and, at the same time, served as pastor of Glennallen's Holy Family parish. He next spent a sabbatical year, 1971–72, in Rome, taking part in "Movement for a Better World" and "Continuing Theological Education" programs. His sabbatical over, he was back at St. Mary's Mission High School as teacher and counselor, from 1972–75.

During the fall semester of 1975, Father Mueller was accepted as a graduate student at the University of Alaska–**Fairbanks**. He graduated at the end of December with an M.A. degree in Guidance and Counseling. From January to July 1976, he was half-time chaplain to students at the UA–F, and half-time pastor at Sacred Heart Cathedral, Fairbanks. After spending the month of July at Notre Dame University, he became pastor of the "Railbelt" communities. From July 1976 to August 1984, he was pastor of St. Theresa's parish in **Nenana**, and visiting priest and auxiliary chaplain to communities and military installations strung out for 110 miles along the Parks Highway and the Alaska Railroad from Nenana all the way to Cantwell. While serving his stretched out parish, he spent much "time at the wheel." This left him less time for prayer-book prayers, so he prayed the rosary as he drove. Father Mueller had a special devotion to Mary the Mother of the Lord.

The year 1980 was a milestone year in the life of Father Mueller. On June 18th of that year, he celebrated his silver jubilee as a priest, and on August 5th, he had the joy of witnessing the pouring of the slab for the new, much-needed church at **Healy**. This was to have a worship area upstairs and priest's quarters and a meeting hall downstairs. Father Mueller was put in charge of the whole construction project, including the financing of it. It should be remembered that, in addition to the building project, he still had his regular pastoral duties. Nevertheless, he himself put in much time at the construction site, as carpenter, electrician, furnace man, and jack-of-all trades. With his contributed labor, and that of others, mostly volunteer, the new church was ready to be blessed and formally dedicated— under the title of Holy Mary of Guadalupe, at Father Mueller's insistence—on Pentecost Sunday, May 30, 1982.

The building of the church and all the traveling that was a continuing part of his life took their toll on Father Mueller. He requested another sabbatical, for the year 1984–85. He spent the autumn part of that year at the "Guelph Center of Spirituality" in Guelph, Ontario, and the rest of it in Tacoma, Washington, where he worked with "street people" at Nativity House.

From Chicago, on November 22, 1984, Father Mueller wrote to relatives and friends: "On leav-

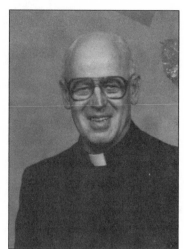

Father Paul B. Mueller, S.J. *LRC.*

ing Nenana last June, I received a special treat from my former parishioners there. They gave me the fare for a round-trip ticket to Germany." While in Germany, he attended his cousin's golden wedding anniversary, and made a retreat at the monastery of the Holy Cross Sisters on the shores of Lake Constance. From Germany, he brought back "lasting memories."

From 1985–88, Father Mueller was stationed at **Holy Spirit Center**, **Anchorage**, engaged in giving retreats and spiritual direction. In 1988, after having served long years and in various capacities in Alaska, he left it, because of deteriorating health. During his Alaskan years, in addition to filling, for the most part, the roles of pastor and teacher, he had been engaged also in a great variety of other activities. For over eleven years, he was Director of the Pontifical Association of the Holy Childhood for the Diocese of Fairbanks. Beginning in 1960, he was a chaplain of the Civil Air Patrol, leaving it some twenty years later with the rank of major. Being a ham radio operator, he served the CAP as a Radio Communications Officer. He served on the mental health boards both in Bethel and in Fairbanks. In Bethel, and again in Nenana, he was a volunteer firetruck driver.

From 1988 on, until his death, Father Mueller was stationed in Spokane. For some years, he served as associate pastor of St. Aloysius parish, until failing health made parish work impossible for him.

Already in the spring of 1985, he had been found to be suffering from Parkinson's disease. He made his last trip to Alaska in May 1992, courtesy of the parishioners of the Healy parish. In Holy Mary of Guadalupe Church, on May 30, the tenth anniversary of the dedication of the parish, he was the principal celebrant at a concelebrated Mass, as well as the homilist. On January 25, 1993, he celebrated his 50th anniversary as a Jesuit. He spent much of the winter 1993–94 in Phoenix, Arizona, at Brophy College Prep. The previous winter he had suffered much from his disease, aggravated by the cold in Spokane. Superiors thinking that the warmer, drier climate would do him good, made it possible for him to go there. He found the Arizona climate "heavenly!"

By 1995, Father Mueller was in total retirement from any active ministry. In the Oregon Province catalog, he was now listed as "praying for the Church and the Society."

In 1992, all the members of the Oregon Province were asked by their Father Provincial to answer the two-fold question: "Where do you see yourself in the year 2000, and what do you see yourself doing?" In answer to the first part of the question, Father Mueller wrote:

> When the year 2000 arrives, I expect to be pushing up daisies. I have Parkinson's disease, and the doctors tell me that from the time the disease is diagnosed, the life expectancy is between two and ten years. Mine was diagnosed in 1985. Add ten years to that and 1995 is all I can expect out of life. But, who knows? Maybe God will fool them all.

The second part of the question he answered somewhat indirectly: " There are several apostolates for which I would like to be remembered. The first one is a prayerful spirit. The Lord God has always been foremost and uppermost in my life. I have always sought His will. His love and grace have always been a motivation force in my life. I believe that comes only through prayer." He wanted to be remembered, too, for his zeal, when it came to the Sacrament of Reconciliation. "I believe that a priest, next to the Holy Sacrifice of the Mass, cannot do any greater work in God's kingdom than to forgive sin."

In the case of Father Mueller, God did fool them all. He lived two years beyond the outside deadline,

1995, given him by his doctors. At the age of 72, in Seattle, Washington, he died of pneumonia, on July 28, 1997. He lies buried in Mount St. Michael's Cemetery, Spokane.

100

Father Ernest H. Muellerleile.
Photo by Br. Charles McBride, C.S.C.

MUELLERLEILE, Father Ernest H.

Ernest H. Muellerleile was born in St. Paul, Minnesota, on June 23, 1919. He was ordained a priest for the Archdiocese of St. Paul, Minnesota, on October 7, 1944. As a young seminarian, he dreamed about being a priest in **Alaska**. However, before moving north to undertake his "dream job," serving what he called "the missions of Alaska," he had first to minister for 25 years, in six different parishes, in his home diocese.

Father Muellerleile spent the year August 1967 to August 1968 in Alaska as a visitor. During the months of November and December 1969, he studied at the University of Alaska–**Fairbanks**. On March 20, 1970, he "came to stay." His first assignment was that of pastor of the **Sitka** parish. There he built a new church, parish hall and convent. He also visited outlying mission stations. November 1972 saw him at **Talkeetna**. From December 1, 1972, to December 1, 1974, he was pastor of **Palmer** and its dependent mission, **Wasilla**. During this time, he served also, for a year, as administrator of the **Glennallen** parish. From December 1, 1974, to Easter 1975, he was associate pastor of St. Benedict's parish in **Anchorage**.

On Easter Sunday 1975, Father Muellerleile became pastor and founder of St. Elizabeth Ann Seton parish in Anchorage. As such, he built the church, school, and parish hall. He was pastor there until 1984. During those years, he served also as organizer of the pilgrimage to the 1976 Eucharistic Congress in Philadelphia and as Diocesan Director of the Campaign for Human Development. In 1976, he became a team priest for Worldwide Marriage Encounter.

After his tenure at St. Elizabeth's, Father Muellerleile went on to found Holy Cross parish in Anchorage. He remained there until his retirement in 2001. His retirement period was of short duration. With smiling resignation, and very much at peace, he awaited his approaching death. This followed only three months after he first learned that he had a serious health problem. He succumbed to kidney cancer on May 16, 2002. On May 22nd, friends and family gathered in Holy Cross Church for the funeral Mass. In Mendota, Minnesota, on May 25th, after a prayer service, held in the same stone church in which he had been baptized some 82 years earlier, he was laid to rest. Not long before his death, he said, "I'll be buried in Minnesota, but my spirit will soar right back to the mountains of Alaska." He loved Alaska's mountains, loved to hike and ski in them.

During his 31 years in Alaska, Father Muellerleile led a simple, joyful, humble life with his people. He was loved for being "the most compassionate and kind-hearted man" that he was. Soft-spoken, open-minded, and accepting of people as they were, he put people at their ease. Being a man of peace, he radiated peace to others.

MURPHY, Brother Alfred T., S.J.

Alfred T. Murphy was born in Calgary, Alberta, Canada, on July 31, 1887. His parents, who were really at home in Everett, Washington, had gone there job hunting. Soon after his birth, they returned to Everett. As a young man, Alfred crossed both the Pacific and Atlantic Oceans, and at least four times sailed to **Alaska**, always as a stowaway. In boxcars, he rode the rails throughout the western states. But, Francis Thompson's poetic "Hound of Heaven" caught up with him, called him to His service. On December 2, 1911, Alfred entered the Jesuit novitiate at Los Gatos, California.

The Father Minister at Los Gatos at the time was Father Michael M. O'Malley, S.J. In his memoirs, he relates the following:

> There was a postulant from **Nome**, Alfred Murphy, to be a Brother. He was versed in many useful trades, and most practical. I gave him many useful jobs to do around the house and outside. He did all well and came for more. He was very happy, too, until he came to me one day scowling, disgusted, ready to quit at once. I asked him what was the sudden trouble. He said, "One can't even smoke in this darned place." Providentially, there happened to be a box of cigars on my desk at the moment. He grinned, took the box, and left the room. A few days later he came back with the box and some of the cigars. He explained, "Fr. Rector was passing my room. He noticed smoke coming out. I was singing. He asked me how I got the cigars. I told him. He told me to take them back to you. So, here's the remainder." He remained and soon became a novice brother.

While still a novice, Alfred Murphy was assigned to Nome. He arrived there on July 31, 1913. The following December, on the 8th, he pronounced his vows as a Jesuit Lay Brother. In Nome, he served as handyman in the parish. Several times he went north to **Marys Igloo** to help Father Joseph **Bernard**, S.J.

On August 4, 1915, Brother Murphy left Nome for his new assignment at St. Mary's Mission, **Akulurak**. He arrived there on the 13th. Except for the year 1929–30, which he spent in Seattle, he was to spend the rest of his life at Akulurak and at the new St. Mary's Mission, **Andreafsky**.

At Akulurak, Brother Murphy did many things, but his chief assignments were prefecting the boys, and maintaining and running the mission boats, first the *Tréca*, then the *Sifton*. As a prefect, he was not a great success. After he had had that job more or less full-time from 1916–28, Alaska Mission Superior Philip I. **Delon**, S.J., wrote to Father Provin-

Brother Alfred T. Murphy, S.J.
JOPA-998.01a.

cial Joseph M. Piet, S.J.: "Brother Murphy, when it comes to prefecting the boys, is not all that could be desired. He has a remarkable hold on the boys, but he has no idea of discipline. You know he never had any himself, when he was a boy."

However, it was not as a prefect of the boys that Brother Murphy was to make his major contribution to St. Mary's Mission. His specialty was the mission boats: maintaining them and operating them on their countless trips to fish camps, or up the Yukon to gather drift logs for firewood, or up the Yukon all the way to **Holy Cross Mission** to deliver fish in exchange for vegetables, or to **Hamilton** to pick up freight, or to deliver and pick up mail or passengers. As captain of the boats, according to Father Paul C. **O'Connor**, S.J., who knew him well, "he never spoke much, seldom even raised his voice, yet all his old school boys jumped at his command."

During the 1940s, Father Segundo **Llorente**, S.J., was Brother Murphy's Superior at Akulurak. He wrote of him:

As the years were going by, he developed the belief that he would work in the summer, but spend the winter reading magazines. His reading became a drug, an addiction. He could not recall anything he read. He had to read for the sake of reading. During the summer, he gathered from his friends piles of pulp magazines to read in the winter. *Argosy* was among them. I was in charge at the time, and I felt that it was my responsibility to put an end to that. So, during his last trip in early October 1943, I had his two sacks of pulp magazines burned. When he came and saw what had happened, he and I went through a very bad half hour. For a week he was moving around in a trance. Slowly he came to his senses. Grace prevailed. Since he had to read, and since our house library had only spiritual books, he read them, and the change in him soon became noticeable. His outlook was more supernatural. He underwent a conversion for the better. He had been using 18 pounds of pipe tobacco every year. Now of his own accord he quit smoking, although he told the Lord that if and when things on the boat became much too hard to handle, he would reserve the privilege of filling his pipe to cool off and get hold of himself. That was what he did. Eventually his eyes began to hurt, when he read, so he quit reading, but not praying. He was so absorbed in God, that it was evident that he was living in the divine presence. He told me that he was saying an average of forty decades of the rosary every day.

On August 3, 1951, St. Mary's Mission was moved from Akulurak to its new site on the Andreafsky River. There Brother Murphy continued to do much as he had been doing now for over 35 years: maintain and run the mission boat. Up to the last year of his life, he was providing wood for the mission's many stoves.

The winter 1953–54 saw Brother Murphy in Seattle for medical attention. While there, he stayed at the Seattle Preparatory School faculty house—and there, with future priest in Alaska, Louis L. **Renner**, S.J., he played some of his last games of chess.

By early March 1954, Brother Murphy was back at St. Mary's Mission. There, a short six months later, he died, on August 27, 1954. Of his suffering and death, Father O'Connor, who was his Superior at the time, wrote, "During his illness he never complained. Brother Murphy died as he lived, very quietly." Father Llorente, his previous Superior, wrote, "A short time before Bro. Murphy's death, Fr. O'Connor and I anointed him. When he died, he looked like a saint to me."

Brother Alfred T. Murphy, S.J., lies buried in the cemetery at St. Mary's Mission on the banks of the Andreafsky River, the first Religious to be buried there.

MURPHY, Father Cornelius K., S.J.

Cornelius K. "Neil" Murphy was born in Butte, Montana, on June 28, 1911. His father, Dennis, worked at first in the Butte copper mines, then on the Road Commission. His mother's maiden name was Mary O'Houlihan. For his elementary schooling, Neil attended Immaculate Conception Grade School; for his secondary, Central Catholic High School, staffed by the Christian Brothers. During the years 1929–31, he attended Mount St. Charles College—later renamed Carroll College—in Helena, Montana. The president of the college described Neil as "a serious and quiet young man, a consistent plodder."

Meanwhile, young men coming home from Gonzaga University in Spokane, Washington, were talking about the Jesuits. In Neil, they found an enthusiastic listener. On August 3, 1931, he entered the Jesuit novitiate at Sheridan, Oregon. There, after completing his two-year noviceship, he spent an additional two years studying the classics and humanities. From 1935–38, he made his philosophical studies at Mount St. Michael's in Spokane. For the next two years, he taught English and French at Bellarmine Preparatory in Tacoma, Washington. During the years 1940–42, he was at **Holy Cross Mission, Alaska**, serving mainly as prefect of the boys in the boarding school. When he left Holy Cross, he brought south with him, to Butte, Robert F. **Corrigal**, to live with the Murphy family, while he received his secondary education at Butte's Central Catholic High School.

From 1942–46, Neil was at Alma College, Los Gatos, California, engaged in theological studies. He was ordained a priest in San Francisco on June 16, 1945. His tertianship he made at Auriesville, New York, 1946–47.

Father Murphy returned to Alaska in 1947. From September to November of that year, he was at **Nulato**; then in **Nome**, from November 19, 1947, to February 1948. He was at Holy Cross from Feb-

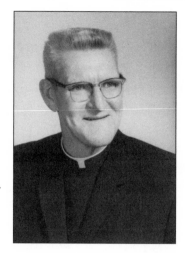

Father Cornelius K. Murphy, S.J. *DFA*.

ruary 1948 to September 1948, after which he returned to Nome to be pastor until September 1956. Before Father Murphy had spent a full year in Nome, Father **Thomas P. Cunningham**, S.J., was able to write to Francis D. **Gleeson**, S.J., Vicar Apostolic of Alaska at the time: "Fr. Murphy continues to do very excellent work in Nome." At the end of Father Murphy's years in Nome, Father **George E. Carroll**, S.J., on September 18, 1956, wrote in the Nome house diary: "Father Murphy, after eight years at Nome, departs to his new assignment at **Fairbanks**. Father made many friends here, and many regretted his departure."

From 1956–65, Father Murphy was assistant pastor at Fairbanks' Immaculate Conception parish. As such, he was also "Spiritual Father" for the children attending Fairbanks' Immaculate Conception Grade School. This meant that he visited each grade for half an hour each week. He was a tall, gaunt, stern looking man with sharp features, and an equally sharp gaze; but, given his kind smile and gentle touch, the children did not find him all that intimidating.

During the years 1965–68, Father Murphy was stationed in **Bethel**. From there, he returned to Fairbanks, to Immaculate Conception Church, where he was to live out the rest of his life, serving now as assistant pastor, now as pastor. During the year 1973–74, he was Rector of the recently established Sacred Heart Cathedral parish, but he continued to reside at "the Immaculate," "the little church," where his heart had been all along.

Both in his capacity as pastor and as assistant pastor, Father Murphy—being the "quintessentially quiet man" that he was, who, according to a confrere, "opened his mouth only to say Mass or to bid at bridge"—did much listening, whether in the parlor, or in the confessional, or on the telephone, or at the bedside of the sick or the dying. He was highly esteemed as a counselor and consoler. He was not given to a lot of talk; but, when he spoke, people knew that he meant what he said. He put much thought, effort and prayer into his preaching. He gave his hearers something to remember—and pray over.

As a young man, Father Murphy was athletic, skilled both when it came to pitching a baseball from the mound or a horseshoe from peg to peg. In later years, he began to suffer from declining health. This gave him a special tolerance for the human weaknesses and the pain of others. He was able to touch the hurts and depressions of many with his healing spirit and understanding love.

Father Murphy's last long illness gave revealing glimpses into the character of the man. Referring to a medical report he had just received, he said—with a twinkle in his eyes, and a shy, but knowing smile—to one of his fellow Jesuits visiting him, "I suppose you've heard the news. Did you know they found the tumors on Good Friday?" He had accepted the verdict with a sense of relief, as a release from his medical problems.

Father Murphy died in Fairbanks Memorial Hospital on Easter Friday morning, April 16, 1982. He lies buried in Birch Hill Cemetery, Fairbanks. "Murphy Hall," in the basement of Immaculate Conception Church, Fairbanks, is named for him.

MUSET, Father Paul, S.J.

Paul Muset was born on July 3, 1854, in Cambrai, Nord, France. Not much is known about his early life. He entered the Champagne Province of the Society of Jesus on September 28, 1873. He was a diligent student. Being adventurous as well, he volunteered for the Rocky Mountain Mission. He made his tertianship at DeSmet Mission, Idaho. In

1889, he went to **Alaska**. By November 30th of that year, after a 17-day trip by dogsled from **St. Michael**, he was at **Tununak**, a Central Yup'ik Eskimo village near Cape Vancouver on Nelson Island, where he was awaited by Father Joseph M. **Tréca**, S.J.

Father Muset was a gifted linguist. He soon had a working command of the Native language. He was also a gifted musician, with a voice described as "glorious." He set about putting parts of the catechism into verse, which he then set to music and taught to the children. Soon he and Father Tréca had the people rehearsed well enough to sing their parts of a Latin High Mass.

Father Muset's stay at Tununak was a relatively short one. Around the middle of September 1891, he arrived at **Holy Cross Mission**. He was "enjoying very good health," according to the entry in the mission diary. He had come to Holy Cross "to make his Profession," that is, to take his final vows as a Jesuit. This he did on the Feast of All Saints, November 1st.

In January of 1892, beginning on the 7th, he gave the Sisters of St. **Ann** their annual retreat. Then, on the 17th, he left Holy Cross, with the intention of doing some missionary work on the Kuskokwim River before going on to Tununak. However, by February 6th, he was back at Holy Cross, "in very poor condition," according to a letter written by Father Paschal **Tosi**, S.J., at Holy Cross on February 25, 1892. In that same letter, Father Tosi went on to write: "He is not a strong man, and his constitution cannot stand the hardships and privations of the sledge traveling." He decided to keep Father Muset at Holy Cross.

At Holy Cross, Father Muset did much of the routine priestly work connected with a boarding school mission. He conducted catechism classes for both children and adults. Again, as at Tununak, he used his gift for music and song to make the teaching effective. He also made some missionary excursions. From June 6th to July 1st of 1892, he was on a missionary excursion to the Kuskokwim River. On July 19th of that year, he was named Superior of Holy Cross.

For reasons of health, Father Muset was out of Alaska by 1893. His heart, however, remained in the North. In a letter to one of his Superiors, dated April 15, 1894, he wrote, "I intended always to go back to Alaska." He recalled the four years he spent there as "years of happiness." But, he was never to see Alaska again. After several years of work on different Indian missions in the Northwest, he was assigned to Missoula, Montana. There, in his 44th year, he died, on September 7, 1897. Many people of the Missoula parish, to show their appreciation for what he had done for them, accompanied his body to St. Ignatius Mission, some distance north of Missoula, where it was taken to be buried.

NAWN, Father Francis X., S.J.

Francis X. Nawn was born in Milwaukee, Wisconsin, on January 1, 1919. He was schooled in Milwaukee: at the Gesu Grade School, at Marquette High, and for two years at Marquette University. He entered the Jesuit novitiate at Florissant, Missouri, as a candidate for the Wisconsin Province, on September 1, 1938. After completing his two-year noviceship at Florissant, he made his "collegiate studies" at St. Louis University from 1942–45. He next taught at Campion High School in Prairie du Chien, Wisconsin, from 1945–48. His four years of theological studies he made at St. Mary's, Kansas. There he was ordained a priest on June 14, 1951. Father Nawn made his tertianship at Decatur, Illinois, 1952–53. Beginning in 1953, he taught physics successively at Regis University in Denver, at Marquette High in Milwaukee, and at Creighton University in Omaha.

Having volunteered to serve on the **Alaska** Mission, Father Nawn first came to Alaska in 1962. On May 30, 1973, in keeping with his wishes, he was transcribed from the Wisconsin Province to the Oregon Province. This assured him of being allowed to stay on in Alaska. For his first two years in Alaska, he was stationed at **Holy Cross**. He then served at **Chevak**, 1964–68. He held station—except for a sabbatical year, 1980–81, at Fordham University, Bronx, New York—at **Alakanuk** from 1968–83. During his Alakanuk years, he had the care also of **Emmonak** and **Nunam Iqua** (Sheldon Point). From 1983–87, he had the care of **St. Michael** and **Stebbins**. He spent his last year of active ministry at St. Mary's, **Andreafsky**.

During his Alakanuk years, Father Nawn engaged in commercial fishing, to share more closely the lives of his people and to earn some money for his mission. He enjoyed the fishing, and was successful at it, and had to admit that, even though it was hard work, he was soon "hooked" on it. "At the end of every season," he wrote, "I have heaved a sigh of relief and said, 'Never again!'—only to find myself the next spring as eager as the Natives to get back out on the river." Though he enjoyed the fishing, and made some money at it, he was motivated to take it up and stay with it primarily by the realization: "If you are not fishing, or connected in some way with fishing, you are just out of communication with village life."

Father Nawn was a practical man, at home with motors and electrical things. He was a ham radio operator, KL7EPN. While he treated the Sisters stationed at the Alakanuk parish "like queens," in the words of one of them, his own lifestyle was simple. Father Louis L. **Renner**, S.J., who substituted for him during the Christmas of 1981, found that his living quarters—outfitted, as they were, with every kind of tool, a workbench, hardware and electrical items of all kinds—resembled more a handyman's workshop than a parish rectory.

The people of Alakanuk, and the Sisters who were stationed there for a time with him, found Father Nawn a quiet man, a kind man with a gentle disposition, easy to get along with. He was a highly competent, dedicated, hard worker, both in the material and in the spiritual realm. In matters theological and liturgical, he was somewhat on the conservative side, but he was not contentious about it. He wanted the people to take responsibility for their parish life. He did not push himself or religion upon the people. The poor and needy were of particular concern to him. In his quiet way, he was always available to all, old and young alike. The children especially were very much drawn to him and were relentless visitors. He played games with them, went skating with them.

That the people appreciated Father Nawn's concern for them became strikingly obvious by the way they responded, when he had his heart attack in August 1980. They were shocked at the news, and for 24 hours, while he was having open heart surgery, they kept a spontaneous vigil of prayers for him. When he returned to Alakanuk in May 1981, after a sabbatical year at Fordham University, the people put on a special, unprecedented potluck to welcome him home. During his absence, other priests stood in for him at Alakanuk. Of them people said, "The other priests were nice, but nothing like Father Nawn. He really understands us."

In 1983, Father Nawn was transferred to St. Michael. Some years later, one of his Alakanuk parishioners, Monica Shelden-Murphy, wrote: "I sorely missed him, when he was transferred. It seemed as if an important part of my life was suddenly gone." Recalling her wedding day, she wrote: "I got married right out of high school, and it was Father Francis Xavier Nawn, S.J., who was the presider at my wedding. The special blessing he gave to each of us, to my husband and me, reached all the way down to my toes. He seemed to have touched a chord deep within me, and my whole being resonated with a joyful sound."

For a time, in 1986, Father Nawn's first stroke laid him low in **Anchorage**. The year 1988–89 found him in Tacoma, Washington, living in the Bellarmine High School community and helping out in various parishes. While in Tacoma, he was felled by another stroke. In 1989, he was moved to the Loyola Hall infirmary at Seattle University, where he was until 1992, when he was transferred to the Jesuit House infirmary at Gonzaga University in Spokane. Though mostly paralyzed by this time, he was able to make it on his own to the dining room and chapel. He bore his paralysis patiently, speaking only with gestures and his smile. He died in Spokane, on October 1, 1992, and lies buried in the Jesuit cemetery at Mount St. Michael's, Spokane.

NAYAGAK, Deacon Michael

He could neither read nor write, neither English nor his native language, Central Yup'ik Eskimo. The

Deacon Michael Nayagak. *DFA.*

exact date of his birth is unknown. He spent his whole life in the Yukon-Kuskokwim Delta in western **Alaska**. And yet, when he died, Rome and its cardinals took note.

Michael Nayagak was born sometime during the first decade of the twentieth century in the **Kashunuk** area. He spent his early years at Kashunuk, a small village about 35 miles southeast of **Hooper Bay**. In the late 1940s, the Kashunuk villagers moved to a nearby site called "Old **Chevak**." By 1950, they had all moved again, to the present Chevak. Michael made the moves with his people. Except for some trips made during his last years to other villages in the delta area, he spent his whole life within a 40-mile radius of those three villages.

Father **John P. Fox**, S.J., came to Alaska in 1927. Two years later, at Kashunuk, on November 6, 1929, he was the officiating priest, when Michael Nayagak married Clotilda Chunaoyarak. Some 40 years after the event, when Michael was preparing for the diaconate, with the hope of also being ordained a priest, Father Fox wrote concerning him: "All the missionaries that know him agree that he is a holy man. He is a born leader, and his village now has about 500 souls. When lay deacons were decided on, his village elected him as one of the two deacons for his village. I have never heard of him being accused of anything wrong."

In October 1970, contemplating the road to the

diaconate that lay before him, Michael wrote, through another, to Robert L. **Whelan**, S.J., Bishop of Fairbanks at the time:

> When I think of all the things we have to learn, it seems real hard for me. But if God helps me, I'll probably understand most of it. I can't seem to find a rightful way to lead people. But be assured I'll be of help to you. Since I started to get this kind of schooling, I seem to be a guy that has his eyes closed. But I will always follow you till our meeting last. Ever since I started working in the church, even though I have never seen our Popes, I try my best to help them all I can. It seems that I had known all along that I'd be working to be a deacon. You'll probably won't understand it, but I'm saying these the best I can.

Michael's loyalty to the Church and his willingness to serve was noticed already, when he was still a young man.

In December 1970, in a letter Michael had some one write for him to Bishop Whelan, he thanked him for "a very nice and thoughtful Christmas card." Michael added: "I am working very fine as a deacon here, and I will continue to put my heart into the work that is so joyous to me." This he wrote five years before he was ordained a deacon. In 1973, Father Fox wrote: "Michael has served as a deacon for several years already, with everything except the actual ordination."

In November 1973, while Michael was undergoing a more formal kind of training for the role of deacon, Bishop Whelan wrote to Agnelo Cardinal Rossi, Prefect of the Sacred Congregation for the Evangelization of Peoples, in Rome:

> In one of the native villages of this diocese in western Alaska, there is an Eskimo widower by the name of Michael Nayagak, a man of deep faith and fervent practice of the Catholic religion. He has been the village chief for many years and is esteemed by his people because of his wisdom and leadership qualities. He is one of the deacons who will soon be ordained. I request he be allowed to go further and be ordained to the priesthood with a minimum of theological training. One or two of our older missionaries could provide the necessary instruction for this man to celebrate Mass and to hear confessions.

Cardinal Rossi replied: "Considering the special circumstances in Alaska and the growing need of priests, as well as the guarantees Your Excellency gives to ensure the worthy exercise of the Holy Priesthood by this exemplary Christian, this Sacred Congregation has decided to grant your wish."

In referring to "older missionaries," Bishop Whelan clearly had in mind Father Fox, who by that time was 81 years old and had spent 46 years in Alaska. To him, Bishop Whelan wrote in December 1973:

> Almost since the beginning of our Diaconate Program, the suggestion has frequently been made that Michael Nayagak is such an outstanding person in his village, that it would be more reasonable to ordain him a priest rather than a deacon. You will see from the enclosed copy of a letter that I received from Cardinal Rossi that we have permission to proceed along these lines. My concern now is how to train Michael in those things that he would have to know in order to be a good priest for his village. I have talked to him about it and he is quite receptive. You are the only one I can think of who would be able to communicate well enough with him. Would you be willing to undertake this chore?

Willingly, Father Fox accepted to be Michael's trainer. He moved to Chevak and, looking beyond Michael's upcoming ordination to the diaconate, began to prepare him for the priesthood. Language and literacy problems were gradually overcome with the help of tapes, translations and interpreters.

Throughout 1974, Father Fox worked closely with Michael in Chevak. On February 8, 1975, Michael took his first formal steps toward Holy Orders, when, in **Marshall**, Bishop Whelan conferred upon him the ministries of Lector and Acolyte. The following month, in a letter to Bishop Whelan, Michael again expressed his desire to continue studies and training so that, "with God's help," he might some day be ordained a priest.

In June 1975, Father René **Astruc**, S.J., Co-director of the **Eskimo Deacon Program**, visited Chevak and "found Michael quite enthusiastic and eager to work." One of the parishioners was helping him with the Yup'ik deacon service and the Mass. To Father Astruc the parish council expressed itself quite anxious to see Michael ordained a deacon and proceed toward ordination to the priesthood. Understanding that the ordination to the priesthood would take place in Chevak, the people of Chevak readily accepted the decision that Michael would be ordained to the diaconate in Nyac, a gold mining camp northeast of **Bethel**. On August 22, 1975, in Nyac, Michael was ordained a deacon by Bishop Whelan. He was the third Eskimo to be ordained a deacon. Present to share with him the joy of his ordination were his three daughters. This meant a great deal to him, since he had lost his wife some years earlier to an illness, and a son in a hunting accident. The setting for the ordination was simple but devout. Wild flowers decorated the make-shift altar. The bishop's throne was a folding chair. The assembled Eskimo congregation did the singing. There was no organ.

That was in August. All expected Deacon Michael Nayagak to continue on with his training for the priesthood. It was not meant to be.

With a heavy heart Bishop Whelan wrote to Cardinal Rossi on October 30, 1975:

On the 22nd of August I ordained Michael Nayagak to the diaconate, and it was a beautiful and joyous occasion for him and his children., two of whom are married. Michael was most conscientious in his preparation for the diaconate and his continuing studies. On the evening of October 3rd he died very suddenly. It was only 42 days after the date of his ordination to the diaconate. He had apparently been in good health right up to the end of his life.

Cardinal Rossi responded: "I shall be grateful if you will transmit our prayerful sentiments of condolences to his family, while assuring them that their father, because of his great ecclesial dedication in life, occupies a special place in the history of the Church in Alaska. May he rest in peace and inspire many to follow his example!"

In another letter, Bishop Whelan gave further details surrounding Deacon Michael Nayagak's death:

Michael seemed to have a premonition of his death. He told his youngest daughter, Charlotte, before she left for school at St. Mary's Mission that he would not see her again, and other things that he said seemed to indicate this premonition. In spite of all this, he was in the best of spirits. He had gone to Bethel, where one of his daughters gave birth to a second child. The doctor told him that he was in good health. He returned to his village of Chevak and had been around during the day, but suddenly he died about nine o'clock that night.

Deacon James Gump of Hooper Bay has left a written account of Michael's last hours. James described Michael as a man who "really know well

how to pray well in Yup'ik." According to James, Michael was "with his rosary as like gear or guide always on hand." Sometimes Michael invited James to visit him in Chevak. The two were close friends.

The day Michael died, James "woke up for a beautiful calm sunshine weather," wondering what he might do that day. "Finally," he wrote,

I start think of M. Nayagak, maybe I visit M. Nayagak and stay overnight in Chevak. After I get to Chevak I see M. Nayagak walk on sidewalk the way he use to walk. He look happy and look he not sick. And then the afternoon continue, and late afternoon two woman come to me and ask me can you pray because M. Nayagak is not feel well. And then I go to him, as I go M. Nayagak is lay on his bed. He look not too strong, well. So he give me the church key, and tell me he want to receive communion. And after that I spend my time in the steambath as I use to for the end of a long day work. I spend in steam house maybe two, three hours, until I satisfied. I after go in the house where I stay. They tell me M. Nayagak was passed away. That is the day what honor the first friday of the month. And the people tell me they see the light above the village as like a poured down. And I was attended at his funeral. And I was feel like happy and glad that I was with him on his last day and no worry for him after all.

Deacon Michael Nayagak was the first of the Eskimo deacons to die. Bishop Whelan summarized: "We feel a great loss in Michael's death. He was a very simple and holy man, truly a spiritual leader of his people."

If Alaska's Eskimo deacons have a patron saint, it is Deacon Michael Nayagak.

145

NENANA

Nenana, at the junction of the Nenana and Tanana Rivers, is a true crossroads town, situated, as it is, along both the George Parks Highway, which connects **Fairbanks** with **Anchorage**, and the Alaska Railroad. It is 58 road miles southwest of Fairbanks. The Athabaskan Indian name for Nenana translates roughly: "a good place to camp between the rivers." Even though Nenana's population is only about 50 percent Alaska Native, Nenana is considered a "Native town." It was at Nenana that, on July 15, 1923, President Warren G. Harding drove the golden spike, signaling the completion of the 471-mile Alaska Railroad, which links Fairbanks to the port of **Seward**. The Nenana post office was established in 1908. In 1910, Nenana's population was 190; in 1920, 634; in 1930, 291; in 1939, 231; in 1950, 242; and in the year 2000, 402.

The first church in Nenana was built by Father Francis M. **Monroe**, S.J., during the year 1917–18. According to *The Official Catholic Directory* the Nenana mission was founded in 1922. The 1923 issue of that same publication lists Nenana for the first time, and gives the name of that mission as St. Theresa, the name by which that mission has been known ever since. St. Therese of Lisieux, "the Little Flower," was not canonized until 1925. It is not clear, whether the patroness of the Nenana mission has, from the outset, been St. Therese, or was, at first, St. Theresa of Avila. For many years now, St. Therese, "the Little Flower," has been presumed to be the patroness of the Nenana Catholic community.

The Catholic community in Nenana has always been small. Up to the 1960s, it was served at irregular intervals by priests stationed in Fairbanks. Bishop Francis D. **Gleeson**, S.J., Vicar Apostolic of Alaska at the time, began to visit it about 1950. On December 19, 1952, the Monroe-built church burned down to its foundation. Lost in that fire was the pectoral cross that at one time had belonged to Archbishop Charles J. **Seghers** and had been passed on down to Bishop Gleeson. By late October 1953, the church was replaced, on the same foundation, with a new one.

The first priest stationed full-time in Nenana was Father Wallace M. Olson, from 1962–65. Fathers Francis P. Ready and Georges E. Bourque, O.P., filled in during the

St. Theresa's Church, Nenana.
Photo by Madeleine Betz.

year 1965–66. Father Robert F. Dunn was there beginning in March 1966 until about 1970.

The St. Theresa of Lisieux parish was formally erected as a parish on December 8, 1970, by Robert L. **Whelan**, S.J., Bishop of Fairbanks at the time. The above mentioned four priests were followed by Jesuit Fathers William C. **Dibb**, 1970–72; Lawrence A. **Nevue**, 1974–76; and **Paul B. Mueller**, 1976–84. They, as did the priests before and after them, served not only the Nenana Catholic community, but also other Catholic communities located along the "Railbelt," among them: Anderson, Clear Air Force Base, **Healy**, McKinley Park, and Cantwell.

No priest was assigned to Nenana during the years 1972–74. It was visited at different times by one or other of the following three: Fathers Donald E. Henkes, Michael P. Murphy, and William A. Zorichak.

From 1984–88, Father J. Albert **Levitre** was stationed at Nenana. During the year 1988–89, it was served out of Fairbanks by Father William T. **Burke**, S.J. Father Gerhard J. Wallner held station at Nenana from 1989–91, Father John A. **Hinsvark** from 1991–94, and Father Jack **de Verteuil** from 1991–96. Beginning in 1996, and as of the year 2004, Nenana was visited out of Healy by Father de Verteuil.

The Nenana parish has seen the service also of Sisters. During the years 1989–91, Sister Patricia

Ann Miller, O.P., served it as Pastoral Administrator. From 1991–2002, Sister Agnes Anne Wilcox, S.M.S.M., served there in the same capacity.

61, 206

NEVUE, Father Lawrence A., S.J.

Lawrence A. Nevue was born in Yakima, Washington, on August 19, 1911. There he attended St. Paul's Grade School and Marquette High School. From 1929–30, he attended St. Joseph's Minor Seminary in Mountain View, California. He entered the Jesuit novitiate at Sheridan, Oregon, on July 29, 1932. After completing his two-year noviceship and two years of classical and humanities studies, he went to Mount St. Michael's, Spokane, Washington, where he studied philosophy from 1936–39. He spent the years 1939–42 at Sacred Heart Mission, DeSmet, Idaho. His theological studies he made at Alma College, Los Gatos, California, from 1942–46. He was ordained a priest in San Francisco, on June 16, 1945. He made his tertianship at Port Townsend, Washington, 1946–47.

Father Nevue's first assignment in **Alaska** was **Juneau**. He arrived on June 23, 1947, and served there till August. From August 4, 1947, to August 14, 1952, he was pastor of the **Sitka** parish. As such, he had two bedrooms, a kitchen, and a small living room added to the parish facilities. The year 1952–53 saw him assistant pastor of St. Francis Xavier's parish in Missoula, Montana. He then returned to Alaska to be assistant pastor at Immaculate Conception Church and hospital chaplain at St. Joseph's Hospital, both in **Fairbanks**, from 1953–56.

From September 1956 to July 1964, he was pastor of St. Joseph's parish in **Nome**. While serving as such, he also visited its dependent missions of **Teller** and **Little Diomede** Island. Regarding Father Nevue's stay on Little Diomede, Father Segundo **Llorente**, S.J., in a letter dated June 28, 1965, wrote to Francis D. **Gleeson**, S.J., Bishop of Fairbanks at the time, "The Little Diomeders talk very highly of Fr. Nevue, who used to go hunting with them on the ice floes. Fr. N. certainly endeared himself to them."

Father Lawrence A. Nevue, S.J. *LRC.*

From 1964–66, Father Nevue was stationed at **Nulato**. There he won the hearts of the people not only by his gentleness and kindness, but also by his sympathetic understanding of their traditional feast for the dead, the "stickdance" ceremonials. From Nulato he returned to Fairbanks for the years 1966–73. The year 1973–74 found him on sabbatical leave at the Jesuit School of Theology at Berkeley, California. Back in Alaska, he spent the years 1974–76 as pastor of **Nenana** and its dependent "Railbelt" stations, the communities strung out for 110 miles along the Parks Highway and the Alaska Railroad from Nenana all the way to Cantwell. He then returned again to Fairbanks for the years 1976–79. After that, he cared for the "highway" parishes, **Delta Junction**, **Tok**, and **Northway**, during the years 1979–82. Both the Railbelt and the highway parishes demanded a great deal of driving. His years of active ministry ended in Fairbanks. From 1982–84, he was pastor again of Immaculate Conception parish.

From February 1960 to August 1971, Father Nevue was a chaplain in the Alaska National Guard. He left the Guard with the rank of major.

In February 1984, Father Nevue had the joy of visiting Europe and the Holy Land. The following month, he suffered an incapacitating stroke. A year of therapy in Fairbanks followed.

During this he edified all who worked with him, or visited him, by his humility, patience, serenity and sense of humor. His life-long, charming boyish manner continued to endear him to one and all. He made good progress, but never fully recovered. On March 10, 1985, he left Alaska for the Jesuit House infirmary at Gonzaga University in Spokane. He died in Spokane on August 21, 1987, and lies buried in the Jesuit cemetery at Mount St. Michael's.

142

Holy Family Church, Newtok. *DFA.*

NEW KNOCK HOCK

The former Central Yup'ik Eskimo village of New Knock Hock was located on the right bank of the Black River, about eight miles northwest of Kusilvak Mountain in the Yukon-Kuskokwim Delta. There were 27 cabins at New Knock Hock in 1947. A new church, dedicated to St. John the Baptist, was built there in 1949 by Father Norman E. **Donohue**, S.J. The village had a population of 122 in 1950, all living in "about 30 new homes" provided through the instrumentality of Father Paul C. **O'Connor**, S.J., chairman of the Alaska Housing Authority. On September 1, 1951, a post office was established at New Knock Hock. Twenty-eight children of school age were noted for the year 1951. And yet, by 1957, the village was completely abandoned, the entire Black River drainage population having moved either to villages on the lower Yukon River—**Alakanuk**, **Emmonak**, **Mountain Village**, **Nunam Iqua** (Sheldon Point)—or to **Scammon Bay**. The Black River was too shallow during most of the open-water months for barge service, so no government schools were constructed along its route.

Father Donohue visited New Knock Hock out of **Akulurak** from 1946–50. Father Segundo **Llorente**, S.J., did likewise during the year 1950–51, then out of Alakanuk till New Knock Hock was totally abandoned.

During one stay at New Knock Hock of "exactly eighty-six days with their nights," Father Llorente had with him as his interpreter William **Tyson**, "a former Akulurak pupil who without any doubt became the best interpreter in the land. He was so good that while he spoke the eyes of the people were fixed on him as though he were an apparition from heaven."

64

NEWTOK

The Central Yup'ik Eskimo village of Newtok is located on the Kealavik River, a little north of Nelson Island, in the Yukon-Kuskokwim Delta. In its earlier days, it was referred to also as "New **Keyaluvik**." It came into existence in 1949, when people moved from Keyaluvik, ten air miles distant, to this new site. In 1951, Father Paul C. **O'Connor**, S.J., wrote, "This is the second year that the people have lived in the new village of Newktok. They comprise all the people formerly living in Keyaluvik and those scattered over the tundra. There are 118 people there and 32 children of school age." The people made the move to Newtok—properly pronounced "Newktok"—to escape the seasonal flooding at Keyaluvik. One anthropologist described the Newtok site as "a flat, soggy, wilderness of tundra, moss and berries, surrounded by show-and-sink lakes." Newtok had a population of 148 in 1973, of 207 in 1990, and 321 in the year 2000.

In Holy Family Church, Newtok, Central Yup'ik Eskimo children crowd around Bishop Michael J. Kaniecki, S.J., after he finished hearing Confessions on April 21, 1991. *LR.*

The Catholic Faith came to the Keyaluvik–Newtok people as early as around 1895, mainly through the work of the roving missionary Father Joseph M. **Tréca**, S.J. Around 1955, Father **John J. Wood**, S.J., built a new church in Newtok. This burned to the ground in August 1974. A new church, dedicated to the Holy Family, was blessed by Robert L. **Whelan**, S.J., Bishop of Fairbanks at the time, on July 26, 1978.

The following Jesuit priests either visited or were in residence at Newtok: Wood, 1952–59; Bernard F. **McMeel**, 1959–64; Francis X. **Nawn**, 1964–66; Francis J. **Fallert**, 1966–75, 1986–87, and 1988–90; Norman E. **Donohue**, 1975–76; Thomas G. **Provinsal**, 1976–77, 1979–86 and 1990–91; Richard D. **Case**, 1977–79; Henry G. **Hargreaves**, 1987–88; Eugene P. **Delmore**, 1991–94; Paul M. **Cochran**, 1994–97 and 2001 to the present (2004); Mark A. **Hoelsken**, 1997–2001.

Eskimo Deacons, too, served and were serving their Newtok parish as of the year 2004: Nicholas Tommy (deceased and buried at Newtok), Larry Charles and Mark Tom (retired).

During the summer of 1973, Sisters Pauline Higgins and Paula Cosko, Sisters of **Providence** stationed in **Fairbanks**, taught catechism classes in Newtok.

NIGHTMUTE

The Central Yup'ik Eskimo village of Nightmute is located on the Toksook River on Nelson Island in the Yukon-Kuskokwim Delta. Nightmute is properly pronounced "nickt mute." The village is nestled near the foothills of the Kaluyut Mountains. The frequent gusty, turbulent winds blowing off the mountains onto the village gave the place its Eskimo name, *Nikhta*, meaning "pressed down." The inhabitants of Nightmute are, therefore, "the people of the pressed down place." The village had a population of 78 in 1939, 27 in 1950, and 237 in 1960. In 1964, many of the people moved west to a new location named **Toksook Bay**. Nightmute's population numbered 153 in 1990, and 208 in the year 2000.

Catholic missionaries were active on Nelson Island as early as 1889, mainly at **Tununak**. Then, for roughly four decades, the area was only visited from time to time. In September 1929, Simeon Sipary—"the sterling catechist," and stepfather of Ivan **Sipary**—began evangelizing the people of Nightmute. He is given credit for the conversion of many of the Nelson Islanders, the people of Nightmute included. He died at Nightmute on May 13, 1931.

In 1931, a crew from **Holy Cross Mission**, traveling on the mission boat, the *Little Flower*, and consisting of Father John L. **Lucchesi**, S.J., Jesuit seminarian **Thomas P. Cunningham**, Brother John

(*right*) Our Lady of Perpetual Help Church, Nightmute. *PP.*

(*below*) Nightmute (pronounced Nikt Mute) as it appeared in 1972. The village is nestled near the foothills of the Kaluyut Mountains on the banks of the Toksook River. The frequent gusty, turbulent winds blowing off the mountains onto the village gave the place its Eskimo name, Nikhta, meaing "pressed down." The inhabitants of Nightmute are "the people of the pressed down place." *DFA.*

Hess, S.J., and "some of the big boys from Holy Cross," put up a chapel at Nightmute. A small addition was built on to this in 1938 to provide living quarters for the visiting priest. In 1949, Father Paul C. **Deschout**, S.J., built a new church at Nightmute. The Nightmute parish is dedicated under the title of Our Lady of Perpetual Help.

In connection with Nightmute should be mentioned **Umkumiut**, once an inhabited village site, but today only the spring sealing and the summer fishing camp of people from Nightmute.

The people of Nightmute have been served by the following Jesuit Fathers: **John P. Fox**, out of **Hooper Bay**, 1931–34; Deschout, out of Tununak, 1934–35, 1936–59, and 1960–61; Paul H. **Linssen**, out of **Chefornak**, 1959–60; James E. **Jacobson**, out of Chefornak, 1961–66; Francis J. **Fallert**, out of Toksook Bay, 1966–75; Daniel J. **Tainter**, out of Toksook Bay, 1975–77; Bernard F. **McMeel**, out of Hooper Bay, 1977–78; Richard L. **McCaffrey**, out of Toksook Bay, 1978–79; Richard D. **Case**, out of Tununak, 1979–84; Thomas G. **Provinsal**, out

St. Peter the Apostle Church, Ninilchik. *Photo by Annemiek J. Brunklaus.*

of Chefornak, 1986–91; Eugene P. **Delmore**, out of Toksook Bay, 1991–94; Henry G. **Hargreaves**, out of Toksook Bay, 1994–98; Mark A. **Hoelsken**, out of Chefornak, 1998–99; and David J. **Anderson**, out of Toksook Bay, 1999 to the present (2004). For the years 1984–86, no priest is listed as visiting Nightmute.

Eskimo Deacons, too, served and were serving their Nightmute parish as of the year 2004: Maxie Altsik (deceased and buried at Nightmute), Thomas Jumbo, Ignatius Matthias, and Camillus Tulik.

Sisters Jeannette LaRose and Patricia Richard, both Sisters of St. **Ann**, split their time, during the years 1983–88, between Nightmute and Chefornak. Regarding their mission in those two villages, Sister Jeannette wrote, "It is to impart Adult Religious Education, to prepare catechists, and to minister in any other way opened to us at the moment." As need arose, the two also did some substitute teaching in the school—"our favorite way of reaching the children."

NINILCHIK

The town of Ninilchik, a one-time fishing and fur-farming village, is located on the west coast of the Kenai Peninsula, 38 miles southwest of **Kenai**. In 1890, its population numbered 81; in 1920, 87; in 1930, 124; in 1967, 169; and in the year 2000, 772.

A post office was established there in the early 1940s.

When, in the fall of 1950, the road from **Seward** to **Homer** was opened, Father Martin G. Borbeck, S.J., stationed in Seward at the time, began to make monthly visits to Ninilchik, Homer, and **Soldotna**. He offered Mass in a private home for three families. Father Arnold L. **Custer**, S.J., stationed in Seward from 1952–61, continued Father Borbeck's practice of monthly visits to Ninilchik. When the Ninilchik Catholic congregation had grown to around 40, the American Legion Hall was used for Catholic services. Then a small Quonset hut, set up near the old post office, served as a church.

In 1961, Redemptorist Fathers from the Oakland Province began ministry to the Catholic communities on the Kenai Peninsula. The first three, all head-quartered in Seward to begin with, were Fathers Edward C. **O'Neill**, pastor of the Seward parish, James Van Hoomissen, and Robert L. Woodruff. Out of Seward they began to care for the Kenai Peninsula missions of Homer, Kenai, Ninilchik, **Seldovia**, and Soldotna. It was they who saw to the building of a new church in Ninilchik, St. Peter the Apostle, finished and dedicated in 1964. As facilities were constructed at the various missions, the Fathers began to reside there. Ninilchik never had a resident pastor. Different Redemptorist Fathers continued to care for the Ninilchik mission, at first out of Seward, then later, generally, out of either Homer or Soldotna, until 1992, when all but one of their Congregation left Alaska. By that time, a total of 19 Redemptorist priests had helped maintain a constant Redemptorist presence on the Kenai Peninsula, ministering to and building churches for its ever-growing population. The last Redemptorist to leave Alaska, in August, 2002, was Father Richard G. **Strass**. He was also the last of their number to serve Ninilchik, out of Homer. Two Redemptorists lie buried in Soldotna: Fathers Thaddeus Dean and Robert J. Wells. Father Dean tended to the Ninilchik mission for a number of years.

Since the Redemptorists left Alaska, the Ninilchik mission, along with other Kenai Peninsula missions—except for **Cooper Landing**, which has been cared for by the pastor of Seward—has been shepherded by "supply priests" out of Anchorage. Lay people have served as local Parish Administrators and in similar capacities.

15

NOME

As in the case of many early-day Alaskan cities and towns, so also in the case of Nome—a city along Norton Sound, on the southern coast of the Seward Peninsula, in northwestern **Alaska**—it was gold that put the city on the map. In the summer of 1898, a major discovery of gold was made on Anvil Creek near what today is the city of Nome. In June 1899, gold was found also on the beaches of Nome, and in such abundance that the place was, for a time, referred to as "the poor man's paradise." By early summer 1900, the rush was on. At the peak of that summer, there were 30,000 people at Nome. Nome incorporated as a city on April 9, 1901. Its population, however, began to decline rapidly. By 1920, for some time already a mix of Inupiat Eskimos and whites, it was down to 852. Then it began gradually to increase. In 1950, Nome had a population of 1,876. Its population continued to increase during the latter half of the 1900s. People relocating from **King Island** to Nome contributed to this. In the year 2000, Nome's population numbered 3,505, with Eskimos in the majority. As the third millennium dawned, Nome was serving as a transportation and commercial hub for 17 villages of northwestern Alaska. It had also become a center for Eskimo crafts and for tourism. Since 1973, Nome has been familiar to many worldwide as the finish line of the annual **Iditarod** Trail Sled Dog Race.

Catholic history in Nome began in August 1899, when Father John B. **René**, S.J., visited it briefly. People pleaded with him to send a priest, as well as Sisters to open a hospital. Father Joseph M. **Tréca**, S.J., spent short periods of time there the following month, September, and again in February 1900. (Father Tréca was an assistant pastor in Nome, 1915–18. Some time during those years, he took excellent photos of posing Eskimo family groups.) The Nome parish was officially established on July 4, 1901, by Father Aloysius **Jacquet**, S.J. By September 17th, he and his assistant, Father John **Van der Pol**, S.J., were able to sleep in the newly constructed parish rectory. The new church, dedicated to St. Joseph, was blessed on November 17th. Crowning this westernmost church in North America was a steeple that dominated the Nome skyline. It was topped off with a cross lined with rows of electric lights. The cross seemed to hang by an invisible thread in the dark arctic sky. This "white man's star," as the Eskimos called it, measuring six feet by eight, was visible for a distance of more than 20 miles. It was illuminated each evening at the town's expense to serve as a beacon to many a weary miner or musher groping his way home through winter darkness or a blizzard.

The speedy bringing about of the parish church, rectory and social hall for young men cost Father Jacquet, a master fund-raiser and public relations man, dearly. Before the year 1901 was out, he was declared so legally insane that he had to be institutionalized.

Many priests have staffed St. Joseph's parish since its founding in 1901. That same year Father Rogatien **Camille**, S.J., replacing Father Jacquet, joined Father Van der Pol. The year 1902–03 saw Jesuit Fathers Joseph M. **Cataldo** and Edward J. **Devine** at St. Joseph's.

Four Sisters of **Providence** arrived in Nome on June 19, 1902, and a fifth on October 1st. Before the year was out, they had established Holy Cross Hospital in a renovated building in the center of town. On November 24, 1906, the Sisters and their

patients moved into the newly built three-story hospital next to the parish rectory. This hospital was closed in September 1918, when the Sisters left Nome. It was reopened briefly later that year under the supervision of Father Frederick A. **Ruppert**, S.J.—assistant pastor in Nome, 1918–21, and 1922–23—to accommodate victims of the influenza epidemic. Father **Paul B. Mueller**, S.J., pastor of St. Joseph's 1965–66, oversaw the demolition of the hospital in 1966. The Sisters of Providence staffed also a parochial school in Nome, from the fall of 1904 to May 1918. Nome saw the Sisters of Providence again in the summers of 1951–57, when they taught catechism classes there. Sister Paula Cosko, a Sister of Providence, was in Nome during the years 1969–72 engaged in educational and other ministries. Nome was further blessed by a Sis-

ter's presence when **Ursuline** Sister Cecilia Huber was pastorally involved with St. Joseph's parish from 1989–91.

On July 16, 1903, there arrived in Nome Father Bellarmine **Lafortune**, S.J. He was to spend 28 of his 44 Alaskan years as pastor or assistant pastor of St. Joseph's. He was originally scheduled for **Holy Cross Mission**, but, upon his arrival in Nome, was kept there "to take the charge of the Eskimos." In 1905, he had a special combination chapel–workshop building constructed in back of the church "just for the Eskimos." In 1913, sleds for Vilhjalmur Stefansson's third polar expedition were built by Father Lafortune and his Eskimos in this shop. The shop flourished, and was enlarged in 1916. In September 1921, the building was converted into a "native school." While Father Lafortune did devote the

(*opposite*) Nome in April 1948. The first St. Joseph's Church can be seen at the extreme right and upper part of this aerial view. The steeple is gone. The second St. Joseph's Church can be seen in front of old Holy Cross Hospital, middle right. The old rectory is still standing to right of the hospital. *Photo by William A. Shepherd/Dr. Dorothy Jean Ray Collection.*

(*right*) St. Joseph's Church, Nome. *MK.*

majority of his time to the Nome and Seward area Eskimos, especially those of King Island, and came to be hailed as "the Little Father of the Eskimos," he did, nevertheless, minister for many years, and most faithfully, also to the parish's non-Native people.

During the first quarter of its existence, the Nome parish saw a fair number of pastors and assistant pastors come and go. One of the more colorful ones among them was Father John **Forhan**, S.J., in Nome from 1908–14. He was a spell-binding preacher. People waited all week to hear his Sunday sermon. However, he was incapable of tolerating anything or anybody not one hundred percent Holy Roman Catholic. Father Lafortune wrote of him: "I am afraid that he might be too brusque, too impatient with the class of sinners we have up this way." Father Forhan, finding Nome "not a locality in which the exercise of ministry gives any very great consolation," sailed south on the *Victoria* on September 8, 1914, never to return.

Beginning in 1935—by which time the Nome parish had seen the coming and going of 18 different priests—and ending in 1951, Father **Thomas P. Cunningham**, S.J., served the Nome parish on and off for a total of five years. Few of Nome's former pastors are better and more fondly remembered, by whites and Eskimos alike, than "Father Tom," as he was generally known. He soon spoke Eski-

mo fluently, and learned how to hunt with the best of them. His easy-going, friendly, tolerant ways endeared him to all, no matter of what faith, or of none. He was "a natural" for Nome, a station many of his predecessors—because of its remoteness, its frontier atmosphere and mentality, its harsh weather conditions, its disharmonious mixture of Eskimos and whites—had found a formidable challenge, a burden greater than some were able to bear for more than a year or two. After Father Cunningham's first year in Nome, Father Lafortune, who knew well what kind of priest the Seward Peninsula area needed, urged Bishop Joseph R. **Crimont**, S.J., Vicar Apostolic of Alaska at the time, to stop off in Ireland on his way to Rome to find "a Father like Fr. Th. Cunningham."

Father Edmund A. **Anable**, S.J., pastor of St. Joseph's from 1943–47, left his mark on the parish inasmuch as in 1945–46 he replaced the original church and rectory with a new church and rectory built out of two military surplus buildings. The new church was opened on Easter Sunday 1946. The old church, having been built on unstable ground, needed annual re-leveling, as did many of Nome's buildings. The steeple had started to separate from the main structure. The church had become unsafe, too big for its purpose, difficult to heat. The steeple was removed and the building sold in 1946 to the U.S.

Smelting, Refining and Mining Company, which moved it to the northern edge of Nome, where it served as a warehouse for half a century. In 1996, it was moved to a new site, restored, given a new steeple, and, as a visitor center, given a new lease on life.

Father **Cornelius K. Murphy**, S.J., was pastor of St. Joseph's from 1947–56. He was followed by Father Lawrence A. **Nevue**, S.J., 1956–64. Prior to 1966, in addition to the priests already mentioned, other priests and Jesuit Lay Brothers, too numerous to mention all by name, served the Nome parish in one capacity or another, most all of them for only three years or less.

The **Little Sisters of Jesus** first came to Nome in 1952. While an integral part of St. Joseph's parish life, they never formally served as parish staff members. Theirs was, in keeping with their Congregation's basic charism, a ministry of prayerful presence and friendship.

In 1966, Father James E. **Poole**, S.J., "a man of dreams and drive," took over as pastor of the Nome parish. By then, he had for some years already dreamt of establishing a radio station in western Alaska, and of being a "missionary by microphone." On July 14, 1971, his dream became a reality, when radio station **KNOM** went on the air and began a long history of award-winning broadcasting. In both his parish and radio ministry, Father Poole received the indispensable, generous assistance of numerous members of the **Jesuit Volunteer Corps** and of the KNOM Volunteers, along with that of members of the Brothers of Christian Instruction (**F.I.C.**).

From 1969–83, Father Harold J. **Greif**, S.J., was assistant pastor to Father Poole. In 1980, Father Poole was freed of his responsibilities as pastor of St. Joseph's, but he continued on as the director of the radio station until 1988, when he left Alaska. Even after his departure, KNOM continued to flourish under its exceptionally competent General Manager, Thomas A. **Busch**.

Except for Father Francis P. Ready, at St. Joseph's 1963–65, diocesan priests did not start serving the Nome parish until 1985, when Father Joseph G. **Stolz** was assigned there. He was followed by Fathers James E. **Falsey**, Jack **de Verteuil**, and Andrzej Maslanka. It was during Father Falsey's

pastorate, 1990–94, that the third St. Joseph's Church was constructed. This was dedicated on March 19, 1994, by Michael J. **Kaniecki**, S.J., Bishop of **Fairbanks** at the time. Father John A. **Hinsvark** became pastor of St. Joseph's parish in August 1994, and was still its pastor a decade later.

But, what are shepherds without sheep? What are pastors without parishioners? Ultimately, it was the Catholic community of Nome that first put St. Joseph's parish on Alaska's spiritual map over a century ago, and it is that same community that has continued to keep it there.

A chronological sequence of discontinuous entries made by various hands from September 29, 1901, to May 26, 1974, in the house diary kept at Nome's St. Joseph's parish weaves the following rich tapestry of day-to-day life in that parish:

～

The first Mass was said in our chapel . . . Death of McKinley announced . . . house warming . . . Fr. Jacquet, in mounting his horse, fell and hurt his little finger . . . The steeple is being put up . . . Fr. Jacquet visited the S.S. St. Paul to collect from outgoing passengers . . . Rev. Fr. Jacquet was declared insane by the civil authorities . . . First rehearsal of our choir . . . Ice stopped running yesterday . . . —28: Nome people do not like to get up early . . . All our wine is frozen in our pantry . . . Fr. Camille took his last vows . . . Frank Hardy the condemned murderer is hanged today. Fr. Cataldo assisted him to the scaffold. He had previously given him Communion in his cell . . . The heaviest blizzard of the season began today. It is really a fierce one . . . Peter Bernard and his partner launched their two-masted schooner. Father Devine christened the vessel and broke the traditional bottle of champagne on the bow. A thousand thirsty Nomeites looking on thought it was a crying shame . . . At 4:30 fire gutted the Lawrence Hotel . . . Fr. Crimont does not feel very well . . . 9 Eskimos from Marys Igloo were baptized . . . Father Lafortune starts with nine dogs and a load of provisions on a missionary trip to Cape Prince of Wales . . . The big dog race to Candle starts . . . Up this way, most of our marriages are mixed, and sometimes it's a queer mixture . . . One of our miners was killed this morning by the falling of a bucket in a mine . . . The cold is dreadful. The water freezes in one's basin . . . This presbytery of ours has a rickety foundation. In a strong wind, it wobbles in a most alarming manner . . . Fr. Lafortune set out this morning with 7 dogs, and will make Sinrock tonight . . . Today, the brother put up our circular or rosette window in the façade of the church . . . Phonograph was played at noon in honor of Fr. **Bernard**'s visit . . . Sleds for Stefansson expedition finished at last . . . This morning some rain fell. There was a real white rainbow . . . The chief of King Island died this morning . . . The sea has been wild these days . . . Father Tréca took pictures of the 1st Communion class . . . Anna Stevens is cured from a severe attack of rheumatism by the Little Flower . . . Sr. Berchmans received a scalp wound by the accidental discharge of a shotgun . . . Cardinal Ratti has been chosen pope . . . I buried Utizoak . . . My dogs got in a fight and killed my leader 'Wolfe' . . . and the year 1922 comes to a close . . . W. Marsh, in returning from Ear Mountain, fell down a very high bluff, buffeted by the storm, was hurt badly and froze to death . . . Owing to the death of Fr. Ruppert, no card party will be given before spring . . . Nothing could be found of the box of oranges . . . Bernadette Eugnak, the very devoted organist, dies . . . The Boxer takes the Diomeders to their country . . . Yesterday morning Amundsen arrived

(*opposite*) Holy Cross Hospital, Nome, built in 1906. To its right stand the parish rectory and St. Joseph's Church, built in 1901. *JOPA-408.2.01.*

(*right*) The second St. Joseph's Church, Nome. Built by Father Edmund A. Anable, S.J., out of military surplus buildings, it served from 1946–94. *DFA.*

The Eskimo chapel in Nome, 1917.
JOPA-408.3.05.

from Teller . . . arrival of numerous puffins . . . The missionary plane arrived this afternoon from Holy Cross . . . Sad news—Kotzebue, Oct. 12, 1930: Fr. **Delon**, Fr. Walsh and Ralph Wien killed in plane at 3:45 this afternoon . . . Mail arrived today by plane and dogteam . . . Woodley seeing coast clear landed at King Island where Fr. Lafortune is . . . This day [Sept. 17, 1934] will go down in the annals of Nome as the day of the 'big fire' . . . The Northland arrives. Aboard the ship were Rev. Fr. **Hubbard**, S.J., the glacier priest . . . Fr. Cunningham with a few King Islanders start for Sledge Island to make a provision of eggs . . . a certain Father Murray, a scientist (?) from Notre Dame University, passes here on his way to St. Lawrence Island with the view of finding in the dumps of the Eskimos a trace of some ancient civilization . . . Large crowds have been enjoying skating on the ice in front of town . . . Bro. **Hansen** died suddenly last night at the hospital . . . This is a terrible town with its whites and Eskimo fallen-aways . . . Fr. Tom Cunningham arrived from Diomede; looks thin, or rather emaciated, the eyes sunk and ever shivering. He admits that he has suffered true, real and unadulterated hunger this winter. Being practically penniless, I [Segundo

Llorente, S.J.] loaned him $50 to be paid back within the next 99 years . . . It is quite interesting to see the native women in breeches and smoking . . . I bought one oogruk skin for **Akulurak** where there are no oogruks, and where there are 180 feet to wear and tear mukluks . . . Father Anable goes to Fairbanks for a little rest . . . Father Lafortune was stricken with what seems like a light stroke . . . three and a half altar rails of Communions at the 8 o'clock Mass . . . Sisters begin catechism classes today . . . Father **Convert** receives his citizenship in Nome . . . Father Patrick Peyton speaks on the 'Rosary' over the radio . . . The Little Sisters do a wonderful job cleaning up the church . . . What a surprise! I found out that I buried the wrong 'Tom' . . . Sunday, May 26, 1974, I, Louis L. **Renner**, S.J., arrived here in Nome, last Wednesday, May 22nd. I am here on my way (Deo volente) to King Island to do ground work for my proposed biography of Father Bellarmine Lafortune, S.J."

14, 23, 31, 40, 68, 93, 97, 161, 163

NORTH POLE

North Pole, incorporated as a city in 1953, is located 12 miles southeast of **Fairbanks** along the Richardson Highway. In 1967, it had 615 inhabitants; in the year 2000, 1,570.

On Sunday morning, September 28, 1975, Robert L. **Whelan**, S.J., Bishop of Fairbanks at the time, celebrated a Mass in the North Pole Grange Hall. Concelebrants were Father Richard L. **McCaffrey**, S.J., and Father Louis F. McKernan, C.S.P. Future Paulist James M. **Kolb** assisted. At that Mass, Bishop Whelan formally established the parish of St. Nicholas at North Pole, **Alaska**, and installed Father McKernan as its first pastor.

St. Nicholas Church, North Pole. *LR.*

What became a thriving parish had humble origins. In the mid-1950s, Father Lawrence A. **Nevue**, S.J., stationed at Immaculate Conception parish in Fairbanks at the time, regularly visited the North Pole Catholic community and offered Mass, generally in private homes. During the early 1960s, the Catholic Church bought land in North Pole. Beginning around 1970, Sister Alice Legault, a Sister of St. **Ann**, using the North Pole Grange Hall as a base of operations, began to help gather people together when a priest was coming for Masses, and at other times to build a sense of parish life through Bible study groups, prayer meetings, and Communion Services.

The property the Church originally bought at North Pole was sold. The property on which St. Nicholas parish was subsequently established was donated by Mr. Ken Ulz of Fairbanks in the early 1970s. On it a modular double-wide mobile home unit, 24 × 60', with a large basement, was erected in the summer of 1975 to serve as a temporary church and home for the first pastoral team of St. Nicholas, Father McKernan and seminarian James Kolb. The two had come to North Pole in August of that year.

On May 7, 1978, ground-breaking ceremonies took place on the site where the new St. Nicholas Church was to rise. Father **Francis E. Mueller**, S.J., as Chancellor of the Diocese of Fairbanks, assisted by Father McKernan, officiated at the ceremony. At this time, weekend Masses were being offered

in the basement of the parish house. It was not long before the new church was ready for dedication. Much of the construction work had been done by parishioners. The solemn dedication of St. Nicholas Church took place on December 3, 1978. Bishop Whelan was principal celebrant at the services. Concelebrating with him were Bishop Francis D. **Gleeson**, S.J.; Paulist Fathers, Very Rev. Wilfrid A. Dewan, McKernon, Charles R. Kullmann, and Kolb; and Father William C. **Dibb**, S.J.

A new rectory was added to the parish complex in the fall of 1995.

The following Paulist Fathers, listed in order of service from 1975–95, served St. Nicholas parish: McKernan, Kolb, Kullmann, Vincent G. Wissman, Thomas W. Jones, Theodore A. Vierra, Dennis W. Hickey, Michael J. Martin, and James Fisher.

Father Jack **de Verteuil** served the St. Nicholas parish during the year 1989–90. From 1995–2002, Father J. Albert **Levitre** was pastor there. For a short time, during the year 2002, Father William E. **Cardy**, O.F.M., tended the North Pole parish. Father Ross A. **Tozzi** began as pastor of St. Nicholas in 2002, and was serving as such as of the year 2004.

Rev. Mr. Walter H. Gelinas, as a founding member of its Parish Council, began serving the St. Nicholas Catholic community while it was still in its Grange Hall days. He was ordained to the permanent diaconate on November 1, 1988. On November 2, 2003, Bishop Donald J. **Kettler** celebrated a special Mass commemorating Deacon Walter's 15 years of service to St. Nicholas parish.

NORTHWAY

In the year 2000, Northway, which includes Northway proper, as well as nearby Northway Junction and Northway Village, had a population of 274. It is located near the Alaska Highway, some 80 miles southeast of **Tok** and some 40 miles from the Canadian border.

In the early 1950s, Father John R. **Buchanan**, S.J., headquartered in Tok, built a small log chapel, named for St. Ann, at Northway above the Alaska Highway. This was later dismantled and taken to near Northway Village. When Father Anderson E. **Bakewell**, S.J., arrived on the Northway scene in 1967, he found "a pile of logs covered with snow." He rebuilt the chapel. Before Father Bakewell began to serve the Northway Catholic community on a regular basis out of Tok, **Oblate** Father Henk Huijbers had done so out of Burwash Landing, Yukon Territory, Canada. Subsequently, the Northway Catholic community has always been served by the same priests that have served the Tok Catholic community.

NULATO

Nulato, a Koyukon Athabaskan Indian village on the right bank of the middle Yukon River, takes its name from the Nulato River, a stream flowing into the Yukon about two miles below the village. It was founded in 1838, when the Russians built a trading post at the mouth of this stream. Nulato village is the end result of a movement of the indigenous people away from a semi-nomadic, camp-based existence to a permanent, village-based existence. In 1851, it was the scene of the "Nulato Massacre." The Nulato post office was established in 1897. Nulato's population was 118 in 1890, 230 in 1910, 258 in 1920, 204 in 1930, 113 in 1940, 176 in 1950, 336 in 2000.

In the annals of Catholicity in northern **Alaska**, Nulato deserves to be written large. It has every right to claim the primacy among Catholic missions there. Nulato first saw Catholic missionaries in June 1873, when **Oblate** Bishop Isidore Clut and Father Auguste Lecorre passed by there on their way downriver to **St. Michael**. On July 31, 1877, Charles J. **Seghers**, Bishop of Vancouver Island at the time,

(*left*) St. Ann's Chapel, Northway. *DFA.*

(*opposite*) Our Lady of the Snows Church, Nulato. *MK.*

and Father Joseph M. **Mandart** arrived at Nulato to spend the year in and out of there. The bishop dedicated the mission under the title of *Sancta Maria Ad Nives* ("St. Mary of the Snows"). However, when the Jesuits took over the Nulato mission in 1887, they placed it under the patronage of St. Peter Claver. It was not until 1950 that the original name, slightly modified to "Our Lady of the Snows," was restored to the mission. Since then, the Nulato parish has been known under that title. St. Peter Claver, however, continued to be a secondary patron of the Nulato mission.

As early as 1891, the Jesuits ran a "contract school" at Nulato. On September 19, 1899, three Sisters of St. **Ann** arrived from **Holy Cross Mission** to open a day school. Classes began on November 2nd with eleven pupils. With some slight breaks from time to time, the Sisters of St. Ann served at Nulato in various capacities, though mainly as schoolteachers, until 1983.

For 110 years, from 1887 to 1997, the Nulato mission always had at least one priest stationed there. After that, it was visited, on a regular basis, by priests stationed in **Galena**. The first Jesuit priest to winter at Nulato was Father Paschal **Tosi**, who made it his headquarters for the year 1887–88. The first church at Nulato was built in 1888. This was replaced by a new one in 1915–16. Others followed. The one still in use as of the year 2004 was dedicated on November 10, 1974. A new Fathers House was built in 1930. In 1941, this became the Sisters Convent, and the building that had served as the convent since 1899 became the Fathers House. This, in a state of great dilapidation, was replaced by a new Fathers House in 1953.

Whether Sisters, Brothers, or priests, the missionaries at Nulato led, in large part, as did the people of Nulato, a subsistence lifestyle. During the early part of the 1900s, the Nulato mission had its own herd of reindeer. The Sisters and Brothers gardened. The Brothers also ran a farm for a time, as well as hunted and fished. For some years during the early days, in an effort to support itself, the mission operated a quasi-trading post, was into bartering, trading, and selling. But, it soon became evident that this was not a proper function for a Catholic mission, and the mission got out of that business venture.

As to the kind of people the Jesuits and the Sisters of St. Ann sought to evangelize and teach at Nulato, Father Aloysius A. **Ragaru**, S.J., in 1895, wrote to Father Tosi: "The people of Nulato, it seems after the saying of all, are brighter and fitter for civilization than many other tribes. More good is to be expected, if they turn good—more evil, if they turn bad." In 1928, Father Philip I. **Delon**, S.J., General Superior of the Alaska Mission, wrote to Father Provincial Joseph M. Piet, S.J., concerning the people of Nulato: "Nulato is a place where the people are a critical and criticizing set, very apt to

pick [out] flaws in a man's character and ways. A man with odd mannerisms, or an unprepossessing appearance, would be out of place here."

Unquestionably, much of the success enjoyed by the Jesuit missionaries at Nulato is attributable to the fact that, from the beginning, they regarded communication as the most crucial aspect of their efforts at evangelization. Upon arrival on the middle Yukon, the pioneer missionaries applied themselves to learning the language, Koyukon Athabaskan. Soon grammars, dictionaries, catechisms, prayer books, hymnals, and translations of scriptural and liturgical texts were produced in the Native language. The emphasis, from the outset, on formal schooling, too, contributed to their success. Later missionaries, who were not fluent in Koyukon, had written materials at their disposal, and a generation of Natives to communicate with that knew English. The stumbling block between missionaries and Nulato Natives was not the language barrier, but a misunderstanding, on the part of the missionaries, of traditional Native cultural ceremonials—especially of the "stickdance," or "Feast for the Dead"—and, therefore, opposition to them. Nulato, along with **Kaltag**, is one of the two "stickdance villages."

In the course of its long existence, many, too many to mention all by name, priests, Sisters and Brothers served at the Nulato mission. Certain ones among them, however, are especially notable—for one reason or other, or for length of years at Nulato—and must be mentioned by name. They are: Jesuit Fathers John B. **Baud**, Julius **Jetté**, Joseph F. **McElmeel**, Ragaru and Crispin S. **Rossi**. Father William J. **Loyens**, while never stationed at Nulato in a ministerial capacity, did spend long months there doing field work for a major article and for his doctoral dissertation. Father Charles A. **Saalfeld** was one of the last Jesuit priests stationed at Nulato, and is one of only two Religious buried there, the other being a Sister of St Ann, Sister Mary of the Eucharistic Heart. Father Theodore E. **Kestler** has the distinction of having been the last Jesuit to be stationed at Nulato, from 1982–85. Among the Jesuit Brothers who served at Nulato and stand out are Brothers Carmelo **Giordano** and Edward J. **Horwedel**.

Father William E. **Cardy** and Brother Joseph

Rogenski were the first Franciscans to serve at Nulato, from 1986–92. When the Franciscans first came to the middle Yukon, one of the Native men of Nulato asked one of the Jesuits, "Are these Sanfriscans real priests? Can they say Mass and do baptisms?"

After the Jesuits and Franciscans came the diocesan priests: Father John B. **Martinek**, from 1992–95; and Father James E. **Falsey**, from 1995–98. After 1998, Nulato began to be served only by visiting priests stationed in **Galena**.

Many Sisters of St. Ann also served at Nulato, again too many to mention all by name. Deserving of mention, however, are Sisters Mary Claude and Mary Abigail. The two jointly rendered a total of 36 years of dedicated service at Nulato. Sister Jeannette LaRose has the distinction of having been the last Sister of St. Ann to be stationed at Nulato, during the year 1982–83.

16, 28, 65, 66, 101, 119, 142, 187

NUNAM IQUA

On August 29, 1916, Father Philip I. **Delon**, S.J., wrote to his Father Provincial: "Today a strong headwind and rain storm keep me at a little village the natives call 'Nunam Ikkoa,' the 'End of the Earth.'" For close to a century, that little village was known to non-Natives as "Sheldon's Point." It was so named after a certain Mr. Sheldon, who, in the early 1900s, had a saltry and trading post on the point very near where the village is today located, some ten miles southwest of **Alakanuk** and on the left bank of the Kemeluk Pass on the south mouth of the Yukon River. As of March 6, 2000, Sheldon's, or Sheldon, Point ceased, officially, to exist. On that date, by governmental decree, the original Native name of the village, Nunam Iqua, was restored. In 1950, Nunam Iqua had a population of 43. During the 1950s, some of the people from the Black River region settled also at Nunam Iqua. In 1960, the village had a population of 110; by 1970, 125; by 1979, 143; by 1990, 109; and by the year 2000, 164.

In 1954, Father Segundo **Llorente**, S.J., put up Nunam Iqua's first Catholic church, a small building constructed out of lumber salvaged from buildings taken down at St. Mary's Mission, **Akulurak**.

(*right*) Nulato mission buildings during the early 1900s. *JOPA-510.46.*

(*below*) St. Peter's Church, Nunam Iqua. *LR.*

In 1971, Brother John **Huck**, S.J., and Father Richard L. **McCaffrey**, S.J., built a quality rectory near the church.

At first, the Nunam Iqua parish was dedicated under the title of St. Mary. Since 1983, however, it has been under that of St. Peter.

Nunam Iqua has been served mainly by Jesuit priests stationed at Alakanuk: Llorente, 1954–63; William T. **McIntyre**, 1963–68; Francis X. **Nawn**, 1968–80 and 1981–83; Thomas J. **Hatrel**, 1983–88; René **Astruc**, 1988–89; Thomas N. **Gallagher**, 1989–90; Henry G. **Hargreaves**, 1990–92; and Thomas G. **Provinsal**, beginning in 1992, and as of the year 2004.

Over the years, Nunam Iqua has been served also by Sisters stationed at Alakanuk.

OALARANNA (variously spelled), Mr. John Charles

Wrote Anne Morrow Lindbergh in her book, *North to the Orient*:

> Today they were all down at the wharf, as we were, to see their chief win the kyak [*sic*] race. Of course, he would win. That was why he was chief. He was taller and stronger and stood better and danced better and hunted better than anyone else in the tribe. He seemed quite invincible, as he stood there, his broad shoulders thrown back, his head well set. Even his features were stronger than those of his men: firmer mouth, more pronounced cheekbones, unusually deep-set eyes. He belonged to those born rulers of the earth. The chief won, of course.

Others described him as "powerful and awesome." In matters both secular and sacred (Catholic), he was a foremost, exemplary leader.

Lindbergh made her observations of the "chief" in 1931, when Inupiat Eskimo John Charles Oalaranna, born on **King Island** around 1883 of Kiunana and Arnatok, was about 48 years old. He had been baptized in **Nome** on September 11, 1906, by Father Bellarmine **Lafortune**, S.J., who estimated him to be, at the time, 22 years old.

Little is known of Oalaranna's early years. It is known that he had two brothers. One of them, Ugitkuna, one day went out hunting on the ice, and never came back, leaving his 9-year-old son, Paul **Tiulana**, fatherless. That was in 1930. Oalaranna became a caring father and mentor to his nephew, teaching him the traditional Native way of life, especially in what concerned hunting and surviving on the moving pack ice. Oalaranna himself was an exceptionally gifted hunter, survivor.

From the 1930s to the 1950s, most of what took place on King Island, a rocky granite outcropping in the Bering Sea some 90 miles northwest of Nome, was dominated by the strong personality of Oalaranna. When, in January 1932, the King Islanders tried to get a canned crab industry going, the shareholders chose him to launch the venture. When in June 1932, King Islanders were invited to take part in the production of the movie *Eskimo*, it was Oalaranna who was contacted by representatives of Metro-Goldwyn-Mayer. When, during World War II, the **Alaska** Territorial Guard was established on King Island, he was its captain. He it was who, during his prime, was the cultural broker, the go-between on all occasions, when his traditional Native society came face to face with western society.

In its Indian Reorganization Act of 1934, the U.S. Congress decreed that local village councils be instituted in Alaska's villages, and that the president of each council bear the title of "chief," a term foreign to traditional Eskimo culture. On King Island, the first formal meeting held in keeping with the IRA took place on April 3, 1939. The minutes of that meeting record that Oalaranna, in secret balloting, was elected chief, an office to which he was re-elected at every subsequent election, until that of December 30, 1946. He was a born leader, endowed, as he was, with extraordinary natural gifts, with poise, and with unusual personal charisma.

Oalaranna was endowed also with a sense of propriety, of protocol. In the early 1940s, he made special efforts to teach Philip and Carrie Tate, schoolteachers on King Island from 1943–45, the Eskimo language, visiting them practically every Sunday for two hours. They, however, learned little Eskimo, and found his visits a strain. Father **George E. Carroll**, S.J., priest on the island from 1951–60, who likewise knew little Eskimo, but was, nevertheless, visited officially, formally and faithfully for two hours almost every Sunday afternoon by "the old chief"—

(*above*) Mr. Charles John Oalaranna. *JOPA-171.4.01.*

(*above, right*) "Chief" Charles John Oalaranna kibitzes at a card game in the men's house, aguli-it. Poker was a favorite game with the King Islanders. The men and older boys spent most of their indoor time in men's houses such as this, where they worked on hunting gear, carved ivory, socialized, told stories, politicked, took sweat baths, and engaged in various gymnastics. Eskimo dancing, too, took place in the men's houses. *BH/JOPA-548.6913.11.02.*

as Oalaranna was by now called—too, found the visits a strain.

From the day he was baptized and throughout his long life, Oalaranna remained a devout, exemplary Catholic. On the last day of school, year after year, he gave the children a brief lecture in Eskimo, and then closed the formalities with a prayer. When there was no priest on King Island, he would get up in church and talk about God and lead the prayers, hymns, and rosaries. He also gave religious instruction. Frequently, he would close an evening of Eskimo dancing, or a village council meeting, with a prayer. He himself was an outstanding Eskimo dancer, and a mainstay of the traditional Native culture. He personified a harmonious blend of the new religion, "the Christianity," and the traditional Inupiaq culture.

For decades, Oalaranna was the main "midwife" on King Island, and the godfather of numerous children. He and his wife, Aisenna, had nine children, but only two daughters reached adulthood and married. Aisenna died on July 25, 1956. The following year he "took doctor's orders," and moved to the mainland, where he spent the rest of his days in King Island Village a mile east of Nome. Seven more winters were allotted him. On June 10, 1964, as he was walking home toward King Island Village, a heart attack put an abrupt end to the long and eventful life of this noble man.

110

OBLATES OF MARY IMMACULATE (O.M.I.)

The first Catholic missionary incursions into the Alaskan mainland were made by members of the Religious Congregation of the Missionary Oblates of Mary Immaculate. The first Catholic priest to enter Alaska was the 28-year-old Father Jean Séguin, O.M.I. On September 23, 1862, he arrived at Fort Yukon, a trading post at the time at the confluence of the Yukon and Porcupine Rivers. He dedicated his "mission" there to his patron saint, St. John the Evangelist. He spent a fruitless, humiliating winter. The chief trader at the post did not approve of Catholic activities. While he shared his table with the Anglican minister, he relegated the Oblate Father to the servants' quarters for lodging and meals. The humiliation meant nothing to Father Séguin personally, but the effect of this social snub on his relations with the Indians, who judged by appearances, was damaging. Father Séguin left Fort Yukon, on June 3, 1863, to return to Canada.

During the summer of 1870, Father Émile Petitot spent some time at Fort Yukon. He, too, met with little success in what was by now Anglican territory. It was in response to a call for priests made by François X. Mercier, a devout French-Canadian Catholic trader from Montreal, that the Oblates first entered Alaska. Mercier feared that Protestant missionaries would soon take over the whole Yukon River country.

On September 11, 1872, two years after Father Petitot had returned to Canada, Oblate Bishop Isidore Clut of the Athabaska–MacKenzie diocese, accompanied by future Oblate Father Auguste Lecorre, set out from the mission of Good Hope in Canada for Fort Yukon. One month later, on October 13th, and "extremely tired," they arrived at the fort, where they were cordially received by its officers, most of whom were Catholic. The two spent the winter at the fort, where they devoted most of their time to the study of the Native language. Since the Indians had already been converted to the Anglican Church, there was little missionary work for them to do.

On May 15, 1873, the two left Fort Yukon, with **St. Michael** as their ultimate destination. On May 20th, they arrived at Nuklukayet, today's **Tanana**, where they spent two weeks instructing Indians and baptizing children. Bishop Clut reported "a great victory" there, the baptism of the children of the two most powerful "chiefs," plus that of 26 other children. At Nuklukayet, Bishop Clut celebrated the first Pontifical Mass ever celebrated in Alaska. It was celebrated, according to Mercier, "in the presence of several hundred savages, come from everywhere to sell me their furs. My house being too small to hold so many people, this beautiful ceremony took place in open air, in front of my house, on the bank of the Youkon [sic], and produced a strong impression on the spirit of the savages, who had never seen anything so beautiful."

In the company of Mercier, and on his boat, Bishop Clut and Father Lecorre, on June 4th, left Nuklukayet for St. Michael. Along the way they baptized 116 children. On June 20th, the party reached St. Michael, where the bishop spent two weeks. After studying the situation, he concluded that St. Michael would be an excellent place for the establishment of a permanent mission in that part of Alaska. Two advantages in particular recommended St. Michael as a headquarters for Catholic missionary activity: there were at the time neither Russian nor Protestant ministers active in the area; and Mercier, as the newly appointed chief agent for the Alaska Commercial Company, would be making St. Michael his center of operations. Leaving Father Lecorre in charge at St. Michael, Bishop Clut, on July 7, 1873, departed again upriver for Canada. He was the first Catholic bishop to set foot in Alaska. At the time of his Alaskan trip, he was Auxiliary Bishop to the Vicar Apostolic of Athabaska–Mackenzie.

Father Lecorre, at this time still a diocesan priest, spent the winter 1873–74 at St. Michael. It is reasonably assumed that, while there, he made missionary excursions to lower Yukon River and Yukon Delta villages, as well as to **Unalakleet**. In the summer of 1874, he received letters informing him that Alaska had been placed under the ecclesiastical jurisdiction of the bishop of Vancouver Island, Charles J. **Seghers**, and directing him to choose between serving as a priest at the disposal of Bishop Seghers or returning to his own mission. He chose the latter, and sailed for San Francisco. Some time later he joined the Oblates.

Since the time of those early-day Oblate pioneer Alaskan missionaries, other members of that Congregation have served in Alaska. From February 1931 to January 1932, Father Joseph Allard, O.M.I., was pastor of Sacred Heart parish in **Seward**. After that he worked with the Tlingit Indian people of **Sitka** and **Hoonah**. In the early 1960s, Father Henk Huijbers, O.M.I., out of Burwash Landing, Yukon Territory, Canada, tended to St. Ann's mission at **Northway** on a regular basis.

In more recent years, Oblate priests have served mostly in Southeastern Alaska. Father Edward T. McHugh cared for the Catholic communities in **Haines** and **Petersburg**, from 1971–77. Father Gerard B. Clenaghan was in **Yakutat** during the years 1975–77. Father Gerard Gottenbos was pastor of the **Wrangell** parish from 1985–96. Father Edward Matthews was pastor there from 1996–99. Father Paul Wightman was pastor of the Sitka parish from 1995–99. From 1923–62, Oblate Fathers stationed in Prince Rupert, British Columbia, Canada, cared for St. Margaret's mission at Hyder in Southeastern Alaska.

As of the year 2004, Missionary Oblates of Mary Immaculate were still serving in Alaska. Roger L. **Schwietz**, O.M.I., became Archbishop of **Anchorage** on March 3, 2001. From the outset, he was ably assisted by his fellow Oblate, Brother Craig Bonham. Oblate Father Tom Killeen was pastor of St. Joseph's parish in **Cordova**, and Oblate Father Gerald Brunet pastor of Holy Family parish in **Glennallen**, as well as Native Ministry Director in Anchorage. Oblate Fathers Anthony B. Dummer and James Blaney were serving in the Diocese of **Juneau**: Father Dummer as pastor of St. Paul the Apostle parish, Juneau; Father Blaney as pastor of Sacred Heart parish, **Hoonah**.

22, 74, 174

Father Paul C. O'Connor, S.J. *LRC.*

O'BRIEN, Father Charles, S.J.

Charles O'Brien was born in county Cheshire, England, on November 25, 1879. After serving in the British Navy, he entered the Society of Jesus on September 7, 1900. He studied theology at Woodstock, Maryland, and was ordained a priest in 1916. His tertianship he made at Los Gatos, California, 1919–20. He arrived at St. Mary's Mission, **Akulurak**, Alaska, on September 9, 1921. On March 9, 1922, he left Akulurak for **Tununak**. He returned to Akulurak on April 3rd, after a hard 26-day trip. In early May, he made an overnight trip to Old and New **Hamilton**, from which, according to the Akulurak diarist, he returned with "a very bad cold." On May 29th, the diarist recorded: "Fr. O'Brien laid up by inflammatory general rheumatism, suffering very much, cannot move and must be helped for everything." His condition worsened. On June 15th, he left Akulurak by boat for Old Hamilton and a trip to the States. He died, that June 15, 1922, before the boat reached Old Hamilton—"after having taken more food than he had taken for many days."

He was conscious till the last moment. Father Joseph M. **Tréca**, S.J., was with him, when he died.

Father O'Brien's body was taken back to Akulurak and buried there on the 17th. He was 42 years old, described as an "excellent athlete, tall, well built, but his stomach was weak." It was known that he was "very sensitive to dampness and cold, and that he had rheumatism already in the States." Unable to learn the Central Yup'ik Eskimo language, he had intended, in any case, to leave Alaska.

O'CONNOR, Father Paul C., S.J.

Wrote Sister Margaret Cantwell, a Sister of St. **Ann**: "When I first saw him, standing in the old hallway of the Girls' House at **Holy Cross Mission**, I thought he was, at least, the Governor of **Alaska**!" He was not in Alaska long, before he was referred to as "The Lord's Tramp of the Tundra." He was among the last of the mushing missionaries. He was early on recognized as "an Alaskan missionary *par excellence*," and as "a man of great principle." At the time of his death, his very close friend of many years, Father Segundo **Llorente**, S.J., wrote of him: "His death has left a void in the hearts of his many friends in Alaska, where he spent 40 years." He described him as "a princely priest, built like the legendary Apollo with a striking beauty that lasted well into his old age, who was, nonetheless, known as a priestly priest, a spiritual man, a man of God."

Paul Cornelius O'Connor was born in Herington, Kansas, on June 28, 1897. His father, Maurice, was

Father Paul C. O'Connor, S.J., ca. 1942, enjoying a skate with some of Kotzebue's youngsters. *JOPA-825.02.*

a railroad worker. His mother, Ella Pettit, was a woman with French Huguenot forebears. When Paul was still a young boy, the family moved to Spokane, Washington. There he attended Gonzaga High School. While in high school, he was an amateur boxer. He entered the Jesuit novitiate at Los Gatos, California, on May 29, 1915. After completing his two-year noviceship, he spent three more years there studying the classics and humanities. He then went to Mount St. Michael's, in Spokane, for three years of philosophical studies. He spent the years 1923–26 teaching Latin, Greek, and English, as well as some economics and sociology, at Gonzaga High School. In addition to his teaching, he also directed the Acolytes Sodality at St. Aloysius Church. His regal bearing, his handsome good looks, his excellent singing voice, and his dedicated work as a teacher all made a deep impression on the boys.

In 1926, Paul sailed for Europe for four years of theological studies. He spent two years at Heythrop College, Chipping Norton, England, and two at St. Augustin in Enghien, Belgium. He made the switch for two reasons: the "Britishness" of Heythrop was just too much for him, and he wanted to learn another language, in this case, French, in deference to his mother's French roots. She died while he was at Enghien. He was unable to come home for the funeral. Paul was ordained a priest at Enghien on August 25, 1929.

Upon arriving back in the United States in 1930, Father O'Connor was assigned to Alaska. He began his long years of ministry in Alaska at Holy Cross Mission. Soon he was making excursions to nearby villages. From 1931–33, he made **Pilot Station** his headquarters. Out of there, he visited also its dependent stations: **Mountain Village**, **Marshall**, Takchak, and Chukartulik.

During the year 1933–34, Father O'Connor made his tertianship at Port Townsend, Washington. He then returned to Alaska to begin a seven-year tenure at St. Mary's Mission, **Akulurak**. For six of those years, he was the local Superior. Father Llorente, who met him at Akulurak, wrote of his first impression of him:

> I was convinced that when God made him, God decided to do a good job, and God had succeeded. O'Connor stood about six feet, straight as a pine tree. There wasn't a flaw from head to toe. He was so handsome that when people met him, they stood still in wonderment. But God again, being perfect, did a perfect job with Paul this way: While Paul drew people to him with his irresistible smile, he kept them at arm's distance and even farther with his quick anger. He simply loved to argue and in the course of the argument he would do everything in his power to crush the opponent.

Then and there, Father Llorente made up his mind never to disagree with, never to argue with, never to contradict Father O'Connor. "As a result of this," he could write, "we went happily along together for the next forty years, meeting quite often. In later years he mellowed considerably."

With Father O'Connor, "cleanliness is next to godliness" was more than a trite cliché. Even in bush Alaska, cleanliness and neatness in all things were matters of great importance to him. His personal grooming bordered on the fastidious. Once, after having had to slog through the mud of the Bering Sea coast, he wrote, "I was mud from head to toe—I who hate the very thought of dust or mud on my spic and span clericals." It was not long before the old Akulurak mission, under Father O'Connor's eye, and paint brush, was spic-er and span-er than it had been for quite some time. Some of the old-timers there wondered out loud whether his generous application of coats of paint to everything, inside and out, was not a "failure in holy poverty."

At Akulurak, Father O'Connor now found himself in the heart of Central Yup'ik Eskimo country, where English was still pretty much a foreign language. He immediately applied himself to the study of Central Yup'ik Eskimo, which he still knew as "Innuit." For his personal use, he produced what he called a "Private Lexicon." He never became an expert in the language, but he came to esteem it very highly. In his book, *Eskimo Parish*, he wrote, "From a purely aesthetic point of view, Innuit possesses a structural superiority to our language." He found it compared favorably with the richness of Greek. He concluded, "It would be a crime to destroy his [the Native's] beautiful tongue."

Father O'Connor argued not only for the preservation of the Native language, but also for the preservation of the Native culture in general. Finding himself the Superior of a mission boarding school at Akulurak, he wrote, concerning schooling and Native culture:

> There is a rich store of human culture for the educator to work on in the native. A cultured native is not the product of those schools whose principal aim is to transform a native into a white. A cultured native is rather the finished specimen of the school which endeavors to bring out what is best in the native himself, and which gives him an education based on an intelligent understanding both of the native mind and his natural environment. Such a man wins not only the respect of the whites, but he is honored by his own people as well. Let the educator, therefore, not destroy but rather preserve and cultivate the cultural advantages already inherent in the life of the native.

During his Akulurak years, Father O'Connor spent much time in winter on the trail visiting Eskimo villages scattered widely throughout the Akulurak region. According to Father Llorente, "He loved dogs and he loved the trail." In summer, he boated and waded through the various rivers and sloughs to visit the people in their fish camps.

On September 24, 1941, Father O'Connor began his five-year stay in **Kotzebue**. Upon his arrival there, his sensitivities concerning cleanliness and order were very much offended, when he found the "church like a barn." During the following months, he spent much time in cleaning and in applying shellac, paint, kalsomine to floor, walls, and ceiling.

After Father O'Connor had everything in order and under control in Kotzebue, he began to make trips to the nearby reindeer camp and to the villages of Deering, Candle, Kiana, Shungnak, Kivalina, and Selawik. Several times he visited Point Hope. On one major trip, made in September 1943 on the *S.S. Waipio*, he traveled up the Arctic Coast all the way to **Barrow**. In 1942, he spent five weeks in **Nome**. In the summer of 1944, he was in the Pacific Northwest to offer the funeral Mass for his father and to attend to various business matters.

Father O'Connor's years in Kotzebue were not all formal priestly ministry, work, and travel. He found time to organize baseball and hockey games, skiing and ice-skating parties. He himself was an avid cross-country skier and skater. In the Kotzebue diary, he recorded: "Much skiing on nearby hill," "Skating magnificent. I go for miles down the bay." On some of his skating outings he used "a sail unto advantage."

While in Kotzebue, Father O'Connor "hoped to have a moral influence on the whole country." To become better acquainted with the men of the district, he became the book- and timekeeper for "a war project" that was going on there at the time. He also took an active interest in the legal system, doing what he could to bring about fair trials, especially in cases involving Natives.

Rather abruptly, during Holy Week in April 1946, Father O'Connor had to leave Kotzebue for Portland, Oregon, to receive medical attention for a hernia problem.

On August 1, 1946, Father O'Connor, back in Alaska again, relieved Father **John P. Fox**, S.J., at **Hooper Bay**. In addition to tending to this new post, he also visited, on a regular basis, its dependent mission, **Scammon Bay**. Immediately upon his arrival at Hooper Bay, there was a "general cleanup in progress." One of his early letters from there he signed off as "from Hooper Bay mud-hole." In another letter he wrote, "It seems most of my time is spent cooking and cleaning up. One of his first order of temporal business at Hooper Bay was to transform the second story of the building that had served as a convent for the Sisters of Our Lady of the **Snows** into a chapel.

From Hooper Bay, on January 24, 1949, he wrote to Father George T. **Boileau**, S.J.:

It [the Mass] is the one and only action that I never get tired of. Everyday it is a new thrill. For this reason I take complete charge of my own altar and have every thing spic and span. Even here at Hooper Bay, I have a swell little altar—liturgical, too, in the better sense of the word. I have absolutely everything for a fitting celebration of the mass. My little chapel is a gem and I intend to keep it such.

Already during his first year at Hooper Bay, Father O'Connor became deeply involved with the Alaska Housing Authority. He served as Chairman of the Board of Commissioners from the AHA's inception. This meant that he had to make periodic trips to Washington, D.C. In providing housing in Alaska both for white people in the cities and for Native people in the villages, he and the members of the AHA proved to be extraordinarily successful. Their hope was to combat tuberculosis, so prevalent at the time, with better housing. Father O'Connor was instrumental in getting hundreds of new houses for Native people throughout northern Alaska. To his Father Provincial, Leopold J. Robinson, S.J., he wrote, "I have been careful to put these houses in isolated districts, and needless to say have looked to our own missionary villages first." In early 1949, the new Father Provincial, Harold O. Small, S.J., after visiting Father O'Connor at Hooper Bay, reported to the Province that he, "as a member of the Territorial Housing Bureau, commands the highest respect from the Territorial and Federal officials."

In 1950, Father O'Connor served as official census-taker along his stretch of the Bering Sea coast.

In April of that year, at the request of the Governor of the Territory of Alaska and the head of the Democratic Party, he went to Washington, D.C., to testify in favor of statehood for Alaska. That year, too, he was "officially given the title of Captain in the National Guard." As such, he served as chaplain for all the Guard Units up as far as Nome. During his Hooper Bay years, he served also as postmaster.

In spite of all the work and official responsibilities, Father O'Connor did not neglect domestic needs. In 1950, Father Henry G. **Hargreaves**, S.J., noted in the Hooper Bay "History of the House" that Father O'Connor was continuing to build up the house library. Nor did he neglect the children of the village. The following year, Father Hargreaves noted in a letter:

Fr. O'Connor is very successful with the children, has their friendship, and every good day he finds time in the afternoon to go for a walk with a group of them, or play soccer, or ice skate. He coaches them in several plays every year, and encourages the children to learn catechism by prizes and an occasional party. Fr. O'Connor has the faculty of getting on with the old, young and very young.

And, concerning his own case, Father Hargreaves, new to the Alaska missions, could write, "Fr. O'Connor is a great inspiration and support in all this work."

As of July 10, 1953, Father O'Connor was the Superior of St. Mary's Mission, **Andreafsky**. Four years earlier, in a letter to Father James U. **Conwell**, S.J., he had written, "I understand that the bishop does not think I rate as a superior in any capacity." Throughout most of his years in northern Alaska, Father O'Connor was Superior of the places, where he was stationed. For a quarter of a century, he was a Consultor to the General Superior of the Alaska Mission. Some of his fellow Alaskan Jesuits, who knew him well, wondered at times why he was never appointed General Superior, or even Vicar Apostolic of Alaska, when a new bishop was needed. On May 4, 1955, Father Llorente, in a letter written at **Alakanuk** to Father Joseph F. **McElmeel**, S.J., wrote: "Fr. O'Connor is on the race to the Constitutional Convention. It is hoped here that he makes it. How come he never made the Alaska vicariate nor even the General Superiorship? He is a power.

Or was it because he has been too much of a power?" Father O'Connor, by his sheer presence, could be over-powering. He was not elected as a delegate to the Constitutional Convention.

As the man in charge at St. Mary's, Father O'Connor found he had "quite a job—work piled on work, but life is meant to be such, so why complain. With these boys saddled around my neck morning and night, I have hardly time to complain. But things are moving." He found the boys to be "quite a gang, but one has to be on the jump all the time." He was proud of his boys, and of the way he soon had them out-singing the girls. Father Edmund A. **Anable**, S.J., who knew him well, wrote at the time of his death, "He took an interest in the youngsters, was kind to them, but there was order. Classes ran smoothly and on schedule."

Predictably, things at St. Mary's moved along in a very orderly fashion under Father O'Connor's supervision. There was no ambiguity about regulations. The regimentation was tight and perfect, modeled on his own life, which was programmed, more or less, down to the last minute. When he spoke, the matter was settled. It was advisable not to disturb him before breakfast. He did become more amiable "as the coffee sank," in the words of Father Llorente. He loved to play chess, but this, too, was serious business for him. He was a fierce competitor.

Father O'Connor, in 1959, became procurator for the Alaska Mission. As such, he spent a year in Seattle, before moving to Portland, Oregon. As procurator, according to one writer, he was "a combination of St. Nicholas and an efficient quartermaster." His job was to order and ship north food, fuel, and a variety of supplies needed by the different Alaskan missions. "After the food is ordered and freighted to Alaska," he said in an interview, "I look around for the cold cash needed to pay the bills." To raise that "cold cash," he, as a self-described "pickpocket," traveled extensively throughout the 48 states on lecturing and begging tours. His best source of income for the missions, however, was a monthly newsletter sent to benefactors and potential benefactors. In those letters, he informed readers of missionary life and missionary needs in Alaska. After filling the role of procurator successfully for six years, he returned to Alaska.

Father O'Connor spent the year 1965–66 as Superior of **Copper Valley School**. In the yearbook for that year, he stated his view as to what should characterize the school: "academic scholarship and Christian excellence."

From 1966–75, Father O'Connor served as chaplain at **Providence** Hospital in **Anchorage**. As ever, his priestly dedication was total. He made it a point to know as much about a given patient as he possibly could. "Know your patients—you've got to know your people," he insisted. He saw every patient every day. He found a particular satisfaction in delighting the children in pediatrics. He prepared for his visits to them in advance, coming up with conundrums and rhyming riddles to amuse them and shorten their days. During his years as hospital chaplain, cross-country skiing twice a week continued to be his winter recreation. The warmer months of the year saw him tending flowers—many of them started in flats under a lamp in his chaplain's quarters—and the grounds around the hospital. The fragrance of his roses was often mingled with the smell of the smoke of his pipe. He was a faithful puffer of the pipe.

Save for some hernia problems, Father O'Connor had throughout his life always enjoyed vigorous good health. By the end of 1975, however, he had begun to feel his age. He was now nearly 80 years old. In January 1976, therefore, he returned to the Northwest. He spent some months as chaplain at St. Elizabeth Hospital in Baker, Oregon. Next he himself needed to be hospitalized for a combination of phlebitis, anemia and a bleeding stomach ulcer. He then spent the early part of 1977 at Mount St. Michael's in Spokane, "sick with Brain Tumor," in his own words. Soon, however, because of further health complications, he was placed in the Mount St. Vincent Nursing Home in Seattle. His health then improved rather remarkably, so much so that he was able to return to Spokane and become part of the Gonzaga Jesuit Community, where he spent his last days. He died in a Spokane hospital, on March 8, 1979.

After his death, his obituarist, Father Neill R. Meany, S.J., wrote: "When Fr. O'Connor was overtaken by his final illness, it was as if a mighty redwood had crashed to earth. It is no mere poetry to call this man one of the physical and spiritual giants

Bishop Robert Dermot O'Flanagan. *LRC.*

of the Alaska Mission." His long-time friend and admirer, Father Llorente, wrote to Father Louis L. **Renner**, S.J.: "I gave the funeral oration and praised him as he deserved. But after the funeral rites, I felt a sense of loneliness, almost like an orphan."

Father Paul Cornelius O'Connor, S.J., lies buried in the Jesuit cemetery at Mount St. Michael's, Spokane.

76, 94, 95

O'FLANAGAN, Bishop Robert Dermot

Robert Dermot O'Flanagan (he always used only Dermot as a first name) was born on March 9, 1901, at Castle D'Arcy, Lahinch, County Clare, Ireland. He had five brothers and three sisters. He was educated at Belvedere College, Dublin, from 1908–17. On October 4, 1917, he entered the Jesuit novitiate at Tullabeg, County Offaly. After completing his two-year noviceship, he spent an additional year at Tullabeg, studying the classics and humanities. He then taught for a year at the Jesuit school at Clongowes Wood College, Naas, County Kildare. His philosophical studies he made at Milltown Park, Dublin, from 1921–24. He then taught again for two years at Clongowes. From 1926–30, he made his theological studies at St. Ignatius College, Valkenburg, Limburg, Holland. There he was ordained a priest, on August 27, 1929. After completing another year of theology, Father O'Flanagan returned to

Ireland, where he again taught at Clongowes for two years. The year 1932 marked a turning point in his life. In June of that year, he left the Society of Jesus. His reasons for doing so will never be known, because the relevant documents were destroyed by his Father Rector, "in 1940 or 1941, when it seemed a war-related invasion of Ireland was imminent."

Precisely during this crucial year in his life, 1932, a Eucharistic Congress was being held in Dublin. Among those attending, was Father Patrick J. **O'Reilly**, S.J., veteran missionary of the Pacific Northwest and **Alaska**. After hearing Father O'Reilly talk about Alaska, Father O'Flanagan concluded that it was there that his future lay.

In January 1933, Father O'Flanagan arrived in **Juneau**. There he met Joseph R. **Crimont**, S.J., Vicar Apostolic of Alaska at the time, who assigned him, for the time being, to **Seward**. Father O'Flanagan was warmly welcomed by the people of Seward, so much so that he wrote back to Bishop Crimont, "people were falling over themselves trying to help me and make me feel at home—the non-Catholics as much as the Catholics. It was worthwhile leaving Ireland for that alone."

After a short time in Seward, Father O'Flanagan found himself at Holy Family parish in **Anchorage**, relieving the pastor of Holy Family parish for a "temporary stint"—which was to last 18 years, and make him "the best remembered of all the priests in the early history of Anchorage."

It did not take Father O'Flanagan long to become a well-known figure in Anchorage. His reserve, soft-spoken words, and beguiling Irish ways opened doors and hearts to him and to his message. Frequently he visited the sick in the Railroad Hospital. On a winter day, a common sight was that of Father "O" shoveling snow off the rectory porch or church sidewalks. He tended the church and rectory furnaces, and his dusty coveralls became him no less than did his black cassock.

Parishioners remembered him as "a most frugal man, who did his own housekeeping and janitorial work," and as "an ordinary man, who did good for everybody." They were worried, however, that "he didn't eat right." He seemed to live on coffee and sweet rolls.

Father O'Flanagan was, at heart, a pastoral man.

Along with tending to his Holy Family flock, on the third Sunday of each month—or on other occasions, when there was special need—he traveled by train back to Seward to care for the small Catholic community there.

Built in 1915, the original Holy Family Church was, by the mid-1930s, beginning to show its age. It was difficult to heat. There was little about the place as such that would draw people to it. This concerned Father O'Flanagan, and he gave thought to replacing the church. However, owing to the recent Great Depression, money for the new church was still hard to come by.

Meanwhile, not just a new church, but a Catholic hospital for Anchorage was on his mind. He broached the subject of a hospital in Anchorage to Bishop Crimont and the Sisters of **Providence**. To the delight of Father O'Flanagan, the "L" Street Providence Hospital opened on June 29, 1939, and the Sisters of Providence began their long years of hospital ministry in Anchorage. In addition to becoming firmly rooted in Anchorage through his works, Father O'Flanagan became a U.S. Citizen on November 30, 1943.

Mrs. Jack (Audrey) Clawson, among other things, offered to see to the interior design of the proposed new church. With her help and the encouragement of many others, but slowed by World War II, construction of the new church moved along rather haltingly. However, it had progressed, finally, to the stage where, on December 14, 1947, Father O'Flanagan could offer the first Mass in the basement of the long-awaited church. In October 1948, he saw the completion of the new church—with its white beauty and classic lines, a graceful monument on the corner of 5th Avenue and "H" Street.

Momentous news was heard in Southcentral Alaska on the evening of July 18, 1951. On that evening, it was announced that a new diocese had been created in Alaska, the Diocese of Juneau —officially established as of June 23, 1951—and that, on July 9th, Father O'Flanagan had been appointed its first bishop.

In Holy Family Church, Anchorage, on October 3, 1951, Father Dermot O'Flanagan, in solemn ceremonies, was consecrated a bishop by Francis D. **Gleeson**, S.J., Vicar Apostolic of Alaska at the time. Charles D. White, Bishop of Spokane, and Joseph P. Dougherty, Bishop of Yakima, were co-consecrators. Thomas A. Connolly, Archbishop of Seattle, delivered the sermon. Bishop O'Flanagan was the first priest to be consecrated a bishop in Alaska. For his motto he took: *Ut Omnes Unum Sint* ("that all might be one").

After his consecration, *The Anchorage Daily Times* editorialized:

> Bishop O'Flanagan can be remembered by many local residents as a young man who came here fresh from Ireland. His friendliness and humility won him an immediate spot in the hearts of all the people. He extended his three-month visit until it ran into years. His flock prospered and grew under his leadership. The magnificent new Church of the Holy Family will ever be a monument in concrete to the inspiration and spiritual leadership he gave.

With mixed feelings, Bishop O'Flanagan, after 18 years in Anchorage, his "home," left it for Juneau. There, in the small, wooden Church of the Nativity of the Blessed Virgin Mary—now elevated to Cathedral status—he was formally installed as the first Bishop of Juneau on October 7, 1951.

In November 1960, Father Segundo **Llorente**, S.J., with the approval of Bishop Gleeson, was elected by write-in vote to serve in Alaska's newly formed House of Representatives. This meant, of course, that, when the House was in session, he would have to reside in Juneau. Bishop O'Flanagan, according to Father Llorente, "panicked" at the thought of a priest's being in politics. In an official letter, he informed Father Llorente that he was not to be seen in the Cathedral, nor in the rectory with other priests, and had no faculties to hear confessions, and that he could offer only a private Mass in the hospital chapel early in the morning. This Father Llorente did, every morning at 7:00.

The letter in question, according to Father Llorente, was not wholly of Bishop O'Flanagan's inspiration. In keeping with his nobility of character and humility, Bishop O'Flanagan, in a letter to Bishop Gleeson, dated March 6, 1961, wrote: "Father Segundo Llorente appears to be doing very well. He is highly spoken of in town, is conducting himself in an excellent manner, and it looks as proof that my fears about his coming to the Legislature were not too solidly founded. I am most happy to know that I was mistaken."

By 1963, twelve years after Bishop O'Flanagan had become Ordinary of the Diocese of Juneau, the diocese—comprising, at the time, 70, 800 square miles—numbered some 20,000 Catholics in a total population of some 145,000. The diocese was organized into 11 parishes and 12 missions, served by 26 priests. There were two high schools, one elementary school, and four general hospitals under Catholic auspices. Bishop O'Flanagan was happy and proud to be playing a major role in the growth of the Church in Alaska.

In 1968, however, Bishop O'Flanagan, reasoning that it was "time for a younger man to take over," resigned as Ordinary of the Diocese of Juneau, effective as of June 19th. By this time, he had been in Alaska 35 years. He left it for a warmer climate, that of San Diego, California. At Little Flower Haven, a retirement home run by the Carmelite Sisters of the Divine Heart of Jesus, in La Mesa, California, he died on December 31, 1972. With the end of his life, a major chapter in the history of the Catholic Church in Alaska came to an end.

By way of a brief epilogue, the last word here regarding Bishop Dermot O'Flanagan is left to Sister Margaret Cantwell, S.S.A. A long-term resident in Alaska and historian of the Catholic Church in Alaska, she wrote:

> Bishop O'Flanagan, the first big name in Anchorage's ecclesiastical history, seems to have the mystery of Ireland about him—with "little people" (in this case "little things") coloring and molding his life. There is much antithesis in his life also. Although I did not get to know him well, I knew (wondered about) some mystery causing his reticence in later life—so antithetical to his friendliness among the people in early Anchorage. There is his "unknown" about leaving the Jesuits. There is his "chance meeting" with Fr. O'Reilly. There is his separation from the Jesuits—but yet, his long "connection" with the Jesuits in building up the Church in Alaska. And there is his death in California, and his burial in Anchorage, not Juneau.

Bishop Dermot O'Flanagan lies buried in the Catholic plot of Anchorage's Angelus Memorial Park Cemetery.

15

OHAGAMIUT

The one-time Central Yup'ik Eskimo village of Ohagamiut—located on the north bank of the Kuskokwim River, 1.8 miles east of Upper **Kalskag** and some 30 miles west of **Aniak**—had a population of 130 in 1880. It was here that the Catholic Church had its first mission on the Kuskokwim River. In 1891, Father Paschal **Tosi**, S.J., visited the Kuskokwim and hired Nicholaj Dementov, manager of a nearby trading post, to build a mission house at Ohagamiut. The house was built of logs, was one-story high, had five rooms, with a hall through the center. It was finished by October 1892. Father Francis A. **Barnum**, S.J., who visited Ohagamiut soon after the house was finished, described it as "by far the most solid and best constructed building we have." In 1894, Father Aloysius J. **Robaut**, S.J., began to serve the Ohagamiut mission—dedicated to St. Ignatius Loyola—residing there for longer periods of time.

After four years of intermittent work on the Kuskokwim, Father Robaut wrote to his Superior, Father John B. **René**, S.J.:

> St. Ignatius Mission seems to me by far the most destitute of all our places in this country of Alaska. I have yet no church, no accommodations, and no church goods, except my traveling chapel [Mass kit], which is put up in a room serving at one time for a church, at another for a reception room, dining room and kitchen, and at night for a sleeping room. But, on the other hand, things look quite different from the spiritual standpoint. I have no hesitation in saying that, in my opinion, St. Ignatius' Mission on the Kuskokwim is likely to become the very best field for apostolic work we possess in the northern part of **Alaska** territory. Everything here foreshadows important results, and I hope soon to be able to make it an evident fact to you that nowhere else have we greater hope of solid and lasting good.

Tragedy struck St. Ignatius Mission on November 30, 1903. The mission building burned to the ground. Everything was lost, including Father Robaut's irreplaceable language manuscripts. However, the following year, a new structure was put up. Father Robaut continued to serve the Ohagamiut community faithfully until 1916. By that time, most of his congregation had either succumbed to epidemics or relocated elsewhere.

O'MALLEY, Brother Gerald J., S.J.

Gerald J. O'Malley was born on July 19, 1918, and raised in Schenectady, New York, the son of John and Esabel O'Malley. His mother died, when he was still very young. After spending the first grade in a public school, he attended St. Columba grade and high schools, from 1926–37. Soon after graduating from high school, he enlisted in the U.S. Coast Guard, in which he served from 1939–54. Nine of those years he spent in Alaskan waters. Among his memories was "transporting the famous 'Glacier Priest,' Fr. **Hubbard**, and his two dogs" on one of his scientific expeditions to **Alaska**. What the dogs did to the newly painted deck was remembered, but not appreciated.

In the course of his years in the Coast Guard, O'Malley became acquainted with the Jesuit priests stationed in **Sitka**, **Juneau**, and **Ketchikan**. The time came, when he felt he should commit himself to something permanent. "It's gotta be a total commitment," he said, "Not just one foot in." While at Ketchikan, he applied for membership in the Oregon Province of the Society of Jesus as a Lay Brother. He was accepted and, on September 27, 1954, he entered the novitiate at Florissant, Missouri. After taking his vows, he became "plant engineer" at Mount St. Michael's in Spokane, Washington, from 1956–62.

From 1962–79, Brother O'Malley was stationed at St. Mary's Mission on the **Andreafsky** River in western Alaska. There, for 17 years, he was in charge of maintenance and operations. He prided himself—not without a hint of complaint—that he kept the school running "on nothing."

From his first days at St. Mary's, he found himself almost overwhelmed with responsibilities and challenges. In his autobiographical sketch, he wrote: "Here work and responsibilities grew as the plant itself with its various needs grew and changed very rapidly. I started with such things as setting up a cannery line, converting a wood furnace to oil, making adjustments and improvements on the generator, which was becoming too small for the demands being made on it." At the same time as he was attending to the Mission's physical needs, he also tried to prepare the boys at the school, and the men in the village, to be ready for, and to adjust to, the rapidly changing conditions of Eskimo life.

Brother Gerald J. O'Malley, S.J. *LRC.*

The only break Brother O'Malley had during his long years at St. Mary's was in 1967, when, from February to June, he made his tertianship in Cleveland, Ohio. Early in 1979, Superiors decided that a change would do him good, and recommended that, by way of a sabbatical, he take part in Gonzaga University's CREDO Program during the year 1979–80. With negative enthusiasm, he applied to be admitted to the program. "My interest in the CREDO Program is minimal," he said during an interview held on June 22, 1979. "I was told by my Superiors to request admission." Looking back on that event 14 years later, speaking as a sailor, he said of it, "Having nothing to say in the matter, I was shipped off to GU."

After enduring and surviving the program, Brother O'Malley was "homeported" to **Anchorage**, to take up new duties there. He joined the Jesuit Community living in the Birchwood Street residence. At first, his duties were somewhat ill-defined. It was suggested that he "see native students at Alaska Pacific University," a kind of "campus ministry." A priest soon took over this ministry. Brother O'Malley was then assigned "to take care of the house," to maintain it and to operate it as a "rooming house" for people traveling through Anchorage to and from the villages. This he was to do throughout most of the 1980s.

It was in 1981, however, that Brother O'Malley really came into his own. At the request of Francis T. **Hurley**, Archbishop of Anchorage at the time, he became a Port Chaplain. He was delighted at "the chance to get back aboard ships." In 1982, he took a course in port chaplaincy training in Houston, Texas. In 1983, at a special ceremony, he was presented with a Bosn's Pipe. In one year alone, 1985, he boarded 218 vessels. In 1992, he attended the World Congress of the Apostleship of the Sea in Houston. In 1993, he received a letter from the Jesuit Father General, in which he was assured that Father General was praying special blessings upon him and his worthwhile ministry as a Port Chaplain.

Brother O'Malley was described by one interviewer as "erect and barrel-chested." He was a man of strong likes and dislikes. There was a gruffness about him. He was not a man of many words. He summarized his ministry as a Port Chaplain: "As chaplain of the Port of Anchorage, I still consider myself a sailor. I go aboard ships. I don't preach religion. If they find me sincere, they open up. I just respond to questions, and set an example. You project the life you are living." He described his port ministry as "a ministry of presence."

In 1995, in Anchorage, Brother O'Malley underwent drastic treatment for tumors in the kidneys and the brain. He was then moved to the Jesuit House infirmary at Gonzaga University. On October 30, 1996, in Spokane, he died. He lies buried in the Jesuit cemetery at Mount St. Michael's.

O'NEILL, Father Edward C., C.Ss.R.

Edward C. O'Neill was born in Madison, Wisconsin, on July 18, 1903. On June 19, 1924, he entered the novitiate, Mt. St. Clement's College of the Missouri Province of the Congregation of the Most Holy Redeemer, the Redemptorists, in De Soto, Missouri. There he made his Religious profession on August 2, 1925, as a member of the St. Louis Province. He was ordained a priest by Bishop Paul P. Rhode in Immaculate Conception Seminary, Oconomowoc, Wisconsin, on July 2, 1930.

Father O'Neill's first assignment as a priest was as professor at Holy Redeemer College, the Redemptorist minor seminary in Oakland, California. After his years at Holy Redeemer, he served as pastor and rector of Redemptorist parishes in Portland, Oregon, and Whittier, California. As a pastor, he was known to be "always a priest of quiet dignity, earnest rather than spectacular."

At the outbreak of World War II, Father O'Neill

Father Edward C. O'Neill, C. Ss. R. *Courtesy of Redemptorists Denver Province.*

became a chaplain in the U.S. Navy, reaching the rank of Captain. Long after his return to civilian life, he remained active in the Naval Reserve. After the war, he reluctantly accepted an appointment as Rector of Holy Redeemer College.

On September 29, 1961, Father O'Neill began to serve as pastor of Sacred Heart parish in **Seward, Alaska**. On March 27, 1964, he lived through the Good Friday earthquake. In his diary, under that date, he wrote: "EARTHQUAKE. Was here at desk preparing sermon for this evening, when QUAKE began at 5:36 PM. At first thought it was going to be another brief tremor, but very soon realized it was a block-buster. Thought the quakes would never stop."

From July 1968 to August 1969, Father O'Neill was pastor of St. Mary's parish in **Kodiak**. He was pastor of Our Lady of the Angels parish, **Kenai**, from August 1969 to July 1972, when he became pastor of Our Lady of Perpetual Help parish in **Soldotna**. In 1975, he was gratified to see the parish center at Soldotna near its final stages of construction. On November 26, 1977, he was again back in Seward to serve as pastor there for another two years. Then, after several years at Soldotna, he was out of Alaska—"eased out by a younger element." He left Alaska reluctantly and with a heavy heart. After spending his remaining active years at Sacred Heart parish in Seattle, Washington, he voluntarily accepted a final transfer to St. Clement's Health Care Center in Liguori, Missouri. There he died on October 9, 1991, just into his 89th year.

Father O'Neill, an avid bowler and highly skilled bridge player, is remembered as "always a dignified, cultured, gentleman priest." During life, he was admired for being a "priest for all the people," and for his "untiring visits to the sick." He was among the first of the 19 Redemptorists that eventually served in Alaska.

15

O'REILLY, Father Patrick J., S.J.

Patrick J. O'Reilly was born in Kilkee, County Clare, Ireland, to John O'Reilly and Margaret Sexton O'Reilly on February 5, 1872. For his schooling, he attended the Convent National School in Kilkee from 1878–80, the Kilkee National School from 1880–85, and the Kilkee Secondary School from 1885–89. He then came to America to study architecture under his maternal uncle, from 1890–92. After that, for a period of 16 months, he studied Latin and the humanities at Sacred Heart Mission, DeSmet, Idaho. He entered the novitiate of the Turin Province of the Society of Jesus at DeSmet on July 8, 1893. By the time he was ordained a priest in St. Aloysius Church in Spokane, Washington, on May 31, 1906, he had studied and taught various subjects at different Indian missions in Montana and at Gonzaga College in Spokane.

From 1906–07, Father O'Reilly again taught at Gonzaga College; then, the following year, he served there as chaplain to students. He was on the "Mission Band," a group of two or three priests traveling far and wide to preach short missions and retreats, during the year 1908–09. He then interrupted his itinerant preaching ministry to make his tertianship at St. Andrew-on-Hudson, in Poughkeepsie, New York. Following that, and throughout most of his active life as a priest, Father O'Reilly was a member of the Mission Band. As such, he traveled to the island of Molokai in the Hawaiian Islands to preach to the lepers there, to England, and to many parts of the United States.

From 1926–28, Father O'Reilly was pastor of Immaculate Conception parish in **Fairbanks, Alaska**. It is thanks to his efforts that Immaculate Conception Church was adorned with the beautiful stained glass windows that so brightened it ever after. And it is thanks to his efforts that the church did not burn to the ground, in March 1927, when a chimney fire flared up. Having saved the church from going up in smoke, he saw fit to provide it with a brick chimney, as well as with a concrete porch.

In the late summer of 1928, Father O'Reilly was informed by telegram: "You are to leave Fairbanks for Seattle via **Holy Cross**, make observations on the way." On September 11th, he left **Nenana**, on a downriver trip that took him to ten different missions strung out along the Yukon River. Near the mouth of the Yukon, he visited **Akulurak** and **Hamilton**, before going on to visit **St. Michael** and **Unalakleet**. He arrived in **Nome** the last day of September. On October 5th—accompanied by Father Patrick F. Savage, S.J., pastor of St. Joseph's parish in Nome—he left Nome on the *Boxer* for **King Island**. They reached the island the next day. On the 7th, a Sunday, Father O'Reilly had "the privilege of celebrating the first Holy Mass in the first church built on King Island." This first church, built by the Eskimos the year before, was a very modest structure built out of wood salvaged from shipwrecks.

After his King Island visit, Father O'Reilly was able to spend a short time at the **Pilgrim Hot Springs** Mission. He left Nome on November 7th, and arrived in Seattle on November 15th.

In 1932, Father O'Reilly was in Dublin, Ireland, as a delegate to the Eucharistic Congress taking place there. On that occasion, he gave a talk which was heard by Father Dermot **O'Flanagan**. This led to the latter's going to Alaska.

From 1940 to December 1941, Father O'Reilly was pastor of St. Rose of Lima parish in **Wrangell** and visiting priest to its dependent stations. He was pastor of St. Gregory of Nazianzen parish in **Sitka** from December 1941 to January 1947. While stationed in Sitka, he served also as auxiliary chaplain to the Armed Forces in the area.

After leaving Alaska, Father O'Reilly served for a short time as a parish priest in Oregon, then as chaplain to a convent of Sisters in Bellingham, Washington. He again spent a year in England preaching and giving missions. During the first half of the 1950s, he was stationed at Port Townsend, Washington, but devoted most of his time to serving as hospital chaplain in Chehalis, Washington. He spent the final days of his life at the Jesuit novitiate at Sheridan, Oregon, where he died on May 26, 1958.

Jesuit historian Wilfred P. Schoenberg described Father Patrick J. O'Reilly as "the last of the Irish prophets, as fiery and threatening as Moses at the foot of Mount Sinai." Father O'Reilly was a man totally dedicated to his ministry of preaching. He never asked anything for himself—except an audience. He loved to talk.

Father O'Reilly lies buried in the Jesuit cemetery at Mount St. Michael's, Spokane.

176

Father Gerald S. Ornowski, M.I.C. *Courtesy of Fr. Ornowski.*

ORNOWSKI, Father Gerald S., M.I.C.

Gerald S. Ornowski was born in Port Austin, Michigan, on January 18, 1935. There, as a member of St. Michael's parish, he was baptized, received his first Holy Communion, and was confirmed. He received his elementary and part of his secondary schooling in Port Austin's public schools. For the last three years of high school, he attended St. Mary's Preparatory in Orchard Lake, Michigan. At St. Mary's, he excelled in public speaking, and was co-editor of the school's award-winning newspaper and yearbook. He earned varsity letters in basketball and track. It was while attending St. Mary's that he resolved to study for the priesthood. The summer after graduating from high school he spent hitchhiking for 10,000 miles around the U.S., as a "last fling" before entering Religious life. By that time, he had already, with his parents, traveled to Mexico, Canada, and Europe.

On September 24, 1953, Gerald entered the novitiate of the Congregation of Marians of the Immaculate Conception, in Stockbridge, Massachusetts—because he "liked the way they lived as a family in Christ and the variety of ministries they offered." After completing his one-year noviceship, he was sent to pursue studies for the priesthood at the Catholic University of America and at St. Joseph's Seminary, both in Washington, D.C. He was ordained a priest in Washington, at the National Shrine of the Immaculate Conception on June 9, 1962.

After his ordination, Father Ornowski held many administrative posts within his Congregation. He served as Superior, Master of Novices, Vocation Director, Provincial Councilor, editor of the magazine *Marian Helpers*. He founded *Info*, a national magazine for promoting vocations among youth. After graduate studies in Pastoral Theology and Spirituality, he was a theology teacher, retreat director, alcoholism counselor, TV speaker, and member of the national board of World Wide Marriage Encounter. As a priest-writer and tour leader, he visited Africa, South America, and the Holy Land.

Father Ornowski had his first taste of **Alaska** in the summer of 1976, when, from May 26th to mid-July, he served as substitute priest for Father John E. **Gurr**, S.J., pastor at St. Francis Xavier's parish in **Kotzebue**, then, from mid-July to August 31st, as substitute priest for Jesuit Fathers James E. **Poole** and Harold J. **Greif**, pastors at St. Joseph's parish in **Nome**. The following year, he returned to northern Alaska, "for a one-year stay, with the purpose of learning the needs of the Church in Alaska and the demands of ministry with a view to possible establishment of the Marian Congregation in Alaska in the future." In 1977, from June 24th to July 27th, he was on **Little Diomede** Island, and from July 27th to September 7th in Nome. After spending several months in Michigan because of his father's illness and death, he returned to Alaska, to **Bethel**, on December 15, 1977. There, at Immaculate Conception parish, he was associate pastor to Father John A. **Hinsvark** until the summer of 1978.

As associate pastor, he regularly visited Bethel's dependent missions of **Marshall** and **Russian Mission**, and served as Auxiliary Air Force Chaplain for the radar site at Cape Newenham.

After his time in Bethel, Father Ornowski went back to New England, to render various services to his Congregation. In the late summer of 1990, however, he returned to Alaska for a longer stay. From 1990–94, he was pastor of the two Bering Sea coastal villages of **Stebbins** and **St. Michael**. Making Stebbins his home base, he commuted between the two Central Yup'ik Eskimo villages by Honda ATV and snowmachine, depending on the condition of the trail. He divided his time equally between the two villages, spending half a week at each.

In both villages, Father Ornowski found his living conditions in deplorable condition. Some ten years later, both villages were to have new churches and living quarters. At Stebbins–St. Michael, he was 500 miles from the nearest road system, without running water or any modern convenience, maintaining two churches and providing spiritual services for two Catholic communities. Not one to complain about his situation, he told an interviewer, "It challenges me completely—physically, psychologically and spiritually." Considering his spiritual work the most important, he went on to add, "To bring God's word to the people and to make the Eucharist present is my greatest satisfaction." In his 1990 Christmas letter to "Loved Ones," he wrote:

> I am well . . . alone, but not lonely . . . supported by prayers and packages from the Lower 48 . . . provided for here by the people with bread, berries and fish . . . I cook, wash, repair, maintain things myself . . . learn from Natives. I could reflect at length on the curses and blessings of this way of life; but, just let me say that, basically, I am very happy—because I'm convinced that God wants me here, and that God and some people love me.

During the years 1994–97, Father Ornowski was again out of Alaska, more immediately involved with affairs of his Congregation. By now, however, he needed Alaska—and the Missionary Diocese of **Fairbanks** needed him. In 1997, he became pastor of St. Mark's University Parish and Catholic Center in Fairbanks. As such, he served mainly as a chaplain to students and faculty at the University of Alaska–Fairbanks. As of 2004, he still had an office on campus, and all liturgies took place on campus.

Though, as a "bush priest," Father Ornowski enjoyed the natural way of life in remote Eskimo villages and the Native people with whom he shared it, he made the transition to campus life readily enough, accepting it as a new challenge. "I thrive on challenge," he wrote, "and the charisma of my religious community, the Marians of the Immaculate Conception, is to respond to God's will as voiced by the Church's spiritual leaders." The "spiritual leader," in this case, was Michael J. **Kaniecki**, S.J., Bishop of Fairbanks at the time, who asked him to take on the chaplaincy at the UA–F.

As pastor of St. Mark's University Parish, Father Ornowski lived in a small house in woods at the edge of the campus. In winter, moose routinely visited him, eating the dried flowers out of his window boxes. Though living in the city of Fairbanks, he was still only a few minutes' drive from the Alaskan wilderness. "That's fine with me," he wrote, "because I'm a hunter and outdoorsman from way back." As hunter and chaplain, he was frequently able to serve members of the Catholic Student Association not only "food for thought," but also "food from the land"—moose meat bagged by him.

When Father Ornowski first began his campus ministry, he wondered if the gap in age, culture, and psychology between him and the university students might be too great. Time proved his initial fears to have been groundless. By making himself available to all students and staff, regardless of religious persuasion, he was soon accepted on campus not only by the students in general, but also by the university faculty and administration. In the year 2001, looking back on his years at the university, he ended an article by writing:

> The reservations I had four years ago about the transition from the bush to academia are pretty well dissolved. The students have accepted me. I have tried to be friendly, helpful and authentic with them. I trust that my efforts will bear fruit in the long run. Here, too, as in the bush, I have found challenges and beauty and blessing. Thanks be to God!

As of the year 2004, he was still engaged in campus ministry at the University of Alaska–Fairbanks.

PAIMIUT

Paimiut—meaning "people of the stream's mouth"—a former Central Yup'ik Eskimo village, was located 22 miles southwest of **Holy Cross Mission**, on the right bank of the Yukon River. By the mid-1950s, it was nearly abandoned, its people having moved mostly to **Aniak** and Upper **Kalskag**.

Catholic baptisms were performed at Paimiut as early as in the 1890s by Jesuit missionaries. It was routinely visited by priests stationed at Holy Cross, principal among them Father Aloysius J. **Robaut**. However, from 1926, when a mission was built there, to 1928, it had what was described as "a flourishing school," and Father **Edward J. Cunningham**, S.J., was in residence. Tatiana Demientieff and Dora Cristo, two young women from Holy Cross, taught at the Paimiut school. From time to time, Sister Mary Armella, a Sister of St. **Ann**, visited Paimiut.

Mention should be made here of Jake Aloysius, a Paimiut leader. When 20 or so "big boys" and "big girls" with their supervisors came from Holy Cross Mission to set up fish camp for the six-week long king salmon season, he and his family always saw to it that the mission people felt welcome. The mission boys and their supervisors used the old school as their sleeping quarters. The girls and the Sisters lived in the mission house, a rather large "home" with several rooms and an attached chapel/church. Bishop Joseph R. **Crimont**, S.J., had intended at one time to retire here, but never did so. As additional help for the mission crew, Jake provided radio communication with Holy Cross all through the fishing season, shared his expertise, and put his icehouse at the disposal of the mission.

PALMER

The town of Palmer, an agricultural supply town, lies in the Matanuska Valley, 37 miles northeast of **Anchorage**. It was established as a railroad station on the Matanuska Branch of the Alaska Railroad about 1916. A Palmer post office was established in 1917, but discontinued in 1925. A Warton post office was there from 1931–35. Since 1935, it has again been the Palmer post office. In the 1930s, Palmer became the center for the Alaska Rural Rehabilitation Corporation, administered by the U.S. Dept. of the Interior. As such, it served as the supply center of a colony of about 180 farm families from the American Midwest. Palmer's population was 150, in 1939; 890, in 1950; 1,181, in 1967; and 4,533, in the year 2000.

Official Catholic beginnings in Palmer date from May 25, 1935, when Father F. Merrill **Sulzman** first went there to minister to the newly arriving colonists. The first Mass in Palmer was offered by him the following day in the tent of Mr. Leo Jacobs on a makeshift altar made of scrap lumber. Though funds were very limited, the actual construction of Palmer's first Catholic church began on June 2, 1936. Soon funds ran out. Father Sulzman, in January 1937, went back East to solicit funds. During his absence, Father Leo Dufour cared for the Palmer Catholic community out of Anchorage. Father Sulzman was back in Palmer to preside at the formal dedication ceremonies of the new church held on July 24, 1937. The church, with a rectory attached, was built out of logs. It was dedicated under the patronage of St. Michael.

The joy of the dedication, however, was short lived. Architectural flaws in the design of the church began to show up. The heating system proved to be wholly inadequate. Winds blew through chinks between the logs. One Friday night, late in the fall, part of the roof blew off. Costly changes were called for. The money to make them was not at hand. Again Father Sulzman went East on a fund-raising trip. There a doctor found his health to be so deteriorated,

(*top*) St. Michael's Church, Palmer.

(*bottom*) The original St. Michael's Church, Palmer, built in 1936. *Both photos courtesy of St. Michael's parish, Palmer.*

that he recommended a long period of rest in a warmer climate.

About this same time, Bishop Joseph R. **Crimont**, S.J., Vicar Apostolic of **Alaska** at the time, was receiving reports from the valley that some of the parishioners were upset with Father Sulzman's lifestyle and wished his transfer, feeling that another priest might do better at building the parish spirit. Concerned about the reports, and about the health and spiritual good of Father Sulzman, Bishop Cri-

mont agreed to a year of recuperation for him outside Alaska. "Thus," in the words of historian Sister Margaret Cantwell, S.S.A., "Father Sulzman's saga in the Matanuska Valley—one of the most picturesque episodes in the establishment of the Catholic Church within what became the Archdiocese of Anchorage—came to a conclusion. The church was up, the parish begun, the time for change was ripe."

The Reverend Dr. Charles M. van Estvelt, a Hollander, known also as "the Canon," was the second pastor of St. Michael's parish, from September 8, 1938, to June 4, 1939. In October of 1938, he erected the Stations of the Cross in St. Michael's Church.

The third pastor of St. Michael's parish was Father James P. **Snead**, for a period of 27 years, from August 1939 to May 1966. During his first five years as pastor, he lived in Anchorage and commuted to Palmer. September 8, 1952, was for him "a red-letter day," to use his own words. On that day, work on a basement for the church began. However, the completion of the project and the payment for it was delayed for more than a year. In the meantime, Father Snead went to Portland, Oregon, for medical treatment. During his absence of several months, Father Raymond W. **Mosey** replaced him.

In 1960, in an effort to minimize heat loss to the church and rectory, Father Snead had the parish plant stuccoed. Whatever the effects of the stuccoing were, St. Michael's Church lost the log cabin appearance, that had charmed parishioners and visitors alike. While the stuccoing was in progress, Father Snead took a trip around the world. During his last ten years as pastor of St. Michael's, from 1956–66, for reasons of health, he lived in **Providence** Hospital, Anchorage, and commuted to Palmer for confessions and Masses. In 1966, Father Snead, "deservedly the best known and loved by the people of the valley of all the priests who ministered there," according to Sister Margaret, took on a new assignment, that of pastor of St. Benedict's parish in Anchorage. Next to Father Sulzman, Father Snead is remembered as *the* priest of Palmer.

From June 1, 1966, to November 1966, Msgr. John A. **Lunney** was pastor of St. Michael's parish. He was responsible for the building of the present St. Michael's Church and rectory, as well as for the first church in **Big Lake**.

After Msgr. Lunney, the following priests served as pastors of St. Michael's parish: Father Rayner Ziemski, O.F.M. Conv., from November 1966 to October 1967; Msgr. Francis A. Murphy, from October 1967 to March 1970; Father James A. O'Carroll, C.S.Sp., from March 1970 to September 1971; Father Edward J. Stirling, C.S.Sp., from October 1971 to November 1972; Father Ernest H. **Muellerleile**, from November 30, 1972, to November 30, 1974; Father John J. **Marx**—who carried out extensive remodeling of St. Michael's Church—from December 1, 1974, to August 19, 1977; Father Sean O'Donoghue, C.S.Sp.—noted for reducing the parish debt and for teaching many classes to the youth and the adults—from August 20, 1977, to September 17, 1979; and Father **Gerard T. Ryan**, C.S.Sp., from September 18, 1979, to August 1987. Under his direction, St. Michael's Church received some further remodeling. A lofty new entryway, with new bathrooms, was built, and a new kitchen was excavated and built in the church basement.

After Father Ryan, the following served as pastors of St. Michael's parish: Father Michael Shields, August 1987 to May 1994; Father David Cowdan, August 1994 to April 1999; and Father Leo C. **Desso**, beginning on July 1, 1999, and as of the year 2004.

In the course of its long history, St. Michael's parish was blessed also by the ministry of many devoted Sisters, Brothers, and lay people. Over the years, two of its one-time mission stations, St. Bernard's in **Talkeetna** and Sacred Heart in **Wasilla**, evolved into full-fledged parishes.

St. Michael's parish is noted for its hospitality, and for its concern for the poor and needy. But, before all else, this parish in the valley, at the foot of Pioneer Peak, stands as "a symbol of vision, hope, and courage," in the words of Francis T. **Hurley**, retired Archbishop of Anchorage, with the Mass and the Eucharist central to all it is and does.

15, 73

PAQUIN, Brother Ulric, S.J.

Ulric Paquin was born in the Province of Quebec, Canada. He arrived in **Nome, Alaska**, on August 1, 1910. In September, after spending around a month at **Marys Igloo**, he went to **St. Michael**. **Ursuline** Sister Mother Amadeus Dunne, who knew him there, described him as "full of vigor, activity, kindness, energy." On the morning of January 27, 1911, he started out with sled and five dogs from St. Michael with a load of lumber for **Stebbins**, an Eskimo village less than ten miles from St. Michael. He had traveled often between the two communities. On this particular day, he was wearing a parka and mukluks, but he had neither a sleeping bag nor blankets along. A sudden, violent snowstorm came up, and he lost his bearings. He unloaded the lumber and lay down on the sled. When he did not return to St. Michael as expected, a search was organized. On February 3rd, he was found, lying on the sled, his rosary around his neck, his dogs huddled around him, frozen to death. The date of his death is given as January 27, 1911. He was only 36 years old, and had been in the Society of Jesus only nine years. He lies buried at St. Michael.

PARODI, Father Aloysius, S.J.

He was described by Father Francis M. **Ménager**, S.J., as "small of stature, but stocky, with a kind and noble face, and a large Roman nose." Father Francis A. **Barnum**, S.J., remembered him as "a saintly man with a lovable disposition," but as "one who should never have been sent to **Alaska**, for he was utterly unfitted in every way to endure such a hard life as ours."

Aloysius Parodi, born in San Quirico, near Genoa, Italy, on January 28, 1846, entered the Society of Jesus on September 10, 1873. After completing his studies in Nice, France, and in Monaco, he was ordained a priest in St. Louis, Missouri, on September 5, 1878. His tertianship he made at Santa Clara, California, 1887–88. He took his final vows at Sacred Heart Mission, DeSmet, Idaho, on February 2, 1891. Before going to Alaska, he did priestly work in the Pacific Northwest, both among the Indian peoples and the whites. He had a gift for languages, and that very likely accounts for his having been sent to Alaska.

Father Parodi arrived in Alaska in 1892, and spent his first Alaskan winter at the Kanelik mission near **Akulurak**. During that winter, he made a trip to **Tununak** with Father Joseph M. **Tréca**, S.J. Father Parodi was at St. Mary's Mission, Akulurak, from 1893–96. He spent the winter 1896–97 at Tununak, alone. While there, he had "a terrible trial," and was brought back to Akulurak "in a pitiful condition." According to Father Barnum, Father Parodi, while at Tununak, became violently insane,

fell victim to "polar anaemia," an insidious malady. The attack assumed a very violent form, and he developed traits that were just the opposite of his mild and gentle disposition. One day he rushed from the house, in only his underclothes, plunged into the river, crossed it and made his way up into the mountains. Loska [Alexis Kalenin, the Eskimo-Russian trader at Tununak and friend of the Fathers] missed him; and, seeing his clothes thrown around in disorder, he was alarmed and instituted a search. He spent the day dragging the river with fish nets, then concluded that the tide had swept his body out to sea. The next day one of the sharp-eyed natives reported that he had seen some strange object on the side of the mountain. Loska used his field glasses and discovered it was the poor priest. A rescue party was immediately dispatched, but they had immense trouble bringing him back, for he fought like a wildcat. After his return, he would remain perfectly quiet and docile for a week or two, and then another outburst would occur. On these occasions, he would try to drown himself, or to inflict some other injury, so that Loska was obliged to put him under actual restraint. Finally, he became so bad that Loska brought him to his house and kept him in his own room. When at last the summer came, Loska brought him to Akulurak. During the journey, he had to be kept securely tied to prevent him from attempting to jump overboard.

Father Parodi recovered from his mental illness. He spent the year 1897–98 at Akulurak, the year 1898–99 at **Skagway**—where, according to Father Philibert **Turnell**, S.J., he "rendered valuable assistance"—and his last two years in Alaska, 1899–1901, at **Holy Cross Mission**. His major Alaskan Superior, Father Paschal **Tosi**, S.J., found him to be "too good-hearted."

After some time in the Northwest, Father Parodi went to Detroit, Michigan, in 1910, where, for years, he worked among the Italian people. He died in Detroit, on April 15, 1928, in his 83rd year.

Father Normand A. Pepin, S.J. *BR-898033.*

PEPIN, Father Normand A., S.J.

For over 50 years he thanked God daily for calling him to the Society of His Son, to the Society of Jesus. Routinely, on weekends, this Jesuit priest celebrated Mass for the public in three different languages. On weekdays, during the school year, he commuted daily between the **Fairbanks** House of Prayer and the Fairbanks Catholic schools. In the course of his many years as a Jesuit, he served the Lord and His people in his native New England, in the tropics of Brazil, and in the sub-Arctic regions of northern **Alaska**. He lived in or visited all 50 states of the Union. He was equally at home on cross-country skis, at the blackboard, and on the keyboard. His musical compositions were performed in Fairbanks and in Pittsburgh, Pennsylvania. Beginning in 1977, he called Alaska home.

Normand Amadee Pepin was born in Norwood, Massachusetts, on February 26, 1933. He spent all his boyhood in nearby Walpole, where he was baptized and raised in Blessed Sacrament parish. He attended grammar and junior high school in Walpole's public schools. His first contact with the Society of Jesus came in his high school days, when he attended Jesuit-staffed Boston College High School. Shortly after graduating from this in June 1950, he entered the Jesuit novitiate at Shadowbrook, Lenox, Massachusetts, on July 30, 1950. Two years later, on July 31, 1952, the Feast of St. Ignatius Loyola, he became a full-fledged member of the Society of Jesus, when he pronounced his vows of perpetual poverty, chastity and obedience.

Normand spent two more years at Shadowbrook, taking college level courses, mainly in the classics and humanities, before moving on to three years of philosophical studies at Weston College in Weston, Massachusetts. These completed, he taught at Holy Cross College in Worcester, Massachusetts, for a year, then for two at his alma mater, Boston College High. After his teaching years, he returned to Weston to make his theological studies. At the end of his third year there, he was ordained a priest, at Weston, on June 15, 1963. A fourth year of theology at Weston followed. During this, he began looking to overseas missions. He volunteered for Brazil, and was accepted. At Volta Redonda, the "Pittsburgh of Brazil," he made his tertianship. However, he soon discovered that he was unable to endure the tropical climate very well. He was recalled to Boston. He tried a second time to make a go of it in Brazil, but again he was forced to conclude that he would not be able to take the tropical climate. Endowed with a special gift for foreign languages, he was able, while in Brazil, to become quite fluent in Portuguese.

Father Pepin spent the next phase of his career, eight and a half years, at Cheverus High School, in Portland, Maine, where he taught mainly mathematics. He had, by this time, earned an M.A. degree in mathematics at a National Science Foundation Institute. At Cheverus, he was active also in intramural sports and as director of basketball, soccer, football, and street hockey programs. While at Cheverus, he was active, too, in the Model Cities program, in which he directed, both during the winter and the summer months, tutorial and recreational projects for inner-city boys.

Toward the end of his years at Cheverus, Father Pepin again felt himself strongly drawn to missionary work. This time he looked north. During part of the summer of 1976, he was in **Anchorage**, ministering at what was then still St. Paul Miki parish, and is now St. Elizabeth Ann Seton parish. In 1977, he returned to Alaska, to spend the year 1977–78 teaching mathematics and Religion at Monroe Catholic High School in Fairbanks. He next devoted four years, 1978–82, to teaching these same subjects to classes consisting mainly of Central Yup'ik Eskimo students attending St. Mary's Mission boarding school on the banks of the **Andreafsky**

River in western Alaska. When time allowed and conditions were right, he spent many pleasant hours cross-country skiing. His four years at St. Mary's he described, almost two decades later, as the "the happiest of my life." His stay at St. Mary's was followed by a one-year stay in a parish in Spring Hill, Florida, where his musical talents were in demand.

In 1983, Father Pepin returned to Fairbanks, where, for over two decades, he continued to serve in a variety of capacities, but mainly as a teacher and chaplain at the Catholic schools. As a teacher, he routinely taught courses on all levels, courses such as Religion, algebra, French, music and chorus. As chaplain, he offered Mass now in this classroom, now in that, now in the gymnasium. All that changed, to his great joy, on April 14, 2000, when the schools' Holy Family Chapel was formally opened and dedicated. Thereafter, he offered Mass in it almost daily for faculty and students. As chaplain, he also taught Bible studies, accompanied and directed students on annual retreats, and oversaw the annual Holy Week productions of the Living Stations of the Cross. Understandably, his many contributions to the schools over the long years were deeply appreciated by all connected with the schools. Nancy Cook, long-time Director of the Catholic Schools of Fairbanks, wrote, "I can't thank Father Pepin enough for his long-term dedication to our schools. Father is unique. The students, faculty and staff, as well as parents and families of our students are blessed to have him as such an integral part of our community."

For two and a half years, Father Pepin played the organ and directed the choir at Sacred Heart Cathedral, Fairbanks. For many years, in the House of Prayer, Fairbanks, he offered the Tridentine Mass almost every Sunday for a small, but very appreciative congregation. For many years, too, he ministered to the Hispanic community in the Fairbanks area, offering Sunday and feast-day Masses for them. The Portuguese he learned in Brazil, along with a number of summers he spent in Mexico, enabled him to become fluent in Spanish. Likewise for many years, he offered also a variety of adult education courses in Sacred Scripture and the Sacraments, as well as courses based on the New Catechism.

Given the fact that Father Pepin, throughout his

After the premier performance of his oratorio, "Obedient Unto Death," at the University of Alaska–Fairbanks on April 12, 1987, Father Normand A. Pepin, S.J., at the reception held in in the Great Hall, autographs programs. Dr. Suzanne Summerville, director of the performance, holding a bouquet of flowers, is standing behind him. *LR.*

Jesuit life, always had a multiplicity of official assignments and duties, one can only marvel that he found time enough to exercise so productively the very special talent God had bestowed on him, that of composer. During his theological studies, he already composed liturgical music and several organ pieces, which were published. While still at Cheverus, he began work on what he intended to be his life's major, crowning work as a composer, an oratorio on the Passion of Jesus. This, bearing the title "Obedient Unto Death," was first performed on April 12, 1987, by the Fairbanks Choral Society and members of the Fairbanks Symphony Orchestra. The oratorio has been described as "the sublime expression of one priest's love for Christ." Its composer admits to having been moved to tears, as he wrote certain parts of it. People hearing it have likewise been moved to tears.

"Obedient Unto Death" was subsequently performed also by the Pittsburgh Concert Chorale. The *Pittsburgh Post Gazette* referred to it as a "masterpiece." The work was recommended for a Pulitzer Prize in music. All this is the more remarkable, when one considers that Father Pepin never took a class

in composition. He learned composition by analyzing works of other composers. On March, 10, 2002, another of his compositions, "Hadassah," was performed by the Pittsburgh Concert Chorale. On November 23, 2002, in Fairbanks, "before a packed cathedral," his "Requiem" was performed. "What a beautiful piece of music!" said conductor Eduard Zilberkant to Father Pepin after the performance.

From all the foregoing, one can readily, and rightfully, conclude that Father Pepin, a golden jubilarian as a Jesuit as of the year 2000, led a full and rich life. Although he had all along found much consolation and satisfaction in his various ministries as a Jesuit and priest, he also needed to take regular breaks from so demanding a life. This he did religiously. During winter months he found relaxation in cross-country skiing—something he was able to do even while undergoing radiation treatment in Anchorage in the year 2001 for prostate cancer. Over the years, during snow-free months, he took many day-hikes in the rugged wilderness surrounding Fairbanks. His favorite summer vacations, however, consisted of drives of many hundreds of miles along the wilderness highways of northern Alaska and northern Canada. In August 1996, accompanied by Father Louis L. **Renner**, S.J., he drove the Dempster Highway all the way up to the Canadian Arctic coast. The trip was so arranged that the two never missed offering daily Mass. All of Father Pepin's travels were always planned in such a way that he never had to miss offering daily Mass.

No listing of Father Pepin's forms of relaxation would be complete without the mention of one of his favorite pastimes, that of solving crossword puzzles, at which he was a true, recognized whiz. He often created puzzles—not as mere diversionary devices, but as teaching tools—for his students to solve.

Of Father Pepin, Bishop Michael J. **Kaniecki**, S. J., said, "If you want something done, ask a busy man, ask, e.g., Father Pepin—a man of many, many talents!"

As of the year 2004, Father Pepin was still serving as chaplain to Fairbanks' Catholic schools and as director of the House of Prayer.

PERREAULT, Deacon Paul V.

After serving in Vietnam, he, as a chief warrant officer in the U.S. Army, flew CH-54 Sky Crane helicopters in Germany. As a Professional Engineer, he designed and saw to the building of numerous new churches in the villages of northern **Alaska**. As an ordained deacon, he had—as of the year 2004—for nearly 20 years, assisted and preached at Masses, first in Sacred Heart Cathedral, **Fairbanks**, then, in subsequent years, at St. Mark's University Parish at the University of Alaska–Fairbanks, and at St. Theresa's parish in **Nenana**.

Paul V. Perreault was born on February 10, 1947, in Providence, Rhode Island, to Clarence Paul Perreault and Lillie Mae Massotti. From 1952–54, he attended Tyler Catholic School in Providence. In 1954, the family moved to El Cajon, California, where he finished grade school and the first year of high school. For the following two years of high school, he attended St. Augustine Catholic High School in San Diego. In 1964, he graduated from Ballard High School in Seattle. He then attended the University of Washington, in Seattle, for three years, studying Aerospace Engineering. In 1968, he joined the U.S. Army. On March 16, 1968, he married Mary Beth Teuful. In 1969, he entered flight school, where he learned to fly CH-54 Sky Crane helicopters. At first, he flew these in Vietnam, then in Germany.

While Paul was stationed in Germany, what seemed like an Old Testament type of vision and calling came to Mary Beth and him. In October 1973, after a prayer meeting in Wiesbaden, Mary Beth had the vision and heard the calling. The message was: "When you get done with your tour of duty in Germany, get out of the service, go to Seattle, and from there go wherever the Holy Spirit leads you!" Soon the message was also confirmed with Paul.

At this time, Paul was a chief warrant officer. He loved what he was doing; and he was almost six years into what promised to be a highly satisfying 20 to 30 year career. However, his military career was about to end. In his own words: "We discerned the call as carefully as we knew how—checking with each other—checking with our pastor. In peace with the decision to get out of the Army and follow

Deacon Paul V. Perreault, P.E., at the controls of the Cessna 172, which he flew for the Diocese of Fairbanks. *Photo by Fr. Sean Thomson.*

the call, I applied for discharge. Six months of paper work was completed in one month."

On December 3, 1973, Paul and Mary Beth left Germany for Fort Dix, the discharge point. Where was the Holy Spirit leading them? While attending a Mission Sunday Mass the previous October, they had heard the priest in his homily touch on the widespread mission fields extending from "the far reaches of Africa to the Eskimos of Alaska." When they heard "Alaska," Paul and Mary Beth looked at each other and knew that they were being led north and west, to Alaska, to serve the people there.

In July 1974, in a small camper van, with a three-months supply of food, a small tool box, and a Saint Bernard dog, they headed north to the future. They arrived in Fairbanks on August 3, 1974. Fairbanks was the destination of their choice, because they had the names of two people to contact there: D.A. [*sic*] McGilvary and Ruth Regan. Their names had been listed in a charismatic prayer group directory the Perreaults had chanced upon while still in Germany. The four were to become lasting mutual friends.

It was Paul's belief that one should commit oneself to what one does well. In his case, it was construction work. After completing a carpenter apprenticeship program, in August 1981, he continued to work for a total of 15 years as a carpenter. Seeing

Church ministry work as an integral part of what he was, he began serving as a maintenance worker at Sacred Heart Cathedral, Fairbanks; then, also as a lector, and soon thereafter also as a Eucharistic Minister.

In the fall of 1982, Paul began to take part in a newly formed deacon training program in Fairbanks. During the next several years, he gradually became convinced that he was indeed called to be a permanent deacon. In Sacred Heart Cathedral, on July 20, 1986, he was ordained to the permanent diaconate by Michael J. **Kaniecki**, S.J., Bishop of Fairbanks at the time. Until 1999, he served at Sacred Heart Cathedral parish as a deacon. He then began to serve in the same capacity at St. Mark's University Parish at the University of Alaska–Fairbanks.

Meanwhile, having yearned all along to complete his studies for a civil engineering degree, Deacon Paul, in 1983—sixteen years after leaving the University of Washington—resumed his studies for the degree, at the University of Alaska–Fairbanks. In the course of those studies, he was admitted to two engineering honor societies. In June 1987, he graduated with his degree, and was recognized as the outstanding civil engineering student. In January 1993, he earned a Professional Engineering registration; and, by the end of that same year, he completed his Master of Science degree in Civil Engineering, specializing in structural and arctic engineering. He was now Deacon Paul V. Perreault, M.S.C.E., P.E., employed full time, working for private contractors, the City of Fairbanks, and for a private consultant. As such, he was gaining valuable hands-on experience in the many-faceted field of engineering. In 2003, he was accepted by the University of Alaska–Fairbanks as a doctoral candidate. The study of arctic foundations was to be his specialty.

Then, it was a case of "Opportunity knocks!"—in the words of Deacon Paul. Up to this time in his life, he had been following two separate trails at the same time: one as a deacon, the other as an engineer. But now, a kindly Providence so disposed matters that the two trails merged into one. The Catholic Diocese of Northern Alaska had design needs. Some of its engineering projects came to the private consulting firm for which Deacon Paul was working at the time. He recognized that, being both a deacon and a professional engineer, he could do the work directly for the Church at substantial cost savings. He developed a proposed job description. This proved to be mutually acceptable. On July 1, 1994, he began working part-time as Diocesan Engineer for the Diocese of Fairbanks. The position soon developed into full-time.

Deacon Paul's first task: design a prototype church and build it in three villages. On December 10, 1995, the new St. Charles Spinola Church at **Pilot Station** was dedicated. This was the first of a series of village churches he designed and saw built under his direction. Churches at **Marshall**, **Russian Mission**, and **Stebbins** followed. As of late in the year 2004, churches at **St. Michael** and **Ruby** were nearing completion. A new church at **Scammon Bay** was slated to be next.

On April 14, 2000, the Holy Family Chapel at the Catholic schools complex, Fairbanks, was dedicated. Other significant improvements at the schools were made, while the chapel was being constructed. Deacon Paul, as project manager, played a major role in this monumental construction project. His was the responsibility to see to it that construction proceeded on schedule and under budget. The $5 million project was completed on time and under budget.

In addition to designing and seeing to the construction of new churches, Deacon Paul systematically traveled to the far corners of the diocese, visiting about six villages a year, to inspect the condition of its churches and buildings from foundation to roof, and to make sure that they were properly maintained and that safety standards were met.

Making the rounds to the villages on those "risk management" inspection trips entailed for Deacon Paul a considerable amount of travel by air. Flying to "bush" Alaska commercially is complicated, time-consuming, and very expensive. While still a helicopter pilot in Germany, he had already worked toward getting his fixed-wing pilot's license. By the summer of 1995, after a little more training in Fairbanks, he had it.

For several years, Deacon Paul had the use of borrowed planes, but there were serious drawbacks to having to rely on someone else's plane. In 1998, with a generous grant from the Catholic Church

Extension Society, the Diocese of Fairbanks was able to buy and put at his disposal a Cessna 172. In August of that year, he was scheduled to visit and do risk management inspection at a number of villages along the Bering Sea coast. The diocesan treasurer was to have gone with him to do audits of the parish books at those villages; but, being unable to do so, asked Mary Beth, a Certified Public Accountant, to go in his stead. The deacon and wife team on the wing had themselves a wonderful trip, and returned safely to Fairbanks with their dual mission well accomplished. As of the year 2004, Deacon Paul considered himself singularly blessed in having the wife that he had in Mary Beth. Both of the couple's children were adopted boys.

At the end of an autobiographical sketch requested of him by Father Louis L. **Renner**, S.J., Paul V. Perreault, permanent deacon and professional engineer, wrote:

> Pause a moment. Reflect with me. Share the joy. Here I am, a carpenter. And an engineer. And a pilot. And a deacon. Designing mission churches. Flying to and building those churches side by side with the Native people of Alaska. The moment comes. At the door, the keys and the building plans have been passed from the construction team to Bishop. The walls have been blessed. Now, Bishop is consecrating the altar. The chrism is poured. Watch on with me as I stand vested as a deacon, serving at Bishop's side. See the joy in the faces of the people gathered in this new place of worship. Feel the tears well up, as you know the completion of being fully alive in God's service.

81, 82

PERRON, Father Joseph, S.J.

Joseph Perron was born in Chatillion d'Aoste, at the foot of the Alps, at the east side of Mont Blanc, on July 25, 1864. After his elementary schooling, he was tutored for some years by two different priests. By his own admission, as a young man he "developed a strong tendency to irritability and anger." Nevertheless, he aspired to be a priest. He studied in a diocesan seminary for four years, before he entered the novitiate of the Turin Province of the Society of Jesus at Chieri, Italy, on June 2, 1886.

On November 28, 1886, Archbishop Charles J. **Seghers** was shot to death near **Nulato, Alaska**. When, some time after the event, Joseph Perron

Father Joseph Perron, S.J. *LRC.*

heard about it, he considered himself called to serve on the Alaska Mission. After completing his two-year noviceship and two years of classical and humanities studies, he studied philosophy for two years, then taught in the College of St. Thomas in Cuneo, Italy, for a year. From 1893–97, he studied theology at Chieri. He was ordained a priest on July 30, 1896. After a fourth year of theology, Father Perron, in company of Father John L. **Lucchesi**, S.J., sailed for New York in the autumn of 1897. During the year 1897–98, he made his tertianship at Frederick, Maryland.

Early in June 1898, Father Perron, along with Fathers Julius **Jetté**, S.J., and John B. **René**, S.J., sailed from San Francisco for **St. Michael**, where they arrived on June 24th. There they were met by Father Francis A. **Barnum**, S.J., who, about to leave Alaska for good, gave Father Perron his Mass kit. This served Father Perron very well throughout his 22 years of missionary life in Alaska.

Father Perron spent the summer of 1898 at **Holy Cross Mission** as substitute prefect of the boys. At the beginning of October, he was sent to Nulato, where he was to spend the years 1898–1900. His first concern at Nulato was the learning of the local language, Koyukon Athabaskan. For his tutor, he had a blind and epileptic boy who did not speak English. He found "the first year's experiences in Nulato were rather trying." During his second year there, he was able to teach the children catechism in the Native language. By the end of his second year at Nulato, he could claim that he had "mastered the principal difficulties of the Nulato language."

For the years 1900–13, Father Perron was assigned to Holy Cross. He spent part of the summer of 1900 at St. Michael. There, and later that year, in and around Holy Cross, he attended to the many victims of the "Great Sickness" that struck the lower Yukon River region. He cared for the sick to the extent he was able, and with his own hands made coffins, dug graves, and buried the dead.

Father Perron's principal assignment at Holy Cross was to evangelize the people in the Holy Cross area. Recognizing that Koyukon was not intelligible enough to the local people, he began immediately to apply himself to the learning of the local language, in this case Ingalik. For his teacher he had a shaman, to whom he gave a loaf of bread for every lesson taught. "In about six months," he recalled in later years, "I got a pretty fair knowledge of the new dialect." He left various manuscripts in the Ingalik language.

Father Perron found the people in the Holy Cross area, especially those still living in the village of Koserefsky on the other side of the Yukon, "a hard lot to Christianize." It was principally the shamans that persisted in obstructing his missionary efforts. In turn, he was unrelenting in his struggle to weaken their influence on the people. In addition to attending to the Holy Cross Natives, he visited also the villages of Anvik and **Shageluk**.

In 1906, Father Perron saw to the building of the new Holy Cross Church and a new Sisters/Girls House and, in 1911, to the building of the new Fathers/Brothers House.

Since 1899, the post office at Holy Cross had been under the name of "Koserefsky." Father Perron, as postmaster at Holy Cross in 1910, protested to the U.S. Postal Department, and argued that the post office at Holy Cross should be under the name of "Holy Cross." After his repeated requests for a change of name, and after he produced a petition with many signatures requesting a change of name, the name was changed to "Holy Cross" in 1912.

From 1907–09, Father Perron was Vice-Superior of all Jesuits in northern Alaska, though he himself did not consider himself a man suitable to be a Superior of any kind. He recognized that he was

rather self-assertive, rather brusque, when it came to dealing with people. From Holy Cross, on August 26, 1914, Father Philip I. **Delon**, S.J. General Superior of Jesuits in Alaska at the time, wrote to the Father Provincial in Portland, Oregon, Richard Gleeson: "Father Perron—a man than whom I have known none more hated by whites, Indians, and, sorry to say, by many of Ours, Brothers especially. A man of great parts, of course, and virtue—but, for all that, hard-headed, stiff-necked and domineering, a 'king' the whites call him." Yet, in spite of, or perhaps because of, such a temperament, a solemn document honoring him after he had left Holy Cross, proclaimed: "Father Perron deserves the credit of converting the majority of the Natives in the vicinity of Holy Cross."

Late in the winter of 1912–13, Father Perron "suffered quite a good deal from bronchitis." He was, therefore, sent out of Alaska, for two years, to recover. He spent the first of these at St. Ignatius College, in San Francisco, serving there as "Spiritual Father." He also visited parishes and hospitals, gave retreats, and was "Father Confessor" to Sisters in convents. He spent the year 1914–15 at Pendleton, Oregon.

In August 1915, Father Perron returned to Alaska. At first, he was assigned to **Nome**, "to take care of the whites." However, he soon found himself responsible also for the Inupiat Eskimos in Nome. He set about learning their language, but this proved too much for him. On October 8th, he left for St. Michael, on his way to Holy Cross. By this time, however, the Yukon was running ice. He had to wait at St. Michael till travel by dogsled was possible. On New Year's Day 1916, he found himself at **Russian Mission**, brought there by volunteer dog drivers. Later that month, another volunteer driver brought him to Holy Cross. After two months there, he went on to Nulato.

At Nulato, a new church had just been built. Father Perron, with the help of Brother Bartholomew **Keogh**, S.J., undertook to decorate the inside. He himself built the altars. In the Fathers/Brothers House, he fixed up a small chapel for weekday Masses. During this, his second stay at Nulato, he found the Nulato people "very independent and difficult to manage." Twice he called off the Midnight Christmas Mass because they were engaging in "superstitious" practices.

In the summer of 1919, after an absence of six years, Father Perron was again at Holy Cross, for the year 1919–20. Here he found himself quite at home. He advocated mission complexes such as that at Holy Cross: a mission boarding school, a mission church, with land around them owned by the mission, so that the mission had control over who was allowed to settle on that land and to become part of the village growing up around the mission.

Father Perron spent the years 1920–22 downriver, at **Pilot Station**. Then, after spending some of the spring and summer months of the year 1922 at Holy Cross, he left the Alaska mission field for good. For a short time, he worked in Pendleton, Oregon, and in Missoula, Montana, before going south to California, where he spent the rest of his days. The last years of his long, fruitful, priestly life were spent at Sacred Heart Novitiate at Los Gatos, California. There he died, on March 3, 1956, at age 92.

St. Catherine of Siena Church, Petersburg. *DJA.*

PETERSBURG

Petersburg is located on the northern end of Mitkof Island, at the northern entrance to Wrangell Narrows, 32 miles northwest of **Wrangell**. It is inhabited largely by Scandinavians—hence its nickname, the "Little Norway" of **Alaska**—whose chief occupations have over the years been fishing, canning, lumbering, and fur farming. The town grew up around a salmon cannery and a sawmill built between 1897–99 by Peter Buschmann, after whom it is named. The Petersburg post office was established in 1900. In 1950, Petersburg had a population of 1,323; in 1967, 1,592; and in the year 2000, an increase to 3,224.

The Petersburg parish is dedicated under the title of St. Catherine of Siena. For the most part, that parish has never had a resident pastor. During the early days, it was visited by priests stationed in **Ketchikan**. Father William A. **Shepherd**, S.J., in Ketchikan, 1912–13, and 1919–20, visited it "a few times on his way to and from **Juneau**." Father Paul Kern, S.J., in Ketchikan, 1914–19, had services there "once a month." During one of his visits, he noted in his diary the number of Catholics: 29 men, 11 women, and six children. Father Francis M. **Monroe**, S.J., who made Wrangell his headquarters from 1924–39, visited the new Petersburg mission on a more or less regular basis. The room he had in the Mitkof Hotel was his "office," and out of it he taught catechism classes. Sometime before 1939, he built an "Extension Society" church on the corner of 4th and "D" Streets in downtown Petersburg. In 1941, Father Patrick J. **O'Reilly**, S.J., who thought highly of the Petersburg Catholic community, conducted a mission there.

From 1942–59, Father Matthew E. **Hoch** visited Petersburg out of Wrangell at least once a month. Father Raymond W. **Mosey** did likewise, from 1959–63. For roughly the next decade, it continued to be visited by priests stationed in Wrangell. Father Peter C. **Gorges**, stationed in Wrangell at the time, had the pastoral care of the Petersburg mission during the years 1969–72. "I was in Petersburg weekly," he wrote, "from Sunday afternoon until Monday night." From 1972–74, Father James J. **Manske** visited Petersburg out of Wrangell. Father Kevin O'Conor [*sic*], O.M.I., resided in Petersburg during the years 1974–76, as did Msgr. Charles A. **Kekumano** from 1976–81. In 1981, Father Gorges again had the Wrangell–Petersburg assignment. "On my second time around, 1981–85," he wrote, "Petersburg was a parish. I was two weeks in one place and two weeks in the other. That's why I had time to really become part of the Petersburg community also."

After Father Gorges, Fathers Michael Hayden and Cornelius Scanlon each spent a year in Petersburg. Father Michael Nash was responsible for Petersburg from 1988–96. For the following year, Father Gary R. Norman, O.M.I. was assigned there. Father Patrick J. **Travers** tended the Petersburg flock during the years 1997–99. He was followed by Father Michael G. Schwarte, still pastor of the Petersburg parish as of the year 2004.

PETERSON, Father Charles J., S.J.

Charles Jon "Chuck" Peterson was born the younger of two boys to Gustave F. Peterson, Jr., and Margaret Leppert Peterson in Missoula, Montana, on November 26, 1938. There he attended St. Francis Xavier Grade School and Loyola High School, graduating as salutatorian from the latter in 1956. "Drawn to the Jesuit vocation by the example of all the Jesuits staffing the St. Francis Xavier parish–school complex, and attracted to the priesthood by his many years of serving Mass as an acolyte," in his words, he entered the Jesuit novitiate at Sheridan, Oregon, on August 15, 1956. Two years later, having "enjoyed the two years of novitiate formation," he took the simple vows constituting him a Jesuit. He spent two additional years at Sheridan studying the classics and humanities. He did so well in Latin and Greek that he was asked to specialize in those two languages.

In June 1960, Chuck went to West Baden, Indiana, for three years of philosophical studies. By his own admission, he was "a mediocre philosopher, passed everything, but excelled in nothing." Meanwhile, he worked toward a degree in the Classics at Loyola University, Chicago.

Near the end of his elementary schooling, Chuck attended a lecture and saw films about **Alaska** presented by Father Bernard R. **Hubbard**, S.J. This aroused in him a desire to serve one day as a flying missionary priest in Alaska, a desire that never left him. Throughout his high school years, he was fascinated by airplanes and flying. He built and flew many model airplanes. In 1955, he joined the Civil Air Patrol Cadet Corps and won a flight scholarship. However, his hopes of one day being a flying missionary in Alaska came to an abrupt end. When he was about to solo, his ophthalmologist denied

At Woolley Lagoon, some 50 miles northwest of Nome, Father Charles J. Peterson, S.J., has just offered Mass for King Islanders and Little Sisters of Jesus. In the words of his King Island altar boy: "We were having Mass on the beach because the priest did a holy water blessing of the boats, so we would be safe." *Photo by John Zierten, and courtesy of* EXTENSION *Magazine.*

him medical clearance for a general pilot's license. Chuck's eyesight was not adequate enough. Though now resigned not to be doing his own flying in Alaska, his desire to serve as a priest in Alaska never diminished.

It was a happy Chuck Peterson who found himself at **Copper Valley School** during the summer of 1963 ready to begin a two-year stint there as a teacher of Latin, English, and Religion, as well as to serve as prefect of the younger boys and moderator of the Civil Air Patrol Cadet Corps. Recalling his CVS days years later, he remembered as highlights the March 27, 1964, earthquake; his tour around Alaska in the early summer of 1964; and the ordination of Father George T. **Boileau**, S.J., to the rank of bishop on July 31st of that memorable year.

After spending the summer of 1965 at the University of San Francisco completing course work for his Master's degree in the Classics, Chuck went on to teach Latin and Greek at Gonzaga Preparatory in Spokane, Washington, for a year. During that year, he was occupied also as line coach of the junior varsity football team, and coach of the speech and debate teams. After the workload he had had at CVS, he found that "G-Prep was a cakewalk."

In August 1966, Chuck arrived in Toronto, Ontario, Canada, to begin four years of theological studies at Regis College. His favorite studies at Regis were Scripture, Sacramental Theology, and an historical overview of theology. Canon Law and Moral Theology were of lesser interest to him. On June 1, 1969, in St. Anthony's Church in his native city of Missoula he was ordained a priest. A week later, he celebrated his first Solemn High Mass in the church of his childhood, St. Francis Xavier's.

His theological studies completed, Father Peterson was, initially, intended by his Superiors to spend the year 1970–71 teaching at Monroe Catholic High School in **Fairbanks**. However, upon the urging of Father John J. Morris, S.J., the first priest to push seriously, in the late 1960s, for an Alaska Native permanent diaconate program, he was assigned, instead, to **Bethel**, to help further such a program. Though serving as co-pastor of the Bethel parish and of its two dependent missions, **Marshall** and **Russian Mission**, through an all-out effort, Father Peterson was, nevertheless, able to make of the incipient permanent diaconate program a full-fledged reality. While the "push" to inaugurate such a program came from Father Morris originally, it was Father Peterson who brought that "total dedication," in the words of Father Morris, to the program that, in short order, developed into the **Eskimo Deacon Program**. On February 8, 1975, he was present in Marshall to concelebrate at the Mass at which Alvin F. Owletuk of Marshall was ordained to the permanent diaconate. This was the first of many ordinations of a Central Yup'ik Eskimo to the permanent diaconate.

Father Peterson made his tertianship in India during the year 1973–74. During his return trip, while stopping off in Rome, he heard rumors that he might be asked to start a program for the training of Alaska Natives for the priesthood. Upon his arrival in Fairbanks, in August 1974, he learned that that was, indeed, his next assignment. For two years, while serving as Vocation Director for the

Diocese of Fairbanks and as chaplain to Catholic students at the University of Alaska–Fairbanks, he held training workshops for Yup'ik Eskimo deacon candidates, doing most of the teaching himself. In Yup'ik villages, he conducted weekend retreats for young adults to awaken the communities to the need for indigenous ministry in general and for indigenous priestly ministry in particular.

In the fall of 1976, Francis J. **Fallert**, S.J., General Superior of Jesuits in Alaska, ordered Father Peterson to have a seminary for candidates for the priesthood "up and running" by the following year. From October 1976 to April 1977, Father Peterson spent time at Gonzaga University in Spokane, Washington, and at the Jesuit School of Theology at Berkeley, California, seeking advice and help to staff the seminary in question. No staff help was forthcoming. In May, he returned to Fairbanks, where Father Fallert had two Central Yup'ik Eskimo candidates waiting to begin seminary training for the priesthood. A third entered the seminary later, but, by then, the first two had left. The seminary venture, while up, did not run for long. It ended in late 1978. The candidates found life away from their Native environment just too difficult.

From January 1978 to June 1979, Father Peterson, unexpectedly, found himself pastor of **Hooper Bay** and **Scammon Bay**. During that year, he came to see yet more clearly that, in his words, "Native ministry training must take place in the social context of the candidates and of the people whom they serve." The validity of this observation was, at the very time, being concretely underscored by the very successful Eskimo Deacon Program.

From August 1979 through May 1980, Father Peterson again conducted retreats for young adults in villages in the Yukon-Kuskokwim Delta.

On May 19, 1980, Father Peterson's father died suddenly. His mother had died on December 10, 1977. He took time off; went to Portland, Oregon, to work through some grieving and to deal with a serious high blood pressure problem. While in Portland, he developed a program of workshops to be held in several villages for the purpose of helping Alaska Natives to deepen their theological and ministerial skills. When he was back in Alaska, along with continuing to give retreats for young adults, he conducted a series of theological and spirituality workshops during the years 1981–83. All this he did under the title of "Director of the Center of Theology and Spirituality," a named derived from the "seminary experiment." As director of CTS he was headquartered in Fairbanks. He then spent a sabbatical year, 1983–84, at Regis College, where he had made his theology, to "gain more skills in the enculturation directions of the program." His sabbatical ended with a pilgrimage trip to the Holy Land and Spain.

Upon his return to Alaska, Father Peterson found his world "turned upside down." By this time, owing to the settlement in 1976 of the Molly Hootch case which mandated high schools in even relatively small Alaskan villages, high schools had sprung up all over northwestern Alaska, with the result that St. Mary's Mission Boarding School on the **Andreafsky** River was no longer getting the kind of well qualified applicants, nor in sufficient numbers, that had helped to make it such an academic success up to the early 1980s. A student body of diminishing numbers composed of less carefully screened applicants plagued the school with serious social problems, including drugs and suicide. "The viability of St. Mary's was being sorely tested," in the words of Father Peterson. Michael J. **Kaniecki**, S.J., Bishop of Fairbanks as of July 28, 1985, put pressure on Father James A. **Sebesta**, S.J., General Superior of Jesuits in Alaska, to "save the school or close it." Father Peterson was assigned that awesome responsibility. Concerning it, he wrote, "From years of ministry training work to a job as a high school administrator was a big leap into the unknown for me." However, he accepted the challenge.

In 1985, Father Peterson became administrator of St. Mary's. During his first year in that position, along with having on hand a student body far from ideal, he had to contend also with a mutinous group of **Jesuit Volunteer Corps** members, who went so far as to seek his dismissal from the school. However, he survived that first year, and saw to it that this group was replaced with a well prepared new group. From the outset of his tenure at St. Mary's, in addition to running the school, he also conducted an extensive survey of former students and graduates—interviewing, by actual count, 613—to determine whether or not the school could and

should stay open. On the basis of Father Peterson's findings, Bishop Kaniecki determined that the school should be closed. The May 1987 graduation was St. Mary's last. By his own admission, the years 1985–1987 were, as of December 2003, "the toughest apostolic years" of Father Peterson's life.

From August 1987 to August 1989, again unexpectedly, Father Peterson found himself pastor of St. Joseph's parish in **Nome**. As such, he had the care also of its dependent stations: **Little Diomede** Island, **Teller**, and **Unalakleet**. The formation of Native deacons and the training of Native lay ministers that had, all along, been his primary apostolic interests, were now—but only for a time—in other hands.

Father Peterson, in his words, "loved the people and the work" in Nome and at its dependent stations. However, being "a man who could never say 'no,'" the pressures became too great for him. In addition, during his two Nome years, a number of conflicts between him and Bishop Kaniecki surfaced that brought Father Peterson to the point of needing and seeking therapy. From August 1989 to August 1990, while living at Seattle University, he successfully completed a program offered by "Therapy and Renewal Associates."

In August 1990, a renewed Father Peterson was mandated by Bishop Kaniecki to start the Native Ministry Training Program at St. Mary's Mission. He was "delighted" to help again to train Native lay ministers. He headed the program until 1997.

During those seven years, too, in keeping with the wishes of Bishop Kaniecki, Father Peterson started and produced a radio program called "The Lord Be With You!" The program was designed to give spiritual and scriptural inspiration to Native deacons and lay ministers throughout the Yukon-Kuskokwim Delta and to help them with the preparation of their homilies and instructions. The program first went on the air on October 15, 1990. Over the years, and as of the year 2004, it was broadcast four times a week over **KNOM**, the Catholic radio station in Nome. During Father Peterson's seven years with the program, over 700 shows were produced and aired. After he left Alaska, in 1997, first Mr. Patrick C.W. **Tam**, then Father Paul M. **Cochran**, S.J., continued to produce the program.

The years 1990–97 were good years for Father

Peterson. He was happy to be doing the apostolic work of his preference, work that he had undertaken when he first went to Alaska as a young priest in 1970. With the year 1997, his years of fruitful ministry in Alaska came to an end. On August 15th of that year, as Director of the Rocky Mountain Mission, he began to serve the Indian people of the Pacific Northwest. During his first six years in that position, he made Omak, Washington, his headquarters. In December 2003, while still retaining the directorship of the Rocky Mountain Mission, he moved into the Jesuit House Residence at Gonzaga University.

Looking back on his almost 50 years as a Jesuit, Father Peterson reflected:

> The ministries and apostolic missions I felt called to were not necessarily the ones I was assigned to. The Latin and Greek studies I was assigned to, were the last I felt called to. My assignment to teach at Gonzaga Prep was a total surprise. My assignment to start a seminary in Alaska seemed an impossible one to me. My being assigned as pastor to Hooper Bay and Scammon Bay puzzled me. My assignment to administer St. Mary's High School was a bolt out of the blue. My being appointed pastor of Nome was a surprise. Yet, in all those assignments, I found a spiritual energy that complemented the assignments. In the final analysis, they were all in tune with my own aspirations. I had a chance to put into practice the obedience I had vowed all those years.

PILGRIM HOT SPRINGS

The place now commonly known as "Pilgrim Hot Springs"—because of its location on the left bank of the Pilgrim River and the mineral hot springs that well up at the site—became a popular resort and ranch soon after gold was discovered in the **Nome** area around 1900. The Eskimo name for the Pilgrim River is "*Kruzgamepa*," hence, during earlier years, the place was known also as "Kruzgamepa Hot Springs." The property lies some 60 road-miles north of Nome.

Around 1916, Father Bellarmine **Lafortune**, S.J., who had charge of the Seward Peninsula Eskimos at the time, considered **Marys Igloo** to be no longer a suitable center for large-scale missionary activity, including an orphanage. On October 13, 1917, James F. Halpin, representing the Halpin family,

who had bought the "Hot Springs" property with the intention of giving it to the Church, deeded it to Father Lafortune as a gift.

On April 22, 1918, Father Lafortune moved to the Hot Springs ranch to turn it into a mission center and orphanage. During the next several years, much of what was at the Marys Igloo mission was gradually moved to the new mission, including lumber from taken-down buildings—and the name itself of that mission. Pilgrim Hot Springs became the new Our Lady of Lourdes Mission.

The development of the new mission was given particular impetus by the severe influenza epidemic that struck the Seward Peninsula in late 1918. In the Pilgrim Springs house diary, Father Lafortune wrote: "The natives were simply mowed down." The epidemic left many orphans behind. Steadily they were moved from Nome to the new mission–orphanage. On August 15, 1919, Brother John F. **Hansen**, S.J., arrived to join Father **Hubert A. Post**, S.J., who had been at the mission for some time already. Five **Ursuline** Sisters arrived the following day. In October of that year, Brother Peter P. **Wilhalm**, S.J., came to complete the mission staff.

For two decades, the Pilgrim Springs mission flourished, both as a mission center and as a boarding school–orphanage. Its farm and gardens helped to make the mission, in large part, self-supporting. In 1923, it was the scene of bitter-sweet sorrow. On December 15th, Father Frederick A. **Ruppert**, S.J., in his solo attempt to bring a crate of California oranges to the orphans for Christmas, froze to death about four miles up from the mission on the banks of the Pilgrim River. He lies buried at the mission—as do Sister Irene Arvin, O.S.U., who died there on July 25, 1934; Brother Hansen, who died in Nome on January 29, 1938; and Father Edward J. **Cunningham**, S.J., who died at the Springs on January 23, 1941.

On September 29, 1930, a footnote to aviation history was written, when the *Marquette Missionary*—with pilot Brother George J. **Feltes**, S.J., co-pilot Ralph Wien, and Alaska Mission Superior, Father Philip I. **Delon**, S.J., on board—landed at the Hot Springs. This was the first time an airplane landed there. The party had left Nome for **Kotzebue**, with the plan that, if the weather north of the Springs should prove to be unfavorable for flying

(*top*) Our Lady of Lourdes Chapel, Pilgrim Hot Springs. *MK.*

(*bottom*) At the Pilgrim Hot Springs Mission, June 1922,
Ursuline Sisters Mary of the Blessed Sacrament, Theresa,
Rose, and Thecla pose with children, most of them orphans.
JOPA-177.01.

(*opposite*) The Pilgrim Hot Springs Mission with the
Kigluaik Mountains in the background, June 30, 1984. *LR.*

on, they would land at the Springs and attend to business there. Such turned out to be the case.

By 1941, the Pilgrim Springs buildings were in poor repair, firewood in the area had become scarce, and, most important, there were no longer enough orphans to justify the considerable expense of keeping the mission open. In 1935, there were 60 children at the mission, but most of them were non-orphans. On July 31, 1941, Father Edmund A. **Anable**, S.J., who followed Father Cunningham as Superior of the mission, closed it.

In addition to the Jesuit priests and Brothers mentioned above, the following Jesuits also served at the Hot Springs mission: Fathers Peter L. **Baltussen**, John A. **Concannon**, John L. **Lucchesi**, Gabriel M. Ménager, and Aloysius G. **Willebrand**, and Brother Carl F. **Wickart**. Nineteen different Ursuline Sisters, too, served at the Springs.

Though the mission was now closed, the property and the buildings on it continued to belong to the Vicariate of Alaska, then to the Diocese of Fairbanks, after this was established in 1962. At various times and under certain conditions, they were leased out for a number of different purposes. From 1942–45, the U.S. Army housed troops there and built an airstrip. During the 1950s and 60s, several entrepreneurs attempted farming there. In 1969, Pilgrim Springs Ltd. signed a renewable 99-year

lease on the property. In the summer of 1980, scientists from the University of Alaska–**Fairbanks'** Geophysical Institute conducted exploratory studies there to determine if it would be possible to harness geothermal energy from the mineral hot springs. In 1998, Louis Green, Sr., was serving as caretaker of the Springs and gardening there.

On July 30, 2000, Father John A. **Hinsvark**, pastor of St. Joseph's parish, Nome, celebrated a Jubilee 2000 Mass in Our Lady of Lourdes chapel for a group of around 130 people on pilgrimage from the Nome area.

For many years, the Pilgrim Hot Springs mission—described by Father Segundo **Llorente**, S.J., as "an oasis in the heart of the unfriendly Arctic"—has been listed with the National Register of Historic Places.

A chronological sequence of discontinuous entries made by various hands from September 14, 1918, to July 29, 1941, in the house diary kept at the Pilgrim Hot Springs mission weaves the following rich and colorful tapestry of day-to-day life at that mission:

～

We begin the foundation of the barn . . . found wild rice and make our mind to gather lots of it . . . strange how God's Providence twists our plans . . . one of our canines made a dash for the goats. He succeeded to break his collar and was on the point of executing his voracious design, when he was apprehended, given a good lambasting and decorated with 2 collars and 2 chains . . . We chop wood, carry water and hay . . . the choir consists of a few orphans and survivors. May the Child Jesus bless them . . . I milk the cows, a work I had not done for at least 28 years . . . The thermometer is still going down,—68 . . . Our cow, Victoria, dies. God's will be done! . . . May 7, 1919: The birds such as ducks and geese and robins arrived in numbers . . . Aug. 4: Early this morning Messrs Bailey and Ibbetson returned from **Teller** with 12 children. The children are orphans for our care. Almost all were drenched to the skin, but all looked happy . . . the dog Mink broke his chain and jumped Tango . . . The Billy goat died during the night . . . Brother Hansen was hunting and brought home 3 ptarmigans . . . Mary Mosquito made her first Holy Communion this morning . . . Fr. Lafortune and Bro. Hansen went to their fish trap and returned with about 25 lbs. of fish . . . This morning Bro. Hansen and the Sisters renewed their vows . . . Jan. 14, 1920: David Kakarook and Annie Maloney were married . . . Baby Angela died very early this morning and was buried in the afternoon . . . This morning a regular blizzard began and kept up all day. This evening our new building blew over and lies there a sore-looking wreck . . . the children enter very early into the spirit of Holy Week. Some cried during the devotions, saying afterwards that they felt sorry for Jesus . . . Fr. Lafortune left this morning for Noxapaga camps to give the reindeer herders a chance for Easter duty . . . This evening Sr. Berchmans and some children went out to pick salmon berries. They came back with a goodly picking . . . Fr. Ruppert, when found, was all wet and pretty well tired out . . . We hope the Little Flower will help us in getting our electric lights in running order . . . Fr. Lafortune preparing to tan a few skins . . . There was a great and beautiful display of northern lights last night . . . the mule Dan is limping on one foot . . . some of the little girls were troubled with loose teeth, so Fr. Post had to pull them . . . the mosquitoes are fierce . . . This evening Fr. Ruppert arrived in a desolate condition, wet from foot to head and carrying his shoes in his hands . . . The carpenters are building new toilets for the children . . . This morning at 7:15 we felt an earth-tremor . . . Mary of Igloo fame came for a visit . . . The children said the Beads in Eskimo to show how they are trained in their own language . . . Fr. Post began taking photos of the children and Sisters . . . The little girls went to pick willow leaves . . . the bathhouse caught fire . . . A storm blew down the little bell and belfry . . . Coldest night yet, −47 . . . Mary Dosithee is given last Sacraments . . . Mary died this morning . . . the lettering on Fr. Ruppert's cross was done today . . . Dr. Fromm began to look after the teeth of the children . . . The children are being allowed the phonograph, this being carnival . . . Five of the boys amused us with their Eskimo dance

. . . First Friday devotion as customary . . . The mosquitoes are simply wild . . . Bro. Wilhalm made another fruitless search for Fr. Ruppert's sled . . . The girls are keeping the horse Billy busy trotting up and down with some of them on his back . . . After supper we had magic lantern show . . . Some few girls are found writing very silly letters or notes to some boys in the next villages. A very grievous offense, which was not to pass unpunished . . . Emma dies after receiving all the last rites. She was a poor orphan . . . Fr. Post to Nome—replaced by Fr. Lucchesi . . . Fr. Lafortune teaches Eskimo catechism . . . June 7, 1926: Fr. Post arrives with 5 Italian aeronauts, who came from Nome in the dirigible balloon . . . Extra-ordinarily heavy run of salmon . . . July 21, 1927: A great day. Solemn Pontifical Mass at 8 followed by Confirmations. The Bishop gave the community a description of his trip to Lisieux and Rome, and distributed Beads blessed by the Pope and medals of the Little Flower . . . March 9, 1941: Fr. Anable appointed to take Fr. Cunningham's place . . . July 27, 1941: Three children leave for Kotzebue. Two Sisters and 3 children start for outside . . . July 29, 1941: All children walk to station for Nome."

93, 97

PILOT STATION

The Central Yup'ik Eskimo village of Pilot Station is located on the right bank of the lower Yukon River, some 11 miles east of St. Marys, in the Yukon-Kuskokwim Delta. In 1890, it had a population of 103; in 1929, 87; in 1939, 39; in 1950, 52; in 1960, 219; in 1970, 290; in 1979, 301; in 1990, 455; and in the year 2000, 550. Pilot Station received its own post office in 1950.

Baptisms were performed in the Pilot Station area as early as the 1890s by Jesuit missionaries stationed at **Akulurak**. On September 11, 1914, Father Anthony M. **Keyes**, S.J., formally established the Pilot Station mission. This he placed under the patronage of the Jesuit martyr, Blessed Charles Spinola, whose feast day it was. A new church was built by Father **John P. Fox**, S.J., in 1947, and blessed on August 15th of that year. "The patron of the church is St. William," wrote Father Fox, "in memory of William Thomas Sheppard, whose family donated the material for the building." Nevertheless, Blessed Charles Spinola, often referred to as "Saint" Charles Spinola, though he has never been canonized, has all along been the officially recognized patron of the Pilot Station mission.

For half a century, the 1947 church stood and served well the people of Pilot Station. However, the years took their toll. In a 1990 letter, Michael J. **Kaniecki**, S.J., Bishop of **Fairbanks** at the time, described it as "extremely rundown and pathetic." In the summer of 1994, it was taken down. By December 10, 1995, the present church, designed by Deacon Paul V. **Perreault**, P.E., engineer for the Diocese of Fairbanks, was ready to be formally dedicated by Bishop Kaniecki.

The first priest to reside at Pilot Station was Father Keyes, from 1914–21. Father Joseph **Perron**, S.J., was there for the year 1921–22. From 1922–28, Father Keyes visited it out of **Mountain Village**. During the years 1928–29 and 1929–31, it was visited, still out of Mountain Village, by Jesuit Fathers John L. **Lucchesi** and **Edward J. Cunningham** respectively. Father Paul C. **O'Connor**, S.J., made Pilot Station his headquarters for the years 1931–33. During the years 1933–38, it was visited for various periods of time by Jesuit priests stationed elsewhere. They were: Fathers O'Connor, Aloysius G. **Willebrand**, Segundo **Llorente**, and John B. **Sifton**. Father George S. **Endal** visited the Pilot Station mission, out of Mountain Village, from 1938–46.

Pilot Station was visited, likewise out of Mountain Village, from 1946–56, by Father Fox. He was instrumental in bringing electricity to it. He also organized three-day closed retreats for the men and women of Pilot Station, and saw to it that regional "Conventions" were held there on a regular basis. To help him with his Pilot Station ministry, he relied heavily on Native catechists. During the years 1965–68, Father Fox was again named as visiting priest, out of Mountain Village, to Pilot Station.

After Father Fox, Father James E. **Poole**, S.J., residing at Mountain Village, visited Pilot Station during the years 1956–59. The following year, he visited it out of St. Marys. The following Jesuit Fathers, too—some residing at Mountain Village, some at St. Marys—routinely visited Pilot Station: William T. **McIntyre**, 1960–62, and 1969–80; **Paul B. Mueller**, 1962–64; William C. **Dibb**, 1964–65; Paul Jordan, 1968–69; J. Herbert Mead, 1980–81; **Joseph E. Laudwein** and Normand A. **Pepin**, 1981–82; Francis J. **Fallert**, 1982–86; Eugene P. **Delmore**, 1986–91; James A. **Sebesta**, 1991–94; Edward A. Flint, 1994–97; Richard D. **Case**,

St. Charles Spinola Church, Pilot Station. *PP.*

1997–99; Paul M. **Cochran**, 1999–2000. In the most recent years, Pilot Station has been visited only by priests stationed at St. Marys.

Eskimo Deacons, too, served their Pilot Station parish: Norman Kelly (deceased and buried at Pilot Station), and Patrick Edwards, retired as of 1999.

Sister Dorothy Giloley, S.S.J., was at Pilot Station as a Pastoral Facilitator as of the year 2004.

Abe Kelly deserves to be mentioned here for the noble service he rendered the Pilot Station parish, especially at the time of the construction of the new church.

152

PLAMONDON, Father James W., S.J. (Ret.)

James Plamondon was born in Chicago, on January 4, 1918. There he attended Queen of Angels Grade School and Quigley Preparatory Seminary High School. After attending Gonzaga University in Spokane, Washington, during the year 1937–38, he entered the Jesuit novitiate at Sheridan, Oregon, on August 26, 1938. Upon completing his two-year novitiate, he spent an additional two years there studying the classics and humanities. From 1942–45, he was at Mount St. Michael's, in Spokane, for three years of philosophical studies.

The following year, he taught physics and mathematics at Bellarmine Preparatory in Tacoma, Washington. During the year 1946–47, he was at Sacred Heart Mission, DeSmet, Idaho; and, the year after that, at **Holy Cross Mission, Alaska**. He made his theological studies at West Baden College, West Baden Springs, Indiana, from 1948–52. He was ordained a priest on June 13, 1951. His tertianship he made at Port Townsend, Washington, 1952–53.

Father Plamondon spent his first year as a priest in Alaska at **Nulato**. Out of Nulato, he visited the villages of **Galena, Huslia, Kaltag, Koyukuk, Ruby**, and **Tanana**. For the years 1954–62, he was home-based at Galena. There he served also as an auxiliary military chaplain; and, out of there, he visited Huslia, Kaltag, Koyukuk, Ruby, and Tanana. With the help of some of the men of Huslia, he built Huslia's present church, around 1955; and, with the help of Mr. Robert Betz, he also built a church at Koyukuk during the years 1958–62.

In the months of March and April 1958, Father Plamondon was in St. Louis, Missouri, taking flight training at Parks College of Aeronautical Technology. After about five weeks of training, he made some solo flights. However, he never proved qualified enough to receive a pilot's license. By now, however, he did have his amateur radio operator's license. In the winter, he traveled from village to village by snowmachine or on the mail plane. For summer travel, he had a boat of his own, with an outboard. One of his boats he christened *Theotokos* ("God-bearer").

From 1962–65, Father Plamondon was stationed at **St. Michael**, out of which he visited **Stebbins, Chaneliak, Hamilton**, and **Kotlik**. During his last years on the Alaska Mission, he was stationed at Kotlik, from 1965–72. Out of Kotlik, he visited Hamilton and **Emmonak**.

During the early 1970s, Father Plamondon was hoping to move from missionary work into retreat work. With the blessing of his Provincial Superior, he left Alaska in January 1972. His intention was to get into retreat work for a time, and then, with newly acquired skills and experience in spiritual direction, to return to Alaska. To his great disappointment, he found himself, after a few months of training and some experience in retreat work with Father Armand M. Nigro, S.J., reassigned, by an assistant Provincial, to serve as an assistant pastor of St. Jude's parish in Havre, Montana. This he did for two years, from 1972–74. After a year in Havre, he learned that someone had, without his knowledge, removed his name from the list of those attached to the Alaska Mission. This upset him considerably. After two years of what he described as "rather frustrating service in Havre," he requested and received permission to attend the School of Applied Theology in Berkeley California. He was there during the year 1974–75.

In September 1975, Father Plamondon got into the work for which he had left Alaska in the first place by joining the staff of the Cenacle Retreat House in Wayzata, Minnesota. In December of 1975, however, a routine physical examination showed evidence that he was suffering from an aortic aneurysm calling for prompt surgery. This he underwent on December 22nd. After his hospitalization and convalescence, he returned to the Cenacle Retreat House. He was there for the year 1975–76, engaged not only in retreat work, but also in work in the National Marriage Encounter Movement. For the following year, he had no specific assignment. In 1977, under a cloud of general disillusionment and disappointment on his part, he retired from the priesthood, and soon thereafter married. It was a happy marriage. He died on May 25, 1989, and was buried out of St. Joan of Arc's parish, of which he had been a faithful member for over a decade.

POOLE, Father James E. S.J.

As a young man in **Alaska**, he had a great dream—and the drive to eventually realize that dream. He began his missionary work in Alaska as a dogsled missionary, but ended it as a microphone missionary. He did the statewide commentary for television in May 1984, when Pope John Paul II and U.S. President Ronald Reagan visited **Fairbanks**. His portrait is among those of many Alaskan dignitaries in a painting done by artist V. V. Ushanoff depicting the ceremony of the transfer of Alaska from Russia to the United States at **Sitka** on October 18, 1867. Ushanoff included him, because he was "doing marvelous work in the Far North." Francis T. **Hurley**, Archbishop of **Anchorage**, described him as "a dynamic priest, who wedded apostolate and enterprise to preach the word of God and to bring music and information to Eskimo villages." As an old man he could be seen spending much time in the house chapel or pacing back and forth praying the rosary.

James Elwood "Jim" Poole was born in Cle Elum, Washington, on May 18, 1923, to Chester R. Poole and Luella Burke Poole. He had an older brother, Robert, and a younger sister, Helen. For the early grades, he attended schools in Klamath Falls, Oregon, and in Redding, California. "All was happy up to the fifth grade," he painfully recalled in later years, "then social life made it clear that dad was an alcoholic." Taking the three children, and the ten dollars left in her purse, Mrs. Poole boarded the train and went north to live with her parents in Tacoma, Washington.

In Tacoma, Jim completed his elementary education at St. Patrick's Grade School. One of his teachers remembered him as a very ambitious lad who never gave her any trouble. His after-school hours and weekends he spent in scouting activities and in working to earn spending money for himself and for the struggling family.

In 1937, Jim entered Tacoma's Jesuit-staffed Bellarmine Preparatory. The self-confidence that characterized the whole of his adult life came to the fore strikingly already during his high school years. A classmate described him as "one who knew who he was and where he was going," and as "a leader from the word 'go,' who once he set his sights on an idea or an ideal, stayed with it, bulldoggedly, until it was realized."

While he was still in grade school, Jim's special devotion to the Blessed Virgin Mary made itself manifest. At Bellarmine, he was Prefect of Our Lady's Sodality. As such, he displayed his singular talent for fund-raising, by motivating his fellow sodalists to raise enough money to buy a life-size statue of the Virgin Mary for the campus grounds. His boyhood piety and devotion to Mary "did not cramp his style, his zest for enjoying life," according to his sister, Helen. "I don't think he ever missed a dance or a new movie that came to town," she wrote of him. However, she and the girls at the academy she attended thought it strange that he never asked the same girl out twice.

On June 30, 1941, Jim entered the Jesuit novitiate at Sheridan, Oregon. After completing his two-year noviceship, he spent an additional two years there studying the classics and humanities. He next made his philosophical studies at Mount St. Michael's in Spokane, Washington, from 1945–48.

During the years 1948–50, "Mister Poole," as he was now known, served as prefect of the boys at **Holy Cross Mission**, Alaska. At Holy Cross, he was truly in his element. The boarding school and he seemed to have been made for one another. Sister M. George **Edmond**, S.S.A., described life at Holy Cross during the late 1940s as "rough." Of Mr. Poole she wrote, "The smiling, gentlemanly scholastic, because of his happy outlook, his generosity with his time and talents, contributed much to the happiness of the children, as well as to that of the missionaries." Sister M. Ida Brasseur, S.S.A., the cook at Holy Cross at the time, said of him that "he was always trying to brighten everyone's life." For the boys in his charge, his "guys," he begged little extras from the kitchen. With his ghost stories, he held the children spellbound. It was while he was at Holy Cross that he "got the bug" about a real communications network. The mission had an in-house radio station, KAJX. Mostly it was he who operated it. With those two years at Holy Cross began his long love affair with Alaska and its people, especially its Native people.

In the fall of 1950, Mister Poole began his theological studies at Alma College, Los Gatos, California. During his years at Alma, he kept in close touch with Holy Cross through ham radio, and sent literally tons of clothes, candy, and assorted equipment north. In St. Aloysius Church, Spokane, on June 20, 1953, he was ordained a priest. He himself described his ordination day as "the greatest day of my life." Ordination was followed by a fourth year of theology at Alma. Next, working out of Seattle, he spent the year 1954–55 in the Pacific Northwest raising funds for the missions of northern Alaska. The following year, he made his tertianship at Port Townsend, Washington.

By 1956, Father Poole was back in Alaska. His first assignment there as a priest was that of pastor of the lower Yukon River Eskimo villages of **Mountain Village**, **Pilot Station**, and **Marshall**. Of these he made the rounds by dogsled, skiff with outboard motor, and commercial airplane.

While still pastor of those villages, Father Poole, clearly a man to the media born, already had visions of an Alaska-wide Catholic newspaper and a radio station. From Marshall, on April 1, 1959, he wrote to Francis D. **Gleeson**, S.J., Bishop of Northern Alaska at the time, "We have been discussing a radio station. What are your thoughts on the subject?"

In the fall of 1959, Father Poole became Superior of St. Mary's Mission on the **Andreafsky** River. As he had been at Holy Cross, so at St. Mary's, too, he was soon a hit with all at the mission. Brother Robert L. **Benish**, S.J., who was with him at St. Mary's, said of him, "He was interested in everybody, most generous, great with the kids, a great storyteller." As Superior, he had a gift for brightening the days of all by springing unexpected holidays, movies, picnics, joyful surprises on them. He had been happy in the villages; but, being a gregarious, a big-family man, he was even happier at St. Mary's.

While Father Poole was unquestionably a success as a school administrator, he was not, by his own admission, made for the classroom. He was not an educator in the traditional sense of the word. It was through the media, especially through radio, that he saw his chief means of educating, communicating, getting the word, the "Good News," out.

Shortly after arriving at St. Mary's, Father Poole thought to himself: "Instead of addressing only a small congregation on Sunday, why not reach out to the whole village, all week long?" Being a man not only of dreams, but also of determination, he was soon doing just that—through a public address system wired into all the village homes. This, his first major venture into radio, proved to be an immediate success; and led him to ask himself: "Instead of reaching only 30 homes in one village, why not reach out to the many, many villages scattered far and wide throughout western Alaska?" The thought of a Catholic radio station for western Alaska would not go away. Boldly, he wrote to Bishop Gleeson: "Let's get this thing going!" His pleas to Bishop Gleeson did not fall on deaf ears, but they did fall on nearly empty pockets. Nevertheless, Bishop Gleeson, persuaded by the worthiness of Father Poole's proposal, and confident that he had what it took to make a radio station a reality, gave the proposed venture the green light and his blessing. More he could not do. If Father Poole's dream of being "a missionary by microphone" was meant to become a reality, he himself, almost single-handedly, would have to make it such.

In the fall of 1964, Father Poole was unexpectedly called south, to teach at Jesuit High School in Portland, Oregon. Here he found himself in exile. "I really get homesick," he wrote, "for the old icebox and the warmhearted people who live there." However, while in Portland, he kept dreaming about starting a radio station in western Alaska. Thanks to the kindness of a station owner in Portland, he was able to get valuable radio-related experience. In the space of one week, he taped for broadcasting more than 20 short sermons. He also talked with engineers, scouted around for volunteer lay helpers, and collected whatever money he could. Cash began to trickle in. At year's end, he had several thousand dollars banked toward the launching of the hoped-for station.

With almost the same abruptness with which Father Poole had found himself in Portland, he found himself at "the Top of the World," at **Barrow**, Alaska. He arrived there on July 24, 1965. His friendly, out-going nature soon won for him many friends, both Eskimo and white. Six weeks after his arrival in Barrow, he began taking an official census of the town. Census-taking was not a new venture for him, as he had been a census-taker at Holy Cross in 1950. At Barrow, he served also as a member of the Chamber of Commerce and of the Civic Improvement Board. In addition, he was president of the Barrow Youth Committee and scoutmaster.

When Father Poole began the new year 1966 at Barrow, he had no idea how long he would continue on there; nor when, or whether, he might be allowed to take concrete steps toward realizing his dream of establishing a radio station. Meanwhile, money for one kept coming in. By the end of January, he had about $6,500 in his radio fund. He was happy in Barrow, but openly admitted that the radio project was still his main preoccupation. Bishop Gleeson, too, was dreaming the radio dream; and, in hopes of seeing it realized, he reassigned Father Poole, to **Nome**, Alaska. The Nome that Father Poole found in the summer of 1966 was a town of around 2,400, in large part Inupiat Eskimo. Water was still being delivered by the gallon; the "honey bucket" was still the "sewer" system; electrical power was still not very reliable; and none of Nome's streets were paved.

Although Father Poole thought the founding and running of a radio station a more or less full-time job, his primary assignment in Nome was that of pastor of Nome's relatively large St. Joseph's parish. This dual responsibility presented him with a formidable challenge. Typically, he rose to it with enthusiasm. Moreover, he soon joined the Nome Chamber of Commerce and the Rotary Club.

During the fall of 1966, Father Poole spent several weeks traveling widely throughout the Lower 48 renewing old contacts, making new ones, talking radio, attending a radio seminar, begging money and pledges of money, and looking for a key man to handle the technical side of radio. He returned to Nome, highly optimistic that, with a little more financial help, he would be able to "put this thing over the top and on the air by '67."

But, getting his radio station on the air proved to be not all that simple a matter. To make a longish story short: owing to problems concerning land, housing, staffing, equipment, and miles of bureaucratic red tape, it was not until July 14, 1971, that radio **KNOM**, Nome, Alaska, was finally on the air—and on its way to soon becoming a multi-award-winning radio station.

In 1980, Father Poole completed his responsibilities as pastor of St. Joseph's parish, though he continued on as director of KNOM until 1988, when he left Alaska for Portland, Oregon. There he trained as a hospital chaplain. Beginning in 1991, he took up a position as part-time hospital chaplain at Tacoma's St. Joseph's Hospital. At first he lived at the hospital, then with the community at Bellarmine Preparatory. In the latter part of 2003, the Father Provincial of the Oregon Province became aware of allegations that, many years earlier, Father Poole had engaged in sexual misconduct with minors. In keeping with the policies of the Church and the Oregon Province, Father Poole was moved into a monitored environment and removed from ministry while the allegations were being investigated. As of July 2004, the allegations were still in litigation.

While the allegations of misconduct made ambiguous the personal and pastoral role of Father Poole in Alaska, much of his legacy continued on in the work of KNOM, which, now under lay leadership, continued to serve the spiritual needs of much of rural northwestern Alaska.

86, 116

POST, Father Hubert A., S.J.

He was born Hubert A. Poos, on June 12, 1863, in the village of Berbourg, Grand-Duchy of Luxembourg. When he came to America, he changed

ather Hubert A. Post, .J.—sitting up front and ding the "dogomobile"— n his way from Nome to e Pilgrim Hot Springs ission. *LRC.*

Father Hubert A. Post, S.J.
JOPA-906.07a.

his name to Post. He had two sisters and six brothers. When not yet tall enough to reach the top of the altar, he learned to serve Mass. While still in his pre-teens, he wanted to be a priest. He spent the early years of his life in the village of his birth. He then attended the Athenaeum in Luxembourg for four years. After that, he attended the Apostolic School for Foreign Missions in Turnhout, Belgium, for two years. Determined to serve one day as a missionary on the Rocky Mountain Mission, he sailed for America on June 23, 1883. On July 9, 1883, following in the footsteps of his older brother, **John A. Post**, S.J., he entered the Jesuit novitiate at Florissant, Missouri. He taught at St. Ignatius Mission, Montana, from 1888–91, before going on to theological studies at Woodstock, Maryland. He was ordained a priest in 1894.

Beginning in 1895, Father Post spent almost twenty years as a missionary to the Indian peoples of Montana and Idaho. In 1901, he built the first Catholic church in Lewiston, Idaho. He was pastor there for seven years.

On July 25, 1914, Father Post arrived in **Nome, Alaska**, and three days later he became the pastor of St. Joseph's parish there, until 1918. He spent the year 1918–19 in Seattle. He then returned to the Seward Peninsula. This time, however, he was assigned not to Nome, but to the **Pilgrim Hot Springs** Mission north of Nome, where he was

Superior from 1919–25. He was at the Hot Springs, when Father Frederick A. **Ruppert**, S.J., froze to death near there on December 15, 1923. Father Post was next in Nome again for the year 1925–26, and then again at the Hot Springs for the years 1926–30. He spent part of the year 1930 at **Holy Cross Mission**. On September 24, 1930, he had his first airplane ride. On that day, in the new mission plane, the *Marquette Missionary*, he flew from Holy Cross to Nome.

Father Post was in Nome for parts of the years 1930–32. He was in **Kotzebue** from June 1931 to September 1931, when he returned to Nome. By this time, his health was beginning to fail. This so concerned E. J. Beck, Superintendent of the Nome Publics Schools, that he, identifying himself as not a Catholic, took it upon himself to write on December 10, 1931, to Father Joseph M. Piet, S.J., Father Post's Provincial: "It is my opinion that you would not knowingly keep so faithful a soul in this cold country, if you knew of his true condition." Mr. Beck advocated that Father Post be moved to "a warmer clime." He went on to express his high regard for Father Post: "Father Post is one of the most faithful souls to the Church and to humanity that I have ever known. Last year in the hour of my need he was the first to come to my rescue."

Father Post spent the year 1932–33 at Holy Cross, and the following year at **Akulurak**. He was then back again at Holy Cross. During the night of August 26–27, 1935, he suffered a light, but incapacitating, paralytic stroke. In 1936, he went south, to "a warmer clime."

From 1936–39, Father Post was at Port Townsend, Washington. In 1939, he was moved to Mount St. Michael's, in Spokane, Washington, where he died on December 18, 1940. He lies buried in the Jesuit cemetery at Mt. St. Michael's.

POST, Father John A., S.J.

He was born Sheng A. Poos on January 1, 1855, in the village of Berbourg, Grand-Duchy of Luxembourg. When he came to America, he changed his name to John Post. He had two sisters and six brothers. One of them, his younger brother, **Hubert A. Post**, too, became a Jesuit.

John spent his early years in the village of his

birth. At the age of 18, after having completed normal school, he taught for seven years in a school for boys at Senningen. From 1880–82, he attended the Apostolic School for Foreign Missions in Turnhout, Belgium. He then came to America and entered the Jesuit novitiate at Florissant, Missouri, on September 13, 1882. Before finishing his noviceship, he transferred to Woodstock, Maryland, where he took his first vows, in July 1884. He spent the next three years at Woodstock studying philosophy.

Having been accepted for the Rocky Mountain Mission as a volunteer, he spent the year 1887–88 as prefect of the boys at St. Ignatius Mission, Montana, and the following year as a teacher at Gonzaga College in Spokane, Washington. In 1889, he returned to Woodstock for theological studies. These, however, he completed at St. Ignatius, Montana, near the end of 1890. He was ordained to the priesthood on December 8, 1890.

Father Post spent his first year as a priest among the Kootenai Indians, then the years 1891–95 at Sacred Heart Mission, DeSmet, Idaho. His last year there, he made his tertianship. On May 31, 1895, he left DeSmet for **Alaska**.

Father Post spent his first two years in Alaska at **Akulurak**, his second two at **Holy Cross Mission**, and his final two at **St. Michael**. During his Alaskan years, he made some lengthy trips as a missionary. Given his "fondness for order and attention to detail," he left long, detailed accounts of several of those trips.

Father Paschal **Tosi**, S.J., Father Post's Alaskan Superior, described him as "a man of sound judgment, with good administrative quality, who speaks very little, but is always very kind to everybody."

In 1901, Father Post returned to the Northwest. From 1901–05, he was at St. Ignatius Mission, Montana. Thereafter, except for one 14-month period, he was once again at DeSmet, where he spent the remainder of his long life. After a short illness, he died in a Spokane hospital on December 27, 1940. He lies buried in the Sacred Heart Mission cemetery at DeSmet, Idaho.

PRANGE, Father Francis B., S.J.

Francis B. Prange was born in Eugene, Oregon, on March 10, 1893, the middle arrival of seven chil-

Father Francis B. Prange, S.J. *Photo by Bert Perlen/JOPA-1075.02.*

dren, four boys and three girls. One of his brothers, John, four years his junior, also became a Jesuit priest. Francis attended the Sublimity, Oregon, parochial school from 1898–1906. He entered the Jesuit novitiate at Los Gatos, California, on September 15, 1910— incredibly, without having a single day of high school to his credit! After completing his two-year noviceship, he spent an additional three years at Los Gatos studying the classics and humanities. His philosophical studies were begun at Gonzaga University, in Spokane, Washington, and finished at Mount St. Michael's, Spokane, during the years 1915–18. He next taught physics, astronomy and mathematics at Gonzaga University from 1918–21. His theological studies he made in Innsbruck, Austria, from 1921–25. He was ordained a priest in Innsbruck on July 27, 1924. At Exaten bij Baexem, Limburg, Holland, he made his tertianship during the year 1925–26.

After completing the course of his formal Jesuit training, Father Prange spent two years teaching physics at Mount St. Michael's and at Gonzaga University.

In 1928, Father Prange went to **Alaska** for the first time. He spent the years 1928–31 at **Nulato**. Out of there he visited the upriver villages of **Ruby** and **Tanana**, and the downriver village of **Kaltag**. When, in the spring of 1931, Father Bernard R. **Hubbard**, S.J., continued his dogsled trip of over 1,000 miles, Father Prange accompanied him from Nulato to Kaltag.

From 1931–32, Father Prange served at St.

Joseph's parish in Yakima, Washington. Then he was back in mission work again, but not in Alaska. During the year 1932–33, he was at Seattle College as Assistant Mission Procurator. His assignment, as such, was to interest people in the Alaska missions, raise money for the support of the missions, arrange for the shipping of needed supplies to the missions, and to pay the bills. The following year, he was at Port Townsend, Washington, doing the same, but now as head Mission Procurator.

In 1934, Father Prange returned to Alaska. He was stationed at **Holy Cross Mission**; but he spent much time on the trail, visiting **Paimiut** regularly, and various villages on the Kuskokwim River occasionally. From October 10, 1936, to November 25, 1937, he was General Superior of Jesuits in Alaska. Both in his roles as General Superior and as Mission Procurator, he wrote lengthy, detailed reports to the Father Provincial and to the bishop informing them of the conditions the various missions in northern Alaska were in and giving them an overall picture of the financial status of the missions. As General Superior, he also voiced his concern for the men on the missions to higher Superiors, urging them to show more solicitude for the men in their isolation and loneliness. He recommended that they do this through letters of a more personal nature, and by visiting them from time to time at their stations. Known, as he was, for his "bulldog tenacity," for his exterior gruffness, such a show of tender concern on his part made his recommendation all the more forceful.

In 1938, Father Prange left Alaska, to serve once more as Mission Procurator, for two years, while living at Seattle College. He was then again in Yakima, for the years 1940–42; and then again at Port Townsend, for the year 1942–43.

From July 1943 to July 1963, Father Prange served as Catholic chaplain at the United States Federal Penitentiary on McNeil Island near Tacoma, Washington. As such, he lived in the Bellarmine Preparatory community in Tacoma and commuted almost daily to the island. By the time he retired from his ministry as a prison chaplain, he was known nationally. It was he who organized the Self-Improvement Group for the incarcerated. This group put inmates in contact with professional men, who helped them improve themselves while in prison, to build up their self-esteem, to learn skills that would help them find employment after their release from prison.

After his retirement from the prison ministry in 1963, Father Prange spent a year at Seattle Preparatory; and then he was back once more in Alaska, this time serving as chaplain at the **Ketchikan** General Hospital from 1964–67. While stationed in Ketchikan, he also visited Annette Island and Thorne Bay.

From 1967–72, Father Prange, now in semi-retirement, lived in the Bellarmine community.

During the years 1972–75, the last years of life, he lived in full retirement at Maryville Nursing Home in Beaverton, Oregon. After 65 years of selfless, dedicated service as a Jesuit, he died there, of lung cancer, on November 24, 1975. He lies buried in the Jesuit cemetery at Mount St. Michael's.

PRINCE, Brother Joseph J., S.J.

Joseph Prince is the name by which he was known ever since he was a teenager. His real family name, however—as Father Louis L. **Renner**, S.J., learned from Joseph's uncle, Tom Prince, at **Nunam Iqua**, on December 26, 1981—was not Prince, but Yunak. When Joseph began to attend the **Holy Cross Mission** boarding school, he was lumped in with members of the Prince family. The name Prince stuck.

Joseph Prince was born on December 8, 1908, at **St. Michael, Alaska**. Little is known of his early childhood. According to Jesuit Historian Father Wilfred P. Schoenberg, S.J., he was baptized as a child by a Russian Orthodox priest, but later, when he was ten years old, he asked to be received into the Catholic Church. Father Frederick A. **Ruppert**, S.J., sent Joseph, with his parents' permission, to Holy Cross for an education. In 1926, Father Philip I. **Delon**, S.J., General Superior of the Alaska Mission at the time, took Joseph with him, when he went to attend the Eucharistic Congress in Chicago. When Joseph was nineteen, he asked Father Delon if he could become a Jesuit Lay Brother. Father Delon said to him: "I will take you to visit your parents at St. Michael. You must tell them what you wish to do and see how you can stand a long separation from them. If you still wish to go, I will take you to Seattle."

Brother Joseph J. Prince, S.J. *LRC.*

On June 3, 1928, Father Delon, on board the steamer *Gen. Jacobs* headed upriver to **Nulato**, wrote to Father Provincial Joseph M. Piet, S.J., about Joseph Prince, also on board, as follows:

He has had a good test here at Holy Cross. And he gives promise of sticking to it, once he has been admitted. I took him with me as a dog-driver and companion on my 1,200-mile trip this past spring. He was uniformly correct and well behaved and faithful all through. Invariably a daily communicant, he was always edifying in his prayers, as well as in his daily round of tedious duties.

Partly to see Father **Sifton**, but also to give Joseph's vocation a genuine trial, I made a detour after visiting **Akulurak**, and made an extra hundred miles to have Joseph see his mother and sisters and brothers before he would leave the country. I had some apprehension as to the outcome, and I told him so. But he told me that he felt strong enough for the fight that was likely to turn up. So we went. His mother and other relations were down at **Chaneliak**, and Father Sifton was there also. The struggle was even keener than I expected. Even some physical violence was resorted to by the mother. But Joseph, without rough-handling his mother, held his ground and himself firmly. Finally, at the very last moment, as the dog team was hitched up, and she was still holding him, Joseph stepped on the sled-runners, and gave the 'leader' the command 'off!' The team started at a bound, the mother clutched at her boy for three or four steps, as she frantically tried to retain her hold, but the speed of the team was too much for the poor soul (I was going to say pagan soul, as none of the family have yielded themselves to Father Sifton's zeal), and as the sled swung around the corner of the house, she flew off her boy's coat-tail at a tangent, and

rolled on the hard snow. I took just time enough to see that she was not seriously injured, caught up with the sled and sped away. Joseph had not seen, and to this day does not know what befell his mother. He was somewhat shaken and smiling with what seemed to me to be a profound peace and sweet happiness.

Joseph spent his six-month postulancy at Manresa Hall, Port Townsend, Washington. Soon after his arrival there, Father Delon, in a letter to Father Piet, wrote concerning him that "it is reported that he is giving the greatest satisfaction." On December 20, 1928, Joseph entered the Jesuit novitiate at Los Gatos, California. He was very happy there, but he was cold all the time, even in the summer. During the winter of 1929, he suffered a lingering attack of influenza, which soon developed into tuberculosis. He was sent back to Port Townsend in hopes that he would improve; then to the Sisters' Hospital at St. Ignatius Mission, Montana, where, it was thought, the mountain air would help him. But his condition grew only worse.

In December 1930, Joseph received the news that all his family had become Catholic. Father Sifton wrote to him, "The grace, I believe, came to them in no small measure through your prayers and your immolation to God."

When death appeared to be close, Father Walter J. **Fitzgerald**, S.J., Vice-Provincial of the Oregon Vice-Province at the time, sent instructions to the Superior at St. Ignatius Mission that Joseph should be allowed to pronounce his vows as a Jesuit. At ten minutes to nine on the evening of January 6, 1931, Joseph, in a feeble voice, pronounced the words of the vow formula that constituted him a full-fledged member of the Society of Jesus. He thus became the first—and the only—Central Yup'ik Eskimo ever to become a Jesuit Lay Brother. Brother Joseph Prince died two days later. He lies buried in the cemetery at St. Ignatius Mission.

Father Louis Taelman, S.J., who was with Brother Prince during his last days, wrote: "Everybody that visited the Brother during his sickness could not but be edified by his charming religious spirit. He was patient and always cheerfully resigned."

The "Br. Joe Prince Community" at St. Marys on the **Andreafsky** River keeps alive to the present day (2004) the name of Brother Joseph Prince, S.J.

PROVIDENCE, Sisters of

On June 19, 1902, Sisters Mary Conrad (Superior), Rodrigue, Mary Napoleon, and Lambert disembarked in **Nome**. They were the first Sisters of Providence to set foot in **Alaska**. They had come north in response to a formal request from Father John B. **René**, S.J., Prefect Apostolic of Alaska at the time. Several previous attempts, both by prominent individuals and the City Council of Nome, to establish a hospital had been in vain. However, when Father René submitted his request to the Sisters of Providence to open a Nome hospital, their General Administration in Montreal responded affirmatively. The Sisters came to Nome to provide health care, much needed in that gold-feverish town. After preparing to their satisfaction a two-story building located near St. Joseph's Church, which they called Holy Cross Hospital, the Sisters were able to begin their hospital ministry on July 15, 1902, less than a month after their arrival. Other Sisters soon followed to assist or to replace them. Soon the first Holy Cross Hospital proved to be too small. It was replaced by a new, much larger one. Construction of this began on July 3, 1906. By November 24th of that year, it was ready to receive patients.

On September 23, 1904, Sisters Mary Odile and Michael of the Angels arrived in Nome. They were schoolteachers, and they came to Nome to staff St. Joseph's Parochial School, offering grades first through eighth. They, too, were followed by other Sisters of Providence, who came to Nome as teachers.

For roughly a decade and a half, the health care, the education, and social services provided by the Sisters of Providence through the hospital and the school they staffed were very much appreciated by the people of Nome. By the year 1918, however, Nome's white population had decreased to the point, where the Sisters thought it time to close both the hospital and the school. On May 29, 1918, the school was closed. In September of that year, the hospital, too, was closed, in part because of Nome's decreased white population, and, in part, because of the competition provided by a recently opened hospital under the auspices of the Methodist Church. By September 20th, all the Sisters had left Nome.

But, with their departure, Nome did not see the last of the Sisters of Providence. For six years, 1952–57, Sisters stationed at Immaculate Conception School, **Fairbanks**, spent three weeks every summer in Nome teaching children and young adults in Religious Education programs. Sister Paula Cosko was in Nome during the years 1969–72 engaged in educational and other ministries.

On October 1, 1910, six Sisters of Providence arrived in Fairbanks to staff St. Joseph's Hospital. Founded in 1906, this hospital was first staffed by Sisters of St. **Ann**, then by Benedictine Sisters. Among the six was Sister Monaldi, who came from Nome to be Superior of the Fairbanks community—and the "active and decisive administrator" of St. Joseph's Hospital. (Sister Monaldi was one of only three Sisters of Providence to die and be buried in Alaska. She lies buried in the Clay Street Cemetery, Fairbanks. Sisters Gustave Marie and Rita of Charity are also buried there.) The Sisters of Providence staffed the hospital until June 30, 1968. By that time the Congregation had come to the conclusion that it could not bear the costs of the extensive repairs necessitated by Fairbanks' devastating flood of August 1967, nor those of upgrading and expanding the hospital to meet the needs of an ever-growing Fairbanks.

As Nome, so Fairbanks, too, saw first the opening of a hospital, then that of a school. By the early 1940s, the Fairbanks population had grown considerably, and with it a demand for Catholic education. The Sisters of Providence responded by sending north, in 1946, Sisters Joan of Providence and Ignatia Marie. Until 1951, when the new grade school was built, classes were held in the basement of Immaculate Conception Church. From the outset, Immaculate Conception Grade School flourished. The crying need for a Catholic high school was met in 1955, when Monroe Catholic High School enrolled its first freshmen, nine students, and began holding classes in the basement of Immaculate Conception Church. Sister Dorothy of Providence was the first Sister of Providence to teach at Monroe.

By the mid-1960s, there were as many as eight Sisters of Providence teaching in the Fairbanks Catholic schools. The Sisters of Providence remained the dominant Religious community staffing the schools until the early 1970s. In 1974,

(*left*) Sister Florine and Sister Mary Edithe, Sisters of Providence, and pupils gathered in front of St. Joseph's parochial school, Nome, in 1913. *Photo courtesy of Sisters of Providence Archives, Seattle.*

(*above*) Sister Dorothy of Providence, S.P. (Dorothy Lentz)—"with an almost legendary reputation as an excellent teacher," and with M.A. degrees in English and French—was on the faculty of Monroe Catholic High School, Fairbanks, during the first two years of its existence, 1955–57. *Courtesy of MCHS.*

they withdrew from the grade school, and, in 1976, from the high school. For two more years, until 1978, Sisters of Providence continued on in various ministries, mainly those of Religious Education, in and out of Fairbanks. Here it should be mentioned that during the long years the Sisters of Providence were staffing the Catholic schools in Fairbanks and those in **Anchorage**, they were also conducting religious education classes during summers in many towns and villages scattered far and wide throughout northern Alaska, among them: Nome, **Seward**, **Kotzebue**, **Tanana**, **Barrow**, **Galena**, **Ruby**, **Newtok**, and various military bases.

Meanwhile the Sisters of Providence were active also in Anchorage. Their ministry in Anchorage began on June 29, 1939, when they opened Providence Hospital. This, in the course of the years, continued to be upgraded and to expand until today (2004)—at a different site, and with the new name of Providence Alaska Medical Center—it ranks as one of Alaska's major medical facilities.

As in Nome, and as in Fairbanks, so also in Anchorage: first a hospital, then a school. As early as July 1949, the Catholic residents of Anchorage purchased land on which to build a parish school. However, the pastor of Holy Family parish, Anchorage, Father Harley A. **Baker**, was unsuccessful in his efforts to find a community of Sisters available to staff such a school. Lacking a school, he took a different course to assure religious training for the

young. He requested the Sisters of Providence to provide religious education programs for the Catholic children of his parish. A positive response to his request from the Provincial Superior of the Sisters of Providence marked the beginning of a 12-year education ministry in Anchorage by the Sisters of Providence. Near the end of June 1957, six Sisters of Providence arrived in Anchorage and began formal, well-structured summer religious education programs for children. During the five years of their existence, from 1957–61, 27 different Sisters took part in those programs.

Around 1960, assured that they would have a teaching staff provided by the Sisters of Providence, Holy Family and St. Anthony parishes went ahead with their plan to build a junior high school to accommodate grades seven, eight and nine. The plan left open the possibility of expansion later on, so that a new class level could be added each year to create eventually a full-fledged junior-senior high school. Construction began in the spring of 1961. On September 18, 1961, the school, named Central Catholic Junior High School, opened with 107 seventh graders. The faculty consisted of four Sisters of Providence: Mary Armella (principal), Esther, Mary Maurice, and Patricia Maureen.

The school, as new classes were added year after year, continued to grow. By the spring of 1965, however, those principally concerned for the school's future came to a consensus that, chiefly for financial reasons, the plan to complete a senior high school program was no longer feasible. When the 1965–66 school year began, the tenth grade was no longer offered. The school closed after the 1966–67 school year. During the next two years, Sisters of Providence staffed Anchorage's new Catholic primary school, **Hubbard** Memorial School, housed in the same facility that had housed the junior high school. This school closed in 1969. With that closure, the formal education ministry provided by Sisters of Providence in Anchorage came to an end.

By the time the Sisters of Providence, driven by their motto *Caritas Christi urget nos* ("the love of Christ impels us"), celebrated their century of service to the peoples of Alaska in the fields of health care and education, more than one hundred members of that Religious Congregation had committed both short years and long years to those two basic ministries. It was the health care ministry that first brought them to Alaska, to Nome, in 1902, and it was the health care ministry, in Anchorage, that, as of the year 2004, continued to keep them in Alaska.

40, 97, 180, 197

PROVINSAL, Father Thomas G., S.J.

Thomas Gene "Tom" Provinsal—the second of 14 children—was born to John and Mable Bissonette Provinsal in Wendell, Idaho, on September 15, 1944. His parents farmed near Black Diamond, Idaho. Tom began the first grade at St. Joseph's Catholic School in Pocatello, Idaho, in 1950. Because of his father's allergy to dust, the family moved off the farm, and kept moving from place to place, with the result that Tom wound up attend-

Father Thomas G. Provinsal, S.J.
BR-897924.

ing nine different grade schools. He lived in Seattle from 1951 through 1956. For the first year and a half of his high schooling, 1958–60, he attended Bishop White Seminary in Spokane, Washington, then Gonzaga Preparatory, Spokane, from which he graduated in 1962. Thinking of entering the Society of Jesus then, he was advised to wait for a year "to mature a bit." After attending Gonzaga University for a year, he entered the Jesuit Novitiate of St. Francis Xavier, the novitiate of the Oregon Province, at Sheridan, Oregon, on September 7, 1963. He took his first vows on September 8, 1965, after which he spent an additional year at Sheridan studying the classics and humanities.

During the summer of 1966, Tom moved to Mount St. Michael's, on the outskirts of Spokane, to continue his studies of the humanities and to make his philosophical studies. He majored in English and earned a degree in that field. While at Mount St. Michael's, being poetically and artistically gifted and inclined, he directed the play *Becket*.

Tom saw **Alaska** for the first time in the summer of 1968, when he and Rory Miller of the California Province went there to teach catechism under the direction of Father **Paul B. Mueller**, S.J., at **Mountain Village**, **Pilot Station**, **Marshall**, and **Russian Mission**. The two spent a few days also at St. Mary's Mission on the **Andreafsky** River, the gateway to the above villages. When Tom first saw Alaska, he was, in his own words, "fascinated by the vastness of the land." That fascination with Alaska's great wilderness was never to leave him.

In the summer of 1969, having completed his philosophical studies, Tom returned to Alaska. There he spent two years at **Copper Valley School** as a teacher of English, Speech, and Latin, and as "Boys' Dorm Prefect." During the summers of 1970 and '71, he attended the University of Alaska–**Fairbanks**, earning his teaching credentials.

During the year 1971–72, Tom was at Jesuit High School in Portland, Oregon, as a teacher of English. In 1972, he began his theological studies at Regis College in Toronto, Ontario, Canada. He was ordained a priest on June 14, 1975.

Shortly after his ordination, Father Provinsal, more commonly known as "Father Tom," went to **Bethel**, Alaska. By special arrangement with his Superiors, he was to spend two years there studying the Central Yup'ik Eskimo language at the Bethel Community College, a branch of the University of Alaska–Fairbanks, and then to return to Toronto for his fourth year of theology. After being in Bethel for six months, he was sent by Father Francis J. **Fallert**, S.J., his Superior at the time, to serve the people of **Newtok**, with the words, "You can learn Eskimo just as well in the village as in school." In Father Tom's words, "Father Fallert was, however, mistaken. I always regretted I did not stand up to him. But, being Father Fallert, one could never be annoyed at him personally." In 1977, Father Tom, having by then acquired a fairly good speaking knowledge of Eskimo, returned to Toronto to finish his theology. After that he spent five and a half months in Spokane making his tertianship.

Father Tom returned to Alaska in January 1979. From 1979–86, he had the pastoral care of the villages of **Chevak** and Newtok. He commuted between the two "by snowmachine directly in winter, 50 miles; and, at other times, by plane through Bethel, a 220 mile horseshoe." Often he had to overnight in Bethel. On April 13, 1983, he and the people of Chevak had the joy of witnessing the blessing of their new Sacred Heart Church by Robert L. **Whelan**, S.J., Bishop of Fairbanks at the time.

From 1986–90, Father Tom cared for the villages of **Chefornak** and **Nightmute**. During the year 1990–91, in addition to caring for Chefornak and Nightmute, he was responsible also for the villages of Newtok, **Toksook Bay**, and **Tununak**.

During his years in the Nelson Island area, Father Tom occasionally spent some time at the spring and summer sealing and fishing camp of **Umkumiut**. Life at Umkumiut was a good life, for young and old, for people and pastor alike. There, having left all his village cares behind, he enjoyed a life of relative leisure, was free to come and go as he pleased, free to take solitary hikes on the blooming tundra, to pray mind-wandering prayers, to relish the cozy solitude of his $12 \times 16'$ plywood cabin warmed by driftwood burning in his oil-drum stove. An excellent photographer, Father Tom was free to take many quality photographs. He also had a natural gift for Eskimo dancing. "Eskimo dancing," he once wrote, "literally wears out the knees of my pants."

In 1991, Father Tom was assigned to take a sabbatical in Seattle. His Superior wanted him evaluated for anger. After he was tested and counseled by a top neurologist for nine months, it was found that he was not afflicted with that syndrome. In the summer and fall of 1992, in the Jesuit Oregon Province archives at Gonzaga University, he did some research on Father Fallert with a view to writing about him.

From January 1993 to the year 2002, Father Provinsal made his headquarters at **Alakanuk**, taking care of the pastoral needs of that village along with those of its dependent station, **Nunam Iqua**. In November 1995, he took on the responsibility also of **Emmonak**. At the same time, he assisted with the Native Ministry Training Program home-based at St. Mary's Mission. On August 6, 2000, he had the privilege of administering the Last Rites to Michael J. **Kaniecki**, S.J., Bishop of Fairbanks at the time, as he lay dying on the ground near Emmonak's Sacred Heart Church. A year later, at the place where Bishop Kaniecki had died, he had the consolation of concelebrating, with Francis T. **Hurley**, retired Archbishop of **Anchorage** at the time, a memorial Mass on the anniversary day of Bishop Kaniecki's death.

As of the year 2004, Father Provinsal, now home-based in Emmonak since 2002, was providing pastoral care for that village, as well as for Alakanuk, Nunam Iqua, and **Kotlik**.

In early April 2003, Father Tom found himself in the Intensive Care Unit in Providence Hospital, Anchorage, with a mysterious illness that brought him close to death's door. It was never determined

(*far left*) Monica Shelden-Murphy and Edward Aloysius of Alakanuk. They accompanied Father Thomas G. Provinsal, S.J., on his near-fatal roundtrip from Alakanuk to New-tok in March 1994. *LR.*

(*left*) John Pingayak of Chevak. It was he who found Father Thomas G. Provinsal, S.J., while he was stranded near Chevak in a blizzard. *LR.*

just what the illness was. By Easter Sunday, April 20th, however, he had improved to the point where he was able to say Mass in the Alaska Native Hospital. That was not the first time he found himself at death's door. "Father Tom's Ordeal by Blizzard," written by Father Louis L. **Renner**, S.J., recounts that misadventure.

~

A death-like silence came over the diocesan chancery building as Michael J. Kaniecki, S.J., Bishop of Fairbanks, announced over the intercom: "Word has been received that Father Tom Provinsal is lost on the tundra somewhere between Newtok and Chevak. Search and Rescue teams have been out since yesterday evening looking for him. Sub-zero temperatures and high winds in the area are creating chill factors of between 50 and 60 below zero. Please pray that Father Tom may be safe and found soon. Pray also for the safety of those looking for him. I'll keep you posted. Thank you!" The time was early forenoon; the day was March 22, 1994, officially the beginning of spring.

TO NEWTOK

Sometime in January 1994, Father Thomas G. "Father Tom" Provinsal, S.J., mentioned to Monica Shelden-Murphy, Parish Administrator of St. Ignatius parish, Alakanuk, that he had been thinking about making a snowmachine trip to Newtok—a Central Yup'ik Eskimo village just north of Nelson Island and near the Bering Sea in western Alaska—to attend a three-day Songfest. The Songfest would bring the Newtok community and guests together to sing Christian songs and to discuss religious themes and to share religious experiences. It was the "song" part especially that appealed to Father Tom. He has a fine singing voice, and sings well and with pleasure both in English and Eskimo. Monica, wanting to know more about such Songfests,

with a view to possibly holding some in the lower Yukon area, and also eager to see some of the country in which her ancestors had struggled for survival, readily agreed to accompany him.

The projected trip—Alakanuk to St. Marys to Newtok to Alakanuk—would be one of around 300 miles. The direct, 90-mile stretch from St. Marys to Newtok was rarely traveled. There would be no trail. Although Father Tom had traveled parts of that general area often enough, he felt it advisable to have with him an experienced traveling companion. Early on, while planning for the trip, he asked 60-year-old Edward Aloysius—an Eskimo at home in the Yukon-Kuskokwim Delta and long-time friend and helper of priests and the Church in Alakanuk—to accompany him. Edward showed himself eager to make the whole trip. To guide them, Father Tom would have with him a VHF radio, a compass, and a GPS (Global Positioning System), as well as detailed maps. He would also have survival gear along.

During the third week of March, both Monica and Father Tom had Church-related meetings to attend in St. Marys. Monica flew there. Father Tom drove there on his snowmachine, accompanied by Edward driving Monica's.

On Friday, March 18th, at 1:30 P.M., the three left St. Marys, heading, in Monica's words, "down south." "The day," she continued, "started out with blue skies and a brisk north wind, perfect to travel in." When the trio reached the edge of the treeless tundra, they stopped to check their position, using the GPS. The device, because of cold batteries, functioned sluggishly. This was a bulky model which could not easily be kept inside clothing to keep the batteries warm. Father Tom took a compass reading, to confirm the course plotted with the help of the GPS and two Jesuit pilots, Fathers Paul B. **Macke** and James A. **Sebesta**, while the party was still at St. Marys.

The three first headed in the direction of the five volcanoes they knew to be located out on the flat, for the most part relatively featureless, tundra, somewhat over halfway between St. Marys and Newtok. In good time, the volcanoes came into view. "The volcanoes," wrote Monica, "are just northeast of Newtok, 37 miles. By the time we got to them, the sun was sliding down. We headed out in the general direction of Newtok, and by nightfall we were able to see the village lights, and got in without incident."

NEWTOK TO CHEVAK

The Songfest ended Sunday evening, March 20th. According to Monica: "By Monday morning the weather was overcast and hazy. Our next stop was Chevak, which some said was a three- to six-hour ride. It took me 12 hours to get there, and along the way Father Tom and I got separated in a snowstorm that nearly cost him his life . . . I never felt so abandoned as I did then. I had no idea which direction Chevak was, and Father Tom had our survival gear, except for a canvas and sleeping bag, in his sled and the compass."

Recalling that same day's events, Father Tom wrote: "On Monday the day was overcast, but we could actually see the Nelson Island hills clearly for the first time. Deacon David Boyscout was also going to Chevak, but was going to leave later. I decided to leave earlier, as we had to travel slowly. I preferred to go directly to Sheldon Point 120 miles north, but was readily willing to make a stop at Chevak west of our direct line of travel, as that was what Monica wanted. I could visit people too. That should have been the easiest part of the trip. It was frequently traveled and I had made the trip many times before when I was assigned to that region. With the good horizontal vision of Nelson Island, it made sense that we would pick up the mountains behind Chevak, which actually made the trip to Chevak easier than going from it to Newtok. As we got farther from Nelson Island, the hills behind us were clear, and I expected soon to see the mountains in front of us and more easily find Chevak, which rested at the western sight-line of travel. But, instead, the weather began to come down and be hazy and foggy. We never did see them."

DETERIORATING WEATHER

As the day wore on, visibility gradually became poorer. Again there was recourse to the GPS and the compass. Getting the readings, however, exacted a price. "We would stop for GPS and compass reckoning," wrote Father Tom, "which greatly slowed us down. Although I did get position on the GPS, we paid with great delays to track the satellites."

In the afternoon the three found themselves in a worsening "white-out," a weather condition in which—because of soft light and a snowy, foggy haze—sky, horizon, landscape all blend into one uniform, featureless whiteness. This slowed travel still further. According to Father Tom: "With the increasing shadowless white-out conditions of the snow, we had to go still more slowly, because I could hit a bump and fly over an ice ridge at a river crossing without being aware it was there till I was in the air. But, each time we checked our position, we were closer to our goal. But, finally, we were slowed to a mere crawl because of deteriorating conditions. A wind had begun to come up, causing ground drift. We covered about 15 miles in 4 hours, excruciatingly slow as the white weather conditions continued to close down. We made frequent stops to check out our position and reorient our compass direction. Finally we did pass a fish camp, which indicated we were much closer. I was quite confident we would be there soon. Finally, we faced the bluff that runs east and west on a direct line between **Hooper Bay** and Chevak. As we rested at its foot, a yellow snow-machine bobbed and weaved behind us from east to west on the way to Hooper Bay. Though we could easily have caught him, it seemed unnecessary, as we were so close."

Frequent checking of their position with the GPS—time-consuming as this procedure was, because of cold batteries and instrument—showed that the three were getting closer to their destination. The last stop-and-check indicated that they were only 2.4 miles out. "This was our closest marking," wrote Father Tom. "I slowly accelerated and in 3 to 5 minutes was back at the bluff. I turned around in minor triumph. Monica and Ed were gone. I had no idea why they were not with me. The blizzard was between us."

FATHER TOM ALONE

"I had the choice," wrote Father Tom, "of heading into Chevak without them or backtracking on the trail. The batteries on my GPS were giving out again, and this was my fifth and last supply of batteries. I decided to follow my tracks back to them. But the white-out conditions and the hard surface caused by too little snow and slush frozen in the winter and recent powder on top, and the heavy wind, made it difficult to find my trail. It was being blown away. I lost it on an icy patch. I stopped my machine to listen. I could not hear them after I took off my ear caps and took out my ear plugs used to deaden the extreme roar of my little Elan."

Next Father Tom tried to call Chevak on his VHF radio, but was unable to raise anyone. He found out later that he was using the wrong channels. He did not think to try to use the emergency channel used by Search and Rescue teams.

It should be emphasized that Father Tom was not lost, nor did he at any time think himself lost. His narrative continues: "Knowing the compass direction to Chevak, I could still have gone there, but I was ashamed to go in alone without Monica and Ed, who had no compass. I did not know what they could do. I knew that Ed knew how to winter camp, so I was not greatly worried about that. I tried to start my machine and the engine would not turn over. It seemed I was out of gas. I had more in my sled. I decided to camp, as I figured they would, in any event, be near to where we got separated. So, if a search party were sent out, I would not be far from where I had last seen them."

It was now 6 P.M. Setting up a makeshift kind of camp under blizzard conditions would not be easy. Continuing his narrative, Father Tom wrote: "So I got things out of the sled, set up one canvas on the wind side of my sled and laid my sleeping bag and myself inside that wall on my sled mattress, with another canvas around me, and bedded down. I took off my black leather boots and put on sealskin Eskimo boots, and so was snug and warm in my sleeping bag. The blizzard was now so fierce that the powdered snow could find ways into the smallest cracks or opening where the canvas folded together. The snow began to pile up on the downwind side of me in the sled, but this could be an insulation too. I got the canvas around me, so that I was safe, a bit cool on the wind side, but still comfortable. A couple of times, when I looked out, I could see nothing but white powder filling the air. I was in the belly of the blizzard. I worried about Monica and Ed and prayed for them. But I had confidence in Ed, who had been through much in his 60 years of hunting and camping out. During the night I would check the GPS I had in my sleeping bag with me. In the warmth it came up more quickly, and with its lighted face I kept the time and location."

By 2 P.M., Tuesday, March 22nd, Father Tom had been in his snow-covered canvas cocoon for 20 hours, since 6 P.M. of the previous day—"as comfortable as a nervous Gertie like me could be in such close quarters." At that time, he looked out to check his snowmachine. He noticed the engine hood was up, blown open by the force of the wind. It was at this point that he, in his own words, made a "bad decision."

A MAJOR BAD DECISION

"I was not sure where I had put my mittens in the canvas, but thought my knit gloves were in the backpack on my snowmachine handles, so I got out barehanded to close the hood. That was a bad decision, and I knew better of it. When I got to the backpack, having hurried, I found I had dragged my sleeping bag behind me, having entangled my feet in the strings in my haste. My gloves were not in my backpack. I hurried barehanded to close the hood and latch the rubber straps to the notches on the machine. The snow piled inside the hood made it somewhat difficult, and the cold quickly sucked the heat from my hands. In my sealskin boots I slipped as I stepped on the ice. I picked up my sleeping bag and hurried back to the sled. The blizzard had already blown snow into my sleeping space. Instead of immediately searching for my mit-

tens, I decided to arrange my canvas so that my sleeping bag would not melt the new snow. When I first settled in, I had anchored the one canvas under the upwind ski of my sled. So I took it off to wrap around me atop the former sleeping space, but that left me too exposed to the wind. As I wrestled with it flapping horizontally in the wind, my $16 \times 20'$ canvas suddenly stole away from me 30 to 40 feet downwind. I ran to catch it where it lay. (My hands were now feeling the cold and getting a bit numb.) I fought with it against the wind to lay it at the side of the sled to wrap around me. I managed to get my sleeping bag inside, but it was still difficult to get the canvas securely around me, as the force of the wind continued to seize the edges of the canvas. When I was finally secure, I had lost a lot of heat to my hands and never did find a way to get it back. I did get one mitten. I would place my hands under my armpits, between my legs, against my stomach and flex them for circulation. I kept at this for four hours under the tarp. Except for my hands, I was warm. My fur hat beautifully kept my head warm. I was well layered in clothing. During this time I was well aware that people were praying for me."

THE SEARCH FOR FATHER TOM

Father Tom was right in taking it for granted that by this time people throughout western Alaska knew that he was out there somewhere and were looking for him and praying for him. By phone and VHF radios word had gotten around quickly that he was overdue in Chevak. (In fact, already before Monday evening, Chevak people were out looking for all three, considering them overdue. Soon after the party left Newtok, Chevak was informed by radio that the three were on their way.) Because of the severity of the blizzard, people, thinking it too risky to venture out to their local churches, had gathered in homes to pray the rosary for Father Tom's safety. Search and Rescue teams from Chevak, Hooper Bay, and as far away as **Scammon Bay**, were combing the general area in search of him. He knew nothing about the fate of Monica and Edward.

THE FATE OF MONICA AND EDWARD

Monica recounts what happened to her and Edward after they became separated from Father Tom: "When I headed out after him, I was thinking about what he said—that Chevak was around a hill, but I thought he couldn't figure out which hill. He started out toward a hill as far as I could see, and visibility was about 50 feet. I continued along the way I had last seen him go, but never saw him. His trail, due to the storm, was completely obliterated. We came upon a snowmachine trail marker just at a side of the bluff. And before we got there, I saw a commercial plane going in for a landing, but never saw it land, since by that time I could see no more than 20 feet in front of me. Edward and I stopped at the marker, and while there used the marker as a point to look for Father. We had no idea where

he was, and finally decided just to wait there until someone came along. We were there no more than half an
hour, when Dennis Green from Hooper Bay came upon
us. I waved him over and told him what was happening. He brought us into Chevak, and we stopped at his
niece's house, where we warmed up, ate, and got in
touch with the Search and Rescue people, who were
looking for us. I had Mr. Green tell them where he had
picked us up, and that was the general direction they
went to look for Father Tom.

A PRECARIOUS POSITION

Back to Father Tom: "The grace of the moment was
that I did not have to pray for myself. It gave me the
opportunity to pray for others as they prayed for me.
I was also aware of the precarious position I was in.
There was the now real possibility of my hands freezing. They were still flexible but also in cold trouble.
There was the just as real possibility that I could lose
my life. I was not afraid of that, nor did my life flash
before me. But there was a deep sense of having failed
to grieve for others, though I could not identify specific faces or names to that intense emotion. Sometimes
it seemed that I could hear snowmachines in the distance, but I could not be sure. There was nothing to do
but wait, and pray, and deal with the feelings at hand."

In Chevak, staying now in the house of Sister Rose
Beck, S.S.N.D., Pastoral Minister in Chevak, but away
at the time, Monica was on the phone keeping in touch
with everyone and everything relating to Father Tom
and the search for him. (Through Father Mark A.
Hoelsken, S.J., priest for Chevak, Hooper Bay, and
Scammon Bay, she kept in touch with Bishop Kaniecki and Father Theodore E. **Kestler**, S.J., General Superior of the Jesuits in Alaska.) Finally, utterly drained
physically and emotionally, she tried to get some sleep.
However, the steep ice ridges on the riverbanks and
high bluffs in the area kept haunting her imagination.
"I couldn't sleep," she wrote, "because every time I
closed my eyes, I would 'see' Father falling over a high
bluff. Finally, I stayed with my imagination and 'saw'
Father on the tundra plain in a tent, safe and warm. That
was when I was able to get a few hours rest."

JESUIT CONCERN

Among those especially concerned about Father Tom,
besides Bishop Kaniecki, were, of course, his fellow
Jesuits. Father Kestler kept them posted as the anxious
hours slipped by. He, too, saw the whole ordeal as a
moment of grace. Wrote Father Kestler: "When I first
heard that Tom was missing, of course I was very worried—especially when I heard how bad the weather
was. As I waited and worried, it struck me that there
was a very great grace in all this for the Society. How
often we have been with families whose loved ones
were missing and their fate unknown. As we waited
and worried, we were truly in 'solidarity' with them.
We were able to experience first hand the actual pain

and worry that so many of the Native peoples we work
with have been through."

FATHER TOM FOUND

The day was still Tuesday, March 22nd. That day's
weather, according to Monica, "was worsening, with
icing conditions. In the storm I could not see across
the road." Some Search and Rescue team members out
looking for Father were suffering frostbite. Still,
according to Monica, "it was very important they continue searching, because the temperature was steadily
dropping, from 10 degrees above to 10 below." By
Tuesday evening, Father Tom had been exposed to the
elements for over 30 hours, the party having left Newtok at 8:30 A.M. the previous day.

That same Tuesday evening, after school was out,
John Pingayak, schoolteacher in Chevak and leader of
one of Chevak's Search and Rescue teams, gave his
wife, Theresa, a big smile and told her he was going
out to bring Father Tom home.

"Suddenly," wrote Father Tom, recalling the moment
and circumstances of his rescue, "a loud roar of snowmachine and the engine cut off. I threw open the canvas and someone called my name. I said I was all right
except for my hands." It was John Pingayak and his
teammates, Felix Matchian and Norman Pingayak, who
found Father Tom, at 6 that evening. Father Tom's first
question to them was about the safety of Monica and
Edward.

When Monica asked John the next morning how he
had been able to find Father Tom, when so many others had been unable to do so and in such blizzard conditions, he told her: "After I had determined the area in
which to look, and after talking with the guys who had
been out there, I suspected a place, where they hadn't
searched. Since I usually go there to get ice water, I knew
the area well. I, too, nearly overlooked him. If I hadn't
seen the snowmachine, I would not have found him."

Although Father Tom assured his rescuers that he
could easily stand and walk, they had him stay under
the canvas. On his sled, hitched behind one of the snowmachines, he was brought the two-plus miles into
Chevak. The blizzard at this time was so fierce that the
rescuers themselves became a little disoriented as they
made their way to the village.

John brought Father Tom to the Pingayak home. As
the family welcomed him and he thanked his rescuers—other teams had assisted in the rescue—village
health aides were called. They checked him for signs
of hypothermia, took his temperature, pulse, blood
pressure, and gave him fluids intravenously. They
gave his hands nearly the same kind of treatment
given them in the hospital in Anchorage.

John had Father Tom stay with the family overnight.
Theresa fixed him soup and made him sandwiches with
bread just out of the oven. One of the daughters gave
up her room for him. It was 9:00 P.M. before he was

stretched out, relaxed in bed, though his hands were still sore from the cold. As he lay there under the blankets, the family came into the room for family night prayers. Father Tom found this "very touching."

The next morning, John gave Father Tom a pair of his loose-fitting trousers and a sweatshirt. Because of his frostbitten hands, he was having difficulty pulling on his own trousers and buttoning his shirt.

At the Pingayaks' and at the place where Monica was staying the phone kept ringing off the hook. Many people wanted to assure themselves that Father Tom really was all right. The health aides called for him to come to the clinic to have his hands whirlpooled. Then he moved to where Monica and Edward were staying. It was then that he learned how they had become separated. The two versions are in substantial agreement.

CAUSE OF SEPARATION

Monica's: "What happened was when we stopped for a compass reading, I discovered I was low on fuel and said I needed to fuel my machine. I presumed Father heard me. I did not realize he was using ear plugs and couldn't hear me talking to him. While Edward and I were gassing up the machine, Father took off into the storm without us. I hollered out after him, but he continued on his way, never looking back to see whether I was following him."

Father Tom's: "Reunited with Monica and Ed, I found out how we had gotten separated. With my ear plugs in and ear caps on to silence the noise of my snowmachine, I had not heard Monica tell Ed to fill up her gas tank as we stopped for what I thought was an ordinary compass check. We were pretty close to our goal. I pointed out the direction and accelerated slowly. She shouted to me as I left, but I did not hear that either. When I looked back, the blizzard had slipped between us."

The day after Father Tom was found, the storm was so bad that most villagers stayed in their homes. On Thursday, Father Tom was flown out of Chevak to Anchorage to have his hands attended to in the hospital there. His hands will always be acutely sensitive to cold, but will otherwise be more or less normal.

On April 16, three weeks after Father Tom was hospitalized in Anchorage, Bishop Kaniecki visited him there. Two days later he wrote to Monica, "I have never seen Father Tom in a more happy and cheerful spirit than he was in Anchorage. I guess it is like getting a new lease on life and a true meaning for the Resurrection!"

EXPRESSIONS OF GRATITUDE

In letters dated March 24, 1994, and addressed to the people of Chevak and Hooper Bay, Bishop Kaniecki expressed his "very deep gratitude" to all who had helped in the search and rescue of Father Tom. On April 10th, Father Kestler wrote to the members of the Chevak and Hooper Bay Search and Rescue teams, thanking them on behalf of all the Alaskan Jesuits for all they had done for Father Tom under extremely adverse weather conditions. He sent each of the teams a generous check to help with their search and rescue work. He thanked also very sincerely the Chevak health aides—Susie Tall, Rose Kanrilak, Angela Ayuluk, Dorothy Tuluk, and visiting nurses Nancy Robarb and Martha Atti—for the careful treatment they had given Father Tom and assured them that they would be remembered in a special way in the prayers of the Alaskan Jesuits.

FATHER TOM'S REFLECTIONS ON THE ORDEAL

The final words are left to Father Tom. He blames only himself for the party's not coming safely, together, and in good time to Chevak, and for his personal, near fatal ordeal. "What should I have done?" he wrote, thinking back on the whole affair. "1) I should have waited for David Boyscout in Newtok, or have told him we were going to leave early. I wanted to use the GPS. 2) I should have made contact with the man on the yellow snowmachine as Monica suggested. I wanted to get in by myself, since we were close. 3) I should have let Ed Aloysius follow the tracks in, as he was more experienced in that way. Again, I wanted to use the GPS. 4) I should have looked back even at an ordinary compass checkstop. 5) I should have followed the ridge, when I found it a second time. 6) I should have filled my gas tank and gone into Chevak. 7) I should have used my VHF with greater preparation ahead of time, knowing what channels to use. 8) I should have secured both my gloves and mittens. 9) I should have been more familiar with using my winter gear. I was amply and properly supplied. 10) I should have had more regard for myself than for my snowmachine hood."

Father Tom frankly admits that he was caught by some bad decisions on his part. He was sorry and apologetic for having caused so many people such great anxiety and worry, and that some of those searching for him suffered frostbite. However, he was able to conclude the account of his ordeal on an upbeat note: "The trip was in many ways beautiful—for example, as we passed the volcanoes—and fun, as we tried to find our way." Monica fondly remembers "the trip down to Newtok, because one could see forever, and the wind was on our backs and the sun in our faces." Edward enjoyed meeting his Yup'ik cousins for the first time, and planned to return. They no longer seem so far away.

RADICH, Sister Kathleen M., O.S.F.

She was one of the first Franciscan Sisters to serve in **Alaska**. By the time her second decade in Alaska was drawing to a close, she had held positions of major responsibility in all three of Alaska's dioceses. A one-time Chancellor of the Diocese of **Fairbanks** described her as "a phenomenal administrator, an initiator, whose life is deeply rooted in the love of God."

Kathleen Mary "Kathy" Radich, the fifth of nine children, was born to Anthony and Margaret Turina Radich on April 18, 1951, in the fishing town of Astoria, Oregon. She was formed in the Catholic Faith primarily by her parents. Their example also taught her how to live a life of committed service and hospitality. Along with her sisters and brothers, Kathy grew up in Astoria, where she attended St. Mary Star of the Sea Grade School. After finishing the eighth grade, she climbed the stairs to the second floor for four years of high school. In June 1969, she graduated—first in her class.

The Radich parents had "a great belief in education." It was an unspoken expectation in the home that all the children get a college education and that they themselves find the money to pay for it. Accordingly, Kathy spent her first summer after graduating from high school working in a tuna-canning plant. During subsequent summers, she was fortunate enough to earn income as a long-distance telephone operator for "Ma Bell." These jobs, along with accumulated money earned by babysitting, enabled her to enroll at Marylhurst College, a Catholic women's college outside Portland, Oregon, where she majored in mathematics and minored in physical education. At Marylhurst, she was active also in volunteer work and in student government. During her college years, 1969–73, changes in the

Catholic liturgy brought about by the Second Vatican Council were extensive. It was while at Marylhurst that Kathy, by taking part in campus liturgies, developed her love for liturgy and liturgical music.

During Kathy's sophomore year, Sister Loretta Schaff of the Franciscan Provincialate in Portland, asked her whether she had ever considered herself called to Religious life. Kathy's immediate answer was, "No, not me." But, the seed was planted. On August 27, 1973, Kathy—wondering to herself over and over, "What am I doing?"—was airborne, on her way to Aston, Pennsylvania, to join the Sisters of St. Francis of Philadelphia. Upon arriving at the novitiate, she was greeted and wished the grace of perseverance by some 200 strangers speaking in a variety of accents. For dinner, she was served foods she could not identify. It was her first experience of real cultural change. Nevertheless, the grace of perseverance was granted her. After completing a year of candidacy and the two-year noviceship, on August 10, 1976, she took her first vows as a Sister of St. Francis.

For her first assignment, Sister Kathy was sent to St. Thomas the Apostle parish in Riverside, California, to teach junior high math, science, and Religion in the parochial school. Much of her free time she devoted to the parish music program and the parish diocesan youth ministries.

After she had taught for four years in Riverside, Sister Kathy was invited by the pastor of St. Catherine's parish in Rialto, California, to serve as youth director of that parish. Her classroom teaching, which she had assumed would be her life's principal ministry, came to an abrupt end. She spent the next six years building a youth program at St. Catherine's. As an expression of his gratitude to her for what she had done for the youth program,

Phillip F. Straling, Bishop of the newly formed Diocese of San Bernardino in which St. Catherine's now found itself, honored her with the diocesan Our Lady of Guadalupe Award.

Ten years after Sister Kathy took her first vows, an announcement making known the need for someone to minister in the Diocese of **Juneau** caught her eye. Ready for a new challenge, she responded, and, after an interview, was accepted to fill the advertised position. Stepping off the plane in **Ketchikan** in August 1986, she found herself "immediately at home." Soon she and two other Sisters formed the team that staffed the Office of Ministries for the Diocese of Juneau. They served as administrators of, and ministers to, a number of small parishes outside the Juneau area itself. Sister Kathy worked mainly in youth ministry and in Religious education programs. It was she who organized the Diocesan Institute, an adult education conference. She served also as administrator of some parishes and small missions, among them **Skagway**, **Haines**, Angoon, and Hobart Bay. This entailed a considerable amount of traveling, mostly by small, single-engine plane or ferryboat.

In the course of her ministries in small parishes, Sister Kathy began to feel a need to develop better listening and counseling skills, in order to be of greater help to the people she daily dealt with. So, in September 1992, she left her active ministries in Alaska to attend, for two years, the University of Maryland Baltimore School of Social Work to obtain an M.A. degree in clinical social work. Upon graduation, though longing to return to rural Alaska, she went instead to **Anchorage**, where, by serving as Counselor and Director of the Bishop **Whelan** Family Support and Counseling Center, a branch of the Anchorage Archdiocese's Catholic Social Services, she fulfilled a requirement still needed before she could be licensed as a clinical social worker. During the years 1994–7, she worked in the counseling center and traveled twice monthly to **Kenai** and **Wasilla** to provide counseling services.

In 1995, two Sisters of her Franciscan community joined Sister Kathy in Anchorage. Together the three formed a team ministry group. They chose to live in the poorest, most violent part of the city. "Our goal," wrote Sister Kathy, "was to provide a peaceful, prayerful presence. That ministry was truly wonderful. We got to know our neighbors, and we participated in the neighborhood activities and events."

All the while, however, Sister Kathy kept hearing a call, kept feeling a desire to minister in rural Alaska. At this point, a kindly Divine Providence came to her aid. Early in 1997, the Counseling Center in Anchorage had to close; and, in the spring of that year, she received a phone call from Father Theodore E. **Kestler**, S.J., asking her if he could come and speak to the Sisters about ministry in Alaska's Yukon-Kuskokwim Delta area. His plea, "we are desperate," had the Sisters quickly say "Yes!"

In the summer of 1997, Sister Kathy arrived at St. Marys, **Andreafsky**, to begin her years of service as "Coordinator of Rural Ministries: Yukon-Kuskokwim Delta Area," and as overseer of the "Native Ministry Training Program," both headquartered at St. Marys. Father Richard D. **Case**, S.J., a pilot and missionary stationed at St. Marys at the time, recalled some years later Sister Kathy's introduction to that part of Alaska:

> Sister Kathy and I almost immediately flew out to **Chevak** in the Cessna 180. I introduced her to the Yup'ik people and showed her the rhythm of life in the Church. With her experience in the Juneau diocese and in the Anchorage archdiocese, she was well prepared. I was immediately impressed by her flexibility and her organizational skills. That year, she visited all 18 villages of the Yukon-Kuskokwim Delta, and met with the parish councils, the **Eskimo Deacons**, the Eucharistic ministers, and the catechists. She wrote amazing reports on the strengths and needs of the villages. Her leadership style was firm, yet understanding. She gave heart and soul to the support of ministry in the Y-K Delta. As a Franciscan, she epitomized the spirit that filled St. Francis with zeal for ministry to all people.

In September of that year, 1997, Sister Kathy attended a retreat held for the Eskimo deacons and their wives. Seven years later, she still fondly remembered the warm welcome given her by one of the wives, who said simply, "Now you are one of us." That endearing comment made Sister Kathy feel like one who had finally come home to her people in rural Alaska.

Beginning in 1997, and as of the year 2004, St. Marys was the home base of Sister Kathy's ministry among the Central Yup'ik Eskimos of the Yukon-Kuskokwim Delta area. Out of St. Marys, she traveled to 23 different villages to coordinate the vision, ministries, and ministers of the entire region. As coordinator, she also represented Donald J. **Kettler**, Bishop of Fairbanks, implemented diocesan policies, and communicated the pastoral and physical needs of her region to diocesan headquarters.

The vision Sister Kathy embodied, and unerringly kept in focus, was the empowerment of the Native people and of those ministering among and to them to create a truly indigenous Church, a Church integrating in an harmonious manner the traditional Yup'ik culture and Roman Catholicism, a Church truly Yup'ik and, at the same time, truly Catholic.

In the year 2004, Sister Kathleen M. Radich, O.S.F., wrote of her years as Coordinator of Rural Ministries in the Yukon-Kuskokwim Delta:

> My time here among the Yup'ik people has been greatly blessed. I find the Yup'iks to be very much rooted in the same values that Francis of Assisi lived and preached. For me, as a follower of Francis, the way the Yup'iks live out their values of simplicity, love, and respect for creation, joy, and humility has been a wonderful witness and challenge. As I travel and spend time with the people, my prayer is that they also receive Francis' deep-rooted belief in the love God has for each person and for themselves personally.

RAGARU, Father Aloysius A., S.J.

He was seldom on the trail without his medicine kit. He liked to eat lynx meat, and to sing around a campfire. He compiled a notable Koyukon Athabaskan Indian language dictionary. He was, at the same time, both scholarly and practical. A Sister of St. **Ann** referred to him as "a great, holy missionary." His obituarist described him as "a unique and lovable personage."

As he was en route from Helena, Montana Territory, to the Okanogan mission in Washington Territory, he received two letters from Father Joseph M. **Cataldo**, S.J., Superior of the Rocky Mountain Mission at the time. The two letters taken together serve as a classic example of someone's being "volunteered." In the first letter, Father Cataldo

Father Aloysius A. Ragaru, S.J. *JOPA-994.01a.*

asked, "Are you ready to go willingly to **Alaska** with Father **Tosi**? If you are, come to Spokane Falls with your trunk." In the second letter, Cataldo wrote simply, "I am counting on you to go with Father Tosi; I have nobody else to send."

He was born into this world at Grez de Combrée, Maine-et-Loire, France, on November 29, 1847, as Louis-Gonzague Ragaru-Latouche. Throughout his life, however, though he had been a pampered son in a wealthy bourgeois family, he went by the simple name of Aloysius A. Ragaru. After completing elementary and secondary schooling, he studied for three years in the major seminary of the Diocese of Combrée before entering the Society of Jesus, at Angers, on November 10, 1869. As a novice, he served for a time as an ambulance attendant in the Franco-Prussian War. He received his Jesuit training at St. Acheul, Amiens, and in Paris and Laval and Le Mans. He taught at Poitiers. His theological studies were made at St. Helier, Isle of Jersey, Great Britain. There he was ordained a priest on September 10, 1882. After making his tertianship in England, he left from Le Havre, France, on September 19, 1885, for New York, where he arrived ten days later. Here he was still a considerable distance from the Northwest and Alaska, the fields of most of his future labors. After spending some months in the East and among the Indians of the Northwest, he served for a year at Our Lady of Lourdes parish in Spokane Falls.

In 1887, having been "volunteered" for Alaska by Father Cataldo, Father Ragaru, along with Father

Paschal Tosi and Brother Carmelo **Giordano**, S.J., willingly set out for the North. The three entered Alaska via the Chilkoot Trail and the headwaters of the Yukon River. By the time the party reached Nuklukayet, today's **Tanana**, Father Ragaru was so exhausted, that Father Tosi decided that he should spend the winter there. It was a hard winter he had of it! His sojourn at Nuklukayet "proved to be a fiasco." Yet, in spite of that difficult introduction to Alaska, and in spite of the fact that he could easily have gotten out of Alaska—for Father Cataldo had written to him, "Go up there for a year or more. Have a look and write me. We will see about it then."—he stayed on in Alaska. In May 1888, he went downriver to **Nulato**. His stay there proved to be a happy one. The following month, on June 30th, he was able to write to Father Tosi from **St. Michael**, "I find myself happy and most ready to labor and suffer without discouragement, although I well see that the work that offers itself is without limit."

Father Ragaru spent the years 1888 to 1900 at Nulato, with the exception of the years 1893–94 and 1897–98, which he spent at **Holy Cross Mission**. From the outset, he made a concerted effort to learn the local Koyukon Athabaskan Indian language. He left for posterity a fair number of manuscripts in that language. Most of these are of a practical nature, meant to help him and fellow missionaries with everyday, ministry-related, linguistic needs. During his Nulato years, he routinely made visits to upriver and downriver villages and camps. After a few years at Nulato, he wrote to Father Tosi, "I am on the best of terms with Indians." He was on good terms with the Indians, in part, because he respected their traditional beliefs and practices. When given lynx meat to eat, for example, he would return the bones to the donor, so that they would be properly disposed of in keeping with the Native way.

Referring to Father Ragaru, a Sister of St. **Ann**, who observed him help build at Holy Cross during its earliest days, wrote, "The holy missionary was more familiar with his Greek than with the dialect of this tribe; and better at preparing sermons on trees than at building cabins out of them." There was unquestionably a theoretical, scholarly side to Father Ragaru. Evidence thereof is the fact that he kept urging, year after year, for a Catholic day

school at Nulato, till it finally had one in 1899. But, in fairness to him, it must be said that he could also be very practical, see and attend to basic, down-to-earth needs. Another Sister of St. Ann wrote concerning him: "He then laid floorboards, built a storm entrance, and contributed a most important item, a square box with a one-hole perforation in the lid. In the box is placed a bucket, for already there is no possibility of going outside to 'parliament.' The sitting is too cold. We keep the box in the storeroom."

Like many other missionaries in the North, Father Ragaru, too, was an amateur practitioner of medicine. When on the trail, he normally had his medicine kit with him. For eyes inflamed by acute snow-blindness, he had his own special treatment. Upon a disk of lead he folded a little piece of cotton cloth in the shape of a tent, and, after setting fire to it, let it burn out completely. Then, with a wet camel's-hair brush, he gathered up the yellowish residue of the combustion and painted it over the eyes of the sufferer, holding the lids open with thumb and finger. With this treatment, he brought relief to many. It is known that he also performed successful amputations.

Father Ragaru, "for his health," spent the years 1900–03 in the Pacific Northwest. For a short time, he was hospital chaplain at Providence Hospital in Seattle. He next spent a year as pastor of St. Patrick's parish in Spokane, and several years on the Indian missions of Montana and Idaho. Back in Alaska again, he was at Nulato for the year 1903–04. The next two years, 1904–06, saw him upriver, at Tanana. There he established the mission that he named for his patron saint, St. Aloysius. Out of Tanana, he also tended the mission he had newly established at **Kokrines**.

During most of his years at Nulato, Father Ragaru had with him Brother Giordano. Regarding him, he wrote to Father Tosi, "He has become a regular and true Indian in his ways." That Father Ragaru should write this as a negative criticism is all the more surprising in view of the fact that he himself seemed to be quite open to the culture and ways of the Native people. A case in point: whereas some of the Jesuit missionaries serving along the middle Yukon in the course of the years disapproved of the traditional

Native "stickdance," or "Feast for the Dead," Father Ragaru, according to one Koyukon Athabaskan woman, "used to go along with the people."

Reasons of health necessitated Father Ragaru's leaving Alaska in 1906. For the next 13 years he served in various parishes and hospitals in eastern Canada. He never lost his interest in Alaska. During his retirement years he helped Father Francis A. **Barnum**, S.J., compile material and data related to the Alaska mission. In a letter to Father Barnum, he referred to Alaska as "that dear big country."

Father Aloysius A. Ragaru, without ever again having seen the land of his birth, died, at the age of 74 years, in Montreal on May 24, 1921. He lies buried at Sault au Récollet; Quebec, Canada.

Father John B. René, S.J.
JOPA-999.016.

RENÉ, Father John B., S.J.

Jean-Baptiste René was born on August 22, 1841, in Montrevaux, Anjou, France. He entered the Society of Jesus on September 28, 1862. After completing his ecclesiastical studies at Laval, France, and at St. Beunos, Wales, he was ordained a priest at this latter place in 1876. His tertianship was made at Paray-le-Monial. After having served as director of the Apostolic Schools in both Poitiers, France, and in Mungret, Limerick, Ireland, he came to America in 1890.

Father René—described as "a consistently conservative, a rather stiff, autocratic Vendean with a European's infatuation with formality ... very articulate and possessed of a firm and forcible personality"—was also a man of exceptional ability and of true academic accomplishments. On April 2, 1891, he was installed as the third president of Gonzaga College, Spokane. Despite his many accomplishments as such, he held that post for only two years, until March 16, 1893. In 1892, Father René saw to the building of the new wooden St. Aloysius Church in Spokane. Beginning in 1894, he served for a term as an official Consultor to the Superior of the Rocky Mountain Mission.

Father René's nine-year sojourn in **Alaska** began in 1895, when he was assigned to serve as pastor of **Juneau** and outlying towns. He is given credit for having "organized" the Juneau parish. On March 16, 1897, in virtue of a pontifical decree issued in

Rome, he was appointed to succeed Father Paschal **Tosi**, S.J., as Prefect Apostolic of Alaska. At the same time, he was also appointed to succeed him as General Superior of all Jesuits in Alaska. As the incumbent of these two offices, he traveled widely throughout Alaska, but he continued to make Juneau, which he considered centrally located to the Pacific Northwest and northern Alaska, his headquarters.

For the record, it must be mentioned here that, owing to the poor communications of the time, as well as to the pompous and overbearing impression he gave at first meeting, Father René began his terms of office, both as Prefect Apostolic and as Superior of Jesuits in Alaska, not without a considerable amount of misunderstanding and hard feelings on the part of all concerned. However, when the proper documents were adduced, and everything clarified, peace and fraternal charity were again restored in the hearts of all.

In the summer of 1897, Father René visited Father William H. **Judge**, S.J., in Dawson. He greatly admired the man and the hospital work he was doing there. With Father Judge, he recognized the need for expanding the hospital facilities. However, the debt was already considerable, and prospects of soon reducing it not good. Father René, who lacked the ability to spend money he did not have, could not bring himself to give permission to make the needed expansions.

In the summer of 1898, in **Skagway**, Father René

helped Father Philibert **Turnell**, S.J., remodel an empty store into St. Mark's Catholic Church. That same year, the Sisters of St. **Ann**, thanks to his efforts, arrived in Dawson to staff the hospital necessitated by the Klondike gold rush with its attendant health problems. Father René was responsible, too, for getting Sisters of St. Ann to staff the day school at **Nulato**, beginning in 1899.

Father René has the distinction of being the first priest and the first Jesuit to visit **Nome**. This he did in August 1899.

By 1904, Father René's health seemed no longer up to the rigors of the kind of life his duties in Alaska demanded of him. Relieved of his Alaskan responsibilities, he spent the years 1904–15 teaching theology and Hebrew to Jesuit seminarians at Gonzaga College.

Was it really, and solely, for health reasons that Father René found himself out of Alaska by the summer of 1904? It seems not. That same summer, Father Julius **Jetté**, S.J., was passing through Spokane. Under date of June 24, 1904, he wrote to Father Francis A. **Barnum**, S.J.:

> Fr. René is here, a simple private, keeping, as he says, "in a corner." I can tell you, confidentially, that his resignation was not altogether spontaneous, but he takes it cheerfully and buoyantly. He is a man not easily discouraged, as you know, and knows how to make the best of adverse circumstances. I had a long talk with him also, and he showed himself perfectly resigned to give up not only his Prefectship, but also Alaska altogether.

In 1915, Father John B. René, "a man of high intellectual and spiritual attainments," moved to the Jesuit novitiate at Los Gatos, California. There he died on April 6, 1916. He lies buried in the Jesuit cemetery at Santa Clara University.

122, 176

RENNER, Father Louis L., S.J.

Louis Lawrence Renner, the second oldest of eight children, was born to John J. Renner and Rosa Gustin Renner on April 25, 1926, in St. Alexius Hospital in Bismarck, North Dakota. In 1929, the family moved from a farm near St. Anthony to a farm

Father Louis L. Renner, S.J. *MK.*

a few miles north of Flasher. For the first four grades, from 1933–37, Louis attended a boarding school at nearby Fallon staffed by Benedictine Sisters. There he first learned to speak English. In 1937, principally because the Fallon school no longer admitted non-parishioners, but also because of the "dust bowl era" and its negative impact on farmers, the family moved to Tacoma, Washington. For grades five and six, Louis was enrolled in Holy Rosary School, likewise staffed by Benedictine Sisters; and for grades seven and eight, in Sacred Heart School, staffed by Sisters of Providence.

In the fall of 1941, Louis began to attend Tacoma's Jesuit-staffed Bellarmine Preparatory. This marked his first contact with Jesuits. He took the customary courses leading to the classical diploma. But, it was athletics, rather than academics, that mainly interested him. As a sophomore, he was one of two sophomores earning varsity letters in football that year. While at Bellarmine, he was a member of the school's Quill and Scroll Club, a club for aspiring journalists, as well as a half-hearted member of Our Lady's Sodality. For reasons unknown to him at the time, he found himself occasionally attending Mass in the faculty house chapel before morning classes.

Throughout his seven years in Tacoma, 1937–44, Louis earned spending money for himself and the family at odd and part-time jobs such as selling magazines, picking berries, delivering newspapers, pedaling his bike as a Western Union messenger all over

Tacoma, and stocking shelves in a Safeway store. During the summer of 1942, he worked in the lumberyard of the Northern Pacific Railway. He spent the summer of 1943 as a deckhand for the Foss Tug & Barge Company. This was the one job he genuinely loved. The sea, from the time he first read about it, always held a special attraction for him. His last job before his entry into the Society of Jesus was that of a clerk in the parcel post section of Tacoma's downtown post office.

Reflecting on his call to the priesthood as a Jesuit in a homily delivered on the occasion of his golden jubilee as a Jesuit, Father Renner could still give no clear reasons for his having entered the Jesuits. He had had no natural attraction to the Society, nor to the priesthood. His parents had never talked to him about becoming a Religious or a priest. While he had related positively to the Jesuits at Bellarmine and admired certain ones, none of them had so impressed him that he felt drawn to emulate them. The school's "Spiritual Father," Joseph A. Lynch, S.J., alone had ever suggested to him that he "consider the higher life."

During Louis' high school years, World War II was raging. The military draft was in force. Even though he was still only a junior, he would turn 18 on April 25, 1944, and so be subject to the draft. Great turmoil filled his head and heart during the early weeks of 1944. In February, he was inspired to see Father Lynch in hopes that he would put his mind at ease by assuring him that it would be in keeping with God's will for him in the whole matter, if he were to go off to serve his country in the U.S. Navy. Many years later, Louis still distinctly remembered telling Father Lynch twice: "I get this strong urge to join the Navy." But, Father Lynch, being a wise judge of the case, suggested that Louis, instead, apply for admission to the Society of Jesus and, if accepted, enter the Jesuit novitiate at Sheridan, Oregon. Throughout the rest of his life, Louis was deeply grateful for such sage guidance, and never forgot the profound peace that came over him the moment he first walked through the novitiate doors on March 24, 1944. Immediately he was certain that Jesuit life was the only life for him. Seeing no identifiable human motives at play for entering it, he could only conclude that his vocation to

the priestly life as a Jesuit was truly a divine favor, a special gift of grace.

Louis was a happy novice, adapting readily to all aspects of novitiate life, whether temporal or spiritual. On March 25, 1946, he pronounced the simple vows of poverty, chastity and obedience. For his vow crucifix he was given the one that Father John B. **Sifton**, S.J., had left behind when he died at **Hooper Bay**, **Alaska**, in 1940. During the years 1946–48, Louis continued on at Sheridan studying the classics and humanities. He also took summer school courses in French and German.

In the late summer of 1948, Louis moved to Mount St. Michael's, Spokane, Washington, for three years of philosophical studies. Upon his introduction to philosophy, "It was," in his own words, "a case of love at first sight." He chose philosophy for his major. By the end of his third year, he had earned an M.A. degree in it. While at "the Mount," he had various non-academic assignments, among them that of tombstone engraver and "Villa Minister."

Louis had entered the Jesuits with hopes of one day serving on the Alaska Mission, had even corresponded with the Father General in Rome about those hopes. However, during the years following his noviceship, he was drawn more to the academic life. Soon after he began his philosophical studies, Alaska ceased to be on the horizon of his active interests. Accordingly, instead of being assigned to **Holy Cross Mission** for his teaching practicum, he was assigned to teach at Seattle Preparatory for the years 1951–54. There he taught mainly Latin, English, and Religion. He was also the "Property Room Manager." As such, he was responsible for the athletic equipment and accompanied the varsity teams at all their games. While at Seattle Preparatory, he organized the "Orphean Club," a club for students interested in classical music, the arts, and chess.

In the fall of 1954, Louis began his theological studies at Alma College, Los Gatos, California. He was happy to be back full-time in studies, and on the final stretch of the road leading to the priesthood. In St. Aloysius Church, Spokane, on June 15, 1957, he was ordained a priest by Bishop Bernard J. Topel. Then he was again back at Alma for his final year of theology. This he ended, having earned the Licentiate and Master of Sacred Theology degrees.

During the summer of 1958, Father Renner served for six weeks at St. James Cathedral parish in Seattle as chaplain to the surrounding hospitals and as an assistant pastor. At this time, his trunk was packed and addressed to Port Townsend, Washington, where he expected to make his tertianship during the year 1958–59. But, a major, and very welcome, surprise awaited him. On July 31st, Feast of St. Ignatius of Loyola, he learned that he had been assigned to teach at Monroe Catholic High School in **Fairbanks**, Alaska.

When Father Renner left Seattle for studies at Alma, he saw himself going on eventually to get some kind of advanced degree and then spending most of the rest of his life in the classroom. He no longer thought of Alaska as a likely field of future ministry. However, around the mid-1950s, changes were taking place in Fairbanks that reawakened his desire to serve there. Monroe opened in 1955. Teaching there, along with being Newman Club chaplain at the University of Alaska–Fairbanks, would enable him to pursue academic interests and, at the same time, serve in Alaska. The allure of Alaska had never left him. This was known to his Superiors.

By the third week of August 1958, Father Renner, on an Alaska Airlines DC-6 piston-engine plane, was on his way to Fairbanks. The fact that the flight lasted almost eight hours made Alaska seem all the more remote, exotic to him. During later years, he liked to remind people that he was already in Alaska, "back in territorial days, before statehood."

Father Renner found his two years at Monroe most happy, all-around satisfying ones. He taught Religion, English, History and American Government, was Moderator of the Sodality, and "Spiritual Father" to the students. He organized a music appreciation–chess club, helped out in Immaculate Conception parish, and was chaplain to the Catholic students at the UA–F. For his first Alaskan Christmas, he was in **Seward**; and for his first Easter, at the Suntrana coal mining camp near **Healy**. He was moderator of Monroe's first graduating class, that of 1959. During the summer of 1959, he taught German in the Foreign Languages School held at Monroe. In August of that summer, he made his annual retreat at St. Mary's Mission, **Andreafsky**; then, with Father René **Astruc**, S.J., boated downriver to

spend nights at **Hamilton**, **St. Michael**, and **Unalakleet**. He returned to Fairbanks via **Nome**.

During the summer of 1960, Father Renner studied French at the Sorbonne University in Paris for six weeks. He then made his ten-month tertianship at Paray-le-Monial, France. In the course of those ten months, he helped out at U.S. military bases in Germany and gave a three-day retreat in the small French village of Cogny.

Father Renner spent the summer of 1961 in Vienna, Austria, studying German at the university. In October 1961, he began doctoral studies in philosophy at the Ludwig Maximilian University in Munich, Germany. As his philosophical interests had all along been primarily in the field of ethics, he chose for the subject of his dissertation the moral philosophy of the Scottish philosopher Sir W. D. Ross. During the summer of 1962, he was in Oxford, England, doing research in Oxford's Bodleian Library and gathering books by Ross and on Ross-related writings. By the 4th of July, 1965, with doctorate in hand, he was back in Alaska.

In the fall of 1965, Father Renner began his 15-year career as a member of the faculty at the University of Alaska–Fairbanks. He taught mostly German, but also a course in the humanities and courses in Latin. It was he who introduced the university's Latin program. While teaching at the UA–F, he lived in an efficiency apartment a 15-minute walk from there. On an improvised "altar"—a coffee table on top of the dresser—he daily offered morning Mass before going to teach. No matter what the weather, he always walked to and from the university. During his four decades in Alaska, he never suffered frostbite. He knew how to respect and dress for the weather.

In June 1974, Father Renner spent eight days on **King Island** doing research for his proposed biography of Father Bellarmine **Lafortune**, S.J. For the academic year 1975–76, the university granted him sabbatical leave to write the biography. This, his first book, *Pioneer Missionary to the Bering Strait Eskimos: Bellarmine Lafortune, S.J.*, written in collaboration with Dorothy Jean Ray, was published in 1979.

In the summer of 1975, Father Renner accompanied Sister Judy Tralnes, C.S.J.P., and Sister Marie Teresa **Boulet**, O.P., to **Little Diomede** Island, when they went there to teach catechism. He went also to do research for another planned biography, the life of Father **Thomas P. Cunningham**, S.J. This, *"Father Tom" of the Arctic*, was published in 1985. That same year saw the publication also of his *The KNOM/Father Jim Poole Story*.

In the late 1970s, the Diocese of Fairbanks was looking for someone to head up the Alaskan Shepherd fund-raising program. This included also editing *The Alaskan Shepherd*. Father Renner, because of his familiarity with Alaska and his proven ability as a writer, was considered the logical choice. While he had been perfectly happy with his work at the University, he himself, after almost 15 years there, was ready for a change. His career at the university ended on May 11, 1980, with his being appointed "Professor of German Emeritus." The document conferring emeritus status mentions his "commitment to his students," and the fact that he "consistently provided quality instruction" and gave "generously of his time for counseling." His "sustained research," too, is cited.

Father Renner did not immediately take over the Alaskan Shepherd work. From Father Edmund A. **Anable**, S.J., whom he was to replace, he received some on-the-job training. Then, history-minded and adventurous, and wanting to walk in the footsteps of the first Jesuit missionaries to enter Alaska, he, in late June 1980, in company of Fathers **Francis E. Mueller**, S.J., and Richard D. **Tero**, hiked the historic Chilkoot Trail. On the return trip to Fairbanks, he and Father Mueller stopped off

in Dawson to visit the grave of Father William H. **Judge**, S.J., "the saint of Dawson," and the Klondike gold fields.

Father Renner spent a good part of August and most of September 1980 living in a tent in the woods and helping with the building of the new church at Healy. In October, he was in **Kaltag** for a week to help Father James A. **Sebesta**, S.J., lay in a supply of firewood for the winter.

After spending a mini-sabbatical at Gonzaga University in Spokane, Father Renner, in September 1981, took over as director of the Alaskan Shepherd program. In October, he was in **Barrow** for a weekend, supplying for Father Mueller. The latter part of 1981 and the first two days of 1982 saw him at **Alakanuk** and **Nunam Iqua**, where he provided all the priestly services from Christmas Eve to New Year's Day inclusive. From July 1–12, 1982, he was at **Chevak**, replacing the pastor there and helping move building supplies from the riverbank landing to the construction site of the new church. In 1983, he was at Holy Cross for Holy Week and Easter.

At the end of July 1983, Father Renner, while continuing on as director of the Alaskan Shepherd program, began serving as "visiting priest" to **Ruby**,

Father Louis L. Renner, S.J., before Christ the King statue on King Island, June 1974, with the village of Ukivok below him. *LRC.*

commuting there from Fairbanks about every third week.

The year 1984 was one of special highlights for Father Renner. In March, he attended the initial Diocesan Planning meeting at St. Mary's, giving a slide presentation on the history of the Church in Alaska. On May 1st, in Sacred Heart Cathedral, Fairbanks, he was part of the ceremonies at which Michael J. **Kaniecki**, S.J., was ordained a bishop. The following day he was at the Fairbanks International Airport, when Pope John Paul II and President Ronald Reagan spent a number of hours there. He had been part of the Papal Visit Planning Committee. He spent the last days of June and the first days of July in Nome doing research for the above mentioned book on radio station KNOM and Father James E. Poole, S.J. On June 29th, he stood solo on top of the Seward Peninsula's highest peak, 4,714-foot Mt. Osborne. On the 30th, he hiked into the abandoned **Pilgrim Hot Springs** Mission, being the last one to hike over a stretch of tundra to get there. The road all the way in to the mission was completed a short time later.

Other years, too, had their highlights. In April 1985, he attended the traditional Koyukon Athabaskan mortuary feast, the "stickdance," in Kaltag. In June 1986, as part of a group that included Fathers Mueller and Tero, he rubber-rafted for four days down the Copper River from Chitina to near **Cordova**.

From August 1987 to June 1992, Father Renner was visiting priest to **Tanana**. In 1992, wanting more time for writing, he expressed his wish to be freed of the Tanana assignment. His wish was granted. For the next decade, however, he was frequently back on the Yukon, mostly in Ruby for Christmas, Holy Week, and Easter services.

In June 1989, Father Renner spent several weeks camping on the banks of the Nushagak River, a few miles downstream from **Dillingham**. This marked the beginning of a series of annual "working vacations" that lasted until the year 2001 inclusive. (He missed the Dillingham outing only in 1994, the year he celebrated his golden jubilee as a Jesuit.) He was there to help his long-time Alaskan friends— Richard and Gisela Dykema, both of whom, along with two of their daughters, had been in his German classes at the University of Alaska–Fairbanks—set up fish-camp and set-net fish for the king and sockeye salmon that put Dillingham on the map as one of the world's foremost fisheries.

In the fall of 1993, it was made known that priests were needed to do prison ministry in the Fairbanks Correctional Center. Father Renner, though he did not consider himself "a natural" for prison ministry, volunteered; and, for three years, took his monthly turn. Generally, he was accompanied by Mary Therese **Burik**.

On June 6, 1995, a grateful Bishop Kaniecki wrote to Father Renner: "Louie, I can't praise you enough for the fine work you do in the Shepherd Office. Your articles are superb, and I think our reading audience justly recognizes that. Thanks for a superb job, and all the support you have given me."

The Great and Sacred Jubilee Year of Our Lord 2000 brought with it events of major importance for Father Renner and the Diocese of Fairbanks. On April 14th, he concelebrated at the Mass offered on the occasion of the dedication of the Catholic Schools' new Holy Family Chapel. On May 1st, he wrote a lengthy letter to his Father Provincial, Robert E. Grimm, S.J., about the possibility of his eventually moving to Gonzaga University with a view to writing a history of the Catholic Church in Alaska. On August 6th, he learned of the sudden death of Bishop Kaniecki. Very busy days followed upon this. And, all the while, preparations for the Jubilee 2000 celebrations, scheduled to take place in Fairbanks' Carlson Center the last weekend in August, were underway. A major photo exhibit was planned. Father Renner was responsible for selecting photos of all the churches in the Diocese of Fairbanks and of all the men who had held positions of ecclesiastical authority in the diocese, as well as for writing suitable captions. November 2nd was truly a red-letter day in his life. Before the day was out, he had in hand one of the five copies of the *Koyukon Athabaskan Dictionary* to reach Fairbanks. As "Editorial and Bibliographical Consultant" and author of the biographical sketch of Father Julius **Jetté**, S.J., printed in the dictionary, he had invested much time and effort in that monumental work.

With the dawning of the Year of Our Lord 2002,

dawned a year that was to bring about a major change in the life of Father Renner. By the end of February, he had received a letter from Father Grimm informing him: "Now is the time to take up a new mission. On behalf of the Society, I mission you to a ministry of scholarship. I mission you to continue your work writing a history of the Catholic Church in Alaska and ask you to go to Gonzaga University Jesuit Community as a scholar in residence to carry out this ministry."

In an article about Father Renner that appeared in the April 29, 2002, issue of the *Fairbanks Daily News-Miner*, Father Renner is quoted as saying: "I have had but one desire in my life: to fulfill God's plan for me. My whole life has consisted in offering myself totally—bodily, mentally and spiritually—to the will of God. I have no plan for myself. I have only tried to do what God wanted of me."

On Saturday morning, June 8, 2002, Father Renner took a last, slow, nostalgic walk up to the University of Alaska–Fairbanks campus. Late in the evening of the following day, Father **Joseph E. Laudwein**, S.J., drove him to the Fairbanks airport; and, by early Monday morning, June 10th, Father Renner was in Jesuit House at Gonzaga University. He was now out of Alaska—but Alaska was not out of him. At first, he missed it intensely, even to the point of ache. However, he soon got settled in at Gonzaga and on with the writing.

In September 2002, Father Renner received a letter from the Alaska Humanities Forum informing him that he had been "selected to receive the Governor's Award for Friends of the Humanities, awarded to that individual who has advanced the humanities through life-long efforts." The award was presented by Alaska's Governor, Tony Knowles, at a public ceremony held in Anchorage on October 25th. Father Richard D. **Case**, S.J., accepted the award on Father Renner's behalf.

As the year 2004 was beginning to unfold, Father Renner was still working away at what he hoped would, "in due time," be completed and published as *Alaskana Catholica: A History of the Catholic Church in Alaska—A Reference Work in the Format of an Encyclopedia.*

47, 85, 88, 89, 91, 100, 105, 113, 115, 117, 126, 128, 201

RIOBÓ, Fray Juan Antonio García, O.F.M.

On Ascension Thursday, May 13, 1779, Franciscan Fray Juan Antonio García Riobó, assisted by fellow Franciscan priest Matías de Santa Catalina and secular priest Cristóbal Antonio Díaz, offered a Mass of Thanksgiving at Port Santa Cruz, Suemez Island, Bucareli Bay near **Craig**, **Alaska**. This was the first act of formal Catholic worship in Alaska. The three priests were members of the Don Ignacio de Arteaga exploratory expedition that had sailed north from San Blas, Mexico, on the two frigates *La Princesa* and *La Favorita*.

191

ROBAUT, Father Aloysius J., S.J.

The Christmas of 1887 was the young Jesuit missionary priest's first in **Alaska**. By New Year's Eve, however, he was so firmly convinced that it was also his last—the last of his life—that he called to his bedside his companion and instructed him: "Brother, I do not think I will see the New Year Day tomorrow. You will find the old boat. Break it up and make a coffin as best you can, and next spring, when there are long days and a good trail, bring my corpse to **Nulato**. I want to be buried, where Archbishop **Seghers** was killed." The Brother was spared that mournful task, for the young priest recovered, and went on to spend over four decades of fruitful ministry in northern Alaska.

Aloysius J. Robaut was born in Peillon, Alpes-Maritimes, France, on April 12, 1855. He entered the Jesuit Order on March 18, 1873. As a recently ordained priest, he arrived in Spokane, Washington Territory, in 1883. Among his first assignments in the Northwest was St. Francis Regis Mission in Colville, Washington.

In 1886, Father Robaut, along with Father Paschal **Tosi**, S.J., was chosen by Rocky Mountain Mission Superior Father Joseph M. **Cataldo**, S.J., to accompany Archbishop Seghers on his trip to northern Alaska. It was the latter's intention to establish permanent missions there, with Jesuits in charge. Father Cataldo's intention, however, was that the two Jesuits should go with the archbishop merely as companions, "on loan, for a visit to spy out the

Father Aloysius J. Robaut,
S.J. *JOPA-909.01.*

Racket down to **St. Michael**'s, where they reached on
the 14th of June. On the 27th, Fr. Tosi started on the
steamer *Dora* for San Francisco to bring the news there.
Fr. Robaut, after having buried temporarily the Archbishop in the Russian graveyard at St. Michael's, started up the river on the 12th of July, 1887. He arrived at
Anvik the 23rd of July.

Father Tosi went south not only to bring news of
Archbishop Seghers' death, but also to find out from
Father Cataldo what Jesuits should now do concerning Alaska. Father Cataldo's response was
entirely favorable. He decided then and there that
the Jesuits would assume, subject to Rome's
approval, charge of the Alaska Mission. When
Father Tosi, now officially appointed Superior of
the Alaska Mission, went back north that summer,
he took with him Father Aloysius A. **Ragaru**, S.J.,
and Brother Carmelo **Giordano**, S.J.

From Anvik, on July 31st, a wholly disconsolate
and lonely Father Robaut wrote a long letter to the
administrator of the Diocese of Vancouver Island.
"It is with a sick heart and a much felt desponden-
cy of mind that I am now trying to write," he began.
"The fearful news of the horrible murder" made him
feel sick. Father Robaut had come to greatly revere
the archbishop; and, in turn, the latter had come to
regard him as "a very fine fellow." To add to his
dejection, Father Robaut suffered from "a dreadful
felon" on his thumb, so that for nearly two weeks
he had been unable to get any rest whatever.

Yet, despite Father Robaut's general misery, the
thought of his leaving Alaska never so much as
entered his mind. In his ramshackle log cabin, he
began to apply himself "totally to the learning of
the Russian and Indian languages," and he tried "to
keep up the mission Most Rev. Archp. Seghers had
intended to start."

On August 24th, one month after Father Robaut
arrived at Anvik, he took the steamer up to Nuklukayet, today's **Tanana**, which he reached on September 5th. There, on the 21st, "with amazement
and joy," he met Fathers Tosi and Ragaru and
Brother Giordano. The three had just come into
Alaska via the Chilkoot Pass and the upper Yukon.
With Brother Giordano, Father Robaut returned to
Anvik. In late October, he made a trip downriver
to scout out the Koserefsky area. He was well
received by the people there.

land," and "till we [Jesuits] could hear what our
European Superiors would dispose about accepting
missions in Alaska." The three, along with Frank
Fuller, a layman chosen by Archbishop Seghers as
his companion, left Victoria on July 13, 1886.
Almost two months later, via the Inside Passage and
the Chilkoot Pass, they arrived on September 7th
at Harper's Place, a trading post at the confluence
of the Stewart and Yukon Rivers.

It being now relatively late in the season for river
travel, it was decided that the two Jesuits would
spend the winter at Harper's Place, studying the
local language and doing whatever ministerial work
they could. The archbishop, for his part, persisted
in his resolve to continue on downriver with Fuller
to Nulato. Leaving Fathers Tosi and Robaut behind,
with the intention of meeting them downriver in the
spring, Archbishop Seghers and Fuller pushed off
for Nulato. On the north bank of the Yukon River,
about 40 miles upstream from Nulato, early in the
morning of November 28th, a demented Fuller
shot Archbishop Seghers to death.

Writing in the third person, Father Robaut left an
account of the events of the spring and summer of
1887:

> On the following spring the two Fathers left Stewart
> on the 25th of April with the intention of rejoining the
> Bishop and settle affairs with him, but received on their
> way near the old Fort Yukon the first news that Fuller
> had murdered his Lordship: it was on the 6th of June,
> 1887. They continued their way on the steamer *New*

During his stay in Nuklukayet in September, Father Robaut had lived with the trader, Andrew Fredericks. At Anvik, he now had with him the latter's two sons, William and George. He was to teach them English; they were to teach him the local Indian language and act as his interpreters. With one of the boys and an Indian from Anvik as guide, he, in early December, made a dogsled trip to **Shageluk** to get acquainted with the people there. While there, he witnessed "a great Indian feast. Over 500 Indians were gathered to celebrate their great Advent feast they call 'Ayoh'." The feast in question here is the "stickdance," or "Feast for the Dead."

Back at Anvik, Father Robaut spent some of his time instructing the children of the village and teaching them hymns. But the Rev. John W. Chapman, Episcopal missionary at Anvik from 1887 to 1930, had already begun his long and fruitful ministry there, and Father Robaut began to have serious doubts about making Anvik a Catholic mission center. His decision to leave the place was made easy for him by the fact that toward the middle of February 1888 Natives from Koserefsky, who had come to Anvik to trade, invited him to come down and live among them.

"So, considering everything," Father Robaut wrote,

> I thought it a good deal better to give up Anvik and come down 50 miles below, where I knew, from last year, that there was a larger village, with better Indians, and with a much better prospect than at Anvik. Therefore, as soon as I thought it prudent to travel, which was on the 23rd of February, I started for Kosoriffsky [sic], where I was received with open arms by the Indians, who had been urging me the whole winter to come down to them; nay, they themselves, when they heard that I would come, sent me three sleds with eighteen dogs to take me. Since that time I have been here with them and feel most happy.

At Koserefsky, Father Robaut, along with Brother Giordano, spent the first several days living with an Indian family in their cabin. But, seeing that their "scanty little provisions were disappearing a little too fast," they moved into the cabin Father Robaut had purchased the previous autumn. This was not in Koserefsky itself, but on the opposite bank of the Yukon. From there, Father Robaut daily crossed the river on ice to teach the people and to learn their

language. Realizing, however, that his place of residence was not quite fit for a permanent missionary station, he inquired of the Natives, where he might find a location better suited to his purpose. The people seemed at a loss as to what information they could give him concerning this subject.

One day, however, a young man, who had been hired to do some work around the missionaries' cabin, said to Father Robaut: "There would be a good place for a mission not far from here, but the Indians would not suggest it to you, as they believe it is haunted by ghosts." "Will you show it to me?" asked Father Robaut. "Yes," answered the young man, "provided you don't tell the people." "They won't know anything about it," Father Robaut assured him. Accordingly, they climbed up a bluff, and from there the young man showed Father Robaut a level stretch of land, protected on the north by said bluff, and on the west by low, wooded hills, while on the east flowed by silently, majestically, the mighty Yukon. To the south, one could see only forests, dotted here and there with lakes. Father Robaut was pleased with what he saw, and thanked the young man for his help in the matter. Around the middle of June, Father Robaut and Brother Giordano relocated their cabin to what Father Robaut described 21 years later as "a perfect wilderness."

By October 8, 1888, however, there were in this "perfect wilderness" two log houses. One was occupied by three Sisters of St. **Ann** and the three-year-old Anutka Neumann, daughter of the superintendent of the Alaska Commercial Company at St. Michael; and the other by Father Robaut and new arrival Brother John B. **Rosati**, S.J., and a boy from Nulato. By now, this stretch of wilderness had a name: "Mission of the **Holy Cross**."

During his first winter at Holy Cross, Father Robaut made occasional missionary trips to **Paimiut**, where, by March of 1889, he was able to baptize several Eskimos. When spring arrived, he undertook the building of a schoolhouse at Holy Cross. This was ready by the end of September of that year. By then, the mission had 13 boarders. By the following year, life at the newly founded mission, though basic and simple, was supported by a dedication and seriousness of purpose on the part of all involved that gave assurance of the mission's continued prosperity. Accordingly, in 1890, Father

Tosi, no longer considering Father Robaut's presence at Holy Cross essential to its vitality, assigned him to Nulato, where he spent the years 1890–92.

At Nulato, Father Robaut devoted much of his time to the study of the Koyukon language. Struggling with that language, he found that "it has an immense amount of different sounds, which require the ears of a lynx to catch them." Nevertheless, he did gain proficiency in Koyukon. His fellow missionary, Father Ragaru, while working on a dictionary and grammar, turned to him for help. Two decades later, Father Julius **Jetté**, S.J., the most scholarly and best linguist ever of all the Jesuits in Alaska, turned repeatedly to him—to whom he referred, jokingly, yet seriously enough, as his "Source of Knowledge"—for information on fine points of the Koyukon language.

As a linguist, however, Father Robaut made a name for himself not so much for his expertise in Koyukon as for his expertise in the language of the Central Yup'ik Eskimos. He spent many of his active years among them, especially among those of Paimiut and **Ohagamiut**. His Central Yup'ik language contribution has been described as having "great variety and depth, and is considered expert."

In 1892, Father Robaut, though "very happy" at Nulato, was reassigned to Holy Cross. While there, during the next two years, he made missionary journeys to Shageluk, and to the Eskimo villages of **Chaneliak**, **Kotlik** and Ohagamiut.

In the fall of 1892, Father Tosi had a mission house built at Ohagamiut, situated nearly two miles east of Upper **Kalskag** on the north bank of the Kuskokwim River and numbering, in 1880, 130 inhabitants. In 1894, Father Robaut was put in charge of the new mission, dedicated to St. Ignatius, founder of the Jesuit Order. From 1894 to 1916, Father Robaut divided his time more or less equally among the people of Holy Cross, Ohagamiut, and Paimiut. Paimiut, about 25 miles below Holy Cross, served him well as a halfway station between Holy Cross and Ohagamiut.

Most of Father Robaut's missionary excursions were made in the winter, when the people were in their villages, rather than in their widely scattered summer and fall fishing and hunting camps. Naturally, they were made by dogteam. After his first winter in Alaska, he wrote: "For my part I am not a lover of sled and dogs. I got enough of it last winter. Sometimes I would have drowned both dogs and sled, had it been in my power; but, of course, we must get used to it." He did get used to it, and became an expert dog musher. In recognition of his speed when on the trail, the Natives referred to him as "the man who can run."

After four years of intermittent work on the Kuskokwim, Father Robaut was able to write, in 1898, to his ecclesiastical Superior, John B. **René**, S.J.:

> St. Ignatius' Mission seems to me by far the most destitute of all our places in this country of Alaska. I have yet no church, no accommodations, and no church goods, except my traveling chapel [Mass kit], which is put up in a room serving at one time for a church, at another for a reception room, dining room and kitchen, and at night for a sleeping room. But, on the other hand, things look quite different from the spiritual standpoint. I have no hesitation in saying that, in my opinion, St. Ignatius' Mission on the Kuskokwim is likely to become the very best field for apostolic work we possess in the northern part of Alaska territory. Everything here foreshadows important results, and I hope soon to be able to make it an evident fact to you that nowhere else have we greater hope of solid and lasting good.

The winter of 1901–02 was an exceptionally cold one. In the last week of December, while returning from the Kuskokwim to Holy Cross, Father Robaut, according to the Holy Cross Mission house diary, "got his feet frozen badly, and his nose too. He started from his village with only three dogs, hoping to have a good road and make Paimiut in one day; besides, he was not well. He found the tundra very bad, lost his road, was all wet and had to sleep outside without tent and fire, so he got frozen his feet." Several Paimiut men brought him to Holy Cross. His feet were so badly frozen that it was feared at first that he would lose most of his toes. But only the big one on his left foot had to be amputated. The operation was performed by Brother Joseph V. O'Hare, S.J.—with his pocketknife. For the rest of the winter, Father Robaut was unable to be on his feet.

Not long after his trial by frost, Father Robaut had to undergo another trial, this time a trial by fire. In the mission house diary, under date of December 1, 1903, Father John L. **Lucchesi**, S.J., Superior of Holy Cross—writing more in the Italian than in the English idiom—wrote:

At 6 P.M. Fr. Robaut comes from Orarameut [Ohagamiut]. . . . Sad news! Sunday night he woke up and found plenty of thick smoke in the house; went to open the damper and after the inside and outside door, but it was worse! The fire had begun, as it seems, around the stove, burning the socks that were put to dry around, communicated itself to the floor, to the calico hanging on the walls. Fr. could not stand the suffocating smoke; so he runned, as he was only in night shirt, to the village for help, but before he could get any, all house was in fire, and the Indians could save only his trunk with few trifles inside. Everything else in ashes! Let us thank God that Fr. could save his life! He started immediately, borrowing from the Indians parke, pants, shoes, etc.—without not even waiting the end of the fire. His writings, fruit of more than 14 years of hard labour, all also lost!

It was the loss of the priceless, irreplaceable language manuscripts that especially pained Father Robaut. As he stood there in his bare feet in the snow, watching everything go up in flames, he was heard to cry, "My papers! My papers!"

The destruction of the mission dwelling, however, did not interrupt missionary activity on the Kuskokwim for long. "After a few days," according to the mission diary, "Fr. Lucchesi went to the banks of the Kuskokwim and ordered two natives to make habitable that building in which Fr. Robaut kept his carpentry tools. When that was done, Fr. Robaut returned again to his country."

By 1908, Father Robaut was clearly in love with his mission—or "hermitage," as he called it—on the Kuskokwim. In a letter he wrote to Father Jetté in August of that year, he described himself as "an old gray-bearded and bald hermit," and to his mission he referred as "my Kuskokwim home, where my people are dying to have me back with them." A year later, in another letter, he referred to his Kuskokwim station as "my old and beloved mission of St. Ignatius."

Paimiut, rather than Ohagamiut, was Father Robaut's winter residence in 1910. In a letter to his Father Provincial, dated Holy Cross, April 22, 1913, he wrote:

For over 15 years I have been residing most of the time in Kuskokwim, most of the time alone with the Indians [Eskimos], never or scarcely ever hearing a word of English, except when coming to Holy Cross, but now, since three years ago, my residence is down in Pimute, where I have a pretty good and flourishing congregation. I left the old St. Ignatius Mission because most of my old congregation have been swept away by general epidemic, a good many have settled themselves up in Pimute or at Holy Cross, and only a few remain at St. Ignatius, and these I only visit them once in a while.

Father Robaut took his missionary work seriously enough, but himself rather lightly. In that same letter he wrote:

This short account of my solitary and eremitical life away from our own people and civilized world will suffice to enable you to understand the natural fact of my being a regular crank, both in my ways and in my style. Nevertheless, I like my romantic life, and I am never lonesome, and Almighty God has favored me with an excellent health, so that I am not in need of Father to recreate me, nor of Brother to cook for me nor to take care of me. I am sufficient to myself in everything, so far at least. Should I get too old, God will provide.

In that same letter he wrote further: "I like the Indians, and I think I can say that they like me in return; although at times, i.e., when they misbehave, I am worse and more frightful than a grizzly bear. Anyhow, as a rule, they always take well the strokes of my pastoral rod."

By this time, Father Robaut had spent nearly 27 years in the North. He was still able to write that he continued to be "vigorous and robust" and as happy as when he first came into the country—except that then he was "as light and agile as an arctic hare," whereas by this time he had grown "to be a huge mass of flesh, nerves and bones." Nevertheless, the people of Holy Cross continued to call him "the thin priest." His one major regret was that he could no longer run with the dogs on sled trips, and had, instead, often to sit on the sled.

In 1914, after residing in Paimiut for four years, Father Robaut again made Holy Cross his home base for the next two years. He then spent the years 1916–18 at **Akulurak**. While there, on January 15, 1918, he suffered the first of a series of apoplectic strokes. As a result, his memory was, for a time, almost totally gone, and his hands and eyes unsteady and weak. He was unable to do any ministry except offer Mass privately and hear the confessions of his fellow Jesuits there. He spent almost all his time in prayer. However, by April of that year, he was well enough to go to St. Michael. There, over a year later, in August of 1919, he suffered another stroke, his third, that partially paralyzed him, and impaired greatly both his memory and articulation. By September 7th, he was back at Holy Cross, there to spend the rest of his days.

The keepers of the Holy Cross diary had little to record for the years 1919–30 concerning Father Robaut. We read that he once went to the wood camp to offer Mass there, and that he occasionally offered Mass in the church or in one of the mission chapels. In 1922, his whole existence was summed up with the one word, "senex" [old man].

But, there were several highlights during the last decade of Father Robaut's life. On April 17, 1923, he celebrated his golden jubilee as a Jesuit. To make the occasion memorable, a reception was held in the evening in his honor. The chief events of his life, especially as a missionary, were recalled. Several cornet duets and several numbers by the Big Boys Symphony Orchestra lent a musical note to the festive occasion. By way of gifts, Father Robaut received an album of photos from the Sisters, a beaded moose hide cushion from Mr. and Mrs. Ivan Demientieff, and a gold nugget from Mrs. C.P. Gerhart. The evening's festivities ended with Father Robaut's thanking and blessing all present—and announcing a holiday. "A friendly family spirit," recorded the diarist, "was the tone of the evening's doings." On the following day, there was a High Mass in his honor. For his text, the celebrant of the Mass chose the words: "Go out from your father's house, and go into a land which I will show you."

On September 24, 1930, Father Robaut, who had never seen an automobile, was given a ride in an airplane, the *Marquette Missionary*, a plane owned by the Alaska Mission and in the care of Brother George J. **Feltes**, S.J. Recalling Father Robaut's airplane ride, Brother Feltes said, "He got quite a kick out of it."

It was by now late evening in the life of the pioneer Jesuit Alaskan missionary. Less than two months after that memorable airplane ride, the diarist, under date of November 10, 1930, wrote, "Father Robaut goes to the hospital to stay." He received Holy Viaticum on December 12th. The following day: "Fr. Robaut sinking." On the 18th: "Fr. Robaut dies at 9:45 A.M., as easily as if he were falling into a deep sleep." The following day, after the Requiem Mass, his body was buried in the hillside cemetery overlooking the mission he had founded 42 years earlier. According to Father Segundo **Llorente**, S.J., Father Aloysius J. Robaut, S.J., belonged to "the era of giants."

94, 99

ROCCATI, Father Aloysius J., S.J.

Aloysius J. Roccati was born in Turin, Italy, on July 1, 1878, the seventh of eleven children. He entered the novitiate of the Turin Province of the Society of Jesus on August 4, 1894. There he made his novitiate, his classical, humanities, and philosophical studies. For two years he taught in Turin, and for two in Cuneo. He began his theological studies in Chieri, Italy. While in his second year, he volunteered for the Rocky Mountain Mission. In 1906, he came to Spokane, Washington, where he completed his theological studies and was ordained a priest on June 7, 1908. During the year 1908–09, he made his tertianship at Florissant, Missouri.

Father Roccati spent the years 1909–11 in Portland, Oregon, at St. Michael's parish, a parish for Italians. From 1911–15 he was in Spokane, living at Gonzaga University, but ministering to Italians, especially to those living in Spokane's Minnehaha district. On foot, or by streetcar, he commuted between Gonzaga and Minnehaha. He was responsible for getting St. Mary's Church, a mission station of St. Aloysius parish, built there.

In 1915, Father Roccati became pastor of the Nativity of the Blessed Virgin Mary parish in **Juneau, Alaska**, a post he was to hold for ten years. According to historian Gerard G. Steckler, S.J., Father Roccati, as pastor of the Juneau parish, "cemented the unity of the group of buildings on the Catholic block by the erection of a parish school, dedicated in the autumn of 1919." The

Catholic block serves "as a monument to the zeal of Father Roccati, the pastor, and to the devoted cooperation of the Sisters of St. **Ann**. It serves as a school, a parish house and a social and recreational center."

While stationed in Juneau, Father Roccati frequently traveled to other towns in Southeastern Alaska. In 1922, he went to **Sitka** to tear down the old "barn church" and to build a new one.

Once, while trying to find the money needed for his construction projects in Juneau, Father Roccati asked one of the bankers for a loan, but admitted that he had no collateral for it. The banker is said to have replied, "When the very name of Father Roccati is not sufficient collateral, then it is time to close this bank."

During his Juneau years, Father Roccati served also as Chancellor of the Vicariate of Alaska. After his Juneau years, he spent the remaining 40 years of his life, 1925–65, at Holy Family parish in San Jose, California. He died at Santa Cruz, California, on July 2, 1965, and lies buried in the Jesuit cemetery at Santa Clara University.

ROSATI, Brother John B., S.J.

So careful was he in guarding his eyes lest they see something vain, that the Natives called him "Shut Eyes." Sisters of St. **Ann**, with whom he traveled to **Alaska**, said of him that no one could tell the color of his eyes because of the strict guard he kept over them. He was the second Jesuit Lay Brother to serve in Alaska. Brother Carmelo **Giordano** had arrived there in 1887.

John B. Rosati was born in Cosenza, Italy, on March 10, 1856. He entered the Jesuit Order on April 2, 1878. Ten years later, on June 26, 1888, he arrived at **St. Michael**. **Holy Cross Mission** was the scene of most of his Alaskan years. He spent the year 1890–91 at **Tununak**. During that winter, he suffered a great deal. Father Francis A. **Barnum**, S.J., wrote of him that he "fell victim to Polar Anaemia. He became dull and listless and seemed to take no interest in anything. As he became more affected, he began declaring that the devil was constantly around and that he could smell him." Brother Rosati left Alaska in 1895, but then returned to

spend one more year there, 1902–03, in **Juneau**. His Alaskan years may have been difficult ones for him, but they did not shorten his life. He died in San Jose, California, on April 13, 1935, at the age of 79.

ROSHKO, Father Vsevolod

Father Vsevolod Roshko—also, Rochcau and Rochkau—a priest of the Byzantine Rite and a subject of the Sacred Congregation for the Oriental Church, was born in Moscow, Russia, on May 12, 1917. When he was six years old, the family fled Russia for France. He was granted French citizenship and was raised and schooled in France. On June 9, 1946, after completing studies at the *Russicum*, the Russian college in Rome, he was ordained a priest in Rome by Archbishop A. Avreinof. As a young priest, Father Roshko taught in a Paris school for Russian boys. He next spent some time in Chile and North Africa. He was a member of the secular institute of the Little Brothers of Jesus, and had strong inclinations to be a hermit.

Sponsored by Francis D. **Gleeson**, S.J., Vicar Apostolic of **Alaska** at the time, Father Roshko came to Alaska in the summer of 1955. For a short time, he was among "the Oriental people" around Copper Center. On September 30th, he landed for the first time on **Little Diomede** Island, where he spent the next three years engaged in a pastoral ministry.

In the summer of 1958, Father Roshko went to **Dillingham**, where he founded an Eastern Rite mission. He had hoped, at first, to locate in the Eskimo village of Togiak, where he even bought a house. However, within ten days, he realized that there was no meaningful future for him in Togiak. At Dillingham, close to the Catholic mission school, near Squaw Creek, he built, with his own hands, a frame structure church, the Church of the Protective Stole of the Blessed Virgin Mary. This, built in the Byzantine style, had a live tree growing in its center. Attached to the church were his small living quarters.

Father Roshko spent seven years at Dillingham; but, from an apostolic viewpoint, they were not very fruitful years. He described himself as a man more at home with books than with apostolic ministries. He wrote a number of scholarly articles about the Russian Orthodox Church in Alaska. In 1965, he left Alaska for Rome. Later he moved to Jerusalem. He is remembered as "a tall, refined, rather stately priest," with a black beard adding to his appearance.

15

ROSSI, Father Crispin S., S.J.

"Father dry wash," the Koyukon Athabaskan Indian people of **Nulato** called him, because of the way he habitually rubbed his hands when he spoke. But, even 55 years after his death, he was still remembered by the older ones as "a nice priest, a favorite Father." They remembered him and loved him as one who spoke their language well and was understanding of their cultural traditions. Though he was of "commanding stature," they found him "sweet of character and of approachable manner, very fatherly in the confessional." A fellow Jesuit, who knew him well, characterized him as "a man remarkable in prayer, zealous and sacrificed [*sic*] worker, and sublime in humility."

Crispino S. Rossi was born on February 21, 1857, in Genoa, Italy. At an early age, he was ordained a diocesan priest. As such, he then taught for seven years, with great distinction, Latin, Greek, and Rhetoric in the major diocesan seminary in Genoa. His appreciation and love of Italian literature stayed with him throughout his life.

Father Rossi entered the novitiate of the Society of Jesus at Chieri, Italy, on July 28, 1889. After completing his noviceship, he taught at the Jesuit college in Cuneo, Italy. Throughout the years he was teaching—and, at the same time, making a name for himself as an eloquent preacher—he was pleading with Superiors to be sent to the missions of northern **Alaska**. His pleas were heard.

In the summer of 1899, Father Rossi was in Spokane, Washington, learning English. In July 1900, he arrived at **Holy Cross Mission**, where he spent his first Alaskan year. During that year, he distinguished himself by his solicitude and care for the many victims of the epidemic that decimated the Native people along the Yukon.

Father Crispin S. Rossi, S.J. *JOPA-1076.01.*

Father Rossi's next assignment took him to **Nulato**, where he was to spend 23 of his 27 years in Alaska. At Nulato, under the tutelage of Father Julius **Jetté**, S.J., he set about learning the Koyukon Athabaskan Indian language. He gained a good command of it and produced several dictionary manuscripts in it. The people admired him for understanding and speaking their language. They admired him also for the way he traveled up and down the Yukon in his little rowboat, stopping at every fish camp, making all feel at home and happy and better because of his visits. In winter, he traveled by dogsled, visiting outlying villages and hunting and trapping camps. His people were dear to Father Rossi. He would not allow anyone to speak unkindly of his Native flock. Charitably, he would gloss over their shortcomings.

For the year 1918–19, Father Rossi was stationed at St. Mary's Mission, **Akulurak**. There again he worked heroically, this time in caring for the victims of the influenza epidemic that raged throughout most of western Alaska that year.

For health reasons, Father Rossi spent the year 1913–14 not at Nulato, but at Holy Cross. He was then back at Nulato again, until early October 1926, when he was again assigned to Holy Cross. He was in good health at the time, but Holy Cross turned out to be the final scene of his labors. During the latter part of February 1927, he spent two weeks in Bonasila, a village a short distance upriver from

Holy Cross, "instructing the Natives." He returned to Holy Cross with nothing to indicate health problems. However, on March 15th, the following entry was made in the Holy Cross house diary: "Father Rossi unable to say Mass. A pain on the chest and a sharp headache have suddenly come upon him since last night." Three days later, on March 18, 1927, surrounded by the priests and Brothers stationed at the mission, "the end came peacefully."

Father Rossi's death was most unexpected. A few days after it, Father Philip I. **Delon**, S.J., General Superior of the Alaska Mission and at Holy Cross at the time, wrote to the Father Provincial: "He was in perfect health until four days before his death. Up and around and very lively."

Father Crispin Rossi, "a grand old gentleman," as he had been referred to a few years previously by Father S. Aloysius **Eline**, S.J., was laid to rest on March 21st in the Holy Cross Mission cemetery.

(*top*) The new St. Peter-in-Chains Church, Ruby, as it appeared in 2003, not yet finished. The old church, attached to the back of the new, is visible on the left. *LRC.*

(*bottom*) St. Peter-in-Chains Church, Ruby—built by Father James C. Spils, S.J., during the year 1948–49—as it appeared on Christmas Day, 1983. *LR.*

RUBY

Ruby, "The Gem of the Yukon," located on the left bank of the Yukon River, began as a white man's gold-rush community, when gold was discovered on Ruby Creek, close to the site of the present-day Ruby, in 1907. But a town did not develop until 1911, when gold was discovered on nearby Long Creek and a stampede followed. Soon the community numbered over a thousand. A Ruby post office was established in 1912. By 1920, however, Ruby's population was down to 128. In 1939, it had 138 inhabitants; in 1950, 132; in 1960, 179; in 1970, 147; in 1980, 197; and in the year 2000, 188. During the time of the gold-rush boom, Koyukon Athabaskan Indians began to move from **Kokrines** to Ruby. Since shortly after the boom, Ruby's population has consisted largely of Native people.

According to the Ruby diary, Father Hormisdas Ferron, S.J., offered the first Mass ever celebrated in Ruby in the home of Mr. Henry Lovely in August 1912. In September of that year, Father Ferron baptized the first boy born in Ruby, Thomas H. De Vane. The following month, he bought a lot with a one-story frame building on it. This he adapted for use as a church and priest's quarters. The church was placed under the patronage of St. Peter the Apostle. In more recent years, the church has been known as "St. Peter-in-Chains."

During the year 1948–49, Father James C. **Spils**, S.J., built a new church in Ruby. This was built solid, after the image of its builder, and served for over half a century as Ruby's church. On October 26, 1948, Father Spils wrote to Father James U. **Conwell**, S.J.: "You can tell the bishop that my church looks neat and clean inside. It is tight against the winds. In fact, you'd hardly know a blizzard was on until you stepped outside." The following summer, he put "brick paper" on the outside walls and topped the building off with metal roofing. In the autumn of 1982, the priest's quarters were enlarged, when the back of the building was extended. In the summer of 2001, the "Father Spils church" was repositioned to serve as an all-purpose building attached to the new church. The new church was "under cover" by the end of 2002 and scheduled to be dedicated on June 12, 2005.

Over the years, Ruby seldom has had a priest in residence. With rare exceptions, the Ruby parish was served by priests stationed at other middle Yukon villages: notably Kokrines, **Tanana**, **Nulato**, and **Galena**.

The following Jesuit Fathers served the Ruby parish: Julius **Jetté**, during the winter 1912–13, briefly, every month, out of Kokrines; Joseph-Alphonse **Desjardins**, residing in Ruby, for the most part, from April 1913 to July 1915; Jetté, July–August 1915; Crispin S. **Rossi**, during the winter of 1915; Jetté, July–August 1916; John B. **Sifton**, November–December 1916, and in June 1917, and in August 1918; S. Aloysius **Eline**, April and May 1921; Rossi, September 1923, and four days in March 1924; Joseph F. **McElmeel**, briefly in March, July and December 1925, and for longer and shorter periods from 1926–47; Francis B. **Prange**, 1928–31; Spils, 1947–54; James W. **Plamondon**, 1954–62; René **Astruc**, 1962–63; **George E. Carroll**, 1963–69; Charles A. **Saalfeld**, 1969–73; Bernard F. **McMeel**, 1973–76; Thomas W. Fisk, in residence, 1981–83; Louis L. **Renner**, out of **Fairbanks**, 1983–87.

Father Ronald K. **Dunfey**, priest of the Diocese

View of Ruby from the cemetery bluff. *LR*.

of **Juneau**, visited Ruby out of Tanana, 1976–79; and Father William Brunner, S.S.C., out of Galena, 1979–81. Franciscan priests stationed in Galena visited it from 1987–94. Beginning in 1994, and as of the year 2004, Father Joseph **Hemmer**, O.F.M., stationed in **Kaltag**, visited it on a regular basis.

The following Sisters, too, served the Ruby parish: Patricia Ann Miller, O.P., 1983–88; Peggy Glynn, O.P., 1984–88; and Margaret Usuka, S.N.D., 1988–90. Sisters of **Providence** stationed in Fairbanks taught catechism classes in Ruby during the summers of 1970–72.

Brother Kirby **Boone**, C.F.X., was headquartered in Ruby from 1990–96.

Throughout the final two decades of the second millennium, the Ruby parish was served ably and faithfully also by some of its members, notably Harold and Florence **Esmailka** and Katie Kangas. As of the year 2004, Florence and Katie, in the absence of a priest, were still filling the role of Eucharistic Minister.

Father Renner left an account of his first Ruby Christmas, that of 1983:

～

It is early Friday morning, December 23rd. Seven of us, passengers ticketed on the last scheduled pre-Christmas flight to Ruby, are crowded into the small bush air service office on the east ramp of the Fairbanks airport. Heavy snows continue to bury Alaska's interior. Chances of our making it to Ruby for Christmas look bleak. However, the flight is still "on hold," so we continue to nurse diehard hopes. The other six live in Ruby. I am the pastor of St. Peter's parish there, and the people expect me for Christmas. We pass the time making small talk, reading, dozing.

Finally, at 10:48, they decide to "give it a try." According to radio reports, things look a bit better downriver. We are not given much hope, but invited to board. We spring into action. In the pale light of the sub-Arctic dawn, leaning into the driving snow, we single-file our way to the twin-engine Chieftain parked by the hangar and climb in. Our pilot makes the usual comments about seatbelts, smoking, fire extinguishers, survival gear. We taxi out to the runway, are given clearance for takeoff, are airborne.

Through the solid, snow-filled cloud cover we bore our way upward, onward, westward, Ruby-bound. From time to time, we break briefly through the overcast and cruise along above a sea of swirling clouds. A half-hearted winter sun sheds a soft pinkish light on the cloudscape beneath us. Headwinds slow our progress.

We are now 90 minutes into our flight, and should be on the ground at Ruby. However, we have overflown Ruby and are headed for Galena. "So much for Ruby!" I think to myself, resigned. But, our pilot knows what he's doing. He "shoots the approach" to the all-weather field at Galena, plunges down through the cloud cover, makes a 180-degree turn, and doubles back upriver, skimming low along the Yukon through pelting snow. We circle and land. Great sighs of relief!

A pickup truck drives up. We transfer luggage and mail. Two join the driver in the cab; the rest of us pile in back for the two-mile drive down to the village. In the church, Peter Captain, thoughtful as always, has the new electric oil furnace going, "just in case." Church and attached priest's quarters are nice and warm.

It is now mid-afternoon. I phone people and ask them to spread the word that I made it. I grab my plastic water jugs to get water at the village Laundromat. On the way, I drop in at the Trading Post, more to be seen than to buy. People are surprised to see me, and ask, "When you come? Gonna be church tonight?"

Back in my quarters, I boil the kettle on the wood stove, and with a pint of tea wash down some pilot bread and dried salmon, as I sort through a pile of accumulated mail, mostly bulk-rate fire-starter stuff.

I shovel my way to the outhouse and the bell tower. Back inside, I hear a commotion in the church. Two young men have brought in a Christmas tree and are setting it up. We admire the tree, exchange comments about the weather, jokingly weigh the possibilities of a white Christmas. I offer tea, but they decline and go, leaving behind little pools of snowmelt and spruce-scented air smelling of Christmas.

Nora Kangas invites me to a moose stew dinner, and I accept. At 7 o'clock, I ring the bell for a 7:30 Mass. An avalanche of snow off the bell hits me in the neck. The bell's peal is muted by all the snow, but the village canine chorus hears and answers with its well-rehearsed howling. It is close to 8 by the time the last, of the few, drift in. Mass is in my quarters. The service is intimate, devotional.

After Mass, we have tea, then decorate the tree with tinsel and ornaments from Christmases past. This year, for the first time, the people will see lights on the tree in St. Peter's Church. This we owe to Peter, who only yesterday put in an outlet up front.

Before we break up, we discuss the time for Midnight Mass. Mothers with little children might prefer an earlier hour. We come to no conclusion, decide to think about it, to ask around. They go.

The place has cooled down, but I decide to leave the furnace off. It is up against the foot of my bed, and when that gun-fired, hot air hurricane—with its sucking, roaring, blowing—blasts into life, deepest sleep is rudely interrupted. I pay the Lord a brief visit in the church,

St. Peter-in-Chains Church, Ruby. Native beadwork on tanned moosehide trims the altar. The risen Christ, carved out of moose antler, is mounted on a tanned beaver pelt lashed to diamond willow saplings by moose rawhide. *MK.*

retreat into my down-filled sleeping bag, read a little, soon am fast asleep.

It is 9 o'clock, Christmas Eve morning, but still dark, when I wake up. I start a fire in the woodstove, make a short visit in the cold church, snack a breakfast, then settle back to meditate the mysteries of Christmas. The teakettle simmers; the fire, a warm companion, pops and crackles, contented. I nod off.

Confessions are scheduled from 3 to 5 this afternoon. We need heat in the church. I flip the furnace switch to "On." Nothing happens! I go out and check the oil. Plenty. Dusk is already settling. The mercury continues to drop. This furnace is beyond my campfire skills. I phone Peter. "B'right up!" he chirps.

He comes with his tools, whistling. He flips a switch here, presses a button there. No reaction. With wrenches and screwdrivers, he begins the autopsy. He suspects a plugged nozzle. To get at this vital part, he has to disassemble the very heart of our new heating machine. Plying his tools with the skill of surgeon, he soon has the floor littered with assorted pieces of metal.

His diagnosis is correct. A grain too tiny to identify has choked out life. He blows out the nozzle and reassembles everything. I assist by directing the beam of the flashlight to where needed. He presses buttons; I throw the switch. The furnace roars into life. We smile, are grateful. He paper towels up oil, wipes his hands, gathers his tools. I offer tea, but he is in a hurry. I thank him again, then ask when we should have Midnight Mass. "At midnight; it's the custom!" I mention the matter of mothers with small children. "At midnight;

it's the custom!" he repeats. That settles it. I phone the word around and post signs.

Hardly is Peter gone when the first, of the few, come for confession.

I prepare myself a simple Christmas Eve supper, a can of clam chowder and crackers. For dessert I put a badly bruised banana out of its misery. It is now 6:40, the sky clear, cloudless, star-studded, the wind of the afternoon little more than a whisper, the mercury at 3 below. I go out to clear the front steps of the church, and to shovel out again the paths to the outhouse and the bell tower. A thick fog is drifting up the Yukon valley. I pass the early evening hours listening to Handel's *Messiah*, reading, reflecting, nodding off.

As early as 11:08, the first, of the many, announce their arrival at the church entry by stomping snow off their boots. At 11:30, I go out to ring the bell, a mere formality tonight, but it adds a festive note to village life. Inside, the people begin singing carols. Well before midnight, the church is packed. I hear a few last-minute confessions in my quarters, then vest.

It is midnight. I go unto the altar of God. I greet the people: "May the grace and the peace of Christ, the Prince of Peace, Whose birthday we celebrate on this holy night, be with you all!" We pray, we sing, we hear readings about "the kindness and love of God, Our Savior," about angels and shepherds, about good news, peace and joy. Bread and wine are brought forward, offered up, made holy. Many go to Communion. I wish all a joyous Christmas, bless them, dismiss them. On foot and on snowmachines they scurry off into the night.

After Mass, I notice some gift-wrapped packages under the tree. I leave them there. I snack on fruitcake and tea, unwind, turn in. Sleep comes without an effort.

On Christmas Day morning, we have Mass at 11. The crowd is small, yawns a lot. After Mass, we gather in my quarters for tea and cookies. When all have gone, I bring in the presents, open them, and am happy to get wool socks, a velour shirt, jarred salmon strips. As I lunch leisurely, my thoughts turn to parents, brothers, sisters in faraway places, to Christmases of other years.

Katie Kangas has invited me for Christmas dinner. From experience I know that, when Katie invites, it pays to come prepared. No appetizer like a brisk, winter walk.

It is mid-afternoon now, minus 7, no wind. The fog has lifted. Every spruce needle, every birch, willow twig is furred with frost. I move through a world of bluish crystal, as I climb the steep path leading to the cemetery on the bluff overlooking the village. After plowing my way among the graves and praying for the dead, I see down below a snowmachine trail leading out across the river. I go down and follow it.

Gradually I leave the village and its sounds behind. The trail parallels the far bank for a mile, before heading up into the mouth of the Melotzi River. The cold is now more intense. A lone raven in the crown of a spruce tree calls out into the frozen stillness. Isolated stars begin to pop through the pale-blue sky. Time I headed back.

Later, in front of Ivan and me and their three little girls, Katie spreads out a turkey dinner with all the trimmings. We bless and enjoy. Afterwards, I romp with the kids, help them play with their toys.

I step out into the night air. It is laced with the smell of burning spruce and birch. No clouds, no moon, no northern lights. Myriads of stars spangling the black velvet sky above shine to their best advantage. It is now minus 21, but, all caloried up as I am, the night feels almost balmy.

This is a night for cabin-hopping. Behind every door I knock on, I find an unusually warm welcome. Tea, fruitcake, cookies, candy are pressed upon me. Kids show me their gifts. I admire a doll here, a windup robot there. The night wears on. My visits become shorter. Finally, a last "thank-you!" and a last "Merry Christmas!" I head home. Somewhat weary, but soul-satisfied, I enter the church, pray for a brief spell, thank the good Lord for inventing Christmas. I turn off the furnace, slip into the sleeping bag, stretch out, relax—soon wake up in dreamland.

Next thing I know it's Monday, no longer early, 33 below. Frost ferns adorn the window panes. The outhouse door creaks, groans on its frosty hinges. I'm scheduled to return to Fairbanks today. Will I make it? Small planes don't fly, when it gets to be about 40 below. I get ready, just in case. Then snuggle down in my sleeping bag for some reading. Soon I hear the plane buzz the village. The pickup is already outside, honking.

Two teachers and I board the Cessna 207. The pilot adjusts his headset, glances back to see that we are buckled in, turns the key. The engine coughs, catches. We begin to taxi. Full power, and in the dense, brittle-cold air, the 207 roars into the cloudless sky like a homesick angel.

A vast, empty white world slips beneath us, as we drone across the 200-plus miles that separate Ruby from Fairbanks. At 1:09 in the afternoon, we taxi up to the hangar on the east ramp. The pilot chops the power; the plane shudders momentarily, as the prop jerks to a stop. Silence, except for the clicks of rapidly cooling metal. Our pilot logs the flight on his clipboard. We unbuckle, stretch, climb out, and wait for our rides into town. Christmas 1983 is history.

1, 38, 128, 131, 162

In the Ruby cemetery, on February 13, 1984, Father Louis L. Renner, S.J., officiates at the burial of 23-year-old Harvey Albert, a Ruby man who froze to death while on the trail between two cabins on his trap-line. *Photo by Sr. Patricia Ann Miller, O.P.*

RUPPERT, Father Frederick A., S.J.

He had come to **Alaska** from southern California, where the oranges grow. He was the only Alaskan missionary priest to meet death by freezing. Within days of his death, he was hailed as "A Martyr to Charity."

Frederick A. Ruppert was born on February 2, 1879, in Gruensfeld, Baden, Germany. In 1883, his family settled in San Francisco. After completing his elementary schooling, he attended St. Ignatius College in San Francisco. He was admitted into the Society of Jesus on November 3, 1892, at Los Gatos, California. Upon finishing his two-year noviceship and three years of classical studies there, he was sent to St. Louis University in the summer of 1897 to take courses in philosophy. Since he had shown great aptitude for the natural sciences, he was told to prepare himself to teach these. At the end of his three years of philosophical studies, he spent an additional year in studies, before going on to teach physics and chemistry for five years at Santa Clara and in San

(*right*) Father Frederick A. Ruppert, S.J. *JOPA-911.15.*

(*far right*) Mink, the faithful lead-dog that watched protectingly over his frozen master, Father Frederick A. Ruppert, S.J., in December 1923, "lying near him, as if he was trying to keep him warm." *JOPA-911.09.*

Francisco. He next spent four years in Naples, Italy, studying theology. There he was ordained a priest on July 26, 1909. In 1910, he returned to Santa Clara, where he taught chemistry for a year, before making his tertianship at Poughkeepsie, New York. For three years he then taught the natural sciences to Jesuit seminarians at Mount St. Michael's and to students at Gonzaga College in Spokane. In August of 1915, he was appointed Rector of the future Loyola University in Los Angeles. Though he succeeded well as a teacher and administrator, he longed for a more arduous ministry. He asked to be sent to the missions in northern Alaska.

On September 5, 1918, Father Ruppert, described as "a gentle soul and the personification of kindness," arrived on the *Victoria* in **Nome** to minister to the whites in the Nome parish. Within two months, the gentle charity of this newcomer from California was to touch the hearts of many in and around Nome, and within a few short years an artist's conception of the man and his faithful lead-dog was to hang in Rome, and his name to become familiar to millions around the world.

Significant changes were taking place in Nome about this time. Holy Cross Hospital, which had been operated by the Sisters of **Providence** since 1902, was closed shortly after Father Ruppert's arrival. On her southbound trip, the *Victoria* had the last of the Sisters on board, for, by 1918, Nome's population had dwindled to less than a thousand and the Sisters felt that their services were more needed elsewhere.

As the *Victoria* was steaming northward on her last Nome trip of the 1918 season, precautions against an outbreak of the Spanish Influenza were being taken in Nome. Holy Cross Hospital was made ready to receive the *Victoria* passengers, who were to be quarantined in it. The ship arrived on October 20th. Its passengers, though in good health, were, nevertheless, quarantined. Soon, however, the quarantine was lifted, so that the ship could be unloaded. This meant that there was close contact between Nomeites and members of the ship's crew, carriers of the dread disease.

The *Victoria* sailed south on the 28th, leaving behind a white population of around 500 and an equal number of Eskimos. But, while she was still in the Nome roadstead, cases of influenza were already being reported. According to Father Bellarmine **Lafortune**, S.J., "the natives were simply mowed down." On October 31st, the mayor of Nome called a city meeting, at which it was decided that Holy Cross Hospital should be reopened as a hospital, with Father Ruppert in charge.

In the Nome house diary, under dates of November 1st through November 19th, Father Ruppert left an eyewitness account of the events that followed:

Nearly whole congregation ill . . . weather below zero . . . Entire Eskimo population stricken . . . several natives succumb. Hospital increasing number of patients . . . Natives perishing for want of fuel, food and inability to help themselves. Conditions most deplorable . . . More misery among natives discovered . . . Whole families perish . . . Ravages of epidemic without parallel in Nome . . . About 60 deaths among natives . . . Patients coming and going and dying.

Father Ruppert spent the months of November and December of 1918 living in the hospital and running it as the epidemic peaked and declined.

In 1920, Father Ruppert was still the pastor of Nome. Occasionally he visited the **Pilgrim Hot Springs** Mission, some 60 miles north of Nome, generally to make his retreat or to give retreats. One of his trips to the mission was rather memorable. From a letter concerning it, we gain some insight into the kind of man he was, and we learn something about the Pilgrim Springs area terrain. On the trip in question, in company of Bishop Joseph R. **Crimont**, S.J., he met with "various vicissitudes," in Father Ruppert's words. A letter written by Father **Hubert A. Post**, S.J., Superior of the Pilgrim Springs mission at the time, tells what those "vicissitudes" were:

> Bishop Crimont paid us a nice visit, but it came near costing his life . . . They made the Hot Springs Station about 2 P.M. Thence they still had 8 miles to make and his Lordship, being not strong, had to stop several times to catch his breath. Fr. Ruppert came ahead so we might send help, but he too found the road heavy and got lost in the willows after swimming the ice-cold waters of the Pilgrim. . . . Finally they reached us about quarter of twelve.

Father Ruppert spent the year 1921–22 at **Holy Cross Mission**. There he was "given charge of discipline of the boys both junior and senior." He also taught the First Communion class, and served as the stay-at-home priest at the mission.

The new year of 1923 seemed from the outset to have been preordained to be an unusual year, a year whose seasons, weathers, events were destined to be out of joint, not only on the Seward Peninsula, but also in other parts of the world. It was to be a year with signs in the heavens, signs inviting interpretation, signs deceptive in their striking brilliance and beauty.

Blizzards ushered in that fatal year. On April 25th, Father Post noted in the Hot Springs diary: "Quite cold during the night. There are 3 rings about the sun—pointing in different directions about 11 this morning. 2 disappeared shortly and one around the sun remained greater part of afternoon." In the mid-

dle of September, the extraordinary weather conditions of that year were again the subject of a diary entry. With some foreboding, Father Lafortune wrote in the Nome diary: "The summer keeps on. The nights are warm. We learn the destruction [by earthquake] of Yokohama; but here the winter is splendid. Here there is not even white frost. It is most extraordinary. Some people are apprehensive."

On October 8, 1923, Father Ruppert and Bob Ummaok, the mail carrier, left Nome for the Hot Springs. For the next two months, Father Ruppert was preoccupied with retreats. As he began his own, on October 15th, the northern lights seemed to have a message. The following day, Father Post wrote in the diary: "Weather nice. There were northern lights last night." On the 17th: "Last night we had again northern lights display, the most colorful I had ever noticed—four different semi-circles—all in wave and ribbon form. The whole night proved clear as if the moon were up in all its splendor. Even in the early morning lights were still to be seen." On the 18th: "Again northern lights last night, but not so bright." Father Ruppert finished his retreat on October 23rd, after which he gave separate 8-day retreats to the Sisters and the Brothers, with a 3-day retreat for the children in between.

At about 9:45 on the morning of Thursday, December 13th, Father Ruppert and Aloysius, a young man from Nome, left the Hot Springs for Nome. Both were driving a dogteam. Although it had snowed a little the previous night, the trail was still in poor condition for lack of snow. On the 14th, the weather was "cold, but dry," and on the 15th, "–30. Very cold again and clear." On Sunday, the 16th: "It began to blow last night. It is considerably warmer." That Sunday the people at the Hot Springs assumed—wrongly—that Father Ruppert was by then safely in Nome.

"You can imagine our rueful surprise," wrote Father Post to Bishop Crimont on December 21st, 1923, "when on Monday afternoon [the 17th] one of the leaders (Mudd) returned to us half starved." That same afternoon, according to the Hot Springs diary: "At 5:30 old John [Kakaruk] arrived, stating that he had seen tracks of a man and dogs that seemed mysterious to him and he came to report." Old John was invited to spend the night at the mission.

On the 18th, Tuesday, Brothers Peter P. **Wilhalm** and John F. **Hansen**, accompanied by Old John, set out to investigate. They returned, "a little after 3 P.M. with the sad news that they had found Fr. Ruppert's frozen body—carefully watched over by faithful old Mink, who, not recognizing them at first, would not let them approach." With his dogteam, Old John brought the body to the mission, where it was gradually thawed out and readied for burial the next day. Down in Nome no one knew anything as yet about the tragedy.

On December 21st, eight days after Father Ruppert had left the mission for Nome, Father Post wrote the above mentioned letter to Bishop Crimont and hired Fred Topkok with his team to take it to Nome. On December 22nd: "Young Fred Topkok started for Nome. We paid him 40 dollars to carry the sad news of Fr. Ruppert's death to Fr. Lafortune and thence by wire outside."

Topkok arrived in Nome on the 23rd. By the end of the next day, Christmas Eve, word of the mishap had spread throughout most of the world. "Priest dies Martyr of Charity," read the headlines of the Paris edition of the *New York Herald Tribune*. Newspapers of the great cities carried front page accounts of Father Ruppert's death, and preachers, from archbishops to country pastors, told the story on Christmas morning of the "heroic priest" who had caught the spirit of the Christ Child and lived it out to the end.

In the Nome diary, Father Lafortune recorded his reactions to the sad news:

It is an awful day for this mission. Fr. Ruppert leaves the Springs with Bob Ummoak, his brother Norbert, and two boys for Nome. Everything was well as far as Duffy's roadhouse. The next morning the Father made the fatal mistake of starting back alone for the Springs to carry a box of oranges that was at the roadhouse for the children. He was not a dog driver and he knew it; he was hampered by his glasses and he knew it was a great drawback. He knew also that there are always deers in the mountains and my dogs were wild for them. Finally he knew that the children had all the candies and pies and nuts that they wanted. What possessed him to go to the Springs anyway is more than I can say. He had to die on the banks of the Pilgrim River and he could not dodge it. We learnt the news on 23rd Dec. It was a shock all over town. It was the most gloomy Christmas I have ever seen.

Immediately many questions concerning Father Ruppert's death arose. The frozen body, clad, according to the mission diary, in only "shirt sleeves with a short sleeveless sweater, no parka," was found "about 4 miles up river." How did it get there? Where was the parka? And what had become of the sled and the other dogs? How to explain the fact that the two dogs that were accounted for "had no harness and Mudd had not even a collar"?

Concerning the details of that tragic death, Father Post prudently speculated that "the real and full truth will probably never be known." However, the written testimony of persons close to the event and various diary entries make it possible to reconstruct to a large extent the sequence of events and the circumstances that led up to, accompanied, and followed the death of Father Ruppert.

Father Ruppert, with Father Lafortune's team, left the Springs, as noted above, along with Aloysius and his team. They were followed about an hour later by the mail carrier, Bob Ummoak, and his brother Norbert. These Native men had been ordered by Father Post to accompany Father Ruppert all the way to Nome. Father Ruppert was known to be a daring man. He did not hesitate to swim the ice-cold Pilgrim River. But he was also a rather impractical man, a poor dog-musher, a man who got lost occasionally. For these reasons, Father Post made sure that he had a more than adequate escort, when he set out for Nome. In letters to Superiors, Father Post stressed this point.

The travelers spent the night of December 13th at Duffy O'Connor's roadhouse, about 25 miles from the Hot Springs. There they found the box of oranges, which Father Ruppert himself had brought up from Nome on his way to the Hot Springs in October, but could not bring all the way to the mission because of poor trail conditions. The next morning, Friday the 14th, he was determined to bring the oranges to the mission. His Native traveling companions, following the clear instructions they had received from both Fathers Lafortune and Post, made every effort to dissuade him from returning to the mission alone. But, he insisted.

How did Father Ruppert get to that spot in the willows, where he was next seen—in frozen death? In a handwritten account of Father Ruppert's death, written 30 years later, after the sled had been found, Brother Wilhalm provided the answer, as he traced the course Father Ruppert took from the roadhouse to the banks of the Pilgrim:

> He left the roadhouse to come to the mission. He traveled about 12 miles and left the case of oranges on the bank of the river. After going about a mile, he unhitched the dogs, tucked the harness under the bow of the sled and started to walk towards the mission. After walking about 6 miles, he turned off the trail and landed on the Pilgrim River about 3 miles above the mission, and instead of coming down the river, he went up the river.

In a letter Brother Wilhalm wrote on January 6, 1924, he added the detail: "The darkness came on and he got lost in the willows."

The finding of Father Ruppert's sled, in late September 1924, helped further to answer some of the questions surrounding his death. The search for the sled began immediately after the body was found, but remained fruitless, until the following September, when it was found by accident. On September 27th, Brother Hansen started for Nome to have some dental work done. Two days later, the following entry was made in the Nome diary by Father Lafortune:

> Brother Hansen came from the springs. On his way down he found the sled of Fr. Ruppert on the old trail from Iron Creek to the top of Golden Gate pass about 2 miles from the bank of the Pilgrim. The Father evidently turned all his dogs loose. The parka was about 50 feet behind the sled. Along with the sled were two sacks, one empty, the other containing a few articles and $200 in paper money. Nothing could be found of the box of oranges.

All but one of the dogs were eventually accounted for. Mudd returned to the mission. Mink was found with the body. One was found in an abandoned roadhouse 18 miles from the mission. Two others were found about two weeks after the accident at Salmon Lake.

Why did Father Ruppert unhitch the dogs and leave the sled? Brother Wilhalm, in his letter, offers the surmised reason: "The trail was very bad, only a little snow and it was soft. We think that when he got about halfway, the dogs got tired and Father saw it was getting late, so he unhitched the dogs." Poor trail conditions, resulting from lack of snow, may very well, then, have led to the fatigue of the dogs, to the unhitching, to the attempt to walk to the mission, to the getting lost in the willows when darkness came on, to the "mysterious faltering footsteps of a man," to the fatigue of the man, the lying down, and the freezing to death.

What manner of man was Father Ruppert? That he was loved by all at the Hot Springs, where he was a frequent, always welcome visitor, is evident from letters written at the time of his death. He was not yet buried, when **Ursuline** Sister Mary wrote to Bishop Crimont:

> When in October Fr. Ruppert came up from Nome, all the mission rejoiced, as they always did when the word went around "Father Ruppert is here." For how he was loved! Alike by Sisters, Brothers and every little one. Life was much sweeter, when he was about. As Mother once said, "It seems as if nothing can go wrong while he is here," and again at his departure, "It seems as if a lot of holiness goes out of the place when he goes."

Brother Hansen wrote: "He was very much liked by all. Some people even ask for medals or anything he used." On February 4, 1924, Father Crispin S. **Rossi**, S.J., wrote from **Nulato** to seminarian Paul C. **Deschout**, S.J.:

> Fr. Ruppert was a very holy Father, zealous, kind, very charitable, the idol of everyone in Nome since he came there 5 years ago, when under that dreadful Flu that killed so many in Nome and all along the Bering Sea, he truly made himself all to all, working very hard day and night, so that, as the marshal from Nome told me, "both white and red in Nome are ready to kiss the Fr. Ruppert's steps, when he walks through town."

The *Nome Nugget* eulogized:

> [His was] a life that had been spent in doing such great good for others, regardless of race, color or creed. Father Frederick Ruppert was endeared to every man, woman and child who were fortunate enough to make his acquaintance. Only the highest regard was felt for this great dispenser of mercy. The act which cost Father Ruppert his life was being performed by him so that all the little kiddies at the Hot Springs might enjoy the luxury of fresh fruit for Christmas. Never thinking of himself, but of the benefit of others, was the course pursued thru life by this great, good man. It is with heavy heart that the people of this portion of Alaska mourn the death of this great man.

Even Father Lafortune, Father Ruppert's severest critic, knew, nevertheless, how to esteem and praise the sterling qualities of the man, and to mourn his loss. In a letter to Father Martin J. **Lonneux**, S.J., written the day after that "mighty gloomy Christmas," he expressed his opinion of Father Ruppert: "The Father was very good and bright in many ways, but his utter lack of practical sense was the cause of his death, nothing else. His intention was good, but how impractical."

Lastly, it was a dog, Mink, the leader of the team—a brute more noble than many a man—that bore witness to Father Ruppert's heart-winning qualities. Not in words, but in action he showed his affection and fidelity. Sister Mary tells how "the animal had eaten the fur lining out of Father's cap, so starving was it." Yet, he left the body untouched. And, though freezing himself, he stayed and watched protectingly over his master to the last, "lying near him, as if he was trying to keep him warm."

In 1924, the Vatican Mission Exposition opened in Rome. In the hall of North America hung "the most appealing item." It was a painting of a man lying face downward in a snowy waste, with a great dog sitting at his head. It bore the title: "A Martyr to Charity."

Father Frederick A. Ruppert, S.J.: a martyr to charity, or a casualty of his own imprudence? Father Post implied both—much of the former, a little of the latter. "In his case, his ardent charity surpassed his prudence." Was he a victim of his own folly, or a victim of fate? According to Father Lafortune, both played a role in his death. Summarized Father Lafortune: "He had to die on the banks of the Pilgrim River and he could not dodge it."

But, who can safely judge the deep and distant actions of that man, so God-touched, yet so frail? The last word is left to Father Post: "God alone is the knower of the ways of man."

Father Frederick A. Ruppert, S.J., lies buried in the Pilgrim Hot Springs cemetery.

93, 97

Our Lady of Guadalupe Church, Russian Mission. *PP.*

RUSSIAN MISSION

Russian Mission, largely a Central Yup'ik Eskimo village, is located on the west, or right, bank of the Yukon River, 25 miles southeast of **Marshall**, in the Yukon-Kuskokwim Delta. For approximately 150 years, it has been the site of a Russian Orthodox mission. In 1880, Russian Mission had 143 inhabitants; in 1902, 350; in 1929, 54; in 1939, 34; in 1950, 55; in 1960, 102; in 1970, 146; in 1990, 266, and in the year 2000, 296.

Catholic missionaries began visiting the Roman Catholics at Russian Mission, out of **Akulurak**, as early as the 1890s. Later on, they visited them mainly out of **Pilot Station**, **Mountain Village**, and **Bethel**. That was still the case as of 2004. Russian Mission has never had a resident priest.

The Catholic churches at Russian Mission have been dedicated under the title of Our Lady of Quadalupe. A new church was built there in the year 1966–67. This was replaced with the present church, dedicated on October 18, 1998.

During the year 1991–92, Sister Jeannette LaRose, S.S.A., stationed in Mountain Village, visited Russian Mission from time to time as a pastoral minister. Sister Anne Hogan, S.S.J., stationed in **Kalskag**, did likewise during the years 1999–2001. Winnie Pitka, a faithful custodian of the

Russian Mission Catholic church since 1989, continued to be such as of the year 2004.

RUZICKA, Brother Robert J., O.F.M.

Robert Joseph Ruzicka was born in St. Louis, Missouri, on March 31, 1947. In St. Louis, he attended St. Anthony of Padua School for his elementary education. For his secondary education, he attended St. Joseph's Seminary in St. Louis, from which he graduated in 1965. In 1967, he entered the novitiate of the Franciscans, the Order of Friars Minor, to become a member, as a Lay Brother, in that Order's Sacred Heart Province, headquartered in St. Louis. After completing his noviceship at St. Paschal's Friary, in Oak Brook, Illinois, he took his simple vows in 1968.

Brother Robert then went on to receive professional training as a cook and baker at Chicago's Washburn Culinary School, after which he cooked at Our Lady of the Angels Seminary in Quincy, Illinois. In 1971, he made his final profession as a Franciscan Friar. From 1972–76, he was Franciscan Vocation Director in Westmont, Illinois. During the years 1976–86, he was stationed at the Franciscan parish of St. Joseph's in Cleveland, Ohio. There, in addition to cooking for the Friars, he served on the formation team for pre- and post-novitiate candidates, was engaged in ministry to youth and elders, and was spiritual assistant to Secular Franciscans.

In 1985, the Franciscan Friars of Sacred Heart Province were invited by Michael J. **Kaniecki**, S.J., Bishop of **Fairbanks** at the time, to consider ministry among the Koyukon Athabaskan Indian people living in villages along the middle Yukon River in **Alaska**'s northern interior. After the Father Provincial of the Friars visited the area under consideration, and deemed it a field fitting for Franciscan ministry, he made known to the Friars of Sacred Heart Province that he was looking for volunteers "ready, able and willing to answer the call to Alaska, not a place for babes in the woods, but a mission demanding a great deal of self-giving and dedication." Brother Robert, for one, heard and, though not naturally attracted to Alaska, answered the call.

On July 1, 1986, Brother Robert, along with

Brother Robert J. Ruzicka, O.F.M. *LR.*

three other Friars, arrived in Fairbanks. For his first three years in Alaska, he was assigned, as a pastoral assistant, to **Galena**. This he, at first, saw as "a desolate spot midway between Fairbanks and Russia." In addition to doing pastoral ministry in Galena, he also routinely visited **Huslia** to do the same there. Athabaskan elder of Huslia and "pillar" of Huslia's Catholic community, Rose Ambrose, wrote of him: "Brother Robert is handy and helps anyone. He makes people happy. He helps when people are grieving for their lost ones. He has good personality, and good with young children. Plays games with them and teaches catechism. Also visits old people and sick people. I'll say, people have lots of fun with Brother Robert."

It was not long before Brother Robert was acquainted with and at home with interior Alaska and its people. It took him a while, however, to become accustomed to the long summer days. "I almost had to set an alarm clock," he wrote, "to remind me to go to bed." Spending a lot of time outdoors, as he did, and visiting people, he had no trouble coping with the long, dark days of Alaskan winters. Regarding the people he was living with, and with whom he was walking his personal pilgrim way, he wrote, "To my great delight, I met a beautiful, loving, humble (yet very outspoken) people. And to my great relief, the Athabaskans spoke English. They share a rich cultural tradition. I marveled at their great respect for nature and for all of God's creation—so much like St. Francis."

From 1989–94, Brother Robert was stationed at St. Patrick's mission at **Koyukuk**, as Pastoral Administrator. At the same time, he served also as a pastoral assistant at Huslia. From 1994 to the year 2000, he was back again in Galena, as pastoral assistant. During most of these years, he served also as a special Consultor to Bishop Kaniecki.

In the year 2000, Brother Robert, while continuing to be Pastoral Administrator of Koyukuk, became such likewise also of the **Nulato** mission. That same year, he began to serve also as Coordinator of Rural Ministries for seven villages in the middle Yukon area. As of the year 2004, he was still Pastoral Administrator at Nulato and Coordinator of Rural Ministries.

Father Donald A. Doll, S.J., who came to know Brother Robert well during the time the two were together in Alaska, said of him: "Brother Robert is a joy to live and work with. His work is infused with a deep faith in God, and a tremendous optimism. He has a wonderful sense of mission—to be an affirming presence to the people he lives and works with."

As the third millennium dawned, Brother Robert, reflecting on his long years as a Franciscan Friar, almost half of them spent in Alaska, wrote, "God has always directed my life, and prepared me for what I am assigned to do at any given time. If I do my best, God will always be with me and help me. I have always been happy wherever I was assigned. The people of God are wonderful!"

172

Father Gerard T. Ryan, C.S.Sp. *LRC.*

RYAN, Father Gerard T., C.S.Sp.

Father Ryan, an Irish Holy Ghost Father, was born in Dundalk, County Louth, Ireland, on July 17, 1930. He was ordained a priest in Dublin, Ireland, on July 15, 1956. The following year, he was assigned to Nigeria, West Africa. He remained there, mostly in a teaching capacity, until April 1969. During his African years, he experienced 21 months of the 1967–70 Biafra Civil War.

After spending six months in parish work in Ireland, Father Ryan was appointed to St. Agnes parish in Baton Rouge, Louisiana, in November 1969. He was on that assignment for 17 months. He was then recalled to Ireland. After some months of parish work there, he was requested by his Superiors to go to **Alaska**. On November 15, 1971, he arrived in **Anchorage**, where he was immediately assigned as an assistant to Msgr. Francis A. **Cowgill**, pastor of St. Anthony's parish. He served there for 33 months.

On August 18, 1974, Father Ryan became the second pastor of St. Bernard's parish in **Talkeetna**. During his five years there, he ministered also to the people of **Trapper Creek**, **Willow**, and **Big Lake**. At Big Lake, in the latter 1970s, he built Our Lady of the Lake Church to replace the church that had burned to the ground in 1967.

In 1980, Father Ryan was made Archdiocesan Director of Catholic Relief Services; and, beginning in May 1982, he served also as an Archdiocesan Consultor. On January 28, 1982, he received his U.S. citizenship. Soon thereafter, he became a member of the Elks and a Knight of Columbus and a Knight of the Equestrian Order of the Holy Sepulchre of Jerusalem. As of 1995, he was a Grand Officer of the Order.

From September 18, 1979, to August 1987, Father Ryan served as the 12th pastor of St. Michael's parish in **Palmer**. During his pastorate, the church was remodeled and received a lofty new entryway. After some excavation, a new kitchen was built in the church basement. His was the joy of being pastor of St. Michael's parish, when, in 1985, it celebrated the 50th anniversary of its founding.

On April 14, 1987, Father Ryan was appointed pastor of St. Francis Xavier's parish in **Valdez**. During his first winter there, he became afflicted with the "cabin fever syndrome." It was then that he was requested by his Superiors to plan go to Australia. Therefore, after an interim year of helping out in an Anchorage parish, he left for Ireland in June 1989 to spend the summer there. On September 19, 1989, he arrived in Sydney. His first assignment in Australia was that of administrator and assistant pastor at Our Lady's Spiritan Parish, in Ringwood in the Archdiocese of Melbourne. In January 1991, he began to serve at St. Nicholas of Myra parish, in Penrith. On January 13, 1992, he was appointed pastor of St. Monica's parish, in North Parramatta.

Father James P. Ryan.
Courtesy of Fr. Ryan.

RYAN, Father James P.

James P. "Jim" Ryan was born to Daniel I. and Mary Paulbeck Ryan in Plentywood, Montana, on April 14, 1921. At the death of his mother, when he was four years old, he was placed in a convent school staffed by Ursuline nuns in Kenmare, North Dakota, for three years. His elementary schooling he received at Courtney School, a one-room schoolhouse in Sheridan County, Montana, near the farm where he was now living. For his secondary schooling he attended the high school in Plentywood. However, before finishing his senior year, he enlisted in the Civil Conservation Corps. He spent most of his year in the Corps in Glacier National Park, Montana. On July 9, 1942, he enlisted in the U.S. Navy, from which, at war's end, he was honorably discharged. Finding himself "intrigued with the thought of becoming a medical doctor," he enrolled at Seattle College in Seattle, Washington. However, it was not long before his thoughts turned to the priesthood.

On September 21, 1947, Jim entered the Jesuit novitiate at Sheridan, Oregon. After completing his two-year noviceship and two additional years studying the classics and humanities, he made his philosophical studies at Mount Saint Michael's, Spokane, Washington, during the years 1951–54, ending

them with an M.A. degree in Philosophy. From 1954–57, he taught Religion, Latin, Greek, and English at Bellarmine Preparatory in Tacoma, Washington. At the Gregorian University in Rome, Italy, he spent four years in theological studies, from 1957–61. He was ordained a priest in Rome by Cardinal Luigi Traglia on July 9, 1960. After teaching again at Bellarmine Preparatory for two years, he made his tertianship at Port Townsend, Washington, from 1963–64. He took his final vows as a Jesuit on August 15, 1965.

From 1964–70, Father Ryan taught philosophy at what was now Seattle University. In a letter dated June 11, 1970, written by Father Kenneth W. Baker, S.J., then President of Seattle University, Father Ryan was informed that Seattle University would not be renewing his appointment after the academic year 1970–71. He was denied tenure on the basis that his teaching left "something to be desired." He himself, however, saw it otherwise. In his words: "some simulated reasons were given for diminishing my teaching schedule at Seattle U."

This turn of events was extremely upsetting to Father Ryan, so much so that he asked his Father Provincial, Kenneth J. Galbraith, S.J., for a temporary leave of absence from the Society of Jesus. This was granted him on December 22, 1970. He is listed as a Jesuit for the last time in the 1974 issue of the Oregon Province catalog.

Described at the time as "a very apostolic person and very interested in giving of himself and his time to others," Father Ryan spent the year 1971–72 in pastoral ministry at St. John Bosco parish in Tacoma, where he chanced to meet Francis T. **Hurley**, Bishop of **Juneau**, who impressed upon him the need for priests in the Juneau diocese.

On August 15, 1972, Father Ryan arrived in Juneau. He came to regard his move north as an inspired move, guided by Divine Providence. After serving at St. Peter's Church in **Douglas** for a short time, he became pastor of St. Gregory Nazianzen parish in **Sitka**. During his years there, 1972–78, he saw to the completion of the new parish complex begun by Father Ernest H. **Muellerleile**. On September 3, 1973, he witnessed the blessing of the newly completed church.

On May 17, 1978, Father Ryan arrived in **Haines** to take over as pastor of its Sacred Heart parish. As such, he was responsible also for St. Therese of the Child Jesus parish in **Skagway**. In 1981, thanks in large part to his efforts, the new, badly needed Sacred Heart Church in Haines was up.

In Haines, on July 7, 1985, Father Ryan had the joy of celebrating a special Mass of Thanksgiving to God for his 25 years of priesthood. On that occasion, he received the sincere thanks of his parishioners for his years of dedicated service to them. He, in turn, thanked them for their response to his ministry and for their love and respect. During his homily, Michael H. **Kenny**, Bishop of Juneau, likewise thanked Father Ryan for his seven-year pastorate in Haines and commented on Father Ryan's humility, faith, and compassion. Bishop Kenny's admiration for Father Ryan was recorded as "obvious to all."

Retiring from priestly ministry in the Juneau diocese in 1986, Father Ryan moved to Pebble Beach, California. But, retirement for him did not translate into rocking-chair retirement. In a December 9, 1989, letter he wrote: "I continue to help out in parishes as the need arises." Filling in as chaplain at the Carmelite Monastery for nine months he found to be "truly an inspirational time." After ministering to nursing care facilities, especially inasmuch as this involved contact with the elderly, he concluded that "living out one's life into old age is a blessing not to be despised. In these later years, there is plenty of time for prayer and reflection on

what our earthly tour of duty is all about. It's a time for serious reckoning with our heavenly Father's will and what it means to want lovingly to do his will."

As of the year 2004, fifteen years after Father Ryan wrote those edifying words, he was still engaged in part-time ministry, living out his life into old age in Pebble Beach, and lovingly doing his heavenly Father's will.

RYAN, Archbishop Joseph T.

John Joseph Thomas Ryan was born on November 1, 1913, in Albany, New York. His elementary schooling was received at St. Patrick's Institute, and his secondary schooling at Christian Brothers Academy, both schools being in Albany. He then went on to attend Manhattan College in New York City, and St. Joseph's Seminary in Dunwoodie, Yonkers. He was ordained a priest for the Diocese of Albany, in Albany's Cathedral of the Immaculate Conception on June 3, 1939.

Father Ryan's first assignment as a priest was to St. Alphonsus parish, Glens Falls, New York. After spending the summer there, he was transferred to St. Francis de Sales parish in Herkimer, New York, where he spent two years as curate. In 1941, he was assigned to St. Patrick's parish in Troy, New York. During his two years there as assistant priest, he also taught at Catholic Central High School.

From 1943–46, Father Ryan served in the United States Navy, First Marine Division, as a military chaplain. Commissioned a lieutenant (j.g.) in September 1943, he attended the training school for Navy chaplains at William and Mary College, Williamsburg, Virginia. In April 1944, he took ship for the South Pacific. During his 20 months in that combat zone, he received citations for extraordinary valor during the battles on the islands of Peleliu and Okinawa with a Marine artillery regiment.

Upon his return to the Albany diocese in June 1946, Father Ryan was appointed an assistant pastor at St. Mary's parish in Hudson, New York. Eight years later, in July 1954, he became administrator of Our Lady Help of Christians parish in Albany. During this period, he served also as Diocesan Director of Vocations, as moderator of the Communications Arts Guild of the Albany Diocese, and as secretary of the Albany Board of the American Red Cross.

In May 1957, with the blessing of William A. Scully, Bishop of Albany, Francis Cardinal Spellman, Archbishop of New York and Military Vicar for the United States, appointed Father Ryan Chancellor of the Military Ordinariate. As such, Father Ryan made his headquarters in New York City. For the outstanding service he rendered as Chancellor, Pope Pius XII named him, in November 1957, a Papal Chamberlain.

In May 1958, again at the request of Cardinal Spellman, Father Ryan began his ministry with the Catholic Near East Welfare Association (CNEWA) and the Pontifical Mission for Palestine. In his capacity as assistant national secretary of the CNEWA, headquartered in Beirut, Lebanon, he made his first trip to the Near East in late June 1958. On that trip he distributed relief supplies to Palestinian refugees in Lebanon, Syria, Jordan, and the Gaza Strip. For his courageous service in the Near East, he was named a Knight Commander of the Equestrian Order of the Holy Sepulchre in 1958. In November 1960, he was elected National Secretary of the CNEWA.

In recognition of Father Ryan's services and leadership roles with the CNEWA and the Pontifical Mission for Palestine, Pope John XXIII, named him, in 1961, a Domestic Prelate with the title of Right Reverend Monsignor.

When Pope Paul VI made his historic pilgrimage to the Holy Land, January 4–6, 1964, he invited Msgr. Ryan to accompany him as a member of his official party. Msgr. Ryan was the only American so honored. In August 1964, King Hussein of Jordan awarded Msgr. Ryan the "Grand Official Order of Independence" decoration for his work among the many Palestinian refugees in Jordan.

On February 9, 1966, the Archdiocese of **Anchorage, Alaska**, was officially established, and Msgr. Ryan, because of his being "a man of unusual talents, high purpose and sanctity," was named to be its first archbishop. For his motto the archbishopelect chose: *Estote Factores Verbi* ("Be doers of the word"). For the place of his consecration, he chose his hometown of Albany; and for the date of his con-

Archbishop Joseph T. Ryan. *LRC.*

secration March 25, 1966. Cardinal Spellman was the consecrator and principal celebrant of the Pontifical Mass. On Sunday, March 27th, the new archbishop offered his first solemn Pontifical Mass in St. Theresa of Avila Church in his home parish in Albany.

At 3:03, in the afternoon of Tuesday April 12th, Archbishop Ryan arrived in Anchorage. More than 3,000 people were on hand to greet him. In a brief address to the crowd, their new archbishop told them: "It is good to be here. I want to belong and serve everyone, not just Catholics. I feel I am already an Alaskan and am proud to be one. I come as a servant of God to be a doer of His word."

On Thursday, April 14, 1966, at 10:00 A.M., Anchorage's Holy Family Church achieved Cathedral status. At that time, Archbishop Ryan formally took possession of the church as the seat of the new archdiocese. Installation ceremonies took place that same evening at 6:00 in Anchorage's West High School. In addressing the crowd, Archbishop Ryan assured them that holiness of family life would be a dominant theme of his administration. He offered the Holy Family as a model for parents and children.

When Archbishop Ryan was appointed Archbishop of Anchorage, he expected to remain in that position for the rest of his life. However, he remained in it for less than a full decade. On November 4, 1975, it was announced that Pope Paul VI had appointed "the old marine" Coadjutor Archbishop to Terence Cardinal Cooke, Military Vicar of the U.S.

Armed Services. This new appointment, meant that Archbishop Ryan had to leave Anchorage for New York City. While the thought of leaving Anchorage filled him with feelings of sadness—despite the fact that he had experienced there more than his share of frustrations, disappointments, and misunderstandings—he, at the same time, looked forward with joy to his new assignment.

In 1985, what was up to that time known as the Military Ordinariate became the Archdiocese for the Military Services, U.S.A. Archbishop Ryan was appointed its first archbishop on March 16, 1985. He served in that capacity until May 1991, when he retired and returned to the Albany Diocese.

In 1996, Archbishop Ryan began residing at Our Lady of Hope Residence, a retirement facility operated by the Little Sisters of the Poor in Latham, New York. That same year, he visited Anchorage on the occasion of the 30th anniversary of his installation as Archbishop of Anchorage. He visited Anchorage again the following year. In 1998, he broke a hip, but he was soon up and about again. The day before he died, he had "been doing very well," according to the Sister attending him. The day he died, he was sitting at the dinner table awaiting his meal, when he slumped over. He was rushed to his room, where a priest anointed him. He died 15 minutes later. It was October 9, 2000. Archbishop Ryan lies buried in St. Agnes Cemetery in Menands, a suburb of Albany.

"Beginning a new church unit like this Archdiocese in the post-counciliar age," wrote Archbishop Ryan on the Feast of the Holy Family, December 28, 1975, as his stay in Anchorage was near its end, "presented us with a series of challenges and situations that were not experienced by dioceses established in years long past." He went on to mention the "burdens of lack of personnel and financial resources to get a new archdiocese into full efficient operation. These burdens took their toll on all of us."

Humbly, he admitted that "we made some mistakes and met some failures." It must be remembered that the mid-1960s, and the years thereafter, were, by and large, troublous, unsettled times both for the Church and America in general.

In a letter dated February 12, 1996, to his longtime friend and supporter, Father Vincent P. **Kelliher**, S.J., Archbishop Ryan wrote, "I want you to know that you were most helpful to me in the years we spent together in Alaska—helpful during the many trying periods I had while I was there." Reading between these lines and the ones just quoted above, one senses that Archbishop Ryan found his short decade in Anchorage anything but easy and personally satisfying. Yet, one cannot help but marvel at all that he did accomplish during his relatively short term as head of the Anchorage archdiocese, especially in view of the challenges confronting him and the limited resources at his disposal.

"Archbishop Ryan," in the words of his successor, Archbishop Francis T. **Hurley**, "brought to Anchorage a vision that always looked positively and proactively to the future. He never came across as a caretaker." Archbishop Hurley went on to give him credit for "pioneering an archdiocese," for laying the solid foundation—especially by recruiting needed personnel and acquiring property needed for new parishes—upon which the Archdiocese of Anchorage has ever since truly flourished. Archbishop Ryan was a gifted organizer and a competent director of affairs, but, according to Father Richard **Tero**, whom he ordained to the priesthood in 1974, "his success was due in part also to his personality. He was a gracious man, to whom people were readily attracted."

Deservedly, Archbishop Joseph T. Ryan occupies a place of honor in the history of the Catholic Church in Alaska.

SAALFELD, Father Charles A., S.J.

He was a high school science and mathematics teacher, a ham radio operator (KL7DMW), an airplane pilot, a missionary to the Koyukon Athabaskan Indian people, ever a dedicated priest with the Mass the center of his life.

Charles Anthony Saalfeld was born on January 16, 1915, in Cowlitz, Washington. He grew up in Salem, Oregon, where he attended parochial schools. On September 24, 1933, he entered the Jesuit novitiate at Sheridan, Oregon. After completing the two-year noviceship and two years of classical and humanities studies there, he went to Mount St. Michael's, Spokane, Washington, for three years of philosophical studies. From 1940–43, he taught Religion, physics and mathematics at Seattle Preparatory. He made his theological studies at Alma College, Los Gatos, California, from 1943–47. He was ordained a priest on June 13, 1946, in San Francisco. During the year 1947–48, he was a teacher at Bellarmine Preparatory in Tacoma, Washington. His tertianship was made at Port Townsend, Washington. From 1949–56, he taught at Marquette High School in Yakima, Washington. He spent the year 1956–57 studying physics at the University of Wisconsin.

Father Saalfeld first went to **Alaska** in 1957, to continue to teach his specialties, higher mathematics and physics, along with Religion, at Monroe Catholic High School in **Fairbanks**. Upon his arrival there, he designed and equipped the school's science laboratory. By this time, he had a master's degree in higher mathematics. In 1960, he was granted a fellowship by the University of Illinois for further studies in that field. He was a highly competent, no-nonsense teacher, who would have been lost in the classroom without a blackboard. His black cassock was generally white with chalk dust. On weekends, he helped out in the local parish or served as a supply priest at Suntrana (near **Healy**), **Manley Hot Springs**, and **Tanana**. During his latter teaching years, he commuted to these places by flying his own little Taylorcraft.

Father Saalfeld left teaching in 1966 to begin serving as pastor of Tanana. There he managed the construction of a new church in 1967. Flying out of Tanana, he tended also its dependent stations: **Ruby**, **Galena**, **Huslia**, **Koyukuk**, and Manley Hot Springs.

During the year 1973–74, he was on sabbatical leave at the Jesuit School of Theology at Berkeley, California. In 1974, he became pastor of **Nulato**, and its dependent stations, Koyukuk and **Kaltag**.

On Sunday, March 5, 1978, Father Saalfeld offered Mass at Koyukuk. He had been flown there by Father James A. **Sebesta**, S.J. On Monday evening, Father Sebesta flew him back to Nulato. They landed on the frozen Yukon directly in front of the village on a very windy day. Father Sebesta was a little concerned that he might have some difficulty in taking off from Nulato for the remainder of his trip to Kaltag. Father Saalfeld offered to stand by, just in case there was trouble of some kind. Father Sebesta took off successfully. Because of the high wind, the people in Nulato heard neither the plane's landing nor takeoff. Three days later, on the 9th, Father Saalfeld's frozen body was found only a short distance from the spot where Father Sebesta had last seen him wave good-bye. He had been carrying one of the two grips he had taken with him to Koyukuk. An autopsy confirmed that he died of a massive heart attack shortly after seeing the plane take off.

It seems that Father Saalfeld had a premonition

Father Charles A. Saalfeld, S.J. *DFA.*

of his impending death. A few days before it, while visiting one of his women parishioners in Nulato, he "spoke lightly, but confidentially, about death in relation to himself." He was told by this woman that another of his parishioners was afraid of dying and needed to speak to him. He assured her that he would contact the person in question, and remarked how death was "only a way of going home," that it was not to be feared. He added, "I'm ready for it anytime." As he left, he poked his head back in the doorway and said, "Mind you, this is just between the two of us."

As Father Saalfeld had been highly dedicated, serious, and conscientious as a teacher, so was he as a pastor. He was troubled by the fact that the people of Nulato continued to hold the traditional "stickdance," or "Feast for the Dead," ceremonials. He did not see them as reconcilable with Catholic beliefs. He was even more deeply troubled by the abuse of alcohol that he saw in the village, and often spoke out strongly against it. Once, after a general meeting of missionaries in Fairbanks, a frustrated, despondent Father Saalfeld invited Father Louis L. **Renner**, S.J., with whom he had taught for two years at Monroe, out to dinner. He just needed to talk in depth about the drinking problem in Nulato, needed to be assured that he, for his part, was doing all he could to help his people ease the problem.

What people thought of their pastor—at times, a scolding pastor—became clear after his death. With gentle, yet firm, persistence they pleaded with

Father Francis J. **Fallert**, S.J., General Superior of the Alaskan Jesuits, and with Robert L. **Whelan**, S.J., Bishop of Fairbanks, that Father Saalfeld's body be returned to Nulato for burial there among "his people."

The wishes of the people of Nulato were granted. Although prayers and Masses had been offered for Father Saalfeld at the time of his death and burial; nevertheless, on August 5, 1978, Feast of Our Lady of the Snows, patronal feast of the Nulato mission, Bishop Whelan, in a church filled to overflowing, celebrated a memorial Mass for him. With him at the altar were Fathers Fallert, Sebesta, and Donald A. Doll, S.J., a professional photographer on assignment for *National Geographic Magazine*. After the Mass, a solemn procession made its way up to Father Saalfeld's grave site on Cemetery Hill. There the grave was blessed and the gravestone set in place. The rest of the day was marked by celebrations and a potlatch hosted by the people of Nulato. That evening, Benediction was held, with the traditional hymns sung in Latin at the villagers' request. By their reactions to Father Saalfeld's death, the people of Nulato showed that his ministry among them had not been in vain.

142

SANDER, Father Timothy L., O.S.B.

Timothy L. " Tim" Sander, the first of eleven children, was born to Leo B. and Theresa Durrer Sander in Ashland, Oregon, on September 12, 1915. Baptized the day after his birth, he was named Leo Joseph. It was later, while in the seminary, that he took the name Timothy as his Religious name. Why Timothy? As a boy, he knew an Irish policeman, "Officer Tim," whom he liked. He also liked the name Tim.

When Tim was still a young boy, the family moved to Tillamook, Oregon, where Catholic schooling was available to the Sander children. At age seven, he began to attend the same school his father had attended: St. Alphonsus Academy, taught by the Sisters of St. Mary of Beaverton, Oregon. There he received his elementary and two years of his secondary education. When, in 1929, Catholic

Father Timothy L. Sander, O.S.B. *Photo by Curtis Almquist, and courtesy of Fr. Sander.*

schoolchildren in Oregon were no longer allowed to ride public school buses, 14-year-old Tim was provided with a limited driver's license by his father—a dairy farmer—so that he could drive his brothers and sisters to and from school. On the way to school, they stopped at the cheese factory to deliver the milk; on the way home after school, they stopped again to pick up milk cans filled with whey for the pigs.

Tim had a favorite uncle, "Father Louie," a diocesan priest of the Archdiocese of Portland. His inspiring example, along with that of Benedictine priests staffing the Tillamook parish, motivated Tim to enter the seminary high school at Mount Angel, Oregon, in 1931, for the last two years of his secondary education. In 1933, he began studies in the seminary college at Mount Angel. He made his monastic profession on September 8, 1936. By 1938, he had earned his B.S. degree. He then went on to theological studies. He was ordained a priest by Edward D. Howard, Archbishop of Portland, on May 22, 1941. Subsequently, two of his brothers likewise became Benedictine priests and members of Mount Angel Abbey.

In 1942, Father Tim was sent to be a community member of the new Westminster Abbey, first in Burnaby, then in Mission City, British Columbia, Canada. There he taught at Christ the King Seminary until 1956, when he returned to Mount Angel to teach at Mount Angel Prep. From 1961–64, he was its principal. Although Mount Angel Prep was

sold, in 1964, to the Archdiocese of Portland and renamed John F. Kennedy High, he continued on as a teacher and its vice principal during the years 1964–69. When the school was sold again, in 1969, and became a public school, he had his fill of school closings.

During the school year 1969–70, Father Tim's cousin, MaryLee Lowry, was teaching at Monroe Catholic High School in **Fairbanks**, **Alaska**, as a member of the **Jesuit Volunteer Corps**. Contact with her got him thinking north. Processed through the JVC, he found himself in Fairbanks as of August 26, 1970, to begin eight years of teaching and counseling at Monroe. In addition, he was also Superintendent of Catholic Schools during the years 1973–75. By then, he had been a licensed airplane pilot already for twelve years and had taught ground school and flying classes at Mount Angel Prep. In 1966, he had earned an M.A. degree in Education from the University of Oregon.

During his years at Monroe, 1970–78, Father Tim served also as Civilian Chaplain at the Murphy Dome Air Force Station near Fairbanks. In 1971, he became a member of the Alaska Civil Air Patrol. As such, he was involved in many search and rescue operations. As of the year 2004, he was still an active member of the ACAP.

In 1974, Father Tim completed a course in Marriage and Family Counseling at the American Institute of Family Relations in Los Angeles, California. The following year, he received his M.A. degree in Psychology—with emphasis on marriage, family, and child therapy—from Pepperdine University in Los Angeles.

Back in Fairbanks—with the blessing of his Father Abbot, Anselm Galvin, O.S.B.—Father Tim continued his work at Monroe and taught aviation ground school courses, as a Cessna 172 had been made available to the school for flight instruction. Holding an instructor's rating, he helped many students receive their private certificates with land and sea ratings.

At the request of Robert L. **Whelan**, S.J., Bishop of Fairbanks at the time, Father Tim, in 1978, took a position as counselor at Fairbanks Counseling and Adoption. In 1981, he became a member of the American Association for Marriage and Family Therapy, Alaska Division. For a time, he served as its elected president.

In 1983, Father Tim was assigned to offer the Eucharistic and Sacramental liturgies for the Catholic Church North Community that, in 1991, blossomed into St. Raphael's parish. For 12 years, he faithfully served this community. Feeling the weight of his 80 years, he retired from this assignment in 1995. Reflecting on his time at St. Raphael's, he wrote some years later: "It was a time of spiritual growth for me. The community supported me in many ways. They are still family for me. I am one of them." Betty Johnson, Director of Worship for the Diocese of Fairbanks and who played a major role in St. Raphael's coming into being, said of Father Tim: "He was wonderful to work with, always there for us when needed."

After his years of service to St. Raphael's, Father Tim continued his private practice as a marriage and family counselor. He also continued as acting facilitator of Beginning Experience, a Christian support group that facilitates the grief resolution process for adults and children who have suffered a loss through death, divorce, or separation. In a March 17, 2004, letter, Anita Hartmann, a member of the Board of Directors of Beginning Experience, described Father Tim—with the program now for 25 years—as "clearly the rock upon which Beginning Experience rests."

But, more and more, "retirement" began to mean just that for Father Tim. A sign posted in his truck camper read: "Retired. No clock. No address. No phone. No money." In reality, however—even as the third millennium dawned—he did manage to keep busy, mainly as a counselor and Beginning Experience facilitator. Though well into his 80s by then, he still, occasionally, also drove or flew to various outlying places to bring the Mass and Sacraments to Catholic communities without a priest.

In 2002, Father Tim was found to be suffering from prostate cancer. Successful radiation treatment followed. In 2003, he competed in the Senior Olympics held in Fairbanks. He walked away from these with an impressive 15 Gold Medals. The following year, he was still feeling "pretty good." To the question what he yet hoped to accomplish, he replied: "I just want to keep flying, fishing, and serving." In flying he experienced a freedom he found

hard to explain. By "serving," he meant mainly his role in Beginning Experience. "I get a great joy from helping people work through their grieving," he wrote. "That they go on despite the suffering and laugh and feel good again, that is my reward."

As of the year 2004, Father Timothy L. Sander, O.S.B.—who initially had gone to Alaska with a directive from his Father Abbot to "try it for a year"—was still happily in Alaska, in Fairbanks. When asked how it was that he, a Benedictine monk, had wound up ministering in Alaska, of all places, he answered: "I have received the permission of six Abbots to continue my work in Alaska. I have outlived three of them. This is where I need to be."

SAUDIS, Father Richard Bernard Thomas

Richard Bernard Thomas Saudis, the last of three sons, was born to John and Louise Tironas Saudis in Chicago, Illinois, on February 17, 1930. His father was a barber and a musician; his mother a beauty parlor operator. Richard grew up in a very Catholic neighborhood on Chicago's South Side. After graduating from Immaculate Conception Grade School, he entered Quigley Prep Seminary, the minor seminary of the Archdiocese of Chicago. He spent five years there studying the classics and humanities, before going on to philosophical and theological studies at Mundelein, the Archdiocese's major seminary. By the time he finished his seminary training, he had earned a B.A. in Philosophy and a Licentiate in Dogmatic Theology. On May 3, 1955, he was ordained a priest by Samuel Cardinal Stritch.

Father Saudis' first assignment as a priest was to All Saints parish, a small parish on the far south end of Chicago, a parish that included a sizable number of "displaced persons," among them Lithuanian refugees. After serving at All Saints as an associate pastor for five years, he was appointed to the faculty of Quigley Prep Seminary, where, from 1960–68, he taught Latin, mathematics, and social studies, and served as Spiritual Director for the freshman class. While teaching at Quigley, he did graduate studies each summer, studying first classical languages at the University of Notre Dame, then psychology at Loyola University, Chicago.

In 1967, Father Saudis learned that **Joseph T.**

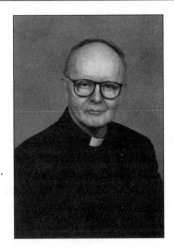

Father Richard B. Saudis.
Courtesy of Fr. Saudis.

Ryan, recently appointed Archbishop of the newly created Archdiocese of **Anchorage**, **Alaska**, was looking for volunteer priests from well-established dioceses to help him "bring into being" the new archdiocese. Father Saudis knew little about Alaska at the time, nor was he curious about it; still, because no one was responding to Archbishop Ryan's request for outside help, he volunteered to serve in the Archdiocese of Anchorage for a possible three-year term.

For his first Alaskan assignment, Father Saudis found himself, not in the Anchorage archdiocese, but in the Diocese of **Juneau**, because of special need there occasioned by the death in **Wrangell** of Father Raymond W. **Mosey**. From July 1968 to June 1969, Father Saudis was pastor of the Wrangell and **Petersburg** parishes. It was during that year that a large parish hall was built next to the church in Wrangell. Looking back on his ministry in Southeastern Alaska, and his getting there, he wrote years later:

> My short stay there was a great introduction to Alaska and its small Catholic communities. That short stay almost never began. Archbishop Ryan—interim administrator of the Juneau diocese after the retirement of its Ordinary, Bishop Dermot **O'Flanagan**—escorted me to Wrangell to install me as pastor. We were flying in from Juneau on an old float plane, a PBY of World War II vintage, when one of the windows imploded. I had just changed seats to the other side of the plane, to get a better view of the scenery, I guess. The shattering glass hit Archbishop Ryan, but he had his hat on in the cold plane and suffered only a superficial cut or two on his head. We went back to Juneau

for another plane, since we couldn't set down in the water with the broken window. We finally came, a few hours late, to my installation.

Not only the getting to Wrangell proved to be an ordeal for Father Saudis, but also his winter there. As the water mains in Wrangell froze up, there was no water in the rectory from Christmas till Easter. For clean, drinking water, the people had to drive to a mountain stream ten miles out of town.

During the summer months of 1969, Father Saudis served at Anchorage's St. Benedict's parish. In the fall, he took up residency at **Copper Valley School**, where he taught sociology. Out of there, he cared for Holy Family parish in **Glennallen**. He found CVS "a unique and exciting place at an exciting time in the history of the Church." In 1970—"at a time, a sad and troubled time," in his words, "when it was decided that the school would close"—he became principal of the school. Copper Valley School closed at the end of the 1970–71 school year.

During his first year back in Anchorage, Father Saudis served as Rector of the Holy Family Cathedral parish; and, briefly, also as Vice-Chancellor to Vincentian Father Francis J. Fish. Upon the sudden death of Father Fish, on April 7, 1972, Father Saudis became Chancellor. From 1973–76, he was Chancellor and, for some of those years, also Vicar General of the Anchorage archdiocese. While serving in those capacities, he resided, for a time, at Holy Spirit Retreat House (known, since 1999, as **Holy Spirit Center**). For a time, too, living at a Stanley Drive address, Father Saudis—"always a good friend of the Sisters of St. **Ann**," in the words of Sister Margaret Cantwell, S.S.A.—offered daily Mass at their convent next door. In 1973, in Rome, Father Saudis attended a three-month course focusing on recent developments in the Church. During his years as Chancellor, he routinely supplied for priests around the archdiocese, at places such as **Cordova**, **Dillingham**, **Palmer**, **Soldotna**, and **Valdez**.

In 1976, Father Saudis, now that Archbishop Ryan was no long Archbishop of Anchorage, was asked by his Ordinary, John Cardinal Cody, to return home, to the Chicago archdiocese. By this time he had come to love Alaska and being part of a frontier archdiocese. He left Alaska with mixed feelings.

Back in his home archdiocese, Father Saudis served at first, and for some four years, as Rector of Niles College of Loyola University, a seminary. He was then appointed pastor of St. Philip the Apostle parish in Northfield, Illinois. After serving in that capacity from 1981–84, he, at the request of Archbishop Ryan, now Ordinary of the Archdiocese for Military Services, U.S.A., headquartered in Washington, D.C., once again was his Chancellor for the years 1985–91.

After his six years in Washington, D.C., Father Saudis returned to his home archdiocese to be associate pastor of St. Odilo parish in Berwyn, Illinois, from 1992–94. After that, at the request of the Chancellor of the Chicago archdiocese, he began to assist at the Archdiocesan Chancery, while continuing to reside at St. Odilo.

As of the year 2004, Father Saudis was still serving in the Archdiocesan Chancery Office, as Associate Vicar General for Canonical Services, "a position," in his words, "that embraces a number of activities as ambiguous as the title."

15

SCAMMON BAY

The Yukon-Kuskokwim Delta village of Scammon Bay (*Marayaaq* in Central Yup'ik Eskimo, which, translated loosely, means "place near the mudflats") is located one mile from the Bering Sea. It lies on the left, the south, bank of the Kun River and at the northern base of the 2,342-foot high Askinuk Mountains. A clear stream flowing year-round out of them provides the villagers with excellent water, a rare blessing in that part of **Alaska**. The village is named after the nearby bay, which honors Captain Charles M. Scammon, who served as marine chief of the Western Union Telegraph Expedition in Alaska. The village was not called Scammon Bay until 1951, when a post office was opened there. In 1950, the village had a population of 103; in 1960, 115; in 1970, 166; in 1979, 193; in 1990, 345. By the year 2000, that number had increased to 465.

The people of Scammon Bay lead, for the most part, a subsistence way of life. They hunt beluga whale, walrus, seal, geese, swans, cranes, ducks, loons and ptarmigan. Fishing yields salmon, whitefish, blackfish, needlefish, herring, humpies, smelt

Blessed Sacrament Church, Scammon Bay. *LR.*

and tomcod. In the fall, a variety of berries are harvested. Scammon Bay's climate is maritime. During the fall and winter months, winds of over 100 miles per hour occasionally lash the village.

Catholicism first touched the Scammon Bay people around 1895, when Jesuit missionaries stationed at **Akulurak**, notable among them Father Joseph M. **Tréca**, began visiting that general area. But it was not until around 1930 that Blessed Sacrament Mission was founded in Scammon Bay. Father Francis M. **Ménager**, S.J., visited the village in 1929, and Father **John P. Fox**, S.J., built a little chapel there in 1932. During the 1930s, George Aluska, of **Tununak**, served as catechist for the people. The Sisters of Our Lady of the **Snows** conducted a little Catholic "school" in Scammon Bay for several years during the 1930s. In the fall of 1946, Father Norman E. **Donohue**, S.J., built a 24 × 12′ church–residence. Father Donohue also brought the Scammon Bay people their first Christmas Mass, "and midnight Mass at that," in his words. During the 1950s, people from the Black River region, from **New Knock Hock**, began to move to Scammon Bay. In 1955, Fathers Henry G. **Hargreaves**, S.J. and **John J. Wood**, S.J., built a new church, which was to serve for nearly half a century. It was to be replaced early in the third millennium.

The Scammon Bay mission has never had a resident pastor. Throughout its history it has been visited mainly by priests stationed at **Hooper Bay**, but also by priests stationed at Akulurak, **Kashunuk**, and **Chevak**.

Eskimo Deacons Dan Akerelrea and Teddy Sundown, too, served their Scammon Bay parish. Both are buried at Scammon Bay. Deacon Francis Charlie was serving there as of the year 2004.

12, 207

SCHWIETZ, Archbishop Roger L., O.M.I.

When he was eight years old, he was out fishing with his aunt and uncle. When asked what he wanted to do when he grew up, without hesitation, he told them that he wanted to be a priest. Then, after thinking a moment, he said, "Maybe I'll even be a bishop."

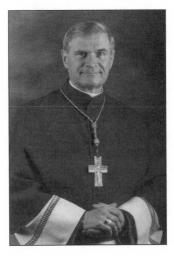

Archbishop Roger L. Schwietz, O.M.I. *Courtesy of Abp. Schwietz.*

Roger L. Schwietz was born on July 3, 1940, in St. Paul, Minnesota, to Archie and Sophie Schwietz, the second of six children. In the fall of 1946, he entered St. Casimir Parish Grade School. He was a good student throughout his years of schooling. At the same time, he was "fun-loving" and took part in a variety of extracurricular activities. He was a member of the Polish Dancers, sang in Glee Clubs, played the accordion, acted in dramas, and got into photography.

After graduating from St. Casimir's, he was still very much interested in becoming a priest, but chose not to attend the minor seminary of the Missionary **Oblates** of Mary Immaculate in Carthage, Missouri. Instead, he enrolled in Cretin High School, a military academy in St. Paul. While at Cretin, he compiled an exemplary record. He was named to the National Honor Society, reached the rank of Major, was awarded the Merit Medal all four years, and served as Associate Editor of the yearbook. As a senior, he was recognized as the one "Most likely to Succeed." The Cretin yearbook noted, too, that he had "an avid desire to become a priest, O.M.I." During his high school years, he had been corresponding with the Oblate Vocation Director.

After graduating from Cretin, having been recommended by the Oblate Provincial Superior as "an excellent prospect," Roger entered Our Lady of the Ozarks College in Carthage on September 1, 1958, to begin preparing for the priesthood as an Oblate. In August 1960, he entered the Oblate novitiate in

Godfrey, Illinois. Following a year of spiritual formation and study, he, on August 15, 1961, took his first vows as a member of the Central United States Province of the Missionary Oblates of Mary Immaculate. Within a month, he was on his way south to Our Lady of the Snows Scholasticate in Pass Christian, Mississippi, to begin his formal studies for the priesthood. After two years, and the completion of a Bachelor's degree, he was recommended to pursue a Master's degree in philosophy at St. Joseph's Scholasticate in Ottawa, Ontario, Canada. By the end of one year, he had completed all the degree requirements but the thesis. Nevertheless, after making his perpetual profession of vows as a Missionary Oblate on September 8, 1964, he was sent to Rome for theological studies at the Gregorian University. These he completed with a Licentiate in Sacred Theology. On December 20, 1967, in Rome, with family members present, Roger was ordained a priest by Archbishop Joseph Fitzgerald, O.M.I.

In September 1968, Father Schwietz began to serve as associate pastor at St. Louis parish in Fond du Lac, Wisconsin. Several months later, he returned to Ottawa to continue his M.A. degree work. In April 1969, he received word that he was being assigned to teach French and music and to be librarian at St. Henry's Preparatory Seminary in Belleville, Illinois. Reluctantly, he left parish work; and, reluctantly, the people of St. Louis parish saw him go. Eighty-three signed a petition requesting that he be allowed to stay on. "In the short time that Fr. Schwietz has been with us," they wrote, "he has acquired the admiration and respect of our people and our school children."

At the end of the school year 1969–70, Father Schwietz was named to the Oblate Province's pre-novitiate formation program at Lewis University in Romeoville, Illinois. While at Lewis, he was also able to teach philosophy part-time and begin class work in Counseling Psychology at Loyola University, Chicago. According to Brother James Gaffney, F.S.C., President of Lewis University:

> Father Schwietz's contacts with the Christian Brothers were numerous and deeply appreciated by the Brothers. His style of liturgical presiding and his homilies manifested a deep, sustaining spirituality, a solidly post-Vatican II theology, and a tremendous sense of Christian community. He generously offered assistance in personal counseling and spiritual direction to our candidates, all of whom found him to be highly competent, understanding, approachable, and exceptionally balanced. In addition, they delighted in his fine sense of humor, his great affability, and his genuine humility.

(Lewis University was to confer an Honorary Doctor of Humanities Degree on him in 1998.) In 1972, Father Schwietz moved to Omaha, Nebraska, when the pre-novitiate program was transferred to Creighton University.

After five years of formation work, Father Schwietz, in 1974, returned to Romeoville. There he taught part-time at Lewis University, did counseling at the Christian Brothers Counseling Center in Westchester, Illinois, and continued work on a Master's degree in Counseling Psychology at Loyola University. By 1975, he finally had the Master's degree in philosophy that he had begun working toward in 1963.

The year 1975 also marked Father Schwietz's return to parish work and to his home state, as well as his first assignment in the Diocese of Duluth. He was named associate pastor of St. Thomas Aquinas Church in International Falls, Minnesota. As one who "enjoyed playing as much as praying," he encouraged parish organizations to invite the entire parish community to participate in the special, and numerous, social activities. Usually, he was there, leading the socializing. At the same time, he and fellow Oblates at St. Thomas Aquinas were, in the words of the parish secretary, "examples of truly spiritual parish and pastoral leaders."

In 1978, Father Schwietz began a five-year term as Superior and Director of the Oblate House of Studies in Omaha. In 1983, he was transferred to Minneapolis to head his Province's Ministry Based Formation Program. As director of this program, he coordinated ministry and community experiences in Oblate parishes and facilities for men who had already graduated from college. When he moved to Duluth in 1984, and became pastor of Holy Family parish, he continued to work with these men by providing them such an experience in his own parish.

The situation at Holy Family was not an easy one to step into. Three parishes were in the process of merging into one. Father Schwietz was largely responsible for helping bring this about. However, with a maximum of tact, he accomplished the task with a minimum of hard feelings on the part of all concerned.

By 1990, Father Schwietz had held many positions of responsibility and filled a variety of roles calling for skills above the average. In addition to those already mentioned, he had served a three-year term on the Provincial Council of the Oblates' Central Province and facilitated a meeting in Rome of Oblate Formators from around the world. In the Diocese of Duluth, he had headed the Office for Liturgy and Spirituality, and had been a member of the Senate of Priests and a Diocesan Consultor.

Father Schwietz's abilities and accomplishments did not go unnoticed in Rome. On December 12, 1989, Pope John Paul II appointed him the seventh Bishop of Duluth. In Duluth's Cathedral of Our Lady of the Rosary, on February 2, 1990, he was ordained a bishop. For his motto he chose: "Jesus Christ is Lord."

During his ten years as Ordinary of the Duluth diocese, Bishop Schwietz wrote three pastoral letters: "A Call to Charity," "A Call to Conversion," and "A Call to Hope." As they had been throughout his years as a priest, so Bishop Schwietz's principal concerns continued to be the liturgy, the laity, youth, and vocations.

On January 18, 2000, Bishop Schwietz was named Coadjutor Archbishop of the Archdiocese of **Anchorage, Alaska**, by Pope John Paul II. The following March, he moved to Anchorage. A year later, on March 3, 2001, upon the retirement of Archbishop Francis T. **Hurley**, he became Archbishop of Anchorage.

Soon after his arrival in Anchorage, Archbishop Schwietz, a pastoral bishop mixing easily with people, began to travel far and wide throughout the vast archdiocese to get to know its people and its remote corners. In hopes of making himself more readily available to the archdiocese's widely scattered, diversified flock, he began pilot training, and to hone his speaking knowledge of Spanish. During his first year in Alaska, he also started a new vocations committee made up of laypeople, seminarians, women Religious, and priests; began exploring possible roles for the archdiocese's 18

deacons; and began meeting with Alaska Native leaders to learn about their needs and their history. Being an enthusiastic outdoorsman, he spent a little time, too, "getting the proper fishing equipment."

In his capacities as Bishop of Duluth and also as Archbishop of Anchorage, Archbishop Schwietz held a number of positions within the National Conference of Catholic Bishops. He was a consultant to the Liturgy Committee from 1991–94. In 1992, he began to serve as a member of the Bishops' Vocation Committee, being elected its chair in 1998. He was a member of the Bishops' Committee on the Laity from 1995–98, and chair of its Subcommittee on Youth from 1993–98. Beginning in 1997, he was also a member of the Catholic Relief Services Board of Directors. During the years 1994–97 and 1998–2002, he was a member of the NCCB Administrative Board. From 1991 on, he was Episcopal Moderator for the Teens Encounter Christ (TEC) movement. He served also as Episcopal Liaison to Region I of the National Association of Catholic Chaplains.

Upon becoming Archbishop of Anchorage, Archbishop Schwietz said: "I look forward with gratitude and joy to years ahead in which I will serve the people of this grand archdiocese as shepherd. I hope to collaborate with the leadership of other faith families, as well as civil authorities, to help promote the God-given dignity of each person, the security of the family, and an ever more just and peaceful society."

SEBESTA, Father James A., S.J.

The takeoff in **Nome, Alaska**, was uneventful. Weather good. **Unalakleet**, 65 miles southwest of **Kaltag**, his destination, was reporting clear skies. **Galena**, however, 65 miles northeast of Kaltag, was reporting "very poor conditions in heavy snow." From experience he knew that the Kaltag weather was generally similar to that of Galena, though that December night there was reason to believe that it might be somewhat better. The attempt to reach Kaltag would involve some risk, he knew, but the risk seemed not too great, and justified. His people were earnestly preparing themselves for Christmas, and were expecting him for Mass the next day, the

Father James A. Sebesta,
S.J. *BR-898052.*

second Sunday of Advent. He did not want to disappoint them.

He made Moses Point, 97 miles east of Nome, with little difficulty. The remaining 94 miles would not be so easy. A range of mountains separating the Yukon River village of Kaltag from the coast had still to be crossed.

He headed out over ice-covered Norton Bay toward Cape Denbigh. The lights of Unalakleet, some 60 miles to the southeast, were still visible, but the weather further to the east was deteriorating noticeably. As he approached the cape, the stars on the horizon began to disappear, and the mountains ahead presented only a faint, blurred outline.

A heading of exactly 92 degrees held the direct course from Moses Point to Kaltag. A check of the ground speed showed 124 mph, indicating a light wind from the southeast. Just before the decision to cross the mountains was made, heading and ground speed were again carefully checked. From now on, the heading had to be held exactly if there was to be any hope of finding Kaltag. It was now 8:52. Twenty-nine minutes would put him directly over Kaltag.

As the Cessna 180 droned along at 7,500 feet, the mountains below faded away in the dark, murky sea of driving snow. Kaltag had to be just 21 minutes dead ahead now. At 9:10 he began his descent to arrive at 5,000 feet above the village. The slanting snow beating against the windshield became denser

by the minute. Hopes of finding Kaltag were growing steadily dimmer; but, with his destination now only five minutes away, he was not about to give up. He continued on course.

9:21. According to all calculations, he had to be directly over Kaltag now. He turned off all lights and peered into the blackness and snow. There, slightly to the right, was the ever so faint glow of a light. He knew that to be the mercury vapor light outside the village electric plant.

He continued his descent, swept past the village, out over the Yukon to the island upriver to get his exact bearings for the final approach and landing. He made his turn, and, aligning himself with the east bank of the island and a spot on the east bank of the river, as he had done so many times before, he corrected the directional gyro to 210 degrees, the runway heading, and slowed to 80 mph. When the east bank of the river passed beneath the airplane, he began the timing, 73 seconds to the end of the runway. After 30 seconds, the village lights rose swiftly out of the swirling snow, and just as swiftly disappeared again, as the village passed under him. Forty-three seconds now to the edge of the runway. He reduced speed still more, and glided down into the white darkness ahead. With 5 seconds to go, he turned on the landing lights. There was a sudden burst of blinding light, as they hit the thick wall of falling snow. A hundred feet ahead, the runway reflectors began to glow. Gently the skis of the 180 settled into the soft cushion of deepening snow.

There was no one at the airstrip to meet the lone pilot and help him secure his plane. But, in the village, a half mile away, Margaret Graue, a member of the **Jesuit Volunteer Corps** stationed in Kaltag, had a warm meal ready. She knew his ways by now.

It was neither a reckless daredevil, nor one of those real lucky "airplane guys" who made that safe landing under truly adverse conditions. It was a well trained, highly skilled pilot with many years of experience. His Nome–Kaltag flight was carefully calculated and involved, in his judgment, little real risk.

James A. "Jim" Sebesta was born in Binghamton, New York, on July 18, 1936—and he was born to fly. In an interview conducted in Kaltag by Father Louis L. **Renner**, S.J., in October 1980, he admit-

(*above*) Father James A. Sebesta, S.J., by the Twin Bonanza Beechcraft at Kaltag on October 14, 1980. *LR.*

(*right*) Father James A. Sebesta, S.J., newly "dressed" for Edgar Kalland at the 1985 Kaltag stickdance. *LR.*

ted that the first clear thought he had ever had was that he wanted to fly. He spent his early years in Norwich, New York, where the family raised chickens. From the chickens he hoped to learn how to fly. While still in the third grade, and dreaming "to fly, like a bird, you know," he fashioned himself a pair of wings and jumped first off the garage roof, then off his neighbor's 3-story chicken coop. In both cases, he went "straight into the ground." Convinced that lack of speed was the basic problem, he took to the road, on his bike, with a pair of wings mounted below the handlebars. That attempt ended with "broken wings and paint and skin all over the road."

It was now time, Jim concluded, to find out how airplanes fly. At the Norwich airport—where he was to work during his high school and college days— he watched planes take off and land. He next got odd jobs at the airport, such as washing the bellies of dirty planes and trimming the grass around the hangars. For this he was rewarded with half-hour airplane rides. By the time he was in the seventh grade, he had a full-time job at the airport. He was given $10.00 and a half-hour flying lesson per

week. He soloed on his sixteenth birthday, and had his private pilot's license by the following year.

While attending Tufts University in Medford, Massachusetts, from which he graduated with a Bachelor of Science degree in physics in 1958, Jim began to do some serious spiritual reading and to ask himself, "What would I really want to have done at the end of my life that would be important?" He considered research in the field of physics, but concluded that working at something that promoted the well-being of other people would be something better to look back on. At that point, the thought of being a priest began to enter his thinking. He could not, however, see himself one of those priests "who went around in a long black dress, tapping little kids on the head and saying, 'there, there, my child!'" The Jesuits, because of the broad scope of their ministries and interests were attractive to him. He learned, too, that Jesuits served on the Alaska missions. It was, then, clearly the Jesuits for him.

On September 7, 1958, with the sole intention of one day serving in Alaska, Jim entered the novitiate of the Maryland Province of the Society of Jesus at

Wernersville, Pennsylvania. After completing his two-year noviceship, he spent an additional two years there studying the classics and humanities. His philosophical studies he made at Loyola Seminary in Shrub Oak, New York, from 1962–64. He then went on to post-graduate studies in physics at Fordham University in the Bronx, New York. These he terminated in 1966 with a Master of Science degree.

Meanwhile, ever since the day Jim first entered the novitiate, he had persisted in making known, "in a whole stack of letters to Superiors, including two to Father General," his hope of being assigned, at first opportunity, to Alaska, a mission field of the Oregon Province. To his great delight, he found himself assigned to **Copper Valley School** for the school year 1966–67 to teach mathematics, physics and general sciences, as well as to serve as moderator of the school's Civil Air Patrol group.

During that year at CVS, Jim was given the use of a J-3 by Pete Huddleston of Copper Center, who owned the plane but was not himself a pilot. The only condition was that Jim had to maintain the plane. So, for about two dollars an hour, he was able to fly. He set about planning an airstrip near the school. "I photographed the whole area from the air," he related in an interview published in 1992, "and designed different places where the airstrip should go. Tony Sipary was the maintenance man there, and he got excited about the airstrip, too. He showed me how to operate the school's D-6 Cat, and I went out every evening after the boys went to bed and started clearing. That was in April, and in May it was finished." By the end of his first year in Alaska, Jim—born to fly, and, according to some who knew him well, a "mechanical and aeronautical genius"—had earned both his commercial and instrument ratings.

From 1967–70, Jim made his theological studies at Weston College, Massachusetts. Father Simon E. Smith, S.J., one of his professors at Weston, remembered him as "a good student, but one who had little use for theological abstractions. He was an eminently practical, pastoral man. Unlike many of his peers in the seminary, Jim always knew where he was going: Alaska! So everything he did—study, fly, work, play, whatever—was ordered clearly to that goal. No identity crisis here!"

During his years at Weston, Jim first earned a flight instructor's rating and then spent much of his free time giving flying lessons. He was the most popular flight instructor at the field and earned enough money to pay for most of his theological studies. He also used part of the money earned from giving flight instructions to get the instrument instructor's and multi-engine ratings. For a time, he was an instructor in Northeastern University's professional pilot program.

On May 23, 1970, in St. Christopher's Church in Binghamton, Jim was ordained a priest by Robert L. **Whelan**, S.J., Bishop of **Fairbanks**. This was Bishop Whelan's first ordination of a man to the priesthood. As an ordination present, Father Jim received a Cessna 180 from Paul Enggaard, his first flight instructor at Mid-State Aviation, Norwich. Of Paul he said in 1980, "Whatever skills in flying I now have I trace to those years of instruction and advice I received from Paul Enggaard." Father Sebesta flew the Cessna 180 to Alaska and signed it over to the Diocese of Fairbanks, but continued for years to fly it to cover his mission stations.

Father Sebesta spent the years 1970–72 in Fairbanks taking courses in cultural anthropology at the University of Alaska–Fairbanks. While in Fairbanks, he also served as campus minister at the university and taught courses in the sciences at Monroe Catholic High School.

In 1972, Father Jim, as pastor of Kaltag, began full-time ministry to the Koyukon Athabaskan Indian people. His first entry into Kaltag was without ceremony—and without style. In a letter to Father Renner, Margaret Graue, in Kaltag at the time, recalled the event vividly:

> I became acquainted with him Christmas Eve, 1970. Fr. Jim arrived in Kaltag at 9:45 P.M. Temperature minus some 40 degrees. Due to the conditions of our airfield, the plane landed in **Nulato**. Fr. Jim came to Kaltag by way of dogsled and Skidoo, 40 miles down the frozen Yukon. He stood on the runners of the sled, the Skidoo driven by one of the villagers. The man was not too happy to make this trip, as this was the second trip he made that day. He told Father to hang on, as he never looks back. When Fr. Jim arrived at my house, I couldn't believe what I saw. His clothes were frozen, face frost bitten. He was cold, tired and hungry. This was Christmas Eve. What was he to do? After some hot coffee and a change of clothing, he celebrated Midnight Mass.

From Father Jim, Father Renner learned that at one point on that trip he had to take one hand off the sled handle to adjust his hat. In doing so, he fell off the runners, but hung on to the sled, and so was dragged some distance, before that driver, who "never looks back," sensed something amiss, stopped, came back and grunted, "Fall off, huh?" On again, gone again.

From 1972–75, Father Jim, while making Kaltag his headquarters, was really a three-rivers pastor. Besides Kaltag on the Yukon, he cared also for **Huslia** on the Koyukuk, 115 air miles northeast of Kaltag, and **McGrath** on the Kuskokwim, 125 air miles southeast of Kaltag. Flying the Cessna 180, he was able to cover all three stations on a weekly basis. For the greater part of those three years, he was involved, too, with the **Eskimo Deacon Program**, flying members of the program—in a twin-engine Beechcraft, a "Twin Bonanza" owned by the Diocese of Fairbanks—from their villages to meeting sites and home again. In addition, he served also as spiritual director of members of the Jesuit Volunteer Corps. During the latter half of 1975, he was Area Director of the Corps in Alaska.

In 1976, from January to June, Father Jim made his tertianship at Leo House in Spokane, Washington. As one of his tertianship "experiments" he was assigned to something he, in his words, "actually dreaded—hospital chaplaincy." He was assigned to the cancer ward. But, after the "experiment" was over, he could say of it, "it turned out to be one of the more valuable experiences of my life. It filled out my own thoughts on the importance of understanding love as the basis for my existence. We are here to discover the fullness of God's love for us."

After completing his tertianship, Father Jim continued on as pastor of Kaltag and its two dependent stations, Huslia and McGrath, for another six years. On February 2, 1977, he was transcribed from the Maryland to the Oregon Province. In the summer of 1982, his tenure in Kaltag came to an end. Looking back on his Kaltag years, he recalled around 1990:

> Being assigned to Kaltag was a positive thing for me, but the initial experience with alcoholism there was depressing. I felt sometimes very discouraged. Finally, I came to the realization that I had to do something.

> I tried a number of things, made mistakes in the process, but learned a great deal. I got very close to the people. What grew was kind of a mutual affection. I look with great fondness on the people down there. Part of that has come from having left behind something of myself.

By the time Father Jim left Kaltag, all the people knew that he was Father "Sebesta," not Father "Asbestos," as some thought, when he first arrived there.

On August 15, 1982, Father Jim became Superior of St. Mary's Mission on the **Andreafsky** River, a position he filled until May 31, 1984, when he was appointed General Superior of Jesuits in Alaska. As such, he continued to reside at St. Mary's, visiting his fellow Jesuits at their stations out of there. From the summer of 1987 to July 31, 1990, when his term as General Superior ended, he made his headquarters in the newly built Jesuit House in Fairbanks. During those three years, he served also as pastor of St. Michael's parish in McGrath, flying his own plane to and from there at regular intervals.

On the night of April 13, 1985, in Kaltag, Father Jim was a key player in the area of intercultural conflict resolution. For generations, Jesuit missionaries stationed in Nulato and Kaltag had opposed the traditional Koyukon Athabaskan "Feast for the Dead," commonly referred to simply as the "stick-dance," on the basis that it was a "superstitious" practice. By the early 1980s, however, they, and most of the Jesuits in Alaska, had come—thanks to post-Vatican II thinking in general and the influence of cultural anthropologist Father William J. **Loyens**, S.J., in particular—to see the "stickdance" in a new light. On that April night, Father Jim, as one who had rendered a significant service to Kaltag resident Edgar **Kalland** at the time of his death, was "dressed" for Edgar by his wife, Virginia. Father Jim was chosen to be "dressed" as an expression of gratitude for what he had done for Edgar during the last hour of his life. He had placed Edgar in the "Twin Bonanza" to ease his breathing with the pure oxygen available in the plane. This was the first "dressing" in keeping with the age-old rites of the Koyukon mortuary feast of a Catholic priest by an Alaskan Native for an Alaskan Native. The fact that Father Jim was General Superior of Jesuits in Alaska, and was being "dressed" with the full approval of Michael J. **Kaniecki**, S.J., Bishop of Fairbanks, also present for the rites, made the whole event all the more significant. After those ceremonies, the Koyukon people had reason to be convinced that their time-honored, sacred mortuary feast would never again meet with clerical disapproval.

Father Jim spent the year 1990–91, residing at St. Mary's Mission working on a "Family Life Program," a program he hoped would "help people lead fuller lives," lives less influenced by alcoholism and the resulting dysfunctional behavior. Alcohol and its deleterious effects on people was one of Father Jim's major concerns throughout his years in Alaska. He was forever urging them and trying to help them to "slack off," as they put it. The negative aspects of life were for him "but one long headwind." All too often it was alcohol that created the "headwind." Much as alcohol abuse exasperated him, he was, according to Sister Dolores Pardini, S.N.D., who worked closely with him in Kaltag, "always extremely patient with the people. No matter how tired or overburdened, he always took time with those who needed it." According to Margaret Graue, who worked with him in Kaltag for over four years, "He always had time for everyone but himself."

During Father Jim's Kaltag days, a row of ceramic and plastic frogs of various kinds and in various postures lined a shelf in the meeting room of his church–residence. They had been given him by different people as their way of teasing him for being "a man always on the hop," always on the come and go. And he was never more a man on the hop than during the years 1991–94, when he was headquartered in **Mountain Village**. His job description in the Oregon Province catalog for those years reads: "Pastoral ministry to the Catholic communities in Mountain Village, **Pilot Station**, **Marshall** and **Russian Mission**. Assisting in Native Ministry Training Program." (One of Father Jim's chief dreams at the time was to see a Native clergy come into being. One of his guiding principles was that people should, in all areas of their lives, be helped to help themselves.). Even given the demands made upon him by this multifold assignment, he found time to fly errands of mercy. No matter how busy he was, or how marginal the weather, when a case

of sickness or an accident, in the judgment of the village health aide, was such as to allow no delay for better weather or a commercial flight, unhesitatingly, he flew the sufferer to the nearest hospital. "It's kind of hard to refuse," he shrugged. Like the Native people he served, he "created" time as needed.

In July 1994, Father Jim left Alaska to spend a sabbatical year at St. Louis University. There he taught part-time in the Aviation Technology Program at the university's Parks College, spent time in private study, and served as a director in the 19th Annotation retreat program, "BRIDGES." From the outset, he found Parks "a great place," and teaching there "very pleasant." Nevertheless, around Christmas time he wrote, "Hearing news from Alaska makes me feel like receiving news from home. Being away makes my heart grow fonder of the people and the country."

Father Jim spent the summer of 1995 in the Bahamas flying Lawrence A. Burke, S.J., Archbishop of Nassau, and his priests from place to place in an Aztec for weekend Masses.

In early August, back in St. Louis, he wrote to Father Renner, "The community here at St. Louis University is very friendly and welcoming. They and the students are very happy to have a Jesuit of my capacity at Parks. But, I do think of Alaska a lot and would very much like to go back. Even with these happy experiences here, I feel Alaska is my home."

In December 2002, Father Jim was still in St. Louis, away from the Alaska he regarded his home, teaching at Parks College, and preparing a course for the graduate school called "Aviation Safety Ethics." This was a wholly new course, intended to be taught "On-Line," meaning it would be offered to students across the country via the WebCT, St. Louis University's medium for "On-Line" courses.

In 2004, ten years after Father Jim left Alaska for his sabbatical, he was still in St. Louis, serving as a professor of aeronautics at Parks. St. Louis University was, to be sure, most pleased to have him stay on and did everything it could to retain him; and he, for his part, was, unquestionably, happy with his lot there. Those two realities notwithstanding, he had hoped, nevertheless, at the end of his sabbatical—and , thereafter, from year to year—to return "home" to Alaska. The question arises: Why was he still in St. Louis as of the year 2004?

In Father Jim's August 1995 letter to Father Renner, we read: "I hope I will not be away from Alaska long, but I still get comments that make me wonder. Someone visiting from the California Province the other day said something like, 'I hear you won't be going back to Alaska, while Kaniecki is bishop.' I don't know where things like that come from, but it is distressing."

Distressing or not, the real reason why Father Jim did not return to Alaska in 1995, or subsequently, was embodied in the one man, Bishop Kaniecki. In the early 1990s, Father Jim, on his "free time," and with the approval of Father Theodore E. **Kestler**, S.J, General Mission Superior, began doing some flying as a commercial pilot for Fairbanks-based Frontier Flying Service, Inc. This was owned by John Hajdukovich, a long-time and close friend of Father Jim's. Father Jim had often spent weekends with the Hajdukovich family at their cabin on Harding Lake, finding relaxation there in swimming and water skiing. On Sundays, he offered Mass for the family and neighbors rounded up by John. Bishop Kaniecki was unable to reconcile Father Jim's role as a commercial pilot with that of a priest serving on the Alaska Mission. There was a falling out between prelate and priest. From the outset, there was more to that sabbatical than what at first met the eye of the general public. Although Bishop Kaniecki did not have the authority to forbid Father Jim to fly as a commercial pilot in the Diocese of Fairbanks, he did have the authority to forbid him to practice routine pastoral ministry in the diocese while keeping his option to fly as a commercial pilot open. Father Jim did not find it in himself to give up commercial piloting in the Diocese of Fairbanks. Even after Bishop Kaniecki's death, on August 6, 2000, Father Jim continued to do some commercial flying, during summers, as the third millennium dawned. Both as man and as priest, he was born to fly.

60, 102, 103, 104, 142

Archbishop Charles John Seghers. *JOPA-7.01.*

SEGHERS, Archbishop Charles John

On the right bank of the Yukon River, 23 miles northeast of **Nulato**, there rises abruptly out of the waters to a height of 300 feet a steep, rocky promontory known to the Koyukon Indians of the area as *Yisletaw*. White men know it as "Bishop Rock," for it was here that the life of Archbishop Charles John Seghers came to an abrupt end.

Charles John Seghers was born in Ghent, Belgium, on December 26, 1839. Tuberculosis was a family scourge. His parents and four siblings died of it. He, too, was infected with it, and for the rest of his life he struggled to survive it. After completing his studies at the College of Saint Barbara in Ghent, he entered the seminary there. Toward the end of his theological studies, however, he felt such a strong attraction for the work of the missions that he decided to transfer to the American Missionary Seminary in Louvain. He was ordained a priest in St. Rombaut's Cathedral, Mechelen, on May 30, 1863.

At this very time, Modeste **Demers**, Bishop of Vancouver Island, B.C., was in Belgium calling for recruits. Father Seghers eagerly answered the call, and was accepted. In November of that year, 1863, he arrived in Victoria on Vancouver Island. In Victoria his talents and zeal were quickly recognized. He was assigned to pastoral work in the city, but served, in effect, during the bishop's many absences, as administrator of the diocese. Bishop Demers considered himself truly blessed to have in Father

Seghers "a true priest of God, an active and zealous worker in the Master's Vineyard, having in view no personal aims, but only the glory of God and the triumph of religion." When Bishop Demers traveled to Rome for the First Vatican Council in 1869, he took Father Seghers with him.

Before Bishop Demers died in 1871, he formally appointed Father Seghers temporary administrator of the diocese. On June 29, 1873, he was consecrated Bishop of the Diocese of Vancouver Island. At the age of 34 years, he was the youngest bishop in America. It was under his ecclesiastical jurisdiction that **Alaska** fell at that time. Three weeks after his consecration, Bishop Seghers made the first of his five trips to Alaska, a trip that took him across Southeastern Alaska and as far west as **Unalaska**. From this time on, Alaska was the principal focus of his pastoral concerns.

In the summer of 1877, Bishop Seghers, accompanied by Father Joseph M. **Mandart**, reached Alaska's northern interior. Via the **Unalakleet–Kaltag** portage, they arrived at Nulato on July 31st. The two made Nulato their headquarters for the year. Out of Nulato, Bishop Seghers roamed far and wide all through that general area, scouting out the country and doing some limited missionary work. On July 11, 1878, Bishop Seghers, full of high hopes and firmly determined to return to establish a permanent central mission at Nulato, sailed from **St. Michael**, along with Father Mandart, for San Francisco. There he received the disquieting news that he had been appointed Coadjutor Archbishop of Oregon City. Bowing to God's will, he reluctantly accepted the appointment. On December 20, 1880, he became Archbishop of Oregon City.

As Archbishop of Oregon City, Archbishop Seghers traveled extensively throughout the vast regions now under his jurisdiction. His heart and hopes, however, continued to remain on Vancouver Island and in Alaska. He saw a chance to return, when the See of Vancouver Island became vacant again during the summer of 1883. In a private audience with Pope Leo XIII, held at the end of December 1883, he made known his reasons for wishing to resign as Archbishop of Oregon City and to be reassigned to Vancouver Island. The Holy Father, greatly edified by the recitation of his reasons, acceded to his wishes and formally appointed him, with the title and privileges of an archbishop, to his former See, the Diocese of Vancouver Island. On April 1, 1885, with great gratitude and joy of heart on the part of all, Seghers, now its archbishop, was welcomed back to Vancouver Island.

Before he had departed Vancouver Island to take over the See of Oregon City, Bishop Seghers made the third of his five trips to Alaska. On April 25, 1879, he set out for **Wrangell**, where he installed his traveling companion, Father John J. **Althoff**, as pastor. The two then visited **Sitka**. His fourth trip to Alaska he made almost immediately after returning to Vancouver Island as its archbishop. On that trip, he visited Sitka and **Juneau**. His fifth, and final, trip to Alaska he was to make a year later.

On July 13, 1886, in company of Jesuit Fathers Paschal **Tosi** and Aloysius J. **Robaut**, and that of a Catholic layman, Frank Fuller, Archbishop Seghers sailed from Victoria, bound for the middle Yukon River valley via Juneau, **Skagway**, the Chilkoot Pass, and the upper Yukon. On September 7th, the party arrived at Harper's Place, a trading post at the confluence of the Yukon and Stewart Rivers. By this time, the leaves on the birches and aspens had turned to gold and begun to fall, the air was cold, the freeze-up not far off. Archbishop Seghers decided that the two priests should spend the winter at Harper's Place, while he and Fuller would press on to Nulato. Father Tosi made known in no uncertain terms the serious misgivings he had about the archbishop's going on alone with Fuller, a drifter with a mysterious personal history, quarrelsome, given to unstable behavior, but who had eagerly offered himself to the archbishop in place of a Jesuit Lay Brother the archbishop had hoped for, but whom Father Joseph M. **Cataldo**, S.J., Superior of the Rocky Mountain Mission at the time, could not spare.

It should be mentioned here that it was with reluctance that Father Cataldo had, in the first place, given Archbishop Seghers even Fathers Tosi and Robaut as traveling companions. They were allowed to go North with the understanding that they were doing so only "on loan, for a visit to spy out the land," and "till we [Jesuits] could hear what our

European Superiors would dispose about accepting Missions in Alaska." At first only one priest had been approved as a traveling companion to the archbishop. But, firmly resolved and clearly intending to finally establish missions in northern Alaska, with Jesuits in charge, the archbishop had insisted on a second priest. Persuasively, he had argued in a letter to Father Cataldo: "It would be unwise to leave one priest by himself in Alaska; and, as my desire is to locate *two* in the interior and then to continue my trip to parts unknown, I beg you to arrange matters so that two Fathers of the Society with one or more Brothers may accompany me."

Despite Father Tosi's protestations and efforts to dissuade the archbishop from continuing on downriver with Fuller, the latter remained unshakable in his determination to do so. Two motives in particular drove him to press on to Nulato, in spite of the lateness of the season and Fuller's unreliability. When he left Nulato eight years earlier, he promised the people there that he would return. But he was motivated even more by his fear that the Episcopal priest, Octavius Parker, reported to be at St. Michael, might get to Nulato before him and establish himself there first. When Archbishop Seghers first learned of that possibility, "it was like a sword piercing his heart."

As Archbishop Seghers and Fuller made their way down the Yukon, traveling conditions, their boat, and Fuller's mind deteriorated rapidly. On October 4th, at the confluence of the Yukon and Tanana Rivers, at Nuklukayet, today's **Tanana**, they abandoned their boat and waited for the river to freeze solid enough for sled travel. By now Archbishop Seghers realized that Fuller was insane. On October 16th, he wrote in his diary: "Peculiar conversation with [Fuller] in which for the third time he gives evidence of his insanity."

On Saturday, November 27th, with Nulato still a good distance off and travel difficult because of deep, soft snow, the archbishop, Fuller and two Indian guides who had joined them at Nuklukayet, decided to spend the night at the fish camp at what is known today as "Bishop Rock." Archbishop Seghers, confident that he would the next day finally reach Nulato, though still some 40 miles downriver, was in good spirits, laughing frequently.

Fuller, by contrast, remained sullen, casting suspicious glances at his companions. Several times that night he got up and moved about.

Sometime between six and seven the next morning, the party rose and prepared to mush the final leg of their arduous journey to Nulato. As the archbishop bent over to pick up his mittens, Fuller, raising the archbishop's .44 caliber Winchester, fired a single shot into the stooping figure. Not yet 47 years old, Archbishop Seghers died instantly. It was Sunday, November 28, 1886. Nulato had, after all, proved to be a destination too far.

The body of the archbishop was taken to St. Michael and buried there for a year. In 1888, it was exhumed and shipped to Victoria, where it found its final resting place in St. Andrew's Cathedral.

To this day the faithful venerate Archbishop Charles John Seghers as "the founder of the Alaska missions," and as "The Apostle of Alaska."

27, 183, 185

SELDOVIA

The historic waterfront town of Seldovia is located on the west coast of the Kenai Peninsula, on the east shore of Seldovia Bay, 16 miles southwest of **Homer**. It is accessible only by air or water. Its population numbered 99 in 1890, 460 in 1967, 479 in 1980, 316 in 1990, and 286 in the year 2000. The Seldovia post office was established in 1898.

Seldovia first saw Catholic priestly ministries in 1950, when Father Martin G. Borbeck, S.J., stationed in **Seward** from 1948–52, began to visit it out of there. From 1952–61, it was visited by Father Arnold L. **Custer**, S.J., likewise out of Seward. Father Borbeck offered Mass for a handful of people in the old schoolhouse in a room that had been transformed into the town library. At first, Father Custer, too, offered Mass in that room. About 1954, he began to offer Mass for around 20 people in the home of Richard and Lynn Inglima, longtime residents of Seldovia. The comfortable Inglima home continued to serve as a place for Mass until 1964.

In 1961, the Redemptorist Fathers from the Oakland Province began to serve the Catholic communities on the Kenai Peninsula. The first three priests, all headquartered in Seward to begin with, were Fathers Edward C. **O'Neill**, pastor of the Seward parish, James Van Hoomissen, and Robert L. Woodruff. One or another of these, or one of their successors, visited Seldovia from time to time for roughly ten years.

By the early 1960s, the Catholics at Seldovia numbered around 40, and had outgrown the Inglima home. Father Woodruff suggested that a Chalet Craft A-Frame structure be erected as a church, and named "St. Mary Star of the Sea." Property for such was donated by Frank Raby. Meanwhile, Mass was offered in the old city hall.

On May 28, 1963, footings were poured for the new church. The building went up, but slowly. Much of the structural work was done by Father Thaddeus Dean and his volunteers. By Christmas 1964, however, the church, named for St. James the Apostle, in keeping with the wishes of Dermot **O'Flanagan**, Bishop of **Juneau**, was far enough along, so that Mass could be offered in it. A decade later, Redemptorist Father Richard G. **Strass** and Max Swick,

helped by volunteers, insulated the floor, walls, and ceiling; paneled the church; put in a bathroom; and made a sleep area in the choir loft.

Throughout most of the 1970s, Seldovia was a mission of **Soldotna**; and, throughout most of the 1980s and as of the year 2004, of Homer. From 1973–92, with the exception of one year, it was principally Father Strass who tended the Seldovia flock. From June 1992 to August 1993, Msgr. Walter F. Jude, a retired priest from the Diocese of Grand Rapids, Michigan, lived in the Seldovia church and offered Mass there every Sunday.

In 1993, Sister Carol Ann Aldrich, R.S.M., began to serve as Pastoral Administrator of the Seldovia mission. As of the year 2004, Ms. Annemiek J. Brunklaus was its Pastoral Minister. Various "circuit rider" priests out of Anchorage visited Seldovia at the turn of the millennium.

15

SEWARD

The town of Seward, on the Kenai Peninsula, at the northwest end of Resurrection Bay, is named for William Henry Seward, U.S. Secretary of State, who negotiated the purchase of **Alaska**. Founded in 1903, by surveyors for the Alaska Railroad (built 1915–23), the town, as the ocean terminus of the railroad and an ice-free harbor, serves as an important supply center for Alaska's interior. A post office was established at Seward in 1895, discontinued in 1896, and reestablished in 1903. Seward's population was 534, in 1910; 652, in 1920; 835, in 1930; 949, in 1939; 2, 114, in 1950; and 2,956, in 1960. Seward was almost completely devastated by the March 27, 1964 earthquake. However, it recovered. By 1992, it had a population of 2, 699; and, by the year 2000, one of 2,830.

Official Catholic ministry in Seward dates from

(*left*) St. James Church, Seldovia.
Photo by Annemiek J. Brunklaus.

(*opposite*) Sacred Heart Church, Seward.
Photo by Deacon Walter Corrigan, Jr.

the summer of 1905. Father Philibert **Turnell**, S.J., arrived there during the latter part of June. By July 4th, a tent chapel was up, and Paulist Father John M. Handly was conducting "a mission" for both Catholics and non-Catholics. Father Turnell had asked his help in getting the Church established in Seward. Late in the fall of 1905, Father Turnell, who was holding services in one tent and living in another, was directed to go to **Juneau**.

Sacred Heart parish in Seward looks upon the year 1910 as the year of its founding. In that year, Father Matthias Schmitt, S.J., put up the 32 × 24′ Sacred Heart Church, the first Catholic church in Seward. At the time, the town was considered "too poor to support a priest." However, when the Federal Government decided to build a railroad from Seward to **Fairbanks**, the town experienced a population increase. Father John B. **Van der Pol**, S.J., who was in Seward a few years after Father Schmitt, enlarged and beautified the church.

The second Sacred Heart Church, the present A-frame church, was already proposed for construction in 1963. The March 27, 1964, earthquake damaged the old original church and rectory beyond repair. On June 16, 1964, ground was broken for the present church, parish hall, and attached rectory. The new church was ready for use by Easter 1965. It was formally dedicated by Archbishop **Joseph T. Ryan** on August 6, 1967. The new parish plant was built during the pastorate, 1961–68, of Father Edward C. **O'Neill**, C.Ss.R.

It was also Father Van der Pol who saw to the construction of Seward's two-story, 25-bed hospital. This was placed under the patronage of St. Francis Xavier, but was called "Seward General Hospital." The hospital, staffed by the Sisters of St. Joseph of Peace–Newark, opened on January 25, 1916. Founding Sisters Margaret Mary, Aloysius, Germaine, and Stephanie were regarded as "heroic pioneers" because of the way in which they coped with disasters and sickness, especially with the 1918 influenza epidemic. The hospital was twice flooded, to such an extent that the Sisters and patients had to evacuate it for a time. It was formally closed on June 7, 1919, because the railroad would not renew its contract, its workers being closer to **Anchorage** by now.

Father William A. **Shepherd**, S.J., was the first priest to perform a baptism in Seward, in 1913. In

An earlier Sacred Heart Church, Seward.
JOPA-423.01.

the course of the almost hundred years of its existence, Seward's Sacred Heart parish has seen the coming and going of around thirty different priests. At times, it was visited by priests stationed in **Cordova**, **Valdez**, or Anchorage. At times, it had a pastor in residence. Some of those priests served for only a short time; some for a longer period. Most of them, while serving as pastor of Sacred Heart parish and residing in Seward, visited its dependent mission stations on the Kenai Peninsula.

As already indicated, Father Turnell was the first priest to visit Seward. After him came the following Jesuit Fathers: Schmitt, in 1910; Shepherd, in 1913; Van der Pol, in 1915; Alphonsus Fletcher, in 1917; and William **McMillan**, in 1918.

There was no resident priest in Seward from 1919–32. During those years, it was visited sporadically out of Anchorage by Fathers Aloysius J. **Markham** and Godfrey Dane, S.J. In 1932, Father Joseph Allard, O.M.I., was resident priest for a brief period. He found the Catholics of Seward to be "a needy flock and a hungry flock." Father F. Merrill **Sulzman** was in Seward during the years 1932, 1933, and 1935. He was "delighted with everything" he found there. During his absences, he was replaced briefly by Father Dermot **O'Flanagan**. The year 1935–36 saw Seward again without a resident priest. Father William Chaput, "a genial host, with the reputation of being an easy mark for 'spongers,'" was in Seward from 1936–48. He has the distinction of having served as pastor in Seward longer than any other priest.

Father Chaput was followed by Father Martin G. Borbeck, S.J. He was in Seward, which he described as an "isolated ice box," from 1948–52. Father Borbeck showed special concern for the religious education of Seward's Catholic children. It was he who had the Sisters of **Providence** come to Seward to conduct summer programs of religious instruction, something they did from 1949–60.

Father Borbeck, in turn, was followed by the last of the Jesuits to serve in Seward, Father Arnold L. **Custer**, S.J., who was there from 1952–1961. Father Custer spent much time on the roads of the Kenai Peninsula visiting the various mission stations dependent on Sacred Heart parish. In passing, it might be mentioned that while he was on the road during Christmas Eve and Christmas Day 1958, Father Louis L. **Renner**, S.J., spent his first Christmas in Alaska replacing him in Seward.

Next it was the Redemptorist Fathers, with several exceptions, who served as pastors of Seward's Sacred Heart parish up to the year 2002. Fathers James Van Hoomissen and Joseph Palmer were the first of their number, arriving in Seward in June 1961. Their tenure was short. In September of that same year, Father O'Neill began his seven-year pastorate. During the year 1968–69, Father Thomas Sloan, a priest from the Archdiocese of Chicago, was pastor. From 1969–72, Redemptorist Father Joseph Elliott was pastor. He was followed, during the years 1972–77, by fellow Redemptorist Father Daniel D.

Debolt. For the years 1977–79, Father O'Neill returned to Seward. During the year 1979–80, Father Bernard Van Hoomissen, C.Ss.R., was pastor. He was followed by Father Paul Miller, C.Ss.R., pastor from 1980–87. His was the privilege of being pastor, when, in 1985, Sacred Heart parish celebrated the 75th anniversary of its founding.

Father Miller was followed by Redemptorist Fathers Joseph Nuttman, 1987–88; and Robert J. Wells, 1988–91. They were followed by diocesan priests: Charles B. Crouse, during the year 1992; and David Means, 1993–95. After them came Redemptorist Fathers Fred Arpin, 1995–96; and Richard G. **Strass**, 1996–2002. Father Richard D. **Tero** began to serve as pastor of Seward's Sacred Heart parish in the year 2002.

15

SHAGELUK

The Ingalik Indian village of Shageluk is located on the east bank of the Innoko River, 20 miles east of Anvik and 34 miles northeast of **Holy Cross**. In 1880, it had 150 inhabitants; in 1920, 130; in 1930, 88; in 1950, 100; in 1970, 167; in 1980, 131; and in the year 2000, 129. A post office was established at Shageluk in 1924.

In December 1887, Father Aloysius J. **Robaut**, S.J., baptized some children at Shageluk. Father William H. **Judge**, S.J., however, is rightly considered the founder of the Shageluk mission. He visited Shageluk out of Holy Cross in February 1891. In August 1892, he began to build there a log-house, "30 x 24 inside and two stories high." The structure was to serve as a church and residence. When the walls were up only seven feet, he had to discontinue building, having been transferred to **Nulato**. By the spring of 1895, however, when he returned to Shageluk, he found that two Lay Brothers had come from Holy Cross, finished the walls, and put a roof on the mission building. He set about finishing the interior. As soon as he had one fourth of the floor of the whole building down, he built an altar in the church part, described as "elegant," and began offering Mass on it. He dedicated the Shageluk mission to the Sacred Heart of Jesus.

According to historical records, "the structure was, in after years, taken to **Paimiut**."

The Shageluk mission has always been served, if only intermittently, by priests stationed at Holy Cross. In 1903, Father Joseph **Perron** bought two houses there. By the summer of 1954, Father Paul H. **Linssen**, before he was assigned to the lower Yukon, had a new Shageluk church well under construction.

The Koyukon "Feast for the Dead," or the "stick-dance," still routinely held in the villages of Nulato and **Kaltag**, is said to have its roots in Shageluk.

49, 142

SHELDON POINT (See Nunam Iqua!)

SHEPHERD, Father William A., S.J.

William Augustine Shepherd was born on June 13, 1874, at the family home in Shepherd's Valley, a valley near Oakland, California, named for the family. William's brother Robert, too, became a Jesuit priest; and his brother James became a Jesuit Lay Brother. Their three sisters became members of the Sisters of Notre Dame de Namur. Their mother, born in Ireland, was Mary Rogers. Their father, born in England, was William J. Shepherd. After his wife's death, and the entrance of all the family into Religious life, William himself entered the Society of Jesus, as a Lay Brother. For a time, he was stationed at the University of Santa Clara. However, his health was found to be too delicate for him to continue on in the Order.

William A. Shepherd, after attending the Hayes Public School near Oakland, from 1886–1894, attended Santa Clara College High School during the year 1894–95. On September 2, 1895, he entered the Jesuit novitiate at Los Gatos, California. He pronounced his first vows on September 8, 1897. Because he had had only one year of high school, he spent the years 1897–1902, still at Los Gatos, studying the classics and humanities. From 1902–05, he made his philosophical studies at Gonzaga College in Spokane, Washington. During the year 1905–06, he taught mathematics at Santa Clara

College. He spent the following two years there teaching Latin and Greek in the high school department, and arithmetic to 7th and 8th graders in the primary division. He then went on to make his theological studies at Gonzaga College from 1908–11. In St. Aloysius Church, Spokane, on June 29, 1911, he was ordained a priest by Bishop Edward J. O'Dea of Seattle. His tertianship was made at St. Stanislaus House of Retreats in Cleveland, Ohio, 1911–12.

In July 1912, Father Shepherd became pastor of Holy Name parish in **Ketchikan**, **Alaska**, with responsibility also for its dependent station, **Wrangell**. For the next two years, 1913–15, he was stationed at **Valdez**. From 1915–19, he was the pioneering pastor of Holy Family parish in **Anchorage**. As such, he saw to the building of the first Holy Family Church. During his Anchorage years, he visited **Seward** from time to time. He it was who performed the first Catholic baptism in Seward, on December 24, 1913, while still stationed at Valdez. For the year 1919–20, he was back again in Ketchikan, where he spent his last year in Alaska.

After his Alaskan years, Father Shepherd spent the year 1920–21 at Holy Family Mission, a Blackfoot Indian mission in Montana. Then, from 1921–27, he was pastor of St. Jude Thaddeus parish in Havre, Montana. Next, for two years, he was assistant pastor of St. Francis Xavier's parish in Missoula, Montana. For the remainder of his long life he ministered in California, the state of his birth. In 1933, he volunteered for the China Mission, but was turned down for reasons of health.

From 1929–40, Father Shepherd served as an assistant pastor at Blessed Sacrament parish in Hollywood. After a year at Alma College, Los Gatos, and two years at Santa Clara University, he went on to found the new parish of St. Rita in San Diego, in 1944. He continued doing parish work in several different places until 1950. From then on, he served mainly as a Father Confessor to fellow Jesuits at Santa Clara University and as a chaplain to Carmelite Nuns.

In the spring of 1957, a severe sickness forced Father Shepherd into more or less total retirement. During his final long battle with cancer, he was cared for by non-Catholic nurses, who let it be known that they were deeply impressed by his heroic patience and resignation. One of them, a Methodist, after caring for him, said, "I am a better person every day for having known him."

Father Shepherd died, in the Santa Clara infirmary, on December 13, 1959. He lies buried in the Jesuit section of the Santa Clara Catholic cemetery.

15

SHIREY, Joseph E., S.J.

Joseph E. "Joe" Shirey, the older of two boys, was born on July 3, 1916, in Fostoria, Ohio, to Karl L. Shirey and Isabel M. Reinhart Shirey. In 1920, the family moved to Roseburg, Oregon. For his first grade, he attended St. Joseph's School. At the end of that school year, the school closed. Thereafter he attended public schools and catechism classes. While in junior high, he received a soprano saxophone. During his junior year in high school, he formed a ten-piece band called "Joe Shirey's Pied Pipers." "This," in his words, "made a big hit with the high school kids and young adults." As a senior, he served as student body president.

After graduating from high school, Joe attended the University of Oregon for three years, majoring in music. In the course of his third year there, he had misgivings about making music a career for life. After praying over the matter, and doing some reading about Religious Orders, he came to the firm conviction that his call in life was to the priesthood, in the Society of Jesus. In September 1940, he was all set to enter the Jesuit novitiate at Sheridan, Oregon.

Then, one morning, Joe received a letter that began with the feared word, "Greetings!" It was from his draft board and informed him that he was due to serve in the U.S. Army for a year. To make that year as painless as possible, he planned to get into an Army band. On March 7, 1941, he left home for the Portland, Oregon, induction station. Exactly nine months later, the Japanese bombed Pearl Harbor. "All thoughts of getting out of the Army and into the novitiate went up in smoke," he wrote. By the time he was given an honorable discharge, on January 7, 1946, he had served as a band leader in the Army and had been to the Philippines and Japan.

Father Joseph E. Shirey, S.J. *JOPA-1077.01.*

Out of the Army now, Joe spent the first part of 1946 at Gonzaga University in Spokane, Washington, studying mainly Latin. On September 7, 1946, he entered the Jesuit Novitiate at Sheridan. After completing his two-year noviceship, he spent a third year there studying the classics and humanities. He next spent three years at Mount St. Michael's, Spokane, studying philosophy. Then he taught for a year at Gonzaga Preparatory in Spokane, before going on to four years of theological studies, from 1953–57, at Alma College, Los Gatos, California. He was ordained a priest in St. Aloysius Church, Spokane, on June 16, 1956.

After a summer at St. Francis Xavier Mission in Montana, Father Shirey spent two years at St. Patrick's parish in Spokane. During the summer of his second year at St. Patrick's, he found himself in **Ketchikan**, **Alaska**, for a few months, to fill in there for the pastor, Father John A. **Concannon**, S.J. This was Father Shirey's first time in Alaska, and he liked what he saw and experienced.

Father Shirey made his tertianship at Port Townsend, Washington, during the year 1959–60, after which he was stationed at St. Joseph's parish in Seattle, Washington, for two years. "It was a great place to work," he recalled years later. During the earlier part of his second year at St. Joseph's, he met Father Robert L. **Whelan**, S.J., pastor of St. Anthony's parish in **Anchorage**, Alaska, who was stop-

ping off in Seattle on his way back to Alaska. The two had a lengthy conversation. When the list of assignments came out that summer, 1962, Father Shirey, to his very pleasant surprise, found himself assigned to serve as Father Whelan's assistant. Ferrying a brand new pickup truck for a dealer to Alaska, he drove the Alaska Highway to Anchorage.

In Anchorage, he found himself immediately at home—even if his physical home was, for a year or so, nothing more than a house trailer shared with Father Whelan. In Father Whelan he had a most congenial co-priest and friend. In Augie Reetz, a St. Anthony's parishioner, he had "a great friend," as well as a pilot and fly-in fishing partner. Father Shirey was an avid fisherman. But, not surprisingly, it was in pastoral ministry that he found his major joys and consolations.

While stationed at St. Joseph's parish in Seattle, Father Shirey had been in charge of the parish's Legion of Mary praesidium. "I developed a great and lasting appreciation of the Legion of Mary," he wrote years later, "and for the very impressive members of that group." Soon after his arrival in Anchorage, in collaboration with a layman, Joe Riendl, he began to organize a Legion of Mary praesidium in St. Anthony's parish. To emphasize the fact that the Legion of Mary was not just a women's organization, the two decided that the first praesidium should have as officers three men and one woman. They stayed with that system for the next two praesidia they organized.

The first praesidium began to meet in December 1962. The meetings were well organized, and everything "worked out beautifully." After three praesidia were busy doing great work for St. Anthony's parish, Msgr. G. Edgar **Gallant**, pastor of Holy Family Cathedral parish in Anchorage, had Father Shirey start a Legion of Mary praesiduim in his parish. Before long, there were six adult praesidia and one junior praesidium in Anchorage.

Early one December morning in 1967, the phone in the St. Anthony's rectory rang. Father Whelan answered it. A minute or so later, he came to Father Shirey's room to announce, "Well, Joe, the honeymoon is over." The phone call was from Washington, D.C., informing Father Whelan that he was the new Bishop of **Fairbanks**. It was news neither priests wanted to hear. The parish was running smoothly; the two liked working together. The phone call meant new assignments for each of them. Years later, both still agreed that the six years they spent together at St. Anthony's had been the best years of their lives as priests.

Bishop-elect Whelan let Father Shirey know that there would be a place for him in the Fairbanks diocese, should he be interested. Father Shirey, however, wary of the cold in northern Alaska, and for other reasons, declined the kind offer, and chose instead to become the pastor of St. Andrew's parish in **Eagle River**. There it was back to house-trailer living, but Father Shirey did not mind. The move was made easier for him by the fact that, for several years, St. Andrew's had been a mission of St. Anthony's and had only recently been elevated to parish status.

Eagle River was, at the time, the fastest growing community in Alaska. On a given weekend, Father Shirey offered as many as six Masses, if one counts the Friday 5:30 P.M. Mass he offered for those wanting to leave town early for their favorite fishing spots.

To no one's surprise, Father Shirey, shortly after he got settled in at St. Andrew's, started the Legion of Mary there, "and as usual," he wrote, "it was a great help." He also did much to improve the Religious Education program at St. Andrew's. When classes were being held, he was always there "to cruise the halls and to pinch hit in case a teacher couldn't make it for some reason. It was a good system."

Again, just when everything was going exceedingly well for Father Shirey, it became time for him to move on. His Provincial Superior asked him to go to St. Ignatius Mission in Montana, to be Superior and co-pastor there. Being, in his own words, "an old fashioned Jesuit," open to the call of obedience, "with a very heavy heart," on June 21, 1972, he left Alaska. About a week later, he drove the '68 Plymouth, in which he had left the Alaska that he loved, under the protective roof of the carport at St. Ignatius Mission. In addition to finding spiritual consolation and satisfaction in successful pastoral ministry at St. Ignatius, Father Shirey found peace and satisfaction also in looking out of his office window toward the beautiful Mission Range and in fishing the teeming trout streams in the immediate vicinity.

On July 1, 1977, Father Shirey became pastor of St. Francis Xavier's parish in Missoula, Montana. During the year 1980–81, he was on sabbatical leave at Gonzaga University taking refresher courses in theology. That sabbatical was topped off with a lengthy pilgrimage to the Holy Land and a week's stay in Rome. His sabbatical over, he was assigned to the Jesuit Missions office in Portland, Oregon. By his own admission, he "would have been happy to spend many years in that assignment." However, "that was not in the deal." At the time, an additional Catholic chaplain was needed at the Veterans Administration Domiciliary at White City, near Medford, Oregon. In 1982, he began to serve as a part-time chaplain there, and, at the same time, as a chaplain at Providence Hospital and Medical Center in Medford. From the outset, he "felt very comfortable with the vets at the domiciliary," being a vet himself. This White City–Medford assignment was to stretch out for over two decades.

In April 2001, Father Shirey wrote: "What comes now, only God knows, and so far He hasn't said anything loudly enough for me to hear. But, convinced that I've been one of God's spoiled brats for almost 85 years, I think it would be pretty dumb to get ulcers worrying about my future." As of the year 2004, he was still on that dual assignment in southern Oregon.

15

SHRINE of St. Therese near Juneau

Nestled in the woods, on a tiny island washed by the rolling tides of Lynn Canal, stands the Shrine of St. Therese, "the Little Flower." It is an oasis of serenity and peace, inviting the pilgrim heart to pause, to find peace of mind and soul in prayerful solitude. This shrine, 23.5 miles north of **Juneau** and reached by the Glacier Highway, was the first major Catholic shrine built in **Alaska**. The shrine, a nearby retreat lodge, and some other buildings are located on a 64.5 acre tract owned by the Diocese of Juneau.

It was Father William G. **Levasseur**, S.J., who first dreamed of building a chapel and retreat lodge in the Juneau area. In 1931, he filed with the U.S. Forest Service for five acres of land at the shrine site. The first logs for the retreat lodge were cut and towed to the site in 1932. That same year, ground was broken and construction on the retreat lodge begun. This was completed in 1935. Originally, plans called also for a log chapel, and, in 1934 and '35, trees for such a chapel were felled in the Eagle River area, some distance from the shrine. Getting the logs to the shrine site, Crow Island, renamed "Shrine Island," however, proved to be a monumental undertaking. Several booms of logs were lost. In 1937, a 400-foot causeway connecting the island, on which the chapel was to be built, with the mainland was constructed. Owing to high tides and severe winter storms, this proved to be quite an engineering feat.

About this time, D. P. "Doc" Holden, a noted stonemason, came to Juneau. It was he who constructed the stone fireplace in the retreat lodge— and brought about a change of plans regarding the building materials to be used for the construction of the chapel. It is thanks to him that today a Nor-man-style chapel, measuring 63 × 28 feet, with a 10 × 10-foot Notre Dame tower 28 feet high—the whole built entirely out of cobble stones gathered from the local beach, embedded in concrete— stands on Shrine Island today. A life-size bronze statue of St. Therese, donated by the Nick Bez family of Seattle in memory of their daughter, stands near the chapel. Surrounding the chapel are the 14 Stations of the Cross, plus a 15th Station honoring the Resurrection of the Lord. When it was first built, the shrine included, in addition to the 32 × 24-foot retreat lodge, also a retreat master's cabin, a Sisters' residence, and a post office. From July 19, 1938 to 1945, there was a "St. Terese, Alaska" post office at the shrine. Father Levasseur was its first postmaster.

While it is clear from the records that it was Father Levasseur who first conceived the idea of there being a chapel and retreat lodge in the Juneau area, it is also clear from the records that, from the outset, his "inspiration and zeal" had the wholehearted support of Bishop Joseph R. **Crimont**, S.J., Vicar Apostolic of Alaska at the time. Given his sin-

Shrine of St. Therese, Juneau. *BH/JOPA-419.3.16.*

gular devotion to St. Therese, under whose patronage he had placed the whole Alaska Mission in 1919, six years before she was officially declared a saint, Bishop Crimont could hardly have been opposed to the construction of a shrine honoring her. On October 30, 1938, the 50th anniversary of his ordination to the priesthood, he laid and blessed the cornerstone of the chapel. The new chapel was dedicated on October 26, 1941, and on that occasion Bishop Crimont offered the first Mass in it. Less than four years later, on May 20, 1945, he died and was laid to rest in the crypt of the chapel. Fifty years later, on March 4, 1995, one of his successors, Bishop Michael H. **Kenny**, was laid to rest next to him. While Bishop Crimont was still alive, the shrine complex was already looked upon by some people as a "white elephant." Proper maintenance of the facilities proved to be quite expensive, and they became rundown. In 1953, Father Joseph F. **McElmeel**, S.J., pastor of Juneau at the time, wrote, "Bishop **O'Flanagan** is making great plans to rehabilitate the Shrine, which has been permitted to run down quite seriously."

The shrine was not allowed to go to ruin. Over the years, it continued to be maintained and upgraded to serve the spiritual needs of many. In 1999, a "new development master plan" was unveiled. This called for renovating the chapel and for modernizing various facilities, as well as for enlarging of the Retreat Center and building new cabins. By this time, the shrine's black granite columbarium, the first such Catholic facility in Southeastern Alaska, was already in use. By June 30, 2001, the newly laid out "Merciful Love Labyrinth," so named in honor of St. Therese, was ready to be blessed. A major Shrine Chapel renovation program was launched in the fall of 2004. Thomas P. Fitterer, Shrine Director as the third millennium began to unfold, deserves a major share of the credit for the renovations and improvements that brought the Shrine into major prominence again.

The Shrine's simple Mission Statement reads:

Located in an area of exceptional beauty and solitude, the Shrine will be a place of Spiritual refuge and retreat for the Diocese of Juneau, other religious groups, and, when possible, for others utilizing it with reverence and care.

Father John B. Sifton, S.J. *JOPA-889.01.*

SIFTON, Father John B., S.J.

One year after his arrival in northern **Alaska**, he wrote to his Father Provincial:

In what I say I am entirely objective. To be candid, Alaska has not taken very kindly to me, and I have become acquainted with more sickness than I suffered in all my previous life. I am bothered with numerous and painful boils, with sore throat, feverish condition and great weakness; it is sheer doggedness that makes me drag myself about to do the necessary routine work. Still, I hope to get used to it all, and what I say is not intended to prepare your Reverence for an approaching petition to be recalled, for I have no idea whatsoever of making such a petition. I offered myself for work in Alaska, and though I did so under a misapprehension, and though I am sorely disappointed and disgusted with the country and the work, I will leave it all to God, and meanwhile do the best I can.

Given such an inauspicious first year in Alaska and such a dismal frame of mind at the end of it, it is remarkable that he went on to spend another 27 years in the North, went on to deserve to belong to what Father Segundo **Llorente**, S.J., described as "the era of the giants." He went on to master the Central Yup'ik Eskimo language, to become so fluent in it that he was given the nickname "the man who speaks" by the Eskimos. He went on to serve as General Superior of the Alaska Mission for more years than anyone before or after him. He became a wholly positive thinker, a man known and esteemed for his wit and sense of humor, and for his ability to cheer people up. Not long after his death, a newly built mission boat was named for him.

John B. Sifton (originally, Sifferlen) was born at Kruth, Haut Rhin (Alsace-Lorraine), France, on November 19, 1871. After attending the French Apostolic School in Little Hampton, England, he entered the Jesuit novitiate at Prairie du Chien, Wisconsin, on September 7, 1889. After his two-year noviceship, he studied the classics and humanities at Sacred Heart Mission, DeSmet, Idaho, before going on to philosophical studies at St. Ignatius Mission, Montana. He next taught for several years at St. Paul's Mission, Hays, Montana. From the fall of 1899 to the summer of 1903, he studied theology at St. Louis University in St. Louis, Missouri. He was ordained a priest on June 28, 1902. He had become a U.S. citizen on December 24, 1901. After making his tertianship at St. Stanislaus, Florissant, Missouri, 1903–04, he spent eight years among the Shoshone and Arapahoe Indians in Wyoming. He had a special gift for learning languages and became fluent in the languages of those tribes.

Father Sifton arrived in Alaska on September 23, 1912, at **St. Michael**, where he was delayed for two months. That meant that he had to get to his first Alaskan assignment, **Nulato**, by dogteam. He referred to his getting there as "my baptism of ice." After spending three months at Nulato, he found himself at **Holy Cross Mission**, his originally intended assignment, for the rest of the year. It was from Holy Cross that he wrote the letter quoted above.

On September 6, 1913, Father Sifton became General Superior of the Alaska Mission. His letters to his successive Father Provincials reveal him to be a shrewd observer of men and situations. He was totally frank and straight forward. To his first Father Provincial he wrote, "The sooner we understand each other, the better." He was looking not for many men, but for men "gifted with a grain of horse sense." He was looking, too, for more American-born men. It rankled him that Northern Alaska was still being referred to by some whites there as "Little Italy."

As General Superior, Father Sifton made Holy Cross his headquarters for the years 1913–16. Thereafter, until the end of his term as General Superior, September 15, 1923, he resided at St. Michael. This continued to be his main station until 1928. As pastor of St. Michael, he was responsible also for its dependent missions: **Stebbins**, **Unalakleet**, **Hamilton**, and **Chaneliak**. In the winter, he visited those missions by dogteam; in the summer, he

The mission boat, the *Sifton*, named for Father John B. Sifton, S.J. *JOPA-889.02.*

generally hitched rides on the riverboats. His upbeat sense of humor, his good relations with the Native deckhands, and his willingness to lend a hand, whenever and wherever needed, made him a favorite of the captains and pilots.

St. Mary's Mission, **Akulurak**, was the next scene of Father Sifton's missionary labors. He was Superior of that mission from 1928–33. During the winter, he visited the villages of that region by dogteam. He spent the years 1933–37 at **Mountain Village**. From there, he visited **Pilot Station**, **Marshall**, and some smaller dependent missions. From July 26, 1933, to October 10, 1936, while attending to his villages, he again served also as General Superior. As such, he "spoke frankly" with his subjects. Though he described himself as "a roughneck," he, nevertheless, "dearly loved," according to Father Paul C. **O'Connor**, S.J., who knew him well, "to bolster up the drooping spirits of his fellow missionaries."

For the years 1937–39, Father Sifton was back at Akulurak. He spent the final year of his life at **Hooper Bay**. There, on October 20, 1940, wholly unexpectedly, according to Father Llorente, "he dropped dead of a heart attack, while he was making his 'evening examen' on his knees leaning on his badly made bed." He was buried at Hooper Bay "in a cemetery of his own," according to Father **John P. Fox**, S.J., at Hooper Bay at the time. For many years his name was kept alive by the newly built mission boat, the *Sifton*, launched in the summer of 1941.

Jesuits are given a crucifix, a "vow crucifix," when they pronounce their first vows. Louis L. **Renner**, was due to pronounce his on March 25, 1946. Because of World War II, metal crucifixes were hard to come by at that time. Father Fox, into whose hands Father Sifton's vow crucifix had come, was made aware of this. He sent it to the novitiate at Sheridan, Oregon, where, on "Brother" Renner's vow day, it was duly blessed and presented to him as now his vow crucifix. From August 1958 to June 10, 2002, it was back in Alaska. As of the year 2004, it was with him at Jesuit House, Gonzaga University, in Spokane, Washington.

SIPARY, Ivan and Maggie

On January 2, 1981, in Holy Family Cathedral, **Anchorage**, **Alaska**, Francis T. **Hurley**, Archbishop of Anchorage, offered a Mass of thanksgiving on behalf of Ivan and Maggie Sipary on the occasion of their 60th wedding anniversary. In his "beautifully simple" talk, he commented on this good Eskimo couple's faithful commitment to one another and their wonderful example to everyone. He thanked them for this and for the work that they had done for the Church along the Bering Sea coast of western Alaska. If the Central Yup'ik Eskimos have a married couple as "patron saints," that couple is Ivan and Maggie Sipary.

In the 1940s, Pope Pius XII sent Ivan and Maggie his Papal Blessings in recognition of the catechetical work they had done among their own people. Ever after that, Maggie's special prayer was that the Pope himself might one day come to Alaska. Every Sunday she lit a candle for that intention. On February 26, 1981, her prayer was answered, when Pope John Paul II came to Anchorage. A copy of the story of her life, taken from her own words, was given to the Holy Father.

Maggie was born at **Kotlik**, on November 23, 1902. Her father, a Kamkoff, was a Russian furtrader; her mother a Central Yup'ik Eskimo. Maggie was baptized in the Russian Orthodox Faith. She attended school in **St. Michael**, living there, from fall to spring, with her older sister. After completing the sixth grade, she had to remain in Kotlik to take care of her bedridden mother during the seven years before she died in 1917. Her father died the following year during the influenza epidemic.

Maggie, as a child, was so extremely bashful and shy, that she never visited anyone, never asked questions. For help, she turned to the Blessed Mother. When she was about 16, and was shopping one day in St. Michael, she looked out the front store window to see a man riding the only bicycle in St. Michael. She heard an inner voice tell her, "You will marry that man." Two years later, she met that man. It was Ivan Sipary.

Ivan was born of Eskimo parents in **Kotzebue**. When he was still very young, his family moved to St. Michael, where he met Father Anthony M. **Keyes**, S. J., and, at the age of eight, became a

Catholic. Following the example of Father Keyes, he became very devoted to the Rosary. For two years, he attended the **Holy Cross Mission** boarding school. Ivan was a very hard worker, always active. He had the first bicycle, the first motor boat, the best dog team in St. Michael.

Maggie's family attended the Russian Orthodox Church faithfully every Saturday and Sunday. Before she married Ivan, however, she joined the Roman Catholic Church. The two were married in the mission church in St. Michael on January 2, 1921. Recalling that day many years later, Maggie recounted how, even on her wedding day, she was so shy that she "didn't know where to look."

From the beginning of their married life, Ivan and Maggie always said the rosary together, and from the missionary in St. Michael at the time, Father John B. **Sifton**, S.J., they tried to learn all they could about the Catholic Faith. "The more we learned," said Maggie, "the more we wanted to know." Both having the faith and zeal of apostolic times, they made serious efforts to share the Faith with their own people, and, as catechists, to spread it among them.

In the summer of 1925, Ivan and Maggie were sent by Father Sifton to **Chaneliak**. That same year, Maggie was taught, in just one week, by an **Ursuline** Sister from the **Pilgrim Hot Springs** Mission to read music and to play the organ. By practicing every day after that on a portable organ loaned her by Father Sifton, she soon learned to play and sing hymns in English and Latin Gregorian chants. Painstakingly she copied down the music and translated many of the hymns into Central Yup'ik Eskimo.

In 1926, Ivan was asked by the Northern Commercial Company to work at **Tununak** on Nelson Island. With Maggie and their three children he moved there for two years. While at Tununak, he was offered a generous promotion by the company, but he turned it down, so that the family, upon the request of Father Martin J. **Lonneux**, S.J.— newly transferred from Tununak to St. Michael and its dependent stations, **Stebbins** and Chaneliak— could return to St. Michael and enable Maggie to serve as Father Lonneux's interpreter. She interpreted for him not only at Masses offered in St. Michael but also at its two dependent stations. This

Maggie Sipary and baby Theresa, at St. Michael, 1931. *BH/JOPA-549.3.50.*

meant much traveling for the family. She was also asked by Father Lonneux to help him write a children's catechism in Eskimo.

Given her limited education, Maggie found the producing of a catechism and the teaching of catechism especially difficult and challenging. Believing that "God asks through the mouth of a priest," she put her confidence in God and in Mary. Before beginning to speak, she prayed "Holy Mother Mary, let me use your tongue to speak right." She "didn't want ever to speak unwisely about such important matters."

Maggie also had a singular devotion to the Blessed Sacrament. It was taught her "from above." One day she heard a voice say to her: "Poor Jesus, always alone in the church. Nobody comes night or day. He waits for people to say hello to Him." After that she always tried to visit Jesus every time she was close to a church.

In 1931, Ivan sold their log home in St. Michael and moved the family to **Hooper Bay**, so that Maggie could be the catechist and interpreter for Father **John P. Fox**, S.J. While at Hooper Bay, Maggie served also as a proficient midwife. Several times she cut up her flannel nightgowns for the newborn. She also began making soap out of seal oil and lye. She wrote letters appealing for clothes for the needy.

In 1932, at the behest of Father Fox, who had complete confidence in them, Ivan and Maggie moved to Tununak to start teaching the Nelson Island people "on their own." They were to continue to build on the foundation laid by Ivan's stepfather, Simeon Sipary. Simeon, "the sterling catechist" who died on May 13, 1931, is given credit for the conversion of many of the Nelson Islanders. At Tununak, Ivan remodeled an old warehouse to use as a little chapel and meeting place. Maggie took along the little organ she had used in St. Michael. Before she went to Tununak, Maggie was told by a teacher's wife, "Don't visit the igloos, or you and your baby will get sick." Maggie answered that she wanted to explain things well, so she had to visit the homes. And this she did—always with her youngest, quiet, on her back. Maggie eventually gave birth to 14 children, nine of whom reached adulthood.

At first, many of the Nelson Islanders did not take too readily to Maggie's teaching, and even complained that she could read their faults, when she told them about sin and hell. When she tried to persuade the people to give up their good luck charms, some threatened to blame her if, after having given them up, they had bad luck. She assured them, "God will take care of all; do not worry." She gave them rosaries, medals, holy pictures, holy water only after they had given up their last charm. For eight years, Ivan and Maggie were on Nelson Island, spending at least one year in each of its several villages.

In an undated letter, written in the early 1940s, Father Paul C. **Deschout**, S.J., wrote from Tununak to Bishop Walter J. **Fitzgerald**, S.J.: "Ivan and Maggie have done so much for these people. After God, they are responsible for the fervor of these people. The good example of such catechists is more eloquent than all my talking."

From Tununak, the Siparys, now a family of ten, returned to Hooper Bay, then went on to serve as catechists at **Scammon Bay** for a short time. The Tununak people wept to see them go, having come to look upon them as their own. After a short stay in Scammon Bay, the Siparys moved to **Hamilton**. Around 1940, Father Paul C. **O'Connor**, S.J., asked them to come to St. Mary's Mission at **Akulurak**. They spent three years there.

After Akulurak, Maggie taught catechism in various villages along the lower Yukon River. In Takchak, a man told Maggie, "You should get pay for this work," and promptly gave her a dollar. Maggie kept it for many years, until the man's death, when she had a Mass offered for his soul.

For about ten years, the Sipary family lived in the new St. Marys on the **Andreafsky** River. There Maggie spent many of her free hours mending sheets and blankets for the mission boarding school, for which she refused to accept pay. All the Sipary children went on to successful careers. Several of the boys became carpenters, another became a highly skilled mechanic, another a professional chef. One of the girls became a schoolteacher, another became a registered nurse, two others of the girls became nurse's aides. In 1965, Ivan and Maggie moved to Anchorage to be nearer some of their family, who by then had settled there.

In Anchorage, Ivan and Maggie continued to be active in apostolic works such as visiting the sick in the hospitals and shut-ins in their homes and in care centers. They assisted Father Fox, also in Anchorage at this time, in his apostolic works. They made and distributed rosaries, along with medals, scapulars, holy cards, Catholic books, and pamphlets. Generously they shared whatever they had, even their little rented mobile home.

Ivan Sipary died on July 19, 1982. Maggie was with him earlier in the day on which he died. She said the rosary out loud, so that he could follow. By now they had prayed a daily rosary together for 62 years. After finishing the rosary, as she left him—not expecting him to die so soon—she said, "I leave you in the hands of Jesus and Mary. Try to think of them." He died peacefully that evening. His life and death reminded many of the life and death of St. Joseph.

On May 2, 1984, Maggie's prayer of the 1940s, that the Pope himself might one day come to Alaska, was answered a second time, when Pope John Paul II made a stop in **Fairbanks**. She was there on that occasion also, sitting among the elderly and infirm. When the Holy Father came to her, he picked up and blessed the well-worn rosary she had been holding. Her rosary, with walrus ivory beads, was a parting gift to her from the Nelson Islanders she had catechized some 50 years earlier.

In 1989, living in a small apartment in Anchorage, Maggie was still listening to interior voices, still praying the rosary, and more than ever enjoying visits from children, grand- and great grandchildren—as well as Native foods. Almost to the end of her life, she continued to be active in the Church, in prayer groups, and in apostolic works, especially those relating to the sick and dying.

Having spent her early years as a member of the Russian Orthodox Church, Maggie felt drawn, during the last decade of her life, to be a parishioner of St. Nicholas of Myra Byzantine Catholic Church in Anchorage. To her last days, she was a very active member of that parish.

On May 16, 1994, Maggie Kamkoff Sipary "fell asleep in the Lord, humbly and quietly." Three days later, in Holy Family Cathedral, the Mass of Christian Burial was offered for her by Archbishop Hurley. Michael J. **Kaniecki**, S.J., Bishop of Fairbanks, and numerous priests concelebrated. Eight of Maggie's children and their families were among the many filling the Cathedral to overflowing. On Sunday, May 22nd, the parish family of St. Nicholas held a special Divine Liturgy for her. Soon after the death of the one-time "simple, little Russian Eskimo girl," there was talk in Byzantine circles about "working on Maggie's cause" for the possibility of her being declared a saint. Maggie lies buried in the Catholic plot of Anchorage's Angelus Memorial Park Cemetery.

SITKA

The town known today as Sitka, **Alaska**, is located on the west coast of Baranof Island, 95 miles southwest of **Juneau**. A Russian settlement, known as New Archangel, was established there in 1804. Tlingit Indians lived in and around Sitka centuries before Russians or Americans ever set foot on the island's rocky shores. In 1808, New Archangel became the headquarters of the Russian American Company and the capital of Russian America, or Alaska. When Alaska was purchased by the United States in 1867, the town was named Sitka, based on the Tlingit Indian name for the site. The transfer of Alaska to the United States took place on Sitka's "Castle Hill" on October 18, 1867. In 1867, Sitka, then the most prosperous fur trading city in the world, had a population of 968; in 1910, 1,039; in 1950, 1,985; and in 1967, 3,237. In the year 2000, the city and borough numbered 8,835. The Sitka post office was established in 1867. Sitka was the capital of Alaska until 1900, when territorial administration was transferred to Juneau.

On December 23rd, the year of the purchase, 120 Sitkan Catholics—"only a few of the many Catholics in Sitka"—signed a petition addressed to Modeste **Demers**, Bishop of Vancouver Island, asking for a priest to minister to them. Sitka's Catholic history began a few months later, when Father Joseph M. **Mandart** was sent from Vancouver Island and remained in Sitka from February to July. In 1873, Charles J. **Seghers**, the newly consecrated Bishop of Vancouver Island, visited Sitka briefly. On May 9, 1879, Seghers, now Archbishop Seghers, accompanied by Father John J. **Althoff**, arrived in Sitka. On that day, he announced to the people of Sitka that the parish was formally established as of that date and placed under the patronage of St. Gregory Nazianzen, and that Father Althoff would henceforth visit them from his mission in **Wrangell**. On May 9, 1979, the parish celebrated the 100th Anniversary of its founding.

In the fall of 1885, Father William L. **Heynen**, another priest from Vancouver Island, went to Sitka. As a temporary church he secured a building known as the Burns Saloon, formerly used as a billiard hall and restaurant. From the Russian Orthodox Church, he also bought an old carriage barn. This he personally planked on the outside and decorated on the inside. He offered his first Mass in the renovated building on December 13th. Father Heynen was recalled from Sitka in 1889.

References to Catholicism in Sitka are scarce. Prior to 1922, services were conducted in the old "carriage barn church." In May 1922, Father Aloysius J. **Roccati**, S.J., was sent from Juneau to Sitka to tear down that church and build a new one. In August of that year, Father G. Edgar **Gallant** went to Sitka on a sick call. While there he blessed the new church under the title of "Star of the Sea." But the original title of St. Gregory of Nazianzen was subsequently restored. A rectory was added to the church in 1943. Thereafter, its sanctuary was enlarged and the seating capacity increased. Some time later, the rectory became an office and a new addition provided quarters for a resident priest. The silver jubilee of that 1922 church was celebrated on November 23, 1947, while Father Lawrence A. **Nevue**, S.J., was pastor. In 1950, the town of Pelican became a dependent mission of the Sitka parish.

Prior to the 1940s, priests from **Skagway** and Juneau visited Sitka at rather infrequent intervals. Just before World War II, in 1940, Father Timothy O. Ryan became the resident pastor. He was followed by Father Patrick J. **O'Reilly**, S.J, in Sitka from December 1941 to January 1947. It was Father O'Reilly who, with the aid of the Seabees, added a new wing and basement to the church and had stained-glass windows installed. After Father O'Reilly left, Father F. Merrill **Sulzman**, just out of military service, spent time in Sitka during the years 1946 and 1947. Father Robert L. **Whelan**, S.J., then came over from Juneau for the Easter of 1947 and stayed till early August.

In 1947, the Mount Edgecumbe government boarding school came into being on Sitka's Japonski Island. From its inception, it was of major concern to the priests serving the Sitka parish. At the girls' dormitory, a chapel for the use of Catholics was opened on the Feast of Christ the King in 1950. The Sisters of St. **Ann** conducted the tuberculosis sanatorium on Alice Island from February 1947 to the end of June 1947. From 1970–72, Father Thomas N. **Gallagher**, S.J., served as a salaried counselor at the Mount Edgecumbe school.

On August 4, 1947, Father Nevue began his five-year tenure in Sitka. This was his first pastoral assignment. He served in Sitka until August 14, 1952. He was responsible for the additions of two bedrooms, a kitchen, and a small living room. The old kitchen was torn out to enlarge the sanctuary. "Across the channel," he said in the homily he gave, when the parish celebrated the 100th Anniversary of its founding, "Lloyd Ripley helped me to convert a part of the basement of the girls' dorm into a chapel for us. The atmosphere for worship was better."

After Father Nevue, the following priests served the Sitka parish: Father John T. O'Brien, S.J., 1952–54; George A. Zelenak, S.J., 1954–56; Joseph F. **McElmeel**, S.J., 1957–60; and Father Michael B. Collins, S.J., 1960–61. To accommodate the growing congregation, Father Collins "converted" the wing to seat another 35. He was followed by Father Maurice F. Corrigan, S.J. During his nine-year stay in Sitka, he bought the property adjoining the parish property, built up a building-fund, and drew up a set of plans for the contemplated new church. However, the church, along with a parish hall and convent, was built by his successor, Father Ernest H. **Muellerleile**, in Sitka from March 20, 1970, to September 20, 1972. His successor, Father **James P. Ryan**, in Sitka from 1972–78, saw to the completion of the new parish complex in 1973. The new St. Gregory's Church was blessed and dedicated by Bishop Francis T. **Hurley** on September 3, 1973. The Bishop **Kenny** Center was completed in 1999. On February 15, 2004, the "old church," now renovated and renamed "Chapel of Our Lady of the Sea," was re-dedicated and blessed by Bishop Michael W. **Warfel**.

Msgr. James F. **Miller** was in Sitka from 1978–85; Father James D. **Cronin** from 1985–87; Father Jerome A. **Frister** from 1984–92; Father Bernard A. **Konda** from 1992–95; and Father Paul Wightman, O.M.I., from 1995–99. Father Peter F. **Gorges**, after serving as pastor of St. Gregory's parish from 1999 to the year 2000, retired in Sitka. Father Matthew Cumberland followed him as pastor of St. Gregory's. As of the year 2004, Father Jean-Paulin Engbanda Lockulu was pastor there.

In 1973, two Holy Family Sisters, Sisters Victor and Anne Marie, came to Sitka. One worked in the parish and set up a catechetical program; the other worked in the surrounding logging camps and towns that had no priest. Sister Margaret Butler, S.S.J., began serving at St. Gregory's parish as a Pastoral Associate in the early 1990s. As such, she was responsible for "religious education, liturgical environment, and women's ministry." The Sitka parish saw the services also of Permanent Deacons Charles Johnson, James Belcher, Otto Gnerich and Francis Mackin.

16

SKAGWAY

The town of Skagway lies on Lynn Canal's uppermost finger, Chilkoot Inlet, the mouth of the Skag-

way River, from which the town derives its name. The name Skagway is a Tlingit Indian word said to mean "home of the northwind." The town, called "The Gateway to the Golden Interior," was founded by Capt. William Moore, who had a cabin there, when gold was first discovered in 1896 near Dawson. The following year, Skagway boomed, became **Alaska**'s largest town as thousands stampeding to Canada's Klondike gold fields made it their base of operations. The Skagway post office was estab-

(*right*) St. Gregory of Nazianzen Church, Sitka. *Photo by Fr. Peter F. Gorges.*

(*below*) The second St. Gregory of Nazianzen Church, Sitka, built by Father Aloysius J. Roccati, S.J., in 1922. When the present St. Gregory's was built in 1973, this second one began to serve as a catechetical center. *JOPA-424.01.*

St. Therese of the Child Jesus Church, Skagway.
Photo by Photography by Otis/LRC.

lished in 1897. The town had a population of 3,117 in 1900. Ninety years later, according to the 1990 census, it had a population of 692, and in the year 2000, 862.

The Catholic Church was not long in establishing itself in Skagway. In March 1898, Father Joseph M. **Tréca**, S.J., offered the first Mass there. That same year, Father Peter C. **Bougis**, S.J., too, visited it, twice and for extended periods of time. On September 8th of that year, Father Philibert **Turnell**, S.J., began his seven-year tenure in Skagway. Fathers Bougis and Turnell first offered Masses in private homes. Then, for a time, the latter offered the Sunday Masses in the schoolhouse. But, before the year was out, he had bought, for $900.00, a store known as the Goldberg Building, a two-story frame structure at the east foot of Fifth Avenue. Part of this building was transformed into St. Mark's Church and was ready for the Christmas 1898 services.

Toward the end of 1898, Father Aloysius **Parodi**, S.J., joined Father Turnell in Skagway, where, according to Father Turnell, he "rendered valuable assistance," before he left in July 1899. During his seven years in Skagway, Father Turnell visited **Haines**, **Sitka**, **Valdez**, and **Seward**. For the years 1905–08, he was replaced in Skagway by Father Bougis. In 1908, Father Turnell returned to Skagway to spend another decade there.

Father Turnell's long years in Skagway came to an end in 1918, when Father G. Edgar **Gallant** replaced him and began his 41-year tenure there. Ever interested in education, Father Gallant, as soon as he was assigned to Skagway, began planning for a boarding school for Indian children of Southeastern Alaska. For such a school, he had the whole-hearted support of Joseph R. **Crimont**, S.J., Vicar Apostolic of Alaska at the time.

In 1930, Father Gallant, while accompanying Bishop Crimont on his official visit to Rome, met a group of American tourists looking for a fourth for a game of bridge. Father Gallant became that fourth. The game affected his whole future, for the bridge players became interested in hearing about his ministry and his dream for a boarding school in Skagway. After the game, a player, John F. O'Dea of Canton, Ohio, drew him aside and offered to donate $30,000 toward the building of the school, on the condition, however, that it be named after the late Pope Pius X.

The cornerstone for Pius X Mission was laid, by Émile M. Buñoz, Bishop of Prince Rupert, on August 30, 1931. By December, the first unit, called Crimont Hall, was ready for use. It was a brick, two-story building, 120 x 57', costing approximately $65,000. Within its walls were 33 rooms, accommodations for 60 children. In 1931, it was the most modern Native school in Alaska. With Sisters of St. **Ann** staffing it, and after opening ceremonies on September 26, 1932, classes began on October 18th, with an enrollment of 42 pupils in grades one to six. Gradually, the other grades were added.

Father Gallant, attracted to the art of weaving, installed looms at the mission on which both he and the children wove items to sell to tourists visiting the mission. Proceeds from the sale of these items contributed to the maintenance of the school. Music, too, flourished at Pius X Mission. In 1939, Father Gallant introduced woodwinds and a few violins. He himself taught some music courses. Soon the Skagway orchestra, directed by Father Gallant, was able to give its first concert. Pius X also had a band. For 20 years, 1939–59, Sister Aimée, S.S.A., played an important role in the mission's music program.

Carving lessons, taught by Samuel Jackson, an expert totem pole carver, were introduced in 1939.

Totem poles and other forms of wood carving were part of the cultural heritage of the children of Southeastern Alaska. In part, the mission school was also supported by its chicken and dairy farms. Working at these gave the older students practical training in farming.

Nor was the spiritual life of the children at Pius X neglected. Devotional exercises received priority: exposition of the Blessed Sacrament, rosary in the chapel, night prayers in common, and litanies. Religious feasts were festively celebrated. Baptisms and first Holy Communions were a commonplace, especially during the mission's earlier years.

On April 14, 1945, the Skagway Sanatorium opened a few miles out of town. Its purpose was to help the Native people, particularly the Aleuts, moved from their homes because of World War II, overcome the widespread tuberculosis that afflicted them. Sisters of St. Ann provided nursing services for it. In February 1947, the sanatorium was moved to **Sitka**.

Disaster struck Pius X Mission on November 16, 1945, when fire destroyed Crimont Hall. No lives were lost. For a short time, children and staff members were housed in various homes and in the empty sanatorium building. On December 14th, the children were moved from the sanatorium building to the Broadway barracks. Classes continued without major interruption, and, in May 1946, seven pupils from grade 8 graduated.

Meanwhile, the construction of a new mission complex was going ahead. On March 19, 1948, a Mass of Thanksgiving was offered in a temporary chapel in the partly restored building. The next day, classes resumed there. High School classes had opened on September 15, 1945, two months before the fire. By May 26, 1948, all were moved into new quarters. Father Gallant was still the main driving force behind the fund-raising for the construction of the new complex.

Around 1950, the mission chapel, dedicated to St. Therese of the Child Jesus, began to serve as the Skagway parish church. Henceforth, the Skagway parish was no longer known as that of St. Mark's, but as that of St. Therese. The old St. Mark's Church was demolished while Father Raymond W. **Mosey** was pastor in Skagway from 1949–52. A

new St. Therese's Church was built in 1975 by the Christian Brothers while Father James D. **Cronin** was pastor of Skagway from 1974–77. It was dedicated on October 3rd by Francis T. **Hurley**, Bishop of **Juneau**.

In the summer of 1959, Father Gallant's long years in Skagway came to an end, when he was named pastor of Holy Family parish in **Anchorage**. During his Skagway years, he had been assisted at various times by other priests, among them: Fathers Mosey; Harley A. **Baker**, from 1941–49; F. Merrill **Sulzman**, during the year 1952–53; and Francis A. **Cowgill**, in Skagway from 1952–59. He served at Pius X Mission as "principal, teacher, good friend of the sisters, and supporter of their work."

After Father Gallant (Msgr. Gallant, as of 1958) left Skagway in 1959, the following priests served Skagway's St. Therese's parish: Francis W. Nugent, 1959–61; James F. **Miller**, 1961–66; Georges E. Bourque, O.P., 1966–67; David A. **Melbourne**, 1967–74; Cronin, 1974–77; **James P. Ryan**, 1977–81; Dennis P. O'Neil, 1981–84; Patrick Hurley, O.S.B., 1984–85; Michael McKeon, O.P., 1985–86; Javier Guttierez, 1986–88; Earl Barcome, 1988–89; Jerome A. **Frister**, 1992–96; Michael Nash, 1996–97; Michael G. Schwarte, 1997–99; Edward Boucher, 1999–2000; and James Blaney, O.M.I., 2000 to July 2004. He was followed by Father Edmund J. Penisten.

Sister Kathy **Radich**, O.S.F., was Parish Administrator from 1989–92, and Sister Judith Gomila, M.S.C., from 1992–98. After them, Sister Jelaine (Jill) Jaeb, O.S.U., began serving the Skagway parish in that capacity.

In December 1959, the mission school in Skagway, now called Pius X School, after limping along for a few months, closed. Differing views on the part of Father Gallant, Dermot **O'Flanagan**, Bishop of **Juneau** at the time, and the Sisters of St. Ann as to what the nature of the school should be were in large part the causes for its closure. By this time, too, Native children from Alaska's interior had **Copper Valley School** as a choice, and Alaska's Southeast villages were getting new public schools of their own. Moreover, Pius X School was beginning to rely too heavily on support from the Bureau of Indian Affairs and the Department of Welfare. It

St. Mark's Church and rectory, Skagway, in about 1950. *Noel Kirshenbaum, Klondike Gold Rush National Historical Park files/LRC.*

was no longer the Catholic School originally intended. According to Father Cowgill, "The Mission had by then served its purpose in time."

The reconstructed Pius X Mission was allowed to fall into a state of disrepair by the Church. In the fall of 1984, the Church made it available to the Skagway volunteer fire department for a training exercise. It was also opened up to the people of Skagway who might want to salvage materials. On March 4, 1985, a several weeks before the building was scheduled to be burned, it "mysteriously" caught fire on a quiet, snowy night and fell victim to the flames.

16

SNEAD, Msgr. James P.

James Prince Snead, born of non-Catholic parents in Atlanta, Georgia, on May 3, 1907, was baptized a Catholic in 1927. He was ordained a priest

for the Vicariate of **Alaska** in Portland, Oregon, on June 3, 1939.

Father Snead arrived in **Anchorage** in late August 1939, with **Palmer** as his first parish assignment. However, during his first five years in Alaska, from 1939–44, he did not live in Palmer. He commuted to there out of Anchorage, where he lived at **Providence** Hospital and served as chaplain. As such, he befriended Walter J. Hickel, an energetic young man with an entrepreneurial spirit, who later became Governor of Alaska, and then U.S. Secretary of the Interior. Father Snead fed Hickel and helped him find a job. Hickel never forgot; and, as he prospered, he became a staunch supporter of Providence Hospital. Along with his ministries as hospital chaplain and as pastor of Palmer, Father Snead also helped out at Anchorage's Fort Richardson Army Base.

In 1944, Father Snead took up residency in Palmer. Next to Father F. Merrill **Sulzman**, founder of St. Michael's parish in Palmer, Father Snead is remembered as *the* priest of Palmer, the parish he served for 27 years.

Statistics left by Father Snead in a small notebook that he carried with him on his commuting trips to and from Palmer show the slow build-up of the parish and some discouraging numbers—and temperatures. The winter of 1946–47 was the coldest in the history of the Matanuska Valley, with temperatures as low as minus 51 degrees. Cold weather, high winds, and icy roads were but some of the hardships of winter in the valley.

September 8, 1952, was "a red-letter day," to use Father Snead's expression. On that day work began on the church basement. The laying of cement blocks signaled a season of hope for better days for the parish. However, completion of the project and payment for it was delayed for more than a year. In the meantime, Father Snead went to Portland, Oregon, for medical treatment. Father Raymond W. **Mosey**, who, in 1953, replaced him at Palmer during his absence for a few months, found him to be

Msgr. James P. Snead. *LRC.*

a notoriously poor housekeeper. Father Snead liked and kept pet animals, among them "Susie," a climbing monkey that left trails throughout the rectory of her comings and goings. Along with being fond of pet animals, Father Snead also engaged in amateur painting and had a great interest in music. Many people came to hear and appreciate his extensive record collection.

Father Snead was not a healthy man. Among other ailments, he suffered from diabetes. In addition to his absences from Palmer for health reasons during 1953, he was away again for two months in 1956, hospitalized after a difficult operation. Even though he struggled for another ten years to serve as pastor of Palmer, poor health forced him to reside in Providence Hospital from 1956–66, during which time he again acted as chaplain. When the new Providence Hospital opened in the fall of 1962, he took up residency there. On Sundays, he drove to Palmer to hear confessions and to offer the two parish Masses.

In an effort to minimize heat loss at the Palmer church and rectory, Father Snead had the parish plant stuccoed in 1960. Whatever the effects of the stuccoing were, St. Michael's Church lost its log cabin appearance, which had so charmed parishioners and visitors alike. While the stuccoing was in progress, he took a trip around the world.

In 1966, Father Snead—"deservedly the best known and loved by the people of the valley of all the priests who ministered there," according to historian Sister Margaret Cantwell, S.S.A.—left the Palmer pastorate to become the first pastor of the new St. Benedict's parish in Anchorage. In 1967, he was raised to the rank of Domestic Prelate and had conferred upon him the title of Monsignor.

St. Benedict's was Msgr. Snead's last assignment as an active parish priest. In 1969, he submitted his letter of resignation to **Joseph T. Ryan**, Archbishop of Anchorage at the time. His decision to relinquish active parochial ministry was prompted primarily by his failing health. With regret, Archbishop Ryan accepted the resignation. Graciously he invited Msgr. Snead to stay on at St. Benedict's as "pastor emeritus" with a regular salary.

In early 1970, Msgr. Snead, after having been hospitalized in Anchorage for four weeks—and after having confided his pet dog, Pierre, to a friend in the dog-grooming business—left Alaska, for Portland, Oregon. At the invitation of Archbishop Ryan, however, he visited Anchorage in the summers of 1972, '73, and '74. Eye cataracts and recurring stages of illness continued to undermine his health, so much so that much of the joint celebration planned for Msgr. Snead and Archbishop Ryan on the occasion of their 35th anniversary of ordination to the priesthood was cancelled.

Msgr. James P. Snead died, in Providence Hospital, Portland, Oregon, on November 13, 1974.

15

SNOWS, Sisters of Our Lady of the

In 1931, Father **John P. Fox**, S.J., found himself stationed at **Hooper Bay**. In addition to being responsible for this Central Yup'ik Eskimo village, he was responsible also for the villages of **Scammon Bay**, **Keyaluvik**, **Tununak**, **Nightmute**, and Old **Chevak**, as well as for the numerous smaller villages scattered throughout a district he described as "300 miles long and 50 miles wide." It was immediately obvious to him that he could not single-handedly be an adequate missionary to so large a district and the many people living in it. He was accustomed to having Native catechists help him; but these, while they rendered most laudable serv-

Bishop Joseph R. Crimont, S[...] and Father John P. Fox, S.J., pose with the Sisters of Our Lady of the Snows in Hoope[r] Bay: Marie Hunter, Annie Sipary, Stella Jimmy, Celest[e] Gump, Ida Hunter, Lizzie Kameroff, and Bernadette A[...] ka. The Sisters were disband[ed] in 1945. *JOPA-267-399.*

ice, had some drawbacks. Often being wives and mothers of families, they could not easily be shifted from one village to another as needs arose. They were also expensive to maintain. Given his sense of justice, he felt that they should be adequately provided for as regards housing and food, and that they should receive some recompense for the important services they rendered. He saw a solution to these two major concerns of his in having as collaborators in his ministry a Congregation of Native Sisters. His plan was to train these Sisters himself, and then put them in pairs in each village to teach catechism and some elementary school courses. In a decree dated September 12, 1933, his plan was formally authorized and blessed by Bishop Joseph R. **Crimont**, S.J., Vicar Apostolic of **Alaska** at the time. Once the plan was implemented, Father Fox was commended on it by the Jesuit Father General in Rome. The idea soon caught on among the Native people.

In 1932, on August 5th, Feast of Our Lady of the Snows, the Congregation of the Sisters of Our Lady of the Snows was officially founded at Hooper Bay. The charter members of the community

were, not surprisingly, two of Father Fox's catechists at the time: Annie Sipary and Clotilda Leo. Other candidates, schooled at St. Mary's Mission, **Akulurak**, and at **Holy Cross Mission**, soon joined the two. The rules of the Congregation were of the kind common to Religious communities dedicated to an active ministry. Some of the rules and practices were taken from the spirit of Jesuit rules and practices and adapted to the circumstances of time and place. Candidates had a two-year noviceship under the spiritual direction and guidance of Father Fox. Daily there were spiritual talks and spiritual reading, and there were annual week-long retreats in total silence. After completing the two-year noviceship satisfactorily, candidates took their vows, but for only one year. Any Sister, then, who did not feel herself called to renewing her vows became automatically free to go on in life as she pleased.

Father Fox soon had the Congregation off to a solid start, and the Sisters were well received in the villages they served. But, a number of his fellow Jesuit missionaries in that general district had misgivings about the whole venture. Some felt he could spend his time as a missionary more profitably. They felt that, given the prevalence of tuberculosis at the time and the early deaths so often resulting from it, he was "building on sand," that he was wasting his time in preparing young women to be Sisters who might soon be dead. His answer to this objection: "Even if the Sisters die early in life, what of it? If the few years they lived, they lived working for their own sanctification and that of their fellow Alaskans, wasn't it worthwhile?" Others thought the whole venture too expensive. And some wondered whether young Native women could be faithful to their vow of chastity, while living and working in a culture which, up to that time, knew only married life as the norm for all. Some of the Sisters did die young, and some left the Congregation on their own accord, and some were advised to leave, to get married and serve as married catechists. The summary records of the Congregation show that, in the end, "the majority of the Sisters were good and loyal. There was not one single scandal."

Those who thought the whole venture too expensive did not know that Father Fox, through his correspondence and newsletters to family, friends and benefactors, was, in reality, able to take care of all his financial needs. He pointed out that the Sisters were also, to some extent, self-supporting, inasmuch as "they hunted rabbits and ptarmigan for the pot and gathered willows for the stove." They helped support themselves, too, by gardening, fishing, gathering eggs and greens in season, and, in general, leading the traditional subsistence way of life.

As the Congregation grew, more space was needed. By 1938, Father Fox was able to provide a two-story convent with a full basement for the Sisters. He tried to visit the Sisters in their outlying villages whenever possible; but, given his many responsibilities, he was able to do this only at relatively infrequent intervals. Accordingly, it was his policy not to leave Sisters—although they were generally in pairs, or, if a Sister was alone, she had a lay woman companion—too long alone in a given village. He had them return to Hooper Bay for community life, Mass and the Sacraments, daily spiritual exercises and priestly instructions. This policy, too, accounted, in part, for the need of more space at Hooper Bay for the Sisters.

As the years went by, it began to seem more and more odd to some that a priest continued to be in charge of the Sisters. It was arranged, therefore, that **Ursuline** Sisters, Mother Mary of the Blessed Sacrament and Mother Scholastica **Lohagen**, should come from Akulurak to Hooper Bay to serve as trainers and spiritual leaders of the Native Sisters. The two were at Hooper Bay from October 1942 to August 1945.

While Father Fox "felt that everything was taking on rosy colors," some of his fellow Jesuits in that part of Alaska continued to have reservations about "this whole Sisters business"—and they were giving voice to their reservations. They were, he recalled, "talking without having seen for themselves. It was all hearsay. I was shouting at the top of my lungs to have them come and see, but nobody would come."

On February 24, 1939, Walter J. **Fitzgerald**, S.J., was consecrated coadjutor to Bishop Crimont. Shortly thereafter, he made the rounds of the missions in northern Alaska. On June 12, 1942, he wrote to Father Fox, "The work of the Native Sisters in instructing the little ones in their prayers and catechism is excellent." Bishop Crimont died on May 20, 1945, "and with him," according to Father Fox, "we lost our best friend." Bishop Fitzgerald was now the man in charge. By 1945, he, seemingly, had forgotten what he had observed three years earlier at Hooper Bay. After having listened for some years to what Jesuits serving in the Yukon-Kuskokwim Delta were saying about the Native Sisterhood, he came to the conclusion that it was "premature," that it was "a liability, rather than an asset." Almost immediately after replacing Bishop Crimont as Vicar Apostolic of Alaska, he "suspended"—in reality, suppressed—the Congregation of the Sisters of Our Lady of the Snows, and dispensed the Sisters from their vows.

August 1945 was a black month for the Native Sisters and Father Fox. On the fourth, he wrote in the Hooper Bay house diary: "Mail arrives. With it an order from Bishop Fitzgerald dispersing (the document says 'suspending') the Native Sisters. The natives, as well as the whites, deeply regret the Bishop's decree killing the community. Fiat!"

The following day, Father Fox read the decree of

suppression to the assembled Sisters. The wording of the decree is rather informal, oblique, and comes at the beginning of what, to all appearances, is a routine letter. The letter, dated **Juneau**, Alaska, August 5, 1945, begins with a greeting and two key sentences:

> Dear Father Fox, Today, the feast day of Our Lady ad Nives [of the Snows], you and the former Sisters of the Snow have been in my prayers that you may sustain the blow of dissolution of the pious association to which you have been so devoted. I trust that it was the guidance of the Holy Spirit that directed the action, and I add my sincere wishes that you and all will take it as coming from the Will of God.

On August 7th, from Hooper Bay, Father Fox wrote to Bishop Fitzgerald: "My dear Bishop: I wish you could have read your document to them yourself. As it was up to me, I read it to seven weeping women. You have no idea of the consternation it caused, even though we all expected this ever since your visit last winter." Then, as if to exonerate to some degree the bishop for the action he had taken, he adds, "However, as in most of this affair, you have been following the lights of others." The "others" were, of course, their fellow Jesuit Alaskan missionaries.

The ex-Sisters, lay women now, returned to secular life. The two Ursuline Sisters returned to Akulurak.

"To me personally," said Father Fox in his later years, "it [the suppression] was a big blow." Even in his old age, he considered Bishop Fitzgerald's decision to have been a wrong one. But, being the obedient man that he was, he had reconciled himself to it as God's will, and, at the time of the suppression, wrote and said little about it, for "the subject was dynamite." Jesuit historian Father Wilfred P. Schoenberg, S.J., wrote, "When these Sisters were gone, there was a kind of emptiness in the Alaskan Church, and no one felt it more keenly than Father John Fox."

During the 13 years the Congregation of the Sisters of Our Lady of the Snows was in existence, a total of 22 candidates were admitted to it. Of these, five died a holy death as Sisters. Eight left of their own accord. Two of these had pronounced temporary vows and had served the missions well for about six years. The other six left as novices. One

had been sent away by Bishop Fitzgerald to take care of her mother. One was advised to go to help her family. One was told to leave. Six were still members of the community, when the Congregation was suppressed. According to Father Fox, "No one ever left the community with hard feelings!"

For the historical record it should be mentioned that, beginning in 1952, at the new St. Mary's Mission on the **Andreafsky** River, another attempt was made at establishing an Alaskan Native Sisterhood. Of this group—named "Oblates of St. Ursula," and often referred to simply as "the Little Sisters"—Father Fox said, "This time I had nothing to do with it except give encouragement." This group did not need to be suppressed. After about ten years, it had gradually disbanded of its own.

A chronological sequence of discontinuous entries made by various hands from September 22, 1932, to April 3, 1945, in the diary kept by the Sisters of Our Lady of the Snows at Hooper Bay weaves the following rich and colorful tapestry:

~

Father Fox arrived from Holy Cross with five postulants . . . Ivan **Sipary** leaves for Tununak. Before going he payed [*sic*] a last visit to our Divine Lord, which was very edifying . . . Feast of the Little Flower and feast of Hooper Bay. Seven girls sang the "Mass of the Holy Angels" . . . Ugly weather . . . We go into retreat tonight. Good-bye for eight days! . . . Clotilda moves downstairs, sick . . . Very stormy and cold. Father's door drifted shut again, so a trapdoor is arranged in the attic so as to get out in the morning . . . Night thief gets into the shed and steals a few fish . . . The people are terribly hungry, and the mission has little to help with . . . People catching more seal and tom cods . . . This morning Clotilda had a spell and we thought she was dying. All the novices were present when she made her vows . . . Clotilda died this morning. After saying the last words of Our Lord on the cross, she died. Her death was a beautiful one . . . Novices go egg hunting, got a little more than a barrel full . . . first lettuce put on table . . . Girls bring up moss to our dormitory to fill the wall on the north side . . . Some villagers caught a walrus nearby . . . Bad trail and dogs absolutely lifeless. Never saw them so skinny . . . Seal fairly plentiful, but very little ammunition can be had anywhere . . . Last night the men shot 46 white whales just in front of the mission on the mud flats . . . Plane arrives with Bishop Crimont. People jubilant. Everybody on beach, all trying to kiss his ring . . . 5 children got into our garden during the night and pulled out a lot of potato plants, cabbages and radishes . . . Berries abundant this year . . . Very high tide and refuge mice everywhere; village practically an island . . . Sr. Sup. goes out for wood with dog team . . . Sisters pretty well frozen in: basins, wash water, holy water all frozen solid. No fire in house all night to save coal . . . Slight earthquake shakes statue of Sacred Heart off altar and breaks . . . Terrible blizzard yesterday . . . Lots of clams from the mud flats . . . Sisters Annie and Martina went for basket grass . . . Sister Martina played on the organ at Benediction for the first time. It was fine . . . Very stormy. At the people's request the bells were rung for travelers who were out. All returned safely . . . Sister Superior shot the first goose and ptarmigans . . . Spent the morning carrying water from the lake . . . Cutting fish all day . . . Sister Celestine went for ice with the team . . . Baking altar bread . . . The two candidates, Maria and Agatha, receive their habits, veils, etc. It was a holiday for the Sisters . . . Rev. Superior gave chocolates to the Sisters . . . Two Sisters went to see the dying old man and said the rosary . . . Sister Mary John died. All the Sisters were present . . . Innuit dance at 7:30. All of us went to see it . . . Two Sisters went out hunting and brought home four emperor geese and one ptarmigan . . . Lessons in Innuit 3:30–4:30 . . . Five Sisters cut up whale meat for dog feed. The skin was given back to the hunter. Father Fox helped us . . . Played "Johnny Got a Zero" on phonograph . . . Took 17 silver salmon and 63 humpbacks . . . Reading of the Passion in Innuit . . . Resumed catechism classes for the children.

Our Lady of Perpetual Help Church, Soldotna. *Photo by Fr. Richard D. Tero.*

SOLDOTNA

Soldotna, located eight miles southeast of **Kenai** on the upper Kenai Peninsula, is one of the youngest towns on the peninsula. It came into being, when the area was opened to homesteading in 1947. In 1967, its population numbered only 32; in the year 2000, 3,759. The Soldotna post office was established in 1949.

During the 1950s, Father Arnold L. **Custer**, S.J., stationed in **Seward** at the time, began to make monthly visits to Soldotna. The name Soldotna, however, does not appear in the *Official Catholic Directory* prior to the 1962 volume, and then as a mission of Sacred Heart parish in **Seward**, staffed, as of the previous year, by Redemptorist Fathers from the Oakland Province. The first three Redemp-

torists stationed in **Alaska**, all headquartered in Seward to begin with, were Fathers Edward C. **O'Neill**, pastor of the Seward parish, James Van Hoomissen, and Robert L. Woodruff.

The first Mass offered in Soldotna by a Redemptorist was celebrated at the Community Center in June 1961 by Father Van Hoomissen, living in a trailer at the time. His first objective was to put up a building that would house a church, rectory, and rooms for parish meetings and catechism classes. In **Anchorage**, he found a big steel building, a Pascoe Building, that had been intended for a brewery. This he was able to obtain for $22,500, provided he would move it. He arranged for its being moved to Soldotna, to a site at the junction of the **Homer** and Kenai roads. The frame of the building was up by Christmas, but the sub-zero weather made this "church" too cold for use for Christmas Mass. Worse, however, was yet to come. In February 1962, the building, under a heavy load of snow saturated by a sudden thaw and a torrential rain, collapsed. Fortunately, no one was in the building just then. From the Pascoe Company, Father Van Hoomissen received a new building. This was transformed into the parish church.

While the church was being constructed, Father

The first Our Lady of Perpetual Help Church, Soldotna. *Courtesy of Redemptorists Denver Province.*

Father Van Hoomissen. Redemptorist Fathers Very Rev. Daniel J. Buckley and Ronald Holdorf resided in Soldotna from 1966–68. Father Buckley was alone there the following year. From 1969–72, Redemptorist Father Daniel D. Debolt was in Soldotna. On October 9, 1970, he saw Our Mother of Perpetual Help achieve parish status. Redemptorist Father O'Neill was pastor from 1972–77. In 1975, he was gratified to see the parish center in Soldotna near its final stages of construction. Father Debolt was pastor again from 1977–80. He was followed by fellow Redemptorist Fathers Richard G. **Strass**, pastor from 1980–88; and Thaddeus Dean, pastor from 1988–91. Father Franklin Wrigley of the Diocese of Oklahoma City filled in for the year 1991–92. From 1992 to the year 2002, Father Richard D. **Tero**, of the Archdiocese of Anchorage, was pastor. It was he who replaced the original church with a new one, dedicated in 1995. As of the year 2004, Father Frank Reitter, S.M., was serving the Soldotna parish.

Redemptorist Fathers Thaddeus Dean and Robert J. Wells are buried in Soldotna, next to the rectory.

15

Van Hoomissen was busy constructing a Redemptorist monastery close to it. Once the concrete floor was put in the basement of the monastery, Masses were offered there for the time being. In August 1962, Father Thaddeus Dean, a fellow Redemptorist, arrived. He helped with the construction of both the church and the monastery. A long "cloister" walk connected the church with the monastery–rectory. On December 25, 1962, the people of Soldotna had the joy of attending Christmas Mass for the first time in their church, dedicated in May 1963. After the monastery was completed, it became a gathering place for the Redemptorist Fathers stationed at various places on the Kenai Peninsula for weekly meetings and community sharing, business, prayer, study, relaxation. Both the monastery and the church were dedicated to Our Mother of Perpetual Help. In 1986, the name was modified to Our Lady of Perpetual Help.

Up until 1966, the Soldotna flock was tended by

SPILS, Father James C., S.J.

The massive hands, with thick, powerful fingers, told much of his story, but not all of it. They were the hands of a builder, but of a builder who was first and foremost a priest of God. They drove many nails, put up many buildings, but they also held and raised up the Body and Blood of Christ, many, many times. Calloused, but consecrated, they were the hands of a priest–builder. Their owner once expressed to God his puzzlement over the seeming paradox of his hands: "Dear Father, these hands you consecrated—but all they do is pound nails. If that's what you want, O.K!"

James C. "Jake" Spils was born in Colton, Washington, on May 23, 1901, the seventh of nine children. His father, Albert, was a farmer. His mother was Mary Hanf. Her father had been killed at Gettysburg. As a boy, Jake was a carefree, outdoors per-

son, addicted to hunting. He attended Holy
Guardian Angels grade school in Colton,
St. Martin's high school in Lacey, Washington, and, from 1920–23, Gonzaga University in Spokane, Washington.

On July 17, 1923, Jake entered the Jesuit
novitiate at Los Gatos, California. After
completing the two-year noviceship and
two years of classical and humanities studies there, he studied philosophy at Mount
St. Michael's, in Spokane, from 1927–30.
He then taught the sciences for three years:
two at Gonzaga and one at Marquette High
School in Yakima, Washington. In 1933, he
was back at Mount St. Michael's for his
theological studies. However, after one
year, he was transferred to the newly
opened Alma College, near Los Gatos. He
was ordained a priest on June 19, 1936. After another year of theology at Alma College, and the year
of tertianship at Port Townsend, Washington,
1937–38, he was sent to **Alaska**. He would have
preferred to teach, but was willing to go where sent.

For his first Alaskan assignment Father Spils had
Holy Cross Mission. Here he found ample opportunity to exercise his practical skills as a building
maintenance man and his skills as a hunter. From
Pius Savage he soon learned how to call geese to
within shooting range. His farm-boy background
had prepared him well to oversee the farming and
gardening at the mission. Under his supervision, the
gardens flourished to such an extent that Holy
Cross, after supplying its own needs and those of
downriver missions, was able to sell a surplus yield
to U.S. Army units based at **Galena**. Profits realized from such sales helped considerably to improve
conditions at the mission, especially during the war
years when, more than ever, it was left to its own
resources. On August 24, 1941, he became Superior of Holy Cross. As such, he made a special effort
to improve the diet of the children, and living conditions in general. With a degree of self-satisfac-
tion and a smile, he told Father Louis L. **Renner**,
S.J., how he raised the daily breakfast ration of one
prune per child to two, and how he built an indoor
toilet for the Sisters of St. **Ann**—"the first flushy
toilet on the Yukon," as he proudly described it.

Father James C. Spils, S.J., chief architect and builder,
in front of St. Mary's Mission constructed during the
years 1949–51. *JOPA-848.03.*

Father Spils spent the years 1947–54, when not
involved with construction work, caring for the missions of Galena, **Kaltag**, **Koyukuk**, **Ruby**, and
Tanana. He made Galena his headquarters. During the year 1948–49, he built a church at Ruby.

In June 1950, Father Spils, with a select crew,
began construction of the new St. Mary's Mission
Boarding School on the **Andreafsky** River. During
the building seasons, work on St. Mary's continued
through the next several years. By July 1951, the
main building was ready for occupancy. However,
much still needed to be done at the mission complex.
On June 9, 1953, Father Paul C. **O'Connor**, S.J.,
Superior of St Mary's at the time, wrote to Father
James U. **Conwell**, S.J., then Chancellor of the Vicariate of Alaska, "My admiration for Fr. Spils is
growing steadily. It is amazing how much the man
knows about constructions and machinery. He is simply a fund of information." It should be remembered
that Father Spils had no formal training whatever as
an architect or construction engineer. He read manuals and learned from hands-on experience.

On January 14, 1952, Father Spils, who had by

then served on the lower and middle Yukon for somewhat over a decade, but was never stationed at Kaltag or **Nulato**, arrived at this latter village to spend a few days with Father John B. **Baud**, S.J. Father Baud was hopeful that his fellow Jesuit would help him dissuade the people from holding the planned traditional Koyukon Athabaskan "stick-dance," or "Feast for the Dead." "Alas," wrote Father Baud, "instead of help, he was the cause that the stick dance really took place by giving encouragement to the people." The dance began the day after Father Spils arrived. Father Spils, who had only a rudimentary understanding of the dance, had a deep, sympathetic understanding of the Koyukon heart. "We are killing the spirit of our natives," he argued, "by trying to abolish their old customs and make white people out of these natives." Father Spils was a man ahead of his times.

By around 1950, the old Holy Cross mission buildings were in such poor condition that they needed either to be replaced or abandoned. Again, Father Spils, "God's builder"—though the St. Mary's project was scarcely completed—was called upon to build elsewhere, from the ground up, yet another whole new boarding school complex. This, known as **Copper Valley School**, opened its doors to its first students in October 1956. Construction did, however, continue on for several more years. People spoke of "the miracle of Copper Valley." What was said of CVS might, with equal validity, have been said of St. Mary's. Bringing into being two such large mission boarding school complexes, in remote Alaskan wilderness settings, with very limited resources, and with almost entirely volunteer crews, did border on the miraculous.

When the Diocese of **Fairbanks** was established in 1962, the need for a cathedral took on special urgency. The diocese needed a cathedral, and the Fairbanks area Catholic community badly needed another church. Its one church, Immaculate Conception Church, had long since become too small for the Catholic population of Fairbanks. Who would build the cathedral? To no one's surprise, it was Father Spils. As in the case of Copper Valley School, so here, too, concrete blocks were made on the site, and, with volunteer help, cemented one on top of the other to provide sturdy walls to support

a wooden roof. The new Sacred Heart of Jesus Cathedral, the largest church in Fairbanks, was ready for services on Palm Sunday 1966. With the completion of the cathedral, Father Spils' career as a builder of major buildings came to an end. It was fitting that a diocesan cathedral should crown his career as a builder for God.

A diocese needs a cathedral, but it also needs some kind of chancery building. Father Spils was approached about building this also, but, reluctantly, he had to decline. At age 66, he was not yet an old man, but advanced arthritis complicated by arteriosclerosis dictated an end to his construction days. He spent the year 1966–67 in Fairbanks, and the following year at Copper Valley School.

The buildings that Father Spils constructed were made in his own image and likeness: large, broad, rough-hewn, sturdy and tough. According to Father Francis J. **Fallert**, S.J., Superior and principal at CVS for some years, "His buildings were like the man himself, solid as a fort." They were built ultimately for God, and they were meant to last. And last they did—with the exception of CVS. This closed its doors in 1971. In 1976, it burned to the ground. Arson was suspected. After the fire, Father Spils said to a disconsolate Sister M. George **Edmond**, S.S.A.—who had put heart and soul into the school as its pioneer Superior and grade school principal for years—"George, God decides the duration of a work. Copper Valley School is finished. We will not talk about it any more." Building for God, as he did, he, too, put heart and soul into what he built, but always with a certain degree of detachment and resignation to God's will in the matter.

For the year 1968–69, Father Spils held the position of Father Minister of the Oregon Province tertianship, relocated from Port Townsend to Seattle. He then returned to Copper Valley School. He was in **Talkeetna**, Alaska, to offer the 1970 Midnight Christmas Mass and to remain through January 1971. During the midnight hours of Sunday, January 24th, he would have lost his life in a fire, had he not made a quick exit from the burning parish trailer. Waking with a start, he had the feeling that something was wrong. He smelled smoke, investigated. Looking into the furnace compartment, he saw flames. Not being able to get to the fire because of the enclosure around the furnace, he grabbed some clothes, his shoes, and dashed out into the minus-40-degree night. In a somewhat distant road-house, he found shelter and summoned help. The church was saved, but the trailer was a total loss. Commenting on his being "fired" from Talkeetna, he wrote:

> I am convinced we are under a kind Providence. When I first went through that house and saw how the furnace was so boxed in, I experienced a very depressed feeling, and I quietly told our dear Lord, as on some other occasions, "I'm in your service, and if you want me now, it's O.K. by me." As I see it, Saint Peter says, "You haven't won your spurs yet. You've got to limp around a bit more."

In 1971, Father Spils went to Cottonwood, Idaho, to be chaplain to the Benedictine Sisters. However, the following year he needed to go into semi-retirement at Gonzaga University. For some years he was available for helping out in parishes on weekends or for longer periods. His homilies were simple and direct, always warm, lacking any hint of severity. He was chided for having many different "variations on his favorite theme, the goodness of God." The Lord was said not to cure or heal limbs, but to "fix" them, when the builder–priest spoke. Father Spils, for all his rough external appearance and manner, was said to have had "a real pastor's heart, was gentle and kind, related beautifully to young people and children."

During Expo '74, the World's Fair in Spokane, Father Spils was named Catholic chaplain to the event. But, on opening day, he suffered an appendix attack. Medics were slow in getting him to a hospital. A ruptured appendix almost cost him his life. Never recovering completely from the ordeal, without complaining, he suffered much pain for the rest of his life.

Father Spils spent his years of total retirement at Gonzaga University, as a member of its Jesuit House community. He was an active community member, readily available and eager for a game of bridge, or pinochle, or cribbage. With little prompting, he would regale any willing listener with stories about Alaska. People sometimes regretted not having a tape recorder going to preserve them for future listeners, so interesting and colorful were many of his stories. Good-naturedly, he would tease people by contradicting them. He enjoyed taking drives. Father Renner took some memorable ones with him: over to Moses Lake, Washington, to visit veteran Alaskan missionary, Father Segundo **Llorente**, S.J., or down to Lewiston, Idaho, to visit relatives. When Father Spils did the driving, and the talking, it was a pleasure to sit back and do the listening. Back in his room, he read a great deal. Some of the heavier theological works he read and re-read. "You now," he said, "some of that stuff is kind of heavy. You can't get it all the first time around."

In 1981, Father Spils made his last trip to Alaska, to **Anchorage**, to see Pope John Paul II— who was stopping off there for a few hours on February 26th—and to attend a Mass celebrated by him. In his homily, the pope emphasized the words, "Abba, Father." To Father Spils, God had always been, before all else, the loving, caring, heavenly Father. Hearing the pope's words, tears filled his eyes. In his declining years, he was hard of hearing. Often, unaware of others in the chapel, he could be heard praying in a low, but audible, voice in tender and loving words. "Father," he would pray, "I'm an old man. I'm tired and want to come home. Take me to be with you." Only the hands of the builder–priest were calloused. The heart became more tender with age.

In the spring of 1981, Gonzaga University awarded Father Spils and his fellow one-time Alaskan missionary, Father **John P. Fox**, S.J.—as well as two veteran Rocky Mountain missionaries—the DeSmet Medal in recognition of his apostolic achievements in Alaska as priest and builder of missions.

Father James C. "Jake" Spils, S.J., died in Spokane, on March 26, 1982, and lies buried in the Jesuit cemetery at Mount St. Michael's.

16, 95, 142

ST. MICHAEL

St. Michael, located on St. Michael Island in Norton Sound, 43 miles southwest of **Unalakleet**, has been on maps since 1833, when the Russian–American Company built Redoubt St. Michael there. In

The new St. Michael's Church, St. Michael. *PP.*

the late 1890s, St. Michael took on great importance as the gateway to interior **Alaska** and the Klondike. As a transfer point, it flourished for several decades. When the Alaska Railroad reached **Nenana** around 1920, St. Michael's days as the main supply center for the interior ended. The St. Michael post office was established in 1897. In 1890, St. Michael's population numbered 101; in 1910, 450; in 1920, 371; in 1930, 147; in 1940, 142; in 1950, 157; in 1970, 207; in 1980, 283; in 1990, 295; and in the year 2000, 368. The Native people of St. Michael are a mixture of Inupiaq-speaking Eskimos from the north and Central Yup'ik-speaking Eskimos from the south.

Catholic missionaries first came to St. Michael in 1873, when **Oblate** Bishop Isidore Clut and future Oblate Father Auguste Lecorre arrived in June. Father Lecorre spent the year 1873–74 there before returning to Canada. In the summer of 1877, Charles J. **Seghers**, Bishop of Vancouver Island at the time, and Father Joseph M. **Mandart** passed through St. Michael en route to the middle Yukon via Unalakleet and the Unalakleet–**Kaltag** portage. In late 1886, the body of Bishop Seghers was brought to St. Michael, where it was stored for a time, then buried for the year 1887–88, before it was disinterred and shipped to Victoria, B.C., Canada.

From 1887 to the year 1899, Jesuit missionaries passed through St. Michael without establishing a permanent mission there. Catholic baptisms, however, were performed there by them during the last decade of the 1800s. St. Michael first appears in the Turin Province catalog of the Society of Jesus for the year 1900–01. Father Joseph M. **Tréca**, S.J., is rightly recognized as the founder, in 1899, of the St. Michael mission. He was there until 1901.

"A handsome church" was built at St. Michael "around 1900." For decades, however, priests stationed at St. Michael complained about how difficult it was to heat this church. Father Martin J. **Lonneux**, S.J., found it "rather a summer building." In 1924, he was told "several times" by Father John B. **Sifton**, S.J., that the church was "a white elephant." Father Lonneux, having been refused permission by Joseph R. **Crimont**, S.J., Vicar Apostolic of Alaska at the time, to take down that church and replace it with a smaller, warmer one, proceeded to build a chapel in the priest's residence to serve as the church. Bishop Crimont wanted the church to continue to stand, "as a monument." In 1953, Father Jules M. **Convert**, S.J., who succeeded Father Lonneux as pastor at St. Michael, built a new St. Michael's Church. Fifty years later, this one— still sporting a Catholic Church Extension Society plaque dated 1953—was replaced by a new one, begun in the year 2000 under the foremanship of

The new St. Bernard's Church. Stebbins. *PP.*

Father Ward Walker. It was dedicated on November 7, 2004, by Bishop Donald J. **Kettler**.

For ten years, from September 26, 1908, to December 9, 1918, when it burned to the ground, the **Ursuline** Sisters had a mission, "St. Ursula's-by-the-Sea," at St. Michael. It served them as a base for teaching school and ministering to the sick.

Until recent years, the St. Michael mission and its two dependent stations, **Stebbins** and Unalakleet, were always staffed by Jesuit priests and Jesuit Lay Brothers. In addition to Father Tréca, the following Jesuits had St. Michael as their headquarters: René **Astruc**, 1956–62; Rogatien **Camille**, 1901–07; Thomas F. **Carlin**, 1995–99; Joseph A. **Chapdelaine**, 1907–09 and 1910–17; Convert, 1949–54; Philip I. **Delon**, 1917–18; George S. **Endal**, 1968–82; Francis J. **Fallert**, 1954–56; Thomas N. **Gallagher**, 1967–68 and 1982–83; Henry G. **Hargreaves**, 1965–66; James E. **Jacobson**, 1966–67; Anthony M. **Keyes**, 1901–02, 1907–10, and 1917; Lonneux, 1928–52; Francis X. **Nawn**, 1983–87; James W. **Plamondon**, 1962–65; **John A. Post**, 1900–01; Aloysius J. **Robaut**, 1918–19; and Sifton, 1916–28.

Father Wallace M. Olson, a diocesan priest, was at St. Michael during the year 1964–65. Father Joseph G. **Stolz**, likewise a diocesan priest, was there from 1987–90. He was followed by Father Gerald

S. **Ornowski**, M.I.C., who visited St. Michael out of Stebbins, from 1990–94. During the year 1994–95, Father James E. **Falsey**, a diocesan priest, visited St. Michael out of Unalakleet. Father Ward Walker, priest of the Diocese of Fairbanks, was at St. Michael from 1999–2002. During the year 2002–03, Jesuit priests stationed in Fairbanks and at St. Marys visited St. Michael from time to time. As of the year 2004, Father Stanislaw Jaszek was tending to the pastoral needs of the St. Michael flock.

The following Jesuit Lay Brothers were stationed at St. Michael: **Bernard I. Cunningham**, 1900–01; Bartholomew **Keogh**, 1901–02 and 1906–10; Felix Montaldo, 1902–04; Joseph V. O'Hare, 1904–05; Ulric **Paquin**, 1910–11; and Hugo Horan, 1919–20.

Sister Dolores Steiner, S.N.D., was at St. Michael in 1981. The first Eskimo to become a Jesuit, Joseph **Prince**, was born at St. Michael. Father Camille and Brother Paquin lie buried at St. Michael. Ivan and Maggie **Sipary** were closely associated with St. Michael.

78, 133

STEBBINS

The name Stebbins first began to appear on maps in 1900. The village of Stebbins is located on St.

Michael Island in Norton Sound, 8 miles from **St. Michael**. Its inhabitants are mostly Central Yup'ik Eskimos from the south, from places such as Nelson Island and Pikmiktalik. At one time, reindeer herding was an important part of the way of life in Stebbins. In 1950, Stebbins had 80 inhabitants; in 1960, 158; in 1970, 231; in 1980, 334; in 1990, 442; and in the year 2000, 547.

The Stebbins mission, under the patronage of St. Bernard, was established in October 1908 by Father Joseph A. **Chapdelaine**, S.J., stationed at St. Michael at the time. On January 27, 1911, Brother Ulric **Paquin**, S.J., while en route from St. Michael with a sled-load of lumber to build a chapel at Stebbins, was caught in a blizzard and froze to death. During the year 1918–19, Father Aloysius J. **Robaut**, S.J., spent longer periods of time at Stebbins. Throughout its history, however, the Stebbins parish has been served almost entirely by priests visiting it out of St. Michael. There is one notable exception: Father Gerald S. **Ornowski**, M.I.C., who made Stebbins his headquarters from 1990–94. As of the year 2004, Father Stanislaw Jaszek was tending to the pastoral needs of the Stebbins flock.

Over the years, the Stebbins parish saw also the services of **Eskimo Deacons** Louie Steve and Charlie Steve. Both lie buried at Stebbins. In recent years, Margaret Marlin has been the faithful Pastoral Administrator of the parish.

November 6, 2002, was a memorable day for the people of St. Bernard's parish, Stebbins. On that day they witnessed the dedication of their new church by Donald J. **Kettler**, Bishop of **Fairbanks**. The new church was built in large part by the people of the community under the foremanship of Leonard Raymond, Project Manager. This new church replaced the old one, put up in the year 1955–56, by Father Francis J. **Fallert**, S.J.

78, 133

STOLZ, Father Joseph G.

Joseph G. Stolz was born in Oberlin, Ohio, on November 4, 1919. He was educated in Elyria, Ohio, and at St. Mary's College in Maryland. He continued his studies first at the Redemptorist Seminary in Esopus, New York, then at St. Mary's Seminary in Cleveland. He was ordained a priest for the Cleveland diocese on May 18, 1963. For the next 22 years, he served in various capacities in different parishes of the Cleveland diocese.

Hearing of the shortage of priests in rural **Alaska**, Father Stolz applied in 1985 to serve in the Missionary Diocese of **Fairbanks**. For a short time, he served at Immaculate Conception parish, Fairbanks. He then became pastor of St. Joseph's parish in **Nome**, a post he held from 1985–87. His next assignment was that of pastor of the **Stebbins** and **St. Michael** missions, from 1987–90. In 1990, he was assigned to **Little Diomede** Island. From there he wrote, in keeping with his sense of humor, that he "saw whales, walrus and ducks go by the rectory. So far none have stopped for a visit." It was while on Little Diomede that, in early March 1991, he suffered a severe heart attack.

Father Stolz spent the next year convalescing, mostly in Fairbanks. He then went to live in St. Nicholas parish, **North Pole**, where he helped out. During the last months of his life, he lived in a cabin in North Pole and spent much of his time writing his memoirs. On January 28, 1993, in the early afternoon, he set out for his customary walk and the praying of the rosary, one of his key devotions. Another heart attack, this time fatal, struck him down near his cabin. His rosary was found next to him.

On February 2nd, at seven in the evening, the Mass of Christian Burial was celebrated in St. Nicholas Church by Michael J. **Kaniecki**, S.J., Bishop of Fairbanks at the time. There were many concelebrants. The church was filled, despite the fact that a new low temperature record of minus 58 degrees had been set that day. Dense ice fog made driving hazardous.

Father Stolz was, in every sense of the word, "a people's priest." He loved being with people and carried on a heavy correspondence. Blessed with a positive outlook on life and a great sense of humor, he was a font of stories, anecdotes and jokes, which he often acted out as he related or told them. Proud of being an Alaskan, he signed many of his letters "Fr. Joe of the North." Sometime before his death, he had told his sister that he hoped to die and be buried in Alaska. Both of these hopes were realized.

He lies buried in Birch Hill Cemetery on the edge of Fairbanks.

133

STRASS, Father Richard G., C.Ss.R

Richard George Strass was born the third child to Edward P. Strass and Agnes Voegtle Strass on August 14, 1933, in Chicago, Illinois. When he was three years old, the family moved to the small farming community of Lombard, Illinois. After attending Sacred Heart Grade School there, he attended the Redemptorist Minor Seminary, St. Joseph's College Preparatory, in Kirkwood, Missouri, for his secondary education and two years of college. After completing his noviceship in De Soto, Missouri, he made his first profession, on September 2, 1958, as a member of the St. Louis Province. His major seminary studies took place at Oconomowoc, Wisconsin. On June 29, 1960, he was ordained a priest by Bishop Joseph E. Kiley.

For some months, as a newly ordained priest, Father Strass did parish work in St. Louis, Missouri. He was then assigned to the Redemptorist Mission in Thailand. There, while studying the language, he worked as the military chaplain for the U.S. Army 809th Engineers. He stayed on as an auxiliary chaplain throughout his first assignment in Thailand. During the Vietnam War, he was stationed "up north," on the Mekong River, taking care of several villages along the river. In his own words, "I loved the rain forest and people of these remote areas." He was their pastor, their only source of medical help, and their guide in agricultural development.

Around 1970, Father Strass was appointed Superior of the mission house of Nongkhai. In 1973, however, along with fellow Redemptorist Robert J. Wells, he was assigned to the Redemptorist Mission on the Kenai Peninsula in **Alaska**. Before going there, he replaced Msgr. Francis A. Murphy, pastor of St. Patrick's parish, Anchorage, for a few months, while Msgr. Murphy made a trip to the Holy Land.

On July 4, 1974, Father Strass became pastor of **Homer** and its dependent stations of **Ninilchik** and **Seldovia**. Among his first concerns was to see to the construction of a Catholic church in Homer. On

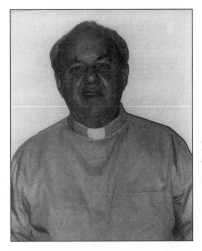

Father Richard G. Strass, C.Ss.R *Courtesy of Redemptorists Denver Province.*

June 21, 1975, the new church, a log church dedicated to St. John the Baptist, was ready to be solemnly blessed by **Joseph T. Ryan**, Archbishop of **Anchorage**. Soon he had churches also in Ninilchik and Seldovia. In addition to attending to these three towns, he made time also "to run around to Port Graham, English Bay, Halibut Cove, and East Homer with small numbers of Catholics scattered around." He also offered the Sacraments to members of the Russian Orthodox Church of the area who rarely saw one of their priests. "It was a great time," he recalled years later, "in those days. With the very small communities one felt like you were part of them and not a distant pastor."

Father Strass was a happy priest and a happy man on the Kenai Peninsula. He "loved to take the hi-school kids camping in the summer, and did a lot of hunting and fishing, cross-country skiing, etc." Soon after arriving in Alaska, he qualified for his private pilot's license and his scuba diving certificate.

In 1979, Father Strass left Homer. For a time, he did pastoral ministry in the Aleutian Islands, mainly at **Unalaska**. He then spent a few months in Thailand with a medical team from Alaska to help with the refugees from the burning fields of Cambodia. From 1980–88, he was pastor of **Soldotna** and its dependent stations.

For the years 1988–92, Father Strass was pastor of Homer again. He was in Great Falls, Montana, from 1992–96, helping to close out the Redemptorist parishes there. He then returned to Alaska to serve as pastor of Sacred Heart parish in **Seward** from 1996 until the year 2002. In August of that year, he returned to Thailand to work at the orphanage at Nongkhai. He had loved Alaska and had mixed feelings about leaving it, but he found "the innocent little ones at the AIDS orphanage a call too hard to resist." His leaving Alaska marked the end of the Redemptorist Congregation's four decades of dedicated service on the Kenai Peninsula.

15

SULZMAN, Father Francis Merrill

Merrill Sulzman (he always went by the name of Merrill) was born on March 16, 1906, the oldest of three children born to Dr. and Mrs. Frank M. Sulzman of Troy, New York. Dr. Sulzman's hobby was travel. From the time his youngest was five years old, the family made extensive trips to faraway places, **Alaska** included. It was while the family was on a trip to Southeastern Alaska in the summer of 1925, that Merrill's vocation to the priesthood began to develop. At **Skagway**, Father G. Edgar **Gallant** met the boat they were on, and showed them what he hoped to do for the Indian children of that town. Merrill had just completed his second year of a pre-medical course at Manhattan College in New York City, but soon thoughts of Skagway and of possibilities for him there began to replace thoughts of medicine. Because he had always enjoyed life in a happy-go-lucky way, his parents were somewhat apprehensive, when he asked to spend the following summer with Father Gallant in Skagway. He did arrive in Skagway as planned, but, somehow, his luggage was not taken off the boat. All he had with him was his saxophone!

After completing certain prescribed studies at Manhattan College, Merrill Sulzman, in 1927, entered St. Michael's Seminary in Toronto, Canada, to study for the priesthood with a view to one day serving as a priest in the Vicariate of Alaska. Joseph R. **Crimont**, S.J., Vicar Apostolic of Alaska at the time, was his sponsor. On February 14, 1931, in the Cathedral in Albany, New York, Merrill Sulzman was ordained a priest by Edmund F. Gibbons, Bishop of the Albany Diocese.

Father Sulzman's first assignment in Alaska was that of assistant to Father Gallant, who had inspired him to become a priest. In Skagway, with his duties in the parish and at Pius X Mission—the new school for children from Southeastern Alaska—as well as at the Chilcoot Barracks, he found himself fully occupied. After a brief "internship" in Skagway, he was transferred to **Seward**.

On May 6, 1935, when the first colonists for the Matanuska Valley arrived at Seward, their attention was soon caught by the figure of a young priest—of medium size, with a lively disposition and engaging smile—who began to move among them, introducing himself, getting to know the different families, asking what he could do to be of service. People, especially the Catholics among them, readily took to him.

Father Sulzman's stay in Seward was a relatively short one. His impulsive request to Bishop Crimont was: "May I be the first priest to volunteer to go with these people?" The bishop's answer was "Yes!" He saw, what other observers, too, were quick to see, that the 29-year-old priest, an outdoorsman type, wiry and tough, would be adaptable to what was sure to be an unordered, difficult beginning in the Matanuska Valley, as people strove to settle in and build a community. When rumors that Father Sulzman was about to be switched to the Matanuska Valley began to circulate, the Seward parish was distraught. But, in Father Sulzman, Bishop Crimont saw the right man for the Matanuska colonists.

Just when Father Sulzman was about to board the train for the slow journey north to the Matanuska Valley, Art Woodley landed at Seward. Hearing of Father Sulzman's intentions, he offered to fly him to the valley. Dressed in hunting clothes, Father Sulzman arrived at the main colonist community, Warton, late Saturday afternoon on May 25, 1935. With him he had his own tent and a few basic supplies. Setting up housekeeping on the carpet of green grass was a simple matter. After meeting several of the leaders of the Matanuska project, Father Sulzman rounded up some of the colonists and made plans for Sunday Mass. That first Mass was offered in a tent on a table made of scrap lumber. Twenty-five people attended. Other Masses followed, wher-

Father Francis Merrill Sulzman. *LRC.*

ever a halfway decent place could be found, but frequently they were offered at the Post Office end of the trading center.

As the fall approached, Father Sulzman pushed for the construction of a wooden house to replace his tent. The one-room, shiplap building, measuring 12 × 15′, was adaptable for all purposes. Mass was offered in it daily for the few people who could come. Sunday Masses were held in the Trading Post.

Early on, during his stay in the Matanuska Valley, Father Sulzman was designated Fire Marshall. On one of his trips to the East, he was given a small car by his father. The words "Fire Chief" were emblazoned on it. He was referred to also as the "Padre of **Palmer**." To relieve the stress brought on the colonists by endless work, many were the Saturday nights that saw Father Sulzman play the saxophone, while colonists and workers danced and relaxed.

Whether it was fighting fires, or playing the saxophone, or settling a dispute, Father Sulzman would drop everything, when the spiritual needs of his flock required his attention. He was first and foremost a priest. A newspaper correspondent said of him: "He has divinity in his soul, but a bit of the devil in his eye."

Along with the Catholic colonists in the Matanuska Valley, at the site of present-day Palmer, Father Sulzman, too, hoped to have a Catholic church up

by the end of May 1936. By the middle of April, about half the number of logs needed for the church had been felled. The actual building of the church began on June 2, 1936. Soon it was realized that the cost of the church would exceed available funds. Accordingly, in January 1937, Father Sulzman went back East to raise funds by lecturing and showing movie clips. His father, aghast at what he considered to be the poor health of his son, took him on a restful three-month "rehabilitation" cruise to the West Indies. On July 24, 1937, the new St. Michael's log church, with rectory attached, was formally dedicated.

The joy of the dedication was short-lived, however. By August, the parish was in debt again. Architectural flaws in the design of the church began to show up. Costly changes were called for. For the first time in his life, Father Sulzman became discouraged. With Bishop Crimont's permission, he again went East to raise funds. There, a doctor friend of the family, after examining him, found his health so deteriorated, that he could not approve of his immediate return to Alaska. Writing to Bishop Crimont, the doctor recommended that Father Sulzman be given a year of absence in a worry-free atmosphere and a warmer climate to regain his health.

About this time also, the bishop was receiving reports from the valley that some of the parishioners were upset at Father's lifestyle and wished for his transfer, feeling that another priest might do better at building the parish spirit. Concerned about the reports and about the health and spiritual good of Father Sulzman, the bishop agreed to a year of recuperation outside Alaska. "Thus," according to historian Sister Margaret Cantwell, S.S.A., "Father Sulzman's saga at Matanuska Valley—one of the most picturesque episodes in the establishment of the Catholic Church within what became the Archdiocese of **Anchorage**, came to a conclusion. The church was up, the parish begun, the time for change was ripe."

Father Sulzman was called back to Alaska, in 1939, to minister for a short time in Skagway. With the outbreak of World War II, he asked to become a military chaplain, and was assigned for a time to Alaska's Annette Island. He was commissioned a first lieutenant in the Army's corps of chaplains, and was ordered to an "undisclosed" place in the Territory of Alaska. This turned out to be the Aleutian Islands. He was involved in the Attu and Kiska battles, and later in the Battle of the Bulge in Europe.

After the war, in January 1946, Father Sulzman was assigned to **Sitka**. Not long there, he fell and broke several ribs. He went to Troy, New York, for medical attention, then returned to Sitka in February 1947 for another brief stay. In 1953, he was in Juneau. A November 1953 Juneau house diary entry reads: "Fr. Sulzman with us, and doing very good work." He remained in Alaska until October 1954.

In May 1955, Father Sulzman was appointed to St. Sylvester parish in New York State. There he celebrated his silver jubilee as a priest. After he had served as an assistant priest in various New York parishes for some years, his health was such that he had to retire altogether. He bought a small house, and settled down to write a book about his Alaskan adventures. Just after starting the introduction to the book, he died of a heart attack on March 13, 1966, three days before his sixtieth birthday.

15

TAINTER, Daniel J., S.J.

He was a rough-and-tumble sort of character, "ready to sleep on the floor at any time." He put on no airs, no pretenses. The Native peoples he ministered to, whether of South Dakota or **Alaska**, found him affable, approachable, courteous. Though called to be a "fisher of men," he was a hunter at heart—and that to the last.

Daniel J. "Dan" Tainter was born on January 21, 1923, in St. Charles, Missouri. His father, Dr. Frank J. Tainter, was a nationally known plastic surgeon; his mother, Louise Rixey, was a convert to the Catholic Faith. Dan was the youngest of six children, of whom three, including himself, entered Religious life. From his earliest years, he took avidly to the outdoors. He loved animals, especially dogs. He was schooled at St. Charles Borromeo Grade School in St. Charles, and at Campion Jesuit High in Prairie du Chien, Wisconsin, where he was active in athletics. He attended St. Louis University for a year.

On August 8, 1942, Dan entered the Jesuit novitiate of the Missouri Province at Florissant, Missouri. After completing his noviceship and studies in the classics and humanities, he went to Mount St. Michael's, Spokane, Washington, for three years of philosophical studies, from 1947–50. While he was at "the Mount," his thoughts kept turning north, to Alaska. In 1954, he wrote to the Father General in Rome, "Even as a small boy I wanted to be an Alaskan missionary."

From 1950–52, Dan taught at Campion. His theological studies were made at St. Mary's, Kansas, from 1952–56. He was ordained a priest on June 16, 1955. For the year 1956–57, he was assistant pastor at St. Malachy's parish in St. Louis. He made his tertianship at Decatur, Illinois, 1957–58, and then went on to 13 years of ministry among the

Oglala Sioux of South Dakota. Twelve of those years were at Holy Rosary Indian Mission at Pine Ridge, and one year, 1959–60, at Mother Butler Center in Rapid City. His warm personality and fondness for people endeared him to all, especially to the Indian children.

Given his love for the outdoors, this life on the Indian missions was made for Father Tainter. On the prairies, he rode horses with the Sioux, and helped them round up and brand their cattle. He hunted antelope successfully. The fruits of a successful hunt he gave to his people. But all the while, he continued to feel himself drawn to serve in Alaska. When he brought the subject up with his Superiors, he was told that "Pine Ridge will be your Alaska." Still, to be ready for Alaska, he took flying lessons—just in case.

Near the end of those hard-lived 13 years among the Sioux, Father Tainter began to be depressed, on the verge of burning out. He needed a change. Superiors realized that Alaska would provide such. On February 2, 1971, in company of his dog, he arrived in Alaska. During his first six months there, he helped out now in this village, now in that. From September 1, 1971, to July 31, 1975, he was headquartered at **Holy Cross**. Out of there, he served also as visiting priest to **Aniak** and **Kalskag**, and, in his own words, "to 10 surrounding smaller villages." With so many stations to care for, his flying skills served him well. In 1973, Father Tainter was transferred from the Missouri Province to the Oregon Province. This was something he had very much desired, for it virtually guaranteed him a future in Alaska.

His next assignment took him to the Central Yup'ik Eskimos on Nelson Island in western Alaska. From July 31, 1975, to November 21, 1977, he was pastor of **Tununak** and its dependent stations,

Father Daniel J. Tainter, S.J. *JOPA-1078.01.*

Toksook Bay and **Nightmute**. He then became pastor of **Hooper Bay** and **Scammon Bay**. While on this assignment, he served also as a National Guard auxiliary chaplain at Cape Romanzof.

It was illness, a proneness to rather severe spells of discouragement and depression, that brought about Father Tainter's leaving Alaska. On October 27, 1978, he took up a new assignment, that of associate pastor of St. John the Baptist parish in Milwaukie, Oregon. During the last year of his life, he was involved in the Marriage Encounter program, and lived at Loyola Retreat House in Portland, Oregon. According to one report, while at the retreat house, "He looked fine and happy and well." That made the news of his death all the more shocking. He died unexpectedly, on November 26, 1980, at the Jesuit villa on the Oregon coast, at Nestucca, near Cloverdale, where he had gone to do some duck hunting with his friend, Father Charles F. Suver, S.J. On Thanksgiving Day morning, November 27th, he was found dead sitting in his room, his bed still made. He had apparently died the night before, while trying to untie his shoe. Given his ardent love for God's creation and the outdoor life, there was something stirringly appropriate about the site of his death. Wrote Father Neill R. Meany, S.J., at the end of his obituary of Father Tainter: "The roar of the ocean, wild and gray in late November, was a fitting Requiem."

Father Tainter lies buried in the Jesuit cemetery at Mount St. Michael's.

TALBOTT, Father Raymond L., S.J.

Raymond L. Talbott was born in Belmont, Washington, on October 10, 1909. His parents were George and Henrietta Meissner Talbott. His elementary and secondary schooling he received in Spokane, Washington, at St. Aloysius and St. Francis Xavier parochial schools and at Gonzaga Preparatory. On July 30, 1927, he entered the Jesuit novitiate at Los Gatos, California. After completing his two-year noviceship, he stayed on an additional two years to study the classics and humanities. From 1931–34, he studied philosophy at Mount St. Michael's in Spokane. He then taught for a year in Yakima, Washington, after which he spent two years at Sacred Heart Mission, DeSmet, Idaho. His theological studies he made at Alma College, Los Gatos, California, from 1937–41. He was ordained a priest in San Francisco on June 27, 1940. He made his tertianship at Port Townsend, Washington, 1941–42.

While still in theological studies, Father Talbott had volunteered to serve in the Armed Forces. In 1942, he joined the U.S. Army as a military chaplain. After he graduated from Chaplains School, his assignments took him to Wales, England; to Normandy and Paris, France; and to Germany. Before he left the Army, he had five battle stars to his credit.

World War II over, Father Talbott, during the latter half of the 1940s, taught rhetoric at Gonzaga University in Spokane, and did parish work at St. Patrick's parish in Spokane's Minnehaha district, and in Harlem, Montana. In 1950, because of the Korean War, he was recalled to military service. This time he served as a chaplain in the U.S. Air Force. As such, he was stationed successively in Spokane, and in **Anchorage** and **Fairbanks, Alaska.**

In the summer of 1953, Father Talbott, now back again in civilian life as of April 1, 1953, became pastor of St. Mary's parish in **Kodiak**, Alaska. What he found there upon his arrival was neither a decent church structure nor any kind of school building. He immediately set about providing these. His appearance on the scene brought about renewed interest in the possibilities of an adequate parish plant. A wholly new church, however, was ruled out by Dermot **O'Flanagan**, Bishop of Juneau at the time, under whose jurisdiction Kodiak fell. Instead, the decision was reached to double the width of the building then in use as a church and to add to its length. By August 30th, the enlarged, renovated structure was ready for use. The parish now had a two-story building with adequate space for priest's quarters on the second floor and for classrooms on the main floor.

With classroom space available, Father Talbott asked himself, "Why not a parochial school?" Under adverse circumstances, the first three grades opened in September 1954. He himself taught the second and third grades. The school was now on its way. A new school was dedicated and blessed on May 7, 1968. By that time, however, he was no longer in Kodiak.

Father Talbott was pastor of Sacred Heart parish, Nespelem, Washington, from 1960–61, and of Sacred Heart Mission, DeSmet, Idaho, from 1961–62. For the years 1962–69, he was stationed at, and worked out of, Port Townsend. From 1969–74, he lived at Seattle University and served as an assistant priest at St. James Cathedral.

From 1974–1992, Father Talbott, while living at Seattle University, was Director of the Chief Seattle Club, a shelter he founded in Seattle's core area. The shelter concerned itself with the plight of homeless Native Americans "bedeviled by alcohol and sunk in poverty." For almost two decades, he dedicated himself totally to the relief of skid row outcasts. The club provided a soup kitchen and a drop-in center, and helped Native Americans find jobs.

In 1992, Father Talbott went into retirement in Portland, where he remained for three years. He was then moved to the Jesuit infirmary at Gonzaga University in Spokane. There, while being read to, he died quietly on November 22, 1995. He lies buried in the Jesuit cemetery at Mount St. Michael's.

Father Talbott is remembered as "a zealous priest, as a humble person with an unwarranted low opinion of himself." He died a solemnly professed Father of the Society of Jesus.

189

TALKEETNA

The town of Talkeetna is located at mile 226.7 on the **Alaska** Railroad, at the junction of the Talkeetna and Susitna Rivers and about 125 road-miles north of **Anchorage**. It developed as a major camp, when the railroad was being built. The Talkeetna post office was established in 1916, and the Talkeetna railroad station opened to traffic in 1920. Talkeetna's population numbered 70 in 1920, 89 in 1930, 136 in 1939, 106 in 1950, 76 in 1967, and 772 in the year 2000.

The Catholic parish at Talkeetna was established in 1970. The church was named for St. Bernard of Menthon, who trained St. Bernard dogs to rescue people lost, or in trouble, in the Swiss Alps. The name was thought appropriate, since Talkeetna is the staging area for climbers of Mount McKinley—Denali, "The Great One."

Father Stanley J. **Allie** was appointed St. Bernard's first administrator, effective as of March 8, 1970. The first Mass in Talkeetna was held in the Federal Aviation Administration laundry room. After Father Allie had his "rectory," a two-bedroom house trailer, set up, Mass was offered in it, on a dresser top. Soon the trailer could barely accommodate the people who came for Mass. By Christmas 1970, however, a church under construction was far enough along to enable Father James C. **Spils**, S.J., filling in temporarily for Father Allie, to offer Midnight Mass in it. During the midnight hours of Sunday, January 24th, Father Spils narrowly escaped with his life, when a fire broke out in the trailer. The unfinished church was saved, but the trailer was a total loss. In 1971, Father Allie, to his considerable relief, witnessed the completion of a combination church and social center at Talkeetna. It was formally dedicated by **Joseph T. Ryan**, Archbishop of Anchorage at the time, on October 20, 1971.

On August 18, 1974, Father **Gerard T. Ryan**, C.S.Sp., succeeded Father Allie as pastor of St. Bernard's. He served as such until September 18, 1979. From 1979–82, it was Father Thomas E. Power who cared for St. Bernard's. He was followed by Father Leo C. **Desso**, there from 1982–84. He, in turn, was followed by Father Urban M. **Bates**, O.P., "supply priest" to Talkeetna from 1984–91. After Father Bates, no priest was formally assigned to care for Talkeetna. It was supplied by various priests, visiting it mostly out of Anchorage. Father Allie, out of **Wasilla**, cared for St. Bernard's during the year 1991–92.

From 1991–95, Sister Louise Tibbetts, S.N.J.M., served as Pastoral Administrator of St. Bernard's.

St. Bernard's Church, Talkeetna. *Courtesy of Renamary Rauchenstein.*

As of the year 2004, St. Bernard's Mission Statement—based on John 21:15-17, "tend my lambs, feed my sheep"—read:

By this we understand that Jesus sent His Spirit to dwell within us that we might continue His work. To "tend" and to "feed" are words with meanings, both secular and spiritual. As individuals and as members of St. Bernard's, we have been given all the gifts and graces necessary to "tend the lambs and feed the sheep" whom the Lord has placed in our care, or under our authority. We resolve to use these gifts and graces as the Lord God directs us, for the good of His people and the glory of God.

15

TAM, Mr. Patrick C.W.

Patrick C. W. Tam, the oldest of three children, was born as "Tam Chun Wah" on June 2, 1958—reckoned on the Chinese calendar as the Year of the Dog—in Kowloon, Hong Kong. Soon after his birth, his mother, Virginia, a convert to Catholicism, had him baptized and named Patrick. In 1965, his family emigrated to the United States, to Rhode Island. There his name was Americanized to "Patrick Chun Wah Tam."

From his earliest youth, his mother's faith made a deep impression on him. He never forgot the stories she told him of having witnessed the persecution of foreign priests and Sisters by the Communists. As a boy, he could see her every morning kneeling in the middle of the living room praying the rosary before a statue of Mary. Her example of faithfully attending Mass, offered in a language she did not understand, so inspired him that he served as an altar boy until he began high school. It was his mother's insistence that her three children receive a Catholic education that most shaped his destiny. While his father worked long hours as a cook in a restaurant, his mother, in addition to keeping house, worked also as a seamstress at home to raise money to pay for tuition.

In Providence, Rhode Island, the three Tam children attended St. Patrick's Grammar School. For his secondary education, Patrick attended LaSalle Academy, likewise in Providence, where, under the strict discipline of the Christian Brothers, he received a solid foundation in the humanities. But, at the same time, he also received crucial spiritual formation through religious education, retreats, guidance from teachers, and the example of the Brothers. His reading of Thomas Merton's *The*

Seven Story Mountain awakened in him a strong and abiding attraction to contemplative spirituality.

After graduating from LaSalle in 1977, Patrick entered the Jesuit-staffed College of the Holy Cross in Worcester, Massachusetts. There he majored in philosophy, and immersed himself in the liberal arts. Annual student retreats based on the Spiritual Exercises of St. Ignatius Loyola, as well as the friendship of his Jesuit teachers, introduced him to the riches of Ignatian spirituality.

While at Holy Cross, Patrick, as a member of a student peace group, participated in a protest against the "christening," in 1979, of the first Trident nuclear submarine in Groton, Connecticut. This action on his part he characterized as "one of the key spiritual events of my life." His decision, made after much prayer and interior struggle, to join in a nonviolent act of civil disobedience woke him up to the gospel call to "hunger and thirst for justice."

In 1981, Patrick graduated, *magna cum laude*, from Holy Cross with a B.A. degree in philosophy. Like many of his classmates, he then weighed his options for the future. A presentation made on campus by a representative of the **Jesuit Volunteer Corps** radically changed his life. Realizing that up to that moment his life had been centered mainly on himself, he felt called to join the JVC. He now wanted a chance to serve God and others, especially the less fortunate. The "preferential option for the poor" principle became a strong undercurrent in his spiritual life. His decision to join the JVC surprised, and disappointed, his parents. Again, he was reminded of "the cost of discipleship."

Having, up to then, resided all his life in urban settings, and wanting to avoid being part of a large JVC community, for fear that that might isolate him from the people he hoped to serve, Patrick opted for rural **Alaska**. In August 1981, he arrived in **Emmonak**, a Central Yup'ik Eskimo village of around 600 near the mouth of the Yukon River in western Alaska. Emmonak became home to him and his JVC partner, Bruce Morrill, a classmate also from Holy Cross. Living in a small room in the back of the "Teen Center" building, which once served as the parish church, the two young men ran Sacred Heart parish's Youth Center and conducted Religious Education classes for high school students.

Mr. Patrick C.W. Tam.
BR-CD 0317-A113.

After one year at Emmonak, Bruce returned to New England, where he became a member of the New England Province of the Society of Jesus. Patrick stayed on—and kept staying on, and on.

After Patrick had served Sacred Heart parish for the years 1981–83 as a member of the JVC, he was hired on as Parish Youth Minister. His decision to continue his stay in Alaska caused his parents much grief and distress. In 1986, he made an extended visit home. By then, just about the time he was getting acclimatized to the Alaskan winters, his parents had moved to Simi Valley, California. His stay in California made him realize beyond a doubt that his life's calling was to the Alaskan bush. While in California, wanting to make the most of his time there, he enrolled in the School of Applied Theology, a lay-ministry training program loosely associated with the Jesuit School of Theology in Berkeley, California. After nine months of study, he announced to his parents his intentions of returning to Alaska. Meanwhile—as his good fortune, or a kindly Providence, would have it—the St. Mary's Mission boarding school on the **Andreafsky** River was due to close permanently in the spring of 1987. Its principal, Sister Angie Pratt, O.S.U., envisioned a youth ministry program built around a traveling retreat team. Patrick was invited to be part of that team. "Of course," he wrote, "I jumped at the invitation, and returned to Emmonak in the summer of 1987." That fall, he and Sister Angie began the work of the Rural Youth Ministry Program, conducting retreats for youths in 18 different villages located in the Yukon-Kuskokwim Delta.

In 1989, Sister Angie left Alaska. Patrick, however, continued to direct the Rural Youth Ministry retreats for about another ten years. Eventually, when he became aware of their spiritual needs, he expanded the program to include out-of-school young adults.

In 1997, Father Charles J. **Peterson**, S.J., who had been responsible for "The Lord Be With You!"—a weekly program broadcast over the Catholic radio station **KNOM, Nome**—left Alaska to take on a new assignment. Before leaving, he asked Patrick to consider replacing him as the producer of the program. For the next three years, Patrick was responsible for the program. This consisted in giving reflections on the given Sunday's gospel reading as a way to help deacons and lay preachers in villages prepare their homilies.

In the spring of 2000, Patrick received some information about Lilly scholarships being offered to lay people wishing to study theology on a graduate level. After much thought and prayer, he applied for and received a scholarship, committing him to two years of study. He promised himself that he was leaving Alaska only to bring back something useful for his ministry among the Yup'ik people. He expected to return to Emmonak, by now his one and only true home.

From the fall of 2000 to the spring of 2002, Patrick attended the Franciscan School of Theology, a member school of the Graduate Theological Union in Berkeley, California. He focused his studies on the issue of inculturation. After successfully completing his thesis—entitled "Ellanguq: The Awakening of the Yup'ik Catholic Imagination"—he graduated in 2002 with a Master of Theological Studies degree.

In the spring of 2002, the Diocese of **Fairbanks** offered Patrick the newly created position of "Adult Faith Developer for the Yukon-Kuskokwim Region," a region covering 24 Yup'ik villages. In June 2002, he returned to Emmonak, stopping off in **Anchorage** to have a last visit with his long-time friend, Father René **Astruc**, S.J., who was dying of cancer. Some time later, Patrick was deeply moved, when he learned that Father Astruc had asked to hear his thesis read to him in the final weeks before his death.

During his first year, 2002–03, as Adult Faith Developer, Patrick settled back into bush life and gave shape to his new ministry. Having learned that interpersonal relationships are at the heart of Yup'ik culture and society, he visited various parishes, to renew old friendships and make new ones. As he went, he tried to affirm and support local efforts at forming small faith-sharing groups by offering suggestions and helpful resource materials. He also conducted parish workshops on bringing together faith and culture. During Lent, he led parish retreats to help Yup'ik adults deepen their prayer lives. Even after some 20 years among the Yup'ik people, Patrick—while marveling at the quick passage of time and the movement of grace in his life from season to season—still considered himself to be merely a student, whose first task was to heed the deep wisdom and spirituality of Yup'ik culture.

190

TANANA

The general area at the confluence of the Tanana and Yukon Rivers, the site of the present-day Tanana, was a traditional, well established seasonal Koyukon Athabaskan Indian settlement and trading location, in earlier days called Nuklukayet. A post office was established there in 1898. In 1890, Tanana had a population of 120; in 1910, 512; in 1950, 228; and in 2000, 308.

The first Catholic missionary to visit Tanana was Father Jean **Séguin**, a member of the Missionary **Oblates** of Mary Immaculate, from 1862–63. Oblate Bishop Isidore Clut and Father Auguste Lecorre visited it in 1873. In the spring of 1878, Archbishop Charles J. **Seghers** and Father Joseph M. **Mandart** spent two months there. Father Aloysius J. **Robaut**, S.J., was there for a time in 1887, and Father Aloysius A. **Ragaru**, S.J., for whose patron saint the mission is named, was stationed there for the year 1887–88. Between the years 1888 and 1904, St. Aloysius Mission in Tanana was visited occasionally by priests from **Nulato**.

From 1904–06, Father Ragaru was stationed in Tanana. In June 1904, he bought a small house with a little annex, which served as a chapel and residence. During his two years at Tanana, he also tended to the mission he had established at **Kokrines**. By this time, Tanana's Native people were almost all Episcopalian. Father Julius **Jetté**, S.J., spent periods of varying length in Tanana during the years 1906–09. In 1909, Father Hormisdas Ferron, S.J., to meet the demands of the whites in Tanana begging for a resident priest, took up residence there. He enlarged the building Father Ragaru had bought and added a tower with a bell. After five years at Tanana, Father Ferron was replaced, in 1914, by Father Jetté, who held station there until October 1922, when he injured himself and was hospitalized. He continued to be the priest assigned to Tanana, for two more years, but was absent the whole time. No one took his place.

St. Aloysius Church, Tanana. *LR.*

Along with mention of Father Jetté and Tanana, mention must be made also of Marian Antoski Edwin of Tanana, venerable Koyukon Athabaskan Indian elder rightly regarded as "a true pillar of the Church." Her beginnings in life were very humble, even precarious. Her very survival was described as "nothing short of miraculous."

Marian was born in a fish camp downriver from Tanana on June 8, 1912. Shortly before her mother was due to give birth, she fell off the ladder leading up to her food cache, injuring herself seriously. Marian was born a "blue baby." Along the Yukon in those days such babies generally died soon after birth. At this time, Father Jetté was responsible for the villages and encampments along that stretch of the Yukon. Because he was knowledgeable also in medical matters, the baby was entrusted to his care. With a U.S. Army soldier he discussed the possibilities of saving the baby's life. "If we can get her to cry," the soldier told Father, "she will live." He told Father to get a spoon, while he would get some whiskey. Marian was given her first "shot," cried— and lived into ripe old age. In his log cabin, Father Jetté kept her warm in the oven of his woodstove.

It is a story Marian loved to recall and tell, with a touch of humor, and in a spirit of gratitude. Marian died on March 2, 2004.

For part of 1924, Father Francis M. **Monroe**, S.J., was stationed in Tanana. During the years 1925–28, it was visited at irregular intervals out of Nulato or **Fairbanks**, and, from 1928–30, only out of Nulato. Father Joseph F. **McElmeel**, S.J., resided in Tanana from 1930–31. For the next three years, no one tended it. It was visited by Father McElmeel out of Nulato from 1934–45, except for the year 1941–42. From 1945–47, he traveled there periodically from **Galena**.

Tanana was cared for by Father James C. **Spils**, S.J., out of Galena during the year 1947–48, then out of Nulato from 1948–52, then again out of Galena during the year 1952–53. Father James W. **Plamondon**, S.J., cared for Tanana out of Nulato, 1953–54, and out of Galena from 1954–62. For a year, 1962–63, Father René **Astruc**, S.J., made trips there out of Galena. For several years, there were no priests specifically assigned to look after the Tanana flock.

In 1966, Father Charles A. **Saalfeld**, S.J., took up residence in Tanana and remained until 1973. While there, he took down the old church and priest's house. In 1967, he saw the new three-sided log church with attached priest's quarters and full basement go up.

During the year 1973–74, Father Bernard F. **McMeel**, S.J., visited Tanana out of Galena. Father Michael J. Morahan, an Irish Province Jesuit, resided in Tanana during the year 1974–75, and Father Ronald K. **Dunfey** did likewise during the years 1976–78. Father Steven C. Moore visited it out of Fairbanks during 1978, and Father Charles E. Brown, likewise out of Fairbanks, from 1978–80. In 1981, Tanana was visited by Father Charles A. **Bartles**, S.J., out of Nulato, and the following year by Father J. Albert **Levitre** out of Fairbanks.

From 1983–87, Father Richard L. **McCaffrey**, S.J., tended the Tanana flock out of Fairbanks faithfully more or less every other week. On his visits, he spent long hours doing also extensive remodeling of the old house behind the church to make it more habitable for the two **Ursuline** Sisters residing in Tanana at the time, Sisters Maria Clarys and Monique Vaernewyck.

The two Sisters were in Tanana from 1983–1996. During their 13 years there, they did much more than merely engage in "a ministry of presence." They served at various times as pastoral and parish Administrators. They held Religion classes for people of all ages. They trained people to become readers and Eucharistic ministers, and to lead Communion Services. Given their artistic talents, they organized sewing and crafts clubs. All the while, they maintained the buildings and grounds, and raised money to help cover parish expenses.

From 1987–92, Father Louis L. **Renner**, S.J., flew to Tanana every other week out of Fairbanks. In 1992, Father **Joseph E. Laudwein**, S.J., began to visit it on a monthly basis, also out of Fairbanks. As of the year 2004, he was still doing so.

Brother Kirby **Boone**, C.F.X., took up station in Tanana in 1996, to serve there as a pastoral minister and Pastoral Administrator, services he was still rendering as of the year 2004.

Sisters of **Providence** stationed in Fairbanks taught catechism courses in Tanana during the summers of 1963–72.

156

St. Aloysius Church and residence in Tanana as it appeared ca. 1920.
JOPA-510.42.

TELLER

Teller, named for the U.S. Senator Henry Moore Teller, is located on a sand spit between Port Clarence and Grantley Harbor, 55 miles southeast of Cape Prince of Wales, on the Seward Peninsula. It is 74 miles by road—50 miles by air—northwest of **Nome**. The Teller site was a traditional Inupiat Eskimo fishing camp, called Nook, before it boomed into existence as a white man's town at the turn of the 19th to the 20th century. The first permanent settlement at Teller was established around 1900, after the Bluestone Placers were discovered 15 miles to the south. During the "boom" years, it became a major regional trading center, attracting Natives from **Little Diomede** Island, **King Island**, **Marys Igloo**, and Wales. The Teller post office was established in 1900, when Teller had an estimated population of 5,000. By 1910, that number had dropped to 125, and by 1930, to only 76. Thereafter, it began to climb again, to 160 in 1950, 220 in 1970,

to 258 in 1979, to 268 in the year 2000. The 1918 influenza epidemic took many lives in the Teller area. International history was made at Teller on May 13, 1926, when the Italian dirigible, *Norge*, on a flight from Norway across the North Pole to Nome, terminated its flight at Teller because of adverse weather conditions.

Teller was first visited by a Catholic priest in 1902, when Father Rogatien **Camille**, S.J., went there out of Nome. For most of its history, the Teller mission has been served out of Nome. Some years, however, it was served out of Marys Igloo, **Pilgrim Hot Springs**, and Little Diomede. Priests have resided at Teller, but for only short times: Father Robert F. Dunn, in 1965; Father Andrew Eördögh, S.J., in 1966; Father Jules M. **Convert**, S.J., 1968–69; Father James E. **Falsey**, 1994–95.

In 1960, Father Lawrence A. **Nevue**, S.J., bought a building at Teller, which two years later began to serve as the church. The old church building then

The Teller Mission when still dedicated to St. Emma.
JOPA-26.01.

St. Ann's Mission, Teller. *MK.*

St. Michael's College in Winooski, Vermont, near Stowe. He graduated in 1965 with a B.A. degree in history. Having been in the Air Force Reserved Officers Training Corps, he was commissioned a second lieutenant, with an entry date of spring 1966 to Air Force active duty.

Hired because of his ten years of sailing experience at Boy Scout camp, Dick was a crew member on a passenger schooner along the coast of Maine during the summer of 1965. In the fall, he worked in Boston, but returned home before Christmas to help his mother get to treatment for breast cancer. She died in May 1967 at the age of 54.

In the military, Dick saw service as an administrative officer with the Strategic Air Command. Assignments were to Walker AFB, Roswell, New Mexico, 1966–67; to Malmstrom AFB, Great Falls, Montana, 1967–68; and to Eielson AFB, **Fairbanks**, **Alaska**, 1969–70. His initial hope had been to be an Air Force pilot. However, failing a critical eye test, that hope was not to be realized.

Dick first came to Alaska by driving up the Alaska Highway from Montana to Fairbanks in January 1969 in minus 50-degree temperatures and ice fog. In spite of its severe winter weather, or maybe because of it, he immediately fell in love with Alaska. In January 1970, knowing that he was soon to complete his four years of active duty, "but," in his own words, "not feeling brave enough to spend 50 more winters in the Far North," he met with **Joseph T. Ryan**, Archbishop of **Anchorage** at the time, to explore the possibilities of his studying to be a priest for the Anchorage archdiocese. After a 20-minute interview with the archbishop, Dick found himself officially a seminarian, scheduled to go, in September 1970, to Holy Trinity Seminary in Dallas, Texas—where Fred T. **Bugarin** was already a seminarian for Anchorage—to begin studies for the priesthood.

From February through April 1970, Dick skied and toured all over Europe, then returned to Fairbanks to do river trips in his kayak with friends. When he had first driven north, as he was going

became "St. Ann's Catholic Church Youth Center." At one time, the Teller mission was known as "St. Emma's." It is now under the title of St. Ann.

TERO, Father Richard D.

Richard D. "Dick" Tero, the third of four sons, was born on February 2, 1943, in Winchendon, Massachusetts, to Leo and Ida Hildreth Tero. Leo's grandfather was born in Canada. Ida's mother, Anne Dougherty, came from Ireland at age 18. Her father was a Yankee. Dick lived half a mile from these grandparents. The faith of his Irish grandmother was a deep source of inspiration to him. Dick's younger brother was mentally handicapped. For six years he was devotedly cared for by Sisters. This, too, was a source of inspiration to Dick and had a big influence on his subsequent vocation to the priesthood.

For his elementary education, Dick attended public schools in Winchendon; for his secondary education, he commuted 18 miles to attend Notre Dame High School—run by the Brothers of the Sacred Heart—in Fitchburg, Massachusetts. Wanting to be on a college ski team, he later enrolled in

(*right*) Father Richard D. Tero. *Photo by Deacon Walter Corrigan, Jr.*

(*far right*) By the bank of the Copper River, on June 10, 1986, Father Richard D. Tero celebrates Mass for members of his rafting party. *LR.*

through the Dawson Creek checkpoint, the elderly inspector checking him to make sure he had adequate winter survival gear, noticed the canoe strapped to the top of his car. He said to Air Force Captain Tero, "Sonny, it will be a while before you can use that canoe up here. The water's a little stiff right now." Canoeing, kayaking, rafting, and sailing were sports that Dick had picked up at scout camp. He was to develop them into major Alaskan adventures.

While in the seminary, Dick spent the summers of 1971–76 serving as director of St. Theresa's Camp at **Soldotna** for the Archdiocese of Anchorage. This was a six-week camp for about 80 youngsters aged 8 to 14.

Dick was ordained a priest on June 4, 1974, in Holy Family Cathedral, Anchorage, by Archbishop Ryan. His first assignment as a priest was that of assistant to Msgr. John A. **Lunney** at Our Lady of Guadalupe parish in the Spenard area of Anchorage. In 1978, Father Tero became pastor of St. Mary's parish in **Kodiak**, which he found to have "a wonderful 100-pupil school, grades 1–8, run by the **Grey Nuns** of the Sacred Heart." During his years in Kodiak, he began planning for a new church. To build up the needed funds, he arranged for the development of some parish lands for a subdivision. He was reassigned before church construction began.

In 1984, Father Tero was named pastor of St.

Patrick's parish, in Muldoon, Anchorage. This was a large city parish of about 800 families, many of them military. Again he was asked to plan for a new church, involving him in fund-raising and building committee meetings. The new St. Patrick's Church was built by his successor, Father Steven C. Moore, in 1996.

After eight years at St. Patrick's, Father Tero, in 1992, was appointed pastor of Our Lady of Perpetual Help parish in Soldotna. There he immediately saw an even more urgent need for a new church. Built in 1962, the old church had poor heat, no bathrooms, and a front door opening directly out to the elements. After pledge drives and more building committee meetings, the Soldotna Catholic community had its new church, dedicated in 1995, and Father Tero was able to enjoy it, for seven years, "with wonderful parishioners."

In September 2002, Father Tero became pastor of Sacred Heart parish in **Seward**, and visiting priest to its dependent station, **Cooper Landing**. At Spring Creek, Alaska's maximum security prison, he began to celebrate Mass every Saturday morning for its inmates and staff. In Seward, too, as he had been on his previous assignments, he was faithful to his ministry to shut-ins, finding his personal spirituality as a priest nourished considerably by praying weekly with the home-bound and bringing them the Sacraments.

It should be mentioned that, at the request of Archbishop Ryan, who had himself been a military chaplain (Navy) during World War II, Father Tero served for many years also as a Reserve Chaplain assigned to Elemendorf AFB, Anchorage. By the time he retired, in 1993, counting his active duty years, he had served in the military for a total of 22 years. His special ministry at Elmendorf was helping the chaplains and, especially, visiting hospital patients and airmen at their job sites, to encourage them in the Faith. In the 1980s, when the Marriage Encounter movement was strong, Father Tero spent many weekends as a team priest heartening couples to live out the Sacrament of Matrimony.

One of Father Tero's consistent joys was sharing his hiking, skiing, and boating interests and skills with his parishioners and others. He led youth groups on canoe trips and hikes on the Kenai Peninsula, and took them on ski tours to the Alyeska ski resort. Hundreds of parishioners and friends, after Sunday Mass, floated the Matanuska and Kenai Rivers with him, their pastor, to enjoy the Alaskan beauties of God's creation.

Father Tero skied many of Alaska's slopes, hiked many of its trails, floated many of its major rivers. Among these latter, to mention but some of them: the Alsek, Yukon, Talkeetna, Charlie, Mulchatna, and the Canning north of the Brooks Range near Prudhoe Bay. Accompanied by Jesuit Fathers **Francis E. Mueller** and Louis L. **Renner**, and friends, he floated the Copper River. Wanting also to walk in the footsteps of the first Jesuit missionaries to enter Alaska, they hiked the historic Chilkoot Trail. Father Tero's Mass kit, carried on his back, was standard equipment on his wilderness outings. On both occasions, Mass was offered. In July 1979, he offered Mass at the site where the first Mass in Alaska had been celebrated 200 years earlier: at Port Santa Cruz, Suemez Island, Bucareli Bay near **Craig**. In 1986, on the banks of the Yukon, he offered Mass at the site where Archbishop Charles J. **Seghers** had been shot to death a hundred years earlier. In Father Tero, the outdoorsman, the historian, and the priest were still, as of the year 2004, harmoniously blended.

15, 126

TIULANA, Mr. Paul

He was born on a mountain rising abruptly out of the Bering Sea 35 miles off the coast of northwestern **Alaska**. As a youth and young man, he hunted seals, walrus, and polar bears on "the ice that never sleeps." He was described as "one of the great chiefs of traditional Eskimo people, who looks at the big picture." He saw service in the U.S. Army during World War II. He danced the Eskimo dance from coast to coast. He spent the last years of his bicultural life in Alaska's largest city, dying there a highly respected Eskimo elder.

Inupiat Eskimo Paul Tiulana was born in the village of Ukivok on **King Island**—a small, steep, rocky outcropping located in the Bering Sea some 90 miles northwest of **Nome**—on June 20, 1921. Tiulana was his Eskimo name; Paul his baptismal name. Throughout his life, he was generally known as Paul. His parents were Ugitkuna and Mitaglaq. As a young boy he was taught to follow all the rules of the village, and to be respectful to others, especially to elders.

When Paul was nine years old, he lost his father. He had gone out hunting on the ice and never came back. His paternal uncle, **Oalaranna**, now became his chief guardian and mentor, teaching him how to hunt and how to survive out on the moving pack ice. Often his uncle kept him walking all day long. During those walks Paul was told to hold his breath for as long as he was able. This was meant to build up his stamina and lung power for the long-distance running, the fast action often demanded of the King Island hunter pursuing or retrieving his prey, or trying to get away from a wounded polar bear, or from deteriorating ice conditions brought about by a sudden change in the direction or velocity of the wind.

When Paul was about 16 years old, his uncle taught him how to maneuver in a kayak, a one-man skin-covered canoe. With that skill acquired, Paul became a full-fledged hunter, able to keep up with the older men, and properly to play his role in a traditional subsistence life-style. The life of the King Island hunter was, by all accounts, a physically and mentally very demanding one of hard work, fraught with many life-threatening dangers. Of that life, Paul said: "It was really hard work, but, magical-

Mr. Paul Tiulana.
JOPA-BH-548.5471.7.18.

ly, I did not feel it. I went out hunting all day long, and I was really tired, when I came in. When I slept, I got all rested up. I did not have feelings of tiredness. When I woke up, I was ready to go out again, whenever the weather was good."

As Paul grew up, he learned, by experience and from his uncle and others, much about the bird and marine life that abounded on and around the island. He was taught how to maintain his hunting equipment: snowshoes, kayak, harpoons, and rifles. His uncle showed him how to "read" the clouds, the winds, and the waves for signs of changing weather and water conditions. From his uncle, Paul learned also what to do, when to do it, and what not to do.

Paul was a very devout, life-long practicing Catholic. He attached great importance to the presence of the statue of Christ the King that had been placed on top of the island in 1937 by Father Bernard R. **Hubbard**, S.J. Regarding the statue, Paul told Father Louis L. **Renner**, S.J., "After the statue was put in place, the powerful demons, that often plagued the King Island men, were never heard again." As a theologian, Paul knew how to keep it simple: "In the way of religion, I would compare King Island beliefs with the religion of the Old Testament." That said it all—and, at the same time, just about nothing. He added, "Christianity brought security to us."

During World War II, in September 1942, Paul was drafted into the Army. In Nome, only one month

later, "there was an accident," he recounted, "that broke my leg. I was helping to unload a transport ship, moving some lumber. The sling slipped out from under some timbers, and the lumber fell on me." He was placed in the Nome hospital, but the doctors did not set the fracture properly, with the result that infection set in. Paul was transferred to Barnes General Hospital in Vancouver, Washington. By that time gangrene had set in. The leg had to be amputated. He was then sent down to Bushnell General Hospital in Brigham City, Utah, to be fitted with a wooden leg. He was there about five months. "I felt that I wanted to die," he recalled some 35 years later. "All my preparation to be a good hunter was lost. I could not go out hunting on the moving ice any more. The Bering Sea ice moves all the time. It is a very dangerous place to be even with two legs."

Paul was then discharged from the Army and sent back home. Twenty-one years old now, in the prime of a hunter's life, he was "just completely disappointed, frustrated and depressed." He felt he had lost everything. His uncle had prepared him to be a polar bear hunter. That was partly what all the running of earlier years was all about, to build his muscles and lungs to run after, or from, polar bears. Polar bear hunting seemed now wholly out of the question for Paul.

A polar bear hunter needed, among other qualifications, two good legs. Paul now had but one good leg. But, he decided he would hunt anyway! "What else could I do?" he asked himself. So, he made himself a pair of sturdy crutches to enable him to walk on the ice; and, one day, when the wind was calm and the current slow, he ventured out on the shorefast ice, and succeeded in getting himself a seal. This picked up his spirits greatly, and emboldened him to continue hunting also on the moving ice. However, one day, while he was on the moving ice, landing a seal at its breathing hole, the ice cracked, opening a 3-foot wide lead between him and his rifle and hunting bag. Handicapped, as he was, he was unable to jump the lead, and so lost both his rifle and hunting bag. Finally, he said to himself, "If I go out hunting on crutches, one day I will not come back. It is too dangerous." He then concluded that he could hunt more safely from a skinboat. Accordingly, with the help of his nephew and brother, he built himself a little skinboat. He had tried a kayak, but, because his good leg was heavier than his wooden one, he could not easily balance himself in it.

In his 16-foot skinboat, Paul became once more a successful hunter, landing various species of seals and walrus—and, one day, even that ultimate trophy, a polar bear. When his mother learned of his success, she cried for joy. By this time, Paul was the manager of the King Island village store; but, and of greater importance to him, he was again what he had all his life prepared to be, a hunter. "I proved myself to be a hunter," he was proud to say, "not a handicapped person, but a hunter."

In Christ the King Church on King Island, on November 25, 1945, Paul Tiulana married Clara Yammana. Eventually five boys and two girls were born to the couple. The family continued to live on King Island until 1956, when they moved to Nome. They moved, in part, because of health problems in the family. Nome had a hospital. In Nome, Paul did some ivory carving and janitorial work, along with offshore hunting, to support his family. The family lived in Nome for 12 years.

In 1967, Paul went to **Anchorage** to represent the northwestern part of Alaska at an Alaska Legal Services meeting. Soon thereafter, he was hired by the Alaska Centennial people to work in tourism. He and Clara decided they could make a living in Anchorage, and the family moved there permanently. They continued, however, to visit Nome and King Island during summers.

After the Centennial events were over, Paul worked for the Alaska Native Welcome Center, and then for the State of Alaska, as an employee interviewer. He next had a job on the Trans-Alaska Pipeline as a counselor at a pump station. He also worked with pipeline superintendents on the Native hire issue, acting as a middleman between supervisors and foremen and Native workers. Being by now solidly bicultural and fluently bilingual, he could competently fill the role of spokesperson, of go-between, of cultural broker, smoothing communications between traditional Native societies and western society. After his jobs on the pipeline, and one as the Seward Skill Center recreation director, he was employed for nearly ten years by the

Cook Inlet Native Association as a cultural coordinator. As such, he helped Alaska Native people adjust to urban life.

One of Paul's major concerns throughout his own urban life was that "we should retain our culture." He tried to communicate this concern for cultural revitalization to all Alaskan Natives, but especially to fellow King Islanders. By this time, a permanent return to King Island was for him and his family no longer a realistic possibility. His own children were by now too urbanized even to consider seriously a return to the traditional King Island subsistence way of life.

As a promoter of Native culture, Paul did his part, and more. He continued to carve ivory, to tell and retell traditional stories, and explain Native ways. In 1980, he built an *umiaq*, a large skinboat, at the Museum of History and Art, Anchorage. But, it was by promoting Eskimo dancing that he made his major contribution to the preservation of Native culture. He made Eskimo drums and masks, taught and organized Eskimo dancing. He himself was a highly accomplished drummer and dancer. Under his direction, the King Island Dancers achieved international fame. In 1982, in Nome, he revived the famous "Wolf Dance." In 1991, it was presented in Anchorage and taped for public television's "Great Performances."

For his contribution to the preservation of Native culture, Paul received well-deserved recognition and awards. In 1983, he was named "Man of the Year" by the Alaska Federation of Natives. The following year, in Washington, D.C., he received the National Heritage Fellowship Award "for being one of our country's living national treasures, carrying on, and preserving, this country's cultural heritage." In 1985, the American Festival of Arts sent Paul and his wife, Clara, to London, England, to demonstrate ethnic arts at the Museum of Mankind. Prince Philip met Paul and Clara at the Museum and, on behalf of Queen Elizabeth, accepted the gifts the Native people of Alaska offered her. In 1988, Paul and the King Island Dancers traveled to Washington, D.C., as honored guest-artists for the opening of the Smithsonian Institution's "Crossroads of Continents" exhibition. Until his death, at the age of 73, Paul continued to work hard to preserve

Native cultural values. He died of cancer, on June 17, 1994, at Anchorage's Native Medical Center, and lies buried in the Catholic plot of Anchorage's Angelus Memorial Park Cemetery next to his wife, Clara.

As stated earlier, Paul was a devout Catholic throughout his life. In his case, his traditional Native culture and Catholicism were so harmoniously interwoven that they formed but one and the same culture. To underscore this by but one example: Before the 1991 performance of the "Wolf Dance," he prayed over the dancers and sprinkled them with holy water to protect them from the dangers associated with the dance.

Most King Islanders have been known for their fidelity to the Catholic Faith. Whether living in Nome, or in **Fairbanks**, or in Anchorage, they—the King Islanders, with a church on their ancestral island dedicated to Christ the King, and a statue of Christ the King atop their island—have gathered annually on the Feast of Christ the King for a special Mass. In Anchorage, it was Paul Tiulana, their leader in things both secular and sacred, who saw to it that the local King Islanders gathered for those special Masses honoring Christ their King.

179

TOK

Tok—"The Gateway to **Alaska!**"—located at the junction of the Alaska and Glenn Highways, takes its name from the nearby stream. The site began to develop in the 1940s with the building of those two highways. The 1960 Census counted only 129 persons for the Tok community. By the year 2000, it had a population of 1,393.

The official Catholic presence in the Tok area dates from September 1949, when Father John R. **Buchanan**, S.J., arrived there to establish a mission. The first Masses offered in Tok were celebrated in the old Tok Road Commission building. In July 1950, Father Buchanan began to build the 20 x 40' log chapel, the original part of today's Holy Rosary Church. The first Mass celebrated in that new log chapel was the Midnight Christmas Mass of 1950. The first baptism in that new chapel, that of an eight-year-old girl, took place on February 14, 1951. In 1954, Father Buchanan left Tok to oversee the construction of **Copper Valley School** near Copper Center.

Since 1954, a considerable variety of priests have served the Tok Catholic community. At first it was Jesuits, who commuted to Tok, mostly from Copper Valley School. During the year 1961–62, Father Joseph L. Asturias, O.P., visited it out of **Delta**

Holy Rosary Church, Tok.
Photo by Madeleine Betz.

Junction, as did Father Patrick S. Duffy the following year. When in Tok, visiting priests either "camped out" in the back of the chapel, or stayed with area families. In 1963, a small sleeping space, with a coal stove, but no water, was added to the chapel. The next year, while Father Georges E. Bourque, O.P., was tending the Tok flock, plumbing was installed. Father Bourque also built the wooden altar that was still in use as of the year 2004. When Father Anderson E. **Bakewell**, S.J, first arrived on the Tok scene in 1967, he found the log church "inadequate in size, heating and facilities." By 1971, he could write, "It now has a log addition as a residence for the priest, an adequate heating system, and proper facilities."

In 1977, David E. Schutt and his wife, Joyce, came to Tok to teach in the local school. They soon became involved in parish life. In 1986, David was ordained to the permanent diaconate. As a deacon, he served as part-time Pastoral Administrator of Holy Rosary parish and conducted Communion services. In 1991, he oversaw the construction of another 20 × 40' log addition to the chapel. This now serves as the church proper.

In September 1995, Sister Linda Hogan, C.S.J., came to Tok as full-time Pastoral Administrator. She set things in motion for providing better living conditions at Tok. Projected was another addition to the church, which was to include a residence with a full basement. The foundation was dug in August 1998. Sister Linda left Tok that year. In August of that same year, Sister Frances McCarron, I.B.V.M., came to Tok as Pastoral Administrator. On September 1, 1999, she was able to move into the new parish residence. On October 17, 1999, Holy Rosary parish celebrated its golden jubilee in spacious, partially new, parish facilities.

Among the priests who have served Tok's Catholic community are Jesuit Fathers: Bakewell, out of Delta Junction, 1967–76; **Joseph L. Hebert**, in residence, 1976–79; Lawrence A. **Nevue**, also in residence, 1979–81, then out of Delta Junction, 1981–82. Father Nevue was the last priest to make Tok his headquarters. His successors have all served Tok out of Delta Junction. They have been: William T. **Burke**, S.J., 1982–87; **Joseph E. Laudwein**, S.J., 1987–94; Don M. **Balquin**, 1994–98. During the years 1999 to 2002, the Tok parish was visited at

irregular intervals out of Fairbanks by Fathers William E. **Cardy**, O.F.M.; Timothy L. **Sander**, O.S.B.; and J. Albert **Levitre**. Father John B. **Martinek** became pastor of the Delta Junction and Tok parishes in the year 2002.

69

TOKSOOK BAY

The Central Yup'ik Eskimo village of Toksook Bay is located in the Yukon-Kuskokwim Delta, on Nelson Island, 6.5 miles southeast of **Tununak**. It was established in 1964, when a number of younger couples from **Nightmute**, some **Chefornak** transplants, and some Tununak and **Newtok** families moved to this new location. In 1990, Toksook Bay had a population of 420. By the year 2000, this had increased to 532.

Catholicism came to the Nightmute people during the early 1900s. Today virtually all the people of Toksook Bay are Catholic, belonging to the parish of St. Peter the Fisherman. The original church was built in 1966. A residence and classroom was built some time later to accommodate Marie Toscana, who ran a Montessori school in Toksook Bay for some time.

The first priest to celebrate Mass in Toksook Bay was Father James E. **Jacobson**, S.J., out of Chefornak, during the year 1964–65. Father Francis J. **Fallert**, S.J., was Toksook Bay's first resident pastor, and there for many years: 1965–75, 1986–87, and 1988–90. He was followed by Jesuit Fathers Daniel J. **Tainter**, 1975–77; Bernard F. **McMeel**, 1977–78; Richard L. **McCaffrey**, 1978–79; Richard D. **Case**, 1979–86; Henry G. **Hargreaves**, 1987–88, and 1994–98; Thomas G. **Provinsal**, 1990–91; Eugene P. **Delmore**, 1991–94; Paul M. **Cochran**, 1994–97; Mark A. **Hoelsken**, 1997–98; and David J. **Anderson**, beginning in 1998, and as of the year 2004.

Eskimo Deacons served, and, as of the year 2004, some were still serving their Toksook Bay parish: Bruno Chakuchin (deceased and buried at Toksook Bay), Nick Therchik, Joseph Asuluk, Gregory Charlie, and James Charlie. James Charlie was one of the first deacons to be appointed a pastoral administrator by Michael J. **Kaniecki**, S.J., Bishop of Fairbanks at the time.

Sister Pauline Igoe, O.P., was "a major influence" in the preparation of catechists at Toksook Bay from 1978–87.

In 1994, Maggie John began to serve as parish administrator. She soon began to prepare others in her region to be parish administrators.

167

TOMKIN, Father Joseph, S.J.

Joseph Tomkin was born in Galway, Wexford, Ireland, on October 3, 1871. He spent his boyhood years on a farm. After completing his elementary schooling at the age of 14, he entered the diocesan seminary in the town of Wexford. After five years of studies there, he was sent to study philosophy in Salamanca, Spain. During his two years in Spain, his teachers were Jesuits, and he felt himself drawn to enter the Society of Jesus. He also felt drawn to be a missionary. Back in Ireland, he applied and was accepted into the Jesuit Order as a candidate for the

Rocky Mountain Mission. On November 3, 1892, he entered the novitiate at DeSmet, Idaho. After completing his two-year noviceship, he was sent to St. Andrew's Mission, near Pendleton, Oregon, on a three-year assignment as a teacher and prefect of the boys. He then spent a year at St. Ignatius Mission, Montana, in philosophical studies. After that, he was at St. Andrew's for another year, before going on to theological studies in Chieri, near Turin, Italy. He was ordained a priest in the summer of 1904.

Before going on to make his tertianship at Poughkeepsie, New York, during the year 1910–11, Father Tomkin was stationed at Gonzaga College, Spokane, Washington, and at various Indian missions and parishes in the Northwest. After tertianship, and before he went to **Alaska**, this was again the case. Except for the seven years he spent as Rector–President of Seattle College, from 1914–21, he was moving from assignment to assignment almost every year. He got used to taking the many changes of status "in stride." It was said of Father Tomkin

Deacon Nick Therchik and wife Laura in front of
St. Peter the Fisherman Church, Toksook Bay. *BR-A10-02.*

Father Joseph Tomkin, S.J. *JOPA-854.04.*

that "he was loyal to his sense of duty," that "he did nothing by halves," that "he sought out and helped the underdog"—and that "he moved quickly."

Father Tomkin was pastor of Holy Name parish in **Ketchikan** during the year 1931–32. On September 17, 1932, he arrived at **Holy Cross Mission** to take over as Superior. From Holy Cross, he wrote two months later, on November 27th, "The Alaska natives are so very different from our redskins of the States: the spirit of work and of prayer seems congenial to them and they are very industrious and in earnest in the performance of both exercises." From 1933 to the time he left Holy Cross, he served also as a Consultor to the General Superior of the Alaska Mission.

Early in the summer of 1936, Father Tomkin began to experience serious health problems. The Sister Infirmarian at Holy Cross diagnosed heart and kidney problems. He spent most of the month of June resting, but no improvement came about. On July 24th, he left for **Fairbanks**. There, while sitting at his desk, he died on October 3, 1936, his 65th birthday. A heart attack was the immediate cause of his death. He had seemed in tolerably good health shortly before his unexpected death. He lies buried in the Clay Street Cemetery in downtown Fairbanks.

TOSI, Father Paschal, S.J.

Father Paschal Tosi was one of the first two Jesuit missionaries—the other being Father Aloy-sius J. **Robaut**—to set foot in **Alaska**. As the first General Superior of Jesuits in Alaska, and as Alaska's first Prefect Apostolic, he is rightly regarded as a true founder and organizer of the Church in northern Alaska.

Paschal Tosi was born April 25, 1837, in the parish of St. Vito, Diocese of Rimini, Italy. After completing studies in the seminary at Bertinoro, he was ordained a diocesan priest in 1861. During his seminary days, he came to know the Jesuits. On October 24, 1862, he entered the Jesuit novitiate in Monaco. In 1865, he arrived in the United States to serve on the Rocky Mountain Mission. For two decades he proved to be an able missionary to the Indian peoples of the American Northwest. He was blessed with a good facility for learning their languages—and yet, he never bothered to learn English well.

When, in 1886, Archbishop Charles John **Seghers** set out for northern Alaska in hopes of establishing permanent missions there, he had with him as traveling companions—in addition to a Catholic layman by the name of Frank Fuller, who was already recognized as being of unsound mind—Fathers Tosi and Robaut. The intention of their Superior, Father Joseph M. **Cataldo**, S.J., Superior of the Rocky Mountain Mission at the time, was that, while they were to go north with the archbishop primarily as his trail companions, they were also "to scout out the country," and then to report back to him their findings. The Jesuits had no intentions at the time of opening a new field of missionary activity in Alaska. However, subsequent events changed their thinking about the whole matter radically.

On September 7th, the Seghers party, by way of **Skagway** and the Chilkoot Pass, reached Harper's Place, a trading post at the confluence of the Yukon and Stewart Rivers. Here they were still in Canada, but, because of the lateness of the season for river travel, it seemed advisable for the four to camp for the winter. Archbishop Seghers, however, was determined to press on downriver, hoping yet to reach **Nulato** before the year was out. Father Tosi made every effort to dissuade him from doing so. After a lengthy discussion—at times rather heated, for both the archbishop and Father Tosi were strong, self-assertive types—it was decided that the two Fathers would spend the winter 1886–87 at Harper's Place, while Archbishop Seghers and Fuller would continue their journey. The understanding on the part of all was that the two priests would meet the archbishop again in the spring, at Nulato.

When the Yukon River ice broke up in the spring of 1887, Fathers Tosi and Robaut, unaware of what had happened to the archbishop in the meanwhile, took passage on Harper's steamer for the descent of the great river. On June 5th, at a point just west of old Fort Yukon, they learned that on November 28th, about 40 river miles above Nulato, a demented Fuller had shot the Archbishop. Father Tosi immediately saw himself to be responsible, at least for the time being, for ecclesiastical affairs in Alaska. That summer, he made a trip to the Pacific Northwest to consult with Father Cataldo, and to urge acceptance by the Jesuits of the Alaska Mission. After some lengthy deliberations and consultations, it was determined that Alaska should be accepted as part of the Rocky Mountain Mission, and that Father Tosi should be formally appointed as Superior of the Alaska Mission, and charged with its systematic development—all this, understandably, on condition that the Father General of the Jesuits in Rome approve. After he was duly apprised of matters in Alaska, Father General did approve, and gave this new Jesuit missionary undertaking in the Far North his blessing.

Back in Alaska, Father Tosi took up station at Nulato. There he built a log cabin church and spent the winter 1887–88. Of all the missions in northern Alaska, Nulato can rightly claim the primacy.

After that first year at Nulato, Father Tosi made **Holy Cross Mission** his headquarters for the remainder of his ten years in northern Alaska. As Superior of the Alaska Mission, he traveled extensively, more to scout out possible future mission sites than to evangelize. His trips—by boat in the summer, by dogteam in the winter—took him to the Kuskokwim River regions, to the Aleutian Islands, and to Southeastern Alaska. During most of the latter half of 1889, he was at **Tununak**, a Central Yup'ik Eskimo village on Nelson Island. He had accompanied Father Joseph M. **Tréca**, S.J., there and had helped him build a log cabin, which was used both as a church and a residence. He left Tununak on December 5th. In March 1891, and again in March 1892, he made trips to Tununak, to

Father Paschal Tosi, S.J.
JOPA-929.01.

visit the three Jesuits now stationed there. On his way to and from, he visited also the many villages scattered throughout the general area between Holy Cross and Tununak.

In the late summer of 1892, Father Tosi traveled to Rome. There Pope Leo XIII, in a private audience, was so moved by Father Tosi's account of the status of the Church in Alaska, that he granted more than what Father Tosi was prepared to ask for. In their native Italian, the Holy Father told him: *"Andate, fate voi da papa in quelle regioni!"* ("Go, and make yourself the Pope in those regions!") He also proposed that Father Tosi be consecrated a bishop. To this, Father Tosi is said to have responded: "Holy Father, in Alaska I travel with dogs. When a storm comes up, I make a hole in the snow and crawl in with the dogs, and live there until the storm blows over. Please don't bring down so low the purple of a bishop." In the spring of 1893, Father Tosi returned to Alaska. On July 17, 1894, the Holy See separated Alaska from the Diocese of Vancouver Island and made it a Prefecture Apostolic with Father Tosi as its first Prefect Apostolic.

During the months of February–April 1895, Father Tosi undertook an extensive trip to **Kotzebue** Sound. In the summers of 1895 and 1896, he traveled to the Pacific Northwest.

Father Paschal Tosi, though unimposing in size and suffering from heart trouble, possessed a strong constitution and immense energy and vitality, so much so that he tended to be impatient with those whose physical weakness prevented them from accomplishing what he expected of them. He was said to have ruled with "Draconian severity." And yet—contrary to what one might, therefore, expect of such a man—by 1897, though only 60 years old, he was physically worn out by his life's labors. In March of that year, while visiting **Akulurak**, he had a paralyzing stroke that left him speechless for several weeks. That same March, he was succeeded, both as General Superior of the Alaska Mission and as Prefect Apostolic, by Father John B. **René**, S.J. Father Tosi was offered the chance to retire to California for the sake of his health. He opted, instead, to go to **Juneau**. From **St. Michael**, on September 13, 1897, Father Tosi, accompanied by Father Tréca, sailed—somewhat reluctantly, for he had hoped to stay on in northern Alaska—for Juneau, where he hoped he would have but a brief stay to recover his health. As the ship, the *Bertha*, left the harbor, a salute of four guns was ordered as a manifestation of the universal esteem in which he was held.

While some of his fellow Jesuits saw in Father Tosi a rather stern, demanding Superior, the public in general held him in highest regard. The captain of the *St. Paul*, the ship on which Father Francis A. **Barnum**, S.J., first came to Alaska, let him know that he was an "ardent admirer of Father Tosi." The Sisters of St. **Ann** all but worshiped him. "As he stood before one," wrote one of them,

> he was small of stature, sun-burned, vested in poor garments; yet he always made an indescribable impression. Something of the simplicity and goodness, the energy and strength of soul of the man called out to the same noble qualities in the souls of others and drew forth their unqualified admiration and reverence. His whole personality radiated the tenderness of his charity. He was a model priest.

Father Wilfred P. Schoenberg, S.J., a noted historian, summarized: "I think it should be stated that Father Tosi, for all his faults, was a great man."

Fathers Tosi and Tréca reached Juneau on October 7th. There Father Tosi's health improved noticeably, at least to appearances. He expressed hopes of soon returning again to the Yukon. But, it was not meant to be. A kindly Providence decreed otherwise. He died early in the morning of January 14, 1898. When he did not appear in the church for Mass that morning, Father Tréca went to look in on him. He found him lying on the floor, dead of a heart

The mission steamer, *Tosi*, on the lower Yukon. *JOPA-555.02*.

attack. Death must have come to him with absolute suddenness, while he was getting dressed, for his face was perfectly calm, and there were no signs of a death agony struggle.

Though Father Tosi had been in Juneau but a short time, he was deeply mourned by the people. The next day, after a Requiem Mass, at which Father Peter C. **Bougis**, S.J., pastor of the Juneau parish at the time, gave an especially moving sermon, the body of Father Tosi was carried by the people—who insisted on doing so—by turns, to the cemetery for burial. Father Tosi was the first Catholic priest to die and be buried in Alaska.

16, 122, 176

Father Ross A. Tozzi.
Courtesy of Dr. Thomas A. Busch.

TOZZI, Father Ross A.

Ross Anthony Tozzi was born to Ezio, a sergeant in the U.S. Army at the time, and Domenica Tozzi on November 24, 1960, in Munich, Germany. As a boy, with his parents and three brothers, he traveled the world, living successively in Germany, Japan, North Carolina, New York, and Maryland. He was schooled in a variety of different institutions. In 1982, he graduated from Loyola College in Baltimore with a B.A. degree in accounting. After graduating with an M.B.A. from the Owen Graduate School of Management at Nashville's Vanderbilt University in 1984, he joined the U.S. Army. For five years, he served as a finance officer: at Burtonwood, England; at Fort Sill, Oklahoma; and at Fort Harrison, Indiana.

In 1989, Ross left the military. That same year, his life's journey took him north. He joined the **Jesuit Volunteer Corps**. As a member of the Corps, he was assigned to serve for a year on the staff that operated Radio **KNOM** in **Nome, Alaska**. However, not knowing, by his own admission, how to say "no," he wound up serving at KNOM for three years. During those three years, he also worked for the Nome-based Northwest Campus of the University of Alaska as its business manager.

Blessed with a generous, volunteering heart, Ross next volunteered his time and talents to the Franciscan Friars in charge of St. Anthony Indian Mission in Zuni, New Mexico. His offer was accepted, and he spent four years, from 1992–1996, in

Zuni. During those years, he took his summer "vacations" in Nome, there helping to close out KNOM's books and to audit its finances for the Diocese of **Fairbanks**.

In 1989, the year he became a member of the JVC, Ross received a letter from Father Brad R. Reynolds, Vocation Director for the Oregon Province of the Society of Jesus, asking him if he would consider a call to priesthood. "I was hot under the collar," recalled Father Ross in his first homily as a priest. "How dare he suggest such a thing!" As Ross's volunteer years followed one after the other, his mother, too, sensed that Ross, as did St. Paul, was "kicking against the goad." "Many times," Ross admitted, "my mother used to ask the same question: 'With all your years as a volunteer, do you ever think of becoming a priest?'" But, he kept turning a deaf ear.

God, however, kept calling out to Ross, in a number of different voices, kept calling him to the priesthood. In the summer of 1993, on one of Ross' many visits to Nome, Father Jack **de Verteuil**, associate pastor of St. Joseph's parish, Nome, at the time, said to him simply, "Ross, forget about marriage; become one of us." And two more times Ross again heard a call to priesthood. In Odenton, Maryland, at the Mass he was attending, the priest began his homily with the rhetorical question, "What is God calling you to do? Is he asking you to give up everything you have and work as a missionary?" At the Zuni mission, Ross yet again heard more or less the same question addressed to him. In the homily he gave at the Mass following the day of his ordination, he told how he answered the question and under what circumstances: "On a dark night, while two of us were driving along a treacherous back road in a blinding snowstorm, I nodded off to sleep, only to awaken suddenly with one word on my mind, 'Yes!'" As a tear trickled down his cheek, Ross understood that he was hearing the voice of God calling him to an unconditional "Yes!"

While Ross was spending Christmas 1995 in Nome, he asked Father John A. **Hinsvark**, Vocation Director for the Diocese of Fairbanks, about becoming a priest for the Diocese of Fairbanks. He was handed an application form, which he filled out and, in so doing, took the first concrete step along the road that was to lead to his being ordained a priest six years later.

In the fall of 1996, Ross began formal studies for the priesthood at Mount Angel Seminary at St. Benedict, Oregon. At the end of the academic year 1999–2000, he graduated with an M.A. degree in Sacred Theology. For his thesis topic he had chosen *The Spirituality of Therese of Lisieux*.

In Fairbanks, on Pentecost Sunday, June 11, 2000, Ross was ordained a transitional deacon by Michael J. **Kaniecki**, S.J., then Bishop of Fairbanks. As a deacon, he still had one more year of preparation before he was ready to be ordained a priest. He spent part of that year "in the field" getting practical, hands-on experience. In addition to two months in Nome, he spent some time assisting at the Downtown Chapel of St. Vincent de Paul parish in Portland, Oregon. Concerning his work there, Father Richard Berg, C.S.C., pastor, wrote: "As much as we will miss him, we're also very pleased to send Ross on to the priesthood. I think he will be an excellent, pastoral priest." A staff member of the Downtown Chapel, who witnessed Deacon Ross in action with the poor, spoke of his "grace, geniality and compassion."

For the date of his ordination to the priesthood, Deacon Ross chose July 14th, a date he considered "very special." In the homily he gave on the day after his ordination, he listed the reasons why he considered July 14th so special. The day marked the 30th anniversary of KNOM's going on the air. It was on July 14, 1947, that Father Bellarmine **Lafortune**,

S.J., missionary for over 40 years to the people of Nome and to the Eskimos of the surrounding area and of **King Island**, collapsed at the altar in the old St. Joseph's Church while offering Mass. And July 14th is also the feast day of Blessed Kateri Tekakwitha, Native American and patroness of ministries to Native Americans. So, it was on July 14, 2001, in the new St. Joseph's Church in Nome, that Ross A. Tozzi was ordained to the priesthood, for the Diocese of Fairbanks, by Francis T. **Hurley**, retired Archbishop of **Anchorage**. That ordination was an historic event. It was the first time ever that a man was ordained a Catholic priest in Nome.

Father Tozzi's first assignment as a priest was that of associate pastor to Father Patrick D. **Bergquist**, pastor of St. Raphael's parish, Fairbanks. As such, he served also occasionally as visiting priest to St. Patrick's parish in **Barrow**. In 2002, Father Tozzi was named pastor of St. Nicholas parish in **North Pole**. As of the year 2004, he was still serving in that capacity.

163

TRAPPER CREEK

The community known officially as Trapper Creek since the middle 1970s lies on the Susitna River some four miles west of **Talkeetna**. During the early days, the only way to get in or out of the settlement was by airplane, or by boat, when the Susitna was open. When the river was frozen over, people walked across it to get to Talkeetna or to make connections with the Alaska Railroad trains. There were no major roads in and out of the area. In the year 2000, the Trapper Creek population numbered 423.

Trapper Creek's roots go back to 1959, when a group of people called the "Michigan 59ers" came into the area in search of homesteading land. A few from Indiana also settled there. In the early 1960s, people from South Dakota, too, filed for property in the area.

When the word was out that a priest was coming to Talkeetna to offer Mass, the boat pilot would come and offer to transport anyone to and from Talkeetna at $5.00 per person for a one-way river-crossing. The first Mass in Talkeetna was held in the Federal Aviation Administration laundry room. There was only one church, a non-denominational church, in Talkeetna at the time.

In the late 1960s, priests from **Palmer** began to come to Trapper Creek to offer Mass in the homes of different people. One of the early homesteaders in the Trapper Creek area had a 14′-square log cabin on his property, which he made available for Mass. Father James A. O'Carroll, C.S.Sp., pastor of St. Michael's parish in Palmer at the time, was the first priest to offer Mass in it.

Father Stanley J. **Allie** became responsible for the Trapper Creek community as of March 8, 1970. Being a pilot, he commuted to it from Talkeetna by air. In 1973, he had a basement hall built at Trapper Creek to serve as a temporary church and meeting place. According to Mary Anna Jurasek, who homesteaded in the Trapper Creek area in July 1959, "The reason for a basement at that time was the fact that there was no place for adults or children to have functions. There was only a one-room schoolhouse. The basement hall was used for movies one Sunday and for bingo the next." Different organizations used the hall for dinners, pancake breakfasts, meetings, and elections. It was used also by the school for its functions. Monies raised were used to pay bills and set aside for the new church. With help from the Catholic Church Extension Society, this was built around the mid-1970s. In keeping with the wishes of benefactors, it was dedicated under the name of St. Philip Benizi.

In August 1974, Father **Gerard T. Ryan**, C.S.Sp., became pastor of St. Bernard's parish in Talkeetna. As such, he became responsible also for the St. Philip Benizi mission in Trapper Creek. Father Ryan was replaced by Father Thomas E. Power, who cared for Trapper Creek from 1979–82. Next, Father Leo C. **Desso** cared for it. He was followed by Father Urban M. **Bates**, O.P., who visited Trapper Creek regularly from 1984–90. Sister Louise Tibbetts, S.N.J.M., was Eucharistic Minister at St. Philip's from 1991–94. Beginning in the mid-1990s, and as of the year 2004, Trapper Creek was served by different priests visiting it about twice a month. Deacons held Eucharistic Service, when no priest was available.

15

TRAVERS, Father Patrick J.

Patrick Joseph "Pat" Travers was born on March 13, 1952, at Scott Air Force Base, Illinois, to William J. and Geraldine Lis Travers. His father, from Philadelphia, Pennsylvania, was a sergeant in the U.S. Air Force. Theirs was a blessed marriage, lasting 52 years. They were dedicated spouses and parents, who provided a happy, stable home for their six children, despite the challenges of military life. Pat was the oldest. His childhood and adolescent years were marked by the frequent moves characteristic of military families. He lived and went to school in Illinois, England, Mississippi, and North Carolina, attending three different high schools.

Pat was very strongly influenced during his childhood by the dedicated Air Force chaplains who helped his family through several trying periods and for whom he frequently served Mass. His first Holy Communion at South Ruislip AFB, England, on May 24, 1959, was, in his words, "an intense experience of the Lord's love for me, the memory of which was to sustain me through the many changes that life was to bring."

During the early 1960s, when his father was stationed in Biloxi, Mississippi, Pat attended the Catholic school operated by the parish of the Nativity of the Blessed Virgin Mary. The young Irish Sisters of Mercy and priests who staffed the school and parish offered him an example of joyful, tireless dedication that inspired him ever after.

In 1968, Pat's father retired from the Air Force, and the family settled in King of Prussia, Pennsylvania, a suburb of Philadelphia, where Pat graduated from high school in June 1969. He then studied at the School of Foreign Service at Georgetown University in Washington, D.C., earning the degree of Bachelor of Science in Foreign Service, *summa cum laude*, in May 1973. He next attended the Harvard Law School in Cambridge, Massachusetts, receiving from it the degree Doctor of Law in June 1976.

After passing the bar examination, Pat began work in Washington, D.C., as an attorney in the Office of General Counsel of the National Oceanic and Atmospheric Administration (NOAA), an agency of the U.S. Department of Commerce. In August 1979, having been appointed NOAA's Regional

Counsel for **Alaska**, he moved to **Juneau**, where he spent the next seven years. His responsibilities were focused on the protection and conservation of marine and coastal resources, especially the establishment of the new Federal regulatory system for marine fisheries in the recently-declared fishery conservation zone extending 200 miles off the coast of Alaska and the rest of the United States, and containing the vast stocks of fish so critical to the Alaskan economy.

While working with NOAA in Alaska, Pat became more and more active in the Cathedral of the Nativity of the Blessed Virgin Mary parish in Juneau. He was inspired especially by the ministry of Michael H. **Kenny**, Bishop of Juneau. He was impressed also by the example set by the young members of the **Jesuit Volunteer Corps**, with some of whom he developed strong friendships. At the suggestion of Father James D. **Cronin**, then Rector of the Cathedral, he began to explore the possibility of his being called to the priesthood. He became a lector and Eucharistic Minister in the Cathedral parish. However, despite much prayer and discernment, a clear sense of being called to take a new course in life seemed to elude him.

In the fall of 1986, Pat accepted a transfer with the NOAA back to Washington, D.C., in the hope that the change might stimulate his discernment process. The following spring, in April 1987, he decided that this would not happen as long as he retained his responsibilities as an assistant General Counsel of NOAA. After ten and a half years of rewarding service with it, he resigned.

Shortly after leaving NOAA, Pat visited a new priory being established in Albuquerque, New Mexico, by members of the Norbertine (Premonstratensian) Order. This small group of priests, with its strong community life and vibrant ministry, attracted Pat greatly. While continuing to discern his calling in life, he went to work as a full-time volunteer for the campaign for Michael Dukakis, a Democratic candidate for the presidency in 1988. He performed a number of tasks in the campaign's Washington office. "The moment of truth," to quote him,

came suddenly, in April 1988, when it became clear that Dukakis would win the Democratic nomination for President, and I had to decide whether or not to commit myself to the election campaign itself, which, at that point, looked very promising for the Democrats. After a week of intense prayer, I knew that the Lord was inviting me to leave the campaign and my former way of life behind and to join the Norbertines in New Mexico.

After completing his one-year noviceship in Albuquerque, "a year filled with prayer and spiritual growth," Pat made profession of simple vows in August 1989. He was then sent to study theology at the Pontifical Gregorian University in Rome, where he lived at the Norbertine Generalate. Returning to school in his late 30s, studying in a foreign language, and living in a highly diverse and structured community presented him with many challenges. Nevertheless, he found study and life in Rome to be "a rewarding experience." Coming from a military family, he saw logic in joining the Chaplain Candidate Program of the U.S. Air Force, and, as a participant in the program, ministered during his vacations at bases in Italy, Germany, the Netherlands, and Turkey.

As time went on, both Pat and the Albuquerque Norbertines saw that he was called to the priesthood, but not to the particular form of community life followed by them. With their help and support, he contacted Bishop Kenny about the possibility of his being ordained a priest for the Diocese of Juneau.

In June 1992, after Pat had earned the degree Bachelor of Sacred Theology at the Gregorian, he returned to Juneau for the first time in six years. At the end of the summer, after his temporary vows with the Norbertines had expired, Bishop Kenny ordained him to the diaconate in the Juneau Cathedral on September 8, 1992. At Bishop Kenny's request, he then returned to the Gregorian to get a licentiate degree in Canon Law. On July 7, 1993, in the Juneau Cathedral, Pat was ordained a priest by Bishop Kenny. This was the first ordination to the priesthood in the Cathedral since that of G. Edgar **Gallant** on March 30, 1918. With his law degree earned, Father Travers returned to Southeastern Alaska permanently in September 1994.

In Juneau, Father Travers served as Judicial Vicar of the Diocese of Juneau, overseeing the Diocesan Tribunal and providing the bishop with advice concerning canon law matters. In December 1996, he was also named Chancellor of the diocese. In the spring of 2003, Michael W. **Warfel**, then Bishop of Juneau, appointed him to the office of Vicar General of the diocese. At the same time, Father Travers served also as Adjutant Judicial Vicar of the Diocese of **Fairbanks**, overseeing the Tribunal of that diocese.

It was, however, pastoral ministry that drew Father Travers to the priesthood in the first place, and in which he found his greatest satisfaction. During the year 1994–95, he administered St. Paul's parish in Juneau, and traveled to **Hoonah** and Gustavus. At the same time, he pioneered a ministry in Spanish to Juneau's increasing number of Hispanic Americans.

Throughout the first decade of his priesthood, Father Travers served as a chaplain in the U.S. Air Force Reserve. From 1994 until the year 2003, he was attached to the chapel staff at Elmendorf AFB, **Anchorage**. In the fall of 2003, he transferred to the reserve unit at McChord AFB near Tacoma, Washington.

From 1997–99, Father Travers was pastor of St. Catherine of Siena parish in **Petersburg**. Beginning in September 1999, and as of the year 2004, he was pastor of Holy Name parish in **Ketchikan**. There he took special satisfaction in working with the children of Holy Name School, the only Catholic school in the Juneau diocese. He found that the "wonderful church and school staff supported and inspired" him in many ways.

As of July 2004, as a chaplain on active duty, with the rank of Captain, Father Travers was serving in the 506th Air Expeditionary Group at Kirkuk Air Base, in Iraq.

TRÉCA, Father Joseph M., S.J.

He spent 36 years in **Alaska**, most of them among the Central Yup'ik Eskimos of western Alaska. He has ever since been recognized as "The Apostle of the Tundra." One historian described him as "a mystic, musician, and hermit by nature." His obituarist hailed him as "one of the most heroic missionary figures of our Northlands." It is said that no one ever saw him angry. When he died, it was said of him that he "died as the saints die." Within two years after his death, a newly built mission boat was named for him. He has gone down in Alaskan

Father Joseph M. Tréca, S.J. *JOPA-830.02.*

Jesuit history as one belonging to the "era of the giants."

Joseph M. Tréca, the second of three children, was born into a tight-knit, bourgeois family in Douai, France, on March 6, 1854. Both his parents were remarkable for their piety and deep love of the Faith. They entrusted Joseph's early training to the care of a holy priest, under whose guidance he progressed rapidly both in virtue and learning.

When, at the age of twelve, Joseph made his first Holy Communion, he received a "special favor." What that special favor was he himself, many years later, told a fellow missionary in Alaska, with the request that he not make it known during Joseph's lifetime. The priest distributing Holy Communion, while still a short distance from little Joseph, accidentally dropped one of the hosts on the sanctuary carpet. Immediately the boy fixed his eyes on the fallen host. To his great surprise, the spot where the host was lying was flooded with light, and from the midst of it the figure of the Infant Jesus appeared, smiling at him, filling his soul with happiness.

When Joseph was about 14 years old, he began attending the Jesuit La Providence College in Amiens. By the time he was nineteen, he had earned his B.A. degree. He now applied for admission into the Society of Jesus, and was accepted. On November 2, 1873, he entered the Jesuit novitiate at St. Acheul, Amiens. After completing his noviceship, he stayed on for two more years to study the classics and humanities. He next spent three years teaching at La Providence College. He then went on to St. Helier, on the British Isle of Jersey, for three years of philosophical studies. After his second year, however, because of health problems, he needed to take a year of rest. After this, he was back at St. Helier to finish philosophy and to make his theological studies. It was during the time of these latter studies that he first, upon reading mission-related material and hearing lectures about missionary life, felt himself attracted to overseas missions. He volunteered for the Rocky Mountain Mission and was accepted. As a newly ordained priest, he arrived in New York in 1885. He spent the year 1885–86 making his tertianship at Santa Clara, California. He was then assigned to DeSmet Mission in Idaho for three years.

On June 14, 1889, Father Tréca sailed from San Francisco on the *Bertha* for Alaska. He landed at **St. Michael** on July 6th. On August 20th, accompanied by Father Paschal **Tosi**, S.J., he arrived at **Tununak**, a Central Yup'ik Eskimo village near Cape Vancouver on Nelson Island, where he founded the first Catholic mission among the Alaskan Eskimos. During September, he and Father Tosi, using locally gathered drift-logs, constructed a small cabin, which served both as church and residence. To make windows for the cabin, Father Tréca scraped the film off photographic plates, which he then mounted in a makeshift frame. By September 29th, the feast of St. Michael, the cabin was finished and blessed, and the first Mass in it offered.

Father Tréca was free now to devote most of his time to the study of the Native language, Central

An early-day Central Yup'ik Eskimo village on the Bering Sea coast.
It was in such villages that Father Joseph M. Tréca, S.J., began the
evangelization of the Central Yup'ik Eskimos. *JOPA*-555.01.

Yup'ik. He seems to have acquired a good working knowledge of it, but left little by way of manuscripts. Around the middle of October, he began a "school" and catechism classes. It was not long before he had organized a choir to sing the various parts of the Latin High Mass. As aids to teaching catechism, he had brought with him large, colored lithographs depicting the more important mysteries of the Catholic Faith. He presented one of these showing the fires of hell. His Eskimo audience cheered, when they saw the fire—even more so, when they saw there was no need of wood to keep the fire going.

After one year at Tununak, having been assisted by Father Paul **Muset**, S.J., who arrived there on November 30th, Father Tréca was able to report: "As the fruit of our labors, we baptized 23 adults on Easter Sunday, and on Whitsunday we administered Holy Communion to 17 first communicants and baptized 15 persons, of whom 13 were adults. From August 1, 1889 to June 1, 1890, we baptized 138 persons, of whom 36 were adults, and have blessed one marriage."

During the year 1891–92, Father Tréca had with him at Tununak Father Francis A. **Barnum**, S.J., new to Alaska. To the length and "death-like" silence of the Alaskan winter Father Barnum ascribed the mental disorder that he termed "polar anaemia." This "insidious malady" afflicted seriously, if only temporarily, some of his fellow missionaries, Father Tréca among them. "As the long dark winter night dragged slowly on," wrote Father Barnum, "he grew taciturn and listless. He would ring the bell at all hours, rousing us up at one or two o'clock in the morning. During the day he would frequently go out and walk around and around the house, talking wildly to himself, until he was half frozen. As the disease progressed, he became more and more eccentric." It was only after Father Tosi, summoned by Father Barnum, arrived that Father Tréca returned to his normal self.

After the Nelson Island mission had been going for three years, it was decided that it was not located centrally enough for missionary work along the Bering Sea coast. In late summer of 1892, Father Tréca relocated to a site near the south mouth of the Yukon River, to Kanelik Pass. Persuaded by his fellow missionaries to do so, he named this mission after St. Joseph, his patron saint. The Kanelik site, too, because of poor ground, had to be abandoned. Both Fathers Tréca and Barnum had advised against this latter site, but Father Tosi had given them "a peremptory order to settle there."

"Thanks for the bomb!" wrote Father Tréca to Father Tosi on August 10, 1892. "My shoulders will not bear it, unless you pray well and have others pray earnestly." Father Tréca had lived in mortal fear of ever being appointed a Superior. Now the "bomb" had fallen. He was named acting Superior by Father Tosi, who was about to make an extended trip to Europe. However, there was a blessing in that bomb. As acting Superior, Father Tréca now had authority to make major decisions. He decided to move the mission of St. Joseph from Kanelik Pass to a new site on the **Akulurak** River.

Father Tréca's heart seems to have remained all along in Tununak. It was with considerable personal reluctance that he had, in the first place, moved away from the original mission at Tununak. Referring to that mission, he wrote, "We *cannot* abandon such a field." He was never again stationed at Tununak, but, out of Akulurak, he visited it often.

Although the Tununak mission was re-established in 1927, by Father Martin J. **Lonneux**, S.J., it was mainly Father Tréca that the Tununak people remembered for generations. They referred to him as "Father *Kutlik*," also as "Father Goodly." The origin or meaning of these names is not clear. They remembered him for his cheerfulness under adverse conditions, for his good sense and balance, and for his readiness to share with them his provisions— which rarely went beyond the bare necessities of life. His generosity and charity were said to be "proverbial." Father Paul C. **Deschout**, S.J., one of his successors at Tununak, wrote to his Father Provincial on April 24, 1938: "Fr. Tréca's name is held in veneration here, as everywhere else along the coast."

Father Tréca wrote the above mentioned 1892 letter, while he was traveling upriver to **Holy Cross Mission**. On August 28th of that year, along with Fathers Tosi, Barnum, and Aloysius J. **Robaut**, S.J., founder of Holy Cross Mission, he visited the place where Archbishop Charles J. **Seghers** had been shot in 1886. There they erected a large wooden cross. This they blessed with all possible solemnity. Then the three each offered Mass in the presence of the many Indians assembled.

By 1894, St. Joseph's mission at Akulurak was a reality, and Father Tréca was recognized as its founder. But the hard work involved in making that mission a reality, along with that of the previous years and exposure while on the trail, had taken their toll on Father Tréca, had undermined his health. In the summer of 1895, in the company of Fathers Tosi and Barnum, he sailed south to California for a year, "to recruit his health."

Father Tréca was back at Akulurak again for the year 1896–97. On September 13, 1897, accompanying Father Tosi, he left St. Michael on the *Bertha* for **Juneau**, where they arrived on October 7th. He served in Juneau and neighboring towns from 1897–99. In Juneau, on June 7, 1899, he became a U.S. citizen.

Father Tréca spent the next two years at St. Michael. From there, in September 1899, he visited **Nome** "for a few days," then again in February of 1900, for "about 18 days." He was only the second priest to visit that new mining camp.

During the year 1901–02, Father Tréca was at Holy Cross, after which he returned once more to Akulurak for the years 1902–1915. Out of Akulurak, he traveled often and far and wide throughout the Yukon-Kuskokwim Delta. On January 2, 1914, as an official Consultor to the General Superior of the Jesuits in Alaska, he wrote from Akulurak: "I have not much to say. As I live here in the wilderness I know very little of what is going on elsewhere."

From 1915–18, Father Tréca was in Nome, having arrived there on October 31st. In Nome, he devoted most of his time to the Eskimos, routinely offering Mass for them in their own little church. In addition to being a good musician, he was also an accomplished photographer. After Mass one day, during his second year in Nome, when the Eskimo people were dressed in their "Sunday best," he took photos of family groups. From the quality of the photos, which he mounted in an old missal serving as a make-do album, it is evident that he saw to it that his subjects posed properly and remained motionless.

After his three years in Nome, Father Tréca, spent the year 1918–19 at Holy Cross. He then returned to his beloved Akulurak, where he spent the remaining years of his life. Staffing that mission during those years, along with Jesuit priests and Lay Brothers, were the **Ursuline** Sisters. One of them wrote about him—who "played so important a part" in the lives of the Sisters—that it was "the eloquence of his life more than his words" that had such a positive influence on people.

By 1925, Father Tréca had spent 35 years in Alaska and was thoroughly attached to it. On September 14, 1925, Father Bellarmine **Lafortune**, S.J., pioneer missionary in Alaska, wrote to Father Lonneux, "When we come to this country, we become glued to it in such a way that we cannot quit anymore. Even poor Father **Jetté** had to come back. They did not make a steel rope strong enough yet to pull Fr. Tréca out."

It was a case of tuberculosis of the hip that finally brought about Father Tréca's departure from Alaska. On July 14, 1926, Father Lonneux wrote in the Akulurak house diary: "The departure of poor Fr. Tréca was a sad one, very hard on the dear old Father, as he had given his life for this part of the country." At 3:30 that afternoon, amid "a terrible suffering," he was carried down to the boat in a chair, bound for the hospital in Seattle.

In Seattle, doctors found the disease far advanced. The Father Superior of Seattle College, William M. Boland, S.J., who was with Father Tréca during his last days, left an account of what transpired: "The holy man, asked by the doctors whether he desired to risk the only very doubtful chance of recovery by the amputation of his tuberculous leg, or die a natural, but lengthy and painful death, he did not want to choose, but left the decision to his Superiors." Surgery was decided upon. Before going into that surgery, Father Tréca took his crucifix, kissed it saying, "I am in the hands of my Lord. His will be done." As Father Boland accompanied him to surgery, Father Tréca said to him: "Father, I think that I shall lay my eyes for the first time upon our Blessed Mother today." The operation was performed about 9:30 A.M., on September 16, 1926. About five minutes to twelve that same morning Father Tréca died.

Father Boland's account adds the further detail: "Such was the esteem the Sisters and people conceived for his virtue even during his short staying at the hospital that, when about dying, the Superioress ordered to ring the bell and the Sisters to be present 'to see how Saints die.'"

Nine years after Father Tréca's death, Father Segundo **Llorente**, S.J., arrived at Akulurak to be Superior. Brother Bartholomew **Keogh**, S.J., a member of the community at the time, who had lived for many years with Father Tréca, told Father Llorente the following:

> One morning Father came for breakfast with a sort of halo, his face flushed with reverential awe and his eyes ablaze with indescribable joy. The two of us were alone in the kitchen. We looked at each other, as if we had never met. Father lowered his voice to a whisper and said, "Brother, this morning at the moment of consecration, as I held the Host, I saw the face of Our Lord smiling at me. It wasn't the first time."

Father Joseph M. Tréca, S.J., "the Apostle of the Tundra," lies buried in the Jesuit cemetery at Mount St. Michael's on the outskirts of Spokane, Washington.

122

On June 7, 1990, St. Joseph's Church, Tununak, is so crowded for the Rite of Christian Burial Mass for Father Francis J. Fallert, S.J., that three little girls find room only up front on the floor. Three altar boys are sitting in the front pew. *LR.*

TUNUNAK

The Central Yup'ik Eskimo village of Tununak is located on the northwest coast of Nelson Island, which lies in the Yukon-Kuskokwim Delta and on the Bering Sea coast. According to the 2000 census, the village had a population of 325.

Tununak is the site of the first Catholic mission among the Central Yup'ik Eskimos. In the fall of 1889, the trader at Tununak, Alexis Kalenin, born of a Russian father and an Eskimo mother, and referred to by the missionaries as "Aluska," brought Jesuit Fathers Joseph M. **Tréca** and Paschal **Tosi** from **St. Michael** to Tununak to establish a mission there. Father Tréca looked upon Nelson Island as a "virgin field." On November 30th, Father Paul **Muset**, S.J., joined him. Their dwelling, hastily constructed by Fathers Tréca and Tosi out of driftwood and sod, was divided into two parts: half for church

and school, half for living quarters. This mission, often referred to as "the coast mission," was first dedicated to the Jesuit Lay Brother St. Alphonsus Rodriguez, then, a few years later, to St. Joseph. It is still dedicated under the title of St. Joseph.

After his first year at Tununak, Father Tréca was able to record the baptism of 43 adults and 128 children. Father Muset's stay there was relatively short. By around the middle of September 1891, he was at **Holy Cross Mission**. For a time, however, while he was at Tununak, he and Father Tréca ran a small school. Brother John B. **Rosati**, S.J., was with the two during the year 1890–91. Father Francis A. **Barnum**, S.J., who described Tununak as the "Siberia" of the Alaskan Mission, and Brother **Bernard I. Cunningham**, S.J., along with Father Tréca, were at Tununak during the year 1891–92.

After 1892, Tununak, because it was so difficult of access, ceased for many years to have a resident missionary. It was visited, however, from time to time by priests stationed at **Akulurak**. In 1927, Father Martin J. **Lonneux**, S.J., moved to Tununak

St. Joseph's Church, Tununak. *MK.*

Father Deschout spent the year 1935–36 making his tertianship at Port Townsend, Washington. During that year, the Siparys were elsewhere; but, in their stead, John Naiyaganik and his wife served as catechists. The Siparys returned to Tununak for the year 1936–37, and Ivan took charge of the building of the new church. Under Father Deschout, a replacement church was built near the end of the 1960s. For a time this was called "St. Peter's." An addition to this was made in 1981, by Brother Ignatius J. **Jakes**, S.J., and Eskimo Deacon Dick Lincoln.

Foremost among the priests who have served the Tununak Catholic community is, of course, Father Deschout. Few Alaskan missionaries have given themselves so totally and for so many years to a community, as he gave himself to the people of Tununak. With him and his people, it was a mutual love affair for more than a quarter of a century. He first met them in 1934, and last saw them in 1961.

Father Deschout was followed at Tununak by Jesuit Fathers James E. **Jacobson**, 1962–66; Francis J. **Fallert**, 1966–74, 1986–87, and 1988–90; Norman E. **Donohue**, 1974–75; Daniel J. **Tainter**, 1975–77; Bernard F. **McMeel**, 1977–78; Richard L. **McCaffrey**, 1978–79; Richard D. **Case**, 1979–86; Henry G. **Hargreaves**, 1987–88, and 1994–98; Thomas G. **Provinsal**, 1990–91; Eugene P. **Delmore**, 1991–94; and David J. **Anderson**, beginning in 1998 and as of the year 2004.

Starting in 1981, the following Eskimo deacons served their Tununak parish: Mike Angaiak (deceased and buried at Tununak), Dick Lincoln, and Thomas Oscar, Sr.

Sister Pauline Igoe, O.P., was "a major influence" in preparing catechists at Tununak from 1978–87. From 1968–76, Marie Toscano, a member of the **Jesuit Volunteer Corps**, conducted a highly successful Montessori School at Tununak.

Father Fallert died in Fairbanks, on June 2, 1990, and was buried at Tununak on June 7th.

34, 72, 122

and put up a small cabin to serve him as a residence and a church. He left in 1928, and again that mission was served only by visiting priests.

In 1934, Father Paul C. **Deschout**, S.J., took up station at Tununak. Father **John P. Fox**, S.J., who accompanied him there, wrote, "I turned the mission over to Father Deschout, in 1934, a big day in Tununak history. They spent an hour in thanksgiving in church, when I arrived with the new pastor, after coming out with boats to meet us in full procession." In his missionary work, Father Deschout was greatly assisted by Ivan and Maggie **Sipary**. Concerning their work as catechists on Nelson Island, he wrote: "Ivan and Maggie have done so much for these people. After God, they are responsible for the fervor of these people. The good example of such catechists is more eloquent than all my talking." Ivan's stepfather, Simeon Sipary, before he died at **Nightmute** on May 13, 1931, had done much to lay a firm foundation for the Catholic Faith on Nelson Island, especially at Nightmute. During the winter 1931–32, George Aluska served as a catechist on Nelson Island.

TURNELL, Father Philibert, S.J.

Born Filiberto Tornielli, he was the son of a count and himself became a count. He was a blood relative of Pope Gregory XVI. **Alaska** was the scene of his ministry; and, even in his old age, "he had a form of obsession that he had to be in Alaska and nowhere else."

Filiberto Tornielli was born in Venice, Italy, on August 14, 1850, son of Count Georgio Tornielli. When he was still a mere boy, his mother died. Shortly after her death, his father left court life and gave up his profession as a lawyer to become a priest. The boy first had a private tutor. At about age 12, he began to attend a seminary school. He next studied law for several years at the University of Padua. Then came the sudden death of his father. During the funeral oration, the first thoughts of himself becoming a priest came to the young count, and future Jesuit. As a young man, Tornielli disliked the Jesuits; but, because he knew that his father had esteemed them highly, he made a retreat under the direction of a Jesuit in Turin. Soon thereafter, on March 24, 1873, he entered the Jesuit novitiate of the Turin Province at Monaco. While he was still a novice, that novitiate was transferred to Chieri, near Turin. After completing his two-year noviceship, he spent another year in Chieri studying the classics and humanities. In Nice, France, he then studied philosophy and theology for two years. He was ordained a priest, on Pentecost Sunday, June 9, 1878, on the Island of Lerins, off the southern coast of France.

Father Tornielli, having volunteered for the Indian missions of the American West, came to the United States the same year he was ordained a priest. He spent several years at Santa Clara College, California, studying English, doing some teaching, and making his tertianship. In 1881, now with his Americanized name of Philibert Turnell, he began almost two decades of work among the Indian peoples of the Pacific Northwest.

On March 4, 1898, Father Turnell sailed from Seattle for Alaska. **Skagway**, the picturesque gold-rush town at the head of Lynn Canal, was his first Alaskan post. When he arrived there, on September 8th, he found no church facilities of any kind. A Catholic family, grateful to have a resident priest in their town, welcomed him into their home. At first, he offered Mass on Sunday mornings in the temporary schoolhouse. Then, a large empty store was purchased and converted into a church. This new church, St. Mark's, dedicated on Christmas Eve, was filled to capacity for the Midnight Mass. Father Turnell served in Skagway, with visits to **Haines**, until 1905. During his first stay in Skagway, he returned to Italy for the beatification of a relative, Blessed Bonaventura Tornielli.

From 1905–08, Father Turnell was stationed in **Valdez** and **Seward**; then he was back in Skagway again for the years 1908–18. He spent the years 1918–26 in **Juneau** and **Douglas**. After a year in **Anchorage**, he was in **Fairbanks** for the years 1927–32.

Wherever he was stationed, Father Turnell was esteemed and well remembered, but it was in Skagway especially that he left lasting impressions. "This faithful servant of God," stated one of his Skagway parishioners, "has earned the respect and good will of every citizen of the town." Father Peter C. **Bougis**, S.J., who replaced him in 1905, said of him, "He bears the reputation of a saintly man, as pure and innocent as a child." When Father Turnell completed his last tenure in Skagway, in 1918, the *Daily Alaskan* noted that "his friends are legion. By his faithful service and kindly ways he has won the esteem and affection of not only his own parishioners but of the whole community. Father Turnell will be long remembered."

By the early 1930s, over three decades of hard work in Alaska began to take their toll on Father Turnell. Failing eyesight necessitated his leaving Alaska in 1932. He spent a year in Port Townsend, Washington, then several at Mount St. Michael's in Spokane, Washington. But, his heart was still in Alaska, and he pleaded with Superiors to be allowed to return. In 1936, he was back in Alaska, in **Ketchikan**. A fall there, however, further weakened his frail health and forced his return to Mount St. Michael's, where he spent the last two years of his long life. He died on October 26, 1938, in Sacred Heart Hospital, Spokane, and lies buried in the Jesuit cemetery at Mount St. Michael's.

For many years after his death, Alaskans and fellow Jesuits "recalled with love the tall, thin, saintly old man of Jovial disposition."

TWOHIG, Brother James, S.J.

For years after his departure from the scene, the incredible deeds of this Jesuit Lay Brother were recounted on **Alaska**'s lower Yukon River. He was "a tough Irishman" with a fiery temper, and a capacity for work so great that he dreaded the arrival of Sunday, "a day of rest." To prove that work does not kill people, he spent three decades in Alaska, working. He lived into his 79th year.

James Twohig was born in Ireland on February 17, 1854. He came to America to seek his fortune. This he did not find. However, he did receive a call from the Lord to serve Him as a Religious Brother. He was accepted as a candidate for the Society of Jesus, and entered the novitiate at Los Gatos, California, on July 22, 1888. For most of his pre-Alaskan years he was at Los Gatos. His last, 1892–93, he spent at St. Ignatius College in San Francisco.

Sailing from San Francisco, on May 19, 1893, on the *Bertha*, Brother Twohig arrived at **St. Michael** on June 21st. His first Alaskan assignment was St. Mary's Mission, **Akulurak**, where he served for the majority of his Alaskan years. For short periods, he was assigned also to **Holy Cross Mission**, **Nulato**, **Pilot Station**, and **Nome**.

Brother Twohig was an able carpenter and blacksmith. He specialized in building, maintaining, and operating the mission steamers. For this he is remembered as "the first Jesuit nautical engineer in Alaska."

Rheumatism, which had troubled Brother Twohig on and off for years, finally forced him to leave Alaska, in 1924. He died in San Francisco on June 27, 1932.

TYSON, Deacon William

He was a man of the tundra, and a man of **Alaska**'s largest city; a man equally at home in the world of the Eskimo, and in the world of the white man. Throughout his long life, he was also "a man for others." He entered this world near the month of the Yukon River; and he left it as an ordained deacon with two bishops, 12 priests and five deacons present at his funeral, held in the Catholic cathedral in **Anchorage**.

According to Church records, William Nugwaralrea Tyson was born to Ignatius Preuchuk and Josephina Tyson on February 23, 1916, at **Akulurak**, and baptized five days later. For most of his years, he lived in the Yukon-Kuskokwim Delta, the traditional land of the Central Yup'ik Eskimo people, to which group he belonged. In those days, there were no large communities, only small, scattered camps, to which people moved in keeping with the season. From his father, William learned the skills needed to survive: hunting, trapping, fishing.

In 1927, at the age of 11, William was sent to St. Mary's Mission boarding school at Akulurak to get some schooling and training from the **Ursuline** Sisters and the Jesuit priests and Lay Brothers staffing the mission. He made his first Holy Communion on February 2, 1928, and was confirmed that same year. Before he received those two Sacraments, he had admired the medicine men, the shamans. But, after receiving his first Holy Communion, "something," in his own words, "went out of me and a great light came in me." He also stated that, at his Confirmation, a great desire to serve his people came into him and that this desire never left him.

William's first wife, Pauline, left him with four children, when she died of tuberculosis. The youngest, a little girl, died a month later. William was to experience more family sorrows before the end of his life. Five sons died under tragic circumstances.

While Pauline was still alive, William traveled all over the Akulurak mission district helping priests, especially by translating for them, as they visited various camps. Father Segundo **Llorente**, S.J., one of the priests for whom William interpreted, said of him: "Without any doubt, William became the best interpreter in the land. He was so good that while he spoke the eyes of the people were fixed on him, as though he were an apparition from heaven." At the same time William was helping the missionaries, he was also supporting his family by hunting and fishing.

On August 31, 1948, William married Maria Arsanyak Julius, a student at the mission school. Soon after, they left for **New Knock Hock** to help Father Norman E. **Donohue**, S.J. William served as teacher, catechist, interpreter, carpenter, post-

Deacon William Tyson.
DFA.

master, store-keeper, and radio operator. Much of his time was with the people. They needed his help; he responded selflessly.

Tuberculosis, so widespread in Alaska at the time, necessitated William's leaving his family in 1950 and going to the sanatorium in **Sitka**. Naturally, he found the separation from his family very painful. With weekly letters, he kept in touch with them. After his return, he made a special point of being always exceptionally close to his family. He was the first to admit that he, by himself, made up only half a person and that his wife Maria made him whole. Maria said, "He taught me never to be alone." The two were happily married for 45 years.

The Tyson children were very well taught and trained by their parents, both in the Native traditions and in the Catholic Faith. Daughter Rose, when interviewed by *Extension* Magazine, recalled, "Being with my dad, holding on to his hand—like when we were going to the store—is my favorite childhood memory." She said, "He passed on his faith just by being who he was."

Eventually the Tyson family moved to St. Marys on the **Andreafsky** River. There William took part in local government. He was active in Eskimo dancing as a choreographer, drummer, singer, and dancer. To the uninitiated, he explained Native customs and the meaning of the dances.

The Tysons were faithful members of the St. Marys parish community. When the **Eskimo Dea-con Program** was started in 1970, William was recommended and advanced by his people as a candidate. He was one of seven in the original group. Another was Michael **Nayagak**. It is William and his wife Maria who deserve credit for the design of the diaconal vestment worn by the Eskimo deacons during liturgical functions. It closely resembles the traditional Eskimo parka. On the outside of the vestment, over his chest, the deacon wears a simple cross hung loosely from the neck.

William was one of the main translators for the deacon workshops and liturgies. In 1971, along with several other Eskimos and two priests, he met in **Tununak** for the purpose of producing an acceptable and polished translation into Eskimo of the common prayers of the Mass and of the Communion liturgies presided over by the deacons-to-be. What they produced was judged "a major achievement." However, three women from **Chefornak**— Adeline Panruk, Mary Tunuchuk, and Agnes Kairaiuak—deserve most of the credit for that "major achievement," for they had laid the foundation of the translation that was, in the end, approved by Eskimo men acknowledged to be translation specialists, among them Leo Moses and William Tyson. It was left to William to attend to fine points concerning orthography, and to type up the Eskimo translations.

While in training for the diaconate, William was involved also with the Alaska Native Land Claims issues. He was an original member of his regional corporation. With other members, he chose "Calista" ("the worker") as a name for the new corporation, indicating thereby again a sense of service to his people. Recognized as an expert translator, he played a major role in the corporation. While on the Calista board, he was sent to Washington, D.C., to sign official documents. Because of his knowledge of the people in his region, he was put in charge of enrollment, distribution of corporation shares, and maintenance of official corporation records. When he had to move to Anchorage, because corporation headquarters were located there, his family followed him.

The 26th of January 1977 was an especially memorable day in the life of William Tyson, for on that day, in Anchorage, he was ordained to the permanent diaconate by the Apostolic Delegate to the United States, Archbishop Jean Jadot. Assisting him were Francis T. **Hurley**, Archbishop of Anchorage; Francis D. **Gleeson**, S.J., retired Bishop of Fairbanks; and Robert L. **Whelan**, S.J., Ordinary of the Diocese of **Fairbanks**, for which William was ordained. William wore a beautiful parka-vestment made for him by Maria for the occasion.

After his ordination, Deacon Tyson continued to attend the Eskimo deacon workshops and the annual retreats held for the Eskimo deacons of the Diocese of Fairbanks. When visiting the villages in connection with his work, he was asked to celebrate liturgies for his people. They appreciated his homilies. During his Anchorage days, he longed to be with his people in their home region. He even talked of going back to the delta of his origins to live in a tent, as he had at times during his younger days.

When Pope John Paul II visited Anchorage on February 26, 1981, Deacon Tyson, as the representative of all the Eskimo deacons, assisted at the altar. In 1983, he was officially appointed to the Office of Native Ministry of the Archdiocese of Anchorage. As such, he was a real inspiration to the Native community, urging them to be true both to their Native roots and to their Catholic Faith. He fostered traditional Eskimo drumming and dancing. With his wife, Maria, he visited the Native Hospital, often acting as an interpreter. Every Sunday, priest or no priest, he gathered the people for prayer and Holy Communion. As long as his health allowed, he and Maria, went to the Highland Mountain Correctional Institution to be available to the inmates for counseling, to share with them traditional stories, to sing, and to dance Eskimo dances for them.

Together, William and Maria Tyson served in many different capacities, generally as bridges between cultures and between the young and Elders. For many years, they were parent volunteers for the Johnson O'Malley Program and board members of the Indian Education parent committee. They worked with students from pre-school through college in preserving Native arts, crafts, clothing, and dancing. They inspired the Greatland Traditional Dancers, who performed throughout Alaska and in the Lower 48.

William Tyson received many awards and was honored both locally and statewide, both for his efforts within the Church and within the Native community. He was named Elder of the Year by the Alaska Federation of Natives, Parent of the Year by the Alaska Native Education Council, and Community Member of the Year by the Cook Inlet Tribal Council/Johnson–O'Malley Program.

"Culingailama wii atuayuitua . . ." sang the singers to the beat of the Eskimo drum as the body of Deacon William Tyson was brought into Holy Family Cathedral in Anchorage on December 30, 1993. William had died of cancer the day after Christmas. When the body was half way down the aisle, Archbishop Hurley sprinkled the casket with holy water, recalling William's baptism. Then the singing and the drumming began again: "I would like to give you my spirit, but I have no drum. I cannot dance. The word of the Creator comes to us over the water. The word of the Creator comes to us through thunder and lightning. I would like to give you my spirit, but I have no drum. I cannot dance." At the end of the song, William's drum was placed on the casket as a reminder of his call: to reach his people through the teaching of his songs.

On the day of William's ordination to the diaconate, Holy Family Cathedral had been filled by his many friends. It was no less so on the day of his funeral. Concelebrating with Archbishop Hurley were Michael J. **Kaniecki**, S.J, Bishop of Fairbanks, twelve priests and five deacons.

Eskimo Deacon William Tyson, as a man of the drum, as a man of the cross, and as "a man for others," touched the lives of many. He will long be remembered as a major figure in the State of Alaska and in the Catholic Church of Alaska. He lies buried in the Catholic plot of Anchorage's Angelus Memorial Park Cemetery.

35, 145, 148

UMKUMIUT

On Nelson Island, in the Yukon-Kuskokwim Delta, situated on a broad, crescent-shaped shelf between the waters of Kangirlvar Bay and the cliffs of two south-facing promontories, lies Umkumiut. For several generations it was an inhabited Central Yup'ik Eskimo village. Father Paul C. **Deschout**, S.J., performed baptisms there from the 1930s to the 1950s. In 1950, it had a population of 99. As of the year 2004, it was only a spring sealing and a summer fishing camp for the people of **Nightmute**, an Eskimo village located 15 miles to the east. A high bank and a barricade of jumbled driftwood logs help to protect the camp, an irregular row of tiny wooden cabins and some white canvas tents, from the waves during storms.

Umkumiut has never had a resident priest, though priests have spent parts of summers there. In 1969, Father John A. **Hinsvark**, with the generous help of volunteers, built Christ the King Church at Umkumiut. The church's unique architectural design was conceived by Father Hinsvark, and the plans for it drawn up by Gordon Gagliano, a member of the **Jesuit Volunteer Corps**. A sum of $20,000 for the church was donated by the Catholic Church Extension Society. In the eyes of Father Louis L. **Renner**, S.J., the architecture of the church, with its "flying buttresses," is "reminiscent of an ancient, many-oared galley, appropriate for coastal peoples." Father Hinsvark, however, interprets the design as "a modified tent, or A-frame structure. The exposed interior trusses remind people of the safety provided by an upturned skiff or Eskimo *umiaq*." Were the church not so remote, surely many people would come to see its unusual, but "architecturally significant style."

UNALAKLEET

The village of Unalakleet is located at the mouth of the Unalakleet River, on Norton Sound. It is an ancient settlement, lying, as it does, at the western terminus of the much used **Kaltag** Portage, which links the coast to the Yukon River and to **Alaska**'s interior. The inhabitants of Unalakleet are mainly Inupiat Eskimos, with also a mix of Athabaskan Indians and Yup'ik Eskimos. Unalakleet means "place where the east wind blows." The Unalakleet post office was established in 1901. In 1880, Unalakleet had a population of 100; in 1910, 247; in 1930, 261; in 1960, 574; in 1970, 434; in 1980, 632; in 1992, 714; and in the year 2000, 747.

Catholic records indicate that Unalakleet was visited as early as 1910, by Father Anthony M. **Keyes**, S.J., stationed at **St. Michael**. In 1949, Father Jules M. **Convert**, S.J., began to visit Unalakleet, likewise out of St. Michael. He built a cabin-church there in 1952. Up until 1956, the Catholic mission in Unalakleet, under the patronage of the Holy Angels, was always cared for by priests stationed at St. Michael. From 1956–63, and during the years 1964–66, Father Convert cared for the Unalakleet mission out of Kaltag. Weather-bound in Unalakleet on December 25, 1962, he offered the first Christmas Midnight Mass ever celebrated there.

Up to the present (2004), various other priests, generally stationed at St. Michael or in **Nome**, have ministered to the Unalakleet Catholic community. With two exceptions, all have done so for only a year or two. Father Thomas F. **Carlin**, S.J., visited it out of St. Michael from 1995–99; and Father George S. **Endal**, S.J., also out of St. Michael, from 1968–82. From 1982–87, he resided in Unalakleet. At his request, the mission of the Holy Angels was

(*top*) Christ the King Church, Umkumiut. *DFA.*

(*bottom*) Church of the Holy Angels, Unalakleet. *MK.*

UNALASKA

The city of Unalaska, 800 air miles southwest of **Anchorage**, is located on the southern shore of Unalaska Bay, Unalaska Island, the second largest island in the Aleutian archipelago. Its industrial seafood processing capabilities are unmatched in Alaska. Unalaska and its port, Dutch Harbor, had a population of 406 in 1880, 317 in 1890, 299 in 1920, 298 in 1939, 173 in 1950, 218 in 1967, and 4,283 in the year 2000. The Ounalaska post office was established in 1888. The name was changed to Unalaska in 1898.

Long before the Catholic community of St. Christopher by the Sea was established at Unalaska, the Latin Rite Mass was offered there by Roman Catholic clergymen passing through that port. The first one to do so was Bishop Charles J. **Seghers**, on his first visit to Alaska in 1873. Others followed him. In May and June 1888, Father Gaspar Genna, S.J., offered Mass at Unalaska for the Sisters of St. **Ann** and Brother John B. **Rosati**, S.J., while they were delayed there en route to the Yukon River. It is safe to assume that after Father Genna other Jesuit priests on their trips north offered Mass at Unalaska. Father Bernard R. **Hubbard**, S.J., had occasion to offer Mass at that locale during his various excursions to the Aleutian Islands.

A more formal Catholic presence at Unalaska began during World War II, when some 60,000 U. S. and Canadian soldiers, along with a few German prisoners of war, were housed there. Catholic chaplains offered Mass in the "Burma Road" interdenominational chapel—which still existed as of the year 2003—for the Catholic soldiers. However, with the departure of the soldiers at the end of the war, the chaplains also left, and the only Church presence that remained was the Russian Orthodox Church.

In 1977, Bernice Gregory, a resident of Unalaska, while on vacation in Hawaii, took advantage of the opportunity to go to confession. When she confessed that it had been three years since her last con-

raised to the rank of a parish in 1982 by Robert L. **Whelan**, S.J., then Bishop of **Fairbanks**. A new "Church of the Holy Angels" was built in 1993–94 to accommodate the Catholic community, which had long since outgrown the small old church.

The Catholic presence in Unalakleet has never been large. Unalakleet has for generations been a stronghold of the Swedish Covenant Church.

fession, the priest chided her for waiting so long. Her response was that neither church nor priest was available where she lived. The priest then commanded her to write to Francis T. **Hurley**, Archbishop of Anchorage at the time, and insist that some ministry be provided the Unalaska Catholic community. Having no priest available for Unalaska, the archbishop sought out Sisters willing to go there.

The first Sister to serve at Unalaska was Sister Marie Ann Brent, S.H.F., who spent the months of June and July 1978 there to see what could be done by way of pastoral ministry and to prepare Bernice Gregory's son for his first Holy Communion. She returned again the following summer, at which time she asked to be assigned to Unalaska permanently. Because of the remoteness of Unalaska, Archbishop Hurley suggested that she go out to that lonely mission for the winter of 1979 "to see how it goes." She was there from November through January 1980, and reported: "Things went extremely well. I loved it." In March of 1980, she returned on a permanent basis and remained until May of 1986. At Unalaska, she at first stayed with the Gregory family for several months. Then the Unalaska Christian Fellowship offered her, rent-free, the apartment over the parsonage's garage. The Fellowship would accept no rent. For the next six years, she lived there rent-free. One of the parishioners paid the oil bill, another the electric bill. It was Sister Marie Ann who arranged with the Fellowship for Mass to be offered in their church building.

In 1986, Sister Ann Christine Pendleton, S.S.N.D., replaced Sister Marie Ann as Pastoral Administrator at Unalaska. She was accompanied by a lay woman, Rosemary Coval, who spoke Polish. The two extended hospitality to a number of Polish seamen who had defected while their ships docked at Dutch Harbor.

Brenda Moscarella cared for the St. Christopher by the Sea mission from 1989–91. Even then, the mission still had no house for a Pastoral Administrator. Because of housing shortages in the city, she

St. Christopher by the Sea Church, Unalaska.
Photo by Fr. Paul Scanlon, O.P.

had to move six times during her two years at Unalaska.

From 1991–93, neither priest nor Pastoral Administrator lived in Unalaska. During the 1980s and 1990s, the Catholic community was served by fly-in priests, who offered Mass for the people one or two weekends a month, weather permitting. Among these was Father Richard G. **Strass**, C.Ss.R. During the later 1980s and the early 1990s, Father **James R. Laudwein**, S.J., visited Unalaska out of Anchorage. He was followed around the mid-1990s by Father James F. **Kelley**, a former Navy chaplain and pilot flying the archdiocesan twin-engine plane. Meanwhile, the Catholic presence at Unalaska was heroically sustained by Catholic stalwarts such as Sandra and Gary Sandness, Annabelle Wilt, Aimee and Rick Kniaziowski, Jack and Marge Fay, Gary and Dana Frojen, among others.

Up until February 2001, Mass was still offered on Saturday evenings at the Christian Fellowship Church and on Sunday mornings at UNISEA, the largest fish cannery in town. However, by 1993, thanks to the efforts of Archbishop Hurley, a lot for a double-width mobile home for the Pastoral

Administrator and the visiting priest had been donated by Toni Stanley. Whenever Father Laudwein was in Unalaska, he helped ready the foundation for the home. "I remember," he wrote, "digging in the rain, sleet, hail and mud to assist with the foundation." In August 1993, Sister Peggy Griffin, O.P., arrived to work as a pastoral minister. The home arrived in two pieces in November. By December 8th, it was assembled and ready for her to move in. With her enthusiastic leadership, the Catholic community began to blossom and grow.

In 1997, Annemiek J. Brunklaus began her years of service at St. Christopher's, taking up the challenge of finding a place for worship that the Catholics could call their own. She was greatly assisted by Father Kelley. During the years before his fatal crash, on March 23, 2002, he looked upon Unalaska as his "home away from home," though he was able to visit it only on the second weekend of a given month. On one other Sunday of a given month, one of the "circuit priests" flying out of Anchorage celebrated the Saturday 7:30 P.M. Mass in the Christian Fellowship Church and the Sunday morning Mass at UNISEA. When no priest was available, the Pastoral Administrator provided the Liturgy of the Word, addressed the assembled, and distributed Communion.

In 2001, Annemiek sold the Pastoral Administrator's modular home. With money derived from that sale, and savings the parishioners had accumulated over the years, plus a donation made in memory of Anne Huot, and help from the Catholic Church Extension Society, she bought a building that was transformed into what, as of the year 2003, was the St. Christopher by the Sea Church Center. The church proper was able to seat 100. The building also had a bedroom for the visiting priest and an apartment for the Pastoral Administrator. In February 2001, Father Kelley celebrated the first Mass in the new church, and, in May 2001, Roger L. **Schwietz**, O.M.I., Archbishop of Anchorage, dedicated it.

After Annemiek left Unalaska in 2002, Charles Takes, accompanied by his wife Gail, served as Pastoral Administrator during the year 2002–03. Father Paul Scanlon, O.P., former pastor of Holy Family Cathedral parish in Anchorage, began to reside in Unalaska on July 5, 2003. Not long after his arrival, he gave the outside of the church a new coat of sea-green paint.

URSULINE (O.S.U.) Sisters in Alaska

The first members of the Order of St. Ursula, Roman Union, to set foot in what is today the State of **Alaska** were Mother Laurentia Walsh (Superior), Sister Mary Claver Driscoll, and Sister Dosithée Leygonie. They arrived at **Akulurak** on September 4, 1905, to staff St. Mary's Mission boarding school. They had been chosen and sent by Rev. Mother Mary Amadeus Dunne, Provincial Superior of the Northern Province of the United States, in response to a request for Ursuline Sisters made by Father Joseph R. **Crimont**, S.J., Prefect Apostolic of Alaska at the time. Under the care of the Ursuline Sisters, working in conjunction with Jesuit priests and Brothers, the boarding school, an institution of basic education and practical training, flourished for close to 50 years. On August 3, 1951, the whole Akulurak mission was relocated to the banks of the **Andreafsky** River as the "New St. Mary's."

During the 46 years of its existence at Akulurak, St. Mary's was staffed by 20 different Ursuline Sisters. Most of them served there for many years. Mother Amadeus herself spent the year 1911–12 there. Mother Laurentia, one of the three original foundresses of that mission and its first Superior, was in charge for over 30 years. Sister Mary Claver, too, served there for many years. Concerning Mother Laurentia as Superior, Father John B. **Sifton**, S.J., wrote from Akulurak, on June 6, 1927: "We all admit that she is too much of a policeman—and yet, stern Mother that she is, she made this place." Mother Laurentia was not one to shrink from getting her hands dirty. Wrote Father Joseph F. **McElmeel**, S.J., about a year later, after observing life at fish camp: "The venerable Mother Laurentia had the sloppiest job of all, washing of the fish, as the boys piled them into the box."

The second Ursuline mission in Alaska was established at **St. Michael**, on September 26, 1908, when Mother Amadeus, along with Sisters Bartholomew Harrison, Margaret Mary, and de

Merici landed there. The mission, a very modest establishment indeed, was named "St. Ursula's-by-the-Sea." For ten years, until it burned to the ground on December 9, 1918, it served the Ursulines as a base for teaching and for ministering to the sick.

While Mother Amadeus was spending the winter 1911–12 at Akulurak, she received word from Father Crimont that she was to go, as soon as possible, to found a house in **Valdez**. Routed by way of Seattle, she arrived in Valdez only on July 22, 1912. She found, to her pleasant surprise, a two-story frame convent, housing Mother Mary of the Angels, Sister Helen, and two postulants, who had arrived on April 16th. The opening of the Valdez novitiate was the realization of what had been one of Mother Amadeus' long-cherished dreams.

During their seven years in Valdez, the Ursulines, in keeping with their traditions, again taught school and cared for the sick. It must be recorded that, all in all, their Valdez venture was not a success. Various misunderstandings soon began to arise between the pastor of Valdez, Father John B. **Van der Pol**, S.J., and the Sisters, between the Sisters and the townspeople, and between the parents of the students and the Sisters. At root of the misunderstandings: the Sisters were just not what the people had expected. They were "just not like other Sisters." Their semi-cloistered life was not well understood by the people of Valdez. The Sisters left Valdez in 1919, the year of the death of Mother Amadeus Dunne, in Seattle, on November 10th.

In October 1917, the **Pilgrim Hot Springs** ranch on the Pilgrim River, some 60 miles north of **Nome**, became the property of the Nome parish. Intentions were to convert it into a mission center with a boarding school and orphanage. Little did anyone at the time realize that just one year later there would be, owing to the great influenza epidemic of 1918,

The first Ursuline Sisters convent at Akulurak. *JOPA-153.1.05.*

Ursuline Sister Frances Connell and St. Mary's Mission girls processing king salmon. Salmon were a staple in the diet at the mission. *DFA.*

orphans in abundance. The first of many sick and orphaned began to arrive at the improvised mission hospital and orphanage in the late fall of 1918. The need for adequate personnel to care for them, and for the many more soon to come, was quite desperate. Throughout the first eight months of 1919, orphans kept arriving at the Pilgrim Hot Springs Mission. For August 16th of that year, the mission diary marked "a notable event, the arrival, namely, of 5 Ursuline Nuns, who came to look after the little orphans." Ursuline records credit only three as being foundresses: Mother Holy Name Besse, Mother Theresa of St. Joseph Rosenberg, and Sister Catherine Finnegan.

During the 22 years that the Pilgrim Hot Springs Mission was open, about 20 different Ursuline Sisters came and went. Two Sisters are especially notable. Sister Thecla Battiston was there the whole time the Ursulines were at the mission, from 1919 to 1941. Sister Irene Arvin is one of only two Ursuline Sisters to die and be buried in Alaska. She died at the mission on July 25, 1934, and lies buried in the cemetery there. Sister Scholastica **Lohagen** died at St. Mary's Mission, Andreafsky, on April 29, 1985, and lies buried in that mission's cemetery.

On March 4, 1939, Father McElmeel wrote in a letter: "Father **E.[dward] Cunningham** at Pilgrim Springs is struggling along with totally unfit buildings and equipment. The devoted Ursulines, almost crowded out by the children, keep on valiantly day after day, though sorely tried." By 1941, the buildings at "the Springs" were in very poor repair. Furthermore, firewood in the area had become scarce. Most important of all, however, there were no longer enough orphans to justify the considerable expense of keeping the mission open. It was closed on July 31, 1941, by Father Edmund A. **Anable**, S.J.

As stated earlier, the Akulurak mission was moved on August 3, 1951, to its new site on the banks of the Andreafsky River. There the mission, still staffed by Ursuline Sisters, Jesuit priests and Brothers, and, in its latter years, also by members of the **Jesuit Volunteer Corps**, continued to flourish. Although the mission at its new site was in no sense a new Ursuline foundation, six Sisters are credited as being its foundresses: Mother Antoinette Johnson (Superior), and Sisters John Frances Mullaney, Athanasius Stevens, Lucy Daly, Thecla Battiston, and Wivina Severins.

During the 36 years of its existence as a boarding school, from 1951–87, the new St. Mary's was to see the service of over 30 different Ursuline Sisters. One of them, Sister Thecla Battiston, spent 28 years there. Those years, plus her years at Akulurak and at Pilgrim Springs, gave her a total of 60 years in Alaska, an Alaskan tenure longer than that of any other Ursuline. Sister Scholastica Lohagen, with 51 years, was the runner-up.

The new St. Mary's school was in large part the creation of the Ursulines. For many of them, the school was the whole of their lives. At the new St. Mary's, the Sisters soon started, and, in large part, staffed, a high school. By 1974, only the four-year high school remained. Gradually this was staffed more and more by non-Ursulines, but they were said to be the "stabilizing influence" that held the school together. The school thrived. In 1980, Bishop Robert L. **Whelan**, S.J., could write: "Throughout the years, St. Mary's students have proved to be a credit to the Church and their school. St. Mary's is a very special kind of school." Nevertheless, on January 27, 1987, Michael J. **Kaniecki**, S.J., successor to Bishop Whelan, announced that St. Mary's High School would close at the end of the 1986–87 school year. While acknowledging that St. Mary's had "a glorious record and a history to be proud of," he was persuaded that the findings of a special task force gave him no choice but to close the school. Among the compelling findings mentioned was that of "severely declining enrollments." This situation was brought about mainly by the settlement, in 1976, of the Molly Hootch case with the enactment of a law that mandated that the State of Alaska erect high schools in Alaska's rural villages.

Dr. Judith Kleinfeld, a professor at the University of Alaska–Fairbanks, who did an in-depth study of St. Mary's High School, equated its closing to "the passing of a very bright era." The school's closing caused its last principal, Ursuline Sister Angie Pratt, genuine pain. Even though she supported the decision to close it, she found the closure "an emotional heartbreak."

In addition to the major and long-lasting Ursuline foundations mentioned so far, there were also some of lesser significance and of shorter duration.

In the early 1940s, Father **John P. Fox**, S.J., requested the help of two Ursuline Sisters to help him at **Hooper Bay** with the training of the Sisters of Our Lady of the **Snows**, a Native Sisterhood he had founded in 1932. Mother Mary of the Blessed Sacrament Hardegon and Sister Scholastica Lohagen, both at Akulurak then, were sent and remained at Hooper Bay from 1942 to September 15, 1945.

From June 1971 to August 1972, Sister Sally Ann Nash served in **Delta Junction** and in **Tok**. In 1973, making **Holy Cross** her headquarters, she served in 14 different coastal villages. From November 1973 to June 1976, she resided at **Toksook Bay**, and served the Nelson Island area villages. In all cases, Religious Education was her ministry.

On August 5, 1968, Sister Maria Clarys arrived at St. Mary's Mission. She was followed a year later by Sister Monique Vaernewyck, who arrived on May 3, 1969. Both came from Belgium and both taught in the mission grade and high schools until 1983. That year they left St. Mary's to take on a new ministry in **Tanana**, "a ministry of presence"—but a ministry of much more. Soon after their arrival in September, each was accepted by the Tanana people as one of them. In the course of their 13 years in Tanana, the Sisters were also at times appointed as pastoral and parish administrators. They held adult Religion classes. Given their artistic talents, they had an organized sewing and crafts club that met one evening weekly. Every day of the week, they taught C.C.D. classes for all ages. They showed parishioners how to instruct their children in the Faith, to become readers and Eucharistic ministers, and to lead Communion Services. They started a parish council and they instructed the parents of children who were to receive the Sacraments of Baptism, First Communion, Confirmation, and Reconciliation. They prepared adults for marriage. All the while, they were maintaining the buildings and grounds, and raising money to help cover parish expenses.

On June 30, 1996, Sisters Maria and Monique moved from Tanana to **Fairbanks**. Their leaving Tanana was a blow to the people. They had come to be regarded as "really everybody's friends," in the words of one Tanana woman. Father **Joseph E. Laudwein**, S.J., visiting priest to Tanana for two of the years the Sisters were there, said of them, "They've been a marvelous presence for the people there, assisting them in counseling situations and helping them to come together to discuss their faith and live their faith." After a sabbatical leave of a year, the Sisters, beginning in October 1997, undertook ministry in Fairbanks, mainly to Alaskan Native people and to the incarcerated. They were still at this ministry as the third millennium began to unfold.

About this same time, after teaching at St. Mary's High School and serving in the St. Mary's parish, Sister Josephine **Aloralrea**, the Order's only Eskimo Sister, undertook parish ministry in the **Juneau** diocese, principally at **Yakutat**. Along with her, also serving in the Juneau diocese, at **Skagway**, was Sister Jelaine (Jill) Jaeb. During the 1990s, Sisters Lorene Griffin and Angie Pratt served in the **Anchorage** archdiocese in social ministries. Sister Lorene was still serving in the archdiocese as of the year 2004.

When, in 1910, Mother Amadeus Dunne first came to Alaska, she had the sincere hope of establishing a mission on **King Island** in Bering Strait, with herself going there to do so. When she learned that no priest would be available to go there to offer daily Mass, she gave up that hope. Eighty years later, however, an Ursuline Sister was to set foot, not on King Island, but on neighboring **Little Diomede** Island. It was Sister Cecilia Huber, who—after teaching at St. Mary's High School during the last years of its operation, and while serving in Nome as Pastoral Minister from 1989–91—made several trips there. By the year 2005, the Sisters of St. Ursula had rendered a century of dedicated, often heroic, service in Alaska.

62, 129

VALDEZ

The city of Valdez, on an excellent, land-locked, ice-free harbor, is located in Southcentral Alaska, at the head of Valdez Arm inside Prince William Sound, 115 miles east of **Anchorage**. The area was explored and named by Spaniards in 1790. Valdez was established in 1898 as a debarkation point for prospectors seeking a route to the Klondike gold fields. The Valdez post office was established the following year. Severely damaged by the March 27, 1964, earthquake, the city was rebuilt about three miles northwest of the old site. Valdez had a population of 810, in 1910; of 466, in 1920; of 442, in 1930; of 529, in 1939; of 554, in 1950; of 555, in 1967; of 4,360, in 1990; and of 4,036, in the year 2000.

Valdez saw its first Catholic priest, when Father Philibert **Turnell**, S.J., visited it for the first time and offered Mass there on the Feast of the Assumption, August 15, 1903. In the spring of 1905, Joseph R. **Crimont**, S.J., then Prefect Apostolic of **Alaska**, decided that a permanent mission should be founded there and that Father Turnell was the one to do this. That same year, Father Turnell, aided by Paulist Father John M. Handly, who was in Valdez preaching "a mission," established the Valdez parish. Father Turnell took up residency there in 1906. By 1908, he had St. Francis Xavier's Church more or less completed. In the spring of that year, Father Matthias Schmitt, S.J., took over as pastor of the Valdez mission. He furnished the church and added more convenient living quarters before leaving Valdez in 1910.

That same year, Father John B. **Van der Pol**, S.J., became pastor of the Valdez mission. He found that Father Turnell, "by his great zeal and charity, his courtesy and earnestness, had laid the foundation broad and sure." At this time, Valdez, now a town of 810, was enjoying economic stability. Its future looked bright. With enthusiasm, Father Van der Pol improved the physical plant. He enlarged the rectory and moved the church to a new location.

It was Father Van der Pol who was instrumental in having the **Ursuline** Sisters come to Valdez to open a house there. Two members of that Order, Mother Mary of the Angels and Sister Helen, along with two postulants, arrived in April 1912. Soon they were housed in a two-story frame building, which served them as a convent and novitiate.

During their seven years in Valdez, the Ursuline Sisters, in keeping with their traditions, taught school and cared for the sick. It must be recorded, however, that, all in all, their Valdez venture turned out to be less than a success. Various misunderstandings soon began to arise between them and Father Van der Pol, the townspeople, and the parents of the students. At the root of the misunderstandings: the Sisters were just not what the people had expected. They were "just not like other Sisters." Their semi-cloistered life was not well understood by the people of Valdez. Consequently, at the end of the 1913–14 school year, they stopped teaching in Valdez. In 1919, they left Valdez altogether. The convent and the property on which it stood were sold to the American Legion.

In 1913, Father Van der Pol, having also **Cordova** and **Seward** to care for, was joined by Father William A. **Shepherd**, S.J., who worked in and out of Valdez until 1916. Father John T. Corbett, S.J., was in Valdez for 1915–16; and Father Alphonsus Fletcher, S.J., for 1916–17. Then it was Father Van der Pol again, for 1917–19. From 1919–25, Father William **McMillan**, S.J., lived in Valdez; from 1925–33, he visited it out of Cordova.

(*left*) St. Francis Xavier's Church, Valdez. *Photo by Dan Stowe.*

(*below*) An earlier St. Francis Xavier's Church, Valdez. *JOPA-425.01.*

After Father McMillan, it was mainly diocesan priests that tended the Valdez flock, either living there, or visiting it from time to time. Father Leo Dufour was responsible for Valdez from 1934–36. Father David A. **Melbourne**, living in Cordova, went to Valdez once a month during the years 1939–59. When he had a priest assistant, that assistant lived at Valdez. Father Emeric Kovach, a priest of the Diocese of **Juneau**, was in Valdez for the year

1953–54. Father Ronald K. **Dunfey** replaced him for the following year. In 1959, Father John A. **Lunney** replaced Father Melbourne as pastor of Cordova–Valdez. He was pastor, when the 1964 earthquake struck. Father John J. **Marx** replaced Father Lunney in 1966. It was he who bought the property for the parish complex in the new town site. That same year, 1966, Father Peter Houck, O.S.B., began his five-year stint in Valdez. In November 1966, St.

Francis Xavier's mission officially became a parish. Father Houck saw to the construction of the new parish complex in the new town site, and witnessed the solemn dedication and blessing of the new St. Francis Xavier's Church on June 20, 1968.

In 1971, Father Eugene P. **Burns**, S.J., became pastor in Valdez. He held station there until 1977. After Father Burns, Father Marx was again in Valdez, as resident pastor, from 1977–82. From 1983–87, Father Michael Shields served as resident pastor of Valdez. For the following year, Father **Gerard T. Ryan**, C.S.Sp., was pastor.

In 1988, priests out of Anchorage began to be the canonical pastors of Valdez. During the years 1988–92, Sister Carol Ann Aldrich, R.S.M., living in Valdez, served St. Francis Xavier's parish as Pastoral Administrator. In 1993, Sister Marie Ann Brent, S.H.F., likewise living in Valdez, began serving the parish in that same capacity.

15

VAN DER POL, John B., S.J.

John B. Van der Pol was born in Osterhout, Netherlands, on January 24, 1862. He entered the novitiate of the Society of Jesus at Florissant, Missouri, on September 24, 1883. After serving among the Colville Indians in Washington Territory, he made his theological studies at Woodstock, Maryland. He was ordained a priest on June 26, 1895. As a young priest, he served among the Indian people of Montana. For his tertianship he was at Florissant, 1900–01.

Father Van der Pol spent his first year in **Alaska** in **Nome**, arriving there on September 13, 1901. It proved to be a difficult year for him. Father Aloysius **Jacquet**, S.J., while in the process of establishing St. Joseph's parish and erecting the parish rectory and church, became mentally so disturbed that he was declared legally insane by civil author-

ities. Father Van der Pol, caught up in "a misfortune that threatened to be a scandal and disgrace," suffered through the ordeal, "the most painful 3 weeks of our life." On August 1, 1902, Father Joseph M. **Cataldo**, S.J., arrived in Nome to replace Father Van der Pol, who had been called to Seattle.

By July 16, 1903, Father Van der Pol was back in Nome, to serve there until 1906. During the summer of 1905, the chapel-workshop building for the Eskimo people, dedicated to the Holy Angels, was put up near St. Joseph's Church. It was designed by Father Van der Pol, a noted designer and builder of chapels, churches and rectories. It was he who bought the machines for the workshop and the furnishings for the chapel. Father Van der Pol was then in **Douglas** for two years.

In 1910, after spending several years in the Pacific Northwest, Father Van der Pol returned north, to Southcentral and Southeastern Alaska. From 1910–19, he was stationed variously in **Cordova**, **Valdez**, and **Seward**. He spent the year 1919–20 in Douglas, then the remainder of his Alaskan years, 1920–24, in **Ketchikan**.

Father Van der Pol was a man of vision, initiative, vitality, and management skills that drove him to accomplish much in the development of the Alaska missions. His correspondence reveals him to have been also a man with a clear, orderly mind who could keep things in proper perspective. He felt that the kind of men needed in Alaska were ones who "have faith and are able to see small things as small things." He was not one to complain. "The solitude, the misunderstandings, the impossible work to be done," he found, "are in the day's work."

Father Van der Pol suffered from rheumatism during his later years. He died in Sacred Heart Hospital, Spokane, Washington, on May 16, 1930, and lies buried in the Jesuit cemetery at Mount St. Michael's near Spokane.

WARFEL, Bishop Michael William

Michael William Warfel, one of five children, two girls and three boys, was born on September 16, 1948, in Elkhart, Indiana, to Robert Warfel and Josephine Rumshas Warfel. His father came from a Pennsylvania Dutch/German background; his mother had Lithuanian roots. His religious roots are unusual. Though his father was a baptized Baptist and his mother had a Catholic background from her Lithuanian ancestry, there was little religion practiced in the home. When young Michael announced he would go to the new Lutheran church being built, within a week he found himself enrolled in catechism classes at the local Catholic parish, St. Vincent de Paul. At the age of twelve, he was baptized in the Catholic Church.

Michael received his early education in Elkhart. While in high school, he participated in cross-country running, track, and field. Wrestling, however, was his sport of choice, and he excelled in competition. Academically, he was heavily involved in the school's music program, singing in its chorus and playing the trumpet in its band. In 1966, after completing high school, he began studies, principally in music, his declared major, at the University of Indiana in Bloomington. However, shortly into his second year, now attending Indiana University at its South Bend campus, he enlisted in the U.S. Army. He served in Vietnam for 18 months and in Korea for 13. He was honorably discharged in 1971.

Following his military service, Michael became interested in Religious life, possibly as a Religious Brother. His pastor, however, urged him to consider the diocesan priesthood instead. Accordingly, in 1972, Michael entered St. Gregory's College Seminary in Cincinnati, Ohio, as a seminarian for the Diocese of Fort Wayne/South Bend in Indiana.

After earning a B.A. degree in philosophy from St. Gregory's, he went on to graduate studies in theology at Mount St. Mary's Seminary of the West, also in Cincinnati.

While Michael was in seminary studies, his sister moved to **Alaska**. There he visited her during summer months. From the outset, he found himself in love with Alaska and its people. When the time came for him to profess candidacy for Holy Orders, a step that formally commits a seminarian to a particular diocese, his heart was in Alaska; and he knew it was in Alaska that he wished to live and minister as a priest. He contacted Francis T. **Hurley**, Archbishop of **Anchorage** at the time, in hopes of being accepted for that archdiocese. Archbishop Hurley, in turn, contacted William E. McManus, Bishop of the Fort Wayne/South Bend diocese, to inquire about the seminarian Michael Warfel. With great generosity of heart, Bishop McManus replied: "He is just the kind of priest I am looking for here; but, if he wants to go, I am willing to make that sacrifice for the mission of Alaska." The change of dioceses took place.

In the summer of 1978, the first one that Michael was affiliated with the Archdiocese of Anchorage, he resided at St. Elizabeth Ann Seton parish in Anchorage and worked for Catholic Social Services. The following summer, he found himself at St. Mary's parish in **Kodiak**. At the end of that summer, in St. Elizabeth Ann Seton Church, Archbishop Hurley ordained him a deacon. During his last year at the seminary, Michael, now a deacon, served for six months at St. Michael's parish in Fort Laramie, Ohio. On April 26, 1980, in St. Matthew's Cathedral in South Bend, Indiana, Michael was ordained a priest for the Archdiocese of Anchorage by Archbishop Hurley. By the end of 1980, Father Warfel had his Master of Divinity degree.

Father Warfel's first assignment as a priest was to St. Benedict's parish in Anchorage, where he was associate pastor under Father Stanley J. **Allie** for four years and under Msgr. Francis A. Murphy for one year. While at St. Benedict's, he served also as visiting priest to St. Michael's parish in **McGrath**, from 1983–85. During his second year as such, he visited McGrath on the third Sunday of every month. He also spent Christmas and Easter there. This he did to "provide a sense of continuity among the people and to give them a sense of belonging."

In 1985, Father Warfel was appointed pastor of Sacred Heart parish in **Wasilla**. After four and a half years there, he, in 1989, became pastor of St. Mary's parish in Kodiak. To be able to minister more effectively to his Hispanic parishioners, he learned Spanish, studying it in Guatemala, the Dominican Republic, and Mexico. Soon fluent in that language, he introduced Masses in Spanish and an outreach program to Kodiak's Spanish-speaking community. In 1995, he was named pastor of Our Lady of Guadalupe parish in Anchorage, where his Spanish language skills also proved to be a most valuable asset.

In addition to his interest in Spanish, Father Warfel had, since seminary days, also a particular interest in and a love for Sacred Scripture. In 1990, specializing in Sacred Scripture, he received an M.A. degree in theology from St. Michael's College in Winooski Park, Vermont. Subsequently, he participated in the Jerusalem Scripture Study Program offered by St. John's University, Collegeville, Minnesota.

On February 19, 1995, the Bishop of Juneau, Michael H. **Kenny**, died suddenly while on a trip to Jordan. The Diocese of Juneau was now vacant. On Tuesday, November 19, 1996, Pope John Paul II announced the appointment of Father Warfel as the fourth Bishop of the Diocese of Juneau. Soon after the appointment became public, Archbishop Hurley made the following comments concerning it: "I am most thankful to Pope John Paul II for selecting Father Warfel to be the next Bishop of Juneau. The Holy Father not only recognizes Father Warfel as an excellent priest, but pays honor to Alaska and to the Archdiocese of Anchorage by selecting one of our own."

On December 17, 1996, in Juneau, Michael

Bishop Michael W. Warfel.
Courtesy of Bp. Warfel.

William Warfel was ordained a bishop by Archbishop Hurley and formally installed as the fourth Bishop of Juneau. For his motto, Bishop Warfel chose: "Always To Walk In Christ." This was the first ordination in Juneau of a Catholic bishop. It was not long before the people of Southeastern Alaska were aware that, in the words of Archbishop Hurley, they had "a pastoral bishop, a zealous and prayerful priest, and a wise and humorous person to carry on the tradition of making the gospel and the Church alive."

From the outset of his tenure as Bishop of Juneau, Bishop Warfel showed himself to be a man of keen insight. He was honest and forthright, easily approachable, a good listener, gifted with a sense of humor that put people at ease in his presence. While taking his responsibilities as a bishop very seriously, he knew, too, how to relax, whether by cross-country skiing or hiking the Alaska wilderness. Early on as bishop, he hiked the historic Chilkoot Trail. The youthful voice that sang well in the chorus during his high school days continued to sing well. His annual celebrations of the Chrism Mass were events of rare liturgical beauty.

On August 6, 2000, Michael J. **Kaniecki**, S.J., died suddenly of a heart attack at **Emmonak**. The Diocese of **Fairbanks** was now without a bishop. Within four days, Father Richard D. **Case**, S.J., was elected by the Diocesan Board of Consultors to serve as Diocesan Administrator until such time as a new bishop would be installed. In the third week of October 2001, Rome saw fit to appoint Bishop Warfel as interim Apostolic Administrator of the Diocese of Fairbanks, while remaining at the same time Bishop of Juneau. As interim Apostolic Administrator, he assumed all the rights, faculties and duties of a diocesan bishop for the Diocese of Fairbanks. The appointment was made in order to lighten the weight of responsibility that had been placed on Father Case, as well as to enable him to resume some of his former pastoral duties. By October 23rd, Bishop Warfel was in Fairbanks, on the first of his more or less monthly visits to Fairbanks, to meet with chancery personnel and other pastoral staff of the Diocese of Fairbanks. He asked Father Case to stay on as his assistant. Father Case found him "easy to work for," adding, "He has a pastoral style that looks for the good of the people he leads. He places great emphasis on evangelization and the proclamation of God's word." At this same time, Bishop Warfel, a member of the United States Conference of Catholic Bishops, also chaired its Committee on Evangelization, and was active on the Administrative Committee for the USCCB.

A month after Bishop Warfel was appointed interim Apostolic Administrator of the Diocese of Fairbanks, he wrote a letter to its people. In it, after a few remarks about how he saw his role as interim Apostolic Administrator, he revealed his pastoral concerns. "As far as my vision for parish life," he wrote, "it is one that provides for authentic and heartfelt worship, especially through liturgy and a level of religious education that is truly formational. Thus inspired, members are moved to acts of charity, justice and peace. Obviously, this is a tall order, but I believe it is the vision that must be kept before the Church." He went on to stress that "ministers in the Church, whether ordained or lay, must strive to be holy," adding, "after all, holiness of life is our greatest and most effective tool, if the Church is going to be effective in its essential mission of evangelization."

Bishop Warfel's added administrative responsibilities, caring for the Fairbanks diocese, were happily concluded for him, when Msgr. Donald J. **Kettler** was ordained and installed as the new Bishop

of Fairbanks on August 22, 2002. As of the year 2004, Bishop Warfel was still the Ordinary of the Juneau diocese.

WASILLA

The City of Wasilla is located in the Matanuska Valley at mile 159.8 on the Alaska Railroad and eleven miles southwest of **Palmer**. Wasilla came into being about 1916, as the name of the station on the railroad. In 1967, its population numbered 112; in the year 2000, 5,469. The Wasilla post office was established in 1917.

Wasilla appears in *The Official Catholic Directory* for the first time in the 1967 edition, as a mission of St. Michael's parish in Palmer. It was not long before the rapidly growing Catholic community in Wasilla began to ask for a church and to become a parish. It was primarily a group of Catholic women, organized as the St. Jude Guild, that took the initiative in bringing about a church in Wasilla. Ground was broken for this in August 1967, but it was almost two years before the church was up. The members of the St. Jude Guild wanted it named in honor of St. Jude, but the Catholic Church Extension Society, which had helped finance the construction of the church, asked that it be named in honor of the Sacred Heart. So it was.

As a mission of St. Michael's parish in Palmer, Sacred Heart was under the care of the pastors of St. Michael's: Msgr. John A. **Lunney**, 1966–67; Msgr. Francis A. Murphy, 1967–70; Father James A. O'Carroll, C.S.Sp., 1970–71; Father Edward J. Stirling, C.S.Sp., 1971–72; Father Ernest H. **Muellerleile**, 1972–74; Father John J. **Marx**, 1974–77; Father Sean O'Donoghue, C.S.Sp., 1977–78; and Father Fred T. **Bugarin**, 1978–79.

In January 1979, Sacred Heart became an independent parish. The first priest to be named its pastor and to reside in Wasilla was Father Bugarin, from 1979–81. It was he who built St. Jude Center in Wasilla.

From 1981–85, there were no priests in residence at Sacred Heart. Instead, Sister Elmer Reisinger, O.S.B., was Parish Administrator. From 1985–89, Father Michael W. **Warfel** was pastor in residence, as was Father Alfred L. Galvan—of the El Paso, Texas, diocese—during the year 1989–90. Deacon

Felix M. Maguire served at Sacred Heart from 1987–89.

In the summer of 1990, Father Stanley J. **Allie** was appointed pastor of Sacred Heart. By that time, the first Sacred Heart Church was much too small to accommodate the parishioners it was meant to serve. He immediately began planning for a new, bigger church. This was somewhat slow in coming into being. The first Mass was offered in it in November 1998. It was dedicated in February 1999.

Father Allie's rather lengthy tenure in Wasilla came to an end in the year 2000. Father Kasparaj Mallavarapu succeeded him, and was still pastor of Sacred Heart as of the year 2004.

15

WHELAN, Bishop Robert L., S.J

It is no exaggeration to say that throughout his long life Robert Louis Whelan was genuinely loved by all who knew him for the man, the priest, the bishop that he was. This zealous, soft-spoken man of quiet, strong demeanor, spent all his active years as a minister of the Church—forty-nine of them— in **Alaska**, serving in all three of the dioceses of Alaska. Upon his retirement as Ordinary of the Diocese of Fairbanks, the Alaska State Legislature, in an official document, honored him as "this special man, who has served the members of his Church with warmth, compassion and understanding, and all Alaskans well."

Robert Louis Whelan was born in Wallace, Idaho, on April 16, 1912. In Wallace he attended, for ten years, Our Lady of Lourdes Academy, staffed by the Sisters of **Providence**. For his last two years of high school, he enrolled as a boarding student at Jesuit-staffed Gonzaga High School in Spokane, Washington. On August 3, 1931, he entered the Jesuit novitiate at Sheridan, Oregon. After completing his two-year noviceship and two years of classical and humanities studies there, he went to Mount St. Michael's in Spokane for three years of philosophical studies. During the academic year 1938–39, he taught at Gonzaga High School and pursued special studies in mathematics and science. He taught from 1939–41 at Bellarmine Preparatory in Tacoma, Washington. From 1941–45 he made

Sacred Heart Church, Wasilla. *Photo by Deacon David E. Schutt.*

Bishop Robert L. Whelan,
S.J. *DFA*.

his theological studies at Alma College, Los Gatos, California. In San Francisco, on June 17, 1944, he was ordained to the priesthood by Archbishop John J. Mitty. Father Whelan made his tertianship, the final year of basic Jesuit training, at Port Townsend, Washington, 1945–46.

On July 10, 1946, Father Whelan arrived in **Juneau**, Alaska, where he was pastor of Nativity of the Blessed Virgin Mary parish for eleven years. As such, he also visited dependent outlying towns and villages. In August 1957, he was named pastor of the newly established Saint Anthony's parish in **Anchorage**. For what he described as "eleven wonderful years" he served in that capacity, building up the new parish both physically and spiritually. During the last six of his eleven years at St. Anthony's, he had with him as his assistant Father Joseph E. **Shirey**, S.J. The two were a perfect match-up. From Father Shirey we know that Father Whelan's favorite outdoor sports were downhill skiing in winter and water skiing in summer. We know, too, that "he carried on a great telephone apostolate. Often, when invited to a parishioner's home for an evening dinner, he could be seen whispering something to the lady of the house, then pick up the phone and call other parishioners." Divulging another Whelan secret, Father Shirey wrote: "He was also known for another of his habits on these home visits. He

would get comfortable in a chair or on a davenport, and in a few minutes be asleep. Knowing smiles and glances signaled that all was well."

The six years the two priests spent together at St. Anthony's were, according to both of them, "about the best years of our lives." But, the togetherness was too good to last.

Early one December morning in 1967, just as Father Whelan was about to go to the church for Mass, the phone rang. He answered it. A short conversation followed. After hanging up, he went and knocked on Father Shirey's door. Invited in, he opened the door and said, "Well, Joe, the honeymoon is over." The call had come from Washington, D.C., informing him that Pope Paul VI, on December 6, 1967, had appointed him Coadjutor Bishop of **Fairbanks** with right of succession.

In Sacred Heart Cathedral, Fairbanks, on February 22, 1968, Father Whelan was ordained to the office of bishop by Archbishop Luigi Raimondi, Apostolic Delegate to the United States. On November 30th of that same year, when Bishop Francis D. **Gleeson**, S.J., Ordinary of the Diocese of Fairbanks, retired, Bishop Whelan succeeded him in that office. In Sacred Heart Cathedral, on February 13, 1969, he was formally installed as the second Bishop of Fairbanks. (When Bishop Gleeson was in the last years of his life, still living in the diocesan chancery building with Bishop Whelan, the latter saw to his every need and with loving solicitude lavished a tender care on him that can fittingly be described only as "maternal.")

As Bishop of Fairbanks, in keeping with the motto on his coat of arms, "Solicitude and Charity," Bishop Whelan was a tireless traveler, visiting by plane, boat, and snowmachine the widely scattered Indian and Eskimo villages of his 409,849-square-mile diocese. Travel became "second nature" to him. He found visiting the various parishes and outlying stations, especially the Native villages and the simple life lived there, to be "an enjoyable experience."

During Bishop Whelan's years in office, the **Eskimo Deacon Program** came into being and to full flower. He ordained 28 Eskimo men to the permanent diaconate, for he considered the ordination of Eskimo men to the diaconate "an important

Bishop Robert L. Whelan, S.J., painting in the one-time barracks building as it is being transformed into the House of Prayer—"a spiritual fitness center"—in Fairbanks. *LR.*

development for the work of the Church in our bush villages, and a morale builder for the Eskimo people." He also ordained a number of men to the priesthood for the diocese. In the cities, towns and villages he visited, he conferred the Sacrament of Confirmation on many. Blessing newly built churches was a true celebration for him. He organized and promoted parish councils in the diocese. It was he who pushed the button, on July 14, 1971, that launched the diocesan Catholic radio station **KNOM, Nome**, on the air. Bishop Whelan was an active shepherd, totally devoted to his flock.

In the early 1980s, Bishop Whelan requested Rome to consider providing him with a coadjutor bishop with right of succession. Rome looked favorably upon his request; and, on May 1, 1984, Bishop Whelan had the joy of ordaining Michael J. **Kaniecki**, S.J., to the office of bishop as his successor. On the following day, the two hosted Pope

John Paul II and President Ronald Reagan during their stopovers in Fairbanks.

On July 28, 1985, Bishop Whelan retired as Bishop of Fairbanks. But, he did not go into rocking-chair retirement. He spent a week on **Little Diomede** Island in Bering Strait, bringing the people there the 1985 Christmas Mass. In 1986, after a sabbatical, he began a new ministry as Director of the House of Prayer, a building situated on the cathedral grounds and placed under the patronage of St. Therese, "the Little Flower." This he termed "a spiritual fitness center." Here, in what he described as "a very peaceful place," he lived. As its director, he organized and directed retreats, prayer sessions, and workshops. He spent much time in personal prayer and on retreats, and in giving spiritual guidance. For physical exercise, he rode his bicycle around the city of Fairbanks. At times, he flew to distant villages to offer Christmas Mass for people who would otherwise have been without it. Christmas 1990 found him offering Mass in the little log church in **McGrath**.

Bishop Whelan liked to keep active, to move about, to be with people, especially young people. They energized him. However, by the early 1990s the years were beginning to weigh somewhat heavily on him, and the first signs of Alzheimer's were beginning to manifest themselves. Fully aware of what might lie ahead for him, and with great generosity of spirit, he offered it all up for the Church and for the Missionary Diocese of Fairbanks.

By 1995, time had come for him to go into full retirement. On August 19th of that year, he offered a special Mass of Thanksgiving for his nearly fifty years in Alaska and for the countless friends he had made there in the course of those years. Festive farewell celebrations followed the Mass. On September 1st, he flew to Spokane to join the Regis Jesuit Community on the Gonzaga University campus. Toward the end of his life, his health had deteriorated to the point where he had to be placed in Spokane's North Central Care Center. There he died in his sleep the evening of September 15, 2001.

In keeping with the express wishes of the people of the Diocese of Fairbanks, the body of Bishop Whelan was brought from Spokane to Sacred Heart Cathedral, Fairbanks, on September 28th. That same evening, a wake was held. The Mass of Christian Burial was celebrated the next day. Present, along with many priests, were Roger L. **Schwietz**, O.M.I., Archbishop of Anchorage, Michael W. **Warfel**, Bishop of Juneau, three Eskimo deacons whom Bishop Whelan had ordained, and as many of the Faithful as could crowd into the Cathedral.

Immediately after the Mass, in Birch Hill Cemetery, Fairbanks, under the birches, on a south-facing slope covered with a carpet of newly fallen autumn leaves—after songs had been song in Latin, Koyukon Athabaskan Indian, and English, and final prayers said and blessings bestowed—Bishop Whelan, "a most thoughtful, kind and gentle man, universally loved," was laid to rest alongside his predecessor, Bishop Francis D. Gleeson, and his successor, Bishop Michael J. Kaniecki.

130, 142, 164

Brother Carl F. Wickart, S.J., a successful hunter. *JOPA-933.1.05.*

WICKART, Brother Carl F., S.J.

Carl Frank Wickart was born in German-speaking Canton Zug, Switzerland, on October 24, 1897. He entered the Jesuit novitiate at Sheridan, Oregon, on March 21, 1932. On July 22, 1935, he arrived at St. Mary's Mission, **Akulurak**. There he proved himself to be a successful hunter of water fowl and rabbits, also a capable mender and handler of fish wheels and fish nets. While at Akulurak, with the gladly-granted permission of his Superior, he went up the Andreafsky River on a brown bear hunt. In the evening of the second day of the hunt, he spotted one, but it was too far away and the light was too poor for a shot. For the next several days he kept looking for the bear, but without success. "Next year!" his Superior consoled him.

From 1938–41, Brother Wickart served at the **Pilgrim Hot Springs** Mission. One of his main chores was to cut firewood for the mission stoves. In December 1941, he began a four-year stay at **Hooper Bay**. There, too, he proved to be a successful hunter of water fowl. On October 30, 1942, he pronounced his final vows as a Jesuit Lay Brother. Hooper Bay turned out to be his last assignment in the Alaskan "bush."

July 10, 1945, was the day of Brother Wickart's memorable arrival in **Juneau**. Sporting a full beard, he hailed a taxi at the airport and directed the driver to take him to the Catholic Church. The driver, concluding from the beard that his fare was a prelate of the Russian Orthodox Church, took him to the church of that denomination. Great was Brother Wickart's surprise, when his knock on the door was answered by another bearded gentleman, who immediately bowed to him, embraced him warmly, and gave him a cordial welcome. The local Orthodox priest had taken him to be the awaited Orthodox bishop.

In Juneau, Brother Wickart served mainly as furnace man, janitor, and custodian at the parish complex and at the parochial school. While in Juneau, he became a U.S. citizen, in January 1951.

That same year, 1951, Brother Wickart was transferred to **Fairbanks**, where he continued to serve as furnace man, janitor and custodian of the parochial school. Being a non-driver, he commuted between the parish rectory and the school on a bicycle. In extreme cold, or when road conditions were too poor for biking, he walked.

Some time during the latter half of 1964, George T. **Boileau**, S.J., newly ordained Coadjutor Bishop of Fairbanks, thoughtfully invited Brother Wickart to join him in Europe. After Bishop Boileau had attended the third session of Vatican II in Rome, he and Brother Wickart met in Switzerland. In the bishop's new VW station wagon, the two drove on to Oberammergau, Germany, where they met Father Louis L. **Renner**, S.J. The three then traveled across Germany, through Luxembourg, toVlijtingen, Belgium, to visit the family of Father William J. **Loyens**, S.J. After overnighting in Brussels, they proceeded on to Paris to spend the night in a hotel and the next day sight-seeing Paris, before driving to Versailles to visit the family of Father René **Astruc**, S.J. Before leaving France, the traveling trio went to Lisieux to pray and offer Mass at the shrine of Ste. Thérèse, patroness of the Alaska missions. After farewells at Le Havre, Father Renner returned to Germany, while Bishop Boileau and Brother Wickart sailed for New York. Brother Wickart was not to see his native land again.

During his later years in Fairbanks, Brother Wickart, relieved of his work at the school, served instead as maintenance man and sacristan of Immaculate Conception Church. People who attended Mass there came to know well the tall, amiable, black-robed Brother with the kindly face and gentle voice, a voice still graced with a touch of Swiss accent. In the church and rectory, he took care of all the little things that needed to be done with an air of quiet dedication right up to the time he was no longer able to climb the stairs.

Early in 1978, Brother Wickart went to Spokane, Washington, for a medical examination. Surgery revealed that he had terminal cancer. Around mid-May, when he was well enough again to travel, he returned to Fairbanks. He wanted to spend his last days where he had spent the last 27 years of his life. On June 7, 1978, in Fairbanks Memorial Hospital, he died "very peacefully." He lies buried in Birch Hill Cemetery, Fairbanks.

WILHALM, Brother Peter P., S.J.

Peter P. Wilhalm was born in Fond du Lac County, Wisconsin, on June 29, 1885. He entered the Jesuit novitiate at Los Gatos, California, on January 19, 1909. From 1910–15, he was in Montana, mostly in Missoula; then, for a year, at Seattle College in Seattle, Washington. In early July 1916, he

Brother Peter P. Wilhalm, S.J.
JOPA-1079.08.

was handed a letter by Joseph R. **Crimont**, S.J., Prefect Apostolic of **Alaska** at the time. Father Crimont had just been in Portland, Oregon, with the Father Provincial, Richard A. Gleeson, author of the letter. "When I opened it," wrote Brother Wilhalm, "I almost fainted, as it was an order to accompany Fr. Crimont to Alaska. I had not even given a thought of ever going to that frozen country."

From 1916–19, Brother Wilhalm served at Immaculate Conception parish in **Fairbanks** as a general handyman. On October 14, 1919, he arrived at the **Pilgrim Hot Springs** Mission, where he was prefect of the boys, gardener, and maintenance man. Father Segundo **Llorente**, S.J., wrote of him: "A pious and hardworking man, he kept the farm at Pilgrim Springs in fine shape and kept constant watch for any deterioration in the buildings to repair it instantly, from doors that did not close tight to leaking roofs or a cracked window. Local Superiors felt more at ease with Brother Wilhalm around." Father Joseph F. **McElmeel**, S.J., said of Brother Wilhalm that "he carried Pilgrim Springs on his shoulders for years." In December 1923, Brother Wilhalm was a member of the party that found the frozen body of Father Frederick A. **Ruppert**, S.J.

When the Pilgrim Springs mission was closed in the summer of 1941, Brother Wilhalm was transferred to St. Mary's mission, **Akulurak**. For five years, he was prefect of the boys and general maintenance man.

Brother Wilhalm spent his last Alaskan years, 1946–48, back where he had spent his first, in Fairbanks. This time he served as janitor of the newly opened parochial school. To drive away the Sunday afternoon blues, he would go to the church choir loft. Accompanying himself on the organ, he would sing his way through the hymnal.

In 1948, Brother Wilhalm's long bout with cancer began, and he had to retire to Mount St. Michael's in Spokane. Cheerful to the end, he died in Sacred Heart Hospital, Spokane, on January 29, 1954. He lies buried in the Jesuit cemetery at Mount St. Michael's.

WILLEBRAND, Father Aloysius G., S.J.

Aloysius Guy Willebrand was born to Henry J. Willebrand and Mabel Montgomery Willebrand in Dayton, Washington, on January 5, 1895. He received almost all his elementary and secondary schooling in the public schools of Clarkston, Washington. For his last semester of high school, he attended Gonzaga High School in Spokane, Washington, from which he graduated in 1915. On July 14, 1915, he entered the Jesuit novitiate at Los Gatos, California. After completing his two-year noviceship, he spent three additional years there studying the classics and humanities. During the years 1920–23, he studied philosophy at Mount St. Michael's in Spokane. Next, he taught at St. Ignatius Mission in Montana for a year, before going on to spend the years 1924–28 at St. Louis University, St. Louis, Missouri, making his theological studies. He was ordained a priest in St. Francis Xavier Church in St. Louis on June 22, 1927.

From 1928–30, Father Willebrand was stationed at St. Mary's Mission, **Akulurak, Alaska**. He was there when, on August 15, 1929, the mission church burned down. After his two years at Akulurak, he spent the year 1930–31 making his tertianship at Port Townsend, Washington. From 1931–33, he was stationed at the **Pilgrim Hot Springs** Mission. There, on October 30, 1932, he took his final vows. During the summer of 1933, he was on temporary assignment in **Kotzebue**. His last year in Alaska,

1933–34, found him in residence at **Pilot Station**, tending to that mission and to its dependent stations.

Father Willebrand spent the remainder of his active life as a priest serving on the Indian missions of the Pacific Northwest. After a drawn-out struggle with cancer of the throat, he died in Sacred Heart Hospital, Spokane, on December 22, 1956. He lies buried in the Jesuit cemetery at Mount St. Michael's.

After Father Willebrand's death, one of his fellow Jesuits wrote of him:

> Father Willebrand had a mind of unusual depth and loved the companionship of his fellow Jesuits, yet all his life as a priest was spent in sacrificing these, teaching numbers and the ABCs and catechism to children when he could have taught in a house of theology. He lived a lonely life on the missions because he saw the need there was for someone to do that work which is so difficult.

WILLOW

Willow is located on the **Alaska** Railroad some 70 highway miles north of **Anchorage**. The Willow post office dates from 1948. In 1967, the town had a population of 78. In the year 2000, its population numbered 1,658.

Mass was first celebrated in Willow in 1964. St. Christopher's parish in Willow was founded in 1967. Vincentian Father Francis J. Fish was its first pastor. For its first church, the parish had a double-wide trailer located on land donated by Mr. and Mrs. Christopher Terry. This served as the parish "church" until the year 2002, when a new church was built—on land donated by Barney Gottstein—and dedicated on June 23, 2002.

Soon after its founding, St. Christopher's became a dependent mission of St. Bernard's parish in **Talkeetna** and was served by priests stationed there. Before St. Bernard's parish was established, priests from **Palmer** used to visit Willow and offer Mass. Among priests that served the Willow community over the decades, in addition to Father Fish, were Fathers Stanley J. **Allie**, Francis A. Murphy, Thomas E. Power, Leo C. **Desso**, Joseph T. Walsh, **Gerard T. Ryan**, C.S.Sp., Urban M. **Bates**, O.P., and LeRoy Clementich, C.S.C.

While the Archdiocese of Anchorage had been and was, as of the year 2004, wholly supportive of them, the people of St. Christopher's were, for the most part, on their own as far as the day to day running of their parish went. "Circuit rider" priests provided the Mass and Sacraments for the people. Occasionally, a deacon visited the parish, when no priest was available. On April 28, 2001, newly appointed Deacon Jay E. Cable began to conduct Eucharistic services at St. Christopher's. In the earlier part of 2002, Deacon David E. Schutt began ministry there.

From 1992–95, Sister Louise Tibbetts, S.N.J.M., served as Pastoral Administrator of St. Christopher's. As of the year 2004, Ray Lizotte was the lay presider at Eucharist services at St. Christopher's. Claire Fitzgaireld was general administrator of the parish.

15

WOOD, Father Gregg D., S.J.

Gregg D. Wood, the oldest of four children, was born on April 15, 1945, at Carlisle Barracks, Pennsylvania, to Gregg D. Wood, Sr., a physician/surgeon in the U.S. Army, and Jeanne L. Fortuna Wood. From infancy on, however, Portland, Oregon, was his home. There he grew up and received his education. From 1950–56, he attended St. Mary

Magdalene Grade School. He completed his elementary education at a public school, after which he attended Jesuit High School in Portland from 1959–63. His collegiate studies were made at Gonzaga University in Spokane, Washington, during the years 1963–67.

Though it was the thinking of his brothers that Gregg was the one to follow in their father's footsteps and minister to the ills of the body, things turned out otherwise. While attending Jesuit High, in his words, he "experienced the beginning of a call to follow the Lord of Life in the Company that bears His name." He was impressed by the discipline, companionship, loyalty, and sense of purpose he witnessed in the Jesuits staffing the school. During his second year at Gonzaga, his calling to be a Jesuit priest came "to full bloom." He went on to finish his collegiate studies, ending them with an undergraduate degree in biology.

On August 21, 1967, Gregg entered the Jesuit Novitiate of St. Francis Xavier at Sheridan, Oregon. His two-year noviceship completed, he studied philosophy during the year 1969–70 at Mount St. Michael's, Spokane. From 1970–72, he taught biology at Seattle Preparatory. From 1972–75, he studied theology at Regis College, Toronto, Ontario, Canada. He was ordained a priest in Seattle on June 21, 1975, by Archbishop Raymond G. Hunthausen.

St. Christopher's Church, Willow. *Courtesy of St. Christopher's parish.*

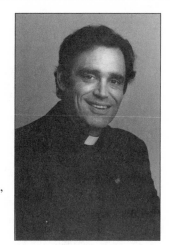

Father Gregg D. Wood,
S.J. *BR-947223*.

During his first year as a priest, Father Wood taught courses in Sacred Scripture and Greek at the Novitiate of St. Francis Xavier, now in Portland, Oregon. After that year, he went on to the California School of Professional Psychology in San Diego, from which he obtained a doctorate in Clinical Psychology in 1984. From 1983–95, he was stationed at Seattle University, where he served as a psychologist in the Counseling Center. For a number of years, he was also the Father Minister of the Jesuit Community.

During the year 1995–96, Father Wood was on a sabbatical, exploring the possibilities of going into ministry to Native Americans, a ministry to which he felt himself being drawn. He also felt called to lead a simpler lifestyle than that of the big city, and he wanted to be more closely connected with nature. Accordingly, he spent time on the Indian missions in eastern Washington and in Montana. For a time, too, he was a member of the Joe **Prince** Community—named for Eskimo Brother Joe Prince—a community composed of the Jesuits ministering in the Yukon-Kuskokwim Delta who, on a regular basis, gathered in a building at St. Mary's Mission on the **Andreafsky** River in western **Alaska**. As a member of that community, he was introduced to the Central Yup'ik Eskimos during an initial two-month visit in **Hooper Bay**. While there, he was shown the movie *The Alaskan Eskimo*, a movie made at Hooper Bay in 1946 by Walt Disney Pro-

ductions. He recalled having seen it in a movie theater as a child.

Happy with his new-found ministry among Native Americans, in this case the Central Yup'ik Eskimos, Father Wood readily consented to replace temporarily Father Mark A. **Hoelsken**, S.J.—the priest then responsible for the villages of Hooper Bay, **Scammon Bay**, and **Chevak**—who was scheduled to be away during the year 1996–97 to make his tertianship in the Philippine Islands. By the time Father Hoelsken returned from the Philippines, Father Wood was so attached to the three villages he was caring for, and so into sharing the lifestyle of the people, that he asked to be allowed to continue on as their priest. As of the year 2004, he was still happily attending to those three villages, even though, after seven years on that three-village assignment, he saw fit to write to Father Louis L. **Renner**, S.J., "The pace here has been relentless, with so many urgent situations that just by their nature take priority."

His being a circuit rider responsible for three villages naturally made for a hectic pace and had its drawbacks. Father Wood, however, being the clinical psychologist and the Jesuit priest that he was, knew how to cope with them. When he was inclined to be discouraged, because things were not happening fast enough and in keeping with his expectations, he had recourse to prayer—"to refocus the situation, to see the big picture." He came to realize that the people to whom he was ministering were ultimately all the Lord's people, that his work was ultimately the Lord's work among them, and that it was the Lord's loving design that was being worked out in them. He humbly admitted to himself that, as a priest, he was only "the Lord's subordinate co-laborer." He found that "witnessing the Lord working in and through His people gladdens the heart."

Whereas others found the Bering Sea coast tundra in winter a bleak, empty, frozen waste, Father Wood found that "time on the tundra is powerful therapy." One day, he and a Jesuit novice were traveling over an icy trail between Scammon Bay and Chevak, a distance of 27 miles. Trail conditions required frequent stops to cool off the snowmachine. During one stop, Father Wood looked out on the frozen tundra, surveyed the panorama, and with excitement said to the young novice, "I do love this! And so it is with my ministry among the people of the North."

207

WOOD, Father John J., S.J.

John J. "Jack" Wood was born in Seattle, Washington, on June 2, 1920. His father was a shipwright. Jack's older brother, Francis, too, was a Jesuit priest; his younger brother, James, a Jesuit Lay Brother. Another brother became a physician, and a sister became a Maryknoll Sister. After receiving his grade school education at St. John's School, Jack attended Seattle Preparatory School from 1934–38. He entered the Jesuit novitiate at Sheridan, Oregon, on August 14, 1938. After completing his two-year noviceship, he spent two years at Sheridan in classical and humanities studies. He made his philosophical studies at Mount St. Michael's, Spokane, Washington, from 1942–45. During the years 1945–47 he was at **Holy Cross Mission, Alaska**. From 1947–51, he studied theology at Alma College, Los Gatos, California. He was ordained a priest in San Francisco, on June 17, 1950. After making his tertianship at Port Townsend, Washington, 1951–52, he returned to Alaska.

Father Wood's first assignment in Alaska as a priest was **Hooper Bay**. Out of there he visited the villages of **Chevak** and **Newtok**. During his Hooper Bay years, 1952–59, he was also a chaplain in the Alaska National Guard and an auxiliary military chaplain to Air Force personnel stationed at Cape Romanzof.

From 1959–62, Father Wood was stationed in **Bethel** as assistant pastor. As such, he traveled to Bethel's dependent missions, among them **Aniak**, **Kalskag**, and **McGrath**.

During the summer of 1959, Father Wood spent six weeks in Tacoma, Washington, taking flight training at Oswald's Flying Service and earning his pilot's license. Later that same summer, ably assisted by his skilled father, he began to build a new church, a log church, at McGrath. The church was ready for "the grand opening," in the words of Father Wood, for the 1960 Christmas Mass.

Father John J. Wood, S.J. *JOPA-1080.01.*

By early 1960, Father Wood had his new airplane, a Cessna 180, christened *Regina Coeli* ("Queen of Heaven"), enabling him to visit his mission stations along the Kuskokwim River more frequently and at less cost. But, his years of flying in Alaska were of short duration.

During the years 1962–64, Father Wood was at Seattle University, suffering already from the onset of multiple sclerosis. He was able, however, to teach evening classes in theology. He returned to Alaska once more in 1964, to serve in Bethel and at McGrath, till deteriorating health necessitated his leaving Alaska permanently in 1966.

The next decade found Father Wood at various places in the Northwest, engaged in such ministries as his health allowed: 1966–70, St. Ignatius parish, Portland; 1970–74, Seattle University; 1974–75, chaplain to the Holy Names Sisters, Spokane; 1975–76, no specific assignment; 1976–77, chaplain at Maryville Nursing Home, Beaverton, Oregon; 1977–88, Mount St. Joseph Residence and Care Center, Portland. From 1988–97, he was at St. Joseph Care Center, Spokane. There he died, on March 11, 1997. He lies buried in the Jesuit cemetery at Mount St. Michael's, Spokane.

Father Wood, according to Father Neill R. Meany, S.J., his obituarist who knew him well, "was a devout Religious, strict, unbending, his strong character a factor in his later sad history. From the outset, he met his failing health condition with denial, refusing to admit his malady and its ever-worsening symptoms." Even when Father Wood was confined to a wheelchair, he was determined that he would "lick" his health problem and "walk tomorrow." He was not the most tractable of patients, but one had to admire his ironclad fortitude and his undying faith in God.

WRANGELL

Wrangell, located on the northwest coast of Wrangell Island in Southeastern **Alaska**, began as Fort Dionysius, a stockade built by the Russians occupying the island in 1834 to prevent encroachment by the Hudson's Bay Company traders. It was named after one of the **Sitka** Russian American Company's chiefs, Baron Von Wrangell. A Tlingit Indian village had occupied the inner harbor long before the Russians arrived. When the United States purchased Alaska in 1867, a military post called Fort Wrangell was established there. It was abandoned in 1877. The Wrangell post office was established in 1902. In 1890, Wrangell had a population of 316; in 1950, 1,162; in 1967, 1,315; and in the year 2000, 2,308. Wrangell's economy is dominated by the fishing and lumbering industries.

On May 3, 1879, Archbishop Charles J. **Seghers** and Father John J. **Althoff** landed in Wrangell. The following day, a Sunday, the first Mass in Wrangell was celebrated in a dance hall. Many whites and 120 Indians attended. On that same day, Archbishop Seghers appointed Father Althoff the first resident priest of the Wrangell parish, which he, the archbishop, placed under the patronage of St. Rose of Lima. This was the first Catholic parish in Alaska. A year later, on May 30, 1880, John B. Brondel, Bishop of Vancouver Island, blessed the church that Father Althoff had built before the year 1879 was out. From that year, to November 1885, Father Althoff made Wrangell his headquarters, out of which he visited Sitka and other places. In November 1885, he moved to **Juneau** to minister to the hundreds who were flocking to Juneau and **Douglas** to work in the gold mines on both sides of the Gastineau Channel. For the next eleven years, until

St. Rose of Lima Church, Wrangell. *DJA.*

he returned to Vancouver Island, Father Althoff continued to make occasional visits to Wrangell.

For a number of years, Wrangell was visited at infrequent intervals by Father Peter C. **Bougis**, S.J., out of Douglas. On July 17, 1907, Father Adrian Sweere, S.J., stationed in **Ketchikan** from 1907–12, made the first of his many visits to Wrangell. The original Wrangell church, having fallen into disrepair, was torn down in April 1898. At the instigation of Joseph R. **Crimont**, S.J., Prefect Apostolic of Alaska at the time, and with the physical help of Father Edward H. **Brown**, S.J., stationed in Juneau from 1904–13, a new church was completed by December 1908. This church was greatly modified by Father Francis M. **Monroe**, S.J., in the mid-1920s. It is not clear what served as a church during the time gap between the first church and the 1908 church.

It was not until 1924 that a resident priest once again served the Wrangell parish and district. Father Monroe made Wrangell his headquarters from 1924–39. During his first year there, he enlarged the entryway to the church, placed a new basement under it, and added a rectory. During the winter of

1935–36, he installed a modern heating plant. In 1939, he began to renovate the interior of the church with a coating of hammered tin. Because of his advanced age and poor health, however, he was unable to finish the project. This was completed by June 2, 1940, Father Monroe's 85th birthday, by Father Edward A. McNamara, S.J., Father Monroe's replacement.

Father Patrick J. **O'Reilly**, S.J., was in Wrangell from 1940 to December 1941, and Father Bernard F. **McMeel**, S.J., from June 1979 to December 1979. Shortly after his arrival there, he was able to write, "the folks seem very friendly." Father Michael J. Taylor, S.J., in Wrangell during the year 1980–81, was the last Jesuit priest to reside and minister in Wrangell.

During the second half of its existence, the Wrangell parish was served mainly by diocesan priests. In January 1942, Father Matthew E. **Hoch** became pastor of St. Rose of Lima parish. As such, he was responsible also for the St. Catherine of Siena mission in **Petersburg**. Upon his arrival in Wrangell, he set to work with all the zeal of a newly ordained priest. Welcomed and accepted, he was appreciated alike by both the Catholics and non-Catholics of the community. Especially concerned about the children, he set up a catechetical program for them. He made weekly trips for Mass and cat-

The city of Wrangell, the first community in Alaska to have a Catholic parish with a resident pastor. *JOPA-426.23.*

echism to the Wrangell Institute, which had opened in 1936. Operated by the Bureau of Indian Affairs, the institute received children from northern Alaska: first as an orphanage, then as a grade school, and finally as a high school. Father Hoch's successors continued to minister to the Institute's staff and children, until it closed on June 30, 1975.

At Wrangell, Father Hoch lived, quite literally, from "hand to mouth," without ever complaining. By 1959, he knew it was time for a change. The faithful people of Wrangell also knew that it was time for their dedicated pastor to move on. He had by then been in Wrangell for 17 years, a period of service to the Wrangell parish unequalled by any previous or subsequent pastor. He had proved himself to be a worthy successor to Fathers Althoff and Monroe.

From 1959–64, Father Raymond W. **Mosey** was pastor of St. Rose of Lima parish. In 1961, with a grant from the Catholic Church Extension Society, he installed a new heating system and applied asbestos shakes to the church and rectory. He was very popular in both Wrangell and Petersburg, where a new St. Catherine of Siena Church was built. Wrangell turned out to be the last scene of his priestly labors. There, on February 2, 1964, he died in his sleep.

During the years 1964–69, the "almost forgotten" Wrangell parish was visited by nearly a dozen different priests for short periods of time. Father Richard B. **Saudis** was in Wrangell from July 1968 to June 1969. It was during his time that a large parish hall was built next to the church.

From May 1969 to September 1972, Father Peter F. **Gorges** was pastor of St. Rose of Lima parish. At that time, it was the parish, with St. Catherine of Siena in Petersburg as its mission. By the time he returned for his second tour in Wrangell, from 1981–85, both were parishes. Concerning Father Gorges' first tour as pastor of Wrangell, historian Msgr. Vincent A. Yzermans wrote:

> He brought a vigor and vitality to the parish that had not been experienced since the death of Mosey. Under his leadership the interior of the church was renovated according to the liturgical norms of the Second Vatican Council. Members of the parish received a new spirit from his youthful zeal and undertook the completion of the new parish hall.

Father James J. **Manske** was pastor of St. Rose of Lima from 1972–76. He was no stranger to the parish. After the death of Father Mosey, Father Manske made frequent trips to Wrangell and Petersburg from Juneau. He was followed by Father Jerome A. **Frister**, in Wrangell from 1976–79. He, in turn, as mentioned above, was followed by Fathers McMeel and Taylor. Msgr. Yzermans was in Wrangell during the late 1970s to write a history of the parish. Father Hugh Robbins, a Viatorian Father, was then pastor for about nine months. Father Donald E. Henkes was there until June 1982.

In June 1982, Father Gorges, who had by then been pastor for a year in Petersburg, began once again to serve both communities, as well as to make monthly visits to Kake and various logging camps in the area. By this time, Petersburg had grown considerably, and St. Catherine of Siena parish was firmly established as an independent parish. Father Gorges split his time, spending two weeks in one parish, then two in the other.

In the summer of 1985, **Oblate** Father Gerard Gottenbos became pastor of St. Rose of Lima parish. He remained pastor until his death in 1996. Under his direction, the St. Rose of Lima Parish Hall was expanded, and a half basement was developed to accommodate a small apartment, a furnace room, and a meeting room. Father Gottenbos, remembered in Wrangell as "the fisherman priest," was very active in AA activities for youth and adults.

Father Edward Matthews, O.M.I., was pastor of the Wrangell parish from 1996–99. He was followed in that role by Father Michael G. Schwarte, who for many years had been working out of the Juneau chancery office as Diocesan Youth Minister. Flying the diocesan airplane, Father Schwarte, still pastor of the Wrangell parish as of the year 2004, was able to provide a full-service of Sunday and weekday Masses in both Wrangell and Petersburg, in addition to making regular visits to Kake. His spiritual and physical energies proved to be a true blessing for that general area.

Y

YAKUTAT

The town of Yakutat, 210 miles northwest of **Juneau**, was originally the principal winter village of the Yakutats, a subtribe of the Tlingit Indians. In 1880, it had a population of 500; in 1890, 300; in 1910, 271; in 1920, 165; in 1939, 292; in 1950, 298; in 1967, 230; and in the year 2000, 680. The Yakitat post office was established in 1892 and discontinued in 1895. It was reestablished as "Yakutat" in 1901.

"On August 24, 1939, Feast of St. Bartholomew Ap.," wrote Msgr. G. Edgar **Gallant** on the fly-leaf of his breviary on October 22, 1971, "I celebrated the first Mass ever celebrated in the Town of Yakutat at the A.N.B. [Alaska Native Brotherhood] Hall. All our boys from the Pius X Mission attended and received Holy Communion." A church structure and resident parish administrator, however, were late in coming to Yakutat.

In 1972, with help from the Catholic Church Extension Society, Yakutat's first Catholic edifice, a little chapel seating about 50 and dedicated to St. Ann, was built, "on a hill in a densely wooded area without any utilities." A volunteer crew of Christian Brothers and a walk-on volunteer, Stuart Shea from New Orleans, Louisiana, "finished the job in one month." The little chapel

was enlarged in 1982, again with help from the Extension Society.

During the early 1970s, Father Kevin O'Conor [*sic*], O.M.I., regularly visited Yakutat. Sister Immaculata of the Presentation Sisters spent two weeks there in July 1974 giving intensive religious education to the children.

In October 1975, Father Gerard B. Clenaghan, O.M.I., arrived in Yakutat, having volunteered to spend two years in the Diocese of **Juneau**. In April 1978, he wrote to Father Louis L. **Renner**, S.J.: "Bishop **Hurley** asked me particularly to endeavor to set up a program whereby the local community would continue to hold a Sunday Eucharistic Service when my two years were up. The Bishop assures me that this is now being done and he is quite pleased with the outcome."

Over the years, various priests have visited Yaku-

St. Ann's Church, Yakutat. *DJA.*

tat, mostly out of Juneau. During the latter part of 1983, Father William C. **Dibb**, S.J., offered monthly Masses at St. Ann's Mission. Father Jerome A. **Frister** made regular fly-in visits to offer Mass there from 1992–97.

Sisters serving as parish administrators and pastoral ministers at St. Ann's resided, for the most part, in Yakutat. Sister Margaret McCarthy, P.B.V.M., was there from 1983–87; Sister Dorothea M. Ross, C.S.J., during the year 1987–88; Sister Helena Fox, P.B.V.M., from 1989–92; Sister Judith Gomila, M.S.C., from 1992–98. In April 1999, Sister Josephine **Aloralrea**, O.S.U., was hired by Michael W. **Warfel**, Bishop of Juneau, as parish administrator of St. Ann's. As of the year 2004, she was still serving in that capacity. Father Perry M. Kenaston was visiting priest to the parish as of the first part of that same year.

BIBLIOGRAPHY

The number(s) at the end of a given entry in *Alaskana Catholica* refer(s) to
the corresponding number(s) of the item(s) listed in this bibliography.

1. Aho, Karen. "Ruby on Road to Recovery," *The Alaskan Shepherd*, Vol. 36, No. 2 (March/April-1998).

2. Anable, Edmund A., S.J., and Margaret Grogan. "Diamond Jubilee," Fairbanks: Immaculate Conception Parish, 1979.

3. Anonymous. *Un Religieux Éducateur: Constantin-Marie, F.I.C. (1874–1926)*. Vannes, France: Librairie Lafolye, 1933.

4. Balcom, Mary G. *The Catholic Church in Alaska*. Chicago: Adams Press, 1970.

5. Barnum, Francis A., S.J. *Grammatical Fundamentals of the Innuit Language as Spoken by Eskimo of the Western Coast of Alaska*. Boston and London: Athenaeum Press, 1901. Reprint: New York: Georg Olms Verlag, 1970.

6. Beck, Mary G. *Holy Name Catholic Church: A History of the Parish of the Holy Name in Ketchikan from 1904–2002*. Ketchikan, Alaska: Pioneer Printing Company, 2002.

7. Betz, Madeleine D., and Louis L. Renner, S.J., in collaboration with Betty J. Johnson. *A Brief Illustrated History of the Diocese of Fairbanks: Profiles of Prelates and Churches, Past and Present in Commemoration of Jubilee 2000)*. Fairbanks: Diocese of Fairbanks, 2001.

8. Bogojavlensky, Sergei. "Imaangmiut Eskimo Careers: Skinboats in Bering Strait." Ph.D. Dissertation, Harvard University, 1969.

9. Bogojavlensky, Sergei and Robert W. Fuller. "Polar Bears, Walrus Hides and Social Solidarity," *The Alaska Journal*, Vol. 3, No.2 (Spring-1973), 66–67.

10. Boone, Kirby, C.F.X. "Brother in Alaska: To Minister, To Wander, to Wonder," *The Alaskan Shepherd*, Vol. 33, No. 5 (Sept./Oct.-1995).

11. Bonner, Dismas, O.F.M. "Franciscans to Northern Alaska," *The Alaskan Shepherd*, Vol. 25, No. 2 (March/April-1987).

12. Brantmeier, Ann. "Scammon Bay," *The Alaskan Shepherd*, Vol. 30, No. 4 (July/Aug.-1992).

13. Buckley, Cornelius M., S.J. *When Jesuits were Giants: Louis-Marie Ruellan, S.J. (1846–1885) and Contemporaries*. San Francisco: Ignatius Press, 1999.

14. Busch, Thomas A. "The Alaska Radio Mission—Station **KNOM**," *The Alaskan Shepherd*, Vol. 35, No. 3 (May/June-1997).

15. Cantwell, Margaret, S.S.A. "The History of the Archdiocese of Anchorage," ms. in the Archives of the Archdiocese of Anchorage, Alaska, 1977

16. _____. in collaboration with Mary George Edmond, S.S.A. *North to Share: The Sisters of Saint Ann in Alaska and the Yukon Territory*. Victoria, B.C., Canada: Sisters of St. Ann, 1992.

17. Cardy, William E., O.F.M. "Twenty-Five Years a Priest: Twelve Years a Tri-Village Bush Pastor," *The Alaskan Shepherd*, Vol. 35, No. 6 (Nov./Dec.-1997).

18. _____. and Joseph Rogenski, O.F.M. "Franciscan Christmas Journal Yukon River: 1986," *The Alaskan Shepherd*, Vol. 25, No. 6 (Nov./Dec.-1987).

19. Carlo, Poldine. *Nulato: An Indian life on the Yukon*. Fairbanks: Poldine Carlo, 1978.

20. Carriker, Robert C. "Father Joseph Bernard among 'les Esquimaux,'" *The Alaska Journal*, Vol. 6, No. 3 (Summer-1976), 161–166.

21. _____. Jennifer Ann Boharski, Eleanor R. Carriker, and Clifford A. Carroll, S.J. *Guide to the Microfilm Edition of the Oregon Province Archives of the Society of Jesus: Alaska Mission Collection*. Spokane, Washington: The Oregon Province of the Society of Jesus, 1980.

22. Champagne, Joseph-Étienne, O.M.I. "First Attempts at the Evangelization of Alaska," *Études Oblates*, Vol. 2, 1943, 13–22.

23. Cole, Terrence M. "A History of the Nome Gold Rush: The Poor Man's Paradise." Ph.D. Dissertation, University of Washington, 1983.

24. Convert, Jules M., S.J. "From Mud Houses to Wood: Kashunak to Chevak," *The Alaska Journal*, Vol. 9, No. 3 (Summer-1979), 24–31.

25. Cook, Nancy. "Excellence in Christian Education: The Catholic Schools of Fairbanks, Alaska," *The Alaskan Shepherd*, Vol. 28, No. 3 (May/June-1990).

26. Crimont, Joseph R., S.J. "A Short Story of a Long-Time Friend: A Retrospect of the 84 Years of the Life of Fr. F. M. Monroe," *Jesuit Seminary News*, 7 (1940), 39–40.

27. De Baets, Maurits. *The Apostle of Alaska: Life of the Most Reverend Charles John Seghers*. Translated from the French by Sister Mary Mildred, S.S.A. Paterson, N.J.: St. Anthony Guild Press, 1943.

28. Desjardins, Joseph-Alphonse, S.J. *En Alaska: Deux mois sous la tente*. Montréal: Imprimerie Du Messager, 1930

29. De Laguna, Frederica. *Tales from the Dena: Indian Stories from the Tanana, Koyukuk, @ Yukon Rivers*. Seattle & London: University of Washington Press, 1995.

30. De Ruyter, Mary Joseph Calasanz (Calasanctius), S.S.A. *The Voice of Alaska*. Lachine, Quebec: St. Ann's Press, 1947.

31. Devine, Edward J., S.J. "Alaskan Letters III–VIII." *The Canadian Messenger of the Sacred Heart*, Vol. 13 (1903) and "Alaskan Letters IX–X, ibid., Vol. 14 (1904).

32. Down, Mary Margaret, S.S.A. *A Century of Service*. Victoria, B.C.: Morriss Printing Co., Ltd., 1996.

33. Dragon, Antonio, S.J. *Enseveli dans les Neiges: Le Père Jules Jetté*. Montréal: Les Éditions Bellarmin, 1951.

34. Fienup-Riordan, Ann. *The Nelson Island Eskimo: Social Structure and Ritual Distribution*. Anchorage: Alaska Pacific University Press, 1983.

35. _____. *Hunting Tradition in a* Changing *World*. Piscataway, New Jersey: Rutgers University Press, 2000.

36. Fortier, Edward J. *One Survived*. Anchorage: Alaska Northwest Publishing Company, 1978.

37. Glody, Robert. *A Shepherd of the far North: The Story of William Francis Walsh (1900–1930)*. San Francisco: Harr Wagner Publishing Co., 1934.

38. Hemmer, Joseph, O.F.M. "Franciscan Ministry to the Athapaskan Indian People Along the Middle Yukon," *The Alaskan Shepherd*, Vol. 38, No. 2 (March/April-2000).

39. Hendry, Simon J., S.J. "A Brief History of the Jesuit Volunteer Corps," ms. (66 pp.) in the Jesuit Oregon Province Archives, 1996.

40. Higgins, Pauline, S.P. *Providence in Alaska: Sisters of Providence: Education Ministry in Alaska, 1902–1978*. Seattle: Sisters of Providence, 1999.

41. Hill, Beth. "The Sisters of St. Ann...they founded schools and hospitals along the Northwest Coast," *The Alaska Journal*, Vol. 7, No. l (Winter-1977), 40–45.

42. Hiller, Carol Louise, O.P. *Gleeson, The Last Vicar Apostolic of all of Alaska: The First Bishop of Fairbanks*. Bloomington, Indiana: lst Books, 2004.

43. Hogan, Anne, S.S.J. "Holy Cross, Alaska: 'The Smile of the Yukon,'" *The Alaskan Shepherd*, Vol. 35, No. 5 (Sept./Oct.-1997).

44. Hubbard, Bernard R., S.J. *Mush, You Malemutes!* New York: America Press, 1932.

45. _____. *Cradle of the Storms*. New York: Dodd, Mead & Co., 1935.

46. Huber, Cecilia, O.S.U. "Little Diomede," *The Alaskan Shepherd*, Vol. 29, No. 1 (Jan./Feb.-1991).

47. Jetté, Julius, S.J., and Eliza Jones. (Editor-in-Chief, James Kari) *Koyukon Athabaskan Dictionary*. Fairbanks: Alaska Native Language Center, University of Alaska Fairbanks, 2000.

48. Joseph, Dorothy Savage. *Fishcamp*. Bend, Oregon: Maverick Publications, 1997.

49. Judge, Charles, S.S. *An American Missionary: A Record of the Work of Rev. William H. Judge, S.J.* 2nd ed. Boston: Catholic Foreign Mission Bureau, 1907.

50. Kalland, Edgar. *Edgar Kallands: A Biography*. Fairbanks, Alaska: Spirit Mountain Press, 1982.

51. Kaniecki, Michael J., S.J. "A Large Country —A Plane Bishop," *The Alaskan Shepherd*, Vol. 28, No. 2 (March/April-1990).

52. _____. "The Catholic Diocese of Fairbanks," *The Alaskan Shepherd*, Vol. 32, No. 1 (Jan./Feb.-1994).

53. _____. "A Missionary in 'the Great Land,'" *The Alaskan Shepherd*, Vol. 36, No. 4 (July/Aug.-1998).

54. _____. "From the Desk—and the Heart—of the Bishop of Alaska's Missionary Diocese," *The Alaskan Shepherd*, Vol. 37, No. 3 (May/June-1999).

55. Kaplan, Lawrence D. *Ugiuvangmiut Quliapyuit: King Island Tales*. Fairbanks: University of Alaska Press. 1988.

56. Kingston, Deanna M. "Returning: Twentieth Century Performances of the King Island Wolf Dance." Ph.D. Dissertation, University of Alaska–Fairbanks, 1999.

57. Kleinfeld, Judith S. *Eskimo School on the Andreafsky: A Study of Effective Bicultural Education*. New York: Praeger Publishers, 1979.

58. LaRose, Jeannette, S.S.A. "A Sister of St. Ann Writes of Her Mission," *The Alaskan Shepherd*, Vol. 23, No. 2 (March/April-1985).

59. L'Ecuyer, Rosalie E. "Mountain Village on the Yukon," *The Alaskan Shepherd*, Vol. 24, No. 3 (May/June-1986).

60. Lester, Jean. *Faces of Alaska from Barrow to Wrangell*. Ester, Alaska: Tanana Yukon Historical Society, Fairbanks Alaska and Poppies Publishing, 1992.

61. Levitre, J. Albert. "The Christmas Diary of a Circuit Rider," *The Alaskan Shepherd*, Vol. 26, No. 6 (Nov./Dec.-1988).

62. Lincoln, Mother Angela, O.S.U. *Life of the Rev. Mother Amadeus*. New York: Paulist Press, 1923.

63. Llorente, Segundo, S.J. *Jesuits in Alaska*. Portland, OR: Service Office, Key Litho, 1969.

64. _____. *Memoirs of a Yukon Priest*. Washington, D.C.: Georgetown University Press, 1990.

65. Loyens, William J., S.J. "The Koyukon Feast for the Dead," *Arctic Anthropology*, Vol. 2, No. 2 (1964): 133–48.

66. _____. "The Changing Culture of the Nulato Koyukon Indians." Ph.D. Dissertation, University of Wisconsin, 1966.

67. Martinek, John B. "Pastor Beyond the Arctic Circle," *The Alaskan Shepherd*, Vol. 37, No. 6 (Nov./Dec.-1999).

68. Maslanka, Andrzej. "Far Away from Poland, My Homeland, the Lord Lead's Me Miraculously," *The Alaskan Shepherd*, Vol. 39, No. 1 (Jan./Feb.-2001).

69. McCarron, Frances, I.B.V.M. "Tok's Holy Rosary Parish Celebrates 50 Golden Years," *The Alaskan Shepherd*, Vol.38, No. 1 (Jan./Feb.-2000).

70. McCullough, Nicole Susan. "The 1951 Bristol Bay Salmon Strike: Isolation, Independence and Illusion on the Last Frontier." M.A. Thesis, University of Alaska–Fairbanks, December, 2001.

71. Medbery, Joan. "Shrine of Saint Terese." *Alaska Magazine*, Vol. 45, no 2 (Feb.-1979), A-4.

72. Ménager, Francis M., S.J. *The Kingdom of the Seal*. Chicago: Loyola University Press, 1962.

73. Miller, Orlando W. *The Frontier in Alaska and the Matanuska Colony*. New Haven and London: Yale University Press, 1975.

74. Mousseau, Gilles, O.M.I. "*L'affaire d'Alaska. À propos du Voyage de Mgr. Clut dans L'Amérique Russe en 1872*," *Études Oblates*, Vol. 5 (1946), 161–88.

75. Muñoz, Juan. "Cliff Dwellers of the Bering Sea," *National Geographic Magazine*, 105 (no. 1), 129–46.

76. O'Connor, Paul C., S.J. *Eskimo Parish*. Milwaukee: The Bruce Publishing Co., 1947.

77. Orth, Donald J. *Dictionary of Alaska Place Names*. Geological Survey Professional Paper 567. Washington, D.C.: U.S. Government Printing Office, 1971.

78. Ornowski, Gerald, M.I.C. "Winter on the Coast of the Bering Sea," *The Alaskan Shepherd*, Vol. 29, No. 6 (Nov./Dec.-1991).

79. _____. "A Bush Priest in Academia," *The Alaskan Shepherd*, Vol. 39, No. 5 (Sept./Oct.-2001).

80. Osentoski, Ann. "Farthest North Paulist: Father James M. Kolb, C.S.P," *The Alaskan Shepherd*, Vol. 26, No. 4 (July/Aug.-1988).

81. Perreault, Mary Beth. "Flying the Alaskan 'Bush'—An Adventure: Part I," *The Alaskan Shepherd*, Vol. 37, No. 4 (July/Aug.-1999).

82. _____. "Flying the Alaskan 'Bush'—An Adventure: Part II," *The Alaskan Shepherd*, Vol. 37, No. 5 (Sept./Oct.-1999).

83. Price, Katherine E. "Adventuring with the 'Glacier Priest': Jesuit Father Bernard R. Hubbard's Alaskan Persona." M.A. Thesis, University of Alaska–Fairbanks, 1999.

84. Provinsal, Thomas G., S.J. "Agnes Matthew: Forever a Child of God," *The Alaskan Shepherd*, Vol. 26, No. 5 (Sept./Oct.-1988).

85. Renner, Louis L., S.J. "The Relaxed Art Lovers," *America*, Vol. 94, No. 12 (Dec. 17, 1955), 33l.

86. _____. "KNOM Helps Make Men Free," *Sign*, Vol. 53, No.4 (Dec. 1973–Jan. 1974), 11–15.

87. _____. "A Footnote to Stefansson's *The Friendly Arctic*," *The Alaska Journal*, Vol. 4, No. 4 (Autumn-1974), 203–4.

88. _____. "The Eskimos Return to King Island," *Catholic Digest*, Vol. 39, No. 5 (March-1975), 46–55.

89. _____. "Return to King Island," *Alaska Magazine*, Vol. XLI, No. 7 (July-1975), 6–8.

90. _____. "Julius Jetté: Distinguished Scholar in Alaska," *The Alaska Journal*, Vol. 5, No. 4 (Autumn-1975), 239–47.

91. _____. "Catechizing the Vikings of Bering Strait," *Eskimo*, 32nd Year, New Series, No. 10 (Fall/Winter-1975–76), 5–20.

92. _____. "The Beginnings of Missionary Aviation in the Arctic: The '*Marquette Missionary*,'" Eskimo, 33rd Year, New Series, No. 11 (Spring/Summer-1976), 8–19.

93. _____. "Fr. Frederick Ruppert, SJ: Martyr of Charity," *Eskimo*, 34th Year, New Series, No. 14 (Fall/Winter-1977–78), 11–22.

94. _____. "The Jesuits and the Yupik Eskimo Language of Southwestern Alaska," *The Alaska Journal*, Vol. 8, No. 1, (Winter-1978), 70–81.

95. _____. "Three Grand Alaskans," *Alaska Magazine*, Vol. XLIV, No. 12 (Dec.-1978), 96.

96. _____. "Father Francis M. Monroe, S.J.: 'The Alaskan Hercules,' and Saint Francis Xavier Mission of Eagle," *Alaska Magazine*, Vol. XLV, No. 4 (April-1979), A 18–25.

97. _____. in collaboration with Dorothy Jean Ray, *Pioneer Missionary to the Bering Strait Eskimos: Bellarmine Lafortune, S.J*. Portland, Oregon: Binford & Mort, 1979.

98. _____. "A Chronicle: The Catholic Church on the Seward Peninsula," Part I, *The Nome Nugget*, Friday, August 3, 1979, p. 5; Part II, ibid., Tuesday, August 7, 1979, pp. 4–5.

99. _____. "Fr. Aloysius Robaut, S.J.: Pioneer Missionary in Alaska," *Eskimo*, 37th Year, New Series, No. 20 (Fall/Winter-1980–81), 5–16.

100. _____. "Our Lady of the Mountain," *Extension Magazine*, Vol. 75, No. 8 (March-1981), 12–18.

101. _____. "Middle Yukon Diary: Part I—Nulato and Koyukuk," *The Alaskan Shepherd*, Vol. 20, No. 2 (March/April-1982).

102. _____. "Middle Yukon Diary: Part II—Kaltag," *The Alaskan Shepherd*, Vol. 20, No. 3, May/June-1982).

103. _____. "Born to Fly: Part I," *The Alaskan Shepherd*, Vol. 20, No. 4 (July/August-1982).

104. _____. "Born to Fly: Part II," *The Alaskan Shepherd*, Vol. 20, No. 5 (Sept./Oct.-1982).

105. _____. "A Christmas diary from Alaska," *Extension Magazine*, Vol. 77, No. 6 (Dec.-1982), 5–11.

106. _____. "The Kaltag Drum Festival," *Alaska Today*, Vol. 10, (Sept. 1982–Aug. 1983), p. 62.

107. _____. "Edgar Kalland, Dog Musher and Boat Captain," *Alaska Native News*, Vol. 1, No. 4, (Feb.-1983), 16–19.

108. _____. "Digging in at Chevak," *Extension Magazine*, Vol. 77, No. 8 (March-1983), 5–10.

109. _____. "The 'Saint of Dawson,'" *North/Nord*, Vol. XXX, No. one, (Spring-1983), 38–43.

110. _____. "Charles Olaranna: Chief of the King Islanders," *The Alaska Journal*, Vol.13. No. 2 (Spring-1983), 14–23.

111. _____. "The Brothers of Christian Instruction in Alaska," *The Alaskan Shepherd*, Vol. 21, No. 2, (March/April-1983).

112. _____. "Tundra Baker," *The Alaskan Shepherd*, Vol. 21, No. 6 (Nov./Dec.-1983).

113. _____. "Alleluia, bush country," *Extension Magazine*, Vol. 78, No. 9 (March–April-1984) 15–18.

114. _____. "A New Alaskan Shepherd: Bishop Michael J. Kaniecki, S.J.," *The Alaskan Shepherd*, Vol. 22, No. 6 (Nov./Dec.-1984).

115. _____. *"Father Tom" of the Arctic.* Portland, Oregon: Binford & Mort, 1985.

116. _____. *The KNOM/Father Jim Poole Story.* Portland, Oregon: Binford & Mort, 1985.

117. _____. "Hiking in the Land of Oz," *Alaska Outdoors*, Vol. VIII, No. 2 (March/April-1985), 66–71.

118. _____. "To fly and to fix," *Company*, Vol. 2, No. 3, (April-1985), 18–19.

119. _____. "The Memory of a Brave Man: The Grave of Lieut. John J. Barnard at Nulato," *The Alaska Journal*, Vol. 15, No. 2, (Spring-1985), 16–21.

120. _____. "A New Church for Galena," *The Alaskan Shepherd*, Vol. 23, No. 5 (Sept./Oct.-1985).

121. _____. "Pastor, Poet, Fisherman: William T. Burke, S.J.," *The Alaskan Shepherd*, Vol. 23, No. 6 (Nov./Dec. 1985).

122. _____. "Francis A. Barnum, S.J.: Pioneer Alaskan Missionary and Linguist," *Alaska History*, Vol. 1, No. 2, (Fall/Winter-1985/86), pp. 19–41.

123. _____. "Father William T. McIntyre, S.J.," *The Alaskan Shepherd*, Vol. 24, No. 1 (Jan./Feb.-1986).

124. _____. "Eskimo Deacons Retreat at Nyac," *The Alaskan Shepherd*, Vol. 24, No. 2 (March/April-1986).

125. _____. "The Bishop Behind Bishop Rock," *The Alaskan Shepherd*, Vol. 24, No. 5 (Sept./Oct.-1986).

126. _____. "Conquering the Copper River," *Alaska Magazine*, Vol. 52, No. 12 (Dec.-1986), 32–35, 53–55.

127. _____. "Father Bernard R. Hubbard, S.J.: 1888–1962," *The Alaskan Shepherd*, Vol. 25, No. 3 (May/June-1987).

128. _____. "The Day We Buried Madeline," *The Alaskan Shepherd*, Vol. 25, No. 4 (July/ Aug.-1987).

129. _____. "A 'Bright Era' in Alaskan Education," *Momentum*, Vol. XVIV, No. 1 (Feb.-1988), 16–17.

130. _____. "The House of Prayer and Bishop Whelan," *The Alaskan Shepherd*, Vol. 26, No. 3 (May/June-1988).

131. _____. "A Ruby Christmas," *Alaska Magazine*, Vol. 54, No. 12 (Dec.-1988), 24–26, 44–45.

132. _____. "Father William Henry Judge, S.J.: 'The Saint of Dawson,'" *The Alaskan Shepherd*, Vol. 27, Nos. 1 and 2 (Jan./Feb. and March/April-1989).

133. _____. "'Father Joe of the North,' The Reverend Joseph G. Stolz: Pastor of St. Michael and Stebbins," *The Alaskan Shepherd*, Vol. 27, No. 5 (Sept./Oct.-1989).

134. _____. "Thomas A. Busch of *KNOM*, Nome, Alaska," *The Alaskan Shepherd*, Vol. 27, No. 6 (Nov./Dec.-1989).

135. _____. "Father Francis J. Fallert, S.J.: 1919–1990," *The Alaskan Shepherd*, Vol. 29, No. 3 (May/June-1991).

136. _____. "Umkumiut," *The Alaskan Shepherd*, Vol. 29, No 4 (July/Aug.-1991).

137. _____. "Father Henry G. Hargreaves, S.J.: 'Dean of Alaskan Missionaries,'" *The Alaskan Shepherd*, Vol. 29, No. 5 (Sept./Oct.-1991).

138. _____. "Confirmations and First Communions in the Kingdom of the Seal," *The Alaskan Shepherd*, Vol. 30, No. 2 (March/April-1992).

139. _____. "St. Patrick's Parish: Barrow, Alaska," *The Alaskan Shepherd*, Vol. 30, No. 6 (Nov./Dec.-1992).

140. _____. "Father Harold J. Greif, S.J.: 1903–1991," *The Alaskan Shepherd*, Vol. 31, No. 1 (Jan./Feb.-1993).

141. _____. "Father Edmund A. Anable, S.J.: 1903–1992," *The Alaskan Shepherd*, Vol. 31, No 2 (March/April-1993).

142. _____. "The Koyukon Athapaskan Stickdance and the Changed Attitude of the Jesuit Missionaries Toward It," *Alaska History*, Vol. 8, No. 1, (Spring-1993), pp. 1–13.

143. _____. "That Man of God with a Caring Ear: Brother Philip Drouin, F.I.C.," *The Alaskan Shepherd*, Vol. 31, No. 4 (July/Aug.-1993).

144. _____. "The Sisters of St. Ann in Alaska and the Yukon Territory: 1886–1993," *The Alaskan Shepherd*, Vol. 31, No. 5 (Sept./Oct.-1993).

145. _____. "Diocese of Fairbanks, Alaska: The Eskimo Diaconate Program," Part I, *Eskimo*, New Series, 50th Year, No. 45 (Spring/Summer-1993), 3–19; Part II, ibid., No. 46 (Fall/Winter-1993), 3–13.

146. _____. "Brother Ignatius J. Jakes, S.J.: 50 Years a Jesuit," *The Alaskan Shepherd*, Vol. 32, No. 2 (March/April-1994).

147. _____. "Alakanuk: St. Ignatius Church Moved," *The Alaskan Shepherd*, Vol. 32, No. 3 (May/June-1994).

148. _____. "Deacon William Tyson, 'A Man for Others': 1916–1993," *The Alaskan Shepherd*, Vol. 32, No. 4 (July/Aug.-1994).

149. _____. "Father Tom's Ordeal by Blizzard: Part I," *The Alaskan Shepherd*, Vol. 33, No. 3 (May/June-1995).

150. _____. "Father Tom's Ordeal by Blizzard: Part II," *The Alaskan Shepherd*, Vol. 33, No. 4 (July/Aug.-1995).

151. _____. "Harry and Rose Ambrose of Huslia," *The Alaskan Shepherd*, Vol. 33, No. 6 (Nov./Dec.-1995).

152. _____. "A New Church for Pilot Station," *The Alaskan Shepherd*, Vol. 34, No. 5 (Sept./Oct.-1996).

153. _____. "*Nucang'in*: Father René Astruc, S.J.," *The Alaskan Shepherd*, Vol. 35, No. 1 (Jan./Feb.-1997).

154. _____. "Father George S. Endal, S.J.: 1902–1996," *The Alaskan Shepherd*, Vol. 35, No. 2 (March/April-1997).

155. _____. "St. Raphael's: A Family Parish on the Northern Edge of Fairbanks," *The Alaskan Shepherd*, Vol. 36, No. 3 (May/June-1998).

156. _____. "Marian Edwin: 'A True Pillar of the Church,'" *The Alaskan Shepherd*, Vol. 36, No. 5 (Sept./Oct.-1998)

157. _____. "Called from the Philippine Islands to the Taiga and Tundra of Northern Alaska: Father Don M. Balquin," *The Alaskan Shepherd*, Vol. 36, No. 6 (Nov./Dec.-1998).

158. _____. "In Pursuit of Excellence: The Catholic Schools of Fairbanks," *The Alaskan Shepherd*, Vol. 37, No. 2 (March/April-1999).

159. _____. "Father Normand Amedee Pepin: 50 Years a Jesuit," *The Alaskan Shepherd*, Vol. 38, No. 5 (Sept./Oct.-2000).

160. _____. "A Good Shepherd Lays Down His Life For His Sheep: Bishop Michael J. Kaniecki, S.J., D.D.: 1935–2000," *The Alaskan Shepherd*, Vol. 38, No. 6 (Nov./Dec.-2000).

161. _____. "St. Joseph Parish, Nome, Alaska: 1901–2001," *The Alaskan Shepherd*, Vol. 39, No. 4 (July/Aug.-2001).

162. _____. "All they want is a simple pine box—and prayers," *Extension Magazine*, Vol. 96, No. 8, (Nov.-2001), 16–19.

163. _____. "The Missionary Diocese of Fairbanks is Blessed with a New Priest: Father Ross A. Tozzi," *The Alaskan Shepherd*, Vol. 39, No. 6 (Nov./Dec.-2001).

164. _____. "Bishop Robert L. Whelan, S.J., D.D.: 1912–2001," *The Alaskan Shepherd*, Vol. 40, No. 1, (Jan./Feb.-2002).

165. _____. with Patricia Walter, "'Holding Down the Fort,' While the Diocese of Fairbanks Awaits a New Bishop: Father Richard D. Case, S.J.," *The Alaskan Shepherd*, Vol. 40, No. 2 (March/April-2002).

166. _____. "ALASKA, Catholic Church in," *The New Catholic Encyclopedia, Second Edition*. Washington, D.C. 2003.

167. Reynolds, Brad, S.J., with photos by Don Doll, S.J. "Eskimo Hunters of the Bering Sea.," *National Geographic Magazine*, Vol. 165, No 6 (June-1984), 814–34.

168. _____. with photos by Don Doll, S.J. "Athapaskans Along the Yukon," *National Geographic Magazine*, Vol. 177, No. 2 (Feb.-1990), 44–69.

169. _____. "Arctic Parish." *Company*, (April, 1985), 2–4.

170. Rogers, Jean, with illustrations by Rie Muñoz. *Goodbye My Island*. New York: Greenwillow Books, 1983.

171. _____. with illustrations by Rie Muñoz. *King Island Christmas*. New York: Greenwillow Books, 1985.

172. Ruzicka, Robert J, O.F.M. "Alaska...One Year Later," *The Alaskan Shepherd*, Vol. 30, No. 1 (Jan./Feb.-1992).

173. Santos, Angel, S.J. *Jesuitas En El Polo Norte: La Mision de Alaska*. Madrid: Graficas Ultra, 1943.

174. Savage, Alma H. *Dogsled Apostles*. New York: Sheed and Ward, 1942.

175. Scarborough, Caprice Murray, with contributions by Deanna M. Kingston and Jeff Kunkel. "The Legacy of the 'Glacier Priest': Bernard R. Hubbard, S.J.," Research Manuscript Series No. 10, 2001, Santa Clara University, Santa Clara, CA.

176. Schoenberg, Wilfred P., S.J. *Paths to the Northwest: A Jesuit History of the Oregon Province*. Chicago: Loyola Press, 1982.

177. _____. "Lay Ministry: The Jesuit Volunteer Corps: The First Thirty Years," unpublished ms. (395 pp.) in the Jesuit Oregon Province Archives, 1986.

178. Schutt, David E. "Eskimo Deacons Retreat At Nyac," *The Alaskan Shepherd*, Vol. 24, No. 2 (March/April-1986).

179. Senungetuk, Vivian and Paul Tiulana. *A Place for Winter: Paul Tiulana's Story*. Anchorage: The Ciri Foundation, 1987.

180. Shideler, John C. and Hal K. Rothman. *Pioneering Spirit: The Sisters of Providence in Alaska*. Anchorage: Providence Hospital, 1987.

181. Spude, Catherine Holder, and Douglas D. Scott and Frank Norris. "Father Turnell's Trash Pit: Klondike Gold Rush," U.S. Dept. of the Interior, National Park Service, Denver Service Center, 1993.

182. Steckler, Gerard G., S.J. "The Diocese of Juneau, Alaska," *Historical Records and Studies of the U.S. Catholic Historical Society*, Vol. XLVII, (1959), 234–54.

183. _____. "The Case of Frank Fuller: Killer of Alaska Missionary Charles Seghers," *Pacific Northwest Quarterly*, Vol. 59, No. 4 (Oct.-1968), pp. 190–202.

184. _____. "The Foundation of the Alaskan Catholic Missions," in *Studies in Mediaevalia and Americana: Essays in Honor of William Lyle Davis, S.J.* Spokane: Gonzaga University Press, 1973, 129–50.

185. _____. *Charles John Seghers, Priest and Bishop in the Pacific Northwest 1839–1886: A Biography.* Fairfield WA: Ye Galleon Press, 1986.

186. Stockton, Jay R. "A Barrow Christmas," *The Alaskan Shepherd*, Vol.30, No. 6 (Nov./Dec.-1992).

187. Stuck, Hudson. *Ten Thousand Miles with a Dogsled: A Narrative of Winter Travels in Interior Alaska.* New York: Charles Scribner's Sons, 1915.

188. Sullivan, Robert J. S.J. *The Ten'a Food Quest.* Anthropological Series, no. 11. Washington D.C.: Catholic University of America Press, 1942.

189. Talbott, Raymond L., S.J. *In Behalf of All: Memoirs of a Northwest Jesuit.* Anchorage, Alaska: BIOP Foundation, 1993.

190. Tam, Patrick, C.W. "Lay Minister to Eskimo Youth and Young Adults," *The Alaskan Shepherd*, Vol. 34, No. 4 (July/Aug.-1996).

191. Tero, Richard D. "Alaska: 1779—Father Riobó's Narrative," *The Alaska Journal*, Vol. 3, No. 2, (Spring-1973), 81–88.

192. Thorpe, Julie Marie, S.N.D. "Sisters Return to Hooper Bay," *The Alaskan Shepherd*, Vol. 28, No. 4 (July/Aug.-1990).

193. Toussaint, Wilda, and Mary Beck, S.S.N.D., and René Astruc, S.J. "Eskimo Deacon Stanley Waska: 1917–1986," *The Alaskan Shepherd*, Vol. 26, No.1 (Jan./Feb.-1988).

194. Usuka, Margaret, S.N.D. "A 'New Church' for Koyukuk," *The Alaskan Shepherd*, Vol. 27, No. 3 (May/June-1989).

195. Vachon, Andrew W., S.J. *Ketchikan Alaskan Sketches.* Seattle: Robert D. Seal, 1959.

196. _____. *Fish without Chips.* Juneau, Alaska: Men of the Cathedral, 1960.

197. Vachon, Merilu, S.P. *The Dear Sourdoughs.* Montreal: Sisters of Providence, 1982.

198. VanStone, James W. *Athapaskan Adaptations: Hunters and Fishermen of the Subarctic Forests.* Chicago: Aldine Publishing Co., 1974.

199. _____. "E.W. Nelson's Notes on the Indians of the Yukon and Innoko Rivers, Alaska," *Fieldiana Anthropology*, Vol. 70 (April 28, 1978). Published by Field Museum of Natural History, Chicago.

200. _____. "Ingalik Contact Ecology: An Ethnohistory of the Lower-Middle Yukon, 1790–1935," *Fieldiana Anthropology*, Vol. 71 (March 29, 1979). Published by Field Museum of Natural History, Chicago.

201. Walter, Patricia. "Priest in Alaska, 1958–2002: Louis L. Renner, S.J.," *The Alaskan Shepherd*, Vol. 40, No. 3 (May–June-2002).

202. _____. "Called to be an Alaskan Shepherd: Bishop Donald J. Kettler," *The Alaskan Shepherd*, Vol. 40, No. 6 (Nov./Dec.-2002).

203. _____. "On the Wing with Bishop Kettler: Part I," *The Alaskan Shepherd*, Vol. 41, No. 1 (Jan./Feb.-2003).

204. _____. "On the Wing with Bishop Kettler: Part II," *The Alaskan Shepherd*, Vol. 41, No. 2 (March/April-2003).

205. Walters, Barbara. "Holy Mary of Guadalupe, Healy, Alaska: 1982–2002," *The Alaskan Shepherd*, Vol. 40, No. 4 (July/Aug.-2002).

206. Wilcox, Agnes Anne S.M.S.M. "Pastoral Administrator to Nenana's 'Lively and Dedicated People,'" *The Alaskan Shepherd*, Vol. 37, No. 1 (Jan./Feb.-1999).

207. Wood, Gregg D., S.J. "Circuit Rider to Three Central Yup'ik Eskimo Villages in Western Alaska," *The Alaskan Shepherd*, Vol. 38, No. 4 (July/Aug.-2000).

208. Yzermans, Vincent A. *Saint Rose of Wrangell: The Church's Beginning in Southeast Alaska.* St. Paul: North Central Publishing Co., 1979.

INDEX

Entries in bold indicate main entries for subject.
Unless otherwise noted, all cities are in Alaska.

430, 435, 449, 450, 456, 480, 484, 485, 488, 497, 521, 523, 530, 558, 561, 567, 571, 582, 584, 592, 598, 603, 607, 613, 628, 645, 648, 665, 669

Anderson, 142, 156, 248, 256

Anderson, Fr. David J., S.J., **32–33**, 142, 156, 248, 256, 258, 464, 630, 644

Andreafsky River, 184, 333, 349

Andreafsky, 5, 6, 14, 18, 23, 38. 58, 61, 82, 99, 106, 108, 111, 121, 144, 151, 239, 255, 271, 376, 377, 391, 393, 483, 530, 536

Andrews, Margaret Koka, 398

Angaiak, Dcn. Mike, 644

Angilbert, Sr. M., S.S.A., 265

Angoon, 530

Aniak Flying Service, 185

Aniak, **33–34**, 66, 93, 115, 121, 141, 221, 239, 243, 317, 322, 357, 429, 438, 615, 672

Ann, Sisters of St., 1, 13, 14, 22, 30, **34–37**, 55, 57, 85, 94, 95, 102, 115, 117, 123, 126, 146, 148, 159, 164, 168, 174, 183, 188, 203, 221, 224, 229, 243, 261, 264, 265, 292, 308, 309–310, 394, 405, 406, 423, 428, 454, 473, 474, 520, 531, 532, 534, 541, 545, 567, 594, 596, 597, 605, 634, 650

Annette Island, 518

Anthropos (magazine), 298

Anvik, 226, 502, 540, 541

Arctic (steamer), 305

Army Intelligence Department, 133

Army Officers' Reserve Corps, 135

Arpin, Fr. Fred, C.Ss.R., 583

Arrupe, Fr. Pedro, S.J., 294

Artim, Fr. Michael, 28

Arvin, Sr. Irene, O.S.U., 507, 654

Arvinak, **37**, 45

Astruc, Fr. René, S.J., 9, 10, 23, **37–40**, 72, 101, 111, 173, 180, 181, 216, 219, 362, 444, 457, 475, 536, 548, 609, 620, 621, 668

Asturias, Fr. Joseph L., O.P., 53, 147, 629–630

Asuluk, Dcn. Joseph, 630

Athabaskan Indians, 15, 251, 259, 261, 649

Atti, Martha, 528

Avugiak, Dcn. Joe, 102

Aylward, Charles and Bridget, 441

Ayuluk, Angela, 528

Babb, Fr. William H., S.J., **41**, 197

Baffaro, Fr. Anthony J., S.J., 335

Bailey, Fr. George M., S.J., 310

Baker, Fr. Harley A., 27, **41–42**, 240, 312, 521, 597

Bakewell, Fr. Anderson E., S.J., **42–43**, 147, 472, 630

Baldwin Peninsula, 363

Balfe, Fr. Joseph A., S.J., 190

Balquin, Fr. Don M., **43–45**, 148, 194, 630

Baltussen, Fr. Peter L., S.J., **45–46**, 364, 509

Baptist, Sr. Mary John, 272

Barcome, Fr. Earl, 240, 597

Bardol, Sr. Diane, G.N.S.H., 236, 354

Barina, Sr. Joan, S.C.M.M., 328

Barnette, E. T., 188

Barnum, Dr. Zenus, 47

Barnum, Fr. Francis A., S.J., **46–52**, 66, 126, 131, 304, 487, 495, 501, 533, 534, 545, 634, 641, 642, 643

Barrow, 14, 44, **52–53**, 132, 137, 366, 420, 422, 446, 482, 514, 521, 537, 636

Barter Island, 134, 135

Bartles, Fr. Charles A., S.J., **54–55**, 67, 219, 281, 622

Bartol, Sr. Carol, G.N.S.H., 236, 354

Bates, Fr. Urban, O.P., 53, **55–56**, 229, 354, 617, 637, 669

Battiston, Sr. Thecla, O.S.U., 8, 508, 654

Baud, Fr. John B., S.J., **56–59**, 121, 183, 184, 273, 318, 354, 474, 606

Baysinger, Sherry, 248

Bayusik, Fr. Robert E., 28, **59**

Beans, Elizabeth, 180

Beans, Dcn. Elmer, 445

Bear (ship), 50

Beck, E. J., 516

Beck, Sr. Mary, S.S.N.D., 174, 244, 363

Beck, Sr. Rose, S.S.N.D., 10, 319, 367, 527

Beech, Ed, 71

Belanger, Dave, 267

Belanger, Priscilla, 267

Belcher, Dcn. James, 595

Belcher, Dixie, 438–439

Benedictine Sisters, 14, 188

Benigno, Dcn. Pasquale, 313

Benish, Br. Robert L., S.J., 2, 8, **59–62**, 514

Bennett, A. A., 437

Berg, Fr. Richard, C.S.C., 636

Berger, Br. Normand, F.I.C., 187

Bergquist, Fr. Patrick D., **62–64**, 194, 196–197, 219, 281, 636

Bering Sea, 175

Bering Strait, 382

Bering, Vitus, 382

Bernard, Fr. Joseph, S.J., 37, **64–66**, 96, 378, 417, 451

Bertha (ship), 440, 634, 640, 642, 646

Bérubé, Br. Raymond, F.I.C., 187

Besse, Mother Holy Name, O.S.U., 654

Bester, Fr. Robert C., 354

Bethel, 33, 55, **66–68**, 99, 121, 141, 144, 151, 155, 160, 178, 179, 182, 199, 216, 222, 237, 239, 243, 244, 255, 286, 293, 317, 321, 340, 357, 381, 382, 391, 414, 420, 424, 429, 437, 448, 449, 453, 491, 505, 523, 556, 672

Betz, Robert, 367, 512

Beuzer, Fr. Vincent J., S.J., 33, **68–70**, 122, 142, 267–268

Bichsel, Fr. William J., S.J., 122

Bickford, Fr. Robert M., S.J., 335

Big Diomede, 382, 384, 386, 388

Big Lake, 17, 18, **70–71**, 495, 558

Bill Moore's Slough, 362

Bill, David and Julia, 244

Birkeland, Leigh, 88

Bishop Whelan Family Support and Counseling Center, 530

Bishop, Katherine, 70, 71

Black River, 173

Blanco, Fr. Vincent, 31

Blaney, Fr. James, O.M.I., 125, 240, 270, 348, 480, 597

Blessed Sacrament Church, Scammon Bay, 568

boating. *See* outdoor sports

Bobka, Rosemary, 292

Boileau, Bp. George T., S.J., 13, 58, 67, **71–73**, 137, 158, 191, 192, 292, 294, 424, 426, 483, 504, 667–668

Boland, Fr. William M., S.J., 642–643

Bolster, Fr. John J., S.J., 335

Bonham, Br. Craig, O.M.I., 480

Bonsecours, Sr. Mary, S.S.A., 309

Boone, Br. Kirby, C.F.X., **73–74**, 221, 425, 549, 622

Borbeck, Fr. Martin G., S.J., 114, 269, 464, 579, 582

Borman, Sr. Cynthia, S.S.N.D., 10, 174